Copyright Law

Cases and Materials   V4.0

Jeanne C. Fromer

Professor, New York University School of
Law, and Co-Director, Engelberg Center on
Innovation Law and Policy

Christopher Jon Sprigman

Murray and Kathleen Bring Professor of Law,
New York University School of Law, and Co-
Director, Engelberg Center on Innovation
Law and Policy

This book is dedicated to our families, and to our students.

We thank Barton Beebe for his guidance with regard to open-source casebooks, Christopher Buccafusco, who gave us helpful comments on an initial draft of this book, as well as a big group of other law professors—too many to name individually—who have given us comments that contributed to this v3.0. We particularly thank Graeme Dinwoodie and Pamela Samuelson, who provided us with sustained chapter-by-chapter comments that helped improve the book. We also thank Madhav Tankha for fantastic graphic and website design, and Rebecca Tushnet for collecting many of the images used in the book. Thanks to Stephen Gray, Tim Keegan, and Krista Staropoli for extraordinary research assistance.

How we've edited the cases that appear in this book: We have numbered paragraphs to ease reference and class discussion. We have also used curly brackets ({ … }) to indicate our own editorial insertions in judicial decisions, as opposed to instances in which we make minor edits or courts themselves edit material that they are quoting, which we indicate with the use of standard brackets ([…]).

VII. Direct and Secondary Liability 507

VIII. Copyright Litigation and Remedies 577

I. Introduction

Some law students come to the subject of copyright law with at least a rough working understanding of what copyright is, and what it does (or is theoretically supposed to do). But for many others, copyright has been, and remains, a subject that they've perhaps heard about but haven't explored too deeply. Whatever level of knowledge you have about copyright at the moment, by the end of this book you will gain a firm grounding in the fundamentals of U.S. copyright law. Let's now begin at the beginning, with a broad statement of what copyright is.

> Copyright is a set of rights of limited scope and duration that are granted by law to the authors of original artistic and literary works, and that arise when such works are fixed in a tangible medium of expression.

We will inquire deeply into each of the elements of that very general definition. But first a short summary of the contents of this casebook:

In the remainder of this **Chapter I**, we'll explore the sources of U.S. copyright law, the history of U.S. copyright, and the theoretical justifications that underlie copyright.

In **Chapter II** we'll examine the subject matter of copyright protection—that is, what sort of "works" copyright protects. We'll also look at the threshold requirements for copyright protection, principally the requirements of *originality* and *fixation*. We'll then explore a central limiting principle of copyright law, the *idea-expression distinction*, which excludes from the scope of copyright protection ideas, facts, procedures, processes, systems, methods of operation, concepts, principles, and discoveries. We'll consider what those categories mean, and examine how the idea-expression distinction has been employed in cases involving a variety of subject matter.

In **Chapter III** we'll look at the meaning of *authorship*, and examine the rules governing copyright *ownership*.

Chapter IV covers copyright *formalities*, the *duration* of the term of copyright, and the rules governing *renewals* and the *termination of transfers of copyright*.

Chapter V details each of the *exclusive rights* granted to copyright owners. For all types of protected works, federal copyright law grants copyright owners the rights to (1) reproduce the work, (2) prepare derivative works based on the work, and (3) publicly distribute copies of the work. Federal law also grants copyright owners of certain types of works the right(s) to publicly display the work or to publicly perform it. For one type of protected work—sound recordings—the Act limits the right of public performance to performance by digital transmission. We explore these rights, including their scope and limitations. We also examine the operation of these rights in a specific context, the music industry, that presents special complexities. Finally, in this chapter we examine the narrow scope of co-called "moral rights" in U.S. copyright law.

In **Chapter VI** we'll examine copyright's *fair use* doctrine, tracing its historical development and modern applications.

Chapter VII details the rules governing *direct liability* for copyright infringement, as well as those defining the various forms of *secondary liability*. This chapter also examines the application of secondary liability rules to *online service providers* and the manufacturers of *devices* that may be used to infringe.

Chapter VIII examines various topics related to *copyright litigation and remedies*, including *subject matter jurisdiction, standing,* the operation of copyright's *statute of limitations,* and the role of the *Copyright Office*. Chapter VIII also details the remedies for copyright infringement, including both *injunctions* and various forms of *monetary relief*. The chapter closes with a brief review of *criminal copyright law*.

Chapter IX reviews the provisions of U.S. copyright law that prohibit the *circumvention of technological protections* for copyrighted works.

Finally, **Chapter X** details the relationship of federal copyright law to contract and other forms of state law.

The remainder of Chapter I presents first a short and general discussion of what sort of subject matter can be protected by copyright law, versus what *patent* and *trademark* laws protect. Patent and trademark laws are, along with copyright law, the principal branches of what's come to be referred to as "intellectual property" law. The chapter then summarizes the sources of copyright law, including a short account of the international framework of copyright treaties. Finally, the chapter reviews the principal theoretical justifications for copyright law.

A. The Categories of Copyrightable Subject Matter

As we will discuss in considerably more detail in Chapter II, section 102 of the Copyright Act sets out the subject matter that copyright protects. The categories of copyrightable subject matter include:

(1) literary works;
(2) musical works, including any accompanying words;
(3) dramatic works, including any accompanying music;
(4) pantomimes and choreographic works;
(5) pictorial, graphic, and sculptural works;
(6) motion pictures and other audiovisual works;
(7) sound recordings; and
(8) architectural works.

We will inquire into the particulars of each of these categories in Chapter II. Suffice now to say that copyright's subject matter can be understood, as a shorthand, to include a range of artistic and literary works. We can distinguish copyright's subject matter from that of patent, which protects scientific and technological inventions. We can also distinguish copyright's subject matter from that of trademark law, which protects words, logos, slogans, designs, domain names, and other symbols or "devices" that uniquely distinguish the goods or services of a firm.

For now, when you think of the subject matter of copyright, think of novels, poems, sculptures, photographs, plays, musical compositions, sound recordings, dances, movies, television shows, buildings, and computer software. Computer software? Yes, software is, somewhat counterintuitively, classified as a "literary work." More on that in Chapter II.

B. The Sources of Copyright Law

1. The U.S. Constitution

Copyright law is predominantly *federal* law. **Article I, Section 8, Clause 8 of the U.S. Constitution** authorizes Congress to create copyright and patent laws. That clause—which is variously referred to as the "Intellectual Property Clause," the "Copyright and Patent Clause," and the "Progress Clause"—provides that

> *Congress shall have Power ... To promote the Progress of Science and useful Arts, by securing for limited Times, to Authors and Inventors, the exclusive Right to their respective Writings and Discoveries.*

We will see as the course proceeds how federal courts have interpreted the meaning of this provision and the scope of the power it grants Congress to make copyright law.

NOTES

1. Which, if any, of the different names for Article I, Section 8, Clause 8 of the Constitution—the "Intellectual Property Clause," the "Copyright and Patent Clause," and the "Progress Clause"—best captures the content and purpose of the clause? What substantive or rhetorical arguments do each of the labels advance?

2. Notice the "parallel" structure of the Copyright and Patent Clause: the clause provides Congress with both copyright and patent lawmaking power, supplies terms that comprise the grant of power for each type of law, and combines those powers in a single clause.

For copyright, the clause can be decomposed to read as follows: *"Congress shall have Power .... To promote the Progress of Science ... by securing for limited Times, to Authors ... the exclusive Right to their ... Writings ...."*

For patent, the clause can be decomposed to read as follows: *"Congress shall have Power ... To promote the Progress of ... useful Arts, by securing for limited Times, to ... Inventors, the exclusive Right to their ... Discoveries."*

For a different, unitary, and thought-provoking reading of this Clause, see Dotan Oliar, *The (Constitutional) Convention on IP: A New Reading,* 57 UCLA L. REV. 421 (2009).

3. It may sound odd, to our modern ears, that the framers identified the purpose of copyright as promoting the progress of "Science." That word sounds more like the domain of patent—laboratories, test tubes, inventions—than copyright. But to the eighteenth-century mind, "science" was a broad term that stood for *learning*, and, as you will see, the English Statute of Anne, the first modern copyright law and a model for both the Copyright and Patent Clause and the first U.S. copyright statute, was entitled "an Act for the encouragement of learning." (Some may also find "useful Arts" a confusing signifier for patents. By "arts," the framers meant "artifices"— that is, machines—and not "art" in the sense that word usually takes in modern language (that is, fine art)).

2. The Copyright Act of 1976

The most important source of law for U.S. copyright is a federal statute, the Copyright Act of 1976, 90 Stat. 2541, which remains in force today with a series of amendments and additions. The Copyright Act is codified in Title 17 of the U.S. Code. Here is a URL for the Copyright Act as it appears on the website of the United States Copyright Office (we'll discuss the Copyright Office separately shortly): www.copyright.gov/title17/

> **PLEASE NOTE:** It is vital to your understanding of copyright that you become familiar both with the overall structure of the Copyright Act, and with the subset of statutory provisions that we will cover in detail in the course. This book will call your attention to particular statutory provisions as they become relevant. Please read them carefully and think about possible areas of incompleteness or imprecision in the statutory text.

3. The Decisions of Federal Courts

Although copyright law is driven by a federal statute, **federal court decisions** are a very important source of copyright law.

Sometimes court decisions are important because they are interpreting the meaning of a provision of the Copyright Act. For example, federal courts applying the fair use provision set out in § 107 of the Copyright Act have interpreted the meaning of that provision, elaborating on the relatively spare guidance found in the statute, and have considered the application of the fair use standard in a wide range of settings.

Sometimes court decisions are important because they establish principles that are later incorporated into the federal copyright statutes. For example, we will see that a limitation to copyright known as the "first sale doctrine" was first established by judicial decision, and only later incorporated into the Copyright Act (specifically, in § 109).

And then sometimes court decisions are important because they establish or articulate elements of copyright law about which the Copyright Act is silent. For example, we will review a number of court decisions that articulate standards for determining whether a work's copyright has been infringed. The standard for determining copyright infringement is a central element of any imaginable copyright system, and yet the Copyright Act says nothing about what the test for infringement is. As we shall see, there are a number of vital issues in copyright law on which the Copyright Act has little or nothing to say, and for which the decisions of federal courts are the sole source of law.

4. Copyright Office Regulations and Guidance

The United States Copyright Office, created by an act of Congress in 1897, is a department within the legislative branch of the U.S. government. The Copyright Office is housed within the Library of Congress, and is headed by a Register of Copyrights, who reports to the Librarian of Congress. The primary function of the Copyright Office is suggested by the title of the official who heads the Office; it is to register claims of copyright, and to serve as a recordkeeper for related functions, such as the recordation of transfers of copyright ownership.

The Copyright Office is granted limited regulatory authority. The Copyright Act provides the Register of Copyrights with authority to "establish regulations not inconsistent with law for the administration of the functions and duties made the responsibility of the Register under this title. All regulations established by the

Register under this title are subject to the approval of the Librarian of Congress." 17 U.S.C. § 702. You can find the regulations at www.copyright.gov/title37.

We note that some have questioned the constitutional basis for *any* regulatory authority granted by Congress to this entity, which itself is a branch of Congress. *See, e.g.*, Andy Gass, *Considering Copyright Rulemaking: The Constitutional Question*, 27 BERKELEY TECH. L.J. 1047 (2012). In any event, the authority granted to the Copyright Office to issue regulations through notice-and-comment rulemaking is directed mostly to the Office's administrative functions and duties, most notably the registration of copyright claims.

In addition to regulations within the area of its authority, the Copyright Office also publishes an important document, the *Compendium of Copyright Office Practices*. The Compendium is a summary of the *practices* of the Copyright Office. It is not a compendium of copyright law generally, or of any aspect of copyright law that lies outside of the Copyright Office's administrative functions. As noted in its introduction, the "primary focus" of the Compendium is "on the registration of copyright claims, documentation of copyright ownership, and recordation of copyright documents, including assignments and licenses." For further clarification, the introduction notes that "[t]he Compendium does not cover every principle of copyright law or detail every aspect of the Office's administrative practices." And, of course, "[t]he Compendium does not override any existing statute or regulation. The policies and practices set forth in the Compendium do not in themselves have the force and effect of law and are not binding upon the Register of Copyrights or U.S. Copyright Office staff." You can find the Compendium at www.copyright.gov/comp3.

5. The International Copyright Regime

There are aspects of international copyright treaties and agreements that bear on U.S. copyright law. This book will discuss the effect of the international regime on particular aspects of U.S. law throughout. Here we offer a short summary of the principal international instruments and institutions that affect U.S. copyright law.

The First Century of U.S. Copyright Law: No Protection for the Works of Foreign Authors

For the first century of U.S. copyright, U.S. law refused to extend protection to the works of foreign authors not domiciled in the United States. During this period, U.S. policy was frankly mercantilist; the United States, as compared with Europe, was not a significant producer of new works of authorship, and it suited American interests to have cheap foreign books readily available. And so publishers in the United States legally "pirated" the works of Charles Dickens, Anthony Trollope, Oscar Wilde, Émile Zola, Stendhal, and other non-U.S. authors.

That changed with the Copyright Act of 1891, which extended U.S. copyright protection to the works of foreign, non-U.S.-domiciled authors if either (1) their home countries accorded U.S. authors comparable protection, or (2) the United States and the author's home country were both signatories to a treaty that guaranteed reciprocal protection. Significantly, the 1891 Act subjected foreign authors to the full range of U.S. copyright formalities (registration, deposit, notice, and renewal, which we will cover in more detail in Chapter IV). It also conditioned protection for foreign (as well as U.S.) works on a requirement that those works be manufactured in the United States. This "manufacturing clause" remained in effect in U.S. copyright law until 1986.

The United States Joins the Berne Convention

The Copyright Act of 1909 and the Copyright Act of 1976 continued to embody the reciprocity principle adopted in the 1891 Act. But as the United States emerged as a major producer and exporter of cultural works, the U.S. interest in more closely aligning with international copyright agreements and norms grew. The United States had long remained outside the principal international copyright treaty, the Berne Convention for the Protection of Literary and Artistic Works (1886), in part because, as will be discussed further in Chapter IV, the Berne Convention was (and is) hostile to formalities that affect "the enjoyment and the exercise" of copyright rights, whereas U.S. copyright law embraced such formalities. However, in the Copyright Act of 1976, Congress began a move away from mandatory formalities that was undertaken with the purpose of eventually acceding to the Berne Convention, a process that culminated in the Berne Convention Implementation Act of 1988.

TRIPS and the WTO

In the wake of its accession to the Berne Convention, the United States joined the European Union and Japan in an effort to strengthen the international intellectual property system by embedding it in a multilateral trade negotiation and trade rule enforcement institution, the World Trade Organization (WTO), which was created in 1994 as part of the Uruguay Round of multilateral trade negotiations. One of the agreements which accompanied the creation of the WTO is the Agreement on Trade Related Aspect of Intellectual Property, or TRIPS. The TRIPS Agreement establishes a set of minimum substantive standards for many areas of intellectual property, including patents, copyrights, trademarks, trade secrets, industrial designs, and geographical indications. Part II of TRIPS focuses on copyright. Of particular importance is Article 9, which adopts the substantive standards of the Berne Convention (except for its moral rights provisions—more on that in Chapter V). The TRIPS Agreement gives teeth to the Berne Convention's substantive standards by making them subject to the WTO dispute resolution process, in which a country can file a complaint against another country for failing to comply with its international obligations.

C. The History of U.S. Copyright Law

The Stationers' Monopoly and the Statute of Anne

The origins of U.S. copyright law lie in England, and, specifically, in the history leading up to the enactment in 1710 of the Statute of Anne, which served as a model for the first U.S. copyright law.

Before the introduction of the printing press in the mid-fifteenth century, there was little need for copyright law. Books were expensive and time-consuming to copy by hand, which made unauthorized copying unattractive. But with the advent of the printing press and of the cheap mass copying that the technology made possible, copying emerged as a concern for book printers. In England, the printers joined together to organize a guild, the Stationers' Company, chartered by the Crown in 1557. The guild, which was focused on controlling copying, entered into a pact with the Crown, which was interested in controlling seditious books. Under the terms of the 1557 charter and a number of licensing acts that followed, the members of the Stationers' Company were granted an exclusive right to print most works within the realm. The Company itself was granted power to search for and destroy books printed by non-guild printers.

This cartel was designed to benefit publishers and the government, and not authors. Eventually, both the Stationers' monopoly and the role of the Stationers' Company in enforcing government censorship of books drew substantial opposition. In his famous polemic *Aereopagitica*, John Milton argued that books should not be subject to pre-publication licensing. His argument has both anti-monopoly and anti-censorship strands. For example, with respect to the Stationers' monopoly:

> *Truth and understanding are not such wares as to be monopoliz'd and traded in by tickets and statutes, and standards. We must not think to make a staple commodity of all the knowledge in the Land, to mark and licence it like our broad cloath, and our wooll packs.*

JOHN MILTON, AREOPAGITICA: A SPEECH FOR THE LIBERTY OF UNLICENSED PRINTING 29 (1644) (H.B. Cotterill ed. 1959). And with respect to the censorship role of the guild:

> *If we think to regulat Printing, thereby to rectifie manners, we must regulat all recreations and pastimes, all that is delightful to man. No musick must be heard, no song be set or sung, but what is grave and Dorick. There must be licencing dancers, that no gesture, motion, or deportment be taught our youth but what by their allowance shall be thought honest; for such Plato was provided of; It will ask more than the work of twenty licencers to examin all the lutes, the violins, and the ghittarrs in every house; they must not be suffer'd to prattle as they doe, but must be licenc'd what they may say. And who shall silence all the airs and madrigalls, that whisper softnes in chambers? ...*

By the 1690s, the Stationers' monopoly had fallen out of favor and Parliament allowed the licensing and censorship provisions that supported that monopoly to lapse.

At that point the Stationers adopted a different tactic: Rather than arguing for a monopoly in their own name, they argued that rights should be given to authors, whom they expected would assign those rights away to the publishers, thereby preserving the Stationers' monopoly in a different form.

The Stationers' new approach contributed to the passage in 1710 of the Statute of Anne. That act, entitled "[a]n act for the encouragement of learning," granted to authors (and not to publishers) an assignable right to control the "printing and reprinting" of books. That right endured for a term of 14 years, renewable once. The right was conditioned, moreover, on the registration of titles for which the author sought protection in the registry maintained by the Stationers' Company.

The 14-year term in the Statute of Anne was, in the publishers' view, simply a supplement, rather than a replacement, for the perpetual monopoly they had been given under the prior Crown system. The publishers' interpretation was defeated, however, in *Donaldson v. Becket*, 98 Eng. Rep. 257 (H.L. 1774). In that case, the House of Lords rejected the publishers' claims of perpetual copyright protection, and made clear that copyrights in published works were established by, and subject to the limits of, the Statute of Anne.

The U.S. Copyright Act of 1790

The Statute of Anne was influential in the framing of the U.S. Constitution's Copyright and Patent Clause. In particular, like the Statute of Anne, which tied copyright to "the encouragement of learning," the clause tied Congress's exercise of its copyright lawmaking power to a public purpose: promotion of progress of knowledge. And again like the Statute of Anne, the clause imposed a temporal limitation on copyright rights, although the precise length of a permissibly "limited" copyright term was left undefined.

The influence of the Statute of Anne is also palpable in the first U.S. copyright statute, the Copyright Act of 1790. The Act, entitled "an Act for the encouragement of learning," applied to maps, charts (that is, maps of water), and books, and provided the copyright owner with the "sole right and liberty of printing, reprinting, publishing and vending" copies for a 14-year term, renewable once for another 14-year term by a surviving author. The 1790 Act also contained a stringent set of formalities. To gain protection under the Act, authors were required to register the title in their works, to publish the registration in a newspaper, and to deposit a copy of the work with the clerk of the local district court and to send another copy within six months of the work's publication to the U.S. Secretary of State.

NOTE

1. As in England following the enactment of the Statute of Anne, U.S. copyright owners following the enactment of the 1790 Act pressed claims in litigation that statutory copyright was merely supplemental to a perpetual right granted by common law. And as in the English *Donaldson* case, those claims were rejected in the United States. In *Wheaton v. Peters*, 33 U.S. (8 Pet.) 591 (1834), the U.S. Supreme Court addressed copyright claims pressed by a private reporter of the Supreme Court's opinions. The Court recognized that the opinions themselves were uncopyrightable, but other material added by the reporter, such as summaries of the arguments presented by the parties to the Court, was eligible for protection. However, the reporter's additions were ineligible for statutory copyright because the reporter had failed to comply with the formalities required to gain protection under the statute. The reporter claimed that his material was nonetheless protectable under the common law, but the Supreme Court rejected that claim:

> That an author, at common law, has a property in his manuscript, and may obtain redress against any one who deprives him of it, or by improperly obtaining a copy endeavours to realise a profit by its publication, cannot be doubted; but this is a very different right from that which asserts a perpetual and exclusive property in the future publication of the work, after the author shall have published it to the world.

> The argument that a literary man is as much entitled to the product of his labour as any other member of society, cannot be controverted. And the answer is, that he realizes this product by the transfer of his manuscripts, or in the sale of his works, when first published....

> That every man is entitled to the fruits of his own labour must be admitted; but he can enjoy them only, except by statutory provision, under the rules of property, which regulate society, and which define the rights of things in general.

The Supreme Court's rejection of common law copyright in published works means that published works are governed exclusively by federal statutory law. That remains the state of copyright today. And as we shall see in Chapter IV, Congress has moved to preempt state protection of unpublished (but fixed) works as well.

Post-1790 Expansion of Copyrightable Subject Matter

As previously mentioned, copyrightable subject matter under the 1790 Act was limited to maps, charts, and books. Over the next century, Congress gradually expanded the categories of eligible subject matter to include engravings, etchings, and prints (1802); musical compositions (1831); dramatic compositions (1856); photographs and negatives (1865); and paintings, drawings, chromolithographs, statuary, and "models or designs intended to be perfected as works of the fine arts" (1870). In 1909, Congress enacted the first major overhaul of federal copyright law. The Copyright Act of 1909 embraced as copyrightable subject matter "all the writings of an author," but then offered a list of specific subject matter protected by copyright, a list which courts interpreted as encompassing all protectable forms of subject matter:

(a)   Books, including composite and cyclopaedic works, directories, gazetteers, and other compilations;

(b)   Periodicals, including newspapers;

(c)   Lectures, sermons, addresses, prepared for oral delivery;

(d)   Dramatic or dramatico-musical compositions;

(e)   Musical compositions;

(f)   Maps;

(g)	Works of art; models or designs for works of art;
(h)	Reproductions of a work of art;
(i)	Drawings or plastic works of a scientific or technical character;
(j)	Photographs;
(k)	Prints and pictorial illustrations.

In 1912, Congress amended this list to include "motion-picture photoplays" and "motion pictures other than photoplays." In 1939, Congress added "prints or labels used for articles of merchandise." In 1971, Congress added sound recordings.

The Copyright Act of 1976

In the 1976 Act—which, as amended, remains the law—Congress sought "to free the courts from rigid or outmoded concepts of the scope of particular [subject matter] categories." H.R. REP. NO. 94-1476, 94th Cong., 2d Sess. 47, at 53 (1976). Toward that end, the 1976 Act veered away from some of the more particular language used in the 1909 Act to describe copyrightable subject matter (such as "lectures, sermons, addresses, prepared for oral delivery") in favor of broad categories of copyrightable subject matter.

Section 102(a) of the 1976 Act listed seven categories, which are deemed to be non-exhaustive of the range of copyrightable subject matter: "(1) literary works; (2) musical works, including any accompanying words; (3) dramatic works, including any accompanying music; (4) pantomimes and choreographic works; (5) pictorial, graphic, and sculptural works; (6) motion pictures and other audiovisual works; and (7) sound recordings." These categories cumulate many of the narrower classes of copyrightable works that the 1909 Act listed separately. And because of the generality of the language that the 1976 Act uses to define categories of subject matter, Congress has avoided the need—at least in many instances—to amend the 1976 Act to account for new technologies. For example, Congress did not need to add new subject matter categories to the 1976 Act to have copyright protection extend to work fixed in digital audio recordings or DVDs; the statutory definitions of "sound recordings" and "audiovisual works" were worded broadly enough to encompass those new media. Since the passage of the 1976 Act, Congress has added, in 1990, only one more category to the list of copyrightable subject matter set forth in § 102(a): architectural works.

Since the 1976 Act, Congress has passed five additional major pieces of copyright-related legislation: the Digital Millennium Copyright Act (DMCA), 112 Stat. 2860 (1998); the Copyright Term Extension Act, 112 Stat. 2827 (1998); the Fairness in Music Licensing Act, *id.*; the Music Modernization Act, Pub. L. 115–264 (2018); and the Copyright Alternative in Small-Claims Enforcement Act (CASE Act), Pub. L. No. 116-260 (2020). We will discuss issues related to the DMCA in Chapter VII when we study the liability of online service providers, and in Chapter IX when we examine the law governing technological protections for copyrighted works. We will discuss the effect and constitutionality of the Copyright Term Extension Act in Chapter IV. We will review in Chapter V the changes to the structure of music industry rights and licensing brought about by the Fairness in Music Licensing Act and the Music Modernization Act. And we will examine the provisions of the CASE Act when we study copyright remedies in Chapter VIII.

D. Why Do We Have Copyright?

As mentioned above, Article I, Section 8, Clause 8, of the U.S. Constitution provides Congress with authority to make copyright law, and links that authority to the accomplishment of a particular purpose—to "promote the Progress of Science." But what exactly does it mean to promote this progress? What role does copyright play in achieving that purpose? And are there justifications for copyright that sound not in utilitarian arguments about promoting progress, but in arguments about authors' rights that are deontic (that is, rights-based and non-consequentialist)?

1. The Utilitarian Account

The dominant justification for copyright, at least in the United States, is **utilitarian**, or **consequentialist**. The claim is that copyright contributes to the "progress of Science" by maintaining adequate incentives to engage in the production of new artistic and literary works. Creating anew is often expensive, and copying, cheap. Without copyright, it is claimed, copyists who don't face the same costs of creation that originators do will underprice originators and compete away the profits from new artistic and literary creativity, thereby suppressing incentives to create new artistic and literary works in the first place.

That is a sensible story. But is it true? On that question, we have little evidence. We are still at an early point in the empirical study of copyright. As some scholars have noted, while there are some helpful empirical studies establishing a link between copyright and creative incentives,[1] thus far the link appears to be considerably less systematically established than theory may have led us to expect. *See generally* Christopher Jon Sprigman, *Copyright and Creative Incentives: What We Know (And Don't)*, 55 HOUSTON L. REV. 451, 454-55 (2017).

Indeed, some suspect that people would create works absent copyright incentives, owing to intrinsic motivation to do so. *See, e.g.,* JESSICA SILBEY, THE EUREKA MYTH: CREATORS, INNOVATORS, AND EVERYDAY INTELLECTUAL PROPERTY (2014); Roberta Rosenthal Kwall, *Inspiration and Innovation: The Intrinsic Dimension of the Artistic Soul*, 81 NOTRE DAME L. REV. 1945 (2006); Rebecca Tushnet, *Economies of Desire: Fair Use and Marketplace Assumptions*, 51 WM. & MARY L. REV. 513 (2009); Diane Leenheer Zimmerman, *Copyrights as Incentives: Did We Just Imagine That?*, 12 THEORETICAL INQUIRIES L. 29 (2011).[2] Others wonder, even so, whether businesses would create distribution channels for these works absent copyright's incentive. *See, e.g.,* Julie E. Cohen, *Copyright as Property in the Post-Industrial Economy: A Research Agenda*, 2011 WISC. L. REV. 141. In fact, an entire subgenre has arisen within the academic literature on copyright documenting creative activity that appears to proceed without, or with little, dependence on formal intellectual property protection. This scholarship, sometimes referred to as the "negative space" literature, and alternatively as "intellectual production without intellectual property" (or "IP without IP"), includes studies of the fashion industry,[3] cuisine,[4] fan fiction,[5] pornography,[6] nineteenth-century U.S. commercial publishing,[7] video games featuring significant

---

[1] Examples include Michela Giorcelli & Petra Moser, *Copyrights and Creativity: Evidence from Italian Operas*, https://papers.ssrn.com/sol3/papers.cfm?abstract_id=2505776, and Rahul Telang & Joel Waldfogel, *Piracy and New Product Creation: A Bollywood Story*, 43 INFO. ECON. & POL'Y 1 (2018).

[2] For a survey of this literature, see Christopher Buccafusco, Zachary C. Burns, Jeanne C. Fromer & Christopher Jon Sprigman, *Experimental Tests of Intellectual Property Law's Creativity Thresholds*, 92 TEX. L. REV. 1921 (2014).

[3] Jonathan Barnett, *Shopping for Gucci on Canal Street: Reflections on Status Consumption, Intellectual Property, and the Incentive Thesis*, 91 VA. L. REV. 1381 (2005); C. Scott Hemphill & Jeannie C. Suk, *The Fashion Originators' Guild of America: Self-Help At The Edge Of IP And Antitrust*, in INTELLECTUAL PROPERTY AT THE EDGE (Rochelle Dreyfuss & Jane Ginsburg eds., 2014); C. Scott Hemphill & Jeannie Suk, *The Law, Culture, and Economics of Fashion*, 61 STAN. L. REV. 1147 (2009); Kal Raustiala & Christopher Jon Sprigman, *The Piracy Paradox: Innovation and Intellectual Property in Fashion Design*, 92 VA. L. REV. 1687 (2006); Kal Raustiala & Christopher Jon Sprigman, *The Piracy Paradox Revisited*, 61 STAN. L. REV. 1201 (2009).

[4] Christopher J. Buccafusco, *On the Legal Consequences of Sauces: Should Thomas Keller's Recipes Be Per Se Copyrightable?*, 24 CARDOZO ARTS & ENT. L. J. 1121 (2007); Emmanuelle Fauchart & Eric von Hippel, *Norms-Based Intellectual Property Systems: The Case of French Chefs*, 19 ORG. SCI. 187 (2008).

[5] Rebecca Tushnet, *Economics of Desire: Fair Use and Marketplace Assumptions*, 51 WM. & MARY L. REV. 513 (2009).

[6] Kate Darling, *IP Without IP? A Study of the Online Adult Entertainment Industry*, 17 STAN. TECH. L. REV. 655 (2014); Kal Raustiala & Christopher Jon Sprigman, *The Second Digital Disruption: Streaming & the Dawn of Data-Driven Creativity*, 94 N.Y.U. L. REV. 1555 (2019).

[7] ROBERT SPOO, WITHOUT COPYRIGHTS: PIRACY, PUBLISHING, AND THE PUBLIC DOMAIN (2013).

user-generated content,[8] stand-up comedy,[9] roller derby,[10] software,[11] jam bands,[12] tattoos,[13] and magic.[14] These studies show the ways in which creative production can flourish in certain contexts with relatively little or no intellectual property protection.[15] Nonetheless, it is unclear whether these negative spaces reflect production and distribution with regard to the range of subject matter that copyright law protects (such as music, books, and movies).

Neil Netanel and others have offered a justification for copyright protection—the "democratic paradigm"—that is a variant of the utilitarian account. In the democratic paradigm, copyright is understood as a tool by which the state recruits market institutions to enhance the democratic character of civil society. According to this justification, both the rights that copyright law grants, and the limitations of those rights, can be understood as an "engine of free expression" that both encourages new speech and limits the extent to which speech relies on state patronage:

> In supporting a market for authors' works, copyright serves two democracy-enhancing functions. The first is a production function. Copyright provides an incentive for creative expression on a wide array of political, social, and aesthetic issues, thus bolstering the discursive foundations for democratic culture and civic association. The second function is structural. Copyright supports a sector of creative and communicative activity that is relatively free from reliance on state subsidy, elite patronage, and cultural hierarchy. The democratic paradigm requires that copyright protection be sufficiently strong to ensure support for copyright's production and structural functions. But at the same time, it would accord authors a limited proprietary entitlement, designed to make room for—and, indeed, to encourage—many transformative and educative uses of existing works.

Neil Weinstock Netanel, *Copyright and a Democratic Civil Society*, 106 YALE L.J. 283, 288 (1996).

Coda: Copyright and the Economics of Non-Rivalry

The Constitution gives Congress power to pass laws establishing copyright rights, but that power is limited to the creation of rights that endure for "limited Times." Why would we limit the term of copyright, especially considering that ordinarily, property rights are not time-limited? Why would we give property rights in a table, or in a plot of land, that last forever and can be passed down from owners to heirs indefinitely, but limit copyright ownership to a finite period?

---

[8] Greg Lastowka, *Minecraft as Web 2.0: Amateur Creativity & Digital Games*, http://papers.ssrn.com/sol3/papers.cfm?abstract_id=1939241.

[9] Dotan Oliar & Christopher Jon Sprigman, *There's No Free Laugh (Anymore): The Emergence of Intellectual Property Norms and the Transformation of Stand-Up Comedy*, 94 VA. L. REV. 1787 (2008).

[10] David Fagundes, *Talk Derby to Me: Intellectual Property Norms Governing Roller Derby Pseudonyms*, 90 TEX. L. REV. 1093 (2012).

[11] YOCHAI BENKLER, THE WEALTH OF NETWORKS: HOW SOCIAL PRODUCTION TRANSFORMS MARKETS AND FREEDOM (2007); Catherine L. Fisk, *Credit Where It's Due: The Law and Norms of Attribution*, 95 GEO. L.J. 49 (2006); Jon M. Garon, *Wiki Authorship, Social Media, and the Curatorial Audience*, 1 HARV. J. SPORTS & ENT. L. 95 (2010); Josh Lerner & Jean Tirole, *The Economics of Technology Sharing: Open Source and Beyond*, 19 J. ECON. PERSP. 99 (2005).

[12] Mark F. Schultz, *Fear and Norms and Rock & Roll: What Jambands Can Teach About Persuading People to Comply with Copyright Law*, 21 BERKELEY TECH. L. J. 651 (2006).

[13] Aaron Perzanowski, *Tattoos and IP Norms*, 98 MINN. L. REV. 511 (2013).

[14] Jacob Loshin, *Secrets Revealed: Protecting Magicians' Intellectual Property Without Law*, in LAW AND MAGIC: A COLLECTION OF ESSAYS 123 (Christine Corcos ed., 2010).

[15] *See also* MAKING AND UNMAKING INTELLECTUAL PROPERTY (Mario Biagioli, Peter Jaszi & Martha Woodmansee eds., 2011).

Chapter I – Introduction

Part of the answer can be found in the difference between **rivalrous** and **non-rivalrous** property. A laptop computer is rivalrous. If you are working on your laptop, I cannot work on it at the same time. In contrast, artistic and literary works are generally considered to be non-rivalrous. Consider a movie broadcast on television. If you turn on your television to view the movie, that doesn't result in my television being switched off. Our consumption of the movie is non-rivalrous. Rivalrousness is closely related to scarcity. Rivalrous goods tend to be scarce. Non-rivalrous goods don't face a scarcity problem. Additional access is always possible.

The law grants property rights in rivalrous goods in part because *property rights help us manage access to scarce goods*. You have a property right in your laptop, and, as a consequence, you can deny me access to it. That's an important right to have, given that if I'm using your laptop it won't be available for your use. Or you can choose to rent the laptop to me for a few hours. Your right to exclude me from your laptop allows you to charge me some price and impose conditions in exchange for allowing access to it.

Again, we grant property rights in rivalrous goods like laptops in part because property rights help us manage access to goods that are scarce. But this "resource allocation" justification for property rights doesn't hold up very well when applied to artistic and literary works. Once such works are created, they are not scarce. If I teach you a song I know, I still know the song, and now you know it as well. Our access to the song is not rivalrous. And the same is true if we both start teaching the song to additional friends. Allowing additional people to have access to the song doesn't reduce its value to us. Indeed, if we enjoy singing in a chorus, having a group of our friends know the song might *increase* its value to us. In this case, the song would be **anti-rivalrous**.

If there's no need to manage scarcity for non-rival goods like literary and artistic works, then why do we grant property rights in them? The utilitarian account says that we grant property rights in literary and artistic works to *maintain adequate incentives to create these works in the first place*. And, importantly, the "incentives" justification does not suggest that copyright should last forever. Rivalrous resources are scarce for as long as they exist, and so the property rights that we create to manage that scarcity must also be perpetual. But copyright rights need not be perpetual in order to create adequate incentives to create new artistic and literary works. Copyright rights need only endure long enough to permit creators to recover enough of the revenues that their work may generate to make the initial act of creation worthwhile.

How long a copyright term is sufficient? That is a surpassingly difficult question to answer with specificity. To set an optimal term, we'd need to know what level of creative output is ideal. And we'd need to know what duration and scope of copyright would produce that level of output. Those questions are theoretically tractable. But we lack the information—about our preferences for consuming literary and artistic works versus other goods, and about how different types of creators respond to incentives—necessary to answer them.

It is vital, moreover, to understand that copyright protection presents tradeoffs. If we increase the term or scope of copyright rights, we might get more new literary and artistic works (we say "might" because, as noted above, the empirical case for the incentives rationale is less than rock-solid). But copyright protection comes at a cost. In preventing competition from copyists, copyright protection allows copyright owners (or, at least that subset of owners that control works for which there is market demand) to charge a supra-competitive price for their artistic and literary works. This has three effects. First, it leads to a transfer of income from consumers to copyright owners; that is indeed the purpose of copyright. Second, it leads to what economists refer to as "deadweight loss." Copyright protection causes some consumers who would have consumed at the competitive price, but who will not consume at the supra-competitive price that the copyright law allows copyright owners to demand, to turn to their second-best consumption choice. This leads to a loss of welfare for those consumers, and for society generally. Third, copyright protection enables copyright owners to charge a high price to subsequent creators who wish to build on existing copyrighted work—or even to bar subsequent creators altogether. Thus, copyright might be used to prevent follow-on creativity that society might value.

In an 1841 speech to the British Parliament, historian and Whig politician Thomas Macaulay put it this way: copyright, Macaulay said, is "a tax on readers for the purpose of giving a bounty to writers." For an economic model of copyright law, see William M. Landes & Richard A. Posner, *An Economic Analysis of Copyright Law*, 18 J. LEGAL STUD. 325 (1989).

Copyright, in short, is a qualified good, and our structuring of copyright law involves a tradeoff. The goal, if we wish to benefit society as a whole, is not the maximal amount of copyright protection, but rather the *optimal* amount. That is, the amount that produces the degree of creative output that achieves the best mix of benefits and costs. Note that this "optimal" creative output is *not* necessarily the same as "more" creative output. Producing more artistic and literary works is not necessarily better; there are only so many poems or movies or computer programs that people are able and willing to consume. (More on this in Chapter II.)

NOTES

1. Assuming that the utilitarian story is, at least in part, correct, do we want to have one set of copyright rights that applies to all sorts of creative work? Or would we be better off creating different rights of different scope or duration for different sorts of creative work? For example, should we protect software differently than motion pictures?

2. What about fine art, like painting and sculpture? Does that need incentive at all to be created? For an argument that fine art does not require copyright incentives, and indeed is impeded by copyright, see Amy Adler, *Why Art Does Not Need Copyright*, 86 GEO. WASH. L. REV. 313 (2018).

3. Some commentators have advanced a different sort of consequentialist argument for intellectual property, and specifically, for copyright: that it is a tool for promoting equality and distributive justice. *See, e.g.*, Justin Hughes & Robert P. Merges, *Copyright and Distributive Justice*, 92 NOTRE DAME L. REV. 513 (2016) (arguing that the success of wealthy Black Americans in "copyright-related industries," such as entertainment and sports, is evidence that copyright promotes distributive justice). But others have argued that intellectual property is unlikely to promote equality. In a recent article, Stephanie Bair argues that the psychological conditions of poverty make intellectual property an ineffective tool for promoting creativity among the poor. Stephanie Plamondon Bair, *Impoverished IP*, 81 OHIO ST. L.J. 523 (2020).

2. Rights-Based Theories

There are, in addition to the incentives-based utilitarian theory, two well-established deontic justifications for copyright.

Lockean Labor Theory

The first deontic justification grows out of the theory of property set out in John Locke's *Two Treatises of Government*. Locke's theory identifies the individual's contribution of labor as the mechanism by which objects are reduced to property, and it focuses on the harm—in terms of fairness rather than wealth maximization—when another deprives the owner of the fruits of that labor. Although Locke himself never applied his **labor-desert theory** beyond real property to creative expression and inventions, others have developed Locke's theory as a non-utilitarian justification for intellectual property rules of varying scope.

Locke's labor-desert theory of property proceeds from the argument that a person who adds their labor to resources that are either unowned or held by all in common has a property right in the product of their efforts. The principal strand of Locke's theory is entirely non-consequentialist. Locke's argument is based primarily in

Chapter I – Introduction

fairness concerns, and is premised on a strong "no-harm" injunction: A person owns their own labor, and that person adds that labor whenever he or she appropriates a thing from the commons. If another takes the object the first person has appropriated, that person also takes the labor that the first person has added to that object in the original act of appropriation. That taking of labor is a harm. People are enjoined not to harm others; the "no-harm" injunction is at the basis of the first person's property right. The right is limited, however, by two provisos. The first is that the appropriation from the commons can result in a property claim only if "enough and as good" is left for others to appropriate. The second is that appropriation must not exceed what can be used: that is, appropriation must not lead to waste. As Locke puts it:

> God, who hath given the World to Men in common, hath also given them reason to make use of it to the best advantage of Life, and convenience....[Y]et being given for the use of Men, there must of necessity be a means to appropriate [the earth and its contents] some way or other before they can be of any use....

> Though the Earth, and all inferior Creatures be common to all Men, yet every Man has a Property in his own Person. This no Body has any Right to but himself. The Labour of his Body, and the Work of his Hands, we may say, are properly his. Whatsover he then removes out of the State that Nature hath provided, and left it in, he hath mixed his Labour with, and joyned to it something that is his own, and thereby makes it his Property....[I]t hath by this labour something annexed to it, that excludes the common right of other Men. For this Labour being the unquestionable Property of the Labourer, no Man but he can have a right to what that is once joyned to, at least where there is enough, and as good left in common for others.

> He that is nourished by the Acorns he pickt up under an Oak, or the Apples he gathered from the Trees in the Wood, has certainly appropriated them to himself....I ask then, When did they begin to be his?...And 'tis plain, if the first gathering made them not his, nothing else could. That labour put a distinction between them and common....And will any one say he had no right to those Acorns or Apples he thus appropriated, because he had not the consent of all Mankind to make them his? Was it a Robbery thus to assume to himself what belonged to all in Common? If such a consent as that was necessary, Man had starved, notwithstanding the Plenty God had given him....

> It will perhaps be objected to this, That if gathering the Acorns, or other Fruits of the Earth, & c. makes a right to them, then any one may in gross as much as he will. To which I Answer, Not so. The same Law of Nature, that does by this means give us Property, does also bound that Property too....As much as any one can make use of to any advantage of life before it spoils; so much he may by his labour fix a Property in. Whatever is beyond this, is more than his share, and belongs to others. Nothing was made by God for Man to spoil or destroy....

JOHN LOCKE, TWO TREATISES ON GOVERNMENT (Book II, Chap. V) (1690). For criticisms of Lockean labor theory as an incoherent idea of property arising from the act of "mixing" labor with objects in the commons, see, for example, ROBERT NOZICK, ANARCHY, STATE AND UTOPIA 174-75 (1974); Jeremy Waldron, *Two Worries About Mixing One's Labour*, 33 PHIL. Q. 37, 37 (1984).

Locke's understanding is, by analogy, an argument for the establishment of some form of property in creative expression. The argument posits first that creative expression is built upon facts and ideas that are in the commons. The labor involved in creating expression based on those common-stock elements is the basis of the laborer's property right in the resulting creative work. And the provisos are, in the view of most scholars applying Lockean theory to intellectual property, easily satisfied. The number of facts and ideas available for other people to use is without limit, so the ability of a first-comer to propertize any particular expression built on those common-stock elements is not substantially limited by the "enough and as good" proviso. It might, however, limit the exclusion of others from certain particular expressions. As to the "anti-waste" proviso, intellectual property can be licensed for money, and it can be held by immortal corporations, or, in the case of ownership by a natural person, transferred or devised so that it may always be actively exploited. It is possible that the anti-waste proviso would counsel that copyright law must contain provisions obliging owners to exploit their property or to license it if there is some demand for access to the particular work at issue. For analyses applying the Lockean framework to self-expression, see Mala Chatterjee, *Lockean Copyright vs. Lockean Property*, 12 J. LEGAL ANALYSIS 136 (2020); Wendy J. Gordon, *A Property Right in Self-Expression: Equality and Individualism in the Natural Law of Intellectual Property*, 102 YALE L.J. 1533 (1993). For an argument that it cannot be so applied, see Seana Shiffrin, *Lockean Arguments for Private Intellectual Property*, in NEW ESSAYS IN THE LEGAL AND POLITICAL THEORY OF PROPERTY 138-67 (Stephen R. Munzer ed., 2001).

Does the Lockean framework readily carry over to the realm of creative expression, or are there further assumptions or arguments one must make to fit the framework to this context? A critical difference between tangible items and intangible ones, like creative expression, raises some questions about applying the Lockean framework to creative expression. The consumption of tangible items is rivalrous, whereas intangible items like ideas and expression are non-rivalrous. So reading a book and accessing its intellectual content is not the same as taking the book itself (the physical item).

For these reasons, the "no-harm" principle is not implicated in the same way when we focus on the "taking" of intellectual property—unlike in the case of tangible property, unauthorized access to an artistic or literary work does not ordinarily result in the owner of that work losing access to it. That is not to say that the no-harm principle has no purchase in the case of intellectual property. Unauthorized consumption of intellectual property might involve deprivation of the possessor's enjoyment of some *profit* from the intellectual property, and that might be the source of the unfairness on which labor theory focuses. This form of unfairness is not the same thing as deprivation of the property itself, but it is nonetheless an important concern. It is also, obviously, precisely the concern that animates the incentives-based utilitarian theory of copyright. There is thus a deeper connection between Lockean and utilitarian analyses of copyright than their respective categorizations might otherwise suggest.

Hegelian/Kantian Personality Theory

A second deontic justification for copyright is found in the idea that because original expression reflects and embodies an author's personality, respect for creators' autonomy requires the recognition of property rights in creative works. This justification grows out of personality-based property theories set out by G.W.F. Hegel and (somewhat more accessibly) Immanuel Kant.

Personality theory is based in the autonomy interests associated with property ownership. The theory posits that property provides an especially powerful mechanism for self-definition, for personal expression, and for society's recognition of the dignity of an individual person. Margaret Radin describes this as a "personhood perspective" based on the view that "to achieve proper self-development—to be a person—an individual needs some control over resources in the external environment." Margaret Jane Radin, *Property and Personhood*, 34 STAN. L. REV. 957, 957 (1982). The best way of providing control over external resources is to recognize property rights, and a particular person's property interest is strongest in the resources that reflect or embody their personality.

Personality theory is appealing in part because it aligns with modern understandings of the importance of property: In a consumer society, we are (in part) what we own. And given popular adherence to a Romantic

Chapter I – Introduction

conception of authorship, Western culture is apt to find a particularly strong link between an individual creator's personality and their creative expression.

Like the Lockean labor theory, the Hegelian/Kantian personality theory provides a distinct deontic justification for the establishment of some form of copyright. But also like the Lockean theory, application of the Hegelian/Kantian justification to particular copyright disputes beneath the most abstract level raises a host of complications. Most significantly, the Hegelian/Kantian system contains no mechanism for reconciling competing personality claims. Think, for example, of the use of another's copyrighted novel to create a movie version of the novel. In this example, the second-comer has made use of something that reflects the personality of the original creator and is therefore, under the Hegelian/Kantian justification, owned by that individual. And yet the second-comer is also a creator, and the movie is a reflection of their personality as well as the original creator's.

The Hegelian/Kantian justification offers no guidance for how property rights must be distributed in such an instance. Is the novelist's right absolute: can the novelist enjoin the moviemaker? Or is the novelist not entitled to stop the movie, but only to share in its profits? Or is the movie a sufficiently independent act of creation such that the moviemaker owes nothing to the novelist?

If one broadens the utilitarian framework beyond seeing copyright as simply a pecuniary incentive to create expressive works, one might reconcile important aspects of the labor and personality theories with utilitarianism. Specifically, these theories can be complementary in important ways because there is a utility to deontic concerns. As evidence from a multitude of vantage points demonstrates, creators of expressive work typically attach great significance to both their labor and personhood interests in their work. As such, the incentive to create ought to be all that much stronger when copyright laws are structured both to protect and to communicate solicitude for authors' labor and personhood interests. The ways in which intellectual property laws can protect creators' labor and personhood interests and employ rhetoric communicating concern for these interests can be seen as **expressive incentives**. The law's careful use of expressive incentives can bolster the utilitarian inducement to create valuable intellectual property. That is, copyright's utilitarian incentives can be pecuniary, expressive, or both. For an exploration of this reconciliation, see Jeanne C. Fromer, *Expressive Incentives in Intellectual Property*, 98 VA. L. REV. 1745 (2012).

The labor and personality theories have had and continue to have more obvious influence in copyright systems outside of the United States, such as Europe, but they are part of the general discussion about the purposes of intellectual property law and the content of intellectual property rules. Query, as we step through the copyright doctrines in the following chapters, whether and how labor theory and personality theory work their way into the otherwise dominant utilitarian approach that U.S. copyright law takes.

II. The Subject Matter of Copyright Protection

Section 102 of the Copyright Act sets out copyright's "subject matter," the types of works that copyright protects. The text of § 102 contains several elements we address in this chapter: the requirements of **fixation** and **originality**, the **idea-expression distinction**, and the **categories of copyrightable subject matter**. (We address the copyrightability of **derivative works and compilations** in section C; section 103 of the Copyright Act addresses derivative works and compilations specifically by building on the more general framework that § 102 provides.)

Because § 102 features heavily throughout this chapter, we set it out in its entirety here, returning to relevant components in the sections that follow.

> *(a) Copyright protection subsists, in accordance with this title, in original works of authorship fixed in any tangible medium of expression, now known or later developed, from which they can be perceived, reproduced, or otherwise communicated, either directly or with the aid of a machine or device. Works of authorship include the following categories:*
>
> > *(1) literary works;*
> > *(2) musical works, including any accompanying words;*
> > *(3) dramatic works, including any accompanying music;*
> > *(4) pantomimes and choreographic works;*
> > *(5) pictorial, graphic, and sculptural works;*
> > *(6) motion pictures and other audiovisual works;*
> > *(7) sound recordings; and*
> > *(8) architectural works.*
>
> *(b) In no case does copyright protection for an original work of authorship extend to any idea, procedure, process, system, method of operation, concept, principle, or discovery, regardless of the form in which it is described, explained, illustrated, or embodied in such work.*

A. Fixation

Section 102 requires, as a pre-condition for copyright protection, that a work be "fixed" in a "tangible medium of expression." There are at least four reasons for this requirement. First and arguably foremost is the high likelihood that the U.S. Constitution requires fixation. The Constitution grants power to Congress to create copyright laws "by securing for limited Times to Authors ... the exclusive Right to their ... Writings." U.S. CONST. art. I, § 8, cl. 8. Although the U.S. Supreme Court has never conclusively ruled that fixation is a constitutional requirement, it has repeatedly suggested or assumed as much. For example, in one case involving recorded music, the Court suggests that a "Writing[]," as used in the Constitution, means "any *physical rendering* of the fruits of creative intellectual or aesthetic labor." Goldstein v. California, 412 U.S. 456, 562 (1983) (emphasis added). By implication, anything that is not physically rendered cannot be a "Writing[]."

Even if fixation were not constitutionally mandated, there are at least three policy reasons that support this requirement. First, recall that a central justification for American copyright law is to encourage the creation and dissemination of artistically and culturally valuable works. A fixation requirement advances these goals by protecting only works that are likely to be preserved—because they are fixed in a tangible medium of expression—and thus more easily disseminated over time and space. By contrast, society is less likely to retain ephemeral works over time and space. An unrecorded performance, for example, is unlikely to be retained other than in the memories of the audience that was there to see it at that moment. On this theory, copyright law provides protection only for fixed works because they are more likely to contribute to preserved knowledge and culture. Malla Pollack, *What Is Congress Supposed to Promote?: Defining "Progress" in Article I, Section 8, Clause 8 of the United States Constitution, or Introducing the Progress Clause*, 80 NEB. L. REV. 754, 773-79 (2001). Are you convinced by this theory? Can you think of whether unfixed works, such as folklore, contribute to a society's knowledge and culture?

Second, copyright fixation serves an evidentiary function. Should a work ever be the subject of an infringement dispute, a fixed copy of the work readily serves as documentary evidence as to what the work is, and what it is not. It is much more difficult to show reliably and precisely what an unfixed work is, and, as a consequence, more difficult reliably to determine whether an unfixed work has been infringed. Douglas Lichtman, *Copyright as a Rule of Evidence*, 52 DUKE L.J. 683, 730-34 (2003); Lydia Pallas Loren, *Fixation as Notice in Copyright Law*, 96 B.U. L. REV. 939 (2016).

Third and relatedly, fixation ensures that a work's (protected) expression is fully delineated, which makes that expression easier to separate from any unprotected "ideas" the work may contain or represent. Lichtman, *supra*, at 731-32. (In section D, below, we delve into this idea-expression distinction.)

Consider now the specific statutory requirements for fixation. Section 102 requires that works be

> *fixed in any tangible medium of expression, now known or later developed, from which they can be perceived, reproduced, or otherwise communicated, either directly or with the aid of a machine or device.*

Section 101 further defines what it means for a work to be "fixed" in a tangible medium of expression:

> *A work is "fixed" in a tangible medium of expression when its embodiment in a copy or phonorecord,*[*] *by or under the authority of the author, is sufficiently permanent or stable to permit it to be perceived, reproduced, or otherwise communicated for a period of more than transitory duration.*

Before delving further into these statutory definitions, a brief word about the history that underlies them. In 1908, the U.S. Supreme Court considered in *White-Smith Music Publishing Co. v. Apollo Co.*, 209 U.S. 1, whether a player piano roll represented a copy of a musical composition. (A player-piano roll is a roll of paper with perforations punched into it. When installed on a player piano, the piano plays notes in sequence as determined by the position and length of the particular perforations. A player piano with an installed piano roll is shown in Figure 1.)

The plaintiff in the case owned copyrights in certain musical compositions, which had been fixed in the form of sheet music. The defendant was in the business of making and selling player pianos and piano rolls. Some of those piano rolls, when installed in the defendant's player pianos, reproduced the plaintiff's compositions. In the resulting suit for infringement, the U.S. Supreme Court was called upon to consider whether the piano rolls were "copies" of the musical composition. (Although this case did not raise issues of fixation of the musical composition in the piano roll as a requisite to copyright protection, it required the Court to ask essentially the same question to ascertain whether the defendant infringed the plaintiff's copyright by creating a copy of the musical composition.)

---

[*] Copies are "material objects, other than phonorecords, in which a work is fixed" as per the statutory definitions. 17 U.S.C. § 101. Phonorecords are "material objects in which sounds, other than those accompanying a motion picture or other audiovisual work, are fixed" as per the statutory definitions. *Id.*

Figure 1: player piano with piano roll

The Supreme Court held that the piano roll was not a copy of the musical composition it represented (and therefore the law did not prohibit this type of reproduction by the defendant). The Court reasoned that the piano roll was not a copy unless it was "put in a form which others [humans] can see and read." Because people did not read piano rolls like many read sheet music, it was not a copy. The Court thought it irrelevant that "[t]hese perforated rolls are parts of a machine which, when duly applied and properly operated in connection with the mechanism to which they are adapted, produce musical tones in harmonious combination." Following this decision, a work was considered fixed only if it existed in a form readable by humans, not just machines.

Although there are arguably justifications for a focus on human readability, the *White-Smith* decision's formalism provoked severe criticism. Even if a person could not read or hear the musical composition encoded in a piano roll, that same person could still consume the work with the help of a player piano. As a functional matter, *White-Smith* meant that copiers could circumvent copyright protections by creating copies of a work that were unreadable by humans, but could be made comprehensible with the aid of a machine.[*]

In its overhaul of copyright law in 1976, Congress instituted fixation as a requisite to copyright protection. (Before the 1976 Act, a work had to be published or registered to get copyright protection. *See infra* Chapter IV.) Congress also overruled *White-Smith* by clarifying that a work is fixed in a tangible medium of expression so long as the work "can be perceived, reproduced, or otherwise communicated, either directly or with the aid of a machine or device." 17 U.S.C. §§ 101 ("copies"; "phonorecords"); 102(a). A legislative report that preceded the new law pointed out that this change was "intended to avoid the artificial and largely unjustifiable distinctions, derived from cases such as *White-Smith* ..., under which statutory copyrightability in certain cases has been made to depend upon the form or medium in which the work is fixed." H.R. REP. NO. 1476, 94th Cong., 2d Sess. 47, at 52 (1976) ("House Report").

With the new language of "fixation" in the 1976 Act, Congress intended to account broadly for existing technologies of fixation (everything from books to sound recordings to the piano roll) as well as then-unknown technologies of fixation. Congress did, however, specifically address one important technology, live

---

[*] The following year, Congress overturned the specific holding of *White-Smith* by granting copyright holders in musical works the right to control the mechanical reproduction of their works and instituting a compulsory-license scheme for manufacturers of piano rolls and other mechanical reproductions. We discuss this legal development further in Chapter V's section on the music industry.

broadcasts. According to the House Report, "the definition of 'fixation' would exclude from the concept purely evanescent or transient reproductions such as those projected briefly on a screen, shown electronically on a television or other cathode ray tube." *Id.* at 53. These representations are not fixed because they are not "sufficiently permanent or stable to permit [them] to be perceived, reproduced, or otherwise communicated for a period of more than transitory duration," as required by § 101. Congress, however, made the choice to protect "live broadcasts—sports, news coverage, live performances of music, etc.—that are reaching the public in unfixed form but that are simultaneously being recorded." H.R. REP. No. 1476, 94th Cong., 2d Sess. 47, at 52 (1976). It did so by adding the following sentence to the statute: "A work consisting of sounds, images, or both, that are being transmitted, is 'fixed' for purposes of this title if a fixation of the work is being made simultaneously with its transmission." 17 U.S.C. § 101.

Congress thought it had resolved a complicated area with its new rules for fixation, but as new technologies developed—and particularly digital technologies—unforeseen complications arose.

> As you read the following case, think about the different copyrights the plaintiff claims to hold and the medium in which each might be fixed. Is there some aspect of video games that might make it difficult to determine whether they are fixed as required by law? What effect does and should the participation of video game players have on the plaintiff's arguments?

Williams Electronics, Inc. v. Artic International, Inc.
685 F.2d 870 (3d Cir. 1982)

SLOVITER, J.: ...

[1] Plaintiff-appellee Williams Electronics, Inc. manufactures and sells coin-operated electronic video games. A video game machine consists of a cabinet containing, *inter alia*, a cathode ray tube (CRT), a sound system, hand controls for the player, and electronic circuit boards. The electronic circuitry includes a microprocessor and memory devices, called ROMs (Read Only Memory), which are tiny computer [chips] containing thousands of data locations which store the instructions and data of a computer program. The microprocessor executes the computer program to cause the game to operate.... [T]he interaction of the program stored in the ROM with the other components of the game produces the sights and sounds of the audiovisual display that the player sees and hears. The memory devices determine not only the appearance and movement of the (game) images but also the variations in movement in response to the player's operation of the hand controls.

[2] ... Williams ... design[ed] a new video game, ... called DEFENDER, which incorporated various original and unique audiovisual features. The DEFENDER game ... has ... achieved great success in the marketplace. In the DEFENDER game, there are symbols of a spaceship and aliens who do battle with symbols of human figures. The player operates the flight of and weapons on the spaceship, and has the mission of preventing invading aliens from kidnapping the humans from a ground plane.

[3] Williams obtained three copyright registrations relating to its DEFENDER game: one covering the computer program; the second covering the audiovisual effects displayed during the game's "attract mode"[2];

---

[2] The "attract mode" refers to the audiovisual effects displayed before a coin is inserted into the game. It repeatedly shows the name of the game, the game symbols in typical motion and interaction patterns, and the initials of previous players who have achieved high scores.

and the third covering the audiovisual effects displayed during the game's "play mode."[3] ...

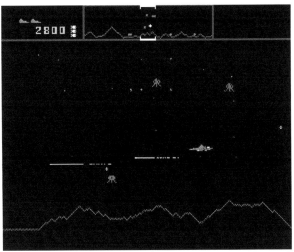

Figure 2: screenshot from Williams Electronics DEFENDER arcade game

[4] Defendant-appellant Artic International, Inc. is a seller of electronic components for video games in competition with Williams.... Artic has sold circuit boards, which contain electronic circuits including a microprocessor and memory devices (ROMs). These memory devices incorporate a computer program which is virtually identical to Williams' program for its DEFENDER game. The result is a circuit board "kit" which is sold by Artic to others and which, when connected to a cathode ray tube, produces audiovisual effects and a game almost identical to the Williams DEFENDER game including both the attract mode and the play mode. The play mode and actual play of Artic's game, entitled "DEFENSE COMMAND," is virtually identical to that of the Williams game, i.e., the characters displayed on the cathode ray tube including the player's spaceship are identical in shape, size, color, manner of movement and interaction with other symbols. Also, the attract mode of the Artic game is substantially identical to that of Williams' game, with minor exceptions such as the absence of the Williams name and the substitution of the terms "DEFENSE" and/or "DEFENSE COMMAND" for the term "DEFENDER" in its display.... [T]he district court found that the defendant Artic had infringed the plaintiff's computer program copyright for the DEFENDER game by selling kits which contain a computer program which is a copy of plaintiff's computer program, and that the defendant had infringed both of the plaintiff's audiovisual copyrights for the DEFENDER game by selling copies of those audiovisual works.

[5] In the appeal before us, defendant does not dispute the findings with respect to copying but instead challenges the conclusions of the district court with respect to copyright infringement and the validity and scope of plaintiff's copyrights....

[6] With respect to the plaintiff's two audiovisual copyrights, defendant contends that there can be no copyright protection for the DEFENDER game's attract mode and play mode because these works fail to meet the statutory requirement of "fixation." ....

[7] Defendant claims that the images in the plaintiff's audiovisual game are transient, and cannot be "fixed." Specifically, it contends that there is a lack of "fixation" because the video game generates or creates "new" images each time the attract mode or play mode is displayed, notwithstanding the fact that the new images are identical or substantially identical to the earlier ones.

---

[3] The "play mode" refers to the audiovisual effects displayed during the actual play of the game, when the game symbols move and interact on the screen, and the player controls the movement of one of the symbols (e.g., a spaceship).

[8] We reject this contention. The fixation requirement is met whenever the work is "sufficiently permanent or stable to permit it to be ... reproduced, or otherwise communicated" for more than a transitory period. Here the original audiovisual features of the DEFENDER game repeat themselves over and over.... The audiovisual work is permanently embodied in a material object, the memory devices, from which it can be perceived with the aid of the other components of the game.

[9] Defendant also apparently contends that the player's participation withdraws the game's audiovisual work from copyright eligibility because there is no set or fixed performance and the player becomes a co-author of what appears on the screen. Although there is player interaction with the machine during the play mode which causes the audiovisual presentation to change in some respects from one game to the next in response to the player's varying participation, there is always a repetitive sequence of a substantial portion of the sights and sounds of the game, and many aspects of the display remain constant from game to game regardless of how the player operates the controls. Furthermore, there is no player participation in the attract mode which is displayed repetitively without change....

[10] [T]he district court's order granting [an] injunction will be affirmed ....

NOTE

1. According to the House Report on the 1976 Act, "the definition of 'fixation' would exclude from the concept purely evanescent or transient reproductions such as those projected briefly on a screen, shown electronically on a ... cathode ray tube, or captured momentarily in the 'memory' of a computer." H.R. REP. NO. 1476, 94th Cong., 2d Sess. 47, at 53 (1976). Can you square this understanding of fixation with the decision in this case?

As you read the following case, think about how long a work must be fixed for it to meet the statutory requirement. How do digital and online technologies make this a complicated question?

Cartoon Network LP v. CSC Holdings, Inc.
536 F.3d 121 (2d Cir. 2008)

WALKER, J.:

[1] Defendant-Appellant Cablevision Systems Corporation wants to market a new "Remote Storage" Digital Video Recorder system ("RS-DVR"), using a technology akin to both traditional, set-top digital video recorders, like TiVo, and the video-on-demand ... services provided by many cable companies. Plaintiffs-Appellees produce copyrighted movies and television programs that they provide to Cablevision pursuant to numerous licensing agreements. They contend that Cablevision, through the operation of its RS-DVR system as proposed, would directly infringe their copyrights ....

[2] Today's television viewers increasingly use digital video recorders ("DVRs") instead of video cassette recorders ("VCRs") to record television programs and play them back later at their convenience. DVRs generally store recorded programming on an internal hard drive rather than a cassette. But, as this case demonstrates, the generic term "DVR" actually refers to a growing number of different devices and systems....

[3] In March 2006, Cablevision, an operator of cable television systems, announced the advent of its new "Remote Storage DVR System." As designed, the RS-DVR allows Cablevision customers who do not have a stand-alone DVR to record cable programming on central hard drives housed and maintained by Cablevision at a "remote" location. RS-DVR customers may then receive playback of those programs through their home television sets, using only a remote control and a standard cable box equipped with the RS-DVR software. Cablevision notified its content providers, including plaintiffs, of its plans to offer RS-DVR, but it did not seek any license from them to operate or sell the RS-DVR.

[4] Plaintiffs, which hold the copyrights to numerous movies and television programs, sued Cablevision for declaratory and injunctive relief. They alleged that Cablevision's proposed operation of the RS-DVR would directly infringe their exclusive rights to both reproduce and publicly perform their copyrighted works....

[5] Cable companies like Cablevision aggregate television programming from a wide variety of "content providers"—the various broadcast and cable channels that produce or provide individual programs—and transmit those programs into the homes of their subscribers via coaxial cable. At the outset of the transmission process, Cablevision gathers the content of the various television channels into a single stream of data....

[6] Under the new RS-DVR, this single stream of data is split into two streams. The first is routed immediately to customers as before. The second stream flows into a device called the Broadband Media Router ("BMR"), which buffers the data stream, reformats it, and sends it to the "Arroyo Server," which consists, in relevant part, of two data buffers and a number of high-capacity hard disks. The entire stream of data moves to the first buffer (the "primary ingest buffer"), at which point the server automatically inquires as to whether any customers want to record any of that programming. If a customer has requested a particular program, the data for that program move from the primary buffer into a secondary buffer, and then onto a portion of one of the hard disks allocated to that customer. As new data flow into the primary buffer, they overwrite a corresponding quantity of data already on the buffer. The primary ingest buffer holds no more than 0.1 seconds of each channel's programming at any moment. Thus, every tenth of a second, the data residing on this buffer are automatically erased and replaced. The data buffer in the BMR holds no more than 1.2 seconds of programming at any time. While buffering occurs at other points in the operation of the RS-DVR, only the BMR buffer and the primary ingest buffer are utilized absent any request from an individual subscriber.

[7] .... To the customer, ... the processes of recording and playback on the RS-DVR are similar to that of a standard set-top DVR. Using a remote control, the customer can record programming by selecting a program in advance from an on-screen guide, or by pressing the record button while viewing a given program.... To begin playback, the customer selects the show from an on-screen list of previously recorded programs. The principal difference in operation is that, instead of sending signals from the remote to an on-set box, the viewer sends signals from the remote, through the cable, to the Arroyo Server at Cablevision's central facility....

[8] As to the buffer data, the district court rejected defendants' argument[] that the data were not "fixed" and therefore were not "copies" as defined in the Copyright Act ....

[9] It is undisputed that Cablevision ... takes the content from one stream of programming, after the split, and stores it, one small piece at a time, in the BMR buffer and the primary ingest buffer. As a result, the information is buffered before any customer requests a recording, and would be buffered even if no such request were made. The question is whether, by buffering the data that make up a given work, Cablevision "reproduce[s]" that work "in copies," 17 U.S.C. §106(1), and thereby infringes the copyright holder's reproduction right.

[10] "Copies," as defined in the Copyright Act, "are material objects ... in which a work is fixed by any method ... and from which the work can be ... reproduced." *Id.* § 101. The Act also provides that a work is "'fixed' in a tangible medium of expression when its embodiment ... is sufficiently permanent or stable to permit it to be ... reproduced ... *for a period of more than transitory duration.*" *Id.* (emphasis added). We believe that this language plainly imposes two distinct but related requirements: the work must be embodied in a medium, i.e., placed in a medium such that it can be perceived, reproduced, etc., from that medium (the "embodiment requirement"), and it must remain thus embodied "for a period of more than transitory duration" (the "duration requirement"). Unless both requirements are met, the work is not "fixed" in the buffer, and, as a result, the buffer data is not a "copy" of the original work whose data is buffered.

[11] The district court mistakenly limited its analysis primarily to the embodiment requirement. As a result of this error, once it determined that the buffer data was "[c]learly ... capable of being reproduced," i.e., that the work was embodied in the buffer, the district court concluded that the work was therefore "fixed" in the buffer, and that a copy had thus been made. In doing so, it relied on a line of cases beginning with *MAI Systems Corp. v. Peak Computer Inc.*, 991 F.2d 511 (9th Cir. 1993) ....

[12] The district court's reliance on cases like *MAI Systems* is misplaced. In general, those cases conclude that an alleged copy is fixed without addressing the duration requirement; it does not follow, however, that those cases assume, much less establish, that such a requirement does not exist. Indeed, the duration requirement, by itself, was not at issue in *MAI Systems* and its progeny. As a result, they do not speak to the issues squarely before us here: If a work is only "embodied" in a medium for a period of transitory duration, can it be "fixed" in that medium, and thus a copy? And what constitutes a period "of more than transitory duration"?

[13] In *MAI Systems*, defendant Peak Computer, Inc., performed maintenance and repairs on computers made and sold by MAI Systems. In order to service a customer's computer, a Peak employee had to operate the computer and run the computer's copyrighted operating system software. The issue in *MAI Systems* was whether, by loading the software into the computer's RAM,[1] the repairman created a "copy" as defined in § 101. The resolution of this issue turned on whether the software's embodiment in the computer's RAM was "fixed," within the meaning of the same section. The Ninth Circuit concluded that

> by showing that Peak loads the software into the RAM and is then able to view the system error log and diagnose the problem with the computer, MAI has adequately shown that the representation created in the RAM is "sufficiently permanent or stable to permit it to be perceived, reproduced, or otherwise communicated for a period of more than transitory duration."

[14] The *MAI Systems* court referenced the "transitory duration" language but did not discuss or analyze it.... This omission suggests that the parties did not litigate the significance of the "transitory duration" language, and the court therefore had no occasion to address it. This is unsurprising, because it seems fair to assume that in these cases the program was embodied in the RAM for at least several minutes.

[15] Accordingly, we construe *MAI Systems* and its progeny as holding that loading a program into a computer's RAM can result in copying that program. We do not read *MAI Systems* as holding that, as a matter of law, loading a program into a form of RAM always results in copying. Such a holding would read the "transitory duration" language out of the definition, and we do not believe our sister circuit would dismiss this statutory language without even discussing it....

---

[1] To run a computer program, the data representing that program must be transferred from a data storage medium (such as a floppy disk or a hard drive) to a form of Random Access Memory ("RAM") where the data can be processed. The data buffers at issue here are also a form of RAM.

[16] Cablevision does not seriously dispute that copyrighted works are "embodied" in the buffer. Data in the BMR buffer can be reformatted and transmitted to the other components of the RS-DVR system. Data in the primary ingest buffer can be copied onto the Arroyo hard disks if a user has requested a recording of that data. Thus, a work's "embodiment" in either buffer "is sufficiently permanent or stable to permit it to be perceived, reproduced," (as in the case of the ingest buffer) "or otherwise communicated" (as in the BMR buffer). The result might be different if only a single second of a much longer work was placed in the buffer in isolation. In such a situation, it might be reasonable to conclude that only a minuscule portion of a work, rather than "a work" was embodied in the buffer. Here, however, where every second of an entire work is placed, one second at a time, in the buffer, we conclude that the work is embodied in the buffer.

[17] Does any such embodiment last "for a period of more than transitory duration"? No bit of data remains in any buffer for more than a fleeting 1.2 seconds. And unlike the data in cases like *MAI Systems*, which remained embodied in the computer's RAM memory until the user turned the computer off, each bit of data here is rapidly and automatically overwritten as soon as it is processed. While our inquiry is necessarily fact-specific, and other factors not present here may alter the duration analysis significantly, these facts strongly suggest that the works in this case are embodied in the buffer for only a "transitory" period, thus failing the duration requirement.

[18] Against this evidence, plaintiffs argue only that the duration is not transitory because the data persist "long enough for Cablevision to make reproductions from them." As we have explained above, however, this reasoning impermissibly reads the duration language out of the statute, and we reject it. Given that the data reside in no buffer for more than 1.2 seconds before being automatically overwritten, and in the absence of compelling arguments to the contrary, we believe that the copyrighted works here are not "embodied" in the buffers for a period of more than transitory duration, and are therefore not "fixed" in the buffers. Accordingly, the acts of buffering in the operation of the RS-DVR do not create copies, as the Copyright Act defines that term....

NOTES

1. In 2011, Victor Whitmill, the artist who had designed and tattooed the face of former boxer Mike Tyson (shown on the left in Figure 3), sued Warner Bros. Entertainment, the distributor of *The Hangover Part II* film, for copyright infringement. He claimed that Warner Bros. infringed his copyright in the tattoo artwork because actor Ed Helms's character sported a similar tattoo on his face in the movie (depicted on the right in Figure 3). Whitmill v. Warner Bros. Ent. Inc., No. 4:11-cv-752 (E.D. Mo. 2011). Warner Bros. argued that Whitmill's tattoo was not fixed as required, because a human body could not and should not be considered a "tangible medium of expression." The case settled without a determination on the question. What do you think of Warner Bros.'s argument as a statutory matter? As a policy or constitutional matter? Are there certain "negative spaces" that copyright law should not reach?

2. The multimedia messaging app Snapchat allows users to send messages, known as snaps, to selected contacts. These snaps can be viewed for between 1 and 10 seconds. After that viewing, Snapchat automatically deletes the snap. (If a snap goes unopened for 30 days, it is also automatically deleted.) Are these snaps fixed, as per copyright law?

3. Might a bowl of perishable Vietnamese food be fixed for purposes of copyright law? One district court recently said no, reasoning that "a bowl of perishable food will, by its terms, ultimately perish," and "a bowl of food which, once it spoils is gone forever, cannot be considered 'fixed.'" Kim Seng Co. v. J & A Importers, Inc., 810 F. Supp. 2d 1046, 1054 (C.D. Cal. 2011). Do you think this result is consistent with *MAI Systems* and *Cartoon Network*? Should it matter whether this bowl of food will endure longer than a program held in a computer's RAM memory, which *MAI Systems* held to be fixed?

Figure 3: Mike Tyson (left) and *The Hangover Part II* movie poster (right)

4. The Uruguay Round Agreements Act, Pub. L. No. 103-465, 108 Stat. 4809 (1994), was passed pursuant to the United States's obligation under the TRIPS Agreement that

> *In respect of a fixation of their performance on a phonogram, performers shall have the possibility of preventing the following acts when undertaken without their authorization: the fixation of their unfixed performances and the reproduction of such fixation.*

Art. 14(1). The Act provides civil and criminal liability for those who, among other things, make or distribute certain audio or video bootlegs (unauthorized copies) of live musical performances, whether or not the performance was fixed by or under the authority of the performer. This law effectively provides "copyright-like" protection to a subset of otherwise copyrightable works that are not fixed. Some criminal defendants accused of violating this Act have challenged its constitutionality, but each court to have considered this challenge has rejected it, reasoning that Congress had the authority to enact the law under the Commerce Clause, even if the Copyright and Patent Clause does not authorize the protection of unfixed works. United States v. Martignon, 492 F.3d 140, 149-52 (2d Cir. 2007); United States v. Moghadam, 175 F.3d 1269, 1280 (11th Cir. 1999); Kiss Catalog, Ltd. v. Passport Int'l Prods., Inc., 405 F. Supp. 2d 1169, 1172-74 (C.D. Cal. 2005). For a contrary view and more on whether Congress can use its other Article I powers to legislate beyond the Copyright and Patent Clause's limitations, see Jeanne C. Fromer, *The Intellectual Property Clause's External Limitations*, 61 DUKE L.J. 1329 (2012).

B. Originality

Section 102 also states that copyright protection attaches to "original works of authorship." The statute is silent as to what an "original work[] of authorship" is. The legislative history of the 1976 Act provides that

> *The phrase "original works of authorship," which is purposely left undefined, is intended to incorporate without change the standard of originality established by the courts under the [1909 Act]. This standard does not include requirements of novelty, ingenuity, or esthetic merit, and there is no intention to enlarge the standard of copyright protection to require them.*

H.R. REP. NO. 1476, 94th Cong., 2d Sess. 47, at 51 (1976). This elaboration states what the originality requirement is *not* without saying precisely what it is.

In the absence of much guidance from Congress, courts have been left to define this central term. As we will see from the cases in this section, courts locate the basis for this originality requirement in the U.S. Constitution's grant of power to Congress to create copyright laws "by securing for limited Times to *Authors* ... the exclusive Right to their ... *Writings*." U.S. CONST. art. I, § 8, cl. 8 (emphases added).

1. Classic Cases

What follows are three classic pre-1976 opinions on originality. These cases set the stage for the Supreme Court's post-1976 definition of originality in *Feist Publications, Inc. v. Rural Telephone Service Co.*, 499 U.S. 340 (1991), which we will read following these important early articulations of the originality standard.

> As you read the next three cases, consider how the different types of works that are at issue—photographs, advertisements containing drawings, and mezzotint versions of paintings—challenge what we understand to be "original." Do all three courts adopt the same or different definitions of originality? If different, how do they differ? Is the originality requirement a stringent one?

Burrow-Giles Lithographic Co. v. Napoleon Sarony
111 U.S. 53 (1884)

MILLER, J.:

[1] .... The suit was commenced by an action at law in which Sarony was plaintiff and the lithographic company was defendant, the plaintiff charging the defendant with violating his copyright in regard to a photograph, the title of which is 'Oscar Wilde, No. 18.' ....

[2] The constitutional question [whether Congress could provide copyright protection for photographs] is not free from difficulty. The eighth section of the first article of the [C]onstitution is the great repository of the powers of [C]ongress, and by the eight[h] clause of that section [C]ongress is authorized "to promote the progress of science and useful arts, by securing, for limited times to authors and inventors the exclusive right to their respective writings and discoveries." The argument here is that a photograph is not a writing nor the production of an author.... It is insisted, in argument, that a photograph being a reproduction, on paper, of the exact features of some natural object, or of some person, is not a writing of which the producer is the author. [The federal statute] places photographs in the same class as things which may be copyrighted with "books, maps, charts, dramatic or musical compositions, engravings, cuts, prints, paintings, drawings, statues, statuary, and models or designs intended to be perfected as works of the fine arts."...

[3] The first [C]ongress of the United States, sitting immediately after the formation of the constitution, enacted that the "author or authors of any map, chart, book, or books, being a citizen or resident of the United States, shall have the sole right and liberty of printing, reprinting, publishing, and vending the same for the period of fourteen years from the recording of the title thereof in the clerk's office, as afterwards directed." This statute not only makes maps and charts subjects of copyright, but mentions them before books in the order of designation. The second section of an act to amend this act, approved April 29, 1802, enacts that ... thereafter he who shall invent and design, engrave, etch, or work, or from his own works shall

cause to be designed and engraved, etched, or worked, any historical or other print or prints, shall have the same exclusive right for the term of 14 years from recording the title thereof as prescribed by law....

Figure 4: Sarony's photograph of Oscar Wilde

[4] The construction placed upon the [C]onstitution by the first act of 1790 and the act of 1802, by the men who were contemporary with its formation, many of whom were members of the convention which framed it, is of itself entitled to very great weight, and when it is remembered that the rights thus established have not been disputed during a period of nearly a century, it is almost conclusive. Unless, therefore, photographs can be distinguished in the classification of this point from the maps, charts, designs, engravings, etchings, cuts, and other prints, it is difficult to see why [C]ongress cannot make them the subject of copyright as well as the others. These statutes certainly answer the objection that books only, or writing, in the limited sense of a book and its author, are within the constitutional provision. Both these words are susceptible of a more enlarged definition than this. An author in that sense is he to whom anything owes its origin; originator; maker; one who completes a work of science or literature. So, also, no one would now claim that the word 'writing' in this clause of the constitution, though the only word used as to subjects in regard to which authors are to be secured, is limited to the actual script of the author, and excludes books and all other printed matter. By writings in that clause is meant the literary productions of those authors, and [C]ongress very properly has declared these to include all forms of writing, printing, engravings, etchings, etc., by which the ideas in the mind of the author are given visible expression. The only reason why photographs were not included in the extended list in the act of 1802 is, probably, that they did not exist, as photography, as an art, was then unknown, and the scientific principle on which it rests, and the chemicals and machinery by which it is operated, have all been discovered long since that statute was enacted....

[5] We entertain no doubt that the [C]onstitution is broad enough to cover an act authorizing copyright of photographs, so far as they are representatives of original intellectual conceptions of the author.

[6] But it is said that an engraving, a painting, a print, does embody the intellectual conception of its author, in which there is novelty, invention, originality, and therefore comes within the purpose of the constitution in securing its exclusive use or sale to its author, while a photograph is the mere mechanical reproduction of the physical features or outlines of some object, animate or inanimate, and involves no originality of thought or any novelty in the intellectual operation connected with its visible reproduction in shape of a picture. That while the effect of light on the prepared plate may have been a discovery in the production of these pictures, and patents could properly be obtained for the combination of the chemicals, for their application to the paper or other surface, for all the machinery by which the light reflected from the object was thrown on the prepared plate, and for all the improvements in this machinery, and in the materials, the remainder of the process is merely mechanical, with no place for novelty, invention, or originality. It is simply the manual operation, by the use of these instruments and preparations, of transferring to the plate the visible representation of some existing object, the accuracy of this representation being its highest merit. This may be true in regard to the ordinary production of a photograph, and that in such case a copyright is no protection. On the question as thus stated we decide nothing....

[7] The [circuit court found], in regard to the photograph in question, that it is a "useful, new, harmonious, characteristic, and graceful picture, and that plaintiff made the same ... entirely from his own original mental conception, to which he gave visible form by posing the said Oscar Wilde in front of the camera, selecting and arranging the costume, draperies, and other various accessories in said photograph, arranging the subject so as to present graceful outlines, arranging and disposing the light and shade, suggesting and evoking the desired expression, and from such disposition, arrangement, or representation, made entirely by plaintiff, he produced the picture in suit." These findings, we think, show this photograph to be an original work of art, the product of plaintiff's intellectual invention, of which plaintiff is the author, and of a class of [creations] for which the [C]onstitution intended that [C]ongress should secure to him the exclusive right to use, publish, and sell, as it has done by [statute]....

George Bleistein v. Donaldson Lithographing Co.
188 U.S. 239 (1903)

HOLMES, J.:

[1] .... The alleged infringements consisted in the copying in reduced form of three chromolithographs prepared by employees of the plaintiffs for advertisements of a circus owned by one Wallace. Each of the three contained a portrait of Wallace in the corner, and lettering bearing some slight relation to the scheme of decoration, indicating the subject of the design and the fact that the reality was to be seen at the circus. One of the designs was of an ordinary ballet, one of a number of men and women, described as the Stirk family, performing on bicycles, and one of groups of men and women whitened to represent statues. The circuit court directed a verdict for the defendant on the ground that the chromolithographs were not within the protection of the copyright law, and this ruling was sustained by the circuit court of appeals....

[2] .... [T]he plaintiff's case is not affected by the fact, if it be one, that the pictures represent actual groups—visible things. They seem from the testimony to have been composed from hints or description, not from sight of a performance. But even if they had been drawn from the life, that fact would not deprive them of protection. The opposite proposition would mean that a portrait by Velasquez or Whistler was common property because others might try their hand on the same face. Others are free to copy the original. They are not free to copy the copy. The copy is the personal reaction of an individual upon nature. Personality always contains something unique. It expresses its singularity even in handwriting, and a very modest grade of art

has in it something irreducible, which is one man's alone. That something he may copyright unless there is a restriction in the words of the act....

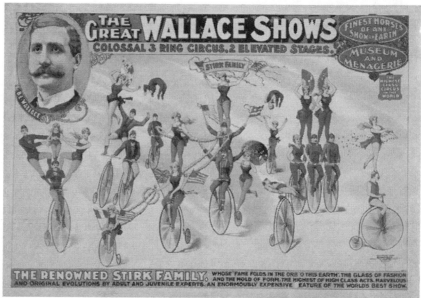

Figure 5: one of Bleistein's three circus posters

[3] We assume that the construction of [the statute] allowing a copyright to the "author, designer, or proprietor ... of any engraving, cut, print ... [or] chromo" is affected by the .... section [which] provides that, "in the construction of this act, the words 'engraving,' 'cut,' and 'print' shall be applied only to pictorial illustrations or works connected with the fine arts."...

[4] These chromolithographs are "pictorial illustrations."... [T]he act ... does not mean that ordinary posters are not good enough to be considered within its scope. The antithesis to "illustrations or works connected with the fine arts" is not works of little merit or of humble degree, or illustrations addressed to the less educated classes .... Certainly works are not the less connected with the fine arts because their pictorial quality attracts the crowd, and therefore gives them a real use—if use means to increase trade and to help to make money. A picture is none the less a picture, and none the less a subject of copyright, that it is used for an advertisement. And if pictures may be used to advertise soap, or the theatre, or monthly magazines, as they are, they may be used to advertise a circus. Of course, the ballet is as legitimate a subject for illustration as any other. A rule cannot be laid down that would excommunicate the paintings of Degas.

[5] Finally, the special adaptation of these pictures to the advertisement of the Wallace shows does not prevent a copyright....

[6] It would be a dangerous undertaking for persons trained only to the law to constitute themselves final judges of the worth of pictorial illustrations, outside of the narrowest and most obvious limits. At the one extreme, some works of genius would be sure to miss appreciation. Their very novelty would make them repulsive until the public had learned the new language in which their author spoke. It may be more than doubted, for instance, whether the etchings of Goya or the paintings of Manet would have been sure of protection when seen for the first time. At the other end, copyright would be denied to pictures which appealed to a public less educated than the judge. Yet if they command the interest of any public, they have a commercial value—it would be bold to say that they have not an aesthetic and educational value—and the taste of any public is not to be treated with contempt. It is an ultimate fact for the moment, whatever may be our hopes for a change. That these pictures had their worth and their success is sufficiently shown by the

desire to reproduce them without regard to the plaintiffs' rights. We are of opinion that there was evidence that the plaintiffs have rights entitled to the protection of the law....

Alfred Bell & Co. v. Catalda Fine Arts
191 F.2d 99 (2d Cir. 1951)

FRANK, J.:

{The plaintiff, a British print producer and dealer, copyrighted in the United States eight mezzotint engravings of well-known paintings from the eighteenth and nineteenth centuries produced at its order by mezzotint engravers. Mezzotint was once a popular process for reproducing paintings by engraving a copper or steel plate that uses, among other things, roughening for shading and smoothing for light areas. The defendants, a color lithographer and a dealer in lithographs, produced and sold color lithographs of these mezzotints. The plaintiff sued for copyright infringement.} ...

Figure 6: original (left) and mezzotint (right) of Thomas Gainsborough's "The Blue Boy"

[1] The defendants' contention apparently results from the ambiguity of the word "original." It may mean startling, novel or unusual, a marked departure from the past.... [By contrast,] "[o]riginal" in reference to a copyrighted work means that the particular work owes its origin to the author. No large measure of novelty is necessary....

[2] .... All that is needed to satisfy both the Constitution and the statute is that the author contributed something more than a merely trivial variation, something recognizably his own. Originality in this context means little more than a prohibition of actual copying. No matter how poor artistically the "author's" addition, it is enough if it be his own. Bleistein v. Donaldson Lithographing Co., 188 U.S. 239, 250 (1903) ....

[3] We consider untenable defendants' suggestion that plaintiff's mezzotints could not validly be copyrighted because they are reproductions of works in the public domain. Not only does the Act include "Reproductions of a work or art," but ... it explicitly provides for the copyrighting of "translations, or other versions of works in the public domain." The mezzotints were such "versions." They "originated" with those who make them,

and ... amply met the standards imposed by the Constitution and the statute.[22] There is evidence that they were not intended to, and did not, imitate the paintings they reproduced. But even if their substantial departures from the paintings were inadvertent, the copyrights would be valid. A copyist's bad eyesight or defective musculature, or a shock caused by a clap of thunder, may yield sufficiently distinguishable variations. Having hit upon such a variation unintentionally, the "author" may adopt it as his and copyright it....

NOTES

1. Consider Justice Holmes's admonition above in *Bleistein*: "It would be a dangerous undertaking for persons trained only to the law to constitute themselves final judges of the work of pictorial illustrations, outside the narrowest and most obvious limits." This assertion is well-known (it is referred to frequently as the *Bleistein* "nondiscrimination principle") and is often invoked in copyright law to state that copyright law should not make its protections depend on the aesthetic worth of the work at issue. That is, there should be no need for aesthetic judgments in copyright law. Is that the natural understanding of what Holmes wrote in *Bleistein*? Keep this principle in mind moving forward, and query whether the opinions excerpted in this book comply with this principle. On whether the copyright statute encodes a nondiscrimination principle and how practically this principle can be enforced, see Amy B. Cohen, *Copyright Law and the Myth of Objectivity: The Idea-Expression Dichotomy and the Inevitability of Artistic Value Judgments*, 66 IND. L.J. 175 (1990), and Robert Kirk Walker & Ben Depoorter, *Unavoidable Aesthetic Judgments in Copyright Law: A Community of Practice Standard*, 109 NW. U. L. REV. 343 (2015). For a reevaluation of Holmes's admonition in *Bleistein* and other aspects of the decision, see Barton Beebe, Bleistein, *the Problem of Aesthetic Progress, and the Making of American Copyright Law*, 117 COLUM. L. REV. 319 (2017).

2. Does *Alfred Bell* suggest that replicas of works in the public domain are always original? If not, what about replicas that have inadvertent minor changes due to the difficulties of replicating with precision?

3. One way to think about originality is by focusing on the work itself. Another way to think about originality is by focusing on the process of creating that work. Do these two different foci yield different results as to whether a work is original? If so, is one more consistent with copyright's utilitarian approach? Lockean labor theory? Kantian/Hegelian personhood theory?

---

[22] *See* COPINGER, THE LAW OF COPYRIGHTS 46 (7th ed. 1936): "Again, an engraver is almost invariably a copyist, but although his work may infringe copyright in the original painting if made without the consent of the owner of the copyright therein, his work may still be original in the sense that he has employed skill and judgment in its production. He produces the resemblance he is desirous of obtaining by means very different from those employed by the painter or draughtsman from whom he copies: means which require great labour and talent. The engraver produces his effects by the management of light and shade, or, as the term of his art expresses it, the chiarooscuro. The due degrees of light and shade are produced by different lines and dots; he who is the engraver must decide on the choice of the different lines or dots for himself, and on his choice depends the success of his print."

2. Contemporary Cases

Fast forward now to the originality requirement as it currently is articulated in § 102 pursuant to the 1976 Act. In reading through the Supreme Court's pronouncement of how to understand the originality requirement under the 1976 Act, consider whether *Burrow-Giles, Bleistein*, and *Alfred Bell* remain good law after this decision. If not, how does the rule articulated here differ? Which theory of copyright law does the Court adopt?

Feist Publications, Inc. v. Rural Telephone Service Co.
499 U.S. 340 (1991)

O'CONNOR, J.:

[1] This case requires us to clarify the extent of copyright protection available to telephone directory white pages.

[2] Rural Telephone Service Company, Inc., is a certified public utility that provides telephone service to several communities in northwest Kansas. It is subject to a state regulation that requires all telephone companies operating in Kansas to issue annually an updated telephone directory. Accordingly, as a condition of its monopoly franchise, Rural publishes a typical telephone directory …. The white pages list in alphabetical order the names of Rural's subscribers, together with their towns and telephone numbers…. Rural distributes its directory free of charge to its subscribers ….

[3] Feist Publications, Inc., is a publishing company that specializes in area-wide telephone directories. Unlike a typical directory, which covers only a particular calling area, Feist's area-wide directories cover a much larger geographical range, reducing the need to call directory assistance or consult multiple directories. The Feist directory that is the subject of this litigation covers 11 different telephone service areas in 15 counties and contains 46,878 white pages listings—compared to Rural's approximately 7,700 listings. Like Rural's directory, Feist's is distributed free of charge ….

[4] As the sole provider of telephone service in its service area, Rural obtains subscriber information quite easily. Persons desiring telephone service must apply to Rural and provide their names and addresses; Rural then assigns them a telephone number. Feist is not a telephone company, let alone one with monopoly status, and therefore lacks independent access to any subscriber information. To obtain white pages listings for its area-wide directory, Feist approached each of the 11 telephone companies operating in northwest Kansas and offered to pay for the right to use its white pages listings.

[5] Of the 11 telephone companies, only Rural refused to license its listings to Feist. Rural's refusal created a problem for Feist, as omitting these listings would have left a gaping hole in its area-wide directory ….

[6] Unable to license Rural's white pages listings, Feist used them without Rural's consent. Feist began by removing several thousand listings that fell outside the geographic range of its area-wide directory, then hired personnel to investigate the 4,935 that remained. These employees verified the data reported by Rural and sought to obtain additional information. As a result, a typical Feist listing includes the individual's street address; most of Rural's listings do not. Notwithstanding these additions, however, 1,309 of the 46,878 listings in Feist's 1983 directory were identical to listings in Rural's 1982–1983 white pages. Four of these were fictitious listings that Rural had inserted into its directory to detect copying.

[7] Rural sued for copyright infringement ....

[8] The *sine qua non* of copyright is originality. To qualify for copyright protection, a work must be original to the author. Original, as the term is used in copyright, means only that the work was independently created by the author (as opposed to copied from other works), and that it possesses at least some minimal degree of creativity. To be sure, the requisite level of creativity is extremely low; even a slight amount will suffice. The vast majority of works make the grade quite easily, as they possess some creative spark, no matter how crude, humble or obvious it might be. Originality does not signify novelty; a work may be original even though it closely resembles other works so long as the similarity is fortuitous, not the result of copying. To illustrate, assume that two poets, each ignorant of the other, compose identical poems. Neither work is novel, yet both are original and, hence, copyrightable.

[9] Originality is a constitutional requirement. The source of Congress' power to enact copyright laws is Article I, §8, cl. 8, of the Constitution, which authorizes Congress to "secur[e] for limited Times to Authors ... the exclusive Right to their respective Writings." In two decisions from the late 19th century—[one being] *Burrow-Giles Lithographic Co. v. Sarony*, 111 U.S. 53 (1884)—this Court defined the crucial terms "authors" and "writings." In so doing, the Court made it unmistakably clear that these terms presuppose a degree of originality....

[10] The originality requirement articulated in [those cases] remains the touchstone of copyright protection today....

[11] It is this bedrock principle of copyright that mandates the law's seemingly disparate treatment of facts and factual compilations. No one may claim originality as to facts. This is because facts do not owe their origin to an act of authorship. The distinction is one between creation and discovery: The first person to find and report a particular fact has not created the fact; he or she has merely discovered its existence. To borrow from *Burrow-Giles*, one who discovers a fact is not its "maker" or "originator." The discoverer merely finds and records. Census takers, for example, do not "create" the population figures that emerge from their efforts; in a sense, they copy these figures from the world around them. Census data therefore do not trigger copyright because these data are not "original" in the constitutional sense. The same is true of all facts—scientific, historical, biographical, and news of the day. They may not be copyrighted and are part of the public domain available to every person.

[12] Factual compilations, on the other hand, may possess the requisite originality. The compilation author typically chooses which facts to include, in what order to place them, and how to arrange the collected data so that they may be used effectively by readers. These choices as to selection and arrangement, so long as they are made independently by the compiler and entail a minimal degree of creativity, are sufficiently original that Congress may protect such compilations through the copyright laws. Thus, even a directory that contains absolutely no protectible written expression, only facts, meets the constitutional minimum for copyright protection if it features an original selection or arrangement....

[13] This inevitably means that the copyright in a factual compilation is thin. Notwithstanding a valid copyright, a subsequent compiler remains free to use the facts contained in another's publication to aid in preparing a competing work, so long as the competing work does not feature the same selection and arrangement....

[14] It may seem unfair that much of the fruit of the compiler's labor may be used by others without compensation.... [H]owever, this is not some unforeseen byproduct of a statutory scheme. It is, rather, the essence of copyright and a constitutional requirement. The primary objective of copyright is not to reward the labor of authors, but "[t]o promote the Progress of Science and useful Arts." Art. I, §8, cl. 8.... As applied to a

factual compilation, assuming the absence of original written expression, only the compiler's selection and arrangement may be protected; the raw facts may be copied at will. This result is neither unfair nor unfortunate. It is the means by which copyright advances the progress of science and art....

[15] This, then, resolves the doctrinal tension: Copyright treats facts and factual compilations in a wholly consistent manner. Facts, whether alone or as part of a compilation, are not original and therefore may not be copyrighted. A factual compilation is eligible for copyright if it features an original selection or arrangement of facts, but the copyright is limited to the particular selection or arrangement. In no event may copyright extend to the facts themselves....

[16] [Some] courts developed a new theory to justify the protection of factual compilations. Known alternatively as "sweat of the brow" or "industrious collection," the underlying notion was that copyright was a reward for the hard work that went into compiling facts....

[17] The "sweat of the brow" doctrine had numerous flaws, the most glaring being that it extended copyright protection in a compilation beyond selection and arrangement—the compiler's original contributions—to the facts themselves....

[18] ... [T]he Copyright Act leave[s] no doubt that originality, not "sweat of the brow," is the touchstone of copyright protection ....

{We return to the copyrightability of the telephone directory listings here below in section C, when we address compilations specifically.}

NOTES

1. In considering the requirement of independent creation that *Feist* articulates, contemplate Judge Learned Hand's statement on the matter: "[I]f by some magic a man who had never known it were to compose anew Keats's *Ode on a Grecian Urn*, he would be an 'author,' and, if he copyrighted it, others might not copy that poem, though they might of course copy Keats's." Sheldon v. Metro-Goldwyn Pictures Corp., 81 F.2d 49, 54 (2d Cir. 1936). How likely is it that someone would independently create Keats's poem? If unlikely, is Hand's statement of any help? Can you explain the rule of independent creation in relation to the utilitarian, Lockean labor, and Kantian/Hegelian personality copyright theories?

2. In *Feist*, the Court states that "the requisite level of creativity is extremely low; even a slight amount will suffice." Compare this threshold requirement to that of patent law, which requires that an invention be both novel and nonobvious to be protectable. 35 U.S.C. §§ 102-103. The requisite level of creativity for an invention to be patentable is much higher. Does copyright law's lower threshold set a target for creativity that results in creators barely clearing the bar? And if the target were set higher, would creators be encouraged to produce more creative work? Some scholars think so. Joseph Scott Miller, *Hoisting Originality*, 31 CARDOZO L. REV. 451, 463-64 (2009); Gideon Parchomovsky & Alex Stein, *Originality*, 95 VA. L. REV. 1505, 1506 (2009). They propose that copyright's creativity threshold be raised to encourage production of more creative works. Others suggest that raising the creativity threshold would require too much undesirable assessment of aesthetic merit or would run counter to how much creativity consumers actually want from artistic and cultural works. Jeanne C. Fromer, *A Psychology of Intellectual Property*, 104 NW. U. L. REV. 1441, 1492-1501 (2010); Erlend Lavik & Stef van Gompel, *On the Prospects of Raising the Originality Requirement in Copyright Law: Perspectives from the Humanities*, 60 J. COPYRIGHT SOC'Y USA 387, 423-24 (2013). There is also empirical work that suggests that providing extrinsic incentives to people to act creatively counterproductively makes them less likely to produce creative works than those without such incentives. Teresa M. Amabile, *Effects of External Evaluation on Artistic Creativity*, 37 J. PERSONALITY & SOC. PSYCHOL. 221, 222 (1979). On the other hand,

an experimental study of creativity thresholds in the context of intellectual property provides evidence that raising the creativity threshold does in fact significantly increase the creativity of the resulting work. Christopher Buccafusco, Zachary C. Burns, Jeanne C. Fromer & Christopher Jon Sprigman, *Experimental Tests of Intellectual Property Laws' Creativity Thresholds*, 92 TEX. L. REV. 1921 (2014).

Think about copyright law's goals. Does keeping the creativity threshold lower or higher better support them? Do we want to encourage the creation of ever more works? Do we want to encourage only works that contribute to aesthetic progress? For more on these questions, see Barton Beebe, Bleistein, *The Problem of Aesthetic Progress, and the Making of American Copyright Law*, 117 COLUM. L. REV. 319 (2017); Jeanne C. Fromer, *An Information Theory of Copyright Law*, 64 EMORY L.J. 71 (2014); Jake Linford, *Copyright and Attention Scarcity*, 41 CARDOZO L. REV. 143 (2020).

3. The 1790 Act discussed in Chapter I covered maps, charts, and books. We just saw in *Feist* that copyright protects certain forms of creative expression, but does not protect facts. But are maps and charts not "facts"? Or, more precisely, do they not represent facts? What elements of a map or chart do you think might be copyrightable expression? For more on these questions, see Isabella Alexander, *Cartography, Empire and Copyright Law in Colonial Australia*, 5 LAW & HISTORY 24 (2018).

To explore more fully the implications of *Feist*, consider this post-*Feist* decision. What role, if any, does a creator's intent play in assessing originality? How do you reconcile this decision with *Alfred Bell*?

Meshwerks, Inc. v. Toyota Motor Sales U.S.A., Inc.
528 F.3d 1258 (10th Cir. 2008)

GORSUCH, J.:

[1] This case calls on us to apply copyright principles to ... digital modeling....

[2] In 2003, and in conjunction with Saatchi & Saatchi, its advertising agency, Toyota began work on its model-year 2004 advertising campaign. Saatchi and Toyota agreed that the campaign would involve, among other things, digital models of Toyota's vehicles for use on Toyota's website and in various other media. These digital models have substantial advantages over the product photographs for which they substitute. With a few clicks of a computer mouse, the advertiser can change the color of the car, its surroundings, and even edit its physical dimensions to portray changes in vehicle styling; before this innovation, advertisers had to conduct new photo shoots of whole fleets of vehicles each time the manufacturer made even a small design change to a car or truck.

[3] To supply these digital models, Saatchi and Toyota hired Grace & Wild, Inc. ("G & W"). In turn, G & W subcontracted with Meshwerks to assist with two initial aspects of the project—digitization and modeling. Digitizing involves collecting physical data points from the object to be portrayed. In the case of Toyota's vehicles, Meshwerks took copious measurements of Toyota's vehicles by covering each car, truck, and van with a grid of tape and running an articulated arm tethered to a computer over the vehicle to measure all points of intersection in the grid. Based on these measurements, modeling software then generated a digital image resembling a wire-frame model. In other words, the vehicles' data points (measurements) were

mapped onto a computerized grid and the modeling software connected the dots to create a "wire frame" of each vehicle.

[4] At this point, however, the on-screen image remained far from perfect and manual "modeling" was necessary. Meshwerks personnel fine-tuned or, as the company prefers it, "sculpted," the lines on screen to resemble each vehicle as closely as possible. Approximately 90 percent of the data points contained in each final model, Meshwerks represents, were the result not of the first-step measurement process, but of the skill and effort its digital sculptors manually expended at the second step. For example, some areas of detail, such as wheels, headlights, door handles, and the Toyota emblem, could not be accurately measured using current technology; those features had to be added at the second "sculpting" stage, and Meshwerks had to recreate those features as realistically as possible by hand, based on photographs. Even for areas that were measured, Meshwerks faced the challenge of converting measurements taken of a three-dimensional car into a two-dimensional computer representation; to achieve this, its modelers had to sculpt, or move, data points to achieve a visually convincing result. The purpose and product of these processes, after nearly 80 to 100 hours of effort per vehicle, were two-dimensional wire-frame depictions of Toyota's vehicles that appeared three-dimensional on screen, but were utterly unadorned-lacking color, shading, and other details....

[5] With Meshwerks' wire-frame products in hand, G & W then manipulated the computerized models by, first, adding detail, the result of which appeared on screen as a "tightening" of the wire frames, as though significantly more wires had been added to the frames, or as though they were made of a finer mesh. Next, G & W digitally applied color, texture, lighting, and animation for use in Toyota's advertisements.... G & W's digital models were then sent to Saatchi to be employed in a number of advertisements prepared by Saatchi and Toyota in various print, online, and television media....

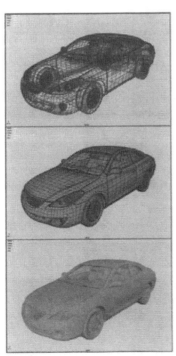 

Figure 7: Meshwerks digital wire-frame models (left) and Toyota finished digital model (right)

[6] This dispute arose because, according to Meshwerks, it contracted with G & W for only a single use of its models—as part of one Toyota television commercial—and neither Toyota nor any other defendant was allowed to use the digital models created from Meshwerks' wire-frames in other advertisements. Thus, Meshwerks contends defendants improperly—in violation of copyright laws as well as the parties' agreement—reused and redistributed the models created by Meshwerks in a host of other media....

[7] In due course, defendants moved for summary judgment on the theory that Meshwerks' wire-frame models lacked sufficient originality to be protected by copyright. Specifically, defendants argued that any original expression found in Meshwerks' products was attributable to the Toyota designers who conceived of the vehicle designs in the first place; accordingly, defendants' use of the models could not give rise to a claim for copyright infringement.

[8] The district court agreed....

[9] The parties focus most of their energy in this case on the question whether Meshwerks' models qualify as independent creations, as opposed to copies of Toyota's handiwork. But what can be said, at least based on received copyright doctrine, to distinguish an independent creation from a copy? And how might that doctrine apply in an age of virtual worlds and digital media that seek to mimic the "real" world, but often do so in ways that undoubtedly qualify as (highly) original? While there is little authority explaining how our received principles of copyright law apply to the relatively new digital medium before us, some lessons may be discerned from how the law coped in an earlier time with a previous revolution in technology: photography....

[10] Applying these principles, evolved in the realm of photography, to the new medium that has come to supplement and even in some ways to supplant it, we think Meshwerks' models are not so much independent creations as (very good) copies of Toyota's vehicles. In reaching this conclusion we rely on (1) an objective assessment of the particular models before us and (2) the parties' purpose in creating them. All the same, we do not doubt for an instant that the digital medium before us, like photography before it, can be employed to create vivid new expressions fully protectable in copyright....

[11] Key to our evaluation of this case is the fact that Meshwerks' digital wire-frame computer models depict Toyota's vehicles without any individualizing features: they are untouched by a digital paintbrush; they are not depicted in front of a palm tree, whizzing down the open road, or climbing up a mountainside. Put another way, Meshwerks' models depict nothing more than unadorned Toyota vehicles—the car as car. And the unequivocal lesson from *Feist* is that works are not copyrightable to the extent they do not involve any expression apart from the raw facts in the world. As Professor Nimmer has commented in connection with the predecessor technology of photography, "[a]s applied to a photograph of a pre-existing product, that bedrock principle [of originality] means that the photographer manifestly cannot claim to have originated the matter depicted therein.... The upshot is that the photographer is entitled to copyright solely based on lighting, angle, perspective, and the other ingredients that traditionally apply to that art-form." Nimmer on Copyright § 3.03[C][3]. It seems to us that exactly the same holds true with the digital medium now before us: the facts in this case unambiguously show that Meshwerks did not make any decisions regarding lighting, shading, the background in front of which a vehicle would be posed, the angle at which to pose it, or the like—in short, its models reflect none of the decisions that can make depictions of things or facts in the world, whether Oscar Wilde or a Toyota Camry, new expressions subject to copyright protection....

[12] ... [W]e hold that the unadorned images of Toyota's vehicles cannot be copyrighted by Meshwerks and ... must be filtered out. To the extent that Meshwerks' digital wire-frame models depict only those unadorned vehicles, having stripped away all lighting, angle, perspective, and "other ingredients" associated with an original expression, we conclude that they have left no copyrightable matter.

[13] Confirming this conclusion as well is the peculiar place where Meshwerks stood in the model-creation pecking order. On the one hand, Meshwerks had nothing to do with designing the appearance of Toyota's vehicles, distinguishing them from any other cars, trucks, or vans in the world. That expressive creation took place before Meshwerks happened along, and was the result of work done by Toyota and its designers .... On the other hand, how the models Meshwerks created were to be deployed in advertising—including the backgrounds, lighting, angles, and colors—were all matters left to those ... who came after Meshwerks left the scene. Meshwerks thus played a narrow, if pivotal, role in the process by simply, if effectively, copying Toyota's vehicles into a digital medium so they could be expressively manipulated by others.[8]

[14] Were we to afford copyright protection in this case, we would run aground on one of the bedrock principles of copyright law—namely, that originality, "as the term is used in copyright, means only that the work was independently created by the author *(as opposed to copied from other works)*." *Feist*, 499 U.S. at 345 (emphasis added). Because our copyright laws protect only "original" expression, the reason for refusing copyright protection to copies is clear, since obviously a copier is not a creator, much less an "independent" creator....

[15] It is certainly true that what Meshwerks accomplished was a peculiar kind of copying. It did not seek to recreate Toyota vehicles outright—steel, rubber, and all; instead, it sought to depict Toyota's three-dimensional physical objects in a two-dimensional digital medium. But we hold, as many before us have already suggested, that, standing alone, the fact that a work in one medium has been copied from a work in another medium does not render it any the less a "copy." After all, the putative creator who merely shifts the medium in which another's creation is expressed has not necessarily added anything beyond the expression contained in the original.

[16] In reaching this conclusion, we do not for a moment seek to downplay the considerable amount of time, effort, and skill that went into making Meshwerks' digital wire-frame models. But, in assessing the originality of a work for which copyright protection is sought, we look only at the final product, not the process, and the fact that intensive, skillful, and even creative labor is invested in the process of creating a product does not guarantee its copyrightability....

[17] Meshwerks' intent in making its wire-frame models provides additional support for our conclusion.... If an artist affirmatively sets out to be unoriginal—to make a copy of someone else's creation, rather than to create an original work—it is far more likely that the resultant product will, in fact, be unoriginal. Of course, this is not to say that the accidental or spontaneous artist will be denied copyright protection for not intending to produce art; it is only to say that authorial intent sometimes can shed light on the question of whether a particular work qualifies as an independent creation or only a copy.

[18] In this case, the undisputed evidence before us leaves no question that Meshwerks set out to copy Toyota's vehicles, rather than to create, or even to add, any original expression. The purchase order signed by G & W asked Meshwerks to "digitize and model" Toyota's vehicles, and Meshwerks' invoice submitted to G & W for payment reflects that this is exactly the service Meshwerks performed. Meshwerks itself has consistently described digitization and modeling as an attempt accurately to depict real-world, three-dimensional objects as digital images viewable on a computer screen. The parties thus intended to have Meshwerks create base-layer digital models to which the original and creative elements viewers would see in actual advertisements could be added by others in subsequent processes....

---

[8] We are not called upon to, and do not, express any view on the copyrightability of the work products produced by those who employed and adorned Meshwerks' models.

Chapter II – Subject Matter

[19] Although we hold that Meshwerks' digital, wire-frame models are insufficiently original to warrant copyright protection, we do not turn a blind eye to the fact that digital imaging is a relatively new and evolving technology and that Congress extended copyright protection to "original works of authorship fixed in any tangible medium of expression, *now known or later developed*." 17 U.S.C. § 102(a) (emphasis added). A Luddite might make the mistake of suggesting that digital modeling, as was once said of photography, allows for nothing more than "mechanical reproduction of the physical features or outlines of some object ... and involves no originality of thought or any novelty in the intellectual operation connected with its visible reproduction in the shape of a picture." *Burrow-Giles*, 111 U.S. at 59. Clearly, this is not so.

[20] Digital modeling can be, surely is being, and no doubt increasingly will be used to create copyrightable expressions. Yet, just as photographs can be, but are not per se, copyrightable, the same holds true for digital models. There's little question that digital models can be devised of Toyota cars with copyrightable features, whether by virtue of unique shading, lighting, angle, background scene, or other choices. The problem for Meshwerks in this particular case is simply that the uncontested facts reveal that it wasn't involved in any such process, and indeed contracted to provide completely unadorned digital replicas of Toyota vehicles in a two-dimensional space. For this reason, we do not envision any "chilling effect" on creative expression based on our holding today, and instead see it as applying to digital modeling the same legal principles that have come, in the fullness of time and with an enlightened eye, to apply to photographs and other media....

NOTES

1. What if Meshwerks had created these same works instead for an art show (perhaps to comment on the role of technology or the car in society)? Consider Marcel Duchamp's Fountain in Figure 8, which is made up of a pre-existing porcelain urinal that he signed "R. Mutt." Is that work original, as per *Meshwerks*?

Figure 8: Marcel Duchamp's *Fountain*

2. Consider the originality of photographs in light of *Burrow-Giles* and *Meshwerks*. Pictured in Figure 9 is Thomas Mangelsen's photograph *Catch of the Day*, which captures a salmon jumping into the gaping mouth of a brown bear in a national park in Alaska. How is this photograph different than the one at issue in *Burrow-*

Giles? What, if anything, makes, Mangelsen's photograph original? More generally, are there different ways in which photographs can be original?

Figure 9: Thomas Mangelsen's *Catch of the Day*

3. In recent years, the Copyright Office has refused to issue copyright registration in various instances involving business logos, including the Tommy Hilfiger flag logo shown on the left in Figure 10, as well as other works, such as the Fuck Snow Globe shown on the right in Figure 10.

Figure 10: Tommy Hilfiger flag logo (left) and Fuck Snow Globe (right)

In these instances, the Copyright Office and its Review Board have stated that these works' respective combinations of commonplace geometric shapes, coloring, or wording are not original under *Feist*. Do you agree? As you proceed through this book, ponder why a business might want copyright protection for its logo in addition to trademark protection, which it presumably could have.

4. The Copyright Office has also issued bright-line regulations that certain material is "not subject to copyright" and therefore "applications for registration of such works cannot be entertained." 37 C.F.R. § 202.1. On this list is "[w]ords and short phrases such as names, titles, and slogans," as well as "mere listing of ingredients or contents." Is it true that these categories of works always lack the requisite modicum of creativity? By contrast to the Copyright Office, some courts have ruled that such material might sometimes be copyrightable. For instance, the Ninth Circuit recently ruled that nine words of lyrics from 3LW's 2001 song

"Playas Gon' Play"—"Playas, they gonna play / And haters, they gonna hate"—might be original in an infringement lawsuit against Taylor Swift for somewhat similar lyrics in her song "Shake It Off," thereby reversing the district court's dismissal of the complaint on the ground that the lyrics lack originality. Hall v. Swift, 786 Fed. Appx. 711 (9th Cir. 2019).

The next case concerns both the fixation and originality requirements. Can works of nature ever be fixed or original? Is there more to the originality requirement than the rule articulated in Feist?

Chapman Kelley v. Chicago Park District
635 F.3d 290 (7th Cir. 2011)

SYKES, J.:

[1] Chapman Kelley is a nationally recognized artist known for his representational paintings of landscapes and flowers—in particular, romantic floral and woodland interpretations set within ellipses. In 1984 he received permission from the Chicago Park District to install an ambitious wildflower display at the north end of Grant Park, a prominent public space in the heart of downtown Chicago. "Wildflower Works" was thereafter planted: two enormous elliptical flower beds, each nearly as big as a football field, featuring a variety of native wildflowers and edged with borders of gravel and steel.

Figure 11: park before alteration

[2] Promoted as "living art," Wildflower Works received critical and popular acclaim, and for a while Kelley and a group of volunteers tended the vast garden, pruning and replanting as needed. But by 2004 Wildflower Works had deteriorated, and the City's goals for Grant Park had changed. So the Park District dramatically modified the garden, substantially reducing its size, reconfiguring the oval flower beds into rectangles, and changing some of the planting material.

[3] Kelley sued the Park District {for violating his moral rights under the Visual Artists Rights Act (VARA), something we study in Chapter V, and which provides protection to certain works of visual art} ....

[4] The district court .... rejected Kelley's moral-rights claim ....

[5] .... [F]or reasons relating to copyright's requirements of expressive authorship and fixation, a living garden like Wildflower Works is not copyrightable....

[6] .... The district court held that although Wildflower Works was both a painting and a sculpture, it was ineligible for copyright because it lacked originality. There is a contradiction here. As we have explained, VARA supplements general copyright protection and applies only to artists who create the specific subcategories of art enumerated in the statute. VARA-eligible paintings and sculptures comprise a discrete subset of otherwise copyrightable pictorial and sculptural works; the statute designates these works of fine art as worthy of special protection. If a work is so lacking in originality that it cannot satisfy the basic requirements for copyright, then it can hardly qualify as a painting or sculpture eligible for *extra* protection under VARA.

[7] That point aside, the district court's conclusion misunderstands the originality requirement....

[8] The district court took the position that Wildflower Works was not original because Kelley was not "the first person to ever conceive of and express an arrangement of growing wildflowers in ellipse-shaped enclosed area[s]." This mistakenly equates originality with novelty; the law is clear that a work can be original even if it is not novel. No one argues that Wildflower Works was copied; it plainly possesses more than a little creative spark....

[9] The real impediment to copyright here is not that Wildflower Works fails the test for originality (understood as "not copied" and "possessing some creativity") but that a living garden lacks the kind of authorship and stable fixation normally required to support copyright. Unlike originality, authorship and fixation are *explicit* constitutional requirements; the Copyright Clause empowers Congress to secure for "authors" exclusive rights in their "writings." U.S. CONST. art 1, § 8, cl. 8. The originality requirement is implicit in these express limitations on the congressional copyright power. *See Feist*, 499 U.S. at 346 (The constitutional reference to "authors" and "writings" "presuppose[s] a degree of originality."). The Supreme Court has repeatedly construed all three terms in relation to one another [or] perhaps has collapsed them into a single concept; therefore, writings are what authors create, but for one to be an author, the writing has to be original.

[10] Without fixation, moreover, there cannot be a "writing." ...

[11] Finally, authorship is an entirely human endeavor. Authors of copyrightable works must be human; works owing their form to the forces of nature cannot be copyrighted. [S]ee also U.S. COPYRIGHT OFFICE, COMPENDIUM II: COPYRIGHT OFFICE PRACTICES § 503.03(a) (1984) ("[A] work must be the product of human authorship" and not the forces of nature.); *id.* § 202.02(b).

[12] Recognizing copyright in Wildflower Works presses too hard on these basic principles. We fully accept that the artistic community might classify Kelley's garden as a work of postmodern conceptual art. We acknowledge as well that copyright's prerequisites of authorship and fixation are broadly defined. But the law must have some limits; not all conceptual art may be copyrighted. In the ordinary copyright case, authorship and fixation are not contested; most works presented for copyright are unambiguously authored and unambiguously fixed. But this is not an ordinary case. A living garden like Wildflower Works is neither "authored" nor "fixed" in the senses required for copyright.

[13] Simply put, gardens are planted and cultivated, not authored. A garden's constituent elements are alive and inherently changeable, not fixed. Most of what we see and experience in a garden—the colors, shapes, textures, and scents of the plants—originates in nature, not in the mind of the gardener. At any given moment in time, a garden owes most of its form and appearance to natural forces, though the gardener who plants and tends it obviously assists. All this is true of Wildflower Works, even though it was designed and planted by an artist.

[14] Of course, a human "author"—whether an artist, a professional landscape designer, or an amateur backyard gardener—determines the initial arrangement of the plants in a garden. This is not the kind of authorship required for copyright. To the extent that seeds or seedlings can be considered a "medium of expression," they originate in nature, and natural forces—not the intellect of the gardener—determine their form, growth, and appearance. Moreover, a garden is simply too changeable to satisfy the primary purpose of fixation; its appearance is too inherently variable to supply a baseline for determining questions of copyright creation and infringement. If a garden can qualify as a "work of authorship" sufficiently "embodied in a copy," at what point has fixation occurred? When the garden is newly planted? When its first blossoms appear? When it is in full bloom? How—and at what point in time—is a court to determine whether infringing copying has occurred?

[15] In contrast, when a landscape designer conceives of a plan for a garden and puts it in writing—records it in text, diagrams, or drawings on paper or on a digital-storage device—we can say that his intangible intellectual property has been embodied in a fixed and tangible "copy." This writing is a sufficiently permanent and stable copy of the designer's intellectual expression and is vulnerable to infringing copying, giving rise to the designer's right to claim copyright. The same cannot be said of a garden, which is not a fixed copy of the gardener's intellectual property.... Seeds and plants in a garden are naturally in a state of perpetual change; they germinate, grow, bloom, become dormant, and eventually die. This life cycle moves gradually, over days, weeks, and season to season, but the real barrier to copyright here is not temporal but essential. The essence of a garden is its vitality, not its fixedness. It may endure from season to season, but its nature is one of dynamic change...

NOTE

1. In *Kelley*, the Seventh Circuit relied on principles of fixation to resolve the case, whereas the district court rested on originality doctrine. Do you think there might be other principles at play here (at least tacitly), such as whether a garden is a permissible category of copyrightable subject matter? We explore the categories of copyrightable subject matter in section E.

C. Derivative Works and Compilations

This section explores derivative works and compilations, two classes of works that are based in part on preexisting material sometimes copyrightable in their own right. They raise distinct questions of originality.

According to § 101, a **derivative work** is

> *a work based upon one or more preexisting works, such as a translation, musical arrangement, dramatization, fictionalization, motion picture version, sound recording, art reproduction, abridgment, condensation, or any other form in which a work may be recast, transformed, or adapted.*

For example, the film *Harry Potter and the Chamber of Secrets*, based on J.K. Rowling's book of the same name is a derivative work, as is a French translation of that book, originally written in English. As per § 101, a **compilation** is

> *a work formed by the collection and assembling of preexisting materials or of data that are selected, coordinated, or arranged in such a way that the resulting work as a whole constitutes an original work of authorship. The term "compilation" includes collective works.*

A **collective work** is further defined in § 101 as

> *a work, such as a periodical issue, anthology, or encyclopedia, in which a number of contributions, constituting separate and independent works in themselves, are assembled into a collective whole.*

Section 103(a) of the Copyright Act provides for the copyrightability of derivative works and compilations:

> *The subject matter of copyright as specified by section 102 includes compilations and derivative works, but protection for a work employing preexisting material in which copyright subsists does not extend to any part of the work in which such material has been used unlawfully.*

That said, the Copyright Act accounts for the fact that these works are based in part on preexisting materials, sometimes copyrightable in their own right, by specifying in section 103(b) that

> *The copyright in a compilation or derivative work extends only to the material contributed by the author of such work, as distinguished from the preexisting material employed in the work, and does not imply any exclusive right in the preexisting material. The copyright in such work is independent of, and does not affect or enlarge the scope, duration, ownership, or subsistence of, any copyright protection in the preexisting material.*

This section considers the meaning of these statutory provisions, as well as the standard of originality in derivative works and compilations. Because of their basis in or incorporation of preexisting material sometimes copyrightable in their own right, they raise additional questions as to their own copyrightability.

1. Derivative Works

The statute says nothing about the threshold of originality required of a derivative work, as compared with the underlying original work. The following cases explore whether a second comer has added enough new, original content to a pre-existing work such that the resulting work is a copyrightable derivative work.

> As you read the following case, consider how, if at all, the court's test for originality differs from how the requirement was articulated outside of the context of derivative works. If the test is different, why do you think that is?

L. Batlin & Son, Inc. v. Jeffrey Snyder

536 F.2d 486 (2d Cir. 1976) (en banc)

OAKES, J.: ...

[1] Uncle Sam mechanical banks have been on the American scene at least since June 8, 1886, when Design Patent No. 16,728, issued on a toy savings bank of its type. The basic delightful design has long since been in

the public domain. The banks are well documented in collectors' books and known to the average person interested in Americana. A description of the bank is that Uncle Sam, dressed in his usual stove pipe hat, blue full dress coat, starred vest and red and white striped trousers, and leaning on his umbrella, stands on a four- or five-inch wide base, on which sits his carpetbag. A coin may be placed in Uncle Sam's extended hand. When a lever is pressed, the arm lowers, and the coin falls into the bag, while Uncle Sam's whiskers move up and down. The base has an embossed American eagle on it with the words "Uncle Sam" on streamers above it, as well as the word "Bank" on each side. Such a bank is listed in a number of collectors' books, ... and is said to be not particularly rare.

[2] Appellant Jeffrey Snyder ... obtained a registration of copyright on a plastic "Uncle Sam bank" .... [H]e had seen a cast metal antique Uncle Sam bank with an overall height of the figure and base of 11 inches.... [H]e flew to Hong Kong to arrange for the design and eventual manufacture of replicas of the bank as Bicentennial items, taking the cast metal Uncle Sam bank with him.... Snyder wanted his bank to be made of plastic and to be shorter than the cast metal sample "in order to fit into the required price range and quality and quantity of material to be used." The figure of Uncle Sam was thus shortened from 11 to nine inches, and the base shortened and narrowed. It was also decided ... to change the shape of the carpetbag and to include the umbrella in a one-piece mold for the Uncle Sam figure, "so as not to have a problem with a loose umbrella or a separate molding process." [Snyder's Hong Kong] representative made his sketches while looking at the cast metal bank. After a clay model was made, a plastic prototype was approved by Snyder and his order placed ....

[3] Appellee Batlin is also in the novelty business and ... ordered 30 cartons of cast iron Uncle Sam mechanical banks from Taiwan where its president had seen the bank made. When he became aware of the existence of a plastic bank, which he considered an almost identical copy of the cast iron bank, Batlin's trading company in Hong Kong procured a manufacturer and the president of Batlin ordered plastic copies also.... Batlin was notified by the United States Customs Service that the plastic banks it was receiving were covered by appellants' copyright. In addition the Customs Service was ... refusing entry to cast iron banks previously ordered, according to ... Batlin .... Thus Batlin instituted suit for a judgment declaring appellants' copyright void ....

[4] This court has examined both the appellants' plastic Uncle Sam bank made under Snyder's copyright and the uncopyrighted model cast iron mechanical bank which is itself a reproduction of the original public domain Uncle Sam bank. Appellant Snyder claims differences not only of size but also in a number of other very minute details: the carpetbag shape of the plastic bank is smooth, the iron bank rough; the metal bank bag is fatter at its base; the eagle on the front of the platform in the metal bank is holding arrows in his talons while in the plastic bank he clutches leaves, this change concededly having been made, however, because "the arrows did not reproduce well in plastic on a smaller size." The shape of Uncle Sam's face is supposedly different, as is the shape and texture of the hats, according to the Snyder affidavit. In the metal version the umbrella is hanging loose while in the plastic item it is included in the single mold. The texture of the clothing, the hairline, shape of the bow ties and of the shirt collar and left arm as well as the flag carrying the name on the base of the statue are all claimed to be different, along with the shape and texture of the eagles on the side. Many of these differences are not perceptible to the casual observer....

[5] .... [T]he Snyder bank is extremely similar to the cast iron bank, save in size and material with the only other differences, such as the shape of the satchel and the leaves in the eagle's talons being by all appearances, minor. Similarities include, more importantly, the appearance and number of stripes on the trousers, buttons on the coat, and stars on the vest and hat, the attire and pose of Uncle Sam, the decor on his base and bag, the overall color scheme, the method of carpetbag opening, to name but a few....

[6] ... [T]he appellants' plastic version reproduces the cast iron bank except that it proportionately reduces the height from approximately eleven inches to approximately nine inches with trivial variations.... [T]he

variations found in appellants' plastic bank were merely trivial and ... it was a reproduction of the metal bank made as simply as possible for the purposes of manufacture. In other words, there were no elements of difference that amounted to significant alteration or that had any purpose other than the functional one of making a more suitable (and probably less expensive) figure in the plastic medium.

Figure 12: public domain cast iron Uncle Sam bank, 1886 (left) and Snyder's plastic version, 1975 (right)

[7] What the leading authority has called "the one pervading element prerequisite to copyright protection regardless of the form of the work" is the requirement of originality that the work be the original product of the claimant. 1 M. NIMMER, THE LAW OF COPYRIGHT s 10, at 32 (1975). This derives from the fact that, constitutionally, copyright protection may be claimed only by authors. Thus, one who has slavishly or mechanically copied from others may not claim to be an author. Since the constitutional requirement must be read into the Copyright Act, the requirement of originality is also a statutory one.... [I]n order to obtain a copyright upon a reproduction of a work of art ... the work [must] contain some substantial, not merely trivial originality.

[8] The test of originality is concededly one with a low threshold in that "[a]ll that is needed . . . is that the 'author' contributed something more than a 'merely trivial' variation, something recognizably 'his own.'" Alfred Bell & Co. v. Catalda Fine Arts, Inc., 191 F.2d at 103. But ... while a copy of something in the public domain will not, if it be merely a copy, support a copyright, a distinguishable variation will.

[9] .... The requirement of substantial as opposed to trivial variation and the prohibition of mechanical copying, both of which are inherent in and subsumed by the concept of originality, apply .... There is implicit in that concept a minimal element of creativity over and above the requirement of independent effort....

[10] A reproduction of a work of art obviously presupposes an underlying work of art.... [I]t has been established that mass-produced commercial objects with a minimal element of artistic craftsmanship may satisfy the statutory requirement of such a work. So, too, a toy which qualifies as a work of art such as the

original Uncle Sam mechanical bank may qualify as a work of art .... The underlying work of art may as here be in the public domain. But even to claim the more limited protection given to a reproduction of a work of art (that to the distinctive features contributed by the reproducer), the reproduction must contain an original contribution not present in the underlying work of art and be more than a mere copy.

[11] .... [T]o support a copyright there must be at least some substantial variation, not merely a trivial variation such as might occur in the translation to a different medium.

[12] Nor can the requirement of originality be satisfied simply by the demonstration of physical skill or special training which, to be sure, ... was required for the production of the plastic molds that furnished the basis for appellants' plastic bank. A considerably higher degree of skill is required, true artistic skill, to make the reproduction copyrightable. Thus in *Alfred Bell & Co. v. Catalda Fine Arts, Inc.*, Judge Frank pointed out that the mezzotint engraver's art there concerned required "great labour and talent" to effectuate the "management of light and shade ... produced by different lines and dots ...," means "very different from those employed by the painter or draughtsman from whom he copies...." Here on the basis of appellants' own expert's testimony it took [Snyder's Hong Kong] representative "[a]bout a day and a half, two days work" to produce the plastic mold sculpture from the metal Uncle Sam bank. If there be a point in the copyright law pertaining to reproductions at which sheer artistic skill and effort can act as a substitute for the requirement of substantial variation, it was not reached here.

[13] Appellants rely heavily upon *Alva Studios, Inc. v. Winninger*, the "Hand of God" case, where the court held that "great skill and originality (were required) to produce a scale reduction of a great work with exactitude." 177 F. Supp. 265, 267 (S.D.N.Y. 1959). There, the original sculpture was, "one of the most intricate pieces of sculpture ever created" with "[i]nnumerable planes, lines and geometric patterns ... interdependent in [a] multi-dimensional work." Originality was found by the district court to consist primarily in the fact that "[i]t takes 'an extremely skilled sculptor' many hours working directly in front of the original" to effectuate a scale reduction. The court, indeed, found the exact replica to be so original, distinct, and creative as to constitute a work of art in itself. The complexity and exactitude there involved distinguishes that case amply from the one at bar. As appellants themselves have pointed out, there are a number of trivial differences or deviations from the original public domain cast iron bank in their plastic reproduction. Thus concededly the plastic version is not, and was scarcely meticulously produced to be, an exactly faithful reproduction. Nor is the creativity in the underlying work of art of the same order of magnitude as in the case of the "Hand of God." Rodin's sculpture is, furthermore, so unique and rare, and adequate public access to it such a problem that a significant public benefit accrues from its precise, artistic reproduction. No such benefit can be imagined to accrue here from the "knock-off" reproduction of the cast iron Uncle Sam bank. Thus appellants' plastic bank is neither in the category of exactitude required by Alva Studios nor in a category of substantial originality; it falls within what has been suggested by the amicus curiae is a copyright no-man's land.

[14] Absent a genuine difference between the underlying work of art and the copy of it for which protection is sought, the public interest in promoting progress in the arts indeed, the constitutional demand, could hardly be served. To extend copyrightability to minuscule variations would simply put a weapon for harassment in the hands of mischievous copiers intent on appropriating and monopolizing public domain work....

NOTE

1. In discussing the relevance of the skill employed to create a replica of an existing work, the court invokes a (smaller) replica of Auguste Rodin's *Hand of God* sculpture (the original and the replica are shown in Figure 13). The court thought the replica was categorically different than Snyder's Uncle Sam banks. In stating that, the court cited to a previous case assessing the copyrightability of the replica. In that case, the district court had reasoned that the replica of *Hand of God* "embodies and resulted from [the replica maker's] skill and

originality in producing an accurate scale reproduction of the original. In a work of sculpture, this reduction requires far more than an abridgment of a written classic; great skill and originality is called for when one seeks to produce a scale reduction of a great work with exactitude." Alva Studios, Inc. v. Winninger, 177 F. Supp. 265, 267 (S.D.N.Y. 1959). The court also thought that originality came from turning a work that was originally 37 inches into one that is 18½ inches and in changing the rear side of the sculpture's base. Finally, the court credited the fact that the sculpture's owner granted permission to the replica maker to make its replicas as a sign that the replica maker's work "bears the stamp of originality and skill." Is the court's reasoning (and *L. Batlin & Son*'s reliance on it to distinguish the Uncle Sam bank replicas) persuasive? How does this reasoning hold up post-*Feist*?

Figure 13: Rodin's *Hand of God* sculpture (left) and Alva Studios replica (right)

In reading the following case, consider how the underlying work differs from the one in the previous case. Does that and should that reflect the assessment of originality in the derivative work? In practice, what does the court's ruling mean for the originality requirement for derivative works?

Daniel Schrock v. Learning Curve International, Inc.
586 F.3d 513 (7th Cir. 2009)

SYKES, J.: ...

[1] HIT is the owner of the copyright in the "Thomas & Friends" properties, and Learning Curve is a producer and distributor of children's toys. HIT and Learning Curve entered into a licensing agreement granting Learning Curve a license to create and market toys based on HIT's characters. HIT and Learning Curve maintain ... that HIT retained all intellectual-property rights in the works produced under the license....

[2] In 1999 Learning Curve retained Daniel Schrock to take product photographs of its toys, including those based on HIT's characters, for use in promotional materials. On numerous occasions during the next four years, Schrock photographed several lines of Learning Curve's toys, including many of the "Thomas & Friends" toy trains, related figures, and train-set accessories.... Schrock invoiced Learning Curve for this work,

and some of the invoices included "usage restrictions" purporting to limit Learning Curve's use of his photographs to two years. Learning Curve paid the invoices in full—in total more than $400,000.

[3] Learning Curve stopped using Schrock's photography services in mid-2003 but continued to use some of his photos in its printed advertising, on packaging, and on the internet. In 2004 Schrock registered his photos for copyright protection and sued HIT and Learning Curve for infringement .... HIT and Learning Curve moved for summary judgment, arguing primarily that Schrock's photos were derivative works and not sufficiently original to claim copyright protection, and that neither HIT nor Learning Curve ever authorized Schrock to copyright the photos. They argued in the alternative that Schrock granted them an unlimited oral license to use the photos.

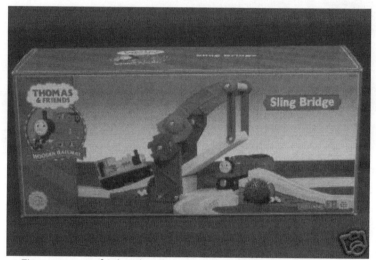

Figure 14: one of Schrock's Thomas & Friends product photographs

[4] The district court granted summary judgment for the defendants.... The judge focused ... on whether the photos were derivative works under the Copyright Act and concluded that they were. Then, following language in *Gracen* [*v. Bradford Exchange*, 698 F.2d 300 (7th Cir.1983)], the judge held that Learning Curve's permission to make the photos was not enough to trigger Schrock's copyright in them; the judge said Schrock must also have Learning Curve's permission to copyright the photos. Schrock did not have that permission, so the judge concluded that Schrock had no copyright in the photos and dismissed his claim for copyright infringement. Schrock appealed....

[5] Schrock argues that the district judge mistakenly classified his photos as derivative works and misread or misapplied *Gracen*. He contends that his photos are not derivative works, and even if they are, his copyright is valid and enforceable because he had permission from Learning Curve to photograph the underlying copyrighted works and his photos contained sufficient incremental original expression to qualify for copyright. HIT and Learning Curve defend the district court's determination that the photos are derivative works and argue that the court properly read *Gracen* to require permission to copyright as well as permission to make the derivative works. Alternatively, they maintain that Schrock's photographs contain insufficient originality to be copyrightable .... Finally, the defendants ask us to affirm on the independent ground that Schrock orally granted them an unlimited license to use his works....

[6] Much of the briefing on appeal—and most of the district court's analysis—concerned the classification of the photos as derivative works.... The Copyright Act specifically grants the author of a derivative work copyright protection in the incremental original expression he contributes as long as the derivative work does not infringe the underlying work. The copyright in a derivative work, however, "extends only to the material

contributed by the author of such work, as distinguished from the preexisting material employed in the work." 17 U.S.C. § 103(b)....

[7] Whether photographs of a copyrighted work are derivative works is the subject of deep disagreement among courts and commentators alike....

[8] We need not resolve the issue definitively here. The classification of Schrock's photos as derivative works does not affect the applicable legal standard for determining copyrightability, although as we have noted, it does determine the scope of copyright protection. Accordingly, we will assume without deciding that each of Schrock's photos qualifies as a derivative work within the meaning of the Copyright Act....

[9] Our review of Schrock's photographs convinces us that they do not fall into the narrow category of photographs that can be classified as slavish copies, lacking any independently created expression. To be sure, the photographs are accurate depictions of the three-dimensional "Thomas & Friends" toys, but Schrock's artistic and technical choices combine to create a two-dimensional image that is subtly but nonetheless sufficiently his own.[3] This is confirmed by Schrock's deposition testimony describing his creative process in depicting the toys. Schrock explained how he used various camera and lighting techniques to make the toys look more "life like," "personable," and "friendly." He explained how he tried to give the toys "a little bit of dimension" and that it was his goal to make the toys "a little bit better than what they look like when you actually see them on the shelf." The original expression in the representative sample is not particularly great (it was not meant to be), but it is enough under the applicable standard to warrant the limited copyright protection accorded derivative works under § 103(b).

[10] Aside from arguing that the works fail under the generally accepted test for originality, Learning Curve and HIT offer two additional reasons why we should conclude that Schrock's photographs are not original. First, they claim that the photos are intended to serve the "purely utilitarian function" of identifying products for consumers. The purpose of the photographs, however, is irrelevant. *See* Bleistein v. Donaldson Lithographing Co., 188 U.S. 239, 251-52 (1903).

[11] The defendants' second and more substantial argument is that it is not enough that Schrock's photographs might pass the ordinary test for originality; they claim that as derivative works, the photos are subject to a higher standard of originality. A leading copyright commentator disagrees. The Nimmer treatise maintains that the quantum of originality required for copyright in a derivative work is the same as that required for copyright in any other work. *See* 1 NIMMER ON COPYRIGHT § 3.01, at 3-2, § 3.03[A], at 3-7. More particularly, Nimmer says the relevant standard is whether a derivative work contains a "nontrivial" variation from the preexisting work "sufficient to render the derivative work distinguishable from [the] prior work in any meaningful manner." *Id.* § 3.03[A], at 3-10. The caselaw generally follows this formulation.

[12] Learning Curve and HIT argue that our decision in *Gracen* established a more demanding standard of originality for derivative works. *Gracen* involved an artistic competition in which artists were invited to submit paintings of the character Dorothy from the Metro-Goldwyn-Mayer ("MGM") movie *The Wizard of Oz*. Participating artists were given a still photograph of Dorothy from the film as an exemplar, and the paintings were solicited and submitted with the understanding that the best painting would be chosen for a series of collector's plates. Plaintiff Gracen prevailed in the competition, but she refused to sign the contract allowing her painting to be used in the collector's plates. The competition sponsor commissioned another artist to create a similar plate, and Gracen sued the sponsor, MGM, and the artist for copyright infringement. We held

---

[3] We note, however, that a mere shift in medium, without more, is generally insufficient to satisfy the requirement of originality for copyright in a derivative work.

that Gracen could not maintain her infringement suit because her painting, a derivative work, was not "substantially different from the underlying work to be copyrightable." ...

[13] The concern expressed in *Gracen* was that a derivative work could be so similar in appearance to the underlying work that in a subsequent infringement suit brought by a derivative author, it would be difficult to separate the original elements of expression in the derivative and underlying works in order to determine whether one derivative work infringed another. The opinion offered the example of artists A and B who both painted their versions of the Mona Lisa, a painting in the public domain. "[I]f the difference between the original and A's reproduction is slight, the difference between A's and B's reproductions will also be slight, so that if B had access to A's reproductions the trier of fact will be hard-pressed to decide whether B was copying A or copying the Mona Lisa itself." *Id.* [at 304.]

[14] No doubt this concern is valid. But nothing in the Copyright Act suggests that derivative works are subject to a more exacting originality requirement than other works of authorship. Indeed, we have explained since *Gracen* that the only "originality" required for a new work to by copyrightable is enough expressive variation from public-domain or other existing works to enable the new work to be readily distinguished from its predecessors. We emphasized ... that this standard does not require a high degree of incremental originality.

[15] .... [We make clear] the following general principles: (1) the originality requirement for derivative works is not more demanding than the originality requirement for other works; and (2) the key inquiry is whether there is sufficient nontrivial expressive variation in the derivative work to make it distinguishable from the underlying work in some meaningful way. This focus on the presence of nontrivial "distinguishable variation" adequately captures the concerns articulated in *Gracen* without unduly narrowing the copyrightability of derivative works. It is worth repeating that the copyright in a derivative work is thin, extending only to the incremental original expression contributed by the author of the derivative work.

[16] As applied to photographs, we have already explained that the original expression in a photograph generally subsists in its rendition of the subject matter. If the photographer's rendition of a copyrighted work varies enough from the underlying work to enable the photograph to be distinguished from the underlying work (aside from the obvious shift from three dimensions to two), then the photograph contains sufficient incremental originality to qualify for copyright. Schrock's photos of the "Thomas & Friends" toys are highly accurate product photos but contain minimally sufficient variation in angle, perspective, lighting, and dimension to be distinguishable from the underlying works; they are not slavish copies. Accordingly, the photos qualify for the limited derivative-work copyright provided by § 103(b). However narrow that copyright might be, it at least protects against the kind of outright copying that occurred here....

[17] To be copyrightable, a derivative work must not be infringing. *See* 17 U.S.C. § 103(a)....

[18] .... [T]here is nothing in the Copyright Act requiring the author of a derivative work to obtain permission to copyright his work from the owner of the copyright in the underlying work. To the contrary, the Act provides that copyright in a derivative work, like copyright in any other work, arises by operation of law once the author's original expression is fixed in a tangible medium. "Copyright protection subsists ... in original works of authorship fixed in any tangible medium of expression," 17 U.S.C. § 102(a), and "[t]he subject matter of copyright ... includes ... derivative works," *id.* § 103(a). "Copyright in a work protected under this title vests initially in the author or authors of the work." *Id.* § 201(a)....

[19] ... [B]ecause the owner of a copyrighted work has the exclusive right to control the preparation of derivative works, the owner could limit the derivative-work author's intellectual-property rights in the contract, license, or agreement that authorized the production of the derivative work....

[20] In this case, the evidence submitted with the summary-judgment motion does not establish as a matter of law that the parties adjusted Schrock's rights by contract .... [F]urther development of the record might resolve the remaining liability questions as a matter of law. It is undisputed that Schrock was authorized to photograph the "Thomas & Friends" toys, and as the creator of the photos, Schrock's copyright arose by operation of law. We cannot tell, however, whether the parties altered this default rule in their agreements....

[21] .... Learning Curve argues in the alternative that Schrock granted it an unlimited license to use his photos, but on this issue the record is also ambiguous. We leave it to the district court to sort out [these issues].

NOTES

1. The court here assumes without deciding that photographs can qualify as derivative works. Can you think of reasons why photographs might qualify as derivative works? Can you think of reasons why they might not?

Figure 15: Gracen's painting (left) and Judy Garland in *The Wizard of Oz* Movie (right)

2. The court discusses *Gracen v. Bradford Exchange*, 698 F.2d 300 (7th Cir. 1983), at length. Consider plaintiff Jorie Gracen's painting of Dorothy as played by Judy Garland in *The Wizard of Oz* movie, shown on the left in Figure 15. The painting is not of any particular scene that actually appears in the movie. Consider also a still photograph from the film of Judy Garland, shown on the right in Figure 15. Does Gracen's painting meet *Schrock*'s originality standard? Should it?

3. We return to consider derivative works in the context of a copyright owner's exclusive right to prepare derivative works based on the owner's work (Chapter V). In that context, we also consider whether the rights to derivative works are more properly vested in the creator of the underlying work or subsequent creators.

2. Compilations

Just as the statute says nothing about the threshold of originality required of a derivative work, the statute is silent on the threshold of originality required of a compilation. We return to the *Feist* decision to explore how to assess the originality of compilations.

Does the Court think that compilations of facts can be copyrightable? To what extent? Will the protection offered, if any, be thick or thin?

Feist Publications, Inc. v. Rural Telephone Service Co.
499 U.S. 340 (1991)

O'CONNOR, J.: ...

[1] The mere fact that a work is copyrighted does not mean that every element of the work may be protected. Originality remains the sine qua non of copyright; accordingly, copyright protection may extend only to those components of a work that are original to the author. Thus, if the compilation author clothes facts with an original collocation of words, he or she may be able to claim a copyright in this written expression. Others may copy the underlying facts from the publication, but not the precise words used to present them.... Where the compilation author adds no written expression but rather lets the facts speak for themselves, the expressive element is more elusive. The only conceivable expression is the manner in which the compiler has selected and arranged the facts. Thus, if the selection and arrangement are original, these elements of the work are eligible for copyright protection.... No matter how original the format, however, the facts themselves do not become original through association.

[2] This inevitably means that the copyright in a factual compilation is thin. Notwithstanding a valid copyright, a subsequent compiler remains free to use the facts contained in another's publication to aid in preparing a competing work, so long as the competing work does not feature the same selection and arrangement....

[3] The definition of "compilation" is found in § 101 of the 1976 Act. It defines a "compilation" in the copyright sense as "a work formed by the collection and assembling of preexisting materials or of data *that* are selected, coordinated, or arranged *in such a way that* the resulting work as a whole constitutes an original work of authorship" (emphasis added).

[4] The purpose of the statutory definition is to emphasize that collections of facts are not copyrightable *per se*. It conveys this message through its tripartite structure, as emphasized above by the italics. The statute identifies three distinct elements and requires each to be met for a work to qualify as a copyrightable compilation: (1) the collection and assembly of pre-existing material, facts, or data; (2) the selection, coordination, or arrangement of those materials; and (3) the creation, by virtue of the particular selection, coordination, or arrangement, of an "original" work of authorship....

[5] The third requirement is ... illuminating. It emphasizes that a compilation, like any other work, is copyrightable only if it satisfies the originality requirement .... Although § 102 states plainly that the originality requirement applies to all works, the point was emphasized with regard to compilations to ensure that courts would not repeat the mistake of the "sweat of the brow" courts by concluding that fact-based works are treated differently and measured by some other standard.

[6] The key to the statutory definition is the second requirement. It instructs courts that, in determining whether a fact-based work is an original work of authorship, they should focus on the manner in which the collected facts have been selected, coordinated, and arranged. This is a straightforward application of the originality requirement. Facts are never original, so the compilation author can claim originality, if at all, only in the way the facts are presented. To that end, the statute dictates that the principal focus should be on whether the selection, coordination, and arrangement are sufficiently original to merit protection.

[7] Not every selection, coordination, or arrangement will pass muster. This is plain from the statute. It states that, to merit protection, the facts must be selected, coordinated, or arranged "in such a way" as to render the work as a whole original. This implies that some "ways" will trigger copyright, but that others will not....

[8] ... [H]owever, the originality requirement is not particularly stringent. A compiler may settle upon a selection or arrangement that others have used; novelty is not required. Originality requires only that the author make the selection or arrangement independently (i.e., without copying that selection or arrangement from another work), and that it display some minimal level of creativity. Presumably, the vast majority of compilations will pass this test, but not all will. There remains a narrow category of works in which the creative spark is utterly lacking or so trivial as to be virtually nonexistent. Such works are incapable of sustaining a valid copyright.

[9] Even if a work qualifies as a copyrightable compilation, it receives only limited protection. This is the point of § 103 of the Act. Section 103 explains that "[t]he subject matter of copyright ... includes compilations," § 103(a), but that copyright protects only the author's original contributions—not the facts or information conveyed ....

[10] As § 103 makes clear, copyright is not a tool by which a compilation author may keep others from using the facts or data he or she has collected.... Rather, the facts contained in existing works may be freely copied because copyright protects only the elements that owe their origin to the compiler—the selection, coordination, and arrangement of facts....

[11] There is no doubt that Feist took from the white pages of Rural's directory a substantial amount of factual information. At a minimum, Feist copied the names, towns, and telephone numbers of 1,309 of Rural's subscribers....

[12] The question is whether .... Feist, by taking 1,309 names, towns, and telephone numbers from Rural's white pages, cop[ied] anything that was "original" to Rural? Certainly, the raw data does not satisfy the originality requirement. Rural may have been the first to discover and report the names, towns, and telephone numbers of its subscribers, but this data does not "ow[e] its origin" to Rural. *Burrow-Giles*, 111 U.S. at 58. Rather, these bits of information are uncopyrightable facts; they existed before Rural reported them and would have continued to exist if Rural had never published a telephone directory....

[13] The question that remains is whether Rural selected, coordinated, or arranged these uncopyrightable facts in an original way.... [T]he selection and arrangement of facts cannot be so mechanical or routine as to require no creativity whatsoever. The standard of originality is low, but it does exist....

[14] The selection, coordination, and arrangement of Rural's white pages do not satisfy the minimum constitutional standards for copyright protection. As mentioned at the outset, Rural's white pages are entirely typical. Persons desiring telephone service in Rural's service area fill out an application and Rural issues them a telephone number. In preparing its white pages, Rural simply takes the data provided by its subscribers and lists it alphabetically by surname. The end product is a garden-variety white pages directory, devoid of even the slightest trace of creativity.

[15] Rural's selection of listings could not be more obvious: It publishes the most basic information—name, town, and telephone number—about each person who applies to it for telephone service. This is "selection" of a sort, but it lacks the modicum of creativity necessary to transform mere selection into copyrightable expression. Rural expended sufficient effort to make the white pages directory useful, but insufficient creativity to make it original....

[16] Nor can Rural claim originality in its coordination and arrangement of facts. The white pages do nothing more than list Rural's subscribers in alphabetical order. This arrangement may, technically speaking, owe its origin to Rural; no one disputes that Rural undertook the task of alphabetizing the names itself. But there is nothing remotely creative about arranging names alphabetically in a white pages directory. It is an age-old practice, firmly rooted in tradition and so commonplace that it has come to be expected as a matter of course. It is not only unoriginal, it is practically inevitable. This time-honored tradition does not possess the minimal creative spark required by the Copyright Act and the Constitution.

[17] We conclude that the names, towns, and telephone numbers copied by Feist were not original to Rural and therefore were not protected by the copyright in Rural's combined white and yellow pages directory....

NOTES

1. In the wake of *Feist*, Congress proposed various bills to protect databases more comprehensively, although none of them passed into law. *See, e.g.*, Database and Collections of Information Misappropriation Act, H.R. 3261, 108th Cong. (2003) (proposing the "prohibit[ion of] the misappropriation of certain databases"); Database Investment and Intellectual Property Antipiracy Act of 1996, H.R. 3531, 104th Cong. (1996) (proposing a statutory amendment "to promote investment and prevent intellectual property piracy with respect to databases"). Those bills generally relied on the Commerce Clause for their authority because the Copyright and Patent Clause had been ruled off-limits by *Feist* for noncreative databases. For differing views about whether Congress has authority to enact database protection laws post-*Feist*, compare Jane C. Ginsburg, *No "Sweat"? Copyright and Other Protection of Works of Information after* Feist v. Rural Telephone, 92 COLUM. L. REV. 338 (1992), with Jeanne C. Fromer, *The Intellectual Property Clause's External Limitations*, 61 DUKE L.J. 1329 (2012). Are there other ways to protect databases if not through federal laws?

Regardless of constitutional authority, is it good policy to protect databases from copying? The European Union thinks so. In 1996, it adopted a Database Directive that gives *sui generis* protection, with some exception, to "the maker of a database which shows that there has been qualitatively and/or quantitatively a substantial investment in either the obtaining, verification or presentation of the contents to prevent extraction and/or re-utilization of the whole or of a substantial part, evaluated qualitatively and/or quantitatively, of the contents of that database." Directive 96/9, of the European Parliament and of the Council of 11 March 1996 on the Legal Protection of Databases, 1996 O.J. (L 77) 20, 25 (EC). Additionally, in 2016, Congress itself enacted the Defend Trade Secrets Act, which provides federal civil remedies for the misappropriation of trade secrets, much like state laws long have. Databases maintained as trade secrets thus now have some form of federal protection.

That said, there are continuing doubts about the wisdom of database protection. In 2005, the European Union conducted a study of its 1996 rule granting protection to databases. The study concluded that the economic impact of the new protections was "unproven," and that, although the new rule "was introduced to stimulate the production of databases in Europe, the new instrument has had no proven impact on the production of databases." Indeed, by 2004, database production in the European Union had fallen below 1998 levels, which was just before the EU rule took effect across the entire community. In other words, the implementation of the new protection against copying correlated with a decline in production, not an increase. And, perhaps more significant, the European Union's share of the global database market has stagnated. In 1992, about 26% of all online databases were produced by European firms, while about 60% were of North American origin. By 2005, North American production had swelled to approximately 70% of the global total. The European Union's share had barely budged, and, by some measures, had even declined slightly. In essence, while database production in the United States and Canada (which, like the United States, lacks protection for fact-based databases) has continued to grow, database production in the European Union has stayed at best constant, and more likely has slowed a bit.

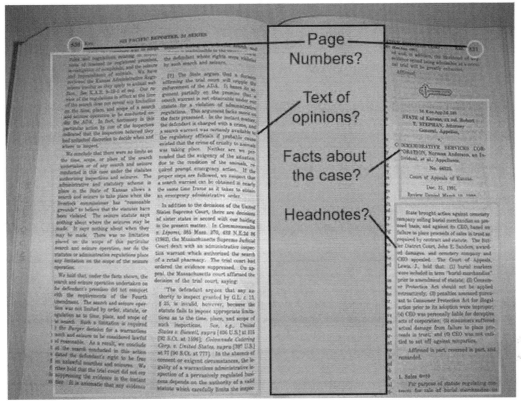

Figure 16: West case reporter

2. Consider whether different aspects of West's case reporters (as exemplified in Figure 16) are protectable by copyright: (a) the text of a case opinion; (b) the facts about a case (such as the party names, the court, and an opinion date); (c) the case headnotes; (d) the page numbers; and (e) the compilation of all of this material. West has sued others for using its "star pagination," pagination keyed to West's case reporters. In one pre-*Feist* decision, it won its claim to copyright protection. West Publishing Co. v. Mead Data Central, Inc. 799 F.2d 1219 (8th Cir. 1986). In another decision, this time post-*Feist*, it lost. Matthew Bender & Co. v. West Pub. Co., 158 F.3d 693 (2d Cir. 1998). Does West have an argument to victory post-*Feist*? What competitive interests are at stake in protecting or denying protection to West for its pagination? Were similar interests at stake in *Feist*?

3. Is a greeting card, like the one shown in Figure 17 on the left, copyrightable? Consider first whether the text and artwork are each independently copyrightable. If not (or even if so), are they altogether copyrightable as a compilation? In a suit by Roth Greeting Cards, maker of this card, against United Card Co. (maker of the card in the same figure on the right), the Ninth Circuit concluded that "[c]onsidering all of these elements together, th[is] card[is] ... both original and copyrightable." Roth Greeting Cards v. United Card Co., 429 F.2d 1106, 1109 (9th Cir. 1970). *Is Roth* good law after *Feist*?

Should we treat this type of work as a compilation? Or something else? If this greeting card qualifies as a compilation, can you imagine a work that would not?

4. Consider a real estate ownership map that covers a county and pictorially shows the location, size, and shape of surveys; land grants; tracts; and various topological features within the county. Numbers and words on the map identify deeds, abstract numbers, acreage, and owners. A sample map excerpt is shown in Figure 18. The map creator assembled this information from county tax, deed, and survey records; river authority data; state survey records, maps and abstracts of land titles; other title and subdivision information; and city and national maps. What evidence might the map creator cite to show that this work is original? Might this

map be protectable as a compilation? Or some other type of work? For the Fifth Circuit's take on this issue, see Mason v. Montgomery Data, Inc., 967 F.2d 135 (5th Cir. 1992).

Figure 17: Roth Greeting Card card (left) and United Card Co. card (right)

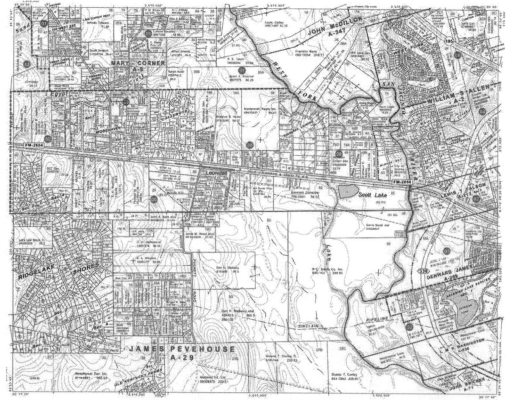

Figure 18: sample county real estate ownership map

5. In its *Compendium of U.S. Copyright Office Practices*, the Copyright Office states that "the Office generally will not register a compilation containing only two or three elements, because the selection is necessarily *de minimis*." § 312.2. To support this rule, the Copyright Office cites the legislative history leading up to the 1976 Act: The House of Representatives Report observes that a work "where relatively few separate elements have been brought together," such as "a composition consisting of words and music, a work published with illustrations or front matter, or three one-act plays," would not be considered a collective work. H.R. REP. NO. 1476, 94th Cong., 2d Sess. 47, at 122 (1976). Does the statutory definition of "compilation" or "collective work" justify or cut against the legislative history (or the Copyright Office's understanding)? How would Roth Greeting Cards and Mason each fare under the Copyright Office rule? As a matter of policy, does the Copyright Office's rule make sense?

6. Consider what makes the selection, coordination, or arrangement of data original. In a Sixth Circuit case alleging copyright infringement of an automobile transmissions catalog with illustrations and a numbering system for transmission parts, the court held that the catalog is not protectable as an original compilation of data. ATC Distribution Grp., Inc. v. Whatever It Takes Transmissions & Parts, Inc., 402 F.3d 700 (6th Cir. 2005). The court reasoned that the selection of data on transmission parts could not supply the requisite creativity because "ATC included in its catalog every transmission part available." As to the arrangement of this data, the court reasoned that even though "the creativity bar has been set extremely low," the catalog at issue "does not even have this minimal level of creativity, ... because the only aspect of the catalog that differs from [a previous transmissions] catalog is the choice of headings and arrangement of the parts into categories— two minor differences that [are] insufficiently creative to justify copyright protection." Even if this sequence of information were new to the industry, the court reasoned that so long as it is "typical, if not inevitable," it lacks the requisite degree of creativity. By contrast, in a case involving a guide to used car values, the Second Circuit held that "the fact that an arrangement of data responds *logically* to the needs of the market for which the compilation was prepared does not negate originality. To the contrary, the use of logic to solve the problems of how best to present the information being compiled is independent creation." CCC Info. Servs., Inc. v. Maclean Hunter Mkt. Reports, Inc., 44 F.3d 61, 67 (2d Cir. 1994). The court proceeded to find originality in this compilation because it divided the used car market into geographical regions, selected optional features for inclusion, adjusted for mileage in 5,000-mile increments, used the abstract concept of the "average vehicle" in each category as the subject of valuation, and decided how many years' models to include in the guide. How do you think the logic of selecting and arranging data should affect the determination of originality? As you read the next section about copyright's idea-expression distinction, think back and ask yourself whether *ATC* or *CCC* represents the better understanding of the scope of copyrightable subject matter.

D. Idea-Expression Distinction

The copyrightability requirements we have looked at thus far in § 102(a) set out affirmative requirements. In contrast, § 102(b)'s withdrawal of protection for certain elements of works is expressed as a limitation on the scope of copyright protection:

> *In no case does copyright protection for an original work of authorship extend to any idea, procedure, process, system, method of operation, concept, principle, or discovery, regardless of the form in which it is described, explained, illustrated, or embodied in such work.*

This section makes clear that copyright law does not protect ideas, procedures, and so forth. However, ideas and the like must be expressed in some way, and the *expression* of an idea is protected matter. Section 102(b) thus sets up a distinction between protectable expression and unprotectable ideas, which has come to be known as the "idea-expression distinction." The idea-expression distinction is shorthand for the entire list of matter that section 102(b) states lies outside the scope of copyright, including procedures, processes, systems, methods of operation, concepts, principles, and discoveries, not just ideas. In enacting this provision in the 1976 Act, the legislative history emphasizes that § 102(b) is meant to codify common law development of the idea-expression distinction. H.R. REP. NO. 1476, 94th Cong., 2d Sess. 47, at 57 (1976).

In this section, we will consider three opinions, each of which help us get at a form of the idea-expression distinction: the **process-expression distinction**, the **idea-expression distinction**, and the **historical fact-expression distinction**, respectively. The policies underlying a denial of protection for each of these three categories are somewhat distinct. That said, underpinning the idea-expression distinction generally is a judgment that ideas, processes, facts, and the like ought to be in the public domain. As one of us has written, "the basic building blocks of expression ought to be left freely available for anyone to use. It would be both inefficient and unfair to grant rights in these basic components that so many authors will need just because one person happened to employ them first. Doing otherwise would ultimately be detrimental to generating a robust body of authored works." Jeanne C. Fromer, *An Information Theory of Copyright Law*, 64 EMORY L.J. 71, 98 (2014).

1. Process-Expression Distinction

The following case is considered the foundational case on the idea-expression distinction. Yet it might be better addressed to a process-expression distinction. As you read this case, consider—in addition to the policy just discussed—whether there are any other reasons copyright law might prefer to exclude from protection procedures, processes, systems, and methods of operation. Also, is everything about Selden's work unprotectable by copyright law? By other laws?

W.C.M. Baker v. Charles Selden
101 U.S. 99 (1879)

BRADLEY, J.:

[1] Charles Selden, the testator of the complainant in this case, in the year 1859 took the requisite steps for obtaining the copyright of a book, entitled "Selden's Condensed Ledger, or Book-keeping Simplified," the object of which was to exhibit and explain a peculiar system of book-keeping. In 1860 and 1861, he took the copyright of several other books, containing additions to and improvements upon the said system. The bill of complaint was filed against the defendant, Baker, for an alleged infringement of these copyrights. The latter, in his answer, denied that Selden was the author or designer of the books, and denied the infringement charged, and contends on the argument that the matter alleged to be infringed is not a lawful subject of copyright....

[2] The book or series of books of which the complainant claims the copyright consists of an introductory essay explaining the system of book-keeping referred to, to which are annexed certain forms or blanks, consisting of ruled lines, and headings, illustrating the system and showing how it is to be used and carried out in practice. This system effects the same results as book-keeping by double entry; but, by a peculiar arrangement of columns and headings, presents the entire operation, of a day, a week, or a month, on a single page, or on two pages facing each other, in an account-book. The defendant uses a similar plan so far as results are concerned; but makes a different arrangement of the columns, and uses different headings. If

the complainant's testator had the exclusive right to the use of the system explained in his book, it would be difficult to contend that the defendant does not infringe it, notwithstanding the difference in his form of arrangement; but if it be assumed that the system is open to public use, it seems to be equally difficult to contend that the books made and sold by the defendant are a violation of the copyright of the complainant's book considered merely as a book explanatory of the system. Where the truths of a science or the methods of an art are the common property of the whole world, any author has the right to express the one, or explain and use the other, in his own way. As an author, Selden explained the system in a particular way. It may be conceded that Baker makes and uses account-books arranged on substantially the same system; but the proof fails to show that he has violated the copyright of Selden's book, regarding the latter merely as an explanatory work; or that he has infringed Selden's right in any way, unless the latter became entitled to an exclusive right in the system.

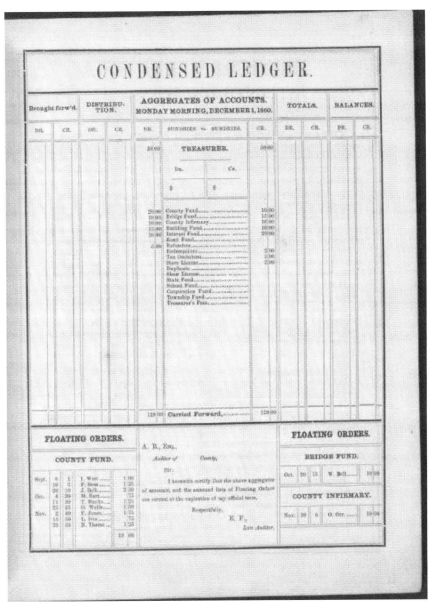

Figure 19: page from *Selden's Condensed Ledger*

[3] The evidence of the complainant is principally directed to the object of showing that Baker uses the same system as that which is explained and illustrated in Selden's books. It becomes important, therefore, to

determine whether, in obtaining the copyright of his books, he secured the exclusive right to the use of the system or method of book-keeping which the said books are intended to illustrate and explain. It is contended that he has secured such exclusive right, because no one can use the system without using substantially the same ruled lines and headings which he was appended to his books in illustration of it. In other words, it is contended that the ruled lines and headings, given to illustrate the system, are a part of the book, and, as such, are secured by the copyright; and that no one can make or use similar ruled lines and headings, or ruled lines and headings made and arranged on substantially the same system, without violating the copyright. And this is really the question to be decided in this case. Stated in another form, the question is, whether the exclusive property in a system of book-keeping can be claimed, under the law or copyright, by means of a book in which that system is explained? ...

[4] There is no doubt that a work on the subject of book-keeping, though only explanatory of well-known systems, may be the subject of a copyright; but, then, it is claimed only as a book. Such a book may be explanatory either of old systems, or of an entirely new system; and, considered as a book, as the work of an author, conveying information on the subject of book-keeping, and containing detailed explanations of the art, it may be a very valuable acquisition to the practical knowledge of the community. But there is a clear distinction between the book, as such, and the art which it is intended to illustrate. The mere statement of the proposition is so evident, that it requires hardly any argument to support it. The same distinction may be predicated of every other art as well as that of book-keeping. A treatise on the composition and use of medicines, be they old or new; on the construction and use of ploughs, or watches, or churns; or on the mixture and application of colors for painting or dyeing; or on the mode of drawing lines to produce the effect of perspective—would be the subject of copyright; but no one would contend that the copyright of the treatise would give the exclusive right to the art or manufacture described therein. The copyright of the book, if not pirated from other works, would be valid without regard to the novelty, or want of novelty, of its subject-matter. The novelty of the art or thing described or explained has nothing to do with the validity of the copyright. To give to the author of the book an exclusive property in the art described therein, when no examination of its novelty has ever been officially made, would be a surprise and a fraud upon the public. That is the province of letters-patent, not of copyright. The claim to an invention or discovery of an art or manufacture must be subjected to the examination of the Patent Office before an exclusive right therein can be obtained; and it can only be secured by a patent from the government.

[5] The difference between the two things, letters-patent and copyright, may be illustrated by reference to the subjects just enumerated. Take the case of medicines. Certain mixtures are found to be of great value in the healing art. If the discoverer writes and publishes a book on the subject (as regular physicians generally do), he gains no exclusive right to the manufacture and sale of the medicine; he gives that to the public. If he desires to acquire such exclusive right, he must obtain a patent for the mixture as a new art, manufacture, or composition of matter. He may copyright his book, if he pleases; but that only secures to him the exclusive right of printing and publishing his book. So of all other inventions or discoveries.

[6] The copyright of a book on perspective, no matter how many drawings and illustrations it may contain, gives no exclusive right to the modes of drawing described, though they may never have been known or used before. By publishing the book, without getting a patent for the art, the latter is given to the public. The fact that the art described in the book by illustrations of lines and figures which are reproduced in practice in the application of the art, makes no difference. Those illustrations are the mere language employed by the author to convey his ideas more clearly. Had he used words of description instead of diagrams (which merely stand in the place of words), there could not be the slightest doubt that others, applying the art to practical use, might lawfully draw the lines and diagrams which were in the author's mind, and which he thus described by words in his book.

[7] The copyright of a work on mathematical science cannot give to the author an exclusive right to the methods of operation which he propounds, or to the diagrams which he employs to explain them, so as to prevent an engineer from using them whenever occasion requires. The very object of publishing a book on science or the useful arts is to communicate to the world the useful knowledge which it contains. But this object would be frustrated if the knowledge could not be used without incurring the guilt of piracy of the book. And where the art it teaches cannot be used without employing the methods and diagrams used to illustrate the book, or such as are similar to them, such methods and diagrams are to be considered as necessary incidents to the art, and given therewith to the public; not given for the purpose of publication in other works explanatory of the art, but for the purpose of practical application....

[8] Of course, these observations are not intended to apply to ornamental designs, or pictorial illustrations addressed to the taste. Of these it may be said, that their form is their essence, and their object, the production of pleasure in their contemplation. This is their final end. They are as much the product of genius and the result of composition, as are the lines of the poet or the historian's period. On the other hand, the teachings of science and the rules and methods of useful art have their final end in application and use; and this application and use are what the public derive from the publication of a book which teaches them. But as embodied and taught in a literary composition or book, their essence consists only in their statement. This alone is what is secured by the copyright. The use by another of the same methods of statement, whether in words or illustrations, in a book published for teaching the art, would undoubtedly be an infringement of the copyright.

[9] ... Charles Selden, by his books, explained and described a peculiar system of book-keeping, and illustrated his method by means of ruled lines and blank columns, with proper headings on a page, or on successive pages. Now, whilst no one has a right to print or publish his book, or any material part thereof, as a book intended to convey instruction in the art, any person may practise and use the art itself which he has described and illustrated therein. The use of the art is a totally different thing from a publication of the book explaining it. The copyright of a book on book-keeping cannot secure the exclusive right to make, sell, and use account-books prepared upon the plan set forth in such book. Whether the art might or might not have been patented, is a question which is not before us. It was not patented, and is open and free to the use of the public. And, of course, in using the art, the ruled lines and headings of accounts must necessarily be used as incident to it.

[10] The plausibility of the claim put forward by the complainant in this case arises from a confusion of ideas produced by the peculiar nature of the art described in the books which have been made the subject of copyright. In describing the art, the illustrations and diagrams employed happen to correspond more closely than usual with the actual work performed by the operator who uses the art. Those illustrations and diagrams consist of ruled lines and headings of accounts; and it is similar ruled lines and headings of accounts which, in the application of the art, the book-keeper makes with his pen, or the stationer with his press; whilst in most other cases the diagrams and illustrations can only be represented in concrete forms of wood, metal, stone, or some other physical embodiment. But the principle is the same in all. The description of the art in a book, though entitled to the benefit of copyright, lays no foundation for an exclusive claim to the art itself. The object of the one is explanation; the object of the other is use. The former may be secured by copyright. The latter can only be secured, if it can be secured at all, by letters-patent....

[11] The conclusion to which we have come is, that blank account-books are not the subject of copyright; and that the mere copyright of Selden's book did not confer upon him the exclusive right to make and use account-books, ruled and arranged as designated by him and described and illustrated in said book....

NOTES

1. For an in-depth consideration of how Congress codified *Baker* in §102(b), see Pamela Samuelson, *Why Copyright Law Excludes Systems and Processes from the Scope of Its Protection*, 85 TEX. L. REV. 1921 (2007).

2. Is a sequence of twenty-six yoga poses and two breathing exercises, as developed by Bikram Choudhury and described in his 1979 book *Bikram's Beginning Yoga Class*, copyrightable? The book contains descriptions, photographs, and drawings of the sequence's poses and exercises. In a copyright infringement lawsuit over unauthorized use of the sequence in a competitor's yoga classes, the Ninth Circuit held that the sequence is not copyrightable. Bikram's Yoga Coll. of India, LP v. Evolation Yoga, Inc., 803 F.3d 1032 (9th Cir. 2015). It reasoned that the sequence is "a healing art: a system designed to yield physical benefits and a sense of well-being," and that the sequence's claim to "produce spiritual and psychological benefits makes it no less a ... system[] or process." Importantly, the court also thought it irrelevant that the sequence's poses might be beautiful or graceful, particularly because

> [t]he performance of many ideas, systems, or processes may be beautiful: a surgeon's intricate movements, a book-keeper's careful notations, or a baker's kneading might each possess a certain grace for at least some viewers. Indeed, from Vermeer's milkmaid to Lewis Hine's power house mechanic, the individual engrossed in a process has long attracted artistic attention. But the beauty of the process does not permit one who describes it to gain, through copyright, the monopolistic power to exclude all others from practicing it. This is true even where, as here, the process was conceived with at least some aesthetic considerations in mind.

3. In what is known as the "blank form" doctrine, the Copyright Office has specified it will not register

> Blank forms, such as time cards, graph paper, account books, diaries, bank checks, scorecards, address books, report forms, order forms and the like, which are designed for recording information and do not in themselves convey information.

37 C.F.R. § 202.1(c). Does the Copyright Office's rule follow from *Baker*? Can you think of any blank forms which should qualify for copyright protection?

4. A critical implication of the idea-expression distinction is the **merger doctrine**. To get a sense of this doctrine, consider *Morrissey v. Proctor & Gamble Co.*, 379 F.2d 675 (1st Cir. 1967). Frank Morrissey owned a copyright in a set of rules for a sweepstakes involving the Social Security numbers of the participants. He sued Proctor & Gamble for copying almost precisely the rules for entry in a sweepstakes contest for Tide detergent. Compare Morrissey's Rule 1 (left) to Proctor & Gamble's (right):

1. Entrants should print name, address and social security number on a boxtop, or a plain paper. Entries must be accompanied by ... boxtop or by plain paper on which the name ... is copied from any source. Official rules are explained on .. packages or leaflets obtained from dealer. If you do not have a social security number you may use the name and number of any member of your immediate family living with you. Only the person named on the entry will be deemed an entrant and may qualify for prize.

Use the correct social security number belonging to the person named on entry ... wrong number will be disqualified.

1. Entrants should print name, address and Social Security number on a Tide boxtop, or on (a) plain paper. Entries must be accompanied by Tide boxtop (any size) or by plain paper on which the name 'Tide' is copied from any source. Official rules are available on Tide Sweepstakes packages, or on leaflets at Tide dealers, or you can send a stamped, self-addressed envelope to: Tide 'Shopping Fling' Sweepstakes, P.O. Box 4459, Chicago 77, Illinois.

If you do not have a Social Security number, you may use the name and number of any member of your immediate family living with you. Only the person named on the entry will be deemed an entrant and may qualify for a prize.

Use the correct Social Security number, belonging to the person named on the entry—wrong numbers will be disqualified.

Baker makes clear that copyright protects original expression describing unprotected contest rules. Although the First Circuit held that there was original expression in Morrissey's rules, it nonetheless denied him copyright protection on them pursuant to the merger doctrine. The court reasoned that when there is "one form of expression, [or] at best only a limited number [of ways to express an idea or system], to permit copyrighting would mean that a party or parties, by copyrighting a mere handful of forms, could exhaust all possibilities of future use of the substance." Put another way, the limited number of ways to express an idea indicates that the idea has merged with the expression itself. Protecting the expression in such circumstances would effectively provide copyright protection for the idea, something copyright law prohibits. In those circumstances, copyright protection ought to be denied to the expression as well.

Instead of denying protection for expression in these circumstances, some courts instead provide what is called **"thin protection,"** wherein only exact or near-exact copying will be prohibited as infringing. For more on the different ways in which courts understand the merger doctrine, see Pamela Samuelson, *Reconceptualizing Copyright's Merger Doctrine*, 63 J. COPYRIGHT SOC'Y U.S.A. 417 (2016).

2. Idea-Expression Distinction

Turning now to a case that applies the idea-expression more canonically, consider what particular policy justifications might undergird copyright law's refusal to protect ideas. What is the connection between the idea-expression distinction and merger doctrine in this case?

ATC Distribution Group, Inc. v. Whatever It Takes Transmissions & Parts, Inc.
402 F.3d 700 (6th Cir. 2005)

BOGGS, C.J.:

[1] Appellant, ATC Distribution Group, Inc., appeals the district court's grant of summary judgment in favor of the Appellees. ATC sells transmission parts. One of ATC's employees, Kenny Hester, left ATC to form his own transmission parts company, Whatever It Takes Transmissions ("WITT"). WITT hired away several of ATC's other employees and created a transmission parts catalog that was almost identical to the ATC catalog, on which Hester had worked while he was with ATC. ATC sued WITT and several of its former employees, including Hester, alleging ... intellectual property ... claims. The district court granted summary judgment in favor of WITT and the other defendants on almost all of ATC's claims.... For the reasons set forth below, we affirm the judgment of the district court in its entirety....

[2] ... This case began with the merger of two companies in 1994. ATC Technology Group, ATC's predecessor-in-interest, acquired Hester Transmission Parts ("HTP"), along with ... the right to use HTP's transmission parts catalog, which HTP had originally acquired from McCarty, a printing company. ATC also acquired the services of Kenny Hester ..., who had worked at HTP ....

[3] Hester eventually left ATC in October 1999 .... Hester started a new transmission parts distributor, WITT, in Louisville, Kentucky in November 1999....

Chapter II – Subject Matter

[4] ... In 1995, ATC first published a transmission parts catalog that Hester had worked on since his days at HTP, a catalog that ATC hoped would become the industry standard. This and subsequent catalogs were distributed throughout the industry. The ATC catalog and the parts numbering system used in the catalog were based on an original catalog and numbering system that McCarty, the printing company, had distributed to several parts wholesalers, each with the wholesaler's own name on it.... After Hester left ATC in 1999, he obtained an electronic copy of the ATC catalog, on which he based a new catalog used by WITT salespeople. According to Hester, no copies of this catalog have ever been distributed outside WITT, but WITT does use many of ATC's part numbers in advertising and in its internal processes.

[5] ATC brought suit against WITT, Hester, and [others] in the United States District Court for the Western District of Kentucky in June 2000, alleging ... copyright infringement (by WITT and Hester), in the form of copying without permission ATC's catalog and the part numbers and illustrations contained in the catalog [among other claims]. All parties moved for summary judgment.

[6] The court granted summary judgment in favor of all named defendants on ATC's claims for copyright infringement ....

[7] The district court ... agreed that the catalog ... lacked the originality required for copyright protection ....

[8] .... ATC argues that its catalog is a creative classification scheme, or taxonomy, which sorts parts into categories and sub-categories, and allocates numbers to each part. Under this theory, the individual part numbers would be protected as the copyrightable expressions of the overall taxonomy....

[9] ATC's parts-classification scheme divides transmission parts into a series of categories and sub-categories. There are three basic categories: brand, transmission type, and type of part. In addition, a suffix field is available to further sub-divide a particular part when appropriate. Within each category, several sub-categories have been created. In the brand category the sub-categories are relatively obvious: the transmissions are listed by manufacturer. In the part category the sub-categories are less obvious, and require decisions such as whether to have a single category of rings, of which some are sealing rings and some are O-rings, or to have two distinct categories, sealing rings and O-rings. Each of the three basic categories and the optional suffix are represented in each part number by a two-digit or three-digit field (with the occasional letter), within which the transmission types or parts are numbered in order, with gaps being left in each sub-category to accommodate new parts in the future. Although all parts within a sub-category are numbered sequentially, the ordering of the sub-categories within a field, or the parts within a sub-category appears to be random. As such, the fact that an "O-ring pump" and an "O-ring pump bolt" are in the same general range of numbers is no accident. But the fact that O-rings in general are numbered in the 300's, and the fact that these two parts are numbered 311 and 312 rather than 341 and 342, are accidental. Each discrete transmission part will have a number that is between five and nine digits and/or letters.

[10] ATC claims that its numbering scheme involves several different types of creativity: (1) deciding what kind of information to convey in part numbers; (2) predicting future developments in the transmission parts industry and deciding how many slots to leave open in a given sub-category to allow for those developments; (3) deciding whether an apparently novel part that does not obviously fit in any of the existing classifications should be assigned a new category of its own or placed in an existing category, and, if the latter, which one; (4) designing the part numbers; and (5) devising the overall taxonomy of part numbers that places the parts into different categories. An example of this last type of creativity would be the decision to include in the catalog entries for "Pressure Plate, Intermediate (Top)" (assigned number 144) and "Pressure Plate, Intermediate (Bottom)" (145), as opposed to using one unitary entry for "Pressure Plate, Intermediate," but adding a suffix to that part number that differentiates between top (1441) and bottom (1442) plates....

[11] Classification schemes can in principle be creative enough to satisfy the originality requirement of copyright protection. *See* Am. Dental Ass'n v. Delta Dental Plans Ass'n, 126 F.3d 977 (7th Cir. 1997) ("Facts do not supply their own principles of organization. Classification is a creative endeavor…. There can be multiple, and equally original, biographies of the same person's life, and multiple original taxonomies of a field of knowledge."). None of ATC's claimed creative endeavors seem particularly creative when compared to a great painting or novel, but the Supreme Court has made clear that only a bare minimum amount of creativity is required to satisfy the constitutional originality requirement. *See* Feist, 499 U.S. at 345. At least some of the decisions made by ATC are arguably non-obvious choices made from among more than a few options.

[12] Original and creative *ideas*, however, are not copyrightable, because 17 U.S.C. § 102(b) provides that "in no case does copyright protection for an original work of authorship extend to any idea, procedure, process, system, method of operation, concept, principle, or discovery, regardless of [its] form." Section 102(b) codifies the common-law principle that unlike a patent, a copyright gives no exclusive right to the art disclosed; protection is given only to the expression of the idea—not the idea itself. And all of the creative aspects of the ATC classification scheme are just that: ideas. ATC cannot copyright its prediction of how many types of sealing ring will be developed in the future, its judgment that O-rings and sealing rings should form two separate categories of parts, or its judgment that a new part belongs with the retainers as opposed to the pressure plates.[4]

[13] The *expression* of ATC's ideas about part classification and the future of the transmission parts market is not barred from copyright protection by the idea-expression distinction. It is barred, however, in part by the "merger doctrine," and in part by the originality requirement. For almost all of the types of creativity claimed by ATC, there is only one reasonable way to express the underlying idea. For example, the only way to express the prediction that a maximum of four additional types of sealing ring might be developed is to leave four numbers unallocated, and the only way to express the idea that a novel part should be placed with the sealing rings rather than with the gaskets is to place that part with the sealing rings. Under the merger doctrine, when there is essentially only one way to express an idea, the idea and its expression are inseparable, and copyright is no bar to copying that expression.

[14] The only aspect of the numbering system that does not merge with the underlying idea is the allocation of numbers to each sub-category, and ultimately to each part. ATC argues that its individual part numbers are copyright protected as expressions of the catalog as a whole, and cites as authority the Seventh Circuit's holding in *American Dental*, which held that the American Dental Association's Code on Dental Procedures and Nomenclature was copyrightable. The Code classified dental procedures into groups, with each procedure receiving a number, a short description, and a long description. For example, number 04267 was assigned to the short description "guided tissue regeneration-nonresorbable barrier, per site, per tooth (includes membrane removal)." The Seventh Circuit held that the numbers assigned to each procedure were copyrightable, in addition to the long and short descriptions of each procedure.

[15] The *American Dental* court's rationale for holding that the individual procedure numbers were copyrightable is rather opaque:

> Number 04267 reads "guided tissue regeneration-nonresorbable barrier, per site, per tooth" but could have read "regeneration of tissue, guided by nonresorbable barrier, one site and tooth per entry". Or "use of barrier to guide regeneration of tissue, without regard to the number of sites per tooth and whether or not the barrier is resorbable". The first variation is linguistic, the

---

[4] As the district court notes, permitting copyright protection for ATC's choice of where in the catalog to locate a new part would be akin to granting copyright protection to a grocer who decides to display a new type of heirloom tomato with the gourmet produce, as opposed to with the other tomatoes or the locally grown produce.

second substantive; in each case the decision to use the actual description is original to the ADA, not knuckling under to an order imposed on language by some "fact" about dental procedures. Blood is shed in the ADA's committees about which description is preferable. The number assigned to any one of the three descriptions could have had four or six digits rather than five; guided tissue regeneration could have been placed in the 2500 series rather than the 4200 series; again any of these choices is original to the author of a taxonomy, and another author could do things differently. Every number in the ADA's Code begins with zero, assuring a large supply of unused numbers for procedures to be devised or reclassified in the future; an author could have elected instead to leave wide gaps inside the sequence. A catalog that initially assigns 04266, 04267, 04268 to three procedures will over time depart substantively from one that initially assigns 42660, 42670, and 42680 to the same three procedures. So all three elements of the Code-numbers, short descriptions, and long descriptions, are copyrightable subject matter under 17 U.S.C. § 102(a).

Almost all of this passage concerns either the wording of the descriptions, or the creative thought that went into the underlying taxonomy, such as the decision to leave gaps in the numbering system. The discussion of the numbers themselves is limited to two immaterial observations: that numbers in the 4200's rather than the 2500's were assigned to guided tissue regeneration; and that the numbers assigned to a particular procedure in a catalog will differ depending on the prior allocation of numbers to other procedures. Neither of these facts evidences any creativity by the ADA that would render the numbers eligible for copyright protection. The mere fact that numbers are attached to, or are a by-product of categories and descriptions that are copyrightable does not render the numbers themselves copyrightable. *See* Southco, Inc. v. Kanebridge Corp., 258 F.3d 148 (3d Cir. 2001) ("For purposes of copyright law ... [a] numbering system itself and the actual numbers produced by the system are two very different works," such that even if the underlying system is original and creative, the numbers themselves are not copyrightable unless they are assigned to parts in a creative way).

[16] Even assuming, arguendo, that some strings of numbers used to designate an item or procedure could be sufficiently creative to merit copyright protection, the parts numbers at issue in the case before us do not evidence any such creativity. ATC's allocation of numbers to parts was an essentially random process, serving only to provide a useful shorthand way of referring to each part. The only reason that a "sealing ring, pump slide" is allocated number 176 is the random ordering of sub-categories of parts, and the random ordering of parts within that sub-category. Were it not for a series of random orderings within each category field, a given part could be 47165 or 89386. As such, the particular numbers allocated to each part do not express any of the creative ideas that went into the classification scheme in any way that could be considered eligible for copyright protection. These numbers are no more copyrightable than would be the fruit of an author's labors if she wrote a book and then "translated" it into numbers using a random number generator for each letter in every word. Even if the text in English was copyrightable, the randomly generated list of numbers that comprised the "translation" could not be....

[17] As a last resort, ATC suggested during oral argument that even if neither the ideas that gave rise to the parts numbers, nor the individual part numbers, *qua* expressions of those ideas, are copyrightable, the part numbers taken as a whole were somehow copyrightable as a middle ground between the two, much in the same way that while neither the basic idea behind a novel nor the individual words used to write it are protected, the story that those words form when taken together is copyrightable. The flaw in this argument is that there is no such middle ground in this case. Unlike the words that comprise a novel, which add up to a story, the numbers used in ATC's catalog only add up to a long list of numbers. Putting all the numbers together does not make them expressive in the way that putting words together makes a narrative....

NOTES

1. The First Amendment is often cited as a basis for the idea-expression distinction. As the Supreme Court observed in *Feist*, copyright law "assures authors the right to their original expression, but encourages others to build freely upon the ideas and information conveyed by a work." Feist Publ'ns, Inc. v. Rural Tel. Serv. Co., 499 U.S. 340, 349-50 (1991). For an exploration and criticism of this justification vis-à-vis First Amendment values, see Neil Weinstock Netanel, *Locating Copyright Within the First Amendment Skein*, 54 STAN. L. REV. 1 (2001).

2. To assess whether something is an unprotectable idea, one must first specify a work's idea (or ideas). Courts frequently note how difficult it is to distinguish between idea and expression, *see, e.g.*, Nichols v. Universal Pictures Corp., 45 F.2d 119, 121 (2d Cir.1930), and there is little to no guiding doctrine on how to ascertain a work's idea (or ideas). For a rare judicial meditation on this essential issue, consider this reflection on how to ascertain the idea of Peter Kaplan's disturbing photograph, shown in Figure 20:

> *[W]hat is the "idea" of Kaplan's photograph? Is it (1) a businessman contemplating suicide by jumping from a building, (2) a businessman contemplating suicide by jumping from a building, seen from the vantage point of the businessman, with his shoes set against the street far below, or perhaps something more general, such as (3) a sense of desperation produced by urban professional life?*

Mannion v. Coors Brewing Co., 377 F. Supp. 2d 444, 456 (S.D.N.Y. 2005). How does the precise articulation of the idea affect copyrightability? The opinion goes on to suggest that one can ascertain the idea of a literary work much more easily than the idea of a photograph or other visual arts. Is that correct?

Figure 20: Peter Kaplan photograph

3. An extension of the merger doctrine is the doctrine of **scènes à faire**, which applies primarily to fictional works (but also, as we shall see, to computer software). As explained by one court, the doctrine bars protection of the "incidents, characters or settings which are as a practical matter indispensable, or at least standard in the treatment of a given topic." Atari, Inc. v. N. Am. Phillips Consumer Elecs. Corp., 672 F.2d 607, 616 (7th Cir. 1982). The animating principle is the same as with the merger doctrine: To give protection to these character or plot elements would counterproductively bar others from writing similar settings, even when those settings are standard for the genre. Consider one (era-specific) application of this doctrine: "Elements such as drunks, prostitutes, vermin and derelict cars would appear in any realistic work about the

work of policemen in the South Bronx." Walker v. Time Life Films, Inc., 784 F.2d 44, 50 (2d Cir. 1986).

---

3. Historical Fact-Expression Distinction

Consider now a third category of unprotectable matter: historical facts. As you read this opinion, reflect on the reasons that historical facts are unprotectable. Does § 102(b) forbid their protection? What incentives does the historical fact-expression distinction provide to historians?

A.A. Hoehling v. Universal City Studios, Inc.
618 F.2d 972 (2d Cir. 1980)

KAUFMAN, C.J.: ...

[1] This litigation arises from three separate accounts of the triumphant introduction, last voyage, and tragic destruction of the Hindenburg, the colossal dirigible constructed in Germany during Hitler's reign. The zeppelin, the last and most sophisticated in a fleet of luxury airships, which punctually floated its wealthy passengers from the Third Reich to the United States, exploded into flames and disintegrated in 35 seconds as it hovered above the Lakehurst, New Jersey Naval Air Station at 7:25 p. m. on May 6, 1937. Thirty-six passengers and crew were killed but, fortunately, 52 persons survived. Official investigations conducted by both American and German authorities could ascertain no definitive cause of the disaster, but both suggested the plausibility of static electricity or St. Elmo's Fire, which could have ignited the highly explosive hydrogen that filled the airship. Throughout, the investigators refused to rule out the possibility of sabotage.

[2] The destruction of the Hindenburg marked the concluding chapter in the chronicle of airship passenger service, for after the tragedy at Lakehurst, the Nazi regime permanently grounded the Graf Zeppelin I and discontinued its plan to construct an even larger dirigible, the Graf Zeppelin II.

[3] The final pages of the airship's story marked the beginning of a series of journalistic, historical, and literary accounts devoted to the Hindenburg and its fate. Indeed, weeks of testimony by a plethora of witnesses before the official investigative panels provided fertile source material for would-be authors. Moreover, both the American and German Commissions issued official reports, detailing all that was then known of the tragedy. A number of newspaper and magazine articles had been written about the Hindenburg in 1936, its first year of trans-Atlantic service, and they, of course, multiplied many fold after the crash. In addition, two passengers Margaret Mather and Gertrud Adelt published separate and detailed accounts of the voyage, C.E. Rosendahl, commander of the Lakehurst Naval Air Station and a pioneer in airship travel himself, wrote a book titled *What About the Airship?*, in which he endorsed the theory that the Hindenburg was the victim of sabotage. In 1957, Nelson Gidding, who would return to the subject of the Hindenburg some 20 years later, wrote an unpublished "treatment" for a motion picture based on the deliberate destruction of the airship.... In 1962, Dale Titler released *Wings of Mystery*, in which he too devoted a chapter to the Hindenburg.[1]

[4] Appellant A.A. Hoehling published *Who Destroyed the Hindenburg?*, a full-length book based on his exhaustive research in 1962. Mr. Hoehling studied the investigative reports, consulted previously published articles and books, and conducted interviews with survivors of the crash as well as others who possessed

---

[1] Titler's account was published after the release of appellant's book. In an affidavit in this litigation, Titler states that he copied Hoehling's theory of sabotage. Hoehling, however, has never instituted a copyright action against Titler.

information about the Hindenburg. His book is presented as a factual account, written in an objective, reportorial style.

[5] The first half recounts the final crossing of the Hindenburg, from Sunday, May 2, when it left Frankfurt, to Thursday, May 6, when it exploded at Lakehurst. Hoehling describes the airship, its role as an instrument of propaganda in Nazi Germany, its passengers and crew, the danger of hydrogen, and the ominous threats received by German officials, warning that the Hindenburg would be destroyed. The second portion, headed *The Quest*, sets forth the progress of the official investigations, followed by an account of Hoehling's own research. In the final chapter, spanning eleven pages, Hoehling suggests that all proffered explanations of the explosion, save deliberate destruction, are unconvincing. He concludes that the most likely saboteur is one Eric Spehl, a "rigger" on the Hindenburg crew who was killed at Lakehurst.

[6] According to Hoehling, Spehl had motive, expertise, and opportunity to plant an explosive device, constructed of dry-cell batteries and a flashbulb, in "Gas Cell 4," the location of the initial explosion. An amateur photographer with access to flashbulbs, Spehl could have destroyed the Hindenburg to please his ladyfriend, a suspected communist dedicated to exploding the myth of Nazi invincibility.

[7] Ten years later appellee Michael MacDonald Mooney published his book, *The Hindenburg*. Mooney's endeavor might be characterized as more literary than historical in its attempt to weave a number of symbolic themes through the actual events surrounding the tragedy. His dominant theme contrasts the natural beauty of the month of May, when the disaster occurred, with the cold, deliberate progress of "technology." The May theme is expressed not simply by the season, but also by the character of Spehl, portrayed as a sensitive artisan with needle and thread. The Hindenburg, in contrast, is the symbol of technology, as are its German creators and the Reich itself. The destruction is depicted as the ultimate triumph of nature over technology, as Spehl plants the bomb that ignites the hydrogen. Developing this theme from the outset, Mooney begins with an extended review of man's efforts to defy nature through flight, focusing on the evolution of the zeppelin. This story culminates in the construction of the Hindenburg, and the Nazis' claims of its indestructibility. Mooney then traces the fateful voyage, advising the reader almost immediately of Spehl's scheme. The book concludes with the airship's explosion.

[8] Mooney acknowledges, in this case, that he consulted Hoehling's book, and that he relied on it for some details. He asserts that he first discovered the "Spehl-as-saboteur" theory when he read Titler's *Wings of Mystery*. Indeed, Titler concludes that Spehl was the saboteur, for essentially the reasons stated by Hoehling. Mooney also claims to have studied the complete National Archives and New York Times files concerning the Hindenburg, as well as all previously published material. Moreover, he traveled to Germany, visited Spehl's birthplace, and conducted a number of interviews with survivors.

[9] After Mooney prepared an outline of his anticipated book, his publisher succeeded in negotiations to sell the motion picture rights to appellee Universal City Studios. Universal then commissioned a screen story by writers Levinson and Link, best known for their television series, *Columbo*, in which a somewhat disheveled, but wise detective unravels artfully conceived murder mysteries. In their screen story, Levinson and Link created a Columbo-like character who endeavored to identify the saboteur on board the Hindenburg. Director Robert Wise, however, was not satisfied with this version, and called upon Nelson Gidding to write a final screenplay. Gidding, it will be recalled, had engaged in preliminary work on a film about the Hindenburg almost twenty years earlier.

[10] The Gidding screenplay follows what is known in the motion picture industry as a "Grand Hotel" formula, developing a number of fictional characters and subplots involving them. This formula has become standard fare in so-called "disaster" movies .... In the film, which was released in late 1975, a rigger named "Boerth," who has an anti-Nazi ladyfriend, plans to destroy the airship in an effort to embarrass the Reich. Nazi officials,

vaguely aware of sabotage threats, station a Luftwaffe intelligence officer on the zeppelin, loosely resembling a Colonel Erdmann who was aboard the Hindenburg. This character is portrayed as a likable fellow who soon discovers that Boerth is the saboteur. Boerth, however, convinces him that the Hindenburg should be destroyed and the two join forces, planning the explosion for several hours after the landing at Lakehurst, when no people would be on board. In Gidding's version, the airship is delayed by a storm, frantic efforts to defuse the bomb fail, and the Hindenburg is destroyed. The film's subplots involve other possible suspects, including a fictional countess who has had her estate expropriated by the Reich, two fictional confidence men wanted by New York City police, and an advertising executive rushing to close a business deal in America.

[11] Upon learning of Universal's plans to release the film, Hoehling instituted this action against Universal [and Mooney] for copyright infringement ....

[12] Hoehling's principal claim is that both Mooney and Universal copied the essential plot of his book i.e., Eric Spehl, influenced by his girlfriend, sabotaged the Hindenburg by placing a crude bomb in Gas Cell 4.... [A]ppellees have labored to convince us that their plots are not substantially similar to Hoehling's. While Hoehling's Spehl destroys the airship to please his communist girlfriend, Mooney's character is motivated by an aversion to the technological age. Universal's Boerth, on the other hand, is a fervent anti-fascist who enlists the support of a Luftwaffe colonel who, in turn, unsuccessfully attempts to defuse the bomb at the eleventh hour.

[13] .... [A]ppellees further argue that Hoehling's plot is an idea, and ideas are not copyrightable as a matter of law.

[14] Hoehling, however, correctly rejoins that while ideas themselves are not subject to copyright, his "expression" of his idea is copyrightable....

[15] [In] works of fiction, ... the distinction between an idea and its expression is especially elusive. But, where, as here, the idea at issue is an interpretation of an historical event, ... such interpretations are not copyrightable as a matter of law.... [Even when] the plots of ... two works were necessarily similar, there could be no infringement because of the public benefit in encouraging the development of historical and biographical works and their public distribution. To avoid a chilling effect on authors who contemplate tackling an historical issue or event, broad latitude must be granted to subsequent authors who make use of historical subject matter, including theories or plots....

[16] [T]he hypothesis that Eric Spehl destroyed the Hindenburg is based entirely on the interpretation of historical facts, including Spehl's life, his girlfriend's anti-Nazi connections, the explosion's origin in Gas Cell 4, Spehl's duty station, discovery of a dry-cell battery among the wreckage, and rumors about Spehl's involvement dating from a 1938 Gestapo investigation. Such an historical interpretation, whether or not it originated with Mr. Hoehling, is not protected by his copyright and can be freely used by subsequent authors....

[17] The same reasoning governs Hoehling's claim that a number of specific facts, ascertained through his personal research, were copied by appellees.[6] ... [F]actual information is in the public domain. Each appellee had the right to avail himself of the facts contained in Hoehling's book and to use such information, whether

---

[6] .... The following ten examples ... are illustrative: (1) Eric Spehl's age and birthplace; (2) Crew members had smuggled monkeys on board the Graf Zeppelin; (3) Germany's ambassador to the United States dismissed threats of sabotage; (4) A warning letter had been received from a Mrs. Rauch; (5) The Hindenburg's captain was constructing a new home in Zeppelinheim; (6) Eric Spehl was a photographer; (7) The airship flew over Boston; (8) The Hindenburg was "tail heavy" before landing; (9) A member of the ground crew had etched his name in the zeppelin's hull; and (10) The navigator set the Hindenburg's course by reference to various North Atlantic islands.

correct or incorrect, in his own literary work.... [W]e refuse to subscribe to the view that an author is absolutely precluded from saving time and effort by referring to and relying upon prior published material. It is just such wasted effort that the proscription against the copyright of ideas and facts are designed to prevent.

[18] The remainder of Hoehling's claimed similarities relate to random duplications of phrases and sequences of events. For example, all three works contain a scene in a German beer hall, in which the airship's crew engages in revelry prior to the voyage. Other claimed similarities concern common German greetings of the period, such as "Heil Hitler," or songs, such as the German National anthem. These elements, however, are merely scenes a faire, that is, incidents, characters or settings which are as a practical matter indispensable, or at least standard, in the treatment of a given topic. Because it is virtually impossible to write about a particular historical era or fictional theme without employing certain stock or standard literary devices, ... scenes a faire are not copyrightable as a matter of law....

[19] All of Hoehling's allegations of copying, therefore, encompass material that is non-copyrightable as a matter of law .... We are aware, however, that in distinguishing between themes, facts, and scenes a faire on the one hand, and copyrightable expression on the other, courts may lose sight of the forest for the trees. By factoring out similarities based on non-copyrightable elements, a court runs the risk of overlooking wholesale usurpation of a prior author's expression. A verbatim reproduction of another work, of course, even in the realm of nonfiction, is actionable as copyright infringement. Thus, ... courts should assure themselves that the works before them are not virtually identical. In this case, it is clear that all three authors relate the story of the Hindenburg differently.

[20] In works devoted to historical subjects, it is our view that a second author may make significant use of prior work, so long as he does not bodily appropriate the expression of another. This principle is justified by the fundamental policy undergirding the copyright laws the encouragement of contributions to recorded knowledge. The financial reward guaranteed to the copyright holder is but an incident of this general objective, rather than an end in itself. Knowledge is expanded as well by granting new authors of historical works a relatively free hand to build upon the work of their predecessors.[7] ...

NOTES

1. The producer of the *Seinfeld* television series sued the publisher of *The Seinfeld Aptitude Test*, a book filled with trivia questions about the series. The book publisher argued in its defense that it did not copy any protected expression, but rather asked trivia questions about the series' underlying (and unprotected) facts. For example, one multiple-choice question asked:

> To impress a woman, George passes himself off as
> a)   a gynecologist
> b)   a geologist
> c)   a marine biologist
> d)   a meteorologist

Then-district court Judge Sotomayor rejected the defendant's characterization, ruling that these purported facts are not historical facts, but **created facts**:

---

[7] We note that publication of Mooney's book and release of the motion picture revived long dormant interest in the Hindenburg. As a result, Hoehling's book, which had been out of print for some time, was actually re-released after the film was featured in theaters across the country.

> *[The trivia book] does not pose "factual" questions about the Seinfeld show; it does not ask who acts in the program, who directs or produces the show, how many seasons it has run, etc. Instead, [it] poses questions about the events depicted during episodes of the Seinfeld show. The facts depicted in a Seinfeld episode, however, are quite unlike the facts depicted in a biography, historical text, or compilation. Seinfeld is fiction; both the "facts" in the various Seinfeld episodes, and the expression of those facts, are plaintiff's creation. Thus, ... [the book] is devoted to questions concerning creative components of Seinfeld. In other words, by copying "facts" that plaintiff invented, [the book] appropriates [the] plaintiff's original contributions.*

Castle Rock Ent. v. Carol Pub. Group, Inc., 955 F. Supp. 260, 266 (S.D.N.Y. 1997), aff'd, 150 F.3d 132 (2d Cir. 1998). "Created facts" as a category is thus a misnomer. The material that then-Judge Sotomayor refers to as "created facts" is, rather, simply copyrightable expression (though a type of expression that might be especially likely to qualify as fair use (Chapter VI)). For more on created facts, see Justin Hughes, *Created Facts and the Flawed Ontology of Copyright Law*, 83 NOTRE DAME L. REV. 43 (2007).

2. In addition to historical facts, some cases focus on expression based on unprotectable **natural facts** (that is, facts about natural objects). In a lawsuit by artist Richard Satava against artist Christopher Lowry, the Ninth Circuit held that Satava's glass-in-glass jellyfish sculptures were not copyrightable. Satava v. Lowry, 323 F.3d 805 (9th Cir. 2003). The court reasoned that a realistic depiction of jellyfish, in a clear outer layer of glass which took the shape of the jellyfish, is not protectable: "These elements are so commonplace in glass-in-glass sculpture and so typical of jellyfish physiology that to recognize copyright protection in their combination effectively would give Satava a monopoly on lifelike glass-in-glass sculptures of single jellyfish with vertical tentacles." Can you envision a jellyfish sculpture in a glass-in-glass structure that is copyrightable?

 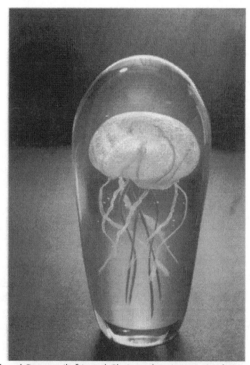

Figure 21: glass-in-glass jellyfish sculptures by Richard Satava (left) and Christopher Lowry (right)

3. Another complicated issue arises with regard to so-called **opinion-based facts**. In one decision on the copyrightability of *Automobile Red Book* valuations, the Second Circuit found the valuations to be protectable because they "were neither reports of historical prices nor mechanical derivations of historical prices or other

data." CCC Info. Servs., Inc. v. Maclean Hunter Mkt. Reports, Inc., 44 F.3d 61, 67 (2d Cir. 1994). Instead, the court understood them to "represent[] predictions by the *Red Book* editors of future prices estimated to cover specified geographic regions .... based not only on a multitude of data sources, but also on professional judgment and expertise." By contrast, the Second Circuit denied copyrightability to a mercantile exchange's settlement prices that it produced to value customers' open positions. N.Y. Mercantile Exch., Inc. v. Intercontinental Exchange, Inc., 497 F.3d 109, 114 (2d Cir. 2007). The Second Circuit noted that the exchange acts more as "a census taker, copying the market's valuation of futures contracts" than as a "creat[or of] the settlement prices." N.Y. Mercantile Exch., Inc. v. Intercontinental Exchange, Inc., 497 F.3d 109, 114 (2d Cir. 2007).

Figure 22: sample pages from *The Automobile Red Book*

4. Not only does copyright law not protect historical facts, but courts also generally refuse to protect aspects of a work that are held out as factual even if these aspects are actually fictional. This doctrine is frequently known as **copyright estoppel,** though the Ninth Circuit has referred to it as the "asserted truths" doctrine. Corbello v. Valli, 974 F.3d 965 (9th Cir. 2020). The exclusion does not depend on whether the facts are objectively or scientifically true. It depends on whether the author holds them out as true. For example, this doctrine has been applied to bar protection for a work the author claimed was dictated to him by the spirit of a dead person. Oliver v. St. Germain Found., 41 F. Supp. 296 (S.D. Cal. 1941). The author's subjective belief regarding the truth or falsity of elements of a work presented as factual is also irrelevant; if the author represents elements to be facts, then the author is estopped from later claiming copyright protection for those "facts." The Ninth Circuit has explained that "It would hinder, not promote the progress of science and useful arts to allow a copyright owner to spring an infringement suit on subsequent authors who built freely on a work held out as factual, contending after the completion of the copyrighted work, and against the work's own averments, that the purported truths were actually fictions." *Corbello*, 974 F.3d at 979. How should this doctrine handle fictional works that use claims to truthfulness as a literary device, like the Orson Welles radio broadcast of "War of the Worlds"?

E. Copyrightable Subject Matter

This section considers the range of copyrightable subject matter. After introducing the categories of copyrightable subject matter, it discusses a mass exclusion of government works from protection and then three particular categories of subject matter—useful articles, architectural works, and computer software—that raise special concerns about the boundaries of copyrightability.

1. Introduction to Categories

Section 102(a) lists different types of works of authorship that copyright law protects:

> *Works of authorship include the following categories:*
>
> *(1) literary works;*
> *(2) musical works, including any accompanying words;*
> *(3) dramatic works, including any accompanying music;*
> *(4) pantomimes and choreographic works;*
> *(5) pictorial, graphic, and sculptural works;*
> *(6) motion pictures and other audiovisual works;*
> *(7) sound recordings; and*
> *(8) architectural works.*

Note that the statutory language suggests that this list is not exhaustive, because in listing these categories, the section says "include." That said, the Copyright Office has expressed the view that only Congress, and not the courts, can provide for the copyrightability of works falling outside the enumerated categories. COPYRIGHT OFFICE COMPENDIUM (THIRD) §§ 307, 313.3. And no court has yet found copyrightable any work falling outside the enumerated categories. For example, the Second Circuit has held that basketball games are not copyrightable subject matter, reasoning that the enumerated "list does not include athletic events, and, although the list is concededly non-exclusive, such events are neither similar nor analogous to any of the listed categories." Nat'l Basketball Ass'n v. Motorola, Inc., 105 F.3d 841, 846 (2d Cir. 1997). This doctrinal development might be explained in several ways. Perhaps courts have not yet found fixed and original works of authorship outside of the broad illustrative categories that Congress established. Or perhaps courts lack a clear method to determine whether a new subject matter category ought to qualify. Alternatively, maybe courts mistakenly believe they cannot protect under copyright law any matter outside of the illustrative categories listed in the Act. Reconsider the Seventh Circuit's *Kelley* decision, which you read in section B to hold that a garden is not fixed. Do you think a garden is copyrightable subject matter?

The statutory category into which a work falls can matter. As we shall see, the category can determine which rights a copyright holder gets. Moreover, courts can apply different approaches to different categories, as we just saw with regard to compilations. Relatedly, a work (or a work's components) can fall into more than one category at a time.

Before delving into the more complicated categories in the sections below, it is helpful to get a sense of how these enumerated categories have been defined. Section 101 defines some of them. In particular, it defines **literary works** as

> *works, other than audiovisual works, expressed in words, numbers, or other verbal or numerical symbols or indicia, regardless of the nature of the material objects, such as books, periodicals, manuscripts, phonorecords, film, tapes, disks, or cards, in which they are embodied.*

This category includes, as expected, material like novels. In addition, perhaps less intuitively, it also includes material that humans typically do not read, such as computer software code, as discussed in more detail in section 5 below.

Based on the list in § 102(a), note that there are two copyrights that generally attach to a song: The first is the **musical work**, which is the song composition itself—the arrangement of notes, chords, rhythms, and other compositional elements. The second is the **sound recording**—the actual fixed performance of the song. As defined by § 101, sound recordings are

> *works that result from the fixation of a series of musical, spoken, or other sounds, but not including the sounds accompanying a motion picture or other audiovisual work, regardless of the nature of the material objects, such as disks, tapes, or other phonorecords, in which they are embodied.*

Until 2018, sound recordings were eligible for federal copyright protection only if fixed on or after February 15, 1972 (when sound recordings were added as a § 102(a) category). The Sound Recording Amendment of 1971, Pub. L. No. 92-140, 85 Stat. 391. In 2018, Congress extended much of federal copyright's protections to pre-1972 sound recordings. The Orrin G. Hatch-Bob Goodlatte Music Modernization Act, Pub. L. No. 115-264, 132 Stat. 3676 (2018).

Pictorial, graphic, and sculptural works are another category of copyrightable works. Section 101 defines them as

> *two-dimensional and three-dimensional works of fine, graphic, and applied art, photographs, prints and art reproductions, maps, globes, charts, diagrams, models, and technical drawings, including architectural plans.*

Copyright protection for this category of works is limited by the **useful articles doctrine**, which we explore in detail below in section 3.

Section 101 defines **motion pictures** as

> *audiovisual works consisting of a series of related images which, when shown in succession, impart an impression of motion, together with accompanying sounds, if any.*

It further defines **audiovisual works** as

> *works that consist of a series of related images which are intrinsically intended to be shown by the use of machines, or devices such as projectors, viewers, or electronic equipment, together with accompanying sounds, if any, regardless of the nature of the material objects, such as films or tapes, in which the works are embodied.*

We defer the definition of architectural works until our deeper discussion of them below in section 5.

2. Exclusion of Government Works

Before exploring further some of the most difficult categories of copyrightable subject matter, this section sets out one wholesale exclusion from the categories of protectable subject matter: that of certain government works. Section 105 sets out that

Copyright protection under this title is not available for any work of the United States Government, but the United States Government is not precluded from receiving and holding copyrights transferred to it by assignment, bequest, or otherwise.

This provision encodes more systematically what has long been a prohibition under the common law from obtaining copyright protection for government edicts. In particular, the U.S. Supreme Court long ago stated that copyright cannot be claimed in federal judicial opinions. Wheaton v. Peters, 33 U.S. (8 Pet.) 591 (1834). The Supreme Court has recently more broadly clarified that as per the **government edicts doctrine**, "copyright does not vest in works that are (1) created by judges and legislators (2) in the course of their judicial and legislative duties," extending *Wheaton*'s reasoning to state judicial opinions and federal and state statutes, not to mention judicial concurrences and dissents and annotations contained in a state's official annotated code. Georgia v. Public.Resource.Org, Inc., 140 S. Ct. 1498, 1508 (2020). The Court explained that "judges, acting as judges, cannot be 'authors' because of their authority to make and interpret the law," just as "legislators, acting as legislators, cannot be either."

This restriction on copyright protection for government edicts is grounded in constitutional and policy considerations. First, denying copyright protection maximizes access to the law and government information so that citizens can know, discuss, use, and seek to change the law and the government's operation. This reasoning is grounded in the right to free speech, due process rights, and policies related to ensuring a democratic government. Second, government works are typically paid for with public funds, which might imply public ownership of those works, or at least no need for a second subsidy of those works via copyright protection. Query whether the typical reasons for copyright protection apply to government works. For more on these issues, see Shyamkrishna Balganesh, *Authoring the Law*, 69 J. COPYRIGHT SOC'Y U.S.A. (forthcoming 2022); Shubha Ghosh, *Legal Code and the Need for a Broader Functionality Doctrine in Copyright*, 50 J. COPYRIGHT SOC'Y U.S.A. 71 (2003); Samuel E. Trosow, *Copyright Protection for Federally Funded Research: Necessary Incentive or Double Subsidy?*, 22 CARDOZO ARTS & ENT. L.J. 613 (2004); Note, Andrea Simon, *A Constitutional Analysis of Copyrighting Government-Commissioned Work*, 84 COLUM. L. REV. 425 (1984).

Even though court decisions barring protection for government edicts refer to federal and state governmental works interchangeably, § 105—by its terms—forbids copyright protection only for federal government works. In particular, § 101 defines a "work of the United States Government" as "a work prepared by an officer or employee of the United States Government as part of that person's official duties." Yet in another way, this statutory bar sweeps more broadly than the narrower common law government edicts doctrine: "That bar applies to works created by all federal 'officer[s] or employee[s],' without regard for the nature of their position or scope of their authority.... Th[e narrower government edicts] doctrine does not apply to non-lawmaking [state] officials, leaving States free to assert copyright in the vast majority of expressive works they produce, such as those created by their universities, libraries, tourism offices, and so on." *Georgia*, 140 S. Ct. at 1510.*

By the statutory terms, § 105 also does not bar copyright in works specially commissioned by the federal government from independent contractors. H.R. REP. NO. 1476, 94th Cong., 2d Sess. 47, at 59 (1976). Similarly, federally funded works are not excluded from obtaining copyright protection. Schnapper v. Foley, 667 F.2d 102 (D.C. Cir. 1981). Note also that § 105 expressly allows for the federal government to hold copyright in works for which copyright has been transferred to the federal government by assignment,

---

* That said, in 2019, Congress carved out a narrow exception to provide that "a civilian member of the faculty of [certain military] institution[s]" "owns the copyright" to "a literary work produced by [the member] in the course of employment [such an] institution for publication by a scholarly press or journal." 17 U.S.C. §§ 105(b)-(c). Congress went on to provide that "[t]he Secretary of Defense may direct [such authors of such works] to provide the Federal Government with an irrevocable, royalty-free, world-wide, nonexclusive license to reproduce, distribute, perform, or display such covered work for purposes of the United States Government." *Id.* § 105(c).

bequest, or otherwise. Together, these provisions open up the possibility for the federal government to subvert the prohibition on copyright by hiring independent contractors to create a copyrightable work, for which they transfer their copyright to the federal government. *See, e.g.*, United States v. Wash. Mint, LLC, 115 F. Supp. 2d 1089 (D. Minn. 2000).

What does the Supreme Court's rule in *Georgia* mean for model codes drafted by a private organization that are then adopted as law in one or more jurisdictions? The First Circuit had previously ruled that in such a situation the code enters the public domain once it is adopted into law, reasoning that:

> *Due process requires people to have notice of what the law requires of them so that they may obey it and avoid its sanctions. So long as the law is generally available for the public to examine, then everyone may be considered to have constructive notice of it; any failure to gain actual notice results from simple lack of diligence. But if access to the law is limited, then the people will or may be unable to learn of its requirements and may be thereby deprived of the notice to which due process entitles them.*

Building Officials & Code Adm'rs Int'l, Inc. v. Code Tech., Inc., 628 F.2d 730, 734 (1st Cir. 1980).

The law remains less clear-cut for private materials incorporated in part into state or local law. For example, the Second Circuit has held that "a state's [mere] reference to a copyrighted work as a legal standard for valuation" does not prohibit an assertion of copyright. CCC Info. Servs., Inc. v. Maclean Hunter Mkt. Reports, Inc., 44 F.3d 61, 74 (2d Cir. 1994). The Fifth Circuit has observed that materials created privately for reasons other than adoption or incorporation into law might provide more justification in favor of copyrightability. *Veeck*, 293 F.3d at 805. The Second Circuit has ruled that two factors govern copyrightability: "(1) whether the entity or individual who created the work needs an economic incentive to create or has a proprietary interest in creating the work and (2) whether the public needs notice of this particular work to have notice of the law." County of Suffolk, N.Y. v. First Am. Real Estate Solutions, 261 F.3d 179, 194 (2d Cir. 2001). Does this reasoning remain valid following the Supreme Court's rule in *Georgia*? *See* Int'l Code Council, Inc. v. UpCodes, Inc., No. 17 Civ. 6261 (VM), 2020 WL 2750636 (S.D.N.Y. May 27, 2020) (distinguishing *Suffolk* post-*Georgia*, saying that "where due process concerns are particularly high, as where a work is itself 'the law,' an author's economic incentives play a particularly low role in the analysis, if any").

Similar to § 105, some foreign governments deny copyright protection to their own government works. 1 NIMMER ON COPYRIGHT § 5.13[E] (2021). Less clear is whether U.S. copyright law denies protection to foreign government works. The Berne Convention leaves that question to the U.S. government to decide. Berne Convention (Paris text), art. 2(4) ("It shall be a matter for legislation in the countries of the Union to determine the protection to be granted to official texts of a legislative, administrative and legal nature, and to official translations of such texts."). Section 105 does not address this category of works, but the same due process concerns arise if the conduct of U.S. persons is made subject to a foreign law, as is likely to happen when a U.S. person travels to a foreign jurisdiction.

3. Useful Articles

The issue of copyright protection for useful articles arises for the variety of pictorial, graphic, or sculptural works that also serve some useful purpose. For a straightforward example, think of a chair. A chair is a sculptural work. It is also useful. Does copyright protect the shape of the chair? Typically, as you shall see, copyright law does not protect the pictorial, graphic, or sculptural features of useful articles, unless those features are "separable" from the useful article's utilitarian aspects.

As you read this foundational Supreme Court decision, consider why copyright law might want to forbid protection for useful articles. Do these motivations connect to other doctrines we have already explored?

Mazer v. Stein
347 U.S. 201 (1954)

REED, J.:

[1] This case involves the validity of copyrights obtained by respondents for statuettes of male and female dancing figures made of semivitreous china. The controversy centers around the fact that although copyrighted as 'works of art,' the statuettes were intended for use and used as bases for table lamps, with electric wiring, sockets and lamp shades attached.

[2] Respondents are partners in the manufacture and sale of electric lamps. One of the respondents created original works of sculpture in the form of human figures by traditional clay-model technique. From this model, a production mold for casting copies was made. The resulting statuettes, without any lamp components added, were submitted by the respondents to the Copyright Office for registration as 'works of art' or reproductions thereof under [the Copyright Act of 1909], and certificates of registration issued.... Thereafter, the statuettes were sold in quantity throughout the country both as lamp bases and as statuettes. The sales in lamp form accounted for all but an insignificant portion of respondents' sales.

Figure 23: one of Stein's ballet dancer statuettes/lamp bases

[3] Petitioners [also] make and sell lamps. Without authorization, they copied the statuettes, embodied them in lamps and sold them.

[4] ... [T]he District Court dismissed the complaint [of copyright infringement against the petitioners]. The Court of Appeals reversed and held the copyrights valid. It said: 'A subsequent utilization of a work of art in an article of manufacture in no way affects the right of the copyright owner to be protected against infringement of the work of art itself.'

[5] Petitioners ... seek here a reversal of the Court of Appeals decree upholding the copyrights. Petitioners in their petition for certiorari present a single question:

> 'Can statuettes be protected in the United States by copyright when the copyright applicant intended primarily to use the statuettes in the form of lamp bases to be made and sold in quantity and carried the intentions into effect?
>
> 'Stripped down to its essentials, the question presented is: Can a lamp manufacturer copyright his lamp bases?'

[6] The first paragraph accurately summarizes the issue. The last gives it a quirk that unjustifiably, we think, broadens the controversy. The case requires an answer, not as to a manufacturer's right to register a lamp base but as to an artist's right to copyright a work of art intended to be reproduced for lamp bases. As petitioners say in their brief, their contention 'questions the validity of the copyright based upon the actions of respondents.' Petitioners question the validity of a copyright of a work of art for 'mass' production. 'Reproduction of a work of art' does not mean to them unlimited reproduction. Their position is that a copyright does not cover industrial reproduction of the protected article. Thus their reply brief states:

> 'When an artist becomes a manufacturer or a designer for a manufacturer he is subject to the limitations of design patents and deserves no more consideration than any other manufacturer or designer.' ...

[7] ... In recent years the question as to utilitarian use of copyrighted articles has been much discussed.

[8] .... In 1790 the First Congress conferred a copyright on 'authors of any map, chart, book or books already printed'. Later, designing, engraving and etching were included; in 1831 musical composition; dramatic compositions in 1856; and photographs and negatives thereof in 1865.

[9] The Act of 1870 defined copyrightable subject matter as:

> '* * * any book, map, chart, dramatic or musical composition, engraving, cut, print, or photograph or negative thereof, or of a painting, drawing, chromo, *statue, statuary, and of models or designs intended to be perfected as works of the fine arts*'. (Emphasis supplied.)

[10] The italicized part added three-dimensional work of art to what had been protected previously. In 1909 Congress again enlarged the scope of the copyright statute. The new Act provided in [section] 4:

> 'That the works for which copyright may be secured under this Act shall include all the writings of an author.'

[11] Some writers interpret this section as being coextensive with the constitutional grant, but the House Report, while inconclusive, indicates that it was 'declaratory of existing law' only.... Significant for our purposes was the deletion of the fine-arts clause of the 1870 Act. Verbal distinctions between purely aesthetic articles and useful works of art ended insofar as the statutory copyright language is concerned.

[12] The practice of the Copyright Office, under the 1870 and 1874 Acts and before the 1909 Act, was to allow registration 'as works of the fine arts' of articles of the same character as those of respondents now under challenge.... The current pertinent regulation ... reads thus:

> 'Works of art (Class G)—(a)—In General. This class includes works of artistic craftsmanship, in so far as their form but not their mechanical or utilitarian aspects are concerned, such as artistic jewelry, enamels, glassware, and tapestries, as well as all works belonging to the fine arts, such as paintings, drawings and sculpture.'

[13] So we have a contemporaneous and long-continued construction of the statutes by the agency charged to administer them that would allow the registration of such a statuette as is in question here....

[14] The successive acts, the legislative history of the 1909 Act and the practice of the Copyright Office unite to show that 'works of art' and 'reproductions of works of art' are terms that were intended by Congress to include the authority to copyright these statuettes. Individual perception of the beautiful is too varied a power to permit a narrow or rigid concept of art. As a standard we can hardly do better than the words of the present Regulation, naming the things that appertain to the arts. They must be original, that is, the author's tangible expression of his ideas. Such expression, whether meticulously delineating the model or mental image or conveying the meaning by modernistic form or color, is copyrightable. What cases there are confirm this coverage of the statute.

[15] The conclusion that the statues here in issue may be copyrighted goes far to solve the question whether their intended reproduction as lamp stands bars or invalidates their registration. This depends solely on statutory interpretation. Congress may after publication protect by copyright any writing of an author. Its statute creates the copyright. It did not exist at common law even though he had a property right in his unpublished work.

[16] But petitioners assert that congressional enactment of the design patent laws should be interpreted as denying protection to artistic articles embodied or reproduced in manufactured articles....

[17] Their argument is that design patents require the critical examination given patents to protect the public against monopoly. Attention is called to *Gorham Mfg. Co. v. White*, 81 U.S. 511 (1871), interpreting the design patent law of 1842, granting a patent to anyone who by 'their own industry, genius, efforts, and expense, may have invented or produced any new and original design for a manufacture.' A pattern for flat silver was there upheld. As petitioner sees the effect of the design patent law:

> 'If an industrial designer can not satisfy the novelty requirements of the design patent laws, then his design as used on articles of manufacture can be copied by anyone.'

[18] Petitioner has furnished the Court a booklet of numerous design patents for statuettes, bases for table lamps and similar articles for manufacture, quite indistinguishable in type from the copyrighted statuettes here in issue. Petitioner urges that overlapping of patent and copyright legislation so as to give an author or inventor a choice between patents and copyrights should not be permitted. We assume petitioner takes the position that protection for a statuette for industrial use can only be obtained by patent, if any protection can be given.

[19] As we have held the statuettes here involved copyrightable, we need not decide the question of their patentability. Though other courts have passed upon the issue as to whether allowance by the election of the author or patentee of one bars a grant of the other, we do not. We do hold that the patentability of the statuettes, fitted as lamps or unfitted, does not bar copyright as works of art. Neither the Copyright Statute nor any other says that because a thing is patentable it may not be copyrighted. We should not so hold.

[20] Unlike a patent, a copyright gives no exclusive right to the art disclosed; protection is given only to the expression of the idea—not the idea itself.... The dichotomy of protection for the aesthetic is not beauty and utility but art for the copyright and the invention of original and ornamental design for design patents. We find nothing in the copyright statute to support the argument that the intended use or use in industry of an article eligible for copyright bars or invalidates its registration. We do not read such a limitation into the copyright law....

[21] The copyright law, like the patent statutes, makes reward to the owner a secondary consideration. However, it is intended definitely to grant valuable, enforceable rights to authors, publishers, etc., without burdensome requirements; to afford greater encouragement to the production of literary (or artistic) works of lasting benefit to the world.

[22] The economic philosophy behind the clause empowering Congress to grant patents and copyrights is the conviction that encouragement of individual effort by personal gain is the best way to advance public welfare through the talents of authors and inventors in 'Science and useful Arts.' Sacrificial days devoted to such creative activities deserve rewards commensurate with the services rendered....

DOUGLAS, J., in which Mr. Justice BLACK concurs:

[23] An important constitutional question underlies this case—a question which was stirred on oral argument but not treated in the briefs. It is whether these statuettes of dancing figures may be copyrighted. Congress has provided that 'works of art', 'models or designs for works of art', and 'reproductions of a work of art' may be copyrighted, and the Court holds that these statuettes are included in the words 'works of art'. But may statuettes be granted the monopoly of the copyright?

[24] Article I, s 8 of the Constitution grants Congress the power 'To promote the Progress of [] Science and useful Arts, by securing for limited Times to Authors the exclusive Right to their respective Writings.' The power is thus circumscribed: it allows a monopoly to be granted only to 'authors' for their 'writings.' Is a sculptor an 'author' and is his statute a 'writing' within the meaning of the Constitution? We have never decided the question....

[25] The interests involved in the category of 'works of art,' as used in the copyright law, are considerable. The Copyright Office has supplied us with a long list of such articles which have been copyrighted—statuettes, book ends, clocks, lamps, door knockers, candlesticks, inkstands, chandeliers, piggy banks, sundials, salt and pepper shakers, fish bowls, casseroles, and ash trays. Perhaps these are all 'writings' in the constitutional sense. But to me, at least, they are not obviously so. It is time that we came to the problem full face. I would accordingly put the case down for reargument.

Congress sought to codify what it understood to be *Mazer*'s holding in the 1976 Act. In its definition of "pictorial, graphic, and sculptural works" in § 101, Congress stated that

> *Such works shall include works of artistic craftsmanship insofar as their form but not their mechanical or utilitarian aspects are concerned; the design of a useful article, as defined in this section, shall be considered a pictorial, graphic, or sculptural work only if, and only to the extent that, such design incorporates pictorial, graphic, or sculptural features that can be identified separately from, and are capable of existing independently of, the utilitarian aspects of the article.*

Section 101 further defines a "useful article" as

an article having an intrinsic utilitarian function that is not merely to portray the appearance of the article or to convey information. An article that is normally a part of a useful article is considered a "useful article."

Congress understood *Mazer*'s holding to suggest that the statuette was **separable** from and capable of existing independently of the lamp, which it encoded in the statute. H.R. REP. NO. 1476, 94th Cong., 2d Sess. 47, at 55 (1976) (indicating that there is the requisite separability when "a statute or carving is ... incorporated into a product without losing its ability to exist independently as a work of art"). Note that pursuant to the statutory language, Stein would get copyright protection only for that which is separable—the statuette—rather than the entire lamp as a whole.

The legislative history enumerated further the statutory line Congress sought to draw between protectable and unprotectable matter in this context:

> *In adopting this ... language, [Congress] is seeking to draw as clear a line as possible between copyrightable works of applied art and uncopyrighted works of industrial design. A two-dimensional painting, drawing, or graphic work is still capable of being identified as such when it is printed on or applied to utilitarian articles such as textile fabrics, wallpaper, containers, and the like.... On the other hand, although the shape of an industrial product may be aesthetically satisfying and valuable, the ... intention is not to offer it copyright protection under the bill. Unless the shape of an automobile, airplane, ladies' dress, food processor, television set, or any other industrial product contains some element that, physically or conceptually, can be identified as separable from the utilitarian aspects of that article, the design would not be copyrighted under the bill.*

This legislative history states that there are two types of separability: physical and conceptual. Physical separability refers to situations in which one can actually remove an expressive work from a functional work, as is possible with the jaguar-shaped sculpture attached to a Jaguar automobile. The sculpture can be physically removed from the automobile and is thus "separable."

The meaning of "conceptual" separability has been less clear. Over the years, courts struggled with how to understand this category of separable works and articulated different, often conflicting, tests. In 2017, the Supreme Court stepped in to resolve the confusion.

As you read the Supreme Court's decision, focus on the differences between the majority and the dissent with regard to how each understands the statute and copyright policy underpinning it. Is the majority's separability test one that will be satisfied easily or with great difficulty? Can you reconcile it with *Bleistein*'s nondiscrimination principle?

Star Athletica, LLC v. Varsity Brands, Inc.
137 S. Ct. 1002 (2017)

THOMAS, J.:

[1] Congress has provided copyright protection for original works of art, but not for industrial designs. The line between art and industrial design, however, is often difficult to draw. This is particularly true when an industrial design incorporates artistic elements. Congress has afforded limited protection for these artistic

elements by providing that "pictorial, graphic, or sculptural features" of the "design of a useful article" are eligible for copyright protection as artistic works if those features "can be identified separately from, and are capable of existing independently of, the utilitarian aspects of the article." 17 U.S.C. § 101.

[2] We granted certiorari to resolve widespread disagreement over the proper test for implementing § 101's separate-identification and independent-existence requirements. We hold that a feature incorporated into the design of a useful article is eligible for copyright protection only if the feature (1) can be perceived as a two- or three-dimensional work of art separate from the useful article and (2) would qualify as a protectable pictorial, graphic, or sculptural work—either on its own or fixed in some other tangible medium of expression—if it were imagined separately from the useful article into which it is incorporated. Because that test is satisfied in this case, we affirm....

[3] Respondents Varsity Brands, Inc., Varsity Spirit Corporation, and Varsity Spirit Fashions & Supplies, Inc., design, make, and sell cheerleading uniforms. Respondents have obtained or acquired more than 200 U.S. copyright registrations for two-dimensional designs appearing on the surface of their uniforms and other garments. These designs are primarily "combinations, positionings, and arrangements of elements" that include "chevrons ..., lines, curves, stripes, angles, diagonals, inverted [chevrons], coloring, and shapes." At issue in this case are Designs 299A, 299B, 074, 078, and 0815.

[4] Petitioner Star Athletica, L.L.C., also markets and sells cheerleading uniforms. Respondents sued petitioner for infringing their copyrights in the five designs. The District Court entered summary judgment for petitioner on respondents' copyright claims on the ground that the designs did not qualify as protectable pictorial, graphic, or sculptural works. It reasoned that the designs served the useful, or "utilitarian," function of identifying the garments as "cheerleading uniforms" and therefore could not be "physically or conceptually" separated under § 101 "from the utilitarian function" of the uniform.

[5] The Court of Appeals for the Sixth Circuit reversed. In its view, the "graphic designs" were "separately identifiable" because the designs "and a blank cheerleading uniform can appear side by side—one as a graphic design, and one as a cheerleading uniform." And it determined that the designs were "capable of existing independently" because they could be incorporated onto the surface of different types of garments, or hung on the wall and framed as art.

[6] Judge McKeague dissented. He would have held that, because "identifying the wearer as a cheerleader" is a utilitarian function of a cheerleading uniform and the surface designs were "integral to" achieving that function, the designs were inseparable from the uniforms....

[7] Courts, the Copyright Office, and commentators have described the analysis undertaken to determine whether a feature can be separately identified from, and exist independently of, a useful article as "separability." In this case, our task is to determine whether the arrangements of lines, chevrons, and colorful shapes appearing on the surface of respondents' cheerleading uniforms are eligible for copyright protection as separable features of the design of those cheerleading uniforms....

[8] Respondents argue that "[s]eparability is only implicated when a [pictorial, graphic, or sculptural] work is the 'design of a useful article.'" They contend that the surface decorations in this case are "two-dimensional graphic designs that appear *on* useful articles," but are not themselves designs *of* useful articles. Consequently, the surface decorations are protected two-dimensional works of graphic art without regard to any separability analysis under § 101. Under this theory, two-dimensional artistic features on the surface of useful articles are "inherently separable."

Design 078
Registration No. VA 1-417-427

Design 0815
Registration No. VA 1-675-905

Design 299B
Registration No. VA 1-319-226

Design 299A
Registration No. VA 1-319-228

Design 074
Registration No. VA 1-411-535

Figure 24: Varsity Brands' cheerleading uniform designs

[9] This argument is inconsistent with the text of § 101. The statute requires separability analysis for any "pictorial, graphic, or sculptural features" incorporated into the "design of a useful article." ... [T]he words "pictorial" and "graphic" include, in this context, two-dimensional features such as pictures, paintings, or drawings. And the statute expressly defines "[p]ictorial, graphical, and sculptural works" to include "two-dimensional ... works of ... art." § 101. The statute thus provides that the "design of a useful article" can include two-dimensional "pictorial" and "graphic" features, and separability analysis applies to those features just as it does to three-dimensional "sculptural" features....

[10] We must now decide when a feature incorporated into a useful article "can be identified separately from" and is "capable of existing independently of" "the utilitarian aspects" of the article. This is not a free-ranging search for the best copyright policy, but rather "depends solely on statutory interpretation." *Mazer v. Stein*, 347 U.S. 201, 214 (1954). The controlling principle in this case is the basic and unexceptional rule that courts must give effect to the clear meaning of statutes as written. We thus begin and end our inquiry with the text, giving each word its ordinary, contemporary, common meaning....

[11] The statute provides that a "pictorial, graphic, or sculptural featur[e]" incorporated into the "design of a useful article" is eligible for copyright protection if it (1) "can be identified separately from," and (2) is "capable of existing independently of, the utilitarian aspects of the article." § 101. The first requirement—separate identification—is not onerous. The decisionmaker need only be able to look at the useful article and spot some two- or three-dimensional element that appears to have pictorial, graphic, or sculptural qualities.

[12] The independent-existence requirement is ordinarily more difficult to satisfy. The decisionmaker must determine that the separately identified feature has the capacity to exist apart from the utilitarian aspects of the article. In other words, the feature must be able to exist as its own pictorial, graphic, or sculptural work as defined in § 101 once it is imagined apart from the useful article. If the feature is not capable of existing as a pictorial, graphic, or sculptural work once separated from the useful article, then it was not a pictorial, graphic, or sculptural feature of that article, but rather one of its utilitarian aspects.

[13] Of course, to qualify as a pictorial, graphic, or sculptural work on its own, the feature cannot itself be a useful article or "[a]n article that is normally a part of a useful article" (which is itself considered a useful article). § 101. Nor could someone claim a copyright in a useful article merely by creating a replica of that article in some other medium—for example, a cardboard model of a car. Although the replica could itself be copyrightable, it would not give rise to any rights in the useful article that inspired it....

[14] .... The ultimate separability question, then, is whether the feature for which copyright protection is claimed would have been eligible for copyright protection as a pictorial, graphic, or sculptural work had it originally been fixed in some tangible medium other than a useful article before being applied to a useful article....

[15] This interpretation is also consistent with the history of the Copyright Act....

[16] Two of *Mazer*'s holdings are relevant here. First, the Court held that the respondents owned a copyright in the statuette even though it was intended for use as a lamp base. In doing so, the Court approved the Copyright Office's regulation extending copyright protection to works of art that might also serve a useful purpose. *See* 37 C.F.R. § 202.8(a) (1949) (protecting "works of artistic craftsmanship, in so far as their form but not their mechanical or utilitarian aspects are concerned").

[17] Second, the Court held that it was irrelevant to the copyright inquiry whether the statuette was initially created as a freestanding sculpture or as a lamp base. *Mazer* thus interpreted the 1909 Act consistently with the rule discussed above: If a design would have been copyrightable as a standalone pictorial, graphic, or sculptural work, it is copyrightable if created first as part of a useful article.

[18] Shortly thereafter, the Copyright Office enacted a regulation implementing the holdings of *Mazer*. As amended, the regulation introduced the modern separability test to copyright law:

> *"If the sole intrinsic function of an article is its utility, the fact that the article is unique and attractively shaped will not qualify it as a work of art. However, if the shape of a utilitarian article incorporates features, such as artistic sculpture, carving, or pictorial representation, which can be identified separately and are capable of existing independently as a work of art, such features will be eligible for registration." 37 C.F.R. § 202.10(c) (1960) (punctuation altered).*

[19] Congress essentially lifted the language governing protection for the design of a useful article directly from the post-*Mazer* regulations and placed it into § 101 of the 1976 Act. Consistent with *Mazer*, the approach we outline today interprets §[] 101 ... in a way that would afford copyright protection to the statuette in *Mazer* regardless of whether it was first created as a standalone sculptural work or as the base of the lamp....

[20] In sum, a feature of the design of a useful article is eligible for copyright if, when identified and imagined apart from the useful article, it would qualify as a pictorial, graphic, or sculptural work either on its own or when fixed in some other tangible medium.

[21] Applying this test to the surface decorations on the cheerleading uniforms is straightforward. First, one can identify the decorations as features having pictorial, graphic, or sculptural qualities. Second, if the arrangement of colors, shapes, stripes, and chevrons on the surface of the cheerleading uniforms were separated from the uniform and applied in another medium—for example, on a painter's canvas—they would qualify as "two-dimensional ... works of ... art," § 101. And imaginatively removing the surface decorations from the uniforms and applying them in another medium would not replicate the uniform itself. Indeed, respondents have applied the designs in this case to other media of expression—different types of clothing— without replicating the uniform. The decorations are therefore separable from the uniforms and eligible for copyright protection.[1]

[22] The dissent argues that the designs are not separable because imaginatively removing them from the uniforms and placing them in some other medium of expression—a canvas, for example—would create "pictures of cheerleader uniforms." Petitioner similarly argues that the decorations cannot be copyrighted because, even when extracted from the useful article, they retain the outline of a cheerleading uniform.

[23] This is not a bar to copyright. Just as two-dimensional fine art corresponds to the shape of the canvas on which it is painted, two-dimensional applied art correlates to the contours of the article on which it is applied. A fresco painted on a wall, ceiling panel, or dome would not lose copyright protection, for example, simply because it was designed to track the dimensions of the surface on which it was painted. Or consider, for example, a design etched or painted on the surface of a guitar. If that entire design is imaginatively removed from the guitar's surface and placed on an album cover, it would still resemble the shape of a guitar. But the image on the cover does not "replicate" the guitar as a useful article. Rather, the design is a two-dimensional work of art that corresponds to the shape of the useful article to which it was applied. The statute protects that work of art whether it is first drawn on the album cover and then applied to the guitar's surface, or vice versa. Failing to protect that art would create an anomaly: It would extend protection to two-dimensional designs that cover a part of a useful article but would not protect the same design if it covered the entire article. The statute does not support that distinction, nor can it be reconciled with the dissent's recognition that "artwork printed on a t-shirt" could be protected.

---

[1] We do not today hold that the surface decorations are copyrightable. We express no opinion on whether these works are sufficiently original to qualify for copyright protection, *see* Feist Publications, Inc. v. Rural Telephone Service Co., 499 U.S. 340, 358–59 (1991), or on whether any other prerequisite of a valid copyright has been satisfied.

[24] To be clear, the only feature of the cheerleading uniform eligible for a copyright in this case is the two-dimensional work of art fixed in the tangible medium of the uniform fabric. Even if respondents ultimately succeed in establishing a valid copyright in the surface decorations at issue here, respondents have no right to prohibit any person from manufacturing a cheerleading uniform of identical shape, cut, and dimensions to the ones on which the decorations in this case appear. They may prohibit only the reproduction of the surface designs in any tangible medium of expression—a uniform or otherwise.[2] ...

[25] Petitioner ... argues that our reading of the statute is missing an important step. It contends that a feature may exist independently only if it can stand alone as a copyrightable work *and* if the useful article from which it was extracted would remain equally useful. In other words, copyright extends only to "solely artistic" features of useful articles. According to petitioner, if a feature of a useful article "advance[s] the utility of the article," then it is categorically beyond the scope of copyright.... Because the uniforms would not be equally useful without the designs, petitioner contends that the designs are inseparable from the "utilitarian aspects" of the uniform.

[26] The Government raises a similar argument, although it reaches a different result. It suggests that the appropriate test is whether the useful article with the artistic feature removed would "remai[n] *similarly* useful." In the view of the United States, however, a plain white cheerleading uniform is "similarly useful" to uniforms with respondents' designs.

[27] The debate over the relative utility of a plain white cheerleading uniform is unnecessary. The focus of the separability inquiry is on the extracted feature and not on any aspects of the useful article that remain after the imaginary extraction. The statute does not require the decisionmaker to imagine a fully functioning useful article without the artistic feature. Instead, it requires that the separated feature qualify as a nonuseful pictorial, graphic, or sculptural work on its own.

[28] Of course, because the removed feature may not be a useful article—as it would then not qualify as a pictorial, graphic, or sculptural work—there necessarily would be some aspects of the original useful article "left behind" if the feature were conceptually removed. But the statute does not require the imagined remainder to be a fully functioning useful article at all, much less an equally useful one. Indeed, such a requirement would deprive the *Mazer* statuette of protection had it been created first as a lamp base rather than as a statuette. Without the base, the "lamp" would be just a shade, bulb, and wires. The statute does not require that we imagine a nonartistic replacement for the removed feature to determine whether that *feature* is capable of an independent existence....

[29] Because we reject the view that a useful article must remain after the artistic feature has been imaginatively separated from the article, we necessarily abandon the distinction between "physical" and "conceptual" separability, which some courts and commentators have adopted based on the Copyright Act's legislative history. *See* H.R. REP. NO. 94–1476, p. 55 (1976). According to this view, a feature is *physically* separable from the underlying useful article if it can "be physically separated from the article by ordinary means while leaving the utilitarian aspects of the article completely intact." COMPENDIUM § 924.2(A)). *Conceptual* separability applies if the feature physically could not be removed from the useful article by ordinary means. *See* COMPENDIUM § 924.2(B).

---

[2] The dissent suggests that our test would lead to the copyrighting of shovels. But a shovel, like a cheerleading uniform, even if displayed in an art gallery, is "an article having an intrinsic utilitarian function that is not merely to portray the appearance of the article or to convey information." 17 U.S.C. § 101. It therefore cannot be copyrighted. A drawing of a shovel could, of course, be copyrighted. And, if the shovel included any artistic features that could be perceived as art apart from the shovel, and which would qualify as protectable pictorial, graphic, or sculptural works on their own or in another medium, they too could be copyrighted. But a shovel as a shovel cannot.

[30] The statutory text indicates that separability is a conceptual undertaking. Because separability does not require the underlying useful article to remain, the physical-conceptual distinction is unnecessary....

[31] Petitioner next argues that we should incorporate two "objective" components into our test to provide guidance to the lower courts: (1) "whether the design elements can be identified as reflecting the designer's artistic judgment exercised independently of functional influence," and (2) whether "there is [a] substantial likelihood that the pictorial, graphic, or sculptural feature would still be marketable to some significant segment of the community without its utilitarian function."

[32] We reject this argument because neither consideration is grounded in the text of the statute....

[33] Finally, petitioner argues that allowing the surface decorations to qualify as a "work of authorship" is inconsistent with Congress' intent to entirely exclude industrial design from copyright. Petitioner notes that Congress refused to pass a provision that would have provided limited copyright protection for industrial designs, including clothing, when it enacted the 1976 Act, and that it has enacted laws protecting designs for specific useful articles—semiconductor chips and boat hulls—while declining to enact other industrial design statutes. From this history of failed legislation petitioner reasons that Congress intends to channel intellectual property claims for industrial design into design patents. It therefore urges us to approach this question with a presumption against copyrightability.

[34] We do not share petitioner's concern. As an initial matter, congressional inaction lacks persuasive significance in most circumstances. Moreover, we have long held that design patent and copyright are not mutually exclusive. Congress has provided for limited copyright protection for certain features of industrial design, and approaching the statute with presumptive hostility toward protection for industrial design would undermine Congress' choice. In any event, as explained above, our test does not render the shape, cut, and physical dimensions of the cheerleading uniforms eligible for copyright protection....

[35] We hold that an artistic feature of the design of a useful article is eligible for copyright protection if the feature (1) can be perceived as a two- or three-dimensional work of art separate from the useful article and (2) would qualify as a protectable pictorial, graphic, or sculptural work either on its own or in some other medium if imagined separately from the useful article. Because the designs on the surface of respondents' cheerleading uniforms in this case satisfy these requirements, the judgment of the Court of Appeals is affirmed....

BREYER, J., with whom Justice KENNEDY joins, dissenting.

[36] I agree with much in the Court's opinion. But I do not agree that the designs that Varsity Brands, Inc., submitted to the Copyright Office are eligible for copyright protection. Even applying the majority's test, the designs *cannot* "be perceived as ... two- or three-dimensional work[s] of art separate from the useful article."

[37] Look at the designs that Varsity submitted to the Copyright Office. You will see only pictures of cheerleader uniforms. And cheerleader uniforms are useful articles. A picture of the relevant design features, whether separately "perceived" on paper or in the imagination, is a picture of, and thereby "replicate[s]," the underlying useful article of which they are a part. Hence the design features that Varsity seeks to protect are not "capable of existing independently o[f] the utilitarian aspects of the article." 17 U.S.C. § 101....

[38] The relevant statutory provision says that the "design of a useful article" is copyrightable "only if, and only to the extent that, such design incorporates pictorial, graphic, or sculptural features that can be identified separately from, and are capable of existing independently of, the utilitarian aspects of the article." But what, we must ask, do the words "identified separately" mean? Just when is a design separate from the

"utilitarian aspect of the [useful] article?" The most direct, helpful aspect of the Court's opinion answers this question by stating:

> "*Nor could someone claim a copyright in a useful article merely by creating a replica of that article in some other medium—for example, a cardboard model of a car. Although the replica could itself be copyrightable, it would not give rise to any rights in the useful article that inspired it.*"

[39] Exactly so. These words help explain the Court's statement that a copyrightable work of art must be "perceived as a two- or three-dimensional work of art separate from the useful article." They help clarify the concept of separateness. They are consistent with Congress' own expressed intent. And they reflect long held views of the Copyright Office. *See* COMPENDIUM OF U.S. COPYRIGHT OFFICE PRACTICES § 924.2(B) (3d ed. 2014).

[40] Consider, for example, the explanation that the House Report for the Copyright Act of 1976 provides. It says:

> "Unless the shape of an automobile, airplane, ladies' dress, food processor, television set, or any other industrial product contains some element that, *physically or conceptually*, can be identified as separable from the utilitarian aspects of that article, the design would not be copyrighted...." H.R. REP., at 55 (emphasis added).

[41] These words suggest two exercises, one physical, one mental. Can the design features (the picture, the graphic, the sculpture) be physically removed from the article (and considered separately), all the while leaving the fully functioning utilitarian object in place? If not, can one nonetheless conceive of the design features separately without replicating a picture of the utilitarian object? If the answer to either of these questions is "yes," then the design is eligible for copyright protection. Otherwise, it is not. The abstract nature of these questions makes them sound difficult to apply. But with the Court's words in mind, the difficulty tends to disappear.

[42] An example will help. Imagine a lamp with a circular marble base, a vertical 10–inch tall brass rod (containing wires) inserted off center on the base, a light bulb fixture emerging from the top of the brass rod, and a lampshade sitting on top. In front of the brass rod a porcelain Siamese cat sits on the base facing outward. Obviously, the Siamese cat is *physically separate* from the lamp, as it could be easily removed while leaving both cat and lamp intact. And, assuming it otherwise qualifies, the designed cat is eligible for copyright protection.

[43] Now suppose there is no long brass rod; instead the cat sits in the middle of the base and the wires run up through the cat to the bulbs. The cat is not physically separate from the lamp, as the reality of the lamp's construction is such that an effort to physically separate the cat and lamp will destroy both cat and lamp. The two are integrated into a single functional object, like the similar configuration of the ballet dancer statuettes that formed the lamp bases at issue in *Mazer v. Stein*. But we can easily imagine the cat on its own, as did Congress when conceptualizing the ballet dancer. *See* H.R. REP., at 55 (the statuette in *Mazer* was "incorporated into a product without losing its ability to exist independently as a work of art"). In doing so, we do not create a mental picture of a lamp (or, in the Court's words, a "replica" of the lamp), which is a useful article. We simply perceive the cat separately, as a small cat figurine that could be a copyrightable design work standing alone that does not replicate the lamp. Hence the cat is *conceptually separate* from the utilitarian article that is the lamp.

Figure 25: cat lamps

[44] Case law, particularly case law that Congress and the Copyright Office have considered, reflects the same approach. Congress cited examples of copyrightable design works, including "a carving on the back of a chair" and "a floral relief design on silver flatware." Copyright Office guidance on copyrightable designs in useful articles include "an engraving on a vase," "[a]rtwork printed on a t-shirt," "[a] colorful pattern decorating the surface of a shopping bag," "[a] drawing on the surface of wallpaper," and "[a] floral relief decorating the handle of a spoon." Courts have found copyrightable matter in a plaster ballet dancer statuette encasing the lamp's electric cords and forming its base, as well as carvings engraved onto furniture, and designs on laminated floor tiles.

[45] By way of contrast, Van Gogh's painting of a pair of old shoes, though beautifully executed and copyrightable as a painting, would not qualify for a shoe design copyright. Courts have similarly denied copyright protection to objects that begin as three-dimensional designs, such as measuring spoons shaped like heart-tipped arrows, candleholders shaped like sailboats, and wire spokes on a wheel cover. None of these designs could qualify for copyright protection that would prevent others from selling spoons, candleholders, or wheel covers with the same design. Why not? Because in each case the design is not separable from the utilitarian aspects of the object to which it relates. The designs cannot be physically separated because they themselves make up the shape of the spoon, candleholders, or wheel covers of which they are a part. And spoons, candleholders, and wheel covers are useful objects, as are the old shoes depicted in Van Gogh's painting. More importantly, one cannot easily imagine or otherwise conceptualize the design of the spoons or the candleholders or the shoes *without that picture, or image, or replica being a picture of spoons, or candleholders, or wheel covers, or shoes*. The designs necessarily bring along the underlying utilitarian object. Hence each design is not conceptually separable from the physical useful object.

[46] The upshot is that one could copyright the floral design on a soupspoon but one could not copyright the shape of the spoon itself, no matter how beautiful, artistic, or esthetically pleasing that shape might be: A picture of the shape of the spoon is also a picture of a spoon; the picture of a floral design is not.

[47] To repeat: A separable design feature must be "capable of existing independently" of the useful article as a separate artistic work that is not itself the useful article. If the claimed feature could be extracted without replicating the useful article of which it is a part, and the result would be a copyrightable artistic work standing alone, then there is a separable design. But if extracting the claimed features would necessarily bring along the underlying useful article, the design is not separable from the useful article. In many or most cases, to

decide whether a design or artistic feature of a useful article is conceptually separate from the article itself, it is enough to imagine the feature on its own and ask, "Have I created a picture of a (useful part of a) useful article?" If so, the design is not separable from the useful article. If not, it is.

[48] In referring to imagined pictures and the like, I am not speaking technically. I am simply trying to explain an intuitive idea of what separation is about, as well as how I understand the majority's opinion. So understood, the opinion puts design copyrights in their rightful place. The law has long recognized that drawings or photographs of real world objects are copyrightable as drawings or photographs, but the copyright does not give protection against others making the underlying useful objects. That is why a copyright on Van Gogh's painting would prevent others from reproducing that painting, but it would not prevent others from reproducing and selling the comfortable old shoes that the painting depicts....

[49] To ask this kind of simple question—does the design picture the useful article?—will not provide an answer in every case, for there will be cases where it is difficult to say whether a picture of the design is, or is not, also a picture of the useful article. But the question will avoid courts focusing primarily upon what I believe is an unhelpful feature of the inquiry, namely, whether the design can be imagined as a "two- or three-dimensional work of art." That is because virtually any industrial design can be thought of separately as a "work of art": Just imagine a frame surrounding the design, or its being placed in a gallery. Consider Marcel Duchamp's "readymades" series, the functional mass-produced objects he designated as art. What is there in the world that, viewed through an esthetic lens, cannot be seen as a good, bad, or indifferent work of art? What design features could not be imaginatively reproduced on a painter's canvas? Indeed, great industrial design may well include design that is inseparable from the useful article—where, as Frank Lloyd Wright put it, "form and function are one." Where they are one, the designer may be able to obtain 15 years of protection through a design patent. But, if they are one, Congress did not intend a century or more of copyright protection....

[50] The conceptual approach that I have described reflects Congress' answer to a problem that is primarily practical and economic. Years ago Lord Macaulay drew attention to the problem when he described copyright in books as a "tax on readers for the purpose of giving a bounty to writers." He called attention to the main benefit of copyright protection, which is to provide an incentive to produce copyrightable works and thereby "promote the Progress of Science and useful Arts." U.S. CONST. art. I, § 8, cl. 8. But Macaulay also made clear that copyright protection imposes costs. Those costs include the higher prices that can accompany the grant of a copyright monopoly. They also can include (for those wishing to display, sell, or perform a design, film, work of art, or piece of music, for example) the costs of discovering whether there are previous copyrights, of contacting copyright holders, and of securing permission to copy. Sometimes, as Thomas Jefferson wrote to James Madison, costs can outweigh "the benefit even of limited monopolies." Letter from Thomas Jefferson to James Madison (July 31, 1788), in 13 PAPERS OF THOMAS JEFFERSON 443 (J. Boyd ed. 1956) (Jefferson Letter). And that is particularly true in light of the fact that Congress has extended the "limited Times" of protection from the "14 years" of Jefferson's day to potentially more than a century today.

[51] The Constitution grants Congress primary responsibility for assessing comparative costs and benefits and drawing copyright's statutory lines. Courts must respect those lines and not grant copyright protection where Congress has decided not to do so. And it is clear that Congress has not extended broad copyright protection to the fashion design industry.

[52] Congress' decision not to grant full copyright protection to the fashion industry has not left the industry without protection. Patent design protection is available. A maker of clothing can obtain trademark protection under the Lanham Act for signature features of the clothing. And a designer who creates an original textile design can receive copyright protection for that pattern as placed, for example, on a bolt of cloth, or anything made with that cloth. ...

[53] The fashion industry has thrived against this backdrop, and designers have contributed immeasurably to artistic and personal self-expression through clothing. But a decision by this Court to grant protection to the design of a garment would grant the designer protection that Congress refused to provide.... That is why I believe it important to emphasize those parts of the Court's opinion that limit the scope of its interpretation. That language, as I have said, makes clear that one may not "claim a copyright in a useful article merely by creating a replica of that article in some other medium," which "would not give rise to any rights in the useful article that inspired it." ...

[54] If we ask the "separateness" question correctly, the answer here is not difficult to find.... Can the design features in Varsity's pictures exist separately from the utilitarian aspects of a dress? Can we extract those features as copyrightable design works standing alone, without bringing along, via picture or design, the dresses of which they constitute a part?

[55] Consider designs 074, 078, and 0815. They certainly look like cheerleader uniforms. That is to say, they look like pictures of cheerleader uniforms, just like Van Gogh's old shoes look like shoes. I do not see how one could see them otherwise. Designs 299A and 299B present slightly closer questions. They omit some of the dresslike context that the other designs possess. But the necklines, the sleeves, and the cut of the skirt suggest that they too are pictures of dresses. Looking at all five of Varsity's pictures, I do not see how one could conceptualize the design features in a way that does not picture, not just artistic designs, but dresses as well.

[56] Were I to accept the majority's invitation to "imaginatively remov[e]" the chevrons and stripes *as they are arranged* on the neckline, waistline, sleeves, and skirt of each uniform, and apply them on a "painter's canvas," that painting would be of a cheerleader's dress. The esthetic elements on which Varsity seeks protection exist only as part of the uniform design—there is nothing to separate out but for dress-shaped lines that replicate the cut and style of the uniforms. Hence, each design is not physically separate, nor is it conceptually separate, from the useful article it depicts, namely, a cheerleader's dress. They cannot be copyrighted.

[57] Varsity, of course, could have sought a design patent for its designs. Or, it could have sought a copyright on a textile design, even one with a similar theme of chevrons and lines.

[58] But that is not the nature of Varsity's copyright claim. It has instead claimed ownership of the particular "'treatment and arrangement'" of the chevrons and lines of the design as they appear at the neckline, waist, skirt, sleeves, and overall cut of each uniform. The majority imagines that Varsity submitted something different—that is, only the surface decorations of chevrons and stripes, as in a textile design. As the majority sees it, Varsity's copyright claim would be the same had it submitted a plain rectangular space depicting chevrons and stripes, like swaths from a bolt of fabric. But considered on their own, the simple stripes are plainly unoriginal. Varsity, then, seeks to do indirectly what it cannot do directly: bring along the design and cut of the dresses by seeking to protect surface decorations whose "treatment and arrangement" are *coextensive with that design and cut*. As Varsity would have it, it would prevent its competitors from making useful three-dimensional cheerleader uniforms by submitting plainly unoriginal chevrons and stripes as cut and arranged on a useful article. But with that cut and arrangement, the resulting pictures on which Varsity seeks protection do not simply depict designs. They depict clothing. They depict the useful articles of which the designs are inextricable parts. And Varsity cannot obtain copyright protection that would give them the power to prevent others from making those useful uniforms, any more than Van Gogh can copyright comfortable old shoes by painting their likeness.

[59] I fear that, in looking past the three-dimensional design inherent in Varsity's claim by treating it as if it were no more than a design for a bolt of cloth, the majority has lost sight of its own important limiting principle. One may not "claim a copyright in a useful article merely by creating a replica of that article in some

other medium," such as in a picture. That is to say, one cannot obtain a copyright that would give its holder "any rights in the useful article that inspired it."

[60] With respect, I dissent.

NOTES

1. To get a feel for *Star Athletica*'s separability test, consider how this work whose copyrightability was litigated pre-*Star Athletica* would fare under the Supreme Court's test: the Brandir RIBBON bicycle rack, as shown in Figure 26 and at issue in *Brandir Int'l, Inc. v. Cascade Pac. Lumber Co.*, 834 F.2d 1142 (2d Cir. 1987). As background, consider the court's explanation of how the bicycle rack came to be:

> *[The bicycle rack's creator] testified, that the original design of the RIBBON Rack stemmed from wire sculptures that [he] had created, each formed from one continuous undulating piece of wire. These sculptures were, he said, created and displayed in his home as a means of personal expression, but apparently were never sold or displayed elsewhere. He also created a wire sculpture in the shape of a bicycle and states that he did not give any thought to the utilitarian application of any of his sculptures until he accidentally juxtaposed the bicycle sculpture with one of the self-standing wire sculptures.... [A] friend, [who was] a bicycle buff and author of numerous articles about urban cycling, ... informed [the creator] that the sculptures would make excellent bicycle racks, permitting bicycles to be parked under the overloops as well as on top of the underloops. Following this meeting, ... [the creator] complet[ed] the designs for the RIBBON Rack by the use of a vacuum cleaner hose, and submit[ted] his drawings to a fabricator complete with dimensions.*

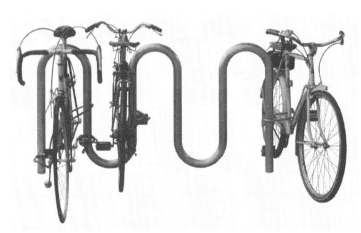

Figure 26: Brandir RIBBON bicycle rack

2. What are the works for which Varsity Brands was seeking copyright protection? The majority opinion understood the work to be "surface designs" consisting primarily of "the arrangement of colors, shapes, stripes, and chevrons on the ...cheerleading uniforms," designs that simply "correspond[ed] to the shape of the useful article[s]." Justice Breyer's dissent, by contrast, conceived of the designs as inescapably depicting cheerleading uniforms, because Varsity Brands did not merely claim a series of chevrons and stripes but instead chevrons and stripes "as they [were] arranged on the neckline, waistline, sleeves, and skirt of each uniform." In contrast, Justice Ginsburg's concurrence (not included above), described the designs as "standalone pictorial and graphic works that [Varsity Brands] reproduce[d] on cheerleading uniforms"—works that did not even require separability analysis because they were not designs of useful articles. How might the understanding of what the work itself is affect the analysis of whether a work is a useful article and whether it

satisfies the separability test? For more on how copyright law's lack of a claiming methodology perpetuates these concerns, see Jeanne C. Fromer & Mark P. McKenna, *Claiming Design*, 167 U. PA. L. REV. 123 (2018).

3. The Supreme Court holds that both two-dimensional and three-dimensional design features must be subjected to separability analysis. It is straightforward to think of three-dimensional design features that are useful or functional. In the context of fashion design, for example, the incorporation of pockets on a pair of trousers is useful because the pockets give the wearer a place for their wallet and keys. Similarly, a shirt sleeve provides a certain degree of warmth, modesty, or ease of movement. Can you think of any two-dimensional design features that are functional?

4. *Star Athletica* does not discuss what makes a feature qualify as functional, or useful, in the first instance. Why might that be important to do? How should one derive that definition? Reconsider § 101's definition of a useful article as "an article having an intrinsic function that is not merely to portray the appearance of the article or to convey information." This definition suggests that a feature is an expressive feature, rather than a functional one, only if the feature serves "merely to portray the appearance of the article or to convey information." A feature with any other purpose is arguably functional as a matter of copyright law. Does this reading mean that design features will qualify as functional more or less frequently?

Can a design feature be simultaneously both expressive and functional? How would § 101 treat such dual-nature features? One possible example of a dual-nature design feature is camouflage. A camouflage pattern might portray its own appearance or convey information. But it also functions to cloak the person or object that it covers in an appropriate environment. Consider, by comparison, the two camouflage patterns in Figure 27. The camouflage pattern on the left was worn by soldiers in the U.S. Army deployed in Afghanistan to cloak them well against their surroundings, whereas the camouflage pattern on the right, worn by North Korean soldiers, does not cloak them, but if anything, makes them easier to see.

Figure 27: good (left) and bad (right) camouflage designs

Consider now optical illusions in fashion. Many features of garment design—line, shape, texture, color, and print—exploit features of human visual perception and optical illusions to influence the way in which the wearer's body is perceived. Importantly, these visual effects can be created with both three-dimensional design techniques such as garment shape and cut as well as with two-dimensional design techniques such as patterns, stripes, and color. For example, consider the Müller-Lyer illusion, as shown in Figure 28 on the left, which causes a line to look longer if it is bracketed on each end by arrow tails and shorter if it is bracketed on each end by arrowheads. This illusion can be incorporated into garment designs to lengthen or contract the body of the wearer through placement of arrow tails or heads, respectively, as shown in Figure 28 on the right. Is that design feature, as it appears on clothing, functional within the meaning of copyright law? Separable? In this vein, reconsider the zig zags, chevrons, and stripes at issue in *Star Athletica*. Might you be able to make the case that they are functional in affecting the perception of the wearer's body?

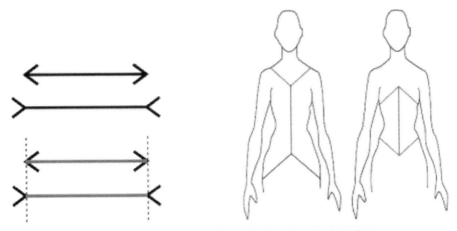

Figure 28: Müller-Lyon Illusion (left) and on body (right)

For more on how to think about this constellation of issues and an argument that much of fashion design is functional as a matter of copyright law, see Christopher Buccafusco & Jeanne C. Fromer, *Fashion's Function in Intellectual Property Law*, 93 NOTRE DAME L. REV. 51 (2017).

5. Consider whether it is good policy to provide copyright protection for fashion designs. Kal Raustiala and Christopher Sprigman suggest that society benefits more by permitting piracy of fashion designs. How so? They explain that "copying may actually promote innovation and benefit originators. We call this the 'piracy paradox.'... [C]opying functions as an important element of—and perhaps even a necessary predicate to—the apparel industry's swift cycle of innovation." Kal Raustiala & Christopher Sprigman, *The Piracy Paradox: Innovation and Intellectual Property in Fashion Design*, 92 VA. L. REV. 1687, 1691 (2006). In their analysis, the value of fashion design is in part status-based and fashion is cyclical. Because of these two features, design copying induces obsolescence of those designs and induces innovation in fashion. To them, if copying is permitted, there will thus be more innovation in fashion design, to the benefit of society. Scott Hemphill and Jeannie Suk Gersen take a stance in favor of protection for "close" copies. To them, "[i]n fashion we observe simultaneously the participation in collective trends and the expression of individuality," which they call "flocking" and "differentiation," respectively. C. Scott Hemphill & Jeannie Suk, *The Law, Culture, and Economics of Fashion*, 61 STAN. L. REV. 1147, 1152 (2009). To encourage both phenomena, they think it is important to forbid close copying of fashion designs or otherwise designers' incentives to create might be undermined. Which view is more convincing? To the extent that fashion designs are in large part about protecting status, or are contemporary forms of sumptuary codes, should copyright law protect them? *See* Barton Beebe, *Intellectual Property Law and the Sumptuary Code*, 123 HARV. L. REV. 809 (2010).

6. Article 25 of the TRIPS Agreement requires protection for industrial designs. Other forms of legal protection are potentially available to those who cannot get copyright protection for a particular design because it is a useful article that fails the separability test. There are three primary other forms of protection in this context: design patents, trade dress protection, and sui generis design protection.

Design patents are available to creators of "any new, original and ornamental design for an article of manufacture." 35 U.S.C. § 171. Design patents provide protection from infringement for fifteen years from the date of patent grant. *Id.* §§ 173, 289. To get a design patent, a design's creator must apply to the Patent and Trademark Office, where the application will be examined for patentability. *Id.* §§ 111, 112, 171.

Product design and product packaging are protectable as trade dress, which, under modern law, is a species of trademark. Wal-Mart Stores, Inc. v. Samara Bros., 529 U.S. 205, 209-16 (2000). Trademark rights arise through use rather than registration. 2 J. THOMAS MCCARTHY, MCCARTHY ON TRADEMARKS & UNFAIR COMPETITION § 16:18 (5th ed. 2018). While the Lanham Act—the governing federal law—creates procedures for federal registration of marks, 15 U.S.C. § 1052, unregistered marks are enforceable under federal law on substantially the same terms as registered marks. *Id.* §§ 1114, 1125(a). Like all marks, to be protectable, product design and packaging must be used in commerce in a way that "identif[ies] and distinguish[es] [a party's goods] from those manufactured or sold by others and ... indicate[s] the source of the goods, even if that source is unknown." *Id.* § 1127. Product packaging is capable of being considered inherently distinctive, but product design is only protectable if it has acquired secondary meaning. *Wal-Mart Stores, Inc.*, 529 U.S. at 210-15. Moreover, trade dress features are not protectable to the extent they are functional, meaning they are "essential to the use or purpose of the article or ... affect[] the cost or quality of the article." TrafFix Dev., Inc. v. Mktg. Displays, Inc., 532 U.S. 23, 33 (2001).

A third possibility is *sui generis* design protection. In the United States, this protection is only of limited availability. The Vessel Hull Design Protection Act protects original ship vessel hulls that are registered for a period of ten years. 17 U.S.C. §§ 1301-1310. The Semiconductor Chip Protection Act protects the visual appearance of semiconductor chips that are registered for a period of ten years. *Id.* §§ 901-914. There have been a number of failed recent attempts to provide *sui generis* protection for fashion designs. Innovative Design Protection and Piracy Protection Act, 111 S. 3728 (2010); Design Piracy Prohibition Act, 110 S. 1957 (2007). The European Union provides *sui generis* design protection for novel designs with individual character. EU: Directive 98/71/EC (Oct. 13, 1998). There are different forms of protection for unregistered and registered designs. *Id.*

Consider now one of the few post-*Star Athletica* circuit court decisions. Does it align with your understanding of how easy or hard protection of useful articles will be under *Star Athletica*? What do you make of the court's analysis of originality, merger, and scenes a faire?

Silvertop Associates Inc. v. Kangaroo Manufacturing Inc.
931 F.3d 215 (3d Cir. 2019)

HARDIMAN, J.:

[1] This ... appeal involves the validity of a copyright in a full-body banana costume. Appellant Kangaroo Manufacturing Inc. concedes that the banana costume it manufactures and sells is substantially similar to the banana costume created and sold by Appellee Rasta Imposta. Yet Kangaroo claims that Rasta cannot hold a valid copyright in such a costume's "pictorial, graphic, or sculptural features." 17 U.S.C. § 101.... We hold that, in combination, the Rasta costume's non-utilitarian, sculptural features are copyrightable, so we will affirm the District Court's preliminary injunction....

[2] This dispute stems from a business relationship that went bad. In 2010, Rasta obtained Copyright Registration No. VA 1-707-439 for its full-body banana costume. Two years later, Rasta began working with a company called Yagoozon, Inc., which purchased and resold thousands of Rasta's banana costumes. Yagoozon's founder, Justin Ligeri, also founded Kangaroo and at all relevant times was aware of Rasta's copyright registration in the banana costume. After the business relationship between Rasta and Yagoozon ended, Rasta's CEO, Robert Berman, discovered Kangaroo selling a costume that resembled his company's without a license.

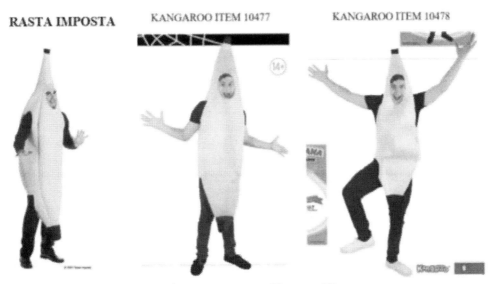

Figure 29: banana costumes of Rasta and Kangaroo

[3] Rasta sued Kangaroo for copyright infringement .... After settlement discussions were unsuccessful, Rasta moved for a preliminary injunction and Kangaroo responded by moving to dismiss. The District Court granted the motion for a preliminary injunction .... Kangaroo appealed ....

[4] Kangaroo claims the injunction should not have issued because Rasta is not likely to succeed on the merits of its copyright infringement claim. According to Kangaroo, Rasta does not hold a valid copyright in its banana costume....

[5] We begin by analyzing whether non-utilitarian, sculptural features of the costume are copyrightable by determining whether those features can be identified separately from its utilitarian features and are capable of existing independently from its utilitarian features. *See* 17 U.S.C. § 101; *Star Athletica*, 137 S. Ct. at 1008. We then consider whether the merger and *scenes a faire* doctrines render the costume ineligible for copyright protection. We conclude that the District Court did not err when it held that Rasta is reasonably likely to prove ownership of a valid copyright....

[6] Having articulated the legal principles that govern our analysis, we turn to the particular facts of this case. To begin with, Rasta's banana costume is a useful article.[4] The artistic features of the costume, in combination, prove both separable and capable of independent existence as a copyrightable work: a sculpture. Those sculptural features include the banana's combination of colors, lines, shape, and length. They do not include the cutout holes for the wearer's arms, legs, and face; the holes' dimensions; or the holes' locations on the costume, because those features are utilitarian.[5] Although more difficult to imagine separately from the costume's non-appearance related utility (i.e., wearability) than many works, one can still imagine the banana apart from the costume as an original sculpture. That sculpted banana, once split from

---

[4] ... [A] costume may serve, aside from its appearance, to clothe the wearer. *Star Athletica* addressed cheerleader uniforms as useful articles. And Rasta concedes its costume is a useful article.

[5] The District Court correctly found that the cutout holes are not, per se, a feature eligible for copyright because they perform a solely utilitarian function. It went on, however, to list the location of the head and arm cutouts which dictate how the costume drapes on and protrudes from a wearer (as opposed to the mere existence of the cutout holes) among the copyrightable features. We disagree with that portion of the District Court's analysis because we must imagine the banana apart from the useful (i.e., wearable) article. Rasta has not identified any artistic aspect to the holes' dimensions or locations except in relation to the wearer. The cutout holes' dimensions and locations on the costume are intrinsically useful (perhaps even necessary) to make the costume wearable like the shape, cut, and dimensions of the cheerleader uniforms in *Star Athletica*, so they cannot be copyrighted.

the costume, is not intrinsically utilitarian and does not merely replicate the costume, so it may be copyrighted.

[7] Kangaroo responds that we must inspect each feature individually, find each one too unoriginal or too utilitarian in isolation for copyright, and decline to protect the whole. But [our case law] forecloses this divide-and-conquer approach by training our focus on the combination of design elements in a work. And the *Star Athletica* Court did not cherry-pick the uniform designs' colors, shapes, or lines; it too evaluated their combination. 137 S. Ct. at 1012 (focusing on "the arrangement of colors, shapes, stripes, and chevrons on the surface of the cheerleading uniforms"). Thus, the separately imagined banana—the sum of its non-utilitarian parts—is copyrightable.

[8] Kangaroo also contends the banana is unoriginal because its designers based the design on a natural banana. They ask us to hold that depictions of natural objects in their natural condition can never be copyrighted. This argument seeks to raise the originality requirement's very low bar, which precedent forecloses for good reason. A judge's own aesthetic judgments must play no role in copyright analysis. Our inquiry is limited to how the article and features are perceived, not how or why they were designed. The cases Kangaroo cites in its brief confirm that whether natural objects are copyrightable depends on the circumstances. *Compare* Satava v. Lowry, 323 F.3d 805, 810 (9th Cir. 2003) (holding that a sculpture of a jellyfish was not copyrightable), *with* Coquico, Inc. v. Rodriguez-Miranda, 562 F.3d 62, 69 (1st Cir. 2009) (holding that several elements of a plush toy depicting a tree frog were copyrightable). The essential question is whether the depiction of the natural object has a minimal level of creativity. Rasta's banana meets those requirements....

[9] We therefore hold that the banana costume's combination of colors, lines, shape, and length (i.e., its artistic features) are both separable and capable of independent existence, and thus are copyrightable....

[10] Lastly, Kangaroo invokes two copyright doctrines—merger and *scenes a faire*—to argue the banana costume is ineligible for protection. Both arguments address the same question: whether copyrighting the banana costume would effectively monopolize an underlying idea, either directly or through elements necessary to that idea's expression....

[11] Here, copyrighting Rasta's banana costume would not effectively monopolize the underlying idea because there are many other ways to make a costume resemble a banana. Indeed, Rasta provided over 20 non-infringing examples. As the District Court observed, one can easily distinguish those examples from Rasta's costume based on the shape, curvature, tips, tips' color, overall color, length, width, lining, texture, and material. We agree and hold the merger doctrine does not apply here....

[12] Here too, copyrighting the banana costume's non-utilitarian features in combination would not threaten ... monopolization [of *scenes a faire*]. Kangaroo points to no specific feature that necessarily results from the costume's subject matter (a banana). Although a banana costume is likely to be yellow, it could be any shade of yellow—or green or brown for that matter. Although a banana costume is likely to be curved, it need not be—let alone in any particular manner. And although a banana costume is likely to have ends that resemble a natural banana's, those tips need not look like Rasta's black tips (in color, shape, or size). Again, the record includes over 20 examples of banana costumes that Rasta concedes would be non-infringing. The *scenes a faire* doctrine does not apply here either....

[13] Because Rasta established a reasonable likelihood that it could prove entitlement to protection for the veritable fruits of its intellectual labor, we will affirm.

4. Computer Software

a. Understanding Computer Software

To study the copyrightability of computer software, it is helpful to first explain some of the terminology in the field. **Software** can generally be understood as the non-tangible component of computers or other hardware that helps direct their operation. This is in contrast to a computer's hardware, such as a processor or disk drive. In modern computers (and other computing devices, such as a smartphone), hardware and software need each other. Neither works without the other. The software instructs the hardware's operation (such as adding two numbers together or saving information to computer memory). Software is stored in computer memory.

Humans write these instructions to the computer in a programming language, using the syntax of the language. These instructions are known as **source code**. Consider the simple example of source code that appears in Figure 30. It is a set of instructions to the computer to display a message of "Good Evening" if it is after 7 pm, a message of "Good Afternoon" if it is before then but after noon, and a message of "Good Morning" if it is earlier than noon.

```
Custom Function #10 -                              ×
IF  TIME[1]  >=  19       ' after 7:00 pm
     SETLCD  1,1,"Good Evening   "
ELSE
     IF  TIME[1]  >=12     ' after 12:00pm
          SETLCD  1,1,  "Good Afternoon"
     ELSE
          SETLCD  1,1,  "Good Morning   "
     ENDIF
ENDIF
```

```
   Select Function      Edit Fn Name       << < > >>
```

Figure 30: source code example

The slightly more complicated example of source code in Figure 31 calculates sales commissions for employees based on specified rates and each employee's total sales and then prints out the sales commissions.

```
#define R  10
Struct Sales {char Name[25], char Dept[8], float Sales};  Sales SalesFile[R];

void main(void)
   {
   int r;
   float MaxSales = 500.00, Rate1 = 0.07, Rate2 = 0.05, Commission, TotalCommission=0;

   GetDataFile(R);
   for(r = 0; r < R; r++)
      if(SalesFile [r].Sales >= MaxSales)
         Commission = SalesFile [r].Sales*Rate1;
      else
         Commission = SalesFile [r].Sales*Rate2;
      TotalCommission += Commission;
      Printf("\n \t %-s \t  %-s   \t %.2f %.2f", SalesFile [r].Name, SalesFile [r].Dept,
             SalesFile [r].Sales, Commission);
      }
   printf("\n\n \t Total Sales Commission: %.2f", TotalCommission);
   }
```

Figure 31: source code example

Source code cannot instruct the computer in and of itself. It first must be converted to a form that a computer can use. Typically, to do that, a program called a compiler converts the source code to instructions that the computer can execute. This conversion happens by breaking down each source code instruction into a set of computer-readable instructions (such as to write a value in memory, then write another value in memory, and then add those values together). This converted code that the computer can "read" or execute is called **object code**, or **machine code**. It is encoded in binary form, or in zeros and ones. A computer can then execute this object code as an **applications program** (such as a word processing program or an internet browser program) in interaction with a computer's **operating system**, which is the software—such as Microsoft's Windows, Apple's Mac OS, the iPhone's iOS, or Linux—that supports a computer's basic functions. This process of a computer's execution of source code instructions is depicted in Figure 32.

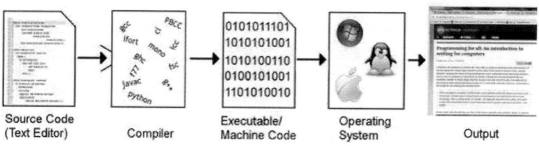

Source Code (Text Editor) — Compiler — Executable/ Machine Code — Operating System — Output

Figure 32: making source code run

Software design principles suggest breaking up software programs into different **modules** that can interact with one another. For example, Figure 33 shows software modules for an accounting software program. One reason modules are helpful is that one can take a module, such as the "Accounts Receivable" module here, and use it as well in a different software program (such as billing software).

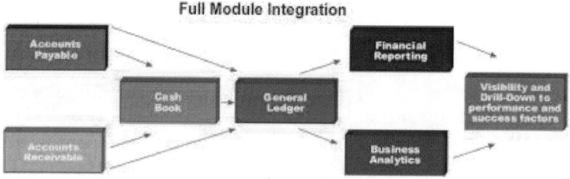

Figure 33: software modules

Finally, what users see in interacting with a software program or operating system is its **user interface**. The user interface of the Microsoft Word word-processing program is depicted in Figure 34.

Figure 34: Microsoft Word user interface

The first general purpose computers became commercially available in the 1950s. During this early era of computing, the computer industry was primarily a hardware business. In fact, IBM and other major mainframe manufacturers provided software to their hardware customers free of charge. In the 1980s, as personal computers, or microcomputers, became widely available, the software sector started to grow. Companies like Microsoft began selling operating system and applications programs independently of hardware. With the growth of the internet in the 1990s, yet more software was developed and distributed by independent software companies. Today, software is widely distributed for many forms of hardware beyond traditional computers, such as phones and refrigerators.

b. Network Effects in Software

One important feature of the software industry to keep in mind as we explore the copyrightability of software are the **network effects** that sometimes drive markets for software. A market exhibits network effects when "the value that consumers place on a good increases as others use the good." Mark A. Lemley & David McGowan, *Legal Implications of Network Economic Effects*, 86 CALIF. L. REV. 479, 481 (1998). As Mark Lemley and David McGowan explain with regard to computer software,

> *An operating system or application program will allow even a single user to perform a variety of tasks regardless whether even a single other consumer owns the software. At the same time, the value of a given program grows considerably as the number of additional purchasers increases. As more consumers adopted WordPerfect, for example, it became easier for each previous user to share files without the need for a conversion program and easier for employees to switch jobs without retraining.*

That is not the only network effect to which software is subject. In addition,

> *software may be subject to "increasing returns" based on positive feedback from the market in the form of complementary goods. Software developers will write more applications programs for an operating system with two-thirds of the market than for a system with one-third because the operating system with the larger share will provide the biggest market for applications*

> *programs. The availability of a broader array of application programs will reinforce the popularity of an operating system, which in turn will make investment in application programs compatible with that system more desirable than investment in programs compatible with less popular systems. Similarly, firms that adopt relatively popular software will likely incur lower costs to train employees and will find it easier to hire productive temporary help than will firms with unpopular software. Importantly, the strength of network effects will vary depending on the type of software in question. Network effects will be materially greater for operating systems software than for applications programs, for example ....*

There are thus many benefits to computer users from the network effects in certain software markets. Having more programs available provides users with more functionality and choice. When network effects drive software markets to standardization, users also may realize a greater ability to exchange data.

Yet the tendency of some software markets to be driven by network effects also raises a number of concerns. Sometimes the power of network effects can trap an industry or a market in an obsolete or less-than-optimal standard because of the difficulties of switching away from it. And sometimes the power of network effects can make the entry of new competitors into software markets more difficult.

Keep in mind the consequences of software's network effects as we consider the policies and doctrines underpinning copyright protection for computer software.

c. Copyright Protection for Software

Copyright law, as reflected in the 1976 Act, says nothing specifically about software. That said, given § 101's expansive definition of "literary work," software would seem to fit into this category of protectable subject matter. The legislative history says as much:

> *The term "literary works" does not connote any criterion of literary merit or qualitative value: it includes catalogs, directories, and similar factual, reference, or instructional works and compilations of data. It also includes computer data bases, and computer programs to the extent that they incorporate authorship in the programmer's expression of original ideas, as distinguished from the ideas themselves.*

H.R. REP. NO. 1476, 94th Cong., 2d Sess. 47, at 54 (1976). Congress deliberately chose not to address computer software explicitly in the 1976 Act. Rather, it decided to give the issue of intellectual property protection for software and other new technologies further attention and established the National Commission on New Technological Uses of Copyrighted Works (CONTU) to study these issues. In 1978, CONTU concluded that computer software should be protected by copyright as a literary work. NATIONAL COMMISSION ON NEW TECHNOLOGICAL USES OF COPYRIGHTED WORKS, FINAL REPORT ON NEW TECHNOLOGICAL USES OF COPYRIGHTED WORKS 11, 14-15, 38, 43-46 (1979). The commission concluded that copyright law's protections and limitations would fit well with software. In particular, it emphasized that

> *The "idea-expression identity" exception provides that copyrighted language may be copied without infringing when there is but a limited number of ways to express a given idea. This rule is the logical extension of the fundamental principle that copyright cannot protect ideas. In the computer context this means that when specific instructions, even though previously copyrighted, are the only and essential means of accomplishing a given task, their later use by another will not amount to an infringement....*

*When other language is available, programmers are free to read copyrighted programs and use
the ideas embodied in them in preparing their own works.*

In 1980, Congress accepted CONTU's recommendation on computer software. It did not expressly change the
subject matter provisions in § 102(a) to allow for software—as it was already considered protectable as a
literary work—but it added two provisions to the statute. First, Congress defined a "computer program" in
§ 101: to be "a set of statements or instructions to be used directly or indirectly in a computer in order to bring
about a certain result." Second, Congress added a defense to copyright infringement in § 117 for limited
categories of copying computer programs, such as when an owner of a copy of computer program copies it
"as an essential step in the utilization of the computer program in conjunction with a machine." For reflections
on CONTU's recommendations and Congress's adoption of them, see Arthur R. Miller, *Copyright Protection for
Computer Programs, Databases, and Computer-Generated Works: Is Anything New Since CONTU?*, 106 HARV. L.
REV. 977 (1993); Pamela Samuelson, *CONTU Revisited: The Case Against Copyright Protection for Computer
Programs in Machine-Readable Form*, 1984 DUKE L.J. 663.

Many preliminary questions about the extent of the copyrightability of computer software nonetheless
remained unresolved. Early cases sought to settle them. In one foundational case, Apple Computer, Inc., sued
Franklin Computer Corporation for copyright infringement. Franklin had made "Apple compatible" computers
by copying the code for the Apple II operating system programs. This enabled Franklin's consumers to use
peripheral equipment and software developed for the Apple II computer. Franklin had copied all of Apple's
code to ensure perfect compatibility. The ensuing Third Circuit decision articulated some fundamental
principles on copyright in software programs. Apple Computer, Inc. v. Franklin Computer Corp., 714 F.2d 1240
(3d Cir. 1983). In addition to source code being copyrightable as a literary work, the Third Circuit ruled that
object code is also copyrightable as a literary work. The court reasoned that "the category of 'literary works'...
is not confined to literature in the nature of Hemingway's *For Whom the Bell Tolls*. The definition of 'literary
works' in section 101 includes expression not only in words but also 'numbers, or other ... numerical symbols
or indicia,' thereby expanding the common usage of 'literary works.'" The court also rejected Franklin's
argument that operating system programs cannot be copyrighted, even if applications programs can. Franklin
had argued that operating system programs were unprotectable as systems or processes pursuant to § 102(b).
The court thought there was no material distinction between operating system programs and applications
programs in this regard, in that both instruct the computer to do something. Finally, the court dismissed
Franklin's argument that the merger doctrine applies to bar protection for Apple's operating system program.
Franklin had maintained that compatibility is important and there are only a few ways to arrange an operating
system to be compatible with Apple's. The Third Circuit disagreed:

> *If other methods of expressing that idea are not foreclosed as a practical matter, then there is
> no merger. Franklin may wish to achieve total compatibility with independently developed
> application programs written for the Apple II, but that is a commercial and competitive
> objective which does not enter into the somewhat metaphysical issue of whether particular
> ideas and expression have merged.*

This was an early case, but over the next few years, all courts agreed that source code and object code, for
both operating systems and applications, were copyrightable.

Despite Congress's determination to include software as copyrightable subject matter, there has been
sustained skepticism regarding whether software is a proper subject of copyright protection. One critique has
been that software code is lacking in the communicative function that copyright is meant to protect. As
CONTU Commissioner John Hersey expressed in his dissent from the commission's report, the other
categories of copyrightable subject matter are "intended to be circulated to human beings and to be used by
them—to be read, heard, or seen, for either pleasurable or practical ends. Computer programs, in their

mature phase, are addressed to machines." NATIONAL COMMISSION ON NEW TECHNOLOGICAL USES OF COPYRIGHTED WORKS, FINAL REPORT ON NEW TECHNOLOGICAL USES OF COPYRIGHTED WORKS 28 (1979). On this front, is software code similar to, or different from, the piano rolls we studied earlier, which are now copyrightable? What to make of the fact that some software code is shared with other programmers, whether to build upon or to learn from it? Another criticism is that object code in particular lacks authorship because it is compiled by a computer from source code. Richard H. Stern, *Another Look at Copyright Protection of Software*, 3 COMPUTER/L. J. 1 (1981). Is that correct? Or does the object code preserve the source code programmer's authorship in its translation? Another related line of criticism is that computer software code has the central aim of functionality, much like things that are patented, and very much unlike the canonical forms of copyrighted works. Jeanne C. Fromer, *A Psychology of Intellectual Property*, 104 NW. U. L. REV. 1441 (2010); Pamela Samuelson, *A Manifesto Concerning the Legal Protection of Computer Programs*, 94 COLUM. L. REV. 2308 (1994). If true, might limitations on copyrightability, such as the idea-expression distinction and the merger doctrine, ensure that functional aspects of programs do not receive protection? Finally, the network effects of software raise some worries that providing too much protection can impede progress in ways that are absent for other categories of copyrightable subject matter that do not produce such network effects. Peter S. Menell, *An Analysis of the Scope of Copyright Protection for Application Programs*, 41 STAN. L. REV.1045, 1066-69 (1989).

The earliest cases protecting software under copyright, like *Apple*, prohibited piracy of computer programs—that is, exact copying. But when cases arose in which claims of copyright infringement rested on copying non-literal elements of computer code, courts had to learn to distinguish idea and process from expression in software.

As you read this case, consider how, if at all, the court takes into account software's unique technical and economic features in establishing the line between protectable expression and unprotectable ideas and processes. Practically, how much do you think will be left as protectable expression in software code after applying the court's framework?

Computer Associates International v. Altai, Inc.
982 F.2d 693 (2d Cir. 1992)

WALKER, J.:

[1] In recent years, the growth of computer science has spawned a number of challenging legal questions, particularly in the field of copyright law. As scientific knowledge advances, courts endeavor to keep pace, and sometimes—as in the area of computer technology—they are required to venture into less than familiar waters. This is not a new development, though. From its beginning, the law of copyright has developed in response to significant changes in technology.

[2] Article I, section 8 of the Constitution authorizes Congress "[t]o promote the Progress of Science and useful Arts, by securing for limited Times to Authors and Inventors the exclusive Right to their respective Writings and Discoveries." The Supreme Court has stated that "[t]he economic philosophy behind the clause ... is the conviction that encouragement of individual effort by personal gain is the best way to advance public welfare...." Mazer v. Stein, 347 U.S. 201, 219 (1954). The author's benefit, however, is clearly a "secondary" consideration. The ultimate aim is, by this incentive, to stimulate artistic creativity for the general public good.

[3] Thus, the copyright law seeks to establish a delicate equilibrium. On the one hand, it affords protection to authors as an incentive to create, and, on the other, it must appropriately limit the extent of that protection so as to avoid the effects of monopolistic stagnation. In applying the federal act to new types of cases, courts must always keep this symmetry in mind.

[4] Among other things, this case deals with the challenging question of whether and to what extent the "non-literal" aspects of a computer program, that is, those aspects that are not reduced to written code, are protected by copyright.... Drawing upon long-standing doctrines of copyright law, we take an approach that we think ... addresses the practical difficulties embedded in these types of cases. In so doing, we have kept in mind the necessary balance between creative incentive and industrial competition....

[5] .... The Copyright Act defines a computer program as "a set of statements or instructions to be used directly or indirectly in a computer in order to bring about a certain result." 17 U.S.C. § 101. In writing these directions, the programmer works from the general to the specific.

[6] The first step in this procedure is to identify a program's ultimate function or purpose. An example of such an ultimate purpose might be the creation and maintenance of a business ledger. Once this goal has been achieved, a programmer breaks down or decomposes the program's ultimate function into simpler constituent problems or "subtasks," which are also known as subroutines or modules. In the context of a business ledger program, a module or subroutine might be responsible for the task of updating a list of outstanding accounts receivable. Sometimes, depending upon the complexity of its task, a subroutine may be broken down further into sub-subroutines.

[7] Having sufficiently decomposed the program's ultimate function into its component elements, a programmer will then arrange the subroutines or modules into what are known as organizational or flow charts. Flow charts map the interactions between modules that achieve the program's end goal.

[8] In order to accomplish these intra-program interactions, a programmer must carefully design each module's parameter list. A parameter list is the information sent to and received from a subroutine. The term "parameter list" refers to the form in which information is passed between modules (e.g. for accounts receivable, the designated time frame and particular customer identifying number) and the information's actual content (e.g. 8/91–7/92; customer No. 3). With respect to form, interacting modules must share similar parameter lists so that they are capable of exchanging information.

[9] The functions of the modules in a program together with each module's relationships to other modules constitute the "structure" of the program. Additionally, the term structure may include the category of modules referred to as "macros." A macro is a single instruction that initiates a sequence of operations or module interactions within the program. Very often the user will accompany a macro with an instruction from the parameter list to refine the instruction (e.g. current total of accounts receivable (macro), but limited to those for 8/91 to 7/92 from customer No. 3 (parameters)).

[10] In fashioning the structure, a programmer will normally attempt to maximize the program's speed, efficiency, as well as simplicity for user operation, while taking into consideration certain externalities such as the memory constraints of the computer upon which the program will be run. This stage of program design often requires the most time and investment.

[11] Once each necessary module has been identified, designed, and its relationship to the other modules has been laid out conceptually, the resulting program structure must be embodied in a written language that the computer can read. This process is called "coding," and requires two steps. First, the programmer must transpose the program's structural blue-print into a source code. This step has been described as comparable to the novelist fleshing out the broad outline of his plot by crafting from words and sentences the paragraphs

that convey the ideas.... Once the source code has been completed, the second step is to translate or "compile" it into object code. Object code is the binary language comprised of zeros and ones through which the computer directly receives its instructions.

[12] After the coding is finished, the programmer will run the program on the computer in order to find and correct any logical and syntactical errors. This is known as "debugging" and, once done, the program is complete....

[13] The subject of this litigation originates with one of CA's marketed programs entitled CA–SCHEDULER. CA–SCHEDULER is a job scheduling program designed for IBM mainframe computers. Its primary functions are straightforward: to create a schedule specifying when the computer should run various tasks, and then to control the computer as it executes the schedule. CA–SCHEDULER contains a sub-program entitled ADAPTER, also developed by CA. ADAPTER is not an independently marketed product of CA; it is a wholly integrated component of CA–SCHEDULER and has no capacity for independent use.

[14] Nevertheless, ADAPTER plays an extremely important role. It is an "operating system compatibility component," which means, roughly speaking, it serves as a translator. An "operating system" is itself a program that manages the resources of the computer, allocating those resources to other programs as needed. The IBM System 370 family of computers, for which CA–SCHEDULER was created, is, depending upon the computer's size, designed to contain one of three operating systems: DOS/VSE, MVS, or CMS. As the district court noted, the general rule is that a program written for one operating system, e.g., DOS/VSE, will not, without modification, run under another operating system such as MVS. ADAPTER's function is to translate the language of a given program into the particular language that the computer's own operating system can understand....

[15] A program like ADAPTER, which allows a computer user to change or use multiple operating systems while maintaining the same software, is highly desirable. It saves the user the costs, both in time and money, that otherwise would be expended in purchasing new programs, modifying existing systems to run them, and gaining familiarity with their operation. The benefits run both ways. The increased compatibility afforded by an ADAPTER-like component, and its resulting popularity among consumers, makes whatever software in which it is incorporated significantly more marketable.

[16] Starting in 1982, Altai began marketing its own job scheduling program entitled ZEKE. The original version of ZEKE was designed for use in conjunction with a VSE operating system. By late 1983, in response to customer demand, Altai decided to rewrite ZEKE so that it could be run in conjunction with an MVS operating system.

[17] At that time, James P. Williams, then an employee of Altai and now its President, approached Claude F. Arney, III, a computer programmer who worked for CA. Williams and Arney were longstanding friends, and had in fact been co-workers at CA for some time before Williams left CA to work for Altai's predecessor. Williams wanted to recruit Arney to assist Altai in designing an MVS version of ZEKE...

[18] Arney ... was intimately familiar with various aspects of ADAPTER....

[19] Once at Altai, Arney and Williams discussed design possibilities for adapting ZEKE to run on MVS operating systems.... Arney persuaded Williams that the best way to make the needed modifications was to introduce a "common system interface" component into ZEKE. He did not tell Williams that his idea stemmed from his familiarity with ADAPTER. They decided to name this new component-program OSCAR.

[20] Arney went to work creating OSCAR at Altai's offices using the ADAPTER source code.... In three months, Arney successfully completed the OSCAR/VSE project. In an additional month he developed an

OSCAR/MVS version. When the dust finally settled, Arney had copied approximately 30% of OSCAR's code from CA's ADAPTER program.

[21] The first generation of OSCAR programs was known as OSCAR 3.4. From 1985 to August 1988, Altai used OSCAR 3.4 in its ZEKE product .... In late July 1988, CA first learned that Altai may have appropriated parts of ADAPTER. After confirming its suspicions, CA secured copyrights on its 2.1 and 7.0 versions of CA–SCHEDULER. CA then brought this copyright and trade secret misappropriation action against Altai.

[22] Apparently, it was upon receipt of the summons and complaint that Altai first learned that Arney had copied much of the OSCAR code from ADAPTER....

[23] Upon advice of counsel, Williams initiated OSCAR's rewrite. The project's goal was to save as much of OSCAR 3.4 as legitimately could be used, and to excise those portions which had been copied from ADAPTER. Arney was entirely excluded from the process, and his copy of the ADAPTER code was locked away. Williams put eight other programmers on the project, none of whom had been involved in any way in the development of OSCAR 3.4. Williams provided the programmers with a description of the ZEKE operating system services so that they could rewrite the appropriate code. The rewrite project took about six months to complete and was finished in mid-November 1989. The resulting program was entitled OSCAR 3.5.

[24] From that point on, Altai shipped only OSCAR 3.5 to its new customers. Altai also shipped OSCAR 3.5 as a "free upgrade" to all customers that had previously purchased OSCAR 3.4....

[25] ... Altai has conceded liability for the copying of ADAPTER into OSCAR 3.4 and raises no challenge to the award of $364,444 in damages on that score. Thus, we address only CA's appeal from the district court's ruling[] that ... Altai was not liable for copyright infringement in developing OSCAR 3.5....

[26] As a general matter, and to varying degrees, copyright protection extends beyond a literary work's strictly textual form to its non-literal components. As we have said, "[i]t is of course essential to any protection of literary property ... that the right cannot be limited literally to the text, else a plagiarist would escape by immaterial variations." Nichols v. Universal Pictures Corp., 45 F.2d 119, 121 (2d Cir.1930) (L. Hand, J.). Thus, where the fundamental essence or structure of one work is duplicated in another, courts have found copyright infringement....

[27] In this case, the hotly contested issues surround OSCAR 3.5. As recounted above, OSCAR 3.5 is the product of Altai's carefully orchestrated rewrite of OSCAR 3.4. After the purge, none of the ADAPTER source code remained in the 3.5 version; thus, Altai made sure that the literal elements of its revamped OSCAR program were no longer substantially similar to the literal elements of CA's ADAPTER.

[28] According to CA, the district court .... committed legal error in analyzing its claims of copyright infringement by failing to find that copyright protects expression contained in the non-literal elements of computer software. We disagree.

[29] CA argues that, despite Altai's rewrite of the OSCAR code, the resulting program remained substantially similar to the structure of its ADAPTER program. As discussed above, a program's structure includes its non-literal components such as general flow charts as well as the more specific organization of inter-modular relationships, parameter lists, and macros. In addition to these aspects, CA contends that OSCAR 3.5 is also substantially similar to ADAPTER with respect to the list of services that both ADAPTER and OSCAR obtain from their respective operating systems. We must decide whether and to what extent these elements of computer programs are protected by copyright law.

[30] ... The Copyright Act affords protection to "original works of authorship fixed in any tangible medium of expression." 17 U.S.C. § 102(a). This broad category of protected "works" includes "literary works," *id.* § 102(a)(1), which are defined by the Act as

> works, other than audiovisual works, expressed in words, numbers, or other verbal or numerical symbols or indicia, regardless of the nature of the material objects, such as books, periodicals, manuscripts, phonorecords, film tapes, disks, or cards, in which they are embodied.

17 U.S.C. § 101. While computer programs are not specifically listed as part of the above statutory definition, the legislative history leaves no doubt that Congress intended them to be considered literary works.

[31] The syllogism that follows from the foregoing premises is a powerful one: if the non-literal structures of literary works are protected by copyright; and if computer programs are literary works, as we are told by the legislature; then the non-literal structures of computer programs are protected by copyright. We have no reservation in joining the company of those courts that have already ascribed to this logic. However, that conclusion does not end our analysis. We must determine the scope of copyright protection that extends to a computer program's non-literal structure....

[32] It is a fundamental principle of copyright law that a copyright does not protect an idea, but only the expression of the idea....

[33] Congress made no special exception for computer programs. To the contrary, the legislative history explicitly states that copyright protects computer programs only "to the extent that they incorporate authorship in programmer's expression of original ideas, as distinguished from the ideas themselves." House Report at 5667; *see also id.* at 5670 ("Section 102(b) is intended ... to make clear that the expression adopted by the programmer is the copyrightable element in a computer program, and that the actual processes or methods embodied in the program are not within the scope of copyright law.") ....

[34] Drawing the line between idea and expression is a tricky business....

[35] The essentially utilitarian nature of a computer program further complicates the task of distilling its idea from its expression. In order to describe both computational processes and abstract ideas, its content combines creative and technical expression. The variations of expression found in purely creative compositions, as opposed to those contained in utilitarian works, are not directed towards practical application. For example, a narration of Humpty Dumpty's demise, which would clearly be a creative composition, does not serve the same ends as, say, a recipe for scrambled eggs—which is a more process oriented text. Thus, compared to aesthetic works, computer programs hover even more closely to the elusive boundary line described in § 102(b).

[36] The doctrinal starting point in analyses of utilitarian works, is the seminal case of *Baker v. Selden*....

[37] To the extent that an accounting text and a computer program are both "a set of statements or instructions ... to bring about a certain result," 17 U.S.C. § 101, they are roughly analogous. In the former case, the processes are ultimately conducted by human agency; in the latter, by electronic means. In either case, as already stated, the processes themselves are not protectable. But the holding in *Baker* goes farther. The Court concluded that those aspects of a work, which "must necessarily be used as incident to" the idea, system or process that the work describes, are also not copyrightable. Selden's ledger sheets, therefore, enjoyed no copyright protection because they were "necessary incidents to" the system of accounting that he described. From this reasoning, we conclude that those elements of a computer program that are necessarily incidental to its function are similarly unprotectable.

[38] While *Baker v. Selden* provides a sound analytical foundation, it offers scant guidance on how to separate idea or process from expression, and moreover, on how to further distinguish protectable expression from that expression which "must necessarily be used as incident to" the work's underlying concept. In the context of computer programs, the Third Circuit's noted decision in *Whelan [Assocs., Inc. v. Jaslow Dental Lab., Inc.,* 797 F.2d 1222 (3d Cir. 1986),] has, thus far, been the most thoughtful attempt to accomplish these ends.

[39] The court in *Whelan* faced substantially the same problem as is presented by this case. There, the defendant was accused of making off with the non-literal structure of the plaintiff's copyrighted dental lab management program, and employing it to create its own competitive version. In assessing whether there had been an infringement, the court had to determine which aspects of the programs involved were ideas, and which were expression. In separating the two, the court settled upon the following conceptual approach:

> [T]he line between idea and expression may be drawn with reference to the end sought to be achieved by the work in question. In other words, the purpose or function of a utilitarian work would be the work's idea, and everything that is not necessary to that purpose or function would be part of the expression of the idea.... Where there are various means of achieving the desired purpose, then the particular means chosen is not necessary to the purpose; hence, there is expression, not idea.

The "idea" of the program at issue in *Whelan* was identified by the court as simply "the efficient management of a dental laboratory."

[40] So far, in the courts, the *Whelan* rule has received a mixed reception. While some decisions have adopted its reasoning, others have rejected it.

[41] *Whelan* has fared even more poorly in the academic community, where its standard for distinguishing idea from expression has been widely criticized for being conceptually overbroad. The leading commentator in the field has stated that "[t]he crucial flaw in [*Whelan's*] reasoning is that it assumes that only one 'idea,' in copyright law terms, underlies any computer program, and that once a separable idea can be identified, everything else must be expression." 3 NIMMER ON COPYRIGHT § 13.03(F), at 13–62.34. This criticism focuses not upon the program's ultimate purpose but upon the reality of its structural design. As we have already noted, a computer program's ultimate function or purpose is the composite result of interacting subroutines. Since each subroutine is itself a program, and thus, may be said to have its own "idea," *Whelan's* general formulation that a program's overall purpose equates with the program's idea is descriptively inadequate.

[42] Accordingly, we think that [the district court] wisely declined to follow *Whelan*....

[43] As discussed herein, we think that district courts would be well-advised to undertake a three-step procedure ... in order to determine whether the non-literal elements of two or more computer programs are substantially similar. This approach breaks no new ground; rather, it draws on such familiar copyright doctrines as merger, scenes a faire, and public domain. In taking this approach, however, we are cognizant that computer technology is a dynamic field which can quickly outpace judicial decisionmaking. Thus, in cases where the technology in question does not allow for a literal application of the procedure we outline below, our opinion should not be read to foreclose the district courts of our circuit from utilizing a modified version.

[44] ... [A] court would first break down the allegedly infringed program into its constituent structural parts. Then, by examining each of these parts for such things as incorporated ideas, expression that is necessarily incidental to those ideas, and elements that are taken from the public domain, a court would then be able to sift out all non-protectable material. Left with a kernel, or possible kernels, of creative expression after following this process of elimination, the court's last step would be to compare this material with the structure of an allegedly infringing program. The result of this comparison will determine whether the

protectable elements of the programs at issue are substantially similar so as to warrant a finding of infringement. It will be helpful to elaborate a bit further.

Step One: Abstraction

[45] As the district court appreciated, the theoretic framework for analyzing substantial similarity expounded by Learned Hand in the *Nichols* case is helpful in the present context. In *Nichols*, we enunciated what has now become known as the "abstractions" test for separating idea from expression:

> Upon any work ... a great number of patterns of increasing generality will fit equally well, as more and more of the incident is left out. The last may perhaps be no more than the most general statement of what the [work] is about, and at times might consist only of its title; but there is a point in this series of abstractions where they are no longer protected, since otherwise the [author] could prevent the use of his "ideas," to which, apart from their expression, his property is never extended.

[46] While the abstractions test was originally applied in relation to literary works such as novels and plays, it is adaptable to computer programs. In contrast to the *Whelan* approach, the abstractions test implicitly recognizes that any given work may consist of a mixture of numerous ideas and expressions.

[47] As applied to computer programs, the abstractions test will comprise the first step in the examination for substantial similarity. Initially, in a manner that resembles reverse engineering on a theoretical plane, a court should dissect the allegedly copied program's structure and isolate each level of abstraction contained within it. This process begins with the code and ends with an articulation of the program's ultimate function. Along the way, it is necessary essentially to retrace and map each of the designer's steps—in the opposite order in which they were taken during the program's creation.

[48] As an anatomical guide to this procedure, the following description is helpful:

> At the lowest level of abstraction, a computer program may be thought of in its entirety as a set of individual instructions organized into a hierarchy of modules. At a higher level of abstraction, the instructions in the lowest-level modules may be replaced conceptually by the functions of those modules. At progressively higher levels of abstraction, the functions of higher-level modules conceptually replace the implementations of those modules in terms of lower-level modules and instructions, until finally, one is left with nothing but the ultimate function of the program.... A program has structure at every level of abstraction at which it is viewed. At low levels of abstraction, a program's structure may be quite complex; at the highest level it is trivial.

Step Two: Filtration

[49] Once the program's abstraction levels have been discovered, the substantial similarity inquiry moves from the conceptual to the concrete. Professor Nimmer suggests, and we endorse, a "successive filtering method" for separating protectable expression from non-protectable material. *See generally* 3 NIMMER § 13.03[F]. This process entails examining the structural components at each level of abstraction to determine whether their particular inclusion at that level was "idea" or was dictated by considerations of efficiency, so as to be necessarily incidental to that idea; required by factors external to the program itself; or taken from the public domain and hence is nonprotectable expression. The structure of any given program may reflect some, all, or none of these considerations. Each case requires its own fact specific investigation.

[50] Strictly speaking, this filtration serves the purpose of defining the scope of plaintiff's copyright. By applying well developed doctrines of copyright law, it may ultimately leave behind a core of protectable material. Further explication of this second step may be helpful.

(a) Elements Dictated by Efficiency ...

[51] CONTU recognized the applicability of the merger doctrine to computer programs. In its report to Congress it stated that:

> [C]opyrighted language may be copied without infringing when there is but a limited number of ways to express a given idea.... In the computer context, this means that when specific instructions, even though previously copyrighted, are the only and essential means of accomplishing a given task, their later use by another will not amount to infringement.

CONTU Report, at 20. While this statement directly concerns only the application of merger to program code, that is, the textual aspect of the program, it reasonably suggests that the doctrine fits comfortably within the general context of computer programs.

[52] Furthermore, when one considers the fact that programmers generally strive to create programs that meet the user's needs in the most efficient manner, the applicability of the merger doctrine to computer programs becomes compelling. In the context of computer program design, the concept of efficiency is akin to deriving the most concise logical proof or formulating the most succinct mathematical computation. Thus, the more efficient a set of modules are, the more closely they approximate the idea or process embodied in that particular aspect of the program's structure.

[53] While, hypothetically, there might be a myriad of ways in which a programmer may effectuate certain functions within a program,—i.e., express the idea embodied in a given subroutine—efficiency concerns may so narrow the practical range of choice as to make only one or two forms of expression workable options. Of course, not all program structure is informed by efficiency concerns. It follows that in order to determine whether the merger doctrine precludes copyright protection to an aspect of a program's structure that is so oriented, a court must inquire whether the use of this particular set of modules is necessary efficiently to implement that part of the program's process being implemented. If the answer is yes, then the expression represented by the programmer's choice of a specific module or group of modules has merged with their underlying idea and is unprotected.

[54] Another justification for linking structural economy with the application of the merger doctrine stems from a program's essentially utilitarian nature and the competitive forces that exist in the software marketplace. Working in tandem, these factors give rise to a problem of proof which merger helps to eliminate.

[55] Efficiency is an industry-wide goal. Since, as we have already noted, there may be only a limited number of efficient implementations for any given program task, it is quite possible that multiple programmers, working independently, will design the identical method employed in the allegedly infringed work. Of course, if this is the case, there is no copyright infringement.

[56] Under these circumstances, the fact that two programs contain the same efficient structure may as likely lead to an inference of independent creation as it does to one of copying. Thus, since evidence of similarly efficient structure is not particularly probative of copying, it should be disregarded in the overall substantial similarity analysis....

(b) Elements Dictated by External Factors

[57] We have stated that where it is virtually impossible to write about a particular historical era or fictional theme without employing certain 'stock' or standard literary devices, such expression is not copyrightable....

[58] Professor Nimmer points out that "in many instances it is virtually impossible to write a program to perform particular functions in a specific computing environment without employing standard techniques." 3 NIMMER § 13.03[F][3], at 13–65. This is a result of the fact that a programmer's freedom of design choice is often circumscribed by extrinsic considerations such as (1) the mechanical specifications of the computer on which a particular program is intended to run; (2) compatibility requirements of other programs with which a program is designed to operate in conjunction; (3) computer manufacturers' design standards; (4) demands of the industry being serviced; and (5) widely accepted programming practices within the computer industry....

[59] ... [W]e conclude that a court must also examine the structural content of an allegedly infringed program for elements that might have been dictated by external factors.

(c) Elements Taken from the Public Domain

[60] Closely related to the non-protectability of scenes a faire, is material found in the public domain. Such material is free for the taking and cannot be appropriated by a single author even though it is included in a copyrighted work. We see no reason to make an exception to this rule for elements of a computer program that have entered the public domain by virtue of freely accessible program exchanges and the like. Thus, a court must also filter out this material from the allegedly infringed program before it makes the final inquiry in its substantial similarity analysis.

Step Three: Comparison

[61] The third and final step of the test for substantial similarity that we believe appropriate for non-literal program components entails a comparison. Once a court has sifted out all elements of the allegedly infringed program which are "ideas" or are dictated by efficiency or external factors, or taken from the public domain, there may remain a core of protectable expression. In terms of a work's copyright value, this is the golden nugget.... {We return to substantial similarity analysis in Chapter V.}

[62] We are satisfied that the three step approach we have just outlined not only comports with, but advances the constitutional policies underlying the Copyright Act. Since any method that tries to distinguish idea from expression ultimately impacts on the scope of copyright protection afforded to a particular type of work, the line it draws must be a pragmatic one, which also keeps in consideration the preservation of the balance between competition and protection.

[63] CA and some amici argue against the type of approach that we have set forth on the grounds that it will be a disincentive for future computer program research and development. At bottom, they claim that if programmers are not guaranteed broad copyright protection for their work, they will not invest the extensive time, energy and funds required to design and improve program structures. While they have a point, their argument cannot carry the day. The interest of the copyright law is not in simply conferring a monopoly on industrious persons, but in advancing the public welfare through rewarding artistic creativity, in a manner that permits the free use and development of non-protectable ideas and processes.

[64] In this respect, our conclusion is informed by Justice Stewart's concise discussion of the principles that correctly govern the adaptation of the copyright law to new circumstances. In *Twentieth Century Music Corp. v. Aiken*, he wrote:

The limited scope of the copyright holder's statutory monopoly, like the limited copyright duration required by the Constitution, reflects a balance of competing claims upon the public interest: Creative work is to be encouraged and rewarded, but private motivation must ultimately serve the cause of promoting broad public availability of literature, music, and the other arts.

The immediate effect of our copyright law is to secure a fair return for an "author's" creative labor. But the ultimate aim is, by this incentive, to stimulate artistic creativity for the general public good.... When technological change has rendered its literal terms ambiguous, the Copyright Act must be construed in light of this basic purpose.

422 U.S. 151, 156 (1975) ....

[65] *Feist* teaches that substantial effort alone cannot confer copyright status on an otherwise uncopyrightable work. As we have discussed, despite the fact that significant labor and expense often goes into computer program flow-charting and debugging, that process does not always result in inherently protectable expression. Thus, *Feist* implicitly undercuts the *Whelan* rationale, which allowed copyright protection beyond the literal computer code in order to provide the proper incentive for programmers by protecting their most valuable efforts.... In view of the Supreme Court's recent holding, however, we must reject the legal basis of CA's disincentive argument.

[66] Furthermore, we are unpersuaded that the test we approve today will lead to the dire consequences for the computer program industry that plaintiff and some amici predict. To the contrary, serious students of the industry have been highly critical of the sweeping scope of copyright protection engendered by the *Whelan* rule, in that it enables first comers to lock up basic programming techniques as implemented in programs to perform particular tasks.

[67] To be frank, the exact contours of copyright protection for non-literal program structure are not completely clear. We trust that as future cases are decided, those limits will become better defined. Indeed, it may well be that the Copyright Act serves as a relatively weak barrier against public access to the theoretical interstices behind a program's source and object codes. This results from the hybrid nature of a computer program, which, while it is literary expression, is also a highly functional, utilitarian component in the larger process of computing.

[68] Generally, we think that copyright registration—with its indiscriminating availability—is not ideally suited to deal with the highly dynamic technology of computer science. Thus far, many of the decisions in this area reflect the courts' attempt to fit the proverbial square peg in a round hole.... [P]atent registration, with its exacting up-front novelty and non-obviousness requirements, might be the more appropriate rubric of protection for intellectual property of this kind....

[69] In the meantime, Congress has made clear that computer programs are literary works entitled to copyright protection. Of course, we shall abide by these instructions, but in so doing we must not impair the overall integrity of copyright law. While incentive based arguments in favor of broad copyright protection are perhaps attractive from a pure policy perspective, ultimately, they have a corrosive effect on certain fundamental tenets of copyright doctrine. If the test we have outlined results in narrowing the scope of protection, as we expect it will, that result flows from applying, in accordance with Congressional intent, long-standing principles of copyright law to computer programs. Of course, our decision is also informed by our concern that these fundamental principles remain undistorted....

[70] The district court had to determine whether Altai's OSCAR 3.5 program was substantially similar to CA's ADAPTER. We note that [the district court]'s method of analysis effectively served as a road map for our own,

with one exception—[the district court] filtered out the non-copyrightable aspects of OSCAR 3.5 rather than those found in ADAPTER, the allegedly infringed program. We think that our approach—i.e., filtering out the unprotected aspects of an allegedly infringed program and then comparing the end product to the structure of the suspect program—is preferable, and therefore believe that district courts should proceed in this manner in future cases.

[71] We opt for this strategy because, in some cases, the defendant's program structure might contain protectable expression and/or other elements that are not found in the plaintiff's program. Since it is extraneous to the allegedly copied work, this material would have no bearing on any potential substantial similarity between the two programs. Thus, its filtration would be wasteful and unnecessarily time consuming. Furthermore, by focusing the analysis on the infringing rather than on the infringed material, a court may mistakenly place too little emphasis on a quantitatively small misappropriation which is, in reality, a qualitatively vital aspect of the plaintiff's protectable expression.

[72] The fact that the district court's analysis proceeded in the reverse order, however, had no material impact on the outcome of this case. Since [the district court] determined that OSCAR effectively contained no protectable expression whatsoever, the most serious charge that can be levelled against him is that he was overly thorough in his examination.

[73] The district court took the first step in the analysis set forth in this opinion when it separated the program by levels of abstraction. The district court stated:

> As applied to computer software programs, this abstractions test would progress in order of "increasing generality" from object code, to source code, to parameter lists, to services required, to general outline. In discussing the particular similarities, therefore, we shall focus on these levels.

[74] While the facts of a different case might require that a district court draw a more particularized blueprint of a program's overall structure, this description is a workable one for the case at hand.

[75] Moving to the district court's evaluation of OSCAR 3.5's structural components, we agree with [the district court]'s systematic exclusion of non-protectable expression. With respect to code, the district court observed that after the rewrite of OSCAR 3.4 to OSCAR 3.5, "there remained virtually no lines of code that were identical to ADAPTER." Accordingly, the court found that the code "present[ed] no similarity at all."

[76] Next, [the district court] addressed the issue of similarity between the two programs' parameter lists and macros. He concluded that, viewing the conflicting evidence most favorably to CA, it demonstrated that "only a few of the lists and macros were similar to protected elements in ADAPTER; the others were either in the public domain or dictated by the functional demands of the program." As discussed above, functional elements and elements taken from the public domain do not qualify for copyright protection. With respect to the few remaining parameter lists and macros, the district court could reasonably conclude that they did not warrant a finding of infringement given their relative contribution to the overall program. In any event, the district court reasonably found that, for lack of persuasive evidence, CA failed to meet its burden of proof on whether the macros and parameter lists at issue were substantially similar.

[77] The district court also found that the overlap exhibited between the list of services required for both ADAPTER and OSCAR 3.5 was "determined by the demands of the operating system and of the applications program to which it [was] to be linked through ADAPTER or OSCAR...." In other words, this aspect of the program's structure was dictated by the nature of other programs with which it was designed to interact and, thus, is not protected by copyright.

[78] Finally, in his infringement analysis, [the district court] accorded no weight to the similarities between the two programs' organizational charts, "because [the charts were] so simple and obvious to anyone exposed to the operation of the program[s]." CA argues that the district court's action in this regard "is not consistent with copyright law"—that "obvious" expression is protected, and that the district court erroneously failed to realize this. However, to say that elements of a work are "obvious," in the manner in which the district court used the word, is to say that they follow naturally from the work's theme rather than from the author's creativity. This is but one formulation of the scenes a faire doctrine, which we have already endorsed as a means of weeding out unprotectable expression....

[79] In adopting the above three step analysis for substantial similarity between the non-literal elements of computer programs, we seek to insure two things: (1) that programmers may receive appropriate copyright protection for innovative utilitarian works containing expression; and (2) that non-protectable technical expression remains in the public domain for others to use freely as building blocks in their own work. At first blush, it may seem counter-intuitive that someone who has benefitted to some degree from illicitly obtained material can emerge from an infringement suit relatively unscathed. However, so long as the appropriated material consists of non-protectable expression, "[t]his result is neither unfair nor unfortunate. It is the means by which copyright advances the progress of science and art." *Feist*....

NOTE

1. In another foundational case involving software, Apple sued Microsoft for copyright infringement for using the "look and feel" of its Macintosh operating system (see Figure 35) in certain versions of the Microsoft Windows operating system (see Figure 36). The Ninth Circuit found only limited copyright protection, such as for Macintosh's particular depiction of a trash can icon. Apple Comput., Inc. v. Microsoft Corp., 35 F.3d 1435 (9th Cir. 1994). The court rejected Apple's argument that analytic dissection of a graphical user interface (GUI) audiovisual work for protectability and infringement was inappropriate, reasoning that "even though GUIs are thought of as the 'look and feel' of a computer, ... copyright protection extends only to protectable elements of expression." With limited exception, the Ninth Circuit found there to be merely unprotectable ideas (such as "use of windows to display multiple images on the computer screen and to facilitate user interaction with the information contained in the windows") or protectable elements that had been licensed to Microsoft for use. The Ninth Circuit further reasoned that "Apple cannot get patent-like protection for the idea of a graphical user interface, or the idea of a desktop metaphor .... It can, and did, put those ideas together creatively with animation, overlapping windows, and well-designed icons; but it licensed the visual displays which resulted." The court further reasoned that copyright is extremely thin "[w]hen the range of protectable and unauthorized expression is narrow," making "the appropriate standard for illicit copying ... virtual identity."

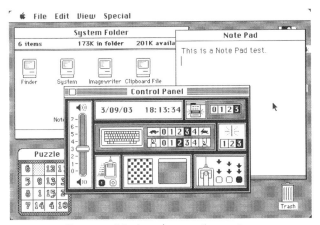

Figure 35: Macintosh operating system

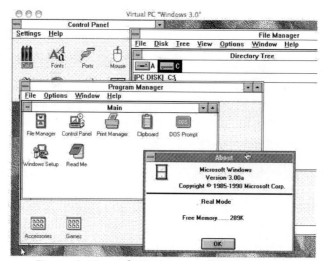

Figure 36: Microsoft Windows 3.0 operating system

Sometimes, a competitor might seek to make its own program compatible with another program, or it might write its own code to make a functionally equivalent program. Does copyright stand in the way of these competitive strategies?

As you read this case, be attentive to what Borland has copied and why it has done so. How do the district court and the First Circuit differ on how they understand the choices that Borland has made? Think about whether copyright doctrines or economic circumstances are driving this decision.

Lotus Development Corp. v. Borland International, Inc.
49 F.3d 807 (1st Cir. 1995)

STAHL, J.:

[1] This appeal requires us to decide whether a computer menu command hierarchy is copyrightable subject matter. In particular, we must decide whether, as the district court held, plaintiff-appellee Lotus Development Corporation's copyright in Lotus 1–2–3, a computer spreadsheet program, was infringed by defendant-appellant Borland International, Inc., when Borland copied the Lotus 1–2–3 menu command hierarchy into its Quattro and Quattro Pro computer spreadsheet programs....

[2] Lotus 1–2–3 is a spreadsheet program that enables users to perform accounting functions electronically on a computer. Users manipulate and control the program via a series of menu commands, such as "Copy," "Print," and "Quit." Users choose commands either by highlighting them on the screen or by typing their first letter. In all, Lotus 1–2–3 has 469 commands arranged into more than 50 menus and submenus.

[3] Lotus 1–2–3, like many computer programs, allows users to write what are called "macros." By writing a macro, a user can designate a series of command choices with a single macro keystroke. Then, to execute that series of commands in multiple parts of the spreadsheet, rather than typing the whole series each time, the user only needs to type the single pre-programmed macro keystroke, causing the program to recall and perform the designated series of commands automatically. Thus, Lotus 1–2–3 macros shorten the time needed to set up and operate the program.

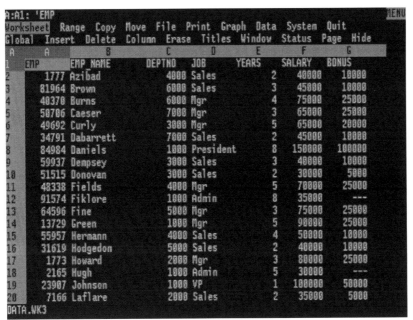

Figure 37: screenshot of Lotus 1-2-3 spreadsheet program

[4] Borland released its first Quattro program to the public in 1987, after Borland's engineers had labored over its development for nearly three years. Borland's objective was to develop a spreadsheet program far superior to existing programs, including Lotus 1–2–3. In Borland's words, "[f]rom the time of its initial release ... Quattro included enormous innovations over competing spreadsheet products."

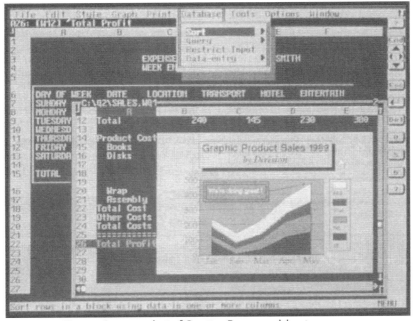

Figure 38: screenshot of Quattro Pro spreadsheet program

[5] The district court found, and Borland does not now contest, that Borland included in its Quattro and Quattro Pro version 1.0 programs a virtually identical copy of the entire 1–2–3 menu tree. In so doing, Borland did not copy any of Lotus's underlying computer code; it copied only the words and structure of Lotus's menu command hierarchy. Borland included the Lotus menu command hierarchy in its programs to make them compatible with Lotus 1–2–3 so that spreadsheet users who were already familiar with Lotus 1–2–3 would be able to switch to the Borland programs without having to learn new commands or rewrite their Lotus macros.

Chapter II – Subject Matter

[6] In its Quattro and Quattro Pro version 1.0 programs, Borland achieved compatibility with Lotus 1–2–3 by offering its users an alternate user interface, the "Lotus Emulation Interface." By activating the Emulation Interface, Borland users would see the Lotus menu commands on their screens and could interact with Quattro or Quattro Pro as if using Lotus 1–2–3, albeit with a slightly different looking screen and with many Borland options not available on Lotus 1–2–3. In effect, Borland allowed users to choose how they wanted to communicate with Borland's spreadsheet programs: either by using menu commands designed by Borland, or by using the commands and command structure used in Lotus 1–2–3 augmented by Borland-added commands.

[7] Lotus filed this action against Borland ....

[8] .... The district court ruled that the Lotus menu command hierarchy was copyrightable expression because

> [a] very satisfactory spreadsheet menu tree can be constructed using different commands and a different command structure from those of Lotus 1–2–3. In fact, Borland has constructed just such an alternate tree for use in Quattro Pro's native mode. Even if one holds the arrangement of menu commands constant, it is possible to generate literally millions of satisfactory menu trees by varying the menu commands employed.

[9] The district court demonstrated this by offering alternate command words for the ten commands that appear in Lotus's main menu. For example, the district court stated that "[t]he 'Quit' command could be named 'Exit' without any other modifications," and that "[t]he 'Copy' command could be called 'Clone,' 'Ditto,' 'Duplicate,' 'Imitate,' 'Mimic,' 'Replicate,' and 'Reproduce,' among others." Because so many variations were possible, the district court concluded that the Lotus developers' choice and arrangement of command terms, reflected in the Lotus menu command hierarchy, constituted copyrightable expression....

[10] .... [T]he court concluded that a jury trial was necessary ... to what extent, if any, functional constraints limited the number of possible ways that the Lotus menu command hierarchy could have been arranged at the time of its creation....

[11] Immediately following the district court's summary judgment decision, Borland removed the Lotus Emulation Interface from its products.... Nonetheless, Borland's programs continued to be partially compatible with Lotus 1–2–3, for Borland retained what it called the "Key Reader" in its Quattro Pro programs. Once turned on, the Key Reader allowed Borland's programs to understand and perform some Lotus 1–2–3 macros.... Accordingly, people who wrote or purchased macros to shorten the time needed to perform an operation in Lotus 1–2–3 could still use those macros in Borland's programs. The district court permitted Lotus to file a supplemental complaint alleging that the Key Reader infringed its copyright...

[12] ... [T]he district court found that "each of the Borland emulation interfaces contains a virtually identical copy of the 1–2–3 menu tree and that the 1–2–3 menu tree is capable of a wide variety of expression."

[13] ... [T]he district court [also] found that Borland's Key Reader file included "a virtually identical copy of the Lotus menu tree structure, but represented in a different form and with first letters of menu command names in place of the full menu command names." In other words, Borland's programs no longer included the Lotus command terms, but only their first letters. The district court held that "the Lotus menu structure, organization, and first letters of the command names ... constitute part of the protectable expression found in [Lotus 1–2–3]." Accordingly, the district court held that with its Key Reader, Borland had infringed Lotus's copyright....

[14] On appeal, ... Borland contends that the Lotus menu command hierarchy is not copyrightable because it is a system, method of operation, process, or procedure foreclosed from protection by 17 U.S.C. § 102(b)....

[15] Whether a computer menu command hierarchy constitutes copyrightable subject matter is a matter of first impression in this court....

[16] Borland vigorously argues, however, that the Supreme Court charted our course more than 100 years ago when it decided *Baker v. Selden*....

[17] We do not think that *Baker v. Selden* is nearly as analogous to this appeal as Borland claims. Of course, Lotus 1–2–3 is a computer spreadsheet, and as such its grid of horizontal rows and vertical columns certainly resembles an accounting ledger or any other paper spreadsheet. Those grids, however, are not at issue in this appeal for, unlike Selden, Lotus does not claim to have a monopoly over its accounting system. Rather, this appeal involves Lotus's monopoly over the commands it uses to operate the computer. Accordingly, this appeal is not, as Borland contends, "identical" to *Baker v. Selden*....

[18] Before we analyze whether the Lotus menu command hierarchy is a system, method of operation, process, or procedure, we first consider the applicability of the test the Second Circuit set forth in *Computer Assoc. Int'l, Inc. v. Altai, Inc*....

[19] In the instant appeal, we are not confronted with alleged nonliteral copying of computer code. Rather, we are faced with Borland's deliberate, literal copying of the Lotus menu command hierarchy. Thus, we must determine not whether nonliteral copying occurred in some amorphous sense, but rather whether the literal copying of the Lotus menu command hierarchy constitutes copyright infringement.

[20] While the *Altai* test may provide a useful framework for assessing the alleged nonliteral copying of computer code, we find it to be of little help in assessing whether the literal copying of a menu command hierarchy constitutes copyright infringement. In fact, we think that the *Altai* test in this context may actually be misleading because, in instructing courts to abstract the various levels, it seems to encourage them to find a base level that includes copyrightable subject matter that, if literally copied, would make the copier liable for copyright infringement.[8] While that base (or literal) level would not be at issue in a nonliteral-copying case like *Altai*, it is precisely what is at issue in this appeal. We think that abstracting menu command hierarchies down to their individual word and menu levels and then filtering idea from expression at that stage, as both the Altai and the district court tests require, obscures the more fundamental question of whether a menu command hierarchy can be copyrighted at all. The initial inquiry should not be whether individual components of a menu command hierarchy are expressive, but rather whether the menu command hierarchy as a whole can be copyrighted....

[21] Borland argues that the Lotus menu command hierarchy is uncopyrightable because it is a system, method of operation, process, or procedure foreclosed from copyright protection by 17 U.S.C. § 102(b). Section 102(b) states: "In no case does copyright protection for an original work of authorship extend to any idea, procedure, process, system, method of operation, concept, principle, or discovery, regardless of the form in which it is described, explained, illustrated, or embodied in such work." Because we conclude that the Lotus menu command hierarchy is a method of operation, we do not consider whether it could also be a system, process, or procedure.

[22] We think that "method of operation," as that term is used in § 102(b), refers to the means by which a person operates something, whether it be a car, a food processor, or a computer. Thus a text describing how to operate something would not extend copyright protection to the method of operation itself; other people

---

[8] We recognize that *Altai* never states that every work contains a copyrightable "nugget" of protectable expression. Nonetheless, the implication is that for literal copying, "it is not necessary to determine the level of abstraction at which similarity ceases to consist of an 'expression of ideas,' because literal similarity by definition is always a similarity as to the expression of ideas." 3 MELVILLE B. NIMMER & DAVID NIMMER, NIMMER ON COPYRIGHT § 13.03[A](2) (1993).

would be free to employ that method and to describe it in their own words. Similarly, if a new method of operation is used rather than described, other people would still be free to employ or describe that method.

[23] We hold that the Lotus menu command hierarchy is an uncopyrightable "method of operation." The Lotus menu command hierarchy provides the means by which users control and operate Lotus 1–2–3. If users wish to copy material, for example, they use the "Copy" command. If users wish to print material, they use the "Print" command. Users must use the command terms to tell the computer what to do. Without the menu command hierarchy, users would not be able to access and control, or indeed make use of, Lotus 1–2–3's functional capabilities.

[24] The Lotus menu command hierarchy does not merely explain and present Lotus 1–2–3's functional capabilities to the user; it also serves as the method by which the program is operated and controlled.... The Lotus menu command hierarchy is ... different from the Lotus screen displays, for users need not "use" any expressive aspects of the screen displays in order to operate Lotus 1–2–3; because the way the screens look has little bearing on how users control the program, the screen displays are not part of Lotus 1–2–3's "method of operation." ... The Lotus menu command hierarchy is also different from the underlying computer code, because while code is necessary for the program to work, its precise formulation is not. In other words, to offer the same capabilities as Lotus 1–2–3, Borland did not have to copy Lotus's underlying code (and indeed it did not); to allow users to operate its programs in substantially the same way, however, Borland had to copy the Lotus menu command hierarchy. Thus the Lotus 1–2–3 code is not a uncopyrightable "method of operation." ...

[25] The district court held that the Lotus menu command hierarchy, with its specific choice and arrangement of command terms, constituted an "expression" of the "idea" of operating a computer program with commands arranged hierarchically into menus and submenus. Under the district court's reasoning, Lotus's decision to employ hierarchically arranged command terms to operate its program could not foreclose its competitors from also employing hierarchically arranged command terms to operate their programs, but it did foreclose them from employing the specific command terms and arrangement that Lotus had used. In effect, the district court limited Lotus 1–2–3's "method of operation" to an abstraction.

[26] Accepting the district court's finding that the Lotus developers made some expressive choices in choosing and arranging the Lotus command terms, we nonetheless hold that that expression is not copyrightable because it is part of Lotus 1–2–3's "method of operation." We do not think that "methods of operation" are limited to abstractions; rather, they are the means by which a user operates something. If specific words are essential to operating something, then they are part of a "method of operation" and, as such, are unprotectable. This is so whether they must be highlighted, typed in, or even spoken, as computer programs no doubt will soon be controlled by spoken words.

[27] The fact that Lotus developers could have designed the Lotus menu command hierarchy differently is immaterial to the question of whether it is a "method of operation." In other words, our initial inquiry is not whether the Lotus menu command hierarchy incorporates any expression. Rather, our initial inquiry is whether the Lotus menu command hierarchy is a "method of operation." Concluding, as we do, that users operate Lotus 1–2–3 by using the Lotus menu command hierarchy, and that the entire Lotus menu command hierarchy is essential to operating Lotus 1–2–3, we do not inquire further whether that method of operation could have been designed differently. The "expressive" choices of what to name the command terms and how to arrange them do not magically change the uncopyrightable menu command hierarchy into copyrightable subject matter.

[28] Our holding that "methods of operation" are not limited to mere abstractions is bolstered by *Baker v. Selden*. In *Baker*, the Supreme Court explained that

the teachings of science and the rules and methods of useful art have their final end in application and use; and this application and use are what the public derive from the publication of a book which teaches them.... The description of the art in a book, though entitled to the benefit of copyright, lays no foundation for an exclusive claim to the art itself. The object of the one is explanation; the object of the other is use. The former may be secured by copyright. The latter can only be secured, if it can be secured at all, by letters-patent.

Lotus wrote its menu command hierarchy so that people could learn it and use it. Accordingly, it falls squarely within the prohibition on copyright protection established in *Baker v. Selden* and codified by Congress in § 102(b).

[29] In many ways, the Lotus menu command hierarchy is like the buttons used to control, say, a video cassette recorder. A VCR is a machine that enables one to watch and record video tapes. Users operate VCRs by pressing a series of buttons that are typically labelled "Record, Play, Reverse, Fast Forward, Pause, Stop/Eject." That the buttons are arranged and labeled does not make them a "literary work," nor does it make them an "expression" of the abstract "method of operating" a VCR via a set of labeled buttons. Instead, the buttons are themselves the "method of operating" the VCR.

[30] When a Lotus 1–2–3 user chooses a command, either by highlighting it on the screen or by typing its first letter, he or she effectively pushes a button. Highlighting the "Print" command on the screen, or typing the letter "P," is analogous to pressing a VCR button labeled "Play."

[31] Just as one could not operate a buttonless VCR, it would be impossible to operate Lotus 1–2–3 without employing its menu command hierarchy. Thus the Lotus command terms are not equivalent to the labels on the VCR's buttons, but are instead equivalent to the buttons themselves. Unlike the labels on a VCR's buttons, which merely make operating a VCR easier by indicating the buttons' functions, the Lotus menu commands are essential to operating Lotus 1–2–3. Without the menu commands, there would be no way to "push" the Lotus buttons, as one could push unlabeled VCR buttons. While Lotus could probably have designed a user interface for which the command terms were mere labels, it did not do so here. Lotus 1–2–3 depends for its operation on use of the precise command terms that make up the Lotus menu command hierarchy....

[32] That the Lotus menu command hierarchy is a "method of operation" becomes clearer when one considers program compatibility. Under Lotus's theory, if a user uses several different programs, he or she must learn how to perform the same operation in a different way for each program used. For example, if the user wanted the computer to print material, then the user would have to learn not just one method of operating the computer such that it prints, but many different methods. We find this absurd. The fact that there may be many different ways to operate a computer program, or even many different ways to operate a computer program using a set of hierarchically arranged command terms, does not make the actual method of operation chosen copyrightable; it still functions as a method for operating the computer and as such is uncopyrightable.

[33] Consider also that users employ the Lotus menu command hierarchy in writing macros. Under the district court's holding, if the user wrote a macro to shorten the time needed to perform a certain operation in Lotus 1–2–3, the user would be unable to use that macro to shorten the time needed to perform that same operation in another program. Rather, the user would have to rewrite his or her macro using that other program's menu command hierarchy. This is despite the fact that the macro is clearly the user's own work product. We think that forcing the user to cause the computer to perform the same operation in a different way ignores Congress's direction in § 102(b) that "methods of operation" are not copyrightable. That programs can offer users the ability to write macros in many different ways does not change the fact that, once written, the macro allows the user to perform an operation automatically. As the Lotus menu command

hierarchy serves as the basis for Lotus 1–2–3 macros, the Lotus menu command hierarchy is a "method of operation." ...

[34] We also note that in most contexts, there is no need to "build" upon other people's expression, for the ideas conveyed by that expression can be conveyed by someone else without copying the first author's expression.[13] In the context of methods of operation, however, "building" requires the use of the precise method of operation already employed; otherwise, "building" would require dismantling, too. Original developers are not the only people entitled to build on the methods of operation they create; anyone can. Thus, Borland may build on the method of operation that Lotus designed and may use the Lotus menu command hierarchy in doing so....

[35] ... [W]e hold that the Lotus menu command hierarchy is uncopyrightable subject matter ....

BOUDIN, J., concurring.

[36] The importance of this case, and a slightly different emphasis in my view of the underlying problem, prompt me to add a few words to the majority's tightly focused discussion....

[37] Most of the law of copyright and the "tools" of analysis have developed in the context of literary works such as novels, plays, and films. In this milieu, the principal problem—simply stated, if difficult to resolve—is to stimulate creative expression without unduly limiting access by others to the broader themes and concepts deployed by the author. The middle of the spectrum presents close cases; but a "mistake" in providing too much protection involves a small cost: subsequent authors treating the same themes must take a few more steps away from the original expression.

[38] The problem presented by computer programs is fundamentally different in one respect. The computer program is a means for causing something to happen; it has a mechanical utility, an instrumental role, in accomplishing the world's work. Granting protection, in other words, can have some of the consequences of patent protection in limiting other people's ability to perform a task in the most efficient manner. Utility does not bar copyright (dictionaries may be copyrighted), but it alters the calculus.

[39] Of course, the argument for protection is undiminished, perhaps even enhanced, by utility: if we want more of an intellectual product, a temporary monopoly for the creator provides incentives for others to create other, different items in this class. But the "cost" side of the equation may be different where one places a very high value on public access to a useful innovation that may be the most efficient means of performing a given task. Thus, the argument for extending protection may be the same; but the stakes on the other side are much higher.

[40] It is no accident that patent protection has preconditions that copyright protection does not—notably, the requirements of novelty and non-obviousness—and that patents are granted for a shorter period than copyrights. This problem of utility has sometimes manifested itself in copyright cases, such as *Baker v. Selden*, and been dealt with through various formulations that limit copyright or create limited rights to copy. But the case law and doctrine addressed to utility in copyright have been brief detours in the general march of copyright law.

[41] Requests for the protection of computer menus present the concern with fencing off access to the commons in an acute form. A new menu may be a creative work, but over time its importance may come to reside more in the investment that has been made by users in learning the menu and in building their own

---

[13] When there are a limited number of ways to express an idea, however, the expression "merges" with the idea and becomes uncopyrightable.

mini-programs—macros—in reliance upon the menu. Better typewriter keyboard layouts may exist, but the familiar QWERTY keyboard dominates the market because that is what everyone has learned to use. The QWERTY keyboard is nothing other than a menu of letters.

[42] Thus, to assume that computer programs are just one more new means of expression, like a filmed play, may be quite wrong. The "form"—the written source code or the menu structure depicted on the screen—look hauntingly like the familiar stuff of copyright; but the "substance" probably has more to do with problems presented in patent law or, as already noted, in those rare cases where copyright law has confronted industrially useful expressions. Applying copyright law to computer programs is like assembling a jigsaw puzzle whose pieces do not quite fit.

[43] All of this would make no difference if Congress had squarely confronted the issue, and given explicit directions as to what should be done. The Copyright Act of 1976 took a different course. While Congress said that computer programs might be subject to copyright protection, it said this in very general terms; and, especially in § 102(b), Congress adopted a string of exclusions that if taken literally might easily seem to exclude most computer programs from protection. The only detailed prescriptions for computers involve narrow issues (like back-up copies) of no relevance here.

[44] Of course, one could still read the statute as a congressional command that the familiar doctrines of copyright law be taken and applied to computer programs, in cookie cutter fashion, as if the programs were novels or play scripts. Some of the cases involving computer programs embody this approach. It seems to be mistaken on two different grounds: the tradition of copyright law, and the likely intent of Congress.

[45] The broad-brush conception of copyright protection, the time limits, and the formalities have long been prescribed by statute. But the heart of copyright doctrine—what may be protected and with what limitations and exceptions—has been developed by the courts through experience with individual cases. Occasionally Congress addresses a problem in detail. For the most part the interstitial development of copyright through the courts is our tradition.

[46] Nothing in the language or legislative history of the 1976 Act, or at least nothing brought to our attention, suggests that Congress meant the courts to abandon this case-by-case approach. Indeed, by setting up § 102(b) as a counterpoint theme, Congress has arguably recognized the tension and left it for the courts to resolve through the development of case law. And case law development is adaptive: it allows new problems to be solved with help of earlier doctrine, but it does not preclude new doctrines to meet new situations....

[47] In this case, the raw facts are mostly, if not entirely, undisputed. Although the inferences to be drawn may be more debatable, it is very hard to see that Borland has shown any interest in the Lotus menu except as a fall-back option for those users already committed to it by prior experience or in order to run their own macros using 1–2–3 commands. At least for the amateur, accessing the Lotus menu in the Borland Quattro or Quattro Pro program takes some effort.

[48] Put differently, it is unlikely that users who value the Lotus menu for its own sake—independent of any investment they have made themselves in learning Lotus' commands or creating macros dependent upon them—would choose the Borland program in order to secure access to the Lotus menu. Borland's success is due primarily to other features. Its rationale for deploying the Lotus menu bears the ring of truth.

[49] Now, any use of the Lotus menu by Borland is a commercial use and deprives Lotus of a portion of its "reward," in the sense that an infringement claim if allowed would increase Lotus' profits. But this is circular reasoning: broadly speaking, every limitation on copyright or privileged use diminishes the reward of the original creator. Yet not every writing is copyrightable or every use an infringement. The provision of reward

is one concern of copyright law, but it is not the only one. If it were, copyrights would be perpetual and there would be no exceptions.

[50] The present case is an unattractive one for copyright protection of the menu. The menu commands (e.g., "print," "quit") are largely for standard procedures that Lotus did not invent and are common words that Lotus cannot monopolize. What is left is the particular combination and sub-grouping of commands in a pattern devised by Lotus. This arrangement may have a more appealing logic and ease of use than some other configurations; but there is a certain arbitrariness to many of the choices.

[51] If Lotus is granted a monopoly on this pattern, users who have learned the command structure of Lotus 1–2–3 or devised their own macros are locked into Lotus, just as a typist who has learned the QWERTY keyboard would be the captive of anyone who had a monopoly on the production of such a keyboard. Apparently, for a period Lotus 1–2–3 has had such sway in the market that it has represented the de facto standard for electronic spreadsheet commands. So long as Lotus is the superior spreadsheet—either in quality or in price—there may be nothing wrong with this advantage.

[52] But if a better spreadsheet comes along, it is hard to see why customers who have learned the Lotus menu and devised macros for it should remain captives of Lotus because of an investment in learning made by the users and not by Lotus. Lotus has already reaped a substantial reward for being first; assuming that the Borland program is now better, good reasons exist for freeing it to attract old Lotus customers: to enable the old customers to take advantage of a new advance, and to reward Borland in turn for making a better product. If Borland has not made a better product, then customers will remain with Lotus anyway.

[53] Thus, for me the question is not whether Borland should prevail but on what basis. Various avenues might be traveled, but the main choices are between holding that the menu is not protectable by copyright and devising a new doctrine that Borland's use is privileged. No solution is perfect and no intermediate appellate court can make the final choice.

[54] To call the menu a "method of operation" is, in the common use of those words, a defensible position. After all, the purpose of the menu is not to be admired as a work of literary or pictorial art. It is to transmit directions from the user to the computer, i.e., to operate the computer. The menu is also a "method" in the dictionary sense because it is a "planned way of doing something," an "order or system," and (aptly here) an "orderly or systematic arrangement, sequence or the like." Random House Webster's College Dictionary 853 (1991).

[55] A different approach would be to say that Borland's use is privileged because, in the context already described, it is not seeking to appropriate the advances made by Lotus' menu; rather, having provided an arguably more attractive menu of its own, Borland is merely trying to give former Lotus users an option to exploit their own prior investment in learning or in macros. The difference is that such a privileged use approach would not automatically protect Borland if it had simply copied the Lotus menu (using different codes), contributed nothing of its own, and resold Lotus under the Borland label.

[56] The closest analogue in conventional copyright is the fair use doctrine....

[57] But a privileged use doctrine would certainly involve problems of its own. It might more closely tailor the limits on copyright protection to the reasons for limiting that protection; but it would entail a host of administrative problems that would cause cost and delay, and would also reduce the ability of the industry to predict outcomes. Indeed, to the extent that Lotus' menu is an important standard in the industry, it might be argued that any use ought to be deemed privileged.

[58] In sum, the majority's result persuades me and its formulation is as good, if not better, than any other that occurs to me now as within the reach of courts. Some solutions (e.g., a very short copyright period for menus) are not options at all for courts but might be for Congress. In all events, the choices are important ones of policy, not linguistics, and they should be made with the underlying considerations in view.

NOTES

1. The First Circuit in *Lotus* makes an analogy to VCRs to explain why it thinks the menu command hierarchy is a method of operation: "Just as one could not operate a buttonless VCR, it would be impossible to operate Lotus 1-2-3 without employing its menu command hierarchy. Thus the Lotus command terms are not equivalent to the labels on the VCR's buttons, but are instead equivalent to the buttons themselves." Consider whether this analogy is apt. Do these labels do anything without the mechanisms underlying them? Is Lotus's complaint that Borland took its menu structure, sequence, and organizations about the location and arrangement of the "buttons" or the "buttons" themselves?

2. Just as there are other forms of protection for industrial designs, there are other forms of protection for computer software: primarily patent and trade secrecy protections. Patent law protects inventions that are novel, nonobvious, and useful. 35 U.S.C. §§ 101-103. Patents are granted after successfully undergoing examination by the Patent and Trademark Office to ascertain that an invention meets patentability conditions and the description in the patent application satisfies certain disclosure requirements. *Id.* §§ 112, 131. The patent right permits the patentee to exclude others from practicing the invention claimed in the patent for a term of typically twenty years from the date the patent application was filed. *Id.* § 154(a). In recent years, the U.S. Supreme Court has made it harder to get software patents by reining in the rules of patentable subject matter. Alice Corp. Pty. Ltd. v. CLS Bank Int'l, 134 S. Ct. 2347 (2017); Bilski v. Kappos, 561 U.S. 593 (2010).

Trade secret law generally protects information (broadly defined) that derives independent economic value from not being generally known or readily ascertainable by others, and is subject to reasonable efforts to maintain its secrecy. UNIFORM TRADE SECRETS ACT § 1(4) (1985). One who has a valid trade secret cannot protect it from use against anyone, but only one who has misappropriated the trade secret. *Id.* §§ 1-3. For example, reverse engineering or independent discovery are legitimate ways to acquire a trade secret. Chicago Lock Co. v. Fanberg, 676 F.2d 400, 405 (9th Cir. 1982). As long as the information stays unknown to the requisite degree, it remains protectable, so trade secret protection can in theory last for a long time. On the attractiveness of using trade secrecy to protect software, see Jeanne C. Fromer, *Machines as the New Oompa-Loompas: Trade Secrecy, the Cloud, Machine Learning, and Automation*, 94 N.Y.U. L. REV. 706 (2019); Sonia K. Katyal, *The Paradox of Source Code Secrecy*, 104 CORNELL L. REV. 1183 (2019).

3. Over the past few decades, **open-source software** has become a prominent part of the world of software. Copyright holders in open-source software releases the source code under a license that grants all users the right to study, modify, and distribute the software. Open-source software authors do not renounce their copyright rights but rather use them to enforce the open availability of the source code. Two of the most popular open-source licenses are the GNU General Public License and the Apache License.

Supporters of the open-source software movement claim multiple advantages over traditional software. First, they claim that open-source software will be of a higher quality because the source code's openness makes it quicker and easier to fix bugs and create ever better variations and versions of the software. Second, open-source proponents argue that open software is cheaper to acquire and maintain. For more on the open-source movement, copyright law, and economics, see Robert W. Gomulkiewicz, *How Copyleft Uses License Rights to Succeed in the Open Source Software Revolution and the Implications for Article 2B*, 36 HOUS. L. REV. 179 (1999); David McGowan, *Legal Implications of Open-Source Software*, 2001 U. ILL. L. REV. 241.

4. In *Oracle America, Inc. v. Google Inc.*, 750 F.3d 1339 (Fed. Cir. 2014), the Federal Circuit understood copyrightability of a "method of operation" differently than the First Circuit had in *Lotus*. In that case, Oracle claimed that Google infringed Oracle's copyrights in its Java Application Program Interface (API) when Google included Oracle's so-called "declaring code" in the implementation of Java that it uses in its Android mobile operating system as a way to achieve some level of compatibility for programmers. The purpose of the Java API is to define and implement in advance a set of common operations that programmers can use in their software. The method's functionality is defined by the method's implementing code, which consists of the step-by-step instructions the computer follows to carry out the declared operation. Oracle's declaring code names each operation (or "method") contained in the API and defines how the methods are organized within Java. The declaring code allows developers to create references to the API methods in their software code, which in turn tell the computer where to go to run the methods. API methods are invoked in a particular format—java.package.Class.method()—which mirrors the organization of the declaring code. Therefore, the APIs can be used in any Java project as long as the declaring code stays constant. Google had copied the declaring code in 37 Java API packages, as listed in Figure 39, into its Android operating system. The Federal Circuit held that the Java declaring code was indeed a method of operation but held that "the [copyright] protection accorded a particular expression of an idea" is not extinguished "merely because that expression is embodied in a method of operation." In the Federal Circuit's view, if the implementation of a particular method of operation involves some creative choice, then it will be copyrightable.

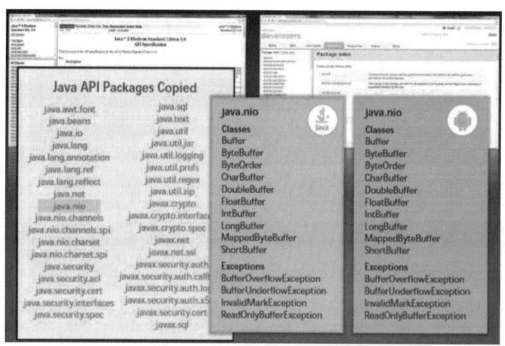

Figure 39: Java API packages at issue

The court also ruled that even though the only way to write Java-compatible APIs is to copy the Java declaring code, the merger doctrine did not bar protection of the declaring code. It explained that "copyrightability and the scope of protectable activity are to be evaluated at the time of creation, not at the time of infringement. The focus is, therefore, on the options that were available to []Oracle at the time it created the API packages. Of course, once []Oracle created 'java.lang.Math.max,' programmers who want to use that particular package have to call it by that name. But ... nothing prevented Google from writing its own declaring code, along with its own implementing code, to achieve the same result. In such circumstances, the chosen expression simply does not merge with the idea being expressed."

Do you agree that the declaring code is a "method of operation"? If so, does § 102 permit that it be protectable by copyright law? (Look carefully at the text of § 102(b), and, in particular, the provision's final clause.) Is the Federal Circuit right to apply the merger doctrine at the moment of copyrightability rather than at the time of copying? The Supreme Court granted certiorari in this case but ultimately ruled in Google's favor on grounds of fair use. (You will read that decision in Chapter VI.) The Federal Circuit's decision is therefore irrelevant, even if it still technically stands. The Supreme Court's decision repeatedly cited *Lotus* approvingly. What does that say about the continuing vitality of the Federal Circuit's decision on copyrightability? For an analysis of the copyrightability following the Supreme Court's fair use ruling, see Mark A. Lemley & Pamela Samuelson, *Interfaces and Interoperability After* Google v. Oracle, 100 TEX. L. REV. 1 (2021).

5. Architectural Works

Until 1990, U.S. copyright law did not specifically provide protection for architectural works. Until that time, in theory, buildings could be protected as pictorial, graphic, or sculptural works, but they were subject to exacting separability analysis as useful articles. Architectural plans and drawings themselves could be protected as pictorial, graphic, or sculptural works, but others could build from these plans and drawings. Imperial Homes Corp. v. Lamont, 458 F.2d 895 (5th Cir. 1972).

That all changed in 1990 when Congress expanded copyright protection by adding § 102(a)(8) with its specific protection for "architectural works" as a category of works of authorship. Architectural Works Copyright Protection Act of 1990, Pub. Law 101-650, 104 Stat. 5089. Congress added this protection to comply with the Berne Convention, which requires protection of architectural works and to which the United States had acceded in 1989. Berne Convention (Paris text), art. 2(1); H.R. REP. NO. 101-735, 101st Cong., 2d Sess. 4 (1990). The new law also added to § 101 a definition of architectural works:

> An "architectural work" is the design of a building as embodied in any tangible medium of expression, including a building, architectural plans, or drawings. The work includes the overall form as well as the arrangement and composition of spaces and elements in the design, but does not include individual standard features.

Although the statute did not define a "building," the legislative history indicates that the term includes "habitable structures such as houses and office buildings. It also covers structures that are used, but not inhabited, by human beings, such as churches, pergolas, gazebos, and garden pavilions." H.R. REP. NO. 101-735, 101st Cong., 2d Sess. 4 (1990).

Note that this new protection applies only to architectural works created on or after December 1, 1990. Architectural Works Copyright Protection Act of 1990, § 706(1).

Additionally, an architectural work need not be built to qualify for copyright protection. It merely needs to be fixed in any tangible medium of expression, as required by § 102(a). Architectural plans thus qualify to fix an architectural work.

As you read this case, think about what the originality requirement means for an architectural work. Consider also whether and how the statutory definition in § 101 limits protection for building designs.

James E. Zalewski v. Cicero Builder Dev., Inc.
754 F.3d 95 (2d Cir. 2014)

WESLEY, J.:

[1] This case calls on us to explore the limits of copyright protection for architectural works. Plaintiffs–Appellants are James Zalewski, an architect, and Draftics, Ltd., the company through which he does business. Zalewski asserts that he created and then licensed numerous designs for colonial homes to two construction companies. He alleges that these companies and their contractors infringed his copyright in these designs by using them in ways the licenses did not permit and after the licenses had expired.... Defendants principally contend that their designs do not copy the protected elements of Plaintiff's designs....

[2] In the 1990s, Plaintiff James Zalewski was self-employed as an architect doing business through the firm Draftics, Ltd. During this period, he granted Defendants T.P. Builders and Cillis Builders licenses to use several colonial home designs he had created. According to Zalewski, after the licenses expired, T.P. hired Defendant V.S. Sofia Engineering and Defendant DeRaven Design & Drafting and Cillis hired DeRaven to customize his designs for their customers and continued marketing his designs, or customized versions thereof, without his consent. Defendant Cicero Builders built two houses using DeRaven designs that were allegedly based on Plaintiff's originals.

[3] Zalewski filed the first of these now consolidated actions in July 2010 in the United States District Court for the Northern District of New York, alleging that Defendants infringed the copyright in his original designs. Zalewski asserts that, in building the homes and customizing the designs, Defendants copied the overall size, shape, and silhouette of his designs as well as the placement of rooms, windows, doors, closets, stairs, and other architectural features....

[4] .... [T]he court granted judgment to all ... defendants and denied Zalewski's cross-motion for summary judgment....

[5] What aspects of Zalewski's designs are protectable? A fundamental rule of copyright law is that it protects only "original works of authorship," those aspects of the work that originate with the author himself. Everything else in the work, the history it describes, the facts it mentions, and the ideas it embraces, are in the public domain free for others to draw upon. It is the peculiar expressions of that history, those facts, and those ideas that belong exclusively to their author. Thus, any author may draw from the history of English-speaking peoples, but no one may copy from *A History of the English-Speaking Peoples*. Any artist may portray the Spanish Civil War, but no one may paint another *Guernica*. And anyone may draw a cartoon mouse, but there can be only one Mickey.

[6] Numerous doctrines separate protectable expression from elements of the public domain. For example, the doctrine of "scènes-à-faire" teaches that elements of a work that are indispensable, or at least standard, in the treatment of a given topic—like cowboys, bank robbers, and shootouts in stories of the American West—get no protection. Similarly, the "merger doctrine" instructs that some ideas can only be expressed in a

limited number of ways—single words or colors for example. When expression is so limited, idea and expression "merge." Expressions merged with ideas cannot be protected, lest one author own the idea itself.

Mirror image of copyrighted DRA217 design

19 Timber Lane infringing design

Figure 40: sample Zalewski design (left) and sample defendant design (right)

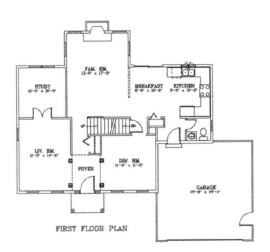
Mirror image of copyrighted DRA217 design

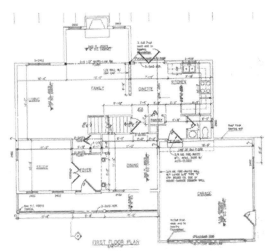
19 Timber Lane infringing design
(Peripheral dimension data cropped to
facilitate side-by-side comparison)

Figure 41: sample Zalewski design (left) and sample defendant design (right)

[7] The central question of this case is how to apply these and related doctrines to separate the protectable from the unprotectable in architectural works. Defendants urge us to chart a different course. They view Plaintiff's designs as a compilation of various architectural features that individually and collectively do not merit copyright protection. They rely on the Eleventh Circuit case of *Intervest Construction, Inc. v. Canterbury Estate Homes, Inc.*, 554 F.3d 914 (11th Cir. 2008), and the Supreme Court's doctrine governing "compilations" set out in *Feist*....

[8] In *Intervest*, the Eleventh Circuit applied [*Feist*] to architecture. It held that all copyrighted works are either "creative, derivative, [or] compiled," that is original, variations on an original, or compilations of unoriginal material. According to *Intervest*, each kind of work gets varying levels of protection. The court then relied on the similarity between the statutory definitions of "compilation" and "architectural work" to conclude that architectural works fall into the "compiled" category, and are thus entitled to only a "thin" copyright based solely on their arrangement and coordination of unoriginal and uncopyrightable elements. On facts similar to

those here, the *Intervest* court held that any copying of the plaintiff's house designs went only to standard architectural features arranged in standard ways. In other words, any copying was not wrongful.

[9] While we agree with the outcome in *Intervest*, we disagree with its reasoning. "Creative," "derivative," and "compiled" may be useful concepts in some cases, but we reject the idea that works always fall neatly into one of these categories. Every kind of work at some level is a compilation, an arrangement of uncopyrightable "common elements." No individual word is copyrightable, but the arrangement of words into a book is. No color is copyrightable, but the arrangement of colors on canvas is. Likewise, doors and walls are not copyrightable, but their arrangement in a building is. Some architectural designs, like that of a single-room log cabin, will consist solely of standard features arranged in standard ways; others, like the Guggenheim, will include standard features, but also present something entirely new. Architecture, in this regard, is like every art form.

[10] Moreover, we see little support in the statute for *Intervest*'s use of categories. Although the statutory definitions of "compilations" and "architectural works" both speak of an "arrangement" or "to arrange" and refer to "standard features" or "preexisting material," architectural works and compilations are not the only works that are defined with reference to their discrete—and perhaps uncopyrightable—elements.[16] For example, the statute defines "Literary works" as "words, numbers, or other ... symbols" arranged in "books, periodicals" or other media; "Sound Recordings" as "a series of musical, spoken, or other sounds"; a "computer program" as "a set of statements or instructions"; and "Motion Pictures" and "Audio Visual works" as "series of related images." As we have explained, the merger doctrine will often render these discrete elements un-copyrightable. Softel v. Dragon Med. & Scientific Commc'ns, 118 F.3d 955, 964 (2d Cir. 1997) (explaining that "the words that constitute a literary work are not copyrightable, yet ... a collection of words" may be).[17]

[11] Labeling architecture a compilation obscures the real issue. Every work of art will have some standard elements, which taken in isolation are un-copyrightable, but many works will have original elements—or original arrangements of elements. The challenge in adjudicating copyright cases is not to determine whether a work is a creative work, a derivative work, or a compilation, but to determine what in it originated with the author and what did not. *Intervest* fails to do this. It compares the floor plans of the two houses, focusing only on the narrow arrangement and coordination of what it deems "standard ... features" and intuits that there was no copying of the arrangement. But it fails to provide any analysis of what made a feature "standard" and unprotectable. Hence, we find it of little assistance here.

[12] Courts should treat architectural copyrights no differently than other copyrights. This is what Congress envisioned, and it is an approach we have employed before....

[13] In *Peter F. Gaito Architecture, LLC v. Simone Development Corp.*, 602 F.3d 57 (2d Cir. 2010), ... we held that copying of architecture that was light, airy, and transparent, as well as design parameters and generalized

---

[16] Additionally, the definitions of "architectural work" and "compilation" have little else in common. The statute defines an "architectural work" as "the design of a building as embodied in any tangible medium of expression, including a building, architectural plans, or drawings. The work includes the overall form as well as the arrangement and composition of spaces and elements in the design, but does not include individual standard features." A "compilation" is a "work formed by the collection and assembling of preexisting materials or of data that are selected, coordinated, or arranged in such a way that the resulting work as a whole constitutes an original work of authorship."

[17] The legislative history also supports this view. When Congress added architectural works to the list of copyrightable subject matter, it made clear that it wanted architectural works analyzed no differently than other works and differentiated between architectural works that present "original design elements" and those that do not. *Intervest* contravenes Congress' intent by treating architectural works differently than other works and failing to determine what in architecture—beyond mere arrangement—is copyrightable.

notions of where to place functional elements, went only to ideas and not protected expression. [Yet] in *Sparaco v. Lawler, Matusky, Skelly, Engineers LLP*, 303 F.3d 460 (2d Cir. 2002), we held that although a construction site preparation plan was preliminary in the sense that it pertained to the early phases of construction, it was extremely detailed and thus more than a mere idea.

[14] Determining the boundaries of copyright protection in non-traditional areas of creative expression, like architecture, is not something new. A number of our cases have applied copyright doctrines in other unusual contexts. In *Altai*, for example, we had to determine for the first time what elements of a computer program are protectable. To do so, we simply applied the usual copyright doctrines of merger, public domain, and scènes-à-faire to these new circumstances. For example, we held that the merger doctrine would apply when "efficiency concerns … so narrow the practical range of [coding options] as to make only one or two forms of expression workable…." Similarly, we applied the doctrine of scènes-à-faire because "in many instances it is virtually impossible to write a program … without employing standard techniques." Consequently, we held that coding dictated by mechanical specifications, industry design standards, market demands, and usual programing practices also did not get copyright protection.

[15] All of these principles apply equally well to architecture. Efficiency is an important architectural concern. Any design elements attributable to building codes, topography, structures that already exist on the construction site, or engineering necessity should therefore get no protection.

[16] There are scènes-à-faire in architecture. Neoclassical government buildings, colonial houses, and modern high-rise office buildings are all recognized styles from which architects draw. Elements taken from these styles should get no protection. Likewise, there are certain market expectations for homes or commercial buildings. Design features used by all architects, because of consumer demand, also get no protection.

[17] Our prior architecture cases support this approach. In *Sparaco*, we held that there can be no copyright in a plan insofar as it merely represents the topography of a building site. Topography is an un-copyrightable "fact."[18] In *Attia* [*v. Society of N.Y. Hospital*, 201 F.3d 50 (2d Cir. 1999),] we recognized that generalized notions of where to place functional elements, how to route the flow of traffic, and methods of construction are un-protectable. Architects cannot claim that good engineering is original to them—or at least can get no copyright protection for it.[19] Finally, in *Gaito Architecture*, we held that there is no copyright in a building plan's design parameters. Constraints placed on an architect by the way her client plans to use the building do not originate with the architect….

[18] After considering these principles and reviewing the designs in question, we conclude that even if Defendants copied Zalewski's plans, they copied only the unprotected elements of his designs. Plaintiff's principal argument is that Defendants' designs are so close to his that Defendants must have infringed. He is correct that the designs are, in many respects, quite close, but this is not enough. It proves at most copying, not wrongful copying.

---

[18] We do not doubt that topography will often inspire, or indeed require, original architectural solutions that will be worthy of copyright. Frank Lloyd Wright's *Fallingwater* is a prominent example. There may also be original ways of representing existing topography. The topography itself, however, is uncopyrightable. If two architects submit competing bids for the same project, one cannot assert that the other's design infringed his copyright because their designs include reference to the same topography or share similarities dictated by that topography. One expects competent architects to accurately represent a construction site.
We note that this only applies to existing topography, however, because existing topography is an uncopyrightable fact. An architect may be able to copyright his original proposals for alterations to the topography. On the other hand, such alterations may be dictated by good engineering practice or a customer requirement, in which case they may not be copyrightable. We leave exploration of these issues to future cases.
[19] The functional aspects of a work are governed by patent law, not copyright law. *See* Baker v. Selden, 101 U.S. 99 (1879).

[19] First, many of the similarities are a function of consumer expectations and standard house design generally. Plaintiff can get no credit for putting a closet in every bedroom, a fireplace in the middle of an exterior wall, and kitchen counters against the kitchen walls. Furthermore, the overall footprint of the house and the size of the rooms are design parameters dictated by consumer preferences and the lot the house will occupy, not the architect.

[20] Finally, most of the similarities between Plaintiff's and Defendants' designs are features of all colonial homes, or houses generally. So long as Plaintiff was seeking to design a colonial house, he was bound to certain conventions. He cannot claim copyright in those conventions. Great artists often express themselves through the vocabulary of existing forms. Shakespeare wrote his Sonnets; Brahms composed his Hungarian Dances; and Plaintiff designed his colonial houses. Because we must preserve these forms for future artists, neither iambic pentameter, nor European folk motifs, nor clapboard siding are copyrightable.

[21] Plaintiff makes no attempt to distinguish those aspects of his designs that were original to him from those dictated by the form in which he worked. For example, Zalewski claims that the "front porches are the same design, size, and in the same location." But a door centered on the front of the house is typical of many homes, and colonials in particular.[20] Moreover, there are subtle differences in the paneling, size, and framing of Plaintiff's and Defendants' doors. These differences are not great, but given the constraints of a colonial design, they are significant. The same is true of the windows and garage doors that Plaintiff claims are identical. They are quite similar in location, size, and general design, but again, the similarities are due primarily to the shared colonial archetype. The window panes, shutters, and garage-door paneling all have subtle differences. Likewise, the designs' shared footprint and general layout are in keeping with the colonial style. There are only so many ways to arrange four bedrooms upstairs and a kitchen, dining room, living room, and study downstairs. Beyond these similarities, Plaintiff's and Defendants' layouts are different in many ways. The exact placement and sizes of doors, closets, and countertops often differ as do the arrangements of rooms.

[22] Although he undoubtedly spent many hours on his designs, and although there is certainly something of Plaintiff's own expression in his work, as long as Plaintiff adhered to a pre-existing style his original contribution was slight—his copyright very thin. Only very close copying would have taken whatever actually belonged to Plaintiff. Copying that is not so close would—and in this case did—only capture the generalities of the style in which Plaintiff worked and elements common to all homes. Defendants' houses shared Plaintiff's general style, but took nothing from his original expression....

[23] For the foregoing reasons, the district court's ... order ... granting summary judgment ... [is] AFFIRMED....

NOTES

1. Originality in some architectural works, such as the Spaceship Earth structure at the Epcot theme park, shown in Figure 42, can readily be established solely based on the "overall form" of the building, as per § 101.

Establishing originality this way is harder for other architectural works. Note how *Zalewski* underscores that the originality of architectural works can also stem from "the arrangement and composition of spaces and elements in the design, but does not include individual standard features," as set out in § 101. This statutory language seems to suggest analysis of originality in a manner akin to compilations, something some courts point out but which *Zalewski* partially resists.

---

[20] Defendants have helpfully included in the record excerpts from several treatises, which describe the basics of colonial architecture. The features of prominent architectural styles, particularly of home designs, are matters with which we are familiar and of which we can take judicial notice. Although Plaintiff insists that his houses are not in the colonial style, he offers no argument or evidence on this point, merely assertion. We find these assertions incredible.

Figure 42: Spaceship Earth structure at Epcot Theme Park

2. One reason that Congress added architectural works as a category of copyrightable subject matter rather than include them as a subcategory of pictorial, graphic, and sculptural works was to avoid the need for a complicated separability analysis for architectural works. H.R. REP. NO. 101-735, 101st Cong., 2d Sess. 4 (1990). Does that mean that functional aspects of architectural works are protectable, so long as they are original? How does *Zalewski* analyze functional elements of architectural works?

3. There are some specific concerns about protecting architectural works under copyright law. For one thing, a building's owner might not own copyright in the building. As such, the building owner might be prohibited from modifying or destroying a protected building. For this reason, Congress provided an exception to copyright law:

> [T]he owners of a building embodying an architectural work may, without the consent of the author or copyright owner of the architectural work, make or authorize the making of alterations to such building, and destroy or authorize the destruction of such building.

17 U.S.C. § 120(b). Another concern with copyright protection for architectural works is that members of the public might not be able to take photographs that include a protected building without infringing the copyright in the building. To avoid such broad liability, Congress provided another exception to copyright law:

> The copyright in an architectural work that has been constructed does not include the right to prevent the making, distributing, or public display of pictures, paintings, photographs, or other pictorial representations of the work, if the building in which the work is embodied is located in or ordinarily visible from a public place.

Id. § 120(a). Note that for this exception to apply, the building must be "located in or ordinarily visible from a public place."

III. Authorship and Ownership

The Copyright Act does not define either "**author**" or "authorship"; those terms can be understood only by implication from various provisions in the statute, and by the interpretation of the meaning of those terms provided in the opinions of federal courts.

Section 201 of the Copyright Act provides for two ways in which initial copyright ownership may arise in a work:

> *(a) Initial Ownership.—*
> *Copyright in a work protected under this title vests initially in the author or authors of the work. The authors of a joint work are coowners of copyright in the work.*
>
> *(b) Works Made for Hire.—*
> *In the case of a work made for hire, the employer or other person for whom the work was prepared is considered the author for purposes of this title, and, unless the parties have expressly agreed otherwise in a written instrument signed by them, owns all of the rights comprised in the copyright....*

The relevant statutory provisions may be summarized as follows: First, ownership vests initially in a work's author or authors. For a work with one author, initial ownership of the work's copyright vests in that author. For a work with more than one author—defined by the statute as a "**joint work**"—ownership of the copyright vests initially in the co-authors of that work as co-owners.

Second, initial ownership in a "**work made for hire**" vests in "the employer or other person for whom the work was prepared." The owner of a work made for hire is also considered the work's author.

We will first discuss authorship and ownership of single-authored works. We will then examine the rules governing authorship and ownership of joint works. Finally, we will examine the Copyright Act's "work made for hire" provisions.

A. The Definition of Authorship

As you read this decision, focus on the concept of "authorship." The Copyright Act does not define that term or tell us how to determine whether someone is an "author," although that determination is absolutely central to copyright law. Does the decision provide a definition of "author" or "authorship"? If so, what is it?

Alexander Lindsay v. The Wrecked and Abandoned Vessel R.M.S. Titanic
52 U.S.P.Q.2d 1609 (S.D.N.Y. 1999)

BAER, J.: ...

[1] In 1994, the plaintiff[, Alexander Lindsay], under contract with a British television company, filmed and directed the British documentary film, "Explorers of the Titanic," a chronicle of defendant [R.M.S. Titanic, Inc.]'s third salvage expedition of the Titanic. To film this documentary, Lindsay sailed with ... the salvage expedition crew to the wreck site and remained at sea for approximately one month. The plaintiff alleges that

during and after filming this documentary in 1994, he conceived a new film project for the Titanic wreck using high illumination lighting equipment....

[2] As part of his pre-production efforts, the plaintiff created various storyboards for the film, a series of drawings which incorporated images of the Titanic by identifying specific camera angles and shooting sequences that reflected [his] creative inspiration and force behind his concept for shooting the Subject Work. The plaintiff also alleges that he, along with members of his film team, designed the huge underwater light towers that were later used to make the film. Lindsay also personally constructed the light towers and thereafter for approximately 3–4 weeks directed, produced, and acted as the cinematographer of the Subject Work, underwater video[]taping of the Titanic wreck site, and otherwise participated in the 1996 salvage operation. He also directed the filming of the wreck site from on board the salvage vessel "Ocean Voyager" after leading daily planning sessions with the crew of the Nautile, the submarine used to transport the film equipment and photographers to the underwater wreck site. The purpose of these sessions was to provide the photographers with detailed instructions for positioning and utilizing the light towers.

[3] The plaintiff now alleges that he was never fully compensated for his services and that, *inter alia*, the defendants are now "unlawfully profiting from the exploitation of the" film project at issue....

[4] .... The defendants ... move ... to dismiss Lindsay's copyright claims, and the plaintiff cross-moves for summary judgment on his copyright ... claim[]....

[5] The defendants first argue that the plaintiff cannot have any protectable right in the illuminated footage since he did not dive to the ship and thus did not himself actually photograph the wreckage. This argument, however, does not hold water.

[6] The Copyright Act of 1976 provides that copyright ownership "vests initially in the author or authors of the work." 17 U.S.C. § 201(a). Generally speaking, the author of a work is the person who actually creates the work, that is, the person who translates an idea into a fixed, tangible expression entitled to copyright protection. In the context of film footage and photography, it makes intuitive sense that the "author" of a work is the individual or individuals who took the pictures, i.e. the photographer. However, the concept is broader than as argued by the defendants.

[7] For over 100 years, the Supreme Court has recognized that photographs may receive copyright protection in "so far as they are representatives of original intellectual conceptions of the author." Burrow-Giles Lithographic Co. v. Sarony, 111 U.S. 53, 58 (1884). An individual claiming to be an author for copyright purposes must show "the existence of those facts of originality, of intellectual production, of thought, and conception." Feist Publications, Inc. v. Rural Telephone Service Company, Inc., 499 U.S. 340, 346–47 (1991) (citing *Burrow-Giles*, 111 U.S. at 59–60). Taken as true, the plaintiff's allegations meet this standard. Lindsay's alleged storyboards and the specific directions he provided to the film crew regarding the use of the light towers and the angles from which to shoot the wreck all indicate that the final footage would indeed be the product of Lindsay's "original intellectual conceptions."

[8] The fact that Lindsay did not literally perform the filming, i.e. by diving to the wreck and operating the cameras, will not defeat his claims of having "authored" the illuminated footage. The plaintiff alleges that as part of his pre-production efforts, he created so-called "storyboards," a series of drawings which incorporated images of the Titanic by identifying specific camera angles and shooting sequences. During the expedition itself, Lindsay claims to have been the director, producer and cinematographer of the underwater footage. As part of this role, Lindsay alleges that he directed daily planning sessions with the film crew to provide them with detailed instructions for positioning and utilizing the light towers. Moreover, the plaintiff actually directed the filming of the Titanic from on board the Ocean Voyager, the salvage vessel that held the crew

and equipment. Finally, Lindsay screened the footage at the end of each day to confirm that he had obtained the images he wanted.

[9] All else being equal, where a plaintiff alleges that he exercised such a high degree of control over a film operation—including the type and amount of lighting used, the specific camera angles to be employed, and other detail-intensive artistic elements of a film—such that the final product duplicates his conceptions and visions of what the film should look like, the plaintiff may be said to be an "author" within the meaning of the Copyright Act....

NOTES

1. Can you extract from this case an understanding of the definition of the term "author"? What is it? Is the definition adequate to determine who is and who is not an "author" across a range of contexts?

2. In *Community for Creative Non-Violence v. Reid*, 490 U.S. 730, 737 (1989), the Supreme Court stated that the author of a work is the person "who actually creates the work, that is, the person who translates an idea into a fixed, tangible expression entitled to copyright protection." (citing 17 U.S.C. § 102). Does this articulation of the definition of authorship align with the holding in *Lindsay*?

As you read the next decision, think again about the definition of "author" that you extracted from *Lindsay* and ask yourself (a) whether the court followed that rule, and (b) if not, why?

Cindy Lee Garcia v. Google, Inc.
786 F.3d 733 (9th Cir. 2014) (en banc)

McKEOWN, J.:

[1] In this case, a heartfelt plea for personal protection is juxtaposed with the limits of copyright law and fundamental principles of free speech. The appeal teaches a simple lesson—a weak copyright claim cannot justify censorship in the guise of authorship....

[2] In July 2011, Cindy Lee Garcia responded to a casting call for a film titled *Desert Warrior*, an action-adventure thriller set in ancient Arabia. Garcia was cast in a cameo role, for which she earned $500. She received and reviewed a few pages of script. Acting under a professional director hired to oversee production, Garcia spoke two sentences: "Is George crazy? Our daughter is but a child?" Her role was to deliver those lines and to seem concerned.

[3] Garcia later discovered that writer-director Mark Basseley Youssef ... had a different film in mind: an anti-Islam polemic renamed *Innocence of Muslims*. The film, featuring a crude production, depicts the Prophet Mohammed as, among other things, a murderer, pedophile, and homosexual. Film producers dubbed over Garcia's lines and replaced them with a voice asking, "Is your Mohammed a child molester?" Garcia appears on screen for only five seconds.

[4] Almost a year after the casting call, in June 2012, Youssef uploaded a 13-minute-and-51-second trailer of *Innocence of Muslims* to YouTube, the video-sharing website owned by Google, Inc., which boasts a global audience of more than one billion visitors per month. After it was translated into Arabic, the film fomented

outrage across the Middle East, and media reports linked it to numerous violent protests. The film also has been a subject of political controversy over its purported connection to the September 11, 2012, attack on the United States Consulate in Benghazi, Libya.

[5] Shortly after the Benghazi attack, an Egyptian cleric issued a fatwa against anyone associated with *Innocence of Muslims*, calling upon the "Muslim Youth in America[] and Europe" to "kill the director, the producer[,] and the actors and everyone who helped and promoted this film." Garcia received multiple death threats.

[6] Legal wrangling ensued. Garcia asked Google to remove the film, asserting it was hate speech and violated her state law rights to privacy and to control her likeness. Garcia also sent Google five takedown notices ..., claiming that YouTube's broadcast of *Innocence of Muslims* infringed her copyright in her audio-visual dramatic performance. Google declined to remove the film....

[7] ... Garcia turned to federal court.... [She] alleged copyright infringement against both defendants ....

[8] Garcia then moved for a temporary restraining order and for an order to show cause on a preliminary injunction .... She sought to bar Google from hosting *Innocence of Muslims* on YouTube or any other Google-run website.

[9] ... [T]he district court denied Garcia's motion for a preliminary injunction.... In particular, the district court found that the nature of Garcia's copyright interest was unclear ...

[10] ... [A divided] panel majority reversed the district court and granted Garcia's preliminary injunction. Despite characterizing Garcia's copyright claim as "fairly debatable," the panel majority nonetheless concluded that Garcia was likely to prevail on her copyright claim as to her individual performance in *Innocence of Muslims*....

[11] We granted rehearing en banc....

[12] .... A plaintiff seeking a preliminary injunction must show[, among other things,] that ... she is likely to succeed on the merits....

[13] The central question is whether the law and facts clearly favor Garcia's claim to a copyright in her five-second acting performance as it appears in *Innocence of Muslims*. The answer is no....

[14] Under the Copyright Act, "[c]opyright protection subsists ... in original works of authorship fixed in any tangible medium of expression ... [including] motion pictures." 17 U.S.C. § 102(a). That fixation must be done "by or under the authority of the author." [*Id.*] § 101. Benchmarked against this statutory standard, the law does not clearly favor Garcia's position.

[15] The statute purposefully left "works of authorship" undefined to provide for some flexibility. Nevertheless, several other provisions provide useful guidance. An audiovisual work is one that consists of "a series of related images which are intrinsically intended to be shown" by machines or other electronic equipment, plus "accompanying sounds." 17 U.S.C. § 101. In turn, a "motion picture" is an "audiovisual work [] consisting of a series of related images which, when shown in succession, impart an impression of motion, together with accompanying sounds, if any." *Id.* These two definitions embody the work here: *Innocence of Muslims* is an audiovisual work that is categorized as a motion picture and is derivative of the script. Garcia is

the author of none of this and makes no copyright claim to the film or to the script.[6] Instead, Garcia claims that her five-second performance itself merits copyright protection.

[16] In the face of this statutory scheme, it comes as no surprise that during this litigation, the Copyright Office found that Garcia's performance was not a copyrightable work when it rejected her copyright application. The Copyright Office explained that its "longstanding practices do not allow a copyright claim by an individual actor or actress in his or her performance contained within a motion picture." Thus, "[f]or copyright registration purposes, a motion picture is a single integrated work.... Assuming Ms. Garcia's contribution was limited to her acting performance, we cannot register her performance apart from the motion picture."

[17] We credit this expert opinion of the Copyright Office—the office charged with administration and enforcement of the copyright laws and registration. The Copyright Office's well-reasoned position reflects a body of experience and informed judgment to which courts and litigants may properly resort for guidance....

[18] Garcia's theory of copyright law would result in [a] legal morass ...—splintering a movie into many different "works," even in the absence of an independent fixation. Simply put, as Google claimed, it "make[s] Swiss cheese of copyrights."

[19] Take, for example, films with a large cast—the proverbial "cast of thousands"—such as *Ben-Hur* or *Lord of the Rings*. The silent epic *Ben-Hur* advertised a cast of 125,000 people. In the *Lord of the Rings* trilogy, 20,000 extras tramped around Middle-Earth alongside Frodo Baggins .... Treating every acting performance as an independent work would not only be a logistical and financial nightmare, it would turn cast of thousands into a new mantra: copyright of thousands....

[20] .... Untangling the complex, difficult-to-access, and often phantom chain of title to tens, hundreds, or even thousands of standalone copyrights is a task that could tie the distribution chain in knots. And filming group scenes like a public parade, or the 1963 March on Washington, would pose a huge burden if each of the thousands of marchers could claim an independent copyright.

[21] Garcia's copyright claim faces yet another statutory barrier: She never fixed her acting performance in a tangible medium, as required ....[13]

[22] For better or for worse, Youssef and his crew "fixed" Garcia's performance in the tangible medium, whether in physical film or in digital form. However one might characterize Garcia's performance, she played no role in fixation. On top of this, Garcia claims that she never agreed to the film's ultimate rendition or how she was portrayed in *Innocence of Muslims*, so she can hardly argue that the film or her cameo in it was fixed "by or under [her] authority." 17 U.S.C. § 101.

[23] In sum, the district court committed no error in its copyright analysis. Issuance of the mandatory preliminary injunction requires more than a possible or fairly debatable claim .... Because neither the Copyright Act nor the Copyright Office's interpretation supports Garcia's claim, this is a hurdle she cannot clear....

---

[6] In another odd twist, one of Garcia's primary objections rests on the words falsely attributed to her via dubbing. But she cannot claim copyright in words she neither authored nor spoke. That leaves Garcia with a legitimate and serious beef, though not one that can be vindicated under the rubric of copyright.

[13] The Copyright Office draws a distinction between acting performances like Garcia's, which are intended to be an inseparable part of an integrated film, and standalone works that are separately fixed and incorporated into a film. We in no way foreclose copyright protection for the latter—any "discrete work in itself that is later incorporated into a motion picture," as the Copyright Office put it.

[24] Privacy laws, not copyright, may offer remedies tailored to Garcia's personal and reputational harms. On that point, we offer no substantive view....

KOZINSKI, J., dissenting:

[25] Garcia's dramatic performance met all of the requirements for copyright protection: It was copyrightable subject matter, it was original and it was fixed at the moment it was recorded. So what happened to the copyright? At times, the majority says that Garcia's performance was not copyrightable at all. And at other times, it seems to say that Garcia just didn't do enough to gain a copyright in the scene. Either way, the majority is wrong and makes a total mess of copyright law, right here in the Hollywood Circuit. In its haste to take internet service providers off the hook for infringement, the court today robs performers and other creative talent of rights Congress gave them. I won't be a party to it....

[26] Youssef handed Garcia a script. Garcia performed it. Youssef recorded Garcia's performance on video and saved the clip. Until today, I understood that the rights in such a performance are determined according to elementary copyright principles: An "original work[] of authorship," 17 U.S.C. §102(a), requires only copyrightable subject matter and a "minimal degree of creativity." Feist Publ'ns, Inc. v. Rural Tel. Serv. Co., 499 U.S. 340, 345 (1991). The work is "fixed" when it is "sufficiently permanent or stable to permit it to be perceived, reproduced, or otherwise communicated for a period of more than transitory duration." 17 U.S.C. §101. And at that moment, the "author or authors of the work" instantly and automatically acquire a copyright interest in it. 17 U.S.C. § 201(a). This isn't exactly String Theory; more like Copyright 101.

[27] Garcia's performance met these minimal requirements; the majority doesn't contend otherwise. The majority nevertheless holds that Garcia's performance isn't a "work," apparently because it was created during the production of a later-assembled film, *Innocence of Muslims*. But if you say something is not a work, it means that it isn't copyrightable by anyone. Under the majority's definition of "work," no one (not even Youssef) can claim a copyright in any part of Garcia's performance, even though it was recorded several months before *Innocence of Muslims* was assembled. Instead, *Innocence of Muslims*—the ultimate film—is the only thing that can be a "work." If this is what my colleagues are saying, they are casting doubt on the copyrightability of vast swaths of material created during production of a film or other composite work.

[28] The implications are daunting. If Garcia's scene is not a work, then every take of every scene of, say, *Lord of the Rings* is not a work, and thus not protected by copyright, unless and until the clips become part of the final movie. If some dastardly crew member were to run off with a copy of the Battle of Morannon, the dastard would be free to display it for profit until it was made part of the final movie. And, of course, the take-outs, the alternative scenes, the special effects never used, all of those things would be fair game because none of these things would be "works" under the majority's definition. And what about a draft chapter of a novel? Is there no copyright in the draft chapter unless it gets included in the published book? Or if part of the draft gets included, is there no copyright in the rest of it?

[29] This is a remarkable proposition, for which the majority provides remarkably little authority.... [A] contribution to a movie can be copyrightable (and thus can be a "work")....

[30] The majority also seems to hold that Garcia is not entitled to copyright protection because she is not an author of the recorded scene. According to the majority, Garcia can't be an author of her own scene because she "played no role in [her performance's] fixation."

[31] But a performer need not operate the recording equipment to be an author of his own performance. Without Garcia's performance, all that existed was a script. To convert the script into a video, there needed to be both an actor physically performing it and filmmakers recording the performance. Both kinds of activities can result in copyrightable expression. Garcia's performance had at least "some minimal degree of creativity"

apart from the script and Youssef's direction. *See Feist*, 499 U.S. at 345. One's "[p]ersonality always contains something unique. It expresses its singularity even in handwriting, and a very modest grade of art has in it something which is one man's alone." Bleistein v. Donaldson Lithographing Co., 188 U.S. 239, 250 (1903). To dispute this is to claim that *Gone With the Wind* would be the same movie if Rhett Butler were played by Peter Lorre.

[32] .... I'd therefore find that Garcia acquired a copyright in her performance the moment it was fixed.... It's not our job to take away from performers rights Congress gave them. Did Jimi Hendrix acquire no copyright in the recordings of his concerts because he didn't run the recorder in addition to playing the guitar? Garcia may not be as talented as Hendrix—who is?—but she's no less entitled to the protections of the Copyright Act....

[33] [U]nder our copyright law, the creators of original, copyrightable material automatically acquire a copyright interest in the material as soon as it is fixed. There's no exception for material created during production of a film or other composite work. When modern works, such as films or plays, are produced, contributors will often create separate, copyrightable works as part of the process. Our copyright law says that the copyright interests in this material vest initially with its creators, who will then have leverage to obtain compensation by contract. The answer to the "Swiss cheese" bugbear isn't for courts to limit who can acquire copyrights in order to make life simpler for producers and internet service providers. It's for the parties to allocate their rights by contract. Google makes oodles of dollars by enabling its users to upload almost any video without pre-screening for potential copyright infringement. Google's business model assumes the risk that a user's upload infringes someone else's copyright, and that it may have to take corrective action if a copyright holder comes forward.

[34] The majority credits the doomsday claims at the expense of property rights that Congress created. Its new standard artificially shrinks authorial rights by holding that a performer must personally record his creative expression in order to retain any copyright interest in it, speculating that a contrary rule might curb filmmaking and burden the internet. But our injunction has been in place for over a year; reports of the internet's demise have been greatly exaggerated....

NOTES

1. Should Garcia be treated as an "author" under the standard set out by *Lindsay*? On what basis did the *Garcia* court hold that Garcia was not an author? For an analogous case reaching a similar result, see 16 Casa Duse, LLC v. Merkin, 791 F.3d 247 (2d Cir. 2015) ("Filmmaking is a collaborative process typically involving artistic contributions from large numbers of people, including—in addition to producers, directors, and screenwriters—actors, designers, cinematographers, camera operators, and a host of skilled technical contributors. If copyright subsisted separately in each of their contributions to the completed film, the copyright in the film itself, which is recognized by statute as a work of authorship, could be undermined by any number of individual claims."). For an investigation whether actors deserve to be treated as authors, see Justin Hughes, *Actors as Authors in American Copyright Law*, 51 CONN. L. REV. 1 (2019).

2. Imagine that a director hires an actor to produce a very short scene—less than one minute—that the director plans to incorporate into a 90-minute movie. The director hands over a script and some money; the actor hires a camera crew, shoots the scene described in the script, and hands the completed scene back to the director. Is the scene itself a "work"? Or is only the completed movie a "work"?

3. In *Naruto v. Slater*, 888 F.3d 418 (9th Cir. 2018), the Ninth Circuit held that the Copyright Act does not recognize claims of authorship or copyright ownership by non-humans. That case involved assertions of copyright ownership on behalf of a monkey, represented on a "next friend" basis by People for the Ethical Treatment of Animals. The monkey (which PETA dubbed "Naruto") happened upon a camera left unattended

by a professional photographer, David Slater. While handling the camera, the monkey repeatedly tripped the shutter and captured several very striking "selfies," including the one shown in Figure 43.

Figure 43: selfie photograph captured by "Naruto"

The Ninth Circuit noted that the Copyright Act is silent with respect to the standing of non-humans to assert claims of authorship or copyright ownership. In the face of that silence, the court refused to presume that Congress intended to provide standing to non-humans to press those claims. The U.S. Copyright Office takes the same position. In its *Compendium of U.S. Copyright Office Practices*, §§ 306, 313.2 (3d ed. 2014), the Copyright Office expressly concluded that the Copyright Act does not recognize non-humans as authors.

4. Can a machine running a computer program be considered an author if the program's operation generates poetry, artwork, or music? If not, who is the author? *See* Annemarie Bridy, *Coding Creativity: Copyright and the Artificially Intelligent Author*, 2012 STAN. TECH. L. REV. 5; Jane C. Ginsburg & Luke Ali Budiardjo, *Authors and Machines*, 34 BERKELEY TECH. L.J. 343 (2019); James Grimmelmann, *There's No Such Thing as a Computer-Authored Work—And It's a Good Thing, Too*, 39 COLUM. J.L. & ARTS 403 (2016); Pamela Samuelson, *Allocating Ownership Rights in Computer-Generated Works*, 47 U. PITT. L. REV. 1185 (1986).

B. Authorship and Ownership in Joint Works

Section 101 of the Copyright Act defines "joint work" as follows:

> A "joint work" is a work prepared by two or more authors with the intention that their contributions be merged into inseparable or interdependent parts of a unitary whole.

Although the Copyright Act explicitly contemplates the existence of a category of joint works, the statute is silent with respect to the nature of the joint-authorship relationship, including the nature of joint authors' co-ownership of the copyright in their joint work. This omission was intentional: According to the Copyright Act's legislative history, "[t]here is ... no need for a specific statutory provision concerning the rights and duties of the coowners of a work; court-made law on this point is left undisturbed. Under the bill, as under the present law, coowners of a copyright would be treated generally as tenants in common, with each coowner having an independent right to use or license the use of a work, subject to a duty of accounting to the other coowners for any profits." H.R. REP. NO. 1476, 94th Cong., 2d Sess. 47, at 121 (1976).

Note that the co-authors' rights as co-owners are simply default rules and may be adjusted by the agreement of the co-authors. For example, in the absence of an agreement to the contrary, each co-author (regardless of how much "authorship" that a particular co-author contributed) will own an equal, undivided fractional interest in the entire work. But co-authors might agree that one of them is entitled to a greater or lesser share of revenues from licensing the work. Similarly, in the absence of an agreement to the contrary, each co-author has an independent right to exercise each of the copyright rights in the work, and to license others to do so. But co-authors might also agree that no one of them may use the work, or may license use of the work, without the other co-author's (or co-authors') agreement. We will return to the issue of licensing in Chapter X.

As you read the following cases, consider the roles that (a) status as an "author" and (b) the parties' "intention" play in the court's understanding of the definition of a "joint work."

Karen Erickson v. Trinity Theatre, Inc.
13 F.3d 1061 (7th Cir. 1994)

RIPPLE, J.: ...

[1] [Karen] Erickson was one of the founders of a theatre company in Evanston, Illinois, that ultimately became known as Trinity Theatre. Between 1981 and January 1991, Ms. Erickson served Trinity in various capacities: as playwright, artistic director, actress, play director, business manager, and member of the board of directors. This suit revolves around Ms. Erickson's role as playwright....

[2] Ms. Erickson left Trinity Theatre in January 1991.... On January 21, 1991, Ms. Erickson's attorneys wrote Trinity a letter demanding that the theatre discontinue performing the plaintiff's plays. Trinity refused to comply with the request.

[3] ... Ms. Erickson filed a ... complaint against Trinity Theatre, members of Trinity's management, and individual Trinity actors ... in which she alleged copyright infringement ....

[4] The [court is] faced with ... establishing the appropriate test for determining whether a work has been prepared as a "joint work" within the meaning of § 101 of the Copyright Act of 1976. The parties suggested different approaches. Trinity maintained that the standard for determining a joint work is "collaboration alone"; because there was collaboration between Ms. Erickson and its members, its members jointly authored the ... plays at issue and share rights to their use and production. Ms. Erickson contended that the appropriate test for a joint work is the "copyrightable subject matter" test. Under the test suggested by Ms. Erickson, none of the plays were joint works because only she was an author; the other actors had not contributed independently copyrightable subject matter....

[5] Even if two or more persons collaborate ..., the product will be considered a "joint work" only if the collaborators can be considered "authors." Courts have applied two tests to evaluate the contributions of authors claiming joint authorship status: Professor Nimmer's de minimis test and Professor Goldstein's copyrightable subject matter ("copyrightability") test. The de minimis and copyrightability tests differ in one fundamental respect. The de minimis test requires that only the combined product of joint efforts must be

copyrightable. By contrast, Professor Goldstein's copyrightability test requires that each author's contribution be copyrightable. We evaluate each of these tests in turn....

[6] [Nimmer's] position has not found support in the courts. The lack of support in all likelihood stems from one of several weaknesses in Professor Nimmer's approach. First, Professor Nimmer's test is not consistent with one of the [Copyright] Act's premises: ideas and concepts standing alone should not receive protection. Because the creative process necessarily involves the development of existing concepts into new forms, any restriction on the free exchange of ideas stifles creativity to some extent. Restrictions on an author's use of existing ideas in a work, such as the threat that accepting suggestions from another party might jeopardize the author's sole entitlement to a copyright, would hinder creativity. Second, contribution of an idea is an exceedingly ambiguous concept. Professor Nimmer provides little guidance to courts or parties regarding when a contribution rises to the level of joint authorship except to state that the contribution must be "more than a word or a line."

[7] .... For these reasons, we, as the majority of the other courts, cannot accept Professor Nimmer's test as an adequate judicial tool to ascertain joint authorship.

[8] The copyrightable subject matter test ... formulated by Professor Paul Goldstein ... has been adopted, in some form, by a majority of courts that have considered the issue. According to Professor Goldstein, "[a] collaborative contribution will not produce a joint work, and a contributor will not obtain a co-ownership interest, unless the contribution represents original expression that could stand on its own as the subject matter of copyright." Professor Goldstein and the courts adopting his test justify this position by noting that § 101's and § 302(b)'s use of the word "authors" suggests that each collaborator's contribution must be a copyrightable "work of authorship" within the meaning of § 102(a).

[9] We agree that the language of the Act supports the adoption of a copyrightability requirement. Section 101 of the Act defines a "joint work" as a "work prepared by two or more *authors*" (emphasis added). To qualify as an author, one must supply more than mere direction or ideas. An author is the party who actually creates the work, that is, the person who translates an idea into a fixed, tangible expression entitled to copyright protection....

[10] The copyrightable subject matter test does not suffer from the same infirmities as Professor Nimmer's de minimis test. The copyrightability test advances creativity in science and art by allowing for the unhindered exchange of ideas, and protects authorship rights in a consistent and predictable manner. It excludes contributions such as ideas which are not protected under the Copyright Act. This test also enables parties to predict whether their contributions to a work will entitle them to copyright protection as a joint author. Compared to the uncertain exercise of divining whether a contribution is more than de minimis, reliance on the copyrightability of an author's proposed contribution yields relatively certain answers. The copyrightability standard allows contributors to avoid post-contribution disputes concerning authorship, and to protect themselves by contract if it appears that they would not enjoy the benefits accorded to authors of joint works under the Act....

[11] In order for the plays to be joint works under the Act, Trinity ... must show that actors' contributions to Ms. Erickson's work could have been independently copyrighted. Trinity cannot establish this requirement for any of the ... works. The actors, on the whole, could not identify specific contributions that they had made to Ms. Erickson's works. Even when [a Trinity Theatre actor] was able to do so, the contributions that he identified were not independently copyrightable. Ideas, refinements, and suggestions, standing alone, are not the subjects of copyrights....

[12] Trinity cannot establish joint authorship to the plays at issue....

Jefri Aalmuhammed v. Spike Lee

202 F.3d 1227 (9th Cir. 1999)

KLEINFELD, J.: ...

[1] In 1991, Warner Brothers contracted with Spike Lee and his production companies to make the movie *Malcolm X*, to be based on the book, *The Autobiography of Malcolm X*. Lee co-wrote the screenplay, directed, and co-produced the movie, which starred Denzel Washington as Malcolm X. Washington asked Jefri Aalmuhammed to assist him in his preparation for the starring role because Aalmuhammed knew a great deal about Malcolm X and Islam. Aalmuhammed, a devout Muslim, was particularly knowledgeable about the life of Malcolm X, having previously written, directed, and produced a documentary film about Malcolm X.

[2] Aalmuhammed joined Washington on the movie set.... Aalmuhammed presented evidence that his involvement in making the movie was very extensive. He reviewed the shooting script for Spike Lee and Denzel Washington and suggested extensive script revisions. Some of his script revisions were included in the released version of the film; others were filmed but not included in the released version. Most of the revisions Aalmuhammed made were to ensure the religious and historical accuracy and authenticity of scenes depicting Malcolm X's religious conversion and pilgrimage to Mecca.

[3] Aalmuhammed submitted evidence that he directed Denzel Washington and other actors while on the set, created at least two entire scenes with new characters, translated Arabic into English for subtitles, supplied his own voice for voice-overs, selected the proper prayers and religious practices for the characters, and edited parts of the movie during post production. Washington testified in his deposition that Aalmuhammed's contribution to the movie was "great" because he "helped to rewrite, to make more authentic." Once production ended, Aalmuhammed met with numerous Islamic organizations to persuade them that the movie was an accurate depiction of Malcolm X's life.

[4] Aalmuhammed never had a written contract with Warner Brothers, Lee, or Lee's production companies, but he expected Lee to compensate him for his work.... Aalmuhammed ultimately received a check for $25,000 from Lee, which he cashed, and a check for $100,000 from Washington, which he did not cash.

[5] During the summer before Malcolm X's November 1992 release, Aalmuhammed asked for a writing credit as a co-writer of the film, but was turned down. When the film was released, it credited Aalmuhammed only as an "Islamic Technical Consultant," far down the list. In November 1995, Aalmuhammed applied for a copyright with the U.S. Copyright Office, claiming he was a co-creator, co-writer, and co-director of the movie. The Copyright Office issued him a "Certificate of Registration," but advised him in a letter that his "claims conflict with previous registrations" of the film.

[6] On November 17, 1995, Aalmuhammed filed a complaint against Spike Lee, his production companies, and Warner Brothers .... The suit sought declaratory relief and an accounting under the Copyright Act.... The district court dismissed some of the claims under Rule 12(b)(6) and the rest on summary judgment....

[7] Aalmuhammed claimed that the movie *Malcolm X* was a "joint work" of which he was an author, thus making him a co-owner of the copyright. He sought a declaratory judgment to that effect, and an accounting for profits. He is not claiming copyright merely in what he wrote or contributed, but rather in the whole work, as a co-author of a "joint work." ...

[8] Aalmuhammed argues that he established a genuine issue of fact as to whether he was an author of a "joint work," *Malcolm X*. The Copyright Act does not define "author," but it does define "joint work":

A "joint work" is a work prepared by two or more authors with the intention that their contributions be merged into inseparable or interdependent parts of a unitary whole.

[9] .... The statutory language establishes that for a work to be a "joint work" there must be (1) a copyrightable work, (2) two or more "authors," and (3) the authors must intend their contributions be merged into inseparable or interdependent parts of a unitary whole. A "joint work" in this circuit requires each author to make an independently copyrightable contribution to the disputed work. *Malcolm X* is a copyrightable work, and it is undisputed that the movie was intended by everyone involved with it to be a unitary whole.... Aalmuhammed has ... submitted evidence that he rewrote several specific passages of dialogue that appeared in *Malcolm X*, and that he wrote scenes relating to Malcolm X's Hajj pilgrimage that were enacted in the movie. If Aalmuhammed's evidence is accepted, as it must be on summary judgment, these items would have been independently copyrightable. Aalmuhammed, therefore, has presented a genuine issue of fact as to whether he made a copyrightable contribution. All persons involved intended that Aalmuhammed's contributions would be merged into interdependent parts of the movie as a unitary whole. Aalmuhammed maintains that he has shown a genuine issue of fact for each element of a "joint work."

[10] But there is another element to a "joint work." A "joint work" includes "two or more authors." Aalmuhammed established that he contributed substantially to the film, but not that he was one of its "authors." We hold that authorship is required under the statutory definition of a joint work, and that authorship is not the same thing as making a valuable and copyrightable contribution. We recognize that a contributor of an expression may be deemed to be the "author" of that expression for purposes of determining whether it is independently copyrightable. The issue we deal with is a different and larger one: is the contributor an author of the joint work within the meaning of 17 U.S.C. § 101.

[11] .... The word "author" is taken from the traditional activity of one person sitting at a desk with a pen and writing something for publication. It is relatively easy to apply the word "author" to a novel. It is also easy to apply the word to two people who work together in a fairly traditional pen-and-ink way, like, perhaps, Gilbert and Sullivan. In the song, "I Am the Very Model of a Modern Major General," Gilbert's words and Sullivan's tune are inseparable, and anyone who has heard the song knows that it owes its existence to both men, Sir William Gilbert and Sir Arthur Sullivan, as its creative originator. But as the number of contributors grows and the work itself becomes less the product of one or two individuals who create it without much help, the word is harder to apply.

[12] Who, in the absence of contract, can be considered an author of a movie? The word is traditionally used to mean the originator or the person who causes something to come into being .... For a movie, that might be the producer who raises the money.... The "auteur" theory suggests that it might be the director, at least if the director is able to impose his artistic judgments on the film. Traditionally, by analogy to books, the author was regarded as the person who writes the screenplay, but often a movie reflects the work of many screenwriters.... [T]he person with creative control tends to be the person in whose name the money is raised, perhaps a star, perhaps the director, perhaps the producer, with control gravitating to the star as the financial investment in scenes already shot grows. Where the visual aspect of the movie is especially important, the chief cinematographer might be regarded as the author. And for, say, a Disney animated movie like *The Jungle Book*, it might perhaps be the animators and the composers of the music.

[13] The Supreme Court dealt with the problem of defining "author" in new media in *Burrow-Giles Lithographic Co. v. Sarony*. The question there was, who is the author of a photograph: the person who sets it up and snaps the shutter, or the person who makes the lithograph from it. Oscar Wilde, the person whose picture was at issue, doubtless offered some creative advice as well. The Court decided that the photographer was the author ...: "the person who has superintended the arrangement, who has actually formed the picture by putting the persons in position, and arranging the place where the people are to be—the man who is the

effective cause of that"; "'author' involves originating, making, producing, as the inventive or master mind, the thing which is to be protected"; "the man who really represents, creates, or gives effect to the idea, fancy, or imagination." The Court said that an "author," in the sense that the Founding Fathers used the term in the Constitution, was "he to whom anything owes its origin; originator; maker; one who completes a work of science or literature."

[14] .... So many people might qualify as an "author" if the question were limited to whether they made a substantial creative contribution that that test would not distinguish one from another. Everyone from the producer and director to casting director, costumer, hairstylist, and "best boy" gets listed in the movie credits because all of their creative contributions really do matter. It is striking in *Malcolm X* how much the person who controlled the hue of the lighting contributed, yet no one would use the word "author" to denote that individual's relationship to the movie. A creative contribution does not suffice to establish authorship of the movie.

[15] *Burrow-Giles*, in defining "author," requires more than a minimal creative or original contribution to the work.... *Burrow-Giles* defines author as the person to whom the work owes its origin and who superintended the whole work, the "master mind." In a movie this definition, in the absence of a contract to the contrary, would generally limit authorship to someone at the top of the screen credits, sometimes the producer, sometimes the director, possibly the star, or the screenwriter—someone who has artistic control. After all, in *Burrow-Giles* the lithographer made a substantial copyrightable creative contribution, and so did the person who posed, Oscar Wilde, but the Court held that the photographer was the author.

[16] Considering *Burrow-Giles* ... and the Gilbert and Sullivan example, several factors suggest themselves as among the criteria for joint authorship, in the absence of contract. First, an author superintends the work by exercising control. This will likely be a person who has actually formed the picture by putting the persons in position, and arranging the place where the people are to be—the man who is the effective cause of that, or the inventive or master mind who creates, or gives effect to the idea. Second, putative coauthors make objective manifestations of a shared intent to be coauthors, as by denoting the authorship of *The Pirates of Penzance* as "Gilbert and Sullivan." We say objective manifestations because, were the mutual intent to be determined by subjective intent, it could become an instrument of fraud, were one coauthor to hide from the other an intention to take sole credit for the work. Third, the audience appeal of the work turns on both contributions and the share of each in its success cannot be appraised. Control in many cases will be the most important factor.

[17] The best objective manifestation of a shared intent, of course, is a contract saying that the parties intend to be or not to be co-authors. In the absence of a contract, the inquiry must of necessity focus on the facts. The factors articulated in this decision ... cannot be reduced to a rigid formula, because the creative relationships to which they apply vary too much. Different people do creative work together in different ways, and even among the same people working together the relationship may change over time as the work proceeds.

[18] Aalmuhammed did not at any time have superintendence of the work. Warner Brothers and Spike Lee controlled it. Aalmuhammed was not the person who has actually formed the picture by putting the persons in position, and arranging the place. Spike Lee was, so far as we can tell from the record. Aalmuhammed ... could make extremely helpful recommendations, but Spike Lee was not bound to accept any of them, and the work would not benefit in the slightest unless Spike Lee chose to accept them. Aalmuhammed lacked control over the work, and absence of control is strong evidence of the absence of co-authorship.

[19] Also, neither Aalmuhammed, nor Spike Lee, nor Warner Brothers, made any objective manifestations of an intent to be coauthors. Warner Brothers required Spike Lee to sign a "work for hire" agreement, so that

even Lee would not be a co-author and co-owner with Warner Brothers. It would be illogical to conclude that Warner Brothers, while not wanting to permit Lee to own the copyright, intended to share ownership with individuals like Aalmuhammed who worked under Lee's control, especially ones who at the time had made known no claim to the role of co-author. No one, including Aalmuhammed, made any indication to anyone prior to litigation that Aalmuhammed was intended to be a co-author and co-owner.

[20] Aalmuhammed offered no evidence that he was the inventive or master mind of the movie.... What Aalmuhammed's evidence showed, and all it showed, was that, subject to Spike Lee's authority to accept them, he made very valuable contributions to the movie. That is not enough for co-authorship of a joint work.

[21] The Constitution establishes the social policy that our construction of the statutory term "authors" carries out. The Founding Fathers gave Congress the power to give authors copyrights in order "[t]o promote the progress of Science and useful arts." Progress would be retarded rather than promoted, if an author could not consult with others and adopt their useful suggestions without sacrificing sole ownership of the work. Too open a definition of author would compel authors to insulate themselves and maintain ignorance of the contributions others might make. Spike Lee could not consult a scholarly Muslim to make a movie about a religious conversion to Islam, and the arts would be the poorer for that....

[22] Because the record before the district court established no genuine issue of fact as to Aalmuhammed's co-authorship of Malcolm X as a joint work, the district court correctly granted summary judgment dismissing his claims for declaratory judgment and an accounting resting on co-authorship....

NOTES

1. Consider the different ways in which *Erickson* and *Aalmuhammed* interpret the meaning and effect of the word "authors" in the statutory definition of joint work. Are the two courts' interpretations reconcilable?

2. *Aalmuhammed* says that an "author" is the "inventive" actor, or the "master mind," exercising creative control over the production of a work. What do those words mean? Think of famous creative duos like W.S. Gilbert and Arthur Sullivan, John Lennon and Paul McCartney, and Charles and Ray Eames. Can you identify a "master mind" in any of these duos? Does that concept fit with the reality of creative collaboration?

3. Does *Aalmuhammed*'s interpretation of the meaning of "author" have roots in the statutory definition of "joint work"?

4. What sort of "intention" is necessary to create a joint work? *Aalmuhammed* suggests that what is required is an intention by each participant to enter into a co-authorship relationship. *Aalmuhammed* further provides that this intent may be demonstrated by "objective manifestations." But the text of § 101 and the legislative history suggest that the requisite intent is focused on a different point. That is, the "intention" required is not to be co-authors, but merely to "merge" the separate contributions of the putative co-authors into a "unitary whole." The legislative history makes this clear: "[A] work is 'joint' if the authors collaborated with each other, or if each of the authors prepared his or her contribution with the knowledge and intention that it would be merged with the contributions of other authors as 'inseparable or interdependent parts of a unitary whole.' The touchstone here is the intention, at the time the writing is done, that the parts be absorbed or combined into an integral unit...." H.R. REP. NO. 1476, 94th Cong., 2d Sess. 47, at 120 (1976).

5. If *Aalmuhammed*'s construction of the meaning of both "authors" and "intention" is not aligned with the statute, what do you suppose led the Ninth Circuit to add its "intent to be co-authors" requirement?

6. Is a Wikipedia entry, or the entirety of Wikipedia, a joint work with all contributors as co-authors? Why or why not? For more on the granularity of authorship and micro-works, see Justin Hughes, *Size Matters (or*

Should) in Copyright Law, 74 FORDHAM L. REV. 575 (2005); Molly Shaffer Van Houweling, *Author Autonomy and Atomism in Copyright Law*, 96 VA. L. REV. 549 (2010).

7. Recently there has been a string of lawsuits filed by paparazzi photographers against celebrities who have posted the pictures paparazzi took of them on their social media accounts. Do the celebrities have a possible claim of co-authorship and co-ownership of those photographs? *See* Jeanne C. Fromer, *The New CopyrightOpportunist*, 67 J. COPYRIGHT SOC'Y 1 (2020).

8. As you read earlier, copyright law's default rule grants all co-authors of joint works an equal co-ownership share. Of course, co-authors can agree to contract around this rule. But the question nonetheless arises whether equal co-ownership is the right default, especially given the possibility that co-authors might make contributions of different magnitude and value. One of the concerns motivating the default rule of equal co-ownership shares must be the cost and difficulty of determining, either ex ante or ex post, the relative importance or value of different co-authors' contributions. Recent empirical scholarship also suggests that, at least for jointly written songs, co-ownership by equal shares actually improves the quality of creativity. *See* Sarah Polcz, *Loyalties vs. Royalties*, 73 HASTINGS L.J. (forthcoming 2022), https://papers.ssrn.com/sol3/papers.cfm?abstract_id=3904499.

C. Authorship and Ownership in Works Made for Hire

As stated above, the Copyright Act of 1976 provides that copyright ownership "vests initially in the author or authors of the work." 17 U.S.C. § 201(a). As a general rule, the author is the party or parties who actually create the work, that is, the person or persons who translate an idea into a fixed, tangible expression entitled to copyright protection. *Id.* § 102. However, the Copyright Act establishes an exception for "works made for hire." If the work is made for hire, "the employer or other person for whom the work was prepared is considered the author," and initially owns the copyright, unless there is a written agreement to the contrary. *Id.* § 201(b).

As we shall see later in this book, a work's status as a "work made for hire" has implications for, among other things, (a) the duration of the copyright term that applies to the work, and (b) whether the author of that work may take advantage of the Copyright Act's termination-of-transfers provision. We'll return to those issues in Chapter IV.

Section 101 of the Copyright Act contains a two-part definition of "work made for hire":

> A *"work made for hire" is*—
>
> > *(1) a work prepared by an employee within the scope of his or her employment; or*
> >
> > *(2) a work specially ordered or commissioned for use as a contribution to a collective work, as a part of a motion picture or other audiovisual work, as a translation, as a supplementary work, as a compilation, as an instructional text, as a test, as answer material for a test, or as an atlas, if the parties expressly agree in a written instrument signed by them that the work shall be considered a work made for hire. For the purpose of the foregoing sentence, a "supplementary work" is a work prepared for publication as a secondary adjunct to a work by another author for the purpose of introducing, concluding, illustrating, explaining, revising, commenting upon, or assisting in the use of the other work, such as forewords, afterwords, pictorial illustrations, maps, charts, tables, editorial notes, musical arrangements, answer material for tests, bibliographies, appendixes, and indexes, and an "instructional text" is a literary, pictorial, or*

graphic work prepared for publication and with the purpose of use in systematic instructional activities.

NOTES

1. What role do the "work made for hire" provisions play in the overall scheme of U.S. copyright law? What are the policy arguments for and against the "work made for hire" provisions?

2. Recall that the Constitution's Copyright and Patent Clause empowers Congress to grant copyrights to "Authors." Is the Copyright Act's "work made for hire" provision constitutional?

1. Works of Employees Operating Within the Scope of Employment

The next two cases focus on the first part of the "work made for hire" definition—the part that classifies as works made for hire "work[s] prepared by an employee within the scope of his or her employment ...." As you read these cases, think about whether the guidance they provide (a) regarding who is an "employee" and (b) whether a particular work falls within the "scope of employment," tracks your intuitions about these concepts.

Community for Creative Non-Violence v. James Earl Reid
490 U.S. 730 (1989)

MARSHALL, J.: ...

[1] Petitioners are the Community for Creative Non–Violence (CCNV), a nonprofit unincorporated association dedicated to eliminating homelessness in America, and Mitch Snyder, a member and trustee of CCNV. In the fall of 1985, CCNV decided to participate in the annual Christmastime Pageant of Peace in Washington, D.C., by sponsoring a display to dramatize the plight of the homeless. As the District Court recounted:

> Snyder and fellow CCNV members conceived the idea for the nature of the display: a sculpture of a modern Nativity scene in which, in lieu of the traditional Holy Family, the two adult figures and the infant would appear as contemporary homeless people huddled on a streetside steam grate. The family was to be black (most of the homeless in Washington being black); the figures were to be life-sized, and the steam grate would be positioned atop a platform pedestal, or base, within which special-effects equipment would be enclosed to emit simulated steam through the grid to swirl about the figures. They also settled upon a title for the work—'Third World America'—and a legend for the pedestal: 'and still there is no room at the inn.'

[2] Snyder made inquiries to locate an artist to produce the sculpture. He was referred to respondent James Earl Reid, a Baltimore, Maryland, sculptor. In the course of two telephone calls, Reid agreed to sculpt the three human figures. CCNV agreed to make the steam grate and pedestal for the statue. Reid proposed that the work be cast in bronze, at a total cost of approximately $100,000 and taking six to eight months to complete. Snyder rejected that proposal because CCNV did not have sufficient funds, and because the statue had to be completed by December 12 to be included in the pageant. Reid then suggested, and Snyder agreed, that the sculpture would be made of a material known as "Design Cast 62," a synthetic substance that could meet CCNV's monetary and time constraints, could be tinted to resemble bronze, and could withstand the

elements. The parties agreed that the project would cost no more than $15,000, not including Reid's services, which he offered to donate. The parties did not sign a written agreement. Neither party mentioned copyright.

[3] After Reid received an advance of $3,000, he made several sketches of figures in various poses. At Snyder's request, Reid sent CCNV a sketch of a proposed sculpture showing the family in a crèche like setting: the mother seated, cradling a baby in her lap; the father standing behind her, bending over her shoulder to touch the baby's foot. Reid testified that Snyder asked for the sketch to use in raising funds for the sculpture. Snyder testified that it was also for his approval. Reid sought a black family to serve as a model for the sculpture. Upon Snyder's suggestion, Reid visited a family living at CCNV's Washington shelter but decided that only their newly born child was a suitable model. While Reid was in Washington, Snyder took him to see homeless people living on the streets. Snyder pointed out that they tended to recline on steam grates, rather than sit or stand, in order to warm their bodies. From that time on, Reid's sketches contained only reclining figures.

[4] Throughout November and the first two weeks of December 1985, Reid worked exclusively on the statue, assisted at various times by a dozen different people who were paid with funds provided in installments by CCNV. On a number of occasions, CCNV members visited Reid to check on his progress and to coordinate CCNV's construction of the base. CCNV rejected Reid's proposal to use suitcases or shopping bags to hold the family's personal belongings, insisting instead on a shopping cart. Reid and CCNV members did not discuss copyright ownership on any of these visits.

Figure 44: "Third World America," by James Earl Reid

[5] On December 24, 1985, 12 days after the agreed-upon date, Reid delivered the completed statue to Washington. There it was joined to the steam grate and pedestal prepared by CCNV and placed on display near the site of the pageant. Snyder paid Reid the final installment of the $15,000. The statue remained on display for a month. In late January 1986, CCNV members returned it to Reid's studio in Baltimore for minor repairs. Several weeks later, Snyder began making plans to take the statue on a tour of several cities to raise money for the homeless. Reid objected, contending that the Design Cast 62 material was not strong enough to withstand the ambitious itinerary. He urged CCNV to cast the statue in bronze at a cost of $35,000, or to create a master mold at a cost of $5,000. Snyder declined to spend more of CCNV's money on the project.

[6] In March 1986, Snyder asked Reid to return the sculpture. Reid refused. He then filed a certificate of copyright registration for "Third World America" in his name and announced plans to take the sculpture on a more modest tour than the one CCNV had proposed. Snyder, acting in his capacity as CCNV's trustee, immediately filed a competing certificate of copyright registration.

[7] Snyder and CCNV then commenced this action against Reid ... seeking return of the sculpture and a determination of copyright ownership. The District Court granted a preliminary injunction, ordering the sculpture's return. After a 2–day bench trial, the District Court declared that "Third World America" was a "work made for hire" under § 101 of the Copyright Act and that Snyder, as trustee for CCNV, was the exclusive owner of the copyright in the sculpture. The court reasoned that Reid had been an "employee" of CCNV within the meaning of § 101(1) because CCNV was the motivating force in the statue's production. Snyder and other CCNV members, the court explained, conceived the idea of a contemporary Nativity scene to contrast with the national celebration of the season, and directed enough of Reid's effort to assure that, in the end, he had produced what they, not he, wanted.

[8] The Court of Appeals for the District of Columbia Circuit reversed and remanded, holding that Reid owned the copyright because "Third World America" was not a work for hire.... Because, under agency law, Reid was an independent contractor, the court concluded that the work was not "prepared by an employee" under § 101(1)....

[9] We granted certiorari to resolve a conflict among the Courts of Appeals over the proper construction of the "work made for hire" provisions of the Act....

[10] The Copyright Act of 1976 provides that copyright ownership "vests initially in the author or authors of the work." As a general rule, the author is the party who actually creates the work, that is, the person who translates an idea into a fixed, tangible expression entitled to copyright protection. The Act carves out an important exception, however, for works made for hire. If the work is for hire, "the employer or other person for whom the work was prepared is considered the author" and owns the copyright, unless there is a written agreement to the contrary....[4]

[11] Section 101 of the 1976 Act provides that a work is for hire under two sets of circumstances:

> (1) a work prepared by an employee within the scope of his or her employment; or

> (2) a work specially ordered or commissioned for use as a contribution to a collective work, as a part of a motion picture or other audiovisual work, as a translation, as a supplementary work, as a compilation, as an instructional text, as a test, as answer material for a test, or as an atlas, if the parties expressly agree in a written instrument signed by them that the work shall be considered a work made for hire.

[12] Petitioners do not claim that the statue satisfies the terms of § 101(2). Quite clearly, it does not. Sculpture does not fit within any of the nine categories of "specially ordered or commissioned" works enumerated in that subsection, and no written agreement between the parties establishes "Third World America" as a work for hire.

[13] The dispositive inquiry in this case therefore is whether "Third World America" is "a work prepared by an employee within the scope of his or her employment" under § 101(1). The Act does not define these terms. In the absence of such guidance, four interpretations have emerged. The first holds that a work is prepared by an employee whenever the hiring party retains the right to control the product. Petitioners take this view. A

---

[4] As of 1955, approximately 40 percent of all copyright registrations were for works for hire, according to a Copyright Office study.... The Copyright Office does not keep more recent statistics on the number of work for hire registrations.

second, and closely related, view is that a work is prepared by an employee under § 101(1) when the hiring party has actually wielded control with respect to the creation of a particular work. This approach [i]s ... adopted ... at times, by petitioners. A third view is that the term "employee" within § 101(1) carries its common-law agency law meaning. This view was endorsed ... by the Court of Appeals below. Finally, respondent and numerous amici curiae contend that the term "employee" only refers to formal, salaried employees.

[14] The starting point for our interpretation of a statute is always its language. The Act nowhere defines the terms "employee" or "scope of employment." It is, however, well established that where Congress uses terms that have accumulated settled meaning under the common law, a court must infer, unless the statute otherwise dictates, that Congress means to incorporate the established meaning of these terms. In the past, when Congress has used the term "employee" without defining it, we have concluded that Congress intended to describe the conventional master-servant relationship as understood by common-law agency doctrine. Nothing in the text of the work for hire provisions indicates that Congress used the words "employee" and "employment" to describe anything other than the conventional relation of employer and employ[ee]. On the contrary, Congress' intent to incorporate the agency law definition is suggested by § 101(1)'s use of the term, "scope of employment," a widely used term of art in agency law. *See* Restatement (Second) of Agency § 228 (1958).

[15] In past cases of statutory interpretation, when we have concluded that Congress intended terms such as "employee," "employer," and "scope of employment" to be understood in light of agency law, we have relied on the general common law of agency ... to give meaning to these terms.... We thus agree with the Court of Appeals that the term "employee" should be understood in light of the general common law of agency.

[16] In contrast, neither test proposed by petitioners is consistent with the text of the Act. The exclusive focus of the right to control the product test on the relationship between the hiring party and the product clashes with the language of § 101(1), which focuses on the relationship between the hired and hiring parties. The right to control the product test also would distort the meaning of the ensuing subsection, § 101(2). Section 101 plainly creates two distinct ways in which a work can be deemed for hire: one for works prepared by employees, the other for those specially ordered or commissioned works which fall within one of the nine enumerated categories and are the subject of a written agreement. The right to control the product test ignores this dichotomy by transforming into a work for hire under § 101(1) any "specially ordered or commissioned" work that is subject to the supervision and control of the hiring party. Because a party who hires a "specially ordered or commissioned" work by definition has a right to specify the characteristics of the product desired, at the time the commission is accepted, and frequently until it is completed, the right to control the product test would mean that many works that could satisfy § 101(2) would already have been deemed works for hire under § 101(1)....

[17] The actual control test fares only marginally better when measured against the language and structure of § 101. Under this test, ... work for hire status under § 101(1) depends on a hiring party's actual control of, rather than right to control, the product.... [T]here is no statutory support for an additional dichotomy between commissioned works that are actually controlled and supervised by the hiring party and those that are not.

[18] We therefore conclude that the language and structure of § 101 of the Act do not support either the right to control the product or the actual control approaches.[8] The structure of § 101 indicates that a work for hire

---

[8] We also reject the suggestion of respondent and amici that the § 101(1) term "employee" refers only to formal, salaried employees. While there is some support for such a definition in the legislative history, the language of § 101(1) cannot support it. The Act does not say "formal" or "salaried" employee, but simply "employee." ...

can arise through one of two mutually exclusive means, one for employees and one for independent contractors, and ordinary canons of statutory interpretation indicate that the classification of a particular hired party should be made with reference to agency law....

[19] ... [P]etitioners' construction of the work for hire provisions would impede Congress' paramount goal in revising the 1976 Act of enhancing predictability and certainty of copyright ownership. In a "copyright marketplace," the parties negotiate with an expectation that one of them will own the copyright in the completed work. With that expectation, the parties at the outset can settle on relevant contractual terms, such as the price for the work and the ownership of reproduction rights.

[20] To the extent that petitioners endorse an actual control test, CCNV's construction of the work for hire provisions prevents such planning. Because that test turns on whether the hiring party has closely monitored the production process, the parties would not know until late in the process, if not until the work is completed, whether a work will ultimately fall within § 101(1). Under petitioners' approach, therefore, parties would have to predict in advance whether the hiring party will sufficiently control a given work to make it the author. If they guess incorrectly, their reliance on work for hire ... may give them a copyright interest that they did not bargain for. This understanding of the work for hire provisions clearly thwarts Congress' goal of ensuring predictability through advance planning....

[21] We turn, finally, to an application of § 101 to Reid's production of "Third World America." In determining whether a hired party is an employee under the general common law of agency, we consider the hiring party's right to control the manner and means by which the product is accomplished. Among the other factors relevant to this inquiry are the skill required; the source of the instrumentalities and tools; the location of the work; the duration of the relationship between the parties; whether the hiring party has the right to assign additional projects to the hired party; the extent of the hired party's discretion over when and how long to work; the method of payment; the hired party's role in hiring and paying assistants; whether the work is part of the regular business of the hiring party; whether the hiring party is in business; the provision of employee benefits; and the tax treatment of the hired party. *See* Restatement § 220(2) (setting forth a nonexhaustive list of factors relevant to determining whether a hired party is an employee). No one of these factors is determinative.

[22] Examining the circumstances of this case in light of these factors, we agree with the Court of Appeals that Reid was not an employee of CCNV but an independent contractor. True, CCNV members directed enough of Reid's work to ensure that he produced a sculpture that met their specifications. But the extent of control the hiring party exercises over the details of the product is not dispositive. Indeed, all the other circumstances weigh heavily against finding an employment relationship. Reid is a sculptor, a skilled occupation. Reid supplied his own tools. He worked in his own studio in Baltimore, making daily supervision of his activities from Washington practically impossible. Reid was retained for less than two months, a relatively short period of time. During and after this time, CCNV had no right to assign additional projects to Reid. Apart from the deadline for completing the sculpture, Reid had absolute freedom to decide when and how long to work. CCNV paid Reid $15,000, a sum dependent on completion of a specific job, a method by which independent contractors are often compensated. Reid had total discretion in hiring and paying assistants. Creating sculptures was hardly regular business for CCNV. Indeed, CCNV is not a business at all. Finally, CCNV did not pay payroll or Social Security taxes, provide any employee benefits, or contribute to unemployment insurance or workers' compensation funds.

[23] Because Reid was an independent contractor, whether "Third World America" is a work for hire depends on whether it satisfies the terms of § 101(2). This petitioners concede it cannot do. Thus, CCNV is not the author of "Third World America" by virtue of the work for hire provisions of the Act. However, ... CCNV nevertheless may be a joint author of the sculpture if, on remand, the District Court determines that CCNV

and Reid prepared the work "with the intention that their contributions be merged into inseparable or interdependent parts of a unitary whole." In that case, CCNV and Reid would be co-owners of the copyright in the work....

NOTES

1. Is the Court's textual argument—that the common law agency approach to determining status as employee or independent contractor is consistent with the Copyright Act's text, and that the other tests ("right to control the product," "actual control," and "formal or salaried employee") are not—convincing?

2. Similarly, the court rejects the "right to control the product" and "actual control" tests in part because those tests would make it difficult for the parties to predict in advance who would end up owning the copyright. Is that a convincing argument? Does the common law agency test fare better on this count?

3. While the *CCNV* case was pending on remand, Mitch Snyder died by suicide. For a respectful appreciation of a complicated life, see https://www.nytimes.com/1990/07/06/obituaries/mitch-snyder-46-advocate-of-homeless.html. The case settled soon thereafter, with the parties agreeing that Reid was the author and copyright owner of "Third World America," but that CCNV was the owner of the physical sculpture. The parties further agreed that CCNV and Reid would each have rights to produce two-dimensional copies (posters and postcards) of the work.

4. If the *CCNV* case had not settled, the district court on remand would have considered whether "Third World America" was a joint work in which Reid and CCNV were co-authors. How do you think this issue should have been decided?

5. For a survey of how courts have used the *CCNV* factors, and, in particular, an analysis of which of the *CCNV* factors is the most important, see Ryan Vacca, *Work Made for Hire—Analyzing the Multifactor Balancing Test*, 42 FLA. ST. L. REV. 197 (2014). Based on his analysis of a dataset of cases applying the *CCNV* factors, Vacca concludes that tax treatment, the provision of employee benefits, and payment method are the most important, followed closely by whether the hiring party has the power to assign additional projects, the skill required, and the source of the instrumentalities and tools. The other *CCNV* factors appear to be less important in driving the analysis of whether a party is an employee or independent contractor.

6. In *JustMed, Inc. v. Byce*, 600 F.3d 1118 (9th Cir. 2010), the Ninth Circuit held that the defendant was an employee despite his argument that the plaintiff did not treat him as an employee for tax purposes. Other *CCNV* factors also weighed against employment. For example, the defendant had been paid in shares of stock, which had not been reported as income by him. Nonetheless, the court reasoned that the business at issue was a technology start-up company rather than an established business, which affected its evaluation of the factors. How should the *CCNV* factors be applied to evaluate employment status for a technology start-up company or other less traditional businesses?

7. In 2005, the American Law Institute adopted the *Restatement (Third) of Agency*. The new Restatement no longer contains the list of factors relied upon in *CCNV* for determining employment status. Instead, it provides that "an employee is an agent whose principal controls or has the right to control the manner and means of the agent's performance of work." RESTATEMENT (THIRD) OF AGENCY §7.07(3)(a). Do you think the result in *CCNV* would come out any differently under the Restatement's revised formulation? Do you think this new standard better comports with current types of employment?

Avtec Systems, Inc. v. Jeffrey G. Peiffer
21 F.3d 568 (4th Cir. 1994)

PHILLIPS, J.: ...

[1] .... Avtec Systems, Inc. markets space-related computer services and products to the federal government. Its services include computerized simulations of satellite orbital patterns. Jeffrey G. Peiffer began working part-time for Avtec while in college and became the company's fifth full-time employee upon his graduation in 1984. During his career with Avtec, his job description included "implement[ing] computer simulation" and, specifically, simulating "satellite orbits."

[2] In 1984, Avtec purchased a Macintosh computer at Peiffer's suggestion. After Peiffer demonstrated the computer's abilities to Avtec President Ronald Hirsch and other employees, it became apparent that the company's orbital simulations would be enhanced in several respects by using a Macintosh. It is disputed whether that idea originated with Peiffer alone or in discussions with other Avtec personnel; it also is disputed whether Avtec authorized Peiffer to begin developing a computer program for that purpose as he did in 1985. Peiffer demonstrated the Program—called "the .309 version"—to Hirsch and others at Avtec that same year, and again during his 1988 performance appraisal as evidence of his initiative on the job.

[3] At that point, Hirsch and another Avtec employee suggested several modifications to enhance the Program's utility as a marketing tool for the company. Peiffer charged time to an Avtec account for making those enhancements. Peiffer also received a $5,000 bonus in early 1989 for helping to land a contract by demonstrating the Program as a unique Avtec service. He performed similar demonstrations for other clients as well. Later that year, Avtec issued a written policy, of which Peiffer was aware, binding employees to duties of confidentiality and nondisclosure respecting the company's proprietary information and trade secrets.

[4] In early 1990, another Avtec employee found some bugs in the Program. After Peiffer fixed them, that other employee presented the corrected version to a client. In 1991, Avtec labeled the Program as a trademark and advertised it as unique to Avtec. At no time before his eventual departure from Avtec did Peiffer represent to his employer or to its potential clients that he had an ownership interest in the Program.

[5] In 1992, however, when Peiffer was asked to demonstrate the Program to NASA as part of a contract bid, he used the old, uncorrected .309 version without informing anyone at Avtec or NASA of that fact. Peiffer concedes that Avtec did not win that contract in part because he showed the outdated version. Shortly thereafter, when Peiffer was again asked to demonstrate the program, he refused and said that he didn't have a copy of it at the office.

[6] Unbeknownst to Avtec, Peiffer had met Paul F. Kisak early in 1989 and granted Kisak's company, Kisak-Kisak, Inc. (KKI) an exclusive license to market the Program. Sales generated $197,000 in gross revenues for KKI, of which Peiffer received approximately half.

[7] Avtec registered for a copyright in the .309 version of the Program on March 27, 1992. Six days later, Avtec commenced this action against Peiffer, Kisak, and KKI charging copyright infringement, misappropriation of trade secrets, and breach of fiduciary duty.... On April 9, Peiffer registered his copyright claim in the .309 version, which he called MacOrbit, and another copyright claim in the 2.05 version, which he called the Orbit Program and identified as derivative of the .309 version. Defendants then counterclaimed for copyright infringement.

[8] After a three-day bench trial, the court found that Peiffer owned copyright in the later version of the Program, reasoning that he had not created it within the scope of his employment as is required by 17 U.S.C.

§ 201(b) in order for copyright to vest in an employer. On that basis, the court denied Avtec relief on Count I and—pursuant to defendants' counterclaim—ordered Avtec to withdraw its registration of copyright....

[9] To recover on its copyright claim, Avtec had to show that it owned a valid copyright in the Program and that defendants encroached upon one of the exclusive rights it conferred....

[10] These rights presumptively vest in the author—the one who translates an original idea into a fixed, tangible means of expression. The presumption of authorial ownership falls, however, if the work is made for hire, such as one prepared by an employee within the scope of his or her employment. Under those circumstances, copyright vests in the employer for whom the work was prepared. This exception is overridden only by a clear writing reserving authorship rights to the employee, 17 U.S.C. § 201(b), which concededly did not exist in this case.

[11] It is essentially undisputed that Peiffer was Avtec's employee at the time of the Program's inception. The contested issue throughout has been whether Peiffer created the Program within the scope of his employment. [*Community for Creative Non-Violence v.*] *Reid* instructs that common-law agency principles govern resolution of that question. As expressed in Section 228 of the *Restatement* [*(Second) of Agency*], the key principle is that a servant's conduct is within the scope of employment "only if: (a) it is of the kind he is employed to perform; (b) it occurs substantially within the authorized time and space limits; [and] (c) it is actuated, at least in part, by a purpose to serve the master."

[12] We agree with the district court that creation of the Program was "of the kind" of work Peiffer was employed to perform. When that element of the *Restatement* test is met, courts have tended not to grant employees authorship rights solely on the basis that the work was done at home on off-hours.

[13] On the other hand, copyright does not vest in the employer solely because the subject matter of the work bears upon or arises out of the employee's activities for his employer. Thus, Avtec had to show that Peiffer was at least appreciably motivated by a desire to further its corporate goals in order to satisfy the third element of the work-for-hire test.

[14] The district court found that Peiffer had not developed version 2.05 of the Program "within Avtec authorized time and space limits ... [and] was [not] motivated, at least in part, by a purpose to serve Avtec." On this basis, the court held that copyright vested in Peiffer, not in Avtec, and accordingly rendered judgment in favor of defendants on Avtec's claim and on their counterclaim....

[15] Instead of focusing upon the question whether the .309 version was created within the scope of Peiffer's employment, however, the district court made a preliminary finding that Avtec used the original version solely as "a demonstration and marketing device," while the later 2.05 version was a "stand-alone software package that could be marketed commercially," which Avtec neither could nor would have developed. Relying on this utilitarian distinction between two versions of the program, the court expressly confined its decision on the question of copyright ownership to "the current 2.05 version" of the Program. Finding dispositive the facts that Peiffer worked on the Program at home, on his own equipment and time, as a "personal hobby, and not to satisfy specific work obligations for Avtec," the court reasoned that "while Peiffer allowed earlier versions of the Orbit Program to be used by Avtec for various client demonstrations, Avtec did not ... persuade the Court that Peiffer's *development of the 2.05 version* ... was actuated by his desire to serve Avtec" and held that Avtec could not "claim complete or joint ownership *of the 2.05 version.*"

[16] Defendants urge us to extend this express language to encompass the .309 version as well....

[17] .... Anticipating our *de novo* review of the legal component of the scope-of-employment issue, the parties emphasize conflicting evidence supporting their respective positions on that issue. Avtec points to evidence

that it authorized Peiffer to work on the project at home during off-hours and contends that Peiffer's resulting behavior compels the inference that he intended the work, at least in part, to contribute to Avtec's successful pursuit of its business objectives. Defendants counter with the evidence relied upon by the district court that Peiffer developed the Program as a hobby and that Avtec failed to exercise significant control or supervision over the project.

[18] ... [W]e ...conclud[e] that the district court's resolution of the scope-of-employment issue was flawed by a misapprehension of the controlling legal principles. We are not in a position to resolve that heavily fact-laden issue in the first instance; among other reasons, credibility could be decisive. Though we regret the necessity, we must instead vacate those portions of the judgment respecting the claim and counterclaim for copyright infringement and remand those claims for reconsideration, in light of this opinion, of the dispositive common issue whether the original Program was created within the scope of Peiffer's employment....

NOTES

1. Again, is the common law agency test predictable in its application? Does the analysis in this case align with your intuitions regarding whether Pfeiffer undertook his work respecting either version of the software program within the scope of his employment with Avtec?

2. How should the district court rule on remand?

3. *Avtec* leans heavily on § 228 of the *Restatement (Second) of Agency*, which states that an employee's conduct is within the scope of employment "only if: (a) it is of the kind he is employed to perform; (b) it occurs substantially within the authorized time and space limits; [and] (c) it is actuated, at least in part, by a purpose to serve the master." Does this formulation fit with the conditions of modern employment (such as the flexible work schedules and ability to telecommute that many employees have)? Note that *Avtec* has arguably adjusted the Restatement's three-part test by refusing to apply the second part literally ("When th[e first] element of the *Restatement* test is met, courts have tended not to grant employees authorship rights solely on the basis that the work was done at home on off-hours.").

4. As noted above, in 2005, the American Law Institute adopted the *Restatement (Third) of Agency*. In § 7.07(2), the new Restatement sets out a different test for scope of employment:

> An employee acts within the scope of employment when performing work assigned by the employer or engaging in a course of conduct subject to the employer's control. An employee's act is not within the scope of employment when it occurs within an independent course of conduct not intended by the employee to serve any purpose of the employer.

Should the result in *Avtec* change if this revised test is applied?

5. What do you think would have happened if *Avtec* had come out in favor of the defendants? It is likely that even if the .309 version of the program was not created within the scope of Avtec's employment, the court would have found that Peiffer implicitly licensed that code to his employer, and that the license endured so long as the code was used by the employer. *See, e.g.,* Effects Assoc., Inc. v. Cohen, 908 F.2d 555 (9th Cir. 1990) (holding that although special effects footage did not qualify as a work made for hire nor was ownership transferred by written agreement, the parties' course of conduct created an implied license to use the footage in the defendant's motion picture).

2. Specially Ordered or Commissioned Works

In addition to works created by employees within the scope of their employment, the Copyright Act defines a second category of works as potential works made for hire: works that are "specially ordered or commissioned." 17 U.S.C. § 101.

The Categories of Works

For a specially ordered or commissioned work to be a work made for hire, two requirements must be fulfilled. First, the work must fit within one of the specified types of works listed in the statute. Under the terms defining work made for hire in § 101, a specially ordered or commissioned work is eligible to be considered a work made for hire if it has been specially ordered or commissioned for use as: (1) a contribution to a collective work, (2) as a part of a motion picture or other audiovisual work, (3) as a translation, (4) as a supplementary work, (5) as a compilation, (6) as an instructional text, (7) as a test, (8) as answer material for a test, or (9) as an atlas.

What distinguishes these categories from other types of specially ordered or commissioned works that are not eligible for work made for hire treatment? (Think of the sculpture in *CCNV v. Reid*, which the Supreme Court said was outside of the list of enumerated categories and thus ineligible for work made for hire treatment as a "specially ordered or commissioned work.") Is the statutory list just an artifact of special-interest lobbying? Or does the list reflect some deeper commonality among works in the enumerated categories that makes these works especially suitable for work made for hire treatment? According to former Register of Copyrights Marybeth Peters, the categories were chosen in response to practical concerns about the consequences of permitting termination of transfers with respect to certain types of works:

> [W]orks included in these categories tend to be works done by freelance authors at the instance, direction, and risk of a publisher or producer where it was argued that it would be unfair to allow such authors to terminate assignments of rights. Other exceptions (contributions to collective works, parts of motion pictures), were based on the fact that the resulting work involved numerous authors and that permitting terminations of grants of rights to such works would cause chaos.

Sound Recordings as Works Made for Hire: Hearings Before the Subcomm. on Courts and Intellectual Property of the H. Comm. on the Judiciary, 106th Cong. 257 (2000).

The Writing Requirement

Second, the parties must agree, in a written instrument signed by both of them, that "the work shall be considered a work made for hire." 17 U.S.C. § 101.

Both requirements must be met in order for a specially ordered or commissioned work to be a work made for hire.

NOTES

1. There is a circuit split about the timing of the writing requirement. The Second Circuit has suggested that the "writing requirement of § 101(2) can be met by a writing executed after the work is created, if the writing confirms a prior agreement, either explicit or implicit, made before the creation of the work." Playboy Enter., Inc. v. Dumas, 53 F.3d 549, 560 (2d Cir. 1995). That approach is contrary to the position taken by the Seventh Circuit, which has held that execution of the writing must occur before creation of the subject work, "in order

to serve its purpose of identifying the (noncreator) owner unequivocally." Schiller & Schmidt, Inc. v. Nordisco Corp., 969 F.2d 410, 413 (7th Cir. 1992). Which view makes more sense as a matter of copyright policy?

2. There has also been some disagreement about whether the written agreement must clearly identify the work as a "work made for hire." The Second Circuit refused to recognize a work as a work made for hire where the writing consisted of a check issued by the commissioning party that bore a check legend that mentioned only "assignment" and did not explicitly identify the payment as being for creation of a work made for hire. *Playboy Enter.*, 53 F.3d at 560. In contrast, the Ninth Circuit does not require any "talismanic words." Warren v. Fox Family Worldwide, Inc., 328 F.3d 1136, 1141 (9th Cir. 2003).

3. There is a longstanding dispute regarding whether commissioned sound recordings qualify as works made for hire, at least when they were contributions to collective works—that is, they were contributions to record albums, which are collections of independent sound recordings. Several courts have expressed skepticism that sound recordings are properly treated as works made for hire under the "specially ordered or commissioned" prong of the definition, and several courts have stated specifically that sound recordings as such are not among any of the nine categories of specially ordered or commissioned works. *See, e.g.*, Staggers v. Real Authentic Sound, 77 F. Supp. 2d 57 (D.D.C. 1999); Ballas v. Tedesco, 41 F. Supp. 2d 531 (D.N.J. 1999); Lulirama Ltd. v. Axcess Broadcast Services, Inc., 128 F.3d 872 (5th Cir. 1997).

In 1999, record companies attempted to settle the controversy by pushing for amendments to the Copyright Act. That effort was initially successful, and sound recordings were added to the list of categories of works made eligible for works made for hire treatment as a specially ordered or commissioned work under 17 U.S.C. § 101(2). *See* S. 1948, 106th Cong. § 1011(d) (1999) (enacted). Congress characterized the addition as a "technical amendment." However, less than one year later, and after an uproar led by musicians, sound recordings were removed from the provision. *See* Work Made for Hire and Copyright Corrections Act, H.R. 5107, 106th Cong., Pub. L. 106–369, 114 Stat. 1444 (2000). The 2000 deletion restored the "works made for hire" provision to the pre-1999 amendment status by repealing the 1999 amendment, and also by adding language to the Copyright Act instructing courts that they should interpret the meaning of the "work made for hire" provision as if the legislation adding and then removing sound recordings from the list had never been passed. *See* 146 Cong. Rec. H7244-02, H7245 (daily ed. Sept. 6, 2000) (statement of Rep. Berman).

IV. Copyright Formalities and Duration

Until now, our study of copyright law has focused principally on metaphysical matters like originality, the difference between idea and expression, and the nature of authorship. In this chapter, we shift to more technical matters related to copyright. This chapter explores the **formalities** that copyright law has long had in place and how they have changed in recent years, as well as the rules and policies underlying copyright **duration**, as well as **renewals** and **terminations of transfer**.

A. Formalities

Copyright law's formalities are procedural mechanisms with which one must or is encouraged to comply. From the very first copyright statute in 1790, Congress required that authors comply with certain formalities, such as registering their copyrights and giving notice of their copyright. Failure to comply with these requirements either terminated the copyright or prevented it from arising in the first place.

However, in a process that began in earnest with the 1976 Act and culminated in successor legislation—most importantly, U.S. accession to the Berne Convention in 1989—Congress pared back, and in some instances entirely discarded, copyright formalities. Under current law, as discussed in Chapter II, copyright arises the moment an original work of authorship is fixed in a tangible medium of expression. Formalities like registration and notice, though encouraged, are not required as conditions of protection.

Beginning with the 1976 Act, then, the United States moved from a "conditional" copyright system that premised the existence and continuation of copyright on compliance with formalities to an "unconditional" system with a reduced set of voluntary formalities that play a more minor role.

Nonetheless, formalities still play an important role in copyright law for two reasons. First, the diminishment of formalities over time applies only prospectively, so older works—those that started copyright protection before these diminishments—continue to be affected by the prior rules. Second, most of these formalities have not disappeared. Even though they are no longer required, there are still sometimes hefty incentives to comply with them. For these reasons, understanding copyright formalities is important to any lawyer working in copyright law. Each subsection below will typically explore three sets of rules: those under the 1909 Act (all works published before January 1, 1978), those under the 1976 Act (all works fixed on or after January 1, 1978 but before U.S. accession to the Berne Convention, and all works fixed but unpublished before January 1, 1978), and those following U.S. accession to the Berne Convention (all works fixed on or after March 1, 1989).

The following sections in turn consider **publication**, copyright **notice**, **registration**, **deposit**, and other formalities. In exploring the legal requirements of each formality, we also consider the policy reasons for and against that formality. That said, there are some policy considerations generally applicable to the role of formalities in a copyright system.

First consider why it might be advisable to diminish, if not eliminate, the importance of formalities in copyright law. Most critically, artists—even sophisticated ones—can inadvertently abandon copyright rights they would prefer to have by overlooking precise compliance with one or more of copyright's formalities. Many artists might not even realize there are formalities with which to comply in the first instance. This might particularly be the case for foreign artists, because foreign countries long ago moved away from copyright formalities. Many foreign artists therefore have long assumed that the United States does not require formalities as prerequisite to securing or maintaining copyright protection. Formalities also make obtaining copyright protection more expensive. Formalities thus undermine any goal of providing copyright protection readily. Moreover, because other countries have moved away from requiring formalities, U.S. formalities undermine efforts at international harmonization of copyright law.

Now consider, by contrast, the useful purposes that formalities can serve. A copyright registry—a centralized database of all copyrighted works—can provide helpful information about these works to third parties. In particular, it enables would-be users of a work to determine quickly and inexpensively whether the work in question is indeed subject to copyright, and, if so, from whom to seek a license. This interest might be more critical than with regard to real estate or personal property. The property interest protected by copyright is intangible. Unlike real estate or personal property, the property embodied in copyright has no unique physical existence. A painting, a book, and an iPhone containing an audio recording are all physical objects, but the expression fixed in each of them may, absent the workings of the law, freely be copied and ownership of copies transferred. Therefore, although the question of who owns a particular copy of a book presents no more difficulty than does ownership of any particular piece of personal property, the question of who owns rights in the expression contained in the book most often cannot be answered simply by understanding who owns the book. Copyright formalities can create the information about ownership that mere possession of a copyrighted work could not.

Formalities also serve the purpose of allowing authors to distinguish between works for which they desire copyright protection—by complying deliberately with copyright formalities—and those for which they do not. This might be especially important given how many copyrightable works we all create constantly.

For more on these policy issues, see Jane C. Ginsburg, *The U.S. Experience with Mandatory Copyright Formalities: A Love/Hate Relationship*, 33 COLUM. J.L. & ARTS 311 (2010); Christopher Jon Sprigman, *Reform(alizing) Copyright*, 57 STAN. L. REV. 485 (2004).

1. Publication

Until January 1, 1978, when the 1976 Act took effect, American federal copyright protection began not with fixation, but with publication of copies of a qualifying work (or registration of an unpublished work). Moreover, until 1978, state law—often but not always common law—would automatically protect unpublished works upon creation without the need to comply with any formalities. This state law protection would last until publication. Upon publication, the work would forfeit state law protection and be protected, if at all, by federal copyright law.

The doctrine that publication divests common law protection had long ago been established by the U.S. Supreme Court in *Wheaton v. Peters*, 33 U.S. (8 Peters) 591 (1834). (Note that following the implementation of the 1976 Act, which expanded federal copyright protection to cover all fixed works (published and unpublished alike), state protection concomitantly contracted to cover only the unfixed works that do not qualify under the expanded federal regime. From then forward, all fixed works fell exclusively under the federal copyright regime. We study the extent of federal copyright law's preemption of state laws in Chapter X.) For a thorough treatment of copyright protection under state law, see 1 MELVILLE B. NIMMER & DAVID NIMMER, NIMMER ON COPYRIGHT § 2.02 (2022).

Under the 1909 Act, one could secure federal protection upon publication only if one complied with all statutory formalities, discussed in the sections that follow. Act of Mar. 4, 1909, ch. 320, §§ 9-22. The implication is that one's published work would (exit state law protection and) fall into the public domain if one did not comply with all statutory formalities.

On or after January 1, 1978, with the switch to fixation as trigger of federal copyright protection, publication became less relevant to establishing a work's status under copyright law. Nonetheless, it remains occasionally relevant, because some of the 1976 Act's provisions turn on whether a work is published. For example, the deposit provision—discussed in section 4—applies only to published works. 17 U.S.C. §§ 407(a)-(d). As another example, the duration rule governing anonymous and pseudonymous works and works made for hire—discussed in section B.1—is applied in part based on the year of first publication of a work. 17 U.S.C. § 302(c). Additionally, the availability of statutory damages and attorney's fees can turn on when a work was registered in relation to the work's publication. *Id.* § 412.

1909 Act	1976 Act	Post-Berne
Publication a requisite to federal copyright protection	Publication sometimes relevant when a specific copyright provision turns on publication or lack thereof	No change from 1976 Act

Table 1: significance of publication

Understanding what does and does not constitute a "publication" remains crucial for works claiming protection under the 1909 Act. The 1909 Act did not define what constitutes a publication. (The only statutory clue to the meaning of "publication" lies in § 26 of the 1909 Act, which stated that the date of publication for a work "of which copies are reproduced for sale or distribution ... shall be held to be the earliest date when copies of the first authorized edition were *placed on sale, sold, or publicly distributed* by the proprietor of the copyright or under his authority." (emphasis added)) Beyond that fragment, which provides only the most general guidance, courts considering when publication takes place under the 1909 Act have had to craft their own rules.

What does and does not constitute a publication is also sometimes relevant for works claiming protection under the 1976 Act. Unlike the 1909 Act, the 1976 Act defines "publication." According to § 101, "publication" is

> the distribution of copies or phonorecords of a work to the public by sale or other transfer of ownership, or by rental, lease, or lending. The offering to distribute copies or phonorecords to a group of persons for purposes of further distribution, public performance, or public display, constitutes publication. A public performance or display of a work does not of itself constitute publication.

As you read the following case construing the 1909 Act, consider how much the court's explication of "publication" matches your intuitive understanding of what a publication is. Which of the policies underlying copyright law is a requirement of publication designed to serve? Should it matter whether Martin Luther King, Jr.'s speech was extemporaneous or planned?

Estate of Martin Luther King, Jr., Inc. v. CBS, Inc.
194 F.3d 1211 (11th Cir. 1999)

ANDERSON, C.J.:

[1] The Estate of Martin Luther King, Jr., Inc. brought this copyright infringement action against CBS, Inc. after CBS produced a video documentary that used, without authorization, portions of civil rights leader Dr. Martin Luther King's famous "I Have a Dream" speech at the March on Washington on August 28, 1963. The

district court granted summary judgment to CBS on the ground that Dr. King had engaged in a general publication of the speech, placing it into the public domain. We now reverse....

[2] The facts underlying this case form part of our national heritage and are well-known to many Americans. On the afternoon of August 28, 1963, the Southern Christian Leadership Conference held the March on Washington to promote the growing civil rights movement. The events of the day were seen and heard by some 200,000 people gathered at the March, and were broadcast live via radio and television to a nationwide audience of millions of viewers. The highlight of the March was a rousing speech that Dr. Martin Luther King, Jr., the SCLC's founder and president, gave in front of the Lincoln Memorial. The Speech contained the famous utterance, "I have a dream ...," which became symbolic of the civil rights movement. The SCLC had sought out wide press coverage of the March and the Speech, and these efforts were successful; the Speech was reported in daily newspapers across the country, was broadcast live on radio and television, and was extensively covered on television and radio subsequent to the live broadcast.

[3] On September 30, 1963, approximately one month after the delivery of the Speech, Dr. King took steps to secure federal copyright protection for the Speech under the Copyright Act of 1909, and a certificate of registration of his claim to copyright was issued by the Copyright Office on October 2, 1963. Almost immediately thereafter, Dr. King filed suit in the Southern District of New York to enjoin the unauthorized sale of recordings of the Speech and won a preliminary injunction on December 13, 1963.

[4] For the next twenty years, Dr. King and the Estate enjoyed copyright protection in the Speech and licensed it for a variety of uses, and renewed the copyright when necessary. In 1994, CBS entered into a contract with the Arts & Entertainment Network to produce a historical documentary series entitled "The 20th Century with Mike Wallace." One segment was devoted to "Martin Luther King, Jr. and The March on Washington." That episode contained material filmed by CBS during the March and extensive footage of the Speech (amounting to about 60% of its total content). CBS, however, did not seek the Estate's permission to use the Speech in this manner and refused to pay royalties to the Estate. The instant litigation ensued.

[5] On summary judgment, the district court framed the issue as "whether the public delivery of Dr. King's speech ... constituted a general publication of the speech so as to place it in the public domain." After discussing the relevant case law, the district court held that Dr. King's "performance coupled with such wide and unlimited reproduction and dissemination as occurred concomitant to Dr. King's speech during the March on Washington can be seen only as a general publication which thrust the speech into the public domain." Thus, the district court granted CBS's motion for summary judgment. The Estate now appeals to this Court....

[6] Because of the dates of the critical events, the determinative issues in this case are properly analyzed under the Copyright Act of 1909, rather than the Copyright Act of 1976 that is currently in effect. The question is whether Dr. King's attempt to obtain statutory copyright protection on September 30, 1963 was effective, or whether it was a nullity because the Speech had already been forfeited to the public domain via a general publication.

[7] Under the regime created by the 1909 Act, an author received state common law protection automatically at the time of creation of a work. This state common law protection persisted until the moment of a general publication.[3] When a general publication occurred, the author either forfeited his work to the public domain, or, if he had therebefore complied with federal statutory requirements, converted his common law copyright into a federal statutory copyright.

---

[3] We stress that in this area of the law the word "publication" is a legal word of art, denoting a process much more esoteric than is suggested by the lay definition of the term.

[8] In order to soften the hardship of the rule that publication destroys common law rights, courts developed a distinction between a "general publication" and a "limited publication." Only a general publication divested a common law copyright. A general publication occurred when a work was made available to members of the public at large without regard to their identity or what they intended to do with the work. Conversely, a non-divesting limited publication was one that communicated the contents of a work to a select group and for a limited purpose, and without the right of diffusion, reproduction, distribution or sale. The issue before us is whether Dr. King's delivery of the Speech was a general publication.

[9] Numerous cases stand for the proposition that the performance of a work is not a general publication.

[10] It appears from the case law that a general publication occurs only in two situations. First, a general publication occurs if tangible copies of the work are distributed to the general public in such a manner as allows the public to exercise dominion and control over the work. Second, a general publication may occur if the work is exhibited or displayed in such a manner as to permit unrestricted copying by the general public. However, the case law indicates that restrictions on copying may be implied, and that express limitations in that regard are deemed unnecessary.

[11] The case law indicates that distribution to the news media, as opposed to the general public, for the purpose of enabling the reporting of a contemporary newsworthy event, is only a limited publication. For example, in *Public Affairs Assoc., Inc. v. Rickover*, 284 F.2d 262 (D.C. Cir. 1960), the court said that general publication occurs only when there is "a studied effort not only to secure publicity for the contents of the addresses through the channels of information, but to *go beyond customary sources of press or broadcasting* in distributing the addresses to any interested individual." (emphasis added) Although the *Rickover* court ultimately held that a general publication had occurred, it contrasted the "limited use of the addresses by the press for fair comment," i.e., limited publication, with "the unlimited distribution to anyone who was interested," i.e., general publication. This rule comports with common sense; it does not force an author whose message happens to be newsworthy to choose between obtaining news coverage for his work and preserving his common-law copyright....

[12] With the above principles in mind, in the summary judgment posture of this case and on the current state of this record, we are unable to conclude that CBS has demonstrated beyond any genuine issue of material fact that Dr. King, simply through his oral delivery of the Speech, engaged in a general publication making the Speech available to members of the public at large without regard to their identity or what they intended to do with the work. A performance, no matter how broad the audience, is not a publication; to hold otherwise would be to upset a long line of precedent. This conclusion is not altered by the fact that the Speech was broadcast live to a broad radio and television audience and was the subject of extensive contemporaneous news coverage. We follow the above cited case law indicating that release to the news media for contemporary coverage of a newsworthy event is only a limited publication.[4] ...

---

[4] We emphasize the summary judgment posture of this case, which necessitates that we disregard evidence that may be important or even dispositive at trial. In other words, in this summary judgment posture, we consider only the evidence with respect to which there is no genuine issue of material fact. This evidence includes only the fact of the oral delivery of the Speech to a large audience and the fact that the sponsors of the event including Dr. King sought and successfully obtained live broadcasts on radio and television and extensive contemporary coverage in the news media. In this regard, we do not consider at this stage of the litigation two potentially important pieces of evidence brought to our attention by CBS. First, an advance text of the Speech was apparently available in a press tent on the day of the speech. According to an eyewitness affidavit submitted by CBS, members of the public at large—not merely the press—were permitted access to the press tent and were given copies of the advance text. However, the Estate has proffered affidavits which contradict the statements of the CBS witness, and suggest that access was controlled by the SCLC within reasonable means. Moreover, the Estate argues that much of the content of the Speech was generated extemporaneously by Dr. King and

[13] The district court held that "the circumstances in this case take the work in question outside the parameters of the 'performance is not a publication' doctrine." These circumstances included "the overwhelmingly public nature of the speech and the fervent intentions of the March organizers to draw press attention." Certainly, the Speech was one of a kind—a unique event in history. However, the features that make the Speech unique—e.g., the huge audience and the Speech's significance in terms of newsworthiness and history—are features that, according to the case law, are not significant in the general versus limited publication analysis. With respect to the huge audience, the case law indicates that the general publication issue depends, not on the number of people involved, but rather on the fact that the work is made available to the public without regard to who they are or what they propose to do with it....

[14] With respect to the significance of the Speech in terms of newsworthiness and history, the case law again suggests that this feature should not play a substantial role in the analysis. As noted above, the D.C. Circuit in *Rickover* indicated that the wide press distribution of the speeches at issue there would not alone have constituted a general publication....

[15] The district court cited *Letter Edged in Black Press, Inc. v. Public Bldg. Comm'n of Chicago,* 320 F. Supp. 1303 (N.D. Ill. 1970), CBS's best case, in support of its reasoning .... In *Letter Edged in Black,* the question was whether the city had dedicated a Picasso sculpture (located in front of the Chicago Civic Center) to the public domain by general publication....

[16] The district court likened the instant case to *Letter Edged in Black* on the ground that there was a lack of restriction on copying and free allowance of reproduction by the press. However, we do not believe the analogy fits—at least not at this summary judgment stage. Significantly, in *Letter Edged in Black* there were manifestations of the city's intent to distribute generally among the public at large that have no parallels in the evidence we can consider in the instant summary judgment posture. The city gave photographs of the sculpture to the public, not merely the press, upon request. The city commercially sold a postcard featuring the sculpture. Copying was apparently widespread at an exhibit of the sculpture, and the city took no action to curtail copying and photographing by the public. At trial, CBS may well produce evidence that brings the instant case on all fours with *Letter Edged in Black,*[6] but the present state of the record does not support the analogy ....

[17] Because there exist genuine issues of material fact as to whether a general publication occurred, we must reverse the district court's grant of summary judgment for CBS.... Of course, we express no opinion on the eventual merits of this litigation. The judgment of the district court is reversed and remanded for further proceedings not inconsistent with this opinion.

---

was not contained in this advance text—an argument that we do not consider but that can be explored by the district court. Finding genuine issues of material fact with respect to the availability of the advance text to the general public, the district court disregarded CBS's allegations in this regard. We agree, and do likewise.

Second, CBS has produced a September 1963 issue of the SCLC's newsletter in which the text of the Speech was reprinted in its entirety, with no copyright notice. The newsletter was widely circulated to the general public. Indeed, at oral argument, the Estate conceded that this reprinting of the Speech and wide distribution of the newsletter would constitute a general publication, if it were authorized by Dr. King. However, the Estate has raised the issue that Dr. King did not authorize this reprinting and distribution of the Speech. Finding genuine issues of fact in this regard, the district court disregarded this evidence. We agree, and do likewise....

[6] For example, if the SCLC's reprinting of the text of the Speech in the September 1963 newsletter was authorized, *see supra* note 4, that reprinting might be analogous to the public distribution of photographs in *Letter Edged in Black.* Similarly, if CBS were to adduce evidence that Dr. King or his agents offered copies of the Speech indiscriminately to any member of the public who requested them, e.g., through the availability of the advance text in the press tent, that would make the facts of the instant case closer to those of *Letter Edged in Black.*

COOK, J., concurring in part and dissenting in part: ...

[18] ... I would hold that no publication, general or limited, occurred because Dr. King's delivery of his "I Have A Dream" speech was a mere performance of that work, and performance simply cannot constitute a publication regardless of (1) the size of the audience involved, or (2) efforts to obtain widespread contemporary news coverage under circumstances that may have allowed the copying of the work. It is my belief that this analysis (1) differs significantly from one which is premised on a limited publication theory, and (2) also avoids the legal fiction of declaring that Dr. King's "I Have A Dream" speech, as a limited publication, was communicated to a select group for a narrow purpose, a holding that has been generally criticized by commentators....

NOTES

1. Noted copyright scholar Benjamin Kaplan bemoaned courts' definitions of publication under the 1909 Act: "The concept of publication has been seriously distorted and now bedevils much of the law of copyright." Benjamin Kaplan, *Publication in Copyright Law: The Question of Phonograph Records*, 103 U. PA. L. REV. 469, 488-89 (1955). One reason that courts' definitions under the 1909 Act were confusing is that courts often sought explicitly to minimize forfeiture of federal copyright. The more readily that an act qualified as publication, the more easily authors could inadvertently lose both their federal rights, by not complying with the requisite formalities, and their state rights by having published the work. Courts sought to prevent such forfeitures by creating the categories of general publication and limited publication. Only a general publication would divest a state law copyright. By contrast, a limited publication would not. Scholars generally understand some of courts' more strained understandings of general and limited publication as courts seeking to avoid forfeiture of copyright. *E.g.*, Jane C. Ginsburg, *The U.S. Experience with Mandatory Copyright Formalities: A Love/Hate Relationship*, 33 COLUM. J.L. & ARTS 311, 322-23 (2010). For an empirical study of judicial decisions on publication, see Deborah R. Gerhardt, *Copyright Publication: An Empirical Study*, 87 NOTRE DAME L. REV. 135 (2011).

2. A second reason that courts' definitions of publication might be confusing is because technologies of dissemination have changed so substantially over time. American copyright law first made publication a key moment in a world of dissemination of works via print, when it was more straightforward to understand what counted as a publication. However, with the advent of non-print forms of dissemination, such as movie theater showings, television broadcasts, and internet websites, it became harder to understand what constitutes a publication. The *King* case demonstrates this growing difficulty with its conclusion that a speech broadcast on television to millions of people does not constitute a general publication.

The legislative history leading up to the 1976 Act emphasizes the outdatedness of the concept of publication as one reason to move away from requiring it as a condition of federal copyright protection. H.R. REP. No. 1476, 94th Cong., 2d Sess. 47, at 129-30 (1976) ("'Publication,' perhaps the most important single concept under the present law, also represents its most serious defect. Although at one time, when works were disseminated almost exclusively through printed copies, 'publication' could serve as a practical dividing line between common law and statutory protection, this is no longer true.").

3. Why did copyright law include a publication requirement in the first place? One reason is that publication tended to correlate with economic exploitation of a work. Another is that publication is a moment that deposit with the Copyright Office (discussed below in section 4) becomes easy. Do copyright's underlying policies coincide with one or both of these explanations? Do these explanations support or undermine a decision to exclude performances of a work from a definition of publication? For more on the rationales for excluding performances from the definition of publication, see 1 NIMMER ON COPYRIGHT § 4.08.

2. Copyright Notice

All U.S. copyright statutes from the first American copyright statute in 1790 through 1976 have included a notice requirement. The legislative history leading up to the 1976 Act listed four purposes of copyright notice:

1. It has the effect of placing in the public domain a substantial body of published material that no one is interested in copyrighting;
2. It informs the public as to whether a particular work is copyrighted;
3. It identifies the copyright owner; and
4. It shows the date of publication.

H.R. REP. NO. 1476, 94th Cong., 2d Sess. 47, at 143 (1976). Weighed against these benefits is the possibility of inadvertent forfeiture of copyright protection should one neglect to include copyright notice. *Id.* As you review the rules for copyright notice under the 1909 Act, the 1976 Act, and following U.S. accession to the Berne Convention, consider how well the rules strike a balance between these various interests.

The 1909 Act required, as a condition of copyright protection, that proper copyright notice be affixed to copies of a work upon publication. 17 U.S.C. §§ 9, 18-20 (1909). To be valid, the notice had to contain (1) the word "Copyright," the abbreviation "Copr.," or the © symbol; (2) the name of the copyright owner; and (3) for printed literary, musical, and dramatic works, the date of first publication. *Id.* § 18. Notice had to appear in a precise location toward the beginning of books, periodicals, and musical works. *Id.* § 19. For other works like motion pictures, the location of the required notice was not prescribed. Coventry Ware, Inc. v. Reliance Frame Co., 288 F.2d 193, 194-95 (2d Cir. 1961). Works lacking valid notice upon publication moved into the public domain.

The 1976 Act principally carried forward the 1909 Act's requirements as to the content of copyright notice, except that the date of first publication became required for all works. 17 U.S.C. § 401(b) (1976). The new law prospectively gave more flexibility as to where notice could be placed by requiring it to "be affixed to ... copies in such manner and location as to give reasonable notice of the claim of copyright." *Id.* § 401(c) (1976). It also continued to require notice upon publication as a condition of copyright protection. *Id.* §§ 401-402 (1976). That said, the Act diminished the consequences of not affixing proper notice: instead of injecting those works into the public domain, the law gave an opportunity to cure defective notice through "a reasonable effort ... made to add notice to all copies ... that are distributed to the public in the United States after the omission has been discovered" and registration within five years after publication without notice. *Id.* § 405(a)(2) (1976).

Because the Berne Convention bars formalities as a condition of copyright protection, Congress changed the rules on notice when the United States acceded to the Berne Convention. Berne Convention Implementation Act of 1988, Pub. L. No. 100-568, § 7. It left the provisions of the 1976 Act governing notice principally intact but prospectively made complying with these provisions optional. 17 U.S.C. § 401(a) ("Whenever a work protected under this title is published in the United States or elsewhere by authority of the copyright owner, a notice of copyright as provided by this section *may* be placed on publicly distributed copies from which the work can be visually perceived, either directly or with the aid of a machine or device." (emphasis added)). As an incentive to provide this optional notice, Congress added that if the copyright owner complies with the notice rules, "no weight shall be given to ... a defendant's interposition of a defense based on innocent infringement in mitigation of actual or statutory damages" with limited exception. *Id.* § 401(d). (We discuss this defense in Chapter VIII. Variations on this defense had been available as well under the 1909 and 1976 Acts for innocent infringers of works that had omitted notice but were excused for doing so.)

1909 Act	1976 Act	Post-Berne
Proper notice required to maintain copyright protection	Proper notice required to maintain copyright protection, but 5-year opportunity to cure inadequate notice	Provision of notice optional, though notice eliminates an innocent infringer defense
Proper notice requires (1) ©, Copr., or Copyright; (2) name of copyright owner; (3) (for some works) date of first publication	Same as 1909 Act, but date of first publication required for all works	No change from 1976 Act
Proper notice must be in a specific location for books, periodicals	Notice must be in a manner and location that gives reasonable notice	No change from 1976 Act

Table 2: notice rules

There are some specialized notice rules for certain types of works. For example, since the 1976 Act, the notice requirement is satisfied for each contribution to a collective work if the collective work as a whole has a single compliant notice. 17 U.S.C. § 404(a).

NOTES

1. The evolution of copyright law's notice rules might seem like minor tweaks to formalities. Arguably, however, the law's changes to notice rules effectuate a much bigger systemic shift: they are key to switching copyright from an opt-in system—in which a work's owner had to act deliberately by affixing notice and registering (as discussed in the next section)—to an opt-out system—in which copyright protection is provided to all copyrightable works whether or not the work's owner desires copyright protection. For an argument that this switch to an opt-out system has been harmful to copyright's goals and that the United States might move back to an opt-in system without running afoul of its Berne Convention obligations, see James Gibson, *Once and Future Copyright*, 81 NOTRE DAME L. REV. 167 (2005); Christopher Jon Sprigman, *Reform(alizing) Copyright*, 57 STAN. L. REV. 485 (2004).

2. Given that works lacking copyright notice can no longer be presumed to be in the public domain, copying such works without a thorough investigation can be dangerous. For some works, known as **orphan works**, their owner cannot be found even after a reasonably diligent search. There have been proposals, thus far unsuccessful, to amend copyright law to allow for the use of orphan works. The issue of orphan works became particularly acute in the context of the Google Book Search project, in which Google scanned books so they could be searched and viewed in part online. (We review litigation regarding this project in Chapter VI.) Many of the books that Google wanted to scan—often out of print and obscure—were orphan works. Omitting these books from the project would diminish the utility of Google's book search software. For an exploration of orphan works, proposed legislation, and the Google Book Search project, see James Grimmelmann, *The Elephantine Google Books Settlement*, 58 J. COPYRIGHT SOC'Y U.S.A. 497 (2011); Pamela Samuelson, *The Google Book Settlement as Copyright Reform*, 2011 WISC. L. REV. 479.

3. Although copyright notice can be helpful for putting the public on notice of copyright interests, what is to stop a publisher from putting a copyright notice on a work that is in the public domain (because it is either uncopyrightable or its copyright has already expired)? The Copyright Act contains no legal disincentive, such

as a fine, for false claims of ownership of public domain materials. For an argument that copyright law should penalize this "copyfraud," particularly because it discourages the public from freely using materials in the public domain, see Jason Mazzone, *Copyfraud*, 81 N.Y.U. L. REV. 1026 (2006). As Mazzone describes it, "[f]alse copyright notices appear on modern reprints of Shakespeare's plays, Beethoven's piano scores, greeting card versions of Monet's Water Lilies, and even the U.S. Constitution. Archives claim blanket copyright in everything in their collections. Vendors of microfilmed versions of historical newspapers assert copyright ownership."

4. Fixation itself might be seen as providing notice that copyright might exist in the fixed work. For an exploration of how well fixation serves the notice functions that copyright can provide, see Lydia Pallas Loren, *Fixation as Notice in Copyright Law*, 96 B.U. L. REV. 939 (2016).

3. Registration

The value of registration has been to provide for third parties a written record of copyright ownership in a work. Over the course of American copyright history, as with the other formalities, registration has moved from being required to increasingly optional.

Under the 1909 Act, registration was optional until the last year of the first copyright term (then twenty-eight years, as discussed below in section B). If registration would occur within that period, the copyright owner would be entitled to a renewal term of an additional twenty-eight years. If not, the work would fall into the public domain upon the end of the first term. Act of Mar. 4, 1909, ch. 320, §§ 23-24. The Copyright Renewal Act of 1992 made the renewal term automatic for all works published from 1964 through 1977, thereby removing the requirement that the renewal term was contingent on registration before the renewal period for these works. Pub. L. 102–307, 106 Stat. 264. Nonetheless, the 1992 law instituted incentives to register copyright before the renewal period, including broader rights over derivative works in the renewal term. 17 U.S.C. § 304(a)(4)(A).

The 1909 Act also made registration of a work a prerequisite to maintaining an infringement action. Act of Mar. 4, 1909, ch. 320, § 12. Under the 1976 Act, copyright registration remained prerequisite to an infringement suit with little exception. 17 U.S.C. § 411(a) (1976).

The 1976 Act also provided incentives to register copyright. For one thing, a copyright owner could recover statutory damages and attorney's fees for infringement of a work only if the owner registered copyright in the work before the infringement began (or within a grace period). *Id.* § 412 (1976). By contrast, under the 1909 Act, a copyright owner could recover statutory damages or attorney's fees without having registered the work before infringement began. A second incentive to register copyright in a work is that the registration provides *prima facie* validity of the copyright so long as registration happens within five years of the work's first publication. *Id.* § 410(c) (1976). Although the 1909 Act had the same evidentiary advantage, it was indifferent to how soon the registration was filed. Act of Mar. 4, 1909, ch. 320, § 55.

Following U.S. accession to the Berne Convention, the 1976 Act's registration rules and incentives principally remain in place with one major exception. Registration is still prerequisite to an infringement lawsuit, but only for "any United States work" made after March 1, 1989. 17 U.S.C. § 411(a). Foreign works made after this time are exempt from registration before an infringement suit over them.

The Copyright Office examines registration applications to ensure that a work at issue is copyrightable and otherwise complies with copyright law. *Id.* § 410(a). If the Office determines that the work has complied with copyright's requirements, it will register copyright in the work and issue a certificate of registration. *Id.*

Otherwise, it will refuse registration. *Id.* § 410(b). That said, if copyrightability is uncertain, the Copyright Office will register the work under a "Rule of Doubt" and rely on subsequent litigation to sort out any problems. COMPENDIUM OF U.S. COPYRIGHT OFFICE PRACTICES § 607.

If registration is denied, the applicant may seek judicial review of the denial in the U.S. District Court for the District of Columbia. 5 U.S.C. §§ 701-706. Alternatively, the applicant can still commence an action for infringement but must serve upon the Register of Copyrights notice of the action with a copy of the complaint. 17 U.S.C. § 411(a). The Register is authorized, but not required, to "become a party to the action with respect to the issue of registrability of the copyright claim by entering an appearance within sixty days after such service, but the Register's failure to become a party shall not deprive the court of jurisdiction to determine that issue." *Id.*

1909 Act	1976 Act	Post-Berne
Registration optional until last year of first copyright term (and only mandatory for renewal of works first published before 1964)	Registration optional, but provides *prima facie* evidence of validity and permits possible recovery of statutory damages and attorney's fees	No change from 1976 Act
Registration a prerequisite to lawsuit	Registration a prerequisite to lawsuit	Registration a prerequisite to lawsuit only for U.S. works

Table 3: registration rules

NOTES

1. Does the 1988 change to registration rules comply with the Berne Convention requirement that copyright not be subject to formalities? Why this change? As David Nimmer explains in his treatise, "although United States citizens were somewhat disadvantaged by Congress's action, at least no non-U.S. Berne claimants could contend that the United States was setting up impermissible formal roadblocks to the protection of their copyrights." 1 NIMMER ON COPYRIGHT § 7.16.

2. How do copyright law's registration rules align with copyright's goals? In evaluating the fit, consider what must be done to register a work: deposit the work (as discussed in the next section), complete an application requiring principally procedural details about the work—such as the copyright owner's name, the work's title, the publication year if published, the year in which the work was completed, and the category of copyrightable subject matter—and pay a fee. 17 U.S.C. §§ 408-409; 37 C.F.R. § 202.3.

Note also that to secure a copyright registration, the applicant is not asked to say anything about the work's content. Does this help or undermine copyright's policy goals? For more on this issue, see Jeanne C. Fromer, *Claiming Intellectual Property*, 76 U. CHI. L. REV. 719 (2009); Jeanne C. Fromer & Mark P. McKenna, *Claiming Design*, 167 U. PA. L. REV. 123 (2018).

3. There had been a circuit split as to whether the "registration of [a] copyright claim has been made" within the meaning of § 411(a) when the copyright holder delivers the required application, deposit, and fee to the Copyright Office, or only once the Copyright Office acts on that application. This determination affects when a copyright holder can bring an infringement lawsuit. The U.S. Supreme Court recently resolved this split, holding that registration of a copyright claim occurs when the Copyright Office registers a copyright, at which

point a copyright holder can file an infringement suit. *Fourth Estate Pub. Benefit Corp. v. Wall-Street.com, LLC*, 139 S. Ct. 881 (2019).

4. The Supreme Court recently clarified that an applicant's "[l]ack of knowledge of either fact or law can excuse an inaccuracy in a copyright registration," meaning that the registration is valid despite the inaccuracy. *Unicolors, Inc. v. H&M Hennes & Mauritz, LP*, 142 S. Ct. 941, 945 (2022) (construing 17 U.S.C. § 411(b)(1) on the validity of a registration certificate).

5. One consequence of a registration scheme is that scholars can study the demographics of copyright registrations, the range of subject matter being registered, and so forth. A recent study analyzing over fifteen million works registered in the Copyright Office from 1978 through 2012 is Robert Brauneis & Dotan Oliar, *An Empirical Study of the Race, Ethnicity, Gender, and Age of Copyright Registrants*, 86 GEO. WASH. L. REV. 46 (2018). Among other data, they report that over two-thirds of authors in registered works are men, that Black authors register music works at rates significantly higher than those of other races and ethnicities, and that the authors of literary works are on average ten years older than the authors of music works.

4. Deposit

Deposit is closely linked to registration, not only because registration of a work requires its deposit but also because its goal is to provide the Library of Congress—via the Copyright Office—copies of copyrighted works to bolster registration's written record.

The 1909 Act required the prompt deposit of two complete copies of the best published edition of the work with the Copyright Office. Act of Mar. 4, 1909, ch. 320, § 12. Like registration, deposit was also a prerequisite to an infringement suit. *Id.* The Copyright Office could also demand deposit. *Id.* § 13. Failure to comply with such a demand in a timely fashion (three months for U.S. works) resulted in forfeiture of the copyright and a fine. *Id.*

The 1976 Act principally carried forward the 1909 Act requirements, 17 U.S.C. §§ 407, 408, 411(a) (1976), with an important exception. Failure to comply with a Copyright Office demand for deposit within three months of the demand no longer resulted in copyright forfeiture but only in a civil fine. *Id.* § 407(d) (1976).

Following U.S. accession to the Berne Convention, deposit is a prerequisite to an infringement lawsuit only for U.S. works. *Id.* §§ 408, 411(a).

1909 Act	1976 Act	Post-Berne
Sanctions for failure to comply with demand for deposit, including copyright forfeiture	Fine is only sanction for failure to comply with demand for deposit	No change from 1976 Act
Deposit a prerequisite to lawsuit	Deposit a prerequisite to lawsuit	Deposit a prerequisite to lawsuit only for U.S. works

Table 4: deposit rules

NOTES

1. A study by the Copyright Office emphasizes another principal purpose of deposit: "it has materially assisted the Library [of Congress] in building its collections on all aspects of American history, literature, law, music, and social culture." ELIZABETH K. DUNNE, DEPOSIT OF COPYRIGHTED WORKS, COPYRIGHT OFFICE STUDY NO. 20, at 30 (Comm. Print 1960). For a further argument that there should be a digital deposit requirement, see Peter S. Menell, *Knowledge Accessibility and Preservation Policy for the Digital Age*, 44 HOUS. L. REV. 1013 (2007).

2. The deposit requirements for a copyrighted work are different for software than for other works. Rather than require deposit of the entire work, as is usually the case when registering copyright in the work, the Copyright Office permits a copyright applicant to submit only small portions of the program and keep the rest secret. In particular, an applicant can satisfy the deposit requirement by submitting "[t]he first and last 25 pages or equivalent units of the source code." 37 C.F.R. § 202.20(c)(2)(vii)(A)(1). If the applicant is also claiming the source code as a trade secret, the applicant can satisfy the deposit requirement by submitting even less code. *Id.* § 202.20(c)(2)(vii)(A)(2). Additionally, the Copyright Office will register copyright in a software program even if only the object code—and not the source code—is provided, but it will register the copyright only under a rule of doubt because it has not examined the source code. *Id.* § 202.20(c)(2)(vii)(B). Is it acceptable to treat computer software differently than other categories of copyrightable subject matter in terms of how much needs to be disclosed to register copyright? For more on this issue, see Pamela Samuelson, *CONTU Revisited: The Case Against Copyright Protection for Computer Programs in Machine-Readable Form*, 1984 DUKE L.J. 663, 715-16.

3. How plausible is it to comply with the deposit requirement for the latest technologies? Consider webpages, online databases, and social media.

5. Other Formalities

This section addresses two other formalities, recordation of transfer and domestic manufacture.

a. Recordation of Transfer

The Copyright Office provides rules on recordation of transfer. According to § 205(a), "[a]ny transfer of copyright ownership or other document pertaining to a copyright may be recorded in the Copyright Office." The Register of Copyrights will record the document, upon receipt with a fee, and return it with a certificate of recordation. Id. § 205(b). So long as the document specifically identifies the work and the work has been registered, the recordation serves as "constructive notice of the facts stated in the recorded document." *Id.* § 205(c). An unrecorded transfer is void against a subsequent bona fide purchaser for value who records first. *Id.* § 205(d).

1909 Act	1976 Act	Post-Berne
Unrecorded transfer void against a subsequent bona fide purchaser for value	No change from 1909 Act	No change from 1909 Act
Recordation not prerequisite to lawsuit	Recordation a prerequisite to lawsuit	Recordation not prerequisite to lawsuit

Table 5: recordation of transfer rules

Under the 1976 Act, recordation of transfer was made a prerequisite to an infringement suit by someone claiming to be copyright owner by virtue of the transfer. 17 U.S.C. § 205(d) (1976). Congress eliminated this requirement when the United States acceded to the Berne Convention. Berne Convention Implementation Act of 1988, Pub. L. No. 100-568, § 5.

b. Domestic Manufacture

The 1909 Act provided that to be protected by copyright, any printed book or periodical in the English language and any printed book or periodical of domestic origin in any language had to be printed within the United States, according to specified requirements regarding type set and the like. Act of Mar. 4, 1909, ch. 320, § 15. The law also provided exemptions for certain categories of works, like those in raised characters for the blind. *Id.* This requirement developed out of earlier prohibitions on copyright protection for foreign authors. For an exploration of the nationalist policies underlying this requirement and other aspects of copyright history, see Graeme W. Austin, *Does the Copyright Clause Mandate Isolationism?*, 26 COLUM. J.L. & ARTS 17 (2002).

Courts tended to read the Act's requirement of domestic manufacture liberally, lest many works be found to be in violation of the requirement. For example, the federal government urged and convinced one court that a copyright owner complied with the requirement so long as the owner first published the work in a domestic manufactured edition and thereafter published it in another country. Hoffenberg v. Kaminstein, 396 F.2d 684 (D.C. Cir. 1968).

In 1955, the United States ratified the Universal Copyright Convention, which prospectively permitted foreign authors of works first printed abroad in the English language to secure copyright protection without running afoul of the manufacture provision. Universal Copyright Convention art. III.1.

A variation of the domestic manufacture requirement carried forward into the 1976 Act. 17 U.S.C. § 601 (1976). It was set to expire—and did—on July 1, 1986. All works on or after this date have complete copyright protection regardless of the location of manufacture.

6. Restoration

As can be seen from the previous sections, before U.S. accession to the Berne Convention, failure to comply with copyright formalities led to the loss of U.S. copyright protection. Yet Article 18 of the Berne Convention requires retroactive protection of foreign works that lost protection for failing to satisfy the formalities imposed by domestic laws.

In 1994, Congress opted to comply with this aspect of the Berne Convention. It passed a law, codified in § 104A, restoring copyright protection for certain works originating from countries that are members of the Berne Convention or the World Trade Organization on January 1, 1996. Uruguay Round Agreement Act, Pub. L. No. 103-465, 108 Stat. 4809. Section 104A applies to "restored works," which it defines in section (h)(6) as:

> *an original work of authorship that— ...*
>
> *(B) is not in the public domain in its source country through expiration of term of protection; [and]*
>
> *(C) is in the public domain in the United States due to—*

(i) noncompliance with formalities imposed at any time by United States copyright law, including failure of renewal, lack of proper notice, or failure to comply with any manufacturing requirements; ... [or]

(iii) lack of national eligibility.

Copyright protection in such a work was restored as of January 1, 1996 (with some exceptions), *id.* § 104A(a)(1)(A), and "shall subsist for the remainder of the term of copyright that the work would have otherwise been granted in the United States if the work never entered the public domain in the United States." *Id.* § 104A(a)(1)(B).

Pursuant to § 104A, copyright was restored to some very prominent works, including J.R.R. Tolkien's *Lord of the Rings* trilogy, Pablo Picasso's *Guernica*, Fritz Lang's *Metropolis*, the works of M.C. Escher, Sergei Prokofiev's *Peter and the Wolf*, the Pippi Longstocking books, and Alfred Hitchcock's films including *The Man Who Knew Too Much*.

Many third parties had relied on these works being in the public domain and had used them accordingly. Although § 104A grants the full panoply of rights and remedies in restored works for infringing acts occurring on or after the date of restoration, *id.* § 104A(d)(1), it also gave "reliance parties" a period of immunity to wind down their activities that were now infringing, *id.* § 104A(d)(2). Specifically, before suing for infringement, the owner of the restored copyright needs to give notice of intent to enforce the restored copyright. This notice can be constructive, by filing with the Copyright Office within twenty-four months of the date of restoration, "a notice of intent to enforce the restored copyright," *id.* § 104A(d)(2)(A)(i), or actual, by serving a reliance party with that notice of intent, *id.* § 104A(d)(2)(B)(i). Then, the owner of the restored copyright must provide twelve months of immunity following notice. *Id.* § 104A(d)(2).

The constitutionality of § 104A was at issue in the U.S. Supreme Court's decision in *Golan v. Holder*, discussed below in section B.2.

B. Duration

This section addresses the rules and policies of copyright duration. We principally explore the very different frameworks for calculating and evaluating duration under the 1909 Act and the 1976 Act, the latter applying to all works created on or after January 1, 1978, and works fixed but not published before that date.

1. Duration Rules

The precise duration of copyright has changed significantly since the first American copyright law in 1790. That law provided 14 years of protection from the date of a work's publication, which was renewable for an additional 14 years if the author survived the first term. Act of May 31, 1790, ch. 15, 1 Stat. 124. Since then, copyright duration has undergone expansion after expansion.

Fast forward to the 1909 Act. It provides protection for 28 years from the date of first publication, before the end of which the copyright holder could renew the copyright for a further term of 28 years. Act of Mar. 4, 1909, ch. 320, § 23. When the 1976 Act was enacted, it tacked on 19 additional years of protection for works published before 1978, to bring duration for pre-1976 Act works into line with those under the 1976 Act. 17 U.S.C. § 304 (1976). In 1998, the Sonny Bono Term Extension Act added another 20 years of protection for these works. Pub. L. No. 105-298, 112 Stat. 2827.

Adding those numbers together (28 + 28 + 19 + 20), the total possible protection for 1909 Act works is 95 years. This calculation is mostly straightforward, except it is important to keep in mind that works that entered the public domain before the enactment of the 1976 Act did not get the 19 additional years of protection. Nor did works that entered the public domain before the 1998 term extension get its 20 additional years of protection. For example, works published in 1922 could have 75 years of protection and fell into the public domain in 1997, thereby not securing the 20-year extension in 1998.

Additionally, as discussed above with regard to registration (section I.A.3), Congress made all renewals automatic in 1992. Before then, many copyright owners had accidentally lost the renewal term by neglecting to register copyright in time. Congress did not retroactively revive protection for works that had already passed into the public domain due to failure to renew copyright. As of 1992, however, a copyright owner did not need to file for renewal. Therefore, works published before 1964 (28 years before 1992) in which the copyright owner did not renew copyright are not protected. By contrast, works published between 1964 and January 1, 1978—works that entered their renewal period automatically once the 1992 change took effect but before the 1976 Act took effect—were renewed automatically and have 95 years of protection, assuming the copyright owner complied with the requisite formalities.

The 1976 Act made two major changes to calculating duration. First, under the 1976 Act, copyright protection starts at fixation (Chapter II) rather than at publication (section A.1). Second, copyright protection under the 1976 Act lasts for the lifetime of the author plus 50 years, instead of a fixed term. 17 U.S.C. § 302 (1976). As with works under the 1909 Act, the Sonny Bono Term Extension Act in 1998 added another 20 years of protection for works under the 1976 Act, bringing copyright duration to lifetime of the author plus 70 years. Pub. L. No. 105-298, 112 Stat. 2827. As 17 U.S.C. § 302 currently spells out:

> Copyright in a work created on or after January 1, 1978, subsists from its creation and, [with some exceptions], endures for a term consisting of the life of the author and 70 years after the author's death.

These two changes under the 1976 Act to when copyright protection starts and how long it lasts raised complexities for certain categories of works: joint works, works created by a pseudonymous or anonymous author, works made for hire (and thus potentially authored by a business entity rather than an individual), and works that were unpublished as of January 1, 1978. None of these works can be handled straightforwardly by § 302. For joint works, it is unclear which of the multiple authors' lifetimes to use to calculate duration. For works by an anonymous or pseudonymous author, one might not know the author's identity to calculate the author's lifetime. For works made for hire, how does and should one compute the lifetime of a business entity? For works that were created but unpublished before the 1976 Act went into effect, should some older ones whose author died more than 50 years earlier fall immediately into the public domain? Because of these complexities, the 1976 Act created special duration rules for each of these categories of works.

For joint works prepared by two or more authors who did not work for hire, § 302(b) provides that

> the copyright endures for a term consisting of the life of the last surviving author and 70 years after such last surviving author's death.

For anonymous works, pseudonymous works, and works made for hire, § 302(c) provides a different formula to calculate duration:

> the copyright endures for a term of 95 years from the year of its first publication, or a term of 120 years from the year of its creation, whichever expires first.

(Section 302(c) specifies one way in which "publication" is still important under the 1976 Act.)

All works that were unpublished as of January 1, 1978, were—by definition—not protected under the 1909 Act. As discussed above in section A.1, some states provided this category of works an infinite term of protection so long as the works remained unpublished. The 1976 Act removed this category of works from the auspices of state law and brought them within its scope. Section 303 provides that the duration rule for this category of works is generally the same as for other works, as set out in § 302. That said, there was a worry that the rules set out in § 302 are unfair when works by authors that had long ago died were brought into the scope of the 1976 Act and therefore might get no protection (such as if the author had died in 1927, more than 50 years before the effective date of the 1976 Act). Congress addressed this issue in § 303(a) by providing a minimum term of copyright protection for previously unpublished works, which in its current form provides:

> Copyright in a work created before January 1, 1978, but not theretofore in the public domain or copyrighted, subsists from January 1, 1978, and endures for the term provided by section 302. In no case, however, shall the term of copyright in such a work expire before December 31, 2002; and, if the work is published on or before December 31, 2002, the term of copyright shall not expire before December 31, 2047.

That is, for this category of works, the duration is based on the relevant rule in § 302, but if that rule would yield an expiration date before December 31, 2002, the copyright will last until December 31, 2002. Congress also provided an additional incentive to publish works created but unpublished as of January 1, 1978, by granting a potential 45 years of additional protection if the work is published on or before December 31, 2002. For an analysis of the large corpus of works that fell into the public domain on January 1, 2003, as a result of this rule, see R. Anthony Reese, *Public but Private: Copyright's New Unpublished Public Domain*, 85 TEX. L. REV. 585 (2007).

For the most part, the 1976 Act switch that keyed duration to the author's lifetime made copyright notice less important, because (except for a limited number of categories of works, such as works made for hire) one can no longer ascertain duration by looking at the publication year in a copyright notice. The Act appreciates that determination of an author's death date can be harder to determine than a work's publication year. Section 302(e) therefore contains a presumption of an author's death:

> After a period of 95 years from the year of first publication of a work, or a period of 120 years from the year of its creation, whichever expires first, any person who obtains from the Copyright Office a certified report that [its] records ... disclose nothing to indicate that the author of the work is living, or died less than 70 years before, is entitled to the benefits of a presumption that the author has been dead for at least 70 years. Reliance in good faith upon this presumption shall be a complete defense to any action for infringement under this title.

In these cases, a third party can presume, without legal consequence, that a work has fallen into the public domain.

One additional change made by the 1976 Act is set out in § 305, which provides that its copyright terms "run to the end of the calendar year in which they would otherwise expire." (Previously, under the 1909 Act, a copyright term had instead expired based on the actual date of publication, rather than at the end of the calendar year at issue. Act of Mar. 4, 1909, ch. 320, § 23.)

In 2018, Congress granted copyright-like protection to pre-1972 sound recordings, and it created specific duration rules for this category of works: 95 years from the first publication, plus a transition period depending on the year of first publication:

- Until December 31, 2021, for sound recordings first published pre-1923;

- 5 years for recordings first published between 1923 and 1946, for a total of 100 years from first publication;
- 15 years for recordings first published between 1947 and 1956, for a total of 110 years from first publication; and
- Until February 15, 2067, for recordings first published between 1957 and February 15, 1972.

The Orrin G. Hatch-Bob Goodlatte Music Modernization Act, Pub. L. No. 115-264, § 1401(a)(2)(B), 132 Stat. 3676 (2018).

Statutory Category	General Duration Rule
1909 Act	28-year term + 28-year renewal term + 19-year extension + 20-year extension = 95 years
1976 Act – general rule	Lifetime of the author + 70 years
1976 Act – joint works	Lifetime of last surviving author + 70 years
1976 Act – anonymous works, pseudonymous works, & works made for hire	Shorter of 95 years from first publication and 120 years from creation
1976 Act – works created and unpublished before January 1, 1978	If not published before the beginning of 2003, the later of the relevant § 302 rule and December 31, 2002. If published before the beginning of 2003, the later of the relevant § 302 rule and December 31, 2047.
Music Modernization Act – pre-1972 sound recordings	95 years from the first publication, plus a transition period depending on the year of first publication

Table 6: duration rules

NOTE

1. Calculate when copyright expires in the following situations:

   a) On February 10, 1945, Allison completes a novel set in the fashion industry. She publishes the novel on February 10, 1948, complying with the requisite formalities. She does not renew the copyright. She dies on March 1, 2020. When does her copyright expire?

   b) Instead, on February 10, 1968, Allison first publishes her novel. She does not renew the copyright. She dies on March 1, 2020. When does her copyright expire?

   c) Instead, on February 10, 1985, Allison writes a novel set in the fashion industry. She publishes the novel on February 10, 1986. She dies on March 1, 2020. When does her copyright expire?

d) Instead, on February 10, 1985, Allison writes half of a book of poetry. On February 10, 2018, she writes the other half. She publishes the book a month later. She dies on March 1, 2020. When does her copyright expire?

e) Instead, on February 10, 1985, Allison performs five poems she has created as part of an improvisational performance for over 100 people. She dies on March 1, 2020. Shortly thereafter, a fan who attended the performance writes up Allison's five poems from memory and posts them online. When does Allison's copyright expire?

f) Instead, on February 10, 1985, Allison writes a book of poetry and publishes it soon after. On April 1, 1990, Emma releases an album comprising twelve of Allison's poems from the book set to Emma's own music. Allison is interviewed discussing how happy she is that Emma released this album. Emma dies on March 1, 2020. Allison dies on March 1, 2050. When do their copyrights expire?

g) Instead, on February 10, 1985, Allison writes a book of poetry and publishes it soon after. On April 1, 1990, Allison hires Emma to set any twelve of her poems to music at Emma's discretion. On May 1, 1990, Emma releases an album comprising twelve of Allison's poems from the book set to Emma's music. Emma dies on March 1, 2020. Allison dies on March 1, 2050. When do their copyrights expire?

h) Instead, on February 10, 1968, Allison writes a novel, which she is too afraid to publish. Upon her death on March 1, 2020, her husband is instructed in her will to publish the novel. He publishes the novel on April 1, 2021. When does copyright in the novel expire?

2. Duration Policy

With copyright's duration rules set out, it is worthwhile to explore the policies underpinning Congress's duration choices over time as well as the constitutionality of repeated extensions of copyright duration.

First, consider why Congress switched from a duration rule based on a fixed term to one based on an author's lifetime. The legislative history underlying the 1976 Act gives many reasons for this change, including accounting for increased average life expectancies for authors and for the longer commercial life of works. H.R. REP. NO. 1476, 94th Cong., 2d Sess. 47, at 134 (1976).

Congress also observed that a "very large majority of the world's countries have adopted a copyright term of the life of the author and 50 years after the author's death." *Id.* at 135. This disparity had already "provoked consider[able] resentment and some proposals for retaliatory legislation." *Id.* Reciprocal protection through conformity with international practice, Congress thought, would redound to the benefit of American authors. *Id.*

Another reason provided is that it would simplify matters. Before, a person inquiring into whether a work was in the public domain for purposes of, for example, licensing, would need to look at the work's date of registration or publication. But now an author's copyrights would all expire simultaneously, a "definite, determinable event, and it would be the only date that a potential user would have to worry about." *Id.* at 134.

But the change also created additional offsetting complications. As the Copyright Office noted, it would be easier to measure copyright duration with a fixed term commencing with the work's creation or publication. REGISTER OF COPYRIGHTS, 87TH CONG., REPORT OF THE REGISTER OF COPYRIGHTS ON THE GENERAL REVISION OF THE

U.S. COPYRIGHT LAW 48 (Comm. Print 1961). While an author is still alive, one could not definitively compute a copyright's duration with a life-plus-years structure. Even when the author has died, information about the author's date of death might not be readily accessible. *Id.* By contrast, one can measure a fixed copyright duration once one knows when the copyright commenced. *Id.* Additionally, a fixed duration could be employed across the board regardless of the type of copyrighted work, whereas a life-plus-years format would necessitate treating certain works—like anonymous works—differently. *Id.* at 48-49.

When Congress switched from a fixed term to a life-plus-years structure, Congress set out to make the new structure statistically equivalent to the fixed term it was providing for certain categories of works like works made for hire. H.R. REP. NO. 1476, 94th Cong., 2d Sess. 47, at 138 (1976). Therefore, the switch from a fixed term was not principally about extending copyright duration, but about changing the way duration is measured.

Jeanne Fromer suggests that this switch can be understood as an **expressive incentive** to authors to induce the creation of valuable works, not by offering a financial motivation, but by protecting creators' labor and personhood interests and employing rhetoric communicating concern for these interests:

> It is often noted that copyright duration is one of copyright law's most visible components to authors, if not the most visible. One way to provide incentive for people to create, then, is to use a durational structure that is particularly salient to creators. The structure of copyright duration can be seen as doing just that by invoking the author's personhood interests as an incentive. By setting the author's lifetime as the essential variable of copyright protection, copyright law shields works in an author-centered way: for the author's lifetime (and a fixed terms of years following that). The author's lifetime is arguably the duration for which the author's personhood interest in his or her works remains most important, in that the author is associating his or her works with self-concept and building a reputation. Duration with a life-plus-years term is keyed to the author himself or herself, also sending a signal of how important the author is in copyright law. For all of these reasons, copyright's durational structure can serve as an expressive incentive, which can be particularly helpful to advancing copyright's goal of encouraging artistic creations.

> Were copyright law to provide a statistically equivalent duration of a fixed term, it might not offer the same incentive to authors because it would not be offering protection for the author's personhood or signaling any solicitude for it. Keying duration to the work's creation or registration, as was once done, signals the work's importance at the author's expense. The current durational structure, by contrast, assures the author that protection will attach for the author's lifetime (and then some). In fact, Professors Avishalom Tor and Dotan Oliar show, in an experiment, that individuals prefer a life-plus-years term like Congress implemented to a comparable fixed term. Avishalom Tor & Dotan Oliar, Incentive to Create Under a "Lifetime-Plus-Years" Copyright Duration: Lessons from a Behavioral Economic Analysis for *Eldred v. Ashchroft, 36 LOY. L.A. L. REV. 437, 480-81 (2002).*

> [This] understanding also makes sense of how authors seem to get treated differently for copyright duration. When two people create nearly identical works at different points in their lifetimes—one, say, the day before death and the other, say, fifty years before death—they will receive different terms of protection (seventy years in the first example and 120 in the second). When the same author creates two works—one early in life and another later on—copyright protection for both will expire at the same time, meaning different protective terms for each work. These results seem unfair from the narrower vantage point of rewarding equal term lengths to all similarly situated people or works. However, by viewing duration as an expressive

incentive, these differential lengths make sense. If protection of the author's personhood interests is an important goal, awarding a term that takes account of the author's particular circumstances fulfills that goal in a way the equivalent fixed term across the board does not.

Jeanne C. Fromer, *Expressive Incentives in Intellectual Property*, 98 VA. L. REV. 1745, 1801-03 (2012). It should be noted that although the switch to a "life plus" structure for the copyright term can be explained by reference to a theory of expressive incentives, that does not explain Congress's repeated extensions of the copyright term. Just as international harmonization was cited as a key motive for switching to a lifetime-plus-50-year term in the 1976 Act, harmonization with the duration rules of the European Union was cited as a principal basis for adding 20 years of protection to the copyright term in the 1998 term extension act. S. REP. NO. 315, 104th Cong. (1996). This act was also sometimes called "The Mickey Mouse Protection Act," because the Walt Disney Company had been lobbying for this term extension to delay the entry into the public domain of Mickey Mouse, who had first appeared in the *Steamboat Willie* film in 1928. Lawrence Lessig, *Copyright's First Amendment*, 48 UCLA L. REV. 1057, 1065 (2001). Instead of falling into the public domain in 2003, the term extension provided Disney with another 20 years of protection until 2023.

As you read the following case that challenges the constitutionality of the 1998 20-year copyright term extension, consider whether the extension fits well with copyright's purposes and whether any lack of fit ought to affect the law's constitutionality. Is the Supreme Court granting appropriate deference to Congress? What are the key disagreements between Justice Ginsburg's majority opinion and Justice Breyer's dissenting opinion? Are copyright protections and the First Amendment in tension?

Eric Eldred v. John D. Ashcroft
537 U.S. 186 (2003)

GINSBURG, J.:

[1] This case concerns the authority the Constitution assigns to Congress to prescribe the duration of copyrights. The Copyright and Patent Clause of the Constitution, Art. I, § 8, cl. 8, provides as to copyrights: "Congress shall have Power ... [t]o promote the Progress of Science ... by securing [to Authors] for limited Times ... the exclusive Right to their ... Writings." In 1998, in the measure here under inspection, Congress enlarged the duration of copyrights by 20 years. Copyright Term Extension Act (CTEA), Pub. L. 105–298, §§ 102(b) and (d), 112 Stat. 2827–28 (amending 17 U.S.C. §§ 302, 304). As in the case of prior extensions, principally in 1831, 1909, and 1976, Congress provided for application of the enlarged terms to existing and future copyrights alike.

[2] Petitioners are individuals and businesses whose products or services build on copyrighted works that have gone into the public domain. They seek a determination that the CTEA fails constitutional review under both the Copyright Clause's "limited Times" prescription and the First Amendment's free speech guarantee. Under the 1976 Copyright Act, copyright protection generally lasted from the work's creation until 50 years after the author's death. Under the CTEA, most copyrights now run from creation until 70 years after the author's death. Petitioners do not challenge the "life-plus-70-years" timespan itself. "Whether 50 years is enough, or 70 years too much," they acknowledge, "is not a judgment meet for this Court." Congress went awry, petitioners maintain, not with respect to newly created works, but in enlarging the term for published works with existing copyrights. The "limited Tim[e]" in effect when a copyright is secured, petitioners urge, becomes the constitutional boundary, a clear line beyond the power of Congress to extend. As to the First Amendment,

petitioners contend that the CTEA is a content-neutral regulation of speech that fails inspection under the heightened judicial scrutiny appropriate for such regulations.

[3] In accord with the District Court and the Court of Appeals, we reject petitioners' challenges to the CTEA. In that 1998 legislation, as in all previous copyright term extensions, Congress placed existing and future copyrights in parity. In prescribing that alignment, we hold, Congress acted within its authority and did not transgress constitutional limitations....

[4] We evaluate petitioners' challenge to the constitutionality of the CTEA against the backdrop of Congress' previous exercises of its authority under the Copyright Clause. The Nation's first copyright statute, enacted in 1790, provided a federal copyright term of 14 years from the date of publication, renewable for an additional 14 years if the author survived the first term. The 1790 Act's renewable 14-year term applied to existing works (*i.e.*, works already published and works created but not yet published) and future works alike. Congress expanded the federal copyright term to 42 years in 1831 (28 years from publication, renewable for an additional 14 years), and to 56 years in 1909 (28 years from publication, renewable for an additional 28 years). Both times, Congress applied the new copyright term to existing and future works; to qualify for the 1831 extension, an existing work had to be in its initial copyright term at the time the Act became effective.

[5] In 1976, Congress altered the method for computing federal copyright terms. For works created by identified natural persons, the 1976 Act provided that federal copyright protection would run from the work's creation, not—as in the 1790, 1831, and 1909 Acts—its publication; protection would last until 50 years after the author's death. In these respects, the 1976 Act aligned United States copyright terms with the then-dominant international standard adopted under the Berne Convention for the Protection of Literary and Artistic Works. For anonymous works, pseudonymous works, and works made for hire, the 1976 Act provided a term of 75 years from publication or 100 years from creation, whichever expired first.

[6] These new copyright terms, the 1976 Act instructed, governed all works not published by its effective date of January 1, 1978, regardless of when the works were created. For published works with existing copyrights as of that date, the 1976 Act granted a copyright term of 75 years from the date of publication, a 19–year increase over the 56–year term applicable under the 1909 Act.

[7] The measure at issue here, the CTEA, installed the fourth major duration extension of federal copyrights. Retaining the general structure of the 1976 Act, the CTEA enlarges the terms of all existing and future copyrights by 20 years. For works created by identified natural persons, the term now lasts from creation until 70 years after the author's death. This standard harmonizes the baseline United States copyright term with the term adopted by the European Union in 1993. For anonymous works, pseudonymous works, and works made for hire, the term is 95 years from publication or 120 years from creation, whichever expires first.

[8] Paralleling the 1976 Act, the CTEA applies these new terms to all works not published by January 1, 1978. For works published before 1978 with existing copyrights as of the CTEA's effective date, the CTEA extends the term to 95 years from publication. Thus, in common with the 1831, 1909, and 1976 Acts, the CTEA's new terms apply to both future and existing copyrights.[3] ...

[9] Petitioners' suit challenges the CTEA's constitutionality under both the Copyright Clause and the First Amendment. On cross-motions for judgment on the pleadings, the District Court entered judgment for the

---

[3] Petitioners argue that the 1790 Act must be distinguished from the later Acts on the ground that it covered existing *works* but did not extend existing *copyrights*. The parties disagree on the question whether the 1790 Act's copyright term should be regarded in part as compensation for the loss of any then existing state- or common-law copyright protections. Without resolving that dispute, we underscore that the First Congress clearly did confer copyright protection on works that had already been created.

Attorney General .... The court held that the CTEA does not violate the "limited Times" restriction of the Copyright Clause because the CTEA's terms, though longer than the 1976 Act's terms, are still limited, not perpetual, and therefore fit within Congress' discretion. The court also held that "there are no First Amendment rights to use the copyrighted works of others."

[10] The Court of Appeals for the District of Columbia Circuit affirmed.... Copyright, the court reasoned, does not impermissibly restrict free speech, for it grants the author an exclusive right only to the specific form of expression; it does not shield any idea or fact contained in the copyrighted work, and it allows for "fair use" even of the expression itself.

[11] A majority of the Court of Appeals also upheld the CTEA against petitioners' contention that the measure exceeds Congress' power under the Copyright Clause. Specifically, the court rejected petitioners' plea for interpretation of the "limited Times" prescription not discretely but with a view to the "preambular statement of purpose" contained in the Copyright Clause: "To promote the Progress of Science." ...

[12] Judge Sentelle dissented in part. He concluded that Congress lacks power under the Copyright Clause to expand the copyright terms of existing works.

[13] We granted certiorari to address two questions: whether the CTEA's extension of existing copyrights exceeds Congress' power under the Copyright Clause; and whether the CTEA's extension of existing and future copyrights violates the First Amendment. We now answer those two questions in the negative and affirm....

[14] We address first the determination of the courts below that Congress has authority under the Copyright Clause to extend the terms of existing copyrights. Text, history, and precedent, we conclude, confirm that the Copyright Clause empowers Congress to prescribe "limited Times" for copyright protection and to secure the same level and duration of protection for all copyright holders, present and future.

[15] The CTEA's baseline term of life plus 70 years, petitioners concede, qualifies as a "limited Tim[e]" as applied to future copyrights. Petitioners contend, however, that existing copyrights extended to endure for that same term are not "limited." Petitioners' argument essentially reads into the text of the Copyright Clause the command that a time prescription, once set, becomes forever "fixed" or "inalterable." The word "limited," however, does not convey a meaning so constricted. At the time of the Framing, that word meant what it means today: "confine[d] within certain bounds," "restrain[ed]," or "circumscribe[d]." S. JOHNSON, A DICTIONARY OF THE ENGLISH LANGUAGE (7th ed. 1785); see T. SHERIDAN, A COMPLETE DICTIONARY OF THE ENGLISH LANGUAGE (6th ed. 1796) ("confine[d] within certain bounds"); WEBSTER'S THIRD NEW INTERNATIONAL DICTIONARY 1312 (1976) ("confined within limits"; "restricted in extent, number, or duration"). Thus understood, a timespan appropriately "limited" as applied to future copyrights does not automatically cease to be "limited" when applied to existing copyrights. And as we observe [below], there is no cause to suspect that a purpose to evade the "limited Times" prescription prompted Congress to adopt the CTEA.

[16] To comprehend the scope of Congress' power under the Copyright Clause, a page of history is worth a volume of logic. History reveals an unbroken congressional practice of granting to authors of works with existing copyrights the benefit of term extensions so that all under copyright protection will be governed evenhandedly under the same regime.... [The] First Congress accorded the protections of the Nation's first federal copyright statute to existing and future works alike. Since then, Congress has regularly applied duration extensions to both existing and future copyrights.

[17] Satisfied that the CTEA complies with the "limited Times" prescription, we turn now to whether it is a rational exercise of the legislative authority conferred by the Copyright Clause. On that point, we defer substantially to Congress.

[18] The CTEA reflects judgments of a kind Congress typically makes, judgments we cannot dismiss as outside the Legislature's domain. As respondent describes, a key factor in the CTEA's passage was a 1993 European Union directive instructing EU members to establish a copyright term of life plus 70 years. Consistent with the Berne Convention, the EU directed its members to deny this longer term to the works of any non-EU country whose laws did not secure the same extended term. By extending the baseline United States copyright term to life plus 70 years, Congress sought to ensure that American authors would receive the same copyright protection in Europe as their European counterparts. The CTEA may also provide greater incentive for American and other authors to create and disseminate their work in the United States.

[19] In addition to international concerns, Congress passed the CTEA in light of demographic, economic, and technological changes, and rationally credited projections that longer terms would encourage copyright holders to invest in the restoration and public distribution of their works.

[20] In sum, we find that the CTEA is a rational enactment; we are not at liberty to second-guess congressional determinations and policy judgments of this order, however debatable or arguably unwise they may be. Accordingly, we cannot conclude that the CTEA—which continues the unbroken congressional practice of treating future and existing copyrights in parity for term extension purposes—is an impermissible exercise of Congress' power under the Copyright Clause....

[21] Petitioners' Copyright Clause arguments rely on several novel readings of the Clause. We next address these arguments and explain why we find them unpersuasive....

[22] Petitioners contend that even if the CTEA's 20-year term extension is literally a "limited Tim[e]," permitting Congress to extend existing copyrights allows it to evade the "limited Times" constraint by creating effectively perpetual copyrights through repeated extensions. We disagree.

[23] As the Court of Appeals observed, a regime of perpetual copyrights "clearly is not the situation before us." Nothing before this Court warrants construction of the CTEA's 20-year term extension as a congressional attempt to evade or override the "limited Times" constraint. Critically, we again emphasize, petitioners fail to show how the CTEA crosses a constitutionally significant threshold with respect to "limited Times" that the 1831, 1909, and 1976 Acts did not. Those earlier Acts did not create perpetual copyrights, and neither does the CTEA....

[24] Petitioners dominantly advance a series of arguments all premised on the proposition that Congress may not extend an existing copyright absent new consideration from the author. They pursue this main theme under three headings. Petitioners contend that the CTEA's extension of existing copyrights (1) overlooks the requirement of "originality," (2) fails to "promote the Progress of Science," and (3) ignores copyright's *quid pro quo*.

[25] Petitioners' "originality" argument draws on *Feist Publications, Inc. v. Rural Telephone Service Co.*, 499 U.S. 340 (1991). In *Feist*, we observed that "[t]he *sine qua non* of copyright is originality," and held that copyright protection is unavailable to "a narrow category of works in which the creative spark is utterly lacking or so trivial as to be virtually nonexistent." Relying on *Feist*, petitioners urge that even if a work is sufficiently "original" to qualify for copyright protection in the first instance, any extension of the copyright's duration is impermissible because, once published, a work is no longer original.

[26] *Feist*, however, did not touch on the duration of copyright protection. Rather, the decision addressed the core question of copyrightability, *i.e.*, the "creative spark" a work must have to be eligible for copyright protection at all. Explaining the originality requirement, *Feist* trained on the Copyright Clause words "Authors" and "Writings. The decision did not construe the "limited Times" for which a work may be protected, and the originality requirement has no bearing on that prescription.

[27] More forcibly, petitioners contend that the CTEA's extension of existing copyrights does not "promote the Progress of Science" as contemplated by the preambular language of the Copyright Clause. To sustain this objection, petitioners do not argue that the Clause's preamble is an independently enforceable limit on Congress's power. Rather, they maintain that the preambular language identifies the sole end to which Congress may legislate; accordingly, they conclude, the meaning of "limited Times" must be "determined in light of that specified end." The CTEA's extension of existing copyrights categorically fails to "promote the Progress of Science," petitioners argue, because it does not stimulate the creation of new works but merely adds value to works already created.

[28] As petitioners point out, we have described the Copyright Clause as both a grant of power and a limitation, and have said that "[t]he primary objective of copyright" is "[t]o promote the Progress of Science," *Feist*, 499 U.S., at 349. The constitutional command, we have recognized, is that Congress, to the extent it enacts copyright laws at all, create a system that promotes the Progress of Science.[18]

[29] We have also stressed, however, that it is generally for Congress, not the courts, to decide how best to pursue the Copyright Clause's objectives. The justifications we earlier set out for Congress' enactment of the CTEA provide a rational basis for the conclusion that the CTEA "promote[s] the Progress of Science." ...

[30] Closely related to petitioners' preambular argument, or a variant of it, is their assertion that the Copyright Clause "imbeds a quid pro quo." They contend, in this regard, that Congress may grant to an "Autho[r]" an "exclusive Right" for a "limited Tim[e]," but only in exchange for a "Writin[g]." Congress' power to confer copyright protection, petitioners argue, is thus contingent upon an exchange: The author of an original work receives an "exclusive Right" for a "limited Tim[e]" in exchange for a dedication to the public thereafter. Extending an existing copyright without demanding additional consideration, petitioners maintain, bestows an unpaid-for benefit on copyright holders and their heirs, in violation of the *quid pro quo* requirement.

[31] We can demur to petitioners' description of the Copyright Clause as a grant of legislative authority empowering Congress to secure a bargain—this for that. But the legislative evolution earlier recalled demonstrates what the bargain entails. Given the consistent placement of existing copyright holders in parity with future holders, the author of a work created in the last 170 years would reasonably comprehend, as the "this" offered her, a copyright not only for the time in place when protection is gained, but also for any renewal or extension legislated during that time. Congress could rationally seek to "promote ... Progress" by including in every copyright statute an express guarantee that authors would receive the benefit of any later legislative extension of the copyright term....

[32] For the several reasons stated, we find no Copyright Clause impediment to the CTEA's extension of existing copyrights....

---

[18] Justice STEVENS' characterization of reward to the author {in an omitted dissent} as "a secondary consideration" of copyright law, understates the relationship between such rewards and the "Progress of Science." As we have explained, "[t]he economic philosophy behind the [Copyright] [C]lause ... is the conviction that encouragement of individual effort by personal gain is the best way to advance public welfare through the talents of authors and inventors." Mazer v. Stein, 347 U.S. 201, 219 (1954). Accordingly, copyright law *celebrates* the profit motive, recognizing that the incentive to profit from the exploitation of copyrights will redound to the public benefit by resulting in the proliferation of knowledge. The profit motive is the engine that ensures the progress of science. Rewarding authors for their creative labor and "promot[ing] ... Progress" are thus complementary; as James Madison observed, in copyright "[t]he public good fully coincides ... with the claims of individuals." Justice BREYER's assertion that "copyright statutes must serve public, not private, ends" similarly misses the mark. The two ends are not mutually exclusive; copyright law serves public ends by providing individuals with an incentive to pursue private ones.

[33] Petitioners separately argue that the CTEA is a content-neutral regulation of speech that fails heightened judicial review under the First Amendment. We reject petitioners' plea for imposition of uncommonly strict scrutiny on a copyright scheme that incorporates its own speech-protective purposes and safeguards. The Copyright Clause and First Amendment were adopted close in time. This proximity indicates that, in the Framers' view, copyright's limited monopolies are compatible with free speech principles. Indeed, copyright's purpose is to *promote* the creation and publication of free expression....

[34] In addition to spurring the creation and publication of new expression, copyright law contains built-in First Amendment accommodations. First, it distinguishes between ideas and expression and makes only the latter eligible for copyright protection. As we [have] said, this idea/expression dichotomy strikes a definitional balance between the First Amendment and the Copyright Act by permitting free communication of facts while still protecting an author's expression. Due to this distinction, every idea, theory, and fact in a copyrighted work becomes instantly available for public exploitation at the moment of publication.

[35] Second, the "fair use" defense allows the public to use not only facts and ideas contained in a copyrighted work, but also expression itself in certain circumstances. Codified at 17 U.S.C. § 107, the defense provides: "[T]he fair use of a copyrighted work, including such use by reproduction in copies ..., for purposes such as criticism, comment, news reporting, teaching (including multiple copies for classroom use), scholarship, or research, is not an infringement of copyright." The fair use defense affords considerable latitude for scholarship and comment and even for parody....

[36] The CTEA .... protects authors' original expression from unrestricted exploitation. Protection of that order does not raise the free speech concerns present when the government compels or burdens the communication of particular facts or ideas. The First Amendment securely protects the freedom to make—or decline to make—one's own speech; it bears less heavily when speakers assert the right to make other people's speeches. To the extent such assertions raise First Amendment concerns, copyright's built-in free speech safeguards are generally adequate to address them. We recognize that the D.C. Circuit spoke too broadly when it declared copyrights "categorically immune from challenges under the First Amendment." But when, as in this case, Congress has not altered the traditional contours of copyright protection, further First Amendment scrutiny is unnecessary....

[37] As we read the Framers' instruction, the Copyright Clause empowers Congress to determine the intellectual property regimes that, overall, in that body's judgment, will serve the ends of the Clause. Beneath the facade of their inventive constitutional interpretation, petitioners forcefully urge that Congress pursued very bad policy in prescribing the CTEA's long terms. The wisdom of Congress' action, however, is not within our province to second-guess. Satisfied that the legislation before us remains inside the domain the Constitution assigns to the First Branch, we affirm the judgment of the Court of Appeals.

It is so ordered.

STEVENS, J.: dissenting. ...

BREYER, J.: dissenting.

[38] The Constitution's Copyright Clause grants Congress the power to "*promote* the *Progress* of Science ... by securing for *limited* Times to *Authors* ... the exclusive Right to their respective Writings." Art. I, § 8, cl. 8 (emphasis added). The statute before us, the 1998 Sonny Bono Copyright Term Extension Act, extends the term of most existing copyrights to 95 years and that of many new copyrights to 70 years after the author's death. The economic effect of this 20-year extension—the longest blanket extension since the Nation's founding—is to make the copyright term not limited, but virtually perpetual. Its primary legal effect is to grant the extended term not to authors, but to their heirs, estates, or corporate successors. And most importantly,

its practical effect is not to promote, but to inhibit, the progress of "Science"—by which word the Framers meant learning or knowledge.

[39] The majority believes these conclusions rest upon practical judgments that at most suggest the statute is unwise, not that it is unconstitutional. Legal distinctions, however, are often matters of degree. And in this case the failings of degree are so serious that they amount to failings of constitutional kind. Although the Copyright Clause grants broad legislative power to Congress, that grant has limits. And in my view this statute falls outside them....

[40] The "monopoly privileges" that the Copyright Clause confers are neither unlimited nor primarily designed to provide a special private benefit. This Court has made clear that the Clause's limitations are judicially enforceable. And, in assessing this statute for that purpose, I would take into account the fact that the Constitution is a single document, that it contains both a Copyright Clause and a First Amendment, and that the two are related.

[41] The Copyright Clause and the First Amendment seek related objectives—the creation and dissemination of information. When working in tandem, these provisions mutually reinforce each other, the first serving as an engine of free expression, the second assuring that government throws up no obstacle to its dissemination. At the same time, a particular statute that exceeds proper Copyright Clause bounds may set Clause and Amendment at cross-purposes, thereby depriving the public of the speech-related benefits that the Founders, through both, have promised.

[42] Consequently, I would review plausible claims that a copyright statute seriously, and unjustifiably, restricts the dissemination of speech somewhat more carefully than reference to this Court's traditional Copyright Clause jurisprudence might suggest. There is no need in this case to characterize that review as a search for congruence and proportionality, or as some other variation of what this Court has called intermediate scrutiny. Rather, it is necessary only to recognize that this statute involves not pure economic regulation, but regulation of expression, and what may count as rational where economic regulation is at issue is not necessarily rational where we focus on expression—in a Nation constitutionally dedicated to the free dissemination of speech, information, learning, and culture. In this sense only, and where line-drawing among constitutional interests is at issue, I would look harder than does the majority at the statute's rationality— though less hard than precedent might justify.

[43] Thus, I would find that the statute lacks the constitutionally necessary rational support (1) if the significant benefits that it bestows are private, not public; (2) if it threatens seriously to undermine the expressive values that the Copyright Clause embodies; and (3) if it cannot find justification in any significant Clause-related objective. Where, after examination of the statute, it becomes difficult, if not impossible, even to dispute these characterizations, Congress' choice is clearly wrong....

[44] This statute, like virtually every copyright statute, imposes upon the public certain expression-related costs in the form of (1) royalties that may be higher than necessary to evoke creation of the relevant work, and (2) a requirement that one seeking to reproduce a copyrighted work must obtain the copyright holder's permission. The first of these costs translates into higher prices that will potentially restrict a work's dissemination. The second means search costs that themselves may prevent reproduction even where the author has no objection. Although these costs are, in a sense, inevitable concomitants of copyright protection, there are special reasons for thinking them especially serious here.

[45] First, the present statute primarily benefits the holders of existing copyrights, i.e., copyrights on works already created. And a Congressional Research Service (CRS) study prepared for Congress indicates that the added royalty-related sum that the law will transfer to existing copyright holders is large. In conjunction with

official figures on copyright renewals, the CRS Report indicates that only about 2% of copyrights between 55 and 75 years old retain commercial value—*i.e.*, still generate royalties after that time. But books, songs, and movies of that vintage still earn about $400 million per year in royalties. Hence, (despite declining consumer interest in any given work over time) one might conservatively estimate that 20 extra years of copyright protection will mean the transfer of several billion extra royalty dollars to holders of existing copyrights— copyrights that, together, already will have earned many billions of dollars in royalty "reward."

[46] The extra royalty payments will not come from thin air. Rather, they ultimately come from those who wish to read or see or hear those classic books or films or recordings that have survived....

[47] A second, equally important, cause for concern arises out of the fact that copyright extension imposes a "permissions" requirement—not only upon potential users of "classic" works that still retain commercial value, but also upon potential users of *any other work* still in copyright....

[48] The ... permissions requirement can inhibit or prevent the use of old works (particularly those without commercial value): (1) because it may prove expensive to track down or to contract with the copyright holder, (2) because the holder may prove impossible to find, or (3) because the holder when found may deny permission either outright or through misinformed efforts to bargain....

[49] ... [T]o some extent costs of this kind accompany any copyright law, regardless of the length of the copyright term. But to extend that term, preventing works from the 1920's and 1930's from falling into the public domain, will dramatically increase the size of the costs just as—perversely—the likely benefits from protection diminish. The older the work, the less likely it retains commercial value, and the harder it will likely prove to find the current copyright holder....

[50] The majority ... invokes the "fair use" exception, and it notes that copyright law itself is restricted to protection of a work's expression, not its substantive content. Neither the exception nor the restriction, however, would necessarily help those who wish to obtain from electronic databases material that is not there—say, teachers wishing their students to see albums of Depression Era photographs, to read the recorded words of those who actually lived under slavery, or to contrast, say, Gary Cooper's heroic portrayal of Sergeant York with filmed reality from the battlefield of Verdun. Such harm, and more will occur despite the 1998 Act's exemptions and despite the other "First Amendment safeguards" in which the majority places its trust....

[51] What copyright-related benefits might justify the statute's extension of copyright protection? First, no one could reasonably conclude that copyright's traditional economic rationale applies here. The extension will not act as an economic spur encouraging authors to create new works. No potential author can reasonably believe that he has more than a tiny chance of writing a classic that will survive commercially long enough for the copyright extension to matter. After all, if, after 55 to 75 years, only 2% of all copyrights retain commercial value, the percentage surviving after 75 years or more (a typical pre-extension copyright term)—must be far smaller.... Using assumptions about the time value of money provided us by a group of economists (including five Nobel prize winners), it seems fair to say that, for example, a 1% likelihood of earning $100 annually for 20 years, starting *75 years into the future*, is worth less than seven cents today.

[52] What potential Shakespeare, Wharton, or Hemingway would be moved by such a sum? What monetarily motivated Melville would not realize that he could do better for his grandchildren by putting a few dollars into an interest-bearing bank account? The Court itself finds no evidence to the contrary....

[53] I am not certain why the Court considers it relevant in this respect that "[n]othing ... warrants construction of the [1998 Act's] 20-year term extension as a congressional attempt to evade or override the 'limited Times' constraint." Of course Congress did not intend to act unconstitutionally. But it may have

sought to test the Constitution's limits. After all, the statute was named after a Member of Congress, who, the legislative history records, "wanted the term of copyright protection to last forever." 144 Cong. Rec. H9952 (daily ed. Oct. 7, 1998) (statement of Rep. Mary Bono)....

[54] In any event, the incentive-related numbers are far too small for Congress to have concluded rationally, even with respect to new works, that the extension's economic-incentive effect could justify the serious expression-related harms earlier described. And, of course, in respect to works already created—the source of many of the harms previously described—*the statute creates no economic incentive at all.*

[55] Second, the Court relies heavily for justification upon international uniformity of terms. Although it can be helpful to look to international norms and legal experience in understanding American law, in this case the justification based upon foreign rules is surprisingly weak. Those who claim that significant copyright-related benefits flow from greater international uniformity of terms point to the fact that the nations of the European Union have adopted a system of copyright terms uniform among themselves. And the extension before this Court implements a term of life plus 70 years that appears to conform with the European standard. But how does "uniformity" help to justify this statute?

[56] Despite appearances, the statute does *not* create a uniform American–European term with respect to the lion's share of the economically significant works that it affects—*all* works made "for hire" and *all* existing works created prior to 1978. With respect to those works the American statute produces an extended term of 95 years while comparable European rights in "for hire" works last for periods that vary from 50 years to 70 years to life plus 70 years. Neither does the statute create uniformity with respect to anonymous or pseudonymous works.

[57] The statute does produce uniformity with respect to copyrights in new, post-1977 works attributed to natural persons. But these works constitute only a subset (likely a minority) of works that retain commercial value after 75 years. And the fact that uniformity comes so late, if at all, means that bringing American law into conformity with this particular aspect of European law will neither encourage creation nor benefit the long-dead author in any other important way....

[58] In sum, the partial, future uniformity that the 1998 Act promises cannot reasonably be said to justify extension of the copyright term for new works. And concerns with uniformity cannot possibly justify the extension of the new term to older works, for the statute there creates no uniformity at all.

[59] ... [S]everal publishers and filmmakers argue that the statute provides incentives to *those who act as publishers* to republish and to redistribute older copyrighted works. This claim cannot justify this statute, however, because the rationale is inconsistent with the basic purpose of the Copyright Clause—as understood by the Framers and by this Court. The Clause assumes an initial grant of monopoly, designed primarily to encourage creation, followed by termination of the monopoly grant in order to promote dissemination of already-created works. It assumes that it is the *disappearance* of the monopoly grant, not its *perpetuation*, that will, on balance, promote the dissemination of works already in existence....

[60] ... [T]he statute's legislative history suggests another possible justification. That history refers frequently to the financial assistance the statute will bring the entertainment industry, particularly through the promotion of exports. I recognize that Congress has sometimes found that suppression of competition will help Americans sell abroad—though it has simultaneously taken care to protect American buyers from higher domestic prices. In doing so, however, Congress has exercised its commerce, not its copyright, power. I can find nothing in the Copyright Clause that would authorize Congress to enhance the copyright grant's monopoly power, likely leading to higher prices both at home and abroad, *solely* in order to produce higher foreign earnings. That objective is not a *copyright* objective. Nor, standing alone, is it related to any other

objective more closely tied to the Clause itself. Neither can higher corporate profits alone justify the grant's enhancement. The Clause seeks public, not private, benefits.

[61] Finally, the Court mentions as possible justifications "demographic, economic, and technological changes"—by which the Court apparently means the facts that today people communicate with the help of modern technology, live longer, and have children at a later age. The first fact seems to argue not for, but instead against, extension. The second fact seems already corrected for by the 1976 Act's life-plus-50 term, which automatically grows with lifespans. And the third fact—that adults are having children later in life—is a makeweight at best, providing no explanation of why the 1976 Act's term of 50 years after an author's death— a longer term than was available to authors themselves for most of our Nation's history—is an insufficient potential bequest. The weakness of these final rationales simply underscores the conclusion that emerges from consideration of earlier attempts at justification: There is no legitimate, serious copyright-related justification for this statute....

[62] The Court is concerned that our holding in this case not inhibit the broad decisionmaking leeway that the Copyright Clause grants Congress. It is concerned about the implications of today's decision for the Copyright Act of 1976—an Act that changed copyright's basic term from 56 years (assuming renewal) to life of the author plus 50 years. It is concerned about having to determine just how many years of copyright is too many—a determination that it fears would require it to find the "right" constitutional number, a task for which the Court is not well suited.

[63] I share the Court's initial concern, about intrusion upon the decisionmaking authority of Congress. But I do not believe it intrudes upon that authority to find the statute unconstitutional on the basis of (1) a legal analysis of the Copyright Clause's objectives; (2) the total implausibility of any incentive effect; and (3) the statute's apparent failure to provide significant international uniformity. Nor does it intrude upon congressional authority to consider rationality in light of the expressive values underlying the Copyright Clause, related as it is to the First Amendment, and given the constitutional importance of correctly drawing the relevant Clause/Amendment boundary. We cannot avoid the need to examine the statute carefully by saying that "Congress has not altered the traditional contours of copyright protection," for the sentence points to the question, rather than the answer. Nor should we avoid that examination here. That degree of judicial vigilance—at the far outer boundaries of the Clause—is warranted if we are to avoid the monopolies and consequent restrictions of expression that the Clause, read consistently with the First Amendment, seeks to preclude....

[64] Neither do I share the Court's aversion to line-drawing in this case. Even if it is difficult to draw a single clear bright line, the Court could easily decide (as I would decide) that this particular statute simply goes too far. And such examples—of what goes too far—sometimes offer better constitutional guidance than more absolute-sounding rules....

[65] This statute will cause serious expression-related harm. It will likely restrict traditional dissemination of copyrighted works. It will likely inhibit new forms of dissemination through the use of new technology. It threatens to interfere with efforts to preserve our Nation's historical and cultural heritage and efforts to use that heritage, say, to educate our Nation's children. It is easy to understand how the statute might benefit the private financial interests of corporations or heirs who own existing copyrights. But I cannot find any constitutionally legitimate, copyright-related way in which the statute will benefit the public. Indeed, in respect to existing works, the serious public harm and the virtually nonexistent public benefit could not be more clear.

[66] I have set forth the analysis upon which I rest these judgments. This analysis leads inexorably to the conclusion that the statute cannot be understood rationally to advance a constitutionally legitimate interest.

The statute falls outside the scope of legislative power that the Copyright Clause, read in light of the First Amendment, grants to Congress. I would hold the statute unconstitutional.

[67] I respectfully dissent....

NOTES

1. Given that Congress did not again extend the copyright term, the works that were due to fall into the public domain in 1999 fell into the public domain in 2019. Without a copyright term extension, are there any things that copyright owners can do for near-expiring works to garner continuing protection? Are there things they should be forbidden from doing? For an exploration of these issues, see Joseph P. Liu, *The New Public Domain*, 2013 U. ILL. L. REV. 1395.

2. Taking Congress's 1998 copyright term extension as a starting point, Richard Posner and William Landes propose indefinitely renewable copyrights (the possibility of an infinite number of finite term extensions). Richard A. Posner & William M. Landes, *Indefinitely Renewable Copyright*, 70 U. CHI. L. REV. 471 (2003). Arguing from an economic vantage point, they maintain that copyrights are unlikely to be renewed infinitely and that having works in the public domain can be economically inefficient. Are you convinced that copyright owners would not renew their copyrights indefinitely under such a system? Is their proposal good or bad copyright policy?

3. In an empirical study of recorded music sales and streaming, Kristelia García and Justin McCrary show that most copyrighted music earns most of its lifetime revenue in the 5-10 years following initial release. Kristelia A. García & Justin McCrary, *A Reconsideration of Copyright's Term*, 71 ALA. L. REV. 351 (2019). Based on their study, they propose that duration rules ought to be "based on the [relatively short] commercial viability of the average work" because "the societal cost of strong copyright protection that goes beyond the point of commercial viability outweighs the benefit to both creators and consumers as the marginal return on this protection decreases sharply." They advocate that in setting duration rules, policymakers ought to focus on the average work rather than the atypical work with long-term commercial viability.

The following case challenges the constitutionality of copyright restoration under § 104A. Consider how this challenge differs from *Eldred*. Should those differences matter as a constitutional matter?

Lawrence Golan v. Eric H. Holder, Jr.
565 U.S. 302 (2012)

GINSBURG, J.:

[1] The Berne Convention for the Protection of Literary and Artistic Works, which took effect in 1886, is the principal accord governing international copyright relations. Latecomer to the international copyright regime launched by Berne, the United States joined the Convention in 1989. To perfect U.S. implementation of Berne, and as part of our response to the Uruguay Round of multilateral trade negotiations, Congress, in 1994, gave works enjoying copyright protection abroad the same full term of protection available to U.S. works. Congress did so in § 514 of the Uruguay Round Agreements Act (URAA), which grants copyright protection to preexisting works of Berne member countries, protected in their country of origin, but lacking

protection in the United States for any of three reasons: The United States did not protect works from the country of origin at the time of publication; the United States did not protect sound recordings fixed before 1972; or the author had failed to comply with U.S. statutory formalities (formalities Congress no longer requires as prerequisites to copyright protection).

[2] The URAA accords no protection to a foreign work after its full copyright term has expired, causing it to fall into the public domain, whether under the laws of the country of origin or of this country. Works encompassed by § 514 are granted the protection they would have enjoyed had the United States maintained copyright relations with the author's country or removed formalities incompatible with Berne. Foreign authors, however, gain no credit for the protection they lacked in years prior to § 514's enactment. They therefore enjoy fewer total years of exclusivity than do their U.S. counterparts. As a consequence of the barriers to U.S. copyright protection prior to the enactment of § 514, foreign works "restored" to protection by the measure had entered the public domain in this country. To cushion the impact of their placement in protected status, Congress included in § 514 ameliorating accommodations for parties who had exploited affected works before the URAA was enacted.

[3] Petitioners include orchestra conductors, musicians, publishers, and others who formerly enjoyed free access to works § 514 removed from the public domain. They maintain that the Constitution's Copyright and Patent Clause, Art. I, § 8, cl. 8, and First Amendment both decree the invalidity of § 514. Under those prescriptions of our highest law, petitioners assert, a work that has entered the public domain, for whatever reason, must forever remain there.

[4] In accord with the judgment of the Tenth Circuit, we conclude that § 514 does not transgress constitutional limitations on Congress' authority. Neither the Copyright and Patent Clause nor the First Amendment, we hold, makes the public domain, in any and all cases, a territory that works may never exit....

[5] Members of the Berne Union agree to treat authors from other member countries as well as they treat their own. Nationals of a member country, as well as any author who publishes in one of Berne's 164 member states, thus enjoy copyright protection in nations across the globe. Each country, moreover, must afford at least the minimum level of protection specified by Berne. The copyright term must span the author's lifetime, plus at least 50 additional years, whether or not the author has complied with a member state's legal formalities. And, as relevant here, a work must be protected abroad unless its copyright term has expired in either the country where protection is claimed or the country of origin.

[6] A different system of transnational copyright protection long prevailed in this country. Until 1891, foreign works were categorically excluded from Copyright Act protection. Throughout most of the 20th century, the only eligible foreign authors were those whose countries granted reciprocal rights to U.S. authors and whose works were printed in the United States. For domestic and foreign authors alike, protection hinged on compliance with notice, registration, and renewal formalities.

[7] The United States became party to Berne's multilateral, formality-free copyright regime in 1989. Initially, Congress adopted a "minimalist approach" to compliance with the Convention. The Berne Convention Implementation Act of 1988 (BCIA), 102 Stat. 2853, made only those changes to American copyright law that [were] clearly required under the treaty's provisions. Despite Berne's instruction that member countries— including "new accessions to the Union"—protect foreign works under copyright in the country of origin, the BCIA accorded no protection for "any work that is in the public domain in the United States." Protection of future foreign works, the BCIA indicated, satisfied Article 18. Congress indicated, however, that it had not definitively rejected "retroactive" protection for preexisting foreign works; instead it had punted on this issue of Berne's implementation, deferring consideration until "a more thorough examination of Constitutional, commercial, and consumer considerations is possible." ...

[8] The landscape changed in 1994. The Uruguay round of multilateral trade negotiations produced the World Trade Organization (WTO) and the Agreement on Trade-Related Aspects of Intellectual Property Rights (TRIPS).... The WTO gave teeth to the Convention's requirements: Noncompliance with a WTO ruling could subject member countries to tariffs or cross-sector retaliation. The specter of WTO enforcement proceedings bolstered the credibility of our trading partners' threats to challenge the United States for inadequate compliance with Article 18....

[9] Congress' response to the Uruguay agreements put to rest any questions concerning U.S. compliance with Article 18. Section 514 of the URAA extended copyright to works that garnered protection in their countries of origin, but had no right to exclusivity in the United States for any of three reasons: lack of copyright relations between the country of origin and the United States at the time of publication; lack of subject-matter protection for sound recordings fixed before 1972; and failure to comply with U.S. statutory formalities (*e.g.*, failure to provide notice of copyright status, or to register and renew a copyright).

[10] Works that have fallen into the public domain after the expiration of a full copyright term—either in the United States or the country of origin—receive no further protection under § 514. Copyrights "restored" under URAA § 514 "subsist for the remainder of the term of copyright that the work would have otherwise been granted ... if the work never entered the public domain." Prospectively, restoration places foreign works on an equal footing with their U.S. counterparts; assuming a foreign and domestic author died the same day, their works will enter the public domain simultaneously. Restored works, however, receive no compensatory time for the period of exclusivity they would have enjoyed before § 514's enactment, had they been protected at the outset in the United States. Their total term, therefore, falls short of that available to similarly situated U.S. works.

[11] The URAA's disturbance of the public domain hardly escaped Congress' attention. Section 514 imposed no liability for any use of foreign works occurring before restoration. In addition, anyone remained free to copy and use restored works for one year following § 514's enactment. Concerns about § 514's compatibility with the Fifth Amendment's Takings Clause led Congress to include additional protections for "reliance parties"—those who had, before the URAA's enactment, used or acquired a foreign work then in the public domain. Reliance parties may continue to exploit a restored work until the owner of the restored copyright gives notice of intent to enforce—either by filing with the U.S. Copyright Office within two years of restoration, or by actually notifying the reliance party. After that, reliance parties may continue to exploit existing copies for a grace period of one year. Finally, anyone who, before the URAA's enactment, created a "derivative work" based on a restored work may indefinitely exploit the derivation upon payment to the copyright holder of "reasonable compensation," to be set by a district judge if the parties cannot agree....

[12] In 2001, petitioners filed this lawsuit challenging § 514. They maintain that Congress, when it passed the URAA, exceeded its authority under the Copyright Clause and transgressed First Amendment limitations. The District Court granted the Attorney General's motion for summary judgment....

[13] The Court of Appeals for the Tenth Circuit affirmed in part. The public domain, it agreed, was not a "threshold that Congress" was powerless to "traverse in both directions." But § 514, as the Court of Appeals read our decision in *Eldred v. Ashcroft*, 537 U.S. 186 (2003), required further First Amendment inspection. The measure "'altered the traditional contours of copyright protection,'" the court said—specifically, the "bedrock principle" that once works enter the public domain, they do not leave. The case was remanded with an instruction to the District Court to address the First Amendment claim in light of the Tenth Circuit's opinion.

[14] On remand, the District Court's starting premise was uncontested: Section 514 does not regulate speech on the basis of its content; therefore the law would be upheld if "narrowly tailored to serve a significant government interest." Summary judgment was due petitioners, the court concluded, because § 514's

constriction of the public domain was not justified by any of the asserted federal interests: compliance with Berne, securing greater protection for U.S. authors abroad, or remediation of the inequitable treatment suffered by foreign authors whose works lacked protection in the United States.

[15] The Tenth Circuit reversed. Deferring to Congress' predictive judgments in matters relating to foreign affairs, the appellate court held that § 514 survived First Amendment scrutiny. Specifically, the court determined that the law was narrowly tailored to fit the important government aim of protecting U.S. copyright holders' interests abroad.

[16] We granted certiorari to consider petitioners' challenge to § 514 under both the Copyright Clause and the First Amendment, and now affirm....

[17] We first address petitioners' argument that Congress lacked authority, under the Copyright Clause, to enact § 514. The Constitution states that "Congress shall have Power ... [t]o promote the Progress of Science ... by securing for limited Times to Authors ... the exclusive Right to their ... Writings." Art. I, § 8, cl. 8. Petitioners find in this grant of authority an impenetrable barrier to the extension of copyright protection to authors whose writings, for whatever reason, are in the public domain. We see no such barrier in the text of the Copyright Clause, historical practice, or our precedents....

[18] The text of the Copyright Clause does not exclude application of copyright protection to works in the public domain. Petitioners' contrary argument relies primarily on the Constitution's confinement of a copyright's lifespan to a "limited Tim[e]." "Removing works from the public domain," they contend, "violates the 'limited [t]imes' restriction by turning a fixed and predictable period into one that can be reset or resurrected at any time, even after it expires."

[19] Our decision in *Eldred* is largely dispositive of petitioners' limited-time argument. There we addressed the question whether Congress violated the Copyright Clause when it extended, by 20 years, the terms of existing copyrights. Ruling that Congress acted within constitutional bounds, we declined to infer from the text of the Copyright Clause "the command that a time prescription, once set, becomes forever 'fixed' or 'inalterable.'" "The word 'limited,'" we observed, "does not convey a meaning so constricted." Rather, the term is best understood to mean "confine[d] within certain bounds," "restrain [ed]," or "circumscribed." The construction petitioners tender closely resembles the definition rejected in *Eldred* and is similarly infirm....

[20] The difference, petitioners say, is that the limited time had already passed for works in the public domain. What was that limited term for foreign works once excluded from U.S. copyright protection? Exactly "zero," petitioners respond. We find scant sense in this argument, for surely a "limited time" of exclusivity must begin before it may end.

[21] Carried to its logical conclusion, petitioners persist, the Government's position would allow Congress to institute a second "limited" term after the first expires, a third after that, and so on. Thus, as long as Congress legislated in installments, perpetual copyright terms would be achievable. As in *Eldred,* the hypothetical legislative misbehavior petitioners posit is far afield from the case before us. In aligning the United States with other nations bound by the Berne Convention, and thereby according equitable treatment to once disfavored foreign authors, Congress can hardly be charged with a design to move stealthily toward a regime of perpetual copyrights....

[22] Petitioners' ultimate argument as to the Copyright and Patent Clause concerns its initial words. Congress is empowered to "promote the Progress of Science and useful Arts" by enacting systems of copyright and patent protection. Perhaps counterintuitively for the contemporary reader, Congress' copyright authority is tied to the progress of science; its patent authority, to the progress of the useful arts.

[23] The "Progress of Science," petitioners acknowledge, refers broadly to "the creation and spread of knowledge and learning." They nevertheless argue that federal legislation cannot serve the Clause's aim unless the legislation "spur[s] the creation of ... new works." Because § 514 deals solely with works already created, petitioners urge, it "provides no plausible incentive to create new works" and is therefore invalid....

[24] The creation of at least one new work, however, is not the sole way Congress may promote knowledge and learning. In *Eldred,* we rejected an argument nearly identical to the one petitioners rehearse. The *Eldred* petitioners urged that the "CTEA's extension of existing copyrights categorically fails to 'promote the Progress of Science,' ... because it does not stimulate the creation of new works." In response to this argument, we held that the Copyright Clause does not demand that each copyright provision, examined discretely, operate to induce new works. Rather, we explained, the Clause "empowers Congress to determine the intellectual property regimes that, overall, in that body's judgment, will serve the ends of the Clause." ...

[25] Considered against this backdrop, § 514 falls comfortably within Congress' authority under the Copyright Clause. Congress rationally could have concluded that adherence to Berne promotes the diffusion of knowledge. A well-functioning international copyright system would likely encourage the dissemination of existing and future works....

[26] .... We have no warrant to reject the rational judgment Congress made....

[27] We next explain why the First Amendment does not inhibit the restoration authorized by § 514....

[28] Petitioners attempt to distinguish their challenge from the one turned away in *Eldred.* First Amendment interests of a higher order are at stake here, petitioners say, because they—unlike their counterparts in *Eldred*—enjoyed "vested rights" in works that had already entered the public domain. The limited rights they retain under copyright law's "built-in safeguards" are, in their view, no substitute for the unlimited use they enjoyed before § 514's enactment. Nor, petitioners urge, does § 514's "unprecedented" foray into the public domain possess the historical pedigree that supported the term extension at issue in *Eldred.*

[29] However spun, these contentions depend on an argument we considered and rejected above, namely, that the Constitution renders the public domain largely untouchable by Congress. Petitioners here attempt to achieve under the banner of the First Amendment what they could not win under the Copyright Clause: On their view of the Copyright Clause, the public domain is inviolable; as they read the First Amendment, the public domain is policed through heightened judicial scrutiny of Congress' means and ends. As we have already shown, the text of the Copyright Clause and the historical record scarcely establish that once a work enters the public domain, Congress cannot permit anyone—not even the creator—to copyright it. And nothing in the historical record, congressional practice, or our own jurisprudence warrants exceptional First Amendment solicitude for copyrighted works that were once in the public domain. Neither this challenge nor that raised in *Eldred,* we stress, allege Congress transgressed a generally applicable First Amendment prohibition; we are not faced, for example, with copyright protection that hinges on the author's viewpoint....

[30] Section 514, we add, does not impose a blanket prohibition on public access. Petitioners protest that fair use and the idea/expression dichotomy "are plainly inadequate to protect the speech and expression rights that Section 514 took from petitioners, or ... the public"—that is, "the unrestricted right to perform, copy, teach and distribute the *entire* work, for any reason." ...

[31] But Congress has not put petitioners in this bind. The question here, as in *Eldred,* is whether would-be users must pay for their desired use of the author's expression, or else limit their exploitation to "fair use" of that work. Prokofiev's *Peter and the Wolf* could once be performed free of charge; after § 514 the right to perform it must be obtained in the marketplace. This is the same marketplace, of course, that exists for the

music of Prokofiev's U.S. contemporaries: works of Copland and Bernstein, for example, that enjoy copyright protection, but nevertheless appear regularly in the programs of U.S. concertgoers....

[32] Congress determined that U.S. interests were best served by our full participation in the dominant system of international copyright protection. Those interests include ensuring exemplary compliance with our international obligations, securing greater protection for U.S. authors abroad, and remedying unequal treatment of foreign authors. The judgment § 514 expresses lies well within the ken of the political branches. It is our obligation, of course, to determine whether the action Congress took, wise or not, encounters any constitutional shoal. For the reasons stated, we are satisfied it does not. The judgment of the Court of Appeals for the Tenth Circuit is therefore

Affirmed.

Justice KAGAN took no part in the consideration or decision of this case.

Justice BREYER, with whom Justice ALITO joins, dissenting.

[33] In order "[t]o promote the Progress of Science" (by which term the Founders meant "learning" or "knowledge"), the Constitution's Copyright Clause grants Congress the power to "secur[e] for limited Times to Authors ... the exclusive Right to their ... Writings." Art. I, § 8, cl. 8. This "exclusive Right" allows its holder to charge a fee to those who wish to use a copyrighted work, and the ability to charge that fee encourages the production of new material. In this sense, a copyright is, in Macaulay's words, a "tax on readers for the purpose of giving a bounty to writers"—a bounty designed to encourage new production. As the Court said in Eldred, "[t]he economic philosophy behind the [Copyright] [C]lause ... is the conviction that encouragement of individual effort by personal gain is the best way to advance public welfare through the talents of authors and inventors."

[34] The statute before us, however, does not encourage anyone to produce a single new work. By definition, it bestows monetary rewards only on owners of old works—works that have already been created and already are in the American public domain. At the same time, the statute inhibits the dissemination of those works, foreign works published abroad after 1923, of which there are many millions, including films, works of art, innumerable photographs, and, of course, books—books that (in the absence of the statute) would assume their rightful places in computer-accessible databases, spreading knowledge throughout the world. In my view, the Copyright Clause does not authorize Congress to enact this statute. And I consequently dissent....

[35] The possibility of eliciting new production is, and always has been, an essential precondition for American copyright protection. The Constitution's words, "exclusive Right," "limited Times," "Progress of Science," viewed through the lens of history underscore the legal significance of what the Court in *Eldred* referred to as the "economic philosophy behind the Copyright Clause." That philosophy understands copyright's grants of limited monopoly privileges to authors as private benefits that are conferred for a public reason—to elicit new creation.

[36] Yet, as the Founders recognized, monopoly is a two-edged sword. On the one hand, it can encourage production of new works. In the absence of copyright protection, anyone might freely copy the products of an author's creative labor, appropriating the benefits without incurring the nonrepeatable costs of creation, thereby deterring authors from exerting themselves in the first place. On the other hand, copyright tends to restrict the dissemination (and use) of works once produced either because the absence of competition translates directly into higher consumer prices or because the need to secure copying permission sometimes imposes administrative costs that make it difficult for potential users of a copyrighted work to find its owner and strike a bargain. Consequently, the original British copyright statute, the Constitution's Framers, and our case law all have recognized copyright's resulting and necessary call for balance.

[37] At the time the Framers wrote the Constitution, they were well aware of Britain's 18th-century copyright statute, the Statute of Anne, 8 Anne, ch. 19 (1710), and they were aware of the legal struggles that produced it. That statute sought in part to control, and to limit, preexisting monopolies that had emerged in the book trade as a result of the Crown's having previously granted special privileges to royal favorites. The Crown, for example, had chartered the Stationers' Company, permitting it to regulate and to censor works on the government's behalf. The Stationers had thereby acquired control over the disposition of copies of published works, from which emerged the Stationers' copyright—a right conferred on company members, not authors, that was deemed to exist in perpetuity.

[38] To prevent the continuation of the booksellers' monopoly and to encourage authors to write new books, Parliament enacted the Statute of Anne. It bore the title: "An Act for the Encouragement of Learning, by vesting the Copies of printed Books in the Authors or Purchasers of such Copies, during the Times therein mentioned." And it granted authors (not publishers) and their assignees the "sole Right and Liberty of printing" their works for limited periods of time *in order to encourage them* "*to compose and write useful Books.*" (emphasis added) As one historian has put it, "[t]he central plank of the ... Act was ... a cultural *quid pro quo*. To encourage 'learned Men to compose and write useful Books' the state would provide a guaranteed, if temporally limited, right to print and reprint those works." Deazley, *The Myth of Copyright at Common Law*, 62 CAMB. L.J. 106, 108 (2003). At first, in their attempts to minimize their losses, the booksellers argued that authors had a perpetual common-law copyright in their works deriving from their natural rights as creators. But the House of Lords ultimately held in *Donaldson v. Beckett,* 1 Eng. Rep. 837 (1774), that the Statute of Anne had transformed any such perpetual common-law copyright into a copyright of a limited term designed to serve the public interest....

[39] The upshot is that text, history, and precedent demonstrate that the Copyright Clause places great value on the power of copyright to elicit new production. Congress in particular cases may determine that copyright's ability to do so outweighs any concomitant high prices, administrative costs, and restrictions on dissemination. And when it does so, we must respect its judgment. But does the Clause empower Congress to enact a statute that withdraws works from the public domain, brings about higher prices and costs, and in doing so seriously restricts dissemination, particularly to those who need it for scholarly, educational, or cultural purposes—all *without providing any additional incentive* for the production of new material? That is the question before us. And, as I have said, I believe the answer is no. Congress in this statute has exceeded what are, under any plausible reading of the Copyright Clause, its permissible limits....

[40] Thus, while the majority correctly observes that the dissemination-restricting harms of copyright normally present problems appropriate for legislation to resolve, the question is whether the Copyright Clause permits Congress seriously to exacerbate such a problem by taking works out of the public domain without a countervailing benefit. This question *is* appropriate for judicial resolution. Indeed, unlike *Eldred* where the Court had to decide a complicated line-drawing question—when is a copyright term too long?— here an easily administrable standard is available—a standard that would require works that have already fallen into the public domain to stay there.

[41] The several, just mentioned features of the present statute are important, for they distinguish it from other copyright laws. By removing material from the public domain, the statute, in literal terms, "abridges" a preexisting freedom to speak....

[42] Taken together, these speech-related harms (*e.g.,* restricting use of previously available material; reversing payment expectations; rewarding rent-seekers at the public's expense) at least show the presence of a First Amendment interest. And that is enough. For present purposes, I need not decide whether the harms to that interest show a violation of the First Amendment. I need only point to the importance of interpreting the Constitution as a single document—a document that we should not read as setting the

Copyright Clause and the First Amendment at cross-purposes. Nor need I advocate the application here of strict or specially heightened review. I need only find that the First Amendment interest is important enough to require courts to scrutinize with some care the reasons claimed to justify the Act in order to determine whether they constitute reasonable copyright-related justifications for the serious harms, including speech-related harms, which the Act seems likely to impose....

[43] The majority makes several other arguments. First, it argues that the Clause does not require the "creation of at least one new work," but may instead "promote the Progress of Science" in other ways. And it specifically mentions the "dissemination of existing and future works" as determinative here.... But ordinarily a copyright—since it is a *monopoly* on copying—*restricts* dissemination of a work once produced compared to a competitive market. And simply making the industry richer does not mean that the industry, when it makes an ordinary *forward-looking* economic calculus, will distribute works not previously distributed....

[44] Moreover, the argument proves too much. It is the kind of argument that the Stationers' Company might well have made and which the British Parliament rejected....

[45] This argument, whatever its intrinsic merits, is an argument that directly concerns a private benefit: how to obtain more money from the sales of existing products. It is not an argument about a public benefit, such as how to promote or to protect the creative process....

[46] ... [T]he majority [also] argues that this statutory provision is necessary to fulfill our Berne Convention obligations. The Treaty, in Article 18, says that the "Convention shall apply to all works which, at the moment of its coming into force [*i.e.,* 1989 in the case of the United States] have not yet fallen into the public domain in the country of origin through the expiry of the term of protection." The majority and Government say that this means we must protect the foreign works at issue here. And since the Berne Convention, taken as a whole, provides incentives for the creation of new works, I am willing to speculate, for argument's sake, that the statute might indirectly encourage production of new works by making the United States' place in the international copyright regime more secure.

[47] Still, I cannot find this argument sufficient to save the statute. For one thing, this is a dilemma of the Government's own making. The United States obtained the benefits of Berne for many years despite its failure to enact a statute implementing Article 18. But in 1994, the United States and other nations signed the Agreement on Trade-Related Aspects of Intellectual Property Rights, which enabled signatories to use World Trade Organization dispute resolution mechanisms to complain about other members' Berne Convention violations. But at that time the Government, although it successfully secured reservations protecting other special features of American copyright law, made no effort to secure a reservation permitting the United States to keep some or all restored works in the American public domain. And it made no effort to do so despite the fact that Article 18 explicitly authorizes countries to negotiate exceptions to the Article's retroactivity principle.

[48] For another thing, the Convention does not require Congress to enact a statute that causes so much damage to public domain material. Article 18(3) also states that "the respective countries shall determine, each in so far as it is concerned, *the conditions of application of this principle.*" Congress could have alleviated many of the costs that the statute imposes by, for example, creating forms of compulsory licensing, requiring "restored copyright" holders to provide necessary administrative information as a condition of protection, or insisting upon "reasonable royalties." ...

[49] The fact that, by withdrawing material from the public domain, the statute inhibits an important preexisting flow of information is sufficient, when combined with the other features of the statute that I have

discussed, to convince me that the Copyright Clause, interpreted in the light of the First Amendment, does not authorize Congress to enact this statute.

[50] I respectfully dissent from the Court's contrary conclusion.

NOTE

1. The *Golan* majority suggests that Congress enacted the URAA, and restored rights in works that had been in the public domain, as part of its effort to comply with the Berne Convention. For an argument that Berne actually provided the United States with substantial latitude to grant a more limited form of protection than Congress granted in § 104A, see Daniel J. Gervais, Golan v. Holder: *A Look at the Constraints Imposed by the Berne Convention*, 64 VAND. L. REV. EN BANC 147 (2011).

C. Renewals

Recall that under the 1909 Act, copyright had to be renewed to get a second 28-year term. While the 1976 Act prospectively created a single copyright term—thus obviating renewal going forward—it retained renewal for works already protected under the 1909 Act. Can you think why Congress retained the renewal structure for 1909 Act works even as it eliminated it for new works?

In addition, for works already under protection, the 1976 Act added 19 years to the renewal term. 17 U.S.C. § 304(a)(3) (1976). Then, the 1998 change added another 20 years to copyright duration for all works. 17 U.S.C. §§ 304(a)(3), (b). Given the total possible copyright term for 1909 Act works, renewals will continue to be relevant until 2072 (95 years after 1977, just before the 1976 Act went into effect).

Congress saw the renewal term as a way to give authors a second bite at the copyright apple. As the legislative history of the 1909 Act explains:

> It not infrequently happens that the author sells his copyright outright to a publisher for a comparatively small sum. If the work proves to be a great success and lives beyond the term of twenty-eight years, ... it should be the exclusive right of the author to take the renewal term, and the law should be framed as is the existing law, so that he could not be deprived of that right.

H.R. REP. NO.2222, 60th Cong., 2d Sess., at 14 (1909). Does it make sense to treat copyright interests differently than other property, for which there is no second bite at the apple?

Under the 1976 Act, § 304(a)(1)(C) sets out who is entitled to rights in the renewal term (aside from special circumstances such as for works made for hire). In its current form, the statute provides:

> In the case of any other copyrighted work, including a contribution by an individual author to a periodical or to a cyclopedic or other composite work—
>
> 1.   the author of such work, if the author is still living,
>
> 2.   the widow, widower, or children of the author, if the author is not living,
>
> 3.   the author's executors, if such author, widow, widower, or children are not living, or

> 4. *the author's next of kin, in the absence of a will of the author,*
>
> *shall be entitled to a renewal and extension of the copyright in such work for a further term of 67 years.*

The section sets out successive classes of people who get the renewal rights, starting with the author if the author is still alive and proceeding through various heirs or executors, if not. The 1909 Act had set out the same successive classes of people entitled to renewal rights. Act of Mar. 4, 1909, ch. 320, § 23.

Two fundamental questions arise with regard to renewals: (1) Should authors and heirs be able to recapture some aspects of the renewal term once it has been assigned? (2) How should the law handle derivative works during the renewal term, when the works were created under an initial grant before the renewal term? The following case addresses both questions. Does the decision strike the right balance between authors and heirs? Does it strike the right balance between initial authors and authors of derivative works? What about the public interest?

James Stewart v. Sheldon Abend
495 U.S. 207 (1990)

O'CONNOR, J.:

[1] The author of a pre-existing work may assign to another the right to use it in a derivative work. In this case the author of a pre-existing work agreed to assign the rights in his renewal copyright term to the owner of a derivative work, but died before the commencement of the renewal period. The question presented is whether the owner of the derivative work infringed the rights of the successor owner of the pre-existing work by continued distribution and publication of the derivative work during the renewal term of the pre-existing work....

[2] Cornell Woolrich authored the story "It Had to Be Murder," which was first published in February 1942 in *Dime Detective Magazine*. The magazine's publisher, Popular Publications, Inc., obtained the rights to magazine publication of the story and Woolrich retained all other rights. Popular Publications obtained a blanket copyright for the issue of *Dime Detective Magazine* in which "It Had to Be Murder" was published.

[3] The Copyright Act of 1909 provided authors a 28-year initial term of copyright protection plus a 28-year renewal term. In 1945, Woolrich agreed to assign the rights to make motion picture versions of six of his stories, including "It Had to Be Murder," to B.G. De Sylva Productions for $9,250. He also agreed to renew the copyrights in the stories at the appropriate time and to assign the same motion picture rights to De Sylva Productions for the 28-year renewal term. In 1953, actor Jimmy Stewart and director Alfred Hitchcock formed a production company, Patron, Inc., which obtained the motion picture rights in "It Had to Be Murder" from De Sylva's successors in interest for $10,000.

[4] In 1954, Patron, Inc., along with Paramount Pictures, produced and distributed "Rear Window," the motion picture version of Woolrich's story "It Had to Be Murder." Woolrich died in 1968 before he could obtain the rights in the renewal term for petitioners as promised and without a surviving spouse or child. He left his property to a trust administered by his executor, Chase Manhattan Bank, for the benefit of Columbia University. On December 29, 1969, Chase Manhattan Bank renewed the copyright in the "It Had to Be

Murder" story .... Chase Manhattan assigned the renewal rights to respondent Abend for $650 plus 10% of all proceeds from exploitation of the story.

[5] "Rear Window" was broadcast on the ABC television network in 1971. Respondent then notified petitioners Hitchcock (now represented by cotrustees of his will), Stewart, and MCA Inc., the owners of the "Rear Window" motion picture and renewal rights in the motion picture, that he owned the renewal rights in the copyright and that their distribution of the motion picture without his permission infringed his copyright in the story. Hitchcock, Stewart, and MCA nonetheless entered into a second license with ABC to rebroadcast the motion picture. In 1974, respondent filed suit against these same petitioners, and others, in the United States District Court for the Southern District of New York, alleging copyright infringement. Respondent dismissed his complaint in return for $25,000.

Figure 45: poster of Alfred Hitchcock's *Rear Window* film

[6] Three years later, the United States Court of Appeals for the Second Circuit decided *Rohauer v. Killiam Shows, Inc.*, 551 F.2d 484 (1977), in which it held that the owner of the copyright in a derivative work may continue to use the existing derivative work according to the original grant from the author of the pre-existing work even if the grant of rights in the pre-existing work lapsed. Several years later, apparently in reliance on *Rohauer*, petitioners re-released the motion picture in a variety of media....

[7] Respondent then brought the instant suit in the United States District Court for the Central District of California against Hitchcock, Stewart, MCA, and Universal Film Exchanges, a subsidiary of MCA and the distributor of the motion picture. Respondent's complaint alleges that the re-release of the motion picture infringes his copyright in the story because petitioners' right to use the story during the renewal term lapsed when Woolrich died before he could register for the renewal term and transfer his renewal rights to them....

[8] …. The District Court granted petitioners' motions for summary judgment based on *Rohauer* …. Respondent appealed to the United States Court of Appeals for the Ninth Circuit ….

[9] The Court of Appeals reversed …. The issue before the court … was whether petitioners were entitled to distribute and exhibit the motion picture without respondent's permission despite respondent's valid copyright in the pre-existing story. Relying on the renewal provision of the 1909 Act, respondent argued before the Court of Appeals that because he obtained from Chase Manhattan Bank, the statutory successor, the renewal right free and clear of any purported assignments of any interest in the renewal copyright, petitioners' distribution and publication of "Rear Window" without authorization infringed his renewal copyright. Petitioners responded that they had the right to continue to exploit "Rear Window" during the 28-year renewal period because Woolrich had agreed to assign to petitioners' predecessor in interest the motion picture rights in the story for the renewal period.

[10] Petitioners also relied, as did the District Court, on the decision in *Rohauer*. In *Rohauer*, the Court of Appeals for the Second Circuit held that statutory successors to the renewal copyright in a pre-existing work … could not "depriv[e] the proprietor of the derivative copyright of a right … to use so much of the underlying copyrighted work as already has been embodied in the copyrighted derivative work, as a matter of copyright law." The Court of Appeals in the instant case rejected this reasoning, concluding that even if the pre-existing work had been incorporated into a derivative work, use of the pre-existing work was infringing unless the owner of the derivative work held a valid grant of rights in the renewal term.

[11] The court relied on *Miller Music Corp. v. Charles N. Daniels, Inc.*, 362 U.S. 373 (1960), in which we held that assignment of renewal rights by an author before the time for renewal arrives cannot defeat the right of the author's statutory successor to the renewal rights if the author dies before the right to renewal accrues. An assignee of the renewal rights takes only an expectancy: "Until [the time for registration of renewal rights] arrives, assignees of renewal rights take the risk that the rights acquired may never vest in their assignors. A purchaser of such an interest is deprived of nothing. Like all purchasers of contingent interests, he takes subject to the possibility that the contingency may not occur." The Court of Appeals reasoned that "[i]f *Miller Music* makes assignment of the full renewal rights in the underlying copyright unenforceable when the author dies before effecting renewal of the copyright, then, *a fortiori*, an assignment of part of the rights in the underlying work, the right to produce a movie version, must also be unenforceable if the author dies before effecting renewal of the underlying copyright." Finding further support in the legislative history of the 1909 Act and rejecting the *Rohauer* court's reliance on the equities and the termination provisions of the 1976 Act, the Court of Appeals concluded that petitioners received from Woolrich only an expectancy in the renewal rights that never matured; upon Woolrich's death, Woolrich's statutory successor, Chase Manhattan Bank, became "entitled to a renewal and extension of the copyright," which Chase Manhattan secured "within one year prior to the expiration of the original term of copyright." Chase Manhattan then assigned the existing rights in the copyright to respondent….

[12] Petitioners would have us read into the Copyright Act a limitation on the statutorily created rights of the owner of an underlying work. They argue in essence that the rights of the owner of the copyright in the derivative use of the pre-existing work are extinguished once it is incorporated into the derivative work, assuming the author of the pre-existing work has agreed to assign his renewal rights. Because we find no support for such a curtailment of rights in either the 1909 Act or the 1976 Act, or in the legislative history of either, we affirm the judgment of the Court of Appeals….

[13] The right of renewal found in § 24 [of the 1909 Act] provides authors a second opportunity to obtain remuneration for their works. Section 24 provides:

> *[T]he author of [a copyrighted] work, if still living, or the widow, widower, or children of the author, if the author be not living, or if such author, widow, widower, or children be not living, then the author's executors, or in the absence of a will, his next of kin shall be entitled to a renewal and extension of the copyright in such work for a further term of twenty-eight years when application for such renewal and extension shall have been made to the copyright office and duly registered therein within one year prior to the expiration of the original term of copyright.*

[14] Since the earliest copyright statute in this country, the copyright term of ownership has been split between an original term and a renewal term. Originally, the renewal was intended merely to serve as an extension of the original term; at the end of the original term, the renewal could be effected and claimed by the author, if living, or by the author's executors, administrators, or assigns. In 1831, Congress altered the provision so that the author could assign his contingent interest in the renewal term, but could not, through his assignment, divest the rights of his widow or children in the renewal term. The 1831 renewal provisions created an entirely new policy, completely dissevering the title, breaking up the continuance and vesting an absolutely new title *eo nomine* in the persons designated. In this way, Congress attempted to give the author a second chance to control and benefit from his work. Congress also intended to secure to the author's family the opportunity to exploit the work if the author died before he could register for the renewal term....

[15] In its debates leading up to the Copyright Act of 1909, Congress elaborated upon the policy underlying a system comprised of an original term and a completely separate renewal term. The renewal term permits the author, originally in a poor bargaining position, to renegotiate the terms of the grant once the value of the work has been tested. "[U]nlike real property and other forms of personal property, [a copyright] is by its very nature incapable of accurate monetary evaluation prior to its exploitation." 2 M. NIMMER & D. NIMMER, NIMMER ON COPYRIGHT § 9.02, p. 9–23 (1989). If the work proves to be a great success and lives beyond the term of twenty-eight years, it should be the exclusive right of the author to take the renewal term, and the law should be framed so that the author could not be deprived of that right. With these purposes in mind, Congress enacted the renewal provision of the Copyright Act of 1909. With respect to works in their original or renewal term as of January 1, 1978, Congress retained the two-term system of copyright protection in the 1976 Act.

[16] Applying these principles in *Miller Music*, this Court held that when an author dies before the renewal period arrives, his executor is entitled to the renewal rights, even though the author previously assigned his renewal rights to another party. An assignment by an author of his renewal rights made before the original copyright expires is valid against the world, if the author is alive at the commencement of the renewal period.... If the author dies before that time, the next of kin obtain the renewal copyright free of any claim founded upon an assignment made by the author in his lifetime. These results follow not because the author's assignment is invalid but because he had only an expectancy to assign; and his death, prior to the renewal period, terminates his interest in the renewal which by § 24 vests in the named classes.... Thus, the renewal provisions were intended to give the author a second chance to obtain fair remuneration for his creative efforts and to provide the author's family a "new estate" if the author died before the renewal period arrived.

[17] An author holds a bundle of exclusive rights in the copyrighted work, among them the right to copy and the right to incorporate the work into derivative works. By assigning the renewal copyright in the work without limitation, as in *Miller Music*, the author assigns all of these rights. After *Miller Music*, if the author dies before the commencement of the renewal period, the assignee holds nothing. If the assignee of all of the renewal rights holds nothing upon the death of the assignor before arrival of the renewal period, then, *a fortiori*, the assignee of a portion of the renewal rights, *e.g.*, the right to produce a derivative work, must also hold nothing. Therefore, if the author dies before the renewal period, then the assignee may continue to use the original work only if the author's successor transfers the renewal rights to the assignee. Application of this rule to this case should end the inquiry. Woolrich died before the commencement of the renewal period in the

story, and, therefore, petitioners hold only an unfulfilled expectancy. Petitioners have been deprived of nothing. Like all purchasers of contingent interests, [they took] subject to the possibility that the contingency may not occur....

[18] The reason that our inquiry does not end here, and that we granted certiorari, is that the Court of Appeals for the Second Circuit reached a contrary result in *Rohauer*. Petitioners' theory is drawn largely from *Rohauer*. The Court of Appeals in *Rohauer* attempted to craft a "proper reconciliation" between the owner of the pre-existing work, who held the right to the work pursuant to *Miller Music*, and the owner of the derivative work, who had a great deal to lose if the work could not be published or distributed. Addressing a case factually similar to this case, the court concluded that even if the death of the author caused the renewal rights in the pre-existing work to revert to the statutory successor, the owner of the derivative work could continue to exploit that work. The court reasoned that the 1976 Act and the relevant precedents did not preclude such a result and that it was necessitated by a balancing of the equities:

> [T]he equities lie preponderantly in favor of the proprietor of the derivative copyright. In contrast to the situation where an assignee or licensee has done nothing more than print, publicize and distribute a copyrighted story or novel, a person who with the consent of the author has created an opera or a motion picture film will often have made contributions literary, musical and economic, as great as or greater than the original author.... [T]he purchaser of derivative rights has no truly effective way to protect himself against the eventuality of the author's death before the renewal period since there is no way of telling who will be the surviving widow, children or next of kin or the executor until that date arrives.

[19] The Court of Appeals for the Second Circuit thereby shifted the focus from the right to use the pre-existing work in a derivative work to a right inhering in the created derivative work itself. By rendering the renewal right to use the original work irrelevant, the court created an exception to our ruling in *Miller Music* and, as petitioners concede, created an "intrusion" on the statutorily created rights of the owner of the pre-existing work in the renewal term.

[20] Though petitioners do not, indeed could not, argue that its language expressly supports the theory they draw from *Rohauer*, they implicitly rely on § 6 of the 1909 Act, which states that "dramatizations ... of copyrighted works when produced with the consent of the proprietor of the copyright in such works ... shall be regarded as new works subject to copyright under the provisions of this title." Petitioners maintain that the creation of the "new," *i.e.*, derivative, work extinguishes any right the owner of rights in the pre-existing work might have had to sue for infringement that occurs during the renewal term.

[21] We think ... that this conclusion is neither warranted by any express provision of the Copyright Act, nor by the rationale as to the scope of protection achieved in a derivative work. It is moreover contrary to the axiomatic copyright principle that a person may exploit only such copyrighted literary material as he either owns or is licensed to use. The aspects of a derivative work added by the derivative author are that author's property, but the element drawn from the pre-existing work remains on grant from the owner of the pre-existing work. So long as the pre-existing work remains out of the public domain, its use is infringing if one who employs the work does not have a valid license or assignment for use of the pre-existing work....

[22] Properly conceding there is no explicit support for their theory in the 1909 Act, its legislative history, or the case law, petitioners contend, as did the court in *Rohauer*, that the termination provisions of the 1976 Act, while not controlling, support their theory of the case. For works existing in their original or renewal terms as of January 1, 1978, the 1976 Act added 19 years to the 1909 Act's provision of 28 years of initial copyright protection and 28 years of renewal protection. For those works, the author has the power to terminate the grant of rights at the end of the renewal term and, therefore, to gain the benefit of that additional 19 years of

protection. *See* § 304(c). In effect, the 1976 Act provides a third opportunity for the author to benefit from a work in its original or renewal term as of January 1, 1978. Congress, however, created one exception to the author's right to terminate: The author may not, at the end of the renewal term, terminate the right to use a derivative work for which the owner of the derivative work has held valid rights in the original and renewal terms. *See* § 304(c)(6)(A). The author, however, may terminate the right to create new derivative works. *Ibid.* For example, if petitioners held a valid copyright in the story throughout the original and renewal terms, and the renewal term in "Rear Window" were about to expire, petitioners could continue to distribute the motion picture even if respondent terminated the grant of rights, but could not create a new motion picture version of the story. Both the court in *Rohauer* and petitioners infer from this exception to the right to terminate an intent by Congress to prevent authors of pre-existing works from blocking distribution of derivative works. In other words, because Congress decided not to permit authors to exercise a third opportunity to benefit from a work incorporated into a derivative work, the Act expresses a general policy of undermining the author's second opportunity. We disagree....

[23] In fact, if the 1976 Act's termination provisions provide any guidance at all in this case, they tilt against petitioners' theory. The plain language of the termination provision itself indicates that Congress assumed that the owner of the pre-existing work possessed the right to sue for infringement even after incorporation of the pre-existing work in the derivative work.

> A derivative work prepared under authority of the grant before its termination may continue to be utilized under the terms of the grant after its termination, but this privilege does not extend to the preparation after the termination of other derivative works based upon the copyrighted work covered by the terminated grant.

[24] Congress would not have stated explicitly in § 304(c)(6)(A) that, at the end of the renewal term, the owner of the rights in the pre-existing work may not terminate use rights in existing derivative works unless Congress had assumed that the owner continued to hold the right to sue for infringement even after incorporation of the pre-existing work into the derivative work.

[25] Accordingly, we conclude that neither the 1909 Act nor the 1976 Act provides support for the theory set forth in *Rohauer*....

[26] Finally, petitioners urge us to consider the policies underlying the Copyright Act. They argue that the rule announced by the Court of Appeals will undermine one of the policies of the Act—the dissemination of creative works—by leading to many fewer works reaching the public. *Amicus* Columbia Pictures asserts that "[s]ome owners of underlying work renewal copyrights may refuse to negotiate, preferring instead to retire their copyrighted works, and all derivative works based thereon, from public use. Others may make demands—like respondent's demand for 50% of petitioners' future gross proceeds in excess of advertising expenses ...—which are so exorbitant that a negotiated economic accommodation will be impossible." These arguments are better addressed by Congress than the courts.

[27] In any event, the complaint that respondent's monetary request in this case is so high as to preclude agreement fails to acknowledge that an initially high asking price does not preclude bargaining. Presumably, respondent is asking for a share in the proceeds because he wants to profit from the distribution of the work, not because he seeks suppression of it....

NOTES

1. If an author can validly assign their renewal rights in advance, even if only as an expectancy, does the renewal term fulfill its purpose? Can you think of how, in the context of *Abend*, B.G. De Sylva Productions

could have ensured its motion picture rights into the renewal term for Cornell Woolrich's story even if Woolrich died before the renewal term?

2. Recall that the 1909 and 1976 Acts both required that application for renewal of copyright be "made to the Copyright Office and duly registered within one year prior to the expiration of the original term of copyright." 17 U.S.C. § 304(a) (1976). Recall also that, for all works published from 1964 through 1977, the Copyright Renewal Act of 1992 removed the requirement that a renewal term of copyright protection was contingent on registration before the renewal period. Pub. L. 102–307, 106 Stat. 264 (codified at 17 U.S.C. § 304(a)(3)(B)). Nonetheless, the new law instituted incentives to register copyright before the renewal period, including one that aligns with the rule articulated in *Abend*. Specifically, 17 U.S.C. § 304(a)(4)(A) provides that if this registration is not made before the renewal period, the *Abend* rule will be reversed:

> a derivative work prepared under authority of a grant of a transfer or license of the copyright that is made before the expiration of the original term of copyright may continue to be used under the terms of the grant during the renewed and extended term of copyright without infringing the copyright, except that such use does not extend to the preparation during such renewed and extended term of other derivative works based upon the copyrighted work covered by such grant.

D. Terminations of Transfer

The 1909 Act made the renewal term revert back to the original author to give him or her a second chance to recapture the copyright and reprice it. The 1976 Act is similarly motivated to protect authors, who often possess less bargaining power than the distributors with whom they transact. H.R. REP. NO. 1476, 94th Cong., 2d Sess. 47, at 124 (1976). However, because there is no renewal period under the 1976 Act, the author must do something to accomplish this recapture of copyright. In that respect, the 1976 Act enables authors to terminate transfers and exclusive and non-exclusive licenses of their copyright.

The termination provisions for works whose copyright is transferred after the effective date of the 1976 Act are set out in 17 U.S.C. § 203:

> (a) Conditions for Termination.—In the case of any work other than a work made for hire, the exclusive or nonexclusive grant of a transfer or license of copyright or of any right under a copyright, executed by the author on or after January 1, 1978, otherwise than by will, is subject to termination under the following conditions:
>
> > (1) In the case of a grant executed by one author, termination of the grant may be effected by that author or, if the author is dead, by the person or persons who, under clause (2) of this subsection, own and are entitled to exercise a total of more than one-half of that author's termination interest. In the case of a grant executed by two or more authors of a joint work, termination of the grant may be effected by a majority of the authors who executed it; if any of such authors is dead, the termination interest of any such author may be exercised as a unit by the person or persons who, under clause (2) of this subsection, own and are entitled to exercise a total of more than one-half of that author's interest....

Section 203(a)(2) goes on to spell out how the termination right can be exercised when the author has died.

Note also that, as specified, transfers of rights in a work made for hire cannot be terminated. Nor can transfers made by will. Nor can transferors subsequent to the author exercise termination rights.

Section 203(a)(3) spells out the precise five-year window in which an author is entitled to exercise termination:

> *Termination of the grant may be effected at any time during a period of five years beginning at the end of thirty-five years from the date of execution of the grant; or, if the grant covers the right of publication of the work, the period begins at the end of thirty-five years from the date of publication of the work under the grant or at the end of forty years from the date of execution of the grant, whichever term ends earlier.*

To terminate a transfer or license, there must be advance notice of the termination, which must meet the conditions specified in § 203(a)(4):

> *The termination shall be effected by serving an advance notice in writing, signed by the number and proportion of owners of termination interests required under clauses (1) and (2) of this subsection, or by their duly authorized agents, upon the grantee or the grantee's successor in title.*

> *(A) The notice shall state the effective date of the termination, which shall fall within the five-year period specified by clause (3) of this subsection, and the notice shall be served not less than two or more than ten years before that date. A copy of the notice shall be recorded in the Copyright Office before the effective date of termination, as a condition to its taking effect.*

> *(B) The notice shall comply, in form, content, and manner of service, with requirements that the Register of Copyrights shall prescribe by regulation.*

The 1976 Act also provides for termination of some transfers and licenses made under the 1909 Act. That said, these terminations are more limited, corresponding to termination's purpose in this context. The 1976 Act's provision of an additional term of 19 years for works protected under the 1909 Act raised questions as to who should have the benefit of this additional term: the author (or the author's heirs), or the holders of rights in the renewal term. As set out in the legislative history, Congress was convinced that "the extended term represents a completely new property right, and there are strong reasons for giving the author, who is the fundamental beneficiary of copyright under the Constitution, an opportunity to share in it." H.R. REP. NO. 1476, 94th Cong., 2d Sess. 47, at 140 (1976).

Section 304(c) was enacted to provide this form of termination right, and it mostly mirrors the provisions of § 203. The important differences are definitional. First, it permits termination of "the exclusive or nonexclusive grant of a transfer or license of the renewal copyright or any right under it, executed before January 1, 1978, by any of the persons designated by subsection (a)(1)(C) of this section, otherwise than by will," of "any copyright subsisting in either its first or renewal term on January 1, 1978, other than a copyright in a work made for hire." 17 U.S.C. § 304(c). Second, it specifies that termination of the grant can happen within a five-year window following what would have been the end of the second copyright term under the 1909 Act: "Termination of the grant may be effected at any time during a period of five years beginning at the end of fifty-six years from the date copyright was originally secured, or beginning on January 1, 1978, whichever is later." *Id.* § 304(c)(3).

When the 1998 copyright term extension of 20 years was enacted into law, Congress similarly provided termination rights for this new term, but only for pre-1978 transfers or licenses that were not already terminated under § 304(c). Section 304(d) sets out this termination provision. It looks like §§ 203 and 304(c) but for its definitional differences. First, it permits termination of "the exclusive or nonexclusive grant of a transfer or license of the renewal copyright or any right under it, executed before January 1, 1978, by any of the persons designated in subsection (a)(1)(C) of this section, other than by will," of "any copyright other than a work made for hire, subsisting in its renewal term on the effective date of the Sonny Bono Copyright Term Extension Act for which the termination right provided in subsection (c) has expired by such date, where the author or owner of the termination right has not previously exercised such termination right." *Id.* § 304(d). Second, it specifies that termination of the grant can happen within a five-year window following what would have been the end of the second copyright term under the 1976 Act: "Termination of the grant may be effected at any time during a period of 5 years beginning at the end of 75 years from the date copyright was originally secured." *Id.* § 304(d)(2).

Importantly, to make it harder—if not impossible—to contract away any of these three termination rights, the 1976 Act seeks to forbid the possibility of advance agreements by an author not to exercise their termination rights:

> *Termination of the grant may be effected notwithstanding any agreement to the contrary, including an agreement to make a will or to make any future grant.*

Id. §§ 203(a)(5), 304(c)(5), 304(d)(1). This provision was a reaction to how readily one could sign away one's renewal rights in advance under judicial interpretations of the 1909 Act (as *Abend* indicates). Although the language seems both broad and clear-cut ("notwithstanding any agreement to the contrary"), some courts understand this provision formalistically. Pertinently, some courts disallow termination when the author or the author's heirs have renegotiated an agreement in advance of termination, which is understood to revoke the first agreement and start the countdown to the termination window all over again. Penguin Group (USA) Inc. v. Steinbeck, 537 F.3d 193 (2d Cir. 2008); Milne v. Stephen Slesinger, Inc., 430 F.3d 1036 (9th Cir. 2005). The Ninth Circuit reasoned in such a case that upholding the renegotiated agreement as against termination advanced the goals of termination rights because "Congress ... anticipated that parties may contract, as an alternative to statutory termination, to revoke a prior grant by replacing it with a new one." *Milne*, 430 F.3d at 1046. The court continued: "Congress sought to foster this purpose by permitting an author's heirs to use the increased bargaining power conferred by the imminent threat of statutory termination to enter into new, more advantageous grants." Others have criticized this reasoning on the ground that the renegotiated agreement is a forbidden "agreement to the contrary." *E.g.*, Lydia Pallas Loren, *Renegotiating the Copyright Deal in the Shadow of the "Inalienable" Right to Terminate*, 62 FLA. L. REV. 1329 (2010); Peter S. Menell & David Nimmer, *Pooh-Poohing Copyright Law's "Inalienable" Termination Rights*, 57 J. COPYRIGHT SOC'Y U.S.A. 799 (2010).

NOTES

1. Consider the policy implications of providing authors with termination rights. The termination right is intended to allow the author to recapture some of the money from successful works to which the author was not originally entitled. Is this fair to the publishers that take the risk of distributing material? Will authors that are unsuccessful ever exercise their termination rights? If not, termination rights can act as a regressive tax in the following sense: Because publishers know authors can terminate transfers down the road, they are willing to pay all authors less for initial rights because the right is not as valuable. Then, the only authors who will want to terminate transfers later on are those authors whose works become successful enough to make it worthwhile. Those authors will then make a lot of money from termination by regaining their rights. For analysis along these lines, see Kate Darling, *Occupy Copyright: A Law & Economic Analysis of U.S. Author Termination Rights*, 63 BUFF. L. REV. 147 (2015); Michael Karas & Roland Kirstein, *Efficient Contracting under the U.S. Copyright Termination Law*, 54 INT'L REV. L. & ECON. 39 (2018); Guy A. Rub, *Stronger than Kryptonite? Inalienable Profit-Sharing Schemes in Copyright Law*, 27 HARV. J.L. & TECH. 49 (2013). Do you think it is plausible that publishers pay less money for initial rights than they would absent a termination right?

2. Related to termination rights are artist **resale royalty rights**, which grant artists a percentage of the proceeds on the resale of their works. Like termination, it allows artists to benefit down the line should their works become more valuable. Unlike termination, it provides this benefit by allowing artists to share in the appreciated value of their work but without any renegotiation. A California law passed in 1976 guarantees artists five percent of the profits in a later sale of their artwork. Cal. Civ. Code § 986(a). In so doing, California followed France and a number of other nations, in which such profit-sharing with artists is legally required. A federal court has held that the California law is almost entirely preempted by the 1976 Act. Close v. Sotheby's, Inc., 894 F.3d 1061 (9th Cir. 2018). (We study preemption in Chapter X.) There have been proposals, thus far unsuccessful, to enact resale royalty rights into federal law. *E.g.,* The American Royalties Too Act of 2014, S. 2045, 113th Cong. (2014); H.R. 4103, 113th Cong. (2014). Commentary on whether resale royalty rights are helpful to artists at recapturing some of the increased value of their works or serve as a regressive tax tend to mirror the policy debates over termination rights. *E.g.,* Brian L. Frye, *Equitable Resale Royalties*, 24 J. INTELL. PROP. L. 237 (2017); Kal Raustiala & Chris Sprigman, *Artist Resale Royalties: Do They Help or Hurt?*, FREAKONOMICS, Dec. 22, 2011, http://freakonomics.com/2011/12/22/artist-resale-royalties-do-they-help-or-hurt; Guy A. Rub, *The Unconvincing Case for Resale Royalties*, 124 YALE L.J. FORUM 1 (2014).

3. The sound recording industry has feared successful musicians exercising their termination rights, particularly starting in 2013 (35 years after the 1976 Act went into effect). Record labels have sought to stave off artists' ability to exercise these rights by explicitly stating in their contracts with artists that recordings are works made for hire. If that were to be the case, then the termination provisions would not apply and artists would have no termination rights to exercise. However, as seen from our study of works made for hire in Chapter III, sound recordings are not on the statutory list of commissioned works that qualify as works made for hire. 17 U.S.C. § 101. Unless these recordings qualify as a contribution to a collective work or as a compilation (and the required written agreement specifying work-made-for-hire status is executed), these sound recordings can qualify as works made for hire only if the recording artists were employees of their associated record labels (or possibly if the recording artist is an employee of a so-called "loan-out corporation" that artists sometimes use (generally for tax reasons) to contract with record labels) at the time they made their recordings. For a sampling of a majority of the commentary that concludes that it will be hard to establish that these sound recordings are works made for hire and therefore for record labels to disqualify artists from exercising termination rights, see Daniel Gould, *Time's Up: Copyright Termination, Work-for-Hire and the Recording Industry*, 31 COLUM. J.L. & ARTS 91 (2007); Mary LaFrance, *Authorship and Termination Rights in Sound Recordings*, 75 S. CAL. L. REV. 375 (2002).

V. Copyright's Exclusive Rights

To mount a successful claim of copyright infringement, a plaintiff needs to establish (1) the plaintiff's ownership of a valid copyright in a work and (2) the defendant's infringement of the copyright. Feist Publ'ns, Inc. v. Rural Tel. Serv. Co., 499 U.S. 340, 361 (1991); *see* 17 U.S.C. §§ 501(a)-(b). In Chapters II through IV, you learned about the first element of an infringement claim: the plaintiff's ownership of copyright in a fixed, original work of authorship, wherein the copyright remains in effect pursuant to the requisite formalities and duration rules. Starting in this chapter and continuing through Chapter VIII, we turn to the second element of the infringement inquiry. In this chapter, you will study the **exclusive rights** that copyright law provides to copyright holders. A defendant infringes by violating any of these exclusive rights without a defense (such as a limitation on infringement or exclusion of certain actions from infringement). We study some of these limitations and exclusions in this chapter, while deferring the most important infringement defense—fair use—to Chapter VI. In Chapter VII, we will turn to direct and secondary liability, and in Chapter VIII, to copyright litigation and remedies.

Specifically, in this chapter, after setting out the **infringement elements** that must be established to prove that any of the exclusive rights has been violated, we study each of the exclusive rights set out in 17 U.S.C. § 106. Section 106 provides:

> Subject to sections 107 through 122, the owner of copyright under this title has the exclusive rights to do and to authorize any of the following:
>
> (1) to **reproduce** the copyrighted work in copies or phonorecords;
>
> (2) to **prepare derivative works** based upon the copyrighted work;
>
> (3) to **distribute** copies or phonorecords of the copyrighted work to the public by sale or other transfer of ownership, or by rental, lease, or lending;
>
> (4) in the case of literary, musical, dramatic, and choreographic works, pantomimes, and motion pictures and other audiovisual works, to **perform the copyrighted work publicly**;
>
> (5) in the case of literary, musical, dramatic, and choreographic works, pantomimes, and pictorial, graphic, or sculptural works, including the individual images of a motion picture or other audiovisual work, to **display the copyrighted work publicly**; and
>
> (6) in the case of **sound recordings**, to **perform the copyrighted work publicly by means of a digital audio transmission**.

Note that all of these exclusive rights are expressly subject to limitations or exclusions set out in 17 U.S.C. §§ 107-122, some of which we explore in this chapter and Chapter VI.

In this chapter, we also address the exclusive rights that copyright owners might have in the **characters** that appear in their works by virtue of §§ 106(1)-(2), the **moral rights** that copyright owners might hold by virtue of §§ 106 and 106A (and other laws), and the exclusive right to **import** copies of a copyrighted work that is corollary to § 106(3) and is found in 17 U.S.C. § 602.

A. Infringement Elements

Before delving into each of the exclusive rights that copyright law confers, it is helpful to identify and distinguish the two constituent elements of infringement of any of the exclusive rights conferred by copyright law: (1) **copying in fact**, and (2) **copying in law**. The element of "copying in fact" is established by showing that the defendant actually used some elements of the plaintiff's work (potentially including use of unprotected elements such as ideas) to make the defendant's allegedly infringing work. That is, the first part of the infringement tests asks whether, as a factual matter, the defendant copied from the plaintiff's work. Assuming the answer to the copying-in-fact inquiry is yes, the copying is nonetheless only actionable if there is also copying in law. "Copying in law" is established when the defendant's copying is sufficient—both quantitatively and qualitatively—to provoke legal liability for infringement.

Courts frequently use other terms to refer to each of these elements. For example, sometimes they call copying in fact "actual copying." Sometimes, they call copying in law "substantial similarity." Sometimes, they don't distinguish between these two copying elements at all. And sometimes, they simply refer to one of the two elements as "copying." These differing labels and lack of distinction between the two inquiries can make it hard to know which element of the infringement analysis a court is referencing, unless the surrounding context is helpful to disambiguate the two elements. Be attentive to disambiguating the two copying elements in your analysis.

Although copying in fact and copying in law must both be shown to establish a defendant's infringement of any of the copyright holder's exclusive rights, we will explore these two elements separately only in the following section, in the context of the reproduction right. **Make sure to include both copying elements in your analysis regardless of which exclusive right is at issue.** With that said, we now turn to look at each of the exclusive rights in turn.

B. Reproduction Right

The copyright holder's right "to reproduce the copyrighted work in copies or phonorecords," set out in § 106(1), is a central right, and the right most commonly asserted in infringement actions. A defendant's work cannot infringe the plaintiff's reproduction right unless the work is fixed, because the plaintiff's reproduction right is infringed only if plaintiff's work is reproduced "in copies or phonorecords." (Recall this fixation requirement discussed in Chapter II.)

As you shall see, the reproduction right is not just the right to make exact copies of a copyrighted work; it also covers partial copying of a plaintiff's work sufficient to make the defendant's work "substantially similar" to the protected elements in the plaintiff's work. In addition, the reproduction right has been typically understood to include copies in a different medium than that of the underlying copyrighted work. Note also that there need not be any distribution to violate the reproduction right. If you make a copy of someone's copyrighted work and lock it up in a desk drawer to gather dust, you will be infringing that person's right of reproduction (absent a valid defense).

In this section, we will at the outset explore the first infringement element—copying in fact—through the lens of the reproduction right. We then turn to the second infringement requirement of copying in law, which we explore in three contexts: de minimis copies, substantially similar copies, and exact copies.

1. Copying in Fact

As you read the following case, take note of how a plaintiff can establish that a defendant copied in fact. Do you find the plaintiff's evidence convincing? Or the defendant's attempts to rebut that evidence? Consider what this opinion suggests about the mens rea required for copyright infringement.

Three Boys Music Corporation v. Michael Bolton
212 F.3d 477 (9th Cir. 2000)

NELSON, J.:

[1] In 1994, a jury found that Michael Bolton's 1991 pop hit, "Love Is a Wonderful Thing," infringed on the copyright of a 1964 Isley Brothers' song of the same name. The district court denied Bolton's motion for a new trial and affirmed the jury's award of $5.4 million....

[2] We affirm....

[3] The Isley Brothers, one of this country's most well-known rhythm and blues groups, have been inducted into the Rock and Roll Hall of Fame. They helped define the soul sound of the 1960s with songs such as "Shout," "Twist and Shout," and "This Old Heart of Mine," and they mastered the funky beats of the 1970s with songs such as "Who's That Lady," "Fight the Power," and "It's Your Thing." In 1964, the Isley Brothers wrote and recorded "Love is a Wonderful Thing" for United Artists. The Isley Brothers received a copyright for "Love is a Wonderful Thing" from the Register of Copyrights on February 6, 1964. The following year, they switched to the famous Motown label and had three top-100 hits including "This Old Heart of Mine."

[4] Hoping to benefit from the Isley Brothers' Motown success, United Artists released "Love is a Wonderful Thing" in 1966. The song was not released on an album, only on a 45-record as a single. Several industry publications predicted that "Love is a Wonderful Thing" would be a hit—"Cash Box" on August 27, 1966, "Gavin Report" on August 26, 1966, and "Billboard" on September 10, 1966. On September 17, 1966, Billboard listed "Love is a Wonderful Thing" at number 110 in a chart titled "Bubbling Under the Hot 100." The song was never listed on any other Top 100 charts. In 1991, the Isley Brothers' "Love is a Wonderful Thing" was released on compact disc.

[5] Michael Bolton is a singer/songwriter who gained popularity in the late 1980s and early 1990s by reviving the soul sound of the 1960s. Bolton has orchestrated this soul-music revival in part by covering old songs such as Percy Sledge's "When a Man Love a Woman" and Otis Redding's "(Sittin' on the) Dock of the Bay." Bolton also has written his own hit songs. In early 1990, Bolton and [co-author Andrew] Goldmark wrote a song called "Love Is a Wonderful Thing." Bolton released it as a single in April 1991, and as part of Bolton's album, "Time, Love and Tenderness." Bolton's "Love Is a Wonderful Thing" finished 1991 at number 49 on Billboard's year-end pop chart.

[6] On February 24, 1992, Three Boys Music Corporation filed a copyright infringement action .... [T]he jury determined that the appellants had infringed the Isley Brothers' copyright.... On May 9, 1994, the district court entered judgment in favor of the Isley Brothers ....

[7] Proof of copyright infringement is often highly circumstantial .... A copyright plaintiff must prove (1) ownership of the copyright; and (2) infringement—that the defendant copied protected elements of the plaintiff's work. Absent direct evidence of copying, proof of infringement involves fact-based showings that [1] the defendant had "access" to [and actually copied from] the plaintiff's work and [2] that the two works are "substantially similar." ...

[8] Proof of access requires an opportunity to view or to copy plaintiff's work. This is often described as providing a reasonable opportunity or reasonable possibility of viewing the plaintiff's work. We have defined reasonable access as more than a bare possibility.

[9] Circumstantial evidence of reasonable access is proven in one of two ways: (1) a particular chain of events is established between the plaintiff's work and the defendant's access to that work (such as through dealings with a publisher or record company), or (2) the plaintiff's work has been widely disseminated....

[10] Proof of widespread dissemination is sometimes accompanied by a theory that copyright infringement of a popular song was subconscious. Subconscious copying has been accepted since Learned Hand embraced it in a 1924 music infringement case: "Everything registers somewhere in our memories, and no one can tell what may evoke it.... Once it appears that another has in fact used the copyright as the source of this production, he has invaded the author's rights. It is no excuse that in so doing his memory has played him a trick." Fred Fisher, Inc. v. Dillingham, 298 F. 145, 147–48 (S.D.N.Y. 1924).

[11] In modern cases, however, the theory of subconscious copying has been applied to songs that are more remote in time. *ABKCO Music, Inc. v. Harrisongs Music, Ltd.*, 722 F.2d 988 (2d Cir.1983), is the most prominent example. In *ABKCO*, the Second Circuit affirmed a jury's verdict that former Beatle George Harrison, in writing the song "My Sweet Lord," subconsciously copied The Chiffons' "He's So Fine," which was released six years earlier. Harrison admitted hearing "He's So Fine" in 1963, when it was number one on the Billboard charts in the United States for five weeks and one of the top 30 hits in England for seven weeks.... In *ABKCO*, ... the court found that "the similarity was so striking and where access was found, the remoteness of that access provides no basis for reversal." Furthermore, the mere lapse of a considerable period of time between the moment of access and the creation of defendant's work does not preclude a finding of copying.

[12] The Isley Brothers' access argument was based on a theory of widespread dissemination and subconscious copying. They presented evidence supporting four principal ways that Bolton and Goldmark could have had access to the Isley Brothers' "Love is a Wonderful Thing":

[13] (1) Bolton grew up listening to groups such as the Isley Brothers and singing their songs. In 1966, Bolton and Goldmark were 13 and 15, respectively, growing up in Connecticut. Bolton testified that he had been listening to rhythm and blues music by black singers since he was 10 or 11, "appreciated a lot of Black singers," and as a youth was the lead singer in a band that performed "covers" of popular songs by black singers. Bolton also testified that his brother had a "pretty good record collection."

[14] (2) Three disk jockeys testified that the Isley Brothers' song was widely disseminated on radio and television stations where Bolton and Goldmark grew up. First, Jerry Blavitt testified that the Isley Brothers' "Love is a Wonderful Thing" was played five or six times during a 13-week period on the television show, "The Discophonic Scene," which he said aired in Philadelphia, New York, and Hartford-New Haven. Blavitt also testified that he played the song two to three times a week as a disk jockey in Philadelphia and that the station is still playing the song today. Second, Earl Rodney Jones testified that he played the song a minimum of four times a day during an eight to 14 to 24 week period on WVON radio in Chicago, and that the station is still playing the song today. Finally, Jerry Bledsoe testified that he played the song on WUFO radio in Buffalo, and WWRL radio in New York was playing the song in New York in 1967 when he went there. Bledsoe also

testified that he played the song twice on a television show, "Soul," which aired in New York and probably in New Haven, Connecticut, where Bolton lived.

[15] (3) Bolton confessed to being a huge fan of the Isley Brothers and a collector of their music. Ronald Isley testified that when Bolton saw Isley at the Lou Rawls United Negro College Fund Benefit concert in 1988, Bolton said, "I know this guy. I go back with him. I have all his stuff." Angela Winbush, Isley's wife, testified about that meeting that Bolton said, "This man needs no introduction. I know everything he's done."

[16] (4) Bolton wondered if he and Goldmark were copying a song by another famous soul singer. Bolton produced a work tape attempting to show that he and Goldmark independently created their version of "Love Is a Wonderful Thing." On that tape of their recording session, Bolton asked Goldmark if the song they were composing was Marvin Gaye's "Some Kind of Wonderful." The district court, in affirming the jury's verdict, wrote about Bolton's Marvin Gaye remark:

> *This statement suggests that Bolton was contemplating the possibility that the work he and Goldmark were creating, or at least a portion of it, belonged to someone else, but that Bolton wasn't sure who it belonged to. A reasonable jury can infer that Bolton mistakenly attributed the work to Marvin Gaye, when in reality Bolton was subconsciously drawing on Plaintiff's song.*

[17] The appellants contend that the Isley Brothers' theory of access amounts to a "twenty-five-years-after-the-fact-subconscious copying claim." Indeed, this is a more attenuated case of reasonable access and subconscious copying than *ABKCO*. In this case, the appellants never admitted hearing the Isley Brothers' "Love is a Wonderful Thing." That song never topped the Billboard charts or even made the top 100 for a single week. The song was not released on an album or compact disc until 1991, a year after Bolton and Goldmark wrote their song....

[18] Despite the weaknesses of the Isley Brothers' theory of reasonable access, the appellants had a full opportunity to present their case to the jury. Three rhythm and blues experts (including legendary Motown songwriter Lamont Dozier of Holland-Dozier-Holland fame) testified that they never heard of the Isley Brothers' "Love is a Wonderful Thing." Furthermore, Bolton produced copies of "TV Guide" from 1966 suggesting that the television shows playing the song never aired in Connecticut. Bolton also pointed out that 129 songs called "Love is a Wonderful Thing" are registered with the Copyright Office, 85 of them before 1964.

[19] The Isley Brothers' reasonable access arguments are not without merit. Teenagers are generally avid music listeners. It is entirely plausible that two Connecticut teenagers obsessed with rhythm and blues music could remember an Isley Brothers' song that was played on the radio and television for a few weeks, and subconsciously copy it twenty years later. Furthermore, Ronald Isley testified that when they met, Bolton said, "I have all his stuff." Finally, as the district court pointed out, Bolton's remark about Marvin Gaye and "Some Kind of Wonderful" indicates that Bolton believed he may have been copying someone else's song....

[20] Although we might not reach the same conclusion as the jury regarding access, we find that the jury's conclusion about access is supported by substantial evidence....

[21] Bolton and Goldmark also contend that their witnesses rebutted the Isley Brothers' prima facie case of copyright infringement with evidence of independent creation. By establishing reasonable access and substantial similarity, a copyright plaintiff creates a presumption of copying. The burden shifts to the defendant to rebut that presumption through proof of independent creation.

[22] The appellants' case of independent creation hinges on three factors: the work tape demonstrating how Bolton and Goldmark created their song [and] Bolton and Goldmark's history of songwriting .... The jury, however, heard the testimony of Bolton [and] Goldmark ... about independent creation. The work tape revealed evidence that Bolton may have subconsciously copied a song that he believed to be written by Marvin Gaye. Bolton and Goldmark's history of songwriting presents no direct evidence about this case.... Once again, we refuse to disturb the jury's determination about independent creation. The substantial evidence of copying based on access and substantial similarity was such that a reasonable juror could reject this defense....

NOTES

1. Some courts have held that in establishing copying in fact via circumstantial evidence of access and similarity, an **"inverse ratio"** rule applies. According to this rule, courts accept "a lower standard of proof of ... similarity when a high degree of access is shown." Rentmeester v. Nike, Inc., 883 F.3d 1111, 1124 (9th Cir. 2018). Similarly, they accept a lesser degree of access when a high degree of similarity is shown. Yet most circuits have by now rejected this rule. As the Ninth Circuit explained in renouncing the rule:

> As we struggled with the inverse ratio rule over the years, the Second Circuit rejected it ..., describing the idea as a "superficially attractive apophthegm which upon examination confuses more than it clarifies." Arc Music Corp. v. Lee, 296 F.2d 186, 187 (2d Cir. 1961). The court reasoned that "access will not supply [similarity's] lack, and an undue stress upon that one feature can only confuse and even conceal this basic requirement." ...

> The Second Circuit also identified the problematic implications of this principle where access is very high and similarity very low: "[t]he logical outcome of the claimed principle is obviously that proof of actual access will render a showing of similarities entirely unnecessary." However, "it does not follow that 'more' access increases the likelihood of copying." David Aronoff, Exploding the "Inverse Ratio Rule," 55 J. COPYRIGHT SOC'Y 125, 126 (2008). Yet that is what the rule compels....

> ... [T]he inverse ratio rule unfairly advantages those whose work is most accessible by lowering the standard of proof for similarity. Thus the rule benefits those with highly popular works ..., which are also highly accessible. But nothing in copyright law suggests that a work deserves stronger legal protection simply because it is more popular or owned by better-funded rights holders....

> .... Access does not obviate the requirement that the plaintiff must demonstrate that the defendant actually copied the work. By rejecting the inverse ratio rule, we are not suggesting that access cannot serve as circumstantial evidence of actual copying in all cases....

Skidmore v. Led Zeppelin, 952 F.3d 1051, 1068-69 (9th Cir. 2020) (en banc). Do you think the "inverse ratio" rule is sensible, or is copyright law better off without it?

2. Does it make sense as a matter of copyright policy for subconscious copying to be actionable? For different perspectives on this issue, see Shyamkrishna Balganesh, Copyright as Market Prospect, 166 U. PA. L. REV. 443, 492-96 (2018); Robin Feldman, The Role of the Subconscious in Intellectual Property Law, 2 HASTINGS SCI. & TECH. L.J. 1, 4-10 (2010); Wendy J. Gordon, Toward a Jurisprudence of Benefits: The Norms of Copyright and the Problem of Private Censorship, 57 U. CHI. L. REV. 1009, 1028-32 (1990); Carrisa L. Alden, Note, A Proposal to Replace the Subconscious Copying Doctrine, 29 CARDOZO L. REV. 1729 (2008).

Should it make a difference if the defendant admits having been aware of the plaintiff's work (even while denying having copied it in fact)? By contrast to *Three Boys Music*, in which Michael Bolton denied having heard the Isley Brothers' song, in *ABKCO Music, Inc. v. Harrisongs Music, Ltd.*—referenced above—George Harrison admitted to being aware of The Chiffons' "He's So Fine," even while denying having copied it.

Should it matter how remote in time a plaintiff's work is from the defendant's in a claim for subconscious copying?

In the internet age, with so much copyrighted material accessible online, is it easier or harder to establish copying in fact if subconscious copying is actionable?

Focus in the following case on the evidence that suffices to show copying in fact. Is the court's rule clear? Is the rule the same across all categories of copyrightable subject matter and genres? Should it be?

Ronald H. Selle v. Barry Gibb
741 F.2d 896 (7th Cir. 1984)

CUDAHY, J.:

[1] The plaintiff, Ronald H. Selle, brought a suit against three brothers, Maurice, Robin and Barry Gibb, known collectively as the popular singing group, the Bee Gees, alleging that the Bee Gees, in their hit tune, "How Deep Is Your Love," had infringed the copyright of his song, "Let It End." The jury returned a verdict in plaintiff's favor on the issue of liability .... The district court ... granted the defendants' motion for judgment notwithstanding the verdict and, in the alternative, for a new trial. We affirm the grant of the motion for judgment notwithstanding the verdict....

[2] Selle composed his song, "Let It End," in one day in the fall of 1975 and obtained a copyright for it on November 17, 1975. He played his song with his small band two or three times in the Chicago area and sent a tape and lead sheet of the music to eleven music recording and publishing companies. Eight of the companies returned the materials to Selle; three did not respond. This was the extent of the public dissemination of Selle's song. Selle first became aware of the Bee Gees' song, "How Deep Is Your Love," in May 1978 and thought that he recognized the music as his own, although the lyrics were different. He also saw the movie, "Saturday Night Fever," the sound track of which features the song "How Deep Is Your Love," and again recognized the music. He subsequently sued the three Gibb brothers; Paramount Pictures Corporation, which made and distributed the movie; and Phonodisc, Inc., now known as Polygram Distribution, Inc., which made and distributed the cassette tape of "How Deep Is Your Love."

[3] The Bee Gees are internationally known performers and creators of popular music.... The Bee Gees, however, do not themselves read or write music. In composing a song, their practice was to tape a tune, which members of their staff would later transcribe and reduce to a form suitable for copyrighting, sale and performance by both the Bee Gees and others.

[4] In addition to their own testimony at trial, the Bee Gees presented testimony by their manager, Dick Ashby, and two musicians, Albhy Galuten and Blue Weaver, who were on the Bee Gees' staff at the time "How

Chapter V – Exclusive Rights

Deep Is Your Love" was composed. These witnesses described in detail how, in January 1977, the Bee Gees and several members of their staff went to a recording studio in the Chateau d'Herouville[,] about 25 miles northwest of Paris. There the group composed at least six new songs and mixed a live album. Barry Gibb's testimony included a detailed explanation of a work tape which was introduced into evidence and played in court. This tape preserves the actual process of creation during which the brothers, and particularly Barry, created the tune of the accused song while Weaver, a keyboard player, played the tune which was hummed or sung by the brothers. Although the tape does not seem to preserve the very beginning of the process of creation, it does depict the process by which ideas, notes, lyrics and bits of the tune were gradually put together.

[5] Following completion of this work tape, a demo tape was made....

[6] The only expert witness to testify at trial was Arrand Parsons, a professor of music at Northwestern University who has had extensive professional experience primarily in classical music. He has been a program annotator for the Chicago Symphony Orchestra and the New Orleans Symphony Orchestra and has authored works about musical theory. Prior to this case, however, he had never made a comparative analysis of two popular songs. Dr. Parsons testified on the basis of several charts comparing the musical notes of each song and a comparative recording prepared under his direction.

[7] According to Dr. Parsons' testimony, the first eight bars of each song (Theme A) have twenty-four of thirty-four notes in plaintiff's composition and twenty-four of forty notes in defendants' composition which are identical in pitch and symmetrical position. Of thirty-five rhythmic impulses in plaintiff's composition and forty in defendants', thirty are identical. In the last four bars of both songs (Theme B), fourteen notes in each are identical in pitch, and eleven of the fourteen rhythmic impulses are identical. Both Theme A and Theme B appear in the same position in each song but with different intervening material.

[8] Dr. Parsons testified that, in his opinion, "the two songs had such striking similarities that they could not have been written independent of one another." He also testified that he did not know of two songs by different composers "that contain as many striking similarities" as do the two songs at issue here. However, on several occasions, he declined to say that the similarities could only have resulted from copying.

[9] Following presentation of the case, the jury returned a verdict for the plaintiff on the issue of liability .... [The district court judge], however, granted the defendants' motion for judgment notwithstanding the verdict and, in the alternative, for a new trial. [The judge] relied primarily on the plaintiff's inability to demonstrate that the defendants had access to the plaintiff's song, without which a claim of copyright infringement could not prevail regardless how similar the two compositions are. Further, the plaintiff failed to contradict or refute the testimony of the defendants and their witnesses describing the independent creation process of "How Deep Is Your Love." ...

[10] Selle's primary contention on this appeal is that the district court misunderstood the theory of proof of copyright infringement on which he based his claim. Under this theory, copyright infringement can be demonstrated when, even in the absence of any direct evidence of access, the two pieces in question are so strikingly similar that access can be inferred from such similarity alone. Selle argues that the testimony of his expert witness, Dr. Parsons, was sufficient evidence of such striking similarity that it was permissible for the jury, even in the absence of any other evidence concerning access, to infer that the Bee Gees had access to plaintiff's song and indeed copied it....

[11] Proof of copying is crucial to any claim of copyright infringement because no matter how similar the two works may be (even to the point of identity), if the defendant did not copy the accused work, there is no infringement. However, because direct evidence of copying is rarely available, the plaintiff can rely upon

circumstantial evidence to prove this essential element, and the most important component of this sort of circumstantial evidence is proof of access....

[12] If, however, the plaintiff does not have direct evidence of access, then an inference of access may still be established circumstantially by proof of similarity which is so striking that the possibilities of independent creation, coincidence and prior common source are, as a practical matter, precluded. If the plaintiff presents evidence of striking similarity sufficient to raise an inference of access, then copying is presumably proved simultaneously .... The theory which Selle attempts to apply to this case is based on proof of copying by circumstantial proof of access established by striking similarity between the two works.

[13] One difficulty with plaintiff's theory is that no matter how great the similarity between the two works, it is not their similarity *per se* which establishes access; rather, their similarity tends to prove access in light of the nature of the works, the particular musical genre involved and other circumstantial evidence of access. In other words, striking similarity is just one piece of circumstantial evidence tending to show access and must not be considered in isolation; it must be considered together with other types of circumstantial evidence relating to access.

[14] As a threshold matter, therefore, it would appear that there must be at least some other evidence which would establish a reasonable possibility that the complaining work was *available* to the alleged infringer. As noted, two works may be identical in every detail, but, if the alleged infringer created the accused work independently or both works were copied from a common source in the public domain, then there is no infringement. Therefore, if the plaintiff admits to having kept his or her creation under lock and key, it would seem logically impossible to infer access through striking similarity. Thus, although it has frequently been written that striking similarity *alone* can establish access, the decided cases suggest that this circumstance would be most unusual. The plaintiff must always present sufficient evidence to support a reasonable possibility of access because the jury cannot draw an inference of access based upon speculation and conjecture alone....

[15] .... Selle's song certainly did not achieve [a great] extent of public dissemination ..., and there was also no evidence that any of the defendants or their associates were in Chicago on the two or three occasions when the plaintiff played his song publicly.... [I]n this case, the availability of Selle's song, as shown by the evidence, was virtually *de minimis*....

[16] [The district court judge] ... based his decision on what he characterized as the plaintiff's inability to raise more than speculation that the Bee Gees had access to his song. The extensive testimony of the defendants and their witnesses describing the creation process went essentially uncontradicted, and there was no attempt even to impeach their credibility.... [The judge]'s conclusions that there was no more than a bare possibility that the defendants could have had access to Selle's song and that this was an insufficient basis from which the jury could have reasonably inferred the existence of access seem correct. The plaintiff has failed to meet even the minimum threshold of proof of the possibility of access ....

As you read the following case, consider whether it is in tension with *Selle* on the "copying in fact" element. If so, how? If not, why not?

Ty, Inc. v. GMA Accessories, Inc.
132 F.3d 1167 (7th Cir. 1997)

POSNER, C.J.:

[1] Ty, the manufacturer of the popular "Beanie Babies" line of stuffed animals, has obtained a preliminary injunction under the Copyright Act against the sale by GMA ... of "Preston the Pig" and "Louie the Cow." These are bean-bag animals manufactured by GMA that Ty contends are copies of its copyrighted pig ("Squealer") and cow ("Daisy"). Ty began selling the "Beanie Babies" line, including Squealer, in 1993, and it was the popularity of the line that induced GMA to bring out its own line of bean-bag stuffed animals three years later. GMA does not contest the part of the injunction that enjoins the sale of Louie, but asks us on a variety of grounds to vacate the other part, the part that enjoins it from selling Preston....

Figure 46: GMA's Preston the Pig (left), Ty's Squealer the Pig (right)

Figure 47: GMA's Preston the Pig (left), Ty's Squealer the Pig (right)

[2] The two pigs are so nearly identical that if the second is a copy of the first, the second clearly infringes Ty's copyright. But identity is not infringement. The Copyright Act forbids only copying; if independent creation

results in an identical work, the creator of that work is free to sell it. The practical basis for this rule is that unlike the case of patents and trademarks, the creator of an expressive work—an author or sculptor or composer—cannot canvass the entire universe of copyrighted works to discover whether his poem or song or, as in this case, "soft sculpture" is identical to some work in which copyright subsists, especially since unpublished, unregistered works are copyrightable. But identity can be powerful evidence of copying. The more a work is both like an already copyrighted work *and*—for this is equally important—unlike anything that is in the public domain, the less likely it is to be an independent creation. As is generally true in the law, circumstantial evidence—evidence merely probabilistic rather than certain—can confer sufficient confidence on an inference, here of copying, to warrant a legal finding.

[3] The issue of copying can be broken down into two subissues. The first is whether the alleged copier had access to the work that he is claimed to have copied; the second is whether, if so, he used his access to copy. It might seem that access could not be an issue where, as in this case, the allegedly copied work is a mass-produced consumer product purchasable for $5. But we shall see that GMA has attempted to make an issue of access.

[4] Obviously, access does not entail copying. An eyewitness might have seen the defendant buy the copyrighted work; this would be proof of access, but not of copying. But copying entails access. If, therefore, two works are so similar as to make it highly probable that the later one is a copy of the earlier one, the issue of access need not be addressed separately, since if the later work was a copy its creator must have had access to the original. Selle v. Gibb, 741 F.2d 896, 901 (7th Cir. 1984). Of course the inference of access, and hence of copying, could be rebutted by proof that the creator of the later work could not have seen the earlier one or (an alternative mode of access) a copy of the earlier one.... [W]e do not read our decision in *Selle* to hold or imply ... that no matter how closely the works resemble each other, the plaintiff must produce some (other) evidence of access. He must produce evidence of access, all right—but, as we have just said, and as is explicit in *Selle* itself, a similarity that is so close as to be highly unlikely to have been an accident of independent creation *is* evidence of access.

[5] What troubled us in *Selle* but is not a factor here is that two works may be strikingly similar—may in fact be identical—not because one is copied from the other but because both are copies of the same thing in the public domain. In such a case—imagine two people photographing Niagara Falls from the same place at the same time of the day and year and in identical weather—there is no inference of access to anything but the public domain, and, equally, no inference of copying from a copyrighted work. A similarity may be striking without being suspicious.

[6] But here it is both. GMA's pig is strikingly similar to Ty's pig but not to anything in the public domain—a real pig, for example .... The parties' bean-bag pigs bear little resemblance to real pigs even if we overlook the striking anatomical anomaly of Preston—he has three toes, whereas real pigs have cloven hooves. We can imagine an argument that the technology of manufacturing bean-bag animals somehow prevents the manufacturer from imitating a real pig. But anyone even slightly familiar with stuffed animals knows that there are many lifelike stuffed pigs on the market, and whether they are stuffed with beans or other materials does not significantly affect their verisimilitude ....

[7] Real pigs are not the only pigs in the public domain. But GMA has not pointed to any fictional pig in the public domain that Preston resembles. Preston resembles only Squealer, and resembles him so closely as to warrant an inference that GMA copied Squealer. In rebuttal all that GMA presented was the affidavit of the designer, Salmon, who swears, we must assume truthfully, that she never looked at a Squealer before submitting her design. But it is not her design drawing that is alleged to infringe the copyright on Squealer; it is the manufactured Preston, the soft sculpture itself, which ... is much more like Squealer than Salmon's drawing is....

[8] We find no error of law, no clear error of fact, and no abuse of discretion in the grant of the preliminary injunction to Ty....

NOTES

1. Do you find *Selle* and *Ty* to be consistent with one another? If so, how do you reconcile them?

2. Judge Posner labels the plaintiff's and defendant's stuffed pigs as "so nearly identical." Is that right (even discounting the differences that appear to have been manufactured by the defendants)? List out the differences that you can spot.

3. After reading these cases, do you think a conclusion of copying in fact is inevitable whenever there are sufficient similarities between a plaintiff's work and a defendant's work? Does the widespread availability of content on the internet affect your thinking? Are there reasons specific to the relevant genre of the plaintiff's and defendant's works in any case that might make it seem as if there were copying in fact when there might not have been?

4. Patent law takes a different approach than copyright law in not requiring any copying in fact to establish patent infringement. That is, independent creation is no defense to patent infringement. Do you think this approach might make sense in copyright law as well? In the patent context, scholars debate whether patent law should include copyright law's requirement of establishing copying in fact as an element of patent infringement. *See, e.g.*, Mark A. Lemley, *Should Patent Infringement Require Proof of Copying?*, 105 MICH. L. REV. 1525 (2007); Stephen M. Maurer & Suzanne Scotchmer, *The Independent Invention Defence in Intellectual Property*, 69 ECONOMICA 535 (2002); Carl Shapiro, *Prior User Rights*, AM. ECON. REV. 92, 95 (2006); Samson Vermont, *Independent Invention as a Defense to Patent Infringement*, 105 MICH. L. REV. 475 (2006).

5. Can you think about how a defendant might go about documenting independent creation? Are there policies businesses can put in place to make it easier to show there has been no copying in fact?

6. Permitting striking similarity in and of itself to establish copying in fact has long roots, going back at least to the Second Circuit's decision in *Arnstein v. Porter*, 154 F.2d 464 (2d Cir. 1946). In that decision, Judge Frank states that "[i]n some cases, the similarities between the plaintiff's and defendant's work are so extensive and striking as, without more, both to justify an inference of copying and to prove improper appropriation." That said, it is little applied. For example, in a copyright infringement lawsuit by the writers of the screenplay *Dodgeball: The Movie* against the producers and distributors of the movie *Dodgeball: A True Underdog Story*, the district court held there could be no striking similarity to establish copying in fact as a matter of law. Price v. Fox Entertainment Group, Inc., 499 F. Supp. 2d 382 (S.D.N.Y. 2007). Even though the judge noted that both works are "about a dodgeball competition in which a team of misfits or underdogs are pitted against a stronger team of bullies," there were also many differences and the similarities were not of the type that would support an inference of copying:

> For example, although dodgeball is the central sport in both works, the sport is not presented and used in the same manner. In the Screenplay, dodgeball is the ... major sport in the town, and the main characters grew up aspiring to be good dodgeball players. Indeed, dodgeball was a major subject of rivalry since childhood between the main character, Matt, and Mitch. In the Movie, by contrast, the characters stumble upon adult dodgeball through a sports magazine that highlights obscure sports. Neither the main character, Peter, nor his rival, White, had ever played dodgeball before, nor was it ever a subject of their rivalry until they enter the tournament.

Moreover, the main character's love interest in the Screenplay shifts from one person, the cheerleader, to another, the coach's sister Sam, whereas in the Movie, the main character's love interest remains constant on Kate, the lawyer who is hired by the rival gym to foreclose the mortgage on Average Joe's gym. Even on a more abstract level, in the Screenplay, Matt's main motivation was to win the affection of Jessica away from Mitch, the stereotypical popular high school jock with his cheerleader girlfriend; saving his friend's mother's bar was secondary. In the Movie, however, there was never any competition on Peter's part to win the affection of Kate from White, because Kate was repulsed by White. Rather, Peter's sole purpose was to keep his gym from being taken over by the corporate Globo Gym.

2. Copying in Law

We now turn to the second infringement element, of copying in law. Recall that the element of "copying in law" is established when the defendant's copying is sufficient, quantitatively and qualitatively, to provoke legal liability for infringement. In this section, we explore copying in law in three different contexts: the **de minimis copy**, the **substantially similar copy**, and the **exact copy**. As you will see, copyright law handles each context somewhat differently.

a. De Minimis Copy

De minimis copying can be found when the defendant's copying is minimal in a legally salient way. Two recurring scenarios that can sometimes be labeled de minimis copying are (1) when the defendant copies the plaintiff's entire work but it appears as an insignificant aspect of the defendant's work, and (2) when the defendant copies but a minimal part of the plaintiff's work.

As you read the following case, think about how to evaluate when copying is minimal enough that it ought not to qualify as copying in law. Also, from whose perspective is this evaluation made?

Itoffee R. Gayle v. Home Box Office, Inc.
126 U.S.P.Q.2d 1760 (S.D.N.Y. 2018)

FURMAN, J.:

[1] Plaintiff Itoffee R. Gayle, proceeding *pro se*, brings this action against Home Box Office, Inc. ("HBO") alleging copyright infringement. Gayle's claims derive from the brief depiction of graffiti in the background of one scene in an episode of the HBO television series *Vinyl*. In the scene, a woman is shown walking down a New York City street and passing a dumpster tagged with graffiti stating "art we all" that Gayle claims is his intellectual property. Gayle alleges that HBO depicted the graffiti without permission, compensation, or attribution and thus infringed his copyright rights....

[2] HBO now moves ... to dismiss Gayle's claims....

Figure 48: scene from HBO's *Vinyl* depicting Gayle's graffiti on the side of a garbage dumpster

Figure 49: Gayle's graffiti on a garbage dumpster

[3] To prevail on his claim of copyright infringement, Gayle must prove that (1) unauthorized copying of the copyrighted work occurred, and (2) the infringing work is substantially similar. Significantly, demonstrating substantial similarity requires showing both that work copied was protected expression and that the amount that was copied is more than *de minimis*. In the copyright arena, *de minimis* can mean what it means in most legal contexts: a technical violation of a right so trivial that the law will not impose legal consequences, or it can mean that copying has occurred to such a trivial extent as to fall below the quantitative threshold of

substantial similarity, which is always a required element of actionable copying. In analyzing similarity, courts assess the extent to which the copyrighted work is copied in the allegedly infringing work, with a work's observability being paramount. Observability turns on the length of time the copyrighted work is observable as well as factors such as focus, lighting, camera angles, and prominence. The assessment is to be made from the viewpoint of an average lay observer.

[4] [This court]'s decision in *Gottlieb [Dev. LLC v. Paramount Pictures Corp.*, 590 F. Supp. 2d 625 (S.D.N.Y. 2008),] provides a helpful illustration of how these principles apply to claims of the sort at issue here. In that case, the plaintiff claimed that the defendant had infringed his copyright ... in a pinball machine by depicting it in the movie *What Women Want* starring Mel Gibson. [The court] dismissed the copyright claim on the ground that the defendant's use of the pinball machine was *de minimis* as a matter of law. [The court] explained:

> The scene in question lasts only three-and-a-half minutes, and the machine appears in the scene sporadically, for no more than a few seconds at a time. More importantly, the pinball machine is always in the background; it is never seen in the foreground. It never appears by itself or in a close-up. It is never mentioned and plays no role in the plot. It is almost always partially obscured (by Gibson and pieces of furniture), and is fully visible for only a few seconds during the entire scene. The Designs (on the backglass and playfield of the pinball machine) are never fully visible and are either out of focus or obscured. Indeed, an average observer would not recognize the Designs as anything other than generic designs in a pinball machine....

[5] If Gottlieb's claims were implausible, Gayle's border on frivolous. Whereas Gottlieb's claims were based on three-and-a-half minutes of film, Gayle's claims are premised on a fleeting shot of barely visible graffiti painted on what appears to be a dumpster in the background of a single scene. The overall scene is brief, and the graffiti at issue appears on screen for no more than two to three seconds. Moreover, the graffiti is never pictured by itself or in a close-up, and it plays absolutely no role in the plot. Instead, the camera is focused on the actress in the foreground, who is well-lit and depicted in an eye-catching bright-red dress. By contrast, the graffiti is, at best, shown in the background at an oblique angle and in low, uneven light such that it is never fully visible, let alone legible. In fact, the graffiti is hard enough to notice when the video is paused at the critical moment. It is next to impossible to notice when viewing the episode in real time. In short, the graffiti was filmed in such a manner and appears so fleetingly that there is no plausible claim for copyright infringement here....

[6] As evidence that his graffiti was visible [and] observable to average lay viewers, Gayle points to an Instagram message from a user named "Goldpoo_" congratulating him on the appearance of the graffiti in the episode of *Vinyl*. But the anonymous "Goldpoo_" is hardly a stand-in for the average lay observer relevant to the copyright inquiry .... Citing a YouTube video featuring members of the series[] production team detailing the importance of graffiti in recreating the 1970s New York City theme, Gayle also asserts that HBO's use of his graffiti cannot be deemed *de minimis* because it was "certainly deliberate" and "very much consequential." But ... HBO's motive in depicting the graffiti is irrelevant to the *de minimis* inquiry. Where the use is *de minimis*, as here, the copying will not be actionable, even where the work was chosen to be in the background for some thematic relevance.

[7] Accordingly, Gayle's copyright ... claim[] must be and [is] dismissed ....

NOTES

1. Does the de minimis rule make sense as a matter of copyright policy? Why or why not? Does your thinking help you make sense of the perspective the court in *Gayle* used to evaluate the degree of copying?

2. In thinking about the ease of drawing the line between de minimis copying and more substantial copying, consider the Second Circuit's decision in *Ringgold v. Black Entertainment Television, Inc.*, 126 F.3d 70 (2d Cir. 1997). As shown in Figure 50, artist Faith Ringgold had painted *Church Picnic Story Quilt*, a "story quilt design," comprised of a silk-screen painting on a silk quilt. A poster of *Church Picnic Story Quilt* appears in the background of an episode of the *Roc* television series set in a Baltimore church hall. The quilt is either fully or partially visible in nine segments of the episode for between 1.86 and 4.16 seconds each time, for a total visibility of 26.75 seconds. (For one such scene, see Figure 51.)

Figure 50: Faith Ringgold's *Church Picnic Story Quilt*

Figure 51: scene from *Roc* television episode with a poster of Ringgold's work in the background

The Second Circuit held that the defendants' use of Ringgold's work was more than de minimis:

> *From the standpoint of a quantitative assessment of the segments, the principal four-to-five-second segment in which almost all of the poster is clearly visible, albeit in less than perfect focus, reenforced by the briefer segments in which smaller portions are visible, all totaling 26 to 27 seconds, are not de minimis copying.*

Defendants further contend that the segments showing any portion of the poster are de minimis from the standpoint of qualitative sufficiency and therefore not actionable copying because no protectable aspects of plaintiff's expression are discernible. In defendants' view, the television viewer sees no more than "some vague stylized [sic] painting that includes black people," and can discern none of Ringgold's particular expression of her subjects. That is about like saying that a videotape of the Mona Lisa shows only a painting of a woman with a wry smile. Indeed, it seems disingenuous for the defendant HBO, whose production staff evidently thought that the poster was well suited as a set decoration for the African-American church scene of a ROC episode, now to contend that no visually significant aspect of the poster is discernible. In some circumstances, a visual work, though selected by production staff for thematic relevance, or at least for its decorative value, might ultimately be filmed at such a distance and so out of focus that a typical program viewer would not discern any decorative effect that the work of art contributes to the set. But that is not this case. The painting component of the poster is recognizable as a painting, and with sufficient observable detail for the average lay observer to discern African-Americans in Ringgold's colorful, virtually two-dimensional style. The de minimis threshold for actionable copying of protected expression has been crossed.

3. Instead of exempting de minimis copying from copyright infringement, would it be equally satisfying to count it as establishing copying in law but to award only trivial damages to the plaintiff?

b. Substantially Similar Copy

Substantial similarity is the flip side of de minimis copying: It is copying that is sufficient to lead to a conclusion of copying in law. As its name suggests, the defendant's copying need not be exact to constitute a substantially similar copy. To get a feel for what constitutes a substantially similar copy, we will consider first some classic cases and then some more contemporary ones. Because the tests for substantial similarity in the Second Circuit and the Ninth Circuit have diverged from one another since the 1970s—at least in the way each is articulated, if not applied—we will read multiple cases from each circuit.

i. Classic Cases

As you read this case, consider why copyright infringement might be found for copying that is not merely exact. Then, consider which similarities between a plaintiff's work and a defendant's work count toward a conclusion of substantial similarity, and thus copying in law.

Anne Nichols v. Universal Pictures Corporation
45 F.2d 119 (2d Cir. 1930)

HAND, J.:

[1] The plaintiff is the author of a play, 'Abie's Irish Rose,' which it may be assumed was properly copyrighted under ... the Copyright Act. The defendant produced publicly a motion picture ..., 'The Cohens and The Kellys,' which the plaintiff alleges was taken from it. As we think the defendant's play too unlike the plaintiff's to be an infringement, we may assume, arguendo, that in some details the defendant used the plaintiff's play, as will subsequently appear, though we do not so decide....

Chapter V – Exclusive Rights

[2] 'Abie's Irish Rose' presents a Jewish family living in prosperous circumstances in New York. The father, a widower, is in business as a merchant, in which his son and only child helps him. The boy has philandered with young women, who to his father's great disgust have always been Gentiles, for he is obsessed with a passion that his daughter-in-law shall be an orthodox Jewess. When the play opens the son, who has been courting a young Irish Catholic girl, has already married her secretly before a Protestant minister, and is concerned to soften the blow for his father, by securing a favorable impression of his bride, while concealing her faith and race. To accomplish this he introduces her to his father at his home as a Jewess, and lets it appear that he is interested in her, though he conceals the marriage. The girl somewhat reluctantly falls in with the plan; the father takes the bait, becomes infatuated with the girl, concludes that they must marry, and assumes that of course they will, if he so decides. He calls in a rabbi, and prepares for the wedding according to the Jewish rite.

[3] Meanwhile the girl's father, also a widower, who lives in California, and is as intense in his own religious antagonism as the Jew, has been called to New York, supposing that his daughter is to marry an Irishman and a Catholic. Accompanied by a priest, he arrives at the house at the moment when the marriage is being celebrated, but too late to prevent it and the two fathers, each infuriated by the proposed union of his child to a heretic, fall into unseemly and grotesque antics. The priest and the rabbi become friendly, exchange trite sentiments about religion, and agree that the match is good. Apparently out of abundant caution, the priest celebrates the marriage for a third time, while the girl's father is inveigled away. The second act closes with each father, still outraged, seeking to find some way by which the union, thus trebly insured, may be dissolved.

[4] The last act takes place about a year later, the young couple having meanwhile been abjured by each father, and left to their own resources. They have had twins, a boy and a girl, but their fathers know no more than that a child has been born. At Christmas each, led by his craving to see his grandchild, goes separately to the young folks' home, where they encounter each other, each laden with gifts, one for a boy, the other for a girl. After some slapstick comedy, depending upon the insistence of each that he is right about the sex of the grandchild, they become reconciled when they learn the truth, and that each child is to bear the given name of a grandparent. The curtain falls as the fathers are exchanging amenities, and the Jew giving evidence of an abatement in the strictness of his orthodoxy.

[5] 'The Cohens and The Kellys' presents two families, Jewish and Irish, living side by side in the poorer quarters of New York in a state of perpetual enmity. The wives in both cases are still living, and share in the mutual animosity, as do two small sons, and even the respective dogs. The Jews have a daughter, the Irish a son; the Jewish father is in the clothing business; the Irishman is a policeman. The children are in love with each other, and secretly marry, apparently after the play opens. The Jew, being in great financial straits, learns from a lawyer that he has fallen heir to a large fortune from a great-aunt, and moves into a great house, fitted luxuriously. Here he and his family live in vulgar ostentation, and here the Irish boy seeks out his Jewish bride, and is chased away by the angry father. The Jew then abuses the Irishman over the telephone, and both become hysterically excited. The extremity of his feelings make the Jew sick, so that he must go to Florida for a rest, just before which the daughter discloses her marriage to her mother.

[6] On his return the Jew finds that his daughter has borne a child; at first he suspects the lawyer, but eventually learns the truth and is overcome with anger at such a low alliance. Meanwhile, the Irish family who have been forbidden to see the grandchild, go to the Jew's house, and after a violent scene between the two fathers in which the Jew disowns his daughter, who decides to go back with her husband, the Irishman takes her back with her baby to his own poor lodgings. The lawyer, who had hoped to marry the Jew's daughter, seeing his plan foiled, tells the Jew that his fortune really belongs to the Irishman, who was also related to the dead woman, but offers to conceal his knowledge, if the Jew will share the loot. This the Jew repudiates, and, leaving the astonished lawyer, walks through the rain to his enemy's house to surrender the property. He arrives in great dejection, tells the truth, and abjectly turns to leave. A reconciliation ensues, the Irishman

agreeing to share with him equally. The Jew shows some interest in his grandchild, though this is at most a minor motive in the reconciliation, and the curtain falls while the two are in their cups, the Jew insisting that in the firm name for the business, which they are to carry on jointly, his name shall stand first.

Figure 52: posters for the works of the plaintiff (left) and the defendant (right)

[7] It is of course essential to any protection of literary property, whether at common-law or under the statute, that the right cannot be limited literally to the text, else a plagiarist would escape by immaterial variations. That has never been the law, but, as soon as literal appropriation ceases to be the test, the whole matter is necessarily at large, so that ... the decisions cannot help much in a new case. When plays are concerned, the plagiarist may excise a separate scene or he may appropriate part of the dialogue. Then the question is whether the part so taken is substantial; it is the same question as arises in the case of any other copyrighted work. But when the plagiarist does not take out a block in suit, but an abstract of the whole, decision is more troublesome. Upon any work, and especially upon a play, a great number of patterns of increasing generality will fit equally well, as more and more of the incident is left out. The last may perhaps be no more than the most general statement of what the play is about, and at times might consist only of its title; but there is a point in this series of abstractions where they are no longer protected, since otherwise the playwright could prevent the use of his ideas, to which, apart from their expression, his property is never extended. Nobody has ever been able to fix that boundary, and nobody ever can.... As respects plays, the controversy chiefly centers upon the characters and sequence of incident, these being the substance....

[8] .... If *Twelfth Night* were copyrighted, it is quite possible that a second comer might so closely imitate Sir Toby Belch or Malvolio as to infringe, but it would not be enough that for one of his characters he cast a riotous knight who kept wassail to the discomfort of the household, or a vain and foppish steward who

became amorous of his mistress. These would be no more than Shakespeare's 'ideas' in the play, as little capable of monopoly as Einstein's Doctrine of Relativity, or Darwin's theory of the Origin of Species. It follows that the less developed the characters, the less they can be copyrighted; that is the penalty an author must bear for marking them too indistinctly.

[9] In the two plays at bar we think both as to incident and character, the defendant took no more—assuming that it took anything at all—than the law allowed. The stories are quite different. One is of a religious zealot who insists upon his child's marrying no one outside his faith; opposed by another who is in this respect just like him, and is his foil. Their difference in race is merely an obbligato to the main theme, religion. They sink their differences through grandparental pride and affection. In the other, zealotry is wholly absent; religion does not even appear. It is true that the parents are hostile to each other in part because they differ in race; but the marriage of their son to a Jew does not apparently offend the Irish family at all, and it exacerbates the existing animosity of the Jew, principally because he has become rich, when he learns it. They are reconciled through the honesty of the Jew and the generosity of the Irishman; the grandchild has nothing whatever to do with it. The only matter common to the two is a quarrel between a Jewish and an Irish father, the marriage of their children, the birth of grandchildren and a reconciliation.

[10] If the defendant took so much from the plaintiff, it may well have been because her amazing success seemed to prove that this was a subject of enduring popularity. Even so, granting that the plaintiff's play was wholly original, and assuming that novelty is not essential to a copyright, there is no monopoly in such a background. Though the plaintiff discovered the vein, she could not keep it to herself; so defined, the theme was too generalized an abstraction from what she wrote. It was only a part of her ideas.

[11] Nor does she fare better as to her characters. It is indeed scarcely credible that she should not have been aware of those stock figures, the low comedy Jew and Irishman. The defendant has not taken from her more than their prototypes have contained for many decades. If so, obviously so to generalize her copyright, would allow her to cover what was not original with her. But we need not hold this as matter of fact, much as we might be justified. Even though we take it that she devised her figures out of her brain de novo, still the defendant was within its rights.

[12] There are but four characters common to both plays, the lovers and the fathers. The lovers are so faintly indicated as to be no more than stage properties. They are loving and fertile; that is really all that can be said of them, and anyone else is quite within his rights if he puts loving and fertile lovers in a play of his own, wherever he gets the cue. The Plaintiff's Jew is quite unlike the defendant's. His obsession in his religion, on which depends such racial animosity as he has. He is affectionate, warm and patriarchal. None of these fit the defendant's Jew, who shows affection for his daughter only once, and who has none but the most superficial interest in his grandchild. He is tricky, ostentatious and vulgar, only by misfortune redeemed into honesty. Both are grotesque, extravagant and quarrelsome; both are fond of display; but these common qualities make up only a small part of their simple pictures, no more than any one might lift if he chose. The Irish fathers are even more unlike; the plaintiff's a mere symbol for religious fanaticism and patriarchal pride, scarcely a character at all. Neither quality appears in the defendant's, for while he goes to get his grandchild, it is rather out of a truculent determination not to be forbidden, than from pride in his progeny. For the rest he is only a grotesque hobbledehoy, used for low comedy of the most conventional sort, which any one might borrow, if he chanced not to know the exemplar.

[13] .... [The plaintiff's] copyright did not cover everything that might be drawn from her play; its content went to some extent into the public domain. We have to decide how much, and while we are as aware as any one that the line, whereever it is drawn, will seem arbitrary, that is no excuse for not drawing it; it is a question such as courts must answer in nearly all cases. Whatever may be the difficulties a priori, we have no question

on which side of the line this case falls. A comedy based upon conflicts between Irish and Jews, into which the marriage of their children enters, is no more susceptible of copyright than the outline of *Romeo and Juliet*....

[14] The plaintiff has prepared an elaborate analysis of the two plays, showing a 'quadrangle' of the common characters, in which each is represented by the emotions which he discovers. She presents the resulting parallelism as proof of infringement, but the adjectives employed are so general as to be quite useless. Take for example the attribute of 'love' ascribed to both Jews. The plaintiff has depicted her father as deeply attached to his son, who is his hope and joy; not so, the defendant, whose father's conduct is throughout not actuated by any affection for his daughter, and who is merely once overcome for the moment by her distress when he has violently dismissed her lover. 'Anger' covers emotions aroused by quite different occasions in each case; so do 'anxiety,' 'despondency' and 'disgust.' It is unnecessary to go through the catalogue for emotions are too much colored by their causes to be a test when used so broadly. This is not the proper approach to a solution; it must be more ingenuous, more like that of a spectator, who would rely upon the complex of his impressions of each character.

[15] We cannot approve the length of the record, which was due chiefly to the use of expert witnesses.... It ought not to be allowed at all; and while its admission is not a ground for reversal, it cumbers the case and tends to confusion, for the more the court is led into the intricacies of dramatic craftsmanship, the less likely it is to stand upon the firmer, if more naive, ground of its considered impressions upon its own perusal. We hope that in this class of cases such evidence may in the future be entirely excluded, and the case confined to the actual issues; that is, whether the defendant copied it, so far as the supposed infringement is identical....

> In the following case, consider the disagreement between Judge Frank writing for the majority and Judge Clark writing for the dissent. From whose perspective does this case ask us to evaluate whether there is substantial similarity?

Ira Arnstein v. Cole Porter
154 F.2d 464 (2d Cir. 1946)

{Plaintiff Ira Arnstein filed suit against defendant Cole Porter for copyright infringement. In particular, he alleged that Porter's songs "Begin the Beguine," "My Heart Belongs to Daddy," "I Love You," "Night and Day," "You'd Be So Nice to Come Home to," and "Don't Fence Me In" infringed various of Arnstein's multiple musical compositions. According to Arnstein, some, but not all, of these compositions of his had been published and sold, one in 2,000 copies and another in one million copies. He alleged that another of his compositions was unsold but had been publicly performed over the radio and that a copy of the song had been stolen from his room. Arnstein further alleged that two other compositions at issue had never been published or publicly performed but had been sent to a movie producer, multiple publishers, and multiple radio stations and band leaders. He also alleged that Porter "had stooges right along to follow me, watch me, and live in the same apartment with me," and that his apartment had been burglarized multiple times. He did not provide direct evidence that Porter saw or heard any of these compositions or that Porter or any of his agents broke in to his apartment. Porter denied having seen or heard any of Arnstein's songs. Arnstein had previously brought and lost five copyright infringement suits against other defendants.}

FRANK, J.: ...

[1] The principal question on this appeal is whether the lower court ... properly deprived plaintiff of a trial of his copyright infringement action.... [I]t is important to avoid confusing two separate elements essential to a

plaintiff's case in such a suit: (a) that defendant copied from plaintiff's copyrighted work and (b) that the copying (assuming it to be proved) went to far as to constitute improper appropriation.

[2] As to the first—copying—.... analysis ('dissection') is relevant, and the testimony of experts may be received to aid the trier of the facts....

[3] If copying is established, then only does there arise the second issue, that of illicit copying (unlawful appropriation). On that issue (as noted more in detail below) the test is the response of the ordinary lay hearer; accordingly, on that issue, 'dissection' and expert testimony are irrelevant....

[4] Each of these two issues—copying and improper appropriation—is an issue of fact. If there is a trial, the conclusions on those issues of the trier of the facts ... bind this court on appeal, provided the evidence supports those findings, regardless of whether we would ourselves have reached the same conclusions....

[5] Assuming that adequate proof is made of copying, that is not enough; for there can be permissible copying, copying which is not illicit. Whether (if he copied) defendant unlawfully appropriated presents, too, an issue of fact. The proper criterion on that issue is not an analytic or other comparison of the respective musical compositions as they appear on paper or in the judgment of trained musicians.[19] The plaintiff's legally protected interest is not, as such, his reputation as a musician but his interest in the potential financial returns from his compositions which derive from the lay public's approbation of his efforts. The question, therefore, is whether defendant took from plaintiff's works so much of what is pleasing to the ears of lay listeners, who comprise the audience for whom such popular music is composed, that defendant wrongfully appropriated something which belongs to the plaintiff.

[6] Surely, then, we have an issue of fact which a jury is peculiarly fitted to determine.[22] Indeed, even if there were to be a trial before a judge, it would be desirable (although not necessary) for him to summon an advisory jury on this question.

[7] We should not be taken as saying that a[n infringement] case can never arise in which absence of similarities is so patent that a summary judgment for defendant would be correct. Thus suppose that Ravel's 'Bolero' or Shostakovitch's 'Fifth Symphony' were alleged to infringe 'When Irish Eyes Are Smiling.'[23] But this is not such a case. For, after listening to the playing of the respective compositions, we are, at this time, unable to conclude that the likenesses are so trifling that, on the issue of misappropriation, a trial judge could legitimately direct a verdict for defendant.

[8] At the trial, plaintiff may play, or cause to be played, the pieces in such manner that they may seem to a jury to be inexcusably alike, in terms of the way in which lay listeners of such music would be likely to react. The plaintiff may call witnesses whose testimony may aid the jury in reaching its conclusion as to the responses of such audiences. Expert testimony of musicians may also be received, but it will in no way be controlling on the issue of illicit copying, and should be utilized only to assist in determining the reactions of lay auditors. The impression made on the refined ears of musical experts or their views as to the musical excellence of plaintiff's or defendant's works are utterly immaterial on the issue of misappropriation; for the views of such persons are caviar to the general—and plaintiff's and defendant's compositions are not caviar....

---

[19] Where plaintiff relies on similarities to prove copying (as distinguished from improper appropriation) paper comparisons and the opinions of experts may aid the court.

[22] It would, accordingly, be proper to exclude tone-deaf persons from the jury.

[23] In such a case, the complete absence of similarity would negate both copying and improper appropriation.

CLARK, J. (dissenting):

[9] While the procedure followed below seems to me generally simple and appropriate, the defendant did make one fatal tactical error. In an endeavor to assist us, he caused to be prepared records of all the musical pieces here involved, and presented these transcriptions through the medium of the affidavit of his pianist. Though he himself did not stress these records and properly met plaintiff's claims as to the written music with his own analysis, yet the tinny tintinnabulations of the music thus canned resounded through the United States Courthouse to the exclusion of all else, including the real issues in the case. Of course, sound is important in a case of this kind, but it is not so important as to falsify what the eye reports and the mind teaches. Otherwise [infringement] would be suggested by the mere drumming of repetitious sound from our usual popular music, as it issues from a piano, orchestra, or hurdy-gurdy—particularly when ears may be dulled by long usage, possibly artistic repugnance or boredom, or mere distance which causes all sounds to merge. And the judicial eardrum may be peculiarly insensitive after long years of listening to the 'beat, beat, beat' (I find myself plagiarizing from defendant and thus in danger of my brothers' doom) of sound upon it, though perhaps no more so than the ordinary citizen juror—even if tone deafness is made a disqualification for jury service, as advocated.

[10] ... [A]fter repeated hearings of the records, I could not find therein what my brothers found. The only thing definitely mentioned seemed to be the repetitive use of the note e^2 in certain places by both plaintiff and defendant, surely too simple and ordinary a device of composition to be significant. In our former musical [infringement] cases we have, naturally, relied on what seemed the total sound effect; but we have also analyzed the music enough to make sure of an intelligible and intellectual decision....

[11] It is true that ... we considered dissection or technical analysis not the proper approach to support a finding of [infringement], and ... that it must be more ingenuous, more like that of a spectator, who would rely upon the complex of his impressions. But in its context that seems to me clearly sound and in accord with what I have in mind. Thus one may look to the total impression to repulse the charge of [infringement] where a minute dissection might dredge up some points of similarity. Hence one cannot use a purely theoretical disquisition to supply a tonal resemblance which does not otherwise exist. Certainly, however, that does not suggest or compel the converse—that one must keep his brain in torpor for fear that otherwise it would make clear differences which do exist. Music is a matter of the intellect as well as the emotions; that is why eminent musical scholars insist upon the employment of the intellectual faculties for a just appreciation of music. Consequently I do not think we should abolish the use of the intellect here even if we could. When, however, we start with an examination of the written and printed material supplied by the plaintiff in his complaint and exhibits, we find at once that he does not and cannot claim extensive copying, measure by measure, of his compositions. He therefore has resorted to a comparative analysis—the dissection found unpersuasive in ... earlier cases—to support his claim of [infringement] of small detached portions here and there, the musical fillers between the better known parts of the melody. And plaintiff's compositions, as pointed out in the cases cited above, are of the simple and trite character where small repetitive sequences are not hard to discover. It is as though we found Shakespeare a[n infringer] on the basis of his use of articles, pronouns, prepositions, and adjectives also used by others. The surprising thing, however, is to note the small amount of even this type of reproduction which plaintiff by dint of extreme dissection has been able to find....

[12] In the light of these utmost claims of the plaintiff, I do not see a legal basis for the claim of [infringement]....

[13] Since the legal issue seems thus clear to me, I am loath to believe that my colleagues will uphold a final judgment of [infringement] on a record such as this. The present holding is therefore one of those procedural mountains which develop where it is thought that justice must be temporarily sacrificed, lest a mistaken precedent be set at large.... But I should not have thought [the jury] pre-eminently fitted to decide questions

of musical values, certainly not so much so that an advisory jury should be brought in if no other is available. And I should myself hesitate to utter so clear an invitation to exploitation of slight musical analogies by clever musical tricks in the hope of getting juries hereafter in this circuit to divide the wealth of Tin Pan Alley. This holding seems to me an invitation to the strike suit par excellence....

[14] .... Here I think we ought to assume the responsibility of decision now. If, however, we are going to the other extreme of having all decisions of musical [infringement] made by ear, the more unsophisticated and musically naive the better, then it seems to me we are reversing our own precedents to substitute chaos, judicial as well as musical.

NOTES

1. Recall from our discussion of computer software in Chapter II, that the Second Circuit, in *Computer Associates International, Inc. v. Altai, Inc.*, 982 F.2d 693 (2d Cir. 1992), derived its abstraction-filtration-comparison test from Judge Hand's analysis in *Nichols*. Do you think the *Altai* framework follows from *Nichols*?

After the Second Circuit applied its abstraction-filtration-comparison test to Computer Associates' ADAPTER software, it concluded that there was no copyright infringement. It found that so little was left after abstraction and filtration that the little that was left was not substantially similar.

2. In *Arnstein*, Judge Frank sets forth that dissection and expert testimony are appropriate for analyzing copying in fact but not copying in law. Does this seem right in view of the goals of copyright law? For a contrary take—that Judge Frank had this wrong for both copying in fact and copying in law—see Mark A. Lemley, *Our Bizarre System for Proving Copyright Infringement*, 57 J. COPYRIGHT SOC'Y U.S.A. 719 (2010).

Are *Nichols* and *Arnstein* consistent in their allowance of dissection of works to evaluate copying in law?

3. Consider the audience *Arnstein* sets out as the vantage point against which to assess substantial similarity, as well as the ones it excludes. How well does this comport with copyright policy? Is the jury well-suited to evaluate substantial similarity? Why or why not? In which ways does Judge Clark in his dissent disagree with the audience framework that Judge Frank sets out in his majority decision?

Although *Arnstein* would seem to exclude expert views on a work in assessing substantial similarity, in rare cases courts step back from that rule and allow expert testimony as to substantial similarity. For example, the Second Circuit observed in *Altai* (in the context of alleged infringement of computer software) that expert testimony might be relevant when dealing with "art forms [that are not] readily comprehensible and generally familiar to the average layperson." *Altai*, 982 F.2d at 713. Similarly, in a copyright infringement suit over a spiritual song, the Fourth Circuit observed that

> When conducting the second prong of the substantial similarity inquiry, a district court must consider the nature of the intended audience of the plaintiff's work. If, as will most often be the case, the lay public fairly represents the intended audience, the court should apply the lay observer formulation of the ordinary observer test. However, if the intended audience is more narrow in that it possesses specialized expertise, relevant to the purchasing decision, that lay people would lack, the court's inquiry should focus on whether a member of the intended audience would find the two works to be substantially similar.

Dawson v. Hinshaw Music Inc., 905 F.2d 731, 736-37 (4th Cir. 1990).

For an evaluation of how copyright law—and other forms of intellectual property—ought to frame the audience against which infringement is measured, see Jeanne C. Fromer & Mark A. Lemley, *The Audience in Intellectual Property Infringement*, 112 MICH. L. REV. 1251 (2014). Fromer and Lemley argue that to achieve copyright law's utilitarian goals, substantial similarity ought to be assessed through the eyes of both a work's consumer and its experts:

> *[Copyright law, as well as other intellectual property regimes,] should find infringement only when the defendant's product is too similar to the plaintiff's in the eyes of both experts and consumers, not just one or the other. Put another way, infringement in an ideal IP regime grounded in utilitarianism should require proof of both sufficient technical similarity and market substitution. Market substitution is important because a use that does not interfere with the plaintiff's market in some way generally does no relevant harm. Technical similarity is also important because not all acts that interfere with a plaintiff's market are problematic. A defendant who enters the market with a different, better product, for instance, may erode the market for the plaintiff's product, but the law should not prohibit that competition.*

> *.... The expert-as-audience approach ensures that we find infringement only when two works are sufficiently similar in their protectable elements. An audience of experts familiar with the subject matter is likely to understand the technical and historical constraints—including those of the particular genre—that led to similarities and to find improper appropriation only when the works bear sufficient technical similarity to each other despite those constraints. Assessing infringement through the expert's eyes thus ensures that the law protects creators only from sufficiently close imitations.*

> *The consumer matters too, because sometimes similarity of expression occurs in such disparate contexts that the two works are not market substitutes at all. Consumers are more likely than domain experts to be sensitive to whether the defendant's work is substituting for the plaintiff's in the marketplace. This consumer vantage point matters because IP laws—with their instrumental incentives—are generally concerned with protecting IP owners only when they have been harmed in the marketplace with regard to their underlying intellectual property.*

Id. at 1255-56; *cf.* Irina D. Manta, *Reasonable Copyright*, 53 B.C. L. REV. 1303 (2012) (arguing that substantial similarity might better be assessed by experts).

4. For works protected under laws predating the 1976 Act, infringement of a musical composition was to be assessed against the plaintiff's sheet music (also known as a composition's "score"), rather than any sound recording based on that composition. Skidmore v. Led Zeppelin, 952 F.3d 1051 (9th Cir. 2020) (en banc). Current law does not require that musical works be fixed in scores, and instead provides that musical works gain copyright protection even if fixed only in "phonorecords"—that is, in the form of a sound recording. In assessing infringement of a musical composition, how do you think a finding can differ if based on reading the corresponding sheet music or based on listening to a recording or performance of the composition? How do the majority and dissent in *Arnstein* differ in their approach? In an empirical study, Jamie Lund finds that "[p]laying the sound recording in a [musical c]omposition [c]opyright case invites the jurors to make the wrong comparison, comparing the sound recordings, rather than the compositional elements underlying each recording." Jamie Lund, *An Empirical Examination of the Lay Listener Test in Music Composition Copyright Infringement*, 11 VA. SPORTS & ENT. L.J. 137 (2011).

ii. Contemporary Cases

As you read this and the following more contemporary decisions within the Second Circuit, consider how faithful they are to *Nichols* and *Arnstein*. In the context of the test these cases articulate for substantial similarity, consider which similarities between the plaintiff's work and the defendant's work affect each court's outcome on substantial similarity.

Saul Steinberg v. Columbia Pictures Industries, Inc.
663 F. Supp. 706 (S.D.N.Y. 1987)

STANTON, J.: ...

[1] .... On March 29, 1976, *The New Yorker* published as a cover illustration the work at issue in this suit, widely known as a parochial New Yorker's view of the world. The magazine registered this illustration with the United States Copyright Office and subsequently assigned the copyright to [artist Saul] Steinberg. Approximately three months later, plaintiff and *The New Yorker* entered into an agreement to print and sell a certain number of posters of the cover illustration.

[2] .... Plaintiff has ... conceded that numerous posters have been created and published depicting other localities in the same manner that he depicted New York in his illustration. These facts, however, are irrelevant to the merits of this case, which concerns only the relationship between plaintiff's and defendants' illustrations.

[3] Defendants' illustration was created to advertise the movie "Moscow on the Hudson," which recounts the adventures of a Muscovite who defects in New York. In designing this illustration, Columbia's executive art director, Kevin Nolan, has admitted that he specifically referred to Steinberg's poster, and indeed, that he purchased it and hung it, among others, in his office. Furthermore, Nolan explicitly directed the outside artist whom he retained to execute his design, Craig Nelson, to use Steinberg's poster to achieve a more recognizably New York look. Indeed, Nelson acknowledged having used the facade of one particular edifice, at Nolan's suggestion that it would render his drawing more "New York-ish." ...[1]

[4] To decide the issue of infringement, it is necessary to consider the posters themselves. Steinberg's illustration presents a bird's eye view across a portion of the western edge of Manhattan, past the Hudson River and a telescoped version of the rest of the United States and the Pacific Ocean, to a red strip of horizon, beneath which are three flat land masses labeled China, Japan and Russia. The name of the magazine, in *The New Yorker*'s usual typeface, occupies the top fifth of the poster, beneath a thin band of blue wash representing a stylized sky.

[5] The parts of the poster beyond New York are minimized, to symbolize a New Yorker's myopic view of the centrality of his city to the world. The entire United States west of the Hudson River, for example, is reduced to a brown strip labeled "Jersey," together with a light green trapezoid with a few rudimentary rock outcroppings and the names of only seven cities and two states scattered across it. The few blocks of Manhattan, by contrast, are depicted and colored in detail. The four square blocks of the city, which occupy the whole lower half of the poster, include numerous buildings, pedestrians and cars, as well as parking lots

---

[1] Nolan claimed also to have been inspired by some of the posters that were inspired by Steinberg's; such secondary inspiration, however, is irrelevant to whether or not the "Moscow" poster infringes plaintiff's copyright by having impermissibly copied it.

and lamp posts, with water towers atop a few of the buildings. The whimsical, sketchy style and spiky lettering are recognizable as Steinberg's.

[6] The "Moscow" illustration depicts the three main characters of the film on the lower third of their poster, superimposed on a bird's eye view of New York City, and continues eastward across Manhattan and the Atlantic Ocean, past a rudimentary evocation of Europe, to a clump of recognizably Russian-styled buildings on the horizon, labeled "Moscow." The movie credits appear over the lower portion of the characters. The central part of the poster depicts approximately four New York city blocks, with fairly detailed buildings, pedestrians and vehicles, a parking lot, and some water towers and lamp posts. Columbia's artist added a few New York landmarks at apparently random places in his illustration, apparently to render the locale more easily recognizable. Beyond the blue strip labeled "Atlantic Ocean," Europe is represented by London, Paris and Rome, each anchored by a single landmark (although the landmark used for Rome is the Leaning Tower of Pisa).

[7] The horizon behind Moscow is delineated by a red crayoned strip, above which are the title of the movie and a brief textual introduction to the plot. The poster is crowned by a thin strip of blue wash, apparently a stylization of the sky. This poster is executed in a blend of styles: the three characters, whose likenesses were copied from a photograph, have realistic faces and somewhat sketchy clothing, and the city blocks are drawn in a fairly detailed but sketchy style. The lettering on the drawing is spiky, in block-printed handwritten capital letters substantially identical to plaintiff's, while the printed texts at the top and bottom of the poster are in the typeface commonly associated with *The New Yorker* magazine.[2] ...

[8] Defendants' access to plaintiff's illustration is established beyond peradventure. Therefore, the sole issue remaining with respect to liability is whether there is such substantial similarity between the copyrighted and accused works as to establish a violation of plaintiff's copyright. The central issue of "substantial similarity," which can be considered a close question of fact, may also validly be decided as a question of law....

[9] The definition of "substantial similarity" in this circuit is whether an average lay observer would recognize the alleged copy as having been appropriated from the copyrighted work. A plaintiff need no longer meet the severe "ordinary observer" test established by Judge Learned Hand .... Under Judge Hand's formulation, there would be substantial similarity only where the ordinary observer, unless he set out to detect the disparities, would be disposed to overlook them, and regard their aesthetic appeal as the same....

[10] There is no dispute that defendants cannot be held liable for using the *idea* of a map of the world from an egocentrically myopic perspective. No rigid principle has been developed, however, to ascertain when one has gone beyond the idea to the expression, and decisions must therefore inevitably be ad hoc....

[11] Even at first glance, one can see the striking stylistic relationship between the posters, and since style is one ingredient of expression, this relationship is significant. Defendants' illustration was executed in the sketchy, whimsical style that has become one of Steinberg's hallmarks. Both illustrations represent a bird's eye view across the edge of Manhattan and a river bordering New York City to the world beyond. Both depict approximately four city blocks in detail and become increasingly minimalist as the design recedes into the background. Both use the device of a narrow band of blue wash across the top of the poster to represent the sky, and both delineate the horizon with a band of primary red.[3]

---

[2] The typeface is not a subject of copyright, but the similarity reinforces the impression that defendants copied plaintiff's illustration.
[3] Defendants claim that since this use of thin bands of primary colors is a traditional Japanese technique, their adoption of it cannot infringe Steinberg's copyright. This argument ignores the principle that while others are free to copy the original they are not free to copy the copy.

Figure 53: Saul Steinberg's *View of the World from 9th Avenue*

Figure 54: Columbia Pictures' movie poster for *Moscow on the Hudson*

[12] The strongest similarity is evident in the rendering of the New York City blocks. Both artists chose a vantage point that looks directly down a wide two-way cross street that intersects two avenues before reaching a river. Despite defendants' protestations, this is not an inevitable way of depicting blocks in a city with a grid-like street system, particularly since most New York City cross streets are one-way. Since even a photograph may be copyrighted ..., one can hardly gainsay the right of an artist to protect his choice of perspective and lay-out in a drawing, especially in conjunction with the overall concept and individual details. Indeed, the fact that defendants changed the names of the streets while retaining the same graphic depiction weakens their case: had they intended their illustration realistically to depict the streets labeled on the poster, their four city blocks would not so closely resemble plaintiff's four city blocks. Moreover, their argument that they intended the jumble of streets and landmarks and buildings to symbolize their Muscovite protagonist's confusion in a new city does not detract from the strong similarity between their poster and Steinberg's.

[13] While not all of the details are identical, many of them could be mistaken for one another; for example, the depiction of the water towers, and the cars, and the red sign above a parking lot, and even many of the individual buildings. The shapes, windows, and configurations of various edifices are substantially similar. The ornaments, facades and details of Steinberg's buildings appear in defendants', although occasionally at other locations. In this context, it is significant that Steinberg did not depict any buildings actually erected in New York; rather, he was inspired by the general appearance of the structures on the West Side of Manhattan to create his own New York-ish structures. Thus, the similarity between the buildings depicted in the "Moscow" and Steinberg posters cannot be explained by an assertion that the artists happened to choose the same buildings to draw. The close similarity can be explained only by the defendants' artist having copied the plaintiff's work. Similarly, the locations and size, the errors and anomalies of Steinberg's shadows and streetlight, are meticulously imitated.

[14] In addition, the Columbia artist's use of the childlike, spiky block print that has become one of Steinberg's hallmarks to letter the names of the streets in the "Moscow" poster can be explained only as copying. There is no inherent justification for using this style of lettering to label New York City streets as it is associated with New York only through Steinberg's poster.

[15] While defendants' poster shows the city of Moscow on the horizon in far greater detail than anything is depicted in the background of plaintiff's illustration, this fact alone cannot alter the conclusion. "Substantial similarity" does not require identity, and duplication or near identity is not necessary to establish infringement. Neither the depiction of Moscow, nor the eastward perspective, nor the presence of randomly scattered New York City landmarks in defendants' poster suffices to eliminate the substantial similarity between the posters. As Judge Learned Hand wrote, "no plagiarist can excuse the wrong by showing how much of his work he did not pirate." Sheldon v. Metro-Goldwyn Pictures Corp., 81 F.2d 49, 56 (2d Cir.), *cert. denied,* 298 U.S. 669 (1936)....

[16] The process by which defendants' poster was created also undermines this argument. The "map," that is, the portion about which plaintiff is complaining, was designed separately from the rest of the poster. The likenesses of the three main characters, which were copied from a photograph, and the blocks of text were superimposed on the completed map.

[17] I also reject defendants' argument that any similarities between the works are unprotectible *scenes a faire,* or incidents, characters or settings which, as a practical matter, are indispensable or standard in the treatment of a given topic. It is undeniable that a drawing of New York City blocks could be expected to include buildings, pedestrians, vehicles, lampposts and water towers. Plaintiff, however, does not complain of defendants' mere use of these elements in their poster; rather, his complaint is that defendants copied his *expression* of those elements of a street scene.

[18] While evidence of independent creation by the defendants would rebut plaintiff's prima facie case, the absence of any countervailing evidence of creation independent of the copyrighted source may well render clearly erroneous a finding that there was not copying....

NOTE

1. Do you view the *Steinberg* court as having protected Saul Steinberg's style of visual art from copying? Is that consistent with copyright law's aims? Based on *Steinberg*, would you find the following three parochial views of the world, respectively in Figure 55 through Figure 57, from Washington, China, and New York based on Apple Maps software, to be substantially similar to Steinberg's *View of the World from 9th Avenue*?

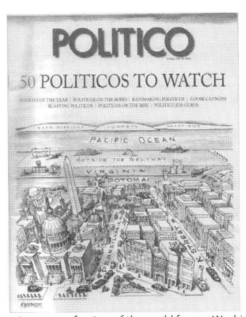

Figure 55: Politico Magazine cover of a view of the world from a Washingtonian's perspective

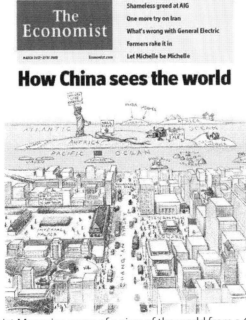

Figure 56: Economist Magazine cover of a view of the world from a Chinese perspective

Figure 57: MAD Magazine parody cover of a New Yorker's view of the world based on Apple Maps software

On whether *Steinberg* protects an artist's style and the status of copyright protection generally for style, see 2 WILLIAM F. PATRY, PATRY ON COPYRIGHT § 4:14 (2018).

In addition to the considerations raised before *Steinberg*, consider whether the Second Circuit's standard of review is desirable.

Judi Boisson v. Banian, Ltd.

273 F.3d 262 (2d Cir. 2001)

CARDAMONE, J.: ...

[1] In 1991 plaintiff [Judi Boisson] designed and produced two alphabet quilts entitled "School Days I" and "School Days II." ... [E]ach consists of square blocks containing the capital letters of the alphabet, displayed in order. The blocks are set in horizontal rows and vertical columns, with the last row filled by blocks containing various pictures or icons. The letters and blocks are made up of different colors, set off by a white border and colored edging....

Figure 58: Boisson "School Days I" quilt

[2] .... [Defendant Banian, Ltd.] imported from India each of the three alphabet quilts at issue in this case[, "ABC Green Version I," "ABC Green Version II," and "ABC Navy"]....

Figure 59: Banian's "ABC Green Version I" (left) and "ABC Navy" (right) quilts

[3] Plaintiffs filed their suit in March 1997 seeking relief from defendants for copyright infringement ....

Chapter V – Exclusive Rights

[4] .... The district court made a finding that actual copying had occurred, and because defendants do not dispute that finding, actual copying is ... established.... Plaintiffs must also demonstrate substantial similarity between defendants' quilts and the *protectible* elements of their own quilts....

[5] .... We review *de novo* the district court's determination with respect to substantial similarity because credibility is not at stake and all that is required is a visual comparison of the products—a task we may perform as well as the district court.

[6] Generally, an allegedly infringing work is considered substantially similar to a copyrighted work if the ordinary observer, unless he set out to detect the disparities, would be disposed to overlook them, and regard their aesthetic appeal as the same.... [A] more refined analysis is required where a plaintiff's work is not wholly original, but rather incorporates elements from the public domain. In these instances, what must be shown is substantial similarity between those elements, and only those elements, that provide copyrightability to the allegedly infringed compilation.... In the case at hand, because the alphabet was taken from the public domain, we must apply the "more discerning" ordinary observer test.

[7] In applying this test, a court is not to dissect the works at issue into separate components and compare only the copyrightable elements. To do so would be to take the "more discerning" test to an extreme, which would result in almost nothing being copyrightable because original works broken down into their composite parts would usually be little more than basic unprotectible elements like letters, colors and symbols. This outcome—affording no copyright protection to an original compilation of unprotectible elements—would be contrary to the Supreme Court's holding in *Feist Publications*.

[8] Although the "more discerning" test has not always been identified by name in our case law, we have nevertheless always recognized that the test is guided by comparing the total concept and feel of the contested works....

[9] In the present case, while use of the alphabet may not provide a basis for infringement, we must compare defendants' quilts and plaintiffs' quilts on the basis of the arrangement and shapes of the letters, the colors chosen to represent the letters and other parts of the quilts, the quilting patterns, the particular icons chosen and their placement. Our analysis of the "total concept and feel" of these works should be instructed by common sense....

[10] "School Days I" consists of six horizontal rows, each row containing five blocks, with a capital letter or an icon in each block. The groupings of blocks in each row are as follows: A–E; F–J; K–O; P–T; U–Y; and Z with four icons following in the last row. The four icons are a cat, a house, a single-starred American flag and a basket. "ABC Green Version I" displays the capital letters of the alphabet in the same formation. The four icons in the last row are a cow jumping over the moon, a sailboat, a bear and a star. "ABC Green Version II" is identical to "ABC Green Version I," except that the picture of the cow jumping over the moon is somewhat altered, the bear is replaced by a teddy bear sitting up and wearing a vest that looks like a single-starred American flag, and the star in the last block is represented in a different color.

[11] All three quilts use a combination of contrasting solid color fabrics or a combination of solid and polka-dotted fabrics to represent the blocks and letters. The following similarities are observed in plaintiffs' and defendants' designs: "A" is dark blue on a light blue background; "B" is red on a white background; "D" is made of polka-dot fabric on a light blue background; "F" on plaintiffs' "School Days I" is white on a pink background, while the "F" on defendants' "ABC Green" versions is pink on a white background; "G" has a green background; "H" and "L" are each a shade of blue on a white background; "M" in each quilt is a shade of yellow on a white background. "N" is green on a white background; "O" is blue on a polka-dot background; "P" is polka-dot fabric on a yellow background; "Q" is brown on a light background; "R" is pink on a

gray/purple background. "S" is white on a red background; "T" is blue on a white background; "U" is gray on a white background; "V" is white on a gray background; "W" is pink on a white background; "X" is purple in all quilts, albeit in different shades, on a light background; "Y" is a shade of yellow on the same light background; and "Z" is navy blue or black, in all the quilts.

[12] Boisson also testified that defendants utilized the same unique shapes as she had given to the letters "J," "M," "N," "P," "R" and "W." With respect to the quilting patterns, "School Days I" and the "ABC Green" versions feature diamond-shaped quilting within the blocks and a "wavy" pattern in the plain white border that surrounds the blocks. The quilts are also edged with a 3/8" green binding.

[13] From this enormous amount of sameness, we think defendants' quilts sufficiently similar to plaintiffs' design as to demonstrate illegal copying. In particular, the overwhelming similarities in color choices lean toward a finding of infringement. Although the icons chosen for each quilt are different and defendants added a green rectangular border around their rows of blocks, these differences are not sufficient to cause even the "more discerning" observer to think the quilts are other than substantially similar insofar as the protectible elements of plaintiffs' quilt are concerned. Moreover, the substitution in "ABC Green Version II" of the teddy bear wearing a flag vest as the third icon causes this version of defendants' quilt to look even more like plaintiffs' quilt that uses a single-starred American flag as its third icon. Consequently, both of defendants' "ABC Green" quilts infringed plaintiffs' copyright on its "School Days I" quilt....

[14] We agree with the district court, however, that [the defendant] did not infringe on plaintiffs' design in "School Days I" when he created "ABC Navy." While both quilts utilize an arrangement of six horizontal rows of five blocks each, "ABC Navy" does not have its four icons in the last row. Rather, the teddy bear with the flag vest is placed after the "A" in the first row, the cow jumping over the moon is placed after the "L" in the third row, the star is placed after the "S" in the fifth row, and the sailboat is placed after the "Z" in the last row. Further, the colors chosen to represent the letters and the blocks in "ABC Navy" are, for the most part, entirely different from "School Days I." Defendants dropped the use of polka-dot fabric, and plaintiffs did not even offer a color comparison in their proposed findings of fact to the district court, as they had with each of the "ABC Green" versions. The quilting pattern in the plain white border is changed to a "zig-zag" in "ABC Navy," as opposed to plaintiffs' "wavy" design. Finally, although defendants use a binding around the edge of their quilt, in this instance it is blue instead of green.

[15] Looking at these quilts side-by-side, we conclude they are not substantially similar to one another. Just as we rejected defendants' earlier argument and held that what few differences existed between "School Days I" and the "ABC Green" quilts could not preclude a finding of infringement, plaintiffs' emphasis on the similarity in style between some of the letters between "School Days I" and "ABC Navy" cannot support a finding of infringement. Because no observer, let alone a "more discerning" observer, would likely find the two works to be substantially similar, no copyright violation could properly be found....

NOTES

1. How often do you envision the ordinary-observer test will be used as compared with the more-discerning-observer test? Of all copyrightable works, how many do you imagine meet *Boisson*'s threshold for switching to the more-discerning-observer test by being "not wholly original, but rather incorporat[ing] elements from the public domain"?

2. In a subsequent decision involving rug designs, the Second Circuit responded to criticism that its more-discerning-observer test is too vague to be helpful:

Some commentators have worried that the "total concept and feel" standard may "invite[] an abdication of analysis," because "feel" can seem a "wholly amorphous referent." 4 MELVILLE B. NIMMER & DAVID NIMMER, NIMMER ON COPYRIGHT § 13.03[A][1][c] (2003). Likewise, one may wonder whether a copyright doctrine whose aspiration is to protect a work's "concept" could end up erroneously protecting "ideas." But our caselaw is not so incautious. Where we have described possible infringement in terms of whether two designs have or do not have a substantially similar "total concept and feel," we generally have taken care to identify precisely the particular aesthetic decisions—original to the plaintiff and copied by the defendant—that might be thought to make the designs similar in the aggregate....

Essentially, the total-concept-and-feel locution functions as a reminder that, while the infringement analysis must begin by dissecting the copyrighted work into its component parts in order to clarify precisely what is not original, infringement analysis is not simply a matter of ascertaining similarity between components viewed in isolation. For the defendant may infringe on the plaintiff's work not only through literal copying of a portion of it, but also by parroting properties that are apparent only when numerous aesthetic decisions embodied in the plaintiff's work of art—the excerpting, modifying, and arranging of public domain compositions, if any, together with the development and representation of wholly new motifs and the use of texture and color, etc.—are considered in relation to one another. The court, confronted with an allegedly infringing work, must analyze the two works closely to figure out in what respects, if any, they are similar, and then determine whether these similarities are due to protected aesthetic expressions original to the allegedly infringed work, or whether the similarity is to something in the original that is free for the taking.

Tufenkian Import/Export Ventures, Inc. v. Einstein Moomjy, Inc., 338 F.3d 127, 134-35 (2d Cir. 2003).

After reading *Boisson* and this excerpt, do you have a sense of how much dissection is appropriate? Consider also that it is juries, and not judges, that often will decide whether a defendant's work is substantially similar to a plaintiff's in "total concept and feel." Is the "total concept and feel" test, as the Second Circuit describes it, administrable by a jury? Or is a jury more likely to take up the seeming linguistic invitation of the "total concept and feel" formulation, which is to consider relevant to infringement mere similarity of ideas, themes, genres, or other unprotected elements?

We turn now to the Ninth Circuit's approach to evaluating substantial similarity. The following case established the contours of the Ninth Circuit test. As you read it, consider its framework and how it differs from the Second Circuit's approach.

Sid & Marty Krofft Television Productions, Inc. v. Mcdonald's Corporation
562 F.2d 1157 (9th Cir. 1977)

CARTER, J.: ...

[1] ... Sid and Marty Krofft ... create[d] a children's television program for exhibition on Saturday morning. The ... [ensuing] H. R. Pufnstuf television show ... was introduced on NBC in September 1969. The series included several fanciful costumed characters, as well as a boy named Jimmy, who lived in a fantasyland called "Living Island," which was inhabited by moving trees and talking books....

Figure 60: still from H. R. Pufnstuf television series

[2] In early 1970, Marty Krofft, the President of both Krofft Television and Krofft Productions and producer of the show, was contacted by an executive from Needham, Harper & Steers, Inc., an advertising agency. He was told that Needham was attempting to get the advertising account of McDonald's hamburger restaurant chain and wanted to base a proposed campaign to McDonald's on the H. R. Pufnstuf characters. The executive wanted to know whether the Kroffts would be interested in working with Needham on a project of this type.

[3] Needham and the Kroffts were in contact by telephone six or seven more times. By a letter dated August 31, 1970, Needham stated it was going forward with the idea of a McDonaldland advertising campaign based on the H. R. Pufnstuf series. It acknowledged the need to pay the Kroffts a fee for preparing artistic designs and engineering plans. Shortly thereafter, Marty Krofft telephoned Needham only to be told that the advertising campaign had been cancelled.

[4] In fact, Needham had already been awarded McDonald's advertising account and was proceeding with the McDonaldland project. Former employees of the Kroffts were hired to design and construct the costumes and sets for McDonaldland. Needham also hired the same voice expert who supplied all of the voices for the Pufnstuf characters to supply some of the voices for the McDonaldland characters. In January 1971, the first of the McDonaldland commercials was broadcast on network television. They continue to be broadcast....

[5] Plaintiffs filed suit .... The complaint alleged ... that the McDonaldland advertising campaign infringed the copyrighted H. R. Pufnstuf television episodes as well as various copyrighted articles of Pufnstuf merchandise....

[6] A verdict in favor of plaintiffs was returned ....

[7] The real task in a copyright infringement action ... is to determine whether there has been copying of the expression of an idea rather than just the idea itself....

Figure 61: stills from McDonaldland advertising campaign

[8] [In t]he test for infringement[,] .... there [therefore] ... must be substantial similarity not only of the general ideas but of the expressions of those ideas as well. Thus two steps in the analytic process are implied by the requirement of substantial similarity.

[9] .... The [first] test[,] for similarity of ideas[,] is ... a factual one, to be decided by the trier of fact.

[10] We shall call this the "extrinsic test." It is extrinsic because it depends not on the responses of the trier of fact, but on specific criteria which can be listed and analyzed. Such criteria include the type of artwork involved, the materials used, the subject matter, and the setting for the subject. Since it is an extrinsic test, analytic dissection and expert testimony are appropriate. Moreover, this question may often be decided as a matter of law.

[11] The determination of when there is substantial similarity between the forms of expression is necessarily more subtle and complex. As Judge Hand candidly observed, "Obviously, no principle can be stated as to when an imitator has gone beyond copying the 'idea,' and has borrowed its 'expression.' Decisions must therefore inevitably be ad hoc." Peter Pan Fabrics, Inc. v. Martin Weiner Corp., 274 F.2d 487, 489 (2d Cir. 1960). If there is substantial similarity in ideas, then the trier of fact must decide whether there is substantial similarity in the expressions of the ideas so as to constitute infringement.

[12] The test to be applied in determining whether there is substantial similarity in expressions shall be labeled an intrinsic one depending on the response of the ordinary reasonable person. It is intrinsic because it does not depend on the type of external criteria and analysis which marks the extrinsic test....

[13] Because this is an intrinsic test, analytic dissection and expert testimony are not appropriate....

[14] In the context of this case, the distinction between these tests is important. Defendants do not dispute the fact that they copied the idea of plaintiffs' Pufnstuf television series basically a fantasyland filled with diverse and fanciful characters in action. They argue, however, that the expressions of this idea are too dissimilar for there to be an infringement. They come to this conclusion by dissecting the constituent parts of the Pufnstuf series characters, setting, and plot and pointing out the dissimilarities between these parts and those of the McDonaldland commercials.

[15] .... Defendants attempt to apply an extrinsic test by the listing of dissimilarities in determining whether the expression they used was substantially similar to the expression used by plaintiffs. That extrinsic test is inappropriate; an intrinsic test must here be used....

[16] Analytic dissection, as defendants have done, is therefore improper....

[17] Since the intrinsic test for expression is uniquely suited for determination by the trier of fact, this court must be reluctant to reverse it....

[18] The H. R. Pufnstuf series became the most popular children's show on Saturday morning television. This success led several manufacturers of children's goods to use the Pufnstuf characters. It is not surprising, then, that McDonald's hoped to duplicate this peculiar appeal to children in its commercials. It was in recognition of the subjective and unpredictable nature of children's responses that defendants opted to recreate the H. R. Pufnstuf format rather than use an original and unproven approach.

[19] Defendants would have this court ignore that intrinsic quality which they recognized to embark on an extrinsic analysis of the two works. For example, in discussing the principal characters Pufnstuf and Mayor McCheese defendants point out:

> "'*Pufnstuf*' wears what can only be described as a yellow and green dragon suit with a blue cummerband from which hangs a medal which says 'mayor'. 'McCheese' wears a version of pink formal dress 'tails' with knicker trousers. He has a typical diplomat's sash on which is written 'mayor', the 'M' consisting of the McDonald's trademark of an 'M' made of golden arches."

[20] So not only do defendants remove the characters from the setting, but dissect further to analyze the clothing, colors, features, and mannerisms of each character. We do not believe that the ordinary reasonable person, let alone a child, viewing these works will even notice that Pufnstuf is wearing a cummerbund while Mayor McCheese is wearing a diplomat's sash....

[21] We have viewed representative samples of both the H. R. Pufnstuf show and McDonaldland commercials. It is clear to us that defendants' works are substantially similar to plaintiffs'. They have captured the "total concept and feel" of the Pufnstuf show. Roth Greeting Cards v. United Card Co., 429 F.2d 1106, 1110 (9th Cir. 1970). We would so conclude even if we were sitting as the triers of fact. There is no doubt that the findings of the jury in this case are not clearly erroneous....

As you read the following case, evaluate how the Ninth Circuit's test has evolved since *Krofft*. Is this refinement a positive development?

Wanda A. Cavalier v. Random House, Inc.
297 F.3d 815 (9th Cir. 2002)

FLETCHER, J.: ...

[1] [Wanda and Christopher] Cavalier[] created copyrighted works involving several characters who are featured in children's stories. Their main character, Nicky Moonbeam, an anthropomorphic moon, teaches children to overcome their fears (including fear of the dark) and encourages children to follow their dreams....

Chapter V – Exclusive Rights

[2] From 1995 through 1998, the Cavaliers submitted more than 280 pages of material, including their copyrighted works, to Random House and [Children's Television Workshop]. The first submission consisted of two stories—*Nicky Moonbeam: The Man in the Moon* and *Nicky Moonbeam Saves Christmas*—and the design for a "moon night light" to be built directly into the back cover of a "board book." A "board book" is a book with sturdy, thick pages, designed for use by young children. Later submissions in 1996 and 1998 consisted of "pitch materials," which included detailed illustrations, ideas for general story lines and television programs, specific traits of the Nicky Moonbeam characters, and goals for the Nicky Moonbeam stories.

[3] After face-to-face meetings with the Cavaliers regarding their submissions, Random House and CTW rejected their works. Soon thereafter, in February 1999, Random House and CTW jointly published the books *Good Night, Ernie* and *Good Night, Elmo* ....

[4] *Nicky Moonbeam: The Man in the Moon* is an approximately 3500-word story. Its main characters are Nicky Moonbeam and Daisy, a five-year-old child. Nicky is a child-like figure drawn with a full moon head, sometimes with and sometimes without a full body. He has egg-shaped eyes, a human-like nose, and a mouth, with moon rocks or craters on his face. Nicky has star friends who have faces drawn in the upper point of the stars, with small, lidded eyes and no nose. In the latest version of the story, Nicky is sad and lonely because he cannot stop dreaming about meeting a child. Nicky sails the Dream Weaver, a sailboat propelled by moonbeams, to Earth where he meets Daisy. After explaining what it is like to be the man-in-the-moon and all the jobs he has, Nicky takes Daisy for a ride in the night sky on his boat. They play in the clouds. Daisy floats on a cloud that looks like a dragon while Nicky balances on an airplane-shaped cloud. After playing all night in the clouds, Nicky and Daisy return to Earth where they play at the beach, building sand castles, playing with crabs, and listening to the waves. Because he is having so much fun, Nicky does not want to return to the sky. But after Daisy explains that disaster would befall the Earth if Nicky did not go back, Nicky returns to the sky and continues to do his "man in the moon" job, comforting and encouraging children. Nicky is happier than he has ever been. He resolves to continue to surround the children with his "moonbeam love," stretching his moonbeam arms to hug the world....

Figure 62: image from Cavalier's Nicky Moonbeam stories

[5] The Cavaliers' "night light in the sky" idea was that the back cover of a board book featuring Nicky Moonbeam would extend some distance beyond the front cover and the pages, so that a portion of the inside of the back cover would be visible on the right-hand side, both when the book was closed and when it was being read. On the extended (visible) portion of the inside back cover would be a night light in the shape of a pearly white moon with black eyes and pink cheeks. Stars would surround the moon night light. The "on" button for the moon night light would be a small circle with a star on it, positioned below and to the right of the night light....

[6] The Cavaliers' proposed art work includes the following illustrations, related to the stories: (1) stars wearing woolen and top hats while relaxing and playing on clouds; (2) a star being polished with cloths by other stars; (3) a smiling moon sending light blue "moonbeams" down to earth, with star dust trail and suggested text, "Nicky ... shines his long beams to earth for a child to walk up, hop on"; and (4) Nicky, as the moon, hanging just outside of a child's bedroom window and sending stars to float around a child's room and glow while the child falls asleep....

[7] *Good Night, Ernie* and *Good Night, Elmo* are both five-page board books featuring *Sesame Street* Muppet characters. In *Good Night, Ernie*, told in 74 words, Ernie wonders about the stars and takes an imaginary journey in the night sky. He wonders how many stars there are, and counts them as he sits on a crescent moon. He wonders where the stars go during the day and he visits them. He wonders how the stars stay bright, and he thinks about helping them shine. All of this "wondering" makes Ernie tired. Ernie returns to his bed which is floating in the sky surrounded by stars. He and the stars wish each other good night. The stars have ping-pong ball-shaped eyes touching a round bulbous nose.

[8] In *Good Night, Elmo*, told in 119 words, Elmo notices the moon shining on his pillow. The moon invites him to "hop on" its moonbeam and "take a ride" through the night sky, where Elmo races a shooting star, sees the cow jumping over the moon, and begins jumping like the cow. All of that jumping tires Elmo, and he rides a moonbeam back to his bed, where he begins to fall asleep as the moon shines through his window. The moon on the cover has ping-pong ball-shaped eyes touching a round bulbous nose.

[9] A star night light, surrounded by stars, is built into the extended inside back cover to the right of the free pages of *Good Night, Ernie*. A comparable moon night light is built into the extended inside back cover of *Good Night, Elmo*. The instructions for the night light are identical for both books: "To turn on Ernie's [Elmo's] night light, press the star button. It turns off by itself." ...

Figure 63: covers of *Good Night, Elmo* and *Good Night, Ernie* board books

[10] The Cavaliers filed in district court ... claims for copyright infringement .... The Cavaliers alleged that Random House and CTW had copied and appropriated their works, including the Nicky Moonbeam characters, illustrations, text, and night light.

[11] The trial court granted Random House and CTW's motion for summary judgment on the following grounds: (1) The Cavaliers' general story lines in which anthropomorphic moon and stars ease children's fears of sleeping in the dark, and the depiction of related scenes and stock characters ("scenes-a-faire"), are not protectible by copyright; [and] (2) *Good Night, Ernie* [and] *Good Night, Elmo* ... were not substantially similar to the copyright-protectible material in the Cavaliers' works .... The Cavaliers timely appealed....

[12] To establish a successful copyright infringement claim, a plaintiff must show that he or she owns the copyright and that defendant copied protected elements of the work. Copying may be established by showing that the infringer had access to plaintiff's copyrighted work and that the works at issue are substantially similar in their protected elements. For purposes of their summary judgment motion, Random House and CTW did not contest ownership or access. The sole issue before us is whether any of Random House's or CTW's works were substantially similar to the Cavaliers' submissions.

[13] We employ a two-part analysis in this circuit—an extrinsic test and an intrinsic test—to determine whether two works are substantially similar. The "extrinsic test" is an objective comparison of specific expressive elements. The test focuses on articulable similarities between the plot, themes, dialogue, mood, setting, pace, characters, and sequence of events in two works. Although originally cast as a "test for similarity of ideas," Sid & Marty Krofft Television Prods., Inc. v. McDonald's Corp., 562 F.2d 1157, 1164 (9th Cir. 1977), the extrinsic test, now encompassing all objective manifestations of *expression*, no longer fits that description. The "intrinsic test" is a subjective comparison that focuses on whether the ordinary, reasonable audience would find the works substantially similar in the total concept and feel of the works.

[14] A court must take care to inquire only whether the *protectible elements, standing alone,* are substantially similar. Therefore, when applying the extrinsic test, a court must filter out and disregard the non-protectible elements in making its substantial similarity determination....

[15] The Cavaliers allege that the following elements of *Good Night, Ernie* were copied by Random House and CTW from their submissions:

> (1) A built-in night light with an "on" button on the inside back cover of a board book, with the light appearing as a moon with eyes, nose, and smiling benevolent expression;
> (2) A character looking into the sky, wondering who and what the stars are;
> (3) A character interacting with smiling, rosy-faced, bright yellow, five-pointed stars;
> (4) A character sitting on a crescent moon;
> (5) Smiling, bright yellow, rosy-cheeked, five-pointed stars playing and lounging on the clouds during the day and wearing colorful woolen hats;
> (6) A character polishing a star with a cloth;
> (7) Smiling, bright yellow, rosy-cheeked, five-pointed stars floating in a child's bedroom, glowing and comforting the child;
> (8) Stars trailed by a distinctive "moondust."

[16] The Cavaliers allege that the following elements of *Good Night, Elmo* were copied:

> (1) A built-in night light comparable to that in *Good Night, Ernie;*
> (2) Moonbeams shining through a window;
> (3) A character saying "hop on a moonbeam and take a ride";

(4) A character interacting with smiling, yellow, rosy-cheeked, five-pointed stars trailing sparkling dust and surrounded by other stars.

[17] We first compare the *Good Night* books to the Nicky Moonbeam stories as literary works, taken as a whole. We then compare individual art work from the *Good Night* books to that in the Cavaliers' submissions....

[18] On summary judgment, only the extrinsic test matters for comparison of literary works. If the Cavaliers can show that there is a triable issue of fact under the extrinsic test, the intrinsic test's subjective inquiry must be left to the jury and Random House and CTW's motion for summary judgment must be denied. Conversely, if the Cavaliers cannot show a triable issue of fact under the extrinsic test, Random House and CTW necessarily prevail on summary judgment. A jury could not find copyright infringement because there can be no substantial similarity without evidence under both the extrinsic and intrinsic tests. We now apply the objective factors of the extrinsic test, considering only the protectible material, to determine whether *Good Night, Ernie* and/or *Good Night, Elmo,* taken as a whole, are sufficiently similar to the Cavaliers' works to raise a triable issue of fact.

[19] The Cavaliers' Nicky Moonbeam stories and *Good Night, Elmo* share the general premise of a child, invited by a moon-type character, who takes a journey through the night sky and returns safely to bed to fall asleep. But basic plot ideas, such as this one, are not protected by copyright law.

[20] Otherwise, the actual narratives in *Good Night, Ernie* and *Good Night, Elmo* do not share much in common with the Nicky Moonbeam stories. The Nicky Moonbeam stories (2000–4000 words each) involve relatively elaborate story lines, while the text in the *Good Night* books (roughly 100 words each) describes a simple, discrete group of scenes. The stories do not share any detailed sequence of events. Moreover, although some of the Cavaliers' illustrations appear to depict events in the Nicky Moonbeam stories, the allegedly copied illustrations appear in a different context in the *Good Night* books.

[21] The principal setting in the *Good Night* books is the night sky, which is also prevalent in the Nicky Moonbeam stories. However, this setting naturally and necessarily flows from the basic plot premise of a child's journey through the night sky; therefore, the night sky setting constitutes scenes-a-faire and cannot support a finding of substantial similarity. Furthermore, neither of the *Good Night* books involves the beach or the North Pole, the venues for significant parts of the Nicky Moonbeam stories.

[22] The pace, dialogue, mood, and theme of the *Good Night* books differ markedly from those of the Nicky Moonbeam stories. In the *Good Night* books, the entire night journey is completed in five simple pages. There is no dialogue in *Good Night, Ernie,* and the dialogue in *Good Night, Elmo* is limited to two simple exchanges. The district court correctly characterized their mood as "fun" and "very lighthearted." There is no focused theme or message in either story.

[23] In contrast, the Nicky Moonbeam stories progress more deliberately, with several contemplative scenes developing thematic details. There is extensive dialogue, especially in *Nicky Moonbeam: Man in the Moon,* where most of the story is based on dialogue between Nicky Moonbeam and Daisy. Although also written for children, the mood in the Nicky Moonbeam stories is more serious and instructional. They contain explicit messages for children, teaching them not to be afraid of the dark, to discover and share their special gifts with the world, and to believe in themselves.

[24] As the Cavaliers acknowledge, the main characters in the *Good Night* books are different—Sesame Street Muppets (Ernie and Elmo) rather than Nicky Moonbeam. Although *Good Night, Elmo* features Mr. Moon, he does not share any of the anthropomorphic characteristics of Nicky Moonbeam, except the ability to talk.

Moreover, a moon character can be considered a stock character for children's literature, and directly flows from the idea of a journey in the night sky. None of the other characters in the Nicky Moonbeam stories are found in the *Good Night* books.

[25] Random House and CTW contend that even if their *Good Night* books contain some protectible elements, such commonalities would not justify a finding of substantial similarity of the works .... We agree.... [A] compilation of random similarities scattered throughout the works is inherently subjective and unreliable. The ... argument is especially strong here since the alleged similarities are selected from over 280 pages of submissions. Further, consideration of the total concept and feel of a work, rather than specific inquiry into plot and character development, is especially appropriate in an infringement action involving children's works. Since the "total concept and feel" of the Cavaliers' stories are, as discussed above, more serious and instructional than defendants' books, a finding of infringement is disfavored in this case. In sum, there is no triable issue of fact on the issue of whether either *Good Night, Ernie* or *Good Night, Elmo* is a substantially similar literary work to the Nicky Moonbeam stories under the extrinsic test....

[26] Even though we hold that the *Good Night* stories, taken as a whole, do not infringe the Cavaliers' copyright, the question remains whether protected parts of the Cavaliers' works have been copied. We therefore consider whether there exists a triable issue of substantial similarity between any of the isolated art work, as freestanding work divorced from the stories. Indeed, almost all of the allegedly copied elements are found in the Cavaliers' art work rather than in the narratives. Three of the art works present a close question of substantial similarity for summary judgment purposes: (1) the moon night light design on the extended inside back cover; (2) the illustration of stars relaxing on clouds; and (3) the illustration of stars being polished.

[27] The basic mode of analysis for comparison of the literary elements applies to comparison of the art work. As with literary works, unprotectible elements should not be considered when applying the extrinsic test to art work. This does not mean that at the end of the day, when the works are considered under the intrinsic test, they should not be compared as a whole. Nor does it mean that infringement cannot be based on original selection and arrangement of unprotected elements. However, the unprotectable elements have to be identified, or filtered, before the works can be considered as a whole. The precise factors evaluated for literary works do not readily apply to art works. Rather, a court looks to the similarity of the objective details in appearance. Although we do not attempt here to provide an exhaustive list of relevant factors for evaluating art work, the subject matter, shapes, colors, materials, and arrangement of the representations may be considered in determining objective similarity in appearance.

[28] It is not clear whether the rule ...—that when comparison of literary works under the extrinsic test presents a triable issue of fact, the question of substantial similarity necessarily survives summary judgment and must go to the jury—applies to art work. The underlying rationale ...—that subjective assessments of similarity in expression are best suited to the trier of fact—appears to favor application of that rule in this case. But we need not decide the issue because we find that a juror could reasonably determine that the first two works at issue—the "moon night light" and "stars relaxing on clouds" (which we find objectively similar under the extrinsic test as discussed below)—were subjectively similar to the Cavaliers' illustrations in "total concept and feel" under the intrinsic test as well.

[29] A comparison of the night light designs reveals obvious similarities. The basic idea—a night light built into the inside back cover of a board book—is the same. In *Good Night, Elmo*, the night light is in the shape of a smiling moon face with pinkish cheeks and black eyes. In *Good Night, Ernie*, the exterior outline of the face on the night light is a star rather than a moon, but the features are the same. Both the moon and star faces in the *Good Night* books share these characteristics with the moon face in the Cavaliers' stories. In both of the *Good Night* books, the stars surround the night light faces in much the same manner as in the Cavaliers' stories. Both lights are positioned in the upper portion of the projecting inside back cover, as they are in the Cavaliers'

design. The shape (a star enclosed in a circle) and positioning of the "on" button to the lower-right is the same. Although the concept of a built-in night light is not protectible under copyright law, the choice of a smiling moon or star face with pinkish cheeks surrounded by stars in a specific configuration, and situated above an encircled star "on" button, constitutes protectible expression. The differences—mainly that the facial features of Random House and CTW's moon and star lights have ping-pong ball-shaped eyes and bulbous nose, compared to plaintiffs' black circles and no nose—are relatively minor and do not support a grant of summary judgment for the defendant on the issue of substantial similarity.

[30] A comparison of the two depictions of stars relaxing on clouds also reveals obvious similarities. The basic concept—stars situated on clouds—is the same. As expressed in their accompanying texts, both illustrations share the theme of exploring the stars' activities during daytime: The Cavaliers' drawing aims "to give you an idea of what stars do during the day when they are 'off work' dressing up or involved in any activity until night"; the text in *Good Night, Ernie* reads "Ernie wonders what the stars do during the day. He thinks about visiting them." Several of the stars in both illustrations are resting on clouds, appearing ready to fall asleep. Most strikingly, several of the stars in both illustrations are wearing red and green woolen (striped and solid) winter or sleeping caps. On the other hand, some of the other details differ. The stars in the Cavaliers' drawing are engaged in various activities—one is wearing a costume, one is dancing in a top hat, one is lounging, and one is yawning. In contrast, none of Random House and CTW's stars are dressed up, and all have sleepy gazes (eyelids drooping). Furthermore, the main characters in each illustration are different (Nicky Moonbeams v. Ernie) and are doing different things (reading vs. flying). Finally, as stated above, the facial features and curves of the stars are different. Despite these differences, the striking similarities in the details of the subject matter, and arrangement of the stars and the clouds, dress of the stars, and accompanying text are sufficient to survive summary judgment on the question of substantial similarity.

[31] Finally, we compare the two depictions of stars being polished. Obvious similarities again appear. The subject matter—a star being polished—is the same. Furthermore, the stars being polished are both five-pointed, yellowish, and smiling. But the basic idea of polishing a star and the depiction of the common features of stars are unprotectible, and the two works differ significantly in the protectible details. Ernie polishes the entire star in *Good Night, Ernie*, while four smaller stars simultaneously polish the points of the star in the Cavaliers' illustration. The curves and facial details of the stars differ, as the *Good Night, Ernie* stars are rounder and have ping-pong ball-shaped eyes and red bulbous noses; moreover, there is a long line of "dirty" stars, as indicated by their brownish tint, waiting to be polished. Ernie also uses sun rays to help him polish. These significant elements are absent from the Cavaliers' work. Thus, we do not find a triable issue of substantial similarity as to this illustration....

Figure 64: images from Cavalier's Nicky Moonbeam stories

Figure 65: images from *Good Night, Ernie* board book

[32] For the foregoing reasons, we AFFIRM the district court's grant of summary judgment on substantial similarity as to the literary works as a whole, ... but REVERSE its grant of summary judgment against plaintiffs' copyright claim with respect to the "moon night light" cover and the "illustration of stars relaxing on clouds."

Do you find the Ninth Circuit's framework in the following case clarifying? Are there particular issues related to photography that make the analysis different?

Jacobus Rentmeester v. Nike, Inc.
883 F.3d 1111 (9th Cir. 2018)

WATFORD, J.:

[1] This is a copyright infringement action brought by the renowned photographer Jacobus Rentmeester against Nike, Inc. The case involves a famous photograph Rentmeester took in 1984 of Michael Jordan, who at the time was a student at the University of North Carolina. The photo originally appeared in *Life* magazine as part of a photo essay featuring American athletes who would soon be competing in the 1984 Summer Olympic Games. We are asked to decide whether Nike infringed Rentmeester's copyright when it commissioned its own photograph of Jordan and then used that photo to create one of its most iconic trademarks....

[2] The allegations in Rentmeester's complaint, which we accept as true at this stage of the proceedings, establish the following. Rentmeester's photograph of Jordan ... is highly original. It depicts Jordan leaping toward a basketball hoop with a basketball raised above his head in his left hand, as though he is attempting to dunk the ball. The setting for the photo is not a basketball court, as one would expect in a shot of this sort. Instead, Rentmeester chose to take the photo on an isolated grassy knoll on the University of North Carolina campus. He brought in a basketball hoop and backboard mounted on a tall pole, which he planted in the ground to position the hoop exactly where he wanted. Whether due to the height of the pole or its placement within the image, the basketball hoop appears to tower above Jordan, beyond his reach.

Figure 66: Rentmeester's photograph

[3] Rentmeester instructed Jordan on the precise pose he wanted Jordan to assume. It was an unusual pose for a basketball player to adopt, one inspired by ballet's *grand jeté*, in which a dancer leaps with legs extended, one foot forward and the other back. Rentmeester positioned the camera below Jordan and snapped the photo at the peak of his jump so that the viewer looks up at Jordan's soaring figure silhouetted against a cloudless blue sky. Rentmeester used powerful strobe lights and a fast shutter speed to capture a sharp image of Jordan contrasted against the sky, even though the sun is shining directly into the camera lens from the lower right-hand corner of the shot.

[4] Not long after Rentmeester's photograph appeared in *Life* magazine, Nike contacted him and asked to borrow color transparencies of the photo. Rentmeester provided Nike with two color transparencies for $150 under a limited license authorizing Nike to use the transparencies "for slide presentation only." It is unclear from the complaint what kind of slide presentation Nike may have been preparing, but the company was then beginning its lucrative partnership with Jordan by promoting the Air Jordan brand of athletic shoes.

[5] In late 1984 or early 1985, Nike hired a photographer to produce its own photograph of Jordan, one obviously inspired by Rentmeester's. In the Nike photo, Jordan is again shown leaping toward a basketball hoop with a basketball held in his left hand above his head, as though he is about to dunk the ball. The photo was taken outdoors and from a similar angle as in Rentmeester's photo, so that the viewer looks up at Jordan's figure silhouetted against the sky. In the Nike photo, though, it is the city of Chicago's skyline that appears in the background, a nod to the fact that by then Jordan was playing professionally for the Chicago Bulls. Jordan wears apparel reflecting the colors of his new team, and he is of course wearing a pair of Nike shoes. Nike used this photo on posters and billboards as part of its marketing campaign for the new Air Jordan brand.

[6] When Rentmeester saw the Nike photo, he threatened to sue Nike for breach of the limited license governing use of his color transparencies. To head off litigation, Nike entered into a new agreement with Rentmeester in March 1985, under which the company agreed to pay $15,000 for the right to continue using the Nike photo on posters and billboards in North America for a period of two years. Rentmeester alleges that Nike continued to use the photo well beyond that period.

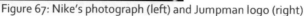

Figure 67: Nike's photograph (left) and Jumpman logo (right)

[7] In 1987, Nike created its iconic "Jumpman" logo, a solid black silhouette that tracks the outline of Jordan's figure as it appears in the Nike photo. Over the past three decades, Nike has used the Jumpman logo in connection with the sale and marketing of billions of dollars of merchandise. It has become one of Nike's most recognizable trademarks.

[8] Rentmeester filed this action in January 2015. He alleges that both the Nike photo and the Jumpman logo infringe the copyright in his 1984 photo of Jordan....

[9] The district court granted Nike's motion to dismiss under Federal Rule of Civil Procedure 12(b)(6). The court dismissed Rentmeester's claims with prejudice after concluding that neither the Nike photo nor the Jumpman logo infringe Rentmeester's copyright as a matter of law. We review that legal determination *de novo*....

[10] To state a claim for copyright infringement, Rentmeester must plausibly allege two things: (1) that he owns a valid copyright in his photograph of Jordan, and (2) that Nike copied protected aspects of the photo's expression.

[11] Although our cases have not always made this point explicit, the second element has two distinct components: "copying" and "unlawful appropriation." Proof of copying by the defendant is necessary because independent creation is a complete defense to copyright infringement. No matter how similar the plaintiff's and the defendant's works are, if the defendant created his independently, without knowledge of or exposure to the plaintiff's work, the defendant is not liable for infringement. Proof of unlawful appropriation—that is, *illicit* copying—is necessary because copyright law does not forbid all copying. The Copyright Act provides that copyright protection does not "extend to any idea, procedure, process, system, method of operation, concept, principle, or discovery, regardless of the form in which it is described, explained, illustrated, or embodied in [the copyrighted] work." 17 U.S.C. § 102(b). Thus, a defendant incurs no liability if he copies only the "ideas" or "concepts" used in the plaintiff's work. To infringe, the defendant must also copy enough of the plaintiff's expression of those ideas or concepts to render the two works substantially similar....

[12] Unfortunately, we have used the same term—"substantial similarity"—to describe both the degree of similarity relevant to proof of copying and the degree of similarity necessary to establish unlawful appropriation. The term means different things in those two contexts. To prove copying, the similarities between the two works need not be extensive, and they need not involve protected elements of the plaintiff's work. They just need to be similarities one would not expect to arise if the two works had been created independently. To prove unlawful appropriation, on the other hand, the similarities between the two works must be "substantial" and they must involve protected elements of the plaintiff's work.

[13] In this case, Rentmeester has plausibly alleged the first element of his infringement claim—that he owns a valid copyright. The complaint asserts that he has been the sole owner of the copyright in his photo since its creation in 1984. And the photo obviously qualifies as an "original work of authorship," given the creative choices Rentmeester made in composing it....

[14] Rentmeester has also plausibly alleged the "copying" component of the second element. He alleges that he provided color transparencies of his photo to Nike's creative director shortly before production of the Nike photo. That allegation establishes that Nike had access to Rentmeester's photo, which in this context means a reasonable opportunity to view it. Nike's access to Rentmeester's photo, combined with the obvious conceptual similarities between the two photos, is sufficient to create a presumption that the Nike photo was the product of copying rather than independent creation.

[15] The remaining question is whether Rentmeester has plausibly alleged that Nike copied enough of the protected expression from Rentmeester's photo to establish unlawful appropriation. To prove this component of his claim, Rentmeester does not have to show that Nike produced an exact duplicate of his photo. But, as mentioned, he does have to show that Nike copied enough of the photo's protected expression to render their works "substantially similar."

[16] In our circuit, determining whether works are substantially similar involves a two-part analysis consisting of the "extrinsic test" and the "intrinsic test." The extrinsic test assesses the objective similarities of the two works, focusing only on the protectable elements of the plaintiff's expression. Before that comparison can be made, the court must "filter out" the unprotectable elements of the plaintiff's work—primarily ideas and concepts, material in the public domain, and *scènes à faire* (stock or standard features that are commonly associated with the treatment of a given subject). The protectable elements that remain are then compared to corresponding elements of the defendant's work to assess similarities in the objective details of the works. The intrinsic test requires a more holistic, subjective comparison of the works to determine whether they are substantially similar in total concept and feel. To prevail, a plaintiff must prove substantial similarity under both tests.

[17] Only the extrinsic test's application may be decided by the court as a matter of law, so that is the only test relevant in reviewing the district court's ruling on a motion to dismiss. Before applying the extrinsic test ourselves, a few words are in order about the filtering process that the test demands.

[18] Certain types of works can be dissected into protected and unprotected elements more readily than others. With novels, plays, and motion pictures, for instance, even after filtering out unprotectable elements like ideas and *scènes à faire*, many protectable elements of expression remain that can be objectively compared. Plot, themes, dialogue, mood, setting, pace, characters, and sequence of events are elements we have previously identified.

[19] Photographs cannot be dissected into protected and unprotected elements in the same way. To be sure, photos can be broken down into objective elements that reflect the various creative choices the photographer made in composing the image—choices related to subject matter, pose, lighting, camera angle, depth of field, and the like. But none of those elements is subject to copyright protection when viewed in isolation. For example, a photographer who produces a photo using a highly original lighting technique or a novel camera angle cannot prevent other photographers from using those same techniques to produce new images of their own, provided the new images are not substantially similar to the earlier, copyrighted photo. With respect to a photograph's subject matter, no photographer can claim a monopoly on the right to photograph a particular subject just because he was the first to capture it on film. A subsequent photographer is free to take her own photo of the same subject, again so long as the resulting image is not substantially similar to the earlier photograph.

[20] That remains true even if, as here, a photographer creates wholly original subject matter by having someone pose in an unusual or distinctive way. Without question, one of the highly original elements of Rentmeester's photo is the fanciful (non-natural) pose he asked Jordan to assume. That pose was a product of Rentmeester's own "intellectual invention," *Burrow-Giles*, 111 U.S. at 60; it would not have been captured on film but for Rentmeester's creativity in conceiving it.

[21] Without gainsaying the originality of the pose Rentmeester created, he cannot copyright the pose itself and thereby prevent others from photographing a person in the same pose. He is entitled to protection only for the way the pose is expressed in his photograph, a product of not just the pose but also the camera angle, timing, and shutter speed Rentmeester chose. If a subsequent photographer persuaded Michael Jordan to assume the exact same pose but took her photo, say, from a bird's eye view directly above him, the resulting image would bear little resemblance to Rentmeester's photo and thus could not be deemed infringing.

[22] What *is* protected by copyright is the photographer's selection and arrangement of the photo's otherwise unprotected elements. If sufficiently original, the combination of subject matter, pose, camera angle, etc., receives protection, not any of the individual elements standing alone. In that respect (although not in others), photographs can be likened to factual compilations. An author of a factual compilation cannot claim copyright protection for the underlying factual material—facts are always free for all to use. If sufficiently original, though, an author's selection and arrangement of the material are entitled to protection. The individual elements that comprise a photograph can be viewed in the same way, as the equivalent of unprotectable "facts" that anyone may use to create new works. A second photographer is free to borrow any of the individual elements featured in a copyrighted photograph, so long as the competing work does not feature the same selection and arrangement of those elements....

[23] This is not to say, as Nike urges us to hold, that all photographs are entitled to only "thin" copyright protection, as is true of factual compilations. A copyrighted work is entitled to thin protection when the range of creative choices that can be made in producing the work is narrow. [For example,] ... there are only so many ways to paint a red bouncy ball on blank canvas.... [C]ontrast[] that with the gazillions of ways to make an aliens-attack movie, a work that would be entitled to "broad" protection given the much wider range of creative choices available in producing it. When only a narrow range of expression is possible, copyright protection is thin because the copyrighted work will contain few protectable features.

[24] Some photographs are entitled to only thin protection because the range of creative choices available in selecting and arranging the photo's elements is quite limited. That was the case in *Ets-Hokin v. Skyy Spirits, Inc.*, 323 F.3d 763 (9th Cir. 2003), where we held that the plaintiff's commercial product shots of a vodka bottle were entitled to only thin protection. Given the constraints imposed by the subject matter and conventions of commercial product shots, there were relatively few creative choices a photographer could make in producing acceptable images of the bottle. As a result, subtle differences in lighting, camera angle, and background were sufficient to render the defendant's otherwise similar-looking photos of the same bottle non-infringing.

[25] With other photographs, however, the range of creative choices available to the photographer will be far broader, and very few of those choices will be dictated by subject matter or convention.... [M]any photos will land more on the "aliens-attack movie" end of the range. As with any other work, the greater the range of creative choices that may be made, the broader the level of protection that will be afforded to the resulting image.

[26] Rentmeester's photo is undoubtedly entitled to broad rather than thin protection. The range of creative choices open to Rentmeester in producing his photo was exceptionally broad; very few of those choices were dictated by convention or subject matter. In fact, Rentmeester's photo is distinctive precisely because he chose *not* to be bound by the conventions commonly followed in photographing a basketball player

attempting to dunk a basketball. Such photos would typically call for a basketball court as the setting, whether indoors or out. Rentmeester chose instead to place Jordan on an open, grassy knoll with a basketball hoop inserted as a prop, whimsically out of place and seeming to tower well above regulation height. Rentmeester also departed from convention by capturing Jordan in a fanciful, highly original pose, one inspired more by ballet's *grand jeté* than by any pose a basketball player might naturally adopt when dunking a basketball. These creative choices—along with the other choices Rentmeester made with respect to lighting, camera angle, depth of field, and selection of foreground and background elements—resulted in a photo with many non-standard elements. Rentmeester's selection and arrangement of those elements produced an image entitled to the broadest protection a photograph can receive.

[27] With those preliminary observations out of the way, we can now turn to whether Rentmeester has plausibly alleged that his photo and the Nike photo are substantially similar under the extrinsic test. As discussed, that inquiry requires us to assess similarities in the selection and arrangement of the photos' elements, as reflected in the objective details of the two works. We do not have a well-defined standard for assessing when similarity in selection and arrangement becomes "substantial," and in truth no hard-and-fast rule could be devised to guide determinations that will necessarily turn on the unique facts of each case. The best we can do is borrow from the standard Judge Learned Hand employed in a case involving fabric designs: The two photos' selection and arrangement of elements must be similar enough that "the ordinary observer, unless he set out to detect the disparities, would be disposed to overlook them."

[28] We conclude that the works at issue here are as a matter of law not substantially similar. Just as Rentmeester made a series of creative choices in the selection and arrangement of the elements in his photograph, so too Nike's photographer made his own distinct choices in that regard. Those choices produced an image that differs from Rentmeester's photo in more than just minor details.

[29] Let's start with the subject matter of the photographs. The two photos are undeniably similar in the subject matter they depict: Both capture Michael Jordan in a leaping pose inspired by ballet's *grand jeté*. But Rentmeester's copyright does not confer a monopoly on that general "idea" or "concept"; he cannot prohibit other photographers from taking their own photos of Jordan in a leaping, *grand jeté*-inspired pose. Because the pose Rentmeester conceived is highly original, though, he is entitled to prevent others from copying the details of that pose as expressed in the photo he took. Had Nike's photographer replicated those details in the Nike photo, a jury might well have been able to find unlawful appropriation even though other elements of the Nike photo, such as background and lighting, differ from the corresponding elements in Rentmeester's photo.

[30] But Nike's photographer did not copy the details of the pose as expressed in Rentmeester's photo; he borrowed only the general idea or concept embodied in the photo. Thus, in each photo Jordan is holding a basketball above his head in his left hand with his legs extended, in a pose at least loosely based on the *grand jeté*. The position of each of his limbs in the two photos is different, however, and those differences in detail are significant because, among other things, they affect the visual impact of the images. In Rentmeester's photo, Jordan's bent limbs combine with the background and foreground elements to convey mainly a sense of horizontal (forward) propulsion, while in the Nike photo Jordan's completely straight limbs combine with the other elements to convey mainly a sense of vertical propulsion. While the photos embody a similar idea or concept, they express it in different ways.

[31] As to the other highly original element of Rentmeester's photo—the unusual outdoor setting he chose— Nike's photographer did not copy the details of that element either. The two photos again share undeniable similarities at the conceptual level: Both are taken outdoors without the usual trappings of a basketball court, other than the presence of a lone hoop and backboard. But when comparing the details of how that concept is expressed in the two photos, stark differences are readily apparent. Rentmeester set his shot on a grassy knoll

with a whimsically out-of-place basketball hoop jutting up from a pole planted in the ground. The grassy knoll in the foreground of Rentmeester's photo is wholly absent from the Nike photo. In fact, in the Nike photo there is no foreground element at all. The positioning of the basketball hoops is also materially different in the two photos. In Rentmeester's photo, the hoop is positioned at a height that appears beyond the ability of anyone to dunk on (even someone as athletic as Jordan), which further contributes to the whimsical rather than realistic nature of the depiction. The hoop in the Nike photo, by contrast, appears to be easily within Jordan's reach.

[32] The other major conceptual similarity shared by the two photos is that both are taken from a similar angle so that the viewer looks up at Jordan's soaring figure silhouetted against a clear sky. This is a far less original element of Rentmeester's photo, as photographers have long used similar camera angles to capture subjects silhouetted against the sky. But even here, the two photos differ as to expressive details in material respects. In Rentmeester's photo, the background is a cloudless blue sky; in the Nike photo, it is the Chicago skyline silhouetted against the orange and purple hues of late dusk or early dawn. In Rentmeester's photo, the sun looms large in the lower right-hand corner of the image; in the Nike photo the sun does not appear at all. And in Rentmeester's photo, parts of Jordan's figure are cast in shadow, while in the Nike photo every inch of Jordan's figure is brightly lit.

[33] Finally, the arrangement of the elements within the photographs is materially different in two further respects. In Rentmeester's photo, Jordan is positioned slightly left of center and appears as a relatively small figure within the frame. In the Nike photo, he is perfectly centered and dominates the frame. In Rentmeester's photo, the basketball hoop stands atop a tall pole planted in the ground, and the hoop's position within the frame balances Jordan's left-of-center placement. In the Nike photo, the hoop takes up the entire right border of the frame, highlighting Jordan's dominant, central position. The hoops are also lit and angled differently toward the viewer, further distinguishing their expressive roles in the photographs.

[34] In our view, these differences in selection and arrangement of elements, as reflected in the photos' objective details, preclude as a matter of law a finding of infringement. Nike's photographer made choices regarding selection and arrangement that produced an image unmistakably different from Rentmeester's photo in material details—disparities that no ordinary observer of the two works would be disposed to overlook. What Rentmeester's photo and the Nike photo share are similarities in general ideas or concepts: Michael Jordan attempting to dunk in a pose inspired by ballet's *grand jeté*; an outdoor setting stripped of most of the traditional trappings of basketball; a camera angle that captures the subject silhouetted against the sky. Rentmeester cannot claim an exclusive right to ideas or concepts at that level of generality, even in combination. Permitting him to claim such a right would withdraw those ideas or concepts from the stock of materials available to other artists, thereby thwarting copyright's fundamental objective of fostering creativity. Copyright promotes the progress of science and the useful arts by encouraging others to build freely upon the ideas and information conveyed by a work. That is all Nike's photographer did here.

[35] If the Nike photo cannot as a matter of law be found substantially similar to Rentmeester's photo, the same conclusion follows ineluctably with respect to the Jumpman logo. The logo is merely a solid black silhouette of Jordan's figure as it appears in the Nike photo, which, as we have said, differs materially from the way Jordan's figure appears in Rentmeester's photo. Isolating that one element from the Nike photo and rendering it in a stylized fashion make the Jumpman logo even less similar to Rentmeester's photo than the Nike photo itself....

[36] ... Rentmeester contends that dismissal at the pleading stage is rarely appropriate in copyright infringement cases and that he should have been allowed to take discovery before the district court assessed substantial similarity. It is true that dismissal of copyright infringement claims occurs more commonly at the summary judgment stage, but dismissal at the pleading stage is by no means unprecedented. Dismissal is

appropriate here because the two photos and the Jumpman logo are properly before us and thus capable of examination and comparison. Nothing disclosed during discovery could alter the fact that the allegedly infringing works are as a matter of law not substantially similar to Rentmeester's photo.

[37] This is not a case in which discovery could shed light on any issues that actually matter to the outcome. In some cases, the defendant claims independent creation as a defense and thus denies having had access to the plaintiff's work. In that scenario, disputed factual issues will often require discovery to flesh out. Here, Nike does not contest that it had access to Rentmeester's photo, so that issue is not in dispute.

[38] In other cases, more may need to be known about the range of creative choices available to the plaintiff photographer in order to determine the breadth of protection available to his work. Here, we have accepted as true all of Rentmeester's allegations concerning the creative choices he made in producing his photograph. But even granting his photo the broad protection it deserves, a comparison of the works at issue makes clear that Nike's photographer made creative choices of his own, which resulted in an image and derivative logo not substantially similar to Rentmeester's photo. Nothing disclosed during discovery could strengthen Rentmeester's arguments on this score....

NOTES

1. Now that you've seen some decisions from both the Second and Ninth Circuits on substantial similarity, how would you say their respective frameworks map onto one another? Are they asking more or less the same questions to analyze copying in law? Or different ones entirely? Is one framework or the other more plaintiff-friendly? What are the advantages and disadvantages of filing an infringement claim in the Second Circuit as compared with the Ninth Circuit?

2. Does reading through these decisions leave you with an impression that there is predictability to the substantial-similarity case law? Or does it seem confusing and unpredictable?

Of the scholars who think that it is confusing and unpredictable, some think it is in part because of a lack of guidelines as to what qualifies as copying in law and in part because of a lack of guidance as to how to distinguish idea from expression. *See, e.g.*, Amy B. Cohen, *Masking Copyright Decisionmaking: The Meaninglessness of Substantial Similarity*, 20 U.C. DAVIS L. REV. 719 (1987). Others think it stems from a lack of attention to how the ordinary reader reads a work of authorship. Zahr K. Said, *A Transactional Theory of the Reader in Copyright Law*, 102 IOWA L. REV. 605 (2017). And others think that treating substantial similarity as a question of law rather than a question of fact would alleviate many of these concerns. Shyamkrishna Balganesh, *The Normativity of Copying in Copyright Law*, 62 DUKE L.J. 203 (2012); Said, *supra*.

3. Now that you have read how different evidence and frameworks are used to assess copying in fact and copying in law, do you think the jury is able to separate out the evidence it properly heard on one such copying element and not allow it to affect its finding on the other inappropriately? In that context, consider the statement made by the jury foreman in *Selle v. Gibb* to the press after the jury rendered a verdict of infringement against the Bee Gees. The foreman revealed that a major factor in the jury's finding of infringement—including copying in law—was that Selle's expert had said that the Bee Gees had not independently created their song and that the Bee Gees had offered no expert testimony to rebut that suggestion. Maurice Possley, *Bee Gees Found Guilty of Plagiarism*, ROLLING STONE, Apr. 14, 1983, at 60, 60. As you now know, expert evidence of the sort may be admitted only as to copying in fact, but not as to copying in law.

Experimental work has shown that subjects' assessments as to copying in law of images shift toward finding copying in law when the subjects are exposed to additional facts about the presence of copying in fact or the creative effort that went into making the first image. Shyamkrishna Balganesh, Irina D. Manta & Tess Wilkinson-Ryan, *Judging Similarity*, 100 IOWA L. REV. 267 (2014).

4. In Chapter IV's consideration of formalities, you read about an incentive for copyright holders to include copyright notice in their works following the U.S. accession to the Berne Convention: the ability to prevent an **innocent infringer defense**. Despite its connotation, this defense does not allow a defendant who copies another's work believing (incorrectly) that their copying is not infringing to negate copying in law. Since 1931, a defendant's mental state as to infringement has been deemed irrelevant. Buck v. Jewell-Lasalle Realty Co., 283 U.S. 191, 198 (1931). Before that time, copyright law was kinder to such an innocent infringer, making it harder—if not impossible—to hold such a person liable for infringement. For more on this history and how circumstances changed, see R. Anthony Reese, *Innocent Infringement in U.S. Copyright Law: A History*, 30 COLUM. J.L. & ARTS 133 (2007).

Instead of providing a general defense to liability, the innocent infringer defense provides for either a limitation on liability or mitigation of actual or statutory damages when notice of copyright was omitted from a defendant's work. By contrast, inclusion of such notice negates the innocent infringer defense. *See* 17 U.S.C. §§ 401(d); 405(b). We delve into this issue more in relation to our study of damages in Chapter VIII.

5. In addition to requiring copying in fact and copying in law to establish infringement, should the plaintiff also be required to prove that the copying is foreseeable, and therefore is the kind of copying that could have affected the original author's ex ante incentives to create? One scholar has proposed that "a new test of 'foreseeable copying' that would require a plaintiff to establish that the defendant's copying was objectively foreseeable at the time of creation—the point at which copyright's incentive structure is meant to have influenced a creator's behavior." Shyamkrishna Balganesh, *Foreseeability and Copyright Incentives*, 122 HARV. L. REV. 1569, 1603 (2009). Balganesh justifies this new element of the plaintiff's prima facie case on the basis that "[i]f the law is willing to assume in other areas that unforeseeable events are not motivational concerns, it would seem inconsistent with this basic premise to have a system of copyright that assumes otherwise. Unforeseeable uses are unlikely to be part of a creator's inducement to create in exactly the same way that unforeseeable consequences are unlikely to be part of an individual's decision whether to act." Are you convinced by this argument?

6. Another scholar has argued that, at least in some cases, a copyright plaintiff should be required to prove that a defendant's copying has *harmed the plaintiff*. The argument suggests that copyright should follow antitrust law in adjusting its liability standard according to whether harm is expected ordinarily to follow from a particular type of infringement:

> First, we should distinguish between conduct we know will harm author incentives over the run of cases, and conduct with more ambiguous effects. So creation and distribution of exact copies of a work should be treated differently than creation of a derivative work. The first we know will almost always be harmful; whether the second is depends on the facts of a particular case.

> Second, we should re-structure copyright's burdens of proof to better filter harmful from harmless uses. This second strategy grows out of and is aimed at implementing the first. For cases involving infringing conduct that is very likely to cause harm, we should preserve copyright's current strict liability rule.... But for cases involving infringing conduct in our second category—i.e., where the effect of the infringing conduct is ambiguous—we should require plaintiffs to prove that they have been harmed in some substantial way.

> There are two principal benefits of such a change. First, by requiring that plaintiffs show substantial actual or likely harm in these "rule of reason" copyright infringement cases, we will

encourage plaintiffs who have suffered substantial harm to come forward, while discouraging suits by rightsholders who suffer no harm, or only speculative harm. Second—and perhaps most importantly—altering the plaintiff's prima facie case in this way will produce information about harms and benefits of different uses of copyrighted works. To do this effectively, the law needs to place the burden on the party most likely to have information about the harm—in virtually all cases, that is likely to be the plaintiff. The law as structured now does not reliably produce this information, with the result that copyright litigation does not help us to know more about how creative incentives are or are not harmed. If we hope to improve our understanding over time, we should re-structure the law so that litigation produces the information about harm that we currently lack.

Christopher Jon Sprigman, *Copyright and the Rule of Reason*, 7 J. TELECOMM. & HIGH TECH. L. 317 (2009); *accord* Christina Bohannan & Herbert Hovenkamp, CREATION WITHOUT RESTRAINT: PROMOTING LIBERTY AND RIVALRY IN INNOVATION 161-99 (2012); Mark A. Lemley & Mark P. McKenna, *Unfair Disruption*, 100 B.U. L. REV. 71 (2020).

7. Should the test for substantial similarity be tailored to the nature of work at issue, be it visual art, music, a novel, or computer software? For an argument that the courts ought to do more tailoring in this regard, see Pamela Samuelson, *A Fresh Look at Tests for Nonliteral Copyright Infringement*, 107 Nw. U. L. REV. 1821 (2013).

8. For infringement claims involving musical works, courts and commentators struggle with which elements of a musical composition ought to be emphasized in findings of substantial similarity and which ought to be deemphasized. Substantial similarity decisions with regard to musical works tend to get more technical in their reliance and evaluation of expert views than decisions for other types of works. *See, e.g.*, Williams v. Gaye, 885 F.3d 1150 (9th Cir. 2018); Swirsky v. Carey, 376 F.3d 841 (9th Cir. 2004); Williams v. Bridgeport Music, Inc., No. LA CV13–06004 JAK (AGRx), 2014 WL 7877773 (C.D. Cal. Oct. 30, 2014). *See also* Gray v. Hudson, 28 F.4th 87 (9th Cir. 2022) (granting the defendant's motion to set aside a jury verdict of infringement, and holding that the "ostinatos [i.e., a continually repeated musical phrase] at issue here consist entirely of commonplace musical elements, and that the similarities between them do not arise out of an original combination of these elements"). One reason this happens is likely because it is difficult to evaluate whether a musical element is similar in two works because it is a stock element for the relevant genre or musical style or because it has been copied. Another reason is because of the difficulty in assessing which elements of a musical work—melody, rhythm, harmony, or organizational structure, to name but a few elements—the law is and ought to be protecting. For an argument that copyright infringement decisions as to musical works tend to emphasize melody to the exclusion of other elements and an analysis of the upshot of deemphasizing other elements of musical works even in genres in which they are more important than melody, see Joseph P. Fishman, *Music as a Matter of Law*, 131 HARV. L. REV. 1861 (2018). For a counterargument that this approach inappropriately emphasizes the visual aspects of music over the aural for reasons related to both cognition and perception of music and the current prominence of African-American-based music, see Olufunmilayo B. Arewa, *A Musical Work Is a Set of Instructions*, 52 HOUS. L. REV. 467 (2014).

c. Exact Copy

Exact copies, except when they involve de minimis copying as explored above in section a, would readily seem to support a conclusion of copying in law. That is very much true for piracy cases. That said, sections 107 through 122 of the Copyright Act set out numerous limitations on liability for certain types of exact copies. To give you a feel for these privileged activities, this section discusses some of the more salient limitations (other than fair use as set out in § 107, which we study in Chapter VI).

Chapter V – Exclusive Rights

Section 108 privileges certain exact copies made by libraries and archives. Section 108 was originally enacted in the Copyright Act of 1976 to address the photocopying possibilities that had become available to libraries, archives, and their patrons. Congress amended § 108 with the Digital Millennium Copyright Act in 1998 to address electronic copies of library materials.

Section 108(a) provides:

> *Except as otherwise provided in this title and notwithstanding the provisions of section 106, it is not an infringement of copyright for a library or archives, or any of its employees acting within the scope of their employment, to reproduce no more than one copy or phonorecord of a work, except as provided in subsections (b) and (c), or to distribute such copy or phonorecord, under the conditions specified by this section, if—*
>
>> *(1) the reproduction or distribution is made without any purpose of direct or indirect commercial advantage;*
>>
>> *(2) the collections of the library or archives are (i) open to the public, or (ii) available not only to researchers affiliated with the library or archives or with the institution of which it is a part, but also to other persons doing research in a specialized field; and*
>>
>> *(3) the reproduction or distribution of the work includes a notice of copyright that appears on the copy or phonorecord that is reproduced under the provisions of this section, or includes a legend stating that the work may be protected by copyright if no such notice can be found on the copy or phonorecord that is reproduced under the provisions of this section.*

As spelled out in this text, libraries and their employees acting within the scope of their employment can claim this privilege. To do so, they must make no more than one copy of a work, that copy must be made without any purpose of commercial advantage, the library's collections must remain open as specified, and there must be notice of copyright on the copy as specified. Moreover, qualifying libraries can also make "three copies or phonorecords of an unpublished work" so long as these copies are "solely for purposes of preservation and security or for deposit for research use in another" qualifying library and the copy being reproduced is "currently in the collection of the library." 17 U.S.C. § 108(b). As to published works, qualifying libraries can make three copies "solely for the purpose of replacement of a copy or phonorecord that is damaged, deteriorating, lost, or stolen, or if the existing format in which the work is stored has become obsolete," so long as "the library ... has, after a reasonable effort, determined that an unused replacement cannot be obtained at a fair price." *Id.* § 108(c). To take advantage of the copying privileges of §§ 108(b) and (c), any digital copy that is made cannot be made available off the library's premises. *Id.* §§ 108(b)-(c). To prevent loopholes, such as mass copying by a group, § 108 has further limitations on these reproduction privileges. *Id.* § 108(g). At the same time, § 108 provides that it should not be understood "to impose liability for copyright infringement upon a library or archives or its employees for the unsupervised use of reproducing equipment located on its premises: *Provided,* That such equipment displays a notice that the making of a copy may be subject to the copyright law." *Id.* § 108(f)(1).

In thinking through copyright policy, why do you suppose that Congress legislated this privilege for these forms of exact copying by libraries? For more on the background of § 108 and its amendment, see Laura N. Gasaway, *Amending the Copyright Act for Libraries and Society: The Section 108 Study Group*, 70 ALB. L. REV. 1331 (2007).

Sections 112 and 118 of the Copyright Act privilege certain exact copies made by broadcasters. Consider § 112. It excludes from infringement liability ephemeral copies made by a broadcaster that already has a license, statutory license, or other allowance to perform or display a work. Section 112(a)(1) provides:

> *Notwithstanding the provisions of section 106, and except in the case of a motion picture or other audiovisual work, it is not an infringement of copyright for a transmitting organization entitled to transmit to the public a performance or display of a work ..., to make no more than one copy or phonorecord of a particular transmission program embodying the performance or display, if—*
>
> > *(A) the copy or phonorecord is retained and used solely by the transmitting organization that made it, and no further copies or phonorecords are reproduced from it; and*
> >
> > *(B) the copy or phonorecord is used solely for the transmitting organization's own transmissions within its local service area, or for purposes of archival preservation or security; and*
> >
> > *(C) unless preserved exclusively for archival purposes, the copy or phonorecord is destroyed within six months from the date the transmission program was first transmitted to the public.*

Note the limitations on this privilege: Broadcasters cannot make ephemeral copies of motion pictures or audiovisual works. For other works being broadcast, only one copy can be made. That copy can be used only for the broadcaster's own transmissions in its service area or for archival or security purposes. And unless the copy is being used for archival purposes, the copy must be destroyed within six months of the date the work was first transmitted to the public.

Why do you think the Copyright Act exempts these ephemeral copies made by broadcasters from infringement liability?

As a final illustration of the Copyright Act's exemptions of some exact copying, consider § 117's exemption of certain copies made in the course of using computer programs (as discussed also in Chapter II's treatment of copyright for computer software). In 1980, following CONTU's recommendation that copyright law be extended to protect computer software, Congress enacted an exemption on certain exact copies in § 117. Most importantly, as currently implemented, it provides that

> *Notwithstanding the provisions of section 106, it is not an infringement for the owner of a copy of a computer program to make or authorize the making of another copy or adaptation of that computer program provided:*
>
> > *(1) that such a new copy or adaptation is created as an essential step in the utilization of the computer program in conjunction with a machine and that it is used in no other manner, or*
> >
> > *(2) that such new copy or adaptation is for archival purposes only and that all archival copies are destroyed in the event that continued possession of the computer program should cease to be rightful.*

Id. § 117(a). This provision exempts a copy of computer programs made automatically by a computer in the course of running the program so long as it is "an essential step in the utilization of the computer program," is not used for any other purpose, and is being made by or on behalf of the owner (rather than, say, a licensee) of the copy of the computer program. It also allows owners of copies of computer programs to make a copy for archival purposes. A subsequent amendment to § 117—following in the wake of *MAI Sys. Corp. v. Peak Comp., Inc.*, 991 F.2d 511 (9th Cir. 1993) (discussed in Chapter II with regard to fixation)—also exempts certain copying made or authorized by owners of copies of computer programs in the course of machine repair or maintenance. 17 U.S.C. § 117(c). For a broader analysis of how copyright law has handled the rise of copy-reliant technologies like the computer, see Matthew Sag, *Copyright and Copy-Reliant Technology*, 103 Nw. U. L. Rev. 1607 (2009).

Why do you think Congress exempted these copies of computer programs from infringement liability?

More generally, taking together § 106(1)'s reproduction right, the judicially-developed "substantial similarity" infringement standard, and the liability exemptions in §§ 107-122, there is a powerful dynamic at play in copyright law. Both the language of § 106(1)'s exclusive right of reproduction and the "substantial similarity" test are constructed such that almost all copying—particularly exact copying—can be actionable unless one of the statutory exemptions applies. The statutory exemptions are each technical and complex, so the precise wording of a particular exemption matters in assessing whether particular copying is exempt from liability.

Is this a good way to construct copyright law—that is, sweeping virtually all copying of protected elements into liability, and then exempting certain sorts of copying? Is there a better way?

C. Distribution (and Importation) Rights

Section 106(3) of the Copyright Act gives copyright owners the exclusive right "to distribute copies or phonorecords of the copyrighted work to the public by sale or other transfer of ownership, or by rental, lease, or lending."

In typical cases, the distribution right functions identically to the reproduction right because most reproduced works are also distributed. The distribution right, however, enables copyright holders to pursue claims against distributors of copies made by someone else. Is it fair to hold liable distributors of copies made by someone else, particularly given that copyright infringement is a strict-liability offense? Does it comport with copyright policy?

Note that this right is limited to the distribution of *copies* (or phonorecords, the term for a copy of a sound recording). It does not reach *streaming*, which does not, in itself, result in the distribution of copies or phonorecords. Why not? Think about how the Copyright Act defines a "copy": "Copies" must be "fixed," as set out in Chapter II. Streaming does not in itself produce a fixed copy.

What does it mean to "distribute" a copy? Does making a copy available constitute distribution? Or must the copy actually be received by another person for distribution to have occurred? Courts have split on that question. *Compare* Capitol Records, Inc. v. Thomas, 579 F. Supp. 2d 1210, 1226 (D. Minn. 2008) (holding that making available copyrighted material does not, without proof that a copy was received, constitute distribution of that work under 17 U.S.C. § 106(3)) , *with* Hotaling v. Church of Jesus Christ of Latter-Day Saints, 118 F.3d 199, 201 (4th Cir. 1997) (holding that "a library distributes a published work, within the meaning of the Copyright Act, when it places an unauthorized copy of the work in its collection, includes the copy in its catalog or index system, and *makes the copy available* to the public") (emphasis added).

Note that even if a plaintiff in a copyright infringement lawsuit is able to show that they have made a copy available but are unable to establish a specific instance of actual distribution, that does not mean that the plaintiff's § 106(3) claim should necessarily be dismissed. If a plaintiff is able to establish that a copy made available in the specific manner at issue in the case is statistically more likely than not to have been actually distributed, that should suffice as proof of distribution; each element of a copyright claim is subject to proof by a preponderance-of-the-evidence standard. So, for example, if data shows that, on average, a copy made available on a particular peer-to-peer system or cyberlocker is likely to have been distributed within a particular amount of time, such evidence should be sufficient to establish that actual distribution of the copy at issue has more likely than not occurred.

The distribution right is subject to an important limitation, the **first-sale doctrine**, which was recognized by U.S. courts at least as far back as the Supreme Court's opinion in *Bobbs-Merrill Co. v. Straus*, 210 U.S. 339 (1908), which you'll read next. As you shall see, Congress codified the first-sale doctrine in § 109 of the Copyright Act.

> As you read the next case, try to fathom the origin of the so-called first-sale doctrine. Is the Supreme Court interpreting the meaning of the copyright law? Or is it importing a common law rule into copyright law? If the latter, what is the common law rule? What social policy does it serve?

Bobbs-Merrill Company v. Isidor Straus
210 U.S. 339 (1908)

DAY, J.:

[1] The complainant in the circuit court, appellant here, the Bobbs-Merrill Company, brought suit against the respondents, appellees here, Isidor Straus and Nathan Straus, partners as R. H. Macy & Company, in the circuit court of the United States for the southern district of New York, to restrain the sale of a copyrighted novel, entitled 'The Castaway,' at retail at less than $1 for each copy. The circuit court dismissed the bill on final hearing. The decree of the circuit court was affirmed on appeal by the circuit court of appeals.

[2] The appellant is the owner of the copyright upon 'The Castaway,' obtained on the 18th day of May, 1904, in conformity to the copyright statutes of the United States. Printed immediately below the copyright notice, on the page in the book following the title page, is inserted the following notice:

> *The price of this book at retail is $1 net. No dealer is licensed to sell it at a less price, and a sale at a less price will be treated as an infringement of the copyright.*
>
> *The Bobbs-Merrill Company.*

[3] Macy & Company, before the commencement of the action, purchased copies of the book for the purpose of selling the same at retail....

[4] The defendants have sold copies of the book at retail at the uniform price of 89 cents a copy, and are still selling, exposing for sale, and offering copies of the book at retail at the price of 89 cents per copy, without the consent of the complainant....

[5] The facts disclose a sale of a book at wholesale by the owners of the copyright, at a satisfactory price, and this without agreement between the parties to such sale obligating the purchaser to control future sales, and where the alleged right springs from the protection of the copyright law alone. It is contended that this power

to control further sales is given by statute to the owner of such a copyright in conferring the sole right to 'vend' a copyrighted book....

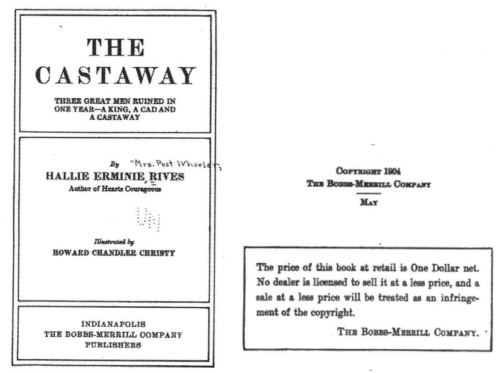

Figure 68: *The Castaway* inside title page (left) and notice (right)

[6] The learned counsel for the appellant in this case, in the argument at bar, disclaims relief because of any contract, and relies solely upon the copyright statutes, and rights therein conferred. The copyright statutes ought to be reasonably construed, with a view to effecting the purposes intended by Congress. They ought not to be unduly extended by judicial construction to include privileges not intended to be conferred, nor so narrowly construed as to deprive those entitled to their benefit of the rights Congress intended to grant....

[7] It is the contention of the appellant that the circuit court erred in failing to ... protect[] the owners of the copyright in the sole right of vending the copyrighted book or other article, and the argument is that the statute vested the whole field of the right of exclusive sale in the copyright owner; that he can part with it to another to the extent that he sees fit, and may withhold to himself, by proper reservations, so much of the right as he pleases.

[8] What does the statute mean in granting 'the sole right of vending the same?' Was it intended to create a right which would permit the holder of the copyright to fasten, by notice in a book or upon one of the articles mentioned within the statute, a restriction upon the subsequent alienation of the subject-matter of copyright after the owner had parted with the title to one who had acquired full dominion over it and had given a satisfactory price for it? It is not denied that one who has sold a copyrighted article, without restriction, has parted with all right to control the sale of it. The purchaser of a book, once sold by authority of the owner of the copyright, may sell it again, although he could not publish a new edition of it.

[9] In this case the stipulated facts show that the books sold by the appellant were sold at wholesale, and purchased by those who made no agreement as to the control of future sales of the book, and took upon themselves no obligation to enforce the notice printed in the book, undertaking to restrict retail sales to a price of $1 per copy.

[10] The precise question, therefore, in this case is, Does the sole right to vend (named in [the copyright statute]) secure to the owner of the copyright right, after a sale of the book to a purchaser, to restrict future sales of the book at retail, to the right to sell it at a certain price per copy, because of a notice in the book that a sale at a different price will be treated as an infringement, which notice has been brought home to one undertaking to sell for less than the named sum? We do not think the statute can be given such a construction, and it is to be remembered that this is purely a question of statutory construction. There is no claim in this case of contract limitation, nor license agreement controlling the subsequent sales of the book.

[11] In our view the copyright statutes, while protecting the owner of the copyright in his right to multiply and sell his production, do not create the right to impose, by notice, such as is disclosed in this case, a limitation at which the book shall be sold at retail by future purchasers, with whom there is no privity of contract. This conclusion is reached in view of the language of the statute, read in the light of its main purpose to secure the right of multiplying copies of the work, a right which is the special creation of the statute. True, the statute also secures, to make this right of multiplication effectual, the sole right to vend copies of the book, the production of the author's thought and conception. The owner of the copyright in this case did sell copies of the book in quantities and at a price satisfactory to it. It has exercised the right to vend. What the complainant contends for embraces not only the right to sell the copies, but to qualify the title of a future purchaser by the reservation of the right to have the remedies of the statute against an infringer because of the printed notice of its purpose so to do unless the purchaser sells at a price fixed in the notice. To add to the right of exclusive sale the authority to control all future retail sales, by a notice that such sales must be made at a fixed sum, would give a right not included in the terms of the statute, and, in our view, extend its operation, by construction, beyond its meaning, when interpreted with a view to ascertaining the legislative intent in its enactment....

NOTE

1. *Bobbs-Merrill* seems to contemplate that parties can contract around the first-sale doctrine. Should the law allow such contracting? Does it make a difference to your analysis if the contract is individually negotiated or is instead provided through a shrinkwrap or clickwrap license made applicable to all would-be purchasers?

The first-sale doctrine is codified in § 109(a) of the Copyright Act:

> *Notwithstanding the provisions of section 106(3), the owner of a particular copy or phonorecord lawfully made under this title, or any person authorized by such owner, is entitled, without the authority of the copyright owner, to sell or otherwise dispose of the possession of that copy or phonorecord....*

Note that by its terms, the protections of § 109(a) extend not only to the sale of copies, but also to other forms of distribution, such as rental, lease, and lending.

> Read the statutory language of § 109(a) carefully before reading the following case. Notice the limitations set out in § 109(a) to the scope of the first-sale doctrine. Has the court in the following case understood and applied those limitations correctly? Is the court's construction of § 109(a) consistent with the common law principle animating the first-sale doctrine?

Capitol Records, LLC v. ReDigi Inc.
910 F.3d 649 (2d Cir. 2018)

LEVAL, J.:

[1] Defendant ReDigi, Inc. ... appeal[s] from the judgment of the United States District Court for the Southern District of New York in favor of Plaintiffs, Capitol Records, LLC ..., finding copyright infringement. Defendants had created an Internet platform designed to enable the lawful resale, under the first sale doctrine, of lawfully purchased digital music files, and had hosted resales of such files on the platform. The district court concluded that, notwithstanding the "first sale" doctrine, codified in the Copyright Act of 1976, 17 U.S.C. § 109(a), ReDigi's Internet system version 1.0 infringed the Plaintiffs' copyrights by enabling the resale of such digital files containing sound recordings of Plaintiffs' copyrighted music. We agree with the district court that ReDigi infringed the Plaintiffs' exclusive rights under 17 U.S.C. § 106(1) to reproduce their copyrighted works. We make no decision whether ReDigi also infringed the Plaintiffs' exclusive rights under 17 U.S.C. § 106(3) to distribute their works....

[2] Plaintiffs are record companies, which own copyrights or licenses in sound recordings of musical performances. Plaintiffs distribute those sound recordings in numerous forms, of which the most familiar twenty years ago was the compact disc. Today, Plaintiffs also distribute their music in the form of digital files, which are sold to the public by authorized agent services, such as Apple iTunes, under license from Plaintiffs. Purchasers from the Apple iTunes online store download the files onto their personal computers or other devices.

[3] ReDigi was founded ... in 2009 with the goal of creating enabling technology and providing a marketplace for the lawful resale of lawfully purchased digital music files. ... During the period addressed by the operative complaint, ReDigi, through its system version 1.0, hosted resales of digital music files containing the Plaintiffs' music by persons who had lawfully purchased the files from iTunes.

[4] Considering the evidence in the light most favorable to ReDigi, ReDigi's system version 1.0 operates as follows.

[5] ... *Music Manager*: A person who owns a digital music file lawfully purchased from iTunes and intends to employ ReDigi's system to resell it must first download and install onto her computer ReDigi's "Music Manager" software program. Once Music Manager has been installed, it analyzes the digital file intended for resale, verifies that the file was originally lawfully purchased from iTunes, and scans it for indications of tampering. If the file was lawfully purchased, Music Manager deems it an "Eligible File" that may be resold.[4]

[6] ... *Data Migration*: The ReDigi user must then cause the file to be transferred to ReDigi's remote server, known as the "Cloud Locker." To effectuate this transfer, ReDigi developed a new method that functions differently from the conventional file transfer. The conventional process is to reproduce the digital file at the receiving destination so that, upon completion of the transfer, the file exists simultaneously on both the

---

[4] Music Manager will deem a file "Eligible" if it was purchased by the user from iTunes or it was purchased by the user through ReDigi, having been originally purchased lawfully by another from iTunes.

receiving device and on the device from which it was transferred. If connectivity is disrupted during such a standard transfer, the process can be repeated because the file remains intact on the sender's device.

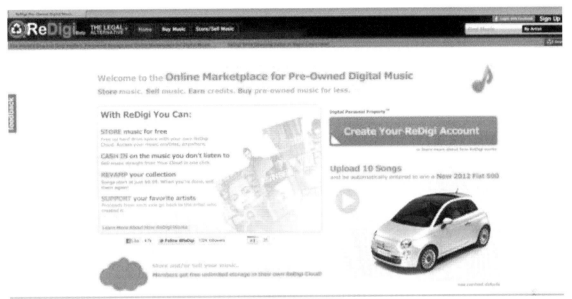

Figure 69: ReDigi screenshot

[7] Under ReDigi's method—which it calls "data migration"—ReDigi's software begins by breaking the digital music file into small blocks of data of roughly four thousand bytes in length. Once the file has been broken into blocks of data ("packets"), ReDigi's system creates a "transitory copy" of each packet in the initial purchaser's computer buffer. Upon copying (or "reading") a packet into the initial purchaser's computer buffer, ReDigi's software sends a command to delete that packet of the digital file from permanent storage on the initial purchaser's device. ReDigi's software then sends the packet to the ReDigi software to be copied into the buffer and deleted from the user's device. During the data migration process, the digital file cannot be accessed, played, or perceived. If connectivity is disrupted during the data migration process, the remnants of the digital file on the user's device are unusable, and the transfer cannot be re-initiated. In such circumstances, ReDigi (according to its brief) bears the cost of the user's loss....

[8] Once all the packets of the source file have been transferred to ReDigi's server, the Eligible File has been entirely removed from the user's device. The packets are then re-assembled into a complete, accessible, and playable file on ReDigi's server.

[9] ReDigi describes its primary technological innovation using the metaphor of a train (the digital file) leaving from one station (the original purchaser's device) and arriving at its destination (in the first instance, ReDigi's server). Under either the typical method or ReDigi's method, packets are sent sequentially, such that, conceptually, each packet is a car moving from the source to the destination device. Once all the packets arrive at the destination device, they are reassembled into a usable file. At that moment, in a typical transfer, the entire digital file in usable form exists on both devices. ReDigi's system differs in that it effectuates a deletion of each packet from the user's device immediately after the "transitory copy" of that packet arrives in the computer's buffer (before the packet is forwarded to ReDigi's server). In other words, as each packet "leaves the station," ReDigi deletes it from the original purchaser's device such that it no longer exists on that device. As a result, the entire file never exists in two places at once.

[10] After the file has reached ReDigi's server but before it has been resold, the user may continue to listen to it by streaming audio from the user's Cloud Locker on ReDigi's server. If the user later re-downloads the file from her Cloud Locker to her computer, ReDigi will delete the file from its own server.

[11] ... *Resale*: Once an Eligible File has "migrated" to ReDigi's server, it can be resold by the user utilizing ReDigi's market function. If it is resold, ReDigi gives the new purchaser exclusive access to the file. ReDigi will (at the new purchaser's option) either download the file to the new purchaser's computer or other device (simultaneously deleting the file from its own server) or will retain the file in the new purchaser's Cloud Locker on ReDigi's server, from which the new purchaser can stream the music. ReDigi's terms of service state that digital media purchases may be streamed or downloaded only for personal use.

[12] ... *Duplicates:* ReDigi purports to guard against a user's retention of duplicates of her digital music files after she sells the files through ReDigi. To that end, Music Manager continuously monitors the user's computer hard drive and connected devices to detect duplicates. When a user attempts to upload an Eligible File to ReDigi's server, ReDigi prompts her to delete any pre-existing duplicates that Music Manager has detected. If ReDigi detects that the user has not deleted the duplicates, ReDigi blocks the upload of the Eligible File. After an upload is complete, Music Manager continues to search the user's connected devices for duplicates. If it detects a duplicate of a previously uploaded Eligible File, ReDigi will prompt the user to authorize ReDigi to delete that duplicate from her personal device and, if authorization is not granted, it will suspend her account.

[13] Plaintiffs point out, and ReDigi does not dispute, that these precautions do not *prevent* the retention of duplicates after resale through ReDigi. Suspension of the original purchaser's ReDigi account does not negate the fact that the original purchaser has both sold and retained the digital music file after she sold it. So long as the user retains previously-made duplicates on devices not linked to the computer that hosts Music Manager, Music Manager will not detect them....

[13] The primary issue on appeal is whether ReDigi's system version 1.0 lawfully enables resales of its users' digital files. Sections 106(1) and (3) of the Copyright Act respectively grant the owner of a copyright the exclusive right to control the reproduction and the distribution of the copyrighted work. Under the first sale doctrine, codified in § 109(a), the rights holder's control *over the distribution* of any particular copy or phonorecord that was lawfully made effectively terminates when that copy or phonorecord is distributed to its first recipient....

[14] ... [I]t is well established that the lawful purchaser of a copy of a book is free to resell, lend, give, or otherwise transfer that copy without violating the copyright holder's exclusive right of distribution. The copy so resold or re-transferred may be re-transferred again and again without violating the exclusive distribution right. It is undisputed that one who owns a digital file from iTunes of music that is fixed in a material object qualifies as "the owner of a particular ... phonorecord lawfully made," and is thus entitled under § 109(a) "to sell or otherwise dispose of the possession of *that*... phonorecord," without violating § 106(3). On the other hand, § 109(a) says nothing about the rights holder's control under § 106(1) over *reproduction* of a copy or phonorecord.

[15] The district court found that resales through ReDigi were infringing for two reasons. The first reason was that, in the course of ReDigi's transfer, the phonorecord has been reproduced in a manner that violates the Plaintiffs' exclusive control of *reproduction* under § 106(1); the second was that the digital files sold through ReDigi, being unlawful reproductions, are not subject to the resale right established by § 109(a), which applies solely to a "particular ... phonorecord ... lawfully made." We agree with the first reason underlying the district court's finding of infringement. As that is a sufficient reason for affirmance of the judgment, we make no ruling on the district court's second reason.

[16] ReDigi argues on appeal that its system effectuates transfer of the *particular* digital file that the user lawfully purchased from iTunes, that it should not be deemed to have reproduced that file, and that it should

therefore come within the protection of 17 U.S.C. § 109(a). ReDigi makes two primary contentions in support of these arguments.

[17] First, ReDigi asserts—as it must for its first sale argument to succeed—that the digital files should be considered "material objects" and therefore, under 17 U.S.C. § 101's definition of "phonorecords" as "material objects," should qualify as "phonorecords" eligible for the protection of § 109(a).

[18] Second, ReDigi argues that from a technical standpoint, its process should not be seen as making a reproduction. ReDigi emphasizes that its system simultaneously causes packets to be removed from the file remaining in the consumer's computer as those packets are copied into the computer buffer and then transferred to the ReDigi server, so that the complete file never exists in more than one place at the same time, and the file on the user's machine continually shrinks in size while the file on the server grows in size. ReDigi points out that the sum of the size of the data stored in the original purchaser's computer and in ReDigi's server never exceeds the size of the original file, which, according to ReDigi, confirms that no reproductions are made during the transfer process.

[19] As for ReDigi's first argument, that the digital file it transfers is a phonorecord protected by § 109(a), we do not decide this issue because we find that ReDigi effectuates an unlawful reproduction even if the digital file itself qualifies as a phonorecord.

[20] As for ReDigi's second argument, we reject it for the following reasons. The Copyright Act defines phonorecords as "material objects in which sounds ... are fixed by any method now known or later developed, and from which the sounds can be perceived, reproduced, or otherwise communicated, either directly or with the aid of a machine or device." 17 U.S.C. § 101. Accordingly, when the purchaser of a digital music file from iTunes possesses that file, embodied for a period of more than transitory duration in a computer or other physical storage device, that device—or at least the portion of it in which the digital music file is fixed (e.g., the location on the hard drive)—becomes a phonorecord. In the course of transferring a digital music file from an original purchaser's computer, through ReDigi, to a new purchaser, the digital file is first received and stored on ReDigi's server and then, at the new purchaser's option, may also be subsequently received and stored on the new purchaser's device. At each of these steps, the digital file is fixed in a new material object "for a period of more than transitory duration." The fixing of the digital file in ReDigi's server, as well as in the new purchaser's device, creates a new phonorecord, which is a reproduction. ReDigi version 1.0's process for enabling the resale of digital files thus inevitably involves the creation of new phonorecords by reproduction, even if the standalone digital file is deemed to be a phonorecord.

[21] As for the argument that, as ReDigi copies a packet of data, it deletes the equivalent packet in the user's device so that the amount of data extant in the transfer process remains constant, this does not rebut or nullify the fact that the eventual receipt and storage of that file in ReDigi's server, as well as in the new purchaser's device (at his option), does involve the making of new phonorecords. Unless the creation of those new phonorecords is justified by the doctrine of fair use, which we discuss and reject in a later {omitted} portion of this opinion, the creation of such new phonorecords involves unauthorized reproduction, which is not protected, or even addressed, by § 109(a).

[22] ReDigi makes several additional arguments designed to characterize its process as involving the transfer of its users' lawfully made phonorecords, rather than the creation of new phonorecords. None of these arguments negates the crucial fact that each transfer of a digital music file to ReDigi's server and each new purchaser's download of a digital music file to his device creates new phonorecords. ReDigi argues, for example, that during a transfer through ReDigi's data migration technology, each packet of data from the original source file resides in a buffer for less than a second before being overwritten, and thus fails to satisfy the requirement that a sound recording must be embodied "for a period of more than transitory duration" to

qualify as a phonorecord. Even if, during transfer, ReDigi's system retains each digital file *in a computer buffer* for a period of no more than transitory duration, those files subsequently become embodied in ReDigi's server and in the new purchaser's device, where they remain for periods "of more than transitory duration." ReDigi's server and the resale purchaser's device on which the digital music files are fixed constitute or contain new phonorecords under the statute.

[23] ReDigi next argues that, in the course of transferring a user's file to ReDigi's own server, and to the resale purchaser's device, ReDigi sees to it that all of the original purchaser's preexisting duplicates are destroyed. As an initial matter, as noted above, ReDigi here overclaims. It does not ensure against retention of duplicate phonorecords created by the original owner.... In addition, even if ReDigi effectively compensated (by offsetting deletions) for the making of unauthorized reproductions in violation of the rights holder's exclusive reproduction right under § 106(1), nonetheless ReDigi's process itself involves the making of unauthorized reproductions that infringe the exclusive reproduction right unless justified under fair use. We are not free to disregard the terms of the statute merely because the entity performing an unauthorized reproduction makes efforts to nullify its consequences by the counterbalancing destruction of the preexisting phonorecords....

[24] Finally, ReDigi argues that the district court's conclusion makes no sense because it would "require a customer to sell her [valuable] computer in order to be able to sell a[n] ... iTunes music file" that was lawfully purchased for under $1.00. Of course it would make no economic sense for a customer to sell her computer or even a $5.00 thumb drive in order to sell "a[n] ... iTunes music file" purchased for $1.00. But ReDigi far overstates its economic argument when it asserts that the "district court's ruling ... eliminat[es] any meaningful competition from resellers" as "no secondary market ... can ever develop if consumers are required to give away their computer hard disks as part of any resale." A secondary market can readily be imagined for first purchasers who cost-effectively place 50 or 100 (or more) songs on an inexpensive device such as a thumb drive and sell it. Furthermore, other technology may exist or be developed that could lawfully effectuate a digital first sale.

[25] We conclude that the operation of ReDigi version 1.0 in effectuating a resale results in the making of at least one unauthorized reproduction. Unauthorized reproduction is not protected by § 109(a)....

[26] We conclude by addressing policy-based arguments raised by ReDigi and its amici. They contend that ReDigi's version 1.0 ought to be validated as in compliance with § 109(a) because it allows for realization of an economically beneficial practice, originally authorized by the courts in the common law development of copyright, and later endorsed by Congress. They also contend that the Copyright Act must be read to vindicate purchasers' ability to alienate digital copyrighted works under the first sale doctrine—emphasizing that § 109(a) is styled as an entitlement rather than a defense to infringement—without regard to technological medium. On this score, they rely heavily on the breadth of the common law first sale doctrine, and on a purported imperative, described as the "principle of technological neutrality" by amici and the "equal treatment principle" by ReDigi, not to disadvantage purchasers of digital copyrighted works, as compared with purchasers of physical copyrighted works.

[27] As for whether the economic consequences of ReDigi's program are beneficial and further the objectives of copyright, we take no position. Courts are poorly equipped to assess the inevitably multifarious economic consequences that would result from such changes of law. So far as we can see, the establishment of ReDigi's resale marketplace would benefit some, especially purchasers of digital music, at the expense of others, especially rightsholders, who, in the sale of their merchandise, would have to compete with resellers of the same merchandise in digital form, which, although second hand, would, unlike second hand books and records, be as good as new.

[28] Furthermore, as to the argument that we should read § 109(a) to accommodate digital resales because the first sale doctrine protects a fundamental entitlement, without regard to the terms of § 109(a) (and incorporated definitions), we think such a ruling would exceed the proper exercise of the court's authority. The copyright statute is a patchwork, sometimes varying from clause to clause, as between provisions for which Congress has taken control, dictating both policy and the details of its execution, and provisions in which Congress approximatively summarized common law developments, implicitly leaving further such development to the courts. The paradigm of the latter category is § 107 on fair use. In the provisions here relevant, Congress dictated the terms of the statutory entitlements. Notwithstanding the purported breadth of the first sale doctrine as originally articulated by the courts, Congress, in promulgating § 109(a), adopted a narrower conception, which negates a claim of unauthorized *distribution* in violation of the author's exclusive right under § 106(3), but not a claim of unauthorized *reproduction* in violation of the exclusive right provided by § 106(1). If ReDigi and its champions have persuasive arguments in support of the change of law they advocate, it is Congress they should persuade. We reject the invitation to substitute our judgment for that of Congress....

NOTES

1. Do you agree with *ReDigi*'s holding that ReDigi infringed the reproduction right? Is *ReDigi*'s ruling on this point required by the text of the Copyright Act? What interpretive methodology is the court applying to the text of the Copyright Act? Can you apply a different interpretive methodology that would reach a different result?

2. Although the Second Circuit did not rule on the issue, the district court in *ReDigi* held that the first-sale doctrine does not apply because the copies produced by the ReDigi service are not "lawfully made." Do you agree with the district court? Why or why not?

3. Soon after Capitol Records filed suit against ReDigi, ReDigi launched ReDigi 2.0, which the district court in the case described as "software that, when installed on a user's computer, purportedly directs the user's new iTunes purchases to upload from iTunes directly to the Cloud Locker. Accordingly, while access may transfer from user to user upon resale, the file is never moved from its initial location in the Cloud Locker." Neither the district court nor the Second Circuit ruled on whether ReDigi 2.0 constitutes copyright infringement. What do you think?

4. Is it good or bad copyright policy to treat physical copies differently than digital ones? For an analysis that a version of the first-sale doctrine ought to apply to digital copies, see Aaron Perzanowski & Jason Schultz, *Legislating Digital Exhaustion*, 29 BERKELEY TECH. L.J. 1535 (2015).

5. Review § 109(b). It limits the protection, for certain categories of works, that § 109(a) provides to the owners of copies. In particular, § 109(b) bans owners of phonorecords and computer programs from engaging in rental, lease, or lending "for direct or indirect commercial advantage" without authorization from the copyright owners. Congress passed limitations on the first-sale doctrine in response to complaints from the recording and software industries that record and software rental was facilitating unlawful copying (via duplication of rented software and taping of rented record albums). Note that these restrictions on the scope of the first-sale doctrine contain some important limitations themselves. By its own terms, § 109(b) does not apply to the lending, lease, or rental of phonorecords by nonprofit libraries and nonprofit educational institutions. 17 U.S.C. § 109(b)(1)(A). Section 109(b) also does not apply to computer programs that are "embodied in a machine or product and which cannot be copied during the ordinary operation or use of the machine or product." *Id.* § 109(b)(1)(B). Additionally, nonprofit libraries are permitted to lend computer programs for nonprofit purposes, provided that "each copy of a computer program which is lent by such library has affixed to the packaging containing the program a warning of copyright." *Id.* § 109(b)(2)(A).

You have doubtless noticed that § 109(b) does not bar the rental, lease, or lending of motion pictures and other audiovisual works. That omission is purposeful. In the past, the motion picture industry has lobbied Congress for its own exception to first sale, but Congress has rebuffed those efforts. The result was a thriving movie rental business (now largely supplanted by streaming, which, as you shall see, constitutes a public performance and thus, unlike most rental of specific copies of motion pictures, is not protected by the first-sale doctrine and must be licensed). Do you think that the availability of movie rentals hurt the motion picture industry? Where would you look for evidence one way or the other on that question? If you conclude that movie rentals were, on balance, not harmful to the motion picture industry, does that suggest anything about the wisdom of Congress's decision to ban (many types) of record and software rentals?

The Copyright Act supplements the § 106(3) distribution right with a provision, set out in § 602, prohibiting unauthorized importation into the United States of copies of a copyrighted work:

> Importation into the United States, without the authority of the owner of copyright under this title, of copies or phonorecords of a work that have been acquired outside the United States is an infringement of the exclusive right to distribute copies or phonorecords under section 106 ....

17 U.S.C. § 602(a)(1). Note that § 602 does not itself provide the copyright holder with a separate exclusive right. Rather, as the Supreme Court held in *Quality King Distributors, Inc. v. L'anza Research Int'l, Inc.*, 523 U.S. 135 (1998), the provision incorporates the § 106(3) distribution right and extends that right to unauthorized importation. As a consequence, § 602 also incorporates the limitations to § 106(3), including the first-sale doctrine set forth in § 109.

> The holding in *Quality King* plays an important role in the Supreme Court's decision in the following case. As you read this case, think about the practical implications of the Supreme Court's holding. If you were counsel for Wiley, how would you advise your client in the wake of the holding?

Supap Kirtsaeng v. John Wiley & Sons, Inc.
568 U.S. 519 (2013)

BREYER, J.:

[1] Section 106 of the Copyright Act grants "the owner of copyright under this title" certain "exclusive rights," including the right "to distribute copies ... of the copyrighted work to the public by sale or other transfer of ownership." 17 U.S.C. § 106(3). These rights are qualified, however, by the application of various limitations set forth in the next several sections of the Act, §§ 107 through 122. Those sections, typically entitled "Limitations on exclusive rights," include, for example, the principle of "fair use" (§ 107), permission for limited library archival reproduction, (§ 108), and the doctrine at issue here, the "first sale" doctrine (§ 109).

[2] Section 109(a) sets forth the "first sale" doctrine as follows:

> "Notwithstanding the provisions of section 106(3) [the section that grants the owner exclusive distribution rights], the owner of a particular copy or phonorecord lawfully made under this title ... is entitled, without the authority of the copyright owner, to sell or otherwise dispose of the possession of that copy or phonorecord." (emphasis added)

[3] Thus, even though § 106(3) forbids distribution of a copy of, say, the copyrighted novel *Herzog* without the copyright owner's permission, § 109(a) adds that, once a copy of *Herzog* has been lawfully sold (or its ownership otherwise lawfully transferred), the buyer of that *copy* and subsequent owners are free to dispose of it as they wish. In copyright jargon, the "first sale" has "exhausted" the copyright owner's § 106(3) exclusive distribution right.

[4] What, however, if the copy of *Herzog* was printed abroad and then initially sold with the copyright owner's permission? Does the "first sale" doctrine still apply? Is the buyer, like the buyer of a domestically manufactured copy, free to bring the copy into the United States and dispose of it as he or she wishes?

[5] To put the matter technically, an "importation" provision, § 602(a)(1), says that

> "[i]mportation into the United States, without the authority of the owner of copyright under this title, of copies ... of a work that have been acquired outside the United States is an infringement of the exclusive right to distribute copies ... under section 106...." (emphasis added)

[6] Thus § 602(a)(1) makes clear that importing a copy without permission violates the owner's exclusive distribution right. But in doing so, § 602(a)(1) refers explicitly to the *§ 106(3)* exclusive distribution right. As we have just said, § 106 is by its terms "[s]ubject to" the various doctrines and principles contained in §§ 107 through 122, including § 109(a)'s "first sale" limitation. Do those same modifications apply—in particular, does the "first sale" modification apply—when considering whether § 602(a)(1) prohibits importing a copy?

[7] In *Quality King Distributors, Inc. v. L'anza Research Int'l, Inc.*, 523 U.S. 135, 145 (1998), we held that § 602(a)(1)'s reference to § 106(3)'s exclusive distribution right incorporates the later subsections' limitations, including, in particular, the "first sale" doctrine of § 109. Thus, it might seem that, § 602(a)(1) notwithstanding, one who buys a copy abroad can freely import that copy into the United States and dispose of it, just as he could had he bought the copy in the United States.

[8] But *Quality King* considered an instance in which the copy, though purchased abroad, was initially manufactured in the United States (and then sent abroad and sold). This case is like *Quality King* but for one important fact. The copies at issue here were manufactured abroad. That fact is important because § 109(a) says that the "first sale" doctrine applies to "a particular copy or phonorecord *lawfully made under this title.*" And we must decide here whether the five words, "lawfully made under this title," make a critical legal difference.

[9] Putting section numbers to the side, we ask whether the "first sale" doctrine applies to protect a buyer or other lawful owner of a copy (of a copyrighted work) lawfully manufactured abroad. Can that buyer bring that copy into the United States (and sell it or give it away) without obtaining permission to do so from the copyright owner? Can, for example, someone who purchases, say at a used bookstore, a book printed abroad subsequently resell it without the copyright owner's permission?

[10] In our view, the answers to these questions are, yes. We hold that the "first sale" doctrine applies to copies of a copyrighted work lawfully made abroad....

[11] Respondent, John Wiley & Sons, Inc., publishes academic textbooks. Wiley obtains from its authors various foreign and domestic copyright assignments, licenses and permissions—to the point that we can, for present purposes, refer to Wiley as the relevant American copyright owner. Wiley often assigns to its wholly owned foreign subsidiary, John Wiley & Sons (Asia) Pte Ltd., rights to publish, print, and sell Wiley's English language textbooks abroad. Each copy of a Wiley Asia foreign edition will likely contain language making clear that the copy is to be sold only in a particular country or geographical region outside the United States.

[12] For example, a copy of Wiley's American edition says, "Copyright © 2008 John Wiley & Sons, Inc. All rights reserved.... Printed in the United States of America." J. WALKER, FUNDAMENTALS OF PHYSICS, p. vi (8th ed. 2008). A copy of Wiley Asia's Asian edition of that book says:

> "Copyright © 2008 John Wiley & Sons (Asia) Pte Ltd[.] All rights reserved. This book is authorized for sale in Europe, Asia, Africa, and the Middle East only and may be not exported out of these territories. Exportation from or importation of this book to another region without the Publisher's authorization is illegal and is a violation of the Publisher's rights. The Publisher may take legal action to enforce its rights.... Printed in Asia." J. Walker, Fundamentals of Physics, p. vi (8th ed. 2008 Wiley Int'l Student ed.)....

[13] The upshot is that there are two essentially equivalent versions of a Wiley textbook, each version manufactured and sold with Wiley's permission: (1) an American version printed and sold in the United States, and (2) a foreign version manufactured and sold abroad. And Wiley makes certain that copies of the second version state that they are not to be taken (without permission) into the United States.

[14] Petitioner, Supap Kirtsaeng, a citizen of Thailand, moved to the United States in 1997 to study mathematics at Cornell University.... While he was studying in the United States, Kirtsaeng asked his friends and family in Thailand to buy copies of foreign edition English-language textbooks at Thai book shops, where they sold at low prices, and mail them to him in the United States. Kirtsaeng would then sell them, reimburse his family and friends, and keep the profit....

[15] In 2008 Wiley brought this federal lawsuit against Kirtsaeng for copyright infringement. Wiley claimed that Kirtsaeng's unauthorized importation of its books and his later resale of those books amounted to an infringement of Wiley's § 106(3) exclusive right to distribute as well as § 602's related import prohibition. Kirtsaeng replied that the books he had acquired were "'lawfully made'" and that he had acquired them legitimately. Thus, in his view, § 109(a)'s "first sale" doctrine permitted him to resell or otherwise dispose of the books without the copyright owner's further permission.

[16] The District Court held that Kirtsaeng could not assert the "first sale" defense because, in its view, that doctrine does not apply to "foreign-manufactured goods" (even if made abroad with the copyright owner's permission). The jury then found that Kirtsaeng had willfully infringed Wiley's American copyrights by selling and importing without authorization copies of eight of Wiley's copyrighted titles. And it assessed statutory damages of $600,000 ($75,000 per work).

[17] On appeal, a split panel of the Second Circuit agreed with the District Court. It pointed out that § 109(a)'s "first sale" doctrine applies only to "the owner of a particular copy ... *lawfully made under this title.*" And, in the majority's view, this language means that the "first sale" doctrine does not apply to copies of American copyrighted works manufactured abroad. A dissenting judge thought that the words "lawfully made under this title" do not refer "to a place of manufacture" but rather "focu[s] on whether a particular copy was manufactured lawfully under" America's copyright statute, and that "the lawfulness of the manufacture of a particular copy should be judged by U.S. copyright law."

[18] We granted Kirtsaeng's petition for certiorari to consider this question in light of different views among the Circuits....

[19] We must decide whether the words "lawfully made under this title" restrict the scope of § 109(a)'s "first sale" doctrine geographically. The Second Circuit, the Ninth Circuit, Wiley, and the Solicitor General (as *amicus*) all read those words as imposing a form of *geographical* limitation. The Second Circuit held that they limit the "first sale" doctrine to particular copies "made in territories *in which the Copyright Act is law,*" which (the Circuit says) are copies "manufactured domestically," not "outside of the United States." Wiley agrees

that those five words limit the "first sale" doctrine "to copies made in conformance with the [United States] Copyright Act *where the Copyright Act is applicable*," which (Wiley says) means it does not apply to copies made "outside the United States" and at least not to "foreign production of a copy for distribution exclusively abroad."...

[20] Kirtsaeng, however, reads the words "lawfully made under this title" as imposing a *non*-geographical limitation. He says that they mean made "in accordance with" or "in compliance with" the Copyright Act. In that case, § 109(a)'s "first sale" doctrine would apply to copyrighted works as long as their manufacture met the requirements of American copyright law. In particular, the doctrine would apply where, as here, copies are manufactured abroad with the permission of the copyright owner.

[21] In our view, § 109(a)'s language, its context, and the common-law history of the "first sale" doctrine, taken together, favor a *non*-geographical interpretation. We also doubt that Congress would have intended to create the practical copyright-related harms with which a geographical interpretation would threaten ordinary scholarly, artistic, commercial, and consumer activities. We consequently conclude that Kirtsaeng's nongeographical reading is the better reading of the Act....

[22] The language of § 109(a) read literally favors Kirtsaeng's nongeographical interpretation, namely, that "lawfully made under this title" means made "in accordance with" or "in compliance with" the Copyright Act. The language of § 109(a) says nothing about geography. The word "under" can mean "[i]n accordance with." 18 OXFORD ENGLISH DICTIONARY 950 (2d ed. 1989). *See also* BLACK'S LAW DICTIONARY 1525 (6th ed. 1990) ("according to"). And a nongeographical interpretation provides each word of the five-word phrase with a distinct purpose. The first two words of the phrase, "lawfully made," suggest an effort to distinguish those copies that were made lawfully from those that were not, and the last three words, "under this title," set forth the standard of "lawful[ness]." Thus, the nongeographical reading is simple, it promotes a traditional copyright objective (combatting piracy), and it makes word-by-word linguistic sense.

[23] The geographical interpretation, however, bristles with linguistic difficulties. It gives the word "lawfully" little, if any, linguistic work to do. (How could a book be *un*lawfully "made under this title"?) It imports geography into a statutory provision that says nothing explicitly about it. And it is far more complex than may at first appear.

[24] To read the clause geographically, Wiley, like the Second Circuit and the Solicitor General, must first emphasize the word "under." Indeed, Wiley reads "under this title" to mean "in conformance with the Copyright Act *where the Copyright Act is applicable*." Wiley must then take a second step, arguing that the Act "is applicable" only in the United States....

[25] One difficulty is that neither "under" nor any other word in the phrase means "where." *See, e.g.,* 18 OXFORD ENGLISH DICTIONARY, *supra*, at 947–952 (definition of "under"). It might mean "subject to," but as this Court has repeatedly acknowledged, the word evades a uniform, consistent meaning.

[26] A far more serious difficulty arises out of the uncertainty and complexity surrounding the second step's effort to read the necessary geographical limitation into the word "applicable" (or the equivalent). Where, precisely, is the Copyright Act "applicable"? The Act does not instantly *protect* an American copyright holder from unauthorized piracy taking place abroad. But that fact does not mean the Act is *inapplicable* to copies made abroad. As a matter of ordinary English, one can say that a statute imposing, say, a tariff upon "any rhododendron grown in Nepal" applies to *all* Nepalese rhododendrons. And, similarly, one can say that the American Copyright Act is *applicable* to *all* pirated copies, including those printed overseas....

[26] The appropriateness of this linguistic usage is underscored by the fact that § 104 of the Act itself says that works "*subject to protection under this title*" include unpublished works "without regard to the nationality or

domicile of the author," and works "first published" in any one of the nearly 180 nations that have signed a copyright treaty with the United States. Thus, ordinary English permits us to say that the Act "applies" to an Irish manuscript lying in its author's Dublin desk drawer as well as to an original recording of a ballet performance first made in Japan and now on display in a Kyoto art gallery.

[27] The Ninth Circuit's geographical interpretation produces still greater linguistic difficulty. As we said, that Circuit interprets the "first sale" doctrine to cover both (1) copies manufactured in the United States and (2) copies manufactured abroad but first sold in the United States with the American copyright owner's permission.

[28] We can understand why the Ninth Circuit may have thought it necessary to add the second part of its definition. As we shall later describe, without some such qualification a copyright holder could prevent a buyer from domestically reselling or even giving away copies of a video game made in Japan, a film made in Germany, or a dress (with a design copyright) made in China, *even* if the copyright holder has granted permission for the foreign manufacture, importation, and an initial domestic sale of the copy. A publisher such as Wiley would be free to print its books abroad, allow their importation and sale within the United States, but prohibit students from later selling their used texts at a campus bookstore. We see no way, however, to reconcile this half-geographical/half-nongeographical interpretation with the language of the phrase, "lawfully made under this title." As a matter of English, it would seem that those five words either do cover copies lawfully made abroad or they do not.

[29] In sum, we believe that geographical interpretations create more linguistic problems than they resolve. And considerations of simplicity and coherence tip the purely linguistic balance in Kirtsaeng's, nongeographical, favor....

[30] Both historical and contemporary statutory context indicate that Congress, when writing the present version of § 109(a), did not have geography in mind. In respect to history, we compare § 109(a)'s present language with the language of its immediate predecessor. That predecessor said:

> "[N]othing in this Act shall be deemed to forbid, prevent, or restrict the transfer of any copy
> of a copyrighted work *the possession of which has been lawfully obtained*." Copyright Act of
> 1909, § 41, 35 Stat. 1084 (emphasis added).

The predecessor says nothing about geography (and Wiley does not argue that it does). So we ask whether Congress, in changing its language implicitly *introduced* a geographical limitation that previously was lacking.

[31] A comparison of language indicates that it did not. The predecessor says that the "first sale" doctrine protects "the transfer of any copy *the possession of which has been lawfully obtained*." The present version says that "*the owner* of a particular copy or phonorecord lawfully made under this title is entitled to sell or otherwise dispose of the possession of that copy or phonorecord." What does this change in language accomplish?

[32] The language of the former version referred to those *who are not owners* of a copy, but mere possessors who "lawfully obtained" a copy. The present version covers only those who are *owners* of a "lawfully made" copy. Whom does the change leave out? Who might have lawfully *obtained* a copy of a copyrighted work but not *owned* that copy? One answer is owners of movie theaters, who during the 1970's (and before) often *leased* films from movie distributors or filmmakers. Because the theater owners had "lawfully obtained" their copies, the earlier version could be read as allowing them to sell that copy, *i.e.*, it might have given them "first sale" protection. Because the theater owners were lessees, not owners, of their copies, the change in language makes clear that they (like bailees and other lessees) cannot take advantage of the "first sale" doctrine....

[33] This objective perfectly well explains the new language of the present version, including the five words here at issue. Section 109(a) now makes clear that a lessee of a copy will *not* receive "first sale" protection but one who *owns* a copy *will* receive "first sale" protection, *provided,* of course, that the copy was "*lawfully made*" and not pirated....

[34] A relevant canon of statutory interpretation favors a nongeographical reading. When a statute covers an issue previously governed by the common law, we must presume that Congress intended to retain the substance of the common law.

[35] The "first sale" doctrine is a common-law doctrine with an impeccable historic pedigree. In the early 17th century Lord Coke explained the common law's refusal to permit restraints on the alienation of chattels. Referring to Littleton, who wrote in the 15th century, Lord Coke wrote:

> "[If] a man be possessed of ... a horse, or of any other chattell ... and give or sell his whole interest ... therein upon condition that the Donee or Vendee shall not alien[ate] the same, the [condition] is voi[d], because his whole interest ... is out of him, so as he hath no possibilit[y] of a Reverter, and it is against Trade and Traffi[c], and bargaining and contracting betwee[n] man and man: and it is within the reason of our Author that it should ouster him of all power given to him." 1 E. COKE, INSTITUTES OF THE LAWS OF ENGLAND § 360, p. 223 (1628).

[36] A law that permits a copyright holder to control the resale or other disposition of a chattel once sold is similarly "against Trade and Traffi[c], and bargaining and contracting." ...

[37] The "first sale" doctrine also frees courts from the administrative burden of trying to enforce restrictions upon difficult-to-trace, readily movable goods. And it avoids the selective enforcement inherent in any such effort. Thus, it is not surprising that for at least a century the "first sale" doctrine has played an important role in American copyright law. *See* Bobbs-Merrill Co. v. Straus, 210 U.S. 339 (1908).

[38] The common-law doctrine makes no geographical distinctions; nor can we find any in *Bobbs-Merrill* (where this Court first applied the "first sale" doctrine) or in § 109(a)'s predecessor provision, which Congress enacted a year later....

[39] Associations of libraries, used-book dealers, technology companies, consumer-goods retailers, and museums point to various ways in which a geographical interpretation would fail to further basic constitutional copyright objectives, in particular "promot[ing] the Progress of Science and useful Arts."

[40] The American Library Association tells us that library collections contain at least 200 million books published abroad (presumably, many were first published in one of the nearly 180 copyright-treaty nations and enjoy American copyright protection under 17 U.S.C. § 104); that many others were first published in the United States but printed abroad because of lower costs; and that a geographical interpretation will likely require the libraries to obtain permission (or at least create significant uncertainty) before circulating or otherwise distributing these books.

[41] How, the American Library Association asks, are the libraries to obtain permission to distribute these millions of books? How can they find, say, the copyright owner of a foreign book, perhaps written decades ago? They may not know the copyright holder's present address. And, even where addresses can be found, the costs of finding them, contacting owners, and negotiating may be high indeed. Are the libraries to stop circulating or distributing or displaying the millions of books in their collections that were printed abroad?

[42] Used-book dealers tell us that, from the time when Benjamin Franklin and Thomas Jefferson built commercial and personal libraries of foreign books, American readers have bought used books published and

printed abroad. But under a geographical interpretation a contemporary tourist who buys, say, at Shakespeare and Co. (in Paris), a dozen copies of a foreign book for American friends might find that she had violated the copyright law. The used-book dealers cannot easily predict what the foreign copyright holder may think about a reader's effort to sell a used copy of a novel. And they believe that a geographical interpretation will injure a large portion of the used-book business.

[43] Technology companies tell us that "automobiles, microwaves, calculators, mobile phones, tablets, and personal computers" contain copyrightable software programs or packaging. Many of these items are made abroad with the American copyright holder's permission and then sold and imported (with that permission) to the United States. A geographical interpretation would prevent the resale of, say, a car, without the permission of the holder of each copyright on each piece of copyrighted automobile software. Yet there is no reason to believe that foreign auto manufacturers regularly obtain this kind of permission from their software component suppliers, and Wiley did not indicate to the contrary when asked. Without that permission a foreign car owner could not sell his or her used car....

[44] Neither Wiley nor any of its many *amici* deny that a geographical interpretation could bring about these "horribles"—at least in principle. Rather, Wiley essentially says that the list is artificially invented. It points out that a federal court first adopted a geographical interpretation more than 30 years ago. Yet, it adds, these problems have not occurred. Why not? Because, says Wiley, the problems and threats are purely theoretical; they are unlikely to reflect reality.

[45] We are less sanguine. For one thing, the law has not been settled for long in Wiley's favor....

[46] For another thing, reliance upon the "first sale" doctrine is deeply embedded in the practices of those, such as booksellers, libraries, museums, and retailers, who have long relied upon its protection. Museums, for example, are not in the habit of asking their foreign counterparts to check with the heirs of copyright owners before sending, *e.g.*, a Picasso on tour. That inertia means a dramatic change is likely necessary before these institutions, instructed by their counsel, would begin to engage in the complex permission-verifying process that a geographical interpretation would demand. And this Court's adoption of the geographical interpretation could provide that dramatic change....

[47] ... Wiley and the dissent claim that a nongeographical interpretation will make it difficult, perhaps impossible, for publishers (and other copyright holders) to divide foreign and domestic markets. We concede that is so. A publisher may find it more difficult to charge different prices for the same book in different geographic markets. But we do not see how these facts help Wiley, for we can find no basic principle of copyright law that suggests that publishers are especially entitled to such rights.

[48] The Constitution describes the nature of American copyright law by providing Congress with the power to "secur[e]" to "[a]uthors" "for limited [t]imes" the "*exclusive [r]ight to their ... [w]ritings.*" ... But the Constitution's language nowhere suggests that its limited exclusive right should include a right to divide markets or a concomitant right to charge different purchasers different prices for the same book, say to increase or to maximize gain. Neither, to our knowledge, did any Founder make any such suggestion. We have found no precedent suggesting a legal preference for interpretations of copyright statutes that would provide for market divisions.

[49] To the contrary, Congress enacted a copyright law that (through the "first sale" doctrine) limits copyright holders' ability to divide domestic markets.... Whether copyright owners should, or should not, have more than ordinary commercial power to divide international markets is a matter for Congress to decide. We do no more here than try to determine what decision Congress has taken....

[50] For these reasons we conclude that the considerations supporting Kirtsaeng's nongeographical interpretation of the words "lawfully made under this title" are the more persuasive. The judgment of the Court of Appeals is reversed, and the case is remanded for further proceedings consistent with this opinion.

It is so ordered.

KAGAN, J. concurring, joined by Justice Alito:

[51] I concur fully in the Court's opinion. Neither the text nor the history of 17 U.S.C. § 109(a) supports removing first-sale protection from every copy of a protected work manufactured abroad. I recognize, however, that the combination of today's decision and *Quality King Distributors, Inc. v. L'anza Research Int'l, Inc.,* 523 U.S. 135 (1998), constricts the scope of § 602(a)(1)'s ban on unauthorized importation. I write to suggest that any problems associated with that limitation come not from our reading of § 109(a) here, but from *Quality King*'s holding that § 109(a) limits § 602(a)(1)....

[52] At bottom, John Wiley (together with the dissent) asks us to misconstrue § 109(a) in order to restore § 602(a)(1) to its purportedly rightful function of enabling copyright holders to segment international markets. I think John Wiley may have a point about what § 602(a)(1) was designed to do; that gives me pause about *Quality King*'s holding that the first-sale doctrine limits the importation ban's scope. But the Court today correctly declines the invitation to save § 602(a)(1) from *Quality King* by destroying the first-sale protection that § 109(a) gives to every owner of a copy manufactured abroad. That would swap one (possible) mistake for a much worse one, and make our reading of the statute only less reflective of Congressional intent. If Congress thinks copyright owners need greater power to restrict importation and thus divide markets, a ready solution is at hand—not the one John Wiley offers in this case, but the one the Court rejected in *Quality King*.

GINSBURG, J. dissenting, joined by Justice Kennedy and, except in ¶¶ 61-63, by Justice Scalia:

[53] In the interpretation of statutes, the function of the courts is easily stated. It is to construe the language so as to give effect to the intent of Congress. Instead of adhering to the Legislature's design, the Court today adopts an interpretation of the Copyright Act at odds with Congress' aim to protect copyright owners against the unauthorized importation of low-priced, foreign-made copies of their copyrighted works....

[54] To justify a holding that shrinks to insignificance copyright protection against the unauthorized importation of foreign-made copies, the Court identifies several "practical problems." The Court's parade of horribles, however, is largely imaginary. Congress' objective in enacting 17 U.S.C. § 602(a)(1)'s importation prohibition can be honored without generating the absurd consequences hypothesized in the Court's opinion....

[55] Because economic conditions and demand for particular goods vary across the globe, copyright owners have a financial incentive to charge different prices for copies of their works in different geographic regions. Their ability to engage in such price discrimination, however, is undermined if arbitrageurs are permitted to import copies from low-price regions and sell them in high-price regions. The question in this case is whether the unauthorized importation of foreign-made copies constitutes copyright infringement under U.S. law....

[56] ... As the Court recognizes, this case turns on the meaning of the phrase "lawfully made under this title" in § 109(a). In my view, that phrase is most sensibly read as referring to instances in which a copy's creation is governed by, and conducted in compliance with, Title 17 of the U.S. Code. This reading is consistent with the Court's interpretation of similar language in other statutes. *See* Fla. Dept. of Revenue v. Piccadilly Cafeterias, Inc., 554 U.S. 33, 52–53 (2008) ("under" in 11 U.S.C. § 1146(a), a Bankruptcy Code provision exempting certain asset transfers from stamp taxes, means "pursuant to"); Ardestani v. INS, 502 U.S. 129, 135 (1991) (the phrase "under section 554" in the Equal Access to Justice Act means "subject to" or "governed by" 5 U.S.C. § 554). It

also accords with dictionary definitions of the word "under." See, *e.g.*, AMERICAN HERITAGE DICTIONARY 1887 (5th ed. 2011) ("under" means, among other things, "[s]ubject to the authority, rule, or control of").

[57] Section 109(a), properly read, affords Kirtsaeng no defense against Wiley's claim of copyright infringement. The Copyright Act, it has been observed time and again, does not apply extraterritorially. The printing of Wiley's foreign-manufactured textbooks therefore was not governed by Title 17. The textbooks thus were not "lawfully made under [Title 17]," the crucial precondition for application of § 109(a). And if § 109(a) does not apply, there is no dispute that Kirtsaeng's conduct constituted copyright infringement under § 602(a)(1)....

[58] The far more plausible reading of §§ 109(a) and 602(a) ... is that Congress intended § 109(a) to apply to copies made in the United States, not to copies manufactured and sold abroad....

[59] I turn now to the Court's justifications for a decision difficult to reconcile with the Copyright Act's text and history....

[60] The Court sees many "horribles" following from a holding that the § 109(a) phrase "lawfully made under this title" does not encompass foreign-made copies. If § 109(a) excluded foreign-made copies, the Court fears, then copyright owners could exercise perpetual control over the downstream distribution or public display of such copies. A ruling in Wiley's favor, the Court asserts, would shutter libraries, put used-book dealers out of business, cripple art museums, and prevent the resale of a wide range of consumer goods, from cars to calculators. Copyright law and precedent, however, erect barriers to the anticipated horribles....

[61] Recognizing that foreign-made copies fall outside the ambit of § 109(a) would not mean they are forever free of the first sale doctrine...

[62] ... [T]he sale of a foreign-manufactured copy in the United States carried out with the copyright owner's authorization would exhaust the copyright owner's right to "vend" that copy. The copy could thenceforth be resold, lent out, or otherwise redistributed without further authorization from the copyright owner.... Thus, ... the first authorized distribution of a foreign-made copy in the United States exhausts the copyright owner's distribution right under § 106(3). After such an authorized distribution, a library may lend, or a used-book dealer may resell, the foreign-made copy without seeking the copyright owner's permission.

[63] For example, if Wiley, rather than Kirtsaeng, had imported into the United States and then sold the foreign-made textbooks at issue in this case, Wiley's § 106(3) distribution right would have been exhausted under the rationale of *Bobbs-Merrill*. Purchasers of the textbooks would thus be free to dispose of the books as they wished without first gaining a license from Wiley....

[64] .... I would therefore affirm the Second Circuit's judgment.

NOTES

1. Did the Court exhaust the possible interpretations of "lawfully made under this title"? If not, what are the additional possible interpretations?

2. The United States has consistently argued in free-trade agreements for rules that would allow a copyright owner to control importation in the way Wiley attempted to do. Is there reason to prefer the result in *Kirtsaeng*, or the U.S. position in trade negotiations? More generally, are the sort of price discrimination schemes that Wiley was seeking in *Kirtsaeng* to defend socially productive or not?

3. Imagine you are counsel for Wiley and the *Kirtsaeng* opinion has just come down. Your client would like to continue to pursue its price discrimination strategy with respect to U.S. versus foreign editions of its texts. What is your advice to your client? Can you suggest some practical steps that Wiley can take that would enable it to continue to price discriminate?

4. Guy Rub theorizes that the result in *Kirtsaeng* provides a major benefit to buyers of copyrighted goods in terms of "a reduction in information costs." Guy A. Rub, *Rebalancing Copyright Exhaustion*, 64 EMORY L.J. 741 (2015). He elaborates:

> *The doctrine helps to create a reasonably clear standard set of rights that buyers receive when they buy copyrighted goods. Because those rights are important in the buyers' buying decision, without copyright exhaustion, they would need to waste resources in verifying their rights, which is inefficient.... [W]ithout copyright exhaustion some markets will include a mix of copyrighted goods that can and cannot be resold, and that in such a case, if the buyers cannot easily distinguish between the various goods, those markets might significantly shrink.*

D. Right to Prepare Derivative Works

Before 1870, American copyright law principally prohibited exact copies of protected works. During this time, for example, a federal court held that a German translation of Harriet Beecher Stowe's *Uncle Tom's Cabin* did not infringe Stowe's copyright in her book, as it was not a copy of her work. Stowe v. Thomas, 23 Fed. Cas. 201 (C.C.E.D. Pa. 1853).

Some courts began to move away from this narrow understanding of copying, but the largest step toward providing copyright holders exclusive rights in derivative works began with the 1870 Copyright Act, which set out that "authors may reserve the right to dramatize or to translate their own works." Act of July 8, 1870, 16 Stat. 212 c. 230 § 86, 35 Cong., 2d Sess. The 1909 Act provided copyright owners with yet more derivative rights, such as to abridgment. Act of March 4, 1909, § 1(b), 60th Cong., 2d Sess. The 1976 Act expanded and generalized these rights, providing in § 106(2) the exclusive right "to prepare derivative works based upon the copyrighted work." Recall § 101's definition of "derivative works" from Chapter II's discussion of the copyrightability of derivative works:

> *A "derivative work" is a work based upon one or more preexisting works, such as a translation, musical arrangement, dramatization, fictionalization, motion picture version, sound recording, art reproduction, abridgment, condensation, or any other form in which a work may be recast, transformed, or adapted. A work consisting of editorial revisions, annotations, elaborations, or other modifications which, as a whole, represent an original work of authorship, is a "derivative work."*

Paul Goldstein has explained the rationale for the provision to copyright holders of the right to prepare derivative works (also sometimes referred to as an adaptation right):

> *The purpose of copyright is to attract private investment to the production of original expression....*
>
> *.... [S]ection 106(2)'s grant of the exclusive right "to prepare derivative works based upon the copyrighted work" enables prospective copyright owners to proportion their investment in a work's expression to the returns expected not only from the market in which the copyrighted*

work is first published, but from other, derivative markets as well. The copyright owners of Gone With the Wind can hope to monopolize not only the sale of the novel's hardcover and paperback editions, but also the use of the novel's expressive elements in translations, motion pictures and countless other derivative formats. Second, just as these owners had a copyright incentive to originate the expression for the novel, Gone With the Wind, section 103—which extends copyright protection to the original elements of derivative works—gives them and their licensees an incentive to add original expression to each derivative work in order to qualify it for copyright protection of its own.

Taken together, sections 102(a) and 103, and sections 106(1) and 106(2), give a prospective copyright owner the incentive to make an original, underlying work, the exclusive right to make new, successive works incorporating expressive elements from the underlying work, and the incentive and exclusive right to make still newer, successive works based on these. The continuum may stretch from an underlying novel or story to the work's adaptation into a motion picture, its transformation into a television series, and the eventual embodiment of its characters in dolls, games and other merchandise. The works at the outer reaches of this continuum, and some intermediate works as well, will frequently bear scant resemblance to the expression or the ideas of the seminal work and will often be connected only by a license authorizing use of a title or character name....

Derivative rights affect the level of investment in copyrighted works by enabling the copyright owner to proportion its investment to the level of expected returns from all markets, not just the market in which the work first appears, as is generally the case with reproduction rights. The publisher who knows that it can license, and obtain payment for, the translation, serialization, condensation and motion picture rights for a novel will invest more in purchasing, producing and marketing the novel than it would if its returns were limited to revenues from book sales in the English language.

Derivative rights also affect the direction of investment in copyrighted works. By spreading the duty to pay over different markets, section 106(2) tends to perfect the information available to the copyright owner respecting the value of its works to different groups of users. It also enables choices in light of that information. Knowing that the French and German language markets belong exclusively to it, a publisher of English language works may decide to invest in works that, once translated, will appeal to these audiences as well. The publisher can acquire a work because of its motion picture potential and can comfortably invest in the work's development and marketing to increase that potential. The publisher may choose either direction, both, or neither; and it can seek returns in other derivative markets, or only in the original market. The important point is that, by securing exclusive rights to all derivative markets, the statute enables the copyright proprietor to select those toward which it will direct investment.

Paul Goldstein, *Derivative Rights and Derivative Works in Copyright*, 30 J. COPYRIGHT SOC'Y U.S.A. 209 (1983).

Why place this right to prepare all of these possible derivative works in the hands of the copyright holder of the underlying work? The rationale seems to be akin to Edmund Kitch's justification of the patent system under prospect theory. Edmund W. Kitch, *The Nature and Function of the Patent System*, 20 J.L. & ECON. 265 (1977). Consider its application to the author of a children's story. In the absence of copyright protection for derivative works, once the story is published and deemed successful, others will quickly race to capitalize on its value. Various authors might publish sequels to the story, while other companies compete to get a movie version into theaters the quickest. Still others may make toys and clothing using the story's characters. All of this investment in design, development, and marketing is potentially wasteful. The world may not need any movie versions of the story, never mind three of them. Moreover, a rational movie studio, knowing the kind of competition it will likely face from others, may simply abandon the project altogether. According to Kitch, by giving a single entity ownership over the whole field of derivative works, copyright law prevents both the wastefulness and the lack of incentives. Coordinated investment in ideas is better than rivalrous investment.

There are numerous concerns with this rationale. For one thing, initial creators are not necessarily going to be the ones with the best ideas for or executions of derivative works. Moreover, there might be inefficient transaction costs for third parties to secure permission to create derivative works. Initial creators might also behave strategically and refuse to allow the creation of certain derivative works, even if they would make society better off. For these reasons, some propose doing away with (or diminishing) copyright law's right to prepare derivative works (and following patent law's rule allowing any improver of a patented invention, including a party other than the patentee, to get a patent in that improvement). *See, e.g.,* Mark A. Lemley, *The Economics of Improvement in Intellectual Property Law*, 75 TEX. L. REV. 989 (1997). For experimental work on sequential creativity in intellectual property, see Stefan Bechtold, Christopher Buccafusco & Christopher Jon Sprigman, *Innovation Heuristics: Experiments on Sequential Creativity in Intellectual Property*, 91 IND. L.J. 1251 (2016).

Either way, given that the reproduction right has expanded well beyond exact copying to cover substantially similar works also, it can be somewhat difficult to understand the need for a separate right to prepare derivative works, or, indeed, whether there is a difference between the reproduction and derivative-work rights at all. The legislative history of the Copyright Act of 1976 sets out the following difference:

> The exclusive right to prepare derivative works, specified separately in clause (2) of section 106, overlaps the exclusive right of reproduction to some extent. It is broader than that right, however, in the sense that reproduction requires fixation in copies or phonorecords, whereas the preparation of a derivative work, such as a ballet, pantomime, or improvised performance, may be an infringement even though nothing is ever fixed in tangible form.

H.R. REP. NO. 1476, 94th Cong., 2d Sess. 47, at 62 (1976). As you read through the cases in this section that set out the contours of the right to prepare derivative works, consider whether this difference is enshrined in the law and whether it is the only difference between the two rights.

In that vein, as you read the following case, consider the court's attempt to distinguish the reproduction right from the right to prepare derivative works. Is its understanding of § 106(2) convincing? How well is it reflected in the statutory language of §§ 106(2) and 101? How are J.K. Rowling's intentions to develop or not develop the derivative market relevant here?

Warner Bros. Entertainment Inc. v. RDR Books
575 F. Supp. 2d 513 (S.D.N.Y. 2008)

PATTERSON, J.: ...

[1] Plaintiff J.K. Rowling is the author of the highly acclaimed *Harry Potter* book series. Written for children but enjoyed by children and adults alike, the *Harry Potter* series chronicles the lives and adventures of Harry Potter and his friends as they come of age at the Hogwarts School of Witchcraft and Wizardry and face the

Chapter V – Exclusive Rights

evil Lord Voldemort. It is a tale of a fictional world filled with magical spells, fantastical creatures, and imaginary places and things....

[2] As a result of the success of the *Harry Potter* books, Plaintiff Warner Bros. Entertainment Inc. obtained from Rowling the exclusive film rights to the entire seven-book *Harry Potter* series. Warner Brothers is the exclusive distributor for worldwide distribution of these films....

[3] In addition, Rowling wrote two short companion books to the *Harry Potter* series, the royalties from which she donated to the charity Comic Relief. The first, *Quidditch Through the Ages* (2001), recounts the history and development of "quidditch," an imaginary sport featured in the *Harry Potter* series that involves teams of witches and wizards on flying broomsticks. The second, *Fantastic Beasts & Where to Find Them* (2001), is an A-to-Z encyclopedia of the imaginary beasts and beings that exist in *Harry Potter'*s fictional world. Both appear in the *Harry Potter* series as textbooks that the students at Hogwarts use in their studies, and the companion books are marketed as such. Neither of the companion books is written in narrative form; instead each book chronicles and expands on the fictional facts that unfold in the *Harry Potter* series....

[4] Rowling has stated on a number of occasions since 1998 that, in addition to the two companion books, she plans to publish a "*Harry Potter* encyclopedia" after the completion of the series and again donate the proceeds to charity. Rowling intends that her encyclopedia contain alphabetical entries for the various people, places and things from the *Harry Potter* novels. While she intends to add new material as well, her encyclopedia is expected to reflect all of the information in the *Harry Potter* series.

[5] Rowling already has begun preparations for work on the encyclopedia by assembling her materials and requesting from her U.K. publisher its "bible" of *Harry Potter* materials. The publisher's "bible" is a catalogue of the people, places, and things from the *Harry Potter* books. (Rowling's U.S. publisher has compiled a similar catalogue of elements from the *Harry Potter* books which Rowling has requested and intends to draw on in creating her encyclopedia. Rowling plans on using an A-to-Z format for her encyclopedia....

[6] Defendant RDR Books is a Michigan-based publishing company that seeks to publish a book entitled "The Lexicon," the subject of this lawsuit. Steven Vander Ark, a former library media specialist at a middle school in Michigan, is the attributed author of the Lexicon. He is also the originator, owner, and operator of "The Harry Potter Lexicon" website, a popular *Harry Potter* fan site from which the content of the Lexicon is drawn....

[7] Vander Ark began work on his website, "The Harry Potter Lexicon," in 1999 and opened the website in 2000. His purpose in establishing the website was to create an encyclopedia that collected and organized information from the *Harry Potter* books in one central source for fans to use for reference. At its launch, the website featured Vander Ark's descriptive lists of spells, characters, creatures, and magical items from *Harry Potter* with hyperlinks to cross-referenced entries. In response to feedback from users of the website, Vander Ark developed an A-to-Z index to each list to allow users to search for entries alphabetically.

[8] The website presently features several indexed lists of people, places, and things from *Harry Potter*, including the "Encyclopedia of Spells," "Encyclopedia of Potions," "Wizards, Witches, and Beings," "The Bestiary," and "Gazetteer of the Wizarding World." In addition to these reference features, the website contains a variety of supplemental material pertaining to *Harry Potter*, including fan art, commentary, essays, timelines, forums, and interactive data. The website is currently run by a staff of seven or eight volunteers, including four primary editors.... The website uses minimal advertising to offset the costs of operation. Use of the website is free and unrestricted.

[9] The content of the encyclopedia entries on the Lexicon website is drawn primarily from the *Harry Potter* series, the companion books, ... and published interviews of Rowling....

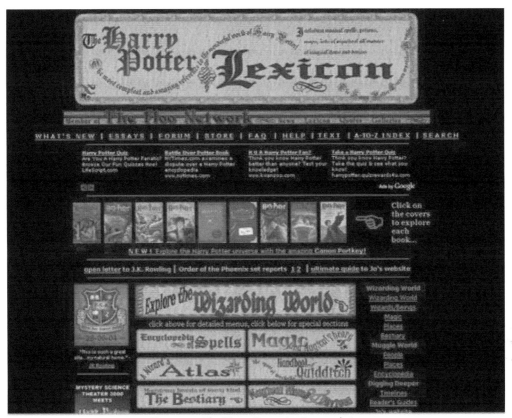

Figure 70: *The Harry Potter Lexicon* website

[10] Vander Ark has received positive feedback, including from Rowling and her publishers, about the value of the Lexicon website as a reference source. In May 2004, Vander Ark read a remark by Rowling posted on her website praising his Lexicon website as follows: "This is such a great site that I have been known to sneak into an internet cafe while out writing and check a fact rather than go into a bookshop and buy a copy of Harry Potter (which is embarrassing). A website for the dangerously obsessive; my natural home." In July 2005, Vander Ark received a note from Cheryl Klein, a Senior Editor at Scholastic Inc., American publisher of the *Harry Potter* series, thanking him and his staff "for the wonderful resource [his] site provides for fans, students, and indeed editors & copyeditors of the Harry Potter series," who "referred to the Lexicon countless times during the editing of [the sixth book in the series], whether to verify a fact, check a timeline, or get a chapter & book reference for a particular event." In September 2006, Vander Ark was invited by Warner Brothers to the set of the film *The Order of the Phoenix*, where he met David Heyman, the producer of all the *Harry Potter* films. Heyman told Vander Ark that Warner Brothers used the Lexicon website almost every day....

[11] Prior to any discussions with RDR Books about publishing portions of the Lexicon website as a book, Vander Ark was aware of Rowling's public statements regarding her intention to write a *Harry Potter* encyclopedia upon completion of the seventh book in the series. In June 2007, just before the release of the seventh book, Vander Ark emailed Christopher Little Literary Agency, Rowling's literary agent in the United Kingdom, and suggested that he would be "a good candidate for work as an editor, given [his] work on the Lexicon," should Rowling start working on an encyclopedia or other reference to the *Harry Potter* series. The literary agency advised him that Rowling intended to work alone and did not require a collaborator....

[12] Roger Rapoport is the president of Defendant RDR Books.... Recognizing a publishing opportunity, Rapoport contacted Vander Ark ... about the possibility of publishing a *Harry Potter* encyclopedia based on some of the materials from the Lexicon website....

Chapter V – Exclusive Rights

[13] At his first meeting with Rapoport in August 2007, Vander Ark raised his concerns regarding the permissibility of publishing the Lexicon in view of Rowling's plan to publish an encyclopedia and her copyrights in the *Harry Potter* books. Prior to August 2007, Vander Ark had developed and circulated the opinion that publishing "any book that is a guide to [the *Harry Potter*] world" would be a violation of Rowling's intellectual property rights. Vander Ark had even stated on a public internet newsgroup that he would not publish the Lexicon "in any form except online" without permission because Rowling, not he, was "entitled to that market." Vander Ark changed his mind about publishing the Lexicon after Rapoport reassured him that he had looked into the legal issue and determined that publication of content from the Lexicon website in book form was legal. Rapoport agreed to stand by this opinion by adding an atypical clause to the publishing contract providing that RDR would defend and indemnify Vander Ark in the event of any lawsuits....

[14] The Lexicon is an A-to-Z guide to the creatures, characters, objects, events, and places that exist in the world of *Harry Potter*.... [T]he Lexicon manuscript is more than 400 type-written pages long and contains 2,437 entries organized alphabetically. The first few pages contain a list of abbreviations used throughout the Lexicon to cite to the original sources of the material.

[15] The Lexicon manuscript was created using the encyclopedia entries from the Lexicon website. Because of space limitations for the printed work, which seeks to be complete but also easy to use, about half of the material from the website was not included in the Lexicon manuscript. The Lexicon itself makes clear that the only source of its content is the work of J.K. Rowling. The first page of the Lexicon manuscript states: "All the information in the Harry Potter Lexicon comes from J.K. Rowling, either in the novels, the 'schoolbooks,' from her interviews, or from material which she developed or wrote herself." ....

[16] The Lexicon entries cull every item and character that appears in the *Harry Potter* works, no matter if it plays a significant or insignificant role in the story. The entries cover every spell (e.g., Expecto Patronum, Expelliarmus, and Incendio), potion (e.g., Love Potion, Felix Felicis, and Draught of Living Death), magical item or device (e.g., Deathly Hallows, Horcrux, Cloak of Invisibility), form of magic (e.g., Legilimency, Occlumency, and the Dark Arts), creature (e.g., Blast-Ended Skrewt, Dementors, and Blood-Sucking Bugbears), character (e.g., Harry Potter, Hagrid, and Lord Voldemort), group or force (e.g., Aurors, Dumbledore's Army, Death Eaters), invented game (e.g., Quidditch), and imaginary place (e.g., Hogwarts School of Witchcraft and Wizardry, Diagon Alley, and the Ministry of Magic) that appear in the *Harry Potter* works....

[17] Each entry, with the exception of the shortest ones, gathers and synthesizes pieces of information relating to its subject that appear scattered across the *Harry Potter* novels, the companion books, ... and published interviews of Rowling. The types of information contained in the entries include descriptions of the subject's attributes, role in the story, relationship to other characters or things, and events involving the subject. Repositories of such information, the entries seek to give as complete a picture as possible of each item or character in the *Harry Potter* world, many of which appear only sporadically throughout the series or in various sources of *Harry Potter* material.

[18] The snippets of information in the entries are generally followed by citations in parentheses that indicate where they were found within the corpus of the *Harry Potter* works. The thoroughness of the Lexicon's citation, however, is not consistent; some entries contain very few citations in relation to the amount material provided. When the Lexicon cites to one of the seven *Harry Potter* novels, the citation provides only the book and chapter number. Vander Ark explained that page numbers were excluded from the citations because the various editions of the *Harry Potter* books have different pagination, but the chapter numbers remain consistent....

[19] While not its primary purpose, the Lexicon includes commentary and background information from outside knowledge on occasion. For example, the Lexicon contains sporadic etymological references, (*e.g.*, entries for "Colloportus," "Lupin, Remus," "Alohamora," "Fidelius Charm"), analogies to characters outside the *Harry Potter* world such as Merlin, and observations of Rowling's allusions to other works of literature such as "the weird sisters" from Shakespeare's Macbeth. The Lexicon also points to the very few "flints," or errors in the continuity of the story, that appear in the *Harry Potter* series.

[20] ... [T]he Lexicon fits in the narrow genre of non-fiction reference guides to fictional works.... [T]he *Harry Potter* series is a multi-volume work of fantasy literature, similar to the works of J.R.R. Tolkien and C.S. Lewis. Such works lend themselves to companion guides or reference works because they reveal an elaborate imaginary world over thousands of pages, involving many characters, creatures, and magical objects that appear and reappear across thousands of pages....

[21] At trial, Rowling testified that the Lexicon took "all the highlights of [her] work, in other words [her] characters' secret history, the jokes certainly, certain exciting narrative twists, all the things that are the highlights of [her] stories." She compared this taking of her work to plundering all of the "plums in [her] cake." At trial, the testimony of Rowling and the expert opinion of [the plaintiffs' expert Jeri] Johnson focused at length on the Lexicon's verbatim copying of language from the *Harry Potter* works. Johnson testified that in particular, entries that deal with invented terms, creatures, places and things from the *Harry Potter* books use "again and again the specific, very colorful, idiosyncratic ... nouns and phrases of Ms. Rowling."

[22] Although it is difficult to quantify how much of the language in the Lexicon is directly lifted from the *Harry Potter* novels and companion books, the Lexicon indeed contains at least a troubling amount of direct quotation or close paraphrasing of Rowling's original language. The Lexicon occasionally uses quotation marks to indicate Rowling's language, but more often the original language is copied without quotation marks, often making it difficult to know which words are Rowling's and which are Vander Ark's.

[23] For example, in the entry for "armor, goblin made," the Lexicon uses Rowling's poetic language nearly verbatim without quotation marks. The original language from *Harry Potter and the Deathly Hallows* reads:

> *"Muggle-borns," he said. "Goblin-made armour does not require cleaning, simple girl. Goblins' silver repels mundane dirt, imbibing only that which strengthens it."*

[24] The Lexicon entry for "armor, goblin made" reads in its entirety:

> *Some armor in the wizarding world is made by goblins, and it is quite valuable. (e.g., HBP20) According to Phineas Nigellus, goblin-made armor does not require cleaning, because goblins' silver repels mundane dirt, imbibing only that which strengthens it, such as basilisk venom. In this context, "armor" also includes blades such as swords.*

[25] Although the Lexicon entry introduces Rowling's language with the phrase, "According to Phineas Nigellus," it does not use quotation marks....

[26] An example of particularly extensive direct quotation is found in the Lexicon entry for "Trelawney, Sibyll Patricia," the professor of Divination at the Hogwarts School who tells two important prophecies in the story. The Lexicon not only reproduces her prophecies word-for-word in their entirety, but in doing so, reveals dramatic plot twists and how they are resolved in the series. For example, the first prophecy reads:

> *"The one with the power to vanquish the Dark Lord approaches.... Born to those who have thrice defied him, born as the seventh month dies ... and the Dark Lord will mark him as his equal, but he will have power the Dark Lord knows not ... and either must die at the hand of the*

other for neither can live while the other survives.... The one with the power to vanquish the Dark Lord will be born as the seventh month dies...."

[27] The Lexicon entry reproduces this prophecy exactly but in italics and indented. The Lexicon entry continues by discussing what happens as a result of this prophecy: "Severus Snape was eavesdropping on this conversation and he reported the first part of the Prophecy to the Dark Lord. Voldemort immediately began searching for this threat, and centered his attention on the child of Lily and James Potter. (OP 37)." The entry then quotes the second prophecy, but without a citation to where it appears in the *Harry Potter* series....

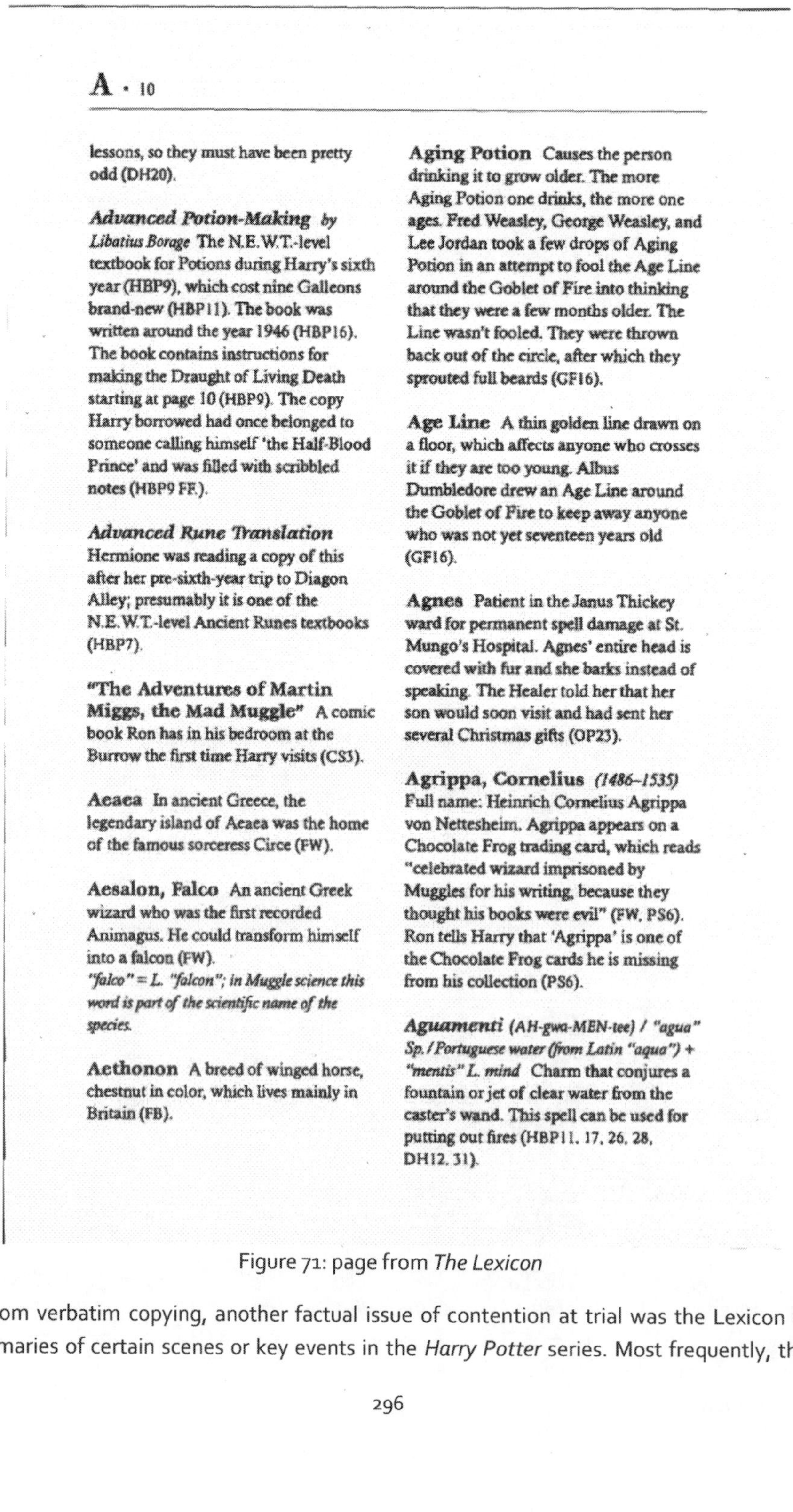

A · 10

lessons, so they must have been pretty odd (DH20).

Advanced Potion-Making *by Libatius Borage* The N.E.W.T.-level textbook for Potions during Harry's sixth year (HBP9), which cost nine Galleons brand-new (HBP11). The book was written around the year 1946 (HBP16). The book contains instructions for making the Draught of Living Death starting at page 10 (HBP9). The copy Harry borrowed had once belonged to someone calling himself 'the Half-Blood Prince' and was filled with scribbled notes (HBP9 FF.).

Advanced Rune Translation Hermione was reading a copy of this after her pre-sixth-year trip to Diagon Alley; presumably it is one of the N.E.W.T.-level Ancient Runes textbooks (HBP7).

"The Adventures of Martin Miggs, the Mad Muggle" A comic book Ron has in his bedroom at the Burrow the first time Harry visits (CS3).

Aeaea In ancient Greece, the legendary island of Aeaea was the home of the famous sorceress Circe (FW).

Aesalon, Falco An ancient Greek wizard who was the first recorded Animagus. He could transform himself into a falcon (FW).
"falco" = L. "falcon"; in Muggle science this word is part of the scientific name of the species.

Aethonon A breed of winged horse, chestnut in color, which lives mainly in Britain (FB).

Aging Potion Causes the person drinking it to grow older. The more Aging Potion one drinks, the more one ages. Fred Weasley, George Weasley, and Lee Jordan took a few drops of Aging Potion in an attempt to fool the Age Line around the Goblet of Fire into thinking that they were a few months older. The Line wasn't fooled. They were thrown back out of the circle, after which they sprouted full beards (GF16).

Age Line A thin golden line drawn on a floor, which affects anyone who crosses it if they are too young. Albus Dumbledore drew an Age Line around the Goblet of Fire to keep away anyone who was not yet seventeen years old (GF16).

Agnes Patient in the Janus Thickey ward for permanent spell damage at St. Mungo's Hospital. Agnes' entire head is covered with fur and she barks instead of speaking. The Healer told her that her son would soon visit and had sent her several Christmas gifts (OP23).

Agrippa, Cornelius *(1486–1535)* Full name: Heinrich Cornelius Agrippa von Nettesheim. Agrippa appears on a Chocolate Frog trading card, which reads "celebrated wizard imprisoned by Muggles for his writing, because they thought his books were evil" (FW, PS6). Ron tells Harry that 'Agrippa' is one of the Chocolate Frog cards he is missing from his collection (PS6).

Aguamenti *(AH-gwa-MEN-tee) / "agua" Sp. / Portuguese water (from Latin "aqua") + "mentis" L. mind* Charm that conjures a fountain or jet of clear water from the caster's wand. This spell can be used for putting out fires (HBP11, 17, 26, 28, DH12, 31).

Figure 71: page from *The Lexicon*

[28] Aside from verbatim copying, another factual issue of contention at trial was the Lexicon entries that contain summaries of certain scenes or key events in the *Harry Potter* series. Most frequently, these are the

longer entries that describe important objects, such as the "Deathly Hallows," or momentous events, such as the "Triwizard Tournament," or that trace the development of an important character, such as Harry Potter, Lord Voldemort, Severus Snape, and Albus Dumbledore. Plaintiffs' expert testified at length that in her opinion these entries constitute "plot summaries," while Defendant's expert characterized them as character studies or analysis.

[29] Neither of these characterizations is exactly apt. Without endorsing one characterization or another, such entries in the Lexicon do encapsulate elements of the very elaborate and wide ranging plot (sometimes in chronological order, sometimes not) confined to the subject of the entry. In the entries for significant characters, these plot elements are occasionally used to support an observation about the character's nature or development.... But other times, the presentation of plot details, in effect, summarizes a vignette or portion of a scene....

[30] .... While acknowledging actual copying, Defendant disputes that the copying amounts to an improper or unlawful appropriation of Rowling's works. Defendant argues that Plaintiffs fail to establish a prima facie case of infringement because they have not shown that the Lexicon is substantially similar to the *Harry Potter* works.

[31] The appropriate inquiry under the substantial similarity test is whether the copying is quantitatively and qualitatively sufficient to support the legal conclusion that infringement (actionable copying) has occurred.[13] The quantitative component addresses the amount of the copyrighted work that is copied, while the qualitative component addresses the copying of protected expression, as opposed to unprotected ideas or facts....

[32] Plaintiffs have shown that the Lexicon copies a sufficient quantity of the *Harry Potter* series[14] to support a finding of substantial similarity between the Lexicon and Rowling's novels. The Lexicon draws 450 manuscript pages worth of material primarily from the 4,100-page *Harry Potter* series. Most of the Lexicon's 2,437 entries contain direct quotations or paraphrases, plot details, or summaries of scenes from one or more of the *Harry Potter* novels.... Although hundreds of pages or thousands of fictional facts may amount to only a fraction of the seven-book series, this quantum of copying is sufficient to support a finding of substantial similarity where the copied expression is entirely the product of the original author's imagination and creation....

[33] As to the qualitative component of the substantial similarity analysis, Plaintiffs have shown that the Lexicon draws its content from creative, original expression in the *Harry Potter* series and companion books. Each of the 2,437 entries in the Lexicon contains "fictional facts" created by Rowling, such as the attributes of imaginary creatures and objects, the traits and undertakings of major and minor characters, and the events surrounding them. The entry for "Boggart," for example, contains the fictional facts that a boggart is "[a] shape shifter that prefers to live in dark, confined spaces, taking the form of the thing most feared by the person it encounters; nobody knows what a boggart looks like in its natural state," and that "Lupin taught his third year Defence Against the Dark Arts class to fight [a boggart] with the Riddikulus spell (PA7), and used a boggart as a substitute for a Dementor in tutoring Harry (PA12)." ... [S]uch invented facts constitute creative

---

[13] The post-trial briefs of the parties both suggest that [the] quantitative/qualitative approach is the applicable test for substantial similarity in this case, and the Court agrees. Since the original and secondary works are of different genres, the question of substantial similarity is difficult to examine using the other tests applied in this Circuit.

[14] The Court analyzes the amount of expression copied from the *Harry Potter* series in the aggregate, rather than from each individual novel in the series .... Cautioning against the aggregate approach ..., the Nimmer treatise warns that the "broader the series, the more all-encompassing plaintiff's copyright becomes, thereby squelching new expression in direct defiance to copyright's mandate of stimulating the production of new works." In this case, however, because the *Harry Potter* novels tell one coherent narrative in a series, rather than tell discrete tales, the danger identified by *Nimmer* is less likely to exist.

expression protected by copyright because characters and events spring from the imagination of the original authors....

[34] Defendant also argues that while a substantial similarity may be found where invented facts are reported and arranged in such a way as to tell essentially the same story as the original, the order in which the fictional facts are presented in the Lexicon bears almost no resemblance to the order in which the fictional facts are arranged to create the story of Harry Potter and the universe he inhabits. Reproducing original expression in fragments or in a different order, however, does not preclude a finding of substantial similarity. Regardless of how the original expression is copied, the standard for determining copyright infringement is not whether the original could be recreated from the allegedly infringing copy, but whether the latter is substantially similar to the former. Here, the Lexicon's rearrangement of Rowling's fictional facts does not alter the protected expression such that the Lexicon ceases to be substantially similar to the original works.

[35] Furthermore, ... the concept of similarity embraces not only global similarities in structure and sequence, but localized similarity in language.... [T]he Lexicon contains a considerable number of direct quotations (often without quotation marks) and close paraphrases of vivid passages in the *Harry Potter* works. Although in these instances, the Lexicon often changes a few words from the original or rewrites original dialogue in the third person, the language is nonetheless substantially similar.

[36] Notwithstanding the dissimilarity in the overall structure of the Lexicon and the original works, some of the Lexicon entries contain summaries of certain scenes or key events in the *Harry Potter* series .... These passages, in effect, retell small portions of the novels, though without the same dramatic effect.... Together these portions of the Lexicon support a finding of substantial similarity....

[37] Plaintiffs allege that the Lexicon not only violates their right of reproduction, but also their right to control the production of derivative works. The Copyright Act defines a "derivative work" as "a work based upon one or more preexisting works, such as a translation, musical arrangement, dramatization, fictionalization, motion picture version, sound recording, art reproduction, abridgment, condensation, or any other form in which a work may be *recast, transformed, or adapted*." 17 U.S.C. § 101 (emphasis added). A work "consisting of editorial revisions, annotations, elaborations, or other modifications which, as a whole, represents an original work of authorship" is also a derivative work. *Id.*

[38] A work is not derivative, however, simply because it is "based upon" the preexisting works.... The statutory language seeks to protect works that are "recast, transformed, or adapted" into another medium, mode, language, or revised version, while still representing the "original work of authorship." ...

[39] .... Given that the Lexicon's use of plot elements is far from an elaborate recounting and does not follow the same plot structure as the *Harry Potter* novels, Plaintiffs' suggestion that these portions of the Lexicon are "unauthorized abridgements" is unpersuasive. Second, and more importantly, although the Lexicon contains a substantial amount of material from the *Harry Potter* works, the material is not merely transformed from one medium to another .... By condensing, synthesizing, and reorganizing the preexisting material in an A-to-Z reference guide, the Lexicon does not recast the material in another medium to retell the story of *Harry Potter*, but instead gives the copyrighted material another purpose. That purpose is to give the reader a ready understanding of individual elements in the elaborate world of *Harry Potter* that appear in voluminous and diverse sources. As a result, the Lexicon no longer "represents [the] original work[s] of authorship." 17 U.S.C. § 101. Under these circumstances, and because the Lexicon does not fall under any example of derivative works listed in the statute, Plaintiffs have failed to show that the Lexicon is a derivative work....

NOTES

1. *Warner Bros.* is one of the few cases that addresses the differences between the reproduction right and the right to prepare derivative works. This paucity of analysis is frustrating for students but is likely because most litigants and courts do not care about the differences so long as they can establish infringement of at least one of these rights. One of the few other decisions addressing the relationship between these two rights is a Second Circuit decision predating *Warner Bros. See* Castle Rock Entm't, Inc. v. Carol Publ'g Grp., Inc., 150 F.3d 132 (2d Cir. 1998). In that case, the court noted in a footnote as an aside that a defendant's work that changes the plaintiff's work so much that it is no longer "substantially similar" violates neither the reproduction right nor the right to prepare derivative works. *See id.* at 143 n.9 ("[I]f the secondary work sufficiently transforms the expression of the original work such that the two works cease to be substantially similar, then the secondary work is not a derivative work and, for that matter, does not infringe the copyright of the original work."). Do you find that view more or less convincing than that taken in *Warner Bros.?*

2. The Second Circuit has made clear that the right to prepare derivative works belongs to the initial creator even when the creator opts not to enter a derivative market. As it reasoned in the context of an infringement lawsuit by the producer of the *Seinfeld* television series against the publisher of *The Seinfeld Aptitude Test*, a book of *Seinfeld* trivia:

> [The Seinfeld Aptitude Test] *substitutes for a derivative market that a television program copyright owner such as Castle Rock would in general develop or license others to develop. Because [the book] borrows exclusively from* Seinfeld *and not from any other television or entertainment programs, [the book] is likely to fill a market niche that Castle Rock[, Seinfeld's producers,] would in general develop.... Although Castle Rock has evidenced little if any interest in exploiting this market for derivative works based on* Seinfeld, *such as by creating and publishing* Seinfeld *trivia books (or at least trivia books that endeavor to satisfy the between-episode cravings of* Seinfeld *lovers), the copyright law must respect that creative and economic choice. It would not serve the ends of the Copyright Act—i.e., to advance the arts—if artists were denied their monopoly over derivative versions of their creative works merely because they made the artistic decision not to saturate those markets with variations of their original.*

Castle Rock Entm't, Inc., 150 F.3d at 145-46. Does the Second Circuit's reasoning accord with copyright policy? Or would it be preferable to allow for either some exceptions or an opposite rule?

3. Is one entitled to copyright protection in the non-infringing portions of a derivative work the creation of which infringes the § 106(2) right of the creator of the underlying work? Recall § 103(a), which provides that "[t]he subject matter of copyright ... includes compilations and derivative works, but protection for a work employing preexisting material in which copyright subsists does not extend to any part of the work in which such material has been used unlawfully."

Consider the following case: In 1992, the musician Prince became the assignee of a copyright in the symbol he had begun using to identify himself, as shown in Figure 72. In 1993, Ferdinand Pickett made a guitar in the shape of this symbol—as shown in Figure 72—which he conceded to be a derivative work of Prince's symbol. Pickett claimed to have shown the guitar to Prince. Shortly thereafter, Prince appeared in public playing a similar guitar, shown in Figure 73.

Figure 72: Prince symbol (left) and Pickett guitar based on the symbol (right)

Pickett sued Prince for copyright infringement. As the Seventh Circuit reviewing the case put it:

> *Pickett claims the right to copyright a work derivative from another person's copyright without that person's permission and then to sue that person for infringement by the person's own derivative work. Pickett's guitar was a derivative work of the copyrighted Prince symbol, and so was Prince's guitar. Since Prince had (or so we must assume) access to Pickett's guitar, and since the two guitars, being derivatives of the same underlying work, are, naturally, very similar in appearance, Pickett has—if he is correct that one can copyright a derivative work when the original work is copyrighted by someone else who hasn't authorized the maker of the derivative work to copyright it—a prima facie case of infringement. Pickett must, he concedes, show that his derivative work has enough originality to entitle him to a copyright, and also that the copyright is limited to the features that the derivative work adds to the original. But he insists that with these limitations his copyright is valid.*

Figure 73: Prince's subsequent guitar (left), as played by him (right)

Pickett v. Prince, 207 F.3d 402, 404-05 (7th Cir. 2000). The Seventh Circuit ruled that, regardless whether Pickett's guitar possessed the requisite originality, he could not claim copyright in his guitar:

> *The Copyright Act grants the owner of a copyright the exclusive right to prepare derivative works based upon the copyrighted work. So Pickett could not make a derivative work based on the Prince symbol without Prince's authorization even if Pickett's guitar had a smidgeon of originality....*

Pickett relies for his ... theory primarily on section 103(a) of the Copyright Act, which provides that while copyright can be obtained in derivative works, "protection for a work employing preexisting material in which copyright subsists does not extend to any part of the work in which such material has been used unlawfully." Pickett reads this as authorizing a person other than the owner of the original work to make a derivative work, merely forbidding him to infringe the original. It is very difficult to see how a derivative work not made by the owner of the original work could fail to infringe it, given the definition of derivative works.... Picket doesn't deny this; ... he is unafraid to acknowledge that he is an infringer and to content himself with arguing that his copyright extends only to the original elements of the infringing work. But we do not read section 103(a) as qualifying the exclusive right of the owner of the copyright of the original work to make derivative works based on that work, the right conferred by section 106(2). Section 103(a) means only, at least so far as bears on this case, that the right to make a derivative work does not authorize the maker to incorporate into it material that infringes someone else's copyright.... But the only copyright that Pickett claims Prince infringed is a copyright that Pickett had no right to obtain, namely a copyright on a derivative work based on Prince's copyrighted symbol.

For a similar result involving a copyright infringement lawsuit against Sylvester Stallone by someone who independently decided to write a treatment for a *Rocky IV* movie based on Sylvester Stallone's description of his idea for that sequel to the media after the *Rocky I, II,* and *III* movies had been made, see Anderson v. Stallone, 11 U.S.P.Q.2d 1161 (C.D. Cal. 1989).

Are these results consistent with the statutory language in § 103(a)? Consider the legislative history set out for that provision:

The second part of the sentence that makes up section 103(a) deals with the status of a compilation or derivative work unlawfully employing preexisting copyrighted material. In providing that protection does not extend to "any part of the work in which such material has been used unlawfully," the bill prevents an infringer from benefiting, through copyright protection, from committing an unlawful act, but preserves protection for those parts of the work that do not employ the preexisting work. Thus, an unauthorized translation of a novel could not be copyrighted at all, but the owner of copyright in an anthology of poetry could sue someone who infringed the whole anthology, even though the infringer proves that publication of one of the poems was unauthorized.

H.R. REP. NO. 1476, 94th Cong., 2d Sess. 47, at 57-58 (1976).

4. For an argument that the right to prepare derivative works should be understood to apply to uses that "transform" preexisting content versus simply "reproducing" that content, see Daniel J. Gervais, *The Derivative Right: Or Why Copyright Law Protects Foxes Better Than Hedgehogs*, 15 VANDERBILT J. ENTER. & TECH. L. 785 (2013).

There are various ways in which a second comer's efforts may recast or transform an initial work. As you read this case and the following one, consider which of these are sufficient to count as creating a derivative work. Can you reconcile the reasoning in the two following cases?

Mirage Editions, Inc. v. Albuquerque A.R.T. Co.
856 F.2d 1341 (9th Cir. 1988)

BRUNETTI, J.: ...

[1] Patrick Nagel was an artist whose works appeared in many media including lithographs, posters, serigraphs, and as graphic art in many magazines, most notably *Playboy*. Nagel died in 1984. His widow Jennifer Dumas owns the copyrights to the Nagel art works which Nagel owned at the time of his death. Mirage is the exclusive publisher of Nagel's works and also owns the copyrights to many of those works. Dumas and Mirage own all of the copyrights to Nagel's works. No one else holds a copyright in any Nagel work. Appellee Alfred Van Der Marck Editions, Inc. is the licensee of Dumas and Mirage and the publisher of the commemorative book entitled *NAGEL: The Art of Patrick Nagel*, which is a compilation of selected copyrighted individual art works and personal commentaries.

Figure 74: cover of Patrick Nagel art book (left) and Nagel print (right)

[2] Since 1984, the primary business of [Albuquerque A.R.T. Co.] has consisted of: 1) purchasing artwork prints or books including good quality artwork page prints therein; 2) gluing each individual print or page print onto a rectangular sheet of black plastic material exposing a narrow black margin around the print; 3) gluing the black sheet with print onto a major surface of a rectangular white ceramic tile; 4) applying a transparent plastic film over the print, black sheet and ceramic tile surface; and 5) offering the tile with artwork mounted thereon for sale in the retail market.

[3] It is undisputed, in this action, that appellant did the above process with the Nagel book. The appellant removed selected pages from the book, mounted them individually onto ceramic tiles and sold the tiles at retail.

[4] Mirage, Dumas and Van Der Marck brought an action alleging infringement of registered copyrights in the artwork of Nagel and in the book....

[5] The district court concluded appellant infringed the copyrights in the individual images through its tile-preparing process and also concluded that the resulting products comprised derivative works.

Figure 75: Albuquerque A.R.T. Co. Nagel print on tile

[6] Appellant contends that there has been no copyright infringement because … its tiles are not derivative works ….

[7] The Copyright Act of 1976, 17 U.S.C. § 101 defines a derivative work as:

> [A] work based upon one or more preexisting works such as a translation, musical arrangement, dramatization, fictionalization, motion picture version, sound recording, art reproduction, abridgment, condensation *or any other form in which a work may be recast, transformed, or adapted*. A work consisting of editorial revisions, annotations, elaborations, or other modifications which, as a whole, represent an original work of authorship is a "derivative work." (emphasis added)

[8] The protection of derivative rights extends beyond mere protection against unauthorized copying to include the right to make other versions of, perform, or exhibit the work.

[9] Melvi[lle] Nimmer in his treatise on copyright law wrote:

> *[A] work will be considered a derivative work only if it would be considered an infringing work if the material which it has derived from a preexisting work had been taken without the consent of a copyright proprietor of such preexisting work.*

1 NIMMER ON COPYRIGHT § 3.01 (1986).

[10] What appellant has clearly done here is to make another version of Nagel's art works, and that amounts to preparation of a derivative work. By borrowing and mounting the preexisting, copyrighted individual art images without the consent of the copyright proprietors … appellant has prepared a derivative work and infringed the subject copyrights.

[11] Appellant's contention that since it has not engaged in "art reproduction" and therefore its tiles are not derivative works is not fully dispositive of this issue. Appellant has ignored the disjunctive phrase "or any other form in which a work may be recast, transformed or adapted." The legislative history of the Copyright Act of 1976 indicates that Congress intended that for a violation of the right to prepare derivative works to occur "the infringing work must incorporate a portion of the copyrighted work in *some form*." 1976 U.S. Code Cong. & Admin. News 5659, 5675. (emphasis added). The language "recast, transformed or adapted" seems to encompass other alternatives besides simple art reproduction. By removing the individual images from the book and placing them on the tiles, perhaps the appellant has not accomplished reproduction. We conclude,

though, that appellant has certainly recast or transformed the individual images by incorporating them into its tile-preparing process....

[12] We recognize that, under the "first sale" doctrine ..., appellant can purchase a copy of the Nagel book and subsequently alienate its ownership in that book. However, the right to transfer applies only to the particular copy of the book which appellant has purchased and nothing else. The mere sale of the book to the appellant without a specific transfer by the copyright holder of its exclusive right to prepare derivative works, does not transfer that right to appellant. The derivative works right, remains unimpaired and with the copyright proprietors .... As we have previously concluded that appellant's tile-preparing process results in derivative works and as the exclusive right to prepare derivative works belongs to the copyright holder, the "first sale" doctrine does not bar the appellees' copyright infringement claims.

Annie Lee v. A.R.T. Company
125 F.3d 580 (7th Cir. 1997)

EASTERBROOK, J.:

[1] Annie Lee creates works of art .... A.R.T. Company [bought some of Lee's notecards and small lithographs,] mounted the works on ceramic tiles (covering the art with transparent epoxy resin in the process)[,] and resold the tiles. Lee contends that these tiles are derivative works, which under 17 U.S.C. § 106(2) may not be prepared without the permission of the copyright proprietor....

[2] Now one might suppose that this is an open and shut case under the doctrine of first sale .... A.R.T. bought the work legitimately, mounted it on a tile, and resold what it had purchased. Because the artist could capture the value of her art's contribution to the finished product as part of the price for the original transaction, the economic rationale for protecting an adaptation as "derivative" is absent. An alteration that includes (or consumes) a complete copy of the original lacks economic significance. One work changes hands multiple times, exactly what § 109(a) permits, so it may lack legal significance too. But § 106(2) creates a separate exclusive right, to "prepare derivative works", and Lee believes that affixing the art to the tile is "preparation," so that A.R.T. would have violated § 106(2) even if it had dumped the finished tiles into the Marianas Trench. For the sake of argument we assume that this is so and ask whether card-on-a-tile is a "derivative work" in the first place.

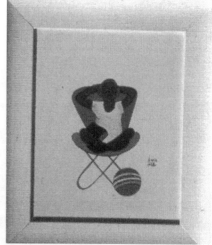

Figure 76: Annie Lee postcards on tile

[3] .... The district court concluded that A.R.T.'s mounting of Lee's works on tile is not an "original work of authorship" because it is no different in form or function from displaying a painting in a frame or placing a medallion in a velvet case. No one believes that a museum violates § 106(2) every time it changes the frame of a painting that is still under copyright, although the choice of frame or glazing affects the impression the art conveys, and many artists specify frames (or pedestals for sculptures) in detail.... [W]e agree. If changing the way in which a work of art will be displayed creates a derivative work, and if Lee is right about what "prepared" means, then the derivative work is "prepared" when the art is mounted .... If the framing process does not create a derivative work, then mounting art on a tile, which serves as a flush frame, does not create a derivative work....

[4] Lee wages a vigorous attack on the district court's conclusion that A.R.T.'s mounting process cannot create a derivative work because the change to the work "as a whole" is not sufficiently original to support a copyright. Cases such as *Gracen v. The Bradford Exchange, Inc.*, 698 F.2d 300 (7th Cir. 1983), show that neither A.R.T. nor Lee herself could have obtained a copyright in the card-on-a-tile, thereby not only extending the period of protection for the images but also eliminating competition in one medium of display.... A.R.T. tried to obtain a copyright in one of its products; the Register of Copyrights sensibly informed A.R.T. that the card-on-a-tile could not be copyrighted independently of the note card itself. But Lee says that this is irrelevant—that a change in a work's appearance may infringe the exclusive right under § 106(2) even if the alteration is too trivial to support an independent copyright. Pointing to the word "original" in the second sentence of the statutory definition, the district judge held that "originality" is essential to a derivative work. This understanding has the support of both cases and respected commentators. *E.g.*, L. Batlin & Son, Inc. v. Snyder, 536 F.2d 486 (2d Cir. 1976); MELVILLE B. NIMMER & DAVID NIMMER, 1 NIMMER ON COPYRIGHTS § 3.03 (1997). Pointing to the fact that the first sentence in the statutory definition omits any reference to originality, Lee insists that a work may be derivative despite the mechanical nature of the transformation. This view, too, has the support of both cases and respected commentators. *E.g.*, Lone Ranger Television, Inc. v. Program Radio Corp., 740 F.2d 718, 722 (9th Cir. 1984); PAUL GOLDSTEIN, COPYRIGHT: PRINCIPLES, LAW AND PRACTICE § 5.3.1 (2d ed. 1996) (suggesting that a transformation is covered by § 106(2) whenever it creates a "new work for a different market").

[5] Fortunately, it is not necessary for us to choose sides. Assume for the moment that the first sentence recognizes a set of non-original derivative works. To prevail, then, Lee must show that A.R.T. altered her works in one of the ways mentioned in the first sentence. The tile is not an "art reproduction"; A.R.T. purchased and mounted Lee's original works. That leaves the residual clause: "any other form in which a work may be recast, transformed, or adapted." None of these words fits what A.R.T. did. Lee's works were not "recast" or "adapted". "Transformed" comes closer .... Yet the copyrighted note cards and lithographs were not "transformed" in the slightest. The art was bonded to a slab of ceramic, but it was not changed in the process. It still depicts exactly what it depicted when it left Lee's studio. If mounting works a "transformation," then changing a painting's frame or a photograph's mat equally produces a derivative work. Indeed, if Lee is right about the meaning of the definition's first sentence, then *any* alteration of a work, however slight, requires the author's permission. We asked at oral argument what would happen if a purchaser jotted a note on one of the note cards, or used it as a coaster for a drink, or cut it in half, or if a collector applied his seal (as is common in Japan); Lee's counsel replied that such changes prepare derivative works, but that as a practical matter artists would not file suit. A definition of derivative work that makes criminals out of art collectors and tourists is jarring despite Lee's gracious offer not to commence civil litigation.

[6] If Lee (and the [N]inth [C]ircuit) are right about what counts as a derivative work, then the United States has established through the back door an extraordinarily broad version of authors' moral rights, under which artists may block any modification of their works of which they disapprove. No European version of *droit moral* goes this far....

NOTE

1. Can you use traditional principles of statutory interpretation to construe the bounds of the right to prepare derivative works, or at least to determine what sort of work qualifies as a "derivative work"? Reconsider § 101's statutory definition. Are derivative works defined broadly? Are there any limiting principles that you can detect? Pamela Samuelson looks to the nine exemplary derivative works listed in § 101's definition. She contends that "[b]y including these nine examples, Congress intended to provide guidance about the types of derivatives covered by this right. To be consistent with the text of the statute, the legislative history, and the constitutional purpose of copyright, derivative work liability should only be imposed under the last [broader] clause of the definition if the plaintiff's claim is analogous to one or more of the exemplary derivatives in the statutory definition." Pamela Samuelson, *The Quest for a Sound Conception of Copyright's Derivative Work Right*, 101 GEO. L.J. 1505, 1511 (2013). With that view in mind, Samuelson proposes that the nine exemplary derivative works can be clustered into three categories: shorter versions of an initial work (abridgements and condensations), faithful renditions of initial works (translations and art reproductions), and a transformation of expression from one medium or genre to another (fictionalizations, dramatizations, motion-picture versions, sound recordings, and musical arrangements). Do you think this is the preferred reading of § 101's definition?

As you read the following case, reconsider whether § 106(2) requires fixation for a work to be a derivative work. How does this decision comport with the legislative history you read earlier this section on that point?

Lewis Galoob Toys, Inc. v. Nintendo of America, Inc.
964 F.2d 965 (9th Cir. 1992)

FARRIS, J.: ...

[1] The Nintendo Entertainment System is a home video game system marketed by Nintendo. To use the system, the player inserts a cartridge containing a video game that Nintendo produces or licenses others to produce. By pressing buttons and manipulating a control pad, the player controls one of the game's characters and progresses through the game. The games are protected as audiovisual works ....

[2] The Game Genie is a device manufactured by Galoob that allows the player to alter up to three features of a Nintendo game. For example, the Game Genie can increase the number of lives of the player's character, increase the speed at which the character moves, and allow the character to float above obstacles. The player controls the changes made by the Game Genie by entering codes provided by the Game Genie Programming Manual and Code Book. The player also can experiment with variations of these codes.

[3] The Game Genie functions by blocking the value for a single data byte sent by the game cartridge to the central processing unit in the Nintendo Entertainment System and replacing it with a new value. If that value controls the character's strength, for example, then the character can be made invincible by increasing the value sufficiently. The Game Genie is inserted between a game cartridge and the Nintendo Entertainment System. The Game Genie does not alter the data that is stored in the game cartridge. Its effects are temporary....

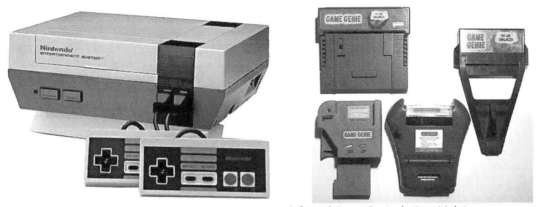
Figure 77: Nintendo Entertainment System (left) and Game Genie devices (right)

Figure 78: Game Genie advertisement

Chapter V – Exclusive Rights

[4] The Copyright Act of 1976 confers upon copyright holders the exclusive right to prepare and authorize others to prepare derivative works based on their copyrighted works. Nintendo argues that the district court erred in concluding that the audiovisual displays created by the Game Genie are not derivative works....

[5] A derivative work must incorporate a protected work in some concrete or permanent "form." The Copyright Act defines a derivative work as follows:

> A "derivative work" is a work based upon one or more preexisting works, such as a translation, musical arrangement, dramatization, fictionalization, motion picture version, sound recording, art reproduction, abridgment, condensation, *or any other form in which a work may be recast, transformed, or adapted*. A work consisting of editorial revisions, annotations, elaborations, or other modifications which, as a whole, represent an original work of authorship, is a "derivative work."

17 U.S.C. § 101 (emphasis added). The examples of derivative works provided by the Act all physically incorporate the underlying work or works. The Act's legislative history similarly indicates that "the infringing work must incorporate a portion of the copyrighted work in some form." 1976 U.S. Code Cong. & Admin. News 5659, 5675.

[6] Our analysis is not controlled by the Copyright Act's definition of "fixed." The Act defines copies as "material objects, other than phonorecords, in which a work is *fixed* by any method." 17 U.S.C. § 101 (emphasis added). The Act's definition of "derivative work," in contrast, lacks any such reference to fixation....

[7] The district court's finding that no independent work is created is supported by the record. The Game Genie merely enhances the audiovisual displays (or underlying data bytes) that originate in Nintendo game cartridges. The altered displays do not incorporate a portion of a copyrighted work in some concrete or permanent *form.* Nintendo argues that the Game Genie's displays are as fixed in the hardware and software used to create them as Nintendo's original displays. Nintendo's argument ignores the fact that the Game Genie cannot produce an audiovisual display; the underlying display must be produced by a Nintendo Entertainment System and game cartridge.... It cannot be a derivative work.

[8] *Mirage Editions* is illustrative. Albuquerque A.R.T. transferred artworks from a commemorative book to individual ceramic tiles. We held that by borrowing and mounting the preexisting, copyrighted individual art images without the consent of the copyright proprietors Albuquerque A.R.T. has prepared a derivative work and infringed the subject copyrights. The ceramic tiles *physically* incorporated the copyrighted works in a form that could be sold. Perhaps more importantly, sales of the tiles supplanted purchasers' demand for the underlying works. Our holding in *Mirage Editions* would have been much different if Albuquerque A.R.T. had distributed lenses that merely enabled users to view several artworks simultaneously.

[9] Nintendo asserted at oral argument that the existence of a $150 million market for the Game Genie indicates that its audiovisual display must be fixed. We understand Nintendo's argument; consumers clearly would not purchase the Game Genie if its display was not "sufficiently permanent or stable to permit it to be perceived ... for a period of more than transitory duration." 17 U.S.C. § 101. But, Nintendo's reliance on the Act's definition of "fixed" is misplaced. Nintendo's argument also proves too much; the existence of a market does not, and cannot, determine conclusively whether a work is an infringing derivative work. For example, although there is a market for kaleidoscopes, it does not necessarily follow that kaleidoscopes create unlawful derivative works when pointed at protected artwork. The same can be said of countless other products that enhance, but do not replace, copyrighted works.

[10] Nintendo also argues that our analysis should focus exclusively on the audiovisual displays created by the Game Genie, *i.e.*, that we should compare the altered displays to Nintendo's original displays. Nintendo

emphasizes that "'[a]udiovisual works' are works that consist of a series of related images ... *regardless of the nature of the material objects ... in which the works are embodied*." 17 U.S.C. § 101 (emphasis added). The Copyright Act's definition of "audiovisual works" is inapposite; the *only* question before us is whether the audiovisual displays created by the Game Genie are "derivative works." The Act does not similarly provide that a work can be a derivative work regardless of the nature of the material objects in which the work is embodied. A derivative work must incorporate a protected work in some concrete or permanent form. We cannot ignore the actual source of the Game Genie's display....

[11] In holding that the audiovisual displays created by the Game Genie are not derivative works, we recognize that technology often advances by improvement rather than replacement. Some time ago, for example, computer companies began marketing spell-checkers that operate within existing word processors by signalling the writer when a word is misspelled. These applications, as well as countless others, could not be produced and marketed if courts were to conclude that the word processor and spell-checker combination is a derivative work based on the word processor alone. The Game Genie is useless by itself, it can only enhance, and cannot duplicate or recast[], a Nintendo game's output. It does not contain or produce a Nintendo game's output in some concrete or permanent form, nor does it supplant demand for Nintendo game cartridges. Such innovations rarely will constitute infringing derivative works under the Copyright Act.

E. Fictional Characters and the Rights of Reproduction and to Prepare Derivative Works

You have read cases involving alleged infringement of expression from movies, plays, music, illustrations, photographs, art works, video games, and even quilts and stuffed animals. The protected expression alleged to be infringed in these cases is all very different. But all of these cases involve material that uncontroversially contains "expression." The cases you're about to read are different. Here the "expression" alleged to be protected by copyright is not text or images or sounds, but is rather a "character." But what precisely is a "character"? A character may be captured in an image or illustration or sculpture—and these are certainly within the categories of copyrightable subject matter set out in 17 U.S.C. § 102(a). Likewise, the attributes of a character may be described in text, and such description is also copyrightable. But what about the character as such? That is, are characters copyrightable apart from their depiction in images or text? The cases considering this question have treated characters as copyrightable in themselves, though they have disagreed over what is required for a character to be copyrightable and not merely "stock." But on what basis have courts held characters as such to be copyrightable subject matter?

Whether characters are copyrightable as such (that is, aside from their textual description or visual depiction) is significant in terms of the scope of ownership that the creator of a character would enjoy. If characters are copyrightable as such, the copyright owner would have the power to prevent use of a copyrighted character in other works. If, on the other hand, characters are not copyrightable as such, the copyright owner would be able to prevent only the use of protectable textual descriptions or visual depictions of the character. But the character as such would be usable by others.

As you read the following cases, review the categories of copyrightable subject matter listed in § 102(a). Into which category, if any, do characters—in themselves and distinct from textual descriptions or visual illustrations of a character—fall?

Warner Bros. Pictures, Inc. v. Columbia Broadcasting System, Inc.
216 F.2d 945 (9th Cir. 1954)

STEPHENS, J:

[1] Dashiell Hammett composed a mystery-detective story entitled 'The Maltese Falcon' which was published serially, and each installment was copyrighted by the publisher. Subsequently, Alfred A. Knopf, Inc., entered into a contract with the author to publish the work in book form, Knopf published the book and, in accord with the terms of the contract, copyrighted it.

[2] In 1930, after publication in book form and after publication of all installments of the first serial thereof, Knopf and Hammett, designated as 'Owners', for a consideration of $8,500.00, granted certain defined rights in and to *The Maltese Falcon* (called 'writings' in the agreement) to Warner Bros., as 'Purchaser'.... Coincidentally, Knopf executed an instrument to Warner called 'Assignment of Copyright' for a nominal consideration. The text of the 'assignment' shows on its face that it is not an assignment of the copyright but that it is a grant to Warner of specified rights to the use of the writings in *The Maltese Falcon*. Both the contract between Hammett-Knopf and Warner, and the 'assignment' from Knopf, purport to grant to Warner certain defined and detailed exclusive rights to the use of *The Maltese Falcon* 'writings' in moving pictures, radio, and television....

Figure 79: movie poster for *The Maltese Falcon* (left), and Humphrey Bogart as Sam Spade (right)

[3] .... [A]t the effective moment of the grants by Hammett and Knopf to Warner, the latter became possessed of the sole and exclusive right to the writing which is within the copyright, less all limiting terms of the grants. The grants are limited to defined uses in motion picture, talking pictures, radio, and television.

[4] It is claimed by Warner that it acquired the exclusive right to the use of the writing, *The Maltese Falcon*, including the individual characters and their names, together with the title, 'The Maltese Falcon', in motion pictures, radio, and television. The use of the title is not in issue, since the grant to Warner specifically includes it.

[5] It is the position of Hammett and the other defendants, all of whom claim some interest under him, that the rights acquired by Warner are those specifically mentioned in the conveying or granting instruments, and that the exclusive right to the use of the characters and/or their names were not mentioned as being granted; that the instruments, properly construed, do not convey any exclusive right to the use of characters with or without names, hence Hammett could use them in other stories....

[6] Hammett did so use the characters with their names and did contract with others for such use. In 1946 he used *The Maltese Falcon* characters including Sam Spade, the detective and the leading character in the Falcon, by name, and granted to third parties the sole and exclusive right, except their use in the Falcon, to use that character by name (later orally enlarged to include other characters of the Falcon) in radio, television, and motion pictures. Under such claimed rights, radio broadcasts of 'Adventures of Sam Spade', including 'The Kandy Tooth' were broadcast in weekly half-hour episodes from 1946 to 1950.

[7] Warner claims infringement of copyright ... by such re-use and, as well, for infringement of parts of the story and the whole of the writing inclusive of characters and their names. Hammett and the other defendants deny infringement ... on any count, and Hammett requests the court to declare his rights in the premises. Knopf is a nominal party asking and claiming nothing, and is made a plaintiff under the right granted Warner in the Hammett-Knopf-Warner contract.

[8] The trial court denied relief to Warner, declared Hammett's rights, and assessed costs against Warner, who appeals.

[9] ... Warner Bros. Corporation ... is a large, experienced moving picture producer. It would seem proper, therefore, to construe the instruments under the assumption that the claimant knew what it wanted and that in defining the items in the instruments which it desired and intended to take, it included all of the items it was contracting to take. We are of the opinion that since the use of characters and character names are nowhere specifically mentioned in the agreements, but that other items, including the title, 'The Maltese Falcon', and their use are specifically mentioned as being granted, that the character rights with the names cannot be held to be within the grants, and that under the doctrine of ejusdem generis, general language cannot be held to include them....

[10] Up to this point we have discussed the points at issue by construing the contract and by seeking the intention of the parties to it, and we have concluded that the parties never intended by their contract to buy and sell the future use of the personalities in the writing.

[11] It will now be profitable to consider whether it was ever intended by the copyright statute that characters with their names should be under its protection.

[12] The practice of writers to compose sequels to stories is old, and the copyright statute, though amended several times, has never specifically mentioned the point. It does not appear that it has ever been adjudicated, although it is mentioned in *Nichols v. Universal Pictures Corp.*, 45 F.2d 119 (2d Cir. 1930).... If Congress had intended that the sale of the right to publish a copyrighted story would foreclose the author's use of its characters in subsequent works for the life of the copyright, it would seem Congress would have made specific provision therefor. Authors work for the love of their art no more than other professional people work in other lines of work for the love of it. There is the financial motive as well. The characters of an author's imagination and the art of his descriptive talent, like a painter's or like a person with his penmanship, are always limited

and always fall into limited patterns. The restriction argued for is unreasonable, and would effect the very opposite of the statute's purpose which is to encourage the production of the arts.

[13] It is our conception of the area covered by the copyright statute that when a study of the two writings is made and it is plain from the study that one of them is not in fact the creation of the putative author, but instead has been copied in substantial part exactly or in transparent re-phrasing to produce essentially the story of the other writing, it infringes.

[14] It is conceivable that the character really constitutes the story being told, but if the character is only the chessman in the game of telling the story he is not within the area of the protection afforded by the copyright....

[15] We conclude that even if the Owners assigned their complete rights in the copyright to the *Falcon*, such assignment did not prevent the author from using the characters used therein, in other stories. The characters were vehicles for the story told, and the vehicles did not go with the sale of the story....

NOTES

1. What does it mean for a character to "constitute[] the story being told," in which case the character is protectable, versus "only a chessman in the game of telling the story," in which case the character is not protectable? Is this test judicially administrable? Is it likely to produce results that are predictable in advance?

2. Is there an economic argument suggesting that characters should or should not be copyrightable? A moral argument? For a cultural and literary approach to the copyrightability of characters, see Zahr K. Said, *Fixing Copyright in Characters: Literary Perspectives on a Legal Problem*, 35 CARDOZO L. REV. 769 (2013).

In its opinion in *DC Comics v. Towle*, 802 F.3d 1012 (9th Cir. 2015), the Ninth Circuit introduced a new test for determining the copyrightability of characters. *Towle* dealt with the copyrightability of an odd sort of "character"—the Batmobile (Batman's car, as shown in Figures 80 and 81), which the defendant had produced as full-sized (and drivable) replicas, as shown in Figure 82. The Ninth Circuit found that the Batmobile was copyrightable as a character. Review the photographs below of the different versions of the Batmobile, and then read the next case, which articulates and applies the *Towle* test in a different context. Then come back to the pictures and ask whether you believe that the *Towle* court correctly applied its own test.

Figure 80: Batmobile as seen in the 1966 television series

Figure 81: Batmobile as seen in the 1989 movie

Figure 82: Mark Towle's replica Batmobiles

Daniels v. Walt Disney Company
958 F.3d 767 (9th Cir. 2020)

McKEOWN, J:

[1] Literary and graphic characters—from James Bond to the Batmobile—capture our creative imagination. These characters also may enjoy copyright protection, subject to certain limitations. Here we consider whether certain anthropomorphized characters representing human emotions qualify for copyright protection. They do not. For guidance, we turn to *DC Comics v. Towle*, our court's most recent explanation of the copyrightability of graphically-depicted characters.

[2] Denise Daniels developed a line of anthropomorphic characters called The Moodsters, which she pitched to entertainment and toy companies around the country, including The Walt Disney Company. Under *Towle*, "lightly sketched" characters such as The Moodsters, which lack "consistent, identifiable character traits and attributes," do not enjoy copyright protection. We affirm the district court's dismissal of Daniels's complaint.

[3] The Moodsters are five characters that are color-coded anthropomorphic emotions, each representing a different emotion: pink (love); yellow (happiness); blue (sadness); red (anger); and green (fear). Daniels initially named The Moodsters Oolvia, Zip, Sniff, Roary, and Shake, although these names changed in each iteration of the characters....

Figure 83: The Moodsters

[4] Daniels ... pitched The Moodsters to numerous media and entertainment companies. One recurring target was The Walt Disney Company and its affiliates, including Pixar. Daniels alleges that she or a member of her team had contact with several different Disney employees between 2005 and 2009....

[5] Disney began development of its movie *Inside Out* in 2010. The movie was released in 2015, and centers on five anthropomorphized emotions that live inside the mind of an 11-year-old girl named Riley. Those emotions are joy, fear, sadness, disgust, and anger. [Pete] Docter, who directed and co-wrote the screenplay, stated that his inspiration for the film was the manner with which his 11-year-old daughter dealt with new emotions as she matured....

Figure 84: *Inside Out* characters

[6] Daniels filed suit against Disney in 2017 for breach of an implied-in-fact contract, arising from Disney's failure to compensate Daniels for the allegedly disclosed material used to develop *Inside Out*. Daniels then

filed an amended complaint, ... alleging copyright infringement of both the individual Moodsters characters and the ensemble of characters as a whole.

[7] Disney filed a motion to dismiss, asserting that Daniels failed to meet the legal standard for copyright in a character .... The district court granted Disney's motion to dismiss, and granted Daniels leave to file an amended complaint on the copyright claims. Disney filed a motion to dismiss the Amended Complaint, which the district court granted on the ground that The Moodsters are not protectable by copyright....

[8] Although characters are not an enumerated copyrightable subject matter under the Copyright Act, *see* 17 U.S.C. § 102(a), there is a long history of extending copyright protection to graphically-depicted characters. However, not every comic book, television, or motion picture character is entitled to copyright protection. A character is entitled to copyright protection if (1) the character has physical as well as conceptual qualities, (2) the character is sufficiently delineated to be recognizable as the same character whenever it appears and displays consistent, identifiable character traits and attributes, and (3) the character is especially distinctive and contains some unique elements of expression. *Towle*....

[9] Disney does not dispute that the individual Moodster characters meet the first prong of the *Towle* test: each has physical as well as conceptual qualities. Because they have physical qualities, The Moodsters are not mere literary characters.

[10] The second prong presents an insurmountable hurdle for Daniels. *Towle* requires that a character must be sufficiently delineated to be recognizable as the same character whenever it appears. Although a character that has appeared in multiple productions or iterations need not have a consistent appearance, it must display consistent, identifiable character traits and attributes such that it is recognizable whenever it appears.

[11] Consistently recognizable characters like Godzilla or James Bond, whose physical characteristics may change over various iterations, but who maintain consistent and identifiable character traits and attributes across various productions and adaptations, meet the test. By contrast, a character that lacks a core set of consistent and identifiable character traits and attributes is not protectable, because that character is not immediately recognizable as the same character whenever it appears.

[12] In addressing The Moodsters, we first distinguish between the idea for a character and the depiction of that character. The notion of using a color to represent a mood or emotion is an idea that does not fall within the protection of copyright.... Color and emotion are ... frequent themes in children's books, such as Dr. Seuss's classic, *My Many Colored Days*, and Anna Llenas's *The Color Monster: A Story of Emotions*.

[13] Notably, colors themselves are not generally copyrightable. Nor is the "idea" of an emotion copyrightable. Taken together, these principles mean that Daniels cannot copyright the idea of colors or emotions, nor can she copyright the idea of using colors to represent emotions where these ideas are embodied in a character without sufficient delineation and distinctiveness.

[14] In analyzing whether The Moodster characters are sufficiently delineated, we carefully examine the graphic depiction of the characters and not the ideas underlying them. We look first to the physical appearance of The Moodsters. Unlike, for example, the Batmobile, which maintained distinct physical and conceptual qualities since its first appearance in the comic books, the physical appearance of The Moodsters changed significantly over time. In [earlier versions dating from 2005 and 2007], the five Moodsters have an insect-like appearance, with skinny bodies, long ears, and tall antennas that act as emotional barometers to form a distinctive shape and glow when an emotion is strongly felt. By the second generation of toys, The Moodsters look like small, loveable bears. They are round and cuddly, have small ears, and each dons a detective's hat and small cape.

Chapter V – Exclusive Rights

[15] Mindful that physical appearance alone is not decisive, we also consider whether The Moodsters have maintained consistent character traits and attributes. Across the various iterations The Moodsters have consistently represented five human emotions, and those emotions have not changed. But other than the idea of color and emotions, there are few other identifiable character traits and attributes that are consistent over the various iterations. In the 2005 [version], each character is described in a few short paragraphs. For example, the Zip character is described as having "an infectious laugh and wakes up each morning with a smile on his face and a friendly attitude." By the 2007 pilot, these characteristics are not mentioned and are not evident from the depiction of Zip. The other four Moodsters similarly lack consistent characteristics and attributes .... Lightly sketched characters of this kind, without identifiable character traits, are not copyrightable under the second prong of *Towle.*

[16] Perhaps the most readily identifiable attribute of The Moodsters is their relationship to emotions. The 2005 [version] explains that each character relates to emotions in its own way when something new happens—the "anger" Moodster might become angry, whereas the "sad" Moodster might become sad. The Moodsters behave in a similar fashion in the 2007 [version], where each character is especially prone to a particular emotion such as anger or sadness. But by 2015, the five Moodsters are "mood detectives," and help a young boy uncover how he feels about situations in his life.

[17] Finally, in every iteration the five Moodsters each have a completely different name. For example, the red/anger Moodster was originally named Roary in the 2005 [version], then Rizzi in the 2007 [version], and as of 2015 was named Razzy .... The other four characters have gone through similar name changes over the three iterations. While a change of name is not dispositive in our analysis, these changes across each iteration further illustrate that Daniels never settled on a well-delineated set of characters beyond their representation of five human emotions.

[18] The Batmobile in *Towle* again provides a useful contrast to this case. There, we recognized that from the time of the 1966 television series to the 1989 motion picture, the Batmobile had numerous identifiable and consistent character traits and attributes. It was always a "crime-fighting car" that allowed Batman to defeat his enemies. It consistently had jet-engines and far more power than an ordinary car, the most up-to-date weaponry, and the ability to navigate through landscapes impassible for an ordinary vehicle. Beyond the emotion it represents, each Moodster lacks comparable identifiable and consistent character traits and attributes across iterations, thus failing the second prong of the *Towle* test.

[19] Finally, even giving Daniels the benefit of the doubt on *Towle's* second prong, we conclude that The Moodsters fail the third prong—they are not especially distinctive and do not contain some unique elements of expression. Daniels identifies The Moodsters as unique in that they each represent a single emotion. But this facet is not sufficient to render them especially distinctive, particularly given their otherwise generic attributes and character traits. In contrast, the Batmobile in *Towle* had a unique and highly recognizable name, unlike each Moodster, which had three entirely different names. Developing a character as an anthropomorphized version of a specific emotion is not sufficient, in itself, to establish a copyrightable character. Taken together, The Moodsters are not especially distinctive, and do not meet the third prong of the *Towle* test....

[20] Since the 1950s, we have also extended copyright protection to characters—both literary and graphic— that constitute "the story being told" in a work. *Warner Bros. Pictures v. Columbia Broad. Sys.,* 216 F.2d 945, 950 (9th Cir. 1954). A character is not copyrightable under this test where "the character is only the chessman in the game of telling the story." This is a high bar, since few characters so dominate the story such that it becomes essentially a character study.

[21] *Warner Brothers* and *Towle* are two different tests for character copyrightability. Thus, we do not embrace the district court's view that *Towle* represents the exclusive test for copyrightability.

[22] The *Warner Brothers* test is therefore available, but it affords no protection to The Moodsters. Neither the [2005 nor 2007 versions] exhibits any prolonged engagement with character development or a character study of The Moodsters. Although the characters are introduced in the [2005 version], along with short descriptions, these pithy descriptions do not constitute the story being told. The [2007 version] contains even less character development—rather, each of The Moodsters serves primarily as a means by which particular emotions are introduced and explored. The Moodsters are mere chessmen in the game of telling the story.

[23] Daniels's final argument is that even if the individual Moodsters are not protectable under the *Towle* or "story being told" regimes, the ensemble of five characters *together* meets one or both of those tests. Daniels's ensemble claim does not change the distinctiveness or degree of delineation of the characters, and so The Moodsters as an ensemble are no more copyrightable than the individual characters.

[24] The district court did not err in dismissing Daniels's claims for copyright infringement....

NOTES

1. Is the three-part test articulated and applied in this case an improvement on the "story being told" test? Is the test specific to the medium in which a character appears?

2. What does it mean for a character to have "physical as well as conceptual qualities"? That criterion was easily satisfied here. But what about characters that are not illustrated? How are they given "physical" qualities? And why is it important that characters be "physical"?

F. Moral Rights

Section 106 of the Copyright Act sets out the exclusive rights of the copyright owner. There is, however, one other set of exclusive rights delineated in another section of the Copyright Act, § 106A. Section 106A provides to authors **rights of attribution and integrity** for a narrow range of works of "visual art." The rights set out in § 106A are often classified within the category of so-called **moral rights**. Moral rights originated in European law. Most countries provide at least some moral rights, which can include the right of attribution (also known as the right of paternity), the right to publish a work anonymously or pseudonymously, and the right to preserve a work's integrity (that is, the right to prevent revision, alteration, distortion, or destruction of a work). Moral rights are often distinguished from "economic rights," of which the exclusive rights contained in § 106 are examples. Article 6*bis* of the Berne Convention requires signatories to provide certain protections for moral rights:

> (1) *Independently of the author's economic rights, and even after the transfer of the said rights, the author shall have the right to claim authorship of the work and to object to any distortion, mutilation or other modification of, or other derogatory action in relation to, the said work, which would be prejudicial to his honor or reputation.*

Article 6*bis*(2) further provides that the two moral rights specified—attribution and integrity—should last at least as long as the author's economic rights. However, the provision allows member states to choose to limit moral rights protection to the author's lifetime.

In contrast to the Berne Convention, the TRIPS Agreement does not require signatories to provide protection for moral rights.

Whether the United States is in compliance with its obligation under the Berne Convention to provide moral rights protections is a matter of considerable debate. The Berne Convention Implementation Act of 1988, Pub. L. No. 100–568, 102 Stat. 2853, contains no provision establishing moral rights protections. Yet § 2(3) of this Act declares that the United States is in compliance: "The amendments made by this Act, together with the law as it exists on the date of the enactment of this Act, satisfy the obligations of the United States in adhering to the Berne Convention and no further rights or interests shall be recognized or created for that purpose." The legislative history of the Act grounds the statute's view that the United States is in compliance with its moral rights obligations on "existing U.S. law[, including] various provisions of the Copyright Act and the Lanham Act, various state statutes, and common law principles such as libel, defamation, misrepresentation, and unfair competition." S. REP. No. 352, 100th Cong., 2d Sess. 9-10 (1988). For analyses of possible gaps between existing U.S. laws and protection of these moral rights, see Roberta Rosenthall Kwall, *Copyright and the Moral Right: Is an American Marriage Possible?*, 38 VAND. L. REV. 1 (1985); John Henry Merryman, *The Refrigerator of Bernard Buffet*, 27 HASTINGS L.J. 1023 (1976).

> As you read the next case, consider whether it provides a basis for Congress's view that existing U.S. law is sufficient to put the United States in compliance with its obligation under the Berne Convention to provide protection for moral rights.

Terry Gilliam v. American Broadcasting Companies, Inc.
538 F.2d 14 (2d Cir. 1976)

LUMBARD, J.:

[1] Plaintiffs, a group of British writers and performers known as "Monty Python," appeal from a denial by Judge Lasker in the Southern District of a preliminary injunction to restrain the American Broadcasting Company (ABC) from broadcasting edited versions of three separate programs originally written and performed by Monty Python for broadcast by the British Broadcasting Corporation (BBC). We agree with Judge Lasker that the appellants have demonstrated that the excising done for ABC impairs the integrity of the original work. We further find that the countervailing injuries that Judge Lasker found might have accrued to ABC as a result of an injunction at a prior date no longer exist. We therefore direct the issuance of a preliminary injunction by the district court.

[2] Since its formation in 1969, the Monty Python group has gained popularity primarily through its thirty-minute television programs created for BBC as part of a comedy series entitled "Monty Python's Flying Circus." In accordance with an agreement between Monty Python and BBC, the group writes and delivers to BBC scripts for use in the television series. This scriptwriters' agreement recites in great detail the procedure to be followed when any alterations are to be made in the script prior to recording of the program. The essence of this section of the agreement is that, while BBC retains final authority to make changes, appellants or their representatives exercise optimum control over the scripts consistent with BBC's authority and only minor changes may be made without prior consultation with the writers. Nothing in the scriptwriters' agreement entitles BBC to alter a program once it has been recorded. The agreement further provides that, subject to the terms therein, the group retains all rights in the script.

[3] Under the agreement, BBC may license the transmission of recordings of the television programs in any overseas territory. The series has been broadcast in this country primarily on non-commercial public broadcasting television stations, although several of the programs have been broadcast on commercial stations in Texas and Nevada. In each instance, the thirty-minute programs have been broadcast as originally recorded and broadcast in England in their entirety and without commercial interruption.

[4] In October 1973, Time-Life Films acquired the right to distribute in the United States certain BBC television programs, including the Monty Python series. Time-Life was permitted to edit the programs only "for insertion of commercials, applicable censorship or governmental … rules and regulations, and National Association of Broadcasters and time segment requirements." No similar clause was included in the scriptwriters' agreement between appellants and BBC. Prior to this time, ABC had sought to acquire the right to broadcast excerpts from various Monty Python programs in the spring of 1975, but the group rejected the proposal for such a disjoined format. Thereafter, in July 1975, ABC agreed with Time-Life to broadcast two ninety-minute specials each comprising three thirty-minute Monty Python programs that had not previously been shown in this country.

[5] Correspondence between representatives of BBC and Monty Python reveals that these parties assumed that ABC would broadcast each of the Monty Python programs "in its entirety." On September 5, 1975, however, the group's British representative inquired of BBC how ABC planned to show the programs in their entirety if approximately 24 minutes of each 90 minute program were to be devoted to commercials. BBC replied on September 12, "we can only reassure you that ABC have decided to run the programmes 'back to back,' and that there is a firm undertaking not to segment them."

[6] ABC broadcast the first of the specials on October 3, 1975. Appellants did not see a tape of the program until late November and were allegedly "appalled" at the discontinuity and "mutilation" that had resulted from the editing done by Time-Life for ABC. Twenty-four minutes of the original 90 minutes of recording had been omitted. Some of the editing had been done in order to make time for commercials; other material had been edited, according to ABC, because the original programs contained offensive or obscene matter.

[7] In early December, Monty Python learned that ABC planned to broadcast the second special on December 26, 1975. The parties began negotiations concerning editing of that program and a delay of the broadcast until Monty Python could view it. These negotiations were futile, however, and on December 15 the group filed this action to enjoin the broadcast and for damages. Following an evidentiary hearing, Judge Lasker found that "the plaintiffs have established an impairment of the integrity of their work" which "caused the film or program … to lose its iconoclastic verve." According to Judge Lasker, "the damage that has been caused to the plaintiffs is irreparable by its nature." Nevertheless, the judge denied the motion for the preliminary injunction on the grounds that it was unclear who owned the copyright in the programs produced by BBC from the scripts written by Monty Python; that there was a question of whether Time-Life and BBC were indispensable parties to the litigation; that ABC would suffer significant financial loss if it were enjoined a week before the scheduled broadcast; and that Monty Python had displayed a "somewhat disturbing casualness" in their pursuance of the matter.

[8] Judge Lasker granted Monty Python's request for more limited relief by requiring ABC to broadcast a disclaimer during the December 26 special to the effect that the group dissociated itself from the program because of the editing. A panel of this court, however, granted a stay of that order until this appeal could be heard and permitted ABC to broadcast, at the beginning of the special, only the legend that the program had been edited by ABC. We heard argument on April 13 and, at that time, enjoined ABC from any further broadcast of edited Monty Python programs pending the decision of the court....

Chapter V – Exclusive Rights

[9] We ... reach the question whether there is a likelihood that appellants will succeed on the merits. In concluding that there is a likelihood of infringement here, we rely especially on the fact that the editing was substantial, i.e., approximately 27 per cent of the original program was omitted, and the editing contravened contractual provisions that limited the right to edit Monty Python material....

[10] Judge Lasker denied the preliminary injunction in part because he was unsure of the ownership of the copyright in the recorded program. Appellants first contend that the question of ownership is irrelevant because the recorded program was merely a derivative work taken from the script in which they hold the uncontested copyright. Thus, even if BBC owned the copyright in the recorded program, its use of that work would be limited by the license granted to BBC by Monty Python for use of the underlying script. We agree....

[11] If the proprietor of the derivative work is licensed by the proprietor of the copyright in the underlying work to vend or distribute the derivative work to third parties, those parties will, of course, suffer no liability for their use of the underlying work consistent with the license to the proprietor of the derivative work. Obviously, it was just this type of arrangement that was contemplated in this instance. The scriptwriters' agreement between Monty Python and BBC specifically permitted the latter to license the transmission of the recordings made by BBC to distributors such as Time-Life for broadcast in overseas territories.

[12] One who obtains permission to use a copyrighted script in the production of a derivative work, however, may not exceed the specific purpose for which permission was granted.... [Appellants] claim that revisions in the script, and ultimately in the program, could be made only after consultation with Monty Python, and that ABC's broadcast of a program edited after recording and without consultation with Monty Python exceeded the scope of any license that BBC was entitled to grant.

[13] .... Whether intended to allow greater economic exploitation of the work ... or to ensure that the copyright proprietor retains a veto power over revisions desired for the derivative work, the ability of the copyright holder to control his work remains paramount in our copyright law. We find, therefore, that unauthorized editing of the underlying work, if proven, would constitute an infringement of the copyright in that work similar to any other use of a work that exceeded the license granted by the proprietor of the copyright.

[14] If the broadcast of an edited version of the Monty Python program infringed the group's copyright in the script, ABC may obtain no solace from the fact that editing was permitted in the agreements between BBC and Time-Life or Time-Life and ABC. BBC was not entitled to make unilateral changes in the script and was not specifically empowered to alter the recordings once made; Monty Python, moreover, had reserved to itself any rights not granted to BBC. Since a grantor may not convey greater rights than it owns, BBC's permission to allow Time-Life, and hence ABC, to edit appears to have been a nullity....

[15] Aside from the question of who owns the relevant copyrights, ABC asserts that the contracts between appellants and BBC permit editing of the programs for commercial television in the United States. ABC argues that the scriptwriters' agreement allows appellants the right to participate in revisions of the script only prior to the recording of the programs, and thus infers that BBC had unrestricted authority to revise after that point. This argument, however, proves too much. A reading of the contract seems to indicate that Monty Python obtained control over editing the script only to ensure control over the program recorded from that script. Since the scriptwriters' agreement explicitly retains for the group all rights not granted by the contract, omission of any terms concerning alterations in the program after recording must be read as reserving to appellants exclusive authority for such revisions.

[16] Finally, ABC contends that appellants must have expected that deletions would be made in the recordings to conform them for use on commercial television in the United States. ABC argues that licensing

in the United States implicitly grants a license to insert commercials in a program and to remove offensive or obscene material prior to broadcast. According to the network, appellants should have anticipated that most of the excised material contained scatological references inappropriate for American television and that these scenes would be replaced with commercials, which presumably are more palatable to the American public.

[17] The proof adduced up to this point, however, provides no basis for finding any implied consent to edit. Prior to the ABC broadcasts, Monty Python programs had been broadcast on a regular basis by both commercial and public television stations in this country without interruption or deletion. Indeed, there is no evidence of any prior broadcast of edited Monty Python material in the United States. These facts, combined with the persistent requests for assurances by the group and its representatives that the programs would be shown intact belie the argument that the group knew or should have known that deletions and commercial interruptions were inevitable.

[18] Several of the deletions made for ABC, such as elimination of the words "hell" and "damn," seem inexplicable given today's standard television fare. If, however, ABC honestly determined that the programs were obscene in substantial part, it could have decided not to broadcast the specials at all, or it could have attempted to reconcile its differences with appellants. The network could not, however, free from a claim of infringement, broadcast in a substantially altered form a program incorporating the script over which the group had retained control.

[19] Our resolution of these technical arguments serves to reinforce our initial inclination that the copyright law should be used to recognize the important role of the artist in our society and the need to encourage production and dissemination of artistic works by providing adequate legal protection for one who submits his work to the public. We therefore conclude that there is a substantial likelihood that, after a full trial, appellants will succeed in proving infringement of their copyright by ABC's broadcast of edited versions of Monty Python programs. In reaching this conclusion, however, we need not accept appellants' assertion that any editing whatsoever would constitute infringement. Courts have recognized that licensees are entitled to some small degree of latitude in arranging the licensed work for presentation to the public in a manner consistent with the licensee's style or standards. That privilege, however, does not extend to the degree of editing that occurred here especially in light of contractual provisions that limited the right to edit Monty Python material....

[20] It also seems likely that appellants will succeed on the theory that, regardless of the right ABC had to broadcast an edited program, the cuts made constituted an actionable mutilation of Monty Python's work. This cause of action, which seeks redress for deformation of an artist's work, finds its roots in the continental concept of droit moral, or moral right, which may generally be summarized as including the right of the artist to have his work attributed to him in the form in which he created it.

[21] American copyright law, as presently written, does not recognize moral rights or provide a cause of action for their violation, since the law seeks to vindicate the economic, rather than the personal, rights of authors. Nevertheless, the economic incentive for artistic and intellectual creation that serves as the foundation for American copyright law cannot be reconciled with the inability of artists to obtain relief for mutilation or misrepresentation of their work to the public on which the artists are financially dependent. Thus courts have long granted relief for misrepresentation of an artist's work by relying on theories outside the statutory law of copyright, such as contract law, or the tort of unfair competition. Although such decisions are clothed in terms of proprietary right in one's creation, they also properly vindicate the author's personal right to prevent the presentation of his work to the public in a distorted form.

[22] Here, the appellants claim that the editing done for ABC mutilated the original work and that consequently the broadcast of those programs as the creation of Monty Python violated the Lanham Act

s 43(a), 15 U.S.C. s 1125(a).[10] This statute, the federal counterpart to state unfair competition laws, has been invoked to prevent misrepresentations that may injure plaintiff's business or personal reputation, even where no registered trademark is concerned. It is sufficient to violate the Act that a representation of a product, although technically true, creates a false impression of the product's origin.

[23] These cases cannot be distinguished from the situation in which a television network broadcasts a program properly designated as having been written and performed by a group, but which has been edited, without the writer's consent, into a form that departs substantially from the original work. To deform his work is to present him to the public as the creator of a work not his own, and thus makes him subject to criticism for work he has not done. In such a case, it is the writer or performer, rather than the network, who suffers the consequences of the mutilation, for the public will have only the final product by which to evaluate the work. Thus, an allegation that a defendant has presented to the public a garbled, distorted version of plaintiff's work seeks to redress the very rights sought to be protected by the Lanham Act, and should be recognized as stating a cause of action under that statute....

[24] During the hearing on the preliminary injunction, Judge Lasker viewed the edited version of the Monty Python program broadcast on December 26 and the original, unedited version. After hearing argument of this appeal, this panel also viewed and compared the two versions. We find that the truncated version at times omitted the climax of the skits to which appellants' rare brand of humor was leading and at other times deleted essential elements in the schematic development of a story line.[12] We therefore agree with Judge Lasker's conclusion that the edited version broadcast by ABC impaired the integrity of appellants' work and represented to the public as the product of appellants what was actually a mere caricature of their talents. We believe that a valid cause of action for such distortion exists and that therefore a preliminary injunction may issue to prevent repetition of the broadcast prior to final determination of the issues.[13] ...

For these reasons we direct that the district court issue the preliminary injunction sought by the appellants.

GURFEIN, J. (concurring): ...

[25] The Copyright Act provides no recognition of the so-called droit moral, or moral right of authors. Nor are such rights recognized in the field of copyright law in the United States. If a distortion or truncation in

---

[10] That statute provides in part: Any person who shall affix, apply, or annex, or use in connection with any goods or services, ... a false designation of origin, or any false description or representation ... and shall cause such goods or services to enter into commerce ... shall be liable to a civil action by any person ... who believes that he is or is likely to be damaged by the use of any such false description or representation.

[12] A single example will illustrate the extent of distortion engendered by the editing. In one skit, an upper class English family is engaged in a discussion of the tonal quality of certain words as "woody" or "tinny." The father soon begins to suggest certain words with sexual connotations as either "woody" or "tinny," whereupon the mother fetches a bucket of water and pours it over his head. The skit continues from this point. The ABC edit eliminates this middle sequence so that the father is comfortably dressed at one moment and, in the next moment, is shown in a soaked condition without any explanation for the change in his appearance.

[13] Judge Gurfein's concurring opinion suggests that since the gravamen of a complaint under the Lanham Act is that the origin of goods has been falsely described, a legend disclaiming Monty Python's approval of the edited version would preclude violation of that Act. We are doubtful that a few words could erase the indelible impression that is made by a television broadcast, especially since the viewer has no means of comparing the truncated version with the complete work in order to determine for himself the talents of plaintiffs. Furthermore, a disclaimer such as the one originally suggested by Judge Lasker in the exigencies of an impending broadcast last December would go unnoticed by viewers who tuned into the broadcast a few minutes after it began.

We therefore conclude that Judge Gurfein's proposal that the district court could find some form of disclaimer would be sufficient might not provide appropriate relief.

connection with a use constitutes an infringement of copyright, there is no need for an additional cause of action beyond copyright infringement. An obligation to mention the name of the author carries the implied duty, however, as a matter of contract, not to make such changes in the work as would render the credit line a false attribution of authorship.

[26] So far as the Lanham Act is concerned, it is not a substitute for droit moral which authors in Europe enjoy. If the licensee may, by contract, distort the recorded work, the Lanham Act does not come into play. If the licensee has no such right by contract, there will be a violation in breach of contract. The Lanham Act can hardly apply literally when the credit line correctly states the work to be that of the plaintiffs which, indeed it is, so far as it goes. The vice complained of is that the truncated version is not what the plaintiffs wrote. But the Lanham Act does not deal with artistic integrity. It only goes to misdescription of origin and the like.

[27] The misdescription of origin can be dealt with, as Judge Lasker did below, by devising an appropriate legend to indicate that the plaintiffs had not approved the editing of the ABC version. With such a legend, there is no conceivable violation of the Lanham Act. If plaintiffs complain that their artistic integrity is still compromised by the distorted version, their claim does not lie under the Lanham Act, which does not protect the copyrighted work itself but protects only against the misdescription or mislabelling.

[28] So long as it is made clear that the ABC version is not approved by the Monty Python group, there is no misdescription of origin. So far as the content of the broadcast itself is concerned, that is not within the proscription of the Lanham Act when there is no misdescription of the authorship....

NOTES

1. The court finds that ABC breached a condition of the license by editing Monty Python's work without approval, and that the breach constitutes a copyright violation. Is there any reason for the court at this point to speak of moral rights? Is there work left for the Lanham Act to do once the court has found that ABC infringed Monty Python's copyrights?

2. More broadly, do moral rights have a role that cannot be fulfilled by some existing body of law? With respect to attribution, copyright's exclusive rights give copyright owners leverage to negotiate to receive attribution in exchange for permission to use their work. Providing attribution via a moral right switches the default: Instead of the copyright owner having to negotiate for attribution, the copyright owner now has an attribution right ab initio. Which is a better arrangement? For an argument that U.S. copyright law may be more efficient, see Christopher Jon Sprigman, Christopher Buccafusco & Zachary Burns, *What's a Name Worth?: Experimental Tests of the Value of Attribution in Intellectual Property*, 93 B.U. L. REV. 1389 (2013).

3. Is a right of attribution a good idea in the first instance? For an argument that it can provide both pecuniary and expressive benefits—such as bolstering an author's reputation or providing a link between an author and their work—see Jeanne C. Fromer, *Expressive Incentives in Intellectual Property*, 98 VA. L. REV. 1745, 1790-98 (2012). *See also* Catherine L. Fisk, *Credit Where It's Due: The Law and Norms of Attribution*, 95 GEO. L.J. 49 (2006); Greg Lastowka, *Digital Attribution: Copyright and the Right to Credit*, 87 B.U. L. REV. 41 (2007). For an argument on the other side that an attribution right is impracticable, see Rebecca Tushnet, *Naming Rights: Attribution and Law*, 2007 UTAH L. REV. 789.

4. What about moral rights protections against "distortion, mutilation or other modification of, or other derogatory action in relation to" a work? As with the attribution right, the copyright owner can restrain distortion or mutilation via contract. That is, in fact, what happened in *Gilliam*. But what about where there isn't a contract? What if, for example, a painting is resold? The second owner is not in contractual privity with the copyright owner, and so the copyright owner cannot, via contract, restrain distortion, mutilation, or

destruction by the new owner. Is there existing law that gives the copyright owner rights in such an instance? *Gilliam* suggests that the Lanham Act may protect integrity rights in situations in which distortion or mutilation could create a false impression about the origin of the work (or the parts of the work that relate to the distortion or mutilation). But does the Lanham Act have anything to say about destruction?

5. Is a robust moral right of integrity consistent with the First Amendment? For an argument that it "threatens art because it fails to recognize the profound artistic importance of modifying, even destroying, works of art, and of freeing art from the control of the artist," see Amy M. Adler, *Against Moral Rights*, 97 CALIF. L. REV. 263 (2009). Picasso is said to have commented that "[t]he urge to destroy is also a creative urge," an aphorism that U.K.-based street-art phenomenon Banksy appears to have taken literally in a recent episode in which Banksy secretly built a shredder mechanism into the frame of a painting with the intent that the painting would be destroyed if it were ever auctioned, leading to the painting's destruction after a successful auction at Sotheby's in 2018. Scott Reyburn, *Banksy Painting Self-Destructs After Fetching $1.4 Million at Sotheby's*, N.Y. TIMES, Oct. 6, 2018, https://www.nytimes.com/2018/10/06/arts/design/uk-banksy-painting-sothebys.html. For a different take—one that it is protective of a more traditional conception of authorial dignity—see Roberta Rosenthal Kwall, *Inspiration and Innovation: The Intrinsic Dimension of the Artistic Soul*, 81 NOTRE DAME L. REV. 1945 (2006).

6. Look at 17 U.S.C. § 1202, enacted in 1998 as part of the Digital Millennium Copyright Act. As discussed further in Chapter IX, § 1202 contains provisions aimed at protecting the integrity of "copyright management information" that is distributed along with copies of a protected work. "Copyright management information" is a category defined to include information such as the title and other information identifying the work (including the information set forth on a notice of copyright); the terms and conditions for use of the work; and the name of, and other identifying information about, the author, the copyright owner, or (with the exception of public performances of works by radio and television broadcast stations) a performer whose performance is fixed in a work other than an audiovisual work, or a writer, performer, or director who is credited in the audiovisual work. This provision, which prohibits the provision of false copyright management information or the removal or alteration of copyright management information without permission by the copyright owner, has been used in a number of recent cases as a tool to obtain attribution. For example, in *Mango v. Buzzfeed, Inc.*, 356 F. Supp. 3d 368 (S.D.N.Y. 2019), the court held that Buzzfeed, an internet news publisher, violated § 1202 by distributing a photographer's photograph after removing the photographer's name that had originally appeared in a gutter credit, a line of text below the photographer's photograph but above the article text with which it had originally been published. The court reasoned that the gutter credit was "copyright management information."

As you read the next case, think about whether the holding in *Gilliam* about the viability of Lanham Act claims aimed at preserving the "integrity" of a work survives.

Dastar Corp. v. Twentieth Century Fox Corp.
539 U.S. 23 (2003)

SCALIA, J.:

[1] In this case, we are asked to decide whether § 43(a) of the Lanham Act, 15 U.S.C. § 1125(a), prevents the unaccredited copying of a work ....

[2] In 1948, three and a half years after the German surrender at Reims, General Dwight D. Eisenhower completed *Crusade in Europe*, his written account of the allied campaign in Europe during World War II. Doubleday published the book, registered it with the Copyright Office in 1948, and granted exclusive television rights to an affiliate of respondent Twentieth Century Fox Film Corporation. Fox, in turn, arranged for Time, Inc., to produce a television series, also called *Crusade in Europe*, based on the book, and Time assigned its copyright in the series to Fox.... In 1975, Doubleday renewed the copyright on the book as the "proprietor of copyright in a work made for hire." Fox, however, did not renew the copyright on the *Crusade* television series, which expired in 1977, leaving the television series in the public domain.

[3] In 1988, Fox reacquired the television rights in General Eisenhower's book, including the exclusive right to distribute the *Crusade* television series on video and to sublicense others to do so. Respondents SFM Entertainment and New Line Home Video, Inc., in turn, acquired from Fox the exclusive rights to distribute Crusade on video. SFM obtained the negatives of the original television series, restored them, and repackaged the series on videotape; New Line distributed the videotapes.

[4] Enter petitioner Dastar. In 1995, Dastar decided to expand its product line from music compact discs to videos. Anticipating renewed interest in World War II on the 50th anniversary of the war's end, Dastar released a video set entitled *World War II Campaigns in Europe*. To make *Campaigns*, Dastar purchased eight beta cam tapes of the *original* version of the *Crusade* television series, which is in the public domain, copied them, and then edited the series. Dastar's *Campaigns* series is slightly more than half as long as the original *Crusade* television series. Dastar substituted a new opening sequence, credit page, and final closing for those of the *Crusade* television series; inserted new chapter-title sequences and narrated chapter introductions; moved the "recap" in the *Crusade* television series to the beginning and retitled it as a "preview"; and removed references to and images of the book. Dastar created new packaging for its *Campaigns* series and (as already noted) a new title.

Figure 85: Twentieth Century Fox's *Crusade in Europe* DVD cover (left), and Dastar's *World War II Campaigns in Europe* VCR tapes (right)

[5] Dastar manufactured and sold the *Campaigns* video set as its own product. The advertising states: "Produced and Distributed by: *Entertainment Distributing*" (which is owned by Dastar), and makes no reference to the *Crusade* television series. Similarly, the screen credits state "DASTAR CORP presents" and "an ENTERTAINMENT DISTRIBUTING Production," and list as executive producer, producer, and associate producer employees of Dastar. The *Campaigns* videos themselves also make no reference to the *Crusade* television series, New Line's *Crusade* videotapes, or the book. Dastar sells its *Campaigns* videos to Sam's Club,

Costco, Best Buy, and other retailers and mail-order companies for $25 per set, substantially less than New Line's video set.

Figure 86: screenshot from Dastar's *World War II Campaigns in Europe*

[6] In 1998, respondents Fox, SFM, and New Line brought this action alleging that Dastar's sale of its *Campaigns* video set infringes Doubleday's copyright in General Eisenhower's book and, thus, their exclusive television rights in the book. Respondents later amended their complaint to add claims that Dastar's sale of *Campaigns* "without proper credit" to the *Crusade* television series constitutes "reverse passing off"[1] in violation of § 43(a) of the Lanham Act and in violation of state unfair-competition law. On cross-motions for summary judgment, the District Court found for respondents on all three counts, treating its resolution of the Lanham Act claim as controlling on the state-law unfair-competition claim because "the ultimate test under both is whether the public is likely to be deceived or confused." The court awarded Dastar's profits to respondents and doubled them pursuant to § 35 of the Lanham Act to deter future infringing conduct by petitioner.

[7] The Court of Appeals for the Ninth Circuit affirmed the judgment for respondents on the Lanham Act claim, but reversed as to the copyright claim and remanded. With respect to the Lanham Act claim, the Court of Appeals reasoned that "Dastar copied substantially the entire *Crusade in Europe* series created by Twentieth Century Fox, labeled the resulting product with a different name and marketed it without attribution to Fox[, and] therefore committed a 'bodily appropriation' of Fox's series." It concluded that "Dastar's 'bodily appropriation' of Fox's original [television] series is sufficient to establish the reverse passing off."[2] The court also affirmed the District Court's award under the Lanham Act of twice Dastar's profits. We granted certiorari....

---

[1] Passing off (or palming off, as it is sometimes called) occurs when a producer misrepresents his own goods or services as someone else's. "Reverse passing off," as its name implies, is the opposite: The producer misrepresents someone else's goods or services as his own.

[2] As for the copyright claim, the Ninth Circuit held that the tax treatment General Eisenhower sought for his manuscript of the book created a triable issue as to whether he intended the book to be a work for hire, and thus as to whether Doubleday properly renewed the copyright in 1976. The copyright issue is still the subject of litigation, but is not before us. We express no opinion as to whether petitioner's product would infringe a valid copyright in General Eisenhower's book.

[8] The Lanham Act was intended to make "actionable the deceptive and misleading use of marks," and "to protect persons engaged in ... commerce against unfair competition." While much of the Lanham Act addresses the registration, use, and infringement of trademarks and related marks, § 43(a) is one of the few provisions that goes beyond trademark protection. As originally enacted, § 43(a) created a federal remedy against a person who used in commerce either "a false designation of origin, or any false description or representation" in connection with "any goods or services." As the Second Circuit accurately observed with regard to the original enactment, however—and as remains true after the 1988 revision—§ 43(a) "does not have boundless application as a remedy for unfair trade practices," Alfred Dunhill, Ltd. v. Interstate Cigar Co., 499 F.2d 232, 237 (2d Cir. 1974). Because of its inherently limited wording, § 43(a) can never be a federal codification of the overall law of unfair competition, but can apply only to certain unfair trade practices prohibited by its text....

[9] ... [T]he gravamen of respondents' claim is that, in marketing and selling *Campaigns* as its own product without acknowledging its nearly wholesale reliance on the *Crusade* television series, Dastar has made a "false designation of origin, false or misleading description of fact, or false or misleading representation of fact, which ... is likely to cause confusion ... as to the origin ... of his or her goods." § 43(a). That claim would undoubtedly be sustained if Dastar had bought some of New Line's *Crusade* videotapes and merely repackaged them as its own. Dastar's alleged wrongdoing, however, is vastly different: It took a creative work in the public domain—the *Crusade* television series—copied it, made modifications (arguably minor), and produced its very own series of videotapes. If "origin" refers only to the manufacturer or producer of the physical "goods" that are made available to the public (in this case the videotapes), Dastar was the origin. If, however, "origin" includes the creator of the underlying work that Dastar copied, then someone else (perhaps Fox) was the origin of Dastar's product. At bottom, we must decide what § 43(a)(1)(A) of the Lanham Act means by the "origin" of "goods." ...

[10] The dictionary definition of "origin" is "[t]he fact or process of coming into being from a source," and "[t]hat from which anything primarily proceeds; source." WEBSTER'S NEW INTERNATIONAL DICTIONARY 1720–1721 (2d ed.1949). And the dictionary definition of "goods" (as relevant here) is "[w]ares; merchandise." *Id.* at 1079. We think the most natural understanding of the "origin" of "goods"—the source of wares—is the producer of the tangible product sold in the marketplace, in this case the physical *Campaigns* videotape sold by Dastar. The concept might be stretched ... to include not only the actual producer, but also the trademark owner who commissioned or assumed responsibility for ("stood behind") production of the physical product. But as used in the Lanham Act, the phrase "origin of goods" is in our view incapable of connoting the person or entity that originated the ideas or communications that "goods" embody or contain. Such an extension would not only stretch the text, but it would be out of accord with the history and purpose of the Lanham Act and inconsistent with precedent.

[11] Section 43(a) of the Lanham Act prohibits actions like trademark infringement that deceive consumers and impair a producer's goodwill.... The consumer who buys a branded product does not automatically assume that the brand-name company is the same entity that came up with the idea for the product, or designed the product—and typically does not care whether it is. The words of the Lanham Act should not be stretched to cover matters that are typically of no consequence to purchasers.

[12] It could be argued, perhaps, that the reality of purchaser concern is different for what might be called a communicative product—one that is valued not primarily for its physical qualities, such as a hammer, but for the intellectual content that it conveys, such as a book or, as here, a video. The purchaser of a novel is interested not merely, if at all, in the identity of the producer of the physical tome (the publisher), but also, and indeed primarily, in the identity of the creator of the story it conveys (the author). And the author, of course, has at least as much interest in avoiding passing off (or reverse passing off) of his creation as does the publisher. For such a communicative product (the argument goes) "origin of goods" in § 43(a) must be

deemed to include not merely the producer of the physical item (the publishing house Farrar, Straus and Giroux, or the video producer Dastar) but also the creator of the content that the physical item conveys (the author Tom Wolfe, or—assertedly—respondents).

[13] The problem with this argument according special treatment to communicative products is that it causes the Lanham Act to conflict with the law of copyright, which addresses that subject specifically. The right to copy, and to copy without attribution, once a copyright has expired, like the right to make an article whose patent has expired—including the right to make it in precisely the shape it carried when patented—passes to the public. In general, unless an intellectual property right such as a patent or copyright protects an item, it will be subject to copying. The rights of a patentee or copyright holder are part of a carefully crafted bargain, under which, once the patent or copyright monopoly has expired, the public may use the invention or work at will and without attribution. Thus, in construing the Lanham Act, we have been careful to caution against misuse or over-extension of trademark and related protections into areas traditionally occupied by patent or copyright. The Lanham Act, we have said, does not exist to reward manufacturers for their innovation in creating a particular device; that is the purpose of the patent law and its period of exclusivity. Federal trademark law has no necessary relation to invention or discovery, but rather, by preventing competitors from copying a source-identifying mark, reduces the customer's costs of shopping and making purchasing decisions, and helps assure a producer that it (and not an imitating competitor) will reap the financial, reputation-related rewards associated with a desirable product. Assuming for the sake of argument that Dastar's representation of itself as the "Producer" of its videos amounted to a representation that it originated the creative work conveyed by the videos, allowing a cause of action under §43(a) for that representation would create a species of mutant copyright law that limits the public's federal right to copy and to use expired copyrights.

[14] When Congress has wished to create such an addition to the law of copyright, it has done so with much more specificity than the Lanham Act's ambiguous use of "origin." The Visual Artists Rights Act of 1990, §603(a), provides that the author of an artistic work "shall have the right ... to claim authorship of that work." 17 U.S.C. §106A(a)(1)(A). That express right of attribution is carefully limited and focused: It attaches only to specified "work[s] of visual art," §101, is personal to the artist, and endures only for "the life of the author." Recognizing in §43(a) a cause of action for misrepresentation of authorship of noncopyrighted works (visual or otherwise) would render these limitations superfluous. A statutory interpretation that renders another statute superfluous is of course to be avoided.

[15] Reading "origin" in §43(a) to require attribution of uncopyrighted materials would pose serious practical problems. Without a copyrighted work as the basepoint, the word "origin" has no discernable limits. A video of the MGM film *Carmen Jones*, after its copyright has expired, would presumably require attribution not just to MGM, but to Oscar Hammerstein II (who wrote the musical on which the film was based), to Georges Bizet (who wrote the opera on which the musical was based), and to Prosper Merimee (who wrote the novel on which the opera was based). In many cases, figuring out who is in the line of "origin" would be no simple task. Indeed, in the present case it is far from clear that respondents have that status. Neither SFM nor New Line had anything to do with the production of the *Crusade* television series—they merely were licensed to distribute the video version. While Fox might have a claim to being in the line of origin, its involvement with the creation of the television series was limited at best. Time, Inc., was the principal, if not the exclusive, creator, albeit under arrangement with Fox. And of course it was neither Fox nor Time, Inc., that shot the film used in the *Crusade* television series. Rather, that footage came from the United States Army, Navy, and Coast Guard, the British Ministry of Information and War Office, the National Film Board of Canada, and unidentified "Newsreel Pool Cameramen." If anyone has a claim to being the *original* creator of the material used in both the *Crusade* television series and the *Campaigns* videotapes, it would be those groups, rather than Fox. We do not think the Lanham Act requires this search for the source of the Nile and all its tributaries.

[16] Another practical difficulty of adopting a special definition of "origin" for communicative products is that it places the manufacturers of those products in a difficult position. On the one hand, they would face Lanham Act liability for *failing* to credit the creator of a work on which their lawful copies are based; and on the other hand they could face Lanham Act liability for *crediting* the creator if that should be regarded as implying the creator's sponsorship or approval of the copy. In this case, for example, if Dastar had simply copied the television series as *Crusade in Europe* and sold it as *Crusade in Europe*, without changing the title or packaging (including the original credits to Fox), it is hard to have confidence in respondents' assurance that they "would not be here on a Lanham Act cause of action."...

[17] In sum, reading the phrase "origin of goods" in the Lanham Act in accordance with the Act's common-law foundations (which were *not* designed to protect originality or creativity), and in light of the copyright and patent laws (which *were*), we conclude that the phrase refers to the producer of the tangible goods that are offered for sale, and not to the author of any idea, concept, or communication embodied in those goods. To hold otherwise would be akin to finding that § 43(a) created a species of perpetual patent and copyright, which Congress may not do. *See* Eldred v. Ashcroft, 537 U.S. 186, 208 (2003).

[18] The creative talent of the sort that lay behind the *Campaigns* videos is not left without protection. The original film footage used in the *Crusade* television series could have been copyrighted, as was copyrighted (as a compilation) the *Crusade* television series, even though it included material from the public domain. Had Fox renewed the copyright in the *Crusade* television series, it would have had an easy claim of copyright infringement. And respondents' contention that *Campaigns* infringes Doubleday's copyright in General Eisenhower's book is still a live question on remand. If, moreover, the producer of a video that substantially copied the *Crusade* series were, in advertising or promotion, to give purchasers the impression that the video was quite different from that series, then one or more of the respondents might have a cause of action—not for reverse passing off under the "confusion ... as to the origin" provision of § 43(a)(1)(A), but for misrepresentation under the "misrepresents the nature, characteristics [or] qualities" provision of § 43(a)(1)(B). For merely saying it is the producer of the video, however, no Lanham Act liability attaches to Dastar....

Justice BREYER took no part in the consideration or decision of this case.

NOTES

1. Does *Dastar* overturn the holding in *Gilliam*? *Dastar* concerns Lanham Act claims in a work in which copyright has expired. *Gilliam* involves a work in which copyright is still in effect. Does *Dastar*'s holding about the permissible scope of Lanham Act claims apply to works that are still protected by copyright? A number of courts have held that it does. *See, e.g.,* Baden Sports, Inc. v. Molten USA, Inc., 556 F.3d 1300, 1306 (Fed. Cir. 2009); General Universal Sys., Inc. v. Lee, 379 F.3d 131, 149 (5th Cir. 2004); Corbis Corp. v. Amazon.com, Inc., 351 F. Supp. 2d 1090, 1116–17 (W.D. Wash. 2004). For an argument that *Gilliam* is still good law after *Dastar*, see Justin Hughes, *American Moral Rights and Fixing the* Dastar *"Gap"*, 2007 UTAH L. REV. 659.

2. Justice Scalia's opinion in *Dastar* raises questions about the breadth of the Supreme Court's holding. Is Justice Scalia simply interpreting the scope of the Lanham Act? Or is the Court offering a broader principle about how to interpret federal laws that might touch upon copyrighted works and copyright law? For an argument that *Dastar* stands for a broad principle that non-copyright statutes should be interpreted, where possible, in a way that avoids burdening access to works in the public domain, see Christopher Jon Sprigman, *Indirect Enforcement of the Intellectual Property Clause*, 30 COLUM. J.L. & ARTS 565 (2007). For a more critical take and why trademark law might play a role for works in the public domain under copyright law, see Laura A. Heymann, *The Trademark/Copyright Divide*, 60 SMU L. REV. 55 (2007).

Chapter V – Exclusive Rights

The **Visual Artists Rights Act (VARA)**, which became law in 1990, grants the author of a "work of visual art" a set of limited moral rights, which include:

(1) ... the right—

> *(A) to claim authorship of that work, and*

> *(B) to prevent the use of his or her name as the author of any work of visual art which he or she did not create;*

(2) ... the right to prevent the use of his or her name as the author of the work of visual art in the event of a distortion, mutilation, or other modification of the work which would be prejudicial to his or her honor or reputation; and

(3) subject to the limitations set forth in section 113(d), ... the right—

> *(A) to prevent any intentional distortion, mutilation, or other modification of that work which would be prejudicial to his or her honor or reputation, and any intentional distortion, mutilation, or modification of that work is a violation of that right, and*

> *(B) to prevent any destruction of a work of recognized stature, and any intentional or grossly negligent destruction of that work is a violation of that right.*

17 U.S.C. § 106A(a). Section 101 defines "work of visual art" as follows:

A "work of visual art" is—

> *(1) a painting, drawing, print or sculpture, existing in a single copy, in a limited edition of 200 copies or fewer that are signed and consecutively numbered by the author, or, in the case of a sculpture, in multiple cast, carved, or fabricated sculptures of 200 or fewer that are consecutively numbered by the author and bear the signature or other identifying mark of the author; or*

> *(2) a still photographic image produced for exhibition purposes only, existing in a single copy that is signed by the author, or in a limited edition of 200 copies or fewer that are signed and consecutively numbered by the author.*

A work of visual art does not include—

> *(A) (i) any poster, map, globe, chart, technical drawing, diagram, model, applied art, motion picture or other audiovisual work, book, magazine, newspaper, periodical, data base, electronic information service, electronic publication, or similar publication;*

> *(ii) any merchandising item or advertising, promotional, descriptive, covering, or packaging material or container;*

> *(iii) any portion or part of any item described in clause (i) or (ii);*

> *(B) any work made for hire; or*

> *(C) any work not subject to copyright protection under this title.*

VARA's scope is narrowed by the provisions limiting coverage to painting, drawings, prints or sculptures produced in a single copy or in certain "limited editions," and photographs hewing to these limitations and which also are produced for "exhibition purposes only." Note that this limitation means that VARA protections apply only to *originals*, or, at most, to a small number of copies produced in "limited editions." VARA protections do not apply to copies outside this narrow category. Perhaps because of the provision's limited scope, there are few cases interpreting VARA. One court has held that VARA's language limiting coverage for photographs to those "produced for exhibition purposes only" means that only photographs intended for exhibition by the author at the time the photographic print was created qualify for protection. Lilley v. Stout, 384 F. Supp. 2d 83 (D.D.C. 2005). VARA's language excluding protection for "any merchandising item or advertising, promotional, descriptive, covering, or packaging material or container" has been enforced with similar stringency. *See, e.g.*, Pollara v. Seymour, 344 F.3d 265 (2d Cir. 2003) (rejecting a VARA claim with respect to a large painting meant to promote a political message). Note also that VARA excludes from protection all works made for hire. Why do you think Congress made that choice?

The rights granted by VARA endure for the life of the author (or for the life of the last surviving author in the case of joint works), and are not transferable but are waiveable "in a written instrument signed by the author." 17 U.S.C. §§ 106A(d)-(e). Section 113(d) addresses waiver in the context of the removal of works of visual art from buildings, providing that waiver after the effective date of VARA may be accomplished only via a writing explicitly providing for waiver and signed by both the building owner and the author. *Id.* § 113(d). Note also that VARA rights are, like other rights granted by the Copyright Act, subject to limitation by the statute's fair use provision, set out in § 107. *Id.* § 106A(a).

Finally, VARA does not grant certain moral rights recognized in other countries. VARA does not provide a right of disclosure (also known as the right of divulgation), protecting an author's authority to prevent third parties from disclosing their work to the public without the author's consent (or under conditions, such as anonymous or pseudonymous publication, that the author specifies). Nor does VARA provide a moral right of withdrawal, granted in the laws of certain other jurisdictions including France, which empowers an author, upon satisfaction of certain conditions, to withdraw his work from the market.

Maria Castillo v. G&M Realty L.P.
950 F.3d 155 (2d Cir. 2020)

PARKER, J.:

[1] Defendants-Appellants G&M Realty L.P … appeal from a judgment of the United States District Court for the Eastern District of New York (Frederic Block, J.). The court concluded that [G&M Realty owner Gerald] Wolkoff violated the Visual Artists Rights Act of 1990 by destroying artwork of Plaintiffs-Appellees, artists who created and displayed their work at the 5Pointz site in Long Island City, New York. We hold that the district court correctly concluded that the artwork created by Appellees was protected by VARA and that Wolkoff's violation of the statute was willful…. Accordingly, we affirm the judgment below.

[2] The facts as found by the district court established that in 2002, Wolkoff undertook to install artwork in a series of dilapidated warehouse buildings that he owned in Long Island City, New York. Wolkoff enlisted Appellee Jonathan Cohen, a distinguished aerosol artist, to turn the warehouses into an exhibition space for artists. Cohen and other artists rented studio spaces in the warehouses and filled the walls with aerosol art, with Cohen serving as curator. Under Cohen's leadership, the site, known as 5Pointz, evolved into a major global center for aerosol art. It attracted thousands of daily visitors, numerous celebrities, and extensive media coverage.

Chapter V – Exclusive Rights

[3] "Creative destruction" was an important feature of the 5Pointz site. Some art at the site achieved permanence, but other art had a short lifespan and was repeatedly painted over. An elaborate system of norms—including Cohen's permission and often consent of the artist whose work was overpainted—governed the painting process. Cohen divided the walls into "short-term rotating walls," where works would generally last for days or weeks, and "longstanding walls," which were more permanent and reserved for the best works at the site. During its lifespan, 5Pointz was home to a total of approximately 10,650 works of art.

[4] In May 2013, Cohen learned that Wolkoff had sought municipal approvals looking to demolish 5Pointz and to build luxury apartments on the site. Seeking to prevent that destruction, Cohen applied to the New York City Landmark Preservation Commission to have 5Pointz designated a site of cultural significance. The application was unsuccessful, as were Cohen's efforts to raise money to purchase the site.

[5] At that point, Cohen, joined by numerous 5Pointz artists, sued under VARA to prevent destruction of the site....

[6] Early in the litigation, Plaintiffs applied for a temporary restraining order to prevent the demolition of the site, which the district court granted. As the TRO expired, Plaintiffs applied for a preliminary injunction. On November 12, 2013, the court denied the application in a minute order but told the parties that a written opinion would soon follow.

[7] That night, Wolkoff began to destroy the artwork. He banned the artists from the site and refused them permission to recover any work that could be removed. Several nights later (and before the district court's written opinion could issue), Wolkoff deployed a group of workmen who, at his instruction, whitewashed the art.

[8] On November 20, 2013, the district court issued its opinion denying the preliminary injunction. Judge Block concluded that, although some of the 5Pointz paintings may have achieved recognized stature, resolution of that question was best reserved for trial. The court also decided that, given the transitory nature of much of the work, preliminary injunctive relief was inappropriate and that the monetary damages available under VARA could remediate any injury proved at trial.

[9] Following the destruction of the art, nine additional artists sued Wolkoff. The two lawsuits were consolidated for trial, which would primarily address whether the artwork had achieved recognized stature and, if it had, the value of the art Wolkoff destroyed....

[10] ... [T]he district court issued its findings of fact and conclusions of law. Drawing on a vast record, the court found that 45 of the works had achieved recognized stature, that Wolkoff had violated VARA by destroying them, and that the violation was willful. More specifically, the court observed that the works "reflect[ed] striking technical and artistic mastery and vision worthy of display in prominent museums if not on the walls of 5Pointz." The findings emphasized Cohen's prominence in the world of aerosol art, the significance of his process of selecting the artists who could exhibit at 5Pointz, and the fact that, while much of the art was temporary, other works were on display for several years. Judge Block credited the artists' evidence of outside recognition of the 5Pointz works and expert testimony as to the works' stature. The court declined to impose liability with respect to the four remaining works because they had not achieved long-term preservation, were insufficiently discussed outside of 5Pointz, and were not modified to the detriment of the artists' reputations.

[11] Where a violation of VARA is established, the statute permits the injured party to recover either actual damages and profits or statutory damages. The statute fixes statutory damages between $750 and $30,000 per work but authorizes damages of up to $150,000 per work if a litigant proves that a violation was "willful." Ultimately, the district court concluded that it could not reliably fix the market value of the destroyed paintings and, for that reason, declined to award actual damages....

"Drunken Bulbs"
by Jonathan Cohen ("Meres One")

"Manga Koi"
by Akiko Miyakami ("Shiro")

"Dream of Oil"
by Francisco Fernandez

Figure 87: sample paintings from 5Pointz

[12] Nonetheless, the court did award statutory damages.... In addition ..., the court found that Wolkoff had acted willfully. This finding was based on Wolkoff's awareness of the ongoing VARA litigation and his refusal to afford the artists the 90-day opportunity provided by the statute to salvage their artwork, some of which

was removable. Judge Block was unpersuaded by Wolkoff's assertion that he whitewashed the artwork to prevent the artists from engaging in disruption and disorderly behavior at the site. Instead, he found that Wolkoff acted out of "pure pique and revenge for the nerve of the plaintiffs to sue to attempt to prevent the destruction of their art." Judge Block awarded the maximum amount of statutory damages: $150,000 for each of the 45 works, for a total of $6.75 million....

[13] VARA creates a scheme of moral rights for artists. The right of attribution generally consists of the right of an artist to be recognized by name as the author of his work or to publish anonymously or pseudonymously. It further includes the right to prevent the artist's work from being attributed to another and to prevent the use of the artist's name on works created by others. The right of integrity allows the artist to prevent any deforming or mutilating changes to his work, even after title in the work has been transferred.[1]

[14] Most importantly for this appeal, VARA gives "the author of a work of visual art" the right "to prevent any destruction of a work of recognized stature" and provides that "any intentional or grossly negligent destruction of that work is a violation of that right." 17 U.S.C. § 106A(a)(3)(B). VARA further permits the artist "to prevent any intentional distortion, mutilation, or other modification of [his or her work] which would be prejudicial to his or her honor or reputation," and provides that "any intentional distortion, mutilation, or modification of that work is a violation of that right." *Id.* § 106A(a)(3)(A). The latter provision applies regardless of a work's stature. These rights may not be transferred, but they "may be waived if the author expressly agrees to such waiver in a written instrument signed by the author." *Id.* § 106A(e)(1).

[15] Additionally, the statute contains specific provisions governing artwork incorporated into a building. If the artwork is incorporated "in such a way that removing the work from the building will cause the destruction, distortion, mutilation, or other modification of the work," then the artist's rights may be waived if and only if he "consented to the installation of the work in the building ... in a written instrument." *Id.* § 113(d)(1). This instrument must be "signed by the owner of the building and the author" and must "specif[y] that the installation of the work may subject the work to destruction, distortion, mutilation, or other modification, by reason of its removal." *Id.* However, "[i]f the owner of a building wishes to remove a work of visual art which is a part of such building and which can be removed from the building without the destruction, distortion, mutilation, or other modification of the work," then the artist's rights prevail unless one of two things has occurred. *Id.* § 113(d)(2). First, the building's owner "has made a diligent, good faith attempt without success to notify the author of the owner's intended action affecting the work of visual art." *Id.* Or second, the owner has "provide[d] such notice in writing and the person so notified failed, within 90 days after receiving such notice, either to remove the work or to pay for its removal." *Id.* ...

[16] The crux of the parties' dispute on this appeal is whether the works at 5Pointz were works of "recognized stature," thereby protected from destruction under § 106A(a)(3)(B). We conclude that a work is of recognized stature when it is one of high quality, status, or caliber that has been acknowledged as such by a relevant community....

[17] The most important component of stature will generally be artistic quality. The relevant community will typically be the artistic community, comprising art historians, art critics, museum curators, gallerists, prominent artists, and other experts. Since recognized stature is necessarily a fluid concept, we can conceive of circumstances under which, for example, a "poor" work by an otherwise highly regarded artist nonetheless merits protection from destruction under VARA. This approach helps to ensure that VARA protects the public

---

[1] The statute recognizes that, unlike novelists or composers, for example, visual artists depend on the integrity of the physical manifestations of their works. Artists' moral rights spring from a belief that an artist in the process of creation injects his spirit into the work and that the artist's personality, as well as the integrity of the work, should therefore be protected and preserved.

interest in preserving the nation's culture. This approach also ensures that the personal judgment of the court is not the determinative factor in the court's analysis.

[18] After all, we are mindful of Justice Holmes's cautionary observation that "[i]t would be a dangerous undertaking for persons trained only to the law to constitute themselves final judges of the worth of [visual art]," Bleistein v. Donaldson Lithographing Co., 188 U.S. 239, 251 (1903). For that reason, aside from the rare case where an artist or work is of such prominence that the issue of recognized stature need not be tried, expert testimony or substantial evidence of non-expert recognition will generally be required to establish recognized stature....

[19] Accordingly, to establish a violation of VARA in this case, the artists were required to demonstrate that their work had achieved recognized stature. Judge Block found that they did so. He concluded that "the plaintiffs adduced such a plethora of exhibits and credible testimony, including the testimony of a highly regarded expert, that even under the most restrictive of evidentiary standards almost all of the plaintiffs' works easily qualify as works of recognized stature." These findings of fact are reviewable only for clear error. Appellants do not hurdle this high bar....

[20] Initially, Wolkoff contends that the great majority of the works in question were temporary ones which, for that reason, could not meet the recognized stature requirement. We disagree. We see nothing in VARA that excludes temporary artwork from attaining recognized stature....

[21] Congress adopted a highly specific definition of visual art. See 17 U.S.C. § 101. In light of this specificity, we see no justification for adopting an additional requirement not included by Congress, even if that requirement is styled as a component of recognized stature. To do so would be to upset the balance achieved by the legislature.

[22] Additionally, at least as recently as 2005, New York City saw a clear instance where temporary artwork achieved recognized stature. That winter, artists Christo Vladimirov Javacheff and Jeanne-Claude Denat, known collectively as "Christo," installed 7,503 orange draped gates in Central Park. This work, known as "The Gates," lasted only two weeks but was the subject of significant critical acclaim and attention, not just from the art world but also from the general public.

[23] In recent years, "street art," much of which is "temporary," has emerged as a major category of contemporary art.... For example, noted street artist Banksy has appeared alongside President Barack Obama and Apple founder Steve Jobs on Time magazine's list of the world's 100 most influential people. Though often painted on building walls where it may be subject to overpainting, Banksy's work is nonetheless acknowledged, both by the art community and the general public, as of significant artistic merit and cultural importance. Famously, Banksy's *Girl with a Balloon* self-destructed after selling for $1.4 million at Sotheby's, but, as with Banksy's street art, the temporary quality of this work has only added to its recognition....

[24] The district court correctly observed that when Congress wanted to impose durational limits on work subject to VARA, it knew how to do so. For example, the statute provides that "[t]he modification of a work of visual art which is a result of the passage of time or the inherent nature of the materials is not a distortion, mutilation, or other modification described in subsection (a)(3)(A)." 17 U.S.C. § 106A(c)(1). For that reason, the gradual erosion of outdoor artwork exposed to the elements or the melting of an ice sculpture does not threaten liability. Congress also imposed a durational limit insofar as the statute protects only works that are "fixed"—"sufficiently permanent ... to be perceived ... for a period of more than transitory duration." *Id.* §§ 101, 102(a). We have held that a work that exists for only 1.2 seconds is of merely transitory duration but have noted with approval cases holding that a work "embodied ... for at least several minutes" is of more than transitory duration. Cartoon Network LP, LLLP v. CSC Holdings, Inc., 536 F.3d 121, 127-28 (2d Cir. 2008). It is

undisputed that the 5Pointz works survived far longer than this and therefore satisfied the statute's minimal durational requirement.

[25] As a variation on the theme that temporary artwork does not merit VARA protection, Wolkoff contends that because the artists were aware that the 5Pointz buildings might eventually be torn down, they should have expected their work to be destroyed. The district court correctly observed, however, that VARA accounts for this possibility. Under § 113(d), if the art at 5Pointz was incorporated into the site such that it could not be removed without being destroyed, then Wolkoff was required to obtain "a written instrument ... that [was] signed by the owner of the building and the [artist] and that specifie[d] that installation of the work may subject the work to destruction, distortion, mutilation, or other modification, by reason of its removal." 17 U.S.C. § 113(d)(1)(B). It is undisputed that no such instrument was executed. If, on the other hand, the 5Pointz art could have been safely removed, then Wolkoff was required to provide written notice of the planned demolition and to allow the artists 90 days to remove the work or to pay for its removal. *See id.* § 113(d)(2)(B). Again, it is undisputed that Wolkoff did none of this....

[26] In addition to his contention that temporary artwork cannot achieve recognized stature, Wolkoff argues that the district court erred in several other respects. He contends that the court erroneously focused on recognized quality, rather than recognized stature, and that, contrary to the approach allegedly taken by the district court, recognized stature must be assessed at the time of a work's destruction, not at the time of trial.... Finally, Wolkoff objects to the district court's reliance on Jonathan Cohen's testimony about his curation of the artwork, as well as its consideration of the overall quality of 5Pointz as a site.

[27] None of these contentions, considered separately or in the aggregate, convinces us that any of Judge Block's findings were clearly erroneous. There is no merit to Wolkoff's contention that the court improperly focused on recognized quality as opposed to recognized stature. The court's detailed findings are dispositive on this point. Nor are we persuaded that the district court evaluated the works' recognition at the time of trial, since it explicitly stated that the "focus of [its] decision was the recognition the works achieved prior to the whitewash." In any event, the quality of a work, assessed by an expert after it has been destroyed, can be probative of its pre-destruction quality, status, or caliber....

[28] ... Appellants object to the district court's reliance on Jonathan Cohen's testimony about his curation of the artwork. The district court reasoned that Cohen's selection process, which involved review of a portfolio of an artist's work and a plan for his or her 5Pointz project, screened for works of stature. Appellants, however, contend that this determination was irrelevant because Cohen made his evaluation before the artists painted their 5Pointz works. Nonetheless, the district court cogently reasoned that a respected aerosol artist's determination that another aerosol artist's work is worthy of display is appropriate evidence of stature. An artist whose merit has been recognized by another prominent artist, museum curator, or art critic is more likely to create work of recognized stature than an artist who has not been screened. This inference is even stronger where, as here, Cohen reviewed a plan for the subject work before allowing it to be painted.[7] Accepting and crediting such testimony easily falls within a district court's trial management responsibilities and in this instance involved no abuse of discretion or clear error.

[29] Finally, Wolkoff contends that the district court erroneously focused on the stature of the 5Pointz site rather than the individual 5Pointz works. Yet again we see no error. The district court did not focus exclusively on the stature of the site. The court considered the individual works at the site and determined that some

---

[7] The House Judiciary Committee Report on VARA confirms our conclusion that an artist's "pre-existing standing in the artistic community" is relevant to "recognized stature." H.R. REP. NO. 101-514 (1990). Indeed, several courts have recognized the possibility that, in extreme cases, an artist's prominence might render all of his work of "recognized stature," even if particular works are unknown to the public.

were not of recognized stature. Setting that aside, we easily conclude that the site of a work is relevant to its recognition and stature and may, in certain cases, render the recognition and stature of a work beyond question. Appearance at a major site—*e.g.*, the Louvre or the Prado—ensures that a work will be recognized, that is, seen and appreciated by the public and the art community. The appearance of a work of art at a curated site such as a museum or 5Pointz means that the work has been deemed meritorious by the curator and therefore is evidence of stature. When the curator is distinguished, his selection of the work is especially probative. Consequently, we see no error when the district court considered the 5Pointz site itself as some evidence of the works' recognized stature....

[30] Appellants next challenge the district court's award of damages....

[31] We review the district court's finding of willfulness for clear error, and we see none. As Judge Block found, Wolkoff admitted his awareness, prior to destroying 5Pointz, that the artists were pressing VARA claims. Additionally, VARA contains provisions limiting artists' rights vis-à-vis building owners when owners give them 90 days' notice and the opportunity to remove their artwork, 17 U.S.C. § 113(d)(2), but Wolkoff testified that, although he was advised by counsel both before and after the destruction, he chose "to hire people to whitewash[] it in one shot instead of waiting for three months." The district court found that this testimony evinced a deliberate choice to violate VARA rather than to follow the statutory notice procedures. Wolkoff did not help his cause when he later reminded the district court that he "would make the same decision today." ... {The Second Circuit also rejected Wolkoff's challenge to the amount of statutory damages awarded. You will study statutory damages and willful infringement in Chapter VIII.}

NOTES

1. Section 501 of the Copyright Act extends copyright's damages provisions to at least certain violations of VARA rights. *See* 17 U.S.C. § 501(a). But at least one court has held that damages may not be available for all violations of VARA rights. In *Massachusetts Museum of Contemporary Art Foundation, Inc. v. Büchel*, 593 F.3d 38 (1st Cir. 2010), an art museum had a series of disputes with an artist over the construction of a large and complex art installation. The artist alleged that the museum made some modifications to the installation during its construction that were contrary to his instructions. Eventually, the conflict worsened to the point that the museum canceled the project. The museum nonetheless chose to mount an exhibition of the partially-completed work, and filed a declaratory judgment action seeking a declaration that it was entitled to present the partial construction to the public. The artist counterclaimed, seeking, among other things, damages and injunctive relief under VARA. The district court granted summary judgment in favor of the museum, after which the museum dismantled the work. On appeal, the First Circuit affirmed the district court's opinion dismissing the artist's attribution claim, but reversed in part, holding that the artist could proceed to trial on his integrity claims. The First Circuit made several important holdings interpreting VARA. In particular, the court held that remedies for successful VARA attribution claim did not include damages. The First Circuit reasoned that the statutory language giving the author the right "to prevent" attribution violations suggested that remedies were limited to injunctions. Do you agree with that interpretation of the statutory language?

2. VARA permits artists to waive their attribution and integrity rights. Moral rights protections in some other countries prohibit waiver. Which position makes more sense, from either an artists'-rights or utilitarian perspective?

3. In *Kelley v. Chicago Park District*, 635 F.3d 290 (7th Cir. 2011), which you read in Chapter II, the Seventh Circuit held that a work cannot be protected by VARA unless it meets the standards for copyright protection, including fixation and originality. That is, as the court explains, VARA "supplements general copyright protection"; it is not a freestanding right.

4. Think back to the cases you read on the right to prepare derivative works—*RDR*, *Mirage*, *Lee*, and *Galoob*. Assuming there is any harm in these scenarios, is having your fictional world summarized, your game play altered, or your artwork laminated on a tile also a "moral" harm? More broadly, do you think there is a good reason that VARA is limited to certain works of visual art rather than encompassing all copyrightable works?

5. A recent dispute involving two outdoor sculptures in New York City raises an interesting issue about the scope of VARA. The dispute involves Charging Bull, a large sculpture that artist Arturo Di Modica placed—without permission—on Wall Street following the 1987 stock market crash.

According to Di Modica, *Charging Bull* was meant to express his sense of confidence in the American economy, and eventually the New York City government found a spot for it in a small plaza in nearby Bowling Green, as shown in Figure 88. The dispute began in 2017, when, on the eve of International Women's Day, *Fearless Girl*, a sculpture by Kristen Visbal intended to speak to the dearth of female executives in New York's financial services industry and shown in Figure 89, was placed across from *Charging Bull*.

Figure 88: *Charging Bull* sculpture

Figure 89: *Fearless Girl* sculpture

Di Modica objected, stating that the placement of *Fearless Girl*, and its visual interaction with *Charging Bull*, changed the meaning of his sculpture. Judge for yourself based on the photograph in Figure 90.

Figure 90: *Charging Bull* and *Fearless Girl* sculptures

Does *Fearless Girl* distort, mutilate, or modify *Charging Bull* in a way that would be actionable under VARA? The statute does not define those terms. If they are construed to include changes to the area around a work that change the "message" of a work, rather than being limited to changes in the work itself, what sorts of claims might that permit? Would museums face potential liability for their decisions to exhibit an artist's work close to the work of other artists in a manner that artist feels may distort the message of their work?

6. A recent case, *Kerson v. Vermont Law School*, No. 5:20-cv-00202-gwc (D. Vt. 2021), raises some questions about the scope of VARA's integrity right. In that case, an artist challenged Vermont Law School's plan to conceal two murals (via permanent installation of a wooden frame with acoustic panels that would surround the murals without damaging them) he had previously been commissioned to paint and install at the law school. According to the school, students had begun to complain about what some perceived as cartoonish, crude depictions in the murals of enslaved Black people. The district court ruled that concealment is not an actionable distortion, mutilation, or modification of a work, and that "the language of the VARA does not include a protection against concealment or removal from display of artworks by the owner."

G. The Rights of Public Performance and Public Display

Section 106(4) of the Copyright Act grants an exclusive right "to perform the copyrighted work publicly" to copyright owners of "literary, musical, dramatic and choreographic works, pantomimes, and motion pictures and other audiovisual works." The Copyright Act separately provides the copyright owners of sound recordings with a narrower public performance right, limited to public performances made "by means of a digital audio transmission," 17 U.S.C. §106(6), which we discuss below in section H.

Section 106(5) of the Copyright Act grants an exclusive right "to display the copyrighted work publicly" to copyright owners of "literary, musical, dramatic and choreographic works, pantomimes, and pictorial, graphic, or sculptural works, including the individual images of a motion picture or other audiovisual work."

Section 101 defines both "perform" and "display":

> To "perform" a work means to recite, render, play, dance, or act it, either directly or by means of any device or process or, in the case of a motion picture or other audiovisual work, to show its images in any sequence or to make the sounds accompanying it audible.

> To "display" a work means to show a copy of it, either directly or by means of a film, slide, television image, or any other device or process or, in the case of a motion picture or other audiovisual work, to show individual images nonsequentially.

Note that the statute gives to copyright owners exclusive rights only with respect to *public* performances or displays. That formulation means that there is a category of *private* performances and displays over which the statute gives a copyright owner no control. How to differentiate performances and displays that are "public" from those that are "private"? Section 101 provides a relevant definition:

> To perform or display a work "publicly" means—

>> (1) to perform or display it at a place open to the public or at any place where a substantial number of persons outside of a normal circle of a family and its social acquaintances is gathered; or

>> (2) to transmit or otherwise communicate a performance or display of the work to a place specified by clause (1) or to the public, by means of any device or process, whether the members of the public capable of receiving the performance or display receive it in the same place or in separate places and at the same time or at different times.[*]

The next three cases you read will concern some of the issues raised by the Copyright Act's definition of what it means to perform or display a work "publicly." Before you read this next case, review the first clause of that definition carefully.

Columbia Pictures Industries, Inc. v. Redd Horne, Inc.

749 F.2d 154 (3d Cir. 1984)

RE, C.J.:

[1] In this copyright infringement case, defendants appeal from an order of the United States District Court for the Western District of Pennsylvania which granted the plaintiffs' motion for summary judgment, and enjoined defendants from exhibiting plaintiffs' copyrighted motion pictures. The defendants, Redd Horne, Inc., Maxwell's Video Showcase, Ltd., Glenn W. Zeny and Robert Zeny, also appeal from the ... award of damages against them in the amount of $44,750.00....

---

[*] Section 101 further defines "transmit": "To 'transmit' a performance or display is to communicate it by any device or process whereby images or sounds are received beyond the place from which they are sent."

[2] Maxwell's Video Showcase, Ltd., operates two stores in Erie, Pennsylvania.... The copyright infringement issue in this case arises from defendants' *exhibition* of video cassettes of the plaintiffs' films, or what defendants euphemistically refer to as their "showcasing" or "in-store rental" concept.

[3] Each store contains a small showroom area in the front of the store, and a "showcase" or exhibition area in the rear. The front showroom contains video equipment and materials for sale or rent, as well as dispensing machines for popcorn and carbonated beverages. Movie posters are also displayed in this front area. In the rear "showcase" area, patrons may view any of an assortment of video cassettes in small, private booths with space for two to four people. There are a total of eighty-five booths in the two stores. Each booth or room is approximately four feet by six feet and is carpeted on the floor and walls. In the front there is a nineteen inch color television and an upholstered bench in the back.

[4] The procedure followed by a patron wishing to utilize one of the viewing booths or rooms is the same at both facilities. The customer selects a film from a catalogue which contains the titles of available films. The fee charged by Maxwell's depends on the number of people in the viewing room, and the time of day. The price is $5.00 for one or two people before 6 p.m., and $6.00 for two people after 6 p.m. There is at all times a $1.00 surcharge for the third and fourth person. The fee also entitles patrons to help themselves to popcorn and soft drinks before entering their assigned rooms. Closing the door of the viewing room activates a signal in the counter area at the front of the store. An employee of Maxwell's then places the cassette of the motion picture chosen by the viewer into one of the video cassette machines in the front of the store and the picture is transmitted to the patron's viewing room....

[5] Access to each room is limited to the individuals who rent it as a group. Although no restriction is placed on the composition of a group, strangers are not grouped in order to fill a particular room to capacity. Maxwell's is open to any member of the public who wishes to utilize its facilities or services....

"To introduce you to the enjoyment of home video movies, Maxwell's would like you to try a showcase promotional screening. Come to Maxwell's and rent any of the 21 private showcase rooms, which hold 2 people comfortably. You pay only for the rental of the showcase room. You have free use of Maxwell's entire library of video films.... See as much as you like—segments of several films or watch a full length movie.... If you already own a video unit and buy a tape from Maxwell's your showcase rental fee is deducted from the price of the tape.... Free popcorn and assorted soft drinks are provided for your pleasure while visiting Maxwell's!"

Figure 91: Maxwell's video screening advertisement

[6] The plaintiffs' complaint is based on their contention that the exhibition or showing of the video cassettes in the private booths on defendants' premises constitutes an unauthorized public performance in violation of plaintiffs' exclusive rights under the federal copyright laws....

[7] It is undisputed that the defendants were licensed to exercise the right of distribution. A copyright owner, however, may dispose of a copy of his work while retaining all underlying copyrights which are not expressly or impliedly disposed of with that copy. Thus, it is clear that the plaintiffs have retained their interest in the other … enumerated rights…. In essence, therefore, the fundamental question is whether the defendants' activities constitute a public performance of the plaintiffs' motion pictures. We agree with the conclusion of the district court that these activities constitute a public performance, and are an infringement.

[8] "To perform a work means … in the case of a motion picture or other audiovisual work, to show its images in any sequence or to make the sounds accompanying it audible." 17 U.S.C. § 101. Clearly, playing a video cassette results in a sequential showing of a motion picture's images and in making the sounds accompanying it audible. Thus, Maxwell's activities constitute a performance under section 101.

[9] The remaining question is whether these performances are public. Section 101 also states that to perform a work "publicly" means "[t]o perform … it at a place open to the public or at any place where a substantial number of persons outside of a normal circle of a family and its social acquaintances is gathered." The statute is written in the disjunctive, and thus two categories of places can satisfy the definition of "to perform a work publicly." The first category is self-evident; it is "a place open to the public." The second category, commonly referred to as a semi-public place, is determined by the size and composition of the audience.

[10] The legislative history indicates that this second category was added to expand the concept of public performance by including those places that, although not open to the public at large, are accessible to a significant number of people. Clearly, if a place is public, the size and composition of the audience are irrelevant. However, if the place is not public, the size and composition of the audience will be determinative.

[11] We find it unnecessary to examine the second part of the statutory definition because we agree with the district court's conclusion that Maxwell's was open to the public. On the composition of the audience, the district court noted that "the showcasing operation is not distinguishable in any significant manner from the exhibition of films at a conventional movie theater." Any member of the public can view a motion picture by paying the appropriate fee. The services provided by Maxwell's are essentially the same as a movie theatre, with the additional feature of privacy. The relevant "place" within the meaning of section 101 is each of Maxwell's two stores, not each individual booth within each store. Simply because the cassettes can be viewed in private does not mitigate the essential fact that Maxwell's is unquestionably open to the public.

[12] The conclusion that Maxwell's activities constitute public performances is fully supported by subsection (2) of the statutory definition of public performance:

> *(2) to transmit or otherwise communicate a performance … of the work to a place specified by clause (1) or to the public, by means of any device or process, whether the members of the public capable of receiving the performance … receive it in the same place or in separate places and at the same time or at different times.*

17 U.S.C. § 101. As explained in the House Report which accompanies the Copyright Revision Act of 1976, "a performance made available by transmission to the public at large is 'public' even though the recipients are not gathered in a single place…. The same principles apply whenever the potential recipients of the transmission represent a limited segment of the public, such as the occupants of hotel rooms …." Thus, the transmission of a performance to members of the public, even in private settings such as hotel rooms or Maxwell's viewing rooms, constitutes a public performance. As the statutory language and legislative history clearly indicate, the fact that members of the public view the performance at different times does not alter this legal consequence.

[13] Professor Nimmer's examination of this definition is particularly pertinent: "*if the same copy* ... of a given work is repeatedly played (*i.e.*, 'performed') by different members of the public, albeit at different times, this constitutes a 'public' performance." .... Although Maxwell's has only one copy of each film, it shows each copy repeatedly to different members of the public. This constitutes a public performance....

[14] The defendants also contend that their activities are protected by the first sale doctrine. The first sale doctrine is codified in section 109(a) of Title 17. This section provides:

> *Notwithstanding the provisions of section 106(3), the owner of a particular copy or phonorecord lawfully made under this title, or any person authorized by such owner, is entitled, without the authority of the copyright owner, to sell or otherwise dispose of the possession of that copy or phonorecord.*

.... The first sale doctrine prevents the copyright owner from controlling the future transfer of a particular copy once its material ownership has been transferred. The transfer of the video cassettes to the defendants, however, did not result in the forfeiture or waiver of all of the exclusive rights found in section 106. The copyright owner's exclusive right "to perform the copyrighted work publicly" has not been affected; only its distribution right as to the transferred copy has been circumscribed.

[15] In essence, the defendants' "first sale" argument is merely another aspect of their argument that their activities are not public performances. For the defendants' argument to succeed, we would have to adopt their characterization of the "showcasing" transaction or activity as an "in-store rental." The facts do not permit such a finding or conclusion. The record clearly demonstrates that showcasing a video cassette at Maxwell's is a significantly different transaction than leasing a tape for home use. Maxwell's never disposed of the tapes in its showcasing operations, nor did the tapes ever leave the store. At all times, Maxwell's maintained physical dominion and control over the tapes. Its employees actually played the cassettes on its machines. The charges or fees received for viewing the cassettes at Maxwell's facilities are analytically indistinguishable from admission fees paid by patrons to gain admission to any public theater. Plainly, in their showcasing operation, the appellants do not sell, rent, or otherwise dispose of the video cassette. On the facts presented, Maxwell's "showcasing" operation is a public performance, which, as a matter of law, constitutes a copyright infringement....

NOTES

1. A performance or display of a copyrighted work is "public" if it occurs at a place "open to the public." *Redd Horne* holds that because the video store is a place "open to the public," the performance of a motion picture inside the video store is a public performance. But why is the video store as a whole the relevant "place"? Why isn't the private room inside the video store—the room where the motion picture is actually performed—the relevant "place"? Does the court give a coherent explanation for why the store, and not the viewing room, is the relevant "place"?

2. Suppose for a moment that the relevant "place" is the screening room, and not the store as a whole. What result then?

3. The court seeks to buttress its holding by arguing that the same facts would lead to a finding that a public performance had taken place under the second part of the statutory definition—the so-called "transmit clause." Do you agree with this? Can you think of a modification to the services provided by Maxwell's video store that would eliminate the prospect of liability under the transmit clause?

4. What if the facts in *Redd Horne* were varied so that instead, a customer would rent a videotape from the store and take it himself or herself to one of the individual viewing booths in the store, where the customer

would place the tape in a VCR and play the tape under the customer's own control? The Third Circuit, in a subsequent case, held that these performances of a motion picture inside the video store are also public. Columbia Pictures Indus., Inc. v. Aveco, Inc., 800 F.2d 59 (3d Cir. 1986). The court reasoned:

> The Copyright Act speaks of performances at a place open to the public. It does not require that the public place be actually crowded with people. A telephone booth, a taxi cab, and even a pay toilet are commonly regarded as "open to the public," even though they are usually occupied only by one party at a time. Our opinion in Redd Horne turned not on the precise whereabouts of the video cassette players, but on the nature of Maxwell's stores. Maxwell's, like [this store], was willing to make a viewing room and video cassette available to any member of the public with the inclination to avail himself of this service. It is this availability that made Maxwell's stores public places, not the coincidence that the video cassette players were situated in the lobby. Because we find Redd Horne indistinguishable from the case at bar, we find that [this store's] operations constituted an authorization of public performances of [the plaintiffs'] copyrighted works.

5. Based on *Redd Horne* and *Aveco*, would it be a public performance for a store to rent videotapes for customers to take home to watch? Why or why not?

6. What if Maxwell's was a hotel instead of a video store? That is, what result if hotel guests rent a DVD from the hotel and play the DVD in an in-room player? The Ninth Circuit held that this situation does not constitute a public performance of the movie. Columbia Pictures Indus., Inc. v. Prof. Real Estate Investors, Inc., 866 F.2d 278 (9th Cir. 1991). In doing so, it didn't disagree with the Third Circuit but found the facts to be distinguishable. How might a hotel and a video store be different?

The next case, which you first encountered in Chapter II, interprets the second part of the statute's language defining when a performance or display is "public." That second part of the definition is often referred to as the "transmit clause." As you read the case, ask yourself whether the court's holding is guided by the statute's text, or whether the statute leaves the court essentially without guidance.

Cartoon Network LP v. CSC Holdings, Inc.
536 F.3d 121 (2d Cir. 2008)

WALKER, J.:

{Recall the facts of this case from Chapter II.} ...

[1] In the district court, plaintiffs successfully argued that Cablevision's proposed system would directly infringe their copyrights in three ways. First, by briefly storing data in the primary ingest buffer and other data buffers integral to the function of the RS-DVR, Cablevision would make copies of protected works and thereby directly infringe plaintiffs' exclusive right of reproduction under the Copyright Act. Second, by copying programs onto the Arroyo Server hard disks (the "playback copies"), Cablevision would again directly infringe the reproduction right. And third, by transmitting the data from the Arroyo Server hard disks to its RS-DVR customers in response to a "playback" request, Cablevision would directly infringe plaintiffs' exclusive right of public performance. Agreeing with all three arguments, the district court awarded summary

declaratory judgment to plaintiffs and enjoined Cablevision from operating the RS-DVR system without obtaining licenses from the plaintiff copyright holders....

[2] ... [A]s to the public performance right, Cablevision conceded that, during the playback, "the streaming of recorded programming in response to a customer's request is a performance." Cablevision contended, however, that the work was performed not by Cablevision, but by the customer, an argument the district court rejected "for the same reasons that [it] reject[ed] the argument that the customer is 'doing' the copying involved in the RS-DVR." Cablevision also argued that such a playback transmission was not "to the public," and therefore not a public performance as defined in the Copyright Act, because it "emanates from a distinct copy of a program uniquely associated with one customer's set-top box and intended for that customer's exclusive viewing in his or her home." The district court disagreed, noting that "Cablevision would transmit *the same program* to members of the public, who may receive the performance at different times, depending on whether they view the program in real time or at a later time as an RS-DVR playback." ...

[3] We review a district court's grant of summary judgment de novo....

[4] Plaintiffs' ... theory is that Cablevision will violate the Copyright Act by engaging in unauthorized public performances of their works through the playback of the RS-DVR copies. The Act grants a copyright owner the exclusive right, "in the case of ... motion pictures and other audiovisual works, to perform the copyrighted work publicly." 17 U.S.C. § 106(4). Section 101, the definitional section of the Act, explains that

> [t]o perform or display a work "publicly" means (1) to perform or display it at a place open to the public or at any place where a substantial number of persons outside of a normal circle of a family and its social acquaintances is gathered; or (2) to transmit or otherwise communicate a performance or display of the work to a place specified by clause (1) or to the public, by means of any device or process, whether the members of the public capable of receiving the performance or display receive it in the same place or in separate places and at the same time or at different times.

[5] The parties agree that this case does not implicate clause (1). Accordingly, we ask whether these facts satisfy the second, "transmit clause" of the public performance definition: Does Cablevision "transmit ... a performance ... of the work ... to the public"? No one disputes that the RS-DVR playback results in the transmission of a performance of a work—the transmission from the Arroyo Server to the customer's television set. Cablevision contends that ... the transmission is not "to the public" under the transmit clause....

[6] The statute itself does not expressly define the term "performance" or the phrase "to the public." It does explain that a transmission may be "to the public ... whether the members of the public capable of receiving the performance ... receive it in the same place or in separate places and at the same time or at different times." This plain language instructs us that, in determining whether a transmission is "to the public," it is of no moment that the potential recipients of the transmission are in different places, or that they may receive the transmission at different times. The implication from this same language, however, is that it is relevant, in determining whether a transmission is made to the public, to discern who is "capable of receiving" the performance being transmitted. The fact that the statute says "capable of receiving the performance," instead of "capable of receiving the transmission," underscores the fact that a transmission of a performance is itself a performance....

[7] ... [I]t is evident that the transmit clause directs us to examine who precisely is "capable of receiving" a particular transmission of a performance. Cablevision argues that, because each RS-DVR transmission is made using a single unique copy of a work, made by an individual subscriber, one that can be decoded exclusively by that subscriber's cable box, only one subscriber is capable of receiving any given RS-DVR

transmission. This argument accords with the language of the transmit clause, which, as described above, directs us to consider the potential audience of a given transmission. We are unpersuaded by the district court's reasoning and the plaintiffs' arguments that we should consider a larger potential audience in determining whether a transmission is "to the public."

[8] The district court, in deciding whether the RS-DVR playback of a program to a particular customer is "to the public," apparently considered all of Cablevision's customers who subscribe to the channel airing that program and all of Cablevision's RS-DVR subscribers who request a copy of that program. Thus, it concluded that the RS-DVR playbacks constituted public performances because "Cablevision would transmit the *same program* to members of the public, who may receive the performance at different times, depending on whether they view the program in real time or at a later time as an RS-DVR playback." In essence, the district court suggested that, in considering whether a transmission is "to the public," we consider not the potential audience of a particular transmission, but the potential audience of the underlying work (i.e., "the program") whose content is being transmitted.

[9] We cannot reconcile the district court's approach with the language of the transmit clause. That clause speaks of people capable of receiving a particular "transmission" or "performance," and not of the potential audience of a particular "work." Indeed, such an approach would render the "to the public" language surplusage. Doubtless the *potential* audience for every copyrighted audiovisual work is the general public. As a result, any transmission of the content of a copyrighted work would constitute a public performance under the district court's interpretation. But the transmit clause obviously contemplates the existence of non-public transmissions; if it did not, Congress would have stopped drafting that clause after "performance."

[10] On appeal, plaintiffs offer a slight variation of this interpretation. They argue that both in its real-time cablecast and via the RS-DVR playback, Cablevision is in fact transmitting the "same performance" of a given work: the performance of the work that occurs when the programming service supplying Cablevision's content transmits that content to Cablevision and the service's other licensees.

[11] Thus, according to plaintiffs, when Congress says that to perform a work publicly means to transmit ... a performance ... to the public, they really meant "transmit ... the 'original performance' ... to the public." The implication of this theory is that to determine whether a given transmission of a performance is "to the public," we would consider not only the potential audience of that transmission, but also the potential audience of any transmission of the same underlying "original" performance.

[12] Like the district court's interpretation, this view obviates any possibility of a purely private transmission. Furthermore, it makes Cablevision's liability depend, in part, on the actions of legal strangers. Assume that HBO transmits a copyrighted work to both Cablevision and Comcast. Cablevision merely retransmits the work from one Cablevision facility to another, while Comcast retransmits the program to its subscribers. Under plaintiffs' interpretation, Cablevision would still be transmitting the performance to the public, solely because Comcast has transmitted the same underlying performance to the public. Similarly, a hapless customer who records a program in his den and later transmits the recording to a television in his bedroom would be liable for publicly performing the work simply because some other party had once transmitted the same underlying performance to the public.

[13] We do not believe Congress intended such odd results. Although the transmit clause is not a model of clarity, we believe that when Congress speaks of transmitting a performance to the public, it refers to the performance created by the act of transmission. Thus, HBO transmits its own performance of a work when it transmits to Cablevision, and Cablevision transmits its own performance of the same work when it retransmits the feed from HBO....

[14] In sum, none of the arguments advanced by plaintiffs or the district court alters our conclusion that, under the transmit clause, we must examine the potential audience of a given transmission by an alleged infringer to determine whether that transmission is "to the public." And because the RS-DVR system, as designed, only makes transmissions to one subscriber using a copy made by that subscriber, we believe that the universe of people capable of receiving an RS-DVR transmission is the single subscriber whose self-made copy is used to create that transmission.

[15] Plaintiffs contend that it is "wholly irrelevant, in determining the existence of a public performance, whether 'unique' *copies* of the same work are used to make the transmissions." But plaintiffs cite no authority for this contention. And our analysis of the transmit clause suggests that, in general, any factor that limits the *potential* audience of a transmission is relevant.

[16] Furthermore, no transmission of an audiovisual work can be made, we assume, without using a copy of that work: to transmit a performance of a movie, for example, the transmitter generally must obtain a copy of that movie. As a result, in the context of movies, television programs, and other audiovisual works, the right of reproduction can reinforce and protect the right of public performance. If the owner of a copyright believes he is injured by a particular transmission of a performance of his work, he may be able to seek redress not only for the infringing transmission, but also for the underlying copying that facilitated the transmission. Given this interplay between the various rights in this context, it seems quite consistent with the Act to treat a transmission made using Copy A as distinct from one made using Copy B, just as we would treat a transmission made by Cablevision as distinct from an otherwise identical transmission made by Comcast. Both factors—the identity of the transmitter and the source material of the transmission—limit the potential audience of a transmission in this case and are therefore germane in determining whether that transmission is made "to the public."

[17] Indeed, we believe that *Columbia Pictures Industries, Inc. v. Redd Horne, Inc.,* 749 F.2d 154 (3d Cir. 1984), relied on by both plaintiffs and the district court, supports our decision to accord significance to the existence and use of distinct copies in our transmit clause analysis....

[18] The Third Circuit found that defendants' conduct constituted a public performance under both clauses of the statutory definition. In concluding that Maxwell's violated the transmit clause, that court explicitly relied on the fact that defendants showed the same copy of a work seriatim to its clientele, and it quoted a treatise emphasizing the same fact:

> Professor Nimmer's examination of this definition is particularly pertinent: "if the same copy ... of a given work is repeatedly played (i.e., 'performed') by different members of the public, albeit at different times, this constitutes a 'public' performance." 2 M. NIMMER, § 8.14[C][3], at 8–142 (emphasis in original).... Although Maxwell's has only one copy of each film, it shows each copy repeatedly to different members of the public. This constitutes a public performance.

[19] Unfortunately, neither the *Redd Horne* court nor Prof. Nimmer explicitly explains *why* the use of a distinct copy affects the transmit clause inquiry. But our independent analysis confirms the soundness of their intuition: the use of a unique copy may limit the potential audience of a transmission and is therefore relevant to whether that transmission is made "to the public." Plaintiffs' unsupported arguments to the contrary are unavailing....

[20] In sum, we find that the transmit clause directs us to identify the potential audience of a given transmission, i.e., the persons "capable of receiving" it, to determine whether that transmission is made "to the public." Because each RS-DVR playback transmission is made to a single subscriber using a single unique copy produced by that subscriber, we conclude that such transmissions are not performances "to the public,"

and therefore do not infringe any exclusive right of public performance. We base this decision on the application of undisputed facts; thus, Cablevision is entitled to summary judgment on this point.

[21] This holding, we must emphasize, does not generally permit content delivery networks to avoid all copyright liability by making copies of each item of content and associating one unique copy with each subscriber to the network, or by giving their subscribers the capacity to make their own individual copies. We do not address whether such a network operator would be able to escape any other form of copyright liability, such as liability for unauthorized reproductions or liability for contributory infringement....

NOTES

1. Why do you think the network plaintiffs brought this claim against Cablevision? What do you think was the basis of the plaintiffs' objection to the Cablevision remote DVR technology?

2. Why do you think Cablevision chose to offer remote DVR technology to its subscribers rather than conventional "customer premises" DVR technology?

3. If a television network transmits a television program but no one ends up watching it, is the transmission a public performance? Compare that result to whether the performance of a work in someone's home to one other person living in that home is public. Do these results juxtaposed together make sense?

As you read the next opinion, consider whether the Second Circuit's decision in *Cartoon Network* is still good law. Also, do you find the majority or dissent's understanding of "perform" more convincing?

American Broadcasting Companies, Inc. v. Aereo, Inc.
573 U.S. 431 (2014)

BREYER, J.:

[1] The Copyright Act of 1976 gives a copyright owner the "exclusive righ[t]" to "perform the copyrighted work publicly." 17 U.S.C. § 106(4). The Act's Transmit Clause defines that exclusive right as including the right to

> "transmit or otherwise communicate a performance ... of the [copyrighted] work ... to the public, by means of any device or process, whether the members of the public capable of receiving the performance ... receive it in the same place or in separate places and at the same time or at different times." § 101.

[2] We must decide whether respondent Aereo, Inc., infringes this exclusive right by selling its subscribers a technologically complex service that allows them to watch television programs over the Internet at about the same time as the programs are broadcast over the air. We conclude that it does....

[3] For a monthly fee, Aereo offers subscribers broadcast television programming over the Internet, virtually as the programming is being broadcast. Much of this programming is made up of copyrighted works. Aereo neither owns the copyright in those works nor holds a license from the copyright owners to perform those works publicly.

[4] Aereo's system is made up of servers, transcoders, and thousands of dime-sized antennas housed in a central warehouse. It works roughly as follows: First, when a subscriber wants to watch a show that is currently being broadcast, he visits Aereo's website and selects, from a list of the local programming, the show he wishes to see.

Figure 92: Aereo advertisement

Figure 93: Aereo advertisement

[5] Second, one of Aereo's servers selects an antenna, which it dedicates to the use of that subscriber (and that subscriber alone) for the duration of the selected show. A server then tunes the antenna to the over-the-air broadcast carrying the show. The antenna begins to receive the broadcast, and an Aereo transcoder translates the signals received into data that can be transmitted over the Internet.

[6] Third, rather than directly send the data to the subscriber, a server saves the data in a subscriber-specific folder on Aereo's hard drive. In other words, Aereo's system creates a subscriber-specific copy—that is, a "personal" copy—of the subscriber's program of choice.

[7] Fourth, once several seconds of programming have been saved, Aereo's server begins to stream the saved copy of the show to the subscriber over the Internet. (The subscriber may instead direct Aereo to stream the program at a later time, but that aspect of Aereo's service is not before us.) The subscriber can watch the streamed program on the screen of his personal computer, tablet, smart phone, Internet-connected television, or other Internet-connected device. The streaming continues, a mere few seconds behind the over-the-air broadcast, until the subscriber has received the entire show.

[8] Aereo emphasizes that the data that its system streams to each subscriber are the data from his own personal copy, made from the broadcast signals received by the particular antenna allotted to him. Its system does not transmit data saved in one subscriber's folder to any other subscriber. When two subscribers wish to watch the same program, Aereo's system activates two separate antennas and saves two separate copies of the program in two separate folders. It then streams the show to the subscribers through two separate transmissions—each from the subscriber's personal copy....

[9] Petitioners are television producers, marketers, distributors, and broadcasters who own the copyrights in many of the programs that Aereo's system streams to its subscribers. They brought suit against Aereo for copyright infringement in Federal District Court. They sought a preliminary injunction, arguing that Aereo was infringing their right to "perform" their works "publicly," as the Transmit Clause defines those terms.

[10] The District Court denied the preliminary injunction. Relying on prior Circuit precedent [*Cartoon Network*], a divided panel of the Second Circuit affirmed. In the Second Circuit's view, Aereo does not perform publicly within the meaning of the Transmit Clause because it does not transmit "to the public." Rather, each time Aereo streams a program to a subscriber, it sends a *private* transmission that is available only to that subscriber.... We granted certiorari.

[11] This case requires us to answer two questions: First, in operating in the manner described above, does Aereo "perform" at all? And second, if so, does Aereo do so "publicly"? We address these distinct questions in turn.

[12] Does Aereo "perform"? Phrased another way, does Aereo "transmit ... a performance" when a subscriber watches a show using Aereo's system, or is it only the subscriber who transmits? In Aereo's view, it does not perform. It does no more than supply equipment that "emulate[s] the operation of a home antenna and [digital video recorder (DVR)]." Like a home antenna and DVR, Aereo's equipment simply responds to its subscribers' directives. So it is only the subscribers who "perform" when they use Aereo's equipment to stream television programs to themselves.

[13] Considered alone, the language of the Act does not clearly indicate when an entity "perform[s]" (or "transmit[s]") and when it merely supplies equipment that allows others to do so. But when read in light of its purpose, the Act is unmistakable: An entity that engages in activities like Aereo's performs....

[14] History makes plain that one of Congress' primary purposes in amending the Copyright Act in 1976 was to overturn this Court's determination that community antenna television (CATV) systems (the precursors of

350

modern cable systems) fell outside the Act's scope. In *Fortnightly Corp. v. United Artists Television, Inc.*, 392 U.S. 390 (1968), the Court considered a CATV system that carried local television broadcasting, much of which was copyrighted, to its subscribers in two cities. The CATV provider placed antennas on hills above the cities and used coaxial cables to carry the signals received by the antennas to the home television sets of its subscribers. The system amplified and modulated the signals in order to improve their strength and efficiently transmit them to subscribers. A subscriber could choose any of the programs he wished to view by simply turning the knob on his own television set. The CATV provider neither edited the programs received nor originated any programs of its own.

[15] Asked to decide whether the CATV provider infringed copyright holders' exclusive right to perform their works publicly, the Court held that the provider did not "perform" at all. The Court drew a line: "Broadcasters perform. Viewers do not perform." And a CATV provider "falls on the viewer's side of the line."

[16] The Court reasoned that CATV providers were unlike broadcasters:

> *"Broadcasters select the programs to be viewed; CATV systems simply carry, without editing, whatever programs they receive. Broadcasters procure programs and propagate them to the public; CATV systems receive programs that have been released to the public and carry them by private channels to additional viewers."*

[17] Instead, CATV providers were more like viewers, for "the basic function [their] equipment serves is little different from that served by the equipment generally furnished by" viewers. "Essentially," the Court said, "a CATV system no more than enhances the viewer's capacity to receive the broadcaster's signals [by] provid[ing] a well-located antenna with an efficient connection to the viewer's television set." ...

{Discussion of similar *Teleprompter* case omitted} ...

[18] In 1976 Congress amended the Copyright Act in large part to reject the Court's holdings in *Fortnightly* and *Teleprompter*. Congress enacted new language that erased the Court's line between broadcaster and viewer, in respect to "perform[ing]" a work. The amended statute clarifies that to "perform" an audiovisual work means "to show its images in any sequence or to make the sounds accompanying it audible." § 101; *see ibid.* (defining "[a]udiovisual works" as "works that consist of a series of related images which are intrinsically intended to be shown by the use of machines ..., together with accompanying sounds"). Under this new language, *both* the broadcaster *and* the viewer of a television program "perform," because they both show the program's images and make audible the program's sounds.

[19] Congress also enacted the Transmit Clause, which specifies that an entity performs publicly when it "transmit[s] ... a performance ... to the public." § 101; *see ibid.* (defining "[t]o 'transmit' a performance" as "to communicate it by any device or process whereby images or sounds are received beyond the place from which they are sent"). Cable system activities, like those of the CATV systems in *Fortnightly* and *Teleprompter*, lie at the heart of the activities that Congress intended this language to cover. The Clause thus makes clear that an entity that acts like a CATV system itself performs, even if when doing so, it simply enhances viewers' ability to receive broadcast television signals....

[20] This history makes clear that Aereo is not simply an equipment provider. Rather, Aereo, and not just its subscribers, "perform[s]" (or "transmit[s]"). Aereo's activities are substantially similar to those of the CATV companies that Congress amended the Act to reach....

[21] Aereo's equipment may serve a "viewer function"; it may enhance the viewer's ability to receive a broadcaster's programs. It may even emulate equipment a viewer could use at home. But the same was true of the equipment that was before the Court, and ultimately before Congress, in *Fortnightly* and *Teleprompter*.

[22] We recognize, and Aereo and the dissent emphasize, one particular difference between Aereo's system and the cable systems at issue in *Fortnightly* and *Teleprompter*. The systems in those cases transmitted constantly; they sent continuous programming to each subscriber's television set. In contrast, Aereo's system remains inert until a subscriber indicates that she wants to watch a program. Only at that moment, in automatic response to the subscriber's request, does Aereo's system activate an antenna and begin to transmit the requested program.

[23] This is a critical difference, says the dissent. It means that Aereo's subscribers, not Aereo, "selec[t] the copyrighted content" that is "perform[ed]," and for that reason they, not Aereo, "transmit" the performance....

[24] In our view, however, ... [g]iven Aereo's overwhelming likeness to the cable companies targeted by the 1976 amendments, this sole technological difference between Aereo and traditional cable companies does not make a critical difference here. The subscribers of the *Fortnightly* and *Teleprompter* cable systems also selected what programs to display on their receiving sets. Indeed, as we explained in *Fortnightly*, such a subscriber "could choose any of the ... programs he wished to view by simply turning the knob on his own television set." The same is true of an Aereo subscriber. Of course, in *Fortnightly* the television signals, in a sense, lurked behind the screen, ready to emerge when the subscriber turned the knob. Here the signals pursue their ordinary course of travel through the universe until today's "turn of the knob"—a click on a website—activates machinery that intercepts and reroutes them to Aereo's subscribers over the Internet. But this difference means nothing to the subscriber. It means nothing to the broadcaster. We do not see how this single difference, invisible to subscriber and broadcaster alike, could transform a system that is for all practical purposes a traditional cable system into [something else].

[25] In other cases involving different kinds of service or technology providers, a user's involvement in the operation of the provider's equipment and selection of the content transmitted may well bear on whether the provider performs within the meaning of the Act. But the many similarities between Aereo and cable companies, considered in light of Congress' basic purposes in amending the Copyright Act, convince us that this difference is not critical here. We conclude that Aereo is not just an equipment supplier and that Aereo "perform[s]." ...

[26] Next, we must consider whether Aereo performs petitioners' works "publicly," within the meaning of the Transmit Clause. Under the Clause, an entity performs a work publicly when it "transmit[s] ... a performance ... of the work ... to the public." § 101. Aereo denies that it satisfies this definition. It reasons as follows: First, the "performance" it "transmit[s]" is the performance created by its act of transmitting. And second, because each of these performances is capable of being received by one and only one subscriber, Aereo transmits privately, not publicly. Even assuming Aereo's first argument is correct, its second does not follow.

[27] We begin with Aereo's first argument. What performance does Aereo transmit? Under the Act, "[t]o 'transmit' a performance ... is to communicate it by any device or process whereby images or sounds are received beyond the place from which they are sent." And "[t]o 'perform'" an audiovisual work means "to show its images in any sequence or to make the sounds accompanying it audible."

[28] Petitioners say Aereo transmits a *prior* performance of their works. Thus when Aereo retransmits a network's prior broadcast, the underlying broadcast (itself a performance) is the performance that Aereo transmits. Aereo, as discussed above, says the performance it transmits is the *new* performance created by its act of transmitting. That performance comes into existence when Aereo streams the sounds and images of a broadcast program to a subscriber's screen.

[29] We assume *arguendo* that Aereo's first argument is correct. Thus, for present purposes, to transmit a performance of (at least) an audiovisual work means to communicate contemporaneously visible images and contemporaneously audible sounds of the work. When an Aereo subscriber selects a program to watch, Aereo streams the program over the Internet to that subscriber. Aereo thereby "communicate[s]" to the subscriber, by means of a "device or process," the work's images and sounds. And those images and sounds are contemporaneously visible and audible on the subscriber's computer (or other Internet-connected device). So under our assumed definition, Aereo transmits a performance whenever its subscribers watch a program.

[30] But what about the Clause's further requirement that Aereo transmit a performance "to the public"? As we have said, an Aereo subscriber receives broadcast television signals with an antenna dedicated to him alone. Aereo's system makes from those signals a personal copy of the selected program. It streams the content of the copy to the same subscriber and to no one else. One and only one subscriber has the ability to see and hear each Aereo transmission. The fact that each transmission is to only one subscriber, in Aereo's view, means that it does not transmit a performance "to the public."

[31] In terms of the Act's purposes, these differences do not distinguish Aereo's system from cable systems, which do perform "publicly." Viewed in terms of Congress' regulatory objectives, why should any of these technological differences matter? They concern the behind-the-scenes way in which Aereo delivers television programming to its viewers' screens. They do not render Aereo's commercial objective any different from that of cable companies. Nor do they significantly alter the viewing experience of Aereo's subscribers. Why would a subscriber who wishes to watch a television show care much whether images and sounds are delivered to his screen via a large multisubscriber antenna or one small dedicated antenna, whether they arrive instantaneously or after a few seconds' delay, or whether they are transmitted directly or after a personal copy is made? And why, if Aereo is right, could not modern CATV systems simply continue the same commercial and consumer-oriented activities, free of copyright restrictions, provided they substitute such new technologies for old? Congress would as much have intended to protect a copyright holder from the unlicensed activities of Aereo as from those of cable companies.

[32] The text of the Clause effectuates Congress' intent. Aereo's argument to the contrary relies on the premise that "to transmit ... a performance" means to make a single transmission. But the Clause suggests that an entity may transmit a performance through multiple, discrete transmissions. That is because one can "transmit" or "communicate" something through a *set* of actions. Thus one can transmit a message to one's friends, irrespective of whether one sends separate identical e-mails to each friend or a single e-mail to all at once....

[33] The fact that a singular noun ("a performance") follows the words "to transmit" does not suggest the contrary. One can sing a song to his family, whether he sings the same song one-on-one or in front of all together. Similarly, one's colleagues may watch a performance of a particular play—say, this season's modern-dress version of "Measure for Measure"—whether they do so at separate or at the same showings. By the same principle, an entity may transmit a performance through one or several transmissions, where the performance is of the same work.

[34] The Transmit Clause must permit this interpretation, for it provides that one may transmit a performance to the public "whether the members of the public capable of receiving the performance ... receive it ... at the same time or at different times." Were the words "to transmit ... a performance" limited to a single act of communication, members of the public could not receive the performance communicated "at different times." Therefore, in light of the purpose and text of the Clause, we conclude that when an entity communicates the same contemporaneously perceptible images and sounds to multiple people, it transmits a performance to them regardless of the number of discrete communications it makes.

[35] We do not see how the fact that Aereo transmits via personal copies of programs could make a difference. The Act applies to transmissions "by means of any device or process." And retransmitting a television program using user-specific copies is a "process" of transmitting a performance. A "cop[y]" of a work is simply a "material objec[t] ... in which a work is fixed ... and from which the work can be perceived, reproduced, or otherwise communicated." So whether Aereo transmits from the same or separate copies, it performs the same work; it shows the same images and makes audible the same sounds. Therefore, when Aereo streams the same television program to multiple subscribers, it "transmit[s] ... a performance" to all of them.

[36] Moreover, the subscribers to whom Aereo transmits television programs constitute "the public." Aereo communicates the same contemporaneously perceptible images and sounds to a large number of people who are unrelated and unknown to each other. This matters because, although the Act does not define "the public," it specifies that an entity performs publicly when it performs at "any place where a substantial number of persons outside of a normal circle of a family and its social acquaintances is gathered." The Act thereby suggests that "the public" consists of a large group of people outside of a family and friends...

[37] Finally, we note that Aereo's subscribers may receive the same programs at different times and locations. This fact does not help Aereo, however, for the Transmit Clause expressly provides that an entity may perform publicly "whether the members of the public capable of receiving the performance ... receive it in the same place or in separate places and at the same time or at different times." In other words, "the public" need not be situated together, spatially or temporally. For these reasons, we conclude that Aereo transmits a performance of petitioners' copyrighted works to the public, within the meaning of the Transmit Clause....

[38] Aereo and many of its supporting *amici* argue that to apply the Transmit Clause to Aereo's conduct will impose copyright liability on other technologies, including new technologies, that Congress could not possibly have wanted to reach. We agree that Congress, while intending the Transmit Clause to apply broadly to cable companies and their equivalents, did not intend to discourage or to control the emergence or use of different kinds of technologies. But we do not believe that our limited holding today will have that effect.

[39] For one thing, the history of cable broadcast transmissions that led to the enactment of the Transmit Clause informs our conclusion that Aereo "perform[s]," but it does not determine whether different kinds of providers in different contexts also "perform." For another, an entity only transmits a performance when it communicates contemporaneously perceptible images and sounds of a work.

[40] Further, we have interpreted the term "the public" to apply to a group of individuals acting as ordinary members of the public who pay primarily to watch broadcast television programs, many of which are copyrighted.... [I]t does not extend to those who act as owners or possessors of the relevant product. And we have not considered whether the public performance right is infringed when the user of a service pays primarily for something other than the transmission of copyrighted works, such as the remote storage of content. In addition, an entity does not transmit to the public if it does not transmit to a substantial number of people outside of a family and its social circle.

[41] We also note that courts often apply a statute's highly general language in light of the statute's basic purposes. Finally, the doctrine of "fair use" can help to prevent inappropriate or inequitable applications of the Clause.

[42] We cannot now answer more precisely how the Transmit Clause or other provisions of the Copyright Act will apply to technologies not before us. We agree with the Solicitor General that "[q]uestions involving cloud computing, [remote storage] DVRs, and other novel issues not before the Court, as to which 'Congress has not plainly marked [the] course,' should await a case in which they are squarely presented." And we note that,

to the extent commercial actors or other interested entities may be concerned with the relationship between the development and use of such technologies and the Copyright Act, they are of course free to seek action from Congress....

[43] For these reasons, we conclude that Aereo "perform[s]" petitioners' copyrighted works "publicly," as those terms are defined by the Transmit Clause. We therefore reverse the contrary judgment of the Court of Appeals, and we remand the case for further proceedings consistent with this opinion....

SCALIA, J., dissenting.

[44] .... The Networks sued Aereo for several forms of copyright infringement, but we are here concerned with a single claim: that Aereo violates the Networks' "exclusive righ[t]" to "perform" their programs "publicly." That claim fails at the very outset because Aereo does not "perform" at all. The Court manages to reach the opposite conclusion only by disregarding widely accepted rules for service-provider liability and adopting in their place an improvised standard ("looks-like-cable-TV") that will sow confusion for years to come....

[45] There are two types of liability for copyright infringement: direct and secondary. As its name suggests, the former applies when an actor personally engages in infringing conduct. Secondary liability, by contrast, is a means of holding defendants responsible for infringement by third parties, even when the defendants have not themselves engaged in the infringing activity. It applies when a defendant intentionally induces or encourages infringing acts by others or profits from such acts while declining to exercise a right to stop or limit them]. {You will learn about direct and secondary liability in detail in Chapter VII.} ...

[46] .... The Networks claim that Aereo *directly* infringes their public-performance right. Accordingly, the Networks must prove that Aereo "perform[s]" copyrighted works when its subscribers log in, select a channel, and push the "watch" button. That process undoubtedly results in a performance; the question is *who* does the performing. If Aereo's subscribers perform but Aereo does not, the claim necessarily fails.

{The dissent goes on to make the case that Aereo's subscribers perform but Aereo does not (because Aereo does not choose the content), so Aereo cannot be held liable for directly infringing the public-performance right.} ...

[47] Making matters worse, the Court provides no criteria for determining when its cable-TV-lookalike rule applies. Must a defendant offer access to live television to qualify? If similarity to cable-television service is the measure, then the answer must be yes. But consider the implications of that answer: Aereo would be free to do exactly what it is doing right now so long as it built mandatory time shifting into its "watch" function.[6] ... Assuming the Court does not intend to adopt such a do-nothing rule (though it very well may), there must be some other means of identifying who is and is not subject to its guilt-by-resemblance regime.

[48] Two other criteria come to mind. One would cover any automated service that captures and stores live television broadcasts at a user's direction. That can't be right, since it is exactly what remote storage digital video recorders (RS-DVRs) do, and the Court insists that its "limited holding" does not decide the fate of those devices. The other potential benchmark is the one offered by the Government: The cable-TV-lookalike rule embraces any entity that "operates an integrated system, substantially dependent on physical equipment that is used in common by [its] subscribers." The Court sensibly avoids that approach because it would sweep in Internet service providers and a host of other entities that quite obviously do not perform.

---

[6] Broadcasts accessible through the "watch" function are technically not live because Aereo's servers take anywhere from a few seconds to a few minutes to begin transmitting data to a subscriber's device. But the resulting delay is so brief that it cannot reasonably be classified as time shifting.

[49] That leaves as the criterion of cable-TV-resemblance nothing but th'ol' totality-of-the-circumstances test (which is not a test at all but merely assertion of an intent to perform test-free, ad hoc, case-by-case evaluation). It will take years, perhaps decades, to determine which automated systems now in existence are governed by the traditional volitional-conduct test and which get the Aereo treatment. (And automated systems now in contemplation will have to take their chances.) The Court vows that its ruling will not affect cloud-storage providers and cable-television systems, but it cannot deliver on that promise given the imprecision of its result-driven rule....

[50] I share the Court's evident feeling that what Aereo is doing (or enabling to be done) to the Networks' copyrighted programming ought not to be allowed. But perhaps we need not distort the Copyright Act to forbid it. As discussed at the outset, Aereo's secondary liability for performance infringement is yet to be determined, as is its primary and secondary liability for reproduction infringement. If that does not suffice, then (assuming one shares the majority's estimation of right and wrong) what we have before us must be considered a "loophole" in the law. It is not the role of this Court to identify and plug loopholes. It is the role of good lawyers to identify and exploit them, and the role of Congress to eliminate them if it wishes. Congress can do that, I may add, in a much more targeted, better informed, and less disruptive fashion than the crude "looks-like-cable-TV" solution the Court invents today.

[51] We came within one vote of declaring the VCR contraband 30 years ago in *Sony Corp. of America v. Universal City Studios, Inc.*, 464 U.S. 417 (1984). {You will read this case in both Chapters VI and VII.} The dissent in that case was driven in part by the plaintiffs' prediction that VCR technology would wreak all manner of havoc in the television and movie industries.

[52] The Networks make similarly dire predictions about Aereo. We are told that nothing less than "the very existence of broadcast television as we know it" is at stake. Aereo and its *amici* dispute those forecasts and make a few of their own, suggesting that a decision in the Networks' favor will stifle technological innovation and imperil billions of dollars of investments in cloud-storage services. We are in no position to judge the validity of those self-interested claims or to foresee the path of future technological development. Hence, the proper course is not to bend and twist the Act's terms in an effort to produce a just outcome, but to apply the law as it stands and leave to Congress the task of deciding whether the Copyright Act needs an upgrade. I conclude, as the Court concluded in *Sony*: "It may well be that Congress will take a fresh look at this new technology, just as it so often has examined other innovations in the past. But it is not our job to apply laws that have not yet been written. Applying the copyright statute, as it now reads, to the facts as they have been developed in this case, the judgment of the Court of Appeals must be [affirmed]."

[53] I respectfully dissent.

NOTES

1. Consider the same question about the plaintiffs' motivations in *Aereo* that was raised above about *Cartoon Network*: What is it about the Aereo service that led the plaintiffs to file a copyright lawsuit? Does the Aereo service threaten the plaintiffs' business model?

2. Does the holding in *Cartoon Network* survive *Aereo*? The majority opinion in *Aereo* does not deal with *Cartoon Network* explicitly. For what it's worth, neither Westlaw nor LEXIS treat *Cartoon Network* as having been overruled. Is this right? If *Cartoon Network* has not been overruled, then what is the holding of *Aereo*?

3. Do you side with the majority or with Justice Scalia regarding whether Aereo "performs" plaintiffs' copyrighted works? What do you think of Justice Scalia's critique of the majority's opinion as "guilt by resemblance"?

4. Justice Scalia also lambastes the majority for departing from copyright precedent regarding "volition"—that is, regarding who is responsible for the creation of the potentially infringing public performances. In Justice Scalia's view, it is Aereo's *customers*, and not Aereo itself, who have exercised the volition that results in the performances that plaintiffs claim infringe. That fact is significant because volition separates *direct* infringers from those who may be *secondarily* liable. As you shall see in Chapter VII, the grounds upon which one may be found secondarily liable for copyright infringement are narrower than the grounds for direct liability.

5. One solution to the concerns posed by new technologies is compulsory licensing. As discussed below in this section, § 111 of the Copyright Act provides compulsory licensing for certain cable retransmissions of broadcast television signals, with the licensing fee set by a statutory formula. Section 119 does the same for satellite retransmissions of local broadcasts. Would a compulsory license be a helpful outcome for Aereo?

The next case concerns public performance/display liability for placing copyrighted material (without authorization) on a publicly-available website. As you likely recall, such unauthorized use may implicate the reproduction, distribution, and derivative-work rights. Here, the court examines potential liability under the public-display right. As you read the case, consider what this case tells you about the likely success of infringement claims against online intermediaries, like search engines or social media platforms, based on claims of unauthorized public display.

Perfect 10, Inc. v. Amazon.com, Inc.

508 F.3d 1146 (9th Cir. 2007)

IKUTA, J.:

[1] In this appeal, we consider a copyright owner's efforts to stop an Internet search engine from facilitating access to infringing images. Perfect 10, Inc. sued Google Inc., for infringing Perfect 10's copyrighted photographs of nude models, among other claims. Perfect 10 brought a similar action against Amazon.com .... The district court preliminarily enjoined Google from creating and publicly displaying thumbnail versions of Perfect 10's images, but did not enjoin Google from linking to third-party websites that display infringing full-size versions of Perfect 10's images. Nor did the district court preliminarily enjoin Amazon.com from giving users access to information provided by Google. Perfect 10 and Google both appeal the district court's order....

[2] The Google search engine that provides responses in the form of images is called "Google Image Search." In response to a search query, Google Image Search identifies text in its database responsive to the query and then communicates to users the images associated with the relevant text. Google's software cannot recognize and index the images themselves. Google Image Search provides search results as a webpage of small images called "thumbnails," which are stored in Google's servers. The thumbnail images are reduced, lower-resolution versions of full-sized images stored on third-party computers.

[3] When a user clicks on a thumbnail image, the user's browser program interprets HTML instructions on Google's webpage. These HTML instructions direct the user's browser to cause a rectangular area (a "window") to appear on the user's computer screen. The window has two separate areas of information. The browser fills the top section of the screen with information from the Google webpage, including the

thumbnail image and text. The HTML instructions also give the user's browser the address of the website publisher's computer that stores the full-size version of the thumbnail. By following the HTML instructions to access the third-party webpage, the user's browser connects to the website publisher's computer, downloads the full-size image, and makes the image appear at the bottom of the window on the user's screen. Google does not store the images that fill this lower part of the window and does not communicate the images to the user; Google simply provides HTML instructions directing a user's browser to access a third-party website. However, the top part of the window (containing the information from the Google webpage) appears to frame and comment on the bottom part of the window. Thus, the user's window appears to be filled with a single integrated presentation of the full-size image, but it is actually an image from a third-party website framed by information from Google's website. The process by which the webpage directs a user's browser to incorporate content from different computers into a single window is referred to as "in-line linking." The term "framing" refers to the process by which information from one computer appears to frame and annotate the in-line linked content from another computer.

[4] Google also stores webpage content in its cache. For each cached webpage, Google's cache contains the text of the webpage as it appeared at the time Google indexed the page, but does not store images from the webpage....

[5] Perfect 10 markets and sells copyrighted images of nude models. Among other enterprises, it operates a subscription website on the Internet. Subscribers pay a monthly fee to view Perfect 10 images in a "members' area" of the site. Subscribers must use a password to log into the members' area. Google does not include these password-protected images from the members' area in Google's index or database. Perfect 10 has also licensed Fonestarz Media Limited to sell and distribute Perfect 10's reduced-size copyrighted images for download and use on cell phones.

[6] Some website publishers republish Perfect 10's images on the Internet without authorization. Once this occurs, Google's search engine may automatically index the webpages containing these images and provide thumbnail versions of images in response to user inquiries. When a user clicks on the thumbnail image returned by Google's search engine, the user's browser accesses the third-party webpage and in-line links to the full-sized infringing image stored on the website publisher's computer. This image appears, in its original context, on the lower portion of the window on the user's computer screen framed by information from Google's webpage....

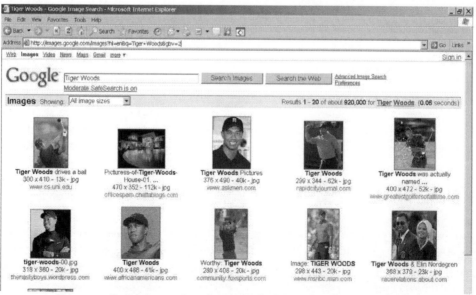

Figure 94: Google Image Search (as it looked during *Perfect 10* litigation)

Figure 95: Google Image Search (as it looked during *Perfect 10* litigation)

[7] Perfect 10 claims that Google's search engine program directly infringes two exclusive rights granted to copyright holders: its display rights and its distribution rights....

[8] The district court held that Perfect 10 was likely to prevail in its claim that Google violated Perfect 10's display right with respect to the infringing thumbnails. However, the district court concluded that Perfect 10 was not likely to prevail on its claim that Google violated either Perfect 10's display or distribution right with respect to its full-size infringing images. We review these rulings for an abuse of discretion....

[9] In considering whether Perfect 10 made a prima facie case of violation of its display right, the district court reasoned that a computer owner that stores an image as electronic information and serves that electronic information directly to the user ... is displaying the electronic information in violation of a copyright holder's exclusive display right. Conversely, the owner of a computer that does not store and serve the electronic information to a user is not displaying that information, even if such owner in-line links to or frames the electronic information. The district court referred to this test as the "server test."

[10] Applying the server test, the district court concluded that Perfect 10 was likely to succeed in its claim that Google's thumbnails constituted direct infringement but was unlikely to succeed in its claim that Google's in-line linking to full-size infringing images constituted a direct infringement. As explained below, because this analysis comports with the language of the Copyright Act, we agree with the district court's resolution of both these issues.

[11] We have not previously addressed the question when a computer displays a copyrighted work for purposes of section 106(5). Section 106(5) states that a copyright owner has the exclusive right "to display the copyrighted work publicly." The Copyright Act explains that "display" means "to show a copy of it, either directly or by means of a film, slide, television image, or any other device or process...." 17 U.S.C. § 101. Section 101 defines "copies" as "material objects, other than phonorecords, in which a work is fixed by any

method now known or later developed, and from which the work can be perceived, reproduced, or otherwise communicated, either directly or with the aid of a machine or device." Finally, the Copyright Act provides that "[a] work is 'fixed' in a tangible medium of expression when its embodiment in a copy or phonorecord, by or under the authority of the author, is sufficiently permanent or stable to permit it to be perceived, reproduced, or otherwise communicated for a period of more than transitory duration."

[12] We must now apply these definitions to the facts of this case. A photographic image is a work that is "'fixed' in a tangible medium of expression," for purposes of the Copyright Act, when embodied (i.e., stored) in a computer's server (or hard disk, or other storage device). The image stored in the computer is the "copy" of the work for purposes of copyright law. The computer owner shows a copy "by means of a ... device or process" when the owner uses the computer to fill the computer screen with the photographic image stored on that computer, or by communicating the stored image electronically to another person's computer. In sum, based on the plain language of the statute, a person displays a photographic image by using a computer to fill a computer screen with a copy of the photographic image fixed in the computer's memory. There is no dispute that Google's computers store thumbnail versions of Perfect 10's copyrighted images and communicate copies of those thumbnails to Google's users.[6] Therefore, Perfect 10 has made a prima facie case that Google's communication of its stored thumbnail images directly infringes Perfect 10's display right.

[13] Google does not, however, display a copy of full-size infringing photographic images for purposes of the Copyright Act when Google frames in-line linked images that appear on a user's computer screen. Because Google's computers do not store the photographic images, Google does not have a copy of the images for purposes of the Copyright Act. In other words, Google does not have any "material objects ... in which a work is fixed ... and from which the work can be perceived, reproduced, or otherwise communicated" and thus cannot communicate a copy.

[14] Instead of communicating a copy of the image, Google provides HTML instructions that direct a user's browser to a website publisher's computer that stores the full-size photographic image. Providing these HTML instructions is not equivalent to showing a copy. First, the HTML instructions are lines of text, not a photographic image. Second, HTML instructions do not themselves cause infringing images to appear on the user's computer screen. The HTML merely gives the address of the image to the user's browser. The browser then interacts with the computer that stores the infringing image. It is this interaction that causes an infringing image to appear on the user's computer screen. Google may facilitate the user's access to infringing images. However, such assistance raises only contributory liability issues and does not constitute direct infringement of the copyright owner's display rights.

[15] Perfect 10 argues that Google displays a copy of the full-size images by framing the full-size images, which gives the impression that Google is showing the image within a single Google webpage. While in-line linking and framing may cause some computer users to believe they are viewing a single Google webpage, the Copyright Act, unlike the Trademark Act, does not protect a copyright holder against acts that cause consumer confusion....

[16] Because Google's cache merely stores the text of webpages, our analysis of whether Google's search engine program potentially infringes Perfect 10's display and distribution rights is equally applicable to Google's cache. Perfect 10 is not likely to succeed in showing that a cached webpage that in-line links to full-size infringing images violates such rights. For purposes of this analysis, it is irrelevant whether cache copies

---

[6] Because Google initiates and controls the storage and communication of these thumbnail images, we do not address whether an entity that merely passively owns and manages an Internet bulletin board or similar system violates a copyright owner's display and distribution rights when the users of the bulletin board or similar system post infringing works.

direct a user's browser to third-party images that are no longer available on the third party's website, because it is the website publisher's computer, rather than Google's computer, that stores and displays the infringing image....

NOTES

1. The court held that under the Copyright Act's plain language, Google does not display full-sized "copies" of plaintiff's images because Google does not *store* full-sized copies of those images; it merely causes a copy stored elsewhere to be displayed on the user's screen. Do you agree with this reading of the statutory text?

2. The Ninth Circuit effectively adopts a "server test"—public display by entity *X* of content stored on entity *Y*'s server is not a public display of a "copy" for which entity *X* can be held liable. If you don't believe that approach is mandated by the text of the Copyright Act (see question 1 above), do you believe the approach is good policy? Should it matter whether the user perceives entity *X* as presenting the display regardless of where the copy is located?

3. Decisions from the U.S. District Court for the Southern District of New York reject the server test, holding instead that the public-display right is violated whenever a defendant "incorporates" a copyrighted image into a public display, even if the image is stored elsewhere. *See* Goldman v. Breitbart News Network, LLC, 302 F. Supp. 3d 585 (S.D.N.Y. 2018); Nicklen v. Sinclair Broad. Grp., 551 F. Supp. 3d 188 (S.D.N.Y. 2021). In *Goldman*, a tweet containing a copyrighted photo was embedded in news stories on the defendants' websites. The court rejected the server test, holding that "the plain language of the Copyright Act, the legislative history undergirding its enactment, and subsequent Supreme Court jurisprudence provide no basis for a rule that allows the physical location or possession of an image to determine who may or may not have 'displayed' a work within the meaning of the Copyright Act." The court also invoked *Aereo*, stating that "[a]t heart, the Court's holding eschewed the notion that Aereo should be absolved of liability based upon purely technical distinctions," and characterizing the "server test" as itself a purely technical distinction. Do you agree with the *Goldman* court's decision? What are its potential practical implications?

In addition to the generally-applicable fair use limitation contained in § 107 that you will learn about in Chapter VI, the Copyright Act contains several specific statutory limitations to the scope of the public-performance and display rights. These are set out in §§ 109(c), 110, 111(d), and 119.

Section 109(c) limits the public-display right as follows:

> *Notwithstanding the provisions of section 106(5), the owner of a particular copy lawfully made under this title, or any person authorized by such owner, is entitled, without the authority of the copyright owner, to display that copy publicly, either directly or by the projection of no more than one image at a time, to viewers present at the place where the copy is located.*

Note that § 109(c) limits the copyright owner's public-display right, but only with respect to displays made by an *owner* of a *lawful* copy of the work, or by those *authorized by such an owner*. One merely in possession of a copy or one who does not have permission from an owner of a lawful copy to display it is not protected by § 109(c). Nor is an owner of a lawful copy permitted to transmit an image of the copy to another location for display. Section 109(c) is essentially a variation on the first-sale doctrine's limitation on the distribution right, but for the public-display right. Because of this limitation, there are few cases alleging infringement of the public-display right.

Section 110's limitations on the public-performance and display rights stem from the history of these rights. The 1909 Copyright Act granted public-performance rights, but only for dramatic and musical compositions, and limited the scope of the right to public performances "for profit." Act of Mar. 4, 1909, ch. 320, § 1. Courts were called upon to answer difficult line-drawing questions about which performances were for profit. Notably, the Supreme Court held that background music played in a restaurant is "for profit" for purposes of the Act. Herbert v. Shanley Co., 242 U.S. 591 (1917). The Court reasoned that even if customers don't pay admission to the restaurant or pay directly for the music, they are paying for the total experience at the restaurant rather than just the food, which can likely be had more cheaply elsewhere. Why do you think the law distinguished between performances for profit and those that were not?

The 1976 Copyright Act removed the "for profit" requirement out of the concern that it was too difficult to determine which performances are for profit. H.R. REP. NO. 1476, 94th Cong., 2d Sess. 47, at 62-63 (1976). As you saw above from your study of the public-performance right as set out in § 106(4), Congress broadened liability under the right. Additionally, Congress opted to provide specific exemptions for performances (and displays) that were customarily regarded as lawful, typically because they were viewed as not being done for profit.

In that vein, § 110 provides a series of exceptions to the public-performance and display rights for certain not-for-profit uses. Perhaps the most consequential of these are the so-called "homestyle" exception contained in § 110(5)(A) and the exception for small commercial establishments contained in § 110(5)(B).

The "homestyle" exception set out in § 110(5)(A) exempts from the public-performance and display rights "communication of a transmission embodying a performance or display of a work by the public reception of the transmission *on a single receiving apparatus of a kind commonly used in private homes*, unless—

> (i) a direct charge is made to see or hear the transmission; or
> (ii) the transmission thus received is further transmitted to the public."

(emphasis added). There has been some litigation over what sort of equipment qualifies as the "kind commonly used in private homes." In *NFL v. McBee & Bruno's, Inc.*, 792 F.2d 726 (8th Cir. 1986), the Eighth Circuit held that bars using a type of satellite reception equipment most commonly used in commercial settings to provide public performances of copyrighted NFL broadcasts were not entitled to claim the shelter of the homestyle provision.

The exception for small commercial establishments set out in § 110(5)(B) provides an exception to the public-performance and display rights limited to "nondramatic musical work[s] intended to be received by the general public, originated by a radio or television broadcast station licensed as such by the Federal Communications Commission, or, if an audiovisual transmission, by a cable system or satellite carrier," if certain conditions are met regarding the total square footage of the establishment's premises and the type of equipment used. Please review § 110(5)(B) for details.

Section 110 also contains other exceptions to the public-performance and display rights, including but not limited to the following:

- Section 110(1): "performance or display of a work by instructors or pupils in the course of face-to-face teaching activities of a nonprofit educational institution, in a classroom or similar place devoted to instruction, unless, in the case of a motion picture or other audiovisual work, the performance, or the display of individual images, is given by means of a copy that was not lawfully made under this title, and that the person responsible for the performance knew or had reason to believe was not lawfully made";
- Section 110(2): performance or display, with certain restrictions, of a work used as part of a governmental or non-profit distance education program;

- Section 110(3): "performance of a nondramatic literary or musical work or of a dramatico-musical work of a religious nature, or display of a work, in the course of services at a place of worship or other religious assembly";
- Section 110(4): performance, without a direct or indirect admission charge and subject to additional conditions, of a nondramatic literary or musical work otherwise than in a transmission to the public, without any purpose of direct or indirect commercial advantage and without payment of any fee or other compensation for the performance to any of its performers, promoters, or organizers;
- Section 110(6): "performance of a nondramatic musical work by a governmental body or a nonprofit agricultural or horticultural organization, in the course of an annual agricultural or horticultural fair or exhibition conducted by such body or organization"
- Section 110(8): "performance of a nondramatic literary work, by or in the course of a transmission specifically designed for and primarily directed to blind or other handicapped persons who are unable to read normal printed material as a result of their handicap, or deaf or other handicapped persons who are unable to hear the aural signals accompanying a transmission of visual signals, if the performance is made without any purpose of direct or indirect commercial advantage and its transmission is made through the facilities of: (i) a governmental body; or (ii) a noncommercial educational broadcast station ...; or (iii) a radio subcarrier authorization ...; or (iv) a cable system";
- Section 110(10): "performance of a nondramatic literary or musical work in the course of a social function which is organized and promoted by a nonprofit veterans' organization or a nonprofit fraternal organization to which the general public is not invited, but not including the invitees of the organizations, if the proceeds from the performance, after deducting the reasonable costs of producing the performance, are used exclusively for charitable purposes and not for financial gain"

Is there any thread that ties these exceptions together coherently? Or are these a hodgepodge of special indulgences that are the product of interest group lobbying?

Section 111 limits public-performance and display rights by subjecting to a compulsory license the retransmission by cable systems of certain distant, non-network broadcast television signals. Section 111 establishes a compulsory license fee, which is calculated according to a formula set out in the statute, and payable by cable operators to the Copyright Office (revenues collected are later divided among broadcasters, professional sports leagues, and individual copyright claimants). Section 119 provides a broadly similar compulsory-license scheme that applies to satellite systems meant for home viewing.

Note that the Second Circuit has held that the § 111 license is not available to internet services that capture broadcast signals and retransmit them to subscribers, because such services do not qualify as "cable system[s]" entitled to access the compulsory license. Section 111(f)(3) defines a "cable system" as:

> a facility, located in any State, territory, trust territory, or possession of the United States, that in whole or in part receives signals transmitted or programs broadcast by one or more television broadcast stations licensed by the Federal Communications Commission, and makes secondary transmissions of such signals or programs by wires, cables, microwave, or other communications channels to subscribing members of the public who pay for such service.

The Second Circuit held, in *WPIX, Inc. v. ivi, Inc.*, 691 F.3d 275 (2d Cir. 2012), that an internet-based service that retransmits broadcast signals does not fall within this definition:

The legislative history indicates that Congress enacted § 111 with the intent to address the issue of poor television reception, or, more specifically, to mitigate the difficulties that certain communities and households faced in receiving over-the-air broadcast signals by enabling the expansion of cable systems.

Through § 111's compulsory license scheme, Congress intended to support localized—rather than nationwide—systems that use cable or optical fibers to transmit signals through a physical, point-to-point connection between a transmission facility and the television sets of individual subscribers.

Congress did not, however, intend for § 111's compulsory license to extend to Internet transmissions. Indeed, the legislative history indicates that if Congress had intended to extend § 111's compulsory license to Internet retransmissions, it would have done so expressly—either through the language of § 111 as it did for microwave retransmissions or by codifying a separate statutory provision as it did for satellite carriers.

Extending § 111's compulsory license to Internet retransmissions, moreover, would not fulfill or further Congress's statutory purpose. Internet retransmission services are not seeking to address issues of reception and remote access to over-the-air television signals. They provide not a local but a nationwide (arguably international) service.

H. Music Industry

No area of copyright law is more complex, or productive of more controversy over recent decades, than the tangle of copyright rules and industry practices that govern the music industry. In this section, we will discuss the provisions of the Copyright Act that bear on the music industry. Just as importantly, we will discuss the institutions that have sprung up within the music industry to facilitate interactions between rightsholders and those who wish to license rights.

Copyright in Musical Compositions Versus Copyright in Sound Recordings

If there is one basic fact that must be absorbed to understand the complex workings of copyright in the music industry, it is the distinction between musical compositions and sound recordings.

One might think of musical compositions—or what people in the industry refer to as "musical works" or "songs"—as the sheet music or the instructions for performing the song.

The sound recording, on the other hand, is a fixation in a phonorecord of a specific performance of a song. Section 101 of the Copyright Act defines "phonorecords" as

> *material objects in which sounds, other than those accompanying a motion picture or other audiovisual work, are fixed by any method now known or later developed, and from which the sounds can be perceived, reproduced, or otherwise communicated, either directly or with the aid of a machine or device.*

Interestingly, sound recordings were not protected at all by federal copyright law until 1972. Before that date, sound recordings were protected, if at all, only by state law, and pre-1972 sound recordings remained protected only by state law until the 2018 passage of the Music Modernization Act ("MMA"), which, as we shall see, establishes a limited *sui generis* right in pre-1972 sound recordings.

Sound recordings "embody" musical compositions. There can be (and often is) more than one sound recording of a particular musical composition. Indeed, for popular compositions, there may be hundreds or even thousands of sound recordings that "embody" that musical composition.

Here's an example. In 1999, Tom Waits and Kathleen Brennan wrote the song "Georgia Lee." Waits and Brennan co-own the copyright in the musical composition (or at least they co-owned that copyright initially and then assigned it to a music publishing company, but more on that shortly). Tom Waits also recorded "Georgia Lee"; it is a track on his 1999 album, *Mule Variations*. Tom Waits owns the copyright in that sound recording (or at least he owned that copyright initially and then assigned it to a record label, but more on that shortly as well).

In 2019, Phoebe Bridgers also recorded a version of "Georgia Lee" (it is a track on the 2019 album, *Come On Up to the House: Women Sing Waits*). Phoebe Bridgers owns the copyright in her sound recording of "Georgia Lee" (or at least she did initially). As you shall see, under the Copyright Act, Bridgers is entitled, once certain conditions are satisfied, to record her own version of the Waits/Brennan musical composition. She need not ask permission of the copyright owners in the Waits/Brennan composition.

This may all be a bit clearer with more detail regarding (1) the rights given to the owners of musical compositions and sound recordings, and (2) the way in which these rights are licensed in the music industry. Take a good look at this chart, which comes from the U.S. Copyright Office, and which sets out the current licensing structure in the music industry.

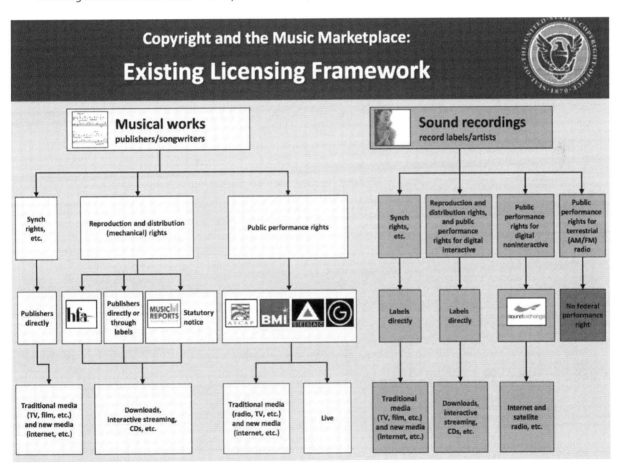

Chapter V – Exclusive Rights

Musical Compositions

Ownership

Initial ownership of copyrights in musical compositions typically vests in the songwriter (or songwriters) as author (or authors) of those works. Sometimes, musical compositions are created as works made for hire by an employee acting within the scope of their employment. In such an instance, the author and initial owner is the songwriter's employer.

Traditionally, songwriters have relied on **music publishing companies** to manage the exploitation of their musical compositions. In the past, songwriters typically transferred ownership of their musical compositions to a music publishing company in exchange for 50% of all licensing royalties. More recently, some songwriters have begun to explore other options, such as the use of publishing "administrators" who handle licensing negotiations, recordkeeping, and collection, but who do not take ownership of the songwriter's copyright.

Statutory Rights of the Copyright Owners in Musical Compositions

The owners of copyrights in musical compositions enjoy all the rights granted in §§ 106(1)-(5)—the exclusive rights to make or authorize reproduction, derivative works, distribution of copies, public performances, and public displays.

Reproduction and Distribution, and the § 115 Compulsory License

The reproduction and distribution rights of copyright owners in *non-dramatic* musical compositions are subject to the **§ 115 compulsory license**. Section 115 does not apply to *dramatic* musical compositions, like operas, in which the main motivation is the telling of a story, and the music serves to enhance the plot. You should review the statutory text of § 115 carefully.

Under the terms of § 115, anyone who wishes to make a **mechanical reproduction** of a copyrighted musical composition—that is, to fix that composition in a phonorecord—is entitled to do so in exchange for payment of a statutory fee. Note that "mechanical reproduction" is a term of art that refers to fixation of a musical composition in any form of phonorecord, whether that phonorecord is made in the form of a CD, a vinyl record, or a download (which § 115 refers to as a "digital phonorecord delivery" or "DPD").

There are two basic scenarios in which mechanical reproductions are made under the terms of the § 115 license. First is when a composition is fixed in a new recording by a recording artist who does not own the copyright in that composition. This is referred to, colloquially, as a **cover**. Second is when an existing recording is reproduced and distributed in the form of a phonorecord by an entity—such as a music download service—that lacks some other form of agreement (such as a direct license from the music publisher that owns the relevant composition copyright) that authorizes this reproduction and distribution.

A § 115 compulsory license for a particular musical composition is available only after that composition has been fixed in a phonorecord created under the authority of the owner of the copyright in the musical composition, and copies of that authorized phonorecord have been distributed to the public. *See* 17 U.S.C. § 115(a)(1).

Once that happens, anyone who wishes to make a sound recording that embodies a copyrighted musical composition—that is, to fix a recording that performs that composition—is entitled to do so without the need to obtain permission from the owner of the copyright in the musical composition. Note that the sound recording made under the authority of the § 115 compulsory license must not "change the basic melody or fundamental character" of the composition it embodies, although the compulsory license "includes the privilege of making a musical arrangement of the work to the extent necessary to conform it to the style or manner of interpretation of the performance involved." *Id.* § 115(a)(2). Note also that any arrangement of the composition made under the authority of § 115 cannot be copyrighted as a derivative work without the consent of the copyright owner in the original composition. *Id.*

The § 115 compulsory license may be obtained by service of a "notice of intention"—often referred to as an NOI—on the owner of the copyright in the musical composition, or, if the owner is unknown, on the Copyright Office. *Id.* § 115(b)(1). Section 115 also provides a set of procedures for paying compulsory license fees to copyright owners. *See Id.* §§ 115(c)(5)-(6). It is important to understand, however, that the specific procedures for obtaining the compulsory license that are set forth in § 115 are *not mandatory.* Section 115 makes clear that copyright owners in nondramatic musical compositions and those who wish to obtain a compulsory license to embody that composition in a phonorecord "may negotiate and agree upon the terms and rates of royalty payments under this section." *Id.* § 115(c)(3)(B). And, as you shall soon see, in practice copyright owners and the recipients of compulsory licenses often do vary those terms and rates.

The statutory fee under § 115 is set currently at 9.1 cents per copy of the sound recording embodying the musical composition or 1.75 cents per minute of playing time (or fraction thereof), whichever is greater. Rates are subject to revision from time to time by Copyright Royalty Judges.

Music Streaming Services and § 115 Compulsory Licenses

Note that recently there has been significant dispute over whether streaming services need to obtain § 115 compulsory licenses. Streaming does not, in itself, involve the reproduction or distribution of fixed copies, and so would not require a mechanical license. The argument that streaming services must obtain mechanical licenses focuses on the services' offering of various forms of temporary downloads— for example, downloads that persist on the user's device for as long as the user remains a subscriber to the streaming service.

The Copyright Office has promulgated regulations regarding such temporary downloads, although it is not clear whether the particular forms of download offered by streaming services fit within the regulatory definitions. In the shadow of this considerable uncertainty, streaming services have been obtaining compulsory licenses according to rates set by the Copyright Royalty Board, a panel comprised of three Copyright Royalty Judges appointed by the Librarian of Congress. There are a number of ongoing lawsuits regarding the means by which certain of the music streaming services have sought to obtain § 115 compulsory licenses.[*]

Intermediaries Aiding in Administration of the § 115 Compulsory License

Some licensees use the statutory NOI process to obtain the § 115 compulsory license, either issuing NOIs themselves or using an agent like Music Reports, Inc. to do so. But most licensees do not obtain the § 115 compulsory license through the NOI process. Instead, they have historically contracted with the Harry Fox Agency, a New York City-based firm, founded in 1927, which has long acted as a middleman between a large number of "affiliated" owners of copyrighted musical compositions and those seeking compulsory licenses. (Note, however, that with the advent of the Music Modernization Act, discussed below, that Harry Fox's role is shrinking.)

---

[*] One of the authors of this casebook (Sprigman) served as counsel to a streaming service involved in this litigation, now settled. Everything that has been written here about this subject comes from publicly-available sources, and not from anything learned in the course of that representation.

Harry Fox offers § 115 compulsory licenses according to terms and rates that differ from the § 115 terms and rates. (Recall that § 115 specifically permits the parties to a compulsory license to negotiate terms and rates that are different from the defaults set out in § 115.) In particular, § 115 compulsory licenses granted through the Harry Fox "affiliate" licensing process do not adhere to the detailed payment and accounting rules set out in § 115. Rather, Harry Fox administers affiliate licenses according to a relatively streamlined payment and accounting process. Additionally, Harry Fox affiliate licenses are often issued at a rate substantially *below* the statutory rate. (Note that for music publishers who are not affiliates, Harry Fox also obtains compulsory licenses for clients using the NOI process, although according to terms that, again, differ in some respects from the statutory default.)

NOTES

1. The Copyright Act provides copyright owners with exclusive rights that are structured as what economists refer to as *property rules*—rules that exclude others from uses that implicate the copyright owner's exclusive rights unless the copyright owner grants permission. That permission is likely to be granted only when the parties agree on a mutually-acceptable licensing fee. On the other hand, the § 115 compulsory license sets up what economists refer to as a *liability rule*—the compulsory license allows use of copyrighted musical compositions without the need to obtain the copyright owner's permission and in exchange for a fee that is set according to a statutory formula. Seen in this perspective, the § 115 license appears anomalous. So why does copyright law have it?

The history behind the compulsory license started in the 1890s, with, of all things, the appearance of the player piano rolls that you read about in Chapter II with regard to fixation. The player piano was the first device for mechanically reproducing music to gain wide distribution in the United States. It is difficult to overstate just how transformative the player piano, and shortly thereafter, the phonograph, were. Before these devices appeared at the end of the nineteenth century, the only way that people ever experienced music was to hear it performed live. And because live performance was so important, there was a thriving business in sheet music—the human-readable instructions for performing musical compositions—to enable those performances.

Recall from Chapter II that player pianos employed a machine-readable form of sheet music, the player piano roll (a scroll of paper with holes punched in it in a sequence that instructed the piano (essentially a mechanical computer) how to perform the musical composition). Recall also that the makers of player pianos refused, for the most part, to pay licensing fees to the owners of copyrights in musical compositions for the reproduction of those compositions in the form of player piano rolls, arguing that the rolls were not "copies" of copyrighted musical compositions because people could not decipher them. The Supreme Court agreed with the player piano manufacturers. *See* White-Smith Publishing Co. v. Apollo Co., 209 U.S. 1 (1908).

Congress overturned the specific result in *White-Smith* within a year. The Copyright Act of 1909 extended the law to cover all "mechanical" reproductions of songs, whether read by people or machines. At the same time, however, Congress mandated that all musical compositions would be subject to a compulsory license allowing anyone to copy the composition without asking permission, so long as they paid a low standardized fee to the songwriter (two cents per copy, originally, and quite a bit *lower*, adjusted for inflation, today). So why did Congress enact the compulsory license? As Kal Raustiala and Christopher Sprigman explain:

> Because it was afraid of one company—Aeolian [then the dominant player piano manufacturer]. That firm is long gone. But in the early part of the 20th century, Congress viewed Aeolian as something like the Microsoft or Google of the nascent player piano market.

Anticipating that Congress would overturn White-Smith Publishing, *Aeolian swiftly bought up song rights from musicians and publishing companies so it could copy them onto player piano rolls. Aeolian's weaker competitors complained to Congress about this attempt to corner the music market.*

So to keep the Aeolian Co. from having a monopoly on the then-crucial player piano roll market, Congress allowed anyone to make a mechanical reproduction of someone else's song. And that doesn't just mean that Aeolian's competitors could make their own piano rolls of popular tunes. Congress's compulsory licensing scheme legalized the cover song—anyone can make their own recording of someone else's song, just so long as a recording of that song has previously been released, and the cover artist pays the required fee.... And the freedom to cover others' songs gave birth to a vibrant culture of continuous musical revival, remaking and reinterpretation, all of which allows good songs to become great and, sometimes, we must admit, classics to be butchered.

It's all in the eye (or ear) of the beholder. But the important point is that because of Aeolian's dominance of a now-defunct technology, we have a musical culture in America in which musicians are free to tweak songs they like—and they do so with great enthusiasm.

Kal Raustiala & Christopher Jon Sprigman, *Scales of Justice: How a Terrible Supreme Court Decision About Player Pianos Made the Cover Song What It Is Today*, Slate, May 12, 2014, http://www.slate.com/articles/technology/history_of_innovation/2014/05/white_smith_music_case_a_terribl e_1908_supreme_court_decision_on_player.html.

2. For an analysis of statutory licenses in the music industry as penalty default licenses that "can encourage more efficient licensing among otherwise divergent parties," see Kristelia A. García, *Penalty Default Licenses: A Case for Uncertainty*, 89 N.Y.U. L. Rev. 1117 (2014). For a different take, arguing that these statutory licenses can ensure access to copyrighted works while still protecting copyright owners' financial incentives, see Jacob Victor, *Reconceptualizing Compulsory Copyright Licenses*, 72 Stan. L. Rev. 915 (2020).

3. As noted above, the compulsory license for musical compositions has led to the growth of a musical culture that tolerates and even celebrates a large measure of appropriation and re-working. Indeed, some the greatest achievements of pop music, jazz, and other music genres are covers (think of Jimi Hendrix's cover of Bob Dylan's "All Along the Watchtower," Patti Smith's take on Van Morrison's "Gloria," Aretha Franklin's version of Otis Redding's "Respect," Aerosmith's cover of The Beatles' "Come Together," Johnny Cash's take on Nine Inch Nails' "Hurt," or John Coltrane's reconceptualization of the Rogers and Hammerstein standard "My Favorite Things"). But the compulsory license also permits the use of copyrighted musical compositions in ways that the copyright owner may never have been willing to approve. (For an example, Google "Paul Anka Smells Like Teen Spirit.") Do you think, on balance, that the compulsory license has been good for musical creativity?

4. Robert Brauneis has argued that the permissive rules governing "cover" recordings of copyrighted musical compositions have disadvantaged black artists, whose work was reproduced in "mirror" versions by white performers for sale to largely white audiences. *See* Robert Brauneis, *Copyright, Music, and Race: The Case of Mirror Cover Recordings*, https://papers.ssrn.com/sol3/papers.cfm?abstract_id=3591113. That said, it is also true that some black artists have benefited from the freedom to cover compositions written by white artists.

5. Does it seem strange that the Copyright Act sets up a compulsory license for the use of *entire* musical compositions, but sets up no compulsory license for the use of *parts* of musical compositions? For that reason, a song that uses a musical theme from a previously-existing copyright composition, but then surrounds that

theme with new material, is infringing unless the limited use is licensed or otherwise allowed.

Public Performance of Copyrighted Musical Compositions, and the "Performance Rights Organizations" (PROs)

Unlike with respect to the § 115 compulsory license for mechanical reproductions of nondramatic musical compositions, which applies to the reproduction and distribution rights, there is no compulsory license provision in the Copyright Act that applies to the copyright owner's § 106(4) right to make or authorize public performances of the work. Every time a sound recording embodying a copyrighted musical composition is played in public, or every time a band performs a copyrighted musical composition in public, that amounts to a public performance of the musical composition. That means that every radio broadcast of a song involves a public performance of the underlying musical composition. And every band performing cover songs in a bar involves a public performance of a musical composition. This creates a need to license the public performance of musical compositions on a very wide scale, and intermediaries—called **performing rights organizations**, or PROs—have arisen to facilitate that form of licensing.

The major performing rights organizations are ASCAP (the American Society of Composers, Authors and Publishers), BMI (Broadcast Music, Inc.), SESAC (originally, Society of European Stage Authors and Composers), and GMR (Global Music Rights). Each of these PROs offers licenses to public-performance rights for a large portfolio of musical compositions that music publishing companies have authorized the PRO to license on their behalf. Crucially, each of the PROs offers licenses on a "blanket" basis. That is, licensees (such as radio stations, concert halls, stadiums, bars, and other venues that play live or recorded music) that pay for a blanket license gain the right to publicly perform every musical composition in the particular PRO's catalog.

Fees for blanket licenses are determined according to complex (and secret) formulas that take into account the expected amount of the licensee's music usage and the size of the audience the licensee is expected to reach. The process for dividing the revenues collected among copyright owners is based on surveys of usage and is similarly shrouded in secrecy.

The two biggest PROs, ASCAP and BMI, operate under antitrust consent decrees with the U.S. Department of Justice Antitrust Division. These consent decrees stem from cases filed by the Antitrust Division in the 1940s and which challenged ASCAP and BMI blanket licenses as unlawful price fixing. The consent decrees are the agreements which arose out of settlement of those cases.

The consent decrees are complex, but their overall aim is to prevent abuse by the two largest PROs of the considerable market power that they possess as a consequence of their exclusive right to license large portfolios of compositions for public performance. Perhaps the most important provision aimed at constraining that market power is the agreement by the PROs that in the event they cannot agree with any particular licensor on the rate for a blanket license, that licensor can go to federal district court (in the Southern District of New York) and have a judge make a binding determination of a reasonable license fee.

The PROs have for more than a half-century been the indispensable intermediaries organizing the market for licensing performance rights of musical compositions. With the explosive growth of digital distribution, however, that market is now shifting, and ASCAP and BMI increasingly are chafing at certain of the provisions of the consent decrees. Recently, major music publishers threatened to withdraw *digital* public performance rights from ASCAP and BMI, claiming that they would prefer to license those directly, but that threat was preempted by a ruling, issued by Judge Cote of the Southern District of New York in a case involving ASCAP, that the consent decrees do not permit the withdrawal by the publishers from ASCAP licensing of only digital public performance rights. *See* In re Pandora Media, Inc., 6 F. Supp. 3d 317 (S.D.N.Y. 2014). That is, the publishers must withdraw all public performance rights or none. In the wake of Judge Cote's ruling, the music publishers asked the Antitrust Division to modify the consent decrees to permit partial withdrawals. In 2016, the DOJ rejected that request. *See* Statement of the Department of Justice on the Closing of the Antitrust Division's Review of the ASCAP and BMI Consent Decrees (Aug. 4, 2016), https://www.justice.gov/atr/file/882101/download.

"Sync" Rights

Finally, there is no specific provision of the Copyright Act that establishes so-called **sync rights**, but within the music industry the term is used to describe the "syncing" of music with an audiovisual work. The process of syncing may implicate the reproduction, distribution, derivative-works, and public-performance rights for both musical compositions and sound recordings. For both compositions and recordings, sync licenses are privately negotiated between music publishers and the television, motion picture, and media users that typically seek licenses for sync rights.

The Music Modernization Act

Passed into law in late 2018, the Music Modernization Act, Public Law 115-264, 132 Stat. 3676, is a collection of three separate reform provisions that together make significant changes to the long-standing rules governing music copyrights. Title I of the MMA, entitled the Musical Works Modernization Act ("MWMA"), makes some changes to the § 115 compulsory license for non-dramatic musical works and establishes a new "mechanical licensing collective" to administer the revised license. Title II of the MMA, the Classics Protection and Access Act ("CPAA"), establishes a new federal *sui generis* system of protection for pre-1972 sound recordings. We will detail the CPAA below when we talk about copyright protection for sound recordings. Title III of the MMA, the Allocation for Music Producers Act ("AMP Act"), revises the compulsory license for non-interactive digital transmissions of sound recordings to direct a small share of compulsory licensing revenues to the producers, mixers, and engineers of sound recordings. In this section, we'll focus on the MWMA, and its revision of the § 115 compulsory license.

The Musical Works Modernization Act

The key provisions of the MWMA provide a "blanket license," similar in concept to the blanket public performance licenses offered by ASCAP, BMI, and other PROs, but which (unlike a PRO license) is granted on a *compulsory* basis. Under 17 U.S.C. § 115(d)(1) as revised by the MWMA, a digital music provider can obtain a compulsory license for "covered activities," which is defined as "making a digital phonorecord delivery of a musical work, including in the form of a permanent download, limited download, or interactive stream." 17 U.S.C. § 115(e)(7). The blanket license came into effect on January 1, 2021. Since then, a compulsory license for mechanical reproduction of a musical composition may be obtained through the same method as before that date—that is, issuance of an NOI. Or, one wishing to make mechanical reproductions may obtain a blanket compulsory license through the new procedures in § 115(d)(2) as revised.

The Blanket License

Under § 115(d) as revised, "[a] digital music provider ... may ... obtain a blanket license from copyright owners through the mechanical licensing collective to make and distribute digital phonorecord deliveries of musical works through one or more covered activities."* 17 U.S.C. §115(d)(1)(A). Except as provided in subsection

---

* Each of the terms employed in this provision is defined in § 115(e). A "digital music provider" is a person who provides a service engaging in "covered activities," and "has a direct contractual, subscription, or other economic relationship with end users of the service" or "exercises direct control over the provision of the service to end users"; "is able to fully report

(d)(1)(C), the blanket license "(i) covers all musical works ... available for compulsory licensing under this section for purposes of engaging in covered activities," and "(ii) includes the making and distribution of server, intermediate, archival, and incidental reproductions of musical works that are reasonable and necessary for the digital music provider to engage in covered activities." *Id.* § 115(d)(1)(B). Note that the blanket license applies solely to the reproduction and distribution of musical works; it covers neither the right of public performance, which must be licensed separately from one or more performance rights organizations, nor synch rights, which must be licensed from the musical composition copyright owner.

A digital music provider that obtains and complies with the terms of a valid blanket license is not subject to actions for infringement of the reproduction and distribution rights for the use of a musical work "to engage in covered activities authorized by such license." *Id.* § 115(d)(1)(D). Failure to follow the procedures for obtaining a blanket license bars the applicant from obtaining a blanket license for a period of three years. *Id.* § 115(b)(4).

The MWMA directs the Copyright Office to establish a new Mechanical Licensing Collective ("MLC") to administer the new blanket license, a task which includes the establishment and maintenance of a musical works database "containing information relating to musical works (and shares of such works) and, to the extent known, the identity and location of the copyright owners of such works (and shares thereof) and the sound recordings in which the musical works are embodied." *Id.* § 115(d)(3)(E)(i). "[T]o the extent practicable," musical work copyright owners have an obligation to "engage in commercially reasonable efforts" to supply such information to the MLC. *Id.* § 115(d)(3)(E)(iv). Congress's goal in establishing the musical works database was to facilitate the matching of sound recordings to musical compositions and buttress the MLC's ability to identify copyright owners so that payment can be made.

To obtain a blanket license, a digital music provider must "submit[] a notice of license to the MLC that specifies the particular covered activities in which the digital music provider seeks to engage." *Id.* § 115(d)(2)(A). Unless the MLC rejects the notice in writing within 30 days, the blanket license will be effective as of the date the notice was sent (but not earlier than January 1, 2021). *Id.* § 115(d)(2)(A)(ii), (d)(2)(B). The MLC may reject a notice only if it fails to meet certain statutory or regulatory requirements, or if the applicant had a blanket license terminated for a default within three years before the MLC receives the notice. *Id.* § 115(d)(2)(A)(iii). If a notice is rejected for the former reason, the MLC must specify the grounds for rejection, and the applicant has 30 calendar days following rejection to submit an amended notice that cures the deficiency. *Id.* § 115(d)(2)(A)(iv). Judicial review of MLC rejections of applications for blanket licenses is available in U.S. District Court. *Id.* § 115(d)(2)(A)(v).

Negotiated Licenses

Subsection (d)(1)(C) allows for negotiated "voluntary" licenses in lieu of the blanket license: "A voluntary license for covered activities entered into by or under the authority of 1 or more copyright owners and 1 or more digital music providers, or authority to make and distribute permanent downloads of a musical work obtained by a digital music provider from a sound recording copyright owner pursuant to an individual download license, shall be given effect in lieu of a blanket license ... with respect to the musical works ... covered by such voluntary license or individual download authority." *Id.* § 115(d)(1)(C).

---

on any revenues and consideration generated by the service"; and "is able to fully report on usage of sound recordings of musical works by the service." 17 U.S.C. § 115(e)(8). A "blanket license" is "a compulsory license to engage in covered activities." Id. § 115(e)(5). The "mechanical licensing collective" is an entity designated by the Register of Copyrights to administer the blanket license. Id. § 115(e)(18). "Digital phonorecord delivery" means "each individual delivery of a phonorecord by digital transmission of a sound recording that results in a specifically identifiable reproduction by or for any transmission recipient of a phonorecord of that sound recording, regardless of whether the digital transmission is also a public performance of the sound recording or any musical work embodied therein, and includes a permanent download, a limited download, or an interactive stream." Id. § 115(e)(10).

"Willing Buyer/Willing Seller"

For compulsory licenses (whether obtained via the current procedures or via the new procedures for blanket licensing), § 115, as amended, specifies that the Copyright Royalty Board "shall establish rates and terms that most clearly represent the rates and terms that would have been negotiated in the marketplace between a willing buyer and a willing seller." *Id.* § 115(c)(1)(F). This is a change in language; before the MWMA, § 810(b) of the statute set out a range of considerations relevant to rate-setting, including maximizing the availability of creative works to the public, providing the copyright owner a fair return, reflecting the relative roles of the copyright owner and the copyright user in making the product available to the public, and minimizing disruptive impact on the industries involved. The new "willing buyer/willing seller" standard is widely expected to result in somewhat higher rates for the compulsory license, but no one knows yet how much higher. Indeed, it will be interesting to see how the Copyright Royalty Board conceptualizes "willing buyer/willing seller" in a market that is dominated by a compulsory license—that is, a market in which "willing buyers" and "willing sellers," if they negotiate at all, do so in the shadow of the compulsory rate.

Sound Recordings

Ownership

Initial ownership of copyrights in a sound recording typically vests in the recording artist (or artists) who create the sound recording, who are the author (or authors) of that work. Sometimes, sound recordings are created as works made for hire by employees acting with the scope of employment. In such an instance, the author and initial owner is the performer's employer.

Traditionally, recording artists have relied on record companies (also known as record labels) to manage the exploitation of their copyrighted sound recordings. In the past, recording artists typically transferred ownership of their sound recordings to a record company, in exchange for an advance as well as a percentage of sales of copies of the sound recording and other royalties (such as royalties for samples and sync rights). Record companies also provided marketing and promotion services. More recently, some recording artists have begun to explore other options, such as the use of intermediaries, like CD Baby, which take on many of the tasks of a record company (aside from marketing and promotion), but which do not take copyright ownership of the recording artist's sound recording.

Exclusive Rights—Limitations on the Scope of Exclusive Rights in Sound Recordings

As with musical compositions, the Copyright Act's treatment of sound recordings is distinctive. In particular, the owners of copyrights in sound recordings have, in general, narrower rights versus the owners of most other forms of copyrighted work.

For one thing, federal copyright rights in sound recordings are of relatively recent vintage. Musical compositions have been protected by federal copyright law since 1831, but sound recordings were not protected by federal copyright law until 1972. In 1971, Congress amended the copyright law to provide federal copyright protection for sound recordings fixed and first published with a statutory copyright notice on or after February 15, 1972. All sound recordings fixed in a phonorecord on or after January 1, 1978, are automatically protected by copyright.

Until Congress's passage in 2018 of the CPAA, sound recordings fixed before February 15, 1972, were protected only by *state* law. In those states that had addressed the issue, copyright owners generally had a right to prevent the reproduction and distribution of such pre-1972 sound recordings. But owners of copyrights in sound recordings had *no general right of public performance* under either state or federal law.

With respect to the federal law, the right of public performance set out in § 106(4) applies to "literary, musical, dramatic, and choreographic works, pantomimes, and motion pictures and other audiovisual works," but not to sound recordings. (Remember that the term "musical" works refers to musical compositions, as distinguished from sound recordings.) The absence of a general right of public performance for sound recordings means that there is no license required from the sound recording copyright owner when a broadcast radio station plays a recording (although a public performance license for the underlying musical composition is required, and is obtained typically via a blanket license from one or more PROs, as you saw above). As you shall see, however, § 106(6) of the Copyright Act does grant sound recording copyright owners a limited public-performance right that covers public performances made via a "digital audio transmission." We'll discuss that right, and the limited compulsory license that applies to it below. The CPAA extends that right to pre-1972 sound recordings, and it also extends to pre-1972 recordings the other rights in § 106 of the Copyright Act that apply to post-1972 sound recordings. (See Chapter IV for a discussion of the term of protection the CPAA provides to pre-1972 sound recordings.)

Section 114 of the Copyright Act contains some additional limitations on the scope of copyright in sound recordings. Section 114(b) provides that the reproduction right "is limited to the right to duplicate the sound recording in the form of phonorecords or copies that directly or indirectly recapture the actual sounds fixed in the recording." 17 U.S.C. § 114(b). This limitation is very important. Its effect is that **sound-alikes** (also known as covers) do not infringe the sound recording copyright owner's reproduction right. The only use of the sound recording that can violate that right is straight-up copying of the actual sounds in the recording—i.e., piracy—or copying of the actual sounds from a discrete piece of the sound recording—i.e., sampling. Section 114(b) applies the same rule to limit the sound recording copyright owner's right to prepare derivative works. Liability for the unauthorized creation of a derivative work is limited to situations in which "the actual sounds fixed in the sound recording are rearranged, remixed, or otherwise altered in sequence or quality." *Id.* § 114(b). In a bid to drive the point home, § 114(b) makes clear that neither the reproduction right nor the derivative-work right "extends to the making of an independent fixation of other sounds, even though such sounds imitate or simulate those in the copyrighted sound recording." *Id.*

The next case involves the practice of **sampling**—copying and remixing sounds from previous sound recordings, and using those (often significantly altered) sounds in new recordings. Sampling implicates the rights of both musical-composition and sound recording copyright owners. In cases like *Newton v. Diamond*, 388 F.3d 1189 (9th Cir. 2004), courts have made clear that samples that appropriate de minimis segments of protected material from copyrighted musical compositions are not actionable. But courts have disagreed over whether the de minimis limitation applies to infringement claims involving samples that are brought by the owners of sound recordings.

As you read the next case, consider carefully whether the Copyright Act's substantial limitations on the scope of sound recording copyright owners' exclusive rights suggests that the usual "de minimis" requirement of the copyright infringement standard should not apply.

VMG Salsoul, LLC v. Madonna Louise Ciccone
824 F.3d 871 (9th Cir. 2016)

GRABER, J.:

[1] In the early 1990s, pop star Madonna Louise Ciccone, commonly known by her first name only, released the song *Vogue* to great commercial success. In this copyright infringement action, Plaintiff VMG Salsoul, LLC, alleges that the producer of *Vogue*, Shep Pettibone, copied a 0.23-second segment of horns from an

earlier song, known as *Love Break*, and used a modified version of that snippet when recording *Vogue*. Plaintiff asserts that Defendants Madonna, Pettibone, and others thereby violated Plaintiff's copyrights to *Love Break*. The district court applied the longstanding legal rule that "de minimis" copying does not constitute infringement and held that, even if Plaintiff proved its allegations of actual copying, the claim failed because the copying (if it occurred) was trivial. The district court granted summary judgment to Defendants .... Plaintiff timely appeals.

[2] Reviewing the summary judgment de novo, we agree with the district court that, as a matter of law, a general audience would not recognize the brief snippet in *Vogue* as originating from *Love Break*. We also reject Plaintiff's argument that Congress eliminated the "de minimis" exception to claims alleging infringement of a sound recording. We recognize that the Sixth Circuit held to the contrary in *Bridgeport Music, Inc. v. Dimension Films*, 410 F.3d 792 (6th Cir. 2005), but—like the leading copyright treatise and several district courts—we find *Bridgeport*'s reasoning unpersuasive. We hold that the "de minimis" exception applies to infringement actions concerning copyrighted sound recordings, just as it applies to all other copyright infringement actions. Accordingly, we affirm the summary judgment in favor of Defendants....

[3] Because this case comes to us on appeal from a grant of summary judgment to Defendants, we recount the facts in the light most favorable to Plaintiff.

[4] In the early 1980s, Pettibone recorded the song *Ooh I Love It (Love Break)*, which we refer to as *Love Break*. In 1990, Madonna and Pettibone recorded the song *Vogue*, which would become a mega-hit dance song after its release on Madonna's albums. Plaintiff alleges that, when recording *Vogue*, Pettibone "sampled" certain sounds from the recording of *Love Break* and added those sounds to *Vogue*. "Sampling" in this context means the actual physical copying of sounds from an existing recording for use in a new recording, even if accomplished with slight modifications such as changes to pitch or tempo. *See* Newton v. Diamond, 388 F.3d 1189, 1192 (9th Cir. 2004) (discussing the term "sampling").

[5] Plaintiff asserts that it holds copyrights to the composition and to the sound recording of *Love Break*. Plaintiff argues that, because *Vogue* contains sampled material from *Love Break*, Defendants have violated both copyrights. Although Plaintiff originally asserted improper sampling of strings, vocals, congas, "vibraslap," and horns from *Love Break* as well as another song, Plaintiff now asserts a sole theory of infringement: When creating two commercial versions of *Vogue*, Pettibone sampled a "horn hit"[1] from *Love Break*, violating Plaintiff's copyrights to both the composition and the sound recording of *Love Break*.

[6] The horn hit appears in *Love Break* in two forms. A "single" horn hit in *Love Break* consists of a quarter-note chord comprised of four notes—E-flat, A, D, and F—in the key of B-flat. The single horn hit lasts for 0.23 seconds. A "double" horn hit in *Love Break* consists of an eighth-note chord of those same notes, followed immediately by a quarter-note chord of the same notes. Plaintiff's expert identified the instruments as "predominantly" trombones and trumpets.

[7] The alleged source of the sampling is the "instrumental" version of *Love Break*,[2] which lasts 7 minutes and 46 seconds. The single horn hit occurs 27 times, and the double horn hit occurs 23 times. The horn hits occur at intervals of approximately 2 to 4 seconds in two different segments: between 3:11 and 4:38, and from 7:01 to the end, at 7:46. The general pattern is single-double repeated, double-single repeated, single-single-

---

[1] Plaintiff prefers the label "horn part," but the label has no effect on the legal analysis. For simplicity, we follow the district court's convention.

[2] The label "instrumental" is misleading: The recording contains many vocals. But again we adopt the terminology used by the district court.

double repeated, and double-single repeated. Many other instruments are playing at the same time as the horns.

[8] The horn hit in *Vogue* appears in the same two forms as in *Love Break*: single and double. A "single" horn hit in *Vogue* consists of a quarter-note chord comprised of four notes—E, A-sharp, D-sharp, and F-sharp—in the key of B-natural.[3] A double horn hit in *Vogue* consists of an eighth-note chord of those same notes, followed immediately by a quarter-note chord of the same notes.

[9] The two commercial versions of *Vogue* that Plaintiff challenges are known as the "radio edit" version and the "compilation" version. The radio edit version of *Vogue* lasts 4 minutes and 53 seconds. The single horn hit occurs once, the double horn hit occurs three times, and a "breakdown" version of the horn hit occurs once.[4] They occur at 0:56, 1:02, 3:41, 4:05, and 4:18. The pattern is single-double-double-double-breakdown. As with *Love Break*, many other instruments are playing at the same time as the horns.

[10] The compilation version of *Vogue* lasts 5 minutes and 17 seconds. The single horn hit occurs once, and the double horn hit occurs five times. They occur at 1:14, 1:20, 3:59, 4:24, 4:40, and 4:57. The pattern is single-double-double-double-double-double. Again, many other instruments are playing as well.

[11] One of Plaintiff's experts transcribed the composition of the horn hits in the two songs as follows.

Love Break's single horn hit:

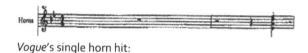

Vogue's single horn hit:

Love Break's double horn hit:

Vogue's double horn hit:

[12] In a written order, the district court granted summary judgment to Defendants on two alternative grounds. First, neither the composition nor the sound recording of the horn hit was "original" for purposes of copyright law. Second, the court ruled that, even if the horn hit was original, any sampling of the horn hit was "de minimis or trivial." ...

[13] Plaintiff has submitted evidence of actual copying. In particular, Tony Shimkin has sworn that he, as Pettibone's personal assistant, helped with the creation of *Vogue* and that, in Shimkin's presence, Pettibone directed an engineer to introduce sounds from *Love Break* into the recording of *Vogue*. Additionally, Plaintiff

---

[3] In musical terms, assuming that the composition was copied, Pettibone "transposed" the horn hit in *Love Break* by one-half step, resulting in notes that are half a step higher in *Vogue*.

[4] The record does not appear to disclose the meaning of a "breakdown" version of the horn hit, and neither party attributes any significance to this form of the horn hit.

submitted reports from music experts who concluded that the horn hits in *Vogue* were sampled from *Love Break*. Defendants do not concede that sampling occurred, and they have introduced much evidence to the contrary.[5] But for purposes of summary judgment, Plaintiff has introduced sufficient evidence (including direct evidence) to create a genuine issue of material fact as to whether copying in fact occurred. Taking the facts in the light most favorable to Plaintiff, Plaintiff has demonstrated actual copying. Accordingly, our analysis proceeds to the next step.

[14] Our leading authority on actual copying is *Newton*, 388 F.3d 1189. We explained in *Newton* that proof of actual copying is insufficient to establish copyright infringement:

> *For an unauthorized use of a copyrighted work to be actionable, the use must be significant enough to constitute infringement. This means that even where the fact of copying is conceded, no legal consequences will follow from that fact unless the copying is substantial. The principle that trivial copying does not constitute actionable infringement has long been a part of copyright law. Indeed, as [a judge] observed over 80 years ago: "Even where there is some copying, that fact is not conclusive of infringement. Some copying is permitted. In addition to copying, it must be shown that this has been done to an unfair extent."* West Publ'g Co. v. Edward Thompson Co., 169 F. 833, 861 (E.D.N.Y. 1909). *This principle reflects the legal maxim,* de minimis non curatlex *(often rendered as, "the law does not concern itself with trifles").*

In other words, to establish its infringement claim, Plaintiff must show that the copying was greater than de minimis.

[15] Plaintiff's claim encompasses two distinct alleged infringements: infringement of the copyright to the *composition* of *Love Break* and infringement of the copyright to the *sound recording* of Love Break. We squarely held in *Newton* that the de minimis exception applies to claims of infringement of a copyrighted composition. But it is an open question in this circuit whether the exception applies to claims of infringement of a copyrighted sound recording....

[16] A use is de minimis only if the average audience would not recognize the appropriation. Accordingly, we must determine whether a reasonable juror could conclude that the average audience would recognize the appropriation. We will consider the composition and the sound recording copyrights in turn.

1. Alleged Infringement of the Composition Copyright

[17] When considering an infringement claim of a copyrighted musical composition, what matters is not how the musicians actually played the notes but, rather, a "generic rendition of the composition." *Newton*, 388 F.3d at 1194; *see id.* at 1193 (holding that, when considering infringement of the composition copyright, one "must remove from consideration all the elements unique to [the musician's] performance"). That is, we must compare the written compositions of the two pieces.

[18] Viewing the evidence in the light most favorable to Plaintiff, Defendants copied two distinct passages in the horn part of the score for *Love Break*. First, Defendants copied the quarter-note single horn hit. But no additional part of the score concerning the single horn hit is the same, because the single horn hit appears at a different place in the measure. In *Love Break*, the notes for the measure are: half-note rest, quarter-note rest, single horn hit. In *Vogue*, however, the notes for the measure are: half-note rest, eighth-note rest, single horn hit, eighth-note rest. Second, Defendants copied a full measure that contains the double horn hit. In both

---

[5] For example, Plaintiff hired Shimkin and then brought this action, raising doubts about Shimkin's credibility; Pettibone and others testified that Shimkin was not present during the creation of *Vogue* and was not even employed by Pettibone at that time; and Defendants' experts dispute the analysis and conclusions of Plaintiff's experts.

songs, the notes for the measure are: half-note rest, eighth-note rest, eighth-note horn hit, quarter-note horn hit. In sum, Defendants copied, at most, a quarter-note single horn hit and a full measure containing rests and a double horn hit.

[19] After listening to the recordings, we conclude that a reasonable jury could *not* conclude that an average audience would recognize the appropriation of the composition. Our decision in *Newton* is instructive. That case involved a copyrighted composition of "a piece for flute and voice." The defendants used a six-second sample that "consist[ed] of three notes, C—D flat—C, sung over a background C note played on the flute." The composition also "require[d] overblowing the background C note that is played on the flute." The defendants repeated a six-second sample "throughout [the song], so that it appears over forty times in various renditions of the song." After listening to the recordings, we affirmed the grant of summary judgment because "an average audience would not discern [the composer's] hand as a composer."

[20] The snippets of the composition that were (as we must assume) taken here are much smaller than the sample at issue in *Newton*. The copied elements from the *Love Break* composition are very short, much shorter than the six-second sample in *Newton*. The single horn hit lasts less than a quarter-second, and the double horn hit lasts—even counting the rests at the beginning of the measure—less than a second. Similarly, the horn hits appear only five or six times in *Vogue*, rather than the dozens of times that the sampled material in *Newton* occurred in the challenged song in that case. Moreover, unlike in *Newton*, in which the challenged song copied *the entire composition* of the original work for the given temporal segment, the sampling at issue here involves only *one instrument group* out of many. As noted above, listening to the audio recordings confirms what the foregoing analysis of the composition strongly suggests: A reasonable jury could not conclude that an average audience would recognize an appropriation of the *Love Break* composition.

2. Alleged Infringement of the Sound Recording Copyright

[21] When considering a claimed infringement of a copyrighted sound recording, what matters is how the musicians *played* the notes, that is, how their rendition distinguishes the recording from a generic rendition of the same composition. Viewing the evidence in the light most favorable to Plaintiff, by accepting its experts' reports, Pettibone sampled one single horn hit, which occurred at 3:35 in *Love Break*. Pettibone then used that sampled single horn hit to create the double horn hit used in *Vogue*.

[22] The horn hit itself was not copied precisely. According to Plaintiff's expert, the chord "was modified by transposing it upward, cleaning up the attack slightly in order to make it punchier [by truncating the horn hit] and overlaying it with other sounds and effects. One such effect mimicked the reverse cymbal crash.... The reverb/delay 'tail' ... was prolonged and heightened." Moreover, as with the composition, the horn hits are not isolated sounds. Many other instruments are playing at the same time in both *Love Break* and *Vogue*.

[23] In sum, viewing the evidence in the light most favorable to Plaintiff, Pettibone copied one quarter-note of a four-note chord, lasting 0.23 seconds; he isolated the horns by filtering out the other instruments playing at the same time; he transposed it to a different key; he truncated it; and he added effects and other sounds to the chord itself. For the double horn hit, he used the same process, except that he duplicated the single horn hit and shortened one of the duplicates to create the eighth-note chord from the quarter-note chord. Finally, he overlaid the resulting horn hits with sounds from many other instruments to create the song *Vogue*.

[24] After listening to the audio recordings submitted by the parties, we conclude that a reasonable juror could *not* conclude that an average audience would recognize the appropriation of the horn hit. That common-sense conclusion is borne out by dry analysis. The horn hit is very short—less than a second. The horn hit occurs only a few times in *Vogue*. Without careful attention, the horn hits are easy to miss. Moreover, the horn hits in *Vogue* do not sound identical to the horn hits from *Love Break*. As noted above, assuming that

the sampling occurred, Pettibone truncated the horn hit, transposed it to a different key, and added other sounds and effects to the horn hit itself. The horn hit *then* was added to *Vogue* along with many other instrument tracks. Even if one grants the dubious proposition that a listener recognized some similarities between the horn hits in the two songs, it is hard to imagine that he or she would conclude that sampling had occurred.

[25] A quirk in the procedural history of this case is illuminating on this point. Plaintiff's primary expert originally *misidentified* the source of the sampled double horn hit. In his original report, the expert concluded that both a single horn hit *and a double horn hit* were sampled from *Love Break*. The parties later discovered the original tracks to *Vogue* and were able to listen to the horn hits without interference from the many other instruments. After listening to those tracks, the expert decided that he had erred in opining that a double horn hit was sampled. He concluded instead that only a single horn hit was sampled, which was used to create the double horn hit in *Vogue*. In other words, a highly qualified and trained musician listened to the recordings with the express aim of discerning which parts of the song had been copied, and he could not do so accurately. An average audience would not do a better job.

[26] In sum, the district court correctly held that summary judgment to Defendants was appropriate on the issue of de minimis copying....

[27] Plaintiff argues, in the alternative, that even if the copying here is trivial, that fact is irrelevant because the de minimis exception does not apply to infringements of copyrighted sound recordings. Plaintiff urges us to follow the Sixth Circuit's decision in *Bridgeport Music, Inc. v. Dimension Films*, 410 F.3d 792 (6th Cir. 2005), which adopted a bright-line rule: For copyrighted sound recordings, any unauthorized copying—no matter how trivial—constitutes infringement.

[28] The rule that infringement occurs only when a substantial portion is copied is firmly established in the law. The leading copyright treatise traces the rule to the mid-1800s. 4 MELVILLE B. NIMMER & DAVID NIMMER, NIMMER ON COPYRIGHT § 13.03[A][2][a], at 13-56 to 13-57, 13-57 n.102 (2013). We recognized the rule as early as 1977: "If copying is established, then only does there arise the second issue, that of illicit copying (unlawful appropriation). On that issue the test is the response of the ordinary lay hearer...." Sid & Marty Krofft Television Prods., Inc. v. McDonald's Corp., 562 F.2d 1157, 1164 (9th Cir. 1977). The reason for the rule is that the plaintiff's legally protected interest is the potential financial return from his compositions which derive from the lay public's approbation of his efforts. If the public does not recognize the appropriation, then the copier has not benefitted from the original artist's expressive content. Accordingly, there is no infringement.

[29] Other than *Bridgeport* and the district courts following that decision, we are aware of no case that has held that the de minimis doctrine does not apply in a copyright infringement case. Instead, courts consistently have applied the rule in *all* cases alleging copyright infringement. Indeed, we stated in dictum in *Newton* that the rule "applies *throughout the law of copyright*, including cases of music sampling." (emphasis added).

[30] Plaintiff nevertheless argues that Congress intended to create a special rule for copyrighted sound recordings, eliminating the de minimis exception. We begin our analysis with the statutory text.

[31] Title 17 U.S.C. § 102, titled "Subject matter of copyright: In general," states, in relevant part:

> (a) Copyright protection subsists, in accordance with this title, in original works of authorship fixed in any tangible medium of expression, now known or later developed, from which they can be perceived, reproduced, or otherwise communicated, either directly or with the aid of a machine or device. Works of authorship include the following categories:
>
> (1) literary works;

(2) musical works, including any accompanying words;

(3) dramatic works, including any accompanying music;

(4) pantomimes and choreographic works;

(5) pictorial, graphic, and sculptural works;

(6) motion pictures and other audiovisual works;

(7) *sound recordings*; and

(8) architectural works.

(Emphasis added). That provision treats sound recordings identically to all other types of protected works; nothing in the text suggests differential treatment, for any purpose, of sound recordings compared to, say, literary works. Similarly, nothing in the neutrally worded statutory definition of "sound recordings" suggests that Congress intended to eliminate the de minimis exception. *See id.* § 101 ("'Sound recordings' are works that result from the fixation of a series of musical, spoken, or other sounds, but not including the sounds accompanying a motion picture or other audiovisual work, regardless of the nature of the material objects, such as disks, tapes, or other phonorecords, in which they are embodied.").

[32] Title 17 U.S.C. § 106, titled "Exclusive rights in copyrighted works," states:

> Subject to sections 107 through 122, the owner of copyright under this title has the exclusive rights to do and to authorize any of the following:
>
> > (1) to reproduce the copyrighted work in copies or phonorecords;
> >
> > (2) to prepare derivative works based upon the copyrighted work;
> >
> > (3) to distribute copies or phonorecords of the copyrighted work to the public by sale or other transfer of ownership, or by rental, lease, or lending;
> >
> > (4) in the case of literary, musical, dramatic, and choreographic works, pantomimes, and motion pictures and other audiovisual works, to perform the copyrighted work publicly;
> >
> > (5) in the case of literary, musical, dramatic, and choreographic works, pantomimes, and pictorial, graphic, or sculptural works, including the individual images of a motion picture or other audiovisual work, to display the copyrighted work publicly; and
> >
> > (6) in the case of sound recordings, to perform the copyrighted work publicly by means of a digital audio transmission.

[33] Again, nothing in that provision suggests differential treatment of de minimis copying of sound recordings compared to, say, sculptures. Although subsection (6) deals exclusively with sound recordings, that subsection concerns public performances; nothing in its text bears on de minimis copying.

[34] Instead, Plaintiff's statutory argument hinges on the third sentence of 17 U.S.C. § 114(b), which states:

> The exclusive rights of the owner of copyright in a sound recording under clauses (1) and (2) of section 106 do not extend to the making or duplication of another sound recording that consists entirely of an independent fixation of other sounds, even though such sounds imitate or simulate those in the copyrighted sound recording.

[35] Like all the other sentences in § 114(b), the third sentence imposes an express *limitation* on the rights of a copyright holder: "The exclusive rights of the owner of a copyright in a sound recording ... *do not extend* to the making or duplication of another sound recording [with certain qualities]." *Id.* (emphasis added); *see id.* (first sentence: "exclusive rights ... do not extend" to certain circumstances; second sentence: "exclusive rights ... do not extend" to certain circumstances; fourth sentence: "exclusive rights ... do not apply" in certain

circumstances). We ordinarily would hesitate to read an *implicit expansion* of rights into Congress' statement of an *express limitation* on rights. Given the considerable background of consistent application of the de minimis exception across centuries of jurisprudence, we are particularly hesitant to read the statutory text as an unstated, implicit elimination of that steadfast rule.

[36] A straightforward reading of the third sentence in § 114(b) reveals Congress' intended limitation on the rights of a sound recording copyright holder: A new recording that mimics the copyrighted recording is not an infringement, even if the mimicking is very well done, so long as there was no actual copying. That is, if a band played and recorded its own version of *Love Break* in a way that sounded very similar to the copyrighted recording of *Love Break*, then there would be no infringement so long as there was no actual copying of the recorded *Love Break*. But the quoted passage does not speak to the question that we face: whether Congress intended to eliminate the longstanding de minimis exception for sound recordings in all circumstances even where, as here, the new sound recording as a whole sounds nothing like the original.

[37] Even if there were some ambiguity as to congressional intent with respect to § 114(b), the legislative history clearly confirms our analysis on each of the above points. Congress intended § 114 to limit, not to expand, the rights of copyright holders: "The approach of the bill is to set forth the copyright owner's exclusive rights in broad terms in section 106, and then to provide various limitations, qualifications, or exemptions in the 12 sections that follow. Thus, everything in section 106 is made 'subject to sections 107 through 118,' and must be read in conjunction with those provisions." H.R. REP. NO. 94-1476, at 61 (1976).

[38] With respect to § 114(b) specifically, a House Report stated:

> Subsection (b) of section 114 makes clear that statutory protection for sound recordings extends only to the particular sounds of which the recording consists, and would not prevent a separate recording of another performance in which those sounds are imitated. Thus, infringement takes place whenever all or any substantial portion of the actual sounds that go to make up a copyrighted sound recording are reproduced in phonorecords by repressing, transcribing, recapturing off the air, or any other method, or by reproducing them in the soundtrack or audio portion of a motion picture or other audiovisual work. Mere imitation of a recorded performance would not constitute a copyright infringement even where one performer deliberately sets out to simulate another's performance as exactly as possible.

Id. at 106 (emphasis added). That passage strongly supports the natural reading of § 114(b), discussed above. Congress intended to make clear that imitation of a recorded performance cannot be infringement so long as no actual copying is done. There is no indication that Congress intended, through § 114(b), to expand the rights of a copyright holder to a sound recording.

[39] Perhaps more importantly, the quoted passage articulates the principle that "infringement takes place whenever all *or any substantial portion* of the actual sounds ... are reproduced." *Id.* (emphasis added). That is, when enacting this specific statutory provision, Congress clearly understood that the de minimis exception applies to copyrighted sound recordings, just as it applies to all other copyrighted works. In sum, the statutory text, confirmed by the legislative history, reveals that Congress intended to maintain the de minimis exception for copyrighted sound recordings.

[40] In coming to a different conclusion, the Sixth Circuit reasoned as follows:

> [T]he rights of sound recording copyright holders under clauses (1) and (2) of section 106 "do not extend to the making or duplication of another sound recording that consists entirely of an independent fixation of other sounds, even though such sounds imitate or simulate those in the copyrighted sound recording." 17 U.S.C. § 114(b) (emphasis added). The significance of this

provision is amplified by the fact that the Copyright Act of 1976 added the word "entirely" to this language. Compare Sound Recording Act of 1971, Pub. L. 92-140, 85 Stat. 391 (Oct. 15, 1971) (adding subsection (f) to former 17 U.S.C. § 1) ("does not extend to the making or duplication of another sound recording that is an independent fixation of other sounds"). In other words, a sound recording owner has the exclusive right to "sample" his own recording.

[41] We reject that interpretation of § 114(b). *Bridgeport* ignored the statutory structure and § 114(b)'s express *limitation* on the rights of a copyright holder. *Bridgeport* also declined to consider legislative history on the ground that "digital sampling wasn't being done in 1971." But the state of technology is irrelevant to interpreting Congress' intent as to statutory structure. Moreover, as Nimmer points out, *Bridgeport*'s reasoning fails on its own terms because contemporary technology plainly allowed the copying of small portions of a protected sound recording. NIMMER § 13.03[A][2][b], at 13-62 n.114.16.

[42] Close examination of *Bridgeport*'s interpretive method further exposes its illogic. In effect, *Bridgeport* inferred from the fact that "exclusive rights ... *do not extend* to the making or duplication of another sound recording that *consists* entirely of an independent fixation of other sounds," 17 U.S.C. § 114(b) (emphases added), the conclusion that exclusive rights *do extend* to the making of another sound recording that *does not consist* entirely of an independent fixation of other sounds. As pointed out by Nimmer, *Bridgeport*'s interpretive method "rests on a logical fallacy." NIMMER § 13.03[A][2][b], at 13-61. A statement that rights do not extend to a particular circumstance does not automatically mean that the rights extend to all other circumstances. In logical terms, it is a fallacy to infer the inverse of a conditional from the conditional.

[43] For example, take as a given the proposition that "if it has rained, then the grass is not dry." It does not necessarily follow that "if it has not rained, then the grass is dry." Someone may have watered the lawn, for instance. We cannot infer the second if-then statement from the first. The first if-then statement does not tell us *anything* about the condition of the grass if it has not rained. Accordingly, even though it is true that, "if the recording consists entirely of independent sounds, then the copyright does not extend to it," that statement does not necessarily mean that "if the recording does not consist entirely of independent sounds, then the copyright does extend to it."

[44] The Sixth Circuit also looked beyond the statutory text, to the nature of a sound recording, and reasoned:

> *[E]ven when a small part of a sound recording is sampled, the part taken is something of value. No further proof of that is necessary than the fact that the producer of the record or the artist on the record intentionally sampled because it would (1) save costs, or (2) add something to the new recording, or (3) both. For the sound recording copyright holder, it is not the "song" but the sounds that are fixed in the medium of his choice. When those sounds are sampled they are taken directly from that fixed medium. It is a physical taking rather than an intellectual one.*

[45] We disagree for three reasons. *First*, the possibility of a "physical taking" exists with respect to other kinds of artistic works as well, such as photographs, as to which the usual de minimis rule applies. A computer program can, for instance, "sample" a piece of one photograph and insert it into another photograph or work of art. We are aware of no copyright case carving out an exception to the de minimis requirement in that context, and we can think of no principled reason to differentiate one kind of "physical taking" from another. *Second*, even accepting the premise that sound recordings differ qualitatively from other copyrighted works and therefore *could warrant* a different infringement rule, that theoretical difference does not mean that Congress *actually adopted* a different rule. *Third*, the distinction between a "physical taking" and an "intellectual one," premised in part on "sav[ing] costs" by not having to hire musicians, does not advance the Sixth Circuit's view. The Supreme Court has held unequivocally that the Copyright Act protects only the expressive aspects of a copyrighted work, and *not* the "fruit of the [author's] labor." Feist Publ'ns, Inc. v. Rural

Tel. Serv. Co., 499 U.S. 340, 349 (1991). Indeed, the Supreme Court in *Feist* explained at length why, though that result may seem unfair, protecting only the expressive aspects of a copyrighted work is actually a key part of the design of the copyright laws. Accordingly, all that remains of *Bridgeport*'s argument is that the second artist has taken some expressive content from the original artist. But that is always true, regardless of the nature of the work, and the de minimis test nevertheless applies.

[46] Because we conclude that Congress intended to maintain the "de minimis" exception for copyrights to sound recordings, we take the unusual step of creating a circuit split by disagreeing with the Sixth Circuit's contrary holding in *Bridgeport*. We do so only after careful reflection ....

[47] Finally, Plaintiff advances several reasons why *Bridgeport*'s rule is superior *as a matter of policy*. For example, the Sixth Circuit opined that its bright-line rule was easy to enforce; that "the market will control the license price and keep it within bounds"; and that "sampling is never accidental" and is therefore easy to avoid. Those arguments are for a legislature, not a court. They speak to what Congress *could decide*; they do not inform what Congress *actually decided*.[11]

[48] We hold that the "de minimis" exception applies to actions alleging infringement of a copyright to sound recordings....

SILVERMAN, J., dissenting:

[49] The plaintiff is the owner of a copyright in a fixed sound recording. This is a valuable property right, the stock-in-trade of artists who make their living recording music and selling records. The plaintiff alleges that the defendants, without a license or any sort of permission, physically copied a small part of the plaintiff's sound recording—which, to repeat, is property belonging to the plaintiff—and, having appropriated it, inserted into their *own* recording. If the plaintiff's allegations are to be believed, the defendants deemed this maneuver preferable to paying for a license to use the material, or to hiring their own musicians to record it. In any other context, this would be called theft. It is no defense to theft that the thief made off with only a "de minimis" part of the victim's property.

[50] The majority chooses to follow the views of a popular treatise instead of an on-point decision of the Sixth Circuit, a decision that has governed the music industry in Nashville—"Music City"—and elsewhere for over a decade without causing either the sky to fall in, or Congress to step in. And just exactly what is the Sixth Circuit's radical holding in *Bridgeport Music, Inc. v. Dimension Films* that the majority finds so distasteful? It's this: if you want to use an *identical copy* of a portion of a copyrighted fixed sound recording—we're not talking about "substantially similar" tunes or rhythms, but an actual *identical copy* of a sound that has already been recorded in a fixed medium—get a license. You can't just take it.

[51] As the majority acknowledges, after *Newton v. Diamond*, 388 F.3d 1189 (9th Cir. 2003), it is an "open question" in the Ninth Circuit whether a de minimis defense applies to fixed sound recordings as it does to less tangible works. The *Bridgeport* court explained why it should not.

---

[11] It also is not clear that the cited policy reasons are necessarily persuasive. For example, this particular case presents an example in which there is uncertainty as to enforcement—musical experts disagree as to whether sampling occurred. As another example, it is not necessarily true that the market will keep license prices "within bounds"—it is possible that a bright-line rule against sampling would unduly stifle creativity in certain segments of the music industry because the licensing costs would be too expensive for the amateur musician. In any event, even raising these counter-points demonstrates that the arguments, as Plaintiff concedes, rest on policy considerations, not on statutory interpretation. One cannot answer questions such as how much licensing cost is too much without exercising value judgments—matters generally assigned to the legislature.

[52] First, by statute, sound recording copyright holders have an *exclusive* right to sample their *own* recordings. It's an exclusive right; the statute does not give that right to others. Under 17 U.S.C. §§ 106 and 114, the holder of a copyright in a sound recording (but not others) has the exclusive right to reproduce the work in copies or records "that directly or indirectly recapture the actual sounds fixed in the recording," as well as the exclusive right to prepare derivative works "in which the actual sounds fixed in the sound recording are rearranged, remixed, or otherwise altered in sequence or quality." 17 U.S.C. §§ 106(1) and (2); 114(b). Congress clearly qualified these exclusive rights, writing that "another sound recording that consists entirely of an independent fixation of other sounds, even though such sounds imitate or simulate those in the copyrighted sound recording" are not within the scope of the copyright holder's exclusive rights. 17 U.S.C. § 114(b). In other words, the world at large is free to imitate or simulate the creative work fixed in the recording (like a tribute band, for example) so long as an actual copy of the sound recording itself is not made.

[53] The majority rejects this straightforward reading, explaining by way of a rhetorical exercise that *Bridgeport*'s reading of § 114(b) is a logical fallacy, expanding the rights of copyright holders beyond that allowed under the judicial de minimis rule. As I see it, it is the majority that tortures the natural reading of these provisions. Bear in mind that § 114(b) simply explains the scope of exclusive rights already granted to copyright holders under § 106. These two provisions must be read together, as the Sixth Circuit did. When read together, their message is clear: copyright holders have exclusive rights to their recordings, but cannot be heard to complain (i.e., there can be no infringement of those exclusive rights) where a new recording consists *entirely* of independently created sounds, such as might be found in a very good imitation. By the same token, if a new recording includes something other than independently created sounds, such as a blatant copy, the copyright holder whose work was sampled has a legitimate gripe. That right was not invented by the Sixth Circuit: it already exists in the statutes. And these statutes say nothing about the de minimis exception.

[54] The second reason the Sixth Circuit gave for not adopting the de minimis rule is that sound recordings are different than their compositional counterparts: when a defendant copies a recording, he or she takes not the song but the sounds as they are fixed in the medium of the copyright holders' choice. In other words, the very nature of digital sampling makes a de minimis analysis inapplicable, since sampling or pirating necessarily involves copying a fixed performance. The defendants wanted horns to punctuate their song, so they took the plaintiff's copyrighted recording of horns. The horn hit is brief, but clearly perceptible and does its job. This is unlike indiscernible photographs used, not for their content (which cannot be made out), but to dress a movie set.

[55] This is a physical taking, not an intellectual one. Sampling is never accidental. As the Sixth Circuit observed, it is not like the case of a composer who has a melody in his head, perhaps not even realizing that the reason he hears this melody is that it is the work of another that he has heard before. When you sample a sound recording you know you are taking another's work product. Accordingly, the pertinent inquiry in a sampling case is not whether a defendant sampled a little or a lot, but whether a defendant sampled at all.

[56] Again, the majority disagrees, rejecting *Bridgeport*'s characterization of a sample as a "physical taking" on the basis that copyright protection extends only to expressive aspects of a work, not the fruit of the author's labor. According to the majority, copyright protection doesn't extend to the sweat of an author's brow. But that's irrelevant here, since there is no question that the underlying sound recording can be copyrighted, and it is the taking of that protectable work that is at issue.

[57] I find *Bridgeport*'s arguments well-reasoned and persuasive. Equally compelling is, I think, Congress's silence in the wake of *Bridgeport*, especially in light of the fact that the Sixth Circuit explicitly invited Congress to clarify or change the law if *Bridgeport*'s bright-line rule was not what Congress intended. While it's true that congressional inaction in the face of judicial interpretation is not ironclad evidence of Congressional approval,

it's not chopped liver either. In this case *Bridgeport* has not been hiding out in the woods, waiting to be found: it has been governing the music industry in Nashville and elsewhere for eleven years. The majority now proposes to introduce a different rule for this circuit, creating a circuit split, and providing a lower level of protection for copyright holders in a different area of the country. This inconsistent approach is plainly in contravention of Congressional intent that copyright laws be predictable and uniform, yet the majority defends its rogue path on the ground that Congress must have intended something other than what the Sixth Circuit has concluded, even though we've heard not a peep from Congress, or for that matter the Supreme Court, in the eleven years since *Bridgeport* has been on the books.

[58] In short, the majority's fuzzy approach would require a factual and largely visceral inquiry into whether each and every instance of sampling was "substantial," whereas *Bridgeport* provides in the case of a fixed sound recording a bright-line rule, and I quote: "Get a license or do not sample." True, *Get a license or do not sample* doesn't carry the same divine force as *Thou Shalt Not Steal*, but it's the same basic idea. I would hold that the de minimis exception does not apply to the sampling, copying, stealing, pirating, misappropriation—call it what you will—of copyrighted fixed sound recordings. Once the sound is fixed, it is tangible property belonging to the copyright holder, and no one else has the right to take even a little of it without permission. I therefore respectfully dissent.

NOTES

1. For most copyrighted works, the reproduction and derivative-work rights protect not only against literal duplication, but also against "imitation"—at least if the elements of the copyright owner's work that are imitated are protectable and not excluded by the idea-expression distinction or other doctrines such as merger or scenes a faire. Why do you think that the Copyright Act treats sound recordings differently?

2. Recall that sound recordings were not even protected by federal copyright law until 1972. Before that time, sound recordings were protected solely by state law. Why do you think that sound recordings came so late to federal copyright protection? And why do you think that, even after sound recordings were protected by federal law, that protection did not include an exclusive right to make or to authorize public performances?

3. What is the purpose of sampling? Is the answer the same from the sampling musician's point of view and from a consumer's perspective? Also, why do musicians sample preexisting sound recordings rather than record their own sound-alike version? Based on your thoughts on these questions, do you think the Ninth Circuit is asking the right question by focusing on whether what was copied from the plaintiff's work is indistinguishable to an average audience? And should your thoughts on sampling make the treatment of musical compositions the same as sound recordings?

4. The courts in *VMG Salsoul* and *Bridgeport Music* (discussed in *VMG Salsoul*) disagree over whether those who copy the sounds from copyrighted sound recordings can be held liable even for copying that is de minimis. But curiously, that debate is largely absent from "personal" copying of musical works and sound recordings. For years before the rise of streaming services made the practice less relevant, people engaged freely in the process of ripping CDs to copy music onto mobile devices such as MP3 players and, later, cell phones. Nothing in the Copyright Act expressly immunizes such personal copying, and whether this sort of personal use is sheltered by the fair use doctrine remains largely untested. The seeming immunity of personal copying of music to copyright challenge appears to arise more from norms and social expectations than from law, strictly speaking. (For how copyright law ought to think about such tolerated uses, see Tim Wu, *Tolerated Use*, 31 COLUM. J.L. & ARTS 617 (2008).)

That said, immunity for personal copying of music is possibly linked to expectations formed in part by the Audio Home Recording Act of 1992 (AHRA), Pub. L. No. 102-563, 106 Stat. 4237. The AHRA regulated a technology, digital audio tape (or DAT), that in 1992 was expected to be a significant new technology for distributing music. But DAT never panned out; it was quickly superseded by other forms of digital storage and then by online distribution.

The AHRA requires manufacturers of digital audio recorders and tapes to embed technology that permits the creation only of first-generation copies. The AHRA includes prohibitions on circumventing the copy-control technology and on marketing technology designed to circumvent that copying-control technology.

The AHRA also enacts a royalty pooling and distribution scheme. DAT manufacturers pay statutory royalties on both recording devices and recording media. The royalties are pooled and subsequently divided among copyright owners of musical works, copyright owners of sound recordings, and recording artists.

Perhaps the most significant element of the AHRA is an exemption from copyright infringement liability for consumers engaged in noncommercial use. Section 1008 provides:

> No action may be brought under this title alleging infringement of copyright based on ... the noncommercial use by a consumer of ... a [recording] device or medium for making digital musical recordings or analog musical recordings.

17 U.S.C. § 1008. Before the AHRA, the recording industry took the position, at least in public, that copies made for personal use were infringing. That position was seemingly contrary to Congress's intent. When Congress passed legislation in 1971 extending copyright protection to sound recordings, it indicated that such protection was not intended "to restrain the home recording, from broadcast or from tapes or records, of recorded performances, where home recording is for private use and with no purpose of reproducing or otherwise capitalizing commercially on it." H.R. Rep. No. 487, 92d Cong., 1st Sess. 7 (1971). Congress's intent may have been clear, but the law as of 1992 was not—not least because there was no judicial authority exempting personal copying of music. Section 1008 made explicit Congress's intent to exempt personal use, at least with respect to the covered recording devices and media. Note, however, that the AHRA specifically exempts from its coverage general purpose computers. That means that for most of the personal copying of music that happens today—personal copying using general purpose computers rather than the devices covered by the AHRA—there is no explicit exemption. But the expectations that animated the exemption for personal use in the AHRA appear to have broadened to encompass all personal copying of music. That expectation is likely bolstered by language in cases like *RIAA v. Diamond Multimedia Systems, Inc.* 180 F.3d 1072 (9th Cir. 1999), suggesting (albeit not holding) that personal copying, even using devices not covered by the AHRA, was immunized as a fair use. The *Diamond* case involved the Rio, an early MP3 player. As the court reasoned:

> In fact, the Rio's operation is entirely consistent with the [AHRA's] main purpose—the facilitation of personal use. As the Senate Report explains, "[t]he purpose of [the Act] is to ensure the right of consumers to make analog or digital audio recordings of copyrighted music for their private, noncommercial use." S. Rep. 102-294, at 86. The Act does so through its home taping exemption, which "protects all noncommercial copying by consumers of digital and analog musical recordings," H.R. Rep. 102-873(I), at 59. The Rio merely makes copies in order to render portable, or "space-shift", those files that already reside on a user's hard drive. Cf. Sony Corp. of America v. Universal City Studios, 464 U.S. 417, 455 (1984) (holding that "time-shifting" of copyrighted television shows with VCR's constitutes fair use under the Copyright Act, and thus is not an infringement). Such copying is paradigmatic non-commercial personal use entirely consistent with the purposes of the Act.

Id. at 1079. *But cf.* A&M Records, Inc. v. Napster, Inc., 239 F.3d 1004, 1024 (9th Cir. 2001) ("[T]he Audio Home Recording Act does not cover the downloading of MP3 files to computer hard drives.... [N]otwithstanding Napster's claim that computers are 'digital audio recording devices,' computer do not make 'digital music recordings' as defined by the Audio Home Recording Act."). *See also* Alliance of Artists & Recording Cos., Inc. v. Denso Int'l Am., Inc., 947 F.3d 849 (D.C. Cir. 2020) (holding that CD-copying devices installed in automobiles were not "digital audio recording devices" subject to AHRA).

The § 106(6) Right to Make or Authorize Public Performance by Means of a Digital Audio Transmission, and the § 114 Compulsory License

As has been mentioned, the § 106(4) public-performance right does not apply to sound recordings, and, as a consequence, sound recording copyright owners enjoy no general right to control public performances. However, under § 106(6), added to the Copyright Act in 1995, sound recording copyright owners are granted a narrower right to control public performances made "by means of a digital audio transmission." 17 U.S.C. § 106(6). Why do you think Congress added this new right?

The § 106(6) right is further limited by § 114, which codifies both a major exemption and a statutory license. Please review § 114.

Sections 114(d)(1)(A)-(B) exempt "nonsubscription broadcast transmissions" from the scope of the § 106(6) right, which means that free, over-the-air digital broadcasts by FCC-licensed broadcasters do not need public-performance licenses from the owners of copyrighted sound recordings that they play on the air. (As discussed above, such broadcasts do require licenses from the owners of copyrights in the underlying musical compositions; these licenses are obtained through one or more PROs.) Note that the exemption only covers "broadcast" transmissions—that is, those made over-the-air. The exemption does not cover non-subscription internet transmissions. Internet radio stations—also known as webcasters—as opposed to traditional over-the-air stations, are subject to the § 106(6) right, although they can qualify, as you shall now see, for a statutory license.

Section 114 also establishes a statutory license that applies to digital audio transmissions that are deemed to be non-interactive. The statute also identifies an intermediary, SoundExchange, which is made responsible for the collection and distribution of statutory digital performance royalties. By contrast, "interactive" transmissions do not qualify for the statutory license, so those engaged in digital audio transmissions that fall into the "interactive" category must seek negotiated licenses with the owners of sound recording copyrights that they wish to publicly perform.

Distinguishing digital audio transmissions that are "interactive" from those that are not was initially a vexing task, but one which has become clearer over time. There is a principle that underlies the distinction between interactive and non-interactive: the interactive variety of digital audio transmission is expected to interfere more with the then-existing market for sound recordings, as compared with the non-interactive variety. That is, interactive services are expected to displace more record sales than non-interactive ones.

You can see this principle at play in § 114's definition of "interactive." An interactive digital audio transmission is one that

> *enables a member of the public to receive a transmission of a program specially created for the recipient, or on request, a transmission of a particular sound recording, whether or not as part of a program, which is selected by or on behalf of the recipient.*

17 U.S.C. § 114(j)(7). You can probably see that a service like Spotify, Apple Music, or Google Play falls into the "interactive" category. Interactive services must negotiate a license with the sound recording copyright owner.

In contrast, a service like Pandora is not "interactive," because it does not transmit programs specially created for the recipient, nor does it permit the recipient to request the transmission of a particular sound recording. Non-interactive services like Pandora may be eligible under § 114(d) to obtain statutory licenses to publicly perform copyrighted musical compositions by means of a digital audio transmission, with fees for the license set according to industry negotiations, with the option of appealing to the judges of the Copyright Royalty Board if those negotiations reach an impasse.

Eligibility for the statutory license is conditioned on a non-interactive service complying with a number of conditions, including (1) not cooperating in efforts by the transmission recipient to engage in automated scanning intended to result in the selected of a particular sound recording for transmission to the recipient; (2) not pre-announcing the schedule on which particular songs will be transmitted; (3) including various sorts of information about the sound recordings being transmitted, to the extent technically feasible; and (4) not violating the "sound recording performance complement." *Id.* § 114(d)(2)(C). The sound recording performance complement is defined as

> the transmission during any 3-hour period, on a particular channel used by a transmitting entity, of no more than—

>> (A) 3 different selections of sound recordings from any one phonorecord lawfully distributed for public performance or sale in the United States, if no more than 2 such selections are transmitted consecutively; or

>> (B) 4 different selections of sound recordings—
>> (i) by the same featured recording artist; or
>> (ii) from any set or compilation of phonorecords lawfully distributed together as a unit for public performance or sale in the United States,
>> if no more than three such selections are transmitted consecutively.

Id. § 114(j)(13). A non-interactive service that fails to observe the limits of the sound recording performance complement may still qualify for the statutory license if the violations were "not willfully intended to avoid the numerical limitations prescribed." *Id.*

It is fair to say that the market has responded to the § 114 arrangements in ways that were not anticipated by many experts. Back in 1995 when § 106(6) and the § 114 statutory license were inserted into the Copyright Act, many believed that the key to success in the digital music streaming market was designing an attractive service that qualified as "non-interactive," and thus eligible for the statutory license. But more than two decades later, it is the *interactive* services, such as Spotify, Apple Music, and Google Play, that have emerged as the most powerful competitors in music streaming. Why is that? So far, these services have been able to strike license deals with the record companies that allow them to offer music at a price that many are willing to pay. And the choice and flexibility of the interactive services appears to be powerfully attractive to consumers. Meanwhile the non-interactive services, such as Pandora, have been consumed in long-running and ruinously expensive disputes over the statutory licensing rate. A full account of those battles is well beyond the scope of an introductory copyright course. Suffice for now to say that they have enriched lawyers while sapping the vitality of the non-interactive services, which, at least for the moment, appear to be losing the competitive battle.

VI. Fair Use

In Chapter V, you read about the exclusive rights of copyright holders and how third parties might infringe those rights. You also learned about some limitations on infringement liability, such as the first-sale doctrine and the rule for soundalike recordings. The limitations discussed in Chapter V are principally bright-line rules. Many are technical and complex, such as § 110's provisions permitting certain small business to transmit musical works.

In this chapter, you will learn about **fair use**, the most wide-ranging limitation on copyright protection. It is unlike the limitations in Chapter V; unlike those relatively narrow, rule-like limitations, fair use is encoded as a standard and it is not always clear-cut to apply. As you'll see, courts develop it on a case-by-case basis, though there are recognizable categories of fair use cases and outcomes within each category are far from random. As you read through the statutory section encoding the fair use standard and the cases that analyze it, think about whether it is preferable to implement fair use as a standard or as a set of rules, be they simple or complex. (In general, rules are costlier to promulgate but are easier and clearer to apply than standards. For that reason, individuals can typically structure their own behavior more readily in the face of clearer-to-apply rules than less-clearer-to-apply standards. Standards are thought to be better suited to doing justice across a range of situations that might not be as easily covered by rules. *See generally* Louis Kaplow, *Rules Versus Standards: An Economic Analysis*, 42 DUKE L.J. 557 (1992).)

In the United States, fair use often is said to have originated with Justice Joseph Story's opinion in *Folsom v. Marsh*, 9 F. Cas. 342 (C.C.D. Mass. 1841), although intimations of fair use can be discerned in opinions before Story's and in earlier English case law. *See* Matthew Sag, *The Pre-History of Fair Use*, 76 BROOK. L. REV. 1371 (2011). In *Folsom*, the plaintiffs had published a 12-volume, 7,000-page book of George Washington's correspondence. The defendants published a 2-volume, 866-page biography of George Washington, which relied heavily on his correspondence. The defendants' book was intended for less specialized readers. Of the 866 pages in the defendants' book, 388 were copied verbatim from the plaintiffs' book. In ruling on the plaintiffs' ensuing copyright infringement claim against the defendants, Justice Story first notes that deciding whether there is infringement is a result of a "balance" of factors. He subsequently observes:

> The question, then, is, whether this is a justifiable use of the original materials, such as the law recognizes as no infringement of the copyright of the plaintiffs.... [W]e must often, in deciding questions of this sort, look to the nature and objects of the selections made, the quantity and value of the materials used, and the degree in which the use may prejudice the sale, or diminish the profits, or supersede the objects, of the original work.

Justice Story elaborates:

> Thus, for example, no one can doubt that a reviewer may fairly cite largely from the original work, if his design be really and truly to use the passages for the purposes of fair and reasonable criticism. On the other hand, it is as clear, that if he thus cites the most important parts of the work, with a view, not to criticise, but to supersede the use of the original work, and substitute the review for it, such a use will be deemed in law a piracy. A wide interval might, of course, exist between these two extremes, calling for great caution and involving great difficulty ....

Courts developed these factors into an analytical framework that defendants could use in appropriate cases to avoid infringement liability by demonstrating their use of a plaintiff's copyrighted work was fair. *See, e.g.,* Loew's Inc. v. Columbia Broadcasting Sys., 131 F. Supp. 165 (S.D. Cal. 1955); N.Y. Tribune v. Otis & Co., 39 F. Supp. 67 (S.D.N.Y. 1941).

Congress subsequently codified these factors in the 1976 Act in § 107:

> *Notwithstanding the provisions of sections 106 and 106A, the fair use of a copyrighted work, including such use by reproduction in copies or phonorecords or by any other means specified by that section, for purposes such as criticism, comment, news reporting, teaching (including multiple copies for classroom use), scholarship, or research, is not an infringement of copyright. In determining whether the use made of a work in any particular case is a fair use the factors to be considered shall include—*
>
> > *(1) the purpose and character of the use, including whether such use is of a commercial nature or is for nonprofit educational purposes;*
> >
> > *(2) the nature of the copyrighted work;*
> >
> > *(3) the amount and substantiality of the portion used in relation to the copyrighted work as a whole; and*
> >
> > *(4) the effect of the use upon the potential market for or value of the copyrighted work.*
>
> *The fact that a work is unpublished shall not itself bar a finding of fair use if such finding is made upon consideration of all the above factors.*

Note that all four listed factors must be considered by courts entertaining a fair use defense. Yet courts can consider additional factors too because the listed factors are set out as non-exhaustive: the § 107 preamble states that "the factors to be considered *shall include* ...," and the language "shall include" is understood to invite consideration of any facts, evidence, or arguments that a court would find germane to the fair use analysis in a particular case. As you read through the cases in this chapter, consider whether factors beyond the four set out in § 107 are or ought to be considered.

In the sections that follow, we consider fair use cases, first in foundational cases followed by more recent ones that try to make sense of the now-central notion of **transformativeness**. These cases cover traditional media, such as magazine articles, books, songs, and visual art, as well as software and internet media.

A. Foundational Cases

As you read the following Supreme Court decision, consider why copyright law provides a fair use defense in the first instance. Pay attention to how the Court analyzes each of the four statutory fair use factors and how it derives an ultimate conclusion as to fair use.

Harper & Row, Publishers, Inc. v. Nation Enterprises
471 U.S. 539 (1985)

O'CONNOR J.: ...

[1] In February 1977, shortly after leaving the White House, former President Gerald R. Ford contracted with petitioners Harper & Row and Reader's Digest, to publish his as yet unwritten memoirs. The memoirs were to contain significant hitherto unpublished material concerning the Watergate crisis, Mr. Ford's pardon of former

President Nixon and Mr. Ford's reflections on this period of history, and the morality and personalities involved. In addition to the right to publish the Ford memoirs in book form, the agreement gave petitioners the exclusive right to license prepublication excerpts, known in the trade as "first serial rights." Two years later, as the memoirs were nearing completion, petitioners negotiated a prepublication licensing agreement with *Time*, a weekly news magazine. *Time* agreed to pay $25,000, $12,500 in advance and an additional $12,500 at publication, in exchange for the right to excerpt 7,500 words from Mr. Ford's account of the Nixon pardon. The issue featuring the excerpts was timed to appear approximately one week before shipment of the full length book version to bookstores. Exclusivity was an important consideration; Harper & Row instituted procedures designed to maintain the confidentiality of the manuscript, and *Time* retained the right to renegotiate the second payment should the material appear in print prior to its release of the excerpts.

[2] Two to three weeks before the *Time* article's scheduled release, an unidentified person secretly brought a copy of the Ford manuscript to Victor Navasky, editor of *The Nation*, a political commentary magazine. Mr. Navasky knew that his possession of the manuscript was not authorized and that the manuscript must be returned quickly to his source to avoid discovery. He hastily put together what he believed was "a real hot news story" composed of quotes, paraphrases, and facts drawn exclusively from the manuscript.... The 2,250-word article ... appeared on April 3, 1979. As a result of *The Nation*'s article, *Time* canceled its piece and refused to pay the remaining $12,500.

Figure 96: Gerald Ford's autobiography (left) and *The Nation*'s article about the book (right)

[3] Petitioners brought suit ..., alleging ... violations of the Copyright Act.... The District Court rejected respondents' argument that The Nation's piece was a "fair use" sanctioned by § 107 of the Act....

[4] A divided panel of the Court of Appeals for the Second Circuit reversed....

[5] ... [C]opyright is intended to increase and not to impede the harvest of knowledge. But .... [t]he rights conferred by copyright are designed to assure contributors to the store of knowledge a fair return for their labors....

[6] .... The monopoly created by copyright thus rewards the individual author in order to benefit the public. This principle applies equally to works of fiction and nonfiction. The book at issue here, for example, was two years in the making, and began with a contract giving the author's copyright to the publishers in exchange for their services in producing and marketing the work. In preparing the book, Mr. Ford drafted essays and word portraits of public figures and participated in hundreds of taped interviews that were later distilled to chronicle his personal viewpoint. It is evident that the monopoly granted by copyright actively served its intended purpose of inducing the creation of new material of potential historical value.

[7] …. The copyright owner's rights, however, are subject to certain statutory exceptions. Among these is § 107 which codifies the traditional privilege of other authors to make "fair use" of an earlier writer's work….

[8] … *The Nation* has admitted to lifting verbatim quotes of the author's original language totaling between 300 and 400 words and constituting some 13% of *The Nation* article. In using generous verbatim excerpts of Mr. Ford's unpublished manuscript to lend authenticity to its account of the forthcoming memoirs, *The Nation* effectively arrogated to itself the right of first publication, an important marketable subsidiary right. For the reasons set forth below, we find that this use of the copyrighted manuscript, even stripped to the verbatim quotes conceded by *The Nation* to be copyrightable expression, was not a fair use within the meaning of the Copyright Act….

[9] Fair use was traditionally defined as a privilege in others than the owner of the copyright to use the copyrighted material in a reasonable manner without his consent. The statutory formulation of the defense of fair use in the Copyright Act reflects the intent of Congress to codify the common-law doctrine. Section 107 requires a case-by-case determination whether a particular use is fair, and the statute notes four nonexclusive factors to be considered. This approach was "intended to restate the [pre-existing] judicial doctrine of fair use, not to change, narrow, or enlarge it in any way." H.R. REP. NO. 94–1476, p. 66 (1976) (hereinafter HOUSE REPORT).

[10] The author's consent to a reasonable use of his copyrighted works had always been implied by the courts as a necessary incident of the constitutional policy of promoting the progress of science and the useful arts, since a prohibition of such use would inhibit subsequent writers from attempting to improve upon prior works and thus frustrate the very ends sought to be attained. [NYU Law] Professor [Alan] Latman, in a study of the doctrine of fair use commissioned by Congress for the revision effort, summarized prior law as turning on the "importance of the material copied or performed from the point of view of the reasonable copyright owner. In other words, would the reasonable copyright owner have consented to the use?"

[11] As early as 1841, Justice Story gave judicial recognition to the doctrine in a case that concerned the letters of another former President, George Washington.

> *"[A] reviewer may fairly cite largely from the original work, if his design be really and truly to use the passages for the purposes of fair and reasonable criticism. On the other hand, it is as clear, that if he thus cites the most important parts of the work, with a view, not to criticise, but to supersede the use of the original work, and substitute the review for it, such a use will be deemed in law a piracy." Folsom v. Marsh, 9 F. Cas. 342, 344–45 (No. 4,901) (CC Mass.).*

[12] As Justice Story's hypothetical illustrates, the fair use doctrine has always precluded a use that "supersede[s] the use of the original."

[13] Perhaps because the fair use doctrine was predicated on the author's implied consent to "reasonable and customary" use when he released his work for public consumption, fair use traditionally was not recognized as a defense to charges of copying from an author's as yet unpublished works. Under common-law copyright, the property of the author in his intellectual creation was absolute until he voluntarily parted with the same. This absolute rule, however, was tempered in practice by the equitable nature of the fair use doctrine. In a given case, factors such as implied consent through *de facto* publication on performance or dissemination of a work may tip the balance of equities in favor of prepublication use. But it has never been seriously disputed that the fact that the plaintiff's work is unpublished is a factor tending to negate the defense of fair use. Publication of an author's expression before he has authorized its dissemination seriously infringes the author's right to decide when and whether it will be made public, a factor not present in fair use of published works. Respondents contend, however, that Congress, in including first publication among the rights enumerated in § 106, which

are expressly subject to fair use under § 107, intended that fair use would apply *in pari materia* to published and unpublished works. The Copyright Act does not support this proposition....

[14] Though the right of first publication, like the other rights enumerated in § 106, is expressly made subject to the fair use provision of § 107, fair use analysis must always be tailored to the individual case. The nature of the interest at stake is highly relevant to whether a given use is fair. From the beginning, those entrusted with the task of revision recognized the overbalancing reasons to preserve the common law protection of undisseminated works until the author or his successor chooses to disclose them. The right of first publication implicates a threshold decision by the author whether and in what form to release his work. First publication is inherently different from other § 106 rights in that only one person can be the first publisher; as the contract with *Time* illustrates, the commercial value of the right lies primarily in exclusivity. Because the potential damage to the author from judicially enforced "sharing" of the first publication right with unauthorized users of his manuscript is substantial, the balance of equities in evaluating such a claim of fair use inevitably shifts....

[15] .... We conclude that the unpublished nature of a work is "[a] key, though not necessarily determinative, factor" tending to negate a defense of fair use. SENATE REPORT, at 64.

[16] We also find unpersuasive respondents' argument that fair use may be made of a soon-to-be-published manuscript on the ground that the author has demonstrated he has no interest in nonpublication. This argument assumes that the unpublished nature of copyrighted material is only relevant to letters or other confidential writings not intended for dissemination. It is true that common-law copyright was often enlisted in the service of personal privacy. In its commercial guise, however, an author's right to choose when he will publish is no less deserving of protection. The period encompassing the work's initiation, its preparation, and its grooming for public dissemination is a crucial one for any literary endeavor. The Copyright Act, which accords the copyright owner the "right to control the first public distribution" of his work, HOUSE REPORT, at 62, echo[e]s the common law's concern that the author or copyright owner retain control throughout this critical stage. The obvious benefit to author and public alike of assuring authors the leisure to develop their ideas free from fear of expropriation outweighs any short-term "news value" to be gained from premature publication of the author's expression. The author's control of first public distribution implicates not only his personal interest in creative control but his property interest in exploitation of prepublication rights, which are valuable in themselves and serve as a valuable adjunct to publicity and marketing. Under ordinary circumstances, the author's right to control the first public appearance of his undisseminated expression will outweigh a claim of fair use....

[17] Respondents, however, contend that First Amendment values require a different rule under the circumstances of this case. The thrust of the decision below is that the scope of fair use is undoubtedly wider when the information conveyed relates to matters of high public concern. Respondents advance the substantial public import of the subject matter of the Ford memoirs as grounds for excusing a use that would ordinarily not pass muster as a fair use—the piracy of verbatim quotations for the purpose of "scooping" the authorized first serialization. Respondents explain their copying of Mr. Ford's expression as essential to reporting the news story it claims the book itself represents. In respondents' view, not only the facts contained in Mr. Ford's memoirs, but the precise manner in which he expressed himself were as newsworthy as what he had to say. Respondents argue that the public's interest in learning this news as fast as possible outweighs the right of the author to control its first publication.

[18] The Second Circuit noted, correctly, that copyright's idea/expression dichotomy strikes a definitional balance between the First Amendment and the Copyright Act by permitting free communication of facts while still protecting an author's expression. No author may copyright his ideas or the facts he narrates.... But copyright assures those who write and publish factual narratives such as "A Time to Heal" that they may at least enjoy the right to market the original expression contained therein as just compensation for their investment.

[19] Respondents' theory, however, would expand fair use to effectively destroy any expectation of copyright protection in the work of a public figure. Absent such protection, there would be little incentive to create or profit in financing such memoirs, and the public would be denied an important source of significant historical information. The promise of copyright would be an empty one if it could be avoided merely by dubbing the infringement a fair use "news report" of the book.

[20] Nor do respondents assert any actual necessity for circumventing the copyright scheme with respect to the types of works and users at issue here. Where an author and publisher have invested extensive resources in creating an original work and are poised to release it to the public, no legitimate aim is served by pre-empting the right of first publication. The fact that the words the author has chosen to clothe his narrative may of themselves be "newsworthy" is not an independent justification for unauthorized copying of the author's expression prior to publication....

[21] In our haste to disseminate news, it should not be forgotten that the Framers intended copyright itself to be the engine of free expression. By establishing a marketable right to the use of one's expression, copyright supplies the economic incentive to create and disseminate ideas...

[22] It is fundamentally at odds with the scheme of copyright to accord lesser rights in those works that are of greatest importance to the public. Such a notion ignores the major premise of copyright and injures author and public alike....

[23] In view of the First Amendment protections already embodied in the Copyright Act's distinction between copyrightable expression and uncopyrightable facts and ideas, and the latitude for scholarship and comment traditionally afforded by fair use, we see no warrant for expanding the doctrine of fair use to create what amounts to a public figure exception to copyright. Whether verbatim copying from a public figure's manuscript in a given case is or is not fair must be judged according to the traditional equities of fair use....

[24] Fair use is a mixed question of law and fact.... [W]hether *The Nation* article constitutes fair use under § 107 must be reviewed in light of the principles discussed above. The factors enumerated in the section are not meant to be exclusive: "[S]ince the doctrine is an equitable rule of reason, no generally applicable definition is possible, and each case raising the question must be decided on its own facts." HOUSE REPORT, at 65. The four factors identified by Congress as especially relevant in determining whether the use was fair are: (1) the purpose and character of the use; (2) the nature of the copyrighted work; (3) the substantiality of the portion used in relation to the copyrighted work as a whole; (4) the effect on the potential market for or value of the copyrighted work. We address each one separately.

[25] *Purpose of the Use.* The Second Circuit correctly identified news reporting as the general purpose of *The Nation*'s use. News reporting is one of the examples enumerated in § 107 to "give some idea of the sort of activities the courts might regard as fair use under the circumstances." SENATE REPORT, at 61.... "[W]hether a use referred to in the first sentence of section 107 is a fair use in a particular case will depend upon the application of the determinative factors, including those mentioned in the second sentence." SENATE REPORT, at 62. The fact that an article arguably is "news" and therefore a productive use is simply one factor in a fair use analysis.

[26] .... *The Nation* has every right to seek to be the first to publish information. But *The Nation* went beyond simply reporting uncopyrightable information and actively sought to exploit the headline value of its infringement, making a "news event" out of its unauthorized first publication of a noted figure's copyrighted expression.

[27] The fact that a publication was commercial as opposed to nonprofit is a separate factor that tends to weigh against a finding of fair use. Every commercial use of copyrighted material is presumptively an unfair

exploitation of the monopoly privilege that belongs to the owner of the copyright. In arguing that the purpose of news reporting is not purely commercial, *The Nation* misses the point entirely. The crux of the profit/nonprofit distinction is not whether the sole motive of the use is monetary gain but whether the user stands to profit from exploitation of the copyrighted material without paying the customary price.

[28] In evaluating character and purpose we cannot ignore *The Nation*'s stated purpose of scooping the forthcoming hardcover and *Time* abstracts. *The Nation*'s use had not merely the incidental effect but the *intended purpose* of supplanting the copyright holder's commercially valuable right of first publication. Also relevant to the character of the use is the propriety of the defendant's conduct. Fair use presupposes good faith and fair dealing. The trial court found that *The Nation* knowingly exploited a purloined manuscript. Unlike the typical claim of fair use, *The Nation* cannot offer up even the fiction of consent as justification....

[29] *Nature of the Copyrighted Work.* Second, the Act directs attention to the nature of the copyrighted work. "A Time to Heal" may be characterized as an unpublished historical narrative or autobiography. The law generally recognizes a greater need to disseminate factual works than works of fiction or fantasy....

[30] Some of the briefer quotes from the memoirs are arguably necessary adequately to convey the facts; for example, Mr. Ford's characterization of the White House tapes as the "smoking gun" is perhaps so integral to the idea expressed as to be inseparable from it. But *The Nation* did not stop at isolated phrases and instead excerpted subjective descriptions and portraits of public figures whose power lies in the author's individualized expression. Such use, focusing on the most expressive elements of the work, exceeds that necessary to disseminate the facts.

[31] The fact that a work is unpublished is a critical element of its nature. Our prior discussion establishes that the scope of fair use is narrower with respect to unpublished works. While even substantial quotations might qualify as fair use in a review of a published work or a news account of a speech that had been delivered to the public or disseminated to the press, the author's right to control the first public appearance of his expression weighs against such use of the work before its release. The right of first publication encompasses not only the choice whether to publish at all, but also the choices of when, where, and in what form first to publish a work.

[32] In the case of Mr. Ford's manuscript, the copyright holders' interest in confidentiality is irrefutable; the copyright holders had entered into a contractual undertaking to "keep the manuscript confidential" and required that all those to whom the manuscript was shown also "sign an agreement to keep the manuscript confidential." While the copyright holders' contract with *Time* required *Time* to submit its proposed article seven days before publication, *The Nation*'s clandestine publication afforded no such opportunity for creative or quality control. It was hastily patched together and contained a number of inaccuracies. A use that so clearly infringes the copyright holder's interests in confidentiality and creative control is difficult to characterize as "fair."

[33] *Amount and Substantiality of the Portion Used.* Next, the Act directs us to examine the amount and substantiality of the portion used in relation to the copyrighted work as a whole. In absolute terms, the words actually quoted were an insubstantial portion of "A Time to Heal." The District Court, however, found that "*[T]he Nation* took what was essentially the heart of the book." We believe the Court of Appeals erred in overruling the District Judge's evaluation of the qualitative nature of the taking. A *Time* editor described the chapters on the pardon as "the most interesting and moving parts of the entire manuscript." .... [*The Nation*] quoted these passages precisely because they qualitatively embodied Ford's distinctive expression.

[34] .... [T]he fact that a substantial portion of the infringing work was copied verbatim is evidence of the qualitative value of the copied material, both to the originator and to the plagiarist who seeks to profit from marketing someone else's copyrighted expression.

[35] Stripped to the verbatim quotes, the direct takings from the unpublished manuscript constitute at least 13% of the infringing article. *The Nation* article is structured around the quoted excerpts which serve as its dramatic focal points. In view of the expressive value of the excerpts and their key role in the infringing work, we cannot agree with the Second Circuit that the "magazine took a meager, indeed an infinitesimal amount of Ford's original language."

[36] *Effect on the Market.* Finally, the Act focuses on "the effect of the use upon the potential market for or value of the copyrighted work." This last factor is undoubtedly the single most important element of fair use. Fair use, when properly applied, is limited to copying by others which does not materially impair the marketability of the work which is copied. The trial court found not merely a potential but an actual effect on the market. *Time*'s cancellation of its projected serialization and its refusal to pay the $12,500 were the direct effect of the infringement.... Rarely will a case of copyright infringement present such clear-cut evidence of actual damage. Petitioners assured *Time* that there would be no other authorized publication of *any* portion of the unpublished manuscript prior to April 23, 1979. *Any* publication of material from chapters 1 and 3 would permit *Time* to renegotiate its final payment. *Time* cited *The Nation*'s article, which contained verbatim quotes from the unpublished manuscript, as a reason for its nonperformance.... [O]nce a copyright holder establishes with reasonable probability the existence of a causal connection between the infringement and a loss of revenue, the burden properly shifts to the infringer to show that this damage would have occurred had there been no taking of copyrighted expression. Petitioners established a prima facie case of actual damage that respondents failed to rebut.

[37] More important, to negate fair use one need only show that if the challenged use should become widespread, it would adversely affect the *potential* market for the copyrighted work...

[38] Placed in a broader perspective, a fair use doctrine that permits extensive prepublication quotations from an unreleased manuscript without the copyright owner's consent poses substantial potential for damage to the marketability of first serialization rights in general. Isolated instances of minor infringements, when multiplied many times, become in the aggregate a major inroad on copyright that must be prevented....

[39] The Court of Appeals erred in concluding that *The Nation*'s use of the copyrighted material was excused by the public's interest in the subject matter. It erred, as well, in overlooking the unpublished nature of the work and the resulting impact on the potential market for first serial rights of permitting unauthorized prepublication excerpts under the rubric of fair use. Finally, in finding the taking "infinitesimal," the Court of Appeals accorded too little weight to the qualitative importance of the quoted passages of original expression. In sum, the traditional doctrine of fair use, as embodied in the Copyright Act, does not sanction the use made by *The Nation* of these copyrighted materials. Any copyright infringer may claim to benefit the public by increasing public access to the copyrighted work. But Congress has not designed, and we see no warrant for judicially imposing, a "compulsory license" permitting unfettered access to the unpublished copyrighted expression of public figures.

[40] .... [W]e find that *The Nation*'s use of these verbatim excerpts from the unpublished manuscript was not a fair use ....

BRENNAN, J., dissenting, in which Justice White and Justice Marshall joined.

[41] The Court holds that *The Nation*'s quotation of 300 words from the unpublished 200,000-word manuscript of President Gerald R. Ford infringed the copyright in that manuscript, even though the quotations related to a historical event of undoubted significance—the resignation and pardon of President Richard M. Nixon. Although the Court pursues the laudable goal of protecting "the economic incentive to create and disseminate ideas," this zealous defense of the copyright owner's prerogative will, I fear, stifle the broad dissemination of

ideas and information copyright is intended to nurture. Protection of the copyright owner's economic interest is achieved in this case through an exceedingly narrow definition of the scope of fair use. The progress of arts and sciences and the robust public debate essential to an enlightened citizenry are ill served by this constricted reading of the fair use doctrine. I therefore respectfully dissent....

[42] In my judgment, the Court's fair use analysis has fallen to the temptation to find copyright violation based on a minimal use of literary form in order to provide compensation for the appropriation of information from a work of history. The failure to distinguish between information and literary form permeates every aspect of the Court's fair use analysis and leads the Court to the wrong result in this case. Application of the statutorily prescribed analysis with attention to the distinction between information and literary form leads to a straightforward finding of fair use within the meaning of § 107....

[43] The Court's exceedingly narrow approach to fair use permits Harper & Row to monopolize information. This holding effects an important extension of property rights and a corresponding curtailment in the free use of knowledge and of ideas. The Court has perhaps advanced the ability of the historian—or at least the public official who has recently left office—to capture the full economic value of information in his or her possession. But the Court does so only by risking the robust debate of public issues that is the essence of self-government. *The Nation* was providing the grist for that robust debate. The Court imposes liability upon *The Nation* for no other reason than that *The Nation* succeeded in being the first to provide certain information to the public. I dissent.

NOTES

1. Given *The Nation*'s status as a non-profit entity, what do you make of the Court's analysis of whether the magazine's use of Ford's autobiography was commercial (as part of its analysis of the first fair use factor)?

2. As a matter of copyright policy, should bad faith be relevant to a determination of fair use? And by what metric is a court to determine "bad faith"? Is *The Nation*'s conduct in reporting on the Ford manuscript "bad faith" by the standards of American journalism? Are you comfortable with a group of lawyers articulating norms for journalists?

3. How does the *Harper & Row* majority view the purpose of fair use? By contrast, how does the dissent view its purpose?

4. Do you have a sense after reading *Harper & Row* whether any particular factor is more important than others to a conclusion of fair use? If so, in all contexts or only in the specific context at issue here?

5. *Harper & Row* emphasized the unpublished nature of the plaintiff's work as a critical aspect weighing against fair use. In this regard, consider *Salinger v. Random House, Inc.*, 811 F.2d 90 (2d Cir. 1987), decided after *Harper & Row*. In *Salinger*, Ian Hamilton had written a biography of the famously reclusive author J.D. Salinger. In the biography, Hamilton relied heavily on unpublished letters that Salinger had written and sent to others, including Learned Hand, Ernest Hemingway, and Whit Burnett. Hamilton gained access to most, if not all, of these letters through various university libraries, to which the recipients had donated the letters. The biography relies on 44 such letters, which Hamilton mostly paraphrases closely and occasionally quotes. For example, in a 1943 letter to Burnett, Salinger expresses his disapproval over the marriage of his ex-girlfriend Oona O'Neill to Charlie Chaplin:

> *I can see them at home evenings. Chaplin squatting grey and nude, atop his chiffonier, swinging his thyroid around his head by his bamboo cane, like a dead rat. Oona in an aquamarine gown, applauding madly from the bathroom. Agnes (her mother) in a Jantzen bathing suit, passing*

> *between them with cocktails. I'm facetious, but I'm sorry. Sorry for anyone with a profile as young*
> *and lovely as Oona's.*

In reliance on this letter, Hamilton wrote in his biography:

> *At one point in a letter to Whit Burnett, he provides a pen portrait of the Happy Hour Chez*
> *Chaplin: the comedian, ancient and unclothed, is brandishing his walking stick—attached to the*
> *stick, and horribly resembling a lifeless rodent, is one of Chaplin's vital organs. Oona claps her*
> *hands in appreciation and Agnes, togged out in a bathing suit, pours drinks. Salinger goes on to*
> *say he's sorry—sorry not for what he has just written, but for Oona: far too youthful and exquisite*
> *for such a dreadful fate.*

Salinger sued Hamilton and Random House, the book's publisher, for copyright infringement. The Second Circuit held in favor of Salinger, finding infringement and no fair use. After noting that *Harper & Row* "underscored the idea that unpublished letters normally enjoy insulation from fair use copying," the Second Circuit reasoned that "the tenor of the Court's entire discussion of unpublished works conveys the idea that such works normally enjoy complete protection against copying any protected expression."

Many understood *Salinger* and other similar post-*Harper & Row* decisions to establish an absolute bar on finding fair use of unpublished works. In response, in 1992, Congress amended § 107 by adding the following sentence after its listing of the four statutory factors: "The fact that a work is unpublished shall not itself bar a finding of fair use if such finding is made upon consideration of all the above factors." Act of Oct. 24, 1992, Pub. L. No. 102-492, 106 Stat. 3145. Was this amendment good copyright policy?

As you read the following case, consider whether and how consumer home video recording of broadcast television shows is different than excerpts of material from a biography in a magazine article.

Sony Corporation of America v. Universal City Studios, Inc.
464 U.S. 417 (1984)

STEVENS, J.:

[1] Petitioners manufacture and sell home video tape recorders. Respondents own the copyrights on some of the television programs that are broadcast on the public airwaves. Some members of the general public use video tape recorders sold by petitioners to record some of these broadcasts, as well as a large number of other broadcasts. The question presented is whether the sale of petitioners' copying equipment to the general public violates any of the rights conferred upon respondents by the Copyright Act.

[2] Respondents commenced this copyright infringement action against petitioners .... Respondents alleged that some individuals had used Betamax video tape recorders (VTR's) to record some of respondents' copyrighted works which had been exhibited on commercially sponsored television and contended that these individuals had thereby infringed respondents' copyrights....

[3] Petitioner Sony manufactures millions of Betamax video tape recorders ....

[4] Several capabilities of the machine are noteworthy. The separate tuner in the Betamax enables it to record a broadcast off one station while the television set is tuned to another channel, permitting the viewer, for example, to watch two simultaneous news broadcasts by watching one "live" and recording the other for later viewing. Tapes may be reused, and programs that have been recorded may be erased either before or after viewing. A timer in the Betamax can be used to activate and deactivate the equipment at predetermined times, enabling an intended viewer to record programs that are transmitted when he or she is not at home. Thus a person may watch a program at home in the evening even though it was broadcast while the viewer was at work during the afternoon. The Betamax is also equipped with a pause button and a fast-forward control. The pause button, when depressed, deactivates the recorder until it is released, thus enabling a viewer to omit a commercial advertisement from the recording, provided, of course, that the viewer is present when the program is recorded. The fast forward control enables the viewer of a previously recorded program to run the tape rapidly when a segment he or she does not desire to see is being played back on the television screen.

[5] The respondents and Sony both conducted surveys of the way the Betamax machine was used by several hundred owners during a sample period in 1978. Although there were some differences in the surveys, they both showed that the primary use of the machine for most owners was "time-shifting"—the practice of recording a program to view it once at a later time, and thereafter erasing it. Time-shifting enables viewers to see programs they otherwise would miss because they are not at home, are occupied with other tasks, or are viewing a program on another station at the time of a broadcast that they desire to watch. Both surveys also showed, however, that a substantial number of interviewees had accumulated libraries of tapes.[3] Sony's survey indicated that over 80% of the interviewees watched at least as much regular television as they had before owning a Betamax.[4] Respondents offered no evidence of decreased television viewing by Betamax owners.

[6] Sony introduced considerable evidence describing television programs that could be copied without objection from any copyright holder, with special emphasis on sports, religious, and educational programming. For example, their survey indicated that 7.3% of all Betamax use is to record sports events, and representatives of professional baseball, football, basketball, and hockey testified that they had no objection to the recording of their televised events for home use.

[7] Respondents offered opinion evidence concerning the future impact of the unrestricted sale of VTR's on the commercial value of their copyrights. The District Court found, however, that they had failed to prove any likelihood of future harm from the use of VTR's for time-shifting....

[8] The [copyright] privileges that Congress may authorize are neither unlimited nor primarily designed to provide a special private benefit. Rather, the limited grant is a means by which an important public purpose may be achieved. It is intended to motivate the creative activity of authors and inventors by the provision of a special reward, and to allow the public access to the products of their genius after the limited period of exclusive control has expired....

---

[3] As evidence of how a VTR may be used, respondents offered the testimony of William Griffiths. Griffiths, although named as an individual defendant, was a client of plaintiffs' law firm. The District Court summarized his testimony as follows: "He owns approximately 100 tapes. When Griffiths bought his Betamax, he intended not only to time-shift (record, play-back and then erase) but also to build a library of cassettes. Maintaining a library, however, proved too expensive, and he is now erasing some earlier tapes and reusing them." ...

[4] The District Court summarized some of the findings in these surveys as follows: "According to plaintiffs' survey, 75.4% of the VTR owners use their machines to record for time-shifting purposes half or most of the time. Defendants' survey showed that 96% of the Betamax owners had used the machine to record programs they otherwise would have missed. When plaintiffs asked interviewees how many cassettes were in their library, 55.8% said there were 10 or fewer. In defendants' survey, of the total programs viewed by interviewees in the past month, 70.4% had been viewed only that one time and for 57.9%, there were no plans for further viewing."

Figure 97: advertisement for Sony's Betamax player

Figure 98: advertisement for Sony's Betamax player

401

[9] The Copyright Act provides the owner of a copyright with a potent arsenal of remedies against an infringer of his work, including an injunction to restrain the infringer from violating his rights {something we study later in Chapter VIII} ....

[10] The two respondents in this case do not seek relief against the Betamax users who have allegedly infringed their copyrights. Moreover, this is not a class action on behalf of all copyright owners who license their works for television broadcast, and respondents have no right to invoke whatever rights other copyright holders may have to bring infringement actions based on Betamax copying of their works. As was made clear by their own evidence, the copying of the respondents' programs represents a small portion of the total use of VTR's. It is, however, the taping of respondents' own copyrighted programs that provides them with standing to charge Sony with contributory infringement. To prevail, they have the burden of proving that users of the Betamax have infringed their copyrights and that Sony should be held responsible for that infringement....

[11] The question [whether there is secondary liability {something we study later in Chapter VII, when we revisit this case}] is ... whether the Betamax is capable of commercially significant noninfringing uses. In order to resolve that question, we need not explore *all* the different potential uses of the machine and determine whether or not they would constitute infringement. Rather, we need only consider whether on the basis of the facts as found by the district court a significant number of them would be non-infringing. Moreover, in order to resolve this case we need not give precise content to the question of how much use is commercially significant. For one potential use of the Betamax plainly satisfies this standard, however it is understood: private, noncommercial time-shifting in the home. It does so both (A) because respondents have no right to prevent other copyright holders from authorizing it for their programs, and (B) because the District Court's factual findings reveal that even the unauthorized home time-shifting of respondents' programs is legitimate fair use....

[12] .... [T]he findings of the District Court make it clear that time-shifting may enlarge the total viewing audience and that many producers are willing to allow private time-shifting to continue, at least for an experimental time period.

[13] The District Court found:

> Even if it were deemed that home-use recording of copyrighted material constituted infringement, the Betamax could still legally be used to record noncopyrighted material or material whose owners consented to the copying. An injunction would deprive the public of the ability to use the Betamax for this noninfringing off-the-air recording.
>
> Defendants introduced considerable testimony at trial about the potential for such copying of sports, religious, educational and other programming. This included testimony from representatives of the Offices of the Commissioners of the National Football, Basketball, Baseball and Hockey Leagues and Associations, the Executive Director of National Religious Broadcasters and various educational communications agencies. Plaintiffs attack the weight of the testimony offered and also contend that an injunction is warranted because infringing uses outweigh noninfringing uses....

[14] Even unauthorized uses of a copyrighted work are not necessarily infringing.... [T]he definition of exclusive rights in § 106 of the present Act is prefaced by the words "subject to sections 107 through 118." Those sections describe a variety of uses of copyrighted material that "are not infringements of copyright notwithstanding the provisions of § 106." The most pertinent in this case is § 107, the legislative endorsement of the doctrine of "fair use."

[15] .... Although not conclusive, the first factor requires that "the commercial or nonprofit character of an activity" be weighed in any fair use decision. If the Betamax were used to make copies for a commercial or profit-making purpose, such use would presumptively be unfair. The contrary presumption is appropriate here, however, because the District Court's findings plainly establish that time-shifting for private home use must be characterized as a noncommercial, nonprofit activity. Moreover, when one considers the nature of a televised copyrighted audiovisual work and that timeshifting merely enables a viewer to see such a work which he had been invited to witness in its entirety free of charge, the fact that the entire work is reproduced does not have its ordinary effect of militating against a finding of fair use.[33]

[16] This is not, however, the end of the inquiry because Congress has also directed us to consider "the effect of the use upon the potential market for or value of the copyrighted work." The purpose of copyright is to create incentives for creative effort. Even copying for noncommercial purposes may impair the copyright holder's ability to obtain the rewards that Congress intended him to have. But a use that has no demonstrable effect upon the potential market for, or the value of, the copyrighted work need not be prohibited in order to protect the author's incentive to create. The prohibition of such noncommercial uses would merely inhibit access to ideas without any countervailing benefit.

[17] Thus, although every commercial use of copyrighted material is presumptively an unfair exploitation of the ... privilege that belongs to the owner of the copyright, noncommercial uses are a different matter. A challenge to a noncommercial use of a copyrighted work requires proof either that the particular use is harmful, or that if it should become widespread, it would adversely affect the potential market for the copyrighted work. Actual present harm need not be shown; such a requirement would leave the copyright holder with no defense against predictable damage. Nor is it necessary to show with certainty that future harm will result. What is necessary is a showing by a preponderance of the evidence that *some* meaningful likelihood of future harm exists. If the intended use is for commercial gain, that likelihood may be presumed. But if it is for a noncommercial purpose, the likelihood must be demonstrated.

[18] In this case, respondents failed to carry their burden with regard to home time-shifting. The District Court described respondents' evidence as follows:

> *Plaintiffs' experts admitted at several points in the trial that the time-shifting without librarying would result in 'not a great deal of harm.' Plaintiffs' greatest concern about time-shifting is with 'a point of important philosophy that transcends even commercial judgment.' They fear that with any Betamax usage, 'invisible boundaries' are passed: 'the copyright owner has lost control over his program.'*

---

[33] It has been suggested that consumptive uses of copyrights by home VTR users are commercial even if the consumer does not sell the homemade tape because the consumer will not buy tapes separately sold by the copyright holder. Furthermore, the error in excusing such theft as noncommercial, we are told, can be seen by simple analogy: jewel theft is not converted into a noncommercial veniality if stolen jewels are simply worn rather than sold. The premise and the analogy are indeed simple, but they add nothing to the argument. The use to which stolen jewel[]ry is put is quite irrelevant in determining whether depriving its true owner of his present possessory interest in it is venial; because of the nature of the item and the true owner's interests in physical possession of it, the law finds the taking objectionable even if the thief does not use the item at all. Theft of a particular item of personal property of course may have commercial significance, for the thief deprives the owner of his right to sell that particular item to any individual. Timeshifting does not even remotely entail comparable consequences to the copyright owner. Moreover, the timeshifter no more steals the program by watching it once than does the live viewer, and the live viewer is no more likely to buy pre-recorded videotapes than is the timeshifter. Indeed, no live viewer would buy a pre-recorded videotape if he did not have access to a VTR.

[19] Later in its opinion, the District Court observed:

> Most of plaintiffs' predictions of harm hinge on speculation about audience viewing patterns and ratings, a measurement system which Sidney Sheinberg, MCA's president, calls a 'black art' because of the significant level of imprecision involved in the calculations....

[20] On the question of potential future harm from time-shifting, the District Court offered a more detailed analysis of the evidence. It rejected respondents' fear that persons watching the original telecast of a program will not be measured in the live audience and the ratings and revenues will decrease" by observing that current measurement technology allows the Betamax audience to be reflected.[36] It rejected respondents' prediction that live television or movie audiences will decrease as more people watch Betamax tapes as an alternative, with the observation that there is no factual basis for the underlying assumption.[37] It rejected respondents' fear that time-shifting will reduce audiences for telecast reruns, and concluded instead that given current market practices, this should aid plaintiffs rather than harm them.[38] And it declared that respondents' suggestion that theater or film rental exhibition of a program will suffer because of time-shift recording of that program lacks merit.[39]

[21] After completing that review, the District Court [concluded that] .... [h]arm from time-shifting is speculative and, at best, minimal....

[22] The District Court's conclusions are buttressed by the fact that to the extent time-shifting expands public access to freely broadcast television programs, it yields societal benefits....

[23] When these factors are all weighed in the ... balance, we must conclude that this record amply supports the District Court's conclusion that home time-shifting is fair use...

---

[36] .... [T]he District Court rejected plaintiffs' suggestion that the commercial attractiveness of television broadcasts would be diminished because Betamax owners would use the pause button or fast-forward control to avoid viewing advertisements: "It must be remembered, however, that to omit commercials, Betamax owners must view the program, including the commercials, while recording. To avoid commercials during playback, the viewer must fast-forward and, for the most part, guess as to when the commercial has passed. For most recordings, either practice may be too tedious. As defendants' survey showed, 92% of the programs were recorded with commercials and only 25% of the owners fast-forward through them. Advertisers will have to make the same kinds of judgments they do now about whether persons viewing televised programs actually watch the advertisements which interrupt them."

[37] [The district court stated:] "Here plaintiffs assume that people will view copies when they would otherwise be watching television or going to the movie theater. There is no factual basis for this assumption. It seems equally likely that Betamax owners will play their tapes when there is nothing on television they wish to see and no movie they want to attend. Defendants' survey does not show any negative effect of Betamax ownership on television viewing or theater attendance."

[38] [The district court stated:] "The underlying assumptions here are particularly difficult to accept. Plaintiffs explain that the Betamax increases access to the original televised material and that the more people there are in this original audience, the fewer people the rerun will attract. Yet current marketing practices, including the success of syndication, show just the opposite. Today, the larger the audience for the original telecast, the higher the price plaintiffs can demand from broadcasters from rerun rights. There is no survey within the knowledge of this court to show that the rerun audience is comprised of persons who have not seen the program. In any event, if ratings can reflect Betamax recording, original audiences may increase and, given market practices, this should aid plaintiffs rather than harm them."

[39] [According to the district court,] "This suggestion lacks merit. By definition, time-shift recording entails viewing and erasing, so the program will no longer be on tape when the later theater run begins. Of course, plaintiffs may fear that the Betamax will keep the tapes long enough to satisfy all their interest in the program and will, therefore, not patronize later theater exhibitions. To the extent this practice involves librarying, it is addressed [elsewhere]. It should also be noted that there is no evidence to suggest that the public interest in later theatrical exhibitions of motion pictures will be reduced any more by Betamax recording than it already is by the television broadcast of the film."

BLACKMUN, J., dissenting, joined by Justices Marshall, Powell, and Rehnquist:

[24] The making of a videotape recording for home viewing is an ordinary rather than a productive use of the Studios' copyrighted works. The District Court found that "Betamax owners use the copy for the same purpose as the original. They add nothing of their own." Although applying the fair use doctrine to home VTR recording, as Sony argues, may increase public access to material broadcast free over the public airwaves, I think Sony's argument misconceives the nature of copyright. Copyright gives the author a right to limit or even to cut off access to his work. A VTR recording creates no public benefit sufficient to justify limiting this right. Nor is this right extinguished by the copyright owner's choice to make the work available over the airwaves. Section 106 of the 1976 Act grants the copyright owner the exclusive right to control the performance and the reproduction of his work, and the fact that he has licensed a single television performance is really irrelevant to the existence of his right to control its reproduction. Although a television broadcast may be free to the viewer, this fact is equally irrelevant; a book borrowed from the public library may not be copied any more freely than a book that is purchased....

[25] I recognize, nevertheless, that there are situations where permitting even an unproductive use would have no effect on the author's incentive to create, that is, where the use would not affect the value of, or the market for, the author's work. Photocopying an old newspaper clipping to send to a friend may be an example; pinning a quotation on one's bulletin board may be another. In each of these cases, the effect on the author is truly *de minimis*. Thus, even though these uses provide no benefit to the public at large, no purpose is served by preserving the author's monopoly, and the use may be regarded as fair.

[26] Courts should move with caution, however, in depriving authors of protection from unproductive "ordinary" uses.... [E]ven in the case of a productive use, § 107(4) requires consideration of "the effect of the use upon the *potential* market for or value of the copyrighted work" (emphasis added). A particular use which may seem to have little or no economic impact on the author's rights today can assume tremendous importance in times to come. Although such a use may seem harmless when viewed in isolation, isolated instances of minor infringements, when multiplied many times, become in the aggregate a major inroad on copyright that must be prevented.

[27] I therefore conclude that, at least when the proposed use is an unproductive one, a copyright owner need prove only a *potential* for harm to the market for or the value of the copyrighted work. Proof of actual harm, or even probable harm, may be impossible in an area where the effect of a new technology is speculative, and requiring such proof would present the real danger of confining the scope of an author's rights on the basis of the present technology so that, as the years go by, his copyright loses much of its value because of unforeseen technical advances. Infringement thus would be found if the copyright owner demonstrates a reasonable possibility that harm will result from the proposed use. When the use is one that creates no benefit to the public at large, copyright protection should not be denied on the basis that a new technology that may result in harm has not yet done so.

[28] The Studios have identified a number of ways in which VTR recording could damage their copyrights. VTR recording could reduce their ability to market their works in movie theaters and through the rental or sale of pre-recorded videotapes or videodiscs; it also could reduce their rerun audience, and consequently the license fees available to them for repeated showings. Moreover, advertisers may be willing to pay for only "live" viewing audiences, if they believe VTR viewers will delete commercials or if rating services are unable to measure VTR use; if this is the case, VTR recording could reduce the license fees the Studios are able to charge

even for first-run showings. Library-building may raise the potential for each of the types of harm identified by the Studios, and time-shifting may raise the potential for substantial harm as well.[35]

[29] Although the District Court found no likelihood of harm from VTR use, I conclude that it applied an incorrect substantive standard and misallocated the burden of proof....

[30] The District Court's reluctance to engage in prediction in this area is understandable, but, in my view, the court was mistaken in concluding that the Studios should bear the risk created by this uncertainty. The Studios have demonstrated a potential for harm, which has not been, and could not be, refuted at this early stage of technological development.

[31] The District Court's analysis of harm, moreover, failed to consider the effect of VTR recording on "the *potential* market for or the value of the copyrighted work," as required by § 107(4)...

[32] In this case, the Studios and their *amici* demonstrate that the advent of the VTR technology created a potential market for their copyrighted programs. That market consists of those persons who find it impossible or inconvenient to watch the programs at the time they are broadcast, and who wish to watch them at other times. These persons are willing to pay for the privilege of watching copyrighted work at their convenience, as is evidenced by the fact that they are willing to pay for VTRs and tapes; undoubtedly, most also would be willing to pay some kind of royalty to copyright holders. The Studios correctly argue that they have been deprived of the ability to exploit this sizable market.

[33] It is thus apparent from the record and from the findings of the District Court that time-shifting does have a substantial adverse effect upon the "potential market for" the Studios' copyrighted works. Accordingly, even under the formulation of the fair use doctrine advanced by Sony, time-shifting cannot be deemed a fair use....[44]

NOTES

1. In economics, **market failure** is understood to be a situation in which the market does not allocate goods or services efficiently, typically leading to a net loss of social welfare. As one example outside the context of copyright law, even though there is great social cost from pollution, absent market intervention, businesses might rationally be disposed to pollute as a byproduct of manufacturing, for example, because their private cost of doing so is low when no law forces them to pay the external social cost of pollution. Law can intervene

---

[35] A VTR owner who has taped a favorite movie for repeated viewing will be less likely to rent or buy a tape containing the same movie, watch a televised rerun, or pay to see the movie at a theater. Although time-shifting may not replace theater or rerun viewing or the purchase of prerecorded tapes or discs, it may well replace rental usage; a VTR user who has recorded a first-run movie for later viewing will have no need to rent a copy when he wants to see it. Both library-builders and time-shifters may avoid commercials; the library builder may use the pause control to record without them, and all users may fast-forward through commercials on playback.

The Studios introduced expert testimony that both time-shifting and librarying would tend to decrease their revenue from copyrighted works. The District Court's findings also show substantial library-building and avoidance of commercials. Both sides submitted surveys showing that the average Betamax user owns between 25 and 32 tapes. The Studios' survey showed that at least 40% of users had more than 10 tapes in a "library"; Sony's survey showed that more than 40% of users planned to view their tapes more than once; and both sides' surveys showed that commercials were avoided at least 25% of the time.

[44] Sony asserts that much or most television broadcasting is available for home recording because ... no copyright owner other than the Studios has brought an infringement action .... The ... assertion[] is irrelevant; Sony's liability does not turn on the fact that only two copyright owners thus far have brought suit. The amount of infringing use must be determined through consideration of the television market as a whole....

to ameliorate this problem by requiring businesses to internalize the social costs of pollution—for example, by imposing taxes on emissions—thereby reducing this externality problem.

In the context of copyright, one can similarly probe whether copyright markets are sometimes causing net social losses. As Wendy Gordon explained in the seminal work on this issue:

> Though the copyright law ... has provided mechanisms to facilitate consensual transfers, at times bargaining may be exceedingly expensive or it may be impractical to obtain enforcement against nonpurchasers, or other market flaws might preclude achievement of desirable consensual exchanges. In those cases, the market cannot be relied on to mediate public interests in dissemination and private interests in remuneration. In extreme instances, Congress may correct for market distortions by imposing a regulatory solution such as a compulsory licensing scheme. Thus, to avoid threatened monopolistic control over the manufacture of piano rolls and other mechanical recordings, Congress provided that any person who wished could make and sell recordings of copyrighted music, so long as he paid to the copyright owner an amount determined under the statute. But the broad brush of this regulatory solution is too sweeping for most cases.
>
> Fair use is one label courts use when they approve a user's departure from the market. A useful starting place for analysis of when fair use is appropriate is therefore an identification of when flaws in the market might make reliance on the judiciary's own analysis of social benefit appropriate. By making such an identification, a measure of coherence can be brought to the doctrine of fair use.... [T]here are certain conditions of perfect competition—or assumptions about how a proper transactional setting should look—whose failure is particularly likely to trigger in the courts an unwillingness to rely on the owner's market right to achieve dissemination.

Wendy J. Gordon, *Fair Use as Market Failure*, 82 COLUM. L. REV. 1600, 1613-14 (1982).

What can cause this sort of market failure that might justify a finding of fair use? Gordon identifies some possibilities. First, **transaction costs** can make it impossible or impracticable for a would-be user of a copyrighted work to reach a deal with the copyright holder. Gordon explains that "[i]f transaction costs exceed anticipated benefits, ... no transactions will occur. Thus, the confluence of two variables is likely to produce a market barrier: high transaction costs and low anticipated profits." When this happens, some socially valuable transfers might not happen if copyright is enforced.

Additionally, **positive externalities** that society can experience from the use of copyrighted works but which are not appropriately valued, or internalized, in the marketplace might also prevent copyright transactions. In particular, as Gordon elaborates, "teaching and scholarship may yield significant 'external benefits'; all of society benefits from having an educated citizenry and from advances in knowledge, yet teacher salaries and revenues from scholarly articles are arguably smaller than such benefit would warrant. When a defendant's works yield such 'external benefits,' the market cannot be relied upon as a mechanism for facilitating socially desirable transactions." In these cases, the potential user might not be able to afford the use of the copyrighted work through the market, even though society would benefit greatly from that potential use. That inability, to Gordon, "may signal to the court that it should investigate whether the social costs of relying on the market are unacceptably high" in analyzing fair use.

Finally, copyright owners might express **anti-dissemination** preferences in some contexts: for example, to prevent criticism of their works. In this situation, Gordon reasons that "[b]ecause the owner's antidissemination motives make licensing unavailable in the consensual market, and because the free flow of information is at stake, a strong case for fair use can be advanced in these cases."

Think through whether you are persuaded by Gordon's framework for assessing fair use and whether you can understand *Sony* as a way to address a market failure.

2. Market facts and technological facts can change over time. Consider the evidence that the copyright holder plaintiffs introduced in *Sony* as to the harms to their revenues from commercial advertisements caused by VCR recording. Consider also whether there was a market in prerecorded VCR tapes of television programs. Additionally, consider whether it was plausible at the time of the litigation to license VCR recordings of television programs. How have these facts changed over the intervening years? If you were to substitute evidence from the year 2000 or the present day on these issues, how would this case be decided? If you thought that market failure explains *Sony*'s outcome, does that market failure continue to exist as time passes? What do your answers suggest for the stability of fair use determinations over time?

3. Around the time of the *Sony* litigation, Jack Valenti, then-president of the Motion Picture Association of America, testified before Congress that "the VCR is to the American film producer and the American public as the Boston Strangler is to the woman alone." Reflected in both Valenti's statement and content owners' decision to sue Sony for copyright infringement is a fear that VCR technology would undercut content owners' businesses. That fear was unfounded, and the *Sony* plaintiffs are surely happy they lost their case. The reason is that content owners started to make significant money through prerecorded video sales, which probably would not have happened had they won the case. Do you think these developments subsequent to *Sony* suggest anything about how well copyright owners can assess their business interests in deciding whether to license their works or sue for infringement?

In reading the following opinion, consider the purpose the Court articulates for fair use. How is the Court's understanding of the four factors different, if at all, than in *Harper & Row* and *Sony*? Also, how does the Court distinguish parody from satire? How does the characterization of a use as parody affect the multi-factor analysis?

Luther R. Campbell v. Acuff–Rose Music, Inc.
510 U.S. 569 (1994)

SOUTER, J.: ...

[1] In 1964, Roy Orbison and William Dees wrote a rock ballad called "Oh, Pretty Woman" and assigned their rights in it to respondent Acuff-Rose Music, Inc. Acuff-Rose registered the song for copyright protection.

[2] Petitioners Luther R. Campbell, Christopher Wongwon, Mark Ross, and David Hobbs are collectively known as 2 Live Crew, a popular rap music group. In 1989, Campbell wrote a song entitled "Pretty Woman," which he later described in an affidavit as intended, "through comical lyrics, to satirize the original work...." On July 5, 1989, 2 Live Crew's manager informed Acuff-Rose that 2 Live Crew had written a parody of "Oh, Pretty Woman," that they would afford all credit for ownership and authorship of the original song to Acuff-Rose, Dees, and Orbison, and that they were willing to pay a fee for the use they wished to make of it. Enclosed with the letter were a copy of the lyrics and a recording of 2 Live Crew's song. Acuff-Rose's agent refused permission, stating that "I am aware of the success enjoyed by 'The 2 Live Crews', but I must inform you that we cannot permit the use of a parody of 'Oh, Pretty Woman.'" Nonetheless, in June or July 1989, 2 Live Crew released records, cassette tapes, and compact discs of "Pretty Woman" in a collection of songs entitled "As Clean As

They Wanna Be." The albums and compact discs identify the authors of "Pretty Woman" as Orbison and Dees and its publisher as Acuff-Rose.

[3] Almost a year later, after nearly a quarter of a million copies of the recording had been sold, Acuff-Rose sued 2 Live Crew and its record company, Luke Skyywalker Records, for copyright infringement. The District Court granted summary judgment for 2 Live Crew ....

[4] The Court of Appeals for the Sixth Circuit reversed and remanded....

[5] We granted certiorari to determine whether 2 Live Crew's commercial parody could be a fair use....

[6] It is uncontested here that 2 Live Crew's song would be an infringement of Acuff-Rose's rights in "Oh, Pretty Woman," under the Copyright Act of 1976 but for a finding of fair use through parody. From the infancy of copyright protection, some opportunity for fair use of copyrighted materials has been thought necessary to fulfill copyright's very purpose, "[t]o promote the Progress of Science and useful Arts...." U.S. CONST., Art. I, § 8, cl. 8....

[7] .... The fair use doctrine ... permits and requires courts to avoid rigid application of the copyright statute when, on occasion, it would stifle the very creativity which that law is designed to foster.

[8] The task [of adjudging fair use] is not to be simplified with bright-line rules, for the statute, like the doctrine it recognizes, calls for case-by-case analysis. The text employs the terms "including" and "such as" in the preamble paragraph to indicate the "illustrative and not limitative" function of the examples given, § 101, which thus provide only general guidance about the sorts of copying that courts and Congress most commonly had found to be fair uses. Nor may the four statutory factors be treated in isolation, one from another. All are to be explored, and the results weighed together, in light of the purposes of copyright.[10] ...

[9] The first factor in a fair use enquiry is "the purpose and character of the use, including whether such use is of a commercial nature or is for nonprofit educational purposes." § 107(1).... The enquiry here may be guided by the examples given in the preamble to § 107, looking to whether the use is for criticism, or comment, or news reporting, and the like. The central purpose of this investigation is to see, in Justice Story's words, whether the new work merely supersedes the objects of the original creation or instead adds something new, with a further purpose or different character, altering the first with new expression, meaning, or message; it asks, in other words, whether and to what extent the new work is "transformative." Pierre N. Leval, *Toward a Fair Use Standard*, 103 HARV. L. REV. 1105, 1111 (1990). Although such transformative use is not absolutely necessary for a finding of fair use,[11] the goal of copyright, to promote science and the arts, is generally furthered by the creation of transformative works. Such works thus lie at the heart of the fair use doctrine's guarantee of breathing space within the confines of copyright, and the more transformative the new work, the less will be the significance of other factors, like commercialism, that may weigh against a finding of fair use.

[10] .... [P]arody has an obvious claim to transformative value .... Like less ostensibly humorous forms of criticism, it can provide social benefit, by shedding light on an earlier work, and, in the process, creating a new one....

---

[10] Because the fair use enquiry often requires close questions of judgment as to the extent of permissible borrowing in cases involving parodies (or other critical works), courts may also wish to bear in mind that the goals of the copyright law, to stimulate the creation and publication of edifying matter, are not always best served by automatically granting injunctive relief when parodists are found to have gone beyond the bounds of fair use.

[11] The obvious statutory exception to this focus on transformative uses is the straight reproduction of multiple copies for classroom distribution.

[11] .... For the purposes of copyright law, ... the heart of any parodist's claim to quote from existing material, is the use of some elements of a prior author's composition to create a new one that, at least in part, comments on that author's works. If, on the contrary, the commentary has no critical bearing on the substance or style of the original composition, which the alleged infringer merely uses to get attention or to avoid the drudgery in working up something fresh, the claim to fairness in borrowing from another's work diminishes accordingly (if it does not vanish), and other factors, like the extent of its commerciality, loom larger.[14] Parody needs to mimic an original to make its point, and so has some claim to use the creation of its victim's (or collective victims') imagination, whereas satire can stand on its own two feet and so requires justification for the very act of borrowing.[15]

[12] The fact that parody can claim legitimacy for some appropriation does not, of course, tell either parodist or judge much about where to draw the line. Like a book review quoting the copyrighted material criticized, parody may or may not be fair use, and petitioners' suggestion that any parodic use is presumptively fair has no more justification in law or fact than the equally hopeful claim that any use for news reporting should be presumed fair, see *Harper & Row*, 471 U.S. at 561. The Act has no hint of an evidentiary preference for parodists over their victims, and no workable presumption for parody could take account of the fact that parody often shades into satire when society is lampooned through its creative artifacts, or that a work may contain both parodic and nonparodic elements. Accordingly, parody, like any other use, has to work its way through the relevant factors, and be judged case by case, in light of the ends of the copyright law.

[13] Here, the District Court held, and the Court of Appeals assumed, that 2 Live Crew's "Pretty Woman" contains parody, commenting on and criticizing the original work, whatever it may have to say about society at large. As the District Court remarked, the words of 2 Live Crew's song copy the original's first line, but then "quickly degenerat[e] into a play on words, substituting predictable lyrics with shocking ones ... [that] derisively demonstrat[e] how bland and banal the Orbison song seems to them." Judge Nelson, dissenting below, came to the same conclusion, that the 2 Live Crew song "was clearly intended to ridicule the white-bread original" and "reminds us that sexual congress with nameless streetwalkers is not necessarily the stuff of romance and is not necessarily without its consequences. The singers (there are several) have the same thing on their minds as did the lonely man with the nasal voice, but here there is no hint of wine and roses." Although the majority below had difficulty discerning any criticism of the original in 2 Live Crew's song, it assumed for purposes of its opinion that there was some.

[14] We have less difficulty in finding that critical element in 2 Live Crew's song than the Court of Appeals did, although having found it we will not take the further step of evaluating its quality. The threshold question when fair use is raised in defense of parody is whether a parodic character may reasonably be perceived.[16] Whether, going beyond that, parody is in good taste or bad does not and should not matter to fair use. As Justice Holmes explained, "[i]t would be a dangerous undertaking for persons trained only to the law to constitute themselves

---

[14] A parody that more loosely targets an original than the parody presented here may still be sufficiently aimed at an original work to come within our analysis of parody. If a parody whose wide dissemination in the market runs the risk of serving as a substitute for the original or licensed derivatives, it is more incumbent on one claiming fair use to establish the extent of transformation and the parody's critical relationship to the original. By contrast, when there is little or no risk of market substitution, whether because of the large extent of transformation of the earlier work, the new work's minimal distribution in the market, the small extent to which it borrows from an original, or other factors, taking parodic aim at an original is a less critical factor in the analysis, and looser forms of parody may be found to be fair use, as may satire with lesser justification for the borrowing than would otherwise be required.

[15] Satire has been defined as a work "in which prevalent follies or vices are assailed with ridicule," OXFORD ENGLISH DICTIONARY, or are "attacked through irony, derision, or wit," AMERICAN HERITAGE DICTIONARY.

[16] The only further judgment, indeed, that a court may pass on a work goes to an assessment of whether the parodic element is slight or great, and the copying small or extensive in relation to the parodic element, for a work with slight parodic element and extensive copying will be more likely to merely supersede the objects of the original.

final judges of the worth of [a work], outside of the narrowest and most obvious limits. At the one extreme some works of genius would be sure to miss appreciation. Their very novelty would make them repulsive until the public had learned the new language in which their author spoke." Bleistein v. Donaldson Lithographing Co., 188 U.S. 239, 251 (1903).

[15] While we might not assign a high rank to the parodic element here, we think it fair to say that 2 Live Crew's song reasonably could be perceived as commenting on the original or criticizing it, to some degree. 2 Live Crew juxtaposes the romantic musings of a man whose fantasy comes true, with degrading taunts, a bawdy demand for sex, and a sigh of relief from paternal responsibility. The later words can be taken as a comment on the naiveté of the original of an earlier day, as a rejection of its sentiment that ignores the ugliness of street life and the debasement that it signifies. It is this joinder of reference and ridicule that marks off the author's choice of parody from the other types of comment and criticism that traditionally have had a claim to fair use protection as transformative works.

[16] The Court of Appeals, however, immediately cut short the enquiry into 2 Live Crew's fair use claim by confining its treatment of the first factor essentially to one relevant fact, the commercial nature of the use. The court then inflated the significance of this fact by applying a presumption ... that every commercial use of copyrighted material is presumptively unfair. In giving virtually dispositive weight to the commercial nature of the parody, the Court of Appeals erred.

[17] The language of the statute makes clear that the commercial or nonprofit educational purpose of a work is only one element of the first factor enquiry into its purpose and character. Section 107(1) uses the term "including" to begin the dependent clause referring to commercial use, and the main clause speaks of a broader investigation into "purpose and character." As we explained in *Harper & Row*, Congress resisted attempts to narrow the ambit of this traditional enquiry by adopting categories of presumptively fair use, and it urged courts to preserve the breadth of their traditionally ample view of the universe of relevant evidence. Accordingly, the mere fact that a use is educational and not for profit does not insulate it from a finding of infringement, any more than the commercial character of a use bars a finding of fairness. If, indeed, commerciality carried presumptive force against a finding of fairness, the presumption would swallow nearly all of the illustrative uses listed in the preamble paragraph of § 107, including news reporting, comment, criticism, teaching, scholarship, and research, since these activities are generally conducted for profit in this country. Congress could not have intended such a rule, which certainly is not inferable from the common-law cases, arising as they did from the world of letters in which Samuel Johnson could pronounce that "[n]o man but a blockhead ever wrote, except for money."

[18] *Sony* itself called for no hard evidentiary presumption. There, we emphasized the need for a "sensitive balancing of interests," noted that Congress had "eschewed a rigid, bright-line approach to fair use," and stated that the commercial or nonprofit educational character of a work is "not conclusive," but rather a fact to be "weighed along with other[s] in fair use decisions." The Court of Appeals's elevation of one sentence from *Sony* [(that "every commercial use ... is presumptively ... unfair")] to a *per se* rule thus runs as much counter to *Sony* itself as to the long common-law tradition of fair use adjudication. Rather, as we explained in *Harper & Row*, *Sony* stands for the proposition that the "fact that a publication was commercial as opposed to nonprofit is a separate factor that tends to weigh against a finding of fair use." But that is all, and the fact that even the force of that tendency will vary with the context is a further reason against elevating commerciality to hard presumptive significance. The use, for example, of a copyrighted work to advertise a product, even in a parody,

will be entitled to less indulgence under the first factor of the fair use enquiry than the sale of a parody for its own sake, let alone one performed a single time by students in school.[18] ...

[19] The second statutory factor, "the nature of the copyrighted work," § 107(2), ... calls for recognition that some works are closer to the core of intended copyright protection than others, with the consequence that fair use is more difficult to establish when the former works are copied. We agree with both the District Court and the Court of Appeals that the Orbison original's creative expression for public dissemination falls within the core of the copyright's protective purposes. This fact, however, is not much help in this case, or ever likely to help much in separating the fair use sheep from the infringing goats in a parody case, since parodies almost invariably copy publicly known, expressive works....

[20] The third factor asks whether "the amount and substantiality of the portion used in relation to the copyrighted work as a whole," § 107(3) .... Here, attention turns to the persuasiveness of a parodist's justification for the particular copying done, and the enquiry will harken back to the first of the statutory factors, for, as in prior cases, we recognize that the extent of permissible copying varies with the purpose and character of the use. The facts bearing on this factor will also tend to address the fourth, by revealing the degree to which the parody may serve as a market substitute for the original or potentially licensed derivatives....

[21] ... [T]his factor calls for thought not only about the quantity of the materials used, but about their quality and importance, too.... [W]hether a substantial portion of the infringing work was copied verbatim from the copyrighted work is a relevant question, for it may reveal a dearth of transformative character or purpose under the first factor, or a greater likelihood of market harm under the fourth; a work composed primarily of an original, particularly its heart, with little added or changed, is more likely to be a merely superseding use, fulfilling demand for the original.

[22] .... Parody presents a difficult case. Parody's humor, or in any event its comment, necessarily springs from recognizable allusion to its object through distorted imitation. Its art lies in the tension between a known original and its parodic twin. When parody takes aim at a particular original work, the parody must be able to conjure up at least enough of that original to make the object of its critical wit recognizable. What makes for this recognition is quotation of the original's most distinctive or memorable features, which the parodist can be sure the audience will know. Once enough has been taken to assure identification, how much more is reasonable will depend, say, on the extent to which the song's overriding purpose and character is to parody the original or, in contrast, the likelihood that the parody may serve as a market substitute for the original. But using some characteristic features cannot be avoided.

[23] We think the Court of Appeals was insufficiently appreciative of parody's need for the recognizable sight or sound when it ruled 2 Live Crew's use unreasonable as a matter of law. It is true, of course, that 2 Live Crew copied the characteristic opening bass riff (or musical phrase) of the original, and true that the words of the first line copy the Orbison lyrics. But if quotation of the opening riff and the first line may be said to go to the "heart" of the original, the heart is also what most readily conjures up the song for parody, and it is the heart at which parody takes aim. Copying does not become excessive in relation to parodic purpose merely because the

---

[18] Finally, regardless of the weight one might place on the alleged infringer's state of mind, *compare Harper & Row* (fair use presupposes good faith and fair dealing), *with* Folsom v. Marsh, 9 F.Cas. 342, 349 (No. 4,901) (CCD Mass.1841) (good faith does not bar a finding of infringement); Leval (good faith irrelevant to fair use analysis), we reject Acuff–Rose's argument that 2 Live Crew's request for permission to use the original should be weighed against a finding of fair use. Even if good faith were central to fair use, 2 Live Crew's actions do not necessarily suggest that they believed their version was not fair use; the offer may simply have been made in a good-faith effort to avoid this litigation. If the use is otherwise fair, then no permission need be sought or granted. Thus, being denied permission to use a work does not weigh against a finding of fair use.

portion taken was the original's heart. If 2 Live Crew had copied a significantly less memorable part of the original, it is difficult to see how its parodic character would have come through.

[24] This is not, of course, to say that anyone who calls himself a parodist can skim the cream and get away scot free. In parody, as in news reporting, context is everything, and the question of fairness asks what else the parodist did besides go to the heart of the original. It is significant that 2 Live Crew not only copied the first line of the original, but thereafter departed markedly from the Orbison lyrics for its own ends. 2 Live Crew not only copied the bass riff and repeated it, but also produced otherwise distinctive sounds, interposing scraper noise, overlaying the music with solos in different keys, and altering the drum beat. This is not a case, then, where a substantial portion of the parody itself is composed of a verbatim copying of the original. It is not, that is, a case where the parody is so insubstantial, as compared to the copying, that the third factor must be resolved as a matter of law against the parodists.

[25] Suffice it to say here that, as to the lyrics, we think ... that no more was taken than necessary, but just for that reason, we fail to see how the copying can be excessive in relation to its parodic purpose, even if the portion taken is the original's "heart." As to the music, we express no opinion whether repetition of the bass riff is excessive copying, and we remand to permit evaluation of the amount taken, in light of the song's parodic purpose and character, its transformative elements, and considerations of the potential for market substitution sketched more fully below....

[26] The fourth fair use factor is "the effect of the use upon the potential market for or value of the copyrighted work." § 107(4). It requires courts to consider not only the extent of market harm caused by the particular actions of the alleged infringer, but also whether unrestricted and widespread conduct of the sort engaged in by the defendant would result in a substantially adverse impact on the potential market for the original. The enquiry must take account not only of harm to the original but also of harm to the market for derivative works.

[27] Since fair use is an affirmative defense, its proponent would have difficulty carrying the burden of demonstrating fair use without favorable evidence about relevant markets.[21] ...

[28] No presumption or inference of market harm ... is applicable to a case involving something beyond mere duplication for commercial purposes.... [W]hen ... the second use is transformative, market substitution is at least less certain, and market harm may not be so readily inferred. Indeed, as to parody pure and simple, it is more likely that the new work will not affect the market for the original in a way cognizable under this factor, that is, by acting as a substitute for it .... This is so because the parody and the original usually serve different market functions.

[29] We do not, of course, suggest that a parody may not harm the market at all, but when a lethal parody, like a scathing theater review, kills demand for the original, it does not produce a harm cognizable under the Copyright Act. Because parody may quite legitimately aim at garroting the original, destroying it commercially as well as artistically, the role of the courts is to distinguish between biting criticism that merely suppresses demand and copyright infringement, which usurps it.

[30] This distinction between potentially remediable displacement and unremediable disparagement is reflected in the rule that there is no protectible derivative market for criticism. The market for potential derivative uses includes only those that creators of original works would in general develop or license others to

[21] Even favorable evidence, without more, is no guarantee of fairness. Judge Leval gives the example of the film producer's appropriation of a composer's previously unknown song that turns the song into a commercial success; the boon to the song does not make the film's simple copying fair. This factor, no less than the other three, may be addressed only through a sensitive balancing of interests. Market harm is a matter of degree, and the importance of this factor will vary, not only with the amount of harm, but also with the relative strength of the showing on the other factors.

develop. Yet the unlikelihood that creators of imaginative works will license critical reviews or lampoons of their own productions removes such uses from the very notion of a potential licensing market.... Thus, to the extent that the opinion below may be read to have considered harm to the market for parodies of "Oh, Pretty Woman," the court erred.

[31] In explaining why the law recognizes no derivative market for critical works, including parody, we have, of course, been speaking of the later work as if it had nothing but a critical aspect. But the later work may have a more complex character, with effects not only in the arena of criticism but also in protectible markets for derivative works, too. In that sort of case, the law looks beyond the criticism to the other elements of the work, as it does here. 2 Live Crew's song comprises not only parody but also rap music, and the derivative market for rap music is a proper focus of enquiry. Evidence of substantial harm to it would weigh against a finding of fair use, because the licensing of derivatives is an important economic incentive to the creation of originals. Of course, the only harm to derivatives that need concern us, as discussed above, is the harm of market substitution. The fact that a parody may impair the market for derivative uses by the very effectiveness of its critical commentary is no more relevant under copyright than the like threat to the original market.[24]

[32] Although 2 Live Crew submitted uncontroverted affidavits on the question of market harm to the original, neither they, nor Acuff-Rose, introduced evidence or affidavits addressing the likely effect of 2 Live Crew's parodic rap song on the market for a nonparody, rap version of "Oh, Pretty Woman." And while Acuff-Rose would have us find evidence of a rap market in the very facts that 2 Live Crew recorded a rap parody of "Oh, Pretty Woman" and another rap group sought a license to record a rap derivative, there was no evidence that a potential rap market was harmed in any way by 2 Live Crew's parody, rap version. The fact that 2 Live Crew's parody sold as part of a collection of rap songs says very little about the parody's effect on a market for a rap version of the original, either of the music alone or of the music with its lyrics.... The evidentiary hole will doubtless be plugged on remand....

---

[24] In some cases it may be difficult to determine whence the harm flows. In such cases, the other fair use factors may provide some indicia of the likely source of the harm. A work whose overriding purpose and character is parodic and whose borrowing is slight in relation to its parody will be far less likely to cause cognizable harm than a work with little parodic content and much copying.

APPENDIX A TO OPINION OF THE COURT

"Oh, Pretty Woman" by Roy Orbison and William Dees

Pretty Woman, walking down the street,
Pretty Woman, the kind I like to meet,
Pretty Woman, I don't believe you, you're not the truth,
No one could look as good as you
Mercy
Pretty Woman, won't you pardon me,
Pretty Woman, I couldn't help but see,
Pretty Woman, that you look lovely as can be
Are you lonely just like me?
Pretty Woman, stop a while,
Pretty Woman, talk a while,
Pretty Woman give your smile to me
Pretty Woman, yeah, yeah, yeah
Pretty Woman, look my way,
Pretty Woman, say you'll stay with me
'Cause I need you, I'll treat you right
Come to me baby, Be mine tonight
Pretty Woman, don't walk on by,
Pretty Woman, don't make me cry,
Pretty Woman, don't walk away,
Hey, O.K.
If that's the way it must be, O.K.
I guess I'll go on home, it's late
There'll be tomorrow night, but wait!
What do I see
Is she walking back to me?
Yeah, she's walking back to me!
Oh, Pretty Woman.

APPENDIX B TO OPINION OF THE COURT

"Pretty Woman" as Recorded by 2 Live Crew

Pretty woman walkin' down the street
Pretty woman girl you look so sweet
Pretty woman you bring me down to that knee
Pretty woman you make me wanna beg please
Oh, pretty woman
Big hairy woman you need to shave that stuff
Big hairy woman you know I bet it's tough
Big hairy woman all that hair it ain't legit
'Cause you look like 'Cousin It'
Big hairy woman
Bald headed woman girl your hair won't grow
Bald headed woman you got a teeny weeny afro
Bald headed woman you know your hair could look nice
Bald headed woman first you got to roll it with rice
Bald headed woman here, let me get this hunk of biz for ya
Ya know what I'm saying you look better than rice a roni
Oh bald headed woman
Big hairy woman come on in
And don't forget your bald headed friend
Hey pretty woman let the boys
Jump in
Two timin' woman girl you know you ain't right
Two timin' woman you's out with my boy last night
Two timin' woman that takes a load off my mind
Two timin' woman now I know the baby ain't mine
Oh, two timin' woman
Oh pretty woman

KENNEDY, J. concurring....

[33] The fair use factors thus reinforce the importance of keeping the definition of parody within proper limits. More than arguable parodic content should be required to deem a would-be parody a fair use. Fair use is an affirmative defense, so doubts about whether a given use is fair should not be resolved in favor of the self-proclaimed parodist. We should not make it easy for musicians to exploit existing works and then later claim that their rendition was a valuable commentary on the original. Almost any revamped modern version of a familiar composition can be construed as a "comment on the naiveté of the original," because of the difference in style and because it will be amusing to hear how the old tune sounds in the new genre. Just the thought of a rap version of Beethoven's Fifth Symphony or "Achy Breaky Heart" is bound to make people smile. If we allow any weak transformation to qualify as parody, however, we weaken the protection of copyright. And underprotection of copyright disserves the goals of copyright just as much as overprotection, by reducing the financial incentive to create....

NOTES

1. Following the Supreme Court's decision, Acuff-Rose Music, Inc., and 2 Live Crew settled the suit. Acuff-Rose dismissed its lawsuit, in exchange for 2 Live Crew agreeing to pay some of the proceeds of sales of their song to Acuff-Rose. *Acuff-Rose Settles Suit with Rap Group*, COMMERCIAL APPEAL, at A14, June 5, 1996.

2. As a matter of copyright policy, why might parodies be considered fair use? Can you reconcile fair use for parodies with the rights of copyright owners to prepare derivative works?

3. After reading *Campbell*, do you have a different sense whether any particular factor is more important than others to a conclusion of fair use? If so, in all contexts or only in the specific on at issue here?

4. Very influential on the Court's decision in *Campbell* was a *Harvard Law Review* article on fair use by Judge Pierre Leval of the U.S. Court of Appeals for the Second Circuit. *See* Pierre N. Leval, *Toward a Fair Use Standard*, 103 HARV. L. REV. 1105 (1990). In the article, Judge Leval argued for "transformativeness" as a touchstone in fair use analysis. Can you think of the ways in which, in the context of the fair use analysis, a defendant's work may be said to "transform" a plaintiff's work? Are all forms of transformativeness equal in value?

5. How can a court decide whether something is a parody? Should it be based on the defendant's creative intent? Or how consumers receive the defendant's use? Or expert opinions? Or another way?

In that regard, consider a case brought by photographer Annie Leibovitz against Paramount Pictures, distributor of the film *Naked Gun 33-⅓: The Final Insult*. Leibovitz had photographed a pregnant, nude Demi Moore for the cover of the August 1991 issue of *Vanity Fair* magazine, as shown in Figure 99. The photograph attracted a significant amount of public attention, and that issue became a top-seller for *Vanity Fair*. In 1993, Paramount Pictures released a promotional poster for its upcoming film release, with star Leslie Nielsen's face superimposed on the body of a nude, pregnant model posed in the same position as Moore and the tagline "Due this March," as shown in Figure 99.

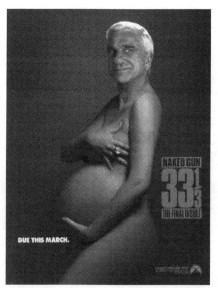

Figure 99: Annie Leibovitz's photograph of Demi Moore (left), and promotional poster for *Naked Gun 33 ⅓: The Final Insult* (right)

Leibovitz sued Paramount Pictures for copyright infringement. The district court granted summary judgment to Paramount, on the ground that its use was fair. The Second Circuit agreed and upheld the district court's ruling. In finding Paramount's poster to be a parody protected by fair use, it reasoned:

> Plainly, the ad adds something new and qualifies as a "transformative" work. Whether it "comments" on the original is a somewhat closer question. Because the smirking face of Nielsen contrasts so strikingly with the serious expression on the face of Moore, the ad may reasonably be perceived as commenting on the seriousness, even the pretentiousness, of the original. The

contrast achieves the effect of ridicule that the Court recognized in Campbell *would serve as a sufficient "comment" to tip the first factor in a parodist's favor.*

In saying this, however, we have some concern about the ease with which every purported parodist could win on the first factor simply by pointing out some feature that contrasts with the original. Being different from an original does not inevitably "comment" on the original. Nevertheless, the ad is not merely different; it differs in a way that may reasonably be perceived as commenting, through ridicule, on what a viewer might reasonably think is the undue self-importance conveyed by the subject of the Leibovitz photograph. A photographer posing a well known actress in a manner that calls to mind a well known painting must expect, or at least tolerate, a parodist's deflating ridicule.

Apart from ridiculing pretentiousness, the ad might also be reasonably perceived as interpreting the Leibovitz photograph to extol the beauty of the pregnant female body, and, rather unchivalrously, to express disagreement with this message. The District Court thought such a comment was reasonably to be perceived from the contrast between "a serious portrayal of a beautiful woman taking great pride in the majesty of her pregnant body ... [and] a ridiculous image of a smirking, foolish-looking pregnant man."

Leibovitz v. Paramount Pictures Corp., 137 F.3d 109, 114-15 (2d Cir. 1996). In light of this case, how do you evaluate Justice Kennedy's concern, expressed in his *Campbell* concurrence, that it might be too easy to claim ex post that the use of a copyrighted work is a parody?

6. After reading *Campbell*, how would you distinguish a parody from a satire for purposes of evaluating fair use?

Consider the following case brought against publishing company Houghton Mifflin Co. by the copyright owners of *Gone with the Wind*, one of the world's best-selling books and which tells the fictional story of Scarlett O'Hara—the spoiled daughter of a wealthy Southern plantation owner—who tries to escape poverty following the American Civil War. Alice Randall wrote a book titled *The Wind Done Gone*, a fictional work based on *Gone with the Wind*. In the book, Randall appropriates characters, plots, and major scenes from *Gone with the Wind* to tell an alternative account of *Gone with the Wind*'s story from the point of view of one of O'Hara's slaves, Cynara, and the daughter of O'Hara's father and Mammy, a slave who was O'Hara's childhood nurse.

In defense of the lawsuit, Randall claimed "that her novel is a critique of [*Gone with the Wind*]'s depiction of slavery and the Civil-War era American South." Suntrust Bank v. Houghton Mifflin Co., 268 F.3d 1257, 1259 (11th Cir. 2001). The Eleventh Circuit characterized Randall's work as a parody, rather than a satire:

> *[T]he parodic character of [*The Wind Done Gone*] is clear. [*The Wind Done Gone*] is not a general commentary upon the Civil-War-era American South, but a specific criticism of and rejoinder to the depiction of slavery and the relationships between blacks and whites in [*Gone with the Wind*]. The fact that Randall chose to convey her criticisms of [*Gone with the Wind*] through a work of fiction, which she contends is a more powerful vehicle for her message than a scholarly article, does not, in and of itself, deprive [*The Wind Done Gone*] of fair-use protection.*

After its analysis of the four statutory factors, the court went on to conclude that the defendants were "entitled to a fair-use defense."

Do you think Randall's work is more appropriately categorized as a parody or a satire? Or is it a frontal attack on the Mitchell novel that does not ridicule, as parody and satire do? Notice how Houghton Mifflin described Randall's book on its cover (shown in Figure 100) as a "parody." Why do you think it did so? Should it matter to a determination of fair use whether a work is categorized as a parody or a satire? We will consider the question again later in this chapter in the context of appropriation art.

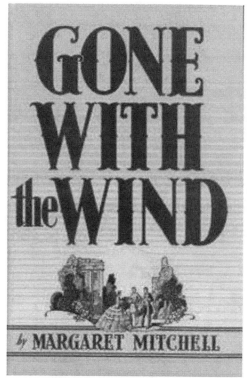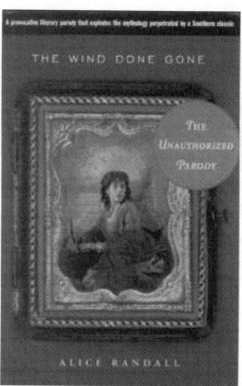

Figure 100: book covers for *Gone with the Wind* (left) and *The Wind Done Gone* (right)

7. After reading *Campbell*, you might think that fair use is asserted as a defense frequently in infringement cases involving music. In an empirical study, Edward Lee finds that outside the context of parody, no court decision has recognized fair use of a plaintiff's musical work in a defendant's musical work. Edward Lee, *Fair Use Avoidance in Music Cases*, 59 B.C. L. REV. 1874 (2018). Moreover, Lee finds that very few of the many infringement cases about music even consider fair use. Lee posits that both musicians and courts are likely avoiding the defense of fair use in this context to make it easier to settle on song credits and royalties, to pursue instead a defense of not having copied protectable material, and to coincide with music industry norms and practices. This avoidance of fair use by litigants means that courts do not have much precedent on which to rely on deciding non-parody fair use music cases.

8. *Campbell* recognizes that certain market effects are irrelevant to the fair use analysis. *Campbell* suggests the exclusion of market effects from consideration under the fourth factor if the effects are unrelated to the protectable aspects of the copyrighted work, such as its ideas or the societal value attributed to the work. In particular, *Campbell* provides that "when a lethal parody, like a scathing theater review, kills demand for the original, it does not produce a harm cognizable under the Copyright Act." The Court there explains that any harm to the copyright holder's market results from the parody's commentary, not its substitutive effect for the copyrighted work. *Campbell* emphasizes that "the role of the courts is to distinguish between biting criticism that merely suppresses demand and copyright infringement, which usurps it." The Court concludes that "[t]he distinction between potentially remediable displacement and unremediable disparagement is reflected in the rule that there is no protectable derivative market for criticism." For an analytical framework on limiting consideration of the fourth factor to copyright-relevant markets, see Jeanne C. Fromer, *Market Effects Bearing on Fair Use*, 90 WASH. L. REV. 615 (2015).

B. Contemporary Cases: What Is Transformativeness?

As you just read, in *Campbell*, the Supreme Court promoted the concept of "transformativeness" as a way of understanding the meaning of the first statutory factor of the fair use standard. The *Campbell* Court employed transformativeness analysis in the context of a parodic use; parody, the Court stated, "has an obvious claim to transformative value." In the years following *Campbell*, courts have employed transformativeness analysis in ways that are almost certainly broader than the Supreme Court's initial use of the analysis in *Campbell*, both in terms of the statutory factors that are affected by a work's transformativeness (or lack of transformativeness) and the kinds of uses that may qualify as "transformative."

1. Historical Research

> As you read the next case, consider the purpose for which and the ways the defendant is using the plaintiff's works and how that ought to affect the analysis of fair use.

Bill Graham Archives v. Dorling Kindersley Limited
448 F.3d 605 (2d Cir. 2006)

RESTANI, J.: ...

[1] In October of 2003, DK [(Dorling Kindersley)] published *Grateful Dead: The Illustrated Trip*, in collaboration with Grateful Dead Productions, intended as a cultural history of the Grateful Dead. The resulting 480-page coffee table book tells the story of the Grateful Dead along a timeline running continuously through the book, chronologically combining over 2000 images representing dates in the Grateful Dead's history with explanatory text. A typical page of the book features a collage of images, text, and graphic art designed to simultaneously capture the eye and inform the reader. Plaintiff BGA [(Bill Graham Archives)] claims to own the copyright to seven images displayed in *Illustrated Trip*, which DK reproduced without BGA's permission.

[2] Initially, DK sought permission from BGA to reproduce the images. In May of 2003, the CEO of Grateful Dead Productions sent a letter to BGA seeking permission for DK to publish the images. BGA responded by offering permission in exchange for Grateful Dead Productions' grant of permission to BGA to make CDs and DVDs out of concert footage in BGA's archives. Next, DK directly contacted BGA seeking to negotiate a license agreement, but the parties disagreed as to an appropriate license fee. Nevertheless, DK proceeded with publication of *Illustrated Trip* without entering a license fee agreement with BGA. Specifically, DK reproduced seven artistic images originally depicted on Grateful Dead event posters and tickets. BGA's seven images are displayed in significantly reduced form and are accompanied by captions describing the concerts they represent.

[3] When DK refused to meet BGA's post-publication license fee demands, BGA filed suit for copyright infringement....

[4] In this case, the district court concluded that the balance of fair use factors weighs in favor of DK.... We agree with the district court that DK's use of the copyrighted images is protected as fair use.

Figure 101: Dorling Kindersley book cover for *Grateful Dead: The Illustrated Trip*

I. Purpose and Character of Use

[5] We first address "the purpose and character of the use, including whether such use is of a commercial nature or is for nonprofit educational purposes." 17 U.S.C. § 107(1). Most important to the court's analysis of the first factor is the "transformative" nature of the work. The question is whether the new work merely supersedes the objects of the original creation, or instead adds something new, with a further purpose or different character, altering the first with new expression, meaning, or message.

[6] Here, the district court determined that *Illustrated Trip* is a biographical work, and the original images are not, and therefore accorded a strong presumption in favor of DK's use. In particular, the district court concluded that DK's use of images placed in chronological order on a timeline is transformatively different from the mere expressive use of images on concert posters or tickets. Because the works are displayed to commemorate historic events, arranged in a creative fashion, and displayed in significantly reduced form, the district court held that the first fair use factor weighs heavily in favor of DK.

[7] Appellant challenges the district court's strong presumption in favor of fair use based on the biographical nature of *Illustrated Trip.* Appellant argues that based on this purported error the district court failed to examine DK's justification for its use of each of the images. Moreover, Appellant argues that as a matter of law merely placing poster images along a timeline is not a transformative use. Appellant asserts that each reproduced image should have been accompanied by comment or criticism related to the artistic nature of the image.

[8] We disagree with Appellant's limited interpretation of transformative use and we agree with the district court that DK's actual use of each image is transformatively different from the original expressive purpose. Preliminarily, we recognize, as the district court did, that *Illustrated Trip* is a biographical work documenting the 30-year history of the Grateful Dead. While there are no categories of presumptively fair use, courts have

frequently afforded fair use protection to the use of copyrighted material in biographies, recognizing such works as forms of historic scholarship, criticism, and comment that require incorporation of original source material for optimum treatment of their subjects. No less a recognition of biographical value is warranted in this case simply because the subject made a mark in pop culture rather than some other area of human endeavor.

Figure 102: Bill Graham Grateful Dead concert poster (top), and use of it in Dorling Kindersley book (bottom)

Figure 103: Bill Graham Grateful Dead concert poster (top), and use of it in Dorling Kindersley book (bottom)

[9] In the instant case, DK's purpose in using the copyrighted images at issue in its biography of the Grateful Dead is plainly different from the original purpose for which they were created. Originally, each of BGA's images fulfilled the dual purposes of artistic expression and promotion. The posters were apparently widely distributed to generate public interest in the Grateful Dead and to convey information to a large number people about the

band's forthcoming concerts. In contrast, DK used each of BGA's images as historical artifacts to document and represent the actual occurrence of Grateful Dead concert events featured on *Illustrated Trip*'s timeline.

[10] In some instances, it is readily apparent that DK's image display enhances the reader's understanding of the biographical text. In other instances, the link between image and text is less obvious; nevertheless, the images still serve as historical artifacts graphically representing the fact of significant Grateful Dead concert events selected by the *Illustrated Trip*'s author for inclusion in the book's timeline. We conclude that both types of uses fulfill DK's transformative purpose of enhancing the biographical information in *Illustrated Trip*, a purpose separate and distinct from the original artistic and promotional purpose for which the images were created. In sum, because DK's use of the disputed images is transformative both when accompanied by referencing commentary and when standing alone, we agree with the district court that DK was not required to discuss the artistic merits of the images to satisfy this first factor of fair use analysis.

[11] This conclusion is strengthened by the manner in which DK displayed the images. First, DK significantly reduced the size of the reproductions. While the small size is sufficient to permit readers to recognize the historical significance of the posters, it is inadequate to offer more than a glimpse of their expressive value. In short, DK used the minimal image size necessary to accomplish its transformative purpose.

[12] Second, DK minimized the expressive value of the reproduced images by combining them with a prominent timeline, textual material, and original graphical artwork, to create a collage of text and images on each page of the book. To further this collage effect, the images are displayed at angles and the original graphical artwork is designed to blend with the images and text. Overall, DK's layout ensures that the images at issue are employed only to enrich the presentation of the cultural history of the Grateful Dead, not to exploit copyrighted artwork for commercial gain.

[13] Third, BGA's images constitute an inconsequential portion of *Illustrated Trip*. The extent to which unlicensed material is used in the challenged work can be a factor in determining whether a biographer's use of original materials has been sufficiently transformative to constitute fair use.... [O]ur circuit has counseled against considering the percentage the allegedly infringing work comprises of the copyrighted work in conducting *third-factor* fair use analysis .... We find this inquiry more relevant in the context of *first-factor* fair use analysis.

[14] In the instant case, the book is 480 pages long, while the BGA images appear on only seven pages. Although the original posters range in size from 13" x 19" to more than 19" x 27," the largest reproduction of a BGA image in *Illustrated Trip* is less than 3" x 4 ½," less than 1/20 the size of the original. And no BGA image takes up more than one-eighth of a page in a book or is given more prominence than any other image on the page. In total, the images account for less than one-fifth of one percent of the book. This stands in stark contrast to ... wholesale takings ..., and we are aware of no case where such an insignificant taking was found to be an unfair use of original materials.

[15] Finally, as to this first factor, we briefly address the commercial nature of *Illustrated Trip*. Even though *Illustrated Trip* is a commercial venture, we recognize that nearly all of the illustrative uses listed in the preamble paragraph of § 107 are generally conducted for profit. Moreover, the crux of the profit/nonprofit distinction is not whether the sole motive of the use is monetary gain but whether the user stands to profit from exploitation of the copyrighted material without paying the customary price. Here, *Illustrated Trip* does not exploit the use of BGA's images as such for commercial gain. Significantly, DK has not used any of BGA's images in its commercial advertising or in any other way to promote the sale of the book. *Illustrated Trip* merely uses pictures and text to describe the life of the Grateful Dead. By design, the use of BGA's images is incidental to the commercial biographical value of the book.

[16] Accordingly, we conclude that the first fair use factor weighs in favor of DK because DK's use of BGA's images is transformatively different from the images' original expressive purpose and DK does not seek to exploit the images' expressive value for commercial gain.

II. Nature of the Copyrighted Work ...

[17] The district court determined that the second factor weighs against DK because the images are creative artworks, which are traditionally the core of intended copyright protection. Nevertheless, the court limited the weight it placed on this factor because the posters have been published extensively. Appellant agrees that the district court properly weighed the second factor against DK, although it questions the lesser protection given to published works. Appellees counter that because the images are mixed factual and creative works and have been long and extensively published, the second factor tilts toward fair use.

[18] We agree with the district court that the creative nature of artistic images typically weighs in favor of the copyright holder. We recognize, however, that the second factor may be of limited usefulness where the creative work of art is being used for a transformative purpose. This is not a case ... in which ... the creative work was being used for the same decorative purpose as the original. Here, we conclude that DK is using BGA's images for the transformative purpose of enhancing the biographical information provided in Illustrated Trip. Accordingly, we hold that even though BGA's images are creative works, which are a core concern of copyright protection, the second factor has limited weight in our analysis because the purpose of DK's use was to emphasize the images' historical rather than creative value.

III. Amount and Substantiality of the Portion Used ...

[19] The district court determined that even though the images are reproduced in their entirety, the third fair use factor weighs in favor of DK because the images are displayed in reduced size and scattered among many other images and texts. In faulting this conclusion, Appellant contends that the amount used is substantial because the images are copied in their entirety. Neither our court nor any of our sister circuits has ever ruled that the copying of an entire work *favors* fair use. At the same time, however, courts have concluded that such copying does not necessarily weigh against fair use because copying the entirety of a work is sometimes necessary to make a fair use of the image. Adopting this reasoning, we conclude that the third-factor inquiry must take into account that the extent of permissible copying varies with the purpose and character of the use.

[20] Here, DK used BGA's images because the posters and tickets were historical artifacts that could document Grateful Dead concert events and provide a visual context for the accompanying text. To accomplish this use, DK displayed reduced versions of the original images and intermingled these visuals with text and original graphic art. As a consequence, even though the copyrighted images are copied in their entirety, the visual impact of their artistic expression is significantly limited because of their reduced size. We conclude that such use by DK is tailored to further its transformative purpose because DK's reduced size reproductions of BGA's images in their entirety displayed the minimal image size and quality necessary to ensure the reader's recognition of the images as historical artifacts of Grateful Dead concert events. Accordingly, the third fair use factor does not weigh against fair use.

IV. Effect of the Use upon the Market for or Value of the Original ...

[21] In the instant case, the parties agree that DK's use of the images did not impact BGA's primary market for the sale of the poster images. Instead, we look to whether DK's unauthorized use usurps BGA's potential to develop a derivative market. Appellant argues that DK interfered with the market for licensing its images for use in books. Appellant contends that there is an established market for licensing its images and it suffered both the loss of royalty revenue directly from DK and the opportunity to obtain royalties from others.

[22] It is indisputable that, as a general matter, a copyright holder is entitled to demand a royalty for licensing others to use its copyrighted work, and that the impact on potential licensing revenues is a proper subject for consideration in assessing the fourth factor. We have noted, however, that were a court automatically to conclude in every case that potential licensing revenues were impermissibly impaired simply because the secondary user did not pay a fee for the right to engage in the use, the fourth fair use factor would *always* favor the copyright holder. Accordingly, we do not find a harm to BGA's license market merely because DK did not pay a fee for BGA's copyrighted images.

[23] Instead, we look at the impact on potential licensing revenues for traditional, reasonable, or likely to be developed markets. In order to establish a traditional license market, Appellant points to the fees paid to other copyright owners for the reproduction of their images in *Illustrated Trip*. Moreover, Appellant asserts that it established a market for licensing its images, and in this case expressed a willingness to license images to DK. Neither of these arguments shows impairment to a traditional, as opposed to a transformative market.

[24] ... [W]e hold that DK's use of BGA's images is transformatively different from their original expressive purpose. In a case such as this, a copyright holder cannot prevent others from entering fair use markets merely by developing or licensing a market for parody, news reporting, educational or other transformative uses of its own creative work. Copyright owners may not preempt exploitation of transformative markets. Moreover, a publisher's willingness to pay license fees for reproduction of images does not establish that the publisher may not, in the alternative, make fair use of those images. Since DK's use of BGA's images falls within a transformative market, BGA does not suffer market harm due to the loss of license fees....

[25] On balance, we conclude, as the district court did, that the fair use factors weigh in favor of DK's use....

NOTE

1. Recall the case discussed in Chapter II with regard to "created facts," in which the producer of the *Seinfeld* television series sued the publisher of *The Seinfeld Aptitude Test*, a book filled with trivia questions about the series. Unlike *Bill Graham Archives*, the Second Circuit held that the defendants infringed the plaintiff's copyrights and did not qualify for a fair use defense. Castle Rock Entm't, Inc. v. Carol Publ'g Grp., Inc., 150 F.3d 132 (2d Cir. 1997). The court did not accept the defendants' characterization that *The Seinfeld Aptitude Test* was a reference or critical work. In analyzing the first fair use factor, it stated:

> Any transformative purpose possessed by The SAT [(The Seinfeld Aptitude Test)] is slight to non-existent. We reject the argument that The SAT was created to educate Seinfeld viewers or to criticize, "expose," or otherwise comment upon Seinfeld. The SAT's purpose, as evidenced definitively by the statements of the book's creators and by the book itself, is to repackage Seinfeld to entertain Seinfeld viewers. The SAT's back cover makes no mention of exposing Seinfeld to its readers, for example, as a pitiably vacuous reflection of a puerile and pervasive television culture, but rather urges SAT readers to "open this book to satisfy [their] between-episode [Seinfeld] cravings." Golub, The SAT's author, described the trivia quiz book not as a commentary or a Seinfeld research tool, but as an effort to "capture Seinfeld's flavor in quiz book fashion." Finally, even viewing The SAT in the light most favorable to defendants, we find scant reason to conclude that this trivia quiz book seeks to educate, criticize, parody, comment, report upon, or research Seinfeld, or otherwise serve a transformative purpose. The book does not contain commentary or analysis about Seinfeld, nor does it suggest how The SAT can be used to research Seinfeld; rather, the book simply poses trivia questions. The SAT's plain purpose, therefore, is not to expose Seinfeld's "nothingness," but to satiate Seinfeld fans' passion for the "nothingness" that Seinfeld has elevated into the realm of protectable creative expression.

As to the fourth fair use factor, the Second Circuit reasoned that "[u]nlike parody, criticism, scholarship, news reporting, or other transformative uses, The SAT substitutes for a derivative market that a television program copyright owner such as Castle Rock would in general develop or license others to develop." *Id.* at 145. Is *Castle Rock* reconcilable with *Bill Graham Archives* on this front?

2. Indexing and Search

As you read the following decision, consider how the court understands transformativeness. Does it use the concept differently in the context at issue here than in previous cases?

Perfect 10, Inc. v. Amazon.com, Inc.
508 F.3d 1146 (9th Cir. 2007)

IKUTA, J.:

{Recall the facts in this case from when you read another excerpt of it earlier in studying the right of public display in Chapter V.} ...

[1] In this case, the district court determined that Google's use of thumbnails was not a fair use ....

[2] *Purpose and character of the use.* ...

[3] Google's use of thumbnails is highly transformative.... Although an image may have been created originally to serve an entertainment, aesthetic, or informative function, a search engine transforms the image into a pointer directing a user to a source of information. Just as a parody has an obvious claim to transformative value because it can provide social benefit, by shedding light on an earlier work, and, in the process, creating a new one, a search engine provides social benefit by incorporating an original work into a new work, namely, an electronic reference tool. Indeed, a search engine may be more transformative than a parody because a search engine provides an entirely new use for the original work, while a parody typically has the same entertainment purpose as the original work. In other words, a search engine puts images in a different context so that they are transformed into a new creation.

[4] The fact that Google incorporates the entire Perfect 10 image into the search engine results does not diminish the transformative nature of Google's use. As the district court correctly noted, ... even making an exact copy of a work may be transformative so long as the copy serves a different function than the original work.... Here, Google uses Perfect 10's images in a new context to serve a different purpose....

[5] In conducting our case-specific analysis of fair use in light of the purposes of copyright, we must weigh Google's superseding and commercial uses of thumbnail images against Google's significant transformative use, as well as the extent to which Google's search engine promotes the purposes of copyright and serves the interests of the public. Although the district court acknowledged the "truism that search engines such as Google Image Search provide great value to the public," the district court did not expressly consider whether this value outweighed the significance of Google's superseding use or the commercial nature of Google's use. The Supreme Court, however, has directed us to be mindful of the extent to which a use promotes the purposes of copyright and serves the interests of the public. *See Campbell; Harper & Row; Sony.*

[6] We note that the superseding use in this case is not significant at present: the district court did not find that any downloads for mobile phone use had taken place [to show that Google's use of thumbnails superseded Perfect 10's right to sell its reduced-size images for use on cell phones]. Moreover, while Google's use of thumbnails to direct users to AdSense partners containing infringing content adds a commercial dimension ..., the district court did not determine that this commercial element was significant. The district court stated that Google's AdSense programs as a whole contributed "$630 million, or 46% of total revenues" to Google's bottom line, but noted that this figure did not "break down the much smaller amount attributable to websites that contain infringing content."

[7] We conclude that the significantly transformative nature of Google's search engine, particularly in light of its public benefit, outweighs Google's superseding and commercial uses of the thumbnails in this case. In reaching this conclusion, we note the importance of analyzing fair use flexibly in light of new circumstances. We are also mindful of the Supreme Court's direction that "the more transformative the new work, the less will be the significance of other factors, like commercialism, that may weigh against a finding of fair use." *Campbell*, 510 U.S. at 579.

[8] Accordingly, we disagree with the district court's conclusion that because Google's use of the thumbnails could supersede Perfect 10's cell phone download use and because the use was ... commercial ..., this fair use factor weighed "slightly" in favor of Perfect 10. Instead, we conclude that the transformative nature of Google's use is more significant than any incidental superseding use or the minor commercial aspects of Google's search engine and website. Therefore, this factor weighs heavily in favor of Google.

[9] *The nature of the copyrighted work....*

[10] Here, the district court found that Perfect 10's images were creative but also previously published.... Once Perfect 10 has exploited this commercially valuable right of first publication by putting its images on the Internet for paid subscribers, Perfect 10 is no longer entitled to the enhanced protection available for an unpublished work. Accordingly the district court did not err in holding that this factor weighed only slightly in favor of Perfect 10.

[11] *The amount and substantiality of the portion used.* .... [Google]'s use of the entire photographic image was reasonable in light of the purpose of a search engine. Specifically, ... it was necessary for [Google] to copy the entire image to allow users to recognize the image and decide whether to pursue more information about the image or the originating website. If [Google] only copied part of the image, it would be more difficult to identify it, thereby reducing the usefulness of the visual search engine.... [T]he district court did not err in finding that this factor favored neither party.

[12] *Effect of use on the market*..... The district court here ... [held] that Google's use of thumbnails did not hurt Perfect 10's market for full-size images. We agree.

[13] Perfect 10 argues that the district court erred because the likelihood of market harm may be presumed if the intended use of an image is for commercial gain. However, this presumption does not arise when a work is transformative because market substitution is at least less certain, and market harm may not be so readily inferred. As previously discussed, Google's use of thumbnails for search engine purposes is highly transformative, and so market harm cannot be presumed.

[14] Perfect 10 also has a market for reduced-size images .... The district court held that "Google's use of thumbnails likely does harm the potential market for the downloading of [Perfect 10's] reduced-size images onto cell phones." The district court reasoned that persons who can obtain Perfect 10 images free of charge from Google are less likely to pay for a download, and the availability of Google's thumbnail images would harm Perfect 10's market for cell phone downloads. As we discussed above, the district court did not make a finding

that Google users have downloaded thumbnail images for cell phone use. This potential harm to Perfect 10's market remains hypothetical. We conclude that this factor favors neither party.

[15] Having undertaken a case-specific analysis of all four factors, we now weigh these factors together in light of the purposes of copyright. In this case, Google has put Perfect 10's thumbnail images (along with millions of other thumbnail images) to a use fundamentally different than the use intended by Perfect 10. In doing so, Google has provided a significant benefit to the public. Weighing this significant transformative use against the unproven use of Google's thumbnails for cell phone downloads, and considering the other fair use factors, all in light of the purpose of copyright, we conclude that Google's use of Perfect 10's thumbnails is a fair use....

NOTE

1. In ruling on the applicability of the fair use defense to Napster's music file-sharing software in a lawsuit brought by music copyright holders, the Ninth Circuit elaborated on how to think about analysis of the first statutory factor with regard to free music downloads through a service that was not charging users:

> A commercial use weighs against a finding of fair use but is not conclusive on the issue. The district court determined that Napster users engage in commercial use of the copyrighted materials largely because (1) "a host user sending a file cannot be said to engage in a personal use when distributing that file to an anonymous requester" and (2) "Napster users get for free something they would ordinarily have to buy." The district court's findings are not clearly erroneous.

> Direct economic benefit is not required to demonstrate a commercial use. Rather, repeated and exploitative copying of copyrighted works, even if the copies are not offered for sale, may constitute a commercial use. In the record before us, commercial use is demonstrated by a showing that repeated and exploitative unauthorized copies of copyrighted works were made to save the expense of purchasing authorized copies. Plaintiffs made such a showing before the district court.

A&M Records, Inc. v. Napster, Inc., 239 F.3d 1004, 1015 (9th Cir. 2001). Do you think this reasoning is sensible? Consider its relevance to *Perfect 10*.

3. Journalism and News

> As you read the following case on news reporting, consider whether it is categorically likelier than other uses not enumerated in the preamble to § 107 to be a fair use. If so, why?

Noelia Lorenzo Monge v. Maya Magazines, Inc.
688 F.3d 1164 (9th Cir. 2012)

McKEOWN, J.:

[1] This appeal reads like a telenovela, a Spanish soap opera. It pits music celebrities, who make money by promoting themselves, against a gossip magazine, that makes money by publishing celebrity photographs,

with a paparazzo, who apparently stole the disputed pictures, stuck in the middle. Noelia Lorenzo Monge and Jorge Reynoso, Latin American celebrities, claim that Maya Magazines, Inc. and Maya Publishing Group, LLC infringed their copyrights by publishing previously unpublished photos of their clandestine wedding in "TVNotas," a Spanish-language celebrity gossip magazine. The district court granted Maya summary judgment on the ground that publication of the images was fair use under the Copyright Act of 1976. We disagree and reverse. The tantalizing and even newsworthy interest in the photos does not trump a balancing of the fair use factors. Simply put, Maya did not sustain its burden of establishing that its wholesale, commercial use of the previously unpublished photos constituted fair use....

[2] Noelia Lorenzo Monge is a pop singer and model. Jorge Reynoso is her manager and husband, and a music producer. Oscar Viqueira is a paparazzo who occasionally worked as a driver and bodyguard for the couple during their visits to Miami. Maya publishes multiple magazines, including the celebrity gossip magazine "TVNotas." In the past, Maya has paid Monge to pose for pictures published in its magazine, "H Para Hombres." Reynoso was paid $25,000 for photos of his wedding to his former wife Pilar Montenegro, as well as $40,000 for photos of his vacation in Paris with Montenegro....

[3] Monge and Reynoso were married at the "Little White Wedding Chapel" in Las Vegas, Nevada on January 3, 2007. Valuing their privacy, and Monge's image as a young, single pop singer, the couple went to great lengths to keep the wedding a secret: only the minister and two chapel employees witnessed the ceremony. Using Monge's camera, chapel employees took three photos of the wedding; later that night at least three more photos of Monge and Reynoso in their nuptial garb were also taken. The pictures were intended for the couple's private use. For two years Monge and Reynoso succeeded in keeping their wedding a secret, even from their families.

[4] In the summer of 2008, Reynoso used Viqueira's sport utility vehicle. Viqueira claims that after Reynoso returned the car, Viqueira found a memory chip in the ashtray. When Viqueira looked at the files on the memory chip, he found the photos of the couple's secret wedding, along with an assortment of other photos and videos. Viqueira tried to capitalize on the files to extort money he claimed Reynoso owed him. When this plan failed, in February 2009, Viqueira sold to Maya all of the electronic files he had taken "to recuperate the payment for [his] work." The price was $1,500. The couple testified, and Maya does not contest, that Viqueira did not have permission to take or sell any of the images on the memory chip....

[5] Reynoso received a phone call from his mother in February 2009, berating him for getting married without telling her. Intent on secrecy, Reynoso denied the marriage to his own mother, but to no avail: She had already seen the wedding photos in a gossip magazine. Maya had published six of the stolen photos—three of the wedding ceremony and three of the wedding night—in Issue 633 of TVNotas. Prior to Issue 633, the photos were unpublished. The headline on the front cover of the magazine stated: "The Secret Wedding of Noelia and Jorge Reynoso in Las Vegas." The byline stated: "We even have photos of their first night as a married couple!" This text was positioned beside the wedding photo on the cover. Three photos were reproduced on the cover: one showing Monge lying on a bed revealing her underwear; one of Reynoso smoking a cigar in front of a neon Playboy logo; and one depicting the newly-married couple.

[6] Inside the magazine, the photos were featured over a two-page spread. "Apparently, the couple married in Las Vegas in January 2007!" was written on the top of the spread. "First and exclusive photos of the secret wedding of Noelia and Jorge Reynoso" was also printed in large font on the spread.

[7] The left side of the spread was comprised of one large wedding photo, a reprint from the cover. Printed on top of this photo was: "Only in TVNotas"; and the caption read: "In fact, a lot has been said about a supposedly secret wedding in Las Vegas, Nevada, that took place in January 2007, but until now, no one had shown photos of that memorable day. TVNotas got a hold of those photos and shows them to you now, exclusively."

[8] The right side of the spread was comprised of four photos. The photos showed the couple next to a priest, kissing in wedding attire, and at a bar. The picture of Monge on a bed with her underwear showing, also published on the cover, was repeated. The footer of this page stated: "Although the couple has declined to confirm their marriage, these photos that we got speak for themselves."

Figure 104: *TVNotas* cover featuring Monge and Reynoso

Figure 105: Photos of Monge and Reynoso wedding, as they appear in *TVNotas*

[9] These six images were the only ones Maya published from the assortment of approximately four hundred images and three videos obtained from Viqueira. Maya did not publish other supporting evidence such as a marriage certificate, choosing instead to rely solely on the sensational photos. The couple claims that the three wedding photos published comprise every wedding photo taken, and that the three photos of the wedding night comprise almost every photo of the wedding night. Maya does not challenge either contention. Nor is there any dispute that Maya generated revenue from sales of Issue 633. Maya also admits that, in the past, it has paid for exclusive rights to publish pictures of celebrity weddings, including other celebrity weddings depicted in Issue 633....

[10] Soon after publication of the pictures, the couple registered copyrights in five of the six published photos— all the published pictures, except the one where the couple appears together in front of a Playboy logo. Monge and Reynoso then filed a complaint against Maya asserting claims for copyright infringement ....

[11] .... The parties filed cross-motions for summary judgment. The district court granted Maya's motion for summary judgment based on fair use ....

A. Purpose and Character of the Use

[12] The first factor includes three principles that simultaneously complement and yet are in tension with one another in this case: news reporting; transformation; and commercial use.

1. News Reporting

[13] The preamble to the fair use statute lists "news reporting" as an illustrative basis supporting fair use under this factor. 17 U.S.C. § 107. We have little doubt that the gossip magazine's sensational coverage of the wedding qualifies as news reporting. Our role in this regard is not as a literary critic. While the parties agree that the pictures at issue are newsworthy, we must nevertheless proceed cautiously because "[t]he promise of copyright would be an empty one if it could be avoided merely by dubbing the infringement a fair use 'news report' of the [work]." *Harper & Row*.

[14] Although news reporting is an example of fair use, it is not sufficient itself to sustain a per se finding of fair use. The fact that an article arguably is 'news' and therefore a productive use is simply one factor in a fair use analysis. In other words, fair use has bounds even in news reporting, and no per se "public interest" exception exists. Because Maya cannot simply take fair use refuge under the umbrella of news reporting, we analyze Maya's coverage in light of two other considerations: the degree of transformation occasioned by Maya's use; and the commercial nature of its use.[6]

2. Transformation ...

[15] Transformation in the news reporting context has been litigated repeatedly in our circuit .... [W]e stated that despite the newsworthiness of ... videos at issue, which documented a beating during a riot in Los Angeles, their mere rebroadcast was not in itself transformative .... Similarly, a news station's broadcast of an extraordinarily timely news segment concerning ongoing riots related to the Rodney King beating was held unfair .... Minor changes, such as placing voice-overs on video clips, do not necessarily transform a work.

[16] Arrangement of a work in a photo montage, however, can be transformative where copyrighted material is incorporated into other material....

[17] The pictures here are a clear, visual recording of the couple's wedding and wedding night. Because publication of photographic evidence that constitutes proof of a newsworthy event is not automatically fair use, we turn to the degree to which Maya's use transformed the works. Each of the individual images was reproduced essentially in its entirety; neither minor cropping nor the inclusion of headlines or captions transformed the copyrighted works. The reasoning regarding voice-overs ... applies with equal vigor to headlines and captions over still images.

---

[6] In evaluating the "purpose and character" factor, we apply the general rule that a party claiming fair use must act in a manner generally compatible with principles of good faith and fair dealing. The couple claims that the magazine acted in bad faith by failing to: seek permission from them; confirm that the copyrights in the images belonged to Viqueira; and seek any documentation as to ownership. Maya presents evidence, however, that it procured a written copyright assignment from Viqueira, and argues that it had no reason to believe that the known paparazzo did not have rights to the photos. While the couple's arguments may call into question Maya's good faith, Maya's actions do not amount to an abuse of the good faith and fair dealing underpinnings of the fair use doctrine. Application of the defense is not foreclosed.

[18] The individual images were marginally transformed, however, in other ways. The text and article accompanying the photos, as well as their arrangement in a photo montage, may give the pictures a further purpose. *Campbell* makes clear that the "heart" of a claim for transformative use is "the use of some elements of a prior author's composition to create a new one that, at least in part, comments on that author's works." Of course, in *Campbell*, the question related to parody, a direct comment aimed at the original song. The dissent's vivid description of the copyrighted photos does not undermine the conclusion that there was no real transformation of the photos themselves. Nor can it be said, as in *Campbell*, that Maya created a new work based on the photos.

[19] Even if the photos were not physically or creatively transformed, Maya claims that publication of the photos as an exposé amounted to transformation. In other words, Maya's publication transformed the photos from their original purpose—images of a wedding night—into newsworthy evidence of a clandestine marriage.[7] In support, Maya relies heavily on *Núñez* [*v. Caribbean Int'l News Corp.*, 235 F.3d 18 (1st Cir. 2000)], a First Circuit case that is distinguishable. In *Núñez*, a photographer sued a newspaper that published his copyrighted images of a woman that had won the title of Miss Universe Puerto Rico. In at least one photo, the woman appeared naked or nearly naked. After a local television station displayed the risqué photographs, the model was interviewed about her fitness to retain the Miss Universe Puerto Rico crown. Soon after, a local newspaper published the photographs without permission, along with several articles about the controversy.

[20] Although *Núñez* also involved news reporting, the similarities end there. The controversy there was whether the salacious photos themselves were befitting a Miss Universe Puerto Rico, and whether she should retain her title. In contrast, the controversy here has little to do with photos; instead, the photos here depict the couple's clandestine wedding. The photos were not even necessary to prove that controverted fact—the marriage certificate, which is a matter of public record, may have sufficed to inform the public that the couple kept their marriage a secret for two years. Indeed, the public interest in the free flow of information is assured by the law's refusal to recognize a valid copyright in facts. Under copyright law, Maya possesses an unfettered right to use any factual information revealed through the photos for the purpose of enlightening its audience, but it can claim no need to bodily appropriate the couple's expression of that information by utilizing portions of the actual photos. Unlike here, in *Núñez* the pictures were the story, and the newspaper in *Núñez* did not seek to manufacture newsworthiness, nor did it scoop the story.[8] Also significant, the work in *Núñez* had already been distributed when the infringement occurred.

[21] We reiterate what the First Circuit emphasized, namely that there is no general newsworthiness exception. In other words, newsworthiness itself does not lead to transformation. The dissent's doomsday prediction about the impact of our decision on investigative journalism is overblown.

[22] Maya's purpose in publishing the photos was to expose the couple's secret wedding, which was at odds with the couple's purpose of documenting their private nuptials. But even an infringer's separate purpose, by itself, does not necessarily create new aesthetics or a new work that alters the first work with new expression,

---

[7] While the couple undisputedly kept the wedding a secret, contrary to the dissent's assertion, the record contains no evidence that the couple made affirmative representations about their marital status. There is no evidence that the couple repeatedly denied their marriage or made other public statements to the contrary. The district court erred in making such factual findings and likewise erred in inferring such representations during the summary judgment proceeding.

[8] Contrary to the dissent's concern, where the content of the work is the story, such as a controversy over a congressman's "salacious" photos or a golf celebrity's "sext" messages, news reporters would have a better claim of transformation, which, far from being determinative, is simply one of the factors we consider in the fair use analysis. In any event, neither example the dissent provides pertains to a "private," unpublished work—both Tiger Woods and Congressman Weiner distributed their "masterpieces" to others.

meaning or message. A difference in purpose is not quite the same thing as transformation, and *Campbell* instructs that transformativeness is the critical inquiry under this factor.

[23] Maya did not transform the photos into a new work, as in *Campbell*, or incorporate the photos as part of a broader work .... Instead, unlike the thumbnail images at issue in *Perfect 10*, Maya left the inherent character of the images unchanged. Maya's use—wholesale copying sprinkled with written commentary—was at best minimally transformative.

3. Commercial Use

[24] Maya's use was undisputedly commercial in nature. The gossip magazine makes no pretense that it is educational. It is a commercial publication.

[25] The Supreme Court has stated that "every commercial use of copyrighted material is presumptively an unfair exploitation of the monopoly privilege that belongs to the owner of the copyright." *Sony*. Commercial use is a factor that tends to weigh against a finding of fair use because the user stands to profit from exploitation of the copyrighted material without paying the customary price. There is no dispute here that Maya is motivated by profits, and in fact profited from the publication of the pictures.

[26] Although Maya's reporting on the clandestine wedding was newsworthy, newsworthiness, by itself, is insufficient to demonstrate fair use. Similarly, exposing truths in the public interest is not a bell weather of fair use. Maya's minimal transformation of the photos is substantially undercut by its undisputed commercial use. On balance, the first factor is at best neutral, and does not support Maya's claim of fair use.

B. Nature of the Copyrighted Work

[27] Under the second factor, we address two aspects of the work: the extent to which it is creative and whether it is unpublished.

[28] Photos are generally viewed as creative, aesthetic expressions of a scene or image and have long been the subject of copyright....

[29] Admittedly, the point-and-shoot images here are hardly the work of famous photographers like Richard Avedon, Diane Arbus, or Annie Liebovitz. But neither are they entirely factual in nature, as Maya argues. Simply because a photo documents an event does not turn a pictorial representation into a factual recitation of the nature referenced in *Harper & Row*. Photos that we now regard as iconic often document an event—whether the flight of the Wright Brothers' airplane, the sailor's kiss in Times Square on V–J Day, the first landing on the moon, or the fall of the Berlin Wall.

[30] Although the published photos were not highly artistic in nature, they do have a defining and common characteristic—until Issue 633 hit the stands, they were unpublished. We pointedly note that we address the unpublished status of the photos only under copyright principles, not privacy law.... We begin with a basic principle: "the unpublished nature of a work is a key, though not necessarily determinative, factor tending to negate a defense of fair use." *Harper & Row*. The Court specifically honed in on the unpublished status of the work, calling it "a critical element of its 'nature.'" Accordingly, "*[u]nder ordinary circumstances*, the author's right to control the first public appearance of his undisseminated expression *will outweigh* a claim of fair use." (emphases added)....

[31] We are unable to discern anything extraordinary about the situation here, and agree with the district court that Maya's "publication undoubtedly supplanted Plaintiffs' right to control the first public appearance of the photographs." This finding further distinguishes *Núñez*, where the works were hardly confidential or secret and

had already been distributed when the infringement occurred. In contrast, Maya's headlines bragged about its exclusive photo spread of never before seen images.

[32] In analyzing the second factor, the nature of the work, we balance the copyright protection received by marginally creative works with the Supreme Court's clear recognition that the unpublished status of the work is a critical element. These aspects counter-balance each other, and because the case is not exceptional, we apply the Supreme Court's admonition that with respect to unpublished works, this factor outweighs Maya's claim of fair use.

C. Amount and Substantiality of the Portion Used

[33] .... We examine both the quantitative and qualitative aspects of the portion of the copyrighted material taken. Quantitatively, every single photo of the wedding and almost every photo of the wedding night were published. With respect to the ceremony, none of the three published photos were heavily cropped. The same is true regarding the remaining photos, with the exception of the image where Reynoso is smoking a cigar. Qualitatively, the minimal cropping of each picture demonstrates that the "heart" of each individual copyrighted picture was published.

[34] The inquiry under this factor is a flexible one, rather than a simple determination of the percentage of the copyrighted work used. But we should be clear, Maya copied 100 percent of the copyrighted photos at issue. While we do not discredit Maya's legitimate role as a news gatherer, its reporting purpose could have been served through publication of the couple's marriage certificate or other sources rather than copyrighted photos. Even absent official documentation, one clear portrait depicting the newly married couple in wedding garb with the priest would certainly have sufficed to verify the clandestine wedding. Maya used far more than was necessary to corroborate its story—all three wedding images and three post-wedding photos. Thus, analyzing both the quantitative and qualitative aspects of the published material, this factor weighs against fair use....

D. Effect upon the Potential Market

[35] The final fair use factor is "the effect of the use upon the *potential market* for or value of the copyrighted work." 17 U.S.C. § 107(4) (emphasis added).... Maya argued, and the district court agreed, that no potential market for the pictures existed because the couple did not intend to sell publication rights to the photos. The district court's legal conclusion that the potential market was destroyed due to the couple's then-present intent regarding publication was in error....

[36] Under section 107, "potential market" means either an immediate or a delayed market, and includes harm to derivative works. Control over the delayed market includes future markets.... Even an author who had disavowed any intention to publish his work during his lifetime was entitled to protection of his copyright, first, because the relevant consideration was the "potential market" and, second, because he has the right to change his mind. The potential market for the photos exists independent of the couple's present intent, and the district court's decision to the contrary was error.

[37] Recognizing that fair use focuses on potential, not just actual, market harm, we note there is little doubt that an actual market exists for the photos. Maya does not offer any evidence of the relevant market or the lack of market harm from its publication other than broad, unsubstantiated statements in its brief. The magazine's failure of proof is hardly surprising: The couple is undisputedly in the business of selling images of themselves and they have done so in the past and Maya itself paid $1,500 for prior photos. Maya's purchase of the pictures unequivocally demonstrates a market for the couple's copyrighted pictures. And Maya is itself a participant in the market for celebrity wedding photos, as Issue 633 also featured pictures of another celebrity wedding with photos that the magazine purchased. The demand for the pictures in the actual market, just as in the potential market, dropped significantly upon Maya's first and exclusive publication.

[38] The impact on the potential market for unpublished works is best illustrated by the Court's analysis in *Harper & Row*: "The right of first publication implicates a threshold decision by the author whether and in what form to release his work." In other words, "[p]ublication of an author's expression before he has authorized its dissemination seriously infringes the author's right to decide when and whether it will be made public, a factor not present in fair use of published works." ... Monge and Reynoso have the right to change their mind. They reasonably could decide to sell the images for profit in the future, as Reynoso has demonstrably done in the past. Similarly, photos of Monge have also been marketed commercially, even to a Maya publication. While Maya boldly emphasized that its publication was "[f]irst and exclusive," the couple's intention at the time of the publication did not give Maya license to forever deprive them of their right to decide when, whether and in what form to release the photos. Thus, Maya's claim that a confidential work receives less copyright protection because its author intends to maintain confidentiality finds no support; to the contrary, it has never been seriously disputed that the fact that the plaintiff's work is unpublished is a factor tending to negate the defense of fair use.

[39] Although the photos were unpublished until Maya printed them for commercial gain, after the publication of Issue 633, the bottom literally dropped out of the market—neither Maya nor anybody else is likely to purchase these pictures from the couple. And it is obvious that any licensing value, to the extent the couple could find a willing licensee, is severely diminished. Maya's un-authorized "first and exclusive" publication of the images substantially harmed the potential market because the publication directly competed with, and completely usurped, the couple's potential market for first publication of the photos.

[40] In addition, to negate fair use one need only show that if the challenged use should become widespread, it would adversely affect the potential market for the copyrighted work. Unrestricted and widespread reproduction of Maya's conduct would not only undermine the ability of celebrities to market images of themselves, but would also create incentives to pirate intellectual property.

[41] Our focus on the usurpation of the market further underscores the limited extent to which Maya transformed the works. In a true transformation, such as the parody in *Campbell*, it is more likely that the new work will not affect the market for the original because the parody and the original usually serve different market functions. Not so here. Maya did not transform the images and create a new work; instead, Maya's mere duplication of the photos serves as a market replacement for the originals, making it likely that cognizable market harm to the originals will occur....

[42] This factor brings us full circle. We recognize that market harm may not be presumed in all instances; however, the harm to both the potential and actual markets based on wholesale copying of unpublished works demonstrates the logic of such a presumption in cases when a commercial use amounts to mere duplication of the entirety of an original. Because the facts demonstrate that Maya's use was akin to mere duplication— affecting both the actual and potential market for the photos—even without the benefit of any presumption, this factor tips against fair use. In this case, the cat is out of the bag....

[43] Waving the news reporting flag is not a get out of jail free card in the copyright arena. Maya's effort to document its exposé does not automatically trump the couple's rights in its unpublished photos. Because the minimal transformation occasioned by Maya's use is amply outweighed by its commercial use, the first factor does not support the magazine. And, even if it did, this factor does not dwarf the effect of the other factors. Upon balancing the copyright protection for these marginally creative works against their unpublished status, we see nothing exceptional about this case, and follow the Supreme Court's direction that the second factor weighs against Maya in this instance. Next, Maya has not demonstrated that the third factor supports fair use. Maya used virtually the entirety of the wedding-related photographs; much more than was necessary to corroborate its story. Finally, the district court further erred by holding, without support, that the couple's then-present intention destroyed the potential market for the photographic works. Maya's use negatively affected

both the potential and actual markets for the couple's photos. Simply because the works were yet unpublished did not give Maya a license to pull the trigger and blow the couple's cover.

[44] The balancing of these factors must be weighed against Maya's burden to establish fair use. Without a single factor tipping in its favor, Maya has not met its burden. Because Maya's affirmative defense of fair use fails as a matter of law, the district court erred by granting summary judgment in favor of Maya on the basis of fair use. Instead, the district court should have granted the couple's summary judgment motion on this issue....

M. SMITH, J., dissenting:

[45] I respectfully dissent. Copyright is not an inviolable right that confers upon creators absolute control and ownership over their creations. Copyright protection was enacted "[t]o promote the Progress of Science and useful Arts" by creating a system in which authors and artists may reap the benefits of their creative contributions. U.S. CONST. art. I, § 8, cl. 8. The fair use doctrine was designed to act as the counterbalance to copyright by permitting courts to avoid rigid application of the copyright statute when, on occasion, it would stifle the very creativity which that law is designed to foster.

[46] The majority's fair use analysis in this case is inconsistent with Supreme Court precedent, and thwarts the public interests of copyright by allowing newsworthy public figures to control their images in the press. The majority contends that the public interest in a free press cannot trump a celebrity's right to control his image and works in the media—even if that celebrity has publicly controverted the very subject matter of the works at issue. Under the majority's analysis, public figures could invoke copyright protection to prevent the media's disclosure of any embarrassing or incriminating works by claiming that such images were intended only for private use. The implications of this analysis undermine the free press and eviscerate the principles upon which copyright was founded. Although newsworthiness alone is insufficient to invoke fair use, public figures should not be able to hide behind the cloak of copyright to prevent the news media from exposing their fallacies. Accordingly, because three of the photos directly proved the fact of the Noelia Monge's and Jorge Reynoso's (the Couple) marriage, I would affirm the district court's finding of fair use as to those wedding photos. However, because the remaining two photos did not directly prove the Couple's wedding and therefore may have been unnecessary to the story, I would remand on the grounds that genuine issues of material fact exist, precluding summary judgment....

A. Purpose and Character of Use

[47] ....The use of photographic evidence to prove a controversial, salacious, or controverted fact weighs in favor of a finding of fair use. In the case of photographic works, a use may be found to be transformative if it complements the original work, rather than supersedes it. Ultimately, the more transformative the use, the less other factors, such as commerciality, weigh against a finding of fair use.

[48] The majority contends that Maya's use of the photos was not transformative because (1) the photos were minimally changed with limited commentary; (2) the photos were offered for the exact same purpose—to document the wedding; and (3) the newsworthiness of the photos was insufficient to support a finding of fair use. I respectfully disagree on all three points.

1. Editing, Arrangement, and Commentary

[49] The majority attempts to diminish the significance of Maya's commentary, cropping, re-sizing, and arrangement of the photos by presenting the publication as little more than a photo album. This is simply not accurate. The February 10, 2009 exposé consisted of a stylized two-page spread: on the left page was a full length image of Reynoso and Noelia embracing in the wedding chapel (originally cropped on the front cover), accompanied by a red text box on the lower left hand corner, with the print:

Definitely, Noelia never ceases to amaze us. Whether it is her fights with her mother, her allegations of sexual abuse, her pornographic videos, her problems with the press or the behavior of her partner, Jorge Reynoso, the Puerto Rican singer always takes over the headlines, and this time is no exception. In fact, a lot has been said about a supposedly secret wedding in Las Vegas, Nevada, that took place in January 2007, but until now, no one had shown photos of that memorable day. TVNotas got a hold of those photos and shows them to you now, exclusively.

[50] The second page consisted of a full page, four-photo montage: first, a different wedding picture of Noelia and Reynoso, next to the minister who married them, in the same wedding clothing, in the same chapel, with the caption, "POSING WITH THE MINISTER OF THEIR MARRIAGE," and accompanying the inset text, "Noelia Lorenzo–Monge and Jorge Reynoso looked happy, she in her stretch mini dress and a garter, he in a suit and tie." To the immediate right of that, a close up photo of Noelia and Reynoso kissing, with two inset captions, above "THEIR FIRST KISS AS MAN AND WIFE" and below, with the accompanying inset text, "After years of a relationship, Reynoso finally came through for her." In the second row, to the left was a photo of Noelia posing next to a seated Reynoso in a bar, his arm around Noelia and a cigar in his hand, with the caption above, "THEY WENT TO A BAR." Finally, to the right of that, a fourth photo of Noelia, laying on the bed in the same stretch white mini dress and black knee high boots, exposing her underwear and looking seductively at the camera, with the above caption, "THIS IS HOW THE SINGER ENDED UP IN THE NUPTIAL SUITE," also accompanied by a smaller caption inset, "Flirty, suggestive and happy, as every wife would be, the Singer posed ready for her wedding night." At the bottom of the page in bold, large black and white print read: "Though they didn't want to confirm their marriage, these images speak for themselves."

[51] Maya's article constituted much more than a haphazard republication of the Couple's photos. Framed around the Couple's refusals to confirm their marriage and to continue to represent Noelia as an "unwed sex symbol," Maya used the images as documentary evidence…. [A] photo montage, with accompanying commentary, may constitute a transformative use. Maya's commentary, editing, and arrangement of the photos added to, and ultimately changed, the original character of the images by advancing them as the basis of an exposé. The extent of Maya's editing, commentary, and arrangement thus weighs in favor of a finding of transformativeness.

2. Different Purpose

[52] The majority contends: "[i]n one sense, the parties' purposes are identical: Photographic documentation of the wedding." However, the majority repeatedly confuses the original subject matter of the photos with the intended use of the images. For the Couple, these were personal images, originally taken to capture the night of their marriage. After they were married, however, the photos were kept secret for the Couple's commercial gain. As Reynoso testified, the images were withheld from the public solely for "marketing" purposes, in order to maintain Noelia's "image of being a single singer appeal to young people."[3] ("Q: Why did you decide to have a secret wedding? A: I just mentioned to you that we're trying to protect her image of being a single singer to appeal to young people … Q: Were there any other reasons? A: No, just marketing reasons."). For Maya, the photos were used as direct, documentary evidence of a clandestine wedding that had been hidden from the public for years, disproving the Couple's representations to the contrary. Indeed, media speculation regarding their relationship—even referring to them as husband and wife—had occurred years before the publication of the TVNotas expose in February 2009. Thus, the exposé served an entirely different purpose—indeed, a purpose contrary to the Couple's original intent to record and conceal their Las Vegas wedding. Accordingly, I

---

[3] Reynoso [has] been linked to other publicity stunts regarding Noelia's image as well, including leaking her sex-tape with former-boyfriend.

would find that the fundamentally different purpose of Maya's use also weighs in favor of a finding of transformativeness.

3. Newsworthiness

[53] The majority misguidedly relies on *Harper & Row* to criticize newsworthiness as a basis for fair use. However, *Harper & Row* is distinguishable on two critical points: (1) the excerpts at issue were soon-to-be published in a hard-cover memoir by their author, President Gerald Ford, and rights to publish excerpts had already been bid on, and sold to, competing magazines; and (2) Ford had never concealed or controverted the facts at issue in the infringing excerpts.

[54] Specifically, *Harper & Row* involved the surreptitious publication by a magazine, *The Nation*, of critical excerpts of Gerald Ford's soon-to-be published memoirs regarding the Nixon pardon. *The Nation* published the excerpts for commercial gain in an effort to "scoop" the hardcover release, as well as its competitors, who had rightfully bid for publication rights. Here, there was no such subterfuge. The Couple had concealed the truth of their relationship from the public, and even from their close friends and family. The photographs proved not only their marriage, but when, where, and how it took place, and for how long the Couple had hidden the truth. In short, Maya's exposé constituted a transformative use because it shed light upon the Couple's covert nuptials.

[55] The majority contends that if a work is created for "private use," and then subsequently published without permission because it is newsworthy, that the publication cannot constitute a fair use. The logical extension of the majority's reasoning could produce absurd results. If public, newsworthy figures were permitted to invoke a "private use" exception, Tiger Woods, for example, could have claimed copyright in his sexting messages and, without fair use, the media would have no right to quote them.[4] Likewise, without a fair use defense, the media would have only been able to describe former Congressman Anthony Weiner's self-portraits, rather than reprint the images themselves. Thus, the majority attempts to distinguish Maya's use of the wedding photos from "legitimate" fair uses—namely, when the "content of the photographs is the story." In so doing, the majority oversimplifies Maya's use of the images and superimposes the court as the final arbiter of what is sufficiently "salacious" or "controversial" to constitute a "legitimately" fair use. This is a dangerous intrusion upon both the sanctity of the free press and copyright.

[56] The majority's proposed test would effectively vest in the courts the power to circumscribe news stories and the sources upon which the media may rely. The line between when a copyrighted work "is the story" and when it is not is not nearly as clear as the majority contends. Thus, if the "story" of Tiger Woods' infidelities was limited to merely exposing his multiple mistresses, the majority's test would still prohibit the "fair use" of his sexts because his liaisons could be proven by other, non-copyrighted sources. Likewise, it is unclear whether republication of former Congressman Weiner's seminude tweets and graphic Facebook messages would be deemed entirely necessary to investigate the organized "cover-up" of his online trysts. News stories have multiple purposes, layers, and facets and, by their nature, evolve over time. Here, while the TVNotas article began as a factual exposé, the story did not end there. Noelia and Reynoso were celebrities who carefully concealed their relationship to maintain Noelia's image as a single sex symbol. Maya's use of the photos was thus integral to exposing to the public the depth of their relationship and the actual events of their secret Vegas

---

[4] The majority implies that Woods' sext messages and former Congressman Weiner's tweets and Facebook messages were public because they "distributed their 'masterpieces' to others." The majority's contention is contrary to well-established copyright law. The Copyright Act defines "Publication" as "the *distribution* of copies or phonorecords of a work to the *public* by sale or other transfer of ownership, or by rental, lease, or lending." 17 U.S.C. § 101 (emphasis added). Merely sending suggestive self-portraits or "sexts" to another, private person does not launch a work into the public domain. Woods's "writings" were likely always intended to be kept secret between author and inspiration. And, but for one rogue tweet, former Congressman Weiner's "works" were kept privately between him and his desired recipients.

wedding night—the venue, the clothing, the after-party. Contrary to the majority's contentions, a mere marriage certificate would not suffice.

[57] Accordingly, I would reject the majority's approach and hold that the fundamentally different purpose underlying Maya's publication of the photos constituted a transformative use, and thus counterbalanced the commerciality of the use such that the first favor weighs in favor of a finding of fair use.

B. Nature of Copyrighted Works

[58] In determining the nature of the original work, we decide first, the extent to which it is a creative work enjoying broader copyright protection as opposed to a factual work requiring broader dissemination, and second, whether it is unpublished, in which case the right of first publication is implicated. Because the law generally recognizes a greater need to disseminate factual works, the "nature of the work" inquiry is designed to distinguish between the levels of "core" protectability of copyright. Indeed, ... where a copyrighted work is informational and factual and news; each characteristic strongly favors a finding of fair use. The tiered approach thus reflects the understanding that certain types of works—namely, fictional, creative, and unpublished works—fall closer to the core of copyright, and other types of works—namely, factual, informative, and published works—enjoy generally less protection.

[59] The majority reasons that the nature of the original photographs weighs against a finding of fair use because they were unpublished. The majority's analysis is flawed on two grounds: (1) the majority ignores the threshold determination that the photos were factual and documentary in nature; and (2) even if the unpublished nature of the work did cut against a finding of fair use, the majority fails to address the fact that the "nature of the work" analysis is much less significant in cases of transformative use.

[60] The majority concedes that the photographs were essentially factual in nature, noting that the images were taken as "[p]hotographic documentation of the wedding" and characterizing the photos as "point-and-shoot," and thus "not highly artistic in nature." Thus, as a threshold matter, the factual and informative nature of the photographs places them outside the core of copyright protection. While the photos were admittedly unpublished, this factor is less significant because the photographs were documentary in nature. Moreover, even if the unpublished nature of the photos did undercut their factual character, any possible impact is further mitigated by the fact that Maya's exposé constituted a transformative use. Although the majority attempts to use the unpublished nature of the works to trump their factual character and Maya's transformative use, we have held in cases of transformative use, the nature of the work carries less significance. Accordingly, I would hold that the second factor weighs either neutrally or slightly in favor of a finding of fair use.

C. Substantiality of Use

[61] When excerpts of a work or compilation of works are taken to tell a narrative different from, and independent of, the collection in its entirety, we may consider the selection and proportion of the excerpts used against the collection as a whole. Although taking the "heart" of a work generally weighs against a finding of fair use, selectivity in using only what is necessary cuts both ways and must be considered in evaluating the amount and substantiality of the use.

[62] The majority concludes that because Maya minimally cropped and altered the five wedding photographs that, qualitatively and quantitatively, the substantiality of the use weighs against a finding of fair use.... The majority's analysis lacks any basis in law or fact.

[63] Contents unseen, Maya purchased a memory disk of four hundred photos and three videos of Noelia and Reynoso. Maya paid for that disk, in its entirety, as a compilation. Indeed, the paparazzo, Oscar Viqueira, received $1,500 for the disk, as a whole. From that disk, Maya culled through, extracted, and ultimately

published five photos from the Couple's secret wedding night to use in its photo montage exposé. Out of all of the possible photos that Maya could have selected from the disk, Maya chose those five because they told the story of the Couple's clandestine nuptials in Las Vegas.

[64] The majority fails to address, let alone refute, the impact of Maya's selectivity because it contends that Maya's use of the photographs must be evaluated individually ....

[65] The reality is that Maya carefully selected the photos out of four hundred possible photos and videos on the disk because it wanted to use them to tell the wedding story. Three of those five photos depicted the wedding itself. The law dictates, at least as to the three photos that depicted the wedding ceremony, that Maya's relative restraint in choosing only those photos supports a finding of fair use. Admittedly, Maya's use of the additional two other photos, of the Couple at the bar, and of Noelia on the nuptial bed, was not necessary to prove the story of their secret wedding. Maya's use of these photos is thus qualitatively distinct from the three images directly depicting the wedding. Accordingly, I would hold that, at least as to the three photos of the wedding ceremony, Maya's selectivity and restraint from using more from the four hundred possible images and videos weighs either neutrally or slightly in favor of a finding of fair use.

D. Harm to Potential and Future Markets

[66] The majority contends that the Couple's intention never to release the photographs, let alone sell them, does not affect our analysis of harm to potential and future markets. The majority relies on ... the proposition that even if an author completely disavowed any intention to publish his work during his lifetime that unauthorized publication of the work by another could still harm potential and future markets. But the majority's selective analysis mischaracterizes our [case law]. In [a previous case], we specifically exempted from the aforementioned reasoning publications involving "market failure," in which an author specifically keeps a work from being published for the purposes of concealing information:

> When an owner refuses to license because he is concerned that defendant's work will substitute for his own work or derivative works, the owner is representing not only his own interest, but also the interest of his potential customers and thus the public interest. Market failure should be found only when the defendant can prove that the copyright owner would refuse to license out of a desire unrelated to the goals of copyright-notably a desire to keep certain information from the public.

[67] Here, the Couple's intention never to publish photos must frame our market harm analysis because their intention was based upon their desire to conceal their secret Las Vegas wedding from the public. The fact that on the date of publication, nearly two years after their wedding, they had still refused to even tell their families, let alone the general public, proves this to be true. The application of the market failure exception makes sense here because the Couple sought to conceal their wedding out of their own interests, namely, to preserve Noelia's image as a "sex symbol," in spite of the common public interest in informing their fans and followers of the event. Accordingly, in light of the Couple's intention to continue to conceal their Las Vegas nuptials, I would hold that the market failure harm exception to the harm to potential and future markets militates toward a finding of fair use....

[68] Overprotecting intellectual property is as harmful as underprotecting it. Creativity is impossible without a rich public domain. To satisfy a celebrity couple's desire to control their public images, the majority extends inapposite case law to undercut the fair use doctrine and the free press. Rather than follow the majority's course, I would affirm the district court's grant of summary judg[]ment on fair use grounds, at least as to the three images of the wedding in the exposé, and remand due to disputed issues of material fact regarding the use of the remaining two nonwedding photos.

NOTE

1. A number of issues arise in the context of journalism as practiced contemporarily. For example, can news reporters claim fair use of photographs of relatively unknown people taken from their social media profiles when news breaks about them? What about professional news organizations' reuse of amateur photography and videography of breaking news posted online?

4. Education

The following case concerns educational uses of copyrighted material. Consider whether it deserves preferential status as a fair use. Do all educational uses deserve preferential status? If not, how would you distinguish those that deserve preferential status from those that do not?

Cambridge University Press v. Carl V. Patton
769 F.3d 1232 (11th Cir. 2014)

TJOFLAT, J.:

[1] Three publishing houses, Cambridge University Press, Oxford University Press, and Sage Publications, Inc. ... allege that members of the Board of Regents of the University System of Georgia and officials at Georgia State University ... infringed Plaintiffs' copyrights by maintaining a policy which allows GSU professors to make digital copies of excerpts of Plaintiffs' books available to students without paying Plaintiffs. Plaintiffs alleged seventy-four individual instances of infringement, which took place during three academic terms in 2009. The District Court issued an order finding that Plaintiffs failed to establish a prima facie case of infringement in twenty-six instances, that the fair use defense applied in forty-three instances, and that Defendants had infringed Plaintiffs' copyrights in the remaining five instances.

[2] .... Because we find that the District Court's fair use analysis was in part erroneous, we reverse the District Court's judgment ....

[3] Like many recent issues in copyright law, this is a case in which technological advances have created a new, more efficient means of delivery for copyrighted works, causing copyright owners and consumers to struggle to define the appropriate boundaries of copyright protection in the new digital marketplace. These boundaries must be drawn carefully in order to assure that copyright law serves its intended purpose, which is to promote the creation of new works for the public good by providing authors and other creators with an economic incentive to create. If copyright's utilitarian goal is to be met, we must be careful not to place overbroad restrictions on the use of copyrighted works, because to do so would prevent would-be authors from effectively building on the ideas of others. Some unpaid use of copyrighted materials must be allowed in order to prevent copyright from functioning as a straightjacket that stifles the very creative activity it seeks to foster. If we allow too much unpaid copying, however, we risk extinguishing the economic incentive to create that copyright is intended to provide.

[4] The fair use doctrine provides a means by which a court may ascertain the appropriate balance in a given case if the market actors cannot do so on their own. Fair use is a defense that can excuse what would otherwise be an infringing use of copyrighted material.... Here, we are called upon to determine whether the unpaid

copying of scholarly works by a university for use by students—facilitated by the development of systems for digital delivery over the Internet—should be excused under the doctrine of fair use....

[5] Plaintiffs do not publish the large, general textbooks commonly used in entry-level university courses. Rather, Plaintiffs publish advanced scholarly works, which might be used in upper-level undergraduate and graduate courses. Cambridge and Oxford publish scholarly books and journals on niche subject areas. Their works involved in this case include research-based monographs, ... instructional books, trade books, and other works on academic topics. Sage primarily publishes books on the social sciences. All three plaintiffs publish, in addition to works by a single author, edited books which feature the contributions of multiple authors.

[6] Plaintiffs market their books to professors who teach at universities and colleges. Cambridge and Oxford regularly send complimentary copies of their publications to professors. Sage provides trial copies upon request. Plaintiffs intend that professors use Plaintiffs' publications in their work and assign them as required reading so that students will purchase them.

[7] Rather than assigning whole books, some professors assign or suggest excerpts from Plaintiffs' books as part of the curriculum for their courses. Professors might do this by putting the work on reserve at the university library so that students can visit the library to read an assigned excerpt. Or, professors might prepare a bound, photocopied, paper "coursepack" containing excerpts from several works for a particular course. Often, a third-party copy shop assembles these coursepacks, performing the copying and binding, obtaining the necessary licenses from publishers, and charging students a fee for the finished coursepack. In recent years, however, universities—following the trend with regard to distribution of many forms of media the world over—have increasingly abandoned paper coursepacks in favor of digital distribution of excerpts over the Internet.

[6] .... GSU maintains two on-campus systems known as "ERes" and "uLearn" for digital distribution of course materials to students....

[7] ERes and uLearn have been popular at GSU. For example, during the Spring 2009 term, paper coursepacks were offered for only about fifteen courses, while instructors in hundreds of courses made readings available on ERes. Thus, the excerpts from larger works that make up some portion of course readings at GSU, and which were once distributed to students via a paper coursepack purchased at the university bookstore, are now largely distributed to students via digital download on the Internet, that the students pay for only indirectly via tuition and fees.

[8] There exists a well-established system for the licensing of excerpts of copyrighted works. Copyright Clearance Center is a not-for-profit corporation .... [that] licenses excerpts from copyrighted works for a fee, acting on behalf of publishers who choose to make their works available through CCC. These licenses are called "permissions." All three Plaintiffs offer excerpt-specific permissions to photocopy or digitally reproduce portions of their works, which may be obtained directly from Plaintiffs or through CCC. Permissions are not, however, available for licensed copying of excerpts from all of Plaintiffs' works.

[9] CCC offers a variety of permissions services to various categories of users, including corporate, educational, and institutional users. One such service, the Academic Permissions Service, licenses educational users to make print copies on a per-use basis. CCC also offers an electronic course content service for licensing of digital excerpts by educational users on a per-use basis, that—in 2008, the year for which evidence on the question was presented—offered only a small percentage of the works that were available through APS. ECCS is designed for electronic reserve systems such as ERes and uLearn. Software is available that would allow GSU library personnel to place an order with CCC for a permission to provide students with a digital copy of an excerpt via ERes. CCC also offers an Academic Repertory License Service which affords subscribers access to excerpts from a set group of about nine million titles, approximately 17 percent of which are available in digital

format. Sage participates in ARLS and did so in 2009, Oxford participated in 2009 with regard to journals but not books, and Cambridge does not participate. GSU did not and does not subscribe to this program.

[10] When the GSU bookstore assembles and sells a paper coursepack containing excerpts from copyrighted works, GSU pays permissions fees for use of the excerpts. The central issue in this case is under what circumstances GSU must pay permissions fees to post a digital copy of an excerpt of Plaintiffs' works to ERes or uLearn....

[11] On April 15, 2008, Plaintiffs filed their original complaint .... Plaintiffs alleged that hundreds of GSU professors have made thousands of copyrighted works—including works owned or controlled by Plaintiffs—available on GSU's electronic reserve systems without obtaining permissions from copyright holders, and that GSU's administration facilitated, encouraged, and induced this practice. Plaintiffs sued Defendants in their official capacities as GSU officials, claiming ... copyright infringement .... Defendants ... assert[ed] a defense of fair use because any alleged use of copyrighted materials was for the purpose of teaching, scholarship or research and for nonprofit educational purposes...

[12] On February 17, 2009, [GSU] announced a new copyright policy ..., which went into effect the same day. Under the 2009 Policy, a revised version of which remains in effect today, GSU professors who wish to post an excerpt of a copyrighted work on ERes or uLearn for distribution to their students must first determine whether they believe that doing so would be fair use. In order to make this determination, professors must fill out a "Fair Use Checklist" for each excerpt.

[13] The Checklist allows GSU professors to perform a version of the analysis a court might perform should the professor claim fair use in a subsequent copyright infringement suit.... For each factor, the Checklist provides several criteria that purportedly weigh either for or against a finding of fair use, each with a corresponding checkbox.[10] The Checklist instructs professors to check each criterion that applies, and then add up the checks to determine whether the factor weighs in favor of or against a finding of fair use. After making this tally, the Checklist explains that "[w]here the factors favoring fair use outnumber those against it, reliance on fair use is justified. Where fewer than half the factors favor fair use, instructors should seek permission from the rights holder." Thus, under the 2009 Policy, a GSU professor may post an excerpt of a copyrighted work on ERes or uLearn without obtaining a permission from the copyright holder if the professor first decides that doing so would be protected by the doctrine of fair use, according to the criteria set forth in the Checklist....

[14] ... [T]he District Court issued an order holding that Defendants had infringed Plaintiffs' copyright in five of the seventy-four instances at issue....

[15] .... The District Court held that the first fair use factor, "the purpose and character of the use, including whether such use is of a commercial nature or is for nonprofit educational purposes," "strongly favor[ed] Defendants" in all instances because "[t]his case involves making copies of excerpts of copyrighted works for teaching students and for scholarship ... [and so] [t]he use is for strictly nonprofit educational purposes."

[16] The District Court held that the second fair use factor, "the nature of the copyrighted work," favored Defendants in all instances because it found—after undertaking an individualized review of all of the works at

---

[10] For example, the Fair Use Checklist provides that the nonprofit educational use of an excerpt favors a finding of fair use, whereas commercial activity weighs against a finding of fair use. Use of a factual or nonfiction work favors a finding of fair use, whereas use of a highly creative work (art, music, novels, films, plays, poetry, fiction) weighs against a finding of fair use. Use of a small portion of a work favors a finding of fair use, whereas use of a large portion or entire work weighs against a finding of fair use. A use that has no significant effect on the market or potential market for the copyrighted work favors a finding of fair use, whereas a use that sign[i]ficantly impairs the market or potential market for the copyrighted work or a derivative weighs against a finding of fair use.

issue for which it found that Plaintiffs had made a prima facie case of infringement—that "the books involved in this case are properly classified as informational in nature, within the spectrum of factual materials and hence favoring fair use."

[17] The District Court held that the third fair use factor, "the amount and substantiality of the portion used in relation to the copyrighted work as a whole," "favor[ed] either Plaintiffs or Defendants, depending on the amount taken from each book."

[18] After hearing testimony from several GSU professors as to the reasoning behind their choice of a particular excerpt and how use of that excerpt furthered the professor's goals for a particular class, the District Court found that all of the selections furthered the legitimate educational purposes of the courses in which they were used. The District Court also found that some professors' educational purposes were furthered by using whole chapters of books, because chapters typically contain a complete treatment of a topic.

[19] The District Court then determined that "[t]he right approach is to select a percentage of pages which reasonably limits copying and to couple that with a reasonable limit on the number of chapters which may be copied." Accordingly, the District Court held that

> [w]here a book is not divided into chapters or contains fewer than ten chapters, unpaid copying of no more than 10 percent of the pages in the book is permissible under factor three.... Where a book contains ten or more chapters, the unpaid copying of up to but no more than one chapter (or its equivalent) will be permissible under fair use factor three.... The chapter or other excerpt must fill a demonstrated, legitimate purpose in the course curriculum and must be narrowly tailored to accomplish that purpose. Where the foregoing limitations are met factor three will favor fair use, i.e., will favor Defendants. Otherwise factor three will favor Plaintiffs....

[20] With regard to the fourth fair use factor, "the effect of the use upon the potential market for or value of the copyrighted work," the District Court found that "Defendants' use of small excerpts did not affect Plaintiffs' actual or potential sales of books" because they do not substitute for the books. However, the District Court found that Defendants' use of excerpts may be at the cost of Plaintiffs' licensing revenues, and so may affect the market for licensing of excerpts. Thus, the District Court concluded that, in reviewing the individual instances of alleged infringement, it would analyze fair use factor four as follows:

> [W]here permissions are readily available from CCC or the publisher for a copy of a small excerpt of a copyrighted book, at a reasonable price, and in a convenient format (in this case, permissions for digital excerpts), and permissions are not paid, factor four weighs heavily in Plaintiffs' favor. Factor four weighs in Defendants' favor when such permissions are not readily available.

[21] .... [I]n cases where no evidence showed whether digital permissions were readily available for excerpts of a particular work, the District Court found that the fourth fair use factor favored Defendants.

[22] The District Court took into account two additional considerations. First, the District Court noted that, based on testimony that "royalties are not an important incentive for academic writers," and on a presumption that that academic authors publish primarily to enhance their professional reputation and contribute to academic knowledge, "[t]here is no reason to believe that allowing unpaid, nonprofit academic use of small excerpts in controlled circumstances would diminish creation of academic works." Second, the District Court found that "it is consistent with the principles of copyright to apply the fair use doctrine in a way that promotes the dissemination of knowledge, and not simply its creation." The District Court noted that the evidence demonstrates that academic permissions income does not represent a significant portion of Plaintiffs' overall revenue. Thus, the District Court found that a slight diminution of Plaintiffs' permissions income caused by the District Court's findings of fair use would not appreciably harm Plaintiffs' ability to publish scholarly works. On

the other hand, the District Court found, "[m]aking small free excerpts available to students would further the spread of knowledge." ...

[23] In weighing the fair use factors to assess each of the forty-eight instances of alleged infringement for which the District Court found that Plaintiffs had established a prima facie case, the District Court held that fair use applied whenever at least three of the four factors favored Defendants. Because the District Court found that factors one and two favored Defendants in all cases, the District Court essentially held that fair use applied each time a professor posted an excerpt that fell within the 10 percent-or-one-chapter limit on allowable copying the District Court had set (such that factor three favored Defendants) and each time there was no evidence that digital permissions were available for excerpts of the work in question (such that factor four favored Defendants).

[24] With regard to factor three, in thirty-five of the forty-eight claims of infringement, the District Court found that the copying was "decidedly small" because it fell within the 10 percent-or-one-chapter limit, and so factor three favored Defendants. In the other thirteen cases, the copying exceeded the 10 percent-or-one-chapter limit, and so the District Court held that factor three favored Plaintiffs.

[25] With regard to factor four, in seventeen of the forty-eight cases, the District Court found that the parties had presented no evidence regarding licensing availability, but because the District Court placed the burden on this issue on Plaintiffs, the District Court found that factor four favored Defendants. In the other thirty-one cases, the District Court found that Plaintiffs had made digital licensing available for excerpts of the work in question, and so, because there was a "ready market for licensed digital excerpts of [the] work in 2009," factor four strongly favored Plaintiffs....

[26] [O]f the forty-eight instances of alleged infringement for which the District Court found that Plaintiffs had established a prima facie case, the District Court held that Defendants had infringed Plaintiffs' copyrights in five instances and that the fair use defense applied in forty-three. The District Court concluded that the 2009 Policy had caused the five instances of infringement. In reaching this conclusion, the District Court noted that the 2009 Policy did not limit copying to excerpts which were "decidedly small," did not prohibit the copying of multiple chapters from the same book, and did not provide sufficient guidance in determining the effect the use of an excerpt may have on the market for or value of the copyrighted work....

[27] .... On appeal, ... Plaintiffs argue that the District Court's application of the fair use factors was legally flawed, and that the District Court consequently erred in finding that the fair use defense applied in forty-three of the forty-eight remaining instances of alleged infringement....

[28] ... [T]he examples enumerated in the preamble of § 107—"criticism, comment, news reporting, teaching (including multiple copies for classroom use), scholarship, or research"—are meant to give some idea of the sort of activities the courts might regard as fair use under the circumstances. This listing was not intended to be exhaustive, or to single out any particular use as presumptively a fair use....

[29] Plaintiffs ... argue that the District Court erred in giving each of the four factors equal weight, essentially taking a mechanical "add up the factors" approach, finding fair use if three factors weighed in favor of fair use and one against and vice versa, and only performing further analysis in case of a "tie." We agree that the District Court's arithmetic approach was improper.

[30] Congress, in the Copyright Act, spoke neither to the relative weight courts should attach to each of the four factors nor to precisely how the factors ought to be balanced. However, the Supreme Court has explained that the four statutory factors may not be treated in isolation, one from another. All are to be explored, and the results weighed together, in light of the purposes of copyright. In keeping with this approach, a given factor may be more or less important in determining whether a particular use should be considered fair under the

specific circumstances of the case. As such, the four factors do not mechanistically resolve fair use issues.... Accordingly, we find that the District Court erred in giving each of the four factors equal weight, and in treating the four factors as a simple mathematical formula. As we will explain, because of the circumstances of this case, some of the factors weigh more heavily on the fair use determination than others...

[31] Plaintiffs [also] argue that the District Court erred in its application of each of the four fair use factors. Plaintiffs' argument centers on a comparison of the circumstances of the instant case to those of the so-called "coursepack cases," in which courts rejected a defense of fair use for commercial copyshops that assembled paper coursepacks containing unlicensed excerpts of copyrighted works for use in university courses.

[32] In *Basic Books, Inc. v. Kinko's Graphics Corp.,* publishing houses sued Kinko's, a commercial copyshop, alleging that Kinko's infringed the publishers' copyrights when it copied excerpts from the publishers' books, without permission and without payment of a license fee, and sold the copies for profit in bound, paper coursepacks to students for use in college courses. 758 F. Supp. 1522, 1526 (S.D.N.Y. 1991). The District Court rejected Kinko's claim that its use of the excerpts was fair use ....

[33] Similarly, in *Princeton University Press v. Michigan Document Services, Inc.,* the Sixth Circuit upheld the District Court's ruling that Michigan Document Services, a commercial copyshop, was not entitled to a fair use defense when it reproduced substantial portions of copyrighted academic works and sold the copies in bound, paper coursepacks to students for use in courses at the University of Michigan, without obtaining permission from the copyright holder. 99 F.3d 1381, 1383 (6th Cir. 1996) (en banc).

[34] In essence, Plaintiffs argue that the coursepack cases should have guided the District Court's analysis in this case, because GSU cannot alter the fair use calculus simply by choosing to distribute course readings in an electronic rather than paper format....

[35] ... [B]ecause the fair use analysis is highly fact-specific and must be performed on a work-by-work basis, the coursepack cases provide guidance but do not dictate the results here, which must be based upon a careful consideration of the circumstances of the individual instances of alleged infringement involved in this case....

[36] Here, Defendants' use of excerpts of Plaintiffs' works is not transformative. The excerpts of Plaintiffs' works posted on GSU's electronic reserve system are verbatim copies of portions of the original books which have merely been converted into a digital format. Although a professor may arrange these excerpts into a particular order or combination for use in a college course, this does not imbue the excerpts themselves with any more than a *de minimis* amount of new meaning. *See Princeton University Press,* 99 F.3d at 1389 ("[I]f you make verbatim copies of 95 pages of a 316-page book, you have not transformed the 95 pages very much—even if you juxtapose them to excerpts from other works.").

[37] Nor do Defendants use the excerpts for anything other than the same intrinsic purpose—or at least one of the purposes—served by Plaintiffs' works: reading material for students in university courses. Although an electronic reserve system may facilitate easy access to excerpts of Plaintiffs' works, it does nothing to transform those works. Rather, Defendants' use of excerpts of Plaintiffs' works supersedes the objects of the original creation. Were this element by itself dispositive, we would be compelled to find that the first factor weighs against a finding of fair use.

[38] However, we must also consider under the first factor whether Defendants' use is for a nonprofit educational purpose, as opposed to a commercial purpose.... Indeed, the Supreme Court has recognized in dicta that nonprofit educational use may weigh in favor of a finding of fair use under the first factor, even when nontransformative. *Campbell,* 510 U.S. at 579 n.11 ("The obvious statutory exception to this focus on transformative uses is the straight reproduction of multiple copies for classroom distribution.").

[39] Because copyright has always been used to promote learning, allowing some leeway for educational fair use furthers the purpose of copyright by providing students and teachers with a means to lawfully access works in order to further their learning in circumstances where it would be unreasonable to require permission. But, as always, care must be taken not to allow too much educational use, lest we undermine the goals of copyright by enervating the incentive for authors to create the works upon which students and teachers depend.

[40] In the coursepack cases, *Princeton University Press* and *Basic Books*, the first factor weighed against a finding of fair use when the nontransformative, educational use in question was performed by a for-profit copyshop, and was therefore commercial.... [T]he[se] court[s] refused to allow the defendants, who were engaged in commercial operations, to stand in the shoes of students and professors in claiming that their making of multiple copies of scholarly works was for nonprofit educational purposes.

[41] However, in both of the coursepack cases, the courts expressly declined to conclude that the copying would fall outside the boundaries of fair use if conducted by professors, students, or academic institutions...

[42] Thus, the question becomes whether Defendants' use of Plaintiffs' works is truly a nonprofit educational use under § 107(1), and if so, whether this places sufficient weight on the first factor scales to justify a finding that this factor favors fair use despite the nontransformativeness of Defendants' use.

[43] GSU is a nonprofit educational institution. While this is relevant, our inquiry does not end there: we must consider not only the nature of the user, but the use itself.

[44] Defendants' use of Plaintiffs' works in the teaching of university courses is clearly for educational purposes. Nevertheless, it is not entirely clear that use by a nonprofit entity for educational purposes is always a "nonprofit" use as contemplated by § 107(1). The Supreme Court has explained that "[t]he crux of the profit/nonprofit distinction is not whether the sole motive of the use is monetary gain but whether the user stands to profit from exploitation of the copyrighted material without paying the customary price." *Harper & Row*, 471 U.S. at 562....

[45] Under [one] line of reasoning, Defendants' educational use of Plaintiffs' works is a for-profit use despite GSU's status as a nonprofit educational institution, and despite the fact that GSU does not directly sell access to Plaintiffs' works on Eres and uLearn. Defendants "exploited" Plaintiffs' copyrighted material for use in university courses without "paying the customary price"—a licensing fee. Defendants profited from the use of excerpts of Plaintiffs' works—however indirectly—because GSU collects money from students in the form of tuition and fees (which students pay in part for access to ERes and uLearn) and reduces its costs by avoiding fees it might have otherwise paid for the excerpts.

[46] However, this reasoning is somewhat circular, and hence of limited usefulness to our fair use inquiry. Of course, any unlicensed use of copyrighted material profits the user in the sense that the user does not pay a potential licensing fee, allowing the user to keep his or her money. If this analysis were persuasive, no use could qualify as "nonprofit" under the first factor. Moreover, if the use is a fair use, then the copyright owner is not entitled to charge for the use, and there is no "customary price" to be paid in the first place...

[47] Although GSU certainly benefits from its use of Plaintiffs' works by being able to provide the works conveniently to students, and profits in the sense that it avoids paying licensing fees, Defendants' use is not fairly characterized as commercial exploitation. Even if Defendants' use profits GSU in some sense, we are not convinced that this type of benefit is indicative of commercial use. There is no evidence that Defendants capture significant revenues as a direct consequence of copying Plaintiffs' works. At the same time, the use provides a broader public benefit—furthering the education of students at a public university.

[48] Thus, we find that Defendants' use of Plaintiffs' works is of the nonprofit educational nature that Congress intended the fair use defense to allow under certain circumstances. Furthermore, we find this sufficiently weighty that the first factor favors a finding of fair use despite the nontransformative nature of the use.

[49] The text of the fair use statute highlights the importance Congress placed on educational use. The preamble to the statute provides that fair uses may include "teaching (including multiple copies for classroom use), scholarship, or research" and the first factor singles out "nonprofit educational purposes." 17 U.S.C. § 107. The legislative history of § 107 further demonstrates that Congress singled out educational purposes for special consideration. In the years leading up to passage of the Copyright Act of 1976 (which introduced § 107), Congress devoted considerable attention to working out the proper scope of the fair use defense as applied to copying for educational and classroom purposes, going so far as to include in a final report the Classroom Guidelines developed by representatives of educator, author, and publisher groups at the urging of Congress....

[50] Accordingly, we find that the District Court did not err in holding that the first factor favors a finding of fair use. Nevertheless, because Defendants' use of Plaintiffs' works is nontransformative, the threat of market substitution is significant. We note that insofar as the first factor is concerned with uses that supplant demand for the original, this factor is closely related to the fourth fair use factor, the effect on the potential market for the work. We will thus revisit this concern when we analyze the fourth factor....

[51] Here, the District Court held that "[b]ecause all of the excerpts are informational and educational in nature and none are fictional, fair use factor two weighs in favor of Defendants." We disagree....

[52] Defendants argue that GSU professors chose the excerpts of Plaintiffs' works for their factual content, not for any expressive content the works may contain, noting that several professors testified that if the use of a particular excerpt was not a fair use, they would have found another source. Of course, other professors testified that they chose particular excerpts because of the author's interpretative originality and significance. Regardless of whether GSU faculty chose the excerpts for their expressive or factual content, the excerpts were copied wholesale—facts, ideas, and original expression alike. Which aspect the secondary user was interested in is irrelevant to the disposition of the second factor.

[53] Accordingly, we find that the District Court erred in holding that the second factor favored fair use in every instance. Where the excerpts of Plaintiffs' works contained evaluative, analytical, or subjectively descriptive material that surpasses the bare facts necessary to communicate information, or derives from the author's experiences or opinions, the District Court should have held that the second factor was neutral, or even weighed against fair use in cases of excerpts that were dominated by such material. That being said, the second fair use factor is of relatively little importance in this case....

[54] Here, the District Court found that the third factor favored fair use in instances where Defendants copied no more than 10 percent of a work, or one chapter in case of a book with ten or more chapters. The District Court's blanket 10 percent-or-one-chapter benchmark was improper. The fair use analysis must be performed on a case-by-case/work-by-work basis. We must avoid hard evidentiary presumptions and eschew a rigid, bright-line approach to fair use. By holding that the third factor favored fair use whenever the amount of copying fell within a 10 percent-or-one-chapter baseline, the District Court abdicated its duty to analyze the third factor for each instance of alleged infringement individually....

[55] Defendants also argue that the District Court's 10 percent-or-one-chapter approach is supported by the record. Defendants' explain that a CCC white paper, *Using Electronic Reserves: Guidelines and Best Practices for Copyright Compliance* (2011), identifies "best practices" for electronic reserves, stating that electronic reserve materials should be limited to "small excerpts" and that "[m]ost experts advise using a single article or ... chapter of a copyrighted work...." However, even if we accept that the 10 percent-or-one-chapter approach

represents a general industry "best practice" for electronic reserves, this is not relevant to an individualized fair use analysis....

[56] Accordingly, ... we find that the District Court erred in applying a 10 percent-or-one-chapter safe harbor in it analysis of the individual instances of alleged infringement. The District Court should have analyzed each instance of alleged copying individually, considering the quantity and the quality of the material taken— including whether the material taken constituted the heart of the work—and whether that taking was excessive in light of the educational purpose of the use and the threat of market substitution....

[57] We agree with the District Court that the small excerpts Defendants used do not substitute for the full books from which they were drawn. Plaintiffs offered no trial testimony or evidence showing that they lost any book sales in or after 2009 on account of any actions by anyone at Georgia State. Thus, the District Court did not err in finding that Defendants' use of small excerpts did not affect Plaintiffs' actual or potential sales of books.

[58] However, CCC's various programs for academic permissions—and Plaintiffs' own permissions programs— constitute a workable market through which universities like GSU may purchase licenses to use excerpts of Plaintiffs' works. Plaintiffs contend that, by failing to purchase digital permissions to use excerpts of Plaintiffs' works on ERes and uLearn, Defendants caused substantial harm to the market for licenses, and that widespread adoption of this practice would cause substantial harm to the potential market. Plaintiffs also argue that, even if a license for a digital excerpt of a work was unavailable, this should not weigh in favor of fair use because the copyright owner is not obliged to accommodate prospective users.

[59] Defendants argue that, because permissions income for academic books represents a miniscule percentage of Plaintiffs' overall revenue, Defendants' practices have not caused substantial harm to the market for Plaintiffs works, and would not do so even if widely adopted. Defendants further argue that unavailability of licensing opportunities for particular works should weigh in favor of fair use.

[60] We note that it is not determinative that programs exist through which universities may license excerpts of Plaintiffs' works. In other words, the fact that Plaintiffs have made paying easier does not automatically dictate a right to payment....

[61] .... [A]bsent evidence to the contrary, if a copyright holder has not made a license available to use a particular work in a particular manner, the inference is that the author or publisher did not think that there would be enough such use to bother making a license available. In such a case, there is little damage to the publisher's market when someone makes use of the work in that way without obtaining a license, and hence the fourth factor should generally weigh in favor of fair use. This is true of Plaintiffs' works for which no license for a digital excerpt was available...

[62] .... A publisher determines the value of a work, which is set by the anticipated demand for the work. Thus, the greater the demand for the work—the greater the market—the more the publisher will pay the author of the work up front, and the more the publisher will endeavor to make the work widely available. If a publisher makes licenses available for some uses but not for others, this indicates that the publisher has likely made a reasoned decision not to enter the licensing market for those uses, which implies that the value of that market is minimal.

[63] With regard to the works for which digital permissions were unavailable, Plaintiffs choose to enter those works into some markets—print copies of the whole work, or perhaps licenses for paper copies of excerpts— but not the digital permission market. This tells us that Plaintiffs likely anticipated that there would be little to no demand for digital excerpts of the excluded works and thus saw the value of that market as de minimis or zero. If the market for digital excerpts were in fact de minimis or zero, then neither Defendants' particular use

nor a widespread use of similar kind would be likely to cause significant market harm. Of course, if publishers choose to participate in the market the calculation will change.

[64] In its individual analysis under the fourth factor of each of the forty-eight works for which it found Plaintiffs had made a prima facie case of infringement, the District Court performed a sufficiently nuanced review of the evidence regarding license availability. Where the evidence showed that there was a ready market for digital excerpts of a work in 2009, the time of the purported infringements, the District Court found that there was small—due to the amount of money involved—but actual damage to the value of Plaintiffs' copyright. The District Court also properly took into account that widespread use of similar unlicensed excerpts could cause substantial harm to the potential market. Thus, where there was a license for digital excerpts available, the District Court generally held that the fourth factor weighed against a finding of fair use. In close cases, the District Court went further and examined the amount of permissions income a work had generated in order to determine how much this particular revenue source contributed to the value of the copyright in the work, noting that where there is no significant demand for excerpts, the likelihood of repetitive unpaid use is diminished. Where there was no evidence in the record to show that a license for digital excerpts was available—as was the case for seventeen works published by Oxford and Cambridge—the District Court held that the fourth factor weighted in favor of fair use. We find that the District Court's analysis under the fourth factor was correct, and that the District Court properly took license availability into account in determining whether the fourth factor weighted for or against fair use....

[65] Accordingly, we REVERSE the judgment of the District Court. We ... REMAND for further proceedings consistent with this opinion.

NOTES

1. On remand, the district court stated that it "estimates the initial, approximate respective weights of the four factors as follows: 25% for factor one, 5% for factor two, 30% for factor three, and 40% for factor four." It then performed individualized inquiries for each work, always having the first factor favor fair use, concluding that 44 of the 48 claims of infringement were fair uses. On appeal again, the Eleventh Circuit remanded again to the district court to revisit its analysis because the court "failed to break free of its erroneous arithmetic approach and to give each excerpt the holistic review the Act demands." Cambridge University Press v. Albert, 906 F.3d 1290, 1300 (11th Cir. 2018). The district court consequently evaluated individually each work used and concluded that the plaintiffs prevailed on 11 of their claims of infringement but the defendants' claims of fair use succeeded as to the 37 other infringement claims. Cambridge Univ. Press v. Becker, 446 F. Supp. 3d 1145 (N.D. Ga. 2020).

2. Do you think fair use analyses ought to distinguish between materials specifically produced for the education market and materials that happen to be used in the course of education? Why, or why not?

3. *Campbell* recognized that many educational uses might not be transformative but still be fair use, pointing to the appearance of making "multiple copies for classroom use" in § 107's preamble. After reading *Cambridge University Press*, do you think that transformativeness plays a key or subsidiary role in fair use determinations regarding education? For varied analyses of how to understand which educational uses of copyrighted material ought to be considered fair (particularly on the ground that they are transformative), see Ann Bartow, *Educational Fair Use in Copyright: Reclaiming the Right to Photocopy Freely*, 60 U. PITT. L. REV. 149 (1998); Brandon Butler, *Transformative Teaching and Educational Fair Use After* Georgia State, 48 CONN. L. REV. 473 (2015); Peter Jaszi, *Fair Use and Education: The Way Forward*, 25 LAW & LITERATURE 33 (2013).

4. Fair use analysis is explicitly sensitive to the market effects of allowing a defendant's use of a copyrighted work by requiring consideration of the fourth statutory factor: "the effect of the use upon the potential market for or value of the copyrighted work." 17 U.S.C. § 107(4).

An important question arises as to which effects are permissible to consider. Pertinently, any copyright plaintiff can assert against a defendant that has used the plaintiff's work without a license that the plaintiff has suffered pecuniary harm from not having obtained a licensing fee for the work. Furthermore, the plaintiff can contend more generally that if the defendant does not have to pay a licensing fee for their use, then other third parties would start using the plaintiff's work in similar contexts without paying, which in turn would harm the defendant's licensing market more broadly. Given that a plaintiff can always assert these market harms, should a court always weigh them against fair use under the fourth factor? *Campbell* suggests that this argument should not always be given much weight: "The market for potential derivative uses includes only those that creators of original works would in general develop or license others to develop." *Campbell*, 510 U.S. at 592. That is, the likelihood of a market's development affects the relevance of its consideration. For scholarship on evaluating the empirical likelihood of a market's development, see Jeanne C. Fromer, *Market Effects Bearing on Fair Use*, 90 WASH. L. REV. 615 (2015); Frank Pasquale, *Breaking the Vicious Circularity:* Sony's Contribution to the Fair Use Doctrine, 55 CASE W. RES. L. REV. 777 (2005).

5. The Second Circuit worked through these principles in American Geophysical Union v. Texaco Inc., 60 F.3d 913 (2d Cir. 1994), in holding that photocopies by a Texaco researcher of technical journal articles are not fair use. The court reasoned that the fourth fair use factor favored the copyright holders even "[t]hough the [journal] publishers still have not established a conventional market for the direct sale and distribution of individual articles." The court elaborated that the publishers "have created, primarily through the [Copyright Clearance Center (CCC)], a workable market for institutional users to obtain licenses for the right to produce their own copies of individual articles via photocopying." Even though the market was not yet "conventional," major businesses used its photocopying licenses, including Texaco. The court concluded that:

> Despite Texaco's claims to the contrary, it is not unsound to conclude that the right to seek payment for a particular use tends to become legally cognizable under the fourth fair use factor when the means for paying for such a use is made easier. This notion is not inherently troubling: it is sensible that a particular unauthorized use should be considered "more fair" when there is no ready market or means to pay for the use, while such an unauthorized use should be considered "less fair" when there is a ready market or means to pay for the use. The vice of circular reasoning arises only if the availability of payment is conclusive against fair use. Whatever the situation may have been previously, before the development of a market for institutional users to obtain licenses to photocopy articles, it is now appropriate to consider the loss of licensing revenues in evaluating "the effect of the use upon the potential market for or value of" journal articles. It is especially appropriate to do so with respect to copying of articles from [the journal at issue in this case], a publication as to which a photocopying license is now available. We do not decide how the fair use balance would be resolved if a photocopying license for [this journal's] articles were not currently available.

Judge Jacobs dissented, criticizing the majority's analysis of the effect on the market as circular. He reasoned that "[t]he CCC scheme is neither traditional nor reasonable; and its development into a real market is subject to substantial impediments. There is a circularity to the problem: the market will not crystallize unless courts reject the fair use argument that Texaco presents; but, under the statutory test, we cannot declare a use to be an infringement unless (assuming other factors also weigh in favor of the secondary user) there is a market to be harmed. At present, only a fraction of journal publishers have sought to exact these fees. I would hold that this fourth factor decisively weighs in favor of Texaco, because there is no normal market in photocopy licenses, and no real consensus among publishers that there ought to be one." Judge Jacobs further noted as to the CCC scheme, "[t]here is nothing workable, and there is no market." Has the Second Circuit broken free of the cicularity involved in analyzing the effect of a use on the market? Or is Judge Jacobs right?

6. Since *Texaco*, courts have elaborated on what constitutes a "traditional, reasonable, or likely to be developed market[]." The Second Circuit has indicated that a copyright owner cannot create a market for criticism and other transformative uses as a way to count that against defendants making such uses:

> *Just as secondary users may not exploit markets that original copyright owners would in general develop or license others to develop even if those owners had not actually done so, copyright owners may not preempt exploitation of transformative markets, which they would not in general develop or license others to develop, by actually developing or licensing others to develop those markets. Thus, by developing or licensing a market for parody, news reporting, educational or other transformative uses of its own creative work, a copyright owner plainly cannot prevent others from entering those fair use markets.*

Castle Rock Entm't, Inc. v. Carol Publ'g Grp., Inc., 150 F.3d 132, 145 n.11 (2d Cir. 1998).

7. Scholars observe that third parties' risk aversion with respect to copyright infringement can cause both copyright protection to grow and fair use to shrink over time. As James Gibson explains, due to risk aversion, "copyright users … seek licenses even when they have a good fair use claim …. This practice of unneeded licensing feeds back into doctrine because … the fair use defense looks to the existence vel non of a licensing market when defining the reach of the copyright entitlement. The result is a steady, incremental, and unintended expansion of copyright, caused by nothing more than ambiguous doctrine and prudent behavior on the part of copyright users." James Gibson, *Risk Aversion and Rights Accretion in Intellectual Property Law*, 116 YALE L.J. 882, 887 (2007).

5. Indexing and Search: Redux

The Authors Guild v. Google, Inc.
804 F.3d 202 (2d Cir. 2015)

LEVAL, J.: …

[1] Google's Library Project, which began in 2004, involves bi-lateral agreements between Google and a number of the world's major research libraries. Under these agreements, the participating libraries select books from their collections to submit to Google for inclusion in the project. Google makes a digital scan of each book, extracts a machine-readable text, and creates an index of the machine-readable text of each book. Google retains the original scanned image of each book, in part so as to improve the accuracy of the machine-readable texts and indices as image-to-text conversion technologies improve.

[2] Since 2004, Google has scanned, rendered machine-readable, and indexed more than 20 million books, including both copyrighted works and works in the public domain. The vast majority of the books are non-fiction, and most are out of print. All of the digital information created by Google in the process is stored on servers protected by the same security systems Google uses to shield its own confidential information.

[3] The digital corpus created by the scanning of these millions of books enables the Google Books search engine. Members of the public who access the Google Books website can enter search words or terms of their own choice, receiving in response a list of all books in the database in which those terms appear, as well as the number of times the term appears in each book. A brief description of each book, entitled "About the Book,"

gives some rudimentary additional information, including a list of the words and terms that appear with most frequency in the book. It sometimes provides links to buy the book online and identifies libraries where the book can be found. The search tool permits a researcher to identify those books, out of millions, that do, as well as those that do not, use the terms selected by the researcher. Google notes that this identifying information instantaneously supplied would otherwise not be obtainable in lifetimes of searching.

[4] No advertising is displayed to a user of the search function. Nor does Google receive payment by reason of the searcher's use of Google's link to purchase the book.

[5] The search engine also makes possible new forms of research, known as "text mining" and "data mining." Google's "ngrams" research tool draws on the Google Library Project corpus to furnish statistical information to Internet users about the frequency of word and phrase usage over centuries. This tool permits users to discern fluctuations of interest in a particular subject over time and space by showing increases and decreases in the frequency of reference and usage in different periods and different linguistic regions. It also allows researchers to comb over the tens of millions of books Google has scanned in order to examine word frequencies, syntactic patterns, and thematic markers and to derive information on how nomenclature, linguistic usage, and literary style have changed over time. The district court gave as an example "track[ing] the frequency of references to the United States as a single entity ('the United States is') versus references to the United States in the plural ('the United States are') and how that usage has changed over time."

[6] The Google Books search function also allows the user a limited viewing of text. In addition to telling the number of times the word or term selected by the searcher appears in the book, the search function will display a maximum of three "snippets" containing it. A snippet is a horizontal segment comprising ordinarily an eighth of a page. Each page of a conventionally formatted book in the Google Books database is divided into eight non-overlapping horizontal segments, each such horizontal segment being a snippet. (Thus, for such a book with 24 lines to a page, each snippet is comprised of three lines of text.) Each search for a particular word or term within a book will reveal the same three snippets, regardless of the number of computers from which the search is launched. Only the first usage of the term on a given page is displayed. Thus, if the top snippet of a page contains two (or more) words for which the user searches, and Google's program is fixed to reveal that particular snippet in response to a search for either term, the second search will duplicate the snippet already revealed by the first search, rather than moving to reveal a different snippet containing the word because the first snippet was already revealed. Google's program does not allow a searcher to increase the number of snippets revealed by repeated entry of the same search term or by entering searches from different computers. A searcher can view more than three snippets of a book by entering additional searches for different terms. However, Google makes permanently unavailable for snippet view one snippet on each page and one complete page out of every ten—a process Google calls "blacklisting."

[7] Google also disables snippet view entirely for types of books for which a single snippet is likely to satisfy the searcher's present need for the book, such as dictionaries, cookbooks, and books of short poems. Finally, since 2005, Google will exclude any book altogether from snippet view at the request of the rights holder by the submission of an online form....

[8] Plaintiffs brought this suit on September 20, 2005, as a putative class action on behalf of similarly situated, rights-owning authors. After several years of negotiation, the parties reached a proposed settlement that would have resolved the claims on a class-wide basis. The proposed settlement allowed Google to make substantially more extensive use of its scans of copyrighted books than contemplated under the present judgment, and provided that Google would make payments to the rights holders in return. On March 22, 2011, however, the district court rejected the proposed settlement as unfair to the class members who relied on the named plaintiffs to represent their interests.

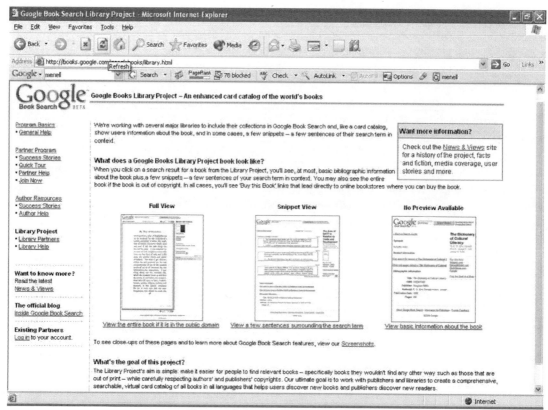

Figure 106: Google Books overview

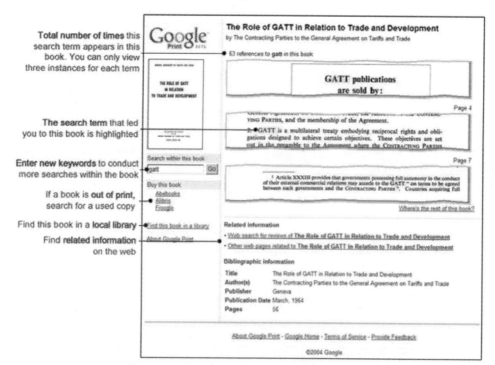

Figure 107: Google Books snippet view overview

[9] On October 14, 2011, Plaintiffs filed a fourth amended class action complaint, which is the operative complaint for this appeal. The district court certified a class on May 31, 2012. Google appealed from the certification, and moved in the district court for summary judgment on its fair use defense. Plaintiffs cross-moved in the district court for summary judgment. On the appeal from the class certification, our court—

questioning whether it was reasonable to infer that the putative class of authors favored the relief sought by the named plaintiffs—provisionally vacated that class certification without addressing the merits of the issue, concluding instead that "resolution of Google's fair use defense in the first instance will necessarily inform and perhaps moot our analysis of many class certification issues."

[10] On November 14, 2013, the district court granted Google's motion for summary judgment, concluding that the uses made by Google of copyrighted books were fair uses, protected by § 107. Upon consideration of the four statutory factors of § 107, the district court found that Google's uses were transformative, that its display of copyrighted material was properly limited, and that the Google Books program did not impermissibly serve as a market substitute for the original works....

II. The Search and Snippet View Functions

A. Factor One

[11] *(1) Transformative purpose.* ... [T]ransformative uses tend to favor a fair use finding because a transformative use is one that communicates something new and different from the original or expands its utility, thus serving copyright's overall objective of contributing to public knowledge.

[12] The word "transformative" cannot be taken too literally as a sufficient key to understanding the elements of fair use. It is rather a suggestive symbol for a complex thought, and does not mean that any and all changes made to an author's original text will necessarily support a finding of fair use.... [T]he would-be fair user of another's work must have justification for the taking. A secondary author is not necessarily at liberty to make wholesale takings of the original author's expression merely because of how well the original author's expression would convey the secondary author's different message. Among the best recognized justifications for copying from another's work is to provide comment on it or criticism of it. A taking from another author's work for the purpose of making points that have no bearing on the original may well be fair use, but the taker would need to show a justification. This part of the Supreme Court's discussion [in *Campbell*] is significant in assessing Google's claim of fair use because, as discussed extensively below, Google's claim of transformative purpose for copying from the works of others is to provide otherwise unavailable information about the originals.

[13] A further complication that can result from oversimplified reliance on whether the copying involves transformation is that the word "transform" also plays a role in defining "derivative works," over which the original rights holder retains exclusive control. Section 106 of the Act specifies the "exclusive right[]" of the copyright owner "(2) to prepare derivative works based upon the copyrighted work." The statute defines derivative works largely by example, rather than explanation. The examples include "translation, musical arrangement, dramatization, fictionalization, motion picture version, sound recording, art reproduction, abridgement, condensation," to which list the statute adds "any other form in which a work may be ... *transformed.*" ... [P]aradigmatic examples of derivative works include the translation of a novel into another language, the adaptation of a novel into a movie or play, or the recasting of a novel as an e-book or an audiobook. While such changes can be described as transformations, they do not involve the kind of transformative purpose that favors a fair use finding. The statutory definition suggests that derivative works generally involve transformations in the nature of *changes of form.* 17 U.S.C. § 101. By contrast, copying from an original for the purpose of criticism or commentary on the original or provision of information about it, tends most clearly to satisfy *Campbell*'s notion of the "transformative" purpose involved in the analysis of Factor One.[18]

---

[18] The Seventh Circuit takes the position that the kind of secondary use that favors satisfaction of the fair use test is better described as a "complementary" use, referring to how a hammer and nail complement one another in that together they

[14] With these considerations in mind, we first consider whether Google's search and snippet views functions satisfy the first fair use factor with respect to Plaintiffs' rights in their books....

[15] *(2) Search Function.* We have no difficulty concluding that Google's making of a digital copy of Plaintiffs' books for the purpose of enabling a search for identification of books containing a term of interest to the searcher involves a highly transformative purpose, in the sense intended by *Campbell*....

[16] ... [T]he purpose of Google's copying of the original copyrighted books is to make available significant information *about those books,* permitting a searcher to identify those that contain a word or term of interest, as well as those that do not include reference to it. In addition, through the ngrams tool, Google allows readers to learn the frequency of usage of selected words in the aggregate corpus of published books in different historical periods. We have no doubt that the purpose of this copying is the sort of transformative purpose described in *Campbell* as strongly favoring satisfaction of the first factor....

[17] *(3) Snippet View.* ... [T]he Google Books search function allows searchers to read snippets from the book searched .... Snippet view adds important value to the basic transformative search function, which tells only whether and how often the searched term appears in the book. Merely knowing that a term of interest appears in a book does not necessarily tell the searcher whether she needs to obtain the book, because it does not reveal whether the term is discussed in a manner or context falling within the scope of the searcher's interest. For example, a searcher seeking books that explore Einstein's theories, who finds that a particular book includes 39 usages of "Einstein," will nonetheless conclude she can skip that book if the snippets reveal that the book speaks of "Einstein" because that is the name of the author's cat. In contrast, the snippet will tell the searcher that this is a book she needs to obtain if the snippet shows that the author is engaging with Einstein's theories.

[18] Google's division of the page into tiny snippets is designed to show the searcher just enough context surrounding the searched term to help her evaluate whether the book falls within the scope of her interest (without revealing so much as to threaten the author's copyright interests). Snippet view thus adds importantly to the highly transformative purpose of identifying books of interest to the searcher. With respect to the first factor test, it favors a finding of fair use (unless the value of its transformative purpose is overcome by its providing text in a manner that offers a competing substitute for Plaintiffs' books, which we discuss under factors three and four below).

[19] *(4) Google's Commercial Motivation.* Plaintiffs also contend that Google's commercial motivation weighs in their favor under the first factor.... Although Google has no revenues flowing directly from its operation of the Google Books functions, Plaintiffs stress that Google is profit-motivated and seeks to use its dominance of book

---

achieve results that neither can accomplish on its own. Ty, Inc. v. Publ'ns Int'l, Ltd., 292 F.3d 512, 517–518 (7th Cir.2002). We do not find the term "complementary" particularly helpful in explaining fair use. The term would encompass changes of form that are generally understood to produce derivative works, rather than fair uses, and, at the same time, would fail to encompass copying for purposes that are generally and properly viewed as creating fair uses. When a novel is converted into film, for example, the original novel and the film ideally complement one another in that each contributes to achieving results that neither can accomplish on its own. The invention of the original author combines with the cinematographic interpretive skills of the filmmaker to produce something that neither could have produced independently. Nonetheless, at least when the intention of the film is to make a "motion picture version" of the novel without undertaking to parody it or to comment on it, the film is generally understood to be a derivative work, which under § 106, falls within the exclusive rights of the copyright owner. Although they complement one another, the film is not a fair use. At the same time, when a secondary work quotes an original for the purpose of parodying it, or discrediting it by exposing its inaccuracies, illogic, or dishonesty, such an undertaking is not within the exclusive prerogatives of the rights holder; it produces a fair use. Yet, when the purpose of the second is essentially to destroy the first, the two are not comfortably described as complementaries that combine to produce together something that neither could have produced independently of the other. We recognize, as just noted above, that the word "transformative," if interpreted too broadly, can also seem to authorize copying that should fall within the scope of an author's derivative rights. Attempts to find a circumspect shorthand for a complex concept are best understood as suggestive of a general direction, rather than as definitive descriptions.

search to fortify its overall dominance of the Internet search market, and that thereby Google indirectly reaps profits from the Google Books functions...

[20] Our court has ... repeatedly rejected the contention that commercial motivation should outweigh a convincing transformative purpose and absence of significant substitutive competition with the original.

[21] While we recognize that in some circumstances, a commercial motivation on the part of the secondary user will weigh against her, especially, as the Supreme Court suggested, when a persuasive transformative purpose is lacking, we see no reason in this case why Google's overall profit motivation should prevail as a reason for denying fair use over its highly convincing transformative purpose, together with the absence of significant substitutive competition, as reasons for granting fair use. Many of the most universally accepted forms of fair use, such as news reporting and commentary, quotation in historical or analytic books, reviews of books, and performances, as well as parody, are all normally done commercially for profit.

B. Factor Two

[22] The second fair use factor directs consideration of the "nature of the copyrighted work." While the "transformative purpose" inquiry discussed above is conventionally treated as a part of first factor analysis, it inevitably involves the second factor as well. One cannot assess whether the copying work has an objective that differs from the original without considering both works, and their respective objectives.

[23] The second factor has rarely played a significant role in the determination of a fair use dispute. The Supreme Court in *Harper & Row* made a passing observation in dictum that, "[t]he law generally recognizes a greater need to disseminate factual works than works of fiction or fantasy." 471 U.S. 539, 563 (1985). Courts have sometimes speculated that this might mean that a finding of fair use is more favored when the copying is of factual works than when copying is from works of fiction. However, while the copyright does not protect facts or ideas set forth in a work, it does protect that author's manner of expressing those facts and ideas. At least unless a persuasive fair use justification is involved, authors of factual works, like authors of fiction, should be entitled to copyright protection of their protected expression. The mere fact that the original is a factual work therefore should not imply that others may freely copy it. Those who report the news undoubtedly create factual works. It cannot seriously be argued that, for that reason, others may freely copy and re-disseminate news reports.[21]

[24] .... While each of the three Plaintiffs' books in this case is factual, we do not consider that as a boost to Google's claim of fair use. If one (or all) of the plaintiff works were fiction, we do not think that would change in any way our appraisal. Nothing in this case influences us one way or the other with respect to the second factor considered in isolation. To the extent that the "nature" of the original copyrighted work necessarily combines with the "purpose and character" of the secondary work to permit assessment of whether the secondary work uses the original in a "transformative" manner, as the term is used in *Campbell*, the second factor favors fair use not because Plaintiffs' works are factual, but because the secondary use transformatively provides valuable information about the original, rather than replicating protected expression in a manner that provides a meaningful substitute for the original.

---

[21] We think it unlikely that the Supreme Court meant in its concise dictum that secondary authors are at liberty to copy extensively from the protected expression of the original author merely because the material is factual. What the *Harper & Row* dictum may well have meant is that, because in the case of factual writings, there is often occasion to test the accuracy of, to rely on, or to repeat their factual propositions, and such testing and reliance may reasonably require quotation (lest a change of expression unwittingly alter the facts), factual works often present well justified fair uses, even if the mere fact that the work is factual does not necessarily justify copying of its protected expression.

C. Factor Three

[25] The third statutory factor instructs us to consider "the amount and substantiality of the portion used in relation to the copyrighted work as a whole." The clear implication of the third factor is that a finding of fair use is more likely when small amounts, or less important passages, are copied than when the copying is extensive, or encompasses the most important parts of the original. The obvious reason for this lies in the relationship between the third and the fourth factors. The larger the amount, or the more important the part, of the original that is copied, the greater the likelihood that the secondary work might serve as an effectively competing substitute for the original, and might therefore diminish the original rights holder's sales and profits.

[26] *(1) Search Function.* The Google Books program has made a digital copy of the entirety of each of Plaintiffs' books. Notwithstanding the reasonable implication of Factor Three that fair use is more likely to be favored by the copying of smaller, rather than larger, portions of the original, courts have rejected any categorical rule that a copying of the entirety cannot be a fair use. Complete unchanged copying has repeatedly been found justified as fair use when the copying was reasonably appropriate to achieve the copier's transformative purpose and was done in such a manner that it did not offer a competing substitute for the original....

[27] .... [N]ot only is the copying of the totality of the original reasonably appropriate to Google's transformative purpose, it is literally necessary to achieve that purpose. If Google copied less than the totality of the originals, its search function could not advise searchers reliably whether their searched term appears in a book (or how many times).

[28] While Google *makes* an unauthorized digital copy of the entire book, it does not reveal that digital copy to the public. The copy is made to enable the search functions to reveal limited, important information about the books. With respect to the search function, Google satisfies the third factor test, as illuminated by the Supreme Court in *Campbell.*

[29] *(2) Snippet View....*

[30] Without doubt, enabling searchers to see portions of the copied texts could have determinative effect on the fair use analysis. The larger the quantity of the copyrighted text the searcher can see and the more control the searcher can exercise over what part of the text she sees, the greater the likelihood that those revelations could serve her as an effective, free substitute for the purchase of the plaintiff's book. We nonetheless conclude that, at least as presently structured by Google, the snippet view does not reveal matter that offers the marketplace a significantly competing substitute for the copyrighted work.

[31] Google has constructed the snippet feature in a manner that substantially protects against its serving as an effectively competing substitute for Plaintiffs' books. In the Background section of this opinion, we describe a variety of limitations Google imposes on the snippet function. These include the small size of the snippets (normally one eighth of a page), the blacklisting of one snippet per page and of one page in every ten, the fact that no more than three snippets are shown—and no more than one per page—for each term searched, and the fact that the same snippets are shown for a searched term no matter how many times, or from how many different computers, the term is searched. In addition, Google does not provide snippet view for types of books, such as dictionaries and cookbooks, for which viewing a small segment is likely to satisfy the searcher's need. The result of these restrictions is, so far as the record demonstrates, that a searcher cannot succeed, even after long extended effort to multiply what can be revealed, in revealing through a snippet search what could usefully serve as a competing substitute for the original.

[32] The blacklisting, which permanently blocks about 22% of a book's text from snippet view, is by no means the most important of the obstacles Google has designed. While it is true that the blacklisting of 22% leaves 78% of a book *theoretically* accessible to a searcher, it does not follow that any large part of that 78% is in fact

accessible. The other restrictions built into the program work together to ensure that, even after protracted effort over a substantial period of time, only small and randomly scattered portions of a book will be accessible. In an effort to show what large portions of text searchers can read through persistently augmented snippet searches, Plaintiffs' counsel employed researchers over a period of weeks to do multiple word searches on Plaintiffs' books. In no case were they able to access as much as 16% of the text, and the snippets collected were usually not sequential but scattered randomly throughout the book. Because Google's snippets are arbitrarily and uniformly divided by lines of text, and not by complete sentences, paragraphs, or any measure dictated by content, a searcher would have great difficulty constructing a search so as to provide any extensive information about the book's use of that term. As snippet view never reveals more than one snippet per page in response to repeated searches for the same term, it is at least difficult, and often impossible, for a searcher to gain access to more than a single snippet's worth of an extended, continuous discussion of the term.

[33] The fact that Plaintiffs' searchers managed to reveal nearly 16% of the text of Plaintiffs' books overstates the degree to which snippet view can provide a meaningful substitute. At least as important as the percentage of words of a book that are revealed is the manner and order in which they are revealed. Even if the search function revealed 100% of the words of the copyrighted book, this would be of little substitutive value if the words were revealed in alphabetical order, or any order other than the order they follow in the original book. It cannot be said that a revelation is "substantial" in the sense intended by the statute's third factor if the revelation is in a form that communicates little of the sense of the original. The fragmentary and scattered nature of the snippets revealed, even after a determined, assiduous, time-consuming search, results in a revelation that is not "substantial," even if it includes an aggregate 16% of the text of the book. If snippet view could be used to reveal a coherent block amounting to 16% of a book, that would raise a very different question beyond the scope of our inquiry.

D. Factor Four

[34] The fourth fair use factor, "the effect of the [copying] use upon the potential market for or value of the copyrighted work," focuses on whether the copy brings to the marketplace a competing substitute for the original, or its derivative, so as to deprive the rights holder of significant revenues because of the likelihood that potential purchasers may opt to acquire the copy in preference to the original. Because copyright is a commercial doctrine whose objective is to stimulate creativity among potential authors by enabling them to earn money from their creations, the fourth factor is of great importance in making a fair use assessment.

[35] *Campbell* stressed the close linkage between the first and fourth factors, in that the more the copying is done to achieve a purpose that differs from the purpose of the original, the less likely it is that the copy will serve as a satisfactory substitute for the original....

[36] However, *Campbell*'s observation as to the likelihood of a secondary use serving as an effective substitute goes only so far. Even if the *purpose* of the copying is for a valuably transformative purpose, such copying might nonetheless harm the value of the copyrighted original if done in a manner that results in widespread revelation of sufficiently significant portions of the original as to make available a significantly competing substitute. The question for us is whether snippet view, notwithstanding its transformative purpose, does that. We conclude that, at least as snippet view is presently constructed, it does not.

[37] Especially in view of the fact that the normal purchase price of a book is relatively low in relation to the cost of manpower needed to secure an arbitrary assortment of randomly scattered snippets, we conclude that the snippet function does not give searchers access to effectively competing substitutes. Snippet view, at best and after a large commitment of manpower, produces discontinuous, tiny fragments, amounting in the aggregate to no more than 16% of a book. This does not threaten the rights holders with any significant harm to the value of their copyrights or diminish their harvest of copyright revenue.

[38] We recognize that the snippet function can cause *some* loss of sales. There are surely instances in which a searcher's need for access to a text will be satisfied by the snippet view, resulting in either the loss of a sale to that searcher, or reduction of demand on libraries for that title, which might have resulted in libraries purchasing additional copies. But the possibility, or even the probability or certainty, of some loss of sales does not suffice to make the copy an effectively competing substitute that would tilt the weighty fourth factor in favor of the rights holder in the original. There must be a meaningful or significant effect "upon the potential market for or value of the copyrighted work."

[39] Furthermore, the type of loss of sale envisioned above will generally occur in relation to interests that are not protected by the copyright. A snippet's capacity to satisfy a searcher's need for access to a copyrighted book will at times be because the snippet conveys a historical fact that the searcher needs to ascertain. For example, a student writing a paper on Franklin D. Roosevelt might need to learn the year Roosevelt was stricken with polio. By entering "Roosevelt polio" in a Google Books search, the student would be taken to (among numerous sites) a snippet from page 31 of Richard Thayer Goldberg's *The Making of Franklin D. Roosevelt* (1981), telling that the polio attack occurred in 1921. This would satisfy the searcher's need for the book, eliminating any need to purchase it or acquire it from a library. But what the searcher derived from the snippet was a historical fact. Author Goldberg's copyright does not extend to the facts communicated by his book. It protects only the author's manner of expression. Google would be entitled, without infringement of Goldberg's copyright, to answer the student's query about the year Roosevelt was afflicted, taking the information from Goldberg's book. The fact that, in the case of the student's snippet search, the information came embedded in three lines of Goldberg's writing, which were superfluous to the searcher's needs, would not change the taking of an unprotected fact into a copyright infringement.

[40] Even if the snippet reveals some authorial expression, because of the brevity of a single snippet and the cumbersome, disjointed, and incomplete nature of the aggregation of snippets made available through snippet view, we think it would be a rare case in which the searcher's interest *in the protected aspect* of the author's work would be satisfied by what is available from snippet view, and rarer still—because of the cumbersome, disjointed, and incomplete nature of the aggregation of snippets made available through snippet view—that snippet view could provide a significant substitute for the purchase of the author's book.

[41] Accordingly, considering the four fair use factors in light of the goals of copyright, we conclude that Google's making of a complete digital copy of Plaintiffs' works for the purpose of providing the public with its search and snippet view functions (at least as snippet view is presently designed) is a fair use and does not infringe Plaintiffs' copyrights in their books....

NOTES

1. Most courts' analyses of the fourth factor focus on the market harms caused to the plaintiff by the defendant's use. Yet the statute frames this factor as an analysis of the "the *effect* of the use upon the potential market for or value of the copyrighted work." 17 U.S.C. § 107(4) (emphasis added). Nowhere does the statute indicate that courts should look just to the "negative effect" of the use. By stating that courts should look to "the effect" generally, should the statute be read as requiring a look at all effects of the use on the potential market for the copyrighted work, both positive and negative? For example, a defendant's use of another's copyrighted work might revive interest in the copyrighted work, boosting sales. Do you see how *Author's Guild* might be read as involving market benefits for the plaintiffs? For an argument that courts ought to weigh both market harms and benefits in assessing the fourth factor, see David Fagundes, *Market Harm, Market Help, and Fair Use*, 17 STAN. TECH. L. REV.359 (2014); Jeanne C. Fromer, *Market Effects Bearing on Fair Use*, 90 WASH. L. REV. 615 (2015); Glynn S. Lunney, Jr., *Fair Use and Market Failure:* Sony Revisited, 82 B.U. L. REV. 975 (2002).

2. Many had thought that *Perfect 10* and *Authors Guild* meant that full copying of copyrighted works for searchable databases of them would now be fair use. The Second Circuit's decision in *Fox News Network, LLC v. TVEyes, Inc.*, 883 F.3d 169 (2d Cir. 2018), demonstrated the sensitivity of those earlier decisions to the facts of the particular case. In this case, as demonstrated by Figure 108, TVEyes "offers a service that enables its clients to easily locate and view segments of televised video programming that are responsive to the clients' interests. It does so by continuously recording vast quantities of television programming, compiling the recorded broadcasts into a database that is text-searchable (based primarily on the closed-captioned text copied from the broadcasts), and allowing its clients to search for and watch (up to) ten-minute video clips that mention terms of interest to the clients." Additionally, "[a] TVEyes client may archive videos permanently on the TVEyes servers and may download videos directly to the client's computer. These services are useful because TVEyes otherwise deletes captured content after thirty-two days. Clients can also email the clips for viewing by others, including those who are not TVEyes clients. And clients can search for videos by date, time, and channel (rather than by keyword). The parties dispute whether clients can watch live broadcasts on TVEyes." Clients include "journalists, government and political organizations, law enforcement, the military, for-profit companies, and non-profits."

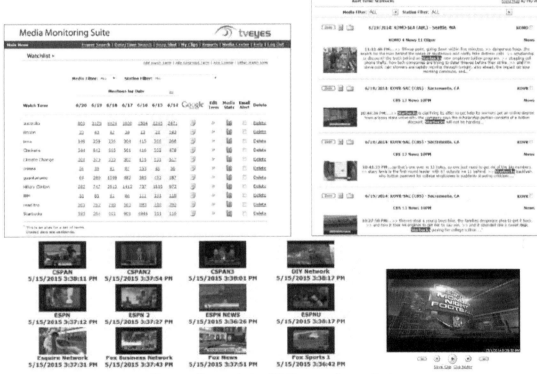

Figure 108: snapshots of TVEyes media monitoring

The Second Circuit ruled that TVEyes is not entitled to claim fair use as to the Watch function it performs (though the district court found TVEyes engaged in fair use by copying material to create its database and providing search functionality, rulings that the parties did not appeal). As to the first fair use factor, the Second Circuit used *Authors Guild* and *Sony* to conclude that TVEyes' use of copyrighted television content is transformative:

> TVEyes's copying of Fox's content for use in the Watch function is similarly transformative insofar as it enables users to isolate, from an ocean of programming, material that is responsive to their interests and needs, and to access that material with targeted precision. It enables nearly instant access to a subset of material—and to information about the material—that would otherwise be irretrievable, or else retrievable only through prohibitively inconvenient or inefficient means....

> *The Watch function certainly qualifies as technology that achieves the transformative purpose of enhancing efficiency: it enables TVEyes's clients to view all of the Fox programming that (over the prior thirty-two days) discussed a particular topic of interest to them, without having to monitor thirty-two days of programming in order to catch each relevant discussion; and it eliminates the clients' need even to view entire programs, because the ten most relevant minutes are presented to them. Much like the television customer in Sony, TVEyes clients can view the Fox programming they want at a time and place that is convenient to them, rather than at the time and place of broadcast. For these reasons, TVEyes's Watch function is at least somewhat transformative.*

Although TVEyes' use was commercial, the court thought that the first factor weighed slightly in favor of TVEyes. The court thought the second factor to be unimportant. Unlike the case on Google Books, the Second Circuit thought that the third factor weighed against TVEyes because "TVEyes makes available virtually the entirety of the Fox programming that TVEyes users want to see and hear." It elaborated that "TVEyes redistributes Fox's news programming in ten-minute clips, which—given the brevity of the average news segment on a particular topic—likely provide TVEyes's users with all of the Fox programming that they seek and the entirety of the message conveyed by Fox to authorized viewers of the original. TVEyes's use of Fox's content is therefore both extensive and inclusive of all that is important from the copyrighted work." The Second Circuit also thought that the fourth factor weighed against TVEyes:

> *The success of the TVEyes business model demonstrates that deep-pocketed consumers are willing to pay well for a service that allows them to search for and view selected television clips, and that this market is worth millions of dollars in the aggregate. Consequently, there is a plausibly exploitable market for such access to televised content, and it is proper to consider whether TVEyes displaces potential Fox revenues when TVEyes allows its clients to watch Fox's copyrighted content without Fox's permission.*

> *Such displacement does occur. Since the ability to re-distribute Fox's content in the manner that TVEyes does is clearly of value to TVEyes, it (or a similar service) should be willing to pay Fox for the right to offer the content. By providing Fox's content to TVEyes clients without payment to Fox, TVEyes is in effect depriving Fox of licensing revenues from TVEyes or from similar entities. And Fox itself might wish to exploit the market for such a service rather than license it to others. TVEyes has thus usurped a market that properly belongs to the copyright-holder. It is of no moment that TVEyes allegedly approached Fox for a license but was rebuffed: the failure to strike a deal satisfactory to both parties does not give TVEyes the right to copy Fox's copyrighted material without payment.*

Are the Second Circuit's analyses of the first and fourth factors reconcilable with prior cases you have read?

In a concurrence, Judge Kaplan cast doubt on the Second Circuit's conclusion that TVEyes' use was at all transformative:

> *Even on the majority's view that TVEyes' Watch function substantially improves the efficiency with which TVEyes customers can access Fox copyrighted broadcasts of possible interest, it does no more than repackage and deliver the original works. It adds no new information, no new aesthetics, and no new insights or understandings. I therefore doubt that it is transformative.*

Does the majority or the concurrence have the better understanding of transformativeness?

6. Software Interoperability

In the Supreme Court's first fair use decision revisiting *Campbell*, consider how it understands transformativeness. Does its reasoning make you reconsider the outcomes in any of the previous circuit court decisions? Also, is there a fair use factor that seems more determinative to the case than the others?

Google LLC v. Oracle America, Inc.

141 S. Ct. 1183 (2021)

BREYER, J.:

[1] Oracle America, Inc., is the current owner of a copyright in Java SE, a computer program that uses the popular Java computer programming language. Google, without permission, has copied a portion of that program, a portion that enables a programmer to call up prewritten software that, together with the computer's hardware, will carry out a large number of specific tasks. The lower courts have considered (1) whether Java SE's owner could copyright the portion that Google copied, and (2) if so, whether Google's copying nonetheless constituted a "fair use" of that material, thereby freeing Google from copyright liability. The Federal Circuit held in Oracle's favor (i.e., that the portion is copyrightable and Google's copying did not constitute a "fair use"). In reviewing that decision, we assume, for argument's sake, that the material was copyrightable. But we hold that the copying here at issue nonetheless constituted a fair use. Hence, Google's copying did not violate the copyright law....

[2] In 2005, Google acquired Android, Inc., a startup firm that hoped to become involved in smartphone software. Google sought, through Android, to develop a software platform for mobile devices like smartphones. A platform provides the necessary infrastructure for computer programmers to develop new programs and applications. One might think of a software platform as a kind of factory floor where computer programmers (analogous to autoworkers, designers, or manufacturers) might come, use sets of tools found there, and create new applications for use in, say, smartphones....

[3] Google envisioned an Android platform that was free and open, such that software developers could use the tools found there free of charge. Its idea was that more and more developers using its Android platform would develop ever more Android-based applications, all of which would make Google's Android-based smartphones more attractive to ultimate consumers. Consumers would then buy and use ever more of those phones. That vision required attracting a sizeable number of skilled programmers.

[4] At that time, many software developers understood and wrote programs using the Java programming language, a language invented by Sun Microsystems (Oracle's predecessor). About six million programmers had spent considerable time learning, and then using, the Java language. Many of those programmers used Sun's own popular Java SE platform to develop new programs primarily for use in desktop and laptop computers. That platform allowed developers using the Java language to write programs that were able to run on any desktop or laptop computer, regardless of the underlying hardware (i.e., the programs were in large part "interoperable"). Indeed, one of Sun's slogans was "'write once, run anywhere.'"

[5] Shortly after acquiring the Android firm, Google began talks with Sun about the possibility of licensing the entire Java platform for its new smartphone technology. But Google did not want to insist that all programs written on the Android platform be interoperable. As Android's founder explained, "[t]he whole idea about [an] open source [platform] is to have very, very few restrictions on what people can do with it," and Sun's interoperability policy would have undermined that free and open business model. Apparently, for reasons related to this disagreement, Google's negotiations with Sun broke down. Google then built its own platform.

[6] The record indicates that roughly 100 Google engineers worked for more than three years to create Google's Android platform software. In doing so, Google tailored the Android platform to smartphone technology, which differs from desktop and laptop computers in important ways. A smartphone, for instance, may run on a more limited battery or take advantage of GPS technology. The Android platform offered programmers the ability to program for that environment. To build the platform, Google wrote millions of lines of new code. Because Google wanted millions of programmers, familiar with Java, to be able easily to work with its new Android platform, it also copied roughly 11,500 lines of code from the Java SE program. The copied lines of code are part of a tool called an Application Programming Interface, or API.

[7] What is an API? The Federal Circuit described an API as a tool that "allow[s] programmers to use ... prewritten code to build certain functions into their own programs, rather than write their own code to perform those functions from scratch." Through an API, a programmer can draw upon a vast library of prewritten code to carry out complex tasks. For lay persons, including judges, juries, and many others, some elaboration of this description may prove useful.

[8] Consider in more detail just what an API does. A computer can perform thousands, perhaps millions, of different tasks that a programmer may wish to use. These tasks range from the most basic to the enormously complex. Ask the computer, for example, to tell you which of two numbers is the higher number or to sort one thousand numbers in ascending order, and it will instantly give you the right answer. An API divides and organizes the world of computing tasks in a particular way. Programmers can then use the API to select the particular task that they need for their programs. In Sun's API (which we refer to as the Sun Java API), each individual task is known as a "method." The API groups somewhat similar methods into larger "classes," and groups somewhat similar classes into larger "packages." This method-class-package organizational structure is referred to as the Sun Java API's "structure, sequence, and organization," or SSO.

[9] For each task, there is computer code, known as "implementing code," that in effect tells the computer how to execute the particular task you have asked it to perform (such as telling you, of two numbers, which is the higher). The implementing code (which Google independently wrote) is not at issue here. For a single task, the implementing code may be hundreds of lines long. It would be difficult, perhaps impossible, for a programmer to create complex software programs without drawing on prewritten task-implementing programs to execute discrete tasks.

[10] But how do you as the programmer tell the computer which of the implementing code programs it should choose, i.e., which task it should carry out? You do so by entering into your own program a command that corresponds to the specific task and calls it up. Those commands, known as "method calls," help you carry out the task by choosing those programs written in implementing code that will do the trick, i.e., that will instruct the computer so that your program will find the higher of two numbers. If a particular computer might perform, say, a million different tasks, different method calls will tell the computer which of those tasks to choose. Those familiar with the Java language already know countless method calls that allow them to invoke countless tasks.

[11] And how does the method call (which a programmer types) actually locate and invoke the particular implementing code that it needs to instruct the computer how to carry out a particular task? It does so through another type of code, which the parties have labeled "declaring code." Declaring code is part of the API. For

each task, the specific command entered by the programmer matches up with specific declaring code inside the API. That declaring code provides both the name for each task and the location of each task within the API's overall organizational system (i.e., the placement of a method within a particular class and the placement of a class within a particular package). In this sense, the declaring code and the method call form a link, allowing the programmer to draw upon the thousands of prewritten tasks, written in implementing code. Without that declaring code, the method calls entered by the programmer would not call up the implementing code.

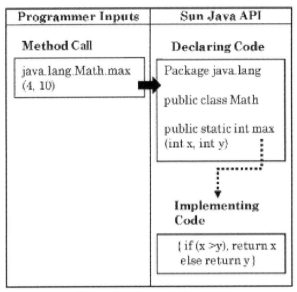

Figure 109: Java API Diagram

[12] The declaring code therefore performs at least two important functions in the Sun Java API. The first, more obvious, function is that the declaring code enables a set of shortcuts for programmers. By connecting complex implementing code with method calls, it allows a programmer to pick out from the API's task library a particular task without having to learn anything more than a simple command. For example, a programmer building a new application for personal banking may wish to use various tasks to, say, calculate a user's balance or authenticate a password. To do so, she need only learn the method calls associated with those tasks. In this way, the declaring code's shortcut function is similar to a gas pedal in a car that tells the car to move faster or the QWERTY keyboard on a typewriter that calls up a certain letter when you press a particular key. As those analogies demonstrate, one can think of the declaring code as part of an interface between human beings and a machine.

[13] The second, less obvious, function is to reflect the way in which Java's creators have divided the potential world of different tasks into an actual world, i.e., precisely which set of potentially millions of different tasks we want to have our Java-based computer systems perform and how we want those tasks arranged and grouped. In this sense, the declaring code performs an organizational function. It determines the structure of the task library that Java's creators have decided to build. To understand this organizational system, think of the Dewey Decimal System that categorizes books into an accessible system or a travel guide that arranges a city's attractions into different categories. Language itself provides a rough analogy to the declaring code's organizational feature, for language itself divides into sets of concepts a world that in certain respects other languages might have divided differently. The developers of Java, for example, decided to place a method called "draw image" inside of a class called "graphics."

[14] Consider a comprehensive, albeit farfetched, analogy that illustrates how the API is actually used by a programmer. Imagine that you can, via certain keystrokes, instruct a robot to move to a particular file cabinet, to open a certain drawer, and to pick out a specific recipe. With the proper recipe in hand, the robot then moves

to your kitchen and gives it to a cook to prepare the dish. This example mirrors the API's task-related organizational system. Through your simple command, the robot locates the right recipe and hands it off to the cook. In the same way, typing in a method call prompts the API to locate the correct implementing code and hand it off to your computer. And importantly, to select the dish that you want for your meal, you do not need to know the recipe's contents, just as a programmer using an API does not need to learn the implementing code. In both situations, learning the simple command is enough.

[15] Now let us consider the example that the District Court used to explain the precise technology here. A programmer wishes, as part of her program, to determine which of two integers is the larger. To do so in the Java language, she will first write **java.lang**. Those words (which we have put in bold type) refer to the "package" (or by analogy to the file cabinet). She will then write **Math**. That word refers to the "class" (or by analogy to the drawer). She will then write **max**. That word refers to the "method" (or by analogy to the recipe). She will then make two parentheses (). And, in between the parentheses she will put two integers, say 4 and 6, that she wishes to compare. The whole expression—the method call—will look like this: "**java.lang.Math.max(4, 6)**." The use of this expression will, by means of the API, call up a task-implementing program that will determine the higher number.

[16] In writing this program, the programmer will use the very symbols we have placed in bold in the precise order we have placed them. But the symbols by themselves do nothing. She must also use software that connects the symbols to the equivalent of file cabinets, drawers, and files. The API is that software. It includes both the declaring code that links each part of the method call to the particular task-implementing program, and the implementing code that actually carries it out.

[17] Now we can return to the copying at issue in this case. Google did not copy the task-implementing programs, or implementing code, from the Sun Java API. It wrote its own task-implementing programs, such as those that would determine which of two integers is the greater or carry out any other desired (normally far more complex) task. This implementing code constitutes the vast majority of both the Sun Java API and the API that Google created for Android. For most of the packages in its new API, Google also wrote its own declaring code. For 37 packages, however, Google copied the declaring code from the Sun Java API. As just explained, that means that, for those 37 packages, Google necessarily copied both the names given to particular tasks and the grouping of those tasks into classes and packages.

[18] In doing so, Google copied that portion of the Sun Java API that allowed programmers expert in the Java programming language to use the "task calling" system that they had already learned. As Google saw it, the 37 packages at issue included those tasks that were likely to prove most useful to programmers working on applications for mobile devices. In fact, three of these packages were fundamental to being able to use the Java language at all. By using the same declaring code for those packages, programmers using the Android platform can rely on the method calls that they are already familiar with to call up particular tasks (e.g., determining which of two integers is the greater); but Google's own implementing programs carry out those tasks. Without that copying, programmers would need to learn an entirely new system to call up the same tasks.

[19] We add that the Android platform has been successful. Within five years of its release in 2007, Android-based devices claimed a large share of the United States market. As of 2015, Android sales produced more than $42 billion in revenue.

[20] In 2010 Oracle Corporation bought Sun. Soon thereafter Oracle brought this lawsuit in the United States District Court for the Northern District of California....

[21] The case has a complex and lengthy history. At the outset Oracle complained that Google's use of the Sun Java API violated both copyright and patent laws. For its copyright claim, Oracle alleged that Google infringed

its copyright by copying, for 37 packages, both the literal declaring code and the nonliteral organizational structure (or SSO) of the API, i.e., the grouping of certain methods into classes and certain classes into packages. For trial purposes the District Court organized three proceedings. The first would cover the copyright issues, the second would cover the patent issues, and the third would, if necessary, calculate damages. The court also determined that a judge should decide whether copyright law could protect an API and that the jury should decide whether Google's use of Oracle's API infringed its copyright and, if so, whether a fair use defense nonetheless applied.

[22] After six weeks of hearing evidence, the jury rejected Oracle's patent claims (which have since dropped out of the case). It also found a limited copyright infringement. It deadlocked as to whether Google could successfully assert a fair use defense. The judge then decided that, regardless, the API's declaring code was not the kind of creation to which copyright law extended its protection. The court noted that Google had written its own implementing code, which constituted the vast majority of its API. It wrote that "anyone is free under the Copyright Act to write his or her own code to carry out exactly the same" tasks that the Sun Java API picks out or specifies. Google copied only the declaring code and organizational structure that was necessary for Java-trained programmers to activate familiar tasks (while, as we said, writing its own implementing code). Hence the copied material, in the judge's view, was a "system or method of operation," which copyright law specifically states cannot be copyrighted.

[23] On appeal, the Federal Circuit reversed. That court held that both the API's declaring code and its organizational structure could be copyrighted. It pointed out that Google could have written its own declaring code just as it wrote its own implementing code. And because in principle Google might have created a whole new system of dividing and labeling tasks that could be called up by programmers, the declaring code (and the system) that made up the Sun Java API was copyrightable.

[24] The Federal Circuit also rejected Oracle's plea that it decide whether Google had the right to use the Sun Java API because doing so was a fair use, immune from copyright liability. The Circuit wrote that fair use "both permits and requires courts to avoid rigid application of the copyright statute when, on occasion, it would stifle the very creativity which that law is designed to foster." But, it added, this "is not a case in which the record contains sufficient factual findings upon which we could base a de novo assessment of Google's affirmative defense of fair use." And it remanded the case for another trial on that question. Google petitioned this Court for a writ of certiorari, seeking review of the Federal Circuit's copyrightability determination. We denied the petition.

[25] On remand the District Court, sitting with a jury, heard evidence for a week. The court instructed the jury to answer one question: Has Google shown by a preponderance of the evidence that its use in Android of the declaring code and organizational structure contained in the 37 Sun Java API packages that it copied constitutes a fair use under the Copyright Act? After three days of deliberation the jury answered the question in the affirmative. Google had shown fair use.

[26] Oracle again appealed to the Federal Circuit. And the Circuit again reversed the District Court. The Federal Circuit assumed all factual questions in Google's favor. But, it said, the question whether those facts constitute a fair use is a question of law. Deciding that question of law, the court held that Google's use of the Sun Java API was not a fair use. It wrote that "[t]here is nothing fair about taking a copyrighted work verbatim and using it for the same purpose and function as the original in a competing platform." It remanded the case again, this time for a trial on damages.

[27] Google then filed a petition for certiorari in this Court. It asked us to review the Federal Circuit's determinations as to both copyrightability and fair use. We granted its petition....

[28] Google's petition for certiorari poses two questions. The first asks whether Java's API is copyrightable. It asks us to examine two of the statutory provisions just mentioned, one that permits copyrighting computer programs and the other that forbids copyrighting, e.g., "process[es]," "system[s]," and "method[s] of operation." Google believes that the API's declaring code and organization fall into these latter categories and are expressly excluded from copyright protection. The second question asks us to determine whether Google's use of the API was a "fair use." Google believes that it was.

[29] A holding for Google on either question presented would dispense with Oracle's copyright claims. Given the rapidly changing technological, economic, and business-related circumstances, we believe we should not answer more than is necessary to resolve the parties' dispute. We shall assume, but purely for argument's sake, that the entire Sun Java API falls within the definition of that which can be copyrighted. We shall ask instead whether Google's use of part of that API was a fair use. Unlike the Federal Circuit, we conclude that it was....

[30] Generically speaking, computer programs differ from books, films, and many other "literary works" in that such programs almost always serve functional purposes. These and other differences have led at least some judges to complain that "applying copyright law to computer programs is like assembling a jigsaw puzzle whose pieces do not quite fit." Lotus Development Corp. v. Borland Int'l, Inc. (Boudin, J., concurring).

[31] These differences also led Congress to think long and hard about whether to grant computer programs copyright protection. In 1974, Congress established a National Commission on New Technological Uses of Copyrighted Works (CONTU) to look into the matter. After several years of research, CONTU concluded that the "availability of copyright protection for computer programs is desirable." At the same time, it recognized that computer programs had unique features. Mindful of not "unduly burdening users of programs and the general public," it wrote that copyright "should not grant anyone more economic power than is necessary to achieve the incentive to create." And it believed that copyright's existing doctrines (e.g., fair use), applied by courts on a case-by-case basis, could prevent holders from using copyright to stifle innovation. Congress then wrote computer program protection into the law.

[32] The upshot, in our view, is that fair use can play an important role in determining the lawful scope of a computer program copyright, such as the copyright at issue here. It can help to distinguish among technologies. It can distinguish between expressive and functional features of computer code where those features are mixed. It can focus on the legitimate need to provide incentives to produce copyrighted material while examining the extent to which yet further protection creates unrelated or illegitimate harms in other markets or to the development of other products. In a word, it can carry out its basic purpose of providing a context-based check that can help to keep a copyright monopoly within its lawful bounds. See H.R. REP. No. 94–1476, pp. 65–66 (1976) (explaining that courts are to "adapt the doctrine [of fair use] to particular situations on a case-by-case basis" and in light of "rapid technological change"); Lexmark Int'l, Inc. v. Static Control Components, Inc., 387 F.3d 522, 543–45 (6th Cir. 2004) (discussing fair use in the context of copying to preserve compatibility); Sony Computer Entertainment, Inc. v. Connectix Corp., 203 F.3d 596, 603–608 (9th Cir. 2000) (applying fair use to intermediate copying necessary to reverse engineer access to unprotected functional elements within a program); Sega Enterprises Ltd. v. Accolade, Inc., 977 F.2d 1510, 1521–1527 (9th Cir. 1992) (holding that wholesale copying of copyrighted code as a preliminary step to develop a competing product was a fair use).

[33] Justice Thomas' thoughtful dissent offers a very different view of how (and perhaps whether) fair use has any role to play for computer programs. We are told that no attempt to distinguish among computer code is tenable when considering "the nature of the work," even though there are important distinctions in the ways that programs are used and designed. We are told that no reuse of code in a new program will ever have a valid "purpose and character," even though the reasons for copying computer code may vary greatly and differ from those applicable to other sorts of works. (accepting that copying as part of "reverse engineer[ing] a system to

ensure compatibility" could be a valid purpose). And we are told that our fair use analysis must prioritize certain factors over others, even though our case law instructs that fair use depends on the context, *see Campbell*.

[34] We do not understand Congress, however, to have shielded computer programs from the ordinary application of copyright's limiting doctrines in this way. By defining computer programs in § 101, Congress chose to place this subject matter within the copyright regime. Like other protected works, that means that the owners of computer programs enjoy the exclusive rights set forth in the Act, including the right to "reproduce [a] copyrighted work" or to "prepare derivative works." 17 U.S.C. § 106. But that also means that exclusive rights in computer programs are limited like any other works. Just as fair use distinguishes among books and films, which are indisputably subjects of copyright, so too must it draw lines among computer programs. And just as fair use takes account of the market in which scripts and paintings are bought and sold, so too must it consider the realities of how technological works are created and disseminated. We do not believe that an approach close to "all or nothing" would be faithful to the Copyright Act's overall design....

[35] At the outset, Google argues that fair use is a question for a jury to decide; here the jury decided the question in Google's favor; and we should limit our review to determining whether "substantial evidence" justified the jury's decision. The Federal Circuit disagreed. It thought that the fair use question was a mixed question of fact and law; that reviewing courts should appropriately defer to the jury's findings of underlying facts; but that the ultimate question whether those facts showed a fair use is a legal question for judges to decide de novo.

[36] We agree with the Federal Circuit's answer to this question. We have said, "[f]air use is a mixed question of law and fact." *Harper & Row*. We have explained that a reviewing court should try to break such a question into its separate factual and legal parts, reviewing each according to the appropriate legal standard. But when a question can be reduced no further, ... the standard of review for a mixed question all depends—on whether answering it entails primarily legal or factual work.

[37] In this case, the ultimate fair use question primarily involves legal work. Fair use was originally a concept fashioned by judges. Our cases still provide legal interpretations of the fair use provision. And those interpretations provide general guidance for future cases. This type of work is legal work.

[38] Applying a legal fair use conclusion may, of course, involve determination of subsidiary factual questions, such as whether there was harm to the actual or potential markets for the copyrighted work or how much of the copyrighted work was copied. In this case the Federal Circuit carefully applied the fact/law principles we set forth ..., leaving factual determinations to the jury and reviewing the ultimate question, a legal question, de novo.

[39] Next, Google argues that the Federal Circuit's approach violates the Seventh Amendment. The Amendment both requires that "the right of trial by jury ... be preserved" and forbids courts to "re-examin[e]" any "fact tried by a jury." The Reexamination Clause is no bar here, however, for, as we have said, the ultimate question here is one of law, not fact. It does not violate the Reexamination Clause for a court to determine the controlling law in resolving a challenge to a jury verdict, as happens any time a court resolves a motion for judgment as a matter of law.

[40] Nor is Google correct that "the right of trial by jury" includes the right to have a jury resolve a fair use defense. That Clause is concerned with the particular trial decision at issue. Even though it is possible to find pre-Revolutionary English cases in which a judge sent related questions like fair abridgment to a jury, those questions were significantly different from the fair use doctrine as courts apply it today. As far as contemporary fair use is concerned, we have described the doctrine as an equitable, not a legal, doctrine. We have found no

case suggesting that application of [our rules] here would fail to preserve the substance of the common-law jury trial right as it existed in 1791....

[41] We turn now to the basic legal question before us: Was Google's copying of the Sun Java API, specifically its use of the declaring code and organizational structure for 37 packages of that API, a fair use[?] In answering this question, we shall consider the four factors set forth in the fair use statute as we find them applicable to the kind of computer programs before us.... For expository purposes, we begin with the second.

A. "The Nature of the Copyrighted Work"

[42] The Sun Java API is a "user interface." It provides a way through which users (here the programmers) can manipulate and control task-performing computer programs via a series of menu commands. The API reflects Sun's division of possible tasks that a computer might perform into a set of actual tasks that certain kinds of computers actually will perform. Sun decided, for example, that its API would call up a task that compares one integer with another to see which is the larger. Sun's API (to our knowledge) will not call up the task of determining which great Arabic scholar decided to use Arabic numerals (rather than Roman numerals) to perform that "larger integer" task. No one claims that the decisions about what counts as a task are themselves copyrightable—although one might argue about decisions as to how to label and organize such tasks (e.g., the decision to name a certain task "max" or to place it in a class called "Math." *Cf.* Baker v. Selden.

[43] As discussed above, ... we can think of the technology as having three essential parts. First, the API includes "implementing code," which actually instructs the computer on the steps to follow to carry out each task. Google wrote its own programs (implementing programs) that would perform each one of the tasks that its API calls up.

[44] Second, the Sun Java API associates a particular command, called a "method call," with the calling up of each task. The symbols **java.lang.**, for example, are part of the command that will call up the program (whether written by Sun or, as here, by Google) that instructs the computer to carry out the "larger number" operation. Oracle does not here argue that the use of these commands by programmers itself violates its copyrights.

[45] Third, the Sun Java API contains computer code that will associate the writing of a method call with particular "places" in the computer that contain the needed implementing code. This is the declaring code. The declaring code both labels the particular tasks in the API and organizes those tasks, or "methods," into "packages" and "classes." We have referred to this organization, by way of rough analogy, as file cabinets, drawers, and files. Oracle does claim that Google's use of the Sun Java API's declaring code violates its copyrights.

[46] The declaring code at issue here resembles other copyrighted works in that it is part of a computer program. Congress has specified that computer programs are subjects of copyright. It differs, however, from many other kinds of copyrightable computer code. It is inextricably bound together with a general system, the division of computing tasks, that no one claims is a proper subject of copyright. It is inextricably bound up with the idea of organizing tasks into what we have called cabinets, drawers, and files, an idea that is also not copyrightable. It is inextricably bound up with the use of specific commands known to programmers, known here as method calls (such as **java.lang.Math.max**, etc.), that Oracle does not here contest. And it is inextricably bound up with implementing code, which is copyrightable but was not copied.

[47] Moreover, the copied declaring code and the uncopied implementing programs call for, and reflect, different kinds of capabilities. A single implementation may walk a computer through dozens of different steps. To write implementing programs, witnesses told the jury, requires balancing such considerations as how quickly a computer can execute a task or the likely size of the computer's memory. One witness described that creativity as "magic" practiced by an API developer when he or she worries "about things like power

470

management" for devices that "run on a battery." This is the very creativity that was needed to develop the Android software for use not in laptops or desktops but in the very different context of smartphones.

[48] The declaring code (inseparable from the programmer's method calls) embodies a different kind of creativity. Sun Java's creators, for example, tried to find declaring code names that would prove intuitively easy to remember. They wanted to attract programmers who would learn the system, help to develop it further, and prove reluctant to use another. Sun's business strategy originally emphasized the importance of using the API to attract programmers. It sought to make the API open and then compete on implementations. The testimony at trial was replete with examples of witnesses drawing this critical line between the user-centered declaratory code and the innovative implementing code.

[49] These features mean that, as part of a user interface, the declaring code differs to some degree from the mine run of computer programs. Like other computer programs, it is functional in nature. But unlike many other programs, its use is inherently bound together with uncopyrightable ideas (general task division and organization) and new creative expression (Android's implementing code). Unlike many other programs, its value in significant part derives from the value that those who do not hold copyrights, namely, computer programmers, invest of their own time and effort to learn the API's system. And unlike many other programs, its value lies in its efforts to encourage programmers to learn and to use that system so that they will use (and continue to use) Sun-related implementing programs that Google did not copy.

[50] Although copyrights protect many different kinds of writing, we have emphasized the need to "recogni[ze] that some works are closer to the core of [copyright] than others," *Campbell*. In our view, for the reasons just described, the declaring code is, if copyrightable at all, further than are most computer programs (such as the implementing code) from the core of copyright. That fact diminishes the fear, expressed by both the dissent and the Federal Circuit, that application of fair use here would seriously undermine the general copyright protection that Congress provided for computer programs. And it means that this factor, "the nature of the copyrighted work," points in the direction of fair use.

B. "The Purpose and Character of the Use"

[51] In the context of fair use, we have considered whether the copier's use adds something new, with a further purpose or different character, altering the copyrighted work with new expression, meaning or message. Commentators have put the matter more broadly, asking whether the copier's use fulfills the objective of copyright law to stimulate creativity for public illumination. In answering this question, we have used the word "transformative" to describe a copying use that adds something new and important. An "'artistic painting'" might, for example, fall within the scope of fair use even though it precisely replicates a copyrighted advertising logo to make a comment about consumerism. Or, as we held in *Campbell*, a parody can be transformative because it comments on the original or criticizes it, for parody needs to mimic an original to make its point.

[52] Google copied portions of the Sun Java API precisely, and it did so in part for the same reason that Sun created those portions, namely, to enable programmers to call up implementing programs that would accomplish particular tasks. But since virtually any unauthorized use of a copyrighted computer program (say, for teaching or research) would do the same, to stop here would severely limit the scope of fair use in the functional context of computer programs. Rather, in determining whether a use is "transformative," we must go further and examine the copying's more specifically described "purpose[s]" and "character." 17 U.S.C. § 107(1).

[53] Here Google's use of the Sun Java API seeks to create new products. It seeks to expand the use and usefulness of Android-based smartphones. Its new product offers programmers a highly creative and innovative tool for a smartphone environment. To the extent that Google used parts of the Sun Java API to

create a new platform that could be readily used by programmers, its use was consistent with that creative progress that is the basic constitutional objective of copyright itself.

[54] The jury heard that Google limited its use of the Sun Java API to tasks and specific programming demands related to Android. It copied the API (which Sun created for use in desktop and laptop computers) only insofar as needed to include tasks that would be useful in smartphone programs. And it did so only insofar as needed to allow programmers to call upon those tasks without discarding a portion of a familiar programming language and learning a new one. To repeat, Google, through Android, provided a new collection of tasks operating in a distinct and different computing environment. Those tasks were carried out through the use of new implementing code (that Google wrote) designed to operate within that new environment. Some of the *amici* refer to what Google did as "reimplementation," defined as the building of a system that repurposes the same words and syntaxes of an existing system—in this case so that programmers who had learned an existing system could put their basic skills to use in a new one.

[55] The record here demonstrates the numerous ways in which reimplementing an interface can further the development of computer programs. The jury heard that shared interfaces are necessary for different programs to speak to each other. It heard that the reimplementation of interfaces is necessary if programmers are to be able to use their acquired skills. It heard that the reuse of APIs is common in the industry. It heard that Sun itself had used pre-existing interfaces in creating Java. And it heard that Sun executives thought that widespread use of the Java programming language, including use on a smartphone platform, would benefit the company....

[56] These and related facts convince us that the "purpose and character" of Google's copying was transformative—to the point where this factor too weighs in favor of fair use.

[57] There are two other considerations that are often taken up under the first factor: commerciality and good faith. The text of § 107 includes various noncommercial uses, such as teaching and scholarship, as paradigmatic examples of privileged copying. There is no doubt that a finding that copying was not commercial in nature tips the scales in favor of fair use. But the inverse is not necessarily true, as many common fair uses are indisputably commercial. For instance, the text of § 107 includes examples like "news reporting," which is often done for commercial profit. So even though Google's use was a commercial endeavor—a fact no party disputed—that is not dispositive of the first factor, particularly in light of the inherently transformative role that the reimplementation played in the new Android system.

[58] As for bad faith, our decision in *Campbell* expressed some skepticism about whether bad faith has any role in a fair use analysis. We find this skepticism justifiable, as copyright is not a privilege reserved for the well-behaved. We have no occasion here to say whether good faith is as a general matter a helpful inquiry. We simply note that given the strength of the other factors pointing toward fair use and the jury finding in Google's favor on hotly contested evidence, that factbound consideration is not determinative in this context.

C. "The Amount and Substantiality of the Portion Used"

[59] If one considers the declaring code in isolation, the quantitative amount of what Google copied was large. Google copied the declaring code for 37 packages of the Sun Java API, totaling approximately 11,500 lines of code. Those lines of code amount to virtually all the declaring code needed to call up hundreds of different tasks. On the other hand, if one considers the entire set of software material in the Sun Java API, the quantitative amount copied was small. The total set of Sun Java API computer code, including implementing code, amounted to 2.86 million lines, of which the copied 11,500 lines were only 0.4 percent.

[60] The question here is whether those 11,500 lines of code should be viewed in isolation or as one part of the considerably greater whole. We have said that even a small amount of copying may fall outside of the scope of fair use where the excerpt copied consists of the "heart" of the original work's creative expression. *Harper &*

Row. On the other hand, copying a larger amount of material can fall within the scope of fair use where the material copied captures little of the material's creative expression or is central to a copier's valid purpose. If a defendant had copied one sentence in a novel, that copying may well be insubstantial. But if that single sentence set forth one of the world's shortest short stories—"When he awoke, the dinosaur was still there."— the question looks much different, as the copied material constitutes a small part of the novel but the entire short story. *See* A. Monterroso, *El Dinosaurio, in* COMPLETE WORKS & OTHER STORIES 42 (E. Grossman transl. 1995). (In the original Spanish, the story reads: "Cuando despertó, el dinosaurio todavía estaba allí.")

[61] Several features of Google's copying suggest that the better way to look at the numbers is to take into account the several million lines that Google did not copy. For one thing, the Sun Java API is inseparably bound to those task-implementing lines. Its purpose is to call them up. For another, Google copied those lines not because of their creativity, their beauty, or even (in a sense) because of their purpose. It copied them because programmers had already learned to work with the Sun Java API's system, and it would have been difficult, perhaps prohibitively so, to attract programmers to build its Android smartphone system without them. Further, Google's basic purpose was to create a different task-related system for a different computing environment (smartphones) and to create a platform—the Android platform—that would help achieve and popularize that objective. The "substantiality" factor will generally weigh in favor of fair use where, as here, the amount of copying was tethered to a valid, and transformative, purpose.

[62] We do not agree with the Federal Circuit's conclusion that Google could have achieved its Java-compatibility objective by copying only the 170 lines of code that are necessary to write in the Java language. In our view, that conclusion views Google's legitimate objectives too narrowly. Google's basic objective was not simply to make the Java programming language usable on its Android systems. It was to permit programmers to make use of their knowledge and experience using the Sun Java API when they wrote new programs for smartphones with the Android platform. In principle, Google might have created its own, different system of declaring code. But the jury could have found that its doing so would not have achieved that basic objective. In a sense, the declaring code was the key that it needed to unlock the programmers' creative energies. And it needed those energies to create and to improve its own innovative Android systems.

[63] We consequently believe that this "substantiality" factor weighs in favor of fair use.

D. Market Effects

[64] The fourth statutory factor focuses upon the "effect" of the copying in the "market for or value of the copyrighted work." Consideration of this factor, at least where computer programs are at issue, can prove more complex than at first it may seem. It can require a court to consider the amount of money that the copyright owner might lose. As we pointed out in *Campbell*, "verbatim copying of the original in its entirety for commercial purposes" may well produce a market substitute for an author's work. Making a film of an author's book may similarly mean potential or presumed losses to the copyright owner. Those losses normally conflict with copyright's basic objective: providing authors with exclusive rights that will spur creative expression.

[65] But a potential loss of revenue is not the whole story. We here must consider not just the amount but also the source of the loss. As we pointed out in *Campbell*, a "lethal parody, like a scathing theatre review," may "kil[l] demand for the original." Yet this kind of harm, even if directly translated into foregone dollars, is not cognizable under the Copyright Act.

[66] Further, we must take into account the public benefits the copying will likely produce. Are those benefits, for example, related to copyright's concern for the creative production of new expression? Are they comparatively important, or unimportant, when compared with dollar amounts likely lost (taking into account as well the nature of the source of the loss)?

[67] We do not say that these questions are always relevant to the application of fair use, not even in the world of computer programs. Nor do we say that these questions are the only questions a court might ask. But we do find them relevant here in helping to determine the likely market effects of Google's reimplementation.

[68] As to the likely amount of loss, the jury could have found that Android did not harm the actual or potential markets for Java SE. And it could have found that Sun itself (now Oracle) would not have been able to enter those markets successfully whether Google did, or did not, copy a part of its API. First, evidence at trial demonstrated that, regardless of Android's smartphone technology, Sun was poorly positioned to succeed in the mobile phone market. The jury heard ample evidence that Java SE's primary market was laptops and desktops. It also heard that Sun's many efforts to move into the mobile phone market had proved unsuccessful. As far back as 2006, prior to Android's release, Sun's executives projected declining revenue for mobile phones because of emerging smartphone technology. When Sun's former CEO was asked directly whether Sun's failure to build a smartphone was attributable to Google's development of Android, he answered that it was not. Given the evidence showing that Sun was beset by business challenges in developing a mobile phone product, the jury was entitled to agree with that assessment.

[69] Second, the jury was repeatedly told that devices using Google's Android platform were different in kind from those that licensed Sun's technology. For instance, witnesses explained that the broader industry distinguished between smartphones and simpler feature phones. As to the specific devices that used Sun-created software, the jury heard that one of these phones lacked a touchscreen, while another did not have a QWERTY keyboard. For other mobile devices, the evidence showed that simpler products, like the Kindle, used Java software, while more advanced technology, like the Kindle Fire, were built on the Android operating system. This record evidence demonstrates that, rather than just repurposing Sun's code from larger computers to smaller computers, Google's Android platform was part of a distinct (and more advanced) market than Java software.

[70] Looking to these important differences, Google's economic expert told the jury that Android was not a market substitute for Java's software. As he explained, "the two products are on very different devices," and the Android platform, which offers "an entire mobile operating stack," is a "very different typ[e] of produc[t]" than Java SE, which is "just an applications programming framework." Taken together, the evidence showed that Sun's mobile phone business was declining, while the market increasingly demanded a new form of smartphone technology that Sun was never able to offer.

[71] Finally, the jury also heard evidence that Sun foresaw a benefit from the broader use of the Java programming language in a new platform like Android, as it would further expand the network of Java-trained programmers. In other words, the jury could have understood Android and Java SE as operating in two distinct markets. And because there are two markets at issue, programmers learning the Java language to work in one market (smartphones) are then able to bring those talents to the other market (laptops). *See* 4 NIMMER ON COPYRIGHT § 13.05[A][4] (explaining that factor four asks what the impact of "widespread conduct of the sort engaged in by the defendant" would be on the market for the present work).

[72] Oracle presented evidence to the contrary. Indeed, the Federal Circuit held that the "market effects" factor militated against fair use in part because Sun had tried to enter the Android market. But those licensing negotiations concerned much more than 37 packages of declaring code, covering topics like the implementation of Java's code and branding and cooperation between the firms. *See also* 4 NIMMER ON COPYRIGHT § 13.05[A][4] (cautioning against the "danger of circularity posed" by considering unrealized licensing opportunities because "it is a given in every fair use case that plaintiff suffers a loss of a potential market if that potential is defined as the theoretical market for licensing the very use at bar"). In any event, the jury's fair use determination means that neither Sun's effort to obtain a license nor Oracle's conflicting evidence

can overcome evidence indicating that, at a minimum, it would have been difficult for Sun to enter the smartphone market, even had Google not used portions of the Sun Java API.

[73] On the other hand, Google's copying helped Google make a vast amount of money from its Android platform. And enforcement of the Sun Java API copyright might give Oracle a significant share of these funds. It is important, however, to consider why and how Oracle might have become entitled to this money. When a new interface, like an API or a spreadsheet program, first comes on the market, it may attract new users because of its expressive qualities, such as a better visual screen or because of its superior functionality. As time passes, however, it may be valuable for a different reason, namely, because users, including programmers, are just used to it. They have already learned how to work with it. *See Lotus Development Corp.* (Boudin, J., concurring).

[74] The record here is filled with evidence that this factor accounts for Google's desire to use the Sun Java API. This source of Android's profitability has much to do with third parties' (say, programmers') investment in Sun Java programs. It has correspondingly less to do with Sun's investment in creating the Sun Java API. We have no reason to believe that the Copyright Act seeks to protect third parties' investment in learning how to operate a created work. *Cf. Campbell* (discussing the need to identify those harms that are "cognizable under the Copyright Act").

[75] Finally, given programmers' investment in learning the Sun Java API, to allow enforcement of Oracle's copyright here would risk harm to the public. Given the costs and difficulties of producing alternative APIs with similar appeal to programmers, allowing enforcement here would make of the Sun Java API's declaring code a lock limiting the future creativity of new programs. Oracle alone would hold the key. The result could well prove highly profitable to Oracle (or other firms holding a copyright in computer interfaces). But those profits could well flow from creative improvements, new applications, and new uses developed by users who have learned to work with that interface. To that extent, the lock would interfere with, not further, copyright's basic creativity objectives. *See Connectix Corp.*, 203 F.3d at 607; *see also Sega Enterprises*, 977 F.2d at 1523–1524 ("An attempt to monopolize the market by making it impossible for others to compete runs counter to the statutory purpose of promoting creative expression"); *Lexmark Int'l*, 387 F.3d at 544 (noting that where a subsequent user copied a computer program to foster functionality, it was not exploiting the programs "commercial value *as a copyrighted work*" (emphasis in original)). After all, copyright supplies the economic incentive to both create and disseminate ideas, and the reimplementation of a user interface allows creative new computer code to more easily enter the market.

[76] The uncertain nature of Sun's ability to compete in Android's market place, the sources of its lost revenue, and the risk of creativity-related harms to the public, when taken together, convince that this fourth factor—market effects—also weighs in favor of fair use....

[77] The fact that computer programs are primarily functional makes it difficult to apply traditional copyright concepts in that technological world. *See Lotus Development Corp.* (Boudin, J., concurring). In doing so here, we have not changed the nature of those concepts. We do not overturn or modify our earlier cases involving fair use—cases, for example, that involve "knockoff" products, journalistic writings, and parodies. Rather, we here recognize that application of a copyright doctrine such as fair use has long proved a cooperative effort of Legislatures and courts, and that Congress, in our view, intended that it so continue. As such, we have looked to the principles set forth in the fair use statute, § 107, and set forth in our earlier cases, and applied them to this different kind of copyrighted work.

[78] We reach the conclusion that in this case, where Google reimplemented a user interface, taking only what was needed to allow users to put their accrued talents to work in a new and transformative program, Google's

copying of the Sun Java API was a fair use of that material as a matter of law. The Federal Circuit's contrary judgment is reversed, and the case is remanded for further proceedings in conformity with this opinion....

Justice BARRETT took no part in the consideration or decision of this case.

Justice THOMAS, with whom Justice ALITO joins, dissenting.

[79] Oracle spent years developing a programming library that successfully attracted software developers, thus enhancing the value of Oracle's products. Google sought a license to use the library in Android, the operating system it was developing for mobile phones. But when the companies could not agree on terms, Google simply copied verbatim 11,500 lines of code from the library. As a result, it erased 97.5% of the value of Oracle's partnership with Amazon, made tens of billions of dollars, and established its position as the owner of the largest mobile operating system in the world. Despite this, the majority holds that this copying was fair use.

[80] The Court reaches this unlikely result in large part because it bypasses the antecedent question clearly before us: Is the software code at issue here protected by the Copyright Act? The majority purports to assume, without deciding, that the code is protected. But its fair-use analysis is wholly inconsistent with the substantial protection Congress gave to computer code. By skipping over the copyrightability question, the majority disregards half the relevant statutory text and distorts its fair-use analysis. Properly considering that statutory text, Oracle's code at issue here is copyrightable, and Google's use of that copyrighted code was anything but fair....

[81] In the 1990s, Oracle created a programming language called Java. Like many programming languages, Java allows developers to prewrite small subprograms called "methods." Methods form the building blocks of more complex programs. This process is not unlike what legislatures do with statutes. To save space and time, legislatures define terms and then use those definitions as a shorthand. For example, the legal definition for "refugee" is more than 300 words long. 8 U.S.C. § 1101(42). Rather than repeat all those words every time they are relevant, the U.S. Code encapsulates them all with a single term that it then inserts into each relevant section. Java methods work similarly. Once a method has been defined, a developer need only type a few characters (the method name and relevant inputs) to invoke everything contained in the subprogram. A programmer familiar with prewritten methods can string many of them together to quickly develop complicated programs without having to write from scratch all the basic subprograms....

[82] Oracle's declaring code was central to its business model. Oracle profited financially by encouraging developers to create programs written in Java and then charging manufacturers a fee to embed in their devices the Java software platform needed to run those programs. To this end, Oracle created a work called Java 2 Platform, Standard Edition, which included a highly organized library containing about 30,000 methods. Oracle gave developers free access to these methods to encourage them to write programs for the Java platform. In return, developers were required to make their programs compatible with the Java platform on any device. Developers were encouraged to make improvements to the platform, but they were required to release beneficial modifications to the public. If a company wanted to customize the platform and keep those customizations secret for business purposes, it had to pay for a separate license.

[83] By 2005, many companies were racing to develop operating systems for what would become modern smartphones. Oracle's strategy had successfully encouraged millions of programmers to learn Java. As a result, Java software platforms were in the vast majority of mobile phones. Google wanted to attract those programmers to Android by including in Android the declaring code with which they were now familiar. But the founder of Android, Andrew Rubin, understood that the declaring code was copyrighted, so Google sought a custom license from Oracle. At least four times between 2005 and 2006, the two companies attempted to negotiate a license, but they were unsuccessful, in part because of trust issues.

[84] When those negotiations broke down, Google simply decided to use Oracle's code anyway. Instead of creating its own declaring code—as Apple and Microsoft chose to do—Google copied verbatim 11,500 lines of Oracle's declaring code and arranged that code exactly as Oracle had done. It then advertised Android to device manufacturers as containing "Core Java Libraries." ...

{The dissent presents its argument that the declaring code is copyrightable.}

[85] .... Three [of the four statutory fair use factors] decisively favor Oracle. And even assuming that the remaining factor favors Google, that factor, without more, cannot legally establish fair use in this context.

[86] .... Tellingly, the majority evaluates the factors neither in sequential order nor in order of importance (at least two factors are more important under our precedent). Instead, it starts with the second factor: the nature of the copyrighted work. It proceeds in this manner in order to create a distinction between declaring and implementing code that renders the former less worthy of protection than the latter. Because the majority's mistaken analysis rests so heavily on this factor, I begin with it as well.

A. The Nature of the Copyrighted Work

[87] This factor requires courts to assess the level of creativity or functionality in the original work. It generally favors fair use when a copyrighted work is more informational or functional than creative. Because code is predominantly functional, this factor will often favor copying when the original work is computer code. But because Congress determined that declaring and implementing code are copyrightable {by deeming computer programs to be copyrightable}, this factor alone cannot support a finding of fair use.

[88] The majority, however, uses this factor to create a distinction between declaring and implementing code that in effect removes copyright protection from declaring code. It concludes that, unlike implementing code, declaring code is far "from the core of copyright" because it becomes valuable only when third parties (computer programmers) value it and because it is "inherently bound together with uncopyrightable ideas."

[89] Congress, however, rejected this sort of categorical distinction that would make declaring code less worthy of protection. The Copyright Act protects code that operates "in a computer in order to bring about a certain result" both "directly" (implementing code) and "indirectly" (declaring code). § 101. And if anything, declaring code is closer to the core of copyright. Developers cannot even see implementing code. Implementing code thus conveys no expression to developers. Declaring code, in contrast, is user facing. It must be designed and organized in a way that is intuitive and understandable to developers so that they can invoke it.

[90] Even setting those concerns aside, the majority's distinction is untenable. True, declaring code is "inherently bound together with uncopyrightable ideas." Is anything not? Books are inherently bound with uncopyrightable ideas—the use of chapters, having a plot, or including dialogue or footnotes. This does not place books far "from the core of copyright." And implementing code, which the majority concedes is copyrightable, is inherently bound up with the division of computing tasks that cannot be copyrighted.[6] We have not discounted a work of authorship simply because it is associated with noncopyrightable ideas. While ideas cannot be copyrighted, expressions of those ideas can.

[91] Similarly, it makes no difference that the value of declaring code depends on how much time third parties invest in learning it. Many other copyrighted works depend on the same. A Broadway musical script needs

---

[6] The majority also belittles declaring code by suggesting it is simply a way to organize implementing code. Not so. Declaring code defines subprograms of implementing code, including by controlling what inputs they can process. Similarly, the majority is wrong to suggest that the purpose of declaring code is to connect pre-existing method calls to implementing code. Declaring code creates the method calls.

actors and singers to invest time learning and rehearsing it. But a theater cannot copy a script—the rights to which are held by a smaller theater—simply because it wants to entice actors to switch theaters and because copying the script is more efficient than requiring the actors to learn a new one.

[92] What the majority says is true of declaring code is no less true of implementing code. Declaring code is how programmers access prewritten implementing code. The value of that implementing code thus is directly proportional to how much programmers value the associated declaring code. The majority correctly recognizes that declaring code "is inextricably bound up with implementing code," but it overlooks the implications of its own conclusion.

[93] Only after wrongly concluding that the nature of declaring code makes that code generally unworthy of protection does the Court move on to consider the other factors. This opening mistake taints the Court's entire analysis.

B. Market Effects

[94] Undoubtedly the single most important element of fair use is the effect of Google's copying upon the potential market for or value of Oracle's copyrighted work. As the Federal Circuit correctly determined, "evidence of actual and potential harm stemming from Google's copying was overwhelming." By copying Oracle's code to develop and release Android, Google ruined Oracle's potential market in at least two ways.

[95] First, Google eliminated the reason manufacturers were willing to pay to install the Java platform. Google's business model differed from Oracle's. While Oracle earned revenue by charging device manufacturers to install the Java platform, Google obtained revenue primarily through ad sales. Its strategy was to release Android to device manufacturers for free and then use Android as a vehicle to collect data on consumers and deliver behavioral ads. With a free product available that included much of Oracle's code (and thus with similar programming potential), device manufacturers no longer saw much reason to pay to embed the Java platform.

[96] For example, before Google released Android, Amazon paid for a license to embed the Java platform in Kindle devices. But after Google released Android, Amazon used the cost-free availability of Android to negotiate a 97.5% discount on its license fee with Oracle. Evidence at trial similarly showed that right after Google released Android, Samsung's contract with Oracle dropped from $40 million to about $1 million. Google contests none of this except to say that Amazon used a different Java platform, Java Micro Edition instead of Java Standard Edition. That difference is inconsequential because the former was simply a smaller subset of the latter. Google copied code found in both platforms. The majority does not dispute—or even mention—this enormous harm.

[97] Second, Google interfered with opportunities for Oracle to license the Java platform to developers of smartphone operating systems. Before Google copied Oracle's code, nearly every mobile phone on the market contained the Java platform. Oracle's code was extraordinarily valuable to anybody who wanted to develop smartphones, which explains why Google tried no fewer than four times to license it. The majority's remark that Google also sought other licenses from Oracle does not change this central fact. Both parties agreed that Oracle could enter Google's current market by licensing its declaring code. But by copying the code and releasing Android, Google eliminated Oracle's opportunity to license its code for that use.

[98] The majority writes off this harm by saying that the jury could have found that Oracle might not have been able to enter the modern smartphone market successfully.[7] But whether Oracle could itself enter that market

---

[7] It also suggests that Oracle may have received some incidental benefit from Android. But even assuming that is true, it would go to the question of damages, not fair use. And there is no evidence that any benefit came even close to offsetting Oracle's enormous loss.

is only half the picture. We look at not only the potential market that creators of original works would in general develop but also those potential markets the copyright holder might license others to develop. A book author need not be able to personally convert a book into a film so long as he can license someone else to do so. That Oracle could have licensed its code for use in Android is undisputed.

[99] Unable to seriously dispute that Google's actions had a disastrous effect on Oracle's potential market, the majority changes course and asserts that enforcing copyright protection could harm the public by giving Oracle the power to "limi[t] the future creativity" of programs on Android. But this case concerns only versions of Android released through November 2014. Google has released six major versions since then. Only about 7.7% of active Android devices still run the versions at issue. The majority's concern about a lock-in effect might carry more weight if this suit concerned versions of Android widely in use or that will be widely in use. It makes little sense in a suit about versions that are close to obsolete.

[100] The majority's concern about a lock-in effect also is speculation belied by history. First, Oracle never had lock-in power. The majority (again) overlooks that Apple and Microsoft created mobile operating systems without using Oracle's declaring code. Second, Oracle always made its declaring code freely available to programmers. There is little reason to suspect Oracle might harm programmers by stopping now. And third, the majority simply assumes that the jury, in a future suit over current Android versions, would give Oracle control of Android instead of just awarding damages or perpetual royalties.

[101] If the majority is going to speculate about what Oracle might do, it at least should consider what Google has done. The majority expresses concern that Oracle might abuse its copyright protection (on outdated Android versions) and "attempt to monopolize the market." But it is Google that recently was fined a record $5 billion [by the European Commission] for abusing Android to violate antitrust laws. Google controls the most widely used mobile operating system in the world. And if companies may now freely copy libraries of declaring code whenever it is more convenient than writing their own, others will likely hesitate to spend the resources Oracle did to create intuitive, well-organized libraries that attract programmers and could compete with Android. If the majority is worried about monopolization, it ought to consider whether Google is the greater threat.

[102] By copying Oracle's work, Google decimated Oracle's market and created a mobile operating system now in over 2.5 billion actively used devices, earning tens of billions of dollars every year. If these effects on Oracle's potential market favor Google, something is very wrong with our fair-use analysis.

C. The Purpose and Character of the Use

[103] The second-most important factor—"the purpose and character of the use, including whether such use is of a commercial nature or is for nonprofit educational purposes"—requires us to consider whether use was commercial and whether it was transformative. Both aspects heavily favor Oracle.

[104] Begin with the overwhelming commercial nature of Google's copying. In 2015 alone, the year before the fair-use trial, Google earned $18 billion from Android. That number has no doubt dramatically increased as Android has grown to dominate the global market share.[9] On this scale, Google's use of Oracle's declaring code weighs heavily—if not decisively—against fair use.

---

[9] The real value also may be much higher because Android indirectly boosts other sources of revenue. For years Google has set its search engine as the default engine on Android. Google can use that engine to collect reams of data used to deliver behavioral advertisements to consumers on desktops. Using control over Android to choose a default search engine may seem trivial, but Google certainly does not think so. According to a Goldman Sachs analysis, Google paid Apple $12 billion

[105] The majority attempts to dismiss this overwhelming commercial use by noting that commercial use does "not necessarily" weigh against fair use. True enough. Commercial use sometimes can be overcome by use that is sufficiently transformative. But we cannot ignore Google's intended purpose of supplanting Oracle's commercially valuable platform with its own. Even if we could, we have never found fair use for copying that reaches into the tens of billions of dollars and wrecks the copyright holder's market.

[106] Regardless, Google fares no better on transformative use. A court generally cannot find fair use unless the copier's use is transformative.... This question is guided by the examples of fair use given in the preamble to § 107. Those examples include: "criticism, comment, news reporting, teaching ..., scholarship, or research." § 107. Although these examples are not exclusive, they are illustrative, and Google's repurposing of Java code from larger computers to smaller computers resembles none of them. Google did not use Oracle's code to teach or reverse engineer a system to ensure compatibility. Instead, to avoid the drudgery in working up something fresh, Google used the declaring code for the same exact purpose Oracle did. As the Federal Circuit correctly determined, "[t]here is nothing fair about taking a copyrighted work verbatim and using it for the same purpose and function as the original in a competing platform."

[107] The majority acknowledges that Google used the copied declaring code "for the same reason" Oracle did. So, by turns, the majority transforms the definition of "transformative." Now, we are told, "transformative" simply means—at least for computer code—a use that will help others "create new products."

[108] That new definition eviscerates copyright. A movie studio that converts a book into a film without permission not only creates a new product (the film) but enables others to "create products"—film reviews, merchandise, YouTube highlight reels, late night television interviews, and the like. Nearly every computer program, once copied, can be used to create new products. Surely the majority would not say that an author can pirate the next version of Microsoft Word simply because he can use it to create new manuscripts.

[109] Ultimately, the majority wrongly conflates transformative use with derivative use. To be transformative, a work must do something fundamentally different from the original. A work that simply serves the same purpose in a new context—which the majority concedes is true here—is derivative, not transformative. Congress made clear that Oracle holds "the exclusive rights ... to prepare derivative works." § 106(2). Rather than create a transformative product, Google profited from exploitation of the copyrighted material without paying the customary price.

D. The Amount and Substantiality of the Portion Used

[110] The statutory fair-use factors also instruct us to consider "the amount and substantiality of the portion used in relation to the copyrighted work as a whole." § 107(3). In general, the greater the amount of use, the more likely the copying is unfair. Ibid. But even if the copier takes only a small amount, copying the "heart" or focal points of a work weighs against fair use, unless no more was taken than necessary for the copier to achieve transformative use.

[111] Google does not dispute the Federal Circuit's conclusion that it copied the heart or focal points of Oracle's work. The declaring code is what attracted programmers to the Java platform and why Google was so interested in that code. And Google copied that code verbatim, which weighs against fair use. The majority does not disagree. Instead, it concludes that Google took no more than necessary to create new products. That analysis fails because Google's use is not transformative. This factor thus weighs against Google.

---

to be the default search engine for Safari, Apple's web browser, for just one year. Google does not appear to have disputed this figure.

[112] Even if Google's use were transformative, the majority is wrong to conclude that Google copied only a small portion of the original work. The majority points out that the 11,500 lines of declaring code—enough to fill about 600 pages in an appendix—were just a fraction of the code in the Java platform. But the proper denominator is declaring code, not all code. A copied work is quantitatively substantial if it could serve as a market substitute for the original work or potentially licensed derivatives of that work. The declaring code is what attracted programmers. And it is what made Android a market substitute for potentially licensed derivatives of Oracle's Java platform. Google's copying was both qualitatively and quantitatively substantial....

[113] In sum, three of the four statutory fair-use factors weigh decidedly against Google. The nature of the copyrighted work—the sole factor possibly favoring Google—cannot by itself support a determination of fair use because holding otherwise would improperly override Congress' determination that declaring code is copyrightable....

NOTES

1. Which fair use factor, if any, was the most important to the Court's conclusion? Why? Is your answer like or unlike your answer for previous cases?

2. Do you think the dissent is right that the majority could not avoid ruling on the copyrightability of the declaring code as a prerequisite to deciding whether Google's use was fair? Note how repeatedly the majority decision approvingly cites Judge Boudin's concurrence in *Lotus Development Corp. v. Borland Int'l, Inc.*, the First Circuit decision on the copyrightability of aspects of a spreadsheet program's user interface you read in Chapter II. Does that suggest anything about the majority's view of copyrightability here?

3. Although the Supreme Court underscores that its ruling is confined to the facts of the case, its multiple supportive citations of two Ninth Circuit decisions involving reverse engineering software for interoperability suggests a possible broader applicability of the fair use decision.

The first of those cases, *Sega Enterprises Ltd. v. Accolade, Inc.*, 977 F.2d 1510 (9th Cir. 1993), involved a copyright infringement lawsuit by Sega, a maker of video game systems and video game cartridges, against Accolade, another maker of video game cartridges, for reverse engineering Sega's programs to discern the requirements to make its own video games compatible with Sega's system. This reverse engineering involved "transform[ing] the machine-readable object code contained in commercially available copies of Sega's game cartridges into human-readable source code using a process called 'disassembly' or 'decompilation.'" Accolade engineers then "experimented to discover the interface specifications for [Sega's] console by modifying the programs and studying the results," from which they created a development manual about how to make a Sega-compatible game. The Ninth Circuit held that this reverse engineering process, which necessarily involved copying Sega's computer programs, constituted fair use. With regard to the first fair use factor, the court emphasized that it weighed in Accolade's favor because Accolade's copying was only to discover the functional requirements for compatibility with Sega's console, aspects that are not copyrightable, and was an intermediate use on the way to creating its own video games. The court emphasized that the second fair use factor "is important to the resolution of cases such as th[is] one." It reasoned that "[b]ecause Sega's video game programs contain unprotected aspects that cannot be examined without copying, we afford them a lower degree of protection than more traditional literary works." The court also found that the third and fourth fair use factors favored Accolade.

In the second Ninth Circuit decision cited approvingly by the Supreme Court, Connectix Corporation had reverse engineered the interoperability specifications for the Sony PlayStation console to enable its games to be run on the Apple iMac computer platform instead of only through the PlayStation console attached to a television. Sony Computer Entertainment, Inc. v. Connectix Corp., 203 F.3d 596 (9th Cir. 2000). Connectix created the Virtual Game Station, a PlayStation emulator for the iMac to emulate the PlayStation's hardware and software. Sony sued Connectix, claiming that when Connectix reverse engineered Sony's PlayStation code during the course of creating the emulator, it infringed Sony's copyright in the code. How is this set of facts and marketplace realities alike or different than in *Sega*? The Ninth Circuit concluded that Connectix's intermediate copies of Sony's copyrighted code that it made in the course of reverse engineering the PlayStation were protected by fair use. In addition to following *Sega*'s analysis, the Ninth Circuit observed that "Connectix's Virtual Game Station is modestly transformative. The product creates a new platform, the personal computer, on which consumers can play games designed for the Sony PlayStation. This innovation affords opportunities for game play in new environments, specifically anywhere a Sony PlayStation console and television are not available, but a computer with a CD-ROM drive is. More important, the Virtual Game Station itself is a wholly new product, notwithstanding the similarity of uses and functions between the Sony PlayStation and the Virtual Game Station."

4. For an analysis of how copyright law ought to handle reverse engineering of others' software, in light of concerns about interoperability and the software marketplace, see Pamela Samuelson & Suzanne Scotchmer, *The Law and Economics of Reverse Engineering*, 111 YALE L.J. 1575 (2002).

5. In *Google*, the district court had asked a jury to rule on fair use. Is fair use an appropriate question to have a jury determine? Do you think a judge or jury is better equipped to assess fair use? As *Google* makes clear, the Supreme Court views fair use as a mixed question of law and fact.

7. Appropriation Art

Over the years, there have been prominent infringement cases about whether a visual artist can use preexisting artwork from another artist for use in subsequent "appropriation art." The Second Circuit decided an important case in this area in *Rogers v. Koons*, 960 F.2d 301 (2d Cir. 1992). In that case, photographer Art Rogers sued artist Jeff Koons for copyright infringement. Koons had created his sculpture "String of Puppies" based on Rogers' photograph "Puppies," which Koons claimed to have purchased in the form of a notecard in a "very commercial, tourist-like card shop." Rogers' photograph and Koons' sculpture are shown in Figure 110.

Koons created "String of Puppies" as one of twenty sculptures for an exhibition he called the *Banality Show*. The Second Circuit recounted Koons' understanding of the show and the pieces he was creating for it:

> He believed [Rogers' photograph] to be typical, commonplace and familiar. The notecard was also similar to other images of people holding animals that Koons had collected. Thus, he viewed the picture as part of the mass culture—"resting in the collective sub-consciousness of people regardless of whether the card had actually ever been seen by such people."

> [Koons] gave his artisans one of Rogers' notecards and told them to copy it. But in order to guide the creation of a three-dimensional sculptural piece from the two-dimensional photograph, Koons communicated extensively with the ... [s]tudio. He visited it once a week during the period the piece was being carved by the workers and gave them written instructions. In his "production notes" Koons stressed that he wanted "Puppies" copied faithfully in the sculpture....

Three of the four copies Koons made sold for a total of $367,000. Koons defended himself against Rogers' claim of infringement by asserting fair use. In particular, he maintained that his sculpture is a protected parody or satire. As explained by the Second Circuit, Koons argued that *his sculpture is a satire or parody of society at large. He insists that "String of Puppies" is a fair social criticism and asserts to support that proposition that he belongs to the school of American artists who believe the mass production of commodities and media images has caused a deterioration in the quality of society, and this artistic tradition of which he is a member proposes through incorporating these images into works of art to comment critically both on the incorporated object and the political and economic system that created it. These themes, Koons states, draw upon the artistic movements of Cubism and Dadaism, with particular influence attributed to Marcel Duchamp, who in 1913 became the first to incorporate manufactured objects (readymades) into a work of art, directly influencing Koons' work and the work of other contemporary American artists.*

Figure 110: Art Rogers "Puppies" photograph (top), and Jeff Koons "String of Puppies" sculpture (bottom)

The Second Circuit refused to accept Koons' characterization of his work as a parody of Rogers':

[T]he copied work must be, at least in part, an object of the parody, otherwise there would be no need to conjure up the original work.

We think this is a necessary rule, as were it otherwise there would be no real limitation on the copier's use of another's copyrighted work to make a statement on some aspect of society at large. If an infringement of copyrightable expression could be justified as fair use solely on the basis of the infringer's claim to a higher or different artistic use—without insuring public awareness of the original work—there would be no practicable boundary to the fair use defense. Koons' claim that his infringement of Rogers' work is fair use solely because he is acting within an artistic tradition of commenting upon the commonplace thus cannot be accepted. The rule's function is to insure that credit is given where credit is due. By requiring that the copied work be an object of the parody, we merely insist that the audience be aware that underlying the parody there is an original and separate expression, attributable to a different artist. This awareness may come from the fact that the copied work is publicly known or because its existence is in some manner acknowledged by the parodist in connection with the parody. Of course, while our view of this matter does not necessarily prevent Koons' expression, although it may, it does recognize that any such exploitation must at least entail paying the customary price.

The problem in the instant case is that even given that "String of Puppies" is a satirical critique of our materialistic society, it is difficult to discern any parody of the photograph "Puppies" itself. We conclude therefore that this first factor of the fair use doctrine cuts against a finding of fair use. The circumstances of this case indicate that Koons' copying of the photograph "Puppies" ... did not constitute a parody of the original work.

The court proceeded to find that Koons was not entitled to a fair use defense, as the other three statutory fair use factors also weighed against Koons.

This decision caused some observers to think that creators of appropriation art would rarely be able to assert fair use as a successful defense unless the appropriated art was itself well-known. *E.g.*, Willajeanne F. McLean, *All's Not Fair in Art and War: A Look at the Fair Use Defense After* Rogers v. Koons, 59 BROOK. L. REV. 373 (1993).

Yet in *Blanch v. Koons*, 467 F.3d 244 (2d Cir. 2006), another infringement lawsuit against Jeff Koons over a decade later, the Second Circuit found fair use. For his "Easyfun-Ethereal" series, "Koons culled images from advertisements or his own photographs, scanned them into a computer, and digitally superimposed the scanned images against backgrounds of pastoral landscapes. He then printed color images of the resulting collages for his assistants to use as templates for applying paint to billboard-sized, 10' x 14' canvasses." One painting in the series, "Niagara," as shown in Figure 111 on the right, "consists of fragmentary images collaged against the backdrop of a landscape. The painting depicts four pairs of women's feet and lower legs dangling prominently over images of confections—a large chocolate fudge brownie topped with ice cream, a tray of donuts, and a tray of apple danish pastries—with a grassy field and Niagara Falls in the background." One of the pairs of legs in "Niagara" came from a photograph by Andrea Blanch, which had appeared in the August 2000 issue of *Allure* magazine as part of a feature on metallic cosmetics and is shown on the left in Figure 111. Blanch sued Koons for copyright infringement.

In concluding that Koons's use of Blanch's photograph was fair, the court found the use to be transformative. Koons had submitted an affidavit that he sought to "comment on the ways in which some of our most basic appetites—for food, play, and sex—are mediated by popular images." "By re-contextualizing these fragments as I do, I try to compel the viewer to break out of the conventional way of experiencing a particular appetite as mediated by mass media." The court reasoned that "Koons is, by his own undisputed description, using Blanch's image as fodder for his commentary on the social and aesthetic consequences of mass media. His stated objective is thus not to repackage Blanch's [photograph], but to employ it in the creation of new information, new aesthetics, new insights and understandings. When, as here, the copyrighted work is used as raw material in the furtherance of distinct creative or communicative objectives, the use is transformative." The court also thought the first fair use factor weighed in favor of Koons even though "'Niagara' … may be better characterized … as satire [than parody]—its message appears to target the genre of which 'Silk Sandals' is typical, rather than the individual photograph itself." The Second Circuit reasoned that "Koons had a genuine creative rationale for borrowing Blanch's image, rather than using it merely" to get attention or avoid doing his own work. The court thought the second factor carried little weight and the third and fourth factors favored Koons.

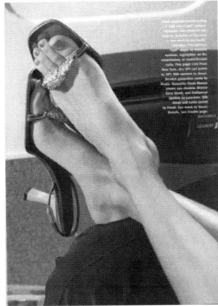

Figure 111: Andrea Blanch's "Silk Sandals by Gucci" photograph (left), and Jeff Koons' "Niagara" (right)

In a subsequent case in the Second Circuit on appropriation art, the court concluded that most, but not necessarily all, of defendant Richard Prince's appropriations of plaintiff Patrick Cariou's photographs were fair use. At issue was the use of Cariou's photographs that he took while he spent six years living with Rastafarians in Jamaica and which were published in a book *Yes Rasta*. An example is shown in Figure 112.

Figure 112: photograph from Patrick Cariou's *Yes Rasta*

Prince bought copies of Cariou's book and used photographs in them to create his *Canal Zone* series. The series has thirty-one pieces of art, thirty of which incorporate whole or partial images from *Yes Rasta*. Two examples of Prince's works from this series are shown in Figure 113.

 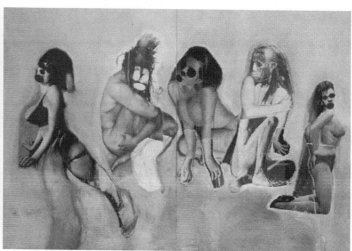

Figure 113: artwork from Richard Prince's *Canal Zone* series

Cariou sued Prince for infringement. As to the first fair use factor, the Second Circuit reasoned:

> [O]ur observation of Prince's artworks themselves convinces us of the transformative nature of all but five.... These twenty-five of Prince's artworks manifest an entirely different aesthetic from Cariou's photographs. Where Cariou's serene and deliberately composed portraits and landscape photographs depict the natural beauty of Rastafarians and their surrounding environs, Prince's crude and jarring works, on the other hand, are hectic and provocative. Cariou's black-and-white photographs were printed in a 9 1/2" x 12" book. Prince has created collages on canvas that incorporate color, feature distorted human and other forms and settings, and measure between ten and nearly a hundred times the size of the photographs. Prince's composition, presentation, scale, color palette, and media are fundamentally different and new compared to the photographs, as is the expressive nature of Prince's work.
>
> Prince's deposition testimony further demonstrates his drastically different approach and aesthetic from Cariou's. Prince testified that he "[doesn't] have any real[] interest in what [another artist's] original intent is because ... what I do is I completely try to change it into something that's completely different.... I'm trying to make a kind of fantastic, absolutely hip, up to date, contemporary take on the music scene." ...
>
> The district court based its conclusion that Prince's work is not transformative in large part on Prince's deposition testimony that he "do[es]n't really have a message," that he was not "trying to create anything with a new meaning or a new message," and that he "do[es]n't have any ... interest in [Cariou's] original intent." On appeal, Cariou argues that we must hold Prince to his testimony and that we are not to consider how Prince's works may reasonably be perceived unless Prince claims that they were satire or parody. No such rule exists, and we do not analyze satire or parody differently from any other transformative use.
>
> It is not surprising that, when transformative use is at issue, the alleged infringer would go to great lengths to explain and defend his use as transformative. Prince did not do so here. However, the fact that Prince did not provide those sorts of explanations in his deposition—which might have lent strong support to his defense—is not dispositive. What is critical is how the work

in question appears to the reasonable observer, not simply what an artist might say about a particular piece or body of work. Prince's work could be transformative even without commenting on Cariou's work or on culture, and even without Prince's stated intention to do so. Rather than confining our inquiry to Prince's explanations of his artworks, we instead examine how the artworks may reasonably be perceived in order to assess their transformative nature....

Cariou v. Prince, 714 F.3d 694, 706-07 (2d Cir. 2013). Should authorial intent be relevant? Should the ordinary observer's reaction be the touchstone of transformativeness? For how *Cariou*'s analytical framework aligns with reader response theory, a literary theory that situates the reader of a work as the focal point through which to assess a work's meaning, see Laura A. Heymann, *Reasonable Appropriation and Reader Response*, 9 U.C. IRVINE L. REV. 343 (2019); Laura A. Heymann, *Everything Is Transformative: Fair Use and Reader Response*, 31 COLUM. J.L. & ARTS 445 (2008).

This series of cases on appropriation art in the Second Circuit culminated in this recent decision. Can you reconcile *Rogers*, *Blanch*, *Cariou*, and this decision? How favorable is the Second Circuit to appropriation art? Is it right to be concerned about the breadth of transformativeness?

Andy Warhol Foundation for the Visual Arts, Inc. v. Lynn Goldsmith
11 F.4th 26 (2d Cir. 2021)

LYNCH, J.:

[1] This case concerns a series of silkscreen prints and pencil illustrations created by the visual artist Andy Warhol based on a 1981 photograph of the musical artist Prince that was taken by Defendant-Appellant Lynn Goldsmith in her studio, and in which she holds copyright. In 1984, Goldsmith's agency, Defendant-Appellant Lynn Goldsmith, Ltd. ("LGL"), then known as Lynn Goldsmith, Inc., licensed the photograph to *Vanity Fair* magazine for use as an artist reference. Unbeknownst to Goldsmith, that artist was Warhol. Also unbeknownst to Goldsmith (and remaining unknown to her until 2016), Warhol did not stop with the image that *Vanity Fair* had commissioned him to create, but created an additional fifteen works, which together became known as the Prince Series.

[2] Goldsmith first became aware of the Prince Series after Prince's death in 2016. Soon thereafter, she notified Plaintiff-Appellee The Andy Warhol Foundation for the Visual Arts, Inc. ("AWF"), successor to Warhol's copyright in the Prince Series, of the perceived violation of her copyright in the photo. In 2017, AWF sued Goldsmith and LGL for a declaratory judgment that the Prince Series works were non-infringing or, in the alternative, that they made fair use of Goldsmith's photograph. Goldsmith and LGL countersued for infringement. The United States District Court for the Southern District of New York granted summary judgment to AWF on its assertion of fair use and dismissed Goldsmith and LGL's counterclaim with prejudice.

[3] Goldsmith and LGL contend that the district court erred in its assessment and application of the four fair-use factors. In particular, they argue that the district court's conclusion that the Prince Series works are transformative was grounded in a subjective evaluation of the underlying artistic message of the works rather than an objective assessment of their purpose and character. We agree. We further agree that the district court's error in analyzing the first factor was compounded in its analysis of the remaining three factors. We conclude upon our own assessment of the record that all four factors favor Goldsmith and that the Prince Series works are not fair use as a matter of law....

Chapter VI – Fair Use

[4] Goldsmith is a professional photographer primarily focusing on celebrity photography, including portrait and concert photography of rock-and-roll musicians. Goldsmith has been active since the 1960s, and her work has been featured widely, including on over 100 record album covers. Goldsmith also founded LGL, the first photo agency focused on celebrity portraiture. LGL represents the work of over two hundred photographers worldwide, including Goldsmith herself.

[5] Andy Warhol ... was an artist recognized for his significant contributions to contemporary art in a variety of media. Warhol is particularly known for his silkscreen portraits of contemporary celebrities. Much of his work is broadly understood as commenting on consumer culture and exploring the relationship between celebrity culture and advertising. AWF is a New York not-for-profit corporation established in 1987 after Warhol's death. AWF holds title to and copyright in much of Warhol's work, which it licenses to generate revenue to further its mission of advancing the visual arts, particularly work that is experimental, under-recognized, or challenging in nature.

[6] On December 3, 1981, while on assignment from Newsweek magazine, Goldsmith took a series of portrait photographs of (then) up-and-coming musician Prince Rogers Nelson (known through most of his career simply as "Prince") in her studio. Goldsmith testified that, prior to Prince's arrival at her studio, she arranged the lighting in a way to showcase his chiseled bone structure. Goldsmith also applied additional makeup to Prince, including eyeshadow and lip gloss, which she testified was intended both to build a rapport with Prince and to accentuate his sensuality. Goldsmith further testified that she was trying to capture Prince's "willing[ness] to bust through what must be [his] immense fears to make the work that [he] wanted to [make]." Goldsmith took black-and-white and color photographs using a Nikon 35-mm camera and a mixture of 85- and 105-mm lenses, which she chose to best capture the shape of Prince's face.

[7] Prince, who according to Goldsmith appeared nervous and uncomfortable, retired to the green room shortly after the session began and ultimately left without allowing Goldsmith to take any additional photographs. During the truncated session, Goldsmith took 23 photographs, 12 in black and white and 11 in color. Goldsmith retained copyright in each of the photographs that she took. Most relevant to this litigation is the following photograph, hereinafter referred to as the "Goldsmith Photograph":

Figure 114: Lynn Goldsmith's photograph of Prince

[8] In 1984, Goldsmith, through LGL, licensed the Goldsmith Photograph to *Vanity Fair* magazine for use as an artist reference. Esin Goknar, who was photo editor at *Vanity Fair* in 1984, testified that the term "artist reference" meant that an artist "would create a work of art based on [the] image reference." The license permitted *Vanity Fair* to publish an illustration based on the Goldsmith Photograph in its November 1984 issue, once as a full page and once as a quarter page. The license further required that the illustration be accompanied by an attribution to Goldsmith. Goldsmith was unaware of the license at the time and played no role in selecting the Goldsmith Photograph for submission to *Vanity Fair*.

[9] *Vanity Fair*, in turn, commissioned Warhol to create an image of Prince for its November 1984 issue. Warhol's illustration, together with an attribution to Goldsmith, was published accompanying an article about Prince by Tristan Vox and appeared as follows:

Figure 115: *Vanity Fair* with Andy Warhol's illustration of Goldsmith's photograph

[10] In addition to the credit that ran alongside the image, a separate attribution to Goldsmith was included elsewhere in the issue, crediting her with the "source photograph" for the Warhol illustration. *Vanity Fair* did not advise Goldsmith that Warhol was the artist for whom her work would serve as a reference, and she did not see the article when it was initially published.

[11] Unbeknownst to Goldsmith and LGL, Warhol created 15 additional works based on the Goldsmith Photograph, known collectively, and together with the *Vanity Fair* image, as the "Prince Series." The Prince Series comprises fourteen silkscreen prints (twelve on canvas, two on paper) and two pencil illustrations, and includes the following images:

Figure 116: some images from Andy Warhol's "Prince Series"

[12] Although the specific means that Warhol used to create the images is unknown (and, perhaps, at this point, unknowable), Neil Printz, the editor of the *Andy Warhol Catalogue Raisonné*, testified that it was Warhol's usual practice to reproduce a photograph as a high-contrast two-tone image on acetate that, after any alterations Warhol chose to make, would be used to create a silkscreen. For the canvas prints, Warhol's general practice was to paint the background and local colors prior to the silkscreen transfer of the image. Paper prints, meanwhile, were generally created entirely by the silkscreen process without any painted embellishments. Finally, Warhol's typical practice for pencil sketches was to project an image onto paper and create a contoured pencil drawing around the projected image.

[13] At some point after Warhol's death, AWF acquired title to and copyright in the Prince Series. Between 1993 and 2004, AWF sold or otherwise transferred custody of 12 of the original Prince Series works to third parties, and, in 1998, transferred custody of the other four works to The Andy Warhol Museum. AWF retains copyright in the Prince Series images and, through The Artist Rights Society (a third-party organization that serves as AWF's agent), continues to license the images for editorial, commercial, and museum usage.

[14] On April 22, 2016, the day after Prince died, Condé Nast, *Vanity Fair*'s parent company, contacted AWF. Its initial intent in doing so was to determine whether AWF still had the 1984 image, which Condé Nast hoped to use in connection with a planned magazine commemorating Prince's life. After learning that AWF had additional images from the Prince Series, Condé Nast ultimately obtained a commercial license, to be exclusive for three months, for a different Prince Series image for the cover of the planned tribute magazine. Condé Nast published the tribute magazine in May 2016 with a Prince Series image on the cover. Goldsmith was not given any credit or attribution for the image, which was instead attributed solely to AWF.

[15] It was at that point that Goldsmith first became aware of the Prince Series. In late July 2016, Goldsmith contacted AWF to advise it of the perceived infringement of her copyright. That November, Goldsmith registered the Goldsmith Photograph with the U.S. Copyright Office as an unpublished work. On April 7, 2017, AWF sued Goldsmith and LGL for a declaratory judgment of non-infringement or, in the alternative, fair use. Goldsmith countersued for copyright infringement ....

[16] On July 1, 2019, the district court granted summary judgment for AWF on its fair-use claim. Upon evaluating the four statutory fair-use factors set forth in 17 U.S.C. § 107, the court concluded that: (1) the Prince Series was "transformative" because, while the Goldsmith Photograph portrays Prince as "not a comfortable person" and a "vulnerable human being," the Prince Series portrays Prince as an "iconic, larger-than-life figure"; (2) although the Goldsmith Photograph is both creative and unpublished, which would traditionally weigh in Goldsmith's favor, this was "of limited importance because the Prince Series works are transformative works"; (3) in creating the Prince Series, Warhol "removed nearly all [of] the [Goldsmith] [P]hotograph's protectible elements"; and (4) the Prince Series works "are not market substitutes that have harmed – or have the potential to harm – Goldsmith". This appeal followed....

[17] As the Supreme Court has held, fair use presents a holistic, context-sensitive inquiry not to be simplified with bright-line rules. All four statutory factors are to be explored, and the results weighed together, in light of the purposes of copyright. Indeed, the Supreme Court has explained that courts must "apply [fair use] in light of the sometimes conflicting aims of copyright law" and that "copyright's protection may be stronger where the copyrighted material ... serves an artistic rather than a utilitarian function." Google v. Oracle.

[18] With those competing goals in mind, we consider each factor to determine whether AWF can avail itself of the fair-use defense in this case. We hold that it cannot.

A. The Purpose and Character of The Use

[19] This factor requires courts to consider the extent to which the secondary work is "transformative," as well as whether it is commercial. We address these considerations separately below.

1. Transformative Works and Derivative Works

[20] Following the Supreme Court's decision in *Campbell*, our assessment of this first factor has focused chiefly on the degree to which the use is "transformative," i.e., "whether the new work merely supersedes the objects of the original creation, or instead adds something new, with a further purpose or different character, altering the first with new expression, meaning, or message." *See also Google* ("[W]e have used the word 'transformative' to describe a copying use that adds something new and important."). We evaluate whether a work is transformative by examining how it may reasonably be perceived. Paradigmatic examples of transformative uses are those Congress itself enumerated in the preamble to § 107: "criticism, comment, news reporting, teaching …, scholarship, or research." And, as the Supreme Court recognized in *Campbell*, parody, which "needs to mimic an original to make its point," is routinely held transformative. These examples are easily understood: the book review excerpting a passage of a novel in order to comment upon it serves a manifestly different purpose from the novel itself.

[21] Although the most straightforward cases of fair use thus involve a secondary work that comments on the original in some fashion, in *Cariou v. Prince*, we rejected the proposition that a secondary work must comment on the original in order to qualify as fair use. In that case, we considered works of appropriation artist Richard Prince that incorporated, among other materials, various black-and-white photographs of Rastafarians taken by Patrick Cariou. After concluding that the district court had imposed a requirement unsupported by the Copyright Act, we conducted our own examination of Prince's works and concluded that twenty-five of the thirty at issue were transformative of Cariou's photographs as a matter of law. In reaching this conclusion, we observed that Prince had incorporated Cariou's "serene and deliberately composed portraits and landscape photographs" into his own "crude and jarring works … [that] incorporate[d] color, feature[d] distorted human and other forms and settings, and measure[d] between ten and nearly a hundred times the size of the photographs." Thus, we concluded that these works "used [Cariou's photographs] as raw material, transformed in the creation of new information, new aesthetics, new insights and understandings," and were transformative within the meaning of this first factor.

[22] In adjudging the Prince Series transformative, the district court relied chiefly on our decision in *Cariou*, which we have previously described as the "high-water mark of our court's recognition of transformative works." TCA Television Corp. v. McCollum, 839 F.3d 168 (2d Cir. 2016). And … that decision has not been immune from criticism. While we remain bound by *Cariou*, and have no occasion or desire to question its correctness on its own facts, our review of the decision below persuades us that some clarification is in order.

[23] … [B]oth the Supreme Court and this Court have emphasized that fair use is a context-sensitive inquiry that does not lend itself to simple bright-line rules. Notwithstanding, the district court appears to have read *Cariou* as having announced such a rule, to wit, that any secondary work is necessarily transformative as a matter of law "[i]f looking at the works side-by-side, the secondary work has a different character, a new expression, and employs new aesthetics with [distinct] creative and communicative results." Although a literal construction of certain passages of *Cariou* may support that proposition, such a reading stretches the decision too far.

[24] Of course, the alteration of an original work with new expression, meaning, or message, whether by the use of new aesthetics, by placing the work in a different context, or by any other means is the sine qua non of transformativeness. It does not follow, however, that any secondary work that adds a new aesthetic or new expression to its source material is necessarily transformative.

[25] Consider the five works at issue in *Cariou* that we did not conclude were transformative as a matter of law. Though varying in degree both amongst themselves and as compared to the works that we did adjudge transformative, each undoubtedly imbued Cariou's work with a "new aesthetic" as that phrase might be colloquially understood. Prince's *Canal Zone* (2007) is a collage of thirty-six of Cariou's photographs, most of which Prince altered by, for example, painting over the faces and bodies of Cariou's subjects, in some instances altering them significantly. In *Graduation*, Prince added blue "lozenges" over the eyes and mouth of Cariou's subject and pasted an image of hands playing a blue guitar over his hands. Both of these works certainly imbued the originals from which they derive with a "new aesthetic;" notwithstanding, we could not confidently make a determination about their transformative nature as a matter of law.

[26] Moreover, there exists an entire class of secondary works that add new expression, meaning, or message to their source material, but may nonetheless fail to qualify as fair use: derivative works. There is some inherent tension in the Copyright Act between derivative works, reserved to the copyright holder, which are defined in part as works that "recast[], *transform*[], or adapt[]" an original work, (emphasis added), and "transformative" fair uses of the copyrighted work by others. Thus, as we have previously observed, an overly liberal standard of transformativeness, such as that employed by the district court in this case, risks crowding out statutory protections for derivative works. *See Authors Guild* ("[T]he word 'transformative,' if interpreted too broadly, can also seem to authorize copying that should fall within the scope of an author's derivative rights.").

[27] We addressed derivative works in *Cariou*, characterizing them as secondary works that merely present "the same material but in a new form" without "add[ing] something new." While that description may be a useful shorthand, it is likewise susceptible to misapplication if interpreted too broadly. Indeed, many derivative works that "add something new" to their source material would not qualify as fair use.

[28] Consider, for example, a film adaptation of a novel. Such adaptations frequently add quite a bit to their source material: characters are combined, eliminated, or created out of thin air; plot elements are simplified or eliminated; new scenes are added; the moral or political implications of the original work may be eliminated or even reversed, or plot and character elements altered to create such implications where the original text eschewed such matters. And all of these editorial modifications are filtered through the creative contributions of the screenwriter, director, cast, camera crew, set designers, cinematographers, editors, sound engineers, and myriad other individuals integral to the creation of a film. It is for that reason that we have recognized that when a novel is converted to a film the invention of the original author combines with the cinematographic interpretive skills of the filmmaker to produce something that neither could have produced independently. Despite the extent to which the resulting movie may transform the aesthetic and message of the underlying literary work, film adaptations are identified as a paradigmatic example of derivative works.

[29] In evaluating the extent to which a work is transformative in the fair use context, we consider the "purpose and character" of the primary and secondary works. Google. In *Bill Graham Archives v. Dorling Kindersley Ltd.*, for example, we held that the reproduction in a book about the Grateful Dead of images of posters originally created to advertise Grateful Dead concerts was transformative because that use was "plainly different from the original purpose for which they were created." Likewise, in [a companion case to *Authors Guild*] we held that the defendants' creation of a searchable "digital corpus" comprising scanned copies of tens of millions of books that enabled researchers, scholars, and others to pinpoint the exact page of any book in the catalogue on which the searched term was used was a "quintessentially transformative use." In *Authors Guild*, we reached the same conclusion when faced with a larger digital corpus complete with tools that enabled researchers to track how a specific word or phrase has been used throughout the development of the English language, despite the fact that ... Google's database also permitted the searcher to view a "snippet" from the original text showing the context in which the word or phrase had appeared. And most recently, in *Google*, the Supreme Court held that fair use protected Google's "precise[]" copying of certain computer programming language in part because Google sought "to create new products ... [and] expand the use and usefulness of ... smartphones"

with it. Thus, the Supreme Court concluded, "the 'purpose and character' of Google's copying was transformative."

[30] But purpose is perhaps a less useful metric where, as here, our task is to assess the transformative nature of works of visual art that, at least at a high level of generality, share the same overarching purpose (i.e., to serve as works of visual art). While this is not the first time we have had to conduct this inquiry, our cases on such works are considerably fewer in number, and a brief review of them yields conflicting guidance. In *Blanch v. Koons*, for example, we adjudged transformative a Jeff Koons painting that incorporated a copyrighted photograph drawn from a fashion magazine where Koons had testified that he intended to "us[e] Blanch's image as fodder for his commentary on the social and aesthetic consequences of mass media." Some time earlier, however, in *Rogers v. Koons*, we denied Koons's fair-use defense as applied to a three-dimensional sculpture recreating a photograph, notwithstanding his claim that he intended his sculpture to serve as a commentary on modern society.[3] And, in *Cariou*, we held twenty-five of Richard Prince's works transformative as a matter of law even though Prince had testified that he "was not 'trying to create anything with a new meaning or a new message.'"

[31] Matters become simpler, however, when we compare the works at issue in each case against their respective source materials. The sculpture at issue in *Rogers* was a three-dimensional colorized version of the photograph on which it was based. In *Blanch*, however, Koons used Blanch's photograph, depicting a woman's legs in high-heeled shoes, as part of a larger work in which he set it alongside several other similar photographs with changes of its colors, the background against which it is portrayed, the medium, the size of the objects pictured, and the objects' details. In so doing, Koons used Blanch's photograph as raw material for an entirely different type of art that commented on existing images by juxtaposing them against others. And in *Cariou*, the copyrighted works found to have been fairly used were, in most cases, juxtaposed with other photographs and obscured and altered to the point that Cariou's original was barely recognizable. The works that were found potentially infringing in *Cariou*, however, were ones in which the original was altered in ways that did not incorporate other images and that superimposed other elements that did not obscure the original image and in which the original image remained, as in the Koons sculpture at issue in *Rogers*, a major if not dominant component of the impression created by the allegedly infringing work.

[32] A common thread running through these cases is that, where a secondary work does not obviously comment on or relate back to the original or use the original for a purpose other than that for which it was created, the bare assertion of a higher or different artistic use is insufficient to render a work transformative. Rather, the secondary work itself must reasonably be perceived as embodying a distinct artistic purpose, one that conveys a new meaning or message separate from its source material. While we cannot, nor do we attempt to, catalog all of the ways in which an artist may achieve that end, we note that the works that have done so thus far have themselves been distinct works of art that draw from numerous sources, rather than works that simply alter or recast a single work with a new aesthetic.

[33] Which brings us back to the Prince Series. The district court held that the Prince Series works are transformative because they "can reasonably be perceived to have transformed Prince from a vulnerable, uncomfortable person to an iconic, larger-than-life figure." That was error.

[34] Though it may well have been Goldsmith's subjective intent to portray Prince as a "vulnerable human being" and Warhol's to strip Prince of that humanity and instead display him as a popular icon, whether a work is transformative cannot turn merely on the stated or perceived intent of the artist or the meaning or impression

---

[3] We note that *Rogers* predates the Supreme Court's formal adoption of the "transformative use" test and thus does not phrase its inquiry in precisely the same manner as the cases that have followed. However, it remains a precedential decision of this Court, and we believe it particularly relevant in this case.

that a critic—or for that matter, a judge—draws from the work. Were it otherwise, the law may well recognize any alteration as transformative.

[35] In conducting this inquiry, however, the district judge should not assume the role of art critic and seek to ascertain the intent behind or meaning of the works at issue. That is so both because judges are typically unsuited to make aesthetic judgments and because such perceptions are inherently subjective. As Goldsmith argues, her own stated intent notwithstanding, "an audience viewing the [Goldsmith] [P]hotograph today, across the vista of the singer's long career, might well see him in a different light than Goldsmith saw him that day in 1981." We agree; it is easy to imagine that a whole generation of Prince's fans might have trouble seeing the Goldsmith Photograph as depicting anything other than the iconic songwriter and performer whose musical works they enjoy and admire.

[36] Instead, the judge must examine whether the secondary work's use of its source material is in service of a fundamentally different and new artistic purpose and character, such that the secondary work stands apart from the raw material used to create it. Although we do not hold that the primary work must be barely recognizable within the secondary work, as was the case with the works held transformative in *Cariou*, the secondary work's transformative purpose and character must, at a bare minimum, comprise something more than the imposition of another artist's style on the primary work such that the secondary work remains both recognizably deriving from, and retaining the essential elements of, its source material.

[37] With this clarification, viewing the works side-by-side, we conclude that the Prince Series is not "transformative" within the meaning of the first factor. That is not to deny that the Warhol works display the distinct aesthetic sensibility that many would immediately associate with Warhol's signature style – the elements of which are absent from the Goldsmith photo. But the same can be said, for example, of the Ken Russell film, from a screenplay by Larry Kramer, derived from D.H. Lawrence's novel, *Women in Love*: the film is as recognizable a "Ken Russell" as the Prince Series are recognizably "Warhols." But the film, for all the ways in which it transforms (that is, in the ordinary meaning of the word, which indeed is used in the very definition of derivative works) its source material, is also plainly an adaptation of the Lawrence novel.

[38] As in the case of such paradigmatically derivative works, there can be no meaningful dispute that the overarching purpose and function of the two works at issue here is identical, not merely in the broad sense that they are created as works of visual art,[5] but also in the narrow but essential sense that they are portraits of the same person.[6] Although this observation does not per se preclude a conclusion that the Prince Series makes fair use of the Goldsmith Photograph, the district court's conclusion rests significantly on the transformative character of Warhol's work. But the Prince Series works can't bear that weight.

[39] Warhol created the series chiefly by removing certain elements from the Goldsmith Photograph, such as depth and contrast, and embellishing the flattened images with loud, unnatural colors. Nonetheless, although we do not conclude that the Prince Series works are necessarily derivative works as a matter of law, they are much closer to presenting the same work in a different form, that form being a high-contrast screenprint, than

[5] The fact that the Goldsmith Photograph and the Prince Series were both created for artistic purposes makes this a different case from, for example, "[a]n artistic painting ... precisely replicat[ing] a copyrighted advertising logo to make a comment about consumerism" (such as Warhol's well-known depictions of Campbell's soup cans), which "might ... fall within the scope of fair use." *Google*.

[6] As much as art critics might distinguish Warhol's aesthetic intentions from those of portrait photographers, Warhol's celebrity prints are invariably identifiable likenesses of their subjects. The district court's description of the Prince Series works as transformative because they "can reasonably be perceived to have transformed Prince from a vulnerable, uncomfortable person to an iconic, larger-than-life figure," rests implicitly on the Warhol depiction being perceived as a recognizable depiction of Prince.

they are to being works that make a transformative use of the original. Crucially, the Prince Series retains the essential elements of the Goldsmith Photograph without significantly adding to or altering those elements.

[40] Indeed, the differences between the Goldsmith Photograph and the Prince Series here are in many respects less substantial than those made to the five works that we could not find transformative as a matter of law in *Cariou*. Unlike the Prince Series, those works unmistakably deviated from Cariou's original portraiture in a manner that suggested an entirely distinct artistic end; rather than recasting those photographs in a new medium, Richard Prince added material that pulled them in new directions. Nevertheless, we could not confidently determine whether those modest alterations amounted to a substantial transformation of the original works of art such that the new works were transformative, and remanded the case to the district court to make that determination in the first instance.

[41] In contrast, the Prince Series retains the essential elements of its source material, and Warhol's modifications serve chiefly to magnify some elements of that material and minimize others. While the cumulative effect of those alterations may change the Goldsmith Photograph in ways that give a different impression of its subject, the Goldsmith Photograph remains the recognizable foundation upon which the Prince Series is built.

[42] Finally, we feel compelled to clarify that it is entirely irrelevant to this analysis that each Prince Series work is immediately recognizable as a "Warhol." Entertaining that logic would inevitably create a celebrity-plagiarist privilege; the more established the artist and the more distinct that artist's style, the greater leeway that artist would have to pilfer the creative labors of others. But the law draws no such distinctions; whether the Prince Series images exhibit the style and characteristics typical of Warhol's work (which they do) does not bear on whether they qualify as fair use under the Copyright Act. As Goldsmith notes, the fact that Martin Scorsese's recent film *The Irishman* is recognizably "a Scorsese" "do[es] not absolve [him] of the obligation to license the original book" on which it is based.

[43] In reaching this conclusion, we do not mean to discount the artistic value of the Prince Series itself. As used in copyright law, the words "transformative" and "derivative" are legal terms of art that do not express the simple ideas that they carry in ordinary usage. We do not disagree with AWF's contention that the cumulative effect of Warhol's changes to the Goldsmith Photograph is to produce a number of striking and memorable images. And our conclusion that those images are closer to what the law deems "derivative" (and not "transformative") does not imply that the Prince Series (or Warhol's art more broadly) is "derivative," in the pejorative artistic sense, of Goldsmith's work or of anyone else's. As Goldsmith succinctly puts it, "[t]here is little doubt ... that the Prince Series reflects Andy Warhol's talent, creativity, and distinctive aesthetic." But the task before us is not to assess the artistic worth of the Prince Series nor its place within Warhol's oeuvre; that is the domain of art historians, critics, collectors, and the museum-going public. Rather, the question we must answer is simply whether the law permits Warhol to claim it as his own, and AWF to exploit it, without Goldsmith's permission. And, at least as far as this aspect of the first factor is concerned, we conclude that the answer to that question is "no."

2. Commercial Use

[44] The statutory language of the first factor also specifically directs courts to consider "whether [the] use is of a commercial nature or is for nonprofit educational purposes." Although finding that a secondary use is commercial tends to weigh against finding that it is fair, we apply the test with caution since nearly all of the illustrative uses listed in the preamble paragraph of § 107 are generally conducted for profit in this country.[7]

---

[7] To recognize this is not to read the commercial/non-profit factor out of the statute. There are other situations in which the absence or presence of a commercial motive may be highly significant. Producing a small number of copies of a short story

And, since the crux of the profit/nonprofit distinction is whether the user stands to profit from exploitation of the copyrighted material without paying the customary price, the commercial nature of a secondary use is of decreased importance when the use is sufficiently transformative such that the primary author should not reasonably expect to be compensated.

[45] We agree with the district court that the Prince Series works are commercial in nature, but that they produce an artistic value that serves the greater public interest. We also agree that, although more relevant to the character of the user than of the use, the fact that AWF's mission is to advance the visual arts, a mission that is doubtless in the public interest, may militate against the simplistic assertion that AWF's sale and licensing of the Prince Series works necessarily derogates from a finding of fair use. Nevertheless, just as we cannot hold that the Prince Series is transformative as a matter of law, neither can we conclude that Warhol and AWF are entitled to monetize it without paying Goldsmith the customary price for the rights to her work, even if that monetization is used for the benefit of the public.

[46] Of course, even where the secondary use is not transformative, the extent to which it serves the public interest, either in and of itself or by generating funds that enable the secondary user to further a public-facing mission, may be highly relevant when assessing equitable remedies, including whether to enjoin the distribution or order the destruction of infringing works. But just as the commercial nature of a transformative secondary use does not itself preclude a finding that the use is fair, the fact that a commercial non-transformative work may also serve the public interest or that the profits from its commercial use are turned to the promotion of non-commercial ends does not factor significantly in favor of finding fair use under the circumstances present here.

B. The Nature of the Copyrighted Work

[47] The second factor directs courts to consider the nature of the copyrighted work, including (1) whether it is expressive or creative or more factual, with a greater leeway being allowed to a claim of fair use where the work is factual or informational, and (2) whether the work is published or unpublished, with the scope of fair use involving unpublished works being considerably narrower.

[48] The district court correctly held that the Goldsmith Photograph is both unpublished and creative but nonetheless concluded that the second factor should favor neither party because LGL had licensed the Goldsmith Photograph to *Vanity Fair* and because the Prince Series was highly transformative. That was error. That Goldsmith, through LGL, made the Goldsmith Photograph available for a single use on limited terms does not change its status as an unpublished work nor diminish the law's protection of her choice of when to make a work public and whether to withhold a work to shore up demand. Further, though we have previously held that this factor may be of limited usefulness where the creative work is being used for a transformative purpose, this relates only to the weight assigned to it, not whom it favors.

[49] Having recognized the Goldsmith Photograph as both creative and unpublished, the district court should have found this factor to favor Goldsmith irrespective of whether it adjudged the Prince Series works transformative within the meaning of the first factor. And, because we disagree that the Prince Series works are transformative, we would accord this factor correspondingly greater weight.

C. The Amount and Substantiality of the Use ...

[50] In this case, AWF argues, and the district court concluded, that this factor weighs in its favor because, by cropping and flattening the Goldsmith Photograph, thereby removing or minimizing its use of light, contrast,

---

to be distributed for free to a high school English class may be quite different from producing a similar number of copies for a lavishly bound and illustrated "limited edition" of the work to be sold in the marketplace at a high price.

shading, and other expressive qualities, Warhol removed nearly all of its copyrightable elements. We do not agree.

[51] We begin with the uncontroversial proposition that copyright does not protect ideas, but only the original or unique way that an author expresses those ideas, concepts, principles, or processes. As applied to photographs, this protection encompasses the photographer's posing the subjects, lighting, angle, selection of film and camera, evoking the desired expression, and almost any other variant involved. The cumulative manifestation of these artistic choices – and what the law ultimately protects – is the image produced in the interval between the shutter opening and closing, i.e., the photograph itself. This is, as we have previously observed, the photographer's particular expression of the idea underlying her photograph.

[52] It is thus easy to understand why AWF's contention misses the mark. The premise of its argument is that Goldsmith cannot copyright Prince's face. True enough. Were it otherwise, nobody else could have taken the man's picture without either seeking Goldsmith's permission or risking a suit for infringement. But while Goldsmith has no monopoly on Prince's face, the law grants her a broad monopoly on its image as it appears in her photographs of him, including the Goldsmith Photograph. And where, as here, the secondary user has used the photograph itself, rather than, for example, a similar photograph, the photograph's specific depiction of its subject cannot be neatly reduced to discrete qualities such as contrast, shading, and depth of field that can be stripped away, taking the image's entitlement to copyright protection along with it.

[53] With that in mind, we readily conclude that the Prince Series borrows significantly from the Goldsmith Photograph, both quantitatively and qualitatively. While Warhol did indeed crop and flatten the Goldsmith Photograph, the end product is not merely a screenprint identifiably based on a photograph of Prince. Rather it is a screenprint readily identifiable as deriving from a specific photograph of Prince, the Goldsmith Photograph. A comparison of the images in the Prince Series makes plain that Warhol did not use the Goldsmith Photograph simply as a reference or aide-mémoire in order to accurately document the physical features of its subject. Instead, the Warhol images are instantly recognizable as depictions or images of the Goldsmith Photograph itself.

[54] To confirm this, one need look no further than the other photographs of Prince that AWF submitted in support of its motion below to evidence its contention that Prince's pose was not unique to the Goldsmith Photograph. Though any of them may have been suitable as a base photograph for Warhol's process, we have little doubt that the Prince Series would be quite different had Warhol used one of them instead of the Goldsmith Photograph to create it. But the resemblance between the Prince Series works and the Goldsmith Photograph goes even further; for example, many of the aspects of Prince's appearance in the Prince Series works, such as the way in which his hair appears shorter on the left side of his face, are present in the Goldsmith Photograph yet absent even from some other photographs that Goldsmith took of Prince during the same photo session. In other words, whatever the effect of Warhol's alterations, the essence of Goldsmith's photograph was copied and persists in the Prince Series. Indeed, Warhol's process had the effect of amplifying, rather than minimizing, certain aspects of the Goldsmith Photograph.[10]

[55] Nor can Warhol's appropriation of the Goldsmith Photograph be deemed reasonable in relation to his purpose. While Warhol presumably required a photograph of Prince to create the Prince Series, AWF proffers no reason why he required Goldsmith's photograph. To the contrary, the evidence in the record suggests that

---

[10] For example, the fact that Prince's mustache appears to be lighter on the right side of his face than the left is barely noticeable in the grayscale Goldsmith Photograph but is quite pronounced in the black-and-white Prince Series screenprints. Moreover, this feature of the Goldsmith Photograph is, again, not common to all other photographs of Prince even from that brief session. The similarity is not simply an artefact of what Prince's facial hair was like on that date, but of the particular effects of light and angle at which Goldsmith captured that aspect of his appearance.

Warhol had no particular interest in the Goldsmith Photograph or Goldsmith herself; *Vanity Fair* licensed a photograph of Prince, and there is no evidence that Warhol (or, for that matter, *Vanity Fair*) was involved in identifying or selecting the particular photograph that LGL provided.

[56] To be clear, we do not hold that this factor will always favor the copyright holder where the work at issue is a photograph and the photograph remains identifiable in the secondary work. But this case is not *Kienitz v. Sconnie Nation LLC*, in which a panel of the Seventh Circuit held that a t-shirt design that incorporated a photograph in a manner that stripped away nearly every expressive element such that, "as with the Cheshire Cat, only the [subject's] smile remain[ed]" was fair use. 766 F.3d 756, 759 (7th Cir. 2014). As discussed, Warhol's rendition of the Goldsmith Photograph leaves quite a bit more detail, down to the glint in Prince's eyes where the umbrellas in Goldsmith's studio reflected off his pupils. Thus, though AWF urges this court to follow the Seventh Circuit's lead, its decision in Kienitz would not compel a different result here, even if it were binding on us—which, of course, it is not.

[57] The district court, reasoning that Warhol had taken only the unprotected elements of the Goldsmith Photograph in service of a transformative purpose, held that this factor strongly favored AWF. Because we disagree on both counts, we conclude that this factor strongly favors Goldsmith.

D. The Effect of the Use on the Market for the Original ...

[58] We agree with the district court that the primary market for the Warhol Prince Series (that is, the market for the original works) and the Goldsmith Photograph do not meaningfully overlap, and Goldsmith does not seriously challenge that determination on appeal. We cannot, however, endorse the district court's implicit rationale that the market for Warhol's works is the market for "Warhols," as doing so would permit this aspect of the fourth factor always to weigh in favor of the alleged infringer so long as he is sufficiently successful to have generated an active market for his own work. Notwithstanding, we see no reason to disturb the district court's overall conclusion that the two works occupy distinct markets, at least as far as direct sales are concerned.

[59] We are unpersuaded, however, by the district court's conclusion that the Prince Series poses no threat to Goldsmith's licensing markets. While Goldsmith does not contend that she has sought to license the Goldsmith Photograph itself, the question under this factor is not solely whether the secondary work harms an existing market for the specific work alleged to have been infringed. Rather, we must also consider whether unrestricted and widespread conduct of the sort engaged in by AWF would result in a substantially adverse impact on the potential market for the Goldsmith Photograph.

[60] As an initial matter, we note that the district court erred in apparently placing the burden of proof as to this factor on Goldsmith. While our prior cases have suggested that the rightsholder bears some initial burden of identifying relevant markets, we have never held that the rightsholder bears the burden of showing actual market harm. Nor would we so hold. Fair use is an affirmative defense; as such, the ultimate burden of proving that the secondary use does not compete in the relevant market is appropriately borne by the party asserting the defense: the secondary user.

[61] In any case, whatever the scope of Goldsmith's initial burden, she satisfied it here. Setting aside AWF's licensing of Prince Series works for use in museum exhibits and publications about Warhol, which is not particularly relevant for the reasons set out in our discussion of the primary market for the works, there is no material dispute that both Goldsmith and AWF have sought to license (and indeed have successfully licensed) their respective depictions of Prince[12] to popular print magazines to accompany articles about him. As

---

[12] In Goldsmith's case, photographs other than the Goldsmith Photograph, which she has withheld from the market.

Goldsmith succinctly states: "both [works] are illustrations of the same famous musician with the same overlapping customer base." Contrary to AWF's assertions, that is more than enough. And, since Goldsmith has identified a relevant market, AWF's failure to put forth any evidence that the availability of the Prince Series works poses no threat to Goldsmith's actual or potential revenue in that market tilts the scales toward Goldsmith.

[62] Further, the district court entirely overlooked the potential harm to Goldsmith's derivative market, which is likewise substantial. Most directly, AWF's licensing of the Prince Series works to Condé Nast without crediting or paying Goldsmith deprived her of royalty payments to which she would have otherwise been entitled. Although we do not always consider lost royalties from the challenged use itself under the fourth factor (as any fair use necessarily involves the secondary user using the primary work without paying for the right to do so), we do consider them where the secondary use occurs within a traditional or reasonable market for the primary work. And here, that market is established both by Goldsmith's uncontroverted expert testimony that photographers generally license others to create stylized derivatives of their work in the vein of the Prince Series, and by the genesis of the Prince Series: a licensing agreement between LGL and *Vanity Fair* to use the Goldsmith Photograph as an artist reference.[13]

[63] We also must consider the impact on this market if the sort of copying in which Warhol engaged were to become a widespread practice. That harm is also self-evident. There currently exists a market to license photographs of musicians, such as the Goldsmith Photograph, to serve as the basis of a stylized derivative image; permitting this use would effectively destroy that broader market, as, if artists could use such images for free, there would be little or no reason to pay for them. This, in turn, risks disincentivizing artists from producing new work by decreasing its value—the precise evil against which copyright law is designed to guard.

[64] Finally, our analysis of the fourth factor also "take[s] into account the public benefits the copying will likely produce." *Google*. AWF argues that weighing the public benefit cuts in its favor because "[d]enying fair-use protection to works like Warhol's will chill the creation of art that employs pre-existing imagery to convey a distinct message." We disagree. Nothing in this opinion stifles the creation of art that may reasonably be perceived as conveying a new meaning or message, and embodying a new purpose, separate from its source material. AWF also lists the possible consequences that it contends will flow if we deny fair use in this case. As discussed *supra*, however, those consequences would be significant to a district court primarily when assessing appropriate equitable relief for a copyright violation. And here, Goldsmith expressly disclaims seeking some of the most extreme remedies available to copyright owners. Moreover, what encroaches on Goldsmith's market is AWF's commercial licensing of the Prince Series, not Warhol's original creation. Thus, art that is not turned into a commercial replica of its source material, and that otherwise occupies a separate primary market, has significantly more breathing space than the commercial licensing of the Prince Series.

[65] Thus, although the primary market for the Goldsmith Photograph and the Prince Series may differ, the Prince Series works pose cognizable harm to Goldsmith's market to license the Goldsmith Photograph to publications for editorial purposes and to other artists to create derivative works based on the Goldsmith Photograph and similar works. Further, the public benefit of the copying at issue in this case does not outweigh the harm identified by Goldsmith. Accordingly, the fourth factor favors Goldsmith.

---

[13] Of course, if a secondary work is sufficiently transformative, the fact that its "raw material" was acquired by means of a limited license will not necessarily defeat a defense of fair use. As discussed *supra*, however, that is not the case here.

E. Weighing the Factors

[66] This court has on numerous occasions resolved fair use determinations at the summary judgment stage where there are no genuine issues of material fact. As no party contends that there exist any issues of material fact in this case, we believe it appropriate to exercise that discretion here.

[67] Having considered each of the four factors, we find that each favors Goldsmith. Further, although the factors are not exclusive, AWF has not identified any additional relevant considerations unique to this case that we should take into account. Accordingly, we hold that AWF's defense of fair use fails as a matter of law.

F. The Effect of *Google*

[68] AWF's petition relies heavily on the Supreme Court's *Google* decision. As AWF notes, *Google* is the Supreme Court's first major decision on fair use in some time, and we granted the petition for rehearing in large part to give careful consideration to that opinion. After such consideration, we emphatically reject AWF's assertion that *Google* "comprehensively refutes the panel's reasoning." To the contrary, as an attentive reading of the discussion above will show, the principles enunciated in *Google* are fully consistent with our original opinion.

[69] AWF's argument that *Google* undermines our analysis rests on a misreading of both the Supreme Court's opinion and ours, misinterpreting both opinions as adopting hard and fast categorical rules of fair use. To the contrary, both opinions recognize that determinations of fair use are highly contextual and fact specific, and are not easily reduced to rigid rules. As the Supreme Court put it, both the historical background of fair use and modern precedent "make[] clear that the concept [of fair use] is flexible, that courts must apply it in light of the sometimes conflicting aims of copyright law, and that its applications may well vary depending upon context." *Google*.

[70] In particular, the Supreme Court in *Google* took pains to emphasize that the unusual context of that case, which involved copyrights in computer code, may well make its conclusions less applicable to contexts such as ours. Thus, while *Google* did indeed find that the precise copying and incorporation of copyrighted code into a new program could (and did, on the particular facts of the case) constitute fair use, the opinion expressly noted that "copyright's protection may be stronger where the copyrighted material ... serves an artistic rather than a utilitarian function." The Court repeatedly emphasized that "[t]he fact that computer programs are primarily functional makes it difficult to apply traditional copyright concepts in that technological world." If the application of traditional copyright concepts to "functional" computer programs is difficult, it follows that a case that addresses fair use in such a novel and unusual context is unlikely to work a dramatic change in the analysis of established principles as applied to a traditional area of copyrighted artistic expression. And indeed, the Supreme Court did not leave that conclusion to inference, expressly advising that in addressing fair use in this new arena, it "ha[d] not changed the nature of those [traditional copyright] concepts."

[71] Just as AWF misreads the fact- and context-specific finding of fair use in *Google* as dictating a result in the very different context before us, it misreads our opinion as "effectively outlawing" an entire "genre" of art "widely viewed as one of the great artistic innovations of the modern era." As any fair reading of our opinion shows, we do not "outlaw" any form of artistic expression, nor do we denigrate any artistic genre; as we explicitly state, it is not the function of judges to decide the meaning and value of art, still less to "outlaw" types of art.

[72] We merely insist that, just as artists must pay for their paint, canvas, neon tubes, marble, film, or digital cameras, if they choose to incorporate the existing copyrighted expression of other artists in ways that draw their purpose and character from that work (as by using a copyrighted portrait of a person to create another portrait of the same person, recognizably derived from the copyrighted portrait, so that someone seeking a

portrait of that person might interchangeably use either one), they must pay for that material as well. As the Supreme Court again recognized in *Google*, the aims of copyright law are "sometimes conflicting." The issue here does not pit novel forms of art against philistine censorship, but rather involves a conflict between artists each seeking to profit from his or her own creative efforts. Copyright law does not provide either side with absolute trumps based on simplistic formulas. Rather, it requires a contextual balancing based on principles that will lead to close calls in particular cases. Like the Supreme Court in *Google*, we have applied those well-established principles to the particular facts before us to conclude that AWF's fair-use defense fails....

JACOBS, J., concurring:

[73] I concur in the opinion of the Court. I write briefly to make a single point....

[74] ... [I]t is useful to emphasize that the holding does not consider, let alone decide, whether the infringement here encumbers the original Prince Series works that are in the hands of collectors or museums, or, in general, whether original works of art that borrow from protected material are likely to infringe.

[75] The sixteen original works have been acquired by various galleries, art dealers, and the Andy Warhol Museum. This case does not decide their rights to use and dispose of those works because Goldsmith does not seek relief as to them. She seeks damages and royalties only for licensed reproductions of the Prince Series.

[76] Although the Andy Warhol Foundation initiated this suit with a request for broader declaratory relief that would cover the original works, Goldsmith did not join issue. The Declaratory Judgment Act is reserved for disputes that are percolating over parties' rights and obligations while harm threatens to accrue. But Goldsmith does not claim that the original works infringe and expresses no intention to encumber them; the opinion of the Court necessarily does not decide that issue.

[77] The issue, however, still looms, and our holding may alarm or alert possessors or creators of other artistic works. Warhol's works are among many pieces that incorporate, appropriate, or borrow from protected material. Risk of a copyright suit or uncertainty about an artwork's status can inhibit the creative expression that is a goal of copyright. So it matters that a key consideration in this case is the harm that the commercial licensing of the Prince Series poses to Goldsmith's market to license her photograph.

[78] As the opinion observes, the photograph and the original Prince Series works have distinct markets. They are not substitutes. An original work of art is marked by the hand or signature of the artist, which is a preponderating factor in its value. But when a work is reproduced, it loses that mystique, as anyone who has browsed a gift shop can appreciate. Thus there is overlap in the licensing markets for the Prince Series and the photograph.

[79] When one of the Prince Series works is licensed to a magazine, it functions as a portrait of the musician Prince—as does Goldsmith's photograph. The Prince Series retains the photograph's expressive capacity for Prince portraiture and is used for that purpose. It may well compete for magazine covers, posters, coffee mugs, and other items featuring the late musician. If the Foundation had refuted the evidence of such market displacement, the weight of the analytical considerations would have changed.

[80] The distinction between the original and licensed Prince Series works is likewise important when it comes to assessing the market effect alongside "the public benefits the copying will likely produce." *Google*. The "public benefits" considered here are those associated with the only use at issue: the Foundation's commercial licensing. This use has nothing to do with copyright's concern for the creative production of new expression. Had the use been Warhol's use of the photograph to construct the modified image, we would need to reassess.

NOTES

1. The Supreme Court has since granted certiorari in *Andy Warhol Foundation*. A decision is expected in 2022-23.

2. Richard Prince is currently the defendant in multiple other copyright infringement lawsuits over his *New Portraits* series. This series consisted almost entirely of other people's Instagram posts, as shown in Figure 117. Richard Prince created the *New Portraits* series by searching other people's Instagram posts; when he found an image he liked, he added his own online comment to the user's post, screen-grabbed the image, and emailed it to an assistant, who had it inkjet-printed and stretched on canvas. The resulting series of six-by-four-foot works sold for $90,000 to $100,000 each. Prince's only changes to the users' Instagram posts (other than printing them out in large format) were the addition of his own brief online comments, alternately salacious and nonsensical, often appropriated from things he heard on television as he found the image. The bulk of the photos he chose from Instagram were vaguely prurient selfies of young, attractive women. They also included a smattering of artists and celebrities like Taylor Swift and Kate Moss. Several of the *New Portraits* were based on photos posted by the Suicide Girls, young women in an alt-porn pin-up collective.

Figure 117: Richard Prince's *New Portraits* series (installation view)

Four different parties whose images Prince appropriated have sued him for copyright infringement. In one of those cases, a district court has denied Prince's motion to dismiss on the ground that Prince's use of the plaintiff's photograph was not transformative as a matter of law—as per *Cariou*—because "Prince's work does not belong to a class of secondary works that are so aesthetically different from the originals that they can pass the Second Circuit's 'reasonable viewer' test as a matter of law." Graham v. Prince, 265 F. Supp. 3d 366, 380 (S.D.N.Y. 2017). As the court explained, Prince "simply reproduces the entirety of Graham's photograph—with some de minimis cropping—in the frame of an Instagram post, along with a cryptic comment written by Prince."

Yet one set of "victims" responded to the appropriation in true Richard Prince spirit. Rather than filing a lawsuit, the Suicide Girls decided to retaliate by reappropriating Prince's appropriations of five of their original images. They then sold the reappropriations themselves online, underselling their copyist in the marketplace. Like Prince, they made a slight alteration to each appropriated image, adding their own comment after Prince's added comment before printing. Their added comment was overtly shaming: "true art." Other than that, they produced works identical to his: inkjet-printed canvases of the same Instagram posts in the same dimensions. The dramatic difference was price. Instead of Prince's $90,000 price tag, the Suicide Girls' nearly identical copies were offered at a mere $90. All profits from their sales went to the nonprofit organization Electronic Frontier

Foundation. Figure 118 shows an image from the Suicide Girls' website advertising one of their reappropriations of Prince's appropriation, side by side.

Figure 118: Suicide Girls' advertisement

The Suicide Girls' move was an instant internet sensation, as bloggers and reporters hailed the Suicide Girls' act of payback. Appealing to the sense of online outrage that Prince's appropriation had caused, the Suicide Girls portrayed themselves as—and indeed might have felt like—online avenging goddesses. Suicide Girls founder Missy Suicide told the press that "The thing about Prince's theft of the images is that it feels like such a violation by someone who doesn't get it." She pondered, "Do we have Mr. Prince's permission to sell these prints? We have the same permission from him that he had from us. ;)." The move elicited not only adoring media coverage. It also generated sales. In one day, the Suicide Girls sold more than 250 prints and soon the entire run sold out. Indeed, Richard Prince himself retweeted their retakings of "his" work, in effect advertising the copies. Instead of seeing the Suicide Girls as siphoning from his profit, Prince welcomed the Suicide Girls on the gravy train, tweeting that the move was "smart."

The Suicide Girls' reappropriation raised money, spread their fame, enacted a sort of public revenge on their appropriator, and vindicated the connection the creators felt to their work. As Missy Suicide explained, "Instagram is such an expression of our identity and to have an old dude steal [our Instagram photos] and get paid such a significant fee for them hurt. We have seen more attention from media and have received tons of messages of support, it has been a little overwhelming, in a good way."

This jiu-jitsu self-help move stood in stark contrast to the conventional litigation route chosen by other unhappy subjects of Prince's works. Unlike litigation, which can be long, expensive, and, as we know from Prince's previous litigation, uncertain in outcome with regard to fair use, the Suicide Girls made a quick and big splash, achieving an immediate sense of vindication, spreading their fame, making money (for charity), and gaining new admirers for their vigilante response. For other examples of people taking copyright law into their own hands and analysis of whether this phenomenon should be celebrated or extinguished, see Amy Adler & Jeanne C. Fromer, *Taking Intellectual Property into Their Own Hands*, 107 CALIF. L. REV. 1455 (2019).

3. For an argument that the transformative test "poses a fundamental threat to art because the test evaluates art by the very criteria that contemporary art rejects," see Amy Adler, *Fair Use and the Future of Art*, 91 N.Y.U. L. REV. 559 (2016). Specifically, Adler argues that "the transformative inquiry asks precisely the wrong questions about contemporary art. It requires courts to search for 'meaning' and 'message' when one goal of so much current art is to throw the idea of stable meaning into play. It requires courts to ask if that message is 'new' when so much contemporary art rejects the goal of newness, using copying as a primary building block of creativity."

4. Now that you've read many copyright decisions on fair use, consider whether you find courts' analyses predictable. Scholars are divided on this question. Some find it to be unpredictable. *See, e.g.*, Deidré A. Keller, *Recognizing the Derivative Works Right as a Moral Right: A Case Comparison and Proposal*, 63 CASE W. RES. L. REV. 511 (2012); Jason Mazzone, *Administering Fair Use*, 51 WM. & MARY L. REV. 395 (2009). Others think that even though fair use comes in many versions, there are patterns and coherence to it. *See, e.g.*, Michael J. Madison, *A Pattern-Oriented Approach to Fair Use*, 45 WM. & MARY L. REV. 1525 (2004); Pamela Samuelson, *Unbundling Fair Uses*, 77 FORDHAM L. REV. 2537 (2009).

Barton Beebe has comprehensively studied all reported federal court decisions on fair use under the 1976 Act. Among other things, Beebe shows that "the outcomes of factors one and four very strongly correlated with the test outcome and fairly strongly correlated with each other, while the outcome of factor two correlated weakly, if at all, with the outcome of the test and with the outcomes of the other factors." Barton Beebe, *An Empirical Study of U.S. Copyright Fair Use Opinions, 1978-2005*, 156 U. PA. L. REV. 549, 584 (2008). Matthew Sag has also shown empirically how significant transformative use is in determining the outcome of fair use cases. Matthew Sag, *Predicting Fair Use*, 73 OHIO ST. L.J. 47 (2012).

5. Jason Mazzone proposes that an administrative body be empowered to help clarify fair use. He proposes "two possible models of agency regulation. In the first model, an agency is responsible for generating regulations that determine what constitutes fair use in specific contexts as well as preventing efforts to interfere with fair uses of copyrighted works. In the second model, an agency issues fair use regulations and determines prior to any copyright infringement claim being brought in court whether the use in question constitutes fair use. Agency regulation can bring much needed clarity and predictability to fair use in ways that neither Congress nor the courts are able to accomplish; an agency can also protect fair use in ways that the market does not." Jason Mazzone, *Administering Fair Use*, 51 WM. & MARY L. REV. 395, 396 (2009). Do you agree with this approach? Is the sort of "fair use agency" that Mazzone proposes vulnerable to regulatory capture, that is to influence by industries that appear regularly before the agency and which may serve as a primary source of employment for officials who have left the agency?

6. Gideon Parchomovsky and Kevin Goldman suggest a different approach to make fair use more certain and predictable: safe harbors. Gideon Parchomovsky & Kevin A. Goldman, *Fair Use Harbors*, 93 VA. L. REV. 1483, 1488-89 (2007). They suggest

> reforming fair use through the recognition of certain types of copying as per se fair. Uses that fall
> within these bounds would not give rise to liability for copyright infringement, so actors who
> engage in them would be categorically immune from suit. Carefully tailored, safe harbors would
> provide much needed certainty to users and potential creators without unduly compromising the

rights of current copyright owners. Thus, the introduction of a bright-line rule component into the doctrine of fair use has the potential to significantly enhance social welfare.

7. Parchomovsky and Goldman's approach is somewhat similar to that adopted in other countries, in which there is a list of exceptions to copyright infringement rather than a general standard like fair use. For example, the European Union's 2019 Directive on Copyright in the Digital Single Market includes an exception from copyright infringement for text and data mining for purposes of scientific research. Article 3. As another illustration, the Directive exempts from infringement uses of copyrighted works for "digital and cross-border teaching activities." Article 5.

VII. Direct and Secondary Liability

In many instances, more than one party may be responsible in some way for the infringement of the copyright in a work. For example, imagine that an individual uses a peer-to-peer file-sharing system to locate and obtain a digital file containing a copyrighted motion picture, which has been made available by another user of the peer-to-peer network without the permission of the copyright owner. Is the user who receives the digital file through the peer-to-peer network liable for infringement? Is the user of the peer-to-peer network who makes the file available liable? Is the firm that creates the software for the peer-to-peer network liable? Are the companies that have made the computers that were used to share files liable? Are businesses that run banner advertisements on the software interface used to operate the peer-to-peer network liable?

As you shall see, copyright law has developed doctrines that determine who can be held liable, either directly or "secondarily," in situations, like the one described above, in which a number of actors may be said to be connected in some way to an act of infringement. This chapter begins by describing the rules governing **direct liability** for copyright infringement. It will then move on to describe the rules of **secondary liability**—liability for those who are not direct infringers, but who somehow assist, encourage, control, benefit from, or otherwise participate in the infringing conduct. The chapter will then consider special rules governing the **liability of online service providers**, as well as the **liability of the manufacturers of devices that can be used for infringement**.

As you read this chapter, pay close attention to the origin of both the direct and secondary liability rules. As you shall see, few of the rules governing either direct or secondary liability are specified in the Copyright Act. These rules have been developed by courts, not Congress. A substantial exception can be found in § 512 of the Copyright Act, which delineates a set of detailed rules limiting the secondary liability of online service providers.

A. Volition as an Element of Direct Liability

As you read the next case, consider whether the concept of "volition" is a good proxy for who is most "directly" responsible for copyright infringement. Are there instances in which you would consider the exercise of volition to be more or less relevant to moral responsibility?

Religious Technology Center v. Netcom On-Line Communication Services, Inc.
907 F. Supp. 1361 (N.D. Cal. 1995)

WHYTE, J.:

[1] This case concerns an issue of first impression regarding intellectual property rights in cyberspace. Specifically, this order addresses whether the operator of a computer bulletin board service ("BBS"), and the large Internet access provider that allows that BBS to reach the Internet, should be liable for copyright infringement committed by a subscriber of the BBS.

[2] Plaintiffs Religious Technology Center and Bridge Publications, Inc. hold copyrights in the unpublished and published works of L. Ron Hubbard, the late founder of the Church of Scientology. Defendant Dennis Erlich is a former minister of Scientology turned vocal critic of the Church, whose pulpit is now the Usenet newsgroup alt.religion.scientology ("a.r.s."), an on-line forum for discussion and criticism of Scientology. Plaintiffs

maintain that Erlich infringed their copyrights when he posted portions of their works on a.r.s. Erlich gained his access to the Internet through defendant Thomas Klemesrud's BBS "support.com." Klemesrud is the operator of the BBS, which is run out of his home and has approximately 500 paying users. Klemesrud's BBS is not directly linked to the Internet, but gains its connection through the facilities of defendant Netcom On-Line Communications, Inc., one of the largest providers of Internet access in the United States.

[3] After failing to convince Erlich to stop his postings, plaintiffs contacted defendants Klemesrud and Netcom. Klemesrud responded to plaintiffs' demands that Erlich be kept off his system by asking plaintiffs to prove that they owned the copyrights to the works posted by Erlich. However, plaintiffs refused Klemesrud's request as unreasonable. Netcom similarly refused plaintiffs' request that Erlich not be allowed to gain access to the Internet through its system. Netcom contended that it would be impossible to prescreen Erlich's postings and that to kick Erlich off the Internet meant kicking off the hundreds of users of Klemesrud's BBS. Consequently, plaintiffs named Klemesrud and Netcom in their suit against Erlich ....

[4] To establish a claim of copyright infringement, a plaintiff must demonstrate (1) ownership of a valid copyright and (2) "copying" of protectable expression by the defendant. Infringement occurs when a defendant violates one of the exclusive rights of the copyright holder.... The court has already determined that plaintiffs have established that they own the copyrights .... The court also found plaintiffs likely to succeed on their claim that defendant Erlich copied the [plaintiffs'] works and was not entitled to a fair use defense. Plaintiffs argue that, although Netcom was not itself the source of any of the infringing materials on its system, it nonetheless should be liable for infringement ... directly ....

[5] The parties do not dispute the basic processes that occur when Erlich posts his allegedly infringing messages to a.r.s. Erlich connects to Klemesrud's BBS using a telephone and a modem. Erlich then transmits his messages to Klemesrud's computer, where they are automatically briefly stored. According to a prearranged pattern established by Netcom's software, Erlich's initial act of posting a message to the Usenet results in the automatic copying of Erlich's message from Klemesrud's computer onto Netcom's computer and onto other computers on the Usenet. In order to ease transmission and for the convenience of Usenet users, Usenet servers maintain postings from newsgroups for a short period of time—eleven days for Netcom's system and three days for Klemesrud's system. Once on Netcom's computers, messages are available to Netcom's customers and Usenet neighbors, who may then download the messages to their own computers. Netcom's local server makes available its postings to a group of Usenet servers, which do the same for other servers until all Usenet sites worldwide have obtained access to the postings, which takes a matter of hours.

[6] Unlike some other large on-line service providers, such as CompuServe, America Online, and Prodigy, Netcom does not create or control the content of the information available to its subscribers. It also does not monitor messages as they are posted. It has, however, suspended the accounts of subscribers who violated its terms and conditions, such as where they had commercial software in their posted files. Netcom admits that, although not currently configured to do this, it may be possible to reprogram its system to screen postings containing particular words or coming from particular individuals. Netcom, however, took no action after it was told by plaintiffs that Erlich had posted messages through Netcom's system that violated plaintiffs' copyrights, instead claiming that it could not shut out Erlich without shutting out all of the users of Klemesrud's BBS....

[7] The Ninth Circuit addressed the question of what constitutes infringement in the context of storage of digital information in a computer's random access memory ("RAM"). *MAI Systems Corp. v. Peak Computer, Inc.*, 991 F.2d 511, 518 (9th Cir. 1993). {You read about this case in Chapter II, on fixation.} In *MAI*, the Ninth Circuit upheld a finding of copyright infringement where a repair person, who was not authorized to use the computer owner's licensed operating system software, turned on the computer, thus loading the operating

system into RAM for long enough to check an "error log." Copyright protection subsists in original works of authorship "*fixed* in any tangible medium of expression, now known or later developed, from which they can be perceived, reproduced, or otherwise communicated, either directly or with the aid of a machine or device." 17 U.S.C. § 102 (emphasis added). A work is "fixed" when its "embodiment in a copy ... is sufficiently permanent or stable to permit it to be perceived, reproduced, or otherwise communicated for a period of more than transitory duration." *Id.* § 101. *MAI* established that the loading of data from a storage device into RAM constitutes copying because that data stays in RAM long enough for it to be perceived.

[8] In the present case, there is no question after *MAI* that "copies" were created, as Erlich's act of sending a message to a.r.s. caused reproductions of portions of plaintiffs' works on both Klemesrud's and Netcom's storage devices. Even though the messages remained on their systems for at most eleven days, they were sufficiently "fixed" to constitute recognizable copies under the Copyright Act.

[9] Accepting that copies were made, Netcom argues that Erlich, and not Netcom, is directly liable for the copying.... [T]he mere fact that Netcom's system incidentally makes temporary copies of plaintiffs' works does not mean Netcom has caused the copying. The court believes that Netcom's act of designing or implementing a system that automatically and uniformly creates temporary copies of all data sent through it is not unlike that of the owner of a copying machine who lets the public make copies with it. Although some of the people using the machine may directly infringe copyrights, courts analyze the machine owner's liability under the rubric of contributory infringement, not direct infringement. Plaintiffs' theory would create many separate acts of infringement and, carried to its natural extreme, would lead to unreasonable liability. It is not difficult to conclude that Erlich infringes by copying a protected work onto his computer and by posting a message to a newsgroup. However, plaintiffs' theory further implicates a Usenet server that carries Erlich's message to other servers regardless of whether that server acts without any human intervention beyond the initial setting up of the system. It would also result in liability for every single Usenet server in the worldwide link of computers transmitting Erlich's message to every other computer. These parties, who are liable under plaintiffs' theory, do no more than operate or implement a system that is essential if Usenet messages are to be widely distributed. There is no need to construe the Act to make all of these parties infringers. Although copyright is a strict liability statute, there should still be some element of volition or causation which is lacking where a defendant's system is merely used to create a copy by a third party.

[10] Plaintiffs point out that the infringing copies resided for eleven days on Netcom's computer and were sent out from it onto the "Information Superhighway." However, under plaintiffs' theory, any storage of a copy that occurs in the process of sending a message to the Usenet is an infringement. While it is possible that less "damage" would have been done if Netcom had heeded plaintiffs' warnings and acted to prevent Erlich's message from being forwarded, this is not relevant to its *direct* liability for copying. The same argument is true of Klemesrud and any Usenet server. Whether a defendant makes a direct copy that constitutes infringement cannot depend on whether it received a warning to delete the message....

[11] *Playboy Enterprises, Inc. v. Frena* involved a suit against the operator of a small BBS whose system contained files of erotic pictures. 839 F. Supp. 1552, 1554 (M.D. Fla. 1993). A subscriber of the defendant's BBS had uploaded files containing digitized pictures copied from the plaintiff's copyrighted magazine, which files remained on the BBS for other subscribers to download. The court did not conclude, as plaintiffs suggest in this case, that the BBS is itself liable for the unauthorized *reproduction* of plaintiffs' work; instead, the court concluded that the BBS operator was liable for violating the plaintiff's right to publicly *distribute and display* copies of its work.

[12] In support of their argument that Netcom is directly liable for copying plaintiffs' works, plaintiffs cite to the court's conclusion that "[t]here is no dispute that [the BBS operator] supplied a product containing unauthorized copies of a copyrighted work. It does not matter that [the BBS operator] claims he did not make

the copies [him]self." It is clear from the context of this discussion that the *Playboy* court was looking only at the exclusive right to distribute copies to the public, where liability exists regardless of whether the defendant makes copies. Here, however, plaintiffs do not argue that Netcom is liable for its public distribution of copies. Instead, they claim that Netcom is liable because its computers in fact made copies. Therefore, the above-quoted language has no bearing on the issue of direct liability for unauthorized reproductions. Notwithstanding *Playboy*'s holding that a BBS operator may be directly liable for *distributing or displaying* to the public copies of protected works, this court holds that the storage on a defendant's system of infringing copies and retransmission to other servers is not a direct infringement by the BBS operator of the exclusive right to *reproduce* the work where such copies are uploaded by an infringing user. *Playboy* does not hold otherwise....

[13] The court is not persuaded by plaintiffs' argument that Netcom is directly liable for the copies that are made and stored on its computer. Where the infringing subscriber is clearly directly liable for the same act, it does not make sense to adopt a rule that could lead to the liability of countless parties whose role in the infringement is nothing more than setting up and operating a system that is necessary for the functioning of the Internet. Such a result is unnecessary as there is already a party directly liable for causing the copies to be made. Plaintiffs occasionally claim that they only seek to hold liable a party that refuses to delete infringing files after they have been warned. However, such liability cannot be based on a theory of direct infringement, where knowledge is irrelevant. The court does not find workable a theory of infringement that would hold the entire Internet liable for activities that cannot reasonably be deterred. Billions of bits of data flow through the Internet and are necessarily stored on servers throughout the network and it is thus practically impossible to screen out infringing bits from noninfringing bits. Because the court cannot see any meaningful distinction (without regard to knowledge) between what Netcom did and what every other Usenet server does, the court finds that Netcom cannot be held liable for direct infringement....

NOTES

1. Who is the direct infringer in *Netcom*? Why do you think the plaintiffs didn't simply sue only the direct infringer?

2. Perhaps the pithiest summary of the court's holding in *Netcom* comes near the end of the opinion, to wit: "The court does not find workable a theory of infringement that would hold the entire Internet liable for activities that cannot reasonably be deterred." Is this a principle that is generally true in copyright law? Remember that copyright infringement is a strict liability tort. As a consequence, a defendant may be liable even for subconscious copyright infringement, such as may occur when a writer or a musician unwittingly copies protected material from a text or a song he or she has previously encountered but does not consciously recall. Does this basic aspect of copyright law fit with the court's holding in *Netcom*? If the two principles are consistent, then it is "volition" that makes the difference. But what sort of "volition" is involved in subconscious copying?

As you read the next case, refer back to the question posed in note 1, above. Why do you think the plaintiffs didn't simply sue as "direct" infringers the individual Cablevision subscribers who made the copies?

Cartoon Network LP v. CSC Holdings, Inc.
536 F.3d 121 (2d Cir. 2008)

WALKER, J.:

{Recall the facts in this case, which you first read with regard to fixation in Chapter II and encountered again with regard to public performance in Chapter V.} ...

[1] In the district court, plaintiffs successfully argued that Cablevision's proposed system would directly infringe their copyrights in three ways. First, by briefly storing data in the primary ingest buffer and other data buffers integral to the function of the RS-DVR, Cablevision would make copies of protected works and thereby directly infringe plaintiffs' exclusive right of reproduction under the Copyright Act. Second, by copying programs onto the Arroyo Server hard disks (the "playback copies"), Cablevision would again directly infringe the reproduction right. And third, by transmitting the data from the Arroyo Server hard disks to its RS-DVR customers in response to a "playback" request, Cablevision would directly infringe plaintiffs' exclusive right of public performance. Agreeing with all three arguments, the district court awarded summary declaratory judgment to plaintiffs and enjoined Cablevision from operating the RS-DVR system without obtaining licenses from the plaintiff copyright holders....

[2] On the issue of whether creation of the playback copies made Cablevision liable for direct infringement, the parties and the district court agreed that the dispositive question was "*who* makes the copies"? Emphasizing Cablevision's "unfettered discretion" over the content available for recording, its ownership and maintenance of the RS-DVR components, and its "continuing relationship" with its RS-DVR customers, the district court concluded that "the copying of programming to the RS-DVR's Arroyo servers ... would be done not by the customer but by Cablevision, albeit at the customer's request."

[3] Finally, as to the public performance right, Cablevision conceded that, during the playback, "the streaming of recorded programming in response to a customer's request is a performance." Cablevision contended, however, that the work was performed not by Cablevision, but by the customer, an argument the district court rejected "for the same reasons that [it] reject [ed] the argument that the customer is 'doing' the copying involved in the RS–DVR." ...

[4] In most copyright disputes, the allegedly infringing act and the identity of the infringer are never in doubt. These cases turn on whether the conduct in question does, in fact, infringe the plaintiff's copyright. In this case, however, the core of the dispute is over the authorship of the infringing conduct. After an RS-DVR subscriber selects a program to record, and that program airs, a copy of the program—a copyrighted work—resides on the hard disks of Cablevision's Arroyo Server, its creation unauthorized by the copyright holder. The question is *who* made this copy. If it is Cablevision, plaintiffs' theory of direct infringement succeeds; if it is the customer, plaintiffs' theory fails because Cablevision would then face, at most, secondary liability, a theory of liability expressly disavowed by plaintiffs.

[5] Few cases examine the line between direct and contributory liability. Both parties cite a line of cases beginning with *Religious Technology Center v. Netcom On–Line Communication Services*, 907 F. Supp. 1361 (N.D. Cal. 1995). In *Netcom*, a third-party customer of the defendant Internet service provider ("ISP") posted a

copyrighted work that was automatically reproduced by the defendant's computer. The district court refused to impose direct liability on the ISP, reasoning that "[a]lthough copyright is a strict liability statute, there should still be some element of volition or causation which is lacking where a defendant's system is merely used to create a copy by a third party." Recently, the Fourth Circuit endorsed the *Netcom* decision, noting that

> to establish direct *liability under ... the Act, something more must be shown than mere ownership of a machine used by others to make illegal copies. There must be actual infringing conduct with a nexus sufficiently close and causal to the illegal copying that one could conclude that the machine owner himself trespassed on the exclusive domain of the copyright owner.*

CoStar Group, Inc. v. LoopNet, Inc., 373 F.3d 544, 550 (4th Cir. 2004).

[6] Here, the district court pigeon-holed the conclusions reached in *Netcom* and its progeny as "premised on the unique attributes of the Internet." While the *Netcom* court was plainly concerned with a theory of direct liability that would effectively "hold the entire Internet liable" for the conduct of a single user, 907 F. Supp. at 1372, its reasoning and conclusions, consistent with precedents of this court and the Supreme Court, and with the text of the Copyright Act, transcend the Internet. Like the Fourth Circuit, we reject the contention that "the *Netcom* decision was driven by expedience and that its holding is inconsistent with the established law of copyright," *CoStar*, 373 F.3d at 549, and we find it "a particularly rational interpretation of § 106," *id.* at 551, rather than a special-purpose rule applicable only to ISPs.

[7] When there is a dispute as to the author of an allegedly infringing instance of reproduction, *Netcom* and its progeny direct our attention to the volitional conduct that causes the copy to be made. There are only two instances of volitional conduct in this case: Cablevision's conduct in designing, housing, and maintaining a system that exists only to produce a copy, and a customer's conduct in ordering that system to produce a copy of a specific program. In the case of a VCR, it seems clear—and we know of no case holding otherwise—that the operator of the VCR, the person who actually presses the button to make the recording, supplies the necessary element of volition, not the person who manufactures, maintains, or, if distinct from the operator, owns the machine. We do not believe that an RS-DVR customer is sufficiently distinguishable from a VCR user to impose liability as a direct infringer on a different party for copies that are made automatically upon that customer's command.

[8] The district court emphasized the fact that copying is "instrumental" rather than "incidental" to the function of the RS-DVR system. While that may distinguish the RS-DVR from the ISPs in *Netcom* and *CoStar*, it does not distinguish the RS-DVR from a VCR, a photocopier, or even a typical copy shop. And the parties do not seem to contest that a company that merely makes photocopiers available to the public on its premises, without more, is not subject to liability for direct infringement for reproductions made by customers using those copiers. They only dispute whether Cablevision is similarly situated to such a proprietor.

[9] The district court found Cablevision analogous to a copy shop that makes course packs for college professors. In the leading case involving such a shop, for example, "[t]he professor [gave] the copyshop the materials of which the coursepack [was] to be made up, and the copyshop [did] the rest." Princeton Univ. Press v. Mich. Document Servs., 99 F.3d 1381, 1384 (6th Cir.1996) (en banc). There did not appear to be any serious dispute in that case that the shop itself was directly liable for reproducing copyrighted works. The district court here found that Cablevision, like this copy shop, would be "doing" the copying, albeit "at the customer's behest."

[10] But because volitional conduct is an important element of direct liability, the district court's analogy is flawed. In determining who actually "makes" a copy, a significant difference exists between making a request to a human employee, who then volitionally operates the copying system to make the copy, and issuing a

command directly to a system, which automatically obeys commands and engages in no volitional conduct. In cases like *Princeton University Press*, the defendants operated a copying device and sold the product they made using that device. Here, by selling access to a system that automatically produces copies on command, Cablevision more closely resembles a store proprietor who charges customers to use a photocopier on his premises, and it seems incorrect to say, without more, that such a proprietor "makes" any copies when his machines are actually operated by his customers....

[11] The district court also emphasized Cablevision's "unfettered discretion in selecting the programming that it would make available for recording." This conduct is indeed more proximate to the creation of illegal copying than, say, operating an ISP or opening a copy shop, where all copied content was supplied by the customers themselves or other third parties. Nonetheless, we do not think it sufficiently proximate to the copying to displace the customer as the person who "makes" the copies when determining liability under the Copyright Act. Cablevision, we note, also has subscribers who use home VCRs or DVRs ..., and has significant control over the content recorded by these customers. But this control is limited to the channels of programming available to a customer and not to the programs themselves. Cablevision has no control over what programs are made available on individual channels or when those programs will air, if at all. In this respect, Cablevision possesses far less control over recordable content than it does in the [video-on-demand] context, where it actively selects and makes available beforehand the individual programs available for viewing. For these reasons, we are not inclined to say that Cablevision, rather than the user, "does" the copying produced by the RS-DVR system. As a result, we find that the district court erred in concluding that Cablevision, rather than its RS-DVR customers, makes the copies carried out by the RS-DVR system.

[12] Our refusal to find Cablevision directly liable on these facts is buttressed by the existence and contours of the Supreme Court's doctrine of contributory liability in the copyright context. After all, the purpose of any causation-based liability doctrine is to identify the actor (or actors) whose "conduct has been so significant and important a cause that [he or she] should be legally responsible." W. PAGE KEETON ET AL., PROSSER AND KEETON ON TORTS § 42, at 273 (5th ed. 1984). But here, to the extent that we may construe the boundaries of direct liability more narrowly, the doctrine of contributory liability stands ready to provide adequate protection to copyrighted works.

[13] Most of the facts found dispositive by the district court—e.g., Cablevision's "continuing relationship" with its RS-DVR customers, its control over recordable content, and the "instrumental[ity]" of copying to the RS-DVR system, seem to us more relevant to the question of contributory liability....

[14] The district court apparently concluded that Cablevision's operation of the RS-DVR system would contribute in such a major way to the copying done by another that it made sense to say that Cablevision was a direct infringer, and thus, in effect, was "doing" the relevant copying.... We need not decide today whether one's contribution to the creation of an infringing copy may be so great that it warrants holding that party directly liable for the infringement, even though another party has actually made the copy. We conclude only that on the facts of this case, copies produced by the RS-DVR system are "made" by the RS-DVR customer, and Cablevision's contribution to this reproduction by providing the system does not warrant the imposition of direct liability. Therefore, Cablevision is entitled to summary judgment on this point, and the district court erred in awarding summary judgment to plaintiffs....

NOTES

1. Think back to the question we asked just before this case: Why didn't the plaintiffs sue the Cablevision subscribers as "direct" infringers? The answer is, because the subscribers, who were recording television programs for personal use, were likely making fair use copies and were not themselves infringers. The Supreme Court so held on similar facts in *Sony Corp. of Am. v. Universal City Studios, Inc.*, 464 U.S. 417, 433

(1984), a case you read in Chapter VI and will revisit later in this chapter. If the Cablevision subscribers are not "direct" infringers, then Cablevision cannot be held liable as a secondary infringer. This fact explains the plaintiffs' attempt to have Cablevision held liable as a direct infringer, an argument that clashed with *Netcom*'s understanding of the sort of volition required for direct infringement.

2. *Netcom* and *Cartoon Network* both suggest that machines cannot possess the requisite volition to infringe copyright, whereas humans can. Is this distinction between human and machine a proper one? For more on this issue, see Mala Chatterjee & Jeanne C. Fromer, *Minds, Machines, and the Law: The Case of Volition in Copyright Law*, 119 COLUM. L. REV. 1887 (2019).

3. Recall *American Broadcasting Cos. v. Aereo, Inc.*, which you read in Chapter V. In particular, consider Justice Scalia's dissent. Does *Aereo* jettison the volition requirement for direct liability found in *Netcom* and *Cartoon Network*? Note that the Second and Ninth Circuits have both found, in decisions after *Aereo*, that the volition criterion for direct liability is still relevant. In *Perfect 10, Inc. v. Giganews, Inc.*, 847 F.3d 657 (9th Cir. 2017), the Ninth Circuit held that "[t]he volitional-conduct requirement is consistent with the *Aereo* majority opinion." The Second Circuit has similarly affirmed the continuing relevance of volition post-*Aereo*. BWP Media USA Inc. v. Polyvore, Inc., 922 F.3d 42 (2d Cir. 2019) (per curiam).

4. Why is the relevant "volition" the choice to make a copy, rather than the choice to build a machine that makes the copy? Think about this question as you read the material, below, on secondary liability.

B. Secondary Liability

Section 501 of the Copyright Act identifies as an infringer "[a]nyone who violates any of the exclusive rights of the copyright owner as provided by section[] 106...." 17 U.S.C. § 501(a). In turn, § 106 states that, with respect to the list of specified rights that you studied in Chapter V, "the owner of copyright ... has the *exclusive rights to do and to authorize*" the activities that implicate those rights. Id. § 106 (emphasis added). The legislative history of the 1976 Act indicates that Congress added the words "to authorize" to § 106 to confirm its intent that contributory infringers be liable under the Act. H.R. REP. NO. 94-1476, 94th Cong., 2d Sess. 61 (1976).

It is clear, in sum, that Congress meant to provide for at least one form of secondary liability for copyright infringement. It is also clear that Congress did not define the standards for secondary liability in the Copyright Act. That job, both prior to and following the enactment of the 1976 Act, has been left to the courts. As we shall see in the following cases, courts have adapted two well-established theories of secondary liability in tort to the copyright context. The first, **contributory liability,** focuses on actors who, while not directly responsible for infringement, nonetheless may be held liable for knowingly assisting or encouraging infringement. The second, **vicarious liability,** focuses on actors who, while again not directly responsible for infringement, nonetheless may be held liable because they benefit from the infringement and have the right or authority to prevent or stop it.

As you read the following cases, pay attention to the ways in which courts adapt the common law secondary liability doctrines to the special context of copyright infringement. In adapting the common law standards, do the courts alter them?

Fonovisa, Inc. v. Cherry Auction, Inc.
76 F.3d 259 (9th Cir. 1996)

SCHROEDER, J.:

[1] This is a copyright ... enforcement action against the operators of a swap meet, sometimes called a flea market, where third-party vendors routinely sell counterfeit recordings that infringe on the plaintiff's copyrights and trademarks. The district court dismissed on the pleadings, holding that the plaintiffs, as a matter of law, could not maintain any cause of action against the swap meet for sales by vendors who leased its premises.... We reverse....

[2] The plaintiff and appellant is Fonovisa, Inc., a California corporation that owns copyrights ... to Latin/Hispanic music recordings. Fonovisa filed this action in district court against defendant-appellee, Cherry Auction, Inc., and its individual operators (collectively "Cherry Auction"). For purposes of this appeal, it is undisputed that Cherry Auction operates a swap meet in Fresno, California, similar to many other swap meets in this country where customers come to purchase various merchandise from individual vendors. The vendors pay a daily rental fee to the swap meet operators in exchange for booth space. Cherry Auction supplies parking, conducts advertising and retains the right to exclude any vendor for any reason, at any time, and thus can exclude vendors for ... infringement. In addition, Cherry Auction receives an entrance fee from each customer who attends the swap meet.

[3] There is also no dispute for purposes of this appeal that Cherry Auction and its operators were aware that vendors in their swap meet were selling counterfeit recordings in violation of Fonovisa's ... copyrights. Indeed, it is alleged that in 1991, the Fresno County Sheriff's Department raided the Cherry Auction swap meet and seized more than 38,000 counterfeit recordings. The following year, after finding that vendors at the Cherry Auction swap meet were still selling counterfeit recordings, the Sheriff sent a letter notifying Cherry Auction of the on-going sales of infringing materials, and reminding Cherry Auction that they had agreed to provide the Sheriff with identifying information from each vendor. In addition, in 1993, Fonovisa itself sent an investigator to the Cherry Auction site and observed sales of counterfeit recordings.

[4] Fonovisa filed its original complaint in the district court ..., and ... the district court granted defendants' motion to dismiss pursuant to Federal Rule of Civil Procedure 12(b)(6). In this appeal, Fonovisa does not challenge the district court's dismissal of its claim for direct copyright infringement, but does appeal the dismissal of its claims for contributory copyright infringement [and] vicarious copyright infringement ....

[5] .... Although the Copyright Act does not expressly impose liability on anyone other than direct infringers, courts have long recognized that in certain circumstances, vicarious or contributory liability will be imposed. *See* Sony Corp. of America v. Universal City Studios, Inc., 464 U.S. 417, 435 (1984) (explaining that "vicarious liability is imposed in virtually all areas of the law, and the concept of contributory infringement is merely a species of the broader problem of identifying circumstances in which it is just to hold one individually accountable for the actions of another")....

Vicarious Copyright Infringement

[6] The concept of vicarious copyright liability was developed in the Second Circuit as an outgrowth of the agency principles of respondeat superior. The landmark case on vicarious liability for sales of counterfeit recordings is *Shapiro, Bernstein and Co. v. H.L. Green Co.*, 316 F.2d 304 (2d Cir. 1963). In *Shapiro*, the court was faced with a copyright infringement suit against the owner of a chain of department stores where a concessionaire was selling counterfeit recordings. Noting that the normal agency rule of respondeat superior imposes liability on an employer for copyright infringements by an employee, the court endeavored to fashion a principle for enforcing copyrights against a defendant whose economic interests were intertwined with the direct infringer's, but who did not actually employ the direct infringer.

[7] The *Shapiro* court looked at the two lines of cases it perceived as most clearly relevant. In one line of cases, the landlord-tenant cases, the courts had held that a landlord who lacked knowledge of the infringing acts of its tenant and who exercised no control over the leased premises was not liable for infringing sales by its tenant. In the other line of cases, the so-called "dance hall cases," the operator of an entertainment venue was held liable for infringing performances when the operator (1) could control the premises and (2) obtained a direct financial benefit from the audience, who paid to enjoy the infringing performance.

[8] From those two lines of cases, the *Shapiro* court determined that the relationship between the store owner and the concessionaire in the case before it was closer to the dance-hall model than to the landlord-tenant model. It imposed liability even though the defendant was unaware of the infringement. *Shapiro* deemed the imposition of vicarious liability neither unduly harsh nor unfair because the store proprietor had the power to cease the conduct of the concessionaire, and because the proprietor derived an obvious and direct financial benefit from the infringement. The test was more clearly articulated in a later Second Circuit case as follows: "even in the absence of an employer-employee relationship one may be vicariously liable if he has the right and ability to supervise the infringing activity and also has a direct financial interest in such activities." Gershwin Publishing Corp. v. Columbia Artists Management, Inc., 443 F.2d 1159, 1162 (2d Cir.1971) ....

[9] The district court in this case agreed with defendant Cherry Auction that Fonovisa did not, as a matter of law, meet either the control or the financial benefit prong of the vicarious copyright infringement test articulated in *Gershwin*. Rather, the district court concluded that based on the pleadings, "Cherry Auction neither supervised nor profited from the vendors' sales." In the district court's view, with respect to both control and financial benefit, Cherry Auction was in the same position as an absentee landlord who has surrendered its exclusive right of occupancy in its leased property to its tenants.

[10] This analogy to absentee landlord is not in accord with the facts as alleged in the district court and which we, for purposes of appeal, must accept. The allegations below were that vendors occupied small booths within premises that Cherry Auction controlled and patrolled. According to the complaint, Cherry Auction had the right to terminate vendors for any reason whatsoever and through that right had the ability to control the activities of vendors on the premises. In addition, Cherry Auction promoted the swap meet and controlled the access of customers to the swap meet area. In terms of control, the allegations before us are strikingly similar to those in *Shapiro* and *Gershwin*...

[11] The district court's dismissal of the vicarious liability claim in this case was therefore not justified on the ground that the complaint failed to allege sufficient control.

[12] We next consider the issue of financial benefit. The plaintiff's allegations encompass many substantive benefits to Cherry Auction from the infringing sales. These include the payment of a daily rental fee by each of the infringing vendors; a direct payment to Cherry Auction by each customer in the form of an admission

fee, and incidental payments for parking, food and other services by customers seeking to purchase infringing recordings.

[13] Cherry Auction nevertheless contends that these benefits cannot satisfy the financial benefit prong of vicarious liability because a commission, directly tied to the sale of particular infringing items, is required. They ask that we restrict the financial benefit prong to the precise facts presented in *Shapiro*, where defendant H.L. Green Company received a 10 or 12 per cent commission from the direct infringers' gross receipts. Cherry Auction points to the low daily rental fee paid by each vendor, discounting all other financial benefits flowing to the swap meet, and asks that we hold that the swap meet is materially similar to a mere landlord. The facts alleged by Fonovisa, however, reflect that the defendants reap substantial financial benefits from admission fees, concession stand sales and parking fees, all of which flow directly from customers who want to buy the counterfeit recordings at bargain basement prices. The plaintiff has sufficiently alleged direct financial benefit.

[14] Our conclusion is fortified by the continuing line of cases, starting with the dance hall cases, imposing vicarious liability on the operator of a business where infringing performances enhance the attractiveness of the venue to potential customers.... In this case, the sale of pirated recordings at the Cherry Auction swap meet is a "draw" for customers, as was the performance of pirated music in the dance hall cases and their progeny.

[15] Plaintiffs have stated a claim for vicarious copyright infringement.

Contributory Copyright Infringement

[16] Contributory infringement originates in tort law and stems from the notion that one who directly contributes to another's infringement should be held accountable. Contributory infringement has been described as an outgrowth of enterprise liability, and imposes liability where one person knowingly contributes to the infringing conduct of another. The classic statement of the doctrine is in *Gershwin*, 443 F.2d 1159, 1162: "[O]ne who, with knowledge of the infringing activity, induces, causes or materially contributes to the infringing conduct of another, may be held liable as a 'contributory' infringer."

[17] There is no question that plaintiff adequately alleged the element of knowledge in this case. The disputed issue is whether plaintiff adequately alleged that Cherry Auction materially contributed to the infringing activity. We have little difficulty in holding that the allegations in this case are sufficient to show material contribution to the infringing activity. Indeed, it would be difficult for the infringing activity to take place in the massive quantities alleged without the support services provided by the swap meet. These services include, *inter alia*, the provision of space, utilities, parking, advertising, plumbing, and customers.

[18] Here again Cherry Auction asks us to ignore all aspects of the enterprise described by the plaintiffs, to concentrate solely on the rental of space, and to hold that the swap meet provides nothing more. Yet Cherry Auction actively strives to provide the environment and the market for counterfeit recording sales to thrive. Its participation in the sales cannot be termed "passive," as Cherry Auction would prefer.

[19] The district court apparently took the view that contribution to infringement should be limited to circumstances in which the defendant expressly promoted or encouraged the sale of counterfeit products, or in some manner protected the identity of the infringers. Given the allegations that the local sheriff lawfully requested that Cherry Auction gather and share basic, identifying information about its vendors, and that Cherry Auction failed to comply, the defendant appears to qualify within the last portion of the district court's own standard that posits liability for protecting infringers' identities. Moreover, we [think] ... that providing the site and facilities for known infringing activity is sufficient to establish contributory liability....

NOTES

1. Do you agree with *Fonovisa*'s holding that the defendant swap-meet operator enjoyed a "direct" financial benefit from the infringement committed by one of the vendors? If the swap meet operator benefited directly, can you give an example of an "indirect" financial benefit?

2. *Fonovisa* holds that "providing the site and facilities for known infringing activity is sufficient to establish contributory liability." Keep this holding in mind as you read the following cases.

3. Refer back to *Netcom* in the previous section. Is there a secondary infringer in *Netcom*? Under which of the two theories discussed in *Fonovisa* (if any) could that party be held secondarily liable?

Perfect 10, Inc. v. Amazon.com, Inc.
508 F.3d 1146 (9th Cir. 2007)

IKUTA, J.:

{Recall the facts of this case from Chapters V and VI.} ...

[1] We now turn to the district court's ruling that Google is unlikely to be secondarily liable for its in-line linking to infringing full-size images under the doctrines of contributory and vicarious infringement. The district court ruled that Perfect 10 did not have a likelihood of proving success on the merits of either its contributory infringement or vicarious infringement claims with respect to the full-size images. In reviewing the district court's conclusions, we are guided by the Supreme Court's recent interpretation of secondary liability, namely: "[o]ne infringes contributorily by intentionally inducing or encouraging direct infringement, and infringes vicariously by profiting from direct infringement while declining to exercise a right to stop or limit it." MGM Studios, Inc. v. Grokster, Ltd., 545 U.S. 913, 930 (2005).

[2] *Direct Infringement by Third Parties.* As a threshold matter, before we examine Perfect 10's claims that Google is secondarily liable, Perfect 10 must establish that there has been direct infringement by third parties. *See* A&M Records, Inc. v. Napster, Inc., 239 F.3d 1004, 1013 n.2 (9th Cir. 2001) ("Secondary liability for copyright infringement does not exist in the absence of direct infringement by a third party.").

[3] Perfect 10 alleges that third parties directly infringed its images in three ways. First, Perfect 10 claims that third-party websites directly infringed its copyright by reproducing, displaying, and distributing unauthorized copies of Perfect 10's images. Google does not dispute this claim on appeal.

[4] Second, Perfect 10 claims that individual users of Google's search engine directly infringed Perfect 10's copyrights by storing full-size infringing images on their computers. We agree with the district court's conclusion that Perfect 10 failed to provide sufficient evidence to support this claim. There is no evidence in the record directly establishing that users of Google's search engine have stored infringing images on their computers, and the district court did not err in declining to infer the existence of such evidence.

[5] Finally, Perfect 10 contends that users who link to infringing websites automatically make "cache" copies of full-size images and thereby directly infringe Perfect 10's reproduction right. The district court rejected this argument, holding that any such reproduction was likely a fair use. The district court reasoned that "[l]ocal caching by the browsers of individual users is noncommercial, transformative, and no more than necessary to achieve the objectives of decreasing network latency and minimizing unnecessary bandwidth usage (essential to the internet). It has a minimal impact on the potential market for the original work." We agree; even assuming such automatic copying could constitute direct infringement, it is a fair use in this context. The

copying function performed automatically by a user's computer to assist in accessing the Internet is a transformative use. Moreover, as noted by the district court, a cache copies no more than is necessary to assist the user in Internet use. It is designed to enhance an individual's computer use, not to supersede the copyright holders' exploitation of their works. Such automatic background copying has no more than a minimal effect on Perfect 10's rights, but a considerable public benefit. Because the four fair use factors weigh in favor of concluding that cache copying constitutes a fair use, Google has established a likelihood of success on this issue. Accordingly, Perfect 10 has not carried its burden of showing that users' cache copies of Perfect 10's full-size images constitute direct infringement.

[6] Therefore, we must assess Perfect 10's arguments that Google is secondarily liable in light of the direct infringement that is undisputed by the parties: third-party websites' reproducing, displaying, and distributing unauthorized copies of Perfect 10's images on the Internet.

A. Contributory Infringement ...

[7] We must ... consider whether Google could be held liable under ... contributory liability ..., that is, the liability that may be imposed for intentionally encouraging infringement through specific acts. *Grokster* {a case you will encounter below in section D} tells us that contribution to infringement must be intentional for liability to arise. However, *Grokster* also directs us to analyze contributory liability in light of "rules of fault-based liability derived from the common law," and common law principles establish that intent may be imputed.... Therefore, under *Grokster*, an actor may be contributorily liable for intentionally encouraging direct infringement if the actor knowingly takes steps that are substantially certain to result in such direct infringement.

[8] Our tests for contributory liability are consistent with the rule set forth in *Grokster*. We have adopted the general rule set forth in *Gershwin Publishing Corp. v. Columbia Artists Management, Inc.*, namely: "one who, with knowledge of the infringing activity, induces, causes or materially contributes to the infringing conduct of another, may be held liable as a 'contributory' infringer," 443 F.2d 1159, 1162 (2d Cir.1971).

[9] We have further refined this test in the context of cyberspace to determine when contributory liability can be imposed on a provider of Internet access or services. In *Napster* {another case you will encounter below in section D}, we considered claims that the operator of an electronic file sharing system was contributorily liable for assisting individual users to swap copyrighted music files stored on their home computers with other users of the system. We stated that "if a computer system operator learns of specific infringing material available on his system and fails to purge such material from the system, the operator knows of and contributes to direct infringement." Because Napster knew of the availability of infringing music files, assisted users in accessing such files, and failed to block access to such files, we concluded that Napster materially contributed to infringement.

[10] The *Napster* test for contributory liability was modeled on the influential district court decision in [*Netcom*] .... *Netcom* held that if plaintiffs could prove that Netcom knew or should have known that the minister infringed plaintiffs' copyrights, "Netcom [would] be liable for contributory infringement since its failure to simply cancel [the former minister's] infringing message and thereby stop an infringing copy from being distributed worldwide constitute[d] substantial participation in [the former minister's] public distribution of the message."

[11] Although neither *Napster* nor *Netcom* expressly required a finding of intent, those cases are consistent with *Grokster* because both decisions ruled that a service provider's knowing failure to prevent infringing actions could be the basis for imposing contributory liability. Under such circumstances, intent may be imputed. In addition, *Napster* and *Netcom* are consistent with the longstanding requirement that an actor's

contribution to infringement must be material to warrant the imposition of contributory liability. Both *Napster* and *Netcom* acknowledge that services or products that facilitate access to websites throughout the world can significantly magnify the effects of otherwise immaterial infringing activities. The Supreme Court has acknowledged that "[t]he argument for imposing indirect liability" is particularly "powerful" when individuals using the defendant's software could make a huge number of infringing downloads every day. *Grokster*, 545 U.S. at 929. Moreover, copyright holders cannot protect their rights in a meaningful way unless they can hold providers of such services or products accountable for their actions pursuant to a test such as that enunciated in *Napster*. *See id.* at 929–30 ("When a widely shared service or product is used to commit infringement, it may be impossible to enforce rights in the protected work effectively against all direct infringers, the only practical alternative being to go against the distributor of the copying device for secondary liability on a theory of contributory or vicarious infringement."). Accordingly, we hold that a computer system operator can be held contributorily liable if it "has *actual* knowledge that *specific* infringing material is available using its system," *Napster*, 239 F.3d at 1022, and can "take simple measures to prevent further damage" to copyrighted works, *Netcom*, 907 F. Supp. at 1375, yet continues to provide access to infringing works.

[12] Here, the district court held that even assuming Google had actual knowledge of infringing material available on its system, Google did not materially contribute to infringing conduct because it did not undertake any substantial promotional or advertising efforts to encourage visits to infringing websites, nor provide a significant revenue stream to the infringing websites. This analysis is erroneous. There is no dispute that Google substantially assists websites to distribute their infringing copies to a worldwide market and assists a worldwide audience of users to access infringing materials. We cannot discount the effect of such a service on copyright owners, even though Google's assistance is available to all websites, not just infringing ones. Applying our test, Google could be held contributorily liable if it had knowledge that infringing Perfect 10 images were available using its search engine, could take simple measures to prevent further damage to Perfect 10's copyrighted works, and failed to take such steps.

[13] The district court did not resolve the factual disputes over the adequacy of Perfect 10's notices to Google and Google's responses to these notices. Moreover, there are factual disputes over whether there are reasonable and feasible means for Google to refrain from providing access to infringing images. Therefore, we must remand this claim to the district court for further consideration whether Perfect 10 would likely succeed in establishing that Google was contributorily liable for in-line linking to full-size infringing images under the test enunciated today.

B. Vicarious Infringement

[14] Perfect 10 also challenges the district court's conclusion that it is not likely to prevail on a theory of vicarious liability against Google.... [O]ne infringes vicariously by profiting from direct infringement while declining to exercise a right to stop or limit it. As this formulation indicates, to succeed in imposing vicarious liability, a plaintiff must establish that the defendant exercises the requisite control over the direct infringer and that the defendant derives a direct financial benefit from the direct infringement.... [T]he "control" element of the vicarious liability test [is directed to] the defendant's right and ability to supervise the direct infringer. Thus, ... a defendant exercises control over a direct infringer when he has both a legal right to stop or limit the directly infringing conduct, as well as the practical ability to do so.

[15] We evaluate Perfect 10's arguments that Google is vicariously liable in light of the direct infringement that is undisputed by the parties, namely, the third-party websites' reproduction, display, and distribution of unauthorized copies of Perfect 10's images on the Internet. In order to prevail at this preliminary injunction stage, Perfect 10 must demonstrate a likelihood of success in establishing that Google has the right and ability to stop or limit the infringing activities of third party websites. In addition, Perfect 10 must establish a

likelihood of proving that Google derives a direct financial benefit from such activities. Perfect 10 has not met this burden.

[16] With respect to the "control" element …, Perfect 10 has not demonstrated a likelihood of showing that Google has the legal right to stop or limit the direct infringement of third-party websites. Unlike *Fonovisa*, where by virtue of a "broad contract" with its vendors the defendant swap meet operators had the right to stop the vendors from selling counterfeit recordings on its premises, Perfect 10 has not shown that Google has contracts with third-party websites that empower Google to stop or limit them from reproducing, displaying, and distributing infringing copies of Perfect 10's images on the Internet. Perfect 10 does point to Google's AdSense agreement, which states that Google reserves "the right to monitor and terminate partnerships with entities that violate others' copyright[s]." However, Google's right to terminate an AdSense partnership does not give Google the right to stop direct infringement by third-party websites. An infringing third-party website can continue to reproduce, display, and distribute its infringing copies of Perfect 10 images after its participation in the AdSense program has ended.

[17] Nor is Google similarly situated to Napster. Napster users infringed the plaintiffs' reproduction and distribution rights through their use of Napster's proprietary music-file sharing system. There, the infringing conduct was the use of Napster's service to download and upload copyrighted music. Because Napster had a closed system requiring user registration, and could terminate its users' accounts and block their access to the Napster system, Napster had the right and ability to prevent its users from engaging in the infringing activity of uploading file names and downloading Napster users' music files through the Napster system. By contrast, Google cannot stop any of the third-party websites from reproducing, displaying, and distributing unauthorized copies of Perfect 10's images because that infringing conduct takes place on the third-party websites. Google cannot terminate those third-party websites or block their ability to host and serve infringing full-size images on the Internet.

[18] Moreover, the district court found that Google lacks the practical ability to police the third-party websites' infringing conduct. Specifically, the court found that Google's supervisory power is limited because "Google's software lacks the ability to analyze every image on the internet, compare each image to all the other copyrighted images that exist in the world … and determine whether a certain image on the web infringes someone's copyright." The district court also concluded that Perfect 10's suggestions regarding measures Google could implement to prevent its web crawler from indexing infringing websites and to block access to infringing images were not workable. Rather, the suggestions suffered from both "imprecision and overbreadth." We hold that these findings are not clearly erroneous. Without image-recognition technology, Google lacks the practical ability to police the infringing activities of third-party websites. This distinguishes Google from the defendants held liable in *Napster* and *Fonovisa*.

[19] Perfect 10 argues that Google could manage its own operations to avoid indexing websites with infringing content and linking to third-party infringing sites. This is a claim of contributory liability, not vicarious liability. Although the lines between direct infringement, contributory infringement, and vicarious liability are not clearly drawn, in general, contributory liability is based on the defendant's failure to stop its own actions which facilitate third-party infringement, while vicarious liability is based on the defendant's failure to cause a third party to stop its directly infringing activities. Google's failure to change its operations to avoid assisting websites to distribute their infringing content may constitute contributory liability. However, this failure is not the same as declining to exercise a right and ability to make third-party websites stop their direct infringement. We reject Perfect 10's efforts to blur this distinction.

[20] Because we conclude that Perfect 10 has not shown a likelihood of establishing Google's right and ability to stop or limit the directly infringing conduct of third-party websites, we agree with the district court's

conclusion that Perfect 10 "has not established a likelihood of proving the [control] prong necessary for vicarious liability."[15] ...

[21] We conclude that .... [t]he district court ... erred in its secondary liability analysis because it failed to consider whether Google ... knew of infringing activities yet failed to take reasonable and feasible steps to refrain from providing access to infringing images. Therefore we must ... reverse the district court's holding that Perfect 10 was unlikely to succeed on the merits of its secondary liability claims .... {Recall that the court found that Google's use of the thumbnail images was fair use, as set out in Chapter VI.}

Perfect 10, Inc. v. Visa International Service, Association
494 F.3d 788 (9th Cir. 2007)

M. SMITH, J.:

[1] Perfect 10, Inc. sued Visa International Service Association, MasterCard International Inc., and several affiliated banks and data processing services, alleging secondary liability under federal copyright ... law .... It sued because Defendants continue to process credit card payments to websites that infringe Perfect 10's intellectual property rights after being notified by Perfect 10 of infringement by those websites. The district court dismissed all causes of action under Federal Rule of Civil Procedure 12(b)(6) for failure to state a claim upon which relief can be granted. We affirm the decision of the district court....

[2] Perfect 10 publishes the magazine "PERFECT10" and operates the subscription website www.perfect10.com, both of which feature tasteful copyrighted images of the world's most beautiful natural models. Perfect 10 claims copyrights in the photographs published in its magazine and on its website .... Perfect 10 alleges that numerous websites based in several countries have stolen its proprietary images, altered them, and illegally offered them for sale online.

[3] Instead of suing the direct infringers in this case, Perfect 10 sued Defendants, financial institutions that process certain credit card payments to the allegedly infringing websites. The Visa and MasterCard entities are associations of member banks that issue credit cards to consumers, automatically process payments to merchants authorized to accept their cards, and provide information to the interested parties necessary to settle the resulting debits and credits. Defendants collect fees for their services in these transactions. Perfect 10 alleges that it sent Defendants repeated notices specifically identifying infringing websites and informing Defendants that some of their consumers use their payment cards to purchase infringing images. Defendants admit receiving some of these notices, but they took no action in response to the notices after receiving them....

[4] Perfect 10 filed suit against Defendants ... alleging contributory and vicarious copyright ... infringement .... The district court granted the Defendants' ... motion [to dismiss] .... Perfect 10 appealed to this court....

[5] Perfect 10 alleges that numerous websites based in several countries—and their paying customers—have directly infringed its rights under the Copyright Act. In the present suit, however, Perfect 10 has sued Defendants, not the direct infringers, claiming contributory and vicarious copyright infringement because Defendants process credit card charges incurred by customers to acquire the infringing images.

[6] We evaluate Perfect 10's claims with an awareness that credit cards serve as the primary engine of electronic commerce and that Congress has determined it to be the "policy of the United States—(1) to

---

[15] Having so concluded, we need not reach Perfect 10's argument that Google received a direct financial benefit.

promote the continued development of the Internet and other interactive computer services and other interactive media [and] (2) to preserve the vibrant and competitive free market that presently exists for the Internet and other interactive computer services, unfettered by Federal or State regulation." 47 U.S.C. §§ 230(b)(1), (2).

1. Contributory Copyright Infringement

[7] Contributory copyright infringement is a form of secondary liability with roots in the tort-law concepts of enterprise liability and imputed intent.... We have found that a defendant is a contributory infringer if it (1) has knowledge of a third party's infringing activity, and (2) induces, causes, or materially contributes to the infringing conduct. In an Internet context, we have found contributory liability when the defendant engages in personal conduct that encourages or assists the infringement.... Most recently, in a case also brought by Perfect 10, we found that "an actor may be contributorily liable ... for intentionally encouraging direct infringement if the actor knowingly takes steps that are substantially certain to result in such direct infringement." *Amazon.com,* 487 F.3d at 727.

[8] .... To find that Defendants' activities fall within the scope of such tests would require a radical and inappropriate expansion of existing principles of secondary liability and would violate the public policy of the United States.

a. Knowledge of the Infringing Activity

[9] Because we find that Perfect 10 has not pled facts sufficient to establish that Defendants ... materially contribute to the infringing activity, Perfect 10's contributory copyright infringement claim fails and we need not address the Defendants' knowledge of the infringing activity.

b. Material Contribution, Inducement, or Causation

[10] To state a claim of contributory infringement, Perfect 10 must allege facts showing that Defendants induce, cause, or materially contribute to the infringing conduct.... Perfect 10 argues that by continuing to process credit card payments to the infringing websites despite having knowledge of ongoing infringement, Defendants induce, enable and contribute to the infringing activity .... We disagree....

[11] The credit card companies cannot be said to materially contribute to the infringement in this case because they have no direct connection to that infringement. Here, the infringement rests on the reproduction, alteration, display and distribution of Perfect 10's images over the Internet. Perfect 10 has not alleged that any infringing material passes over Defendants' payment networks or through their payment processing systems, or that Defendants' systems are used to alter or display the infringing images. In *Fonovisa,* the infringing material was physically located in and traded at the defendant's market. Here, it is not. Nor are Defendants' systems used to locate the infringing images. The search engines in *Amazon.com* provided links to specific infringing images, and the service[] in *Napster* ... allowed users to locate and obtain infringing material. Here, in contrast, the services provided by the credit card companies do not help locate and are not used to distribute the infringing images. While Perfect 10 has alleged that Defendants make it easier for websites to profit from this infringing activity, the issue here is reproduction, alteration, display and distribution, which can occur without payment. Even if infringing images were not paid for, there would still be infringement.

[12] Our analysis is fully consistent with this court's recent decision in *Perfect 10 v. Amazon.com,* where we found that "Google could be held contributorily liable if it had knowledge that infringing Perfect 10 images were available using its search engine, could take simple measures to prevent further damage to Perfect 10's copyrighted works, and failed to take such steps." The dissent claims this statement applies squarely to

Defendants if we just substitute "payment systems" for "search engine." But this is only true if search engines and payment systems are equivalents for these purposes, and they are not. The salient distinction is that Google's search engine itself assists in the distribution of infringing content to Internet users, while Defendants' payment systems do not. The *Amazon.com* court noted that "Google substantially assists websites to distribute their infringing copies to a worldwide market and assists a worldwide audience of users to access infringing materials." Defendants do not provide such a service. They in no way assist or enable Internet users to locate infringing material, and they do not distribute it. They do, as alleged, make infringement more profitable, and people are generally more inclined to engage in an activity when it is financially profitable. However, there is an additional step in the causal chain: Google may materially contribute to infringement by making it fast and easy for third parties to locate and distribute infringing material, whereas Defendants make it easier for infringement to be *profitable*, which tends to increase financial incentives to infringe, which in turn tends to increase infringement.

[13] ... We acknowledge that Defendants' payment systems make it easier for such an infringement to be profitable, and that they therefore have the effect of increasing such infringement, but because infringement of Perfect 10's copyrights can occur without using Defendants' payment system, we hold that payment processing by the Defendants as alleged in Perfect 10's ... Complaint does not constitute a "material contribution" under the test for contributory infringement of copyrights.

[14] Our holding is also fully consistent with and supported by this court's previous holding[] in *Fonovisa* .... While there are some limited similarities between the factual scenario[] in *Fonovisa* ... and the facts in this case, the differences in those scenarios are substantial, and, in our view, dispositive. In *Fonovisa,* we held a flea market proprietor liable as a contributory infringer when it provided the facilities for and benefitted from the sale of pirated works. The court found that the primary infringers and the swap meet were engaged in a mutual enterprise of infringement and observed that "it would be difficult for the infringing activity to take place in the massive quantities alleged without the support services provided by the swap meet. These services include, among other things, the provision of space, utilities, parking, advertising, plumbing, and customers." But the swap meet owner did more to encourage the enterprise. In 1991, the Fresno County Sheriff raided the swap meet and seized 38,000 counterfeit recordings. The Sheriff sent a letter to the swap meet operator the following year notifying it that counterfeit sales continued and reminding it that it had agreed to provide the Sheriff with identifying information from each vendor, but had failed to do so. The *Fonovisa* court found liability because the swap meet operator knowingly provided the "site and facilities" for the infringing activity....

2. Vicarious Copyright Infringement

[15] Vicarious infringement is a concept related to, but distinct from, contributory infringement. Whereas contributory infringement is based on tort-law principles of enterprise liability and imputed intent, vicarious infringement's roots lie in the agency principles of *respondeat superior.* To state a claim for vicarious copyright infringement, a plaintiff must allege that the defendant has (1) the right and ability to supervise the infringing conduct and (2) a direct financial interest in the infringing activity.... Perfect 10 alleges that Defendants have the right and ability to control the content of the infringing websites by refusing to process credit card payments to the websites, enforcing their own rules and regulations, or both. We hold that Defendants' conduct alleged in Perfect 10's ... complaint fails to state a claim for vicarious copyright infringement.

a. Right and Ability to Supervise the Infringing Activity

[16] In order to join a Defendant's payment network, merchants and member banks must agree to follow that Defendant's rules and regulations. These rules, among other things, prohibit member banks from providing services to merchants engaging in certain illegal activities and require the members and member banks to

investigate merchants suspected of engaging in such illegal activity and to terminate their participation in the payment network if certain illegal activity is found. Perfect 10 has alleged that certain websites are infringing Perfect 10's copyrights and that Perfect 10 sent notices of this alleged infringement to Defendants. Accordingly, Perfect 10 has adequately pled that (1) infringement of Perfect 10's copyrights was occurring, (2) Defendants were aware of the infringement, and (3) on this basis, Defendants could have stopped processing credit card payments to the infringing websites. These allegations are not, however, sufficient to establish vicarious liability because even with all reasonable inferences drawn in Perfect 10's favor, Perfect 10's allegations of fact cannot support a finding that Defendants have the right and ability to control the infringing activity.

[17] In reasoning closely analogous to the present case, the *Amazon.com* court held that Google was not vicariously liable for third-party infringement that its search engine facilitates. In so holding, the court found that Google's ability to control its own index, search results, and webpages does not give Google the right to control the infringing acts of third parties even though that ability would allow Google to affect those infringing acts to some degree. Moreover, and even more importantly, the *Amazon.com* court rejected a vicarious liability claim based on Google's policies with sponsored advertisers, which state that it reserves "the right to monitor and terminate partnerships with entities that violate others' copyright[s]." The court found that

> Google's right to terminate an AdSense partnership does not give Google the right to stop direct infringement by third-party websites. An infringing third-party website can continue to reproduce, display, and distribute its infringing copies of Perfect 10 images after its participation in the AdSense program has ended.

This reasoning is equally applicable to the Defendants in this case. Just like Google, Defendants could likely take certain steps that may have the indirect effect of reducing infringing activity on the Internet at large. However, neither Google nor Defendants has any ability to directly control that activity, and the mere ability to withdraw a financial "carrot" does not create the "stick" of "right and ability to control" that vicarious infringement requires. A finding of vicarious liability here, under the theories advocated by the dissent, would also require a finding that Google is vicariously liable for infringement—a conflict we need not create, and radical step we do not take...

[18] Perfect 10 offers [a] counter-argument[]. Perfect 10 ... claims that Defendants' rules and regulations permit them to require member merchants to cease illegal activity—presumably including copyright infringement—as a condition to their continuing right to receive credit card payments from the relevant Defendant entities. Perfect 10 argues that these contractual terms effectively give Defendants contractual control over the *content* of their merchants' websites, and that contractual control over content is sufficient to establish the "right and ability" to control that content for purposes of vicarious liability. In the sense that economic considerations can influence behavior, these contractual rules and regulations do give Defendants some measure of control over the offending websites since it is reasonable to believe that fear of losing access to credit card payment processing services would be a sufficient incentive for at least some website operators to comply with a content-based suggestion from Defendants. But the ability to exert financial pressure does not give Defendants the right or ability to control the actual infringing activity at issue in this case. Defendants have no absolute right[16] to stop that activity—they cannot stop websites from reproducing, altering, or distributing infringing images. Rather, the credit card companies are analogous to Google, which we held was

---

[16] We do not, as the dissent suggests, hold that an absolute right to stop the infringement is a prerequisite for vicarious liability. Rather, we consider the Defendants' inability to directly control the actual infringing activities of third-party websites—reproduction, alteration, display, and distribution over the Internet, not over Defendants' payment systems—as evidence that they, much like Google, lack the right and ability to control those activities.

not liable for vicarious copyright infringement even though search engines could effectively cause a website to disappear by removing it from their search results, and reserve the right to do so.... For vicarious liability to attach, however, the defendant must have the right and ability to *supervise* and *control* the infringement, not just affect it, and Defendants do not have this right or ability....

b. Obvious and Direct Financial Interest in the Infringing Activity

[19] Because Perfect 10 has failed to show that Defendants have the right and ability to control the alleged infringing conduct, it has not pled a viable claim of vicarious liability. Accordingly, we need not reach the issue of direct financial interest....

[20] We decline to create any of the radical new theories of liability advocated by Perfect 10 and the dissent and we affirm the district court's dismissal with prejudice of all causes of action in Perfect 10's complaint for failure to state a claim upon which relief can be granted.

AFFIRMED.

KOZINSKI, J., dissenting for the most part:

[21] Federal law gives copyright owners the exclusive right to "distribute copies [of their works] ... to the public by sale." 17 U.S.C. § 106(3). Plaintiff alleges that certain third parties it refers to as the "Stolen Content Websites" unlawfully copy its protected images and sell them to the public, using defendants' payment systems as financial intermediaries. According to plaintiff, the Stolen Content Websites "maintain no physical presence in the United States in order to evade criminal and civil liability for their illegal conduct." Plaintiff also claims that "Defendants do not enforce their own rules against [the] Stolen Content Websites because Defendants do not want to lose the substantial revenues and profits they receive from the websites." Plaintiff has repeatedly notified defendants that they are abetting the sale of stolen merchandise by "knowingly providing crucial transactional support services for the sale of millions of stolen photos and film clips worth billions of dollars," but to no avail. Frustrated in its effort to protect the rights Congress has given it, plaintiff turns to the federal courts for redress. We should not slam the courthouse door in its face.

[22] Accepting the truth of plaintiff's allegations, as we must on a motion to dismiss, the credit cards are easily liable for indirect copyright infringement: They knowingly provide a financial bridge between buyers and sellers of pirated works, enabling them to consummate infringing transactions, while making a profit on every sale. If such active participation in infringing conduct does not amount to indirect infringement, it's hard to imagine what would. By straining to absolve defendants of liability, the majority leaves our law in disarray.

Contributory Infringement

[23] We have long held that a defendant is liable for contributory infringement if it "materially contributes to the infringing conduct." Our recent opinion in *Perfect 10, Inc. v. Amazon.com, Inc.*, 487 F.3d 701 (9th Cir. 2007), canvasses the caselaw in this area and concludes that Google "could be held contributorily liable if it had knowledge that infringing Perfect 10 images were available using its search engine, could take simple measures to prevent further damage to Perfect 10's copyrighted works, and failed to take such steps." Substitute "payment systems" for "search engine" in this sentence, and it describes defendants here: If a consumer wishes to buy an infringing image from one of the Stolen Content Websites, he can do so by using Visa or MasterCard, just as he can use Google to find the infringing images in the first place. My colleagues engage in wishful thinking when they claim that "Google's search engine itself assists in the distribution of infringing content to Internet users, while Defendants' payment systems do not" and that "[h]elping users to locate an image might substantially assist users to download infringing images, but processing payments does not."

[24] The majority struggles to distinguish *Amazon* by positing an "additional step in the causal chain" between defendants' activities and the infringing conduct. According to the majority, "Google may materially contribute to infringement by making it fast and easy for third parties to locate and distribute infringing material, whereas Defendants make it easier for infringement to be *profitable*, which tends to increase financial incentives to infringe, which in turn tends to increase infringement." The majority is mistaken; there is no "additional step." Defendants participate in every credit card sale of pirated images; the images are delivered to the buyer only after defendants approve the transaction and process the payment. This is not just an economic incentive for infringement; it's an essential step in the infringement process.

[25] In any event, I don't see why it matters whether there is an "additional step." Materiality turns on how significantly the activity helps infringement, not on whether it's characterized as one step or two steps removed from it. The majority recognizes that "Defendants make it easier for websites to profit from this infringing activity," that defendants' conduct "tends to increase infringement," that defendants "have the effect of increasing ... infringement," that "Defendants have the power to undermine the commercial viability of" the Stolen Content Websites and that they "make it easier for websites to profit from this infringing activity," that "Defendants could likely take certain steps that may have the indirect effect of reducing infringing activity on the Internet," and that defendants could "reduce the number of those [infringing] sales." Taking the majority at its word, it sounds like defendants are providing very significant help to the direct infringers.

[26] My colleagues recognize, as they must, that helping consumers locate infringing content can constitute contributory infringement, but they consign the means of payment to secondary status. But why is *locating* infringing images more central to infringement than *paying* for them? If infringing images can't be found, there can be no infringement; but if infringing images can't be paid for, there can be no infringement either. Location services and payment services are equally central to infringement; the majority's contrary assertion is supported largely by disparaging use of "merely," "simply" and "only."...

[27] The majority dismisses the significance of credit cards by arguing that "infringement could continue on a large scale [without them] because other viable funding mechanisms are available." Of course, the same could be said about Google. As the majority admits, if Google were unwilling or unable to serve up infringing images, consumers could use Yahoo!, Ask.com, Microsoft Live Search, A9.com or AltaVista instead. Even if none of these were available, consumers could still locate websites with infringing images through e-mails from friends, messages on discussion forums, tips via online chat, "typo-squatting," peer-to-peer networking using BitTorrent or eDonkey, offline and online advertisements, disreputable search engines hosted on servers in far-off jurisdictions or even old-fashioned word of mouth. The majority's claim that search engines "could effectively cause a website to disappear by removing it from their search results," is quite a stretch...

Vicarious Infringement

[28] A party infringes vicariously by profiting from direct infringement while declining to exercise a right to stop or limit it. There is no doubt that defendants profit from the infringing activity of the Stolen Content Websites; after all, they take a cut of virtually every sale of pirated material. The majority does not dispute this point so I need not belabor it.

[29] Defendants here also have a right to stop or limit the infringing activity, a right they have refused to exercise. As the majority recognizes, "Perfect 10 ... claims that Defendants' rules and regulations permit them to require member merchants to cease illegal activity—presumably including copyright infringement—as a condition to their continuing right to receive credit card payments from the relevant Defendant entities." Assuming the truth of this allegation, the cards have the authority, given to them by contract, to force the Stolen Content Websites to remove infringing images from their inventory as a condition for using

defendants' payment systems. If the merchants comply, their websites stop peddling stolen content and so infringement is stopped or limited. If they don't comply, defendants have the right—and under copyright law the duty—to kick the pirates off their payment networks, forcing them to find other means of getting paid or go out of business. In that case, too, infringement is stopped or limited...

[30] The majority toils to resist this obvious conclusion but its arguments are not persuasive. For example, it makes no difference that defendants control only the means of payment, not the mechanics of transferring the material. In a commercial environment, distribution and payment are (to use a quaint anachronism) like love and marriage—you can't have one without the other. If cards don't process payment, pirates don't deliver booty. The credit cards, in fact, control distribution of the infringing material....

[31] This is an easy case, squarely controlled by our precedent in all material respects. Fairly applying our cases to the facts alleged by Perfect 10, we should reverse the district court and give plaintiff an opportunity to prove its case through discovery and trial. In straining to escape the strictures of our caselaw, the majority draws a series of ephemeral distinctions that are neither required nor permitted; the opinion will prove to be no end of trouble.

NOTES

1. *Perfect 10 v. Amazon* holds "that a computer system operator can be held contributorily liable if it has *actual* knowledge that *specific* infringing material is available using its system, and can take simple measures to prevent further damage to copyrighted works, yet continues to provide access to infringing works." Is this holding consistent with *Fonovisa*'s articulation of the test for contributory infringement? Is it consistent with *Fonovisa*'s application of that test? If the two courts' accounts of contributory infringement liability—either in articulation or application—are inconsistent, is there a good reason to vary the standard as between a brick-and-mortar enterprise like the swap meet in *Fonovisa*, and the sort of online services at issue in *Perfect 10 v. Amazon?*

2. With respect to the "control" prong of the contributory infringement standard as articulated in *Perfect 10 v. Amazon*, does Google enjoy any less "control" over infringers than the swap meet owner in *Fonovisa* did? If Google has knowledge of specific infringing activity, it could remove from its search results sites that host that infringing activity. Why does that not count as the requisite "control"?

3. We should ask the same questions about the holding in *Perfect 10 v. Visa*. The court holds that the credit card companies are not contributory infringers because they do not "materially contribute" to infringement. Can you square that holding with *Fonovisa*'s approach to the "material contribution" prong of contributory infringement?

4. Does the court in *Perfect 10 v. Visa* determine whether Visa directly benefits from infringement? How would you analyze that issue in that case compared with *Fonovisa*, where the court determined that the swap-meet operator benefited directly from infringement?

5. If you believe that the standards for both contributory and vicarious infringement diverge between *Fonovisa* and the *Perfect 10* cases, do you have a theory for why that divergence may be occurring? Would you argue that it is justified?

6. In *UMG Recordings, Inc. v. Shelter Capital Partners, LLC*, 718 F.3d 1006 (9th Cir. 2013), the court considered whether a venture capital firm that had invested in a website that hosted a large amount of infringing content could be held liable as secondary infringers. The court held that they could not:

UMG ... argues that the Investor Defendants "provided Veoh's necessary funding and directed its spending" on "basic operations including ... hardware, software, and employees"— "elements" [that] UMG argues "form 'the site and facilities' for Veoh's direct infringement." UMG thus attempts to liken its case to UMG Recordings, Inc. v. Bertelsmann AG, et al., 222 F.R.D. 408 (N.D. Cal. 2004), *where the district court denied an investor's motion to dismiss claims of contributory infringement. In* Bertelsmann, *however, the investor was Napster's only available source of funding, and thus held significant power and control over Napster's operations. Here, by contrast, there were multiple investors, and none of the Investor Defendants could individually control Veoh. Accordingly, UMG hinges its novel theory of secondary liability on the contention that the three Investor Defendants together took control of Veoh's operations by "obtain[ing] three of the five seats on Veoh's Board of Directors," and effectively provided the "site and facilities" for direct infringement by wielding their majority power to direct spending.*

Even assuming that such joint control, not typically an element of contributory infringement, could satisfy Fonovisa's *site and facilities requirement, UMG's argument fails on its own terms, because the complaint nowhere alleged that the Investor Defendants agreed to work in concert to this end.... [T]hree investors individually acquiring one seat apiece is not the same as agreeing to operate as a unified entity to obtain and leverage majority control.... We therefore affirm the dismissal of UMG's contributory infringement claim.*

[We also] affirm the district court's dismissal of UMG's vicarious liability ... claim[].... UMG's arguments that the Investor Defendants "distribute[d]" Veoh's services and had the right and ability to supervise the infringing users are premised on the unalleged contention that the Investor Defendants agreed to act in concert, and thus together they held a majority of seats on the Board and maintained operational control over the company. We therefore affirm the dismissal of the complaint against the Investor Defendants.

C. Liability of Online Service Providers, and Section 512 Safe Harbors

With the wide public adoption of the internet in the early and mid-1990s, concern grew that companies offering vital online services faced the threat of crippling liability under the traditional doctrines of secondary liability based on the prevalence of direct infringing conduct by their users. Given the scale of user infringement, the difficulty that many online service providers faced in policing that infringement, the simple reluctance of many online service providers to be involved in policing their users, and the inadequacy of indemnification and other contractual mechanisms to reduce the scale of potential secondary liability, Congress debated and eventually passed into law a set of **safe harbors** that protect online service providers against a range of possible secondary infringement claims.

The safe harbors were enacted in 1998 as part of the Digital Millennium Copyright Act, and codified in § 512 of the Copyright Act. Section 512 provides immunity from secondary infringement liability for certain activities of online "service providers" (OSPs), including: (1) transitory digital network communications; (2) system caching; (3) storing information on its systems at the direction of users; and (4) providing information location tools like hypertext links.

For protection under any of the safe harbor provisions, a party must meet the statutory definition of a "service provider." The DMCA provides two definitions, one applicable only to the safe harbor category for transitory digital network communications and the second applicable to all of the other categories. Under § 512(a), the transitory communications provision, "service provider" is defined as "an entity offering the transmission, routing, or providing of connections for digital online communications, between or among points specified by a user, of material of the user's choosing, without modification to the content of the material as sent or received." 17 U.S.C. § 512(k)(1)(A). The remaining three subsections employ a definition of "service provider" that includes "a provider of online services or network access, or the operator of facilities therefor." 17 U.S.C. § 512(k)(1)(B). This definition encompasses, for example, providers offering internet access, email, and chat room and webpage hosting services.

OSPs must comply with certain threshold requirements to qualify for any of the safe harbors. First, OSPs must adopt and reasonably implement a policy that provides for the termination of repeat infringers, and they must inform their users of this policy. 17 U.S.C. § 512(i)(1)(A). Second, OSPs must not interfere with "standard technical measures" applied by copyright owners to protect their works. Id. § 512(i)(1)(B). In addition, each safe harbor has its own requirements that the OSP must meet to qualify for its protection.

The first safe harbor, set out in § 512(a), exempts an OSP from liability for transmitting or transiently storing infringing material. For it to apply, § 512(k)(1) requires that the "service provider" seeking the shelter of the safe harbor be "an entity offering the transmission, routing, or providing of connections for digital online communications, between or among points specified by a user, of material of the user's choosing, without modification to the content of the material as sent or received." Id. § 512(k)(1). In addition, eligibility is conditioned on the following requirements set out in § 512(a):

> (1) the transmission of the material was initiated by or at the direction of a person other than the service provider;
> (2) the transmission, routing, provision of connections, or storage is carried out through an automatic technical process without selection of the material by the service provider;
> (3) the service provider does not select the recipients of the material except as an automatic response to the request of another person;
> (4) no copy of the material made by the service provider in the course of such intermediate or transient storage is maintained on the system or network in a manner ordinarily accessible to anyone other than anticipated recipients, and no such copy is maintained on the system or network in a manner ordinarily accessible to such anticipated recipients for a longer period than is reasonably necessary for the transmission, routing, or provision of connections; and
> (5) the material is transmitted through the system or network without modification of its content.

The second safe harbor, set out in § 512(b), exempts OSPs from liability for caching copies of copyrighted material if the material is made available online by a person other than the OSP and transmitted from that person through the OSP's system or network to a recipient at the recipient's direction, and the storage by the OSP is automatic and done for the purpose of making the material available to other users of the system or network. Id. § 512(b). The OSP must not modify the content of the material, and it must also further comply with a set of specified conditions (including maintaining access controls, such as passwords, that may have been applied to the material). Finally, the OSP must disable access to cached material upon receiving notification that the material infringes copyright, and that either the material has been removed from the originating website or a court has ordered the removal of the material from the originating website. Id. § 512(b)(2).

The third and fourth safe harbors, set out in §§ 512(c)-(d), have emerged as the most crucial for OSPs. The third safe harbor exempts an OSP from liability for infringing materials, such as photographs or sound recordings, that are "hosted" on its servers on behalf of users. *Id.* § 512(c). The fourth safe harbor shelters OSPs that provide links, directories, indices, or other "information location tools" that reference or direct users to infringing material or activity. *Id.* § 512(d).

To qualify for either of these safe harbors, OSPs must designate an agent to receive notification from copyright owners claiming that specific material is infringing. OSPs must file with the Copyright Office information identifying that agent and how the agent may be reached, and must also make the information publicly available. *Id.* § 512(c)(2).

In addition, any OSP that has "actual knowledge" that specific material is infringing or "aware[ness] of facts or circumstances from which infringing activity is apparent," is not eligible for coverage of the safe harbor unless it "acts expeditiously to remove, or disable access to, the material." *Id.* § 512(c)(1)(A).

Additionally, OSPs are ineligible for the safe harbor if they obtain a "financial benefit directly attributable to the infringing activity, in a case in which the service provider has the right and ability to control such activity." *Id.* § 512(c)(1)(B).

Crucially, the third and fourth safe harbors are subject to **"notice and takedown"**—a process which over the past two decades has grown to become the centerpiece of copyright enforcement online. Pursuant to this process, a copyright owner may send a notice of alleged infringement to the OSP's designated agent. *Id.* § 512(c)(3). Detailed rules regarding the form and content of this notice are set out in § 512(c)(3). Most importantly, the notice must identify the specific material alleged to infringe, must provide information sufficient to permit the OSP to locate that specific material (typically, the website link at which it can be found), and must state that the party submitting the notification "has a good faith belief" that the material is infringing. Additionally, the notifying party must affirm under penalty of perjury that he or she is authorized to act on behalf of the copyright owner. Although none of the other required statements in the notice need be made under penalty of perjury, *see id.*, if the notifying party "knowingly materially misrepresents ... that material or activity is infringing," a court may award damages to the alleged infringer or the affected OSP. *Id.* § 512(f).

Section 512(c)(3) provides equally detailed rules defining what OSPs must do upon receipt of such a notice. The protection of the safe harbor is conditioned upon OSPs responding with reasonable dispatch to notices and taking down the material alleged to be infringing. Under the terms of § 512(c)(1)(C), an OSP that receives a proper takedown notice is directed to respond "expeditiously to remove, or disable access to, the material that is claimed to be infringing."

Note that for OSPs that conform to the notice and takedown process, § 512 provides an exemption from liability for "any claim based on" the OSP's good faith takedown. *Id.* § 512(g)(1). This exemption from claims of liability by the users whose material is taken down is conditioned on the OSP "tak[ing] reasonable steps promptly to notify" the user of the takedown. *Id.* § 512(g)(2)(A).

A user who receives a takedown notification from an OSP may file a **"counter-notification"**—a notice that identifies the material taken down; states under penalty of perjury that the notifying party has a good-faith belief that the material was taken down "as a result of mistake or misidentification of the material to be removed or disabled"; and consents to the jurisdiction of the federal district court in the district of the notifying party's contact address, or, for parties who reside outside the United States, where the OSP is located. *Id.* § 512(g)(3). Upon receipt of a proper counter-notification, an OSP must notify the complainant, and must restore the material after ten and within fourteen business days unless it first receives notice that a lawsuit has been filed. *Id.* § 512(g)(2). A party submitting a counter-notification who "knowingly materially misrepresents" that material was removed by mistake will be liable for damages, including costs and attorney's fees, incurred by the copyright owner or its authorized licensee, or by the OSP. *Id.* § 512(f).

Section 512(h) authorizes federal district court clerks to issue subpoenas, upon a copyright owner's request, ordering the identification of individuals who have posted allegedly infringing material. OSPs receiving such subpoenas must "expeditiously disclose" the information. *Id.* § 512(h).

Finally, note that although § 512 shelters an OSP from damages, it does not prevent a court from issuing injunctions and other equitable relief. *See id.* § 512(j). Note also that an OSP has the option either to comply with the requirements and shelter within the § 512 safe harbors, or to *not* comply and to rely instead on the courts' application of the traditional secondary infringement doctrines and the other defenses that might be available to it (for example, fair use). *Id* § 512(l).

NOTES

1. Section 512 has been controversial from the moment it was enacted, but it has thus far lasted for two decades without change. Do you think that § 512 represents a proper balance between the rights of copyright owners and the viability of online service providers? How should we frame a discussion of whether § 512 represents the proper balance? Is the question mostly an economic one? That is, should our inquiry focus on whether § 512 maintains adequate incentives to engage in the production of new copyrighted works while also incentivizing investment in new online services? Or is there a moral dimension to the question, and, if so, does § 512 address it? For an argument that § 512 has displaced substantive copyright law, see Matthew Sag, *Internet Safe Harbors and the Transformation of Copyright Law*, 93 NOTRE DAME L. REV. 499 (2017).

2. If you had the power, what, if anything, would you change about § 512, and why?

3. Who ought to bear the burden of detecting copyright infringement hosted or stored by OSPs: copyright owners or OSPs? For explorations of this issue, see Annemarie Bridy, *Is Online Copyright Enforcement Scalable?*, 13 VAND. J. ENT. & TECH. L. 695 (2011); Lital Helman & Gideon Parchomovsky, *The Best Available Technology Standard*, 111 COLUM. L. REV. 1194 (2011); Sonia K. Katyal & Jason M. Schultz, *The Unending Search for the Optimal Infringement Filter*, 112 COLUM. L. REV. SIDEBAR 83 (2012).

4. The European Union recently initiated a process of significant change to EU-area copyright law with its *Directive on Copyright in the Digital Single Market*, adopted in 2019. EU member states have two years to pass national legislation complying with the Directive. One of the Directive's more controversial provisions, Article 17, requires OSPs to implement "effective and proportionate measures" to prevent copyright infringement. This provision has been interpreted as requiring some form of filtering to block the unauthorized uploading of copyrighted works. *See* Felipe Romero Moreno, *Upload Filters and Human Rights: Implementing Article 17 of the Directive on Copyright in the Digital Single Market*, 34 INT'L REV. L. COMP. & TECH. 153 (2020). What are the arguments for and against requiring upload filtering?

5. After several years of study, including a series of hearings, the U.S. Copyright Office issued a report on § 512. *See* https://www.copyright.gov/policy/section512/section-512-full-report.pdf. Although the Report suggests that § 512 has become unbalanced in favor of OSPs and against the interests of rightsholders, the Copyright Office does not recommend legislation importing the approach of EU Article 17, of mandatory upload filtering. Rather, the Copyright Office recommends to Congress a set of small-scale reforms, including clarifying § 512 "knowledge" requirements—that is, the degree of knowledge of infringement a website operator must have before it is required to take down infringing content as well as the degree of knowledge required to qualify for the safe harbor provisions.

6. In *BMG Rights Mgmt. (US) LLC v. Cox Comm'ns, Inc.*, 881 F.3d 293 (4th Cir. 2018), the Fourth Circuit upheld a district court's finding that internet access provider Cox had failed to fulfill its obligation under 17 U.S.C. § 512(i)(1)(A) to maintain and apply a reasonable repeat-infringer termination policy, and was therefore ineligible for the § 512 safe harbors. BMG had introduced into evidence a number of Cox's internal emails, which featured Cox employees acknowledging that they had received many infringement notices for the same subscriber, given repeated warnings to those subscribers, but never actually terminated them or terminated them only to reconnect them immediately. The emails supported BMG's argument that Cox was only pretending to have a repeat-infringer termination policy; Cox's real policy, BMG said and the Fourth Circuit accepted, was to never terminate subscribers. Note, however, that the Fourth Circuit also acknowledges that mere *accusations* of infringement should not necessarily lead to an obligation to terminate a subscriber. The court states that it is "mindful of the need to afford [O]SPs flexibility in crafting repeat infringer policies, and of the difficulty of determining when it is 'appropriate' to terminate a person's access to the Internet." The court ruled that Cox had lost its safe harbor, not because its termination policy was too lenient, but because it failed to implement its own policy. "Indeed," wrote the court, "in carrying out its thirteen-strike process, Cox very clearly determined not to terminate subscribers who in fact repeatedly violated the policy."

As you read the next case, consider the number of substantial interpretive issues that even a detailed statutory provision like § 512 left for judicial interpretation and "gap filling." Consider also the sheer size of the liability bet that Google made when it acquired YouTube, a deal made before the Second Circuit's decision in the following case.

Viacom International, Inc. v. YouTube, Inc.
676 F.3d 19 (2d Cir. 2012)

CABRANES, J.:

[1] This appeal requires us to clarify the contours of the "safe harbor" provision of the Digital Millennium Copyright Act (DMCA) that limits the liability of online service providers for copyright infringement that occurs "by reason of the storage at the direction of a user of material that resides on a system or network controlled or operated by or for the service provider." 17 U.S.C. § 512(c).

[2] The plaintiffs-appellants in these related actions—Viacom International, Inc., The Football Association Premier League Ltd., and various film studios, television networks, music publishers, and sports leagues—appeal from an August 10, 2010 judgment of the United States District Court for the Southern District of New York, which granted summary judgment to defendants-appellees YouTube, Inc., YouTube, LLC, and Google Inc. The plaintiffs alleged direct and secondary copyright infringement based on the public performance, display, and reproduction of approximately 79,000 audiovisual "clips" that appeared on the YouTube website between 2005 and 2008....

[3] To qualify for protection under any of the safe harbors, a party must meet a set of threshold criteria. First, the party must in fact be a "service provider," defined, in pertinent part, as "a provider of online services or network access, or the operator of facilities therefor." 17 U.S.C. § 512(k)(1)(B). A party that qualifies as a service provider must also satisfy certain "conditions of eligibility," including the adoption and reasonable implementation of a "repeat infringer" policy that "provides for the termination in appropriate circumstances

of subscribers and account holders of the service provider's system or network." *Id.* § 512(i)(1)(A). In addition, a qualifying service provider must accommodate "standard technical measures" that are "used by copyright owners to identify or protect copyrighted works." *Id.* § 512(i)(1)(B), (i)(2).

[4] Beyond the threshold criteria, a service provider must satisfy the requirements of a particular safe harbor. In this case, the safe harbor at issue is § 512(c), which covers infringement claims that arise "by reason of the storage at the direction of a user of material that resides on a system or network controlled or operated by or for the service provider." *Id.* § 512(c)(1). The § 512(c) safe harbor will apply only if the service provider:

> *(A) (i) does not have actual knowledge that the material or an activity using the material on the system or network is infringing;*
>> *(ii) in the absence of such actual knowledge, is not aware of facts or circumstances from which infringing activity is apparent; or*
>> *(iii) upon obtaining such knowledge or awareness, acts expeditiously to remove, or disable access to, the material;*
> *(B) does not receive a financial benefit directly attributable to the infringing activity, in a case in which the service provider has the right and ability to control such activity; and*
> *(C) upon notification of claimed infringement as described in paragraph (3), responds expeditiously to remove, or disable access to, the material that is claimed to be infringing or to be the subject of infringing activity.*

Section 512(c) also sets forth a detailed notification scheme that requires service providers to "designate[] an agent to receive notifications of claimed infringement" and specifies the components of a proper notification, commonly known as a "takedown notice," to that agent. Thus, actual knowledge of infringing material, awareness of facts or circumstances that make infringing activity apparent, or receipt of a takedown notice will each trigger an obligation to expeditiously remove the infringing material.

[5] With the statutory context in mind, we now turn to the facts of this case....

[6] YouTube was founded in February 2005 by Chad Hurley, Steve Chen, and Jawed Karim, three former employees of the internet company Paypal. When YouTube announced the "official launch" of the website in December 2005, a press release described YouTube as a "consumer media company" that "allows people to watch, upload, and share personal video clips at www.YouTube.com." Under the slogan "Broadcast yourself," YouTube achieved rapid prominence and profitability, eclipsing competitors such as Google Video and Yahoo Video by wide margins. In November 2006, Google acquired YouTube in a stock-for-stock transaction valued at $1.65 billion. By March 2010, at the time of summary judgment briefing in this litigation, site traffic on YouTube had soared to more than 1 billion daily video views, with more than 24 hours of new video uploaded to the site every minute.

[7] The basic function of the YouTube website permits users to "upload" and view video clips free of charge. Before uploading a video to YouTube, a user must register and create an account with the website. The registration process requires the user to accept YouTube's Terms of Use agreement, which provides, *inter alia,* that the user "will not submit material that is copyrighted ... unless [he is] the owner of such rights or ha[s] permission from their rightful owner to post the material and to grant YouTube all of the license rights granted herein." When the registration process is complete, the user can sign in to his account, select a video to upload from the user's personal computer, mobile phone, or other device, and instruct the YouTube system to upload the video by clicking on a virtual upload "button."

[8] Uploading a video to the YouTube website triggers a series of automated software functions. During the upload process, YouTube makes one or more exact copies of the video in its original file format. YouTube also

534

makes one or more additional copies of the video in "Flash" format, a process known as "transcoding." The transcoding process ensures that YouTube videos are available for viewing by most users at their request. The YouTube system allows users to gain access to video content by "streaming" the video to the user's computer in response to a playback request. YouTube uses a computer algorithm to identify clips that are "related" to a video the user watches and display links to the "related" clips....

[9] Plaintiff Viacom, an American media conglomerate, and various Viacom affiliates filed suit against YouTube on March 13, 2007, alleging direct and secondary copyright infringement based on the public performance, display, and reproduction of their audiovisual works on the YouTube website. Plaintiff Premier League, an English soccer league, and Plaintiff Bourne Co. filed a putative class action against YouTube on May 4, 2007, alleging direct and secondary copyright infringement on behalf of all copyright owners whose material was copied, stored, displayed, or performed on YouTube without authorization. Specifically at issue were some 63,497 video clips identified by Viacom, as well as 13,500 additional clips identified by the putative class plaintiffs....

[10] ... [T]he District Court ... granted summary judgment to the defendants, finding that YouTube qualified for DMCA safe harbor protection with respect to all claims of direct and secondary copyright infringement. The District Court prefaced its analysis of the DMCA safe harbor by holding that, based on the plaintiffs' summary judgment submissions, "a jury could find that the defendants not only were generally aware of, but welcomed, copyright-infringing material being placed on their website." However, the District Court also noted that the defendants had properly designated an agent pursuant to § 512(c)(2), and "when they received specific notice that a particular item infringed a copyright, they swiftly removed it." Accordingly, the District Court identified the crux of the inquiry with respect to YouTube's copyright liability as follows:

> [T]he critical question is whether the statutory phrases "actual knowledge that the material or an activity using the material on the system or network is infringing," and "facts or circumstances from which infringing activity is apparent" in § 512(c)(1)(A)(i) and (ii) mean a general awareness that there are infringements (here, claimed to be widespread and common), or rather mean actual or constructive knowledge of specific and identifiable infringements of individual items.

[11] After quoting at length from the legislative history of the DMCA, the District Court held that "the phrases 'actual knowledge that the material or an activity' is infringing, and 'facts or circumstances' indicating infringing activity, describe knowledge of specific and identifiable infringements of particular individual items." "Mere knowledge of [the] prevalence of such activity in general," the District Court concluded, "is not enough."

[12] In a final section labeled "Other Points," the District Court rejected two additional claims. First, it rejected the plaintiffs' argument that the replication, transmittal and display of YouTube videos are functions that fall outside the protection § 512(c)(1) affords for "infringement of copyright by reason of ... storage at the direction of the user." Second, it rejected the plaintiffs' argument that YouTube was ineligible for safe harbor protection under the control provision, holding that the "right and ability to control" infringing activity under § 512(c)(1)(B) requires "item-specific" knowledge thereof, because "the provider must know of the particular case before he can control it." ...

A. Actual and "Red Flag" Knowledge: § 512(c)(1)(A)

[13] The first and most important question on appeal is whether the DMCA safe harbor at issue requires "actual knowledge" or "aware[ness]" of facts or circumstances indicating "specific and identifiable

infringements." We consider first the scope of the statutory provision and then its application to the record in this case ....

[14] As in all statutory construction cases, we begin with the language of the statute. Under § 512(c)(1)(A), safe harbor protection is available only if the service provider:

> *(i) does not have actual knowledge that the material or an activity using the material on the system or network is infringing;*
> *(ii) in the absence of such actual knowledge, is not aware of facts or circumstances from which infringing activity is apparent; or*
> *(iii) upon obtaining such knowledge or awareness, acts expeditiously to remove, or disable access to, the material....*

As previously noted, the District Court held that the statutory phrases "actual knowledge that the material ... is infringing" and "facts or circumstances from which infringing activity is apparent" refer to "knowledge of specific and identifiable infringements." For the reasons that follow, we substantially affirm that holding.

[15] Although the parties marshal a battery of other arguments on appeal, it is the text of the statute that compels our conclusion. In particular, we are persuaded that the basic operation of § 512(c) requires knowledge or awareness of specific infringing activity. Under § 512(c)(1)(A), knowledge or awareness alone does not disqualify the service provider; rather, the provider that gains knowledge or awareness of infringing activity retains safe-harbor protection if it "acts expeditiously to remove, or disable access to, the material." 17 U.S.C. § 512(c)(1)(A)(iii). Thus, the nature of the removal obligation itself contemplates knowledge or awareness of specific infringing material, because expeditious removal is possible only if the service provider knows with particularity which items to remove. Indeed, to require expeditious removal in the absence of specific knowledge or awareness would be to mandate an amorphous obligation to take commercially reasonable steps in response to a generalized awareness of infringement. Such a view cannot be reconciled with the language of the statute, which requires "expeditious[]" action to remove or disable "*the material*" at issue. 17 U.S.C. § 512(c)(1)(A)(iii) (emphasis added).

[16] On appeal, the plaintiffs dispute this conclusion by drawing our attention to § 512(c)(1)(A)(ii), the so-called "red flag" knowledge provision. *See id.* § 512(c)(1)(A)(ii) (limiting liability where, "in the absence of such actual knowledge, [the service provider] is not aware of facts or circumstances from which infringing activity is apparent"). In their view, the use of the phrase "facts or circumstances" demonstrates that Congress did not intend to limit the red flag provision to a particular type of knowledge. The plaintiffs contend that requiring awareness of specific infringements in order to establish "aware[ness] of facts or circumstances from which infringing activity is apparent," 17 U.S.C. § 512(c)(1)(A)(ii), renders the red flag provision superfluous, because that provision would be satisfied only when the "actual knowledge" provision is also satisfied. For that reason, the plaintiffs urge the Court to hold that the red flag provision "requires less specificity" than the actual knowledge provision.

[17] This argument misconstrues the relationship between "actual" knowledge and "red flag" knowledge. It is true that we are required to disfavor interpretations of statutes that render language superfluous. But contrary to the plaintiffs' assertions, construing § 512(c)(1)(A) to require actual knowledge or awareness of specific instances of infringement does not render the red flag provision superfluous. The phrase "actual knowledge," which appears in § 512(c)(1)(A)(i), is frequently used to denote subjective belief. By contrast, courts often invoke the language of "facts or circumstances," which appears in § 512(c)(1)(A)(ii), in discussing an objective reasonableness standard.

[18] The difference between actual and red flag knowledge is thus not between specific and generalized knowledge, but instead between a subjective and an objective standard. In other words, the actual knowledge provision turns on whether the provider actually or "subjectively" knew of specific infringement, while the red flag provision turns on whether the provider was subjectively aware of facts that would have made the specific infringement "objectively" obvious to a reasonable person. The red flag provision, because it incorporates an objective standard, is not swallowed up by the actual knowledge provision under our construction of the § 512(c) safe harbor. Both provisions do independent work, and both apply only to specific instances of infringement....

[19] ... [W]e affirm the District Court's holding that actual knowledge or awareness of facts or circumstances that indicate specific and identifiable instances of infringement will disqualify a service provider from the safe harbor....

[20] The corollary question on appeal is whether, under the foregoing construction of § 512(c)(1)(A), the District Court erred in granting summary judgment to YouTube on the record presented. For the reasons that follow, we hold that although the District Court correctly interpreted § 512(c)(1)(A), summary judgment for the defendants was premature....

[21] The plaintiffs argue that, even under the District Court's construction of the safe harbor, the record raises material issues of fact regarding YouTube's actual knowledge or "red flag" awareness of specific instances of infringement. To that end, the plaintiffs draw our attention to various estimates regarding the percentage of infringing content on the YouTube website. For example, Viacom cites evidence that YouTube employees conducted website surveys and estimated that 75–80% of all YouTube streams contained copyrighted material. The class plaintiffs similarly claim that Credit Suisse, acting as financial advisor to Google, estimated that more than 60% of YouTube's content was "premium" copyrighted content—and that only 10% of the premium content was authorized. These approximations suggest that the defendants were conscious that significant quantities of material on the YouTube website were infringing. But such estimates are insufficient, standing alone, to create a triable issue of fact as to whether YouTube actually knew, or was aware of facts or circumstances that would indicate, the existence of particular instances of infringement.

[22] Beyond the survey results, the plaintiffs rely upon internal YouTube communications that do refer to particular clips or groups of clips. The class plaintiffs argue that YouTube was aware of specific infringing material because, *inter alia,* YouTube attempted to search for specific Premier League videos on the site in order to gauge their "value based on video usage." In particular, the class plaintiffs cite a February 7, 2007 e-mail from Patrick Walker, director of video partnerships for Google and YouTube, requesting that his colleagues calculate the number of daily searches for the terms "soccer," "football," and "Premier League" in preparation for a bid on the global rights to Premier League content. On another occasion, Walker requested that any "clearly infringing, official broadcast footage" from a list of top Premier League clubs—including Liverpool Football Club, Chelsea Football Club, Manchester United Football Club, and Arsenal Football Club— be taken down in advance of a meeting with the heads of "several major sports teams and leagues." YouTube ultimately decided not to make a bid for the Premier League rights—but the infringing content allegedly remained on the website.

[23] The record in the *Viacom* action includes additional examples. For instance, YouTube founder Jawed Karim prepared a report in March 2006 which stated that, "[a]s of today[,] episodes and clips of the following well-known shows can still be found [on YouTube]: Family Guy, South Park, MTV Cribs, Daily Show, Reno 911, [and] Dave Chapelle [sic]." Karim further opined that, "although YouTube is not legally required to monitor content ... and complies with DMCA takedown requests, we would benefit from *preemptively* removing content that is blatantly illegal and likely to attract criticism." He also noted that "a more thorough analysis" of the issue would be required. At least some of the TV shows to which Karim referred are owned by Viacom.

A reasonable juror could conclude from the March 2006 report that Karim knew of the presence of Viacom-owned material on YouTube, since he presumably located specific clips of the shows in question before he could announce that YouTube hosted the content "[a]s of today." A reasonable juror could also conclude that Karim believed the clips he located to be infringing (since he refers to them as "blatantly illegal"), and that YouTube did not remove the content from the website until conducting "a more thorough analysis," thus exposing the company to liability in the interim.

[24] Furthermore, in a July 4, 2005 e-mail exchange, YouTube founder Chad Hurley sent an e-mail to his co-founders with the subject line "budlight commercials," and stated, "we need to reject these too." Steve Chen responded, "can we please leave these in a bit longer? another week or two can't hurt." Karim also replied, indicating that he "added back in all 28 bud videos." Similarly, in an August 9, 2005 e-mail exchange, Hurley urged his colleagues "to start being *diligent* about rejecting copyrighted / inappropriate content," noting that "there is a cnn clip of the shuttle clip on the site today, if the boys from Turner would come to the site, they might be pissed?" Again, Chen resisted:

> but we should just keep that stuff on the site. i really don't see what will happen. what?
> someone from cnn sees it? he happens to be someone with power? he happens to want to take
> it down right away. he gets in touch with cnn legal. 2 weeks later, we get a cease & desist
> letter. we take the video down.

And again, Karim agreed, indicating that "the CNN space shuttle clip, I like. we can remove it once we're bigger and better known, but for now that clip is fine."

[25] Upon a review of the record, we are persuaded that the plaintiffs may have raised a material issue of fact regarding YouTube's knowledge or awareness of specific instances of infringement.... [A] reasonable juror could conclude that YouTube had actual knowledge of specific infringing activity, or was at least aware of facts or circumstances from which specific infringing activity was apparent. *See* § 512(c)(1)(A)(i)-(ii). Accordingly, we hold that summary judgment to YouTube on all clips-in-suit, especially in the absence of any detailed examination of the extensive record on summary judgment, was premature.[9]

[26] We hasten to note, however, that although the foregoing e-mails were annexed as exhibits to the summary judgment papers, it is unclear whether the clips referenced therein are among the current clips-in-suit. By definition, only the current clips-in-suit are at issue in this litigation. Accordingly, we vacate the order granting summary judgment and instruct the District Court to determine on remand whether any specific infringements of which YouTube had knowledge or awareness correspond to the clips-in-suit in these actions....

[27] The plaintiffs further argue that the District Court erred in granting summary judgment to the defendants despite evidence that YouTube was "willfully blind" to specific infringing activity. On this issue of first impression, we consider the application of the common law willful blindness doctrine in the DMCA context.

[28] The principle that willful blindness is tantamount to knowledge is hardly novel. A person is "willfully blind" or engages in "conscious avoidance" amounting to knowledge where the person was aware of a high probability of the fact in dispute and consciously avoided confirming that fact. Writing in the trademark

---

[9] We express no opinion as to whether the evidence discussed above will prove sufficient to withstand a renewed motion for summary judgment by YouTube on remand. In particular, we note that there is at least some evidence that the search requested by Walker in his February 7, 2007 e-mail was never carried out. We also note that the class plaintiffs have failed to identify evidence indicating that any infringing content discovered as a result of Walker's request in fact remained on the YouTube website. The class plaintiffs, drawing on the voluminous record in this case, may be able to remedy these deficiencies in their briefing to the District Court on remand.

infringement context, we have held that a service provider is not permitted willful blindness. When it has reason to suspect that users of its service are infringing a protected mark, it may not shield itself from learning of the particular infringing transactions by looking the other way.

[29] The DMCA does not mention willful blindness. As a general matter, we interpret a statute to abrogate a common law principle only if the statute speaks directly to the question addressed by the common law. The relevant question, therefore, is whether the DMCA speaks directly to the principle of willful blindness. The DMCA provision most relevant to the abrogation inquiry is § 512(m), which provides that safe harbor protection shall not be conditioned on "a service provider monitoring its service or affirmatively seeking facts indicating infringing activity, except to the extent consistent with a standard technical measure complying with the provisions of subsection (i)." 17 U.S.C. § 512(m)(1). Section 512(m) is explicit: DMCA safe harbor protection cannot be conditioned on affirmative monitoring by a service provider. For that reason, § 512(m) is incompatible with a broad common law duty to monitor or otherwise seek out infringing activity based on general awareness that infringement may be occurring. That fact does not, however, dispose of the abrogation inquiry; as previously noted, willful blindness cannot be defined as an affirmative duty to monitor. Because the statute does not speak directly to the willful blindness doctrine, § 512(m) limits—but does not abrogate—the doctrine. Accordingly, we hold that the willful blindness doctrine may be applied, in appropriate circumstances, to demonstrate knowledge or awareness of specific instances of infringement under the DMCA.

[30] The District Court cited § 512(m) for the proposition that safe harbor protection does not require affirmative monitoring, but did not expressly address the principle of willful blindness or its relationship to the DMCA safe harbors. As a result, whether the defendants made a deliberate effort to avoid guilty knowledge remains a fact question for the District Court to consider in the first instance on remand.

B. Control and Benefit: § 512(c)(1)(B)

[31] Apart from the foregoing knowledge provisions, the § 512(c) safe harbor provides that an eligible service provider must "not receive a financial benefit directly attributable to the infringing activity, in a case in which the service provider has the right and ability to control such activity." 17 U.S.C. § 512(c)(1)(B). The District Court addressed this issue in a single paragraph, quoting from § 512(c)(1)(B), the so-called "control and benefit" provision, and concluding that "[t]he 'right and ability to control' the activity requires knowledge of it, which must be item-specific." For the reasons that follow, we hold that the District Court erred by importing a specific knowledge requirement into the control and benefit provision, and we therefore remand for further fact-finding on the issue of control....

[32] On appeal, the parties advocate two competing constructions of the "right and ability to control" infringing activity. 17 U.S.C. § 512(c)(1)(B). Because each is fatally flawed, we reject both proposed constructions in favor of a fact-based inquiry to be conducted in the first instance by the District Court.

[33] The first construction, pressed by the defendants, is the one adopted by the District Court, which held that "the provider must know of the particular case before he can control it." The Ninth Circuit recently agreed, holding that until the service provider becomes aware of specific unauthorized material, it cannot exercise its power or authority over the specific infringing item. In practical terms, it does not have the kind of ability to control infringing activity the statute contemplates. The trouble with this construction is that importing a specific knowledge requirement into § 512(c)(1)(B) renders the control provision duplicative of § 512(c)(1)(A). Any service provider that has item-specific knowledge of infringing activity and thereby obtains financial benefit would already be excluded from the safe harbor under § 512(c)(1)(A) for having specific knowledge of infringing material and failing to effect expeditious removal. No additional service provider would be excluded by § 512(c)(1)(B) that was not already excluded by § 512(c)(1)(A). Because statutory

interpretations that render language superfluous are disfavored, we reject the District Court's interpretation of the control provision.

[34] The second construction, urged by the plaintiffs, is that the control provision codifies the common law doctrine of vicarious copyright liability. The common law imposes liability for vicarious copyright infringement when the right and ability to supervise coalesce with an obvious and direct financial interest in the exploitation of copyrighted materials—even in the absence of actual knowledge that the copyright monopoly is being impaired. To support their codification argument, the plaintiffs rely on a House Report relating to a preliminary version of the DMCA: "The 'right and ability to control' language ... codifies the second element of vicarious liability.... Subparagraph (B) is intended to preserve existing case law that examines all relevant aspects of the relationship between the primary and secondary infringer." H.R. REP. NO. 105-551(I), at 26 (1998). In response, YouTube notes that the codification reference was omitted from the committee reports describing the final legislation, and that Congress ultimately abandoned any attempt to "embark[] upon a wholesale clarification" of vicarious liability, electing instead "to create a series of 'safe harbors' for certain common activities of service providers." S. REP. NO. 105–190, at 19.

[35] Happily, the future of digital copyright law does not turn on the confused legislative history of the control provision. The general rule with respect to common law codification is that when Congress uses terms that have accumulated settled meaning under the common law, a court must infer, unless the statute otherwise dictates, that Congress means to incorporate the established meaning of those terms. Under the common law vicarious liability standard, the ability to block infringers' access to a particular environment for any reason whatsoever is evidence of the right and ability to supervise. To adopt that principle in the DMCA context, however, would render the statute internally inconsistent. Section 512(c) actually presumes that service providers have the ability to block access to infringing material. Indeed, a service provider who has knowledge or awareness of infringing material or who receives a takedown notice from a copyright holder is *required* to "remove, or disable access to, the material" in order to claim the benefit of the safe harbor. 17 U.S.C. § 512(c)(1)(A)(iii) & (C). But in taking such action, the service provider would—in the plaintiffs' analysis—be admitting the "right and ability to control" the infringing material. Thus, the prerequisite to safe harbor protection under § 512(c)(1)(A)(iii) & (C) would at the same time be a disqualifier under § 512(c)(1)(B)....

[36] ... [T]he foregoing tension ... is sufficient to establish that the control provision dictates a departure from the common law vicarious liability standard. Accordingly, we conclude that the "right and ability to control" infringing activity under § 512(c)(1)(B) requires something more than the ability to remove or block access to materials posted on a service provider's website. The remaining—and more difficult—question is how to define the "something more" that is required.

[37] To date, only one court has found that a service provider had the right and ability to control infringing activity under § 512(c)(1)(B). In *Perfect 10, Inc. v. Cybernet Ventures, Inc.*, 213 F. Supp. 2d 1146 (C.D. Cal. 2002), the court found control where the service provider instituted a monitoring program by which user websites received "detailed instructions regard[ing] issues of layout, appearance, and content." The service provider also forbade certain types of content and refused access to users who failed to comply with its instructions. Similarly, inducement of copyright infringement ... might also rise to the level of control under § 512(c)(1)(B). Both of these examples involve a service provider exerting substantial influence on the activities of users, without necessarily—or even frequently—acquiring knowledge of specific infringing activity.

[38] In light of our holding that § 512(c)(1)(B) does not include a specific knowledge requirement, we think it prudent to remand to the District Court to consider in the first instance whether the plaintiffs have adduced sufficient evidence to allow a reasonable jury to conclude that YouTube had the right and ability to control the infringing activity and received a financial benefit directly attributable to that activity.

C. "By Reason of" Storage: § 512(c)(1)

[39] The § 512(c) safe harbor is only available when the infringement occurs "by reason of the storage at the direction of a user of material that resides on a system or network controlled or operated by or for the service provider." 17 U.S.C. § 512(c)(1). In this case, the District Court held that YouTube's software functions fell within the safe harbor for infringements that occur "by reason of" user storage. For the reasons that follow, we affirm that holding with respect to three of the challenged software functions—the conversion (or "transcoding") of videos into a standard display format, the playback of videos on "watch" pages, and the "related videos" function. We remand for further fact-finding with respect to a fourth software function, involving the third-party syndication of videos uploaded to YouTube....

[40] The relevant case law makes clear that the § 512(c) safe harbor extends to software functions performed for the purpose of facilitating access to user-stored material.... Transcoding involves making copies of a video in a different encoding scheme in order to render the video viewable over the Internet to most users. The playback process involves delivering copies of YouTube videos to a user's browser cache in response to a user request. The District Court correctly found that to exclude these automated functions from the safe harbor would eviscerate the protection afforded to service providers by § 512(c).

[41] A similar analysis applies to the "related videos" function, by which a YouTube computer algorithm identifies and displays "thumbnails" of clips that are "related" to the video selected by the user. The plaintiffs claim that this practice constitutes content promotion, not "access" to stored content, and therefore falls beyond the scope of the safe harbor.... [T]he related videos function serves to help YouTube users locate and gain access to material stored at the direction of other users. Because the algorithm is closely related to, and follows from, the storage itself, and is narrowly directed toward providing access to material stored at the direction of users, we conclude that the related videos function is also protected by the § 512(c) safe harbor.

[42] The final software function at issue here—third-party syndication—is the closest case. In or around March 2007, YouTube transcoded a select number of videos into a format compatible with mobile devices and "syndicated" or licensed the videos to Verizon Wireless and other companies. The plaintiffs argue—with some force—that business transactions do not occur at the "direction of a user" within the meaning of § 512(c)(1) when they involve the manual selection of copyrighted material for licensing to a third party. The parties do not dispute, however, that none of the clips-in-suit were among the approximately 2,000 videos provided to Verizon Wireless. In order to avoid rendering an advisory opinion on the outer boundaries of the storage provision, we remand for fact-finding on the question of whether any of the clips-in-suit were in fact syndicated to any other third party.

D. Other Arguments ...

[43] The class plaintiffs briefly argue that YouTube failed to comply with the requirements of § 512(i), which conditions safe harbor eligibility on the service provider having "adopted and reasonably implemented ... a policy that provides for the termination in appropriate circumstances of subscribers and account holders of the service provider's system or network who are repeat infringers." 17 U.S.C. § 512(i)(1)(A). Specifically, the class plaintiffs allege that YouTube "deliberately set up its identification tools to try to avoid identifying infringements of class plaintiffs' works." This allegation rests primarily on the assertion that YouTube permitted only designated "partners" to gain access to content identification tools by which YouTube would conduct network searches and identify infringing material.

[44] Because the class plaintiffs challenge YouTube's deployment of search technology, we must consider their § 512(i) argument in conjunction with § 512(m). As previously noted, § 512(m) provides that safe harbor protection cannot be conditioned on "a service provider monitoring its service or affirmatively seeking facts

indicating infringing activity, *except to the extent consistent with a standard technical measure complying with the provisions of subsection (i)."* 17 U.S.C. § 512(m)(1) (emphasis added). In other words, the safe harbor expressly disclaims any affirmative monitoring requirement—except to the extent that such monitoring comprises a "standard technical measure" within the meaning of § 512(i). Refusing to accommodate or implement a "standard technical measure" exposes a service provider to liability; refusing to provide access to mechanisms by which a service provider affirmatively monitors its own network has no such result. In this case, the class plaintiffs make no argument that the content identification tools implemented by YouTube constitute "standard technical measures," such that YouTube would be exposed to liability under § 512(i). For that reason, YouTube cannot be excluded from the safe harbor by dint of a decision to restrict access to its proprietary search mechanisms....

[45] Finally, the plaintiffs argue that the District Court erred in denying summary judgment to the plaintiffs on their claims of direct infringement, vicarious liability, and contributory liability .... In granting summary judgment to the defendants, the District Court held that YouTube "qualif[ied] for the protection of ... § 512(c)," and therefore denied the plaintiffs' cross-motion for summary judgment without comment.

[46] The District Court correctly determined that a finding of safe harbor application necessarily protects a defendant from all affirmative claims for monetary relief. 17 U.S.C. § 512(c)(1). For the reasons previously stated, further fact-finding is required to determine whether YouTube is ultimately entitled to safe harbor protection in this case. Accordingly, we vacate the order denying summary judgment to the plaintiffs and remand the cause without expressing a view on the merits of the plaintiffs' affirmative claims....

NOTES

1. On remand, the district court granted summary judgment for YouTube. On the principal legal issue the Second Circuit left open—the application of the willful blindness doctrine to § 512—the district court ruled that the type of "willful blindness" that can lead to liability is willful blindness respecting a *specific* instance of infringement, as opposed to willful blindness regarding the general incidence of infringement on the service. Viacom Int'l Inc. v. YouTube, Inc., 940 F. Supp. 2d 110, 116 (S.D.N.Y. 2013). In *EMI Christian Music Group v. MP3Tunes, LLC*, 844 F.3d 79 (2d Cir. 2016), the Second Circuit found that a defendant could be found to both have red flag knowledge and to have been willfully blind when the defendant website digitally distributed songs from major labels before 2007 and the defendant was aware that none of the major labels had authorized digital distribution of their sound recordings before 2007. The Second Circuit also held that such a "time-limited, targeted duty—even if encompassing a large number of songs—does not give rise to an 'amorphous' duty to monitor in contravention of [§ 512(m) of] the DMCA."

2. A threshold issue in *Viacom* was whether infringement on the service was "by reason of storage," and therefore eligible for the § 512(c) safe harbor, or whether certain of YouTube's functionality—such as transcoding, playback, and the presentation of "related videos"—were independent of YouTube's storage function, and therefore any infringement committed as a result of these functions would lie outside the safe harbor. The Second Circuit found that "to exclude these automated functions from the safe harbor would eviscerate the protection afforded to service providers by § 512(c)." That may be true, but it doesn't answer the question whether these functions should be grouped under the umbrella of "storage." Can you find an answer to that question in the Second Circuit's opinion? Can you think of one yourself?

3. *Viacom* distinguishes "actual knowledge" under § 512(c) from so-called "red flag" knowledge under that same section—that is, "aware[ness] of facts or circumstances from which infringing activity is apparent." The court holds that the former is *subjective* knowledge of specific infringing activity, while the latter is *objective* knowledge—that is, awareness of facts or circumstances that would put a reasonable person on notice of specific infringing activity. Is this right? Do you see anything in the statutory text that would suggest another

reading? Is there a policy reason to prefer another reading?

Recall that § 512(c) applies to material stored by an OSP on behalf of a user. What does it mean for storage to be "on behalf of" a user? That issue figures prominently in the next case. As you read it, consider whether there is a policy reason to treat an OSP differently based on whether it participates in the decisions that lead to storage or hosting of potentially infringing material.

Mavrix Photographs, LLC v. LiveJournal, Inc. ·
873 F.3d 1045 (9th Cir. 2018)

PAEZ, J.:

[1] Plaintiff Mavrix Photographs appeals the district court's summary judgment in favor of Defendant LiveJournal. Mavrix sued LiveJournal for posting twenty of its copyrighted photographs online. The district court held that the Digital Millennium Copyright Act's § 512(c) safe harbor protected LiveJournal from liability because Mavrix's photographs were stored at the direction of the user.

[2] To be eligible at the threshold for the § 512(c) safe harbor, LiveJournal must show that the photographs were stored at the direction of the user. Although users submitted Mavrix's photographs to LiveJournal, LiveJournal posted the photographs after a team of volunteer moderators led by a LiveJournal employee reviewed and approved them. Whether these photographs were truly stored at the direction of the user, or instead whether LiveJournal is responsible for the photographs, depends on whether the acts of the moderators can be attributed to LiveJournal. The issue we must decide is whether the common law of agency applies to LiveJournal's safe harbor defense. The district court ruled that the common law of agency does not apply to this analysis. We disagree and conclude that it does. As there are genuine factual disputes regarding whether the moderators are LiveJournal's agents, we reverse the district court's summary judgment and remand for trial.

[3] Because the district court ruled on the remaining elements of the safe harbor, we also proceed to discuss those elements in order to provide guidance to the district court and parties on remand. Finally, we vacate the district court's order denying discovery of the moderators' identities because the agency determination may affect this analysis....

[4] LiveJournal is a social media platform. Among other services, it allows users to create and run thematic "communities" in which they post and comment on content related to the theme. LiveJournal communities can create their own rules for submitting and commenting on posts.

[5] LiveJournal set up three types of unpaid administrator roles to run its communities. "Moderators" review posts submitted by users to ensure compliance with the rules. "Maintainers" review and delete posts and have the authority to remove moderators and users from the community. Each community also has one "owner" who has the authority of a maintainer, but can also remove maintainers.

[6] LiveJournal protects against copyright infringement in its communities through various mechanisms. LiveJournal follows the formal notice and takedown procedures outlined in the DMCA by designating an agent and form to report infringement, and by promptly removing infringing posts and prohibiting repeat abusers from the community. 17 U.S.C. § 512(c)(1)(C). LiveJournal's Terms of Service instructs users not to

"[u]pload, post or otherwise transmit any Content that infringes any patent, trademark, trade secret, copyright or other proprietary rights." ...

[7] [Oh No They Didn't! ("ONTD")] is a popular LiveJournal community which features up-to-date celebrity news. Users submit posts containing photographs, videos, links, and gossip about celebrities' lives. ONTD moderators review and publicly post some of the submissions....

[8] Like other LiveJournal communities, ONTD created rules for submitting and commenting on posts. ONTD's rules pertain to both potential copyright infringement and substantive guidance for users.... ONTD's rules also include a list of sources from which users should not copy material. The sources on the list have informally requested that ONTD stop posting infringing material. ONTD has also automatically blocked all material from one source that sent ONTD a cease and desist letter.

[9] ONTD has nine moderators, six maintainers, and one owner. ONTD users submit proposed posts containing celebrity news to an internal queue. Moderators review the submissions and publicly post approximately one-third of them. Moderators review for substance, approving only those submissions relevant to new and exciting celebrity news. Moderators also review for copyright infringement, pornography, and harassment.

[10] When ONTD was created, like other LiveJournal communities, it was operated exclusively by volunteer moderators. LiveJournal was not involved in the day-to-day operation of the site. ONTD, however, grew in popularity to 52 million page views per month in 2010 and attracted LiveJournal's attention. By a significant margin, ONTD is LiveJournal's most popular community and is the only community with a household name. In 2010, LiveJournal sought to exercise more control over ONTD so that it could generate advertising revenue from the popular community. LiveJournal hired a then active moderator, Brendan Delzer, to serve as the community's full time "primary leader." By hiring Delzer, LiveJournal intended to "take over" ONTD, grow the site, and run ads on it.

[11] As the "primary leader," Delzer instructs ONTD moderators on the content they should approve and selects and removes moderators on the basis of their performance. Delzer also continues to perform moderator work, reviewing and approving posts alongside the other moderators whom he oversees. While Delzer is paid and expected to work full time, the other moderators are free to leave and go and volunteer their time in any way they see fit....

[12] Mavrix is a celebrity photography company specializing in candid photographs of celebrities in tropical locations. The company sells its photographs to celebrity magazines. According to Mavrix, infringement of its photographs is particularly devastating to its business model. Since Mavrix's photographs break celebrity news, such as the pregnancy of Beyoncé, infringing posts on sites like ONTD prevent Mavrix from profiting from the sale of the photographs to celebrity magazines....

[13] Mavrix filed an action for damages and injunctive relief against LiveJournal alleging copyright infringement on the basis of twenty Mavrix photographs posted on ONTD. ONTD posted the photographs in seven separate posts between 2010 and 2014.... To the best of his recollection, Delzer did not personally approve the seven posts. LiveJournal has no technological means of determining which moderator approved any given post. Mavrix did not utilize LiveJournal's notice and takedown procedure to notify LiveJournal of the infringements. When Mavrix filed this lawsuit, LiveJournal removed the posts....

[14] LiveJournal moved for summary judgment on the basis of the § 512(c) safe harbor. The district court granted LiveJournal's motion and denied Mavrix's cross-motion for partial summary judgment, concluding that the § 512(c) safe harbor shielded LiveJournal from liability for copyright infringement. Mavrix timely appealed....

[15] .... LiveJournal claimed protection from damages under the § 512(c) safe harbor for "infringement of copyright by reason of the storage [of material] at the direction of a user." 17 U.S.C. § 512(c)(1). To be eligible at the threshold for the § 512(c) safe harbor, a service provider must show that the infringing material was stored "at the direction of the user." If it meets that threshold requirement, the service provider must then show that (1) it lacked actual or red flag knowledge of the infringing material; and (2) it did not receive a "financial benefit directly attributable to the infringing activity, in a case in which the service provider has the right and ability to control such activity." Because the § 512(c) safe harbor is an affirmative defense, LiveJournal must establish beyond controversy every essential element, and failure to do so will render LiveJournal ineligible for the § 512(c) safe harbor's protection. ...

[15] LiveJournal must make a threshold showing that Mavrix's photographs were stored at the direction of the user. "Storage," in this context, has a unique meaning. Congress explained that "[e]xamples of such storage include providing server space for a user's web site, for a chatroom, or other forum in which material may be posted at the direction of users." S. REP. NO. 105-190, at 43 (1998). We have held that storage encompasses the access-facilitating processes in addition to storage itself. We reasoned that rather than requiring that the infringing conduct *be* storage, the statutory language allows for infringement *by reason of the storage* at the direction of a user. The district court held that although moderators screened and publicly posted all of the ONTD posts, the posts were at the direction of the user. The district court focused on the users' submission of infringing photographs to LiveJournal rather than LiveJournal's screening and public posting of the photographs. A different safe harbor, § 512(a), protects service providers from liability for the passive role they play when users submit infringing material to them. The § 512(c) safe harbor focuses on the service provider's role in making material stored by a user publicly accessible on its site. Contrary to the district court's view, public accessibility is the critical inquiry. In the context of this case, that inquiry turns on the role of the moderators in screening and posting users' submissions and whether their acts may be attributed to LiveJournal....

[16] Mavrix, relying on the common law of agency, argues that the moderators are LiveJournal's agents, making LiveJournal liable for the moderators' acts. The district court erred in rejecting this argument.

[17] Statutes are presumed not to disturb the common law, unless the language of a statute is clear and explicit for this purpose. Pursuant to this principle, the Supreme Court and this court have applied common law in cases involving federal copyright law, including the DMCA. The Supreme Court has applied the common law of agency in interpreting the Copyright Act. We have applied the common law of vicarious liability in analyzing the DMCA, reasoning that Congress intended that the DMCA's limitations of liability be interpreted under existing principles of law. We have also applied the common law of agency to determine a service provider's intent to infringe under the DMCA.

[18] Along with other courts, we have applied agency law to questions much like the question of LiveJournal's liability for the moderators' acts. We applied agency law to determine whether a service provider was responsible under the DMCA for copyright infringement by its employees....We therefore have little difficulty holding that common law agency principles apply to the analysis of whether a service provider like LiveJournal is liable for the acts of the ONTD moderators....

[19] In light of the summary judgment record, we conclude that there are genuine issues of material fact as to whether the moderators are LiveJournal's agents. The factual dispute is evident when we apply common law agency principles to the evidentiary record.

[20] Agency is the fiduciary relationship that arises when one person (a principal) manifests assent to another person (an agent) that the agent shall act on the principal's behalf and subject to the principal's control, and the agent manifests assent or otherwise consents so to act. For an agency relationship to exist, an agent must

have authority to act on behalf of the principal and the person represented must have a right to control the actions of the agent.

[21] An agency relationship may be created through actual or apparent authority. Actual authority arises through the principal's assent that the agent take action on the principal's behalf. LiveJournal argues that it did not assent to the moderators acting on its behalf. Mavrix, however, presented evidence that LiveJournal gave its moderators explicit and varying levels of authority to screen posts. Although LiveJournal calls the moderators "volunteers," the moderators performed a vital function in LiveJournal's business model. There is evidence in the record that LiveJournal gave moderators express directions about their screening functions, including criteria for accepting or rejecting posts. Unlike other sites where users may independently post content, LiveJournal relies on moderators as an integral part of its screening and posting business model. LiveJournal also provides three different levels of authority: moderators review posts to ensure they contain celebrity gossip and not pornography or harassment, maintainers delete posts and can remove moderators, and owners can remove maintainers. Genuine issues of material fact therefore exist regarding whether the moderators had actual authority.

[22] Apparent authority arises by a person's manifestation that another has authority to act with legal consequences for the person who makes the manifestation, when a third party reasonably believes the actor to be authorized and the belief is traceable to the manifestation. The principal's manifestations giving rise to apparent authority may consist of direct statements to the third person, directions to the agent to tell something to the third person, or the granting of permission to the agent to perform acts under circumstances which create in him a reputation of authority.

[23] LiveJournal selected moderators and provided them with specific directions. Mavrix presented evidence that LiveJournal users may have reasonably believed that the moderators had authority to act for LiveJournal. One user whose post was removed pursuant to a DMCA notice complained to LiveJournal "I'm sure my entry does not violate any sort of copyright law. ... I followed [ONTD's] formatting standards and the moderators checked and approved my post." The user relied on the moderators' approval as a manifestation that the post complied with copyright law, and the user appeared to believe the moderators acted on behalf of LiveJournal. Such reliance is likely traceable to LiveJournal's policy of providing explicit roles and authority to the moderators. Accordingly, genuine issues of material fact exist regarding whether there was an apparent authority relationship.

[24] Whether an agency relationship exists also depends on the level of control a principal exerts over the agent. Evidence presented by Mavrix shows that LiveJournal maintains significant control over ONTD and its moderators....

[25] On the other hand, ONTD moderators are free to leave and go and volunteer their time in any way they see fit. In addition, the moderators can reject submissions for reasons other than those provided by the rules, which calls into question the level of control that LiveJournal exerts over their conduct. This evidence raises genuine issues of material fact regarding the level of control LiveJournal exercised over the moderators. From the evidence currently in the record, reasonable jurors could conclude that an agency relationship existed....

[26] We turn briefly to a related issue that the fact finder must resolve in the event there is a finding that the moderators are agents of LiveJournal. In that event, the fact finder must assess whether Mavrix's photographs were indeed stored at the direction of the users in light of the moderators' role in screening and posting the photographs. Infringing material is stored at the direction of the user if the service provider played no role in making that infringing material accessible on its site or if the service provider carried out activities that were narrowly directed towards enhancing the accessibility of the posts. Accessibility-enhancing activities include automatic processes, for example, to reformat posts or perform some technological change.

Some manual service provider activities that screen for infringement or other harmful material like pornography can also be accessibility-enhancing. Indeed, § 512(m) of the DMCA provides that no liability will arise from "a service provider monitoring its service or affirmatively seeking facts indicating infringing activity."

[27] The ONTD moderators manually review submissions and publicly post only about one-third of submissions. The moderators review the substance of posts; only those posts relevant to new and exciting celebrity gossip are approved. The question for the fact finder is whether the moderators' acts were merely accessibility-enhancing activities or whether instead their extensive, manual, and substantive activities went beyond the automatic and limited manual activities we have approved as accessibility-enhancing....

[28] Because the district court focused on the users' submission of Mavrix's photographs rather than on ONTD's role in making those photographs publicly accessible and rejected Mavrix's argument that unpaid moderators could be agents of LiveJournal, the district court erred in granting summary judgment to LiveJournal. Genuine issues of material fact exist as to whether the moderators were LiveJournal's agents. Accordingly, remand is warranted. In assessing LiveJournal's threshold eligibility for the § 512(c) safe harbor, the fact finder must resolve the factual dispute regarding the moderators' status as LiveJournal's agents and in light of that determination, whether LiveJournal showed that Mavrix's photographs were stored at the direction of the users....

Review § 512(g), detailed above. Section 512(g) sets out the procedures for seeking to have material that has been taken down restored. In particular, § 512(g) specifies the procedure by which a user objecting to a takedown notice may lodge a counter-notification. Section 512(g) also provides that a user whose materials are removed pursuant to a proper takedown notice cannot sue an OSP if the OSP followed the § 512(g) procedures—including promptly notifying the user whose material has been taken down, and restoring that material upon receiving a proper counter-notification. Nothing in § 512(g)—or indeed in any other part of § 512—prevents a party whose material was wrongfully taken down from suing the party that issued the takedown notice. Indeed, § 512(f) imposes liability on parties who "knowingly materially misrepresent" in a takedown notification that material is infringing, or in a counter-notification that material has been taken down by mistake. As you read the following case, consider whether § 512(f) is likely to have the effect of deterring material misstatements in notifications and counter-notifications.

Stephanie Lenz v. Universal Music Corp.
815 F.3d 1145 (9th Cir. 2016)

TALLMAN, J.:

[1] Stephanie Lenz filed suit under 17 U.S.C. § 512(f)—part of the Digital Millennium Copyright Act—against Universal Music Corp., Universal Music Publishing, Inc., and Universal Music Publishing Group. She alleges Universal misrepresented in a takedown notification that her 29-second home video constituted an infringing use of a portion of a composition by the Artist known as Prince, which Universal insists was unauthorized by the law. Her claim boils down to a question of whether copyright holders have been abusing the extrajudicial takedown procedures provided for in the DMCA by declining to first evaluate whether the content qualifies as fair use. We hold that the statute requires copyright holders to consider fair use before sending a takedown notification, and that in this case, there is a triable issue as to whether the copyright holder formed a

subjective good faith belief that the use was not authorized by law. We affirm the denial of the parties' cross-motions for summary judgment....

[2] .... On February 7, 2007, Lenz uploaded to YouTube a 29-second home video of her two young children in the family kitchen dancing to the song *Let's Go Crazy* by Prince. *Available at* https://www.youtube.com/watch?v=N1KfJHFWlhQ (last visited September 4, 2015). She titled the video "'Let's Go Crazy' # 1." About four seconds into the video, Lenz asks her thirteen month-old son "what do you think of the music?" after which he bobs up and down while holding a push toy.

[3] At the time Lenz posted the video, Universal was Prince's publishing administrator responsible for enforcing his copyrights. To accomplish this objective with respect to YouTube, Robert Allen, Universal's head of business affairs, assigned Sean Johnson, an assistant in the legal department, to monitor YouTube on a daily basis. Johnson searched YouTube for Prince's songs and reviewed the video postings returned by his online search query. When reviewing such videos, he evaluated whether they "embodied a Prince composition" by making "significant use of ... the composition, specifically if the song was recognizable, was in a significant portion of the video or was the focus of the video." According to Allen, "[t]he general guidelines are that ... we review the video to ensure that the composition was the focus and if it was we then notify YouTube that the video should be removed."

[4] Johnson contrasted videos that met this criteria to those "that may have had a second or less of a Prince song, literally a one line, half line of Prince song" or "were shot in incredibly noisy environments, such as bars, where there could be a Prince song playing deep in the background ... to the point where if there was any Prince composition embodied ... in those videos that it was distorted beyond reasonable recognition." None of the video evaluation guidelines explicitly include consideration of the fair use doctrine.

[5] When Johnson reviewed Lenz's video, he recognized *Let's Go Crazy* immediately. He noted that it played loudly in the background throughout the entire video. Based on these details, the video's title, and Lenz's query during the video asking if her son liked the song, he concluded that Prince's song "was very much the focus of the video." As a result, Johnson decided the video should be included in a takedown notification sent to YouTube that listed more than 200 YouTube videos Universal believed to be making unauthorized use of Prince's songs. The notice included a "good faith belief" statement as required by 17 U.S.C. § 512(c)(3)(A)(v): "We have a good faith belief that the above-described activity is not authorized by the copyright owner, its agent, or the law."

[6] After receiving the takedown notification, YouTube removed the video and sent Lenz an email on June 5, 2007, notifying her of the removal. On June 7, 2007, Lenz attempted to restore the video by sending a counter-notification to YouTube pursuant to § 512(g)(3). After YouTube provided this counter-notification to Universal per § 512(g)(2)(B), Universal protested the video's reinstatement because Lenz failed to properly acknowledge that her statement was made under penalty of perjury, as required by § 512(g)(3)(C). Universal's protest reiterated that the video constituted infringement because there was no record that "either she or YouTube were ever granted licenses to reproduce, distribute, publicly perform or otherwise exploit the Composition." The protest made no mention of fair use. After obtaining *pro bono* counsel, Lenz sent a second counter-notification on June 27, 2007, which resulted in YouTube's reinstatement of the video in mid-July....

[7] On February 25, 2010, the district court granted Lenz's partial motion for summary judgment on Universal's six affirmative defenses, including the third affirmative defense that Lenz suffered no damages. Both parties subsequently moved for summary judgment on Lenz's § 512(f) misrepresentation claim. On January 24, 2013, the district court denied both motions in an order that is now before us....

[8] Section 512(c) permits service providers, e.g., YouTube or Google, to avoid copyright infringement liability for storing users' content if—among other requirements—the service provider "expeditiously" removes or disables access to the content after receiving notification from a copyright holder that the content is infringing. Section 512(c)(3)(A) sets forth the elements that such a "takedown notification" must contain. These elements include identification of the copyrighted work, identification of the allegedly infringing material, and, critically, a statement that the copyright holder believes in good faith the infringing material "is not authorized by the copyright owner, its agent, or the law." *Id.* § 512(c)(3)(A). The procedures outlined in § 512(c) are referred to as the DMCA's "takedown procedures."

[9] To avoid liability for disabling or removing content, the service provider must notify the user of the takedown. *Id.* § 512(g)(1)-(2). The user then has the option of restoring the content by sending a counter-notification, which must include a statement of "good faith belief that the material was removed or disabled as a result of mistake or misidentification...." *Id.* § 512(g)(3)(C). Upon receipt of a valid counter-notification, the service provider must inform the copyright holder of the counter-notification and restore the content within "not less than 10, nor more than 14, business days," unless the service provider receives notice that the copyright holder has filed a lawsuit against the user seeking to restrain the user's infringing behavior. *Id.* § 512(g)(2)(B)–(C). The procedures outlined in § 512(g) are referred to as the DMCA's "put-back procedures."

[10] If an entity abuses the DMCA, it may be subject to liability under § 512(f). That section provides: "Any person who knowingly materially misrepresents under this section—(1) that material or activity is infringing, or (2) that material or activity was removed or disabled by mistake or misidentification, shall be liable for any damages...." Subsection (1) generally applies to copyright holders and subsection (2) generally applies to users. Only subsection (1) is at issue here....

[11] We must first determine whether 17 U.S.C. § 512(c)(3)(A)(v) requires copyright holders to consider whether the potentially infringing material is a fair use of a copyright under 17 U.S.C. § 107 before issuing a takedown notification. Section 512(c)(3)(A)(v) requires a takedown notification to include a "statement that the complaining party has a good faith belief that the use of the material in the manner complained of is not authorized by the copyright owner, its agent, or the law." The parties dispute whether fair use is an authorization under the law as contemplated by the statute—which is so far as we know an issue of first impression in any circuit across the nation. Canons of statutory construction dictate that if the language of a statute is clear, we look no further than that language in determining the statute's meaning. A court looks to legislative history only if the statute is unclear. We agree with the district court and hold that the statute unambiguously contemplates fair use as a use authorized by the law.

[12] Fair use is not just excused by the law, it is wholly authorized by the law. In 1976, Congress codified the application of a four-step test for determining the fair use of copyrighted works:

> Notwithstanding the provisions of sections 106 and 106A, *the fair use of a copyrighted work,* ... for purposes such as criticism, comment, news reporting, teaching (including multiple copies for classroom use), scholarship, or research, *is not an infringement of copyright.* In determining whether the use made of a work in any particular case is a fair use the factors to be considered shall include—
>> (1) the purpose and character of the use, including whether such use is of a commercial nature or is for nonprofit educational purposes;
>> (2) the nature of the copyrighted work;
>> (3) the amount and substantiality of the portion used in relation to the copyrighted work as a whole; and
>> (4) the effect of the use upon the potential market for or value of the copyrighted work.
> The fact that a work is unpublished shall not itself bar a finding of fair use if such finding is made upon consideration of all the above factors.

17 U.S.C. § 107 (emphasis added). The statute explains that the fair use of a copyrighted work is permissible because it is a non-infringing use....

[13] ... Universal's sole textual argument is that fair use is not "authorized by the law" because it is an affirmative defense that excuses otherwise infringing conduct. Universal's interpretation is incorrect as it conflates two different concepts: an affirmative defense that is labeled as such due to the procedural posture of the case, and an affirmative defense that excuses impermissible conduct. Supreme Court precedent squarely supports the conclusion that fair use does not fall into the latter camp: "[A]nyone who ... makes a fair use of the work is not an infringer of the copyright with respect to such use." Sony Corp. of Am. v. Universal City Studios, Inc., 464 U.S. 417, 433 (1984).

[14] Given that 17 U.S.C. § 107 expressly authorizes fair use, labeling it as an affirmative defense that excuses conduct is a misnomer:

> *Although the traditional approach is to view "fair use" as an affirmative defense, this writer, speaking only for himself, is of the opinion that it is better viewed as a right granted by the Copyright Act of 1976. Originally, as a judicial doctrine without any statutory basis, fair use was an infringement that was excused—this is presumably why it was treated as a defense. As a statutory doctrine, however, fair use is not an infringement. Thus, since the passage of the 1976 Act, fair use should no longer be considered an infringement to be excused; instead, it is logical to view fair use as a right. Regardless of how fair use is viewed, it is clear that the burden of proving fair use is always on the putative infringer.*

Bateman v. Mnemonics, Inc., 79 F.3d 1532, 1542 n.22 (11th Cir. 1996). We agree. *Cf.* Lydia Pallas Loren, *Fair Use: An Affirmative Defense?*, 90 WASH. L. REV. 685, 688 (2015) ("Congress did not intend fair use to be an affirmative defense—a defense, yes, but not an affirmative defense."). Fair use is therefore distinct from affirmative defenses where a use infringes a copyright, but there is no liability due to a valid excuse, e.g., misuse of a copyright, and laches....

[15] .... Even if, as Universal urges, fair use is classified as an "*affirmative* defense," we hold—for the purposes of the DMCA—fair use is uniquely situated in copyright law so as to be treated differently than traditional affirmative defenses. We conclude that because 17 U.S.C. § 107 created a type of non-infringing use, fair use is "authorized by the law" and a copyright holder must consider the existence of fair use before sending a takedown notification under § 512(c)....

[16] We must next determine if a genuine issue of material fact exists as to whether Universal knowingly misrepresented that it had formed a good faith belief the video did not constitute fair use. This inquiry lies not in whether a court would adjudge the video as a fair use, but whether Universal formed a good faith belief that it was not. Contrary to the district court's holding, Lenz may proceed under an actual knowledge theory, but not under a willful blindness theory....

[17] Though Lenz argues Universal should have known the video qualifies for fair use as a matter of law, we have already decided a copyright holder need only form a subjective good faith belief that a use is not authorized. Rossi v. Motion Picture Ass'n of Am. Inc., 391 F.3d 1000 (9th Cir. 2004). In *Rossi,* we explicitly held that "the 'good faith belief' requirement in § 512(c)(3)(A)(v) encompasses a subjective, rather than objective standard," and we observed that "Congress understands this distinction." We further held:

When enacting the DMCA, Congress could have easily incorporated an objective standard of reasonableness. The fact that it did not do so indicates an intent to adhere to the subjective standard traditionally associated with a good faith requirement.

In § 512(f), Congress included an expressly limited cause of action for improper infringement notifications, imposing liability only if the copyright owner's notification is a knowing misrepresentation. A copyright owner cannot be liable simply because an unknowing mistake is made, even if the copyright owner acted unreasonably in making the mistake. Rather, there must be a demonstration of some actual knowledge of misrepresentation on the part of the copyright owner.

.... We therefore judge Universal's actions by the subjective beliefs it formed about the video....

[18] Universal faces liability if it knowingly misrepresented in the takedown notification that it had formed a good faith belief the video was not authorized by the law, i.e., did not constitute fair use. Here, Lenz presented evidence that Universal did not form any subjective belief about the video's fair use—one way or another—because it failed to consider fair use at all, and knew that it failed to do so. Universal nevertheless contends that its procedures, while not formally labeled consideration of fair use, were tantamount to such consideration. Because the DMCA requires consideration of fair use prior to sending a takedown notification, a jury must determine whether Universal's actions were sufficient to form a subjective good faith belief about the video's fair use or lack thereof.[3]

[19] To be clear, if a copyright holder ignores or neglects our unequivocal holding that it must consider fair use before sending a takedown notification, it is liable for damages under § 512(f). If, however, a copyright holder forms a subjective *good faith* belief the allegedly infringing material does not constitute fair use, we are in no position to dispute the copyright holder's belief even if we would have reached the opposite conclusion. A copyright holder who pays lip service to the consideration of fair use by claiming it formed a good faith belief when there is evidence to the contrary is still subject to § 512(f) liability....

[20] We hold the willful blindness doctrine may be used to determine whether a copyright holder "knowingly materially misrepresent[ed]" that it held a "good faith belief" the offending activity was not a fair use. *See* 17 U.S.C. § 512(c)(3)(A)(v), (f). The willful blindness doctrine may be applied, in appropriate circumstances, to demonstrate knowledge or awareness of specific instances of infringement under the DMCA. But, based on the specific facts presented during summary judgment, we reject the district court's conclusion that Lenz may proceed to trial under a willful blindness theory.

[21] To demonstrate willful blindness a plaintiff must establish two factors: (1) the defendant must subjectively believe that there is a high probability that a fact exists and (2) the defendant must take deliberate actions to avoid learning of that fact. Under this formulation, a willfully blind defendant is one who takes deliberate actions to avoid confirming a high probability of wrongdoing and who can almost be said to have actually known the critical facts. To meet [this] test, Lenz must demonstrate a genuine issue as to whether—before sending the takedown notification—Universal (1) subjectively believed there was a high probability that the video constituted fair use, and (2) took deliberate actions to avoid learning of this fair use.

---

[3] Although the panel agrees on the legal principles we discuss herein, we part company with our dissenting colleague over the propriety of resolving on summary judgment Universal's claim to subjective belief that the copyright was infringed. The dissent would find that no triable issue of fact exists because Universal did not specifically and expressly consider the fair-use elements of 17 U.S.C. § 107. But the question is whether the analysis Universal did conduct of the video was sufficient, not to conclusively establish as a matter of law that the video's use of Let's Go Crazy was fair, but to form a subjective good faith belief that the video was infringing on Prince's copyright. And under the circumstances of this case, that question is for the jury, not this court, to decide.

[22] On summary judgment Lenz failed to meet a threshold showing of the first factor. To make such a showing, Lenz must provide evidence from which a juror could infer that Universal was aware of a high probability the video constituted fair use. But she failed to provide any such evidence. The district court therefore correctly found that "Lenz does not present evidence suggesting Universal subjectively believed either that there was a high probability any given video might make fair use of a Prince composition or her video in particular made fair use of Prince's song 'Let's Go Crazy.'" Yet the district court improperly denied Universal's motion for summary judgment on the willful blindness theory because Universal "has not shown that it *lacked* a subjective belief." By finding blame with Universal's inability to show that it "*lacked* a subjective belief," the district court improperly required Universal to meet its burden of persuasion, even though Lenz had failed to counter the initial burden of production that Universal successfully carried. Lenz may not therefore proceed to trial on a willful blindness theory....

[23] Section 512(f) provides for the recovery of "any damages, including costs and attorneys fees, incurred by the alleged infringer ... who is injured by such misrepresentation, as the result of the service provider relying upon such misrepresentation in removing or disabling access to the material or activity claimed to be infringing." We hold a plaintiff may seek recovery of nominal damages for an injury incurred as a result of a § 512(f) misrepresentation.

[24] Universal incorrectly asserts that Lenz must demonstrate she incurred "actual monetary loss." ... Because Congress specified the recovery of "any damages," we reject Universal's contention that Congress did not indicate its intent to depart from the common law presumption that a misrepresentation plaintiff must have suffered a monetary loss....

[25] The district court therefore properly concluded in its 2010 order:

> The use of "any damages" suggests strongly Congressional intent that recovery be available for damages even if they do not amount to ... substantial economic damages.... Requiring a plaintiff who can [show that the copyright holder knowingly misrepresented its subjective good faith] to demonstrate in addition not only that she suffered damages but also that those damages were economic and substantial would vitiate the deterrent effect of the statute....

[26] .... Because a jury has not yet determined whether Lenz will prevail at trial, we need not decide the scope of recoverable damages, i.e., whether she may recover expenses following the initiation of her § 512(f) suit or *pro bono* costs and attorneys' fees, both of which arose as a result of the injury incurred....

[27] Copyright holders cannot shirk their duty to consider—in good faith and prior to sending a takedown notification—whether allegedly infringing material constitutes fair use, a use which the DMCA plainly contemplates as authorized by the law. That this step imposes responsibility on copyright holders is not a reason for us to reject it. We affirm the district court's order denying the parties' cross-motions for summary judgment....

M. SMITH, J., concurring in part and dissenting in part:

[28] .... I disagree with the majority's conclusion that "whether Universal's actions were sufficient to form a subjective good faith belief about the video's fair use or lack thereof" presents a triable issue of fact. Universal admittedly did not consider fair use before notifying YouTube to take down Lenz's video. It therefore could not have formed a good faith belief that Lenz's video was infringing, and its notification to the contrary was a knowing material misrepresentation. Accordingly, I would hold that Lenz is entitled to summary judgment.

[29] I agree with the majority's conclusion that § 512(c)(3)(A)(v) requires copyright holders to consider whether potentially infringing material is a fair use before issuing a takedown notice. As the majority explains,

a takedown notice must contain "[a] statement that the complaining party has a good faith belief that use of the material in the manner complained of is not authorized by the copyright owner, its agent, or the law." Because fair use of copyrighted material is not an infringement of copyright, such use is "authorized by … the law." *See id.* § 107. Therefore, in order to form "a good faith belief that use of the material in the manner complained of is not authorized by … the law," § 512(c)(3)(A)(v), a party must consider the doctrine of fair use. I also agree with the majority that § 512(f) provides a party injured by a violation of § 512(c)(3)(A)(v) with a right of action for damages, including nominal damages.

[30] However, I part ways with the majority on two issues. First, I would clarify that § 512(f)'s requirement that a misrepresentation be "knowing[]" is satisfied when the party knows that it is ignorant of the truth or falsity of its representation. Second, I would hold that Universal's actions were insufficient as a matter of law to form a subjective good-faith belief that Lenz's video was not a fair use….

[31] Section 512(f) requires that a misrepresentation be "knowing[]" to incur liability. In my view, when the misrepresentation concerns § 512(c)(3)(A)(v), the knowledge requirement is satisfied when the party knows that it has not considered fair use. That is, Universal need not have known that the video was a fair use, or that its actions were insufficient to form a good-faith belief about fair use. It need only have known that it had not considered fair use as such….

[32] One who asserts a belief that a work is infringing without considering fair use lacks a basis for that belief. It follows that one who *knows* that he has not considered fair use *knows* that he lacks a basis for that belief. That is sufficient "actual knowledge of misrepresentation" to meet the scienter requirement of § 512(f). Thus, to be held liable under § 512(f), Universal need only have failed to consider fair use, and known that it had failed to consider fair use….

[33] It is undisputed that Universal's policy was to issue a takedown notice where a copyrighted work was used as "the focus of the video" or "prominently featured in the video." By Universal's own admission, its agents were not instructed to consider whether the use was fair. Instead, Universal directed its agents to spare videos that had "a second or less of a Prince song" or where the song was "distorted beyond reasonable recognition." And yet, from this, the majority concludes that "whether Universal's actions were sufficient to form a subjective good faith belief about the video's fair use or lack thereof" presents a triable issue of fact.

[34] I respectfully disagree. The Copyright Act explicitly enumerates the factors to be considered in assessing whether use of copyrighted material is fair. Universal's policy was expressly to determine whether a video made "significant use"—not *fair* use—of the work. Nothing in Universal's methodology considered the purpose and character of the use, the commercial or noncommercial nature of the use, or whether the use would have a significant impact on the market for the copyrighted work.[4] There is therefore no disputed issue of fact: Universal did *not* consider fair use before issuing a takedown notice.

[35] Moreover, Universal *knew* it had not considered fair use, because § 107 explicitly supplies the factors that "shall" be considered in determining whether a use is fair. I see no reason in law or logic to excuse copyright

---

[4] Had Universal properly considered the statutory elements of fair use, there is no doubt that it would have concluded that Lenz's use of *Let's Go Crazy* was fair. *See, e.g., TCA Television Corp. v. McCollum,* 2015 WL 9255341 (S.D.N.Y. Dec. 17, 2015) (finding on a motion to dismiss that the use in a Broadway show of one minute and seven seconds of the Abbott and Costello routine *Who's On First?* was fair because the use was "highly transformative" and unlikely to usurp the market for the original); *SOFA Entm't, Inc. v. Dodger Prods., Inc.,* 709 F.3d 1273 (9th Cir. 2013) (affirming summary judgment that use of a seven-second clip of *The Ed Sullivan Show* was fair for similar reasons). Universal's "significant use" analysis, by contrast, is more like determining whether a use is *de minimis,* a much more stringent test than fair use. *See Sandoval v. New Line Cinema Corp.,* 147 F.3d 215, 217 (2d Cir. 1998).

holders from the general principle that knowledge of the law is presumed. As explained above, that is sufficient in my view to conclude that Universal's takedown notice was a knowing misrepresentation....

[36] The majority's unfortunate interpretation of § 512(f) would permit a party to avoid liability with only the most perfunctory attention to fair use. Such a construction eviscerates § 512(f) and leaves it toothless against frivolous takedown notices. And, in an era when a significant proportion of media distribution and consumption takes place on third-party safe harbors such as YouTube, if a creative work can be taken down without meaningfully considering fair use, then the viability of the concept of fair use itself is in jeopardy. Such a construction of § 512(f) cannot comport with the intention of Congress.

[37] In sum: Universal represented that it had formed a good-faith belief that Lenz's video was an infringement of copyright—that is, that the video was not fair use. Because Universal did not actually consider the factors constituting fair use, its representation was false—a misrepresentation. Because those factors are set forth in § 107 (and § 107 expressly states that a fair use "is not an infringement of copyright"), Universal's misrepresentation was knowing. And because there is no further disputed issue of fact concerning liability, I respectfully dissent.

NOTES

1. Almost certainly the most important element of *Lenz* is the Ninth Circuit's clear holding that fair use is not merely an "excuse" for infringement, but is rather—as the text of § 107 clearly states—"not an infringement." Note, however, that in its subsequent opinion in *Dr. Seuss Enterprises, L.P. v. ComicMix, LLC*, 983 F.3d 442 (2020), the Ninth Circuit continued to adhere to its prior holding that "the burden of proving fair use is always on the putative infringer."

2. In *Lenz*, the Ninth Circuit cites its prior decision in *Rossi v. Motion Picture Ass'n of Am. Inc.*, 391 F.3d 1000 (9th Cir. 2004), which held that the "good faith belief" requirement in § 512(c)(3)(A)(v) "encompasses a subjective, rather than objective standard." Lenz presented evidence that Universal had failed to consider fair use at all. Universal maintained that its procedures, while not formally considering fair use, were sufficient to allow it to form a good-faith subjective belief about fair use. Noting this dispute, the *Lenz* court held that if, on remand, the jury finds that Universal's procedures were insufficient to allow it to form a good-faith subjective belief about fair use, Universal could be held liable. Does the *Lenz* court's rule provide good incentives for compliance with § 512(f)? What if Universal persists in its apparent prior practice of not explicitly considering fair use when filing takedown notifications? Or what if Universal undertakes the required consideration according to a "subjective" understanding of the boundaries of fair use that are narrower than what courts would otherwise hold? Is that "good faith"?

3. After *Lenz*, do you think it will be possible to have takedown notices sent by robots, and without humans checking to determine whether a particular unauthorized use is a fair use? Could a robot make this determination? For opposing scholarly views on the issue, compare Dan L. Burk, *Algorithmic Fair Use*, 85 U. CHI. L. REV. 283 (2019), with Niva Elkin-Koren, *Fair Use by Design*, 64 UCLA L. REV. 1082 (2017).

4. Note that, at least for YouTube, the notice-and-takedown process has now been supplemented by Google's "Content ID" system. This automated system for detecting potential infringement uses data files supplied by content owners. Content ID automatically scans video content uploaded by users against a database composed of these files to detect potential infringement. If the Content ID system finds what it believes to be a match between video content a user is attempting to upload and a copyrighted work in the Content ID database, Google gives copyright owners the option to block the video from being viewed, to monetize the video by running ads associated with it (in some cases sharing revenue with the uploader), or to track the video's viewership statistics. Access to the Content ID program is limited to major content owners. Note that

Content ID represents a substantial investment by Google and that its viability depends on cooperation by content owners. Do you think that the law should mandate automated filters like Content ID? If the law were to do so, would the need to filter content discourage the entry of new competitors to YouTube and other incumbent online content distributors?

D. Liability of Device Manufacturers

There are many devices in common usage that can be used to infringe copyrights. Every photocopier, camera, or sound recorder can be used to infringe. Of course, many of these devices can also be used to make copies that are perfectly legal—whether because the copying is authorized by the copyright owner, because the material copied is not copyrighted, or because the copying is fair use. The key question is whether the manufacturers of devices that may be used to infringe copyrights can be subject to secondary liability, and, if so, under what circumstances.

> As you read the next case, pay close attention to the source of the rule that the Supreme Court announces. What are the circumstances under which the manufacturer of a device used for infringement may be sued on a theory of secondary liability? And—very importantly—pay close attention to the possible limits of that rule. What are the special features of the device at issue in this case that may make the rule appropriate?

Sony Corporation of America v. Universal City Studios, Inc.
464 U.S. 417 (1984)

STEVENS, J.:

{Recall the facts of this case from Chapter VI.} ...

[1] The Copyright Act does not expressly render anyone liable for infringement committed by another. In contrast, the Patent Act expressly brands anyone who "actively induces infringement of a patent" as an infringer, 35 U.S.C. § 271(b), and further imposes liability on certain individuals labeled "contributory" infringers, id., § 271(c). The absence of such express language in the copyright statute does not preclude the imposition of liability for copyright infringements on certain parties who have not themselves engaged in the infringing activity. For vicarious liability is imposed in virtually all areas of the law, and the concept of contributory infringement is merely a species of the broader problem of identifying the circumstances in which it is just to hold one individual accountable for the actions of another....

[2] Respondents argue ... that supplying the "means" to accomplish an infringing activity and encouraging that activity through advertisement are sufficient to establish liability for copyright infringement. This argument rests on a gross generalization that cannot withstand scrutiny.... Petitioners in the instant case do not supply Betamax consumers with respondents' works; respondents do. Petitioners supply a piece of equipment that is generally capable of copying the entire range of programs that may be televised: those that are uncopyrighted, those that are copyrighted but may be copied without objection from the copyright holder, and those that the copyright holder would prefer not to have copied. The Betamax can be used to make authorized or unauthorized uses of copyrighted works ....

[3] Justice Holmes stated that the producer had "contributed" to the infringement of the copyright, and the label "contributory infringement" has been applied in a number of lower court copyright cases involving an ongoing relationship between the direct infringer and the contributory infringer at the time the infringing conduct occurred. In such cases, as in other situations in which the imposition of vicarious liability is manifestly just, the "contributory" infringer was in a position to control the use of copyrighted works by others and had authorized the use without permission from the copyright owner. This case, however, plainly does not fall in that category. The only contact between Sony and the users of the Betamax that is disclosed by this record occurred at the moment of sale. The District Court expressly found that "no employee of Sony ... had either direct involvement with the allegedly infringing activity or direct contact with purchasers of Betamax who recorded copyrighted works off-the-air." And it further found that "there was no evidence that any of the copies made by ... the other individual witnesses in this suit were influenced or encouraged by [Sony's] advertisements."

[4] If vicarious liability is to be imposed on petitioners in this case, it must rest on the fact that they have sold equipment with constructive knowledge of the fact that their customers may use that equipment to make unauthorized copies of copyrighted material. There is no precedent in the law of copyright for the imposition of vicarious liability on such a theory. The closest analogy is provided by the patent law cases to which it is appropriate to refer because of the historic kinship between patent law and copyright law.

[5] In the Patent Code both the concept of infringement and the concept of contributory infringement are expressly defined by statute. The prohibition against contributory infringement is confined to the knowing sale of a component especially made for use in connection with a particular patent. There is no suggestion in the statute that one patentee may object to the sale of a product that might be used in connection with other patents. Moreover, the Act expressly provides that the sale of a "staple article or commodity of commerce suitable for substantial noninfringing use" is not contributory infringement.

[6] When a charge of contributory infringement is predicated entirely on the sale of an article of commerce that is used by the purchaser to infringe a patent, the public interest in access to that article of commerce is necessarily implicated. A finding of contributory infringement does not, of course, remove the article from the market altogether; it does, however, give the patentee effective control over the sale of that item. Indeed, a finding of contributory infringement is normally the functional equivalent of holding that the disputed article is within the monopoly granted to the patentee.[21]

[7] For that reason, in contributory infringement cases arising under the patent laws the Court has always recognized the critical importance of not allowing the patentee to extend his monopoly beyond the limits of his specific grant. These cases deny the patentee any right to control the distribution of unpatented articles unless they are unsuited for any commercial noninfringing use. Unless a commodity has no use except through practice of the patented method, the patentee has no right to claim that its distribution constitutes contributory infringement....

[8] We recognize there are substantial differences between the patent and copyright laws. But in both areas the contributory infringement doctrine is grounded on the recognition that adequate protection of a monopoly may require the courts to look beyond actual duplication of a device or publication to the products or activities that make such duplication possible. The staple article of commerce doctrine must strike a

---

[21] It seems extraordinary to suggest that the Copyright Act confers upon all copyright owners collectively, much less the two respondents in this case, the exclusive right to distribute VTR's simply because they may be used to infringe copyrights. That, however, is the logical implication of their claim. The request for an injunction below indicates that respondents seek, in effect, to declare VTR's contraband. Their suggestion in this Court that a continuing royalty pursuant to a judicially created compulsory license would be an acceptable remedy merely indicates that respondents, for their part, would be willing to license their claimed monopoly interest in VTR's to petitioners in return for a royalty.

balance between a copyright holder's legitimate demand for effective—not merely symbolic—protection of the statutory monopoly, and the rights of others freely to engage in substantially unrelated areas of commerce. Accordingly, the sale of copying equipment, like the sale of other articles of commerce, does not constitute contributory infringement if the product is widely used for legitimate, unobjectionable purposes. Indeed, it need merely be capable of substantial noninfringing uses....

[9] The question is thus whether the Betamax is capable of commercially significant noninfringing uses. In order to resolve that question, we need not explore *all* the different potential uses of the machine and determine whether or not they would constitute infringement. Rather, we need only consider whether on the basis of the facts as found by the district court a significant number of them would be non-infringing. Moreover, in order to resolve this case we need not give precise content to the question of how much use is commercially significant. For one potential use of the Betamax plainly satisfies this standard, however it is understood: private, noncommercial time-shifting in the home. It does so both (A) because respondents have no right to prevent other copyright holders from authorizing it for their programs, and (B) because the District Court's factual findings reveal that even the unauthorized home time-shifting of respondents' programs is legitimate fair use.

{AUTHORIZED USE AND FAIR USE ANALYSES OMITTED} ...

[10] In summary, the record and findings of the District Court lead us to two conclusions. First, Sony demonstrated a significant likelihood that substantial numbers of copyright holders who license their works for broadcast on free television would not object to having their broadcasts time-shifted by private viewers. And second, respondents failed to demonstrate that time-shifting would cause any likelihood of nonminimal harm to the potential market for, or the value of, their copyrighted works. The Betamax is, therefore, capable of substantial noninfringing uses. Sony's sale of such equipment to the general public does not constitute contributory infringement of respondent's copyrights....

[11] .... One may search the Copyright Act in vain for any sign that the elected representatives of the millions of people who watch television every day have made it unlawful to copy a program for later viewing at home, or have enacted a flat prohibition against the sale of machines that make such copying possible.

[12] It may well be that Congress will take a fresh look at this new technology, just as it so often has examined other innovations in the past. But it is not our job to apply laws that have not yet been written. Applying the copyright statute, as it now reads, to the facts as they have been developed in this case, the judgment of the Court of Appeals must be reversed.

It is so ordered.

BLACKMUN, J., dissenting, joined by Justices Marshall, Powell, and Rehnquist: ...

[13] Sony argues that the manufacturer or seller of a product used to infringe is absolved from liability whenever the product can be put to any substantial noninfringing use.... I do not agree that this technical judge-made doctrine of patent law, based in part on considerations irrelevant to the field of copyright, should be imported wholesale into copyright law. Despite their common constitutional source, patent and copyright protections have not developed in a parallel fashion, and this Court in copyright cases in the past has borrowed patent concepts only sparingly.

[14] I recognize, however, that many of the concerns underlying the "staple article of commerce" doctrine are present in copyright law as well. As the District Court noted, if liability for contributory infringement were imposed on the manufacturer or seller of every product used to infringe—a typewriter, a camera, a photocopying machine—the "wheels of commerce" would be blocked.

[15] I therefore conclude that if a *significant* portion of the product's use is *noninfringing*, the manufacturers and sellers cannot be held contributorily liable for the product's infringing uses. If virtually all of the product's use, however, is to infringe, contributory liability may be imposed; if no one would buy the product for noninfringing purposes alone, it is clear that the manufacturer is purposely profiting from the infringement, and that liability is appropriately imposed. In such a case, the copyright owner's monopoly would not be extended beyond its proper bounds; the manufacturer of such a product contributes to the infringing activities of others and profits directly thereby, while providing no benefit to the public sufficient to justify the infringement.

[16] The Court of Appeals concluded that Sony should be held liable for contributory infringement, reasoning that "[v]ideotape recorders are manufactured, advertised, and sold for the primary purpose of reproducing television programming," and "[v]irtually all television programming is copyrighted material." While I agree with the first of these propositions,[42] the second, for me, is problematic. The key question is not the amount of television programming that is copyrighted, but rather the amount of VTR usage that is infringing.[43] Moreover, the parties and their *amici* have argued vigorously about both the amount of television programming that is covered by copyright and the amount for which permission to copy has been given. The proportion of VTR recording that is infringing is ultimately a question of fact, and the District Court specifically declined to make findings on the "percentage of legal versus illegal home-use recording." In light of my view of the law, resolution of this factual question is essential. I therefore would remand the case for further consideration of this by the District Court....

NOTES

1. Notice that *Sony* was a 5-4 decision. Had one vote gone in the other direction, Sony would have been exposed to potentially crippling secondary infringement liability. What do you think the market's reaction would have been had *Sony* gone the other way? Would VCRs have been withdrawn from the market?

2. Is *Sony*'s rule more protective of copyrighted content or content distribution technologies? What does that emphasis reflect about copyright and innovation policy?

3. How does the rule articulated in *Sony* fit into the traditional tests for secondary liability that you have studied above? Does it negate an element of secondary liability? Is it a third test apart from the traditional tests of secondary liability?

---

[42] Although VTRs also may be used to watch prerecorded video cassettes and to make home motion pictures, these uses do not require a tuner such as the Betamax contains. The Studios do not object to Sony's sale of VTRs without tuners. In considering the noninfringing uses of the Betamax, therefore, those uses that would remain possible without the Betamax's built-in tuner should not be taken into account.

[43] Noninfringing uses would include, for example, recording works that are not protected by copyright, recording works that have entered the public domain, recording with permission of the copyright owner, and, of course, any recording that qualifies as fair use.

As you read the next case, think back to *Sony*, and ask yourself whether there is some feature of the technology in this next case that suggests that the rule developed in *Sony* should not apply. If so, what is that feature? And does it make you more or less willing to impose secondary infringement liability based on the facts of the next case?

A&M Records, Inc. v. Napster, Inc.
239 F.3d 1004 (9th Cir. 2001)

BEEZER, J.:

[1] Plaintiffs are engaged in the commercial recording, distribution and sale of copyrighted musical compositions and sound recordings. The complaint alleges that Napster, Inc. is a contributory and vicarious copyright infringer.... The district court preliminarily enjoined Napster "from engaging in, or facilitating others in copying, downloading, uploading, transmitting, or distributing plaintiffs' copyrighted musical compositions and sound recordings, protected by either federal or state law, without express permission of the rights owner." ...

[2] .... We affirm in part, reverse in part and remand....

[3] Napster facilitates the transmission of MP3 files between and among its users. Through a process commonly called "peer-to-peer" file sharing, Napster allows its users to: (1) make MP3 music files stored on individual computer hard drives available for copying by other Napster users; (2) search for MP3 music files stored on other users' computers; and (3) transfer exact copies of the contents of other users' MP3 files from one computer to another via the Internet. These functions are made possible by Napster's MusicShare software, available free of charge from Napster's Internet site, and Napster's network servers and server-side software....

[4] In order to copy MP3 files through the Napster system, a user must first access Napster's Internet site and download the MusicShare software to his individual computer. Once the software is installed, the user can access the Napster system....

[5] If a registered user wants to list available files stored in his computer's hard drive on Napster for others to access, he must first create a "user library" directory on his computer's hard drive. The user then saves his MP3 files in the library directory, using self-designated file names. He next must log into the Napster system .... His MusicShare software then searches his user library and verifies that the available files are properly formatted. If in the correct MP3 format, the names of the MP3 files will be uploaded from the user's computer to the Napster servers. The content of the MP3 files remains stored in the user's computer.

[6] Once uploaded to the Napster servers, the user's MP3 file names are stored in a server-side "library" under the user's name and become part of a "collective directory" of files available for transfer during the time the user is logged onto the Napster system. The collective directory is fluid; it tracks users who are connected in real time, displaying only file names that are immediately accessible....

[7] Software located on the Napster servers maintains a "search index" of Napster's collective directory. To search the files available from Napster users currently connected to the network servers, the individual user accesses a form in the MusicShare software stored in his computer and enters either the name of a song or an artist as the object of the search. The form is then transmitted to a Napster server and automatically compared to the MP3 file names listed in the server's search index. Napster's server compiles a list of all MP3

file names pulled from the search index which include the same search terms entered on the search form and transmits the list to the searching user....

[8] To transfer a copy of the contents of a requested MP3 file, the Napster server software obtains the Internet address of the requesting user and the Internet address of the "host user" (the user with the available files). The Napster servers then communicate the host user's Internet address to the requesting user. The requesting user's computer uses this information to establish a connection with the host user and downloads a copy of the contents of the MP3 file from one computer to the other over the Internet, "peer-to-peer."...

[9] We ... address plaintiffs' claim that Napster is liable for contributory copyright infringement. Traditionally, one who, with knowledge of the infringing activity, induces, causes or materially contributes to the infringing conduct of another, may be held liable as a contributory infringer. Put differently, liability exists if the defendant engages in personal conduct that encourages or assists the infringement.

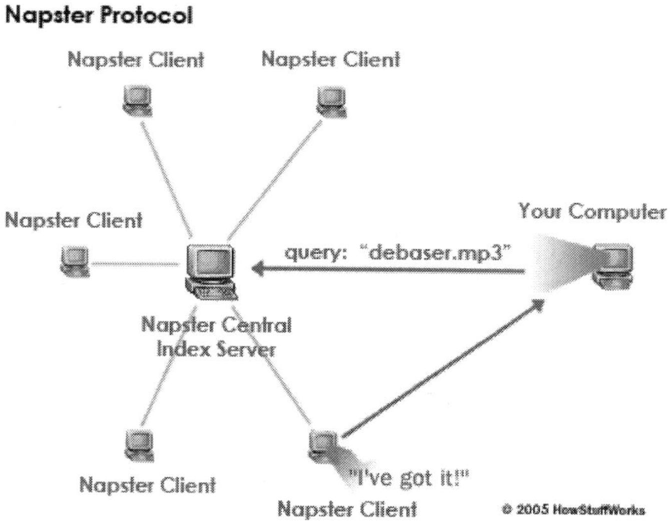

Figure 119: Napster schematic

[10] The district court determined that plaintiffs in all likelihood would establish Napster's liability as a contributory infringer. The district court did not err; Napster, by its conduct, knowingly encourages and assists the infringement of plaintiffs' copyrights....

[11] Contributory liability requires that the secondary infringer know or have reason to know of direct infringement. The district court found that Napster had both actual and constructive knowledge that its users exchanged copyrighted music. The district court also concluded that the law does not require knowledge of specific acts of infringement and rejected Napster's contention that because the company cannot distinguish infringing from noninfringing files, it does not know of the direct infringement.

[12] It is apparent from the record that Napster has knowledge, both actual and constructive, of direct infringement. Napster claims that it is nevertheless protected from contributory liability by the teaching of *Sony Corp. v. Universal City Studios, Inc.*, 464 U.S. 417 (1984). We disagree. We observe that Napster's actual, specific knowledge of direct infringement renders *Sony*'s holding of limited assistance to Napster. We are compelled to make a clear distinction between the architecture of the Napster system and Napster's conduct in relation to the operational capacity of the system.

[13] The *Sony* Court refused to hold the manufacturer and retailers of video tape recorders liable for contributory infringement despite evidence that such machines could be and were used to infringe plaintiffs' copyrighted television shows. *Sony* stated that if liability "is to be imposed on petitioners in this case, it must

rest on the fact that *they have sold equipment with constructive knowledge of the fact that their customers may use that equipment to make unauthorized copies* of copyrighted material." The *Sony* Court declined to impute the requisite level of knowledge where the defendants made and sold equipment capable of both infringing and "substantial noninfringing uses."

[14] We are bound to follow *Sony,* and will not impute the requisite level of knowledge to Napster merely because peer-to-peer file sharing technology may be used to infringe plaintiffs' copyrights. We depart from the reasoning of the district court that Napster failed to demonstrate that its system is capable of commercially significant noninfringing uses. The district court improperly confined the use analysis to current uses, ignoring the system's capabilities. Consequently, the district court placed undue weight on the proportion of current infringing use as compared to current and future noninfringing use. Nonetheless, whether we might arrive at a different result is not the issue here. The instant appeal occurs at an early point in the proceedings and the fully developed factual record may be materially different from that initially before the district court. Regardless of the number of Napster's infringing versus noninfringing uses, the evidentiary record here supported the district court's finding that plaintiffs would likely prevail in establishing that Napster knew or had reason to know of its users' infringement of plaintiffs' copyrights.

[15] This analysis is similar to that of *Religious Technology Center v. Netcom On-Line Communication Services, Inc.,* which suggests that in an online context, evidence of actual knowledge of specific acts of infringement is required to hold a computer system operator liable for contributory copyright infringement....

[16] We agree that if a computer system operator learns of specific infringing material available on his system and fails to purge such material from the system, the operator knows of and contributes to direct infringement. Conversely, absent any specific information which identifies infringing activity, a computer system operator cannot be liable for contributory infringement merely because the structure of the system allows for the exchange of copyrighted material. To enjoin simply because a computer network allows for infringing use would, in our opinion, violate *Sony* and potentially restrict activity unrelated to infringing use.

[17] We nevertheless conclude that sufficient knowledge exists to impose contributory liability when linked to demonstrated infringing use of the Napster system. The record supports the district court's finding that Napster has *actual* knowledge that *specific* infringing material is available using its system, that it could block access to the system by suppliers of the infringing material, and that it failed to remove the material....

[18] Under the facts as found by the district court, Napster materially contributes to the infringing activity.... [T]he district court concluded that "[w]ithout the support services defendant provides, Napster users could not find and download the music they want with the ease of which defendant boasts." We agree that Napster provides the site and facilities for direct infringement....

[19] We affirm the district court's conclusion that plaintiffs have demonstrated a likelihood of success on the merits of the contributory copyright infringement claim....

[20] We turn to the question whether Napster engages in vicarious copyright infringement. Vicarious copyright liability is an "outgrowth" of respondeat superior. In the context of copyright law, vicarious liability extends beyond an employer/employee relationship to cases in which a defendant has the right and ability to supervise the infringing activity and also has a direct financial interest in such activities.

[21] Before moving into this discussion, we note that *Sony*'s "staple article of commerce" analysis has no application to Napster's potential liability for vicarious copyright infringement. The issues of Sony's liability under the "doctrines of 'direct infringement' and 'vicarious liability'" were not before the Supreme Court, although the Court recognized that the "lines between direct infringement, contributory infringement, and vicarious liability are not clearly drawn." Consequently, when the *Sony* Court used the term "vicarious

liability," it did so broadly and outside of a technical analysis of the doctrine of vicarious copyright infringement....

[22] The district court determined that plaintiffs had demonstrated they would likely succeed in establishing that Napster has a direct financial interest in the infringing activity. We agree. Financial benefit exists where the availability of infringing material "acts as a 'draw' for customers." Ample evidence supports the district court's finding that Napster's future revenue is directly dependent upon "increases in userbase." More users register with the Napster system as the "quality and quantity of available music increases." We conclude that the district court did not err in determining that Napster financially benefits from the availability of protected works on its system....

[23] The district court determined that Napster has the right and ability to supervise its users' conduct. We agree in part.

[24] The ability to block infringers' access to a particular environment for any reason whatsoever is evidence of the right and ability to supervise. Here, plaintiffs have demonstrated that Napster retains the right to control access to its system. Napster has an express reservation of rights policy, stating on its website that it expressly reserves the "right to refuse service and terminate accounts in [its] discretion, including, but not limited to, if Napster believes that user conduct violates applicable law ... or for any reason in Napster's sole discretion, with or without cause."

[25] To escape imposition of vicarious liability, the reserved right to police must be exercised to its fullest extent. Turning a blind eye to detectable acts of infringement for the sake of profit gives rise to liability.

[26] The district court correctly determined that Napster had the right and ability to police its system and failed to exercise that right to prevent the exchange of copyrighted material. The district court, however, failed to recognize that the boundaries of the premises that Napster "controls and patrols" are limited. Put differently, Napster's reserved "right and ability" to police is cabined by the system's current architecture. As shown by the record, the Napster system does not "read" the content of indexed files, other than to check that they are in the proper MP3 format.

[27] Napster, however, has the ability to locate infringing material listed on its search indices, and the right to terminate users' access to the system. The file name indices, therefore, are within the "premises" that Napster has the ability to police. We recognize that the files are user-named and may not match copyrighted material exactly (for example, the artist or song could be spelled wrong). For Napster to function effectively, however, file names must reasonably or roughly correspond to the material contained in the files, otherwise no user could ever locate any desired music. As a practical matter, Napster, its users and the record company plaintiffs have equal access to infringing material by employing Napster's "search function."

[28] Our review of the record requires us to accept the district court's conclusion that plaintiffs have demonstrated a likelihood of success on the merits of the vicarious copyright infringement claim. Napster's failure to police the system's "premises," combined with a showing that Napster financially benefits from the continuing availability of infringing files on its system, leads to the imposition of vicarious liability....

NOTE

1. Do you agree with *Napster* that the *Sony* rule does not apply to the technology at issue in that case? Do you agree that Napster's continuing involvement in users' infringing transactions makes Napster fundamentally different from devices—such as photocopiers, VCRs, and, later, DVRs—for which manufacturers have no continuing involvement past the distribution of the device to the public? Consider in particular whether the design, manufacture, and distribution of a device, which the proprietor knows with certainty will be used by a

large number of people to infringe, is categorically different from the operation of an enterprise, like Napster, that facilitates (or that at least arguably could facilitate) both infringing and non-infringing uses, but which depends on the proprietor's continued involvement in user activities that may be infringing.

The next case involves peer-to-peer networks that—unlike Napster—do not rely on a central server or a centralized index of content on the network. Rather, these "true peer-to-peer" services are decentralized and the owner of the network, after distributing the software that permits access, has no continuing involvement in the activities of users. In this way, the distributors of software used to access true peer-to-peer networks are more like the manufacturer of the VCR. Should they be treated the same when it comes to assessing their potential secondary liability for copyright infringement?

Metro-Goldwyn-Mayer Studios Inc. v. Grokster, Ltd.
545 U.S. 913 (2005)

SOUTER, J.:

[1] The question is under what circumstances the distributor of a product capable of both lawful and unlawful use is liable for acts of copyright infringement by third parties using the product. We hold that one who distributes a device with the object of promoting its use to infringe copyright, as shown by clear expression or other affirmative steps taken to foster infringement, is liable for the resulting acts of infringement by third parties....

[2] Respondents, Grokster, Ltd., and StreamCast Networks, Inc., defendants in the trial court, distribute free software products that allow computer users to share electronic files through peer-to-peer networks, so called because users' computers communicate directly with each other, not through central servers....

[3] .... A group of copyright holders (MGM for short, but including motion picture studios, recording companies, songwriters, and music publishers) sued Grokster and StreamCast for their users' copyright infringements, alleging that they knowingly and intentionally distributed their software to enable users to reproduce and distribute the copyrighted works in violation of the Copyright Act....

[4] .... Grokster's eponymous software employs what is known as FastTrack technology, a protocol developed by others and licensed to Grokster. StreamCast distributes a very similar product except that its software, called Morpheus, relies on what is known as Gnutella technology. A user who downloads and installs either software possesses the protocol to send requests for files directly to the computers of others using software compatible with FastTrack or Gnutella. On the FastTrack network opened by the Grokster software, the user's request goes to a computer given an indexing capacity by the software and designated a supernode, or to some other computer with comparable power and capacity to collect temporary indexes of the files available on the computers of users connected to it. The supernode (or indexing computer) searches its own index and may communicate the search request to other supernodes. If the file is found, the supernode discloses its location to the computer requesting it, and the requesting user can download the file directly from the computer located. The copied file is placed in a designated sharing folder on the requesting user's computer, where it is available for other users to download in turn, along with any other file in that folder.

[5] In the Gnutella network made available by Morpheus, the process is mostly the same, except that in some versions of the Gnutella protocol there are no supernodes. In these versions, peer computers using the

protocol communicate directly with each other. When a user enters a search request into the Morpheus software, it sends the request to computers connected with it, which in turn pass the request along to other connected peers. The search results are communicated to the requesting computer, and the user can download desired files directly from peers' computers. As this description indicates, Grokster and StreamCast use no servers to intercept the content of the search requests or to mediate the file transfers conducted by users of the software, there being no central point through which the substance of the communications passes in either direction.

[6] Although Grokster and StreamCast do not therefore know when particular files are copied, a few searches using their software would show what is available on the networks the software reaches. MGM commissioned a statistician to conduct a systematic search, and his study showed that nearly 90% of the files available for download on the FastTrack system were copyrighted works. Grokster and StreamCast dispute this figure, raising methodological problems and arguing that free copying even of copyrighted works may be authorized by the rightholders. They also argue that potential noninfringing uses of their software are significant in kind, even if infrequent in practice. Some musical performers, for example, have gained new audiences by distributing their copyrighted works for free across peer-to-peer networks, and some distributors of unprotected content have used peer-to-peer networks to disseminate files, Shakespeare being an example....

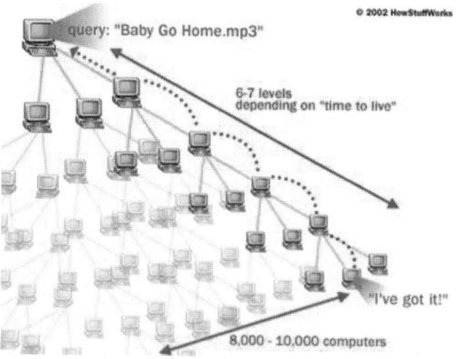

Figure 120: Grokster schematic

[7] As for quantification, the parties' anecdotal and statistical evidence entered thus far to show the content available on the FastTrack and Gnutella networks does not say much about which files are actually downloaded by users, and no one can say how often the software is used to obtain copies of unprotected material. But MGM's evidence gives reason to think that the vast majority of users' downloads are acts of infringement, and because well over 100 million copies of the software in question are known to have been downloaded, and billions of files are shared across the FastTrack and Gnutella networks each month, the probable scope of copyright infringement is staggering.

[8] Grokster and StreamCast concede the infringement in most downloads, and it is uncontested that they are aware that users employ their software primarily to download copyrighted files, even if the decentralized FastTrack and Gnutella networks fail to reveal which files are being copied, and when....

[9] Grokster and StreamCast are not, however, merely passive recipients of information about infringing use. The record is replete with evidence that from the moment Grokster and StreamCast began to distribute their free software, each one clearly voiced the objective that recipients use it to download copyrighted works, and each took active steps to encourage infringement.

[10] After the notorious file-sharing service, Napster, was sued by copyright holders for facilitation of copyright infringement, StreamCast gave away a software program of a kind known as OpenNap, designed as compatible with the Napster program and open to Napster users for downloading files from other Napster and OpenNap users' computers. Evidence indicates that it was always StreamCast's intent to use its OpenNap network to be able to capture email addresses of its initial target market so that it could promote its StreamCast Morpheus interface to them; indeed, the OpenNap program was engineered to leverage Napster's 50 million user base.

[11] StreamCast monitored both the number of users downloading its OpenNap program and the number of music files they downloaded. It also used the resulting OpenNap network to distribute copies of the Morpheus software and to encourage users to adopt it. Internal company documents indicate that StreamCast hoped to attract large numbers of former Napster users if that company was shut down by court order or otherwise, and that StreamCast planned to be the next Napster.... It broadcast banner advertisements to users of other Napster-compatible software, urging them to adopt its OpenNap....

[12] Thus, StreamCast developed promotional materials to market its service as the best Napster alternative. One proposed advertisement read: "Napster Inc. has announced that it will soon begin charging you a fee. That's if the courts don't order it shut down first. What will you do to get around it?" Another proposed ad touted StreamCast's software as the "# 1 alternative to Napster" and asked "[w]hen the lights went off at Napster ... where did the users go?" StreamCast even planned to flaunt the illegal uses of its software; when it launched the OpenNap network, the chief technology officer of the company averred that "[t]he goal is to get in trouble with the law and get sued. It's the best way to get in the new[s]."

[13] The evidence that Grokster sought to capture the market of former Napster users is sparser but revealing, for Grokster launched its own OpenNap system called Swaptor and inserted digital codes into its Web site so that computer users using Web search engines to look for "Napster" or "[f]ree file sharing" would be directed to the Grokster Web site, where they could download the Grokster software. And Grokster's name is an apparent derivative of Napster.

[14] StreamCast's executives monitored the number of songs by certain commercial artists available on their networks, and an internal communication indicates they aimed to have a larger number of copyrighted songs available on their networks than other file-sharing networks. The point, of course, would be to attract users of a mind to infringe, just as it would be with their promotional materials developed showing copyrighted songs as examples of the kinds of files available through Morpheus. Morpheus in fact allowed users to search specifically for "Top 40" songs, which were inevitably copyrighted. Similarly, Grokster sent users a newsletter promoting its ability to provide particular, popular copyrighted materials.

[15] In addition to this evidence of express promotion, marketing, and intent to promote further, the business models employed by Grokster and StreamCast confirm that their principal object was use of their software to download copyrighted works. Grokster and StreamCast receive no revenue from users, who obtain the software itself for nothing. Instead, both companies generate income by selling advertising space, and they

stream the advertising to Grokster and Morpheus users while they are employing the programs. As the number of users of each program increases, advertising opportunities become worth more. While there is doubtless some demand for free Shakespeare, the evidence shows that substantive volume is a function of free access to copyrighted work. Users seeking Top 40 songs, for example, or the latest release by Modest Mouse, are certain to be far more numerous than those seeking a free Decameron, and Grokster and StreamCast translated that demand into dollars.

[16] Finally, there is no evidence that either company made an effort to filter copyrighted material from users' downloads or otherwise impede the sharing of copyrighted files. Although Grokster appears to have sent e-mails warning users about infringing content when it received threatening notice from the copyright holders, it never blocked anyone from continuing to use its software to share copyrighted files. StreamCast not only rejected another company's offer of help to monitor infringement, but blocked the Internet Protocol addresses of entities it believed were trying to engage in such monitoring on its networks....

[17] After discovery, the parties on each side of the case cross-moved for summary judgment.... The District Court held that those who used the Grokster and Morpheus software to download copyrighted media files directly infringed MGM's copyrights, a conclusion not contested on appeal, but the court nonetheless granted summary judgment in favor of Grokster and StreamCast as to any liability arising from distribution of the then-current versions of their software. Distributing that software gave rise to no liability in the court's view, because its use did not provide the distributors with actual knowledge of specific acts of infringement.

[18] The Court of Appeals affirmed. In the court's analysis, a defendant was liable as a contributory infringer when it had knowledge of direct infringement and materially contributed to the infringement. But the court read *Sony Corp. of America v. Universal City Studios, Inc.*, 464 U.S. 417 (1984), as holding that distribution of a commercial product capable of substantial noninfringing uses could not give rise to contributory liability for infringement unless the distributor had actual knowledge of specific instances of infringement and failed to act on that knowledge. The fact that the software was capable of substantial noninfringing uses in the Ninth Circuit's view meant that Grokster and StreamCast were not liable, because they had no such actual knowledge, owing to the decentralized architecture of their software. The court also held that Grokster and StreamCast did not materially contribute to their users' infringement because it was the users themselves who searched for, retrieved, and stored the infringing files, with no involvement by the defendants beyond providing the software in the first place.

[19] The Ninth Circuit also considered whether Grokster and StreamCast could be liable under a theory of vicarious infringement. The court held against liability because the defendants did not monitor or control the use of the software, had no agreed-upon right or current ability to supervise its use, and had no independent duty to police infringement....

[20] One infringes contributorily by intentionally inducing or encouraging direct infringement, and infringes vicariously by profiting from direct infringement while declining to exercise a right to stop or limit it....

[21] Despite the currency of these principles of secondary liability, this Court has dealt with secondary copyright infringement in only one recent case {*Sony*}.... At the trial on the merits, the evidence showed that the principal use of the VCR was for time-shifting, or taping a program for later viewing at a more convenient time, which the Court found to be a fair, not an infringing, use. There was no evidence that Sony had expressed an object of bringing about taping in violation of copyright or had taken active steps to increase its profits from unlawful taping. Although Sony's advertisements urged consumers to buy the VCR to "record favorite shows" or "build a library" of recorded programs, neither of these uses was necessarily infringing.

[22] On those facts, with no evidence of stated or indicated intent to promote infringing uses, the only conceivable basis for imposing liability was on a theory of contributory infringement arising from its sale of VCRs to consumers with knowledge that some would use them to infringe. But because the VCR was capable of commercially significant noninfringing uses, we held the manufacturer could not be faulted solely on the basis of its distribution....

[23] In sum, where an article is "good for nothing else" but infringement, there is no legitimate public interest in its unlicensed availability, and there is no injustice in presuming or imputing an intent to infringe. Conversely, the doctrine absolves the equivocal conduct of selling an item with substantial lawful as well as unlawful uses, and limits liability to instances of more acute fault than the mere understanding that some of one's products will be misused. It leaves breathing room for innovation and a vigorous commerce.

[24] The parties and many of the *amici* in this case think the key to resolving it is the *Sony* rule and, in particular, what it means for a product to be "capable of commercially significant noninfringing uses." MGM advances the argument that granting summary judgment to Grokster and StreamCast as to their current activities gave too much weight to the value of innovative technology, and too little to the copyrights infringed by users of their software, given that 90% of works available on one of the networks was shown to be copyrighted. Assuming the remaining 10% to be its noninfringing use, MGM says this should not qualify as "substantial," and the Court should quantify *Sony* to the extent of holding that a product used "principally" for infringement does not qualify. As mentioned before, Grokster and StreamCast reply by citing evidence that their software can be used to reproduce public domain works, and they point to copyright holders who actually encourage copying. Even if infringement is the principal practice with their software today, they argue, the noninfringing uses are significant and will grow.

[25] We agree with MGM that the Court of Appeals misapplied *Sony*, which it read as limiting secondary liability quite beyond the circumstances to which the case applied. *Sony* barred secondary liability based on presuming or imputing intent to cause infringement solely from the design or distribution of a product capable of substantial lawful use, which the distributor knows is in fact used for infringement. The Ninth Circuit has read *Sony's* limitation to mean that whenever a product is capable of substantial lawful use, the producer can never be held contributorily liable for third parties' infringing use of it; it read the rule as being this broad, even when an actual purpose to cause infringing use is shown by evidence independent of design and distribution of the product, unless the distributors had "specific knowledge of infringement at a time at which they contributed to the infringement, and failed to act upon that information." Because the Circuit found the StreamCast and Grokster software capable of substantial lawful use, it concluded on the basis of its reading of *Sony* that neither company could be held liable, since there was no showing that their software, being without any central server, afforded them knowledge of specific unlawful uses.

[26] This view of *Sony*, however, was error, converting the case from one about liability resting on imputed intent to one about liability on any theory. Because *Sony* did not displace other theories of secondary liability, and because we find below that it was error to grant summary judgment to the companies on MGM's inducement claim, we do not revisit *Sony* further, as MGM requests, to add a more quantified description of the point of balance between protection and commerce when liability rests solely on distribution with knowledge that unlawful use will occur. It is enough to note that the Ninth Circuit's judgment rested on an erroneous understanding of *Sony* and to leave further consideration of the *Sony* rule for a day when that may be required....

[27] *Sony's* rule limits imputing culpable intent as a matter of law from the characteristics or uses of a distributed product. But nothing in *Sony* requires courts to ignore evidence of intent if there is such evidence, and the case was never meant to foreclose rules of fault-based liability derived from the common law. Thus, where evidence goes beyond a product's characteristics or the knowledge that it may be put to infringing

uses, and shows statements or actions directed to promoting infringement, *Sony's* staple-article rule will not preclude liability.

[28] The classic case of direct evidence of unlawful purpose occurs when one induces commission of infringement by another, or entices or persuades another to infringe, as by advertising. Thus at common law a copyright or patent defendant who not only expected but invoked infringing use by advertisement was liable for infringement on principles recognized in every part of the law.

[29] The rule on inducement of infringement as developed in the early cases is no different today. Evidence of active steps taken to encourage direct infringement, such as advertising an infringing use or instructing how to engage in an infringing use, show an affirmative intent that the product be used to infringe, and a showing that infringement was encouraged overcomes the law's reluctance to find liability when a defendant merely sells a commercial product suitable for some lawful use.

[30] For the same reasons that *Sony* took the staple-article doctrine of patent law as a model for its copyright safe-harbor rule, the inducement rule, too, is a sensible one for copyright. We adopt it here, holding that one who distributes a device with the object of promoting its use to infringe copyright, as shown by clear expression or other affirmative steps taken to foster infringement, is liable for the resulting acts of infringement by third parties. We are, of course, mindful of the need to keep from trenching on regular commerce or discouraging the development of technologies with lawful and unlawful potential. Accordingly, just as *Sony* did not find intentional inducement despite the knowledge of the VCR manufacturer that its device could be used to infringe, mere knowledge of infringing potential or of actual infringing uses would not be enough here to subject a distributor to liability. Nor would ordinary acts incident to product distribution, such as offering customers technical support or product updates, support liability in themselves. The inducement rule, instead, premises liability on purposeful, culpable expression and conduct, and thus does nothing to compromise legitimate commerce or discourage innovation having a lawful promise....

[31] .... Here, the summary judgment record is replete with ... evidence that Grokster and StreamCast, unlike the manufacturer and distributor in *Sony*, acted with a purpose to cause copyright violations by use of software suitable for illegal use.

[32] Three features of this evidence of intent are particularly notable. First, each company showed itself to be aiming to satisfy a known source of demand for copyright infringement, the market comprising former Napster users....

[33] Second, this evidence of unlawful objective is given added significance by MGM's showing that neither company attempted to develop filtering tools or other mechanisms to diminish the infringing activity using their software.... [W]e think this evidence underscores Grokster's and StreamCast's intentional facilitation of their users' infringement.[12]

[34] Third, there is a further complement to the direct evidence of unlawful objective. It is useful to recall that StreamCast and Grokster make money by selling advertising space, by directing ads to the screens of computers employing their software. As the record shows, the more the software is used, the more ads are sent out and the greater the advertising revenue becomes. Since the extent of the software's use determines the gain to the distributors, the commercial sense of their enterprise turns on high-volume use, which the record shows is infringing. This evidence alone would not justify an inference of unlawful intent, but viewed in the context of the entire record its import is clear.

---

[12] Of course, in the absence of other evidence of intent, a court would be unable to find contributory infringement liability merely based on a failure to take affirmative steps to prevent infringement, if the device otherwise was capable of substantial noninfringing uses. Such a holding would tread too close to the *Sony* safe harbor.

[35] The unlawful objective is unmistakable....

[36] In addition to intent to bring about infringement and distribution of a device suitable for infringing use, the inducement theory of course requires evidence of actual infringement by recipients of the device, the software in this case. As the account of the facts indicates, there is evidence of infringement on a gigantic scale, and there is no serious issue of the adequacy of MGM's showing on this point in order to survive the companies' summary judgment requests....

[37] In sum, this case is significantly different from *Sony* and reliance on that case to rule in favor of StreamCast and Grokster was error. *Sony* dealt with a claim of liability based solely on distributing a product with alternative lawful and unlawful uses, with knowledge that some users would follow the unlawful course. The case struck a balance between the interests of protection and innovation by holding that the product's capability of substantial lawful employment should bar the imputation of fault and consequent secondary liability for the unlawful acts of others.

[38] MGM's evidence in this case most obviously addresses a different basis of liability for distributing a product open to alternative uses. Here, evidence of the distributors' words and deeds going beyond distribution as such shows a purpose to cause and profit from third-party acts of copyright infringement. If liability for inducing infringement is ultimately found, it will not be on the basis of presuming or imputing fault, but from inferring a patently illegal objective from statements and actions showing what that objective was....

[39] The judgment of the Court of Appeals is vacated, and the case is remanded for further proceedings consistent with this opinion....

GINSBURG, J. concurring, joined by Chief Justice Rehnquist and Justice Kennedy:

[40] I concur in the Court's decision, ... and write separately to clarify why I conclude that the Court of Appeals misperceived, and hence misapplied, our holding in *Sony Corp. of America v. Universal City Studios, Inc.* ...

[41] In *Sony*, the Court considered Sony's liability for selling the Betamax videocassette recorder. It did so enlightened by a full trial record. Drawing an analogy to the staple article of commerce doctrine from patent law, the *Sony* Court observed that the "sale of an article ... adapted to [a patent] infringing use" does not suffice "to make the seller a contributory infringer" if the article "is also adapted to other and lawful uses."

[42] "The staple article of commerce doctrine" applied to copyright, the Court stated, "must strike a balance between a copyright holder's legitimate demand for effective—not merely symbolic—protection of the statutory monopoly, and the rights of others freely to engage in substantially unrelated areas of commerce." "Accordingly," the Court held, "the sale of copying equipment, like the sale of other articles of commerce, does not constitute contributory infringement if the product is widely used for legitimate, unobjectionable purposes. Indeed, it need merely be capable of substantial noninfringing uses." Thus, to resolve the *Sony* case, the Court explained, it had to determine "whether the Betamax is capable of commercially significant noninfringing uses."

[43] To answer that question, the Court considered whether "a significant number of [potential uses of the Betamax were] noninfringing." The Court homed in on one potential use—private, noncommercial time-shifting of television programs in the home (*i.e.*, recording a broadcast TV program for later personal viewing). Time-shifting was noninfringing, the Court concluded, because in some cases trial testimony showed it was authorized by the copyright holder, and in others it qualified as legitimate fair use. Most purchasers used the Betamax principally to engage in time-shifting, a use that "plainly satisfie[d]" the Court's standard. Thus,

there was no need in *Sony* to "give precise content to the question of how much [actual or potential] use is commercially significant." Further development was left for later days and cases....

[44] Even if the absolute number of noninfringing files copied using the Grokster and StreamCast software is large, it does not follow that the products are therefore put to substantial noninfringing uses and are thus immune from liability. The number of noninfringing copies may be reflective of, and dwarfed by, the huge total volume of files shared. Further, the District Court and the Court of Appeals did not sharply distinguish between uses of Grokster's and StreamCast's software products (which this case is about) and uses of peer-to-peer technology generally (which this case is not about).

[45] In sum, when the record in this case was developed, there was evidence that Grokster's and StreamCast's products were, and had been for some time, overwhelmingly used to infringe, and that this infringement was the overwhelming source of revenue from the products. Fairly appraised, the evidence was insufficient to demonstrate, beyond genuine debate, a reasonable prospect that substantial or commercially significant noninfringing uses were likely to develop over time. On this record, the District Court should not have ruled dispositively on the contributory infringement charge by granting summary judgment to Grokster and StreamCast.

[46] If, on remand, the case is not resolved on summary judgment in favor of MGM based on Grokster and StreamCast actively inducing infringement, the Court of Appeals, I would emphasize, should reconsider, on a fuller record, its interpretation of *Sony*'s product distribution holding.

BREYER, J. concurring, joined by Justices Stevens and O'Connor:

[47] I agree with the Court that the distributor of a dual-use technology may be liable for the infringing activities of third parties where he or she actively seeks to advance the infringement. I further agree that, in light of our holding today, we need not now "revisit" *Sony Corp. of America v. Universal City Studios, Inc.* Other Members of the Court, however, take up the *Sony* question: whether Grokster's product is "capable of 'substantial' or 'commercially significant' noninfringing uses." (Ginsburg, J., concurring). And they answer that question by stating that the Court of Appeals was wrong when it granted summary judgment on the issue in Grokster's favor. I write to explain why I disagree with them on this matter....

[48] The Court's opinion in *Sony* and the record evidence (as described and analyzed in the many briefs before us) together convince me that the Court of Appeals' conclusion has adequate legal support....

[49] I begin with *Sony*'s standard. In *Sony*, the Court considered the potential copyright liability of a company that did not itself illegally copy protected material, but rather sold a machine—a videocassette recorder (VCR)—that could be used to do so.... Sony knew many customers would use its VCRs to engage in unauthorized copying and library-building. But that fact, said the Court, was insufficient to make Sony itself an infringer. And the Court ultimately held that Sony was not liable for its customers' acts of infringement.

[50] In reaching this conclusion, the Court recognized the need for the law, in fixing *secondary* copyright liability, to "strike a balance between a copyright holder's legitimate demand for effective—not merely symbolic—protection of the statutory monopoly, and the rights of others freely to engage in substantially unrelated areas of commerce." .... The Court wrote that the sale of copying equipment, "like the sale of other articles of commerce, does not constitute contributory infringement if the product is widely used for legitimate, unobjectionable purposes. *Indeed, it need merely be capable of substantial noninfringing uses.*" The Court ultimately characterized the legal "question" in the particular case as "whether [Sony's VCR] is *capable of commercially significant noninfringing uses*" (while declining to give "precise content" to these terms).

[51] It then applied this standard. The Court had before it a survey (commissioned by the District Court and then prepared by the respondents) showing that roughly 9% of all VCR recordings were of the type—namely, religious, educational, and sports programming—owned by producers and distributors testifying on Sony's behalf who did not object to time-shifting. A much higher percentage of VCR *users* had at one point taped an authorized program, in addition to taping unauthorized programs. And the plaintiffs—not a large class of content providers as in this case—owned only a small percentage of the total available *un*authorized programming. But of all the taping actually done by Sony's customers, only around 9% was of the sort the Court referred to as authorized.

[52] The Court found that the magnitude of authorized programming was "significant," and it also noted the "significant potential for future authorized copying." The Court supported this conclusion by referencing the trial testimony of professional sports league officials and a religious broadcasting representative. It also discussed (1) a Los Angeles educational station affiliated with the Public Broadcasting Service that made many of its programs available for home taping, and (2) *Mr. Rogers' Neighborhood*, a widely watched children's program. On the basis of this testimony and other similar evidence, the Court determined that producers of this kind had authorized duplication of their copyrighted programs "in significant enough numbers to create a *substantial* market for a noninfringing use of the" VCR.

[53] The Court, in using the key word "substantial," indicated that these circumstances alone constituted a sufficient basis for rejecting the imposition of secondary liability. Nonetheless, the Court buttressed its conclusion by finding separately that, in any event, *un*authorized time-shifting often constituted not infringement, but "fair use." ...

[54] When measured against *Sony*'s underlying evidence and analysis, the evidence now before us shows that Grokster passes *Sony*'s test—that is, whether the company's product is capable of substantial or commercially significant noninfringing uses. For one thing, petitioners' (hereinafter MGM) own expert declared that 75% of current files available on Grokster are infringing and 15% are "likely infringing." That leaves some number of files near 10% that apparently are noninfringing, a figure very similar to the 9% or so of authorized time-shifting uses of the VCR that the Court faced in *Sony*....

[55] Importantly, *Sony* also used the word "capable," asking whether the product is "*capable of*" substantial noninfringing uses. Its language and analysis suggest that a figure like 10%, if fixed for all time, might well prove insufficient, but that such a figure serves as an adequate foundation where there is a reasonable prospect of expanded legitimate uses over time. And its language also indicates the appropriateness of looking to potential future uses of the product to determine its "capability."

[56] Here the record reveals a significant future market for noninfringing uses of Grokster-type peer-to-peer software. Such software permits the exchange of *any* sort of digital file—whether that file does, or does not, contain copyrighted material. As more and more uncopyrighted information is stored in swappable form, it seems a likely inference that lawful peer-to-peer sharing will become increasingly prevalent....

[57] There may be other now-unforeseen noninfringing uses that develop for peer-to-peer software, just as the home-video rental industry (unmentioned in *Sony*) developed for the VCR. But the foreseeable development of such uses, when taken together with an estimated 10% noninfringing material, is sufficient to meet *Sony*'s standard. And while *Sony* considered the record following a trial, there are no facts asserted by MGM in its summary judgment filings that lead me to believe the outcome after a trial here could be any different. The lower courts reached the same conclusion.

[58] Of course, Grokster itself may not want to develop these other noninfringing uses. But *Sony*'s standard seeks to protect not the Groksters of this world (which in any event may well be liable under today's holding),

but the development of technology more generally. And Grokster's desires in this respect are beside the point....

[59] The real question here, I believe, is not whether the record evidence satisfies *Sony*. As I have interpreted the standard set forth in that case, it does....

[60] Instead, the real question is whether we should modify the *Sony* standard, as MGM requests, or interpret *Sony* more strictly, as I believe Justice Ginsburg's approach would do in practice.

[61] As I have said, *Sony* itself sought to "strike a balance between a copyright holder's legitimate demand for effective—not merely symbolic—protection of the statutory monopoly, and the rights of others freely to engage in substantially unrelated areas of commerce." Thus, to determine whether modification, or a strict interpretation, of *Sony* is needed, I would ask whether MGM has shown that *Sony* incorrectly balanced copyright and new-technology interests. In particular: (1) Has *Sony* (as I interpret it) worked to protect new technology? (2) If so, would modification or strict interpretation significantly weaken that protection? (3) If so, would new or necessary copyright-related benefits outweigh any such weakening? ...

[62] The first question is the easiest to answer. *Sony*'s rule, as I interpret it, has provided entrepreneurs with needed assurance that they will be shielded from copyright liability as they bring valuable new technologies to market.

[63] Sony's *rule is clear.* That clarity allows those who develop new products that are capable of substantial noninfringing uses to know, *ex ante,* that distribution of their product will not yield massive monetary liability. At the same time, it helps deter them from distributing products that have no other real function than—or that are specifically intended for—copyright infringement, deterrence that the Court's holding today reinforces (by adding a weapon to the copyright holder's legal arsenal).

[64] Sony's *rule is strongly technology protecting.* The rule deliberately makes it difficult for courts to find secondary liability where new technology is at issue. It establishes that the law will not impose copyright liability upon the distributors of dual-use technologies (who do not themselves engage in unauthorized copying) unless the product in question will be used *almost exclusively* to infringe copyrights (or unless they actively induce infringements as we today describe). *Sony* thereby recognizes that the copyright laws are not intended to discourage or to control the emergence of new technologies, including (perhaps especially) those that help disseminate information and ideas more broadly or more efficiently. Thus *Sony*'s rule shelters VCRs, typewriters, tape recorders, photocopiers, computers, cassette players, compact disc burners, digital video recorders, MP3 players, Internet search engines, and peer-to-peer software. But *Sony*'s rule does not shelter descramblers, even if one could *theoretically* use a descrambler in a noninfringing way.

[65] Sony's *rule is forward looking.* It does not confine its scope to a static snapshot of a product's current uses (thereby threatening technologies that have undeveloped future markets). Rather, as the VCR example makes clear, a product's market can evolve dramatically over time. And *Sony*—by referring to a *capacity* for substantial noninfringing uses—recognizes that fact. *Sony*'s word "capable" refers to a plausible, not simply a theoretical, likelihood that such uses will come to pass, and that fact anchors *Sony* in practical reality.

[66] Sony's *rule is mindful of the limitations facing judges where matters of technology are concerned.* Judges have no specialized technical ability to answer questions about present or future technological feasibility or commercial viability where technology professionals, engineers, and venture capitalists themselves may radically disagree and where answers may differ depending upon whether one focuses upon the time of product development or the time of distribution. Consider, for example, the question whether devices can be added to Grokster's software that will filter out infringing files. MGM tells us this is easy enough to do, as do several *amici* that produce and sell the filtering technology. Grokster says it is not at all easy to do, and not an

efficient solution in any event, and several apparently disinterested computer science professors agree. Which account should a judge credit? *Sony* says that the judge will not necessarily have to decide.

[67] Given the nature of the *Sony* rule, it is not surprising that in the last 20 years, there have been relatively few contributory infringement suits—based on a product distribution theory—brought against technology providers (a small handful of federal appellate court cases and perhaps fewer than two dozen District Court cases in the last 20 years). I have found nothing in the briefs or the record that shows that *Sony* has failed to achieve its innovation-protecting objective....

[68] The second, more difficult, question is whether a modified *Sony* rule (or a strict interpretation) would significantly weaken the law's ability to protect new technology. Justice GINSBURG's approach would require defendants to produce considerably more concrete evidence—more than was presented here—to earn *Sony*'s shelter. That heavier evidentiary demand, and especially the more dramatic (case-by-case balancing) modifications that MGM and the Government seek, would, I believe, undercut the protection that *Sony* now offers.

[69] To require defendants to provide, for example, detailed evidence—say, business plans, profitability estimates, projected technological modifications, and so forth—would doubtless make life easier for copyright holder plaintiffs. But it would simultaneously increase the legal uncertainty that surrounds the creation or development of a new technology capable of being put to infringing uses.... The price of a wrong guess—even if it involves a good-faith effort to assess technical and commercial viability—could be large statutory damages (not less than $750 and up to $30,000 *per infringed work*). 17 U.S.C. § 504(c)(1). The additional risk and uncertainty would mean a consequent additional chill of technological development....

[70] The third question—whether a positive copyright impact would outweigh any technology-related loss—I find the most difficult of the three. I do not doubt that a more intrusive *Sony* test would generally provide greater revenue security for copyright holders. But it is harder to conclude that the gains on the copyright swings would exceed the losses on the technology roundabouts.

[71] For one thing, the law disfavors equating the two different kinds of gain and loss; rather, it leans in favor of protecting technology. As *Sony* itself makes clear, the producer of a technology which *permits* unlawful copying does not himself *engage* in unlawful copying—a fact that makes the attachment of copyright liability to the creation, production, or distribution of the technology an exceptional thing. Moreover, *Sony* has been the law for some time. And that fact imposes a serious burden upon copyright holders like MGM to show a need for change in the current rules of the game, including a more strict interpretation of the test.

[72] In any event, the evidence now available does not, in my view, make out a sufficiently strong case for change. To say this is not to doubt the basic need to protect copyrighted material from infringement. The Constitution itself stresses the vital role that copyright plays in advancing the "useful Arts." No one disputes that "reward to the author or artist serves to induce release to the public of the products of his creative genius." And deliberate unlawful copying is no less an unlawful taking of property than garden-variety theft. But these highly general principles cannot by themselves tell us how to balance the interests at issue in *Sony* or whether *Sony*'s standard needs modification. And at certain key points, information is lacking.

[73] Will an unmodified *Sony* lead to a significant diminution in the amount or quality of creative work produced? Since copyright's basic objective is creation and its revenue objectives but a means to that end, this is the underlying copyright question. And its answer is far from clear....

[74] The extent to which related production has actually and resultingly declined remains uncertain, though there is good reason to believe that the decline, if any, is not substantial.

[75] More importantly, copyright holders at least potentially have other tools available to reduce piracy and to abate whatever threat it poses to creative production. As today's opinion makes clear, a copyright holder may proceed against a technology provider where a provable specific intent to infringe (of the kind the Court describes) is present. Services like Grokster may well be liable under an inducement theory.

[76] In addition, a copyright holder has always had the legal authority to bring a traditional infringement suit against one who wrongfully copies. Indeed, since September 2003, the Recording Industry Association of America (RIAA) has filed thousands of suits against people for sharing copyrighted material. These suits have provided copyright holders with damages; have served as a teaching tool, making clear that much file sharing, if done without permission, is unlawful; and apparently have had a real and significant deterrent effect.

[77] Further, copyright holders may develop new technological devices that will help curb unlawful infringement. Some new technology, called "digital watermarking" and "digital fingerprinting," can encode within the file information about the author and the copyright scope and date, which "fingerprints" can help to expose infringers.

[78] At the same time, advances in technology have discouraged unlawful copying by making *lawful* copying (*e.g.*, downloading music with the copyright holder's permission) cheaper and easier to achieve. Several services now sell music for less than $1 per song....

[79] Finally, as *Sony* recognized, the legislative option remains available. Courts are less well suited than Congress to the task of accommodating fully the varied permutations of competing interests that are inevitably implicated by such new technology.

[80] I do not know whether these developments and similar alternatives will prove sufficient, but I am reasonably certain that, given their existence, a strong demonstrated need for modifying *Sony* (or for interpreting *Sony*'s standard more strictly) has not yet been shown. That fact, along with the added risks that modification (or strict interpretation) would impose upon technological innovation, leads me to the conclusion that we should maintain *Sony*, reading its standard as I have read it. As so read, it requires affirmance of the Ninth Circuit's determination of the relevant aspects of the *Sony* question....

[81] For these reasons, I disagree with Justice Ginsburg, but I agree with the Court and join its opinion.

NOTES

1. The Supreme Court's opinion in *Grokster* reminded many that liability for "inducement" is an element of contributory copyright infringement liability. Perhaps that should not have been a surprise, for the inducement prong of contributory infringement liability had figured in the cases for a long time. Here's an example, from *Gershwin Publishing Corp. v. Columbia Artists Management, Inc.*, 443 F.2d 1159, 1162 (2d Cir. 1971): "[O]ne who, with knowledge of the infringing activity, *induces*, causes or materially contributes to the infringing conduct of another, may be held liable as a 'contributory' infringer." (emphasis added)

2. In *Columbia Pictures Industries v. Fung*, 710 F.3d 1020 (9th Cir. 2013), motion picture studios filed suit against Gary Fung and his company, isoHunt Web Technologies, Inc., alleging that the defendants induced third parties to download infringing copies of plaintiffs' copyrighted works. The defendants' websites would use the BitTorrent peer-to-peer file-sharing protocol to collect and distribute content. Each time a torrent file (a file containing information regarding the location of a specific piece of content) would be added to Fung's site, the site would automatically modify the torrent file to make it better able to find the specific content. The defendants also hosted an electronic message board where users could post content, and on which Fung posted comments and also moderated. The Ninth Circuit affirmed a district court opinion holding that (1) the defendants were liable for contributory copyright infringement on an inducement theory, and (2) that

defendants were not entitled to safe harbor protection under the DMCA. On the inducement issue, Fung argued that because he did not develop or distribute any device—that is, the software or technology used for downloading—he is not liable under the inducement rule enunciated in *Grokster*. The Ninth Circuit disagreed, interpreting the rule in *Grokster* to apply to services as well as devices. The Ninth Circuit also found that there was substantial evidence of inducement, including that Fung had encouraged the uploading to his sites of copyrighted content by, among other things, prominently featuring a list of the highest-grossing "Box Office Movies" on his website. On the § 512 issue, the court concluded that Fung was not entitled to safe harbor under § 512(a). That safe harbor, the court held, applies to service providers who act only as conduits for the transmission of information. Fung's sites select which users will communicate with each other; as a consequence, they serve as more than "conduits" between computer users. The court further held that the defendants were not entitled to safe harbor under §§ 512(c) and (d) because safe harbor under those provisions is available only if the service provider does not have actual knowledge that the material or an activity using material on the system or network is infringing. The court stated that Fung had "red flag" knowledge of a broad range of infringing activity.

3. *Napster* and *Grokster* led to the shutdown of several popular peer-to-peer filesharing networks. But of course that did not end filesharing. The BitTorrent network is still very much alive. (Why do you think BitTorrent has not been shut down? Think about the courts' holdings in *Napster* and *Grokster*, and whether they apply to the architecture and conduct of BitTorrent.) And a lot of filesharing is now done through a technology that grew up after peer-to-peer: cyberlockers. Did content owners' campaign against filesharing work? What were the results of that campaign? Would we have gotten iTunes and Spotify and Apple Music without Napster and Grokster? For a broader look at this dynamic, see EDUARDO MOISÉS PEÑALVER & SONIA K. KATYAL, PROPERTY OUTLAWS: HOW SQUATTERS, PIRATES, AND PROTESTERS IMPROVE THE LAW OF OWNERSHIP (2010); KAL RAUSTIALA & CHRISTOPHER JON SPRIGMAN, THE KNOCKOFF ECONOMY (2012) (see particularly, *Epilogue: The Future of Music*).

VIII. Copyright Litigation and Remedies

In this section, we will cover two principal subjects: (1) the various procedural issues that attend copyright infringement litigation, and (2) the remedies available to successful plaintiffs in a copyright infringement action. We will also briefly examine the Copyright Act's provisions regarding *criminal* liability for copyright infringement, and how those provisions have been interpreted, and the new law providing for small claims proceedings before the Copyright Claims Board.

A. Subject Matter Jurisdiction

Under federal law, subject matter jurisdiction over copyright infringement actions is given exclusively to federal courts. The relevant provision, 28 U.S.C. § 1338(a), provides:

> *The district courts shall have original jurisdiction of any civil action arising under any Act of Congress relating to ... copyrights .... No State court shall have jurisdiction over any claim for relief arising under any Act of Congress relating to ... copyrights.*

In most cases, determining whether the cause of action arises under copyright law, and is thus within the exclusive jurisdiction of federal courts, will be unproblematic. But there are some cases in which the determination poses some difficulty. Most of these cases involve so-called "hybrid" claims that raise both copyright and contract law issues. An example is *T.B. Harms Co. v. Eliscu*, 339 F.2d 823 (2d Cir. 1964), which involved a dispute over whether a defendant had assigned his interest in a copyright to the plaintiff, or whether the defendant had retained his interest and assigned it at a later date to a second defendant. The plaintiff advanced no infringement claim and sought no relief grounded in the Copyright Act's remedies provisions. In determining whether the case was properly within the federal courts' jurisdiction, the Second Circuit held that a claim "arises under" the Copyright Act if:

> (1) "[T]he complaint is for a remedy expressly granted by the Act, e.g., a suit for infringement or for the statutory [mechanical] royalties ..."; or
> (2) "[T]he complaint ... asserts a claim requiring construction of the Act ...."

Applying the test, the Second Circuit held that the lawsuit in *T.B. Harms* did not "arise under" the Copyright Act and that the federal courts accordingly lacked subject matter jurisdiction.

NOTES

1. If not all cases connected to copyright law will be heard in federal court, what are the implications for copyright policy?

2. In the Copyright Remedy Clarification Act of 1990 (CRCA), Pub. L. No. 101-553, 104 Stat. 2749 (1990) (codified at 17 U.S.C. §§ 501(a), 511)), Congress amended the Copyright Act to permit copyright infringement suits against states. In *Allen v. Cooper*, 140 S. Ct. 994 (2020), the Supreme Court invalidated the CRCA, holding that Congress lacked the authority to abrogate the states' Eleventh Amendment sovereign immunity from copyright infringement suits via the CRCA. The Court acknowledged that Congress used clear language to abrogate the states' immunity in the CRCA. But the Court held that Congress may not abrogate state sovereign immunity via an exercise of nearly all of its Article I legislative powers, including to provide copyright protection. Nor could the CRCA be justified, the Court held, under Section 5 of the Fourteenth Amendment, which allows Congress to abrogate states' immunity as part of its power to enforce the Amendment's substantive prohibitions. In enacting the CRCA, Congress had failed to identify any pattern of intentional

state infringement for which the infringing state offered no adequate remedy. In the absence of such evidence, the CRCA failed the "congruence and proportionality" test for abrogating state sovereign immunity as an exercise of Section 5.

B. Statute of Limitations

Section 507(b) of the Copyright Act provides that "[n]o civil action shall be maintained under the [Act] unless it is commenced within three years after the claim accrued." That short provision has spawned a surprising number of ambiguities. One such ambiguity is when a copyright infringement claim should be held to have "accrued." A legal claim ordinarily accrues when the conduct that gives rise to the claim occurs. *See* Bay Area Laundry & Dry Cleaning Pension Trust Fund v. Ferbar Corp. of Cal., 522 U.S. 192 (1997). In the case of copyright infringement, under this ordinary understanding—often referred to as the "injury rule"—the claim would "accrue," and the statute of limitations begin to run, when an infringing act occurs. But most courts that have considered the question have abandoned the injury rule in favor of a "discovery rule," holding that a copyright infringement claim "accrues" only when "the plaintiff discovers, or with due diligence should have discovered, the injury that forms the basis for the claim," and that the running of the statute of limitations is therefore "tolled" until the plaintiff discovers the infringement or reasonably should have. *See, e.g.,* William A. Graham Co. v. Haughey, 568 F.3d 425, 433 (3d Cir. 2009).

Note that the Copyright Act's statute of limitations works on a "rolling" basis—that is, for each new act of infringement of a work, even by the same infringer, a new three-year clock begins to run. This means that a particular infringer's liability can potentially continue for decades. Given the "discovery" rule that most courts apply to copyright infringement, what is the argument in favor of a "rolling" statute of limitations for copyright infringement? Does the rolling statute of limitations give copyright owners any benefit that the discovery rule does not in combating infringement that is discovered more than three years after it commences? On the other hand, the rolling statute of limitations does raise the possibility that a rightsholder may delay, possibly for many years, in bringing suit against an open and notorious infringer. Is this fair?

The Supreme Court considered this question in *Petrella v. Metro-Goldwyn-Mayer, Inc.*, 572 U.S. 663 (2014). In particular, the Court considered whether the common law equitable defense of laches should apply to limit copyright infringement claims in which the rightsholder had known about continuing infringement and brought suit only after a lengthy period. Six justices, in an opinion authored by Justice Ginsburg, held that the defense of laches was unavailable in copyright infringement lawsuits:

> If the rule were, as MGM urges, "sue soon, or forever hold your peace," copyright owners would have to mount a federal case fast to stop seemingly innocuous infringements, lest those infringements eventually grow in magnitude. Section 507(b)'s three-year limitations period, however, coupled to the separate-accrual rule, avoids such litigation profusion. It allows a copyright owner to defer suit until she can estimate whether litigation is worth the candle. She will miss out on damages for periods prior to the three-year look-back, but her right to prospective injunctive relief should, in most cases, remain unaltered.

Note, however, that Justice Ginsburg preserved the possibility that defendants may prevail on an equitable estoppel argument "when a copyright owner engages in intentionally misleading representations concerning his abstention from suit, and the alleged infringer detrimentally relies on the copyright owner's deception." In such a case, "the doctrine of estoppel may bar the copyright owner's claims completely, eliminating all potential remedies."

NOTES

1. Do you agree with the Supreme Court's decision in *Petrella* that the equitable defense of laches does not apply to copyright infringement claims? Is there a reason to treat copyright infringement claims differently from other claims?

2. In general, statutes of limitations have two primary purposes: (1) to provide repose—a period after which potential defendants can be assured that they no longer face the threat of legal liability for old acts—and (2) to encourage potential plaintiffs to bring suit in a timely manner, before witnesses and evidence disappear and memories fade. If these are the purposes that underlie statutes of limitations, then how well does the Copyright Act's rolling statute of limitations align with them?

3. Courts in the Ninth Circuit have held that the Supreme Court's decision in *Petrella* did not displace the discovery rule applied by the Ninth Circuit to copyright infringement claims, which serves as "an exception to the three-year damages bar." *E.g.*, Starz Entm't, LLC v. MGM Domestic Television Distrib., LLC, --- F. Supp. 3d ---- (2021). By contrast, the Second Circuit has held that although the discovery rule remains valid post-*Petrella* and is used "to determine when a copyright infringement claim accrues," *Petrella* limits damages claims to "a three-year lookback period from the time a suit is filed to determine the extent of the relief available." Sohm v. Scholastic, Inc., 959 F.3d 39 (2d Cir. 2020). Which approach makes more sense? Does the discovery rule, combined with the rule in *Petrella*, serve the purposes that underlie statutes of limitations?

C. Standing

As you learned in Chapter III, under § 201 of the Copyright Act, copyright ownership "vests initially in the author or authors of the work." Moreover, as you will learn in more detail in Chapter X, assignments or exclusive licenses of copyrights operate as "transfer[s] of copyright ownership." *See* 17 U.S.C. § 101 (defining "transfer of copyright ownership"). In the context of copyright litigation, it is important to understand who is the owner of the copyright rights alleged to have been infringed because under § 501(b) of the Copyright Act, only *copyright owners* have standing to sue for infringement of the copyright(s) they own. Section 501(b) provides as follows:

> The legal or beneficial owner of an exclusive right under a copyright is entitled, subject to the requirements of section 411, to institute an action for any infringement of that particular right committed while he or she is the owner of it. The court may require such owner to serve written notice of the action with a copy of the complaint upon any person shown, by the records of the Copyright Office or otherwise, to have or claim an interest in the copyright, and shall require that such notice be served upon any person whose interest is likely to be affected by a decision in the case. The court may require the joinder, and shall permit the intervention, of any person having or claiming an interest in the copyright.

Section 501(b) gives standing to both "legal" and "beneficial" owners. A legal owner can be the person or entity in which ownership of the copyright originally vested (including in the case of an owner who is not a natural person, via operation of the doctrine of works made for hire, which you learned about in Chapter III). A legal owner can also be a person to whom, or an entity to which, a copyright has been assigned or exclusively licensed. In contrast, a nonexclusive licensee is not a legal owner and does not have standing to sue for infringement.

In the case of an exclusive license, the scope of the licensee's rights, and consequently of the licensee's standing to sue for infringement, will vary according to the terms of the license. A licensee with an exclusive license to the entirety of a copyright will have standing to sue for any act of infringement of that copyright that occurs during the term of the license. A licensee with an exclusive license that conveys less than the entirety of the original copyright owner's rights under the Copyright Act will have standing to sue for acts of infringement that occur during the term of the license *only if those infringing acts implicate the particular rights, or subdivisions of rights, that are conveyed to the licensee via the exclusive license*. For example, a licensee who has an exclusive license to distribute a copyrighted work cannot sue for acts of infringement that involve only unauthorized reproduction, but not distribution. Or consider a licensee who has an exclusive license to reproduce and distribute a copyrighted work east of the Mississippi River. That licensee lacks standing to sue for infringement with respect to unauthorized reproduction and distribution of the work that occurs wholly on the west side of the Mississippi River.

Section 501(b) of the Copyright Act also grants standing to "beneficial" owners of a copyright. As per the Act's legislative history, a "beneficial" owner of copyright includes "an author who ha[s] parted with legal title to the copyright in exchange for percentage royalties based on sales or license fees." H.R. REP. NO. 94-1476, 94th Cong., 2d Sess. 159 (1976). For example, a songwriter who has transferred the copyright in her musical work to a music publishing company in return for a certain percentage of royalties collected from licensing of that work (as has been the typical arrangement in the music industry, as you learned in Chapter V) is a "beneficial" owner who has standing to sue for infringement of that work. That said, often the songwriter will agree, in assigning the copyright to the music publishing company, that the publisher—and not the songwriter—will bring infringement suits respecting the work that has been assigned.

Finally, note that § 501(b) grants standing *only* to legal and beneficial owners. It does not grant standing to parties, like agents, administrators, and others, who are not owners but who may nonetheless have an interest in a copyright—for example, via a contract specifying that the party will provide services related to the copyright, such as negotiating and executing licenses and collecting and remitting royalties, in exchange for fees. A party's interest in a copyright that does not amount to legal or beneficial *ownership* is insufficient to confer standing on that party to sue for infringement of the copyright. For similar reasons, the mere assignment of *the right to sue for infringement* is not sufficient to create standing in the assignee. Righthaven LLC v. Hoehn, 716 F.3d 1166, 1169 (9th Cir. 2013). Only the assignment or exclusive license of a *copyright right* is sufficient. Nor do associations have standing to sue for copyright infringement on behalf of their members. Authors Guild, Inc. v. HathiTrust, 755 F.3d 87, 94 (2d Cir. 2014).

Do you think it is good or bad for copyright policy that a party that acquires a copyright owner's right to sue does not have standing to sue for infringement? For an exploration of this issue, see Shyamkrishna Balganesh, *Copyright Infringement Markets*, 113 COLUM. L. REV. 2277 (2013); Shyamkrishna Balganesh, *The Uneasy Case Against Copyright Trolls*, 86 S. CAL. L. REV. 723 (2013).

NOTES

1. The Copyright Act's legislative history makes the purpose of § 501(b) clear: It was intended to allow "the owner of a particular right to bring an infringement action in that owner's name alone, while at the same time insuring to the extent possible that the other owners whose rights may be affected are notified and given a chance to join the action." H.R. REP. NO. 94-1476, 94th Cong., 2d Sess. 159 (1976). Reread the last two sentences of § 501(b) above to see how Congress effectuated the second purpose it articulated in the legislative history.

2. As you learned in Chapter IV, § 411 of the Copyright Act, which is referenced in § 501(b), requires the owner of any United States work to register the owner's copyright claim in that work before the commencement of an infringement action. (As you also learned, the U.S. Supreme Court recently held that a copyright owner satisfies this requirement only when registration has been *granted or refused by the Copyright Office* prior to

filing suit rather than merely by submitting a registration *application* prior to commencing an infringement action. Fourth Estate Pub. Benefit Corp. v. Wall-Street.com, LLC, 139 S. Ct. 881 (2019).)

3. Parties facing a substantial threat of copyright infringement liability may initiate litigation seeking a declaration that their conduct does not infringe. Under the Declaratory Judgment Act, 28 U.S.C. § 2201, a court has subject matter jurisdiction over an action seeking a declaratory judgment if the party facing a threat of infringement liability—the "declaratory judgment plaintiff"—(1) demonstrates a real and reasonable apprehension that she will be subject to liability if she continues to engage in the potentially infringing conduct, and (2) some statement or action of the copyright owner caused the declaratory judgment plaintiff's apprehension. Shloss v. Sweeney, 515 F. Supp. 2d 1068 (N.D. Cal. 2007).

D. Judicial Deference to the Copyright Office

Copyright is an area of law that interacts with the United States Copyright Office, which is a division of the Library of Congress. The primary function of the Copyright Office is to register claims of copyright in works of authorship. When the Register of Copyrights (the official who heads the Copyright Office) issues a certificate of registration of a claim of copyright in a work before or within five years after the work's publication, the Copyright Act directs courts to treat the certificate as prima facie evidence of the copyright's validity. 17 U.S.C. § 410(c). Of course, the presumption is a limited one; it does not conclusively establish copyrightability but rather shifts to the defendant the burden of proving that the plaintiff's work is not copyrightable. *See* Ets-Hokin v. Skyy Spirits, Inc. 225 F.3d 1068, 1075 (9th Cir. 2000) (explaining that the certificate of registration entitles plaintiff to a "rebuttable presumption of originality").

The Copyright Office is also granted limited regulatory authority. The Copyright Act provides the Register of Copyrights with authority to "establish regulations not inconsistent with law for the administration of the functions and duties made the responsibility of the Register under this title. All regulations established by the Register under this title are subject to the approval of the Librarian of Congress." 17 U.S.C. § 702. Those regulations are made expressly subject to the Administrative Procedures Act. *Id.* § 701(e).

Because the Copyright Office is an arm of Congress and is not part of the executive branch, some have questioned the constitutional basis for *any* regulatory authority granted by Congress to this entity. *See, e.g.,* Andy Gass, *Considering Copyright Rulemaking: The Constitutional Question*, 27 BERKELEY TECH. L.J. 1047 (2012).

In addition to regulations created pursuant to the requirements of the Administrative Procedure Act, the Copyright Office also publishes an important document, the *Compendium of Copyright Office Practices*. The *Compendium* is a summary of the *practices* of the Copyright Office. It is not a compendium of copyright law generally, or of any aspect of copyright law that lies outside of the Copyright Office's administrative functions. As noted in its introduction, the "primary focus" of the Compendium is "on the registration of copyright claims, documentation of copyright ownership, and recordation of copyright documents, including assignments and licenses." For further clarification, the introduction notes that "[t]he Compendium does not override any existing statute or regulation. The policies and practices set forth in the Compendium do not in themselves have the force and effect of law and are not binding upon the Register of Copyrights or U.S. Copyright Office staff."

In its recent decision in *Georgia v. Public.Resource.Org, Inc.*, 140 S. Ct. 1498 (2020), the Supreme Court made clear that the Copyright Office's interpretations of the Copyright Act, as set forth in the *Compendium*, receive no judicial deference: "[T]he Compendium is a non-binding administrative manual that at most merits deference under *Skidmore* v. *Swift & Co.*, 323 U. S. 134 (1944). That means we must follow it only to the extent it has the power to persuade."

NOTES

1. The Register of Copyrights is appointed by (and is removable by) the Librarian of Congress, a presidential appointee. Recently, bills were introduced in both the U.S. House of Representatives and Senate to make the Register a presidential appointee with a fixed term in office. *See* H.R. 1695, Register of Copyrights Selection and Accountability Act of 2017; S. 1010, Register of Copyrights Selection and Accountability Act of 2017. The House of Representatives bill passed there on April 26, 2017, but that bill expired with the election of a new Congress. As of this writing (July 1, 2021), there has been no vote in the Senate on its bill, or on a discussion draft of a successor bill, the Digital Copyright Act of 2021, released in late 2020.

2. The proposal to remove the Register from the control of the Librarian and make the position subject to presidential appointment is generally supported by content owners and opposed by librarians and many content users. Can you think of reasons why that might be so?

3. Is the lack of deference the Copyright Office's pronouncements get (except to the extent they are persuasive) helpful as a matter of copyright policy? In formulating your position, consider the Second Circuit's thinking on this point as it disagreed with the Copyright Office's official position in a report on an aspect of the DMCA's safe harbors: "Although an opinion expressed by the Copyright Office in such a report does not receive *Chevron* deference of the sort accorded to rulemaking by authorized agencies, we do recognize the Copyright Office's intimate familiarity with the copyright statute and would certainly give appropriate deference to its reasonably persuasive interpretations of the Copyright Act. *See* Skidmore v Swift & Co., 323 U.S. 134, 140 (1944) (explaining that the weight of such an interpretation 'will depend upon the thoroughness evident in its consideration, the validity of its reasoning, its consistency with earlier and later pronouncements, and all those facts which give it power to persuade, if lacking power to control')." Capitol Records, LLC v. Vimeo, LLC, 826 F.3d 78, 93 (2d Cir. 2016).

E. Remedies

The Copyright Act makes available a set of powerful civil remedies for infringement. Section 502 furnishes courts the power to "grant temporary and final injunctions on such terms as it may deem reasonable to prevent or restrain infringement of a copyright." Section 503(a) provides that a court

> may order the impounding, on such terms as it may deem reasonable—
>
> > (A) of all copies or phonorecords claimed to have been made or used in violation of the exclusive right of the copyright owner;
> >
> > (B) of all plates, molds, matrices, masters, tapes, film negatives, or other articles by means of which such copies or phonorecords may be reproduced; and
> >
> > (C) of records documenting the manufacture, sale, or receipt of things involved in any such violation, provided that any records seized under this subparagraph shall be taken into the custody of the court.

Section 503(b) further directs that "[a]s part of a final judgment or decree, the court may order the destruction or other reasonable disposition of all copies or phonorecords found to have been made or used in violation of the copyright owner's exclusive rights, and of all plates, molds, matrices, masters, tapes, film negatives, or other articles by means of which such copies or phonorecords may be reproduced."

Section 504 provides for monetary damages, giving successful plaintiffs the option to elect to receive either actual damages and profits as provided in § 504(b), or statutory damages as provided in § 504(c).

Finally, § 505 provides that a court may "in its discretion … allow the recovery of full costs by or against any party other than the United States or an officer thereof. Except as otherwise provided by this title, the court may also award a reasonable attorney's fee to the prevailing party as part of the costs."

1. Injunctive Relief

In cases outside the context of copyright, courts traditionally have required plaintiffs requesting either preliminary or permanent injunctive relief to establish the need for such relief. Courts typically assess the need for permanent injunctive relief according to four factors, which, although phrased with some variation, boil down to a requirement that the plaintiff show:

> *(1) that it has suffered an irreparable injury; (2) that remedies available at law, such as monetary damages, are inadequate to compensate for that injury; (3) that, considering the balance of hardships between the plaintiff and defendant, a remedy in equity is warranted; and (4) that the public interest would not be disserved by a permanent injunction.*

eBay Inc. v. MercExchange, L.L.C., 547 U.S. 388, 391 (2006).

In copyright cases, courts until recently tended to short-circuit this analysis. In particular, most courts were willing to presume irreparable harm based on a showing of likely infringement (in the preliminary injunction context) or proven infringement (in the permanent injunction context). *See, e.g.*, Triad Sys. Corp. v. Southeastern Express Co., 64 F.3d 1330, 1335 (9th Cir. 1995); Video Trip Corp. v. Lightning Video, Inc., 866 F.2d 50, 51-52 (2d Cir. 1989).

The Supreme Court's decision in *eBay* ended this practice. In that case, the Supreme Court ruled that courts could not presume irreparable harm based on the mere fact of infringement, and instead that a plaintiff must establish the need for injunctive relief according to the traditional four-factor test it set out, and, further, that the "decision to grant or deny permanent injunctive relief is an act of equitable discretion by the … court." *eBay* was a patent infringement case, but the Court made clear that its holding applied to copyright infringement cases too, and indeed that its holding was "consistent with [its] treatment of injunctions under the Copyright Act." The Court continued, that it "has consistently rejected invitations to replace traditional equitable considerations with a rule that an injunction automatically follows a determination that a copyright has been infringed." For an empirical study suggesting that *eBay* has had a significant effect in copyright cases, see Matthew Sag & Pamela Samuelson, *Discovering eBay's Impact on Copyright Injunctions Through Empirical Evidence*, https://papers.ssrn.com/sol3/papers.cfm?abstract_id=3898460.

As you read the next case, think about the range of instances in which an injunction may or may not be appropriate. Do you think an injunction would have been ordered, given the facts of the case, even under pre-*eBay* law?

Christopher Phelps & Associates, LLC v. R. Wayne Galloway
492 F.3d 532 (4th Cir. 2007)

NIEMEYER, J.:

[1] After R. Wayne Galloway began construction of his retirement home on Lake Wylie, near Charlotte, North Carolina, using architectural plans designed and copyrighted by Christopher Phelps & Associates, LLC, without permission, Phelps & Associates commenced this action against Galloway for copyright infringement. Phelps & Associates sought damages, disgorgement of profits, and injunctive relief. A jury found that Galloway infringed Phelps & Associates' copyright and awarded it $20,000 in damages, the fee that Phelps & Associates traditionally charged for such plans. The jury also found that Galloway had realized no profits to disgorge. The district court thereafter declined to enter an injunction, finding that the jury verdict had made Phelps & Associates "whole," and entered judgment in favor of Phelps & Associates for $20,000. From that judgment, Phelps & Associates appeals, requesting ... the entry of an injunction prohibiting the future lease or sale of the infringing house and mandating the destruction or return of the infringing plans....

[2] We agree with Galloway's contention that the court in the circumstances presented here did not abuse its discretion in refusing to enter a permanent injunction, as requested by Phelps & Associates, prohibiting Galloway from ever leasing or selling the house. Such an injunction would be overly broad and would unduly restrain the alienation of real property. Other injunctive relief, however, might be available in applying the general principles of equity, as required by *eBay Inc. v. MercExchange*, L.L.C., 547 U.S. 388 (2006), which was decided after the district court's order denying relief in this case. Accordingly, we vacate portions of the district court's order denying injunctive relief and remand for the limited purpose of reconsidering other equitable relief, such as an order requiring Galloway to destroy the infringing plans or return them to Phelps & Associates....

[3] R. Wayne Galloway, in anticipation of retirement, planned to build his "dream home" on a lot that he owned on the North Carolina side of Lake Wylie, southwest of Charlotte, North Carolina. Displeased with the design work done by an architect whom he had hired, Galloway went with his son-in-law to view the designs of homes on Lake Norman, an expensive residential area about 30 miles north of Lake Wylie, where his son-in-law was working as an iron-work subcontractor. There, Galloway saw a French-country style house that he liked. His son-in-law approached the builder of the house, Simonini Builders, Inc., and asked the superintendent for a copy of the plans. The superintendent said that Galloway would have to speak with the owner, Mrs. Gina Bridgeford, because "she purchased the plans, they were actually drawn for her." Galloway contacted Mrs. Bridgeford, who gave Galloway her consent for use of the plans "as long as you don't build in our area." As to her authority to give consent, Mrs. Bridgeford testified at trial, "I felt with all we had paid, we owned the plans at that time." Galloway assured Mrs. Bridgeford that he would not build in the area, telling her that he planned to build on Lake Wylie about 30 miles away. With Mrs. Bridgeford's permission, the superintendent at Simonini Builders gave Galloway a copy of the plans for "The Bridgeford Residence." Each page of the plans included the copyright notice, in small print, of the designing architect as follows:

© 2000 Copyright—Christopher Phelps & Assoc., L.L.C. These plans are protected under the federal copyright laws. The original purchaser of this plan is authorized to construct one and only one home using this plan. Modifications or reuse of this plan is prohibited.

[4] Galloway altered the plans only to cover the name and address of "The Bridgeford Residence" with the name and address of "The Galloway Residence," and then he copied them for constructing his house.

[5] Phelps & Associates, which designed the Bridgeford Residence, is an architectural firm in Charlotte, North Carolina, that designs upscale custom houses. It created the design for the Bridgeford Residence .... The Bridgefords paid Phelps & Associates $20,000 for The Bridgeford Residence design, and the Bridgefords built their house on Lake Norman in accordance with that design.

[6] Acting as his own general contractor, Galloway began construction of his house in September 2001, using the Phelps & Associates plans for the Bridgeford Residence.... Phelps & Associates did not then know that the construction was being pursued without permission. Galloway's framing contractor, who had been asked to do some work for Galloway's brother-in-law using pirated Phelps & Associates plans, surmised that Galloway did not have permission to use the plans and approached Galloway to warn him that he could "get in trouble constructing a copyright plan." Galloway "shrugged his shoulders and said something to the effect: 'They've got to find me, catch me first.'"

[7] Through rumors from subcontractors, Phelps & Associates learned in early 2003 that Galloway was constructing a house using its designs. After confirming that fact, Phelps & Associates sent Galloway a cease and desist letter in July 2003. Upon receipt of the letter, Galloway stopped construction on his house, which was then over half completed. Thereafter, in August 2003, Phelps & Associates registered its plans for The Bridgeford Residence with the Copyright Office and then commenced this action against Galloway for copyright infringement...

[8] At the end of the trial, the jury returned a verdict in favor of Phelps & Associates, finding that Galloway had infringed Phelps & Associate's architectural design copyright; awarding Phelps & Associates $20,000 in actual damages; and finding that Galloway had no profits to disgorge. Thereafter, Phelps & Associates requested injunctive relief from the court (1) ordering that the infringing copy of the plans be returned or destroyed; (2) enjoining completion of the house; and (3) permanently enjoining the lease or sale of the house. The court "in its discretion" denied all injunctive relief, finding that the $20,000 jury award made Phelps & Associates "whole." Accordingly, the court entered judgment in favor of Phelps & Associates for $20,000 in damages.

[9] On appeal, Phelps & Associates contends ... that the district court's refusal to enter an injunction was error as a matter of law because it had proved a past infringement and a likelihood of future infringement.

[10] Phelps & Associates did not obtain an injunction pending appeal, and, according to representations made at oral argument, Galloway has completed the construction of his house, where he now resides. Galloway has also satisfied the $20,000 money judgment....

[11] Phelps & Associates contends that in denying injunctive relief, the district court erred as a matter of law. It argues that the court denied injunctive relief simply because Phelps & Associates received damages and thereby had been made "whole." It maintains that "the mere fact that a copyright owner may recover damages does *not* negate his right to injunctive relief." Phelps & Associates argues affirmatively that when copyright infringement has been proved and there is a threat of continuing infringement, the copyright holder is "*entitled* to an injunction." Because Phelps & Associates says that it made that showing, it claims that it was entitled to injunctive relief.

[12] Insofar as Phelps & Associates suggests that it is *entitled* to injunctive relief, we reject the argument. *See* eBay Inc. v. MercExchange, L.L.C., 547 U.S. 388 (2006). In *eBay*, the Supreme Court rejected any notion that an injunction automatically follows a determination that a copyright has been infringed. The Supreme Court reaffirmed the traditional showing that a plaintiff must make to obtain a permanent injunction in any type of case, including a patent or copyright case:

> *A plaintiff must demonstrate: (1) that it has suffered an irreparable injury; (2) that remedies available at law, such as monetary damages, are inadequate to compensate for that injury; (3) that, considering the balance of hardships between the plaintiff and defendant, a remedy in equity is warranted; and (4) that the public interest would not be disserved by a permanent injunction.*

Moreover, the Court reiterated that even upon this showing, whether to grant the injunction still remains in the equitable discretion of the court.

[13] Rejecting Phelps & Associates' claim to an automatic injunction or an "entitlement" to one, we now apply traditional equity principles to each of Phelps & Associates' requests for injunctive relief to determine whether the district court abused its discretion....

[14] Phelps & Associates' first request, that Galloway be enjoined from completing the house, appears to be moot. At oral argument, the parties represented that the house had been completed....

[15] Phelps & Associates' second request for equitable relief, that Galloway be permanently enjoined from leasing or selling the completed house, is argued with the following syllogism: *First,* the completed house is an infringing copy of Phelps & Associates' copyrighted work. *Second,* as the copyright holder, Phelps & Associates has the exclusive right to "distribute" its copyrighted work "by sale or other transfer of ownership." *Therefore,* Galloway may never lease or sell the house without infringing Phelps & Associates' copyright. Because it is likely that Galloway will lease or sell the house, Phelps & Associates believes this lease or sale should be foreclosed by a permanent injunction.

[16] We agree with Phelps & Associates that Galloway will inevitably sell or transfer his house within the period during which Phelps & Associates still holds the copyright—i.e. 95 years—and that such a sale could, absent this action, expose Galloway to further relief. But Phelps & Associates has requested relief for that inevitable transaction now *in this action,* as part of the panoply of remedies available under the Copyright Act, and therefore entitlement to that relief can be and is resolved in this action under the principles of *eBay*.

[17] The first two *eBay* criteria for injunctive relief—irreparable injury and the inadequacy of monetary damages—have most likely been demonstrated. Irreparable injury often derives from the nature of copyright violations, which deprive the copyright holder of intangible exclusive rights. Damages at law will not remedy the continuing existence of Phelps & Associates' design in the Galloway house. Moreover, while the calculation of future damages and profits for each future sale might be possible, any such effort would entail a substantial amount of speculation and guesswork that renders the effort difficult or impossible in this case. Accordingly, we conclude that Phelps & Associates most likely has satisfied the first two *eBay* factors.

[18] When considering the third and fourth factors, however—the balance of hardships and the public interest—Phelps & Associates' showing has fallen short.

[19] *First,* Phelps & Associates has been fully and adequately compensated for the copying and use of its design as manifested in the single Galloway house .... A sale of the house would not be a second copy or manifestation of the design, but merely a transfer of the structure in which the design was first copied. An injunction against sale would but slightly benefit Phelps & Associates' legitimate entitlements because the

infringing house would retain the same form and location, remaining a permanent nuisance to the copyright regardless of whether there is an injunction. An injunction against sale would neither undo the prior infringement, nor diminish the chances of future copying. At the same time, a permanent injunction would impose a draconian burden on Galloway, effectively creating a *lis pendens* on the house and subjecting him to contempt proceedings simply for selling his own property.

[20] *Second,* a house or building, as an expression of the architect's copyrighted plans, usually has a predominantly functional character. This functional character was the reason American copyright law, pre-Berne Convention, denied protection to constructed architectural works altogether. This is the same reason that Congress manifested an expectation that injunctions will not be routinely issued against substantially completed houses whose designs violated architectural copyrights. H.R. REP. NO. 101-735, at 13–14 (1990) (explaining that buildings "are the only form of copyrightable subject matter that is habitable"). Those considerations are at their strongest when the architectural structure is completed and inhabited by the infringer, as here. While Galloway infringed the copyright, he now is living in a "copy" of the architectural work. His interest in remaining there, with the same rights as other homeowners to alienate his property, is substantial and, in this case, trumps Phelps & Associates' interests in any injunction prohibiting a lease or sale of the house.

[21] *Third,* an injunction against sale of the house would be overbroad, as it would encumber a great deal of property unrelated to the infringement. The materials and labor that went into the Galloway house, in addition to the swimming pool, the fence, and other non-infringing features, as well as the land underneath the house, would be restrained by the requested injunction. As such, the injunction would take on a fundamentally punitive character, which has not been countenanced in the Copyright Act's remedies. In a similar vein, the requested injunction would undermine an ancient reluctance by the courts to restrain the alienability of real property. For these reasons, the public interest would be disserved by the entry of an injunction.

[22] *Finally,* ultimate discretion to grant any such injunctive relief rests with the district court, and for the reasons enumerated, we conclude that deference to the district court's refusal is appropriate in the absence of any showing that such refusal was otherwise an abuse of discretion.

[23] Thus, with respect to the Galloway house as one manifestation of the Phelps & Associates' design, arising from a single infringing transaction, Phelps & Associates is limited to the other relief provided in this case. Upon satisfaction of that relief, Galloway will be entitled to peaceful ownership of the house, with good and marketable title. This is consistent with the result reached when a converter of property satisfies a judgment: if the judgment does not order return of the property, but rather other relief, the converter obtains good and marketable title to the property after satisfying the judgment. The same policies of promoting clear property rights and finality apply in the case of copyright actions involving single copies of completed structures. Indeed, they are perhaps stronger, as we are promoting the alienability of *real* property....

[24] For all of these reasons, we affirm the district court's order denying an injunction against the future lease or sale of Galloway's house....

[25] Finally, Phelps & Associates contends that the district court erred as a matter of law in refusing to grant injunctive relief to require the return or destruction of the infringing plans.

[26] Again, any relief granted in equity is at the discretion of the district court, and a petitioner cannot claim that it was *entitled* to injunctive relief. Nonetheless, the district court, without the benefit of *eBay*, may have denied equitable relief categorically, rather than basing its analysis on the traditional principles of equity.

[27] In denying Phelps & Associates' motion for an injunction, the district court stated:

The court finds that the Plaintiff has been made whole, and in its discretion, declines to order Defendant to destroy all copies of the plans at issue.

[28] Being made whole in the circumstances of this case, however, could only have referred to the jury award of damages for the cost of a license and its finding that Galloway realized no profits for disgorgement. It could not have related to other questions, such as the existence of infringing plans or future acts of infringement.

[29] To explain its ruling, the court stated only,

Evidence at trial revealed that the house is substantially constructed and that only interior finish work remains to be done. Thus, there is no likelihood that completion of the house will result in further infringement.

[30] It does not follow, however, that because the plans were not needed to complete the house, they should not therefore be returned or destroyed, as authorized by 17 U.S.C. § 503(b). The risk of future infringement includes the possible use of plans to build another house, publication of the plans, or other violations of the exclusive rights conferred by 17 U.S.C. § 106.

[31] When Phelps & Associates requested the return or destruction of the infringing plans, the district court was obligated to consider the traditional factors for equitable relief. Yet it appears that the court did not do so. At most, it stated without explanation that it declined "in its discretion ... to order defendant to destroy all copies of the plans at issue." Considering the court's ruling in the context of the admonitions given in *eBay*, we cannot conclude that the district court properly performed its equitable functions. Therefore, we vacate that portion of its order as an abuse of discretion....

NOTES

1. Is the court's refusal to grant an injunction in *Phelps* effectively equivalent to the grant of a compulsory license? Why or why not? If the answer is yes, is that a reason to question the wisdom of the *eBay* rule?

2. In *Metro-Goldwyn-Mayer Studios, Inc. v. Grokster, Ltd.*, 518 F. Supp. 2d 1197 (N.D. Cal. 2007), the court considered whether a defendant's likely inability to pay damages for mass-scale infringement (as found in the Supreme Court's *Grokster* decision, which you read in Chapter VII) amounted to irreparable harm. The court held that an injunction was appropriate, based in part on the plaintiffs' reasonable concern about the defendant's solvency:

Based on the undisputed evidence at summary judgment of massive end-user infringement, it is highly likely that the award of statutory damages that ultimately befalls StreamCast in this case will be enormous (especially considering the potential relationship between inducement and a finding of willfulness), and would far outstrip the amount of revenue the company has garnered in recent years. This Court's conclusion would also be the same even if Plaintiffs chose to forgo a damages award as part of this lawsuit. This is because the amount of infringement that StreamCast could induce in the future is so staggering that the recoverable statutory damages would very probably be well beyond StreamCast's anticipated resources. Because it is extremely unlikely that StreamCast will be able to compensate Plaintiffs monetarily for the infringements it has induced in the past, or the infringements it could induce in the future through Morpheus, Plaintiffs have and will continue to suffer irreparable harm.

As this excerpt shows, the court thinks that a strong likelihood of inability to pay damages can demonstrate the irreparable harm that supports injunctive relief.

3. In *Perfect 10, Inc. v. Google, Inc.*, 653 F.3d 976 (9th Cir. 2011) (recall the case from Chapters V, VI, and VII), the Ninth Circuit considered a situation that was essentially the obverse of *Grokster*. In *Perfect 10*, the plaintiff argued that it would be irreparably harmed, absent a preliminary injunction, because the prospect of continuing infringement would drive it out of business. The Ninth Circuit upheld a district court order denying the plaintiff's request for an injunction:

> *Perfect 10's theory of irreparable harm is that Google's various services provide free access to Perfect 10's proprietary images, and this access has both destroyed its business model and threatened it with financial ruin, since no one would be willing to pay a subscription fee for material that is available without charge.... Given the limited nature of th[e] evidence [the plaintiff presented on this point], the district court did not abuse its discretion in concluding that Perfect 10 failed to establish that Google's operations would cause it irreparable harm. While being forced into bankruptcy qualifies as a form of irreparable harm, Perfect 10 has not established that the requested injunction would forestall that fate. To begin with, Perfect 10 has not alleged that it was ever in sound financial shape.... In sum, Perfect 10 has not shown a sufficient causal connection between irreparable harm to Perfect 10's business and Google's operation of its search engine. Because Perfect 10 has failed to satisfy this necessary requirement for obtaining preliminary injunctive relief, the district court's ruling was not an abuse of discretion.*

2. Actual Damages

Section 504(a) of the Copyright Act provides that

> *an infringer of copyright is liable for either—*
>
> > *(1) the copyright owner's actual damages and any additional profits of the infringer, as provided by subsection (b); or*
> >
> > *(2) statutory damages, as provided by subsection (c).*

Section 504(b) further provides that

> *[t]he copyright owner is entitled to recover the actual damages suffered by him or her as a result of the infringement, and any profits of the infringer that are attributable to the infringement and are not taken into account in computing the actual damages. In establishing the infringer's profits, the copyright owner is required to present proof only of the infringer's gross revenue, and the infringer is required to prove his or her deductible expenses and the elements of profit attributable to factors other than the copyrighted work.*

Although the Copyright Act does not define "actual damages," courts have explained that "an actual damages award looks at the facts from the point of view of the[] copyright owners; it undertakes to compensate the owner for any harm he suffered by reason of the infringer's illegal act." Davis v. Gap, Inc., 246 F.3d 152, 159 (2d Cir. 2001). In the ordinary case, these damages "are usually determined by the loss in the fair market value of the copyright, measured by the profits lost due to the infringement or by the value of the use of the copyrighted work to the infringer." McRoberts Software, Inc. v. Media 100, Inc., 329 F.3d 557, 566 (7th Cir. 2003). Depending on the circumstances in particular cases, courts have awarded as actual damages one or more of: the plaintiff's lost sales profits, the plaintiff's lost licensing profits, or the profits that the plaintiff might have realized from a reasonable royalty if the defendant had taken a license rather than infringed. Courts have also developed rules (or at least guidelines) for proving damages in cases in which the infringed work has been incorporated into a new work that also contains non-infringing material, thus necessitating assessment of the relative importance of infringing and non-infringing content when calculating the percentage of a defendant's profits from the work that were connected to the defendant's infringement of plaintiff's work.

Review §§ 504(a) and (b) carefully before you read next three cases. Pay attention to the burdens of proof with regard to proving damages.

On Davis v. Gap, Inc.
246 F.3d 152 (2d Cir. 2001)

LEVAL, J.:

[1] Plaintiff On Davis appeals from an order of the United States District Court for the Southern District of New York granting summary judgment to the defendant, The Gap, Inc., dismissing plaintiff's claim of copyright infringement.

[2] Davis is the creator and designer of nonfunctional jewelry worn over the eyes in the manner of eyeglasses. The Gap, Inc. is a major international retailer of clothing and accessories marketed largely to a youthful customer base with annual revenues of several billions of dollars. It operates several chains of retail stores, some under the name "Gap." It is undisputed that the Gap, without Davis's permission, used a photograph of an individual wearing Davis's copyrighted eyewear in an advertisement for the stores operating under the "Gap" trademark that was widely displayed throughout the United States. Davis brought this action seeking a declaratory judgment of infringement and damages, including $2,500,000 in unpaid licensing fees, a percentage of the Gap's profits, punitive damages of $10,000,000, and attorney's fees. The district court granted summary judgment for the Gap on the grounds that [among other things,] Davis's claims for actual damages and profits under 17 U.S.C. § 504(b) were too speculative to support recovery ....

[3] Davis has created at least fifteen different designs of eye jewelry, which he markets under the name "Onoculii Designs." Davis describes Onoculii eyewear as "sculptured metallic ornamental wearable art."...

[4] While Davis initially sold his designs on the street, since about 1995 he has marketed his merchandise through boutiques and optical stores. The eyewear sold at a wholesale price of approximately $30–45 a pair. Evidence in the record indicates that it sold at retail for $65–100 a pair in 1995. Davis asserts he has earned approximately $10,000 from sales. He testified that on one occasion he received a $50 fee from *Vibe* magazine for the use of a photograph depicting the musician Sun Ra wearing an Onoculii piece.

[5] In May 1996, prior to Davis's registration of his copyright, the defendant created a series of advertisements showing photographs of people of various lifestyles wearing Gap clothing. The campaign was designed to promote the concept that Gap merchandise is worn by people of all kinds. The ad in question, which bears the caption "fast" emblazoned in red (the "fast" ad), depicts a group of seven young people probably in their twenties, of Asian appearance, standing in a loose V formation staring at the camera with a sultry, pouty, provocative look. The group projects the image of funky intimates of a lively after-hours rock music club. They are dressed primarily in black, exhibiting bare arms and partly bare chests, goatees (accompanied in one case by bleached, streaked hair), large-brimmed, Western-style hats, and distinctive eye shades, worn either over their eyes, on their hats, or cocked over the top of their heads. The central figure, at the apex of the V

formation, is wearing Davis's highly distinctive Onoculii eyewear; he peers over the metal disks directly into the camera lens.

[6] The "fast" photograph was taken by the Gap in May 1996 during a photo shoot in the Tribeca area of Manhattan. The defendant provided the subjects with Gap apparel to wear for the shoot, and a trailer in which to change. The Gap claims that it did not furnish eyewear to any of the subjects, and that the subjects were told to wear their own eyewear, wristwatches, earrings, nose-rings or other incidental items, thereby "permitting each person to project accurately his or her own personal image and appearance."

Figure 121: Gap's "fast" advertisement

[7] The Gap's "fast" advertisement was published in a variety of magazines, including *W*, *Vanity Fair*, *Spin*, *Details*, and *Entertainment Weekly*. Davis claims that the total circulation of these magazines was over 2,500,000. For five weeks during August and September of 1996, the advertisement was displayed on the sides of buses in New York, Boston, Chicago, San Francisco, Atlanta, Washington, D.C., and Seattle. The advertisement may also have been displayed on bus shelters. According to Davis, when used on buses the photograph was cropped so that only the heads and shoulders of the subjects were shown.

[8] Davis submitted evidence showing that during the fourth quarter of 1996, the period that Davis asserts is relevant to the "fast" advertisement, the net annual sales of the parent company, Gap, Inc., increased by about 10 percent, compared to the fourth quarter of 1995, to $1.668 billion dollars. There was no evidence of what portion of the parent company's revenues were attributable to the stores operated under the Gap label, much less what portion was related to the ad in question....

[9] Davis filed this action .... The Gap then filed a motion for summary judgment, arguing, inter alia, that Davis had no entitlement to damages....

[10] ... [T]he district court granted summary judgment for the Gap. As regards damages under 17 U.S.C. § 504(b), the court rejected Davis's claim as unduly speculative ....

[11] 17 U.S.C. § 504 imposes two categories of compensatory damages. Taking care to specify that double recovery is not permitted where the two categories overlap, the statute provides for the recovery of both the infringer's profits and the copyright owner's "actual damages." It is important that these two categories of compensation have different justifications and are based on different financial data. The award of the infringer's profits examines the facts only from the infringer's point of view. If the infringer has earned a profit, this award makes him disgorge the profit to insure that he not benefit from his wrongdoing. The award of the owner's actual damages looks at the facts from the point of view of they copyright owner; it undertakes to compensate the owner for any harm he suffered by reason of the infringer's illegal act.

[12] The district court granted summary judgment dismissing Davis's claims for damages.... With respect to Davis's claim of entitlement to "actual damages" based on the license fee he should have been paid for the Gap's unauthorized use of his copyrighted material, the district court believed that his evidence was too speculative ....

[13] Among the elements Davis sought to prove as damages was the failure to receive a reasonable license fee from the Gap for its use of his copyrighted eyewear. The complaint asserted an entitlement to a $2.5 million licensing fee. The district court rejected the claim .... [finding it] too speculative—that is, insufficiently supported by evidence....

[14] While there was no evidence to support Davis's wildly inflated claim of entitlement to $2.5 million, in our view his evidence did support a much more modest claim of a fair market value for a license to use his design in the ad. In addition to his evidence of numerous instances in which rock music stars wore Onoculii eyewear in photographs exhibited in music publications, Davis testified that on one occasion he was paid a royalty of $50 for the publication by *Vibe* magazine of a photo of the deceased musician Sun Ra wearing Davis's eyewear.

[15] On the basis of this evidence, a jury could reasonably find that Davis established a fair market value of at least $50 as a fee for the use of an image of his copyrighted design. This evidence was sufficiently concrete to support a finding of fair market value of $50 for the type of use made by *Vibe*. And if Davis could show at trial that the Gap used the image in a wider circulation than *Vibe*, that might justify a finding that the market value for the Gap's use of the eyewear was higher than $50. Therefore, to the extent the district court dismissed the

case because Davis's evidence of the market value of a license fee was too speculative, we believe this was error....

[16] To the extent that [previous case law] was based on its observation that the defendant before it was no more inclined to negotiate a purchase price than a "purse snatcher," the facts of our case are significantly different. The Gap was not seeking ... to surreptitiously steal material owned by a competitor. There is no reason to suppose that the Gap's use of Davis's copyrighted eyewear without first receiving his permission was attributable to anything other than oversight or mistake. To the contrary, the facts of this case support the view that the Gap and Davis could have happily discussed the payment of a fee, and that Davis's consent, if sought, could have been had for very little money, since significant advantages might flow to him from having his eyewear displayed in the Gap's ad. Alternatively, if Davis's demands had been excessive, the Gap would in all likelihood have simply eliminated Davis's eyewear from the photograph....

[17] Because [our previous decisions] did not rule on, much less foreclose, the use of a reasonable license fee theory as the measure of damages suffered by Davis when the Gap used his material without payment, we proceed to consider whether that measure of damages is permissible under the statute.

[18] The question is as follows: Assume that the copyright owner proves that the defendant has infringed his work. He proves also that a license to make such use of the work has a fair market value, but does not show that the infringement caused him lost sales, lost opportunities to license, or diminution in the value of the copyright. The only proven loss lies in the owner's failure to receive payment by the infringer of the fair market value of the use illegally appropriated. Should the owner's claim for "actual damages" under § 504(b) be dismissed? Or should the court award damages corresponding to the fair market value of the use appropriated by the infringer?

[19] Neither answer is entirely satisfactory. If the court dismisses the claim by reason of the owner's failure to prove that the act of infringement cause[d] economic harm, the infringer will get his illegal taking for free, and the owner will be left uncompensated for the illegal taking of something of value. On the other hand, an award of damages might be seen as a windfall for an owner who received no less than he would have if the infringer had refrained from the illegal taking. In our view, the more reasonable approach is to allow such an award in appropriate circumstances.

[20] Section 504(a) and (b) employ the broad term "actual damages." Courts and commentators agree it should be broadly construed to favor victims of infringement.

[21] A principal objective of the copyright law is to enable creators to earn a living either by selling or by licensing others to sell copies of the copyrighted work.

[22] If a copier of protected work, instead of obtaining permission and paying the fee, proceeds without permission and without compensating the owner, it seems entirely reasonable to conclude that the owner has suffered damages to the extent of the infringer's taking without paying what the owner was legally entitled to exact a fee for. We can see no reason why, as an abstract matter, the statutory term "actual damages" should not cover the owner's failure to obtain the market value of the fee the owner was entitled to charge for such use....

[23] It is important to note that under the terms of § 504(b), unless such a foregone payment can be considered "actual damages," in some circumstances victims of infringement will go uncompensated. If the infringer's venture turned out to be unprofitable, the owner can receive no recovery based on the statutory award of the "infringer's profits." And in some instances, there will be no harm to the market value of the copyrighted work. The owner may be incapable of showing a loss of either sales or licenses to third parties. To rule that the owner's loss of the fair market value of the license fees he might have exacted of the defendant

do not constitute "actual damages," would mean that in such circumstances an infringer may steal with impunity. We see no reason why this should be so. Of course, if the terms of the statute compelled that result, our perception of inequity would make no difference; the statute would control. But in our view, the statutory term "actual damages" is broad enough to cover this form of deprivation suffered by infringed owners.

[24] We recognize that awarding the copyright owner the lost license fee can risk abuse. Once the defendant has infringed, the owner may claim unreasonable amounts as the license fee—to wit Davis's demand for an award of $2.5 million. The law therefore exacts that the amount of damages may not be based on undue speculation. The question is not what the owner would have charged, but rather what is the fair market value. In order to make out his claim that he has suffered actual damage because of the infringer's failure to pay the fee, the owner must show that the thing taken had a fair market value. But if the plaintiff owner has done so, and the defendant is thus protected against an unrealistically exaggerated claim, we can see little reason not to consider the market value of the uncollected license fee as an element of "actual damages" under § 504(b).

[25] We recognize also that finding the fair market value of a reasonable license fee may involve some uncertainty. But that is not sufficient reason to refuse to consider this as an eligible measure of actual damages. Many of the accepted methods of calculating copyright damages require the court to make uncertain estimates in the realm of contrary to fact. A classic element of the plaintiff's copyright damages is the profits the plaintiff would have earned from third parties, were it not for the infringement. This measure requires the court to explore the counterfactual hypothesis of the contracts and licenses the plaintiff would have made absent the infringement and the costs associated with them. A second accepted method, focusing on the "infringer's profits," similarly requires the court to explore circumstances that are counterfactual. The owner's entitlement to the infringer's profits is limited to the profits "attributable to the infringement." 17 U.S.C. § 504(b). The court, therefore, must compare the defendant's actual profits to what they would have been without the infringement, awarding the plaintiff the difference. Neither of these approaches is necessarily any less speculative than the approach that requires the court to find the market value of the license fee for what the infringer took. Indeed, it may be far less so. Many copyright owners are represented by agents who have established rates that are regularly paid by licensees. In such cases, establishing the fair market value of the license fee of which the owner was deprived is no more speculative than determining the damages in the case of a stolen cargo of lumber or potatoes. Given our long-held view that in assessing copyright damages courts must necessarily engage in some degree of speculation, some difficulty in quantifying the damages attributable to infringement should not bar recovery....

[26] We conclude that Section 504(b) permits a copyright owner to recover actual damages, in appropriate circumstances, for the fair market value of a license covering the defendant's infringing use. Davis adduced sufficiently concrete evidence of a modest fair market value of the use made by the Gap. The Gap's use of the infringed matter was substantial. If Davis were not compensated for the market value of the use taken, he would receive no compensation whatsoever....

Frank Music Corp. v. Metro-Goldwyn-Mayer Inc.
886 F.2d 1545 (9th Cir. 1989)

FLETCHER, J.: ...

[1] .... Plaintiffs are the copyright owners and authors of *Kismet*, a dramatico-musical work. MGM, Inc., under license produced a musical motion picture version of *Kismet*. Beginning April 26, 1974, MGM Grand presented a musical revue entitled *Hallelujah Hollywood* in the hotel's Ziegfeld Theatre. *Hallelujah Hollywood* was largely created by an employee of MGM Grand, Donn Arden, who also staged, produced and directed the show. The

show comprised ten acts, four billed as "tributes" to MGM motion pictures. Act IV was entitled "Kismet," and was a tribute to the MGM movie of that name. It was based almost entirely on music from *Kismet*, and used characters and settings from that musical. Act IV "Kismet" was performed approximately 1700 times, until July 16, 1976, when, under pressure resulting from this litigation, MGM Grand substituted a new Act IV.

Figure 122: MGM *Kismet* movie poster (left), and MGM Grand *Hallelujah Hollywood!* program cover (right)

[2] Plaintiffs filed suit, alleging copyright infringement .... In *Frank Music I* [a previous appeal in this case], we affirmed the district court's conclusion that the use of *Kismet* in *Hallelujah Hollywood* was beyond the scope of MGM Grand's ASCAP license and infringed plaintiffs' copyright. In this appeal, the parties focus on the adequacy of damages ....

A. Apportionment of Profits

1. Direct Profits

[3] In *Frank Music I*, we upheld the district court's conclusion that the plaintiffs failed to prove actual damages arising from the infringement, but vacated the district court's award of $22,000 in apportioned profits as "grossly inadequate," and remanded to the district court for reconsideration.

[4] On remand, the district court calculated MGM Grand's net profit from *Hallelujah Hollywood* at $6,131,606, by deducting from its gross revenues the direct costs MGM Grand proved it had incurred. Neither party challenges this calculation.

[5] In apportioning the profits between Act IV and the other acts in the show, the district court made the following finding:

> *Act IV of "Hallelujah Hollywood" was one of ten acts, approximately a ten minute segment of a 100 minute revue. On this basis, the Court concludes that ten percent of the profits of "Hallelujah Hollywood" are attributable to Act IV.*

[6] Plaintiffs assert that this finding is in error in several respects. First, they point out that on Saturdays *Hallelujah Hollywood* contained only eight acts, not ten, and that on Saturdays the show ran only 75 minutes, not 100. Second, Act IV was approximately eleven and a half minutes long, not ten. Because the show was performed three times on Saturdays, and twice a night on the other evenings of the week, the district court substantially underestimated the running time of Act IV in relation to the rest of the show.[2]

[7] If the district court relied exclusively on a quantitative comparison and failed to consider the relative quality or drawing power of the show's various component parts, it erred. However, the district court's apportionment based on comparative durations would be appropriate if the district court implicitly concluded that all the acts of the show were of roughly equal value. While a more precise statement of the district court's reasons would have been desirable, we find support in the record for the conclusion that all the acts in the show were of substantially equal value.

[8] The district court went on to apportion the parties' relative contributions to Act IV itself:

> The infringing musical material was only one of several elements contributing to the segment. A portion of the profits attributable to Act IV must be allocated to other elements, including the creative talent of the producer and director, the talents of performers, composers, choreographers, costume designers and others who participated in creating Act IV, and the attraction of the unique Ziegfeld Theatre with its elaborate stage effects.... While no precise mathematical formula can be applied, the Court concludes that ... a fair approximation of the value of the infringing work to Act IV is twenty-five percent.

[9] The district court was correct in probing into the parties' relative contributions to Act IV. Where a defendant alters infringing material to suit its own unique purposes, those alterations and the creativity behind them should be taken into account in apportioning the profits of the infringing work. However, the district court appears to have ignored its finding in its previous decision that defendants used not only the plaintiffs' music, but also their lyrics, characters, settings, and costume designs, recreating to a substantial extent the look and sound of the licensed movie version of *Kismet*.

[10] While it was not inappropriate to consider the creativity of producers, performers and others involved in staging and adapting excerpts from *Kismet* for use in *Hallelujah Hollywood*, the district court erred in weighing these contributions so heavily. In performing the apportionment, the benefit of the doubt must always be given to the plaintiff, not the defendant. And while the apportionment may take into account the role of uncopyrightable elements of a work in generating that work's profits, the apportionment should not place too high a value on the defendants' staging of the work, at the expense of undervaluing the plaintiffs' more substantive creative contributions. Production contributions involving expensive costumes and lavish sets will largely be taken into account when deducting the defendants' costs. Indeed, defendants concede that had they produced *Kismet in toto*, it would have been proper for the district court to award 100% of their profits, despite their own creative efforts in staging such a production.

[11] The district court found that defendants' staging of the *Kismet* excerpts was highly significant to Act IV's success. While we believe that a defendant's efforts in staging an infringing production will generally not support more than a *de minimis* deduction from the plaintiff's share of the profits, we cannot say the district court's conclusion that the defendants' contributions were substantial in this case is clearly erroneous. We

---

[2] There were twelve shows weekly which ran for 100 minutes, plus three on Saturdays which ran 75, totalling 1425 minutes per week. Act IV remained constant throughout the week, for a total of approximately 173 minutes. Accordingly, Act IV comprised 12% of the total weekly running time of *Hallelujah Hollywood*. Because the district court's findings differ from those previously found and affirmed in *Frank Music I*, we substitute 12% as the appropriate figure on which we base our subsequent calculations.

recognize that there will be shows in which the attraction of the costumes, scenery or performers outweighs the attraction of the music or dialogue. On the other hand, a producer's ability to stage a lavish presentation, or a performer's ability to fill a hall from the drawing power of her name alone, is not a license to use freely the copyrighted works of others.

[12] We conclude that apportioning 75% of Act IV to the defendants grossly undervalues the importance of the plaintiffs' contributions. Act IV was essentially *Kismet,* with contributions by the defendants; it was not essentially a new work incidentally plagiarizing elements of *Kismet.* A fairer apportionment, giving due regard to the district court's findings, attributes 75% of Act IV to elements taken from the plaintiffs and 25% to the defendants' contributions.[3]

2. Indirect Profits

[13] In *Frank Music I,* we held that the plaintiffs were entitled to recover, in addition to direct profits, a proportion of ascertainable indirect profits from defendants' hotel and gaming operations attributable to the promotional value of *Hallelujah Hollywood.* The district court considered the relative contributions of *Hallelujah Hollywood* and other factors contributing to the hotel's profits, including the hotel's guest accommodations, restaurants, cocktail lounges, star entertainment in the "Celebrity" room, the movie theater, Jai Alai, the casino itself, convention and banquet facilities, tennis courts, swimming pools, gym and sauna, and also the role of advertising and general promotional activities in bringing customers to the hotel. The district court concluded that two percent of MGM Grand's indirect profit was attributable to *Hallelujah Hollywood.* In light of the general promotion and the wide variety of attractions available at MGM Grand, this conclusion is not clearly erroneous.[4]

B. Prejudgment Interest

[14] The district court, without comment, declined to award prejudgment interest. The availability of prejudgment interest under the Copyright Act of 1909 is an issue of first impression in this circuit.

[15] The 1909 Act does not mention prejudgment interest. {The 1976 Act likewise does not mention prejudgment interest.} Nevertheless, courts may allow prejudgment interest even though the governing statute is silent. The goal of compensating the injured party fairly for the loss caused by the defendant's breach of the statutory obligation should be kept in mind. Prejudgment interest compensates the injured party for the loss of the use of money he would otherwise have had.

[16] Defendants argue that Congress did not intend for prejudgment interest to be available under the 1909 Act. They ask us to infer this from the inclusion of prejudgment interest in the Patent Act and the omission of reference to prejudgment interest in either the 1909 Act or the Copyright Act of 1976. Because the Patent and Copyright Acts are similar statutes with similar purposes, defendants argue that differences between the two Acts with respect to prejudgment interest are intentional.

[17] Examination of the history of prejudgment interest in the patent context suggests this argument is flawed. Before Congress enacted 35 U.S.C. § 284, prejudgment interest was generally available in patent infringement cases from the date damages were liquidated, and in exceptional cases from the date of

---

[3] Based on this allocation, plaintiffs are entitled to $551,844.54 as direct profits from the infringement.

[4] We do, however, need to correct an error in calculation or typography noted by the plaintiffs. In subtracting MGM Grand's direct profits of $6,131,606 from its total net profit of approximately $395,000,000, the district court arrived at the figure of $380,868,394. The correct figure is $388,868,394. Plaintiffs are entitled to 9% (75% of 12%) of 2% of this figure, or $699,963.10.

infringement. Such a remedy was available despite the fact that the patent laws then in effect made no mention of prejudgment interest. Indeed, the wording of the relevant patent statute was similar to that of ... the 1909 Copyright Act.

[18] Thus, interpreting the 1909 Act in light of patent law doctrine existing at the time of its enactment and during much of its effective period, we cannot conclude that Congress intended from its silence that prejudgment interest would not be available under the 1909 Act. Just as courts awarded prejudgment interest in order to provide adequate compensation to patent holders before the enactment of 35 U.S.C. § 284, this same remedy should be available to copyright owners for the same purpose.

[19] We therefore hold that prejudgment interest is an available remedy under the 1909 Act. Whether the circumstances of this case warrant the remedy is a separate question. The common-law rule during much of the effective period of the 1909 Act awarded prejudgment interest only on damages that were liquidated or readily ascertainable by mathematical computations and did not rely on opinion or discretion. But even where damages were not liquidated or readily ascertainable, courts had the power to award prejudgment interest on unliquidated damages when necessary to compensate the plaintiff fairly.

[20] Because the 1909 Act allows plaintiffs to recover only the greater of the defendant's profits *or* the plaintiff's actual damages, an award of profits or damages under the 1909 Act will not necessarily be adequate to compensate a prevailing copyright owner. Accordingly, we conclude prejudgment interest ordinarily should be awarded.

[21] Awarding prejudgment interest on the apportioned share of defendant's profits is consistent with the purposes underlying the profits remedy. Profits are awarded to the plaintiff not only to compensate for the plaintiff's injury, but also and primarily to prevent the defendant from being unjustly enriched by its infringing use of the plaintiff's property. For the restitutionary purpose of this remedy to be served fully, the defendant generally should be required to turn over to the plaintiff not only the profits made from the use of his property, but also the interest on these profits, which can well exceed the profits themselves. Indeed, one way to view this interest is as another form of indirect profit accruing from the infringement, which should be turned over to the copyright owner along with other forms of indirect profit. It would be anomalous to hold that a plaintiff can recover, for example, profits derived from the promotional use of its copyrighted material, but not for the value of the use of the revenue generated by the infringement.[10]

[22] We accordingly remand to the district court to enter an award of prejudgment interest.[11] ...

Frederick E. Bouchat v. Baltimore Ravens Football Club

346 F.3d 514 (4th Cir. 2003)

KING, J.:

[1] This appeal arises from the damages phase of a protracted copyright dispute involving the Baltimore Ravens football team. Frederick Bouchat, the holder of the infringed copyright, raises several challenges to the district court's conduct of proceedings that culminated in a jury verdict finding him entitled to no portion

---

[10] Prejudgment interest will, of course, be available on both the direct and indirect profits earned by MGM Grand, since both forms of profit are equally attributable to the infringement.

[11] Plaintiffs requested prejudgment interest only from the date of the last infringing performance. This is an acceptable date from which to start the running of interest. We need not decide in this case whether an award of prejudgment interest from some earlier point in time, such as the first infringement or date of notice, would be appropriate.

of the infringers' profits. In particular, Bouchat asserts that the court erroneously failed to accord him the benefit of a statutory presumption that an infringer's revenues are entirely attributable to the infringement. For the reasons explained below, we affirm....

[2] On November 6, 1995, the National Football League ("NFL") announced that one of its teams, the Cleveland Browns, would shortly be moving to Baltimore. The team was to leave its entire Browns identity in Cleveland, and thus would need a new name and logo when it moved to its new Maryland home. Bouchat, a Baltimore security guard and amateur artist, became interested in the new team, and he began drawing logo designs based on the various names that the team was considering, including the name "Ravens." On or about December 5, 1995, Bouchat created a drawing of a winged shield (the "Shield Drawing") as a "Ravens" logo.

[3] In March of 1996, the Baltimore team adopted the name "Ravens." In early April, Bouchat sent the Shield Drawing via fax to the Maryland Stadium Authority. Beside the Shield Drawing, Bouchat penned a note asking the Chairman of the Authority to send the sketch to the Ravens' president. Bouchat also requested that if the Ravens used the Shield Drawing, they send him a letter of recognition and an autographed helmet.

[4] In a jury trial on the issue of liability, Bouchat's Shield Drawing was found to have been mistakenly used by National Football League Properties, Inc. ("NFLP") in NFLP's production of the Ravens' new logo, the "Flying B."[1] The Ravens had no knowledge that the NFLP had infringed anyone's work and assumed that the Flying B was an original work owned by NFLP. The Ravens used the Flying B as their primary identifying symbol, and the logo appeared in every aspect of the Ravens' activities, including uniforms, stationery, tickets, banners, on-field insignia, and merchandise....

[5] On May 8, 1997, Bouchat filed suit in the District of Maryland, alleging that the Ravens and NFLP ... had infringed his copyright on the Shield Drawing and on several other drawings, and seeking ten million dollars in damages.... On November 3, 1998, the jury found that Bouchat had proven infringement of the Shield Drawing....

[6] Bouchat sought damages from the Ravens and NFLP pursuant to 17 U.S.C. § 504(a)(1), which renders an infringer liable for "the copyright owner's actual damages and any additional profits of the infringer, as provided by [17 U.S.C. § 504(b)]."[2] Section 504(b), in turn, entitles the copyright owner to recover both "the actual damages suffered by him or her as a result of the infringement, and any profits of the infringer that are attributable to the infringement and are not taken into account in computing the actual damages." Because Bouchat made no claim for actual damages, the sole question presented for resolution in the damages trial was the amount, if any, of the Defendants' profits that was attributable to the infringement.

[7] In his complaint, Bouchat contended that some portion of essentially *all* of the Defendants' revenues was attributable to the infringing use of Bouchat's artwork. To satisfy his initial burden under § 504(b), Bouchat presented evidence of the gross receipts from all NFLP and Ravens activities. The district court, however, awarded partial summary judgment to the Defendants with respect to all revenues derived from sources other than (1) sales of merchandise bearing the Flying B logo, and (2) royalties obtained from licensees who sold such merchandise (collectively, the "Merchandise Revenues"). The court reasoned that "[i]f the use of the Flying B logo to designate the Ravens could not reasonably be found to have affected the amount of revenue

---

[1] NFLP is the Ravens' licensing agent: it grants third parties the right to use the logos and trade/service marks of the various NFL teams in connection with a variety of products and services. In this capacity, NFLP both helped to develop the Ravens' new Flying B logo, and sold to third parties the right to incorporate the Flying B in a wide range of merchandise, including apparel, books, athletic bags, and video tapes.

[2] Bouchat was not entitled to pursue statutory damages because the infringement was of an unpublished work and preceded copyright registration. 17 U.S.C. § 412(1).

obtained from an activity, the revenue from that activity could not reasonably be found attributable to the infringement." Concluding that only the Merchandise Revenues could reasonably be found to have been affected by the Defendants' unlawful use of the Flying B, the court excluded, as a matter of law, the remainder of the Defendants' revenues (collectively, the "Non-Merchandise Revenues") from the pool of income that the jury could consider in awarding § 504 damages.[4]

Figure 123: Frederick Bouchat's Baltimore Ravens logo drawing (left), and NFL's Baltimore Ravens logo (right)

Figure 124: Baltimore Ravens game ticket

[8] At the close of discovery, the district court further narrowed the scope of the Defendants' revenues from which the jury would be permitted to award § 504 damages, when it excluded certain portions of the Merchandise Revenues. Specifically, the court awarded partial summary judgment to the Defendants as to Bouchat's claims for profits from "minimum guarantee shortfalls,"[5] "free merchandise,"[6] trading cards, video

---

[4] The Non–Merchandise Revenues would include, for instance, revenues from the sale of game tickets, stadium parking, food, drinks (with the exception of those sold in special logo-bearing cups), broadcast rights, and sponsorships.

[5] Under NFLP's retail licensing agreements, licensed vendors of official, logo-bearing merchandise are required to pay a certain sum each year, regardless of whether any sales of licensed products actually occur. Thus, if actual sales fall short of

games, and game programs (collectively, the "Excluded Merchandise Revenues"). Though it recognized that the Defendants "ha[ve] the burden of proof," the court nonetheless ruled that, with respect to the minimum guarantee shortfalls and the free merchandise, there could be no rational connection between the particular source of revenue and the act of infringement; and that, with respect to the trading cards, video games, and game program sales, the Defendants had produced unrebutted evidence establishing that the revenues received from those sources were not attributable to the infringement.... Both the Non-Merchandise Revenues and a substantial portion of the Merchandise Revenues having thus been excluded, only those revenues derived from the sale of t-shirts, caps, souvenir cups, and other items bearing the Flying B logo (collectively, the "Non-Excluded Merchandise Revenues") would go to the jury for a finding on attributability.

[9] .... [A]t the close of the evidence, the jury was asked to decide whether the Defendants had proven, by a preponderance of the evidence, that the Non-Excluded Merchandise Revenues were attributable entirely to factors other than the Defendants' infringement of Bouchat's copyright. If the jury found that they were not, then it was charged to decide the percentage of the Non-Excluded Merchandise Revenues attributable to factors other than the infringement.

[10] After a full day of deliberations, the jury answered the first question in the affirmative, thereby denying Bouchat any monetary recovery....

[11] Bouchat's primary contention on appeal is that the district court erred in awarding partial summary judgment to the Defendants with respect to certain portions of the Defendants' revenues. In particular, Bouchat asserts that the court failed to give him the benefit of the § 504 statutory presumption that an infringer's revenues are entirely attributable to the infringement. That presumption, he maintains, creates a question of material fact that cannot be resolved on summary judgment. Thus, he asserts, whether any portion of an infringer's revenues are attributable to some source other than the infringement is a question that can be resolved *only* by a jury. As explained below, we disagree....

[12] Bouchat seeks to recover damages pursuant to 17 U.S.C. § 504(b) for the Defendants' infringement of his copyright. Section 504(b) entitles a successful copyright plaintiff to recover "any profits of the infringer that are attributable to the infringement." The statute goes on to specify that,

> *[i]n establishing the infringer's profits, the copyright owner is required to present proof only of the infringer's gross revenue, and the infringer is required to prove his or her deductible expenses and the elements of profit attributable to factors other than the copyrighted work.*

Thus, § 504(b) creates an initial presumption that the infringer's "profits ... attributable to the infringement" are equal to the infringer's gross revenue. Once the copyright owner has established the amount of the infringer's gross revenues, the burden shifts to the infringer to prove either that part or all of those revenues are "deductible expenses" (i.e., are not profits), or that they are "attributable to factors other than the copyrighted work." Although § 504(b) places the burden on the infringer to demonstrate that certain portions of its revenues were due to factors other than the infringement, the infringer need not prove these amounts with mathematical precision....

[13] Despite the existence of § 504(b)'s burden-shifting provision, summary judgment in favor of an infringer with respect to some portion of the infringer's gross revenues may, in the proper circumstances, be appropriate. Though our Court has not spoken directly on this point, several of our sister circuits have

---

what would be required to generate the guaranteed minimum royalty, a vendor must tender payment in the amount needed to make up the difference. This sum is a "minimum guarantee shortfall" payment.

[6] Under NFLP's retail licensing agreements, a licensed vendor of official, logo-bearing merchandise must provide to NFLP, at no cost, a certain quantity of its licensed products each year. These products are referred to as "free merchandise."

awarded partial summary judgment to infringers, excluding as a matter of law certain portions of an infringer's revenues from the jury's § 504(b) attributability inquiry....

[14] ... [T]he Defendants could properly be awarded summary judgment with respect to any given revenue stream if either (1) there exists no conceivable connection between the infringement and those revenues; or (2) despite the existence of a conceivable connection, Bouchat offered only speculation as to the existence of a causal link between the infringement and the revenues. It is to these inquiries that we turn next....

[15] The Defendants derive revenues from six major sources: (1) sponsorships; (2) broadcast and other media licenses; (3) sale of tickets; (4) miscellaneous business activities, which appear to include provision of game-day stadium parking; (5) sale of official team merchandise; and (6) royalties from licensees who sell official team merchandise. The first four of these sources we characterize as the "Non-Merchandise Revenues," while the fifth and sixth are the "Merchandise Revenues."...

[16] Bouchat contends that, because of the Defendants' widespread use of the Flying B as the primary logo— and as an integral marketing tool—for the Baltimore Ravens, some portion of the revenues that the Defendants earned from both the Non-Merchandise Revenues and the Excluded Merchandise Revenues is attributable to the Defendants' infringement of his copyright. When the district court awarded summary judgment to the Defendants as to large segments of their revenues, however, it denied Bouchat the opportunity to prove this contention to the jury. Despite the fact that § 504(b) places on the infringer the burden of proving that revenues are not attributable to the infringement, summary judgment was appropriate with respect to both the Non-Merchandise Revenues and the Excluded Merchandise Revenues.

[17] As detailed above, we analyze the excluded revenue streams in two steps. We first consider whether any of the Non-Merchandise Revenues and the Excluded Merchandise Revenues lacked a conceivable connection to the infringement. If so, summary judgment in favor of the Defendants with respect to those revenues was proper. Turning then to the remaining excluded revenues, we inquire whether, despite the existence of a conceivable connection between those revenues and the infringement, Bouchat offered only speculative evidence of such a causal link in response to a properly supported motion for summary judgment. If so, then summary judgment in favor of the Defendants was appropriate with respect to these revenues as well....

[18] Of all the excluded revenues, only the revenues from minimum guarantee shortfalls and free merchandise lack all conceivable connection to the Defendants' infringement of Bouchat's copyright. Because no rational trier of fact could find that these two subcategories of the Excluded Merchandise Revenues were affected by the Defendants' adoption of the infringing Flying B logo, the court properly removed them from the pool of Defendants' revenues submitted to the jury for consideration under § 504(b).

[19] The levels of each licensee's minimum guarantee and free merchandise obligation were established, *ex ante,* by the terms of the licensee's contract with NFLP; neither figure could fluctuate in response to consumer behavior. As a consequence, the amount of revenue that the Defendants received in the form of minimum guarantee shortfalls and free merchandise was necessarily independent of any reaction that any individual might have had to the Flying B logo. Whereas it is at least hypothetically possible (albeit highly unlikely) that an individual became so enamored of the infringing aspects of the Flying B logo that he was thus inspired to purchase tickets for the Ravens' games, to pay for parking, to buy non-logo-bearing concessions, and thus to boost the Defendants' revenues from these sources, a similar scenario cannot be conjured with respect to revenues whose levels were fixed and immutable before licensees had an opportunity to stock their shelves with logo-bearing goods. No rational trier of fact could find that the infringing Flying B logo enabled the defendants to generate more income from these two sources than they would otherwise have done. Because no portion of the Defendants' gross revenues from minimum guarantee shortfalls and free merchandise could be attributable to the infringement of Bouchat's copyright, the court did not err in awarding summary

judgment to the Defendants with respect to these two sub-categories of the Excluded Merchandise Revenues....

[20] Having concluded that summary judgment in favor of the Defendants was proper with respect to both the minimum guarantee short-falls and the free merchandise, we turn now to the Non-Merchandise Revenues and the remaining sub-categories of the Excluded Merchandise Revenues (i.e., the revenues from trading cards, video games, and game programs). Our inquiry on this point is whether, despite the existence of a conceivable connection between the infringement and the level of revenue that the Defendants earned from these sources, the court was correct in excluding them through summary judgment. Because Bouchat offered only speculative evidence of a causal link between the infringement and the level of the revenues that the Defendants earned from these sources, and because the Defendants' request for summary judgment was supported by unrebutted evidence demonstrating that these revenues were not, in fact, in any way attributable to the infringement, there was no issue of material fact for consideration by the jury. As a result, the court did not err in awarding summary judgment to the Defendants with respect to these remaining categories of revenue.

[21] When they moved for summary judgment, the Defendants successfully carried their initial burden of demonstrating the absence of a genuine issue of material fact. In support of their initial motion for summary judgment, the Defendants proffered affidavits showing that Non-Merchandise Revenues are driven by business and consumer interest in NFL football, and are in no way responsive to logo design. In support of their subsequent summary judgment motion, the Defendants again proffered numerous affidavits, this time showing that sales of trading cards, video games, and game programs are driven by consumer interest in NFL football, and likewise are in no way responsive to logo design. The supporting affidavits established beyond reasonable debate that neither any portion of the Defendants' Non-Merchandise Revenues, nor any portion of their revenues from trading cards, video games, or game programs, was attributable to the Defendants' selection and use of the infringing Flying B rather than some other logo.

[22] Having met their initial burden, the Defendants successfully shifted the onus onto Bouchat to come forward and demonstrate that such an issue does, in fact, exist.... Bouchat, however, produced no specific facts showing that there was a genuine issue for trial; in fact, he declined to respond to the summary judgment motions with any evidence at all, resting instead on his initial, and sole, evidentiary proffer: the total receipts generated by all NFLP and Ravens activities. Because Bouchat failed to offer any nonspeculative evidence demonstrating the existence of a genuine dispute of material fact, the court appropriately awarded summary judgment to the Defendants on the ground that the Non-Merchandise Revenues and the revenues from trading cards, video games, and game programs could not reasonably be found attributable to the infringement....

[23] For the foregoing reasons, the judgment of the district court is affirmed.

NOTES

1. The Ninth Circuit in *Frank Music* reversed the district court's apportionment, holding that the district court's 75-25 split in favor of the defendant was clear error and should be flipped to 25-75 in favor of plaintiff. On what basis did the appellate court make this reallocation? Does a rule emerge from the case regarding how to calculate the relative value of infringing versus non-infringing aspects of the defendant's work for the purpose of apportioning profits?

2. Does copyright policy support awarding a defendant's indirect profits, as the Ninth Circuit did in *Frank Music*? How accurate do you think a court is likely to be in measuring awards of indirect profits?

3. The *Bouchat* court granted summary judgment to the defendants on most of Bouchat's categories of alleged infringement, on the grounds that there could be no conceivable connection between the alleged infringement and revenues. Do you agree with that holding? Even if not, do you agree that Bouchat should recover nothing?

4. Note that the Copyright Act provides for recovery of both actual damages, often equivalent to a reasonable license fee, and *profits* (not already counted in the damages award). Disgorgement of profits prevents defendants from benefiting from their infringement. This award makes sense if we believe that part of the purpose of copyright law is to force parties to channel their transactions through voluntary negotiations, rather than allowing defendants to infringe and then to pay whatever damages the court orders—with the court, in effect, setting the price for the equivalent of a compulsory license. Note, however, that this is not an iron-clad justification for copyright's disgorgement remedy. Sometimes negotiations are expensive, especially when there are many potential plaintiffs, and it would be cheaper to have a court set a price for use of the work. We might label such instances "efficient copyright infringement," and, but for the Copyright Act's disgorgement remedy, we might argue that courts should permit continued infringement, subject to a judicially-determined license price. *See* David Fagundes, *Efficient Copyright Infringement*, 98 IOWA L. REV. 1791 (2013).

5. Some have argued that unlike monetary damages generally, disgorgement under 17 U.S.C. § 504(a) of defendants' profits attributable to infringement is an equitable remedy, and therefore outside the Seventh Amendment jury trial guarantee, which extends to legal but not equitable remedies. The question of whether disgorgement of defendants' profits attributable to infringement must be tried to a jury is not answered by the Copyright Act and has not explicitly been answered by the Supreme Court. A recent district court decision held that an award of defendant's profits in a copyright infringement case was equitable in nature and thus outside the scope of the Seventh Amendment jury guarantee. Fair Isaac Corp. v. Fed. Ins. Co., 468 F. Supp. 3d 1110, 1118 (D. Minn. 2020). For more on disgorgement, see Pamela Samuelson, John M. Golden & Mark P. Gergen, *Recalibrating the Disgorgement Remedy in Intellectual Property Cases*, 100 B.U. L. REV. 1999 (2020).

6. One commentator has proposed conditioning the availability of the disgorgement remedy on timely registration of the work, arguing that this revision to § 504(b) would be a powerful inducement to timely-register commercially valuable works, and is permissible under the rules of international copyright treaties. *See* Christopher Jon Sprigman, *Berne's Vanishing Ban on Formalities*, 28 BERKELEY TECH. L.J. 1565 (2013).

3. Statutory Damages

Section 504(c) makes statutory damages available at a plaintiff's election and in lieu of actual damages and profits. Section 504(c) provides courts discretion to award statutory damages in the following amounts:

> *(1) Except as provided by clause (2) of this subsection, the copyright owner may elect, at any time before final judgment is rendered, to recover, instead of actual damages and profits, an award of statutory damages for all infringements involved in the action, with respect to any one work, for which any one infringer is liable individually, or for which any two or more infringers are liable jointly and severally, in a sum of not less than $750 or more than $30,000 as the court considers just. For the purposes of this subsection, all the parts of a compilation or derivative work constitute one work.*
>
> *(2) In a case where the copyright owner sustains the burden of proving, and the court finds, that infringement was committed willfully, the court in its discretion may increase the award of statutory damages to a sum of not more than $150,000. In a case where the infringer sustains*

*the burden of proving, and the court finds, that such infringer was not aware and had no reason
to believe that his or her acts constituted an infringement of copyright, the court in its discretion
may reduce the award of statutory damages to a sum of not less than $200....*

Why do you think copyright law provides an option for statutory damages in lieu of actual damages and profits? Why might a plaintiff find statutory damages attractive instead of actual damages? Might a defendant prefer statutory damages too?

Note that a plaintiff's ability to recover statutory damages for infringement of a work is conditioned on timely registration of the work (even for non-U.S. works), as you learned in Chapter IV.

The Copyright Act's statutory damages provisions distinguish between ordinary and "willful" infringement, raising the top of the range for willful infringement from $30,000 to $150,000 per work infringed. For infringement to be "willful," it must be done "with knowledge that [one's] conduct constitutes copyright infringement." Princeton Univ. Press v. Mich. Doc. Servs., Inc., 99 F.3d 1381, 1392 (6th Cir. 1996). Does this knowledge justify the five-fold increase in potential maximum statutory damages?

More broadly, notice the wide range of possible statutory damages for infringement. The maximum award for ordinary, non-willful infringement is 40 times the minimum, and the maximum for willful infringement is more than *200 times* the minimum. Why do you think the range is so large? Does the Copyright Act's statutory damages scheme provide predictability for either plaintiffs or defendants? For a critical take on the statutory damages provisions, see Pamela Samuelson & Tara Wheatland, *Statutory Damages in Copyright Law: A Remedy in Need of Reform*, 51 WM. & MARY L. REV. 439 (2009).

How do courts or (more often) juries determine the amount within the wide range the statute makes available that constitutes a "just" award as the statute directs? The appellate courts have provided the district courts with only the most general guidelines. The Second Circuit, for instance, sets forth six factors: (1) the infringer's state of mind; (2) the expenses saved, and profits earned, by the infringer; (3) the revenue lost by the copyright holder; (4) the deterrent effect on the infringer and third parties; (5) the infringer's cooperation in providing evidence concerning the value of the infringing material; and (6) the conduct and attitude of the parties. Bryant v. Media Right Prods., Inc., 603 F.3d 135, 144 (2d Cir. 2010). Other circuits use similar factors.

The Seventh Amendment adds a further wrinkle. While Section 504's reference to "the court" seems to commit a statutory damages determination to the judge, the Supreme Court has held that the Seventh Amendment guarantees a jury trial "on all issues pertinent to an award of statutory damages under § 504(c) of the Copyright Act, including the amount itself." Feltner v. Columbia Pictures Television, Inc., 523 U.S. 340, 355 (1998). Juries enjoy wide latitude in assessing statutory damages. The judge will instruct the jury using the factors mentioned above, but the jury must ultimately decide how to apply these tests on a case-by-case basis. One leading treatise even claims that "it is doubtful that juries can be meaningfully instructed to compare the facts at bar against those of prior cases in order to slot an appropriate award into the scheme of precedent." 4 NIMMER ON COPYRIGHT § 14.04 (2020).

NOTES

1. Note that a finding that infringement is "willful" *raises only the top of the statutory damages range*. It does not change the bottom of the range, which remains $750. Of course, it may be unlikely in most cases that a court would award statutory damages at the bottom of the range for willful infringement, but the option remains available. Note also that the Act provides the possibility of a lower award—as low as $200 per work infringed—for cases of innocent infringement—situations in which the infringer "was not aware and had no reason to believe that his or her acts constituted an infringement of copyright." 17 U.S.C. § 504(c)(2).

2. Section 504(c) gives district courts discretion to award statutory damages within the specified ranges, and appellate review is therefore limited to abuse of discretion. *See* Zomba Enterprises, Inc. v. Panorama Records, Inc., 491 F. 3d 574 (6th Cir. 2007).

3. The Copyright Act directs that a court's award of statutory damages shall be made "with respect to any one work, for which any one infringer is liable" regardless of the number of "infringements involved in the action." 17 U.S.C. § 504(c). What constitutes "one work"? The only guidance the statute provides is that "parts of a compilation or derivative work constitute one work." *Id.*

4. In *Capitol Records, Inc. v. Thomas-Rasset*, 692 F.3d 899 (8th Cir. 2012), the Eighth Circuit held that a statutory damages award of $9,250 for each of twenty-four infringed songs, for a total of $222,000, does not contravene the U.S. Constitution's Due Process Clause. *Thomas-Rasset* held that the Supreme Court's relatively permissive standard in *St. Louis, I. M. & S. Ry. Co. v. Williams,* 251 U.S. 63 (1919), governs statutory damages awards. Under the *Williams* standard, a statutory damages award violates due process only when the defendant shows that it is "so severe and oppressive as to be wholly disproportioned to the offense and obviously unreasonable." Can you imagine a statutory damages award that would meet this standard? What about a case in which there was a willful infringement of a single work that the defendant can show resulted in actual damages of $0.01, but for which a plaintiff is awarded the maximum statutory damages of $150,000? What about a case involving the willful infringement of 100 works that the defendant can show resulted in actual damages of $1.00, but for which a plaintiff is awarded the maximum statutory damages of $15,000,000? And, more broadly, do you agree with *Thomas-Rasset* that the Copyright Act's statutory damages provisions raise no due process concerns because the Act establishes outer limits for such awards? Is the establishment of "outer limits" equivalent to the "fair notice" sufficient to allay due process concerns?

4. Costs and Attorney's Fees

Section 505 of the Copyright Act provides that "[a] court in its discretion may allow the recovery of full costs by or against any party other than the United States or an officer thereof. Except as otherwise provided by this title, the court may also award a reasonable attorney's fee to the prevailing party as part of the costs."

Note that recovery of attorney's fees and other costs for infringement of a work is conditioned on timely registration of the work, as you learned in Chapter IV.

Section 505 makes clear that attorney's fees and other costs may be awarded to any "prevailing party"—that is, to prevailing plaintiffs and defendants alike. *See* Fogerty v. Fantasy, Inc., 510 U.S. 517 (1994). Courts have recognized that an award of attorney's fees to the prevailing party "is the rule rather than the exception, and should be awarded routinely." McGaughey v. Twentieth Century Fox Film Corp., 12 F.3d 62, 65 (5th Cir. 1994). This does not mean, however, that prevailing plaintiffs or defendants are *always* granted attorney's fees. The Supreme Court has made clear that courts have discretion whether to order an award. *Fogerty*, 510 U.S. at 533.

One important question is which factors should inform a court's exercise of discretion in deciding whether to award attorney's fees and costs. In *Kirtsaeng v. John Wiley & Sons, Inc.,* 136 S. Ct. 1979 (2016) ("*Kirtsaeng II*"), the Supreme Court held that a district court should give substantial weight to the objective reasonableness of the losing party's position, while still considering other circumstances relevant to awarding attorney's fees. Those other circumstances include "several nonexclusive factors" identified in *Fogerty*, such as frivolousness, motivation, objective unreasonableness, and the need in particular cases to advance considerations of compensation and deterrence. The Supreme Court directed lower courts to continue to give substantial weight to the reasonableness of the losing party's position. But *Kirtsaeng II* makes clear that objective reasonableness is not the decisive factor:

> *All of that said, objective reasonableness can be only an important factor in assessing fee applications—not the controlling one. As we recognized in* Fogerty, *§ 505 confers broad discretion on district courts and, in deciding whether to fee-shift, they must take into account a range of considerations beyond the reasonableness of litigating positions. That means in any given case a court may award fees even though the losing party offered reasonable arguments (or, conversely, deny fees even though the losing party made unreasonable ones).*

In particular, the Supreme Court observed that notwithstanding a party's reasonableness, a court may order fee-shifting because of a party's litigation misconduct or to deter repeated instances of copyright infringement or overaggressive assertions of copyright claims: "Although objective reasonableness carries significant weight, courts must view all the circumstances of a case on their own terms, in light of the Copyright Act's essential goals."

NOTES

1. Note that the usual rule in U.S. civil litigation is that each party pays its own attorney's fees, win or lose. Why do you think the Copyright Act departs from this so-called "American Rule"? Do you think the departure is justified? What effect do you think the Copyright Act's fee-shifting provision has on who brings copyright infringement litigation, and on what sort of claims are brought?

2. Note again that plaintiffs are eligible to recover attorney's fees only if they have timely registered the infringed work. Is this likely to be a powerful inducement to register? For some works, or for all?

F. Small Claims Proceedings Before the Copyright Claims Board

The Copyright Alternative in Small-Claims Enforcement Act of 2020 ("CASE Act") established the Copyright Claims Board (CCB) as "an alternative forum in which parties may voluntarily seek to resolve certain copyright claims." 17 U.S.C. § 1502(a). Certain small claims—that is, claims for which the copyright owner seeks $30,000 or less in damages, *id.* § 1502(c)—are eligible to be brought in CCB administrative proceedings. Participation in a proceeding before the Board is voluntary: a claimant (which includes both copyright owners claiming infringement as well as any party seeking a declaration of non-infringement, *see id.* § 1501 (defining "claimant")), may choose to commence a proceeding with the CCB instead of filing a lawsuit in federal court, but in no instance is required to do so. *Id.* § 1504(a). The party against whom a claim is made in CCB proceedings has a 60-day period after service of notice within which the party may opt out of CCB proceedings. The opt-out notice must be in writing; once an effective opt-out notice is served, the CCB proceeding is dismissed without prejudice. *Id.* § 1506(i). The law directs the Register of Copyrights to issue regulations allowing libraries and archives to opt out of all CCB proceedings "preemptively" (that is, generally, and in advance of receiving notice from any particular claimant), without paying any fee to do so. *Id.* § 1506(aa).

Section 1504(e) of the Copyright Act sets out the remedies that are available in CCB proceedings. The CCB may award to a copyright owner who establishes infringement "actual damages and profits determined in accordance with section 504(b), with that award taking into consideration, in appropriate cases, whether the infringing party has agreed to cease or mitigate the infringing activity." Alternatively, if the work was timely registered, the copyright owner may elect at any time before a final determination by the CCB to recover "statutory damages, which shall be determined in accordance with section 504(c)." However, the statute places a number of limitations on CCB awards of statutory damages. First, for timely registered works, statutory damages awards "may not exceed $15,000 for each work infringed," up to a maximum award of $30,000. *Id.* §1504(e)(1). In addition, the CCB "may not make any finding that, or consider whether, the infringement was committed willfully," but "may consider, as an additional factor in awarding statutory damages, whether the infringer has agreed to cease or mitigate the infringing activity ...." *Id.*

While statutory damages are available in infringement claims in federal court only if the work infringed was timely registered, the statute empowers the CCB to make statutory damage awards even if the infringed work was not timely registered. If the copyright was *not* timely registered, the CCB may still award statutory damages up to $7500 for each work infringed, subject to a maximum total award of $15,000. *Id.*

The CCB does not have authority to issue injunctions, but a CCB determination "shall include" a requirement to cease the infringing conduct if a party agrees to do so and the agreement is reflected in the record. *Id.* § 1504(e)(2).

Finally, under 17 U.S.C. § 1504(e)(3), parties in proceedings before the CCB "shall bear their own attorneys' fees and costs," with the exception that attorney's fees and costs may be awarded under 17 U.S.C. § 1506(y)(2), with certain limitations, when "a determination is rendered and it is established that a party pursued a claim, counterclaim, or defense for a harassing or other improper purpose, or without a reasonable basis in law or fact." Such awards of fees and costs are not to exceed $5000 in most cases, or $2500 if the adversely affected party is pro se. *Id.* The CCB may, "in the interests of justice," award attorney's fees and costs exceeding these limitations "in extraordinary circumstances, such as where a party has demonstrated a pattern or practice of bad faith conduct." *Id.*

On March 25, 2022, the Copyright Office issued final rules for initiating claims and related procedures before the CCB. *See* https://www.govinfo.gov/content/pkg/FR-2022-03-25/pdf/2022-06264.pdf.

There are substantial questions regarding the constitutionality of the CASE Act. Specifically, it is unclear whether the CASE Act violates Article III of the Constitution by giving adjudicative power to non-Article III judges. Recently, in *Oil States Energy Services, LLC v. Greene's Energy Group, LLC*, 138 S. Ct. 1365 (2017), the Supreme Court upheld "inter partes" review of patents (review by Article I administrative law judges of a patent's validity) based on the finding that adjudication of patent validity involved the determination of so-called "public rights"—that is, "matters arising between the government and others, which from their nature do not require judicial determination and yet are susceptible of it." The Supreme Court had in previous decisions given Congress some latitude to assign adjudication of public rights to non-Article III courts.

In contrast to the inter partes review proceeding upheld in *Oil States*, which involved the validity of a government patent grant to a private owner and therefore fell within the scope of public rights, adjudication of infringement claims under the CASE Act by non-Article III judges seems more clearly to involve a question of private right—a dispute between two private parties, rather than between a private party and the government. *See* Pamela Samuelson & Kathryn Hashimoto, *Scholarly Concerns About a Proposed Copyright Small Claims Tribunal*, 33 BERKELEY TECH. L J. 689 (2018).

G. Criminal Copyright Law

Section 506 of the Copyright Act authorizes criminal liability for "[a]ny person who willfully infringes a copyright" if the infringement was committed:

> *(A) for purposes of commercial advantage or private financial gain;*

(B) by the reproduction or distribution, including by electronic means, during any 180-day period, of 1 or more copies or phonorecords of 1 or more copyrighted works, which have a total retail value of more than $1,000; or

(C) by the distribution of a work being prepared for commercial distribution, by making it available on a computer network accessible to members of the public, if such person knew or should have known that the work was intended for commercial distribution.

The Copyright Act in § 101 defines "financial gain" broadly: "The term 'financial gain' includes receipt, or expectation of receipt, of anything of value, including the receipt of other copyrighted works." The Copyright Act offers no definition of the term "willfully."

The version of the Copyright Act passed in 1976 authorized only misdemeanor criminal liability for infringement (as had the predecessor Copyright Act of 1909). In 1982, Congress reclassified certain commercial-scale infringements of sound recordings and motion pictures as felony criminal violations. In 1992, Congress upgraded to felonies *all* infringements qualifying for criminal prosecution under § 506. Finally, the Protecting Lawful Streaming Act of 2020, part of the Consolidated Appropriations Act of 2021 (Public Law No: 116-260), significantly increases criminal penalties for those who, willfully and for commercial advantage or private financial gain, illegally stream copyrighted material. Previously, illegal streaming was treated as a misdemeanor. Under the new law, the Department of Justice can bring felony charges against providers (as opposed to users) of such illegal services.

Read § 506 carefully, and then also read 18 U.S.C. § 2319, which sets forth the penalties for criminal copyright infringement. As you read the next case, focus on the court's definition of "willfully." Is that term clearly defined? Is the definition sufficient to distinguish between ordinary copyright infringement and infringement that may be prosecuted criminally?

United States of America v. Julius Chow Lieh Liu
731 F.3d 982 (9th Cir. 2013)

NGUYEN, J.:

[1] Julius Liu appeals his convictions and sentence for criminal copyright infringement .... Liu's company, Super DVD, commercially replicated CDs and DVDs for various clients on a scale that subjects him to substantial criminal liability if a client—and, by extension, Liu—lacked permission from the copyright holder to make the copies.

[2] Under the relevant criminal statutes, Liu's guilt turns on whether he acted "willfully".... We hold that the term "willfully" requires the government to prove that a defendant knew he was acting illegally rather than simply that he knew he was making copies.... Because the district court improperly instructed the jury otherwise, we vacate Liu's convictions and remand...

[3] Liu has worked in the replication industry since the early 1990s. In 2000, he founded, and became the CEO of, a DVD-manufacturing company called Super DVD. By 2001, Super DVD employed about 65 people and operated four replication machines at its Hayward, California warehouse....

[4] Meanwhile, the government had become suspicious of Super DVD's operations. In May 2003, Immigration and Customs Enforcement agents raided the warehouse of Vertex International Trading, a computer software reseller based in Coral Springs, Florida, where agents recovered counterfeit copies of the Symantec software "Norton Anti-Virus 2003" and related documentation. The documentation included purchase orders, handwritten notes, and FedEx shipping labels from more than 50 vendors, including Super DVD.

[5] Later that month, private investigator Cynthia Navarro, working on behalf of Symantec, posed as a potential lessee to investigate Super DVD's warehouse. While there, Navarro observed a man using one of two machines that she believed were used for CD or DVD replication. Through a window, she could see into a locked room that was filled wall to wall with spindles of CDs.

[6] At the end of July 2003, agents executed a search warrant on the Super DVD warehouse and recovered thousands of DVDs and CDs. One room stored CDs and DVDs, and another held stampers, artwork, and masters. The CDs included a compilation of rap tracks, *Rap Masters Vol. 2*; three compilations of Latin music tracks, *Los Tucanes de Tijuana: Romanticas, Lo Mejor de la Mafia*, and *3 Reyars* [sic] *del Tex Mex: Romanticas*; and a greatest hits album, *Beatles 1*. The agents also recovered DVD copies of the film *Crouching Tiger, Hidden Dragon*. Liu did not have authorization from the copyright holders to replicate any of these works.

[7] During an interview and at trial, Liu admitted that Super DVD manufactured the *Crouching Tiger* DVDs in 2001 for a company called R & E Trading. R & E gave Super DVD a stamper with the name "Tiger" on it but not the full title of the film. The DVDs were still in Super DVD's warehouse at the time the search warrant was executed because R & E had rejected them, claiming that the movies would freeze. Liu stated that when R & E refused to pay for the order, he became personally involved and realized that R & E did not have the rights to duplicate such a famous movie. Super DVD filed a lawsuit against R & E alleging that R & E deceived it about the copyrights. The lawsuit sought payment from R & E on about 40 invoices totaling approximately $85,000, including work done on the *Crouching Tiger* movie. Super DVD obtained a jury verdict for approximately $600.

[8] Liu generally denied any knowledge of or involvement in replicating the other works. Liu explained that he became involved with the Latin music compilations when one of the former Super DVD engineers introduced Liu to his uncle, Juan Valdez, a famous mariachi singer. Liu and Valdez got together and played music—Liu on the guitar, Valdez singing. Valdez expressed interest in publishing CDs, and Liu told him that he didn't have the facility to do it but suggested companies that could take care of the mastering, printing, and even the sleeve. Liu volunteered to do the overwrapping for Valdez because it only cost him "pennies." Valdez told Liu that he created the tracks by mixing his voice with music from a Karaoke machine and that he had paid for the license. Liu listened to some of the tracks and, believing that it was Valdez's voice, thought that the music "belong[ed] to him." ...

[9] The government charged Liu with three counts of criminal copyright infringement under 17 U.S.C. § 506(a)(1)(A) and 18 U.S.C. § 2319(b)(1) based on the music CDs, the *Crouching Tiger* DVD, and the Norton Anti-Virus software.... Following a three-day jury trial, Liu was convicted on all counts. The district court sentenced Liu to four years in prison followed by three years of supervised release....

[10] .... The [district] court instructed the jury that Liu "willfully infringed" if he "without authorization duplicated, reproduced or sold the copyright belonging to the owners of the works." The court further adopted the government's requested definition of willfully—that "[a]n act is done 'willfully' if the act is done knowingly and intentionally, not through ignorance, mistake or accident." ...

[11] Copyright infringers have been subject to civil liability since the Nation's founding. In a civil suit, liability for copyright infringement is strict. The innocent intent of the defendant constitutes no defense to liability.

[12] Congress first imposed criminal liability for certain types of infringement in the late nineteenth century. The general approach to criminal copyright enforcement—then, as now—has been to punish only those violations that are both willful and economically motivated.

[13] Of the two factors that distinguish criminal from noncriminal copyright violations, willfulness and commerciality, the latter is of little practical importance. The Copyright Act defines "financial gain" broadly to include "receipt, or expectation of receipt, of anything of value, including the receipt of other copyrighted works." 17 U.S.C. § 101. The commerciality requirement thus does not meaningfully winnow down the population of copyright defendants potentially liable to incarceration. The only bar against an overzealous prosecutor criminalizing nearly every copyright infringement case lies in the other prerequisite to criminal liability: willfulness.

[14] But the term "willfully" is ambiguous.[2] To infringe willfully could simply mean to intentionally commit the act that constitutes infringement. Alternatively, it could mean that the defendant must act with a bad purpose or evil motive in the sense that there was an intentional violation of a known legal duty. The 1976 Copyright Act does not define "willfully," and its legislative history offers little guidance.

[15] When faced with a criminal statute containing an ambiguous "willfulness" element, courts normally resolve any doubt in favor of the defendant. Although the general rule is that ignorance of the law or a mistake of law is no defense to criminal prosecution, the modern proliferation of statutes and regulations sometimes makes it difficult for the average citizen to know and comprehend the extent of the duties and obligations imposed by the laws. Thus, the government must prove that the defendant acted "willfully"—that is, with specific intent to violate the law—to be convicted of certain federal criminal offenses.

[16] In reviewing a conviction for criminal copyright infringement, we, and numerous other circuits, have assumed that proof of the defendant's specific intent to violate someone's copyright is required. We now explicitly hold that "willfully" as used in 17 U.S.C. § 506(a) connotes a voluntary, intentional violation of a known legal duty.

[17] The Copyright Act's legislative history supports our interpretation. In 1997, Congress updated the statutory provision governing criminal copyright infringement by inserting the language that Liu requested: "evidence of reproduction or distribution of a copyrighted work, by itself, shall not be sufficient to establish willful infringement." No Electronic Theft (NET) Act, Pub. L. 105–147, § 2(b), 111 Stat. 2678, 2678 (1997) (codified as amended at 17 U.S.C. § 506(c)). This language was in response to the "on-going debate about what precisely is the 'willfulness' standard in the Copyright Act." 143 Cong. Rec. S12,689 (daily ed. Nov. 13, 1997) (statement of Sen. Orrin Hatch); see also id. at 12,690 (statement of Sen. Patrick Leahy) ("This clarification was included to address the concerns expressed ... because the standard of 'willfulness' for criminal copyright infringement is not statutorily defined and the court's interpretation[s] have varied somewhat among the Federal circuits.").[4] Upon passage of the bill in the Senate, Senator Hatch stated that

---

[2] Even within the context of *civil* copyright infringement, we have defined "willful" to mean different things in different contexts. See Barboza v. New Form, Inc. (In re Barboza), 545 F.3d 702, 707–08 (9th Cir. 2008) ("The term 'willful' as used in copyright infringement cases is not equivalent to 'willful' as used in determining whether a debt is nondischargeable under the bankruptcy code.").

[4] Industry representatives and other stakeholders testifying before Congress expressed their hope that the term "willful" would be "given the interpretation that [the majority of] courts ha[d] given [it] in the criminal context," i.e., "that it is not enough for the defendant in a criminal case to have had an intent to copy the work; he must have acted with knowledge that his conduct constituted copyright infringement." *Copyright Piracy, and H.R. 2265, the No Elec. Theft (NET) Act: Hearing Before the Subcomm. on Courts and Intellectual Prop. of the Comm. on the Judiciary H.R.*, 105th Cong. 13–14 (1997) (statement of Marybeth Peters, Register of Copyrights); see id. at 157 (statement of David Nimmer, counsel, United States Telephone Association) ("The courts' divergent interpretations of Section 506(a) yield uncertainty.... Congress should

willful "ought to mean the intent to violate a known legal duty.... As Chairman of the Judiciary Committee, that is the interpretation that I give to this term. Otherwise, I would have objected and not allowed this bill to pass by unanimous consent." 143 Cong. Rec. S12, 689.

[18] As a practical matter, requiring only a general intent to copy as a basis for a criminal conviction would not shield any appreciable amount of infringing conduct from the threat of prosecution. Civil liability will not lie if an author fortuitously creates a work that is substantially similar to another author's copyrighted work. To infringe a copyright, one must *copy* the protected work. Copying is of necessity an intentional act. If we were to read 17 U.S.C. § 506(a)'s willfulness requirement to mean only an intent to copy, there would be no meaningful distinction between civil and criminal liability in the vast majority of cases. That cannot be the result that Congress sought.

[19] In the present case, notwithstanding the parties' agreement to add an instruction that "[e]vidence of reproduction or distribution of a copyrighted work, by itself, shall not be sufficient to establish willful infringement of a copyright," 17 U.S.C. § 506(a)(2), the district court did not include the requested language. In fact, the district court exacerbated the omission by defining willful infringement without the crucial knowledge component:

> In order for the defendant to be found guilty of [copyright infringement], the government must prove each of the following elements beyond a reasonable doubt:

> First, that on a date beginning in 2001 and continuing to on or about July 31, 2003, in the Northern District of California, defendant willfully infringed, that is, without authorization, duplicated, reproduced, or sold compact disks that infringed the copyright belonging to the owners of the works....

By defining "willfully infringed" without any requirement that the defendant knew he was committing copyright infringement, the district court instructed the jury to apply a civil liability standard.

[20] The district court further compounded this error a short time later, instructing the jury that "[a]n act is done 'willfully' if the act is done knowingly and intentionally, not through ignorance, mistake, or accident." We recently considered a virtually identical instruction in *United States v. Berry*, 683 F.3d 1015 (9th Cir. 2012). The district court had instructed the jury that "an act is done willfully if the defendant acted or failed to act knowingly and intentionally and did not act or fail to act through ignorance, mistake, or accident." Finding error, we explained that "the instruction given merged the concepts of 'knowing' and 'willful' without conveying the culpable state of mind that the term 'willfully' is designed to invoke in the criminal arena."

[21] We conclude that the district court in this case erred by defining willfulness such that the jury could have convicted Liu without finding that he knew that his actions were unlawful....

[22] Liu's convictions on the copyright infringement counts cannot stand unless the instructional error was harmless. An error in describing an element of the offense in a jury instruction is harmless only if it is clear beyond a reasonable doubt that a rational jury would have found the defendant guilty absent the error.

[23] The conclusion was irresistible that the infringing CDs and DVDs were replicated in the Super DVD warehouse. The discs all were found there with the exception of the Norton Anti-Virus software, which was

---

specify that 'willful' ... requires a specific intent to violate a known legal duty."); *see also id.* at 37 (statement of Brad Smith, Associate General Counsel, Microsoft Corp.) ("[W]e are *only* talking about *willful infringement* of a copyright holder's rights.... [U]nder criminal law a willful act requires that it be intentionally done with knowledge that it was prohibited by law.").

discovered at the Vertex warehouse along with purchase orders and shipping labels linking it to Liu and Super DVD. Almost all of the music CDs bore Liu's initials, "JL." Liu admitted to reproducing the *Crouching Tiger* DVDs for R & E Trading, and there was a written agreement from early 2001 between Super DVD and R & E to press 2,000 copies of the *Beatles* CD. Although Liu claimed to have no knowledge of how the other discs were made, suggesting that the orders may have been handled by his sales staff, it is unclear whether the jury disbelieved him, thought he had forgotten, or found his employees' acts attributable to him.

[24] Whatever the case, Liu's state of mind was critical. Liu was aware of copyright laws and admittedly had been sued for copyright infringement in the past. His guilt thus hinged on whether he knew that his clients did not have authorization to replicate the disks at issue.

[25] Liu presented evidence that his customers signed agreements stating that they had the copyright to the works in question and promising "to be responsible for all copyright related legal responsibilities." His expert witness testified that other replicators also rely on such agreements rather than carefully investigate each customer. Liu testified that he attempted to verify that there were no copyright violations on the Latin music compilations by listening to the some of the tracks and satisfying himself that it was Valdez's voice. He further claimed that he did not realize R & E's order for *Crouching Tiger* DVDs was unauthorized until he became embroiled in the payment dispute, at which time he filed a lawsuit against R & E. The fact that he initiated a lawsuit over a dispute involving thousands of infringing copies of *Crouching Tiger, Hidden Dragon* that he created is arguably compelling evidence that he did not understand his conduct to have been wrongful.

[26] We cannot say that the jury would not have credited some or all of this evidence had the jury appreciated its relevance. The evidence may have supported a finding that Liu did not know that he was illegally copying copyrighted material and thus he did not willfully infringe the copyrights. Therefore, the failure to provide a proper willfulness instruction was not harmless beyond a reasonable doubt....

[27] Accordingly, we vacate Liu's convictions and sentence for criminal copyright infringement on counts one through three and remand to the district court....

NOTES

1. *Liu* holds that the "willfulness" requirement limits criminal copyright liability to those infringers who are shown to have committed a "voluntary, intentional violation of a known legal duty." That is, the defendant must be shown to have subjectively understood that he or she was committing copyright infringement. What kind of evidence could a prosecutor offer to establish the requisite knowledge and intent?

2. Take another look at 18 U.S.C. § 2319. Do the punishments provided there fit the crime?

3. What is the purpose of criminal copyright liability? Does criminal liability plug some gap in the deterrent effect of civil liability? For an economic analysis of criminal copyright liability, and a (cautious) endorsement of its use in very narrow circumstances, see Christopher Buccafusco & Jonathan S. Masur, *Innovation and Incarceration: An Economic Analysis of Criminal Intellectual Property Law*, 87 S. CAL. L. REV. 275 (2014).

4. Criminal copyright prosecutions have a five-year statute of limitations, 17 U.S.C. § 507(a), as opposed to the three-year statute of limitations applicable to civil copyright claims. Can you think of a reason Congress provided a longer statute of limitations for criminal prosecutions?

IX. Technological Protections for Copyrighted Works

In this chapter, you will learn about the provisions of the Digital Millennium Copyright Act, codified in the Copyright Act principally in §1201, that prohibit certain "circumventions" of technological protection measures that copyright owners may employ to control access to or use of copyrighted works. The §1201 anti-circumvention provisions are one of the two primary changes to copyright law put into place by the Digital Millennium Copyright Act of 1998. The other is the §512 safe-harbor provisions, which you studied in Chapter VII.

A. Early History of Technological Protection Measures

Since at least the early 1980s, some owners of copyrighted content have sought to supplement the rights that copyright provides with **technological protections**—technologies that work to prevent unauthorized access to, or copying of, copyrighted works. One early example was Macrovision, a technology introduced in the mid-1980s and deployed by the motion picture industry to prevent the unauthorized reproduction of pre-recorded videocassettes. Devices were quickly introduced that worked to defeat Macrovision, but these devices never gained widespread distribution, possibly because the incentive to pirate pre-recorded videotapes was blunted by the wide availability of cheap video rentals as well as home taping using the consumer-oriented video cassette recorders (VCRs) that became popular around the same time that Macrovision was introduced. As you read in Chapter VI, the Supreme Court's opinion in *Sony Corp. of America v. Universal City Studios, Inc.*, 464 U.S. 417 (1984), held that VCR taping for the purposes of time shifting constituted fair use.

Also in the 1980s, satellite and cable television broadcasters introduced various forms of encryption to prevent unauthorized access to their services. However, these early cable and satellite technological protections were far from foolproof, and technologies and devices to defeat them were made widely available soon after their introduction. Congress legislated to prohibit unauthorized satellite and cable "black box" decoders, Pub. L. No. 100-667, § 204, 102 Stat. 3935 (codified as amended at 47 U.S.C. § 605(e)(4) (1988)); that law helped limit the availability of the black box devices, though it never succeeded in driving them out of the market entirely.

The most heated battle over technological protections in the 1980s played out in the software industry. Concerned with widespread unauthorized reproduction of their copyrighted programs, software companies began to experiment with a variety of technologies aimed at limiting access and the ability to copy. Some of these technologies frustrated legitimate users, who experienced problems running the programs they'd paid for and even, on occasion, computer crashes. And almost as quickly as software companies introduced new technological protections, hackers developed ways to defeat them. By the early 1990s, the software industry had significantly reduced its reliance on copy-protection technologies. On the other hand, simple access-protection technologies, such as access codes, remained in widespread use.

B. The Audio Home Recording Act

The use of technological protections took an important turn with the introduction, first in Japan and then in the United States, of the digital audiotape (DAT) recording format—the first widely-distributed digital copying technology. After prolonged negotiations, the consumer electronics companies and music and recording industry firms involved in the conception and rollout of DAT coordinated on a technical protocol for DAT copy protection—the so-called Serial Copy Management System (SCMS)—and agreed to include SCMS in all consumer DAT recorders. SCMS allowed the making of first-generation copies (copies made from source material) at the same fidelity as the source material, but blocked subsequent-generation or "serial" copies (copies made from copies).

The firms behind SCMS also sought to have their favored technological protection measure adopted and enforced by law. In 1992, Congress acceded to this desire, passing the Audio Home Recording Act (AHRA), which you first encountered in your study of the music industry in Chapter V. The AHRA requires that all "digital audio recording devices" incorporate SCMS, and it bans the manufacture or distribution of any device or the provision of any service that would circumvent SCMS. 17 U.S.C. § 1002. Note that the statute's definition of "digital audio recording device" limits the AHRA's coverage to devices that are specifically marketed as digital audio recording devices, such as CD-R recorders when marketed as standalone devices. It does not cover general-purpose computers, even though they are often used to copy digital audio files:

> A "digital audio recording device" is any machine or device of a type commonly distributed to individuals for use by individuals, whether or not included with or as part of some other machine or device, the digital recording function of which is designed or marketed for the primary purpose of, and that is capable of, making a digital audio copied recording for private use.

Id. § 1001(3). Thus, the boundary between what is and is not covered by the AHRA is determined by whether or not a particular device is marketed or designed to make audio recordings, not the device's capabilities. An iPhone or Android phone that includes a capability to copy digital audio files is not a "digital audio recording device" under the AHRA, because those devices are not marketed primarily for making copies of music.

Further—as you read in Chapter V—the AHRA requires manufacturers of digital audio recording devices for the consumer market to pay royalties on digital audio recording media and equipment marketed to consumers (as opposed to professionals). Royalties collected under the AHRA scheme are pooled and then divided among copyright owners of sound recordings and musical compositions, as well as featured recording artists, with a small percentage paid to non-featured musicians and vocalists. *Id.* §§ 1003-1007. The AHRA bars infringement actions against consumers for personal, noncommercial copying, and similarly bars actions against manufacturers and distributors of covered digital audio recording devices and media. *Id.* § 1008.

The AHRA's scheme of mandated technical protections against serial copying—a statutory levy that is applied to copying equipment and media, the division of pooled royalties among copyright owners and other market participants, and immunity from suit for use of covered technology—was a unique approach to the copyright issues raised by digital copying technologies. The approach has, however, largely been superseded by technological developments. Most audio (and other) copying these days is undertaken using general-purpose computers and other devices, such as smartphones, rather than the specialized devices covered by the AHRA.

C. The Digital Millennium Copyright Act

Although the rapid technological progression from specialized digital recording devices to the use of general-purpose computers to reproduce, distribute, and modify digital files made the AHRA largely obsolete, content owners remained interested in bolstering federal law with provisions that reinforce technological protections by banning the use or distribution of technologies aimed at circumventing these protections. But opposition from technology companies, librarians, consumer groups, and others was sufficient to counter the push to provide legal anti-circumvention protection. The stalemate was broken in 1996 at the international conference held to draft the World Intellectual Property Organization Copyright Treaty. Representatives at that proceeding agreed to a provision, adopted as Article 11 of the treaty, that mandates the adoption of legal protections against the circumvention of technological protection measures:

Contracting Parties shall provide adequate legal protection and effective legal remedies against the circumvention of effective technological measures that are used by authors in connection with the exercise of their rights under this Treaty or the Berne Convention and that restrict acts, in respect of their works, which are not authorized by the authors concerned or permitted by law.

Their hand strengthened by the treaty mandate, supporters of anti-circumvention protections prevailed in a renewed U.S. lobbying campaign, and the protections were enacted as part of the Digital Millennium Copyright Act of 1998 (DMCA). The DMCA's anti-circumvention provisions were codified principally in 17 U.S.C. § 1201.

1. Section 1201

There are two key distinctions that drive the structure of § 1201. First, § 1201 distinguishes between technologies that control *access* to a copyrighted work and those that control *rights*—that is, technologies that "effectively protect the right of a copyright owner." Second, § 1201 distinguishes between *individual acts of circumvention* and the *distribution of technologies designed to aid in circumvention*.

These two distinctions are reflected in the particular subparts of § 1201, which can be summarized as follows:

1) § 1201(a)(1) prohibits *individual acts* of circumvention of *access controls*;
2) § 1201(a)(2) prohibits *distribution* of technologies designed to aid in circumvention of *access controls*;
3) § 1201(b) prohibits *distribution* of technologies designed to aid in circumvention of *rights controls*; and
4) nothing in § 1201 prohibits *individual acts of* circumvention of *rights controls*.

Violations of § 1201 do not constitute copyright infringement. Rather, they are violations of the DMCA. Section 1203 sets out the civil remedies that provided under the DMCA, and § 1204 does the same for the criminal remedies that the DMCA provides.

Why do you think that copyright holders find it useful to have legal protection against circumvention of their access or rights controls? What might happen without such legal protection? Does the addition of § 1201 raise any worries about upsetting the internal balances of copyright law or of harms to the public that might arise from providing anti-circumvention protections? In particular, what if a member of the public wants to engage in a fair use of a work that is protected by an access control? By a rights control? Note in particular that because § 1201 leaves unregulated individual circumvention of rights controls, an individual who has lawful access to a work is free to circumvent rights controls to make a use permitted by fair use. That same freedom, as we shall see, does not apply to circumvention of *access controls* for the purpose of making a fair use.

2. Section 1201 Triennial Review

Section 1201(a)(1) also includes what Congress characterized as a "fail-safe" mechanism: a triennial review. This review requires the Librarian of Congress, following a rulemaking proceeding held every three years, to exempt from the DMCA's prohibition on circumvention any class of copyrighted works as to which the Librarian has determined that non-infringing uses are, or are likely to be, adversely affected by circumvention prohibition in the succeeding three-year period. The Librarian's determination to grant an exemption is based upon the recommendation of the Register of Copyrights, who conducts the rulemaking proceeding. The Register, in turn, consults with the Assistant Secretary for Communications and Information of the Department of Commerce, who oversees the National Telecommunications and Information Administration.

Chapter IX – Technological Protections

The primary responsibility of the Register and the Librarian in the rulemaking proceeding is to assess whether the implementation of *access controls* within the meaning of § 1201(a)(1) impairs the ability of individuals to make non-infringing uses of copyrighted works. Significantly, the exemptions do not apply to other parts of § 1201. Most notably, exemptions do not apply to § 1201(a)(2), which bars trafficking in products and services used to circumvent access controls, or § 1201(b), which bars trafficking in products and services used to circumvent rights controls. Why do you think that exemptions apply only to access controls? And why do you think they apply only to individual uses of circumvention technologies, and not "trafficking" of those technologies by others?

In considering exemptions, the Register develops a comprehensive administrative record using information submitted by interested members of the public and makes recommendations to the Librarian concerning whether exemptions are warranted based on that record. Under the statutory framework, the Librarian, and thus the Register, must consider "(i) the availability for use of copyrighted works; (ii) the availability for use of works for nonprofit archival, preservation, and educational purposes; (iii) the impact that the prohibition on the circumvention of technological measures applied to copyrighted works has on criticism, comment, news reporting, teaching, scholarship, or research; (iv) the effect of circumvention of technological measures on the market for or value of copyrighted works; and (v) such other factors as the Librarian considers appropriate." 17 U.S.C. § 1201(a)(1)(C).

The most recent triennial review was conducted in 2021. The Library of Congress broadened a variety of exemptions for the diagnosis, maintenance, and repair of consumer devices that rely on software to function, and expanded the categories of people able to take advantage of a previously-granted exemption for reproducing clips of audiovisual works for educational use. The Library also renewed other important exemptions that had previously been granted. For a complete list of exemptions, see https://www.govinfo.gov/content/pkg/FR-2022-03-25/pdf/2022-06264.pdf.

> As you read the next case, think about whether the court has provided an adequate account of its characterization of the technological protection at issue as an access control. Think about whether the characterization of the technological protection as controlling access rather than protecting a copyright owner's rights makes a difference to the outcome of the case.

Universal City Studios, Inc. v. Reimerdes
111 F. Supp. 2d 294 (S.D.N.Y. 2000)

KAPLAN, J.:

[1] Plaintiffs, eight major United States motion picture studios, distribute many of their copyrighted motion pictures for home use on digital versatile disks ("DVDs"), which contain copies of the motion pictures in digital form. They protect those motion pictures from copying by using an encryption system called CSS. CSS-protected motion pictures on DVDs may be viewed only on players and computer drives equipped with licensed technology that permits the devices to decrypt and play—but not to copy—the films.

[2] Late last year, computer hackers devised a computer program called DeCSS that circumvents the CSS protection system and allows CSS-protected motion pictures to be copied and played on devices that lack the licensed decryption technology. Defendants quickly posted DeCSS on their Internet web site, thus making it readily available to much of the world. Plaintiffs promptly brought this action under the Digital Millennium Copyright Act to enjoin defendants from posting DeCSS and to prevent them from electronically "linking"

their site to others that post DeCSS. Defendants responded with what they termed "electronic civil disobedience"—increasing their efforts to link their web site to a large number of others that continue to make DeCSS available.

[3] Defendants contend that their actions do not violate the DMCA and, in any case, that the DMCA, as applied to computer programs, or code, violates the First Amendment....

[4] CSS, or Content Scramble System, is an access control and copy prevention system for DVDs developed by the motion picture companies, including plaintiffs. It is an encryption-based system that requires the use of appropriately configured hardware such as a DVD player or a computer DVD drive to decrypt, unscramble and play back, but not copy, motion pictures on DVDs. The technology necessary to configure DVD players and drives to play CSS-protected DVDs has been licensed to hundreds of manufacturers in the United States and around the world.

[5] DeCSS is a software utility, or computer program, that enables users to break the CSS copy protection system and hence to view DVDs on unlicensed players and make digital copies of DVD movies. The quality of motion pictures decrypted by DeCSS is virtually identical to that of encrypted movies on DVD....

[6] Plaintiffs are eight major motion picture studios....

[7] Defendant Eric Corley is viewed as a leader of the computer hacker community and goes by the name Emmanuel Goldstein, after the leader of the underground in George Orwell's classic, *1984*.... In addition, defendants operate a web site located at <http://www.2600.com> ....

[8] Prior to January 2000, when this action was commenced, defendants posted the source and object code for DeCSS on the 2600.com web site, from which they could be downloaded easily. At that time, 2600.com contained also a list of links to other web sites purporting to post DeCSS....

[9] The major motion picture studios typically distribute films in a sequence of so-called windows, each window referring to a separate channel of distribution and thus to a separate source of revenue. The first window generally is theatrical release, distribution, and exhibition. Subsequently, films are distributed to airlines and hotels, then to the home market, then to pay television, cable and, eventually, free television broadcast. The home market is important to plaintiffs, as it represents a significant source of revenue.

[10] Motion pictures first were, and still are, distributed to the home market in the form of video cassette tapes. In the early 1990's, however, the major movie studios began to explore distribution to the home market in digital format, which offered substantially higher audio and visual quality and greater longevity than video cassette tapes. This technology, which in 1995 became what is known today as DVD, brought with it a new problem—increased risk of piracy by virtue of the fact that digital files, unlike the material on video cassettes, can be copied without degradation from generation to generation....

[11] Discussions among the studios with the goal of organizing a unified response to the piracy threat began in earnest in late 1995 or early 1996.... In 1996, Matsushita Electric Industrial Co. and Toshiba Corp., presented—and the studios adopted—CSS....

[12] CSS involves encrypting, according to an encryption algorithm, the digital sound and graphics files on a DVD that together constitute a motion picture. A CSS-protected DVD can be decrypted by an appropriate decryption algorithm that employs a series of keys stored on the DVD and the DVD player. In consequence, only players and drives containing the appropriate keys are able to decrypt DVD files and thereby play movies stored on DVDs.

[13] As the motion picture companies did not themselves develop CSS and, in any case, are not in the business of making DVD players and drives, the technology for making compliant devices, i.e., devices with CSS keys, had to be licensed to consumer electronics manufacturers. In order to ensure that the decryption technology did not become generally available and that compliant devices could not be used to copy as well as merely to play CSS-protected movies, the technology is licensed subject to strict security requirements. Moreover, manufacturers may not, consistent with their licenses, make equipment that would supply digital output that could be used in copying protected DVDs....

[14] With CSS in place, the studios introduced DVDs on the consumer market in early 1997. All or most of the motion pictures released on DVD were, and continue to be, encrypted with CSS technology....

[15] In late September 1999, Jon Johansen, a Norwegian subject then fifteen years of age, and two individuals he "met" under pseudonyms over the Internet, reverse engineered a licensed DVD player and discovered the CSS encryption algorithm and keys. They used this information to create DeCSS, a program capable of decrypting or "ripping" encrypted DVDs, thereby allowing playback on non-compliant computers as well as the copying of decrypted files to computer hard drives. Mr. Johansen then posted the executable code on his personal Internet web site and informed members of an Internet mailing list that he had done so. Neither Mr. Johansen nor his collaborators obtained a license from the DVD [Copy Control Association administering CSS].

[16] Although Mr. Johansen testified at trial that he created DeCSS in order to make a DVD player that would operate on a computer running the Linux operating system, DeCSS is a Windows executable file; that is, it can be executed only on computers running the Windows operating system. Mr. Johansen explained the fact that he created a Windows rather than a Linux program by asserting that Linux, at the time he created DeCSS, did not support the file system used on DVDs. Hence, it was necessary, he said, to decrypt the DVD on a Windows computer in order subsequently to play the decrypted files on a Linux machine. Assuming that to be true, however, the fact remains that Mr. Johansen created DeCSS in the full knowledge that it could be used on computers running Windows rather than Linux. Moreover, he was well aware that the files, once decrypted, could be copied like any other computer files....

[17] In November 1999, defendants' web site began to offer DeCSS for download. It established also a list of links to several web sites that purportedly "mirrored" or offered DeCSS for download. The links on defendants' mirror list fall into one of three categories. By clicking the mouse on one of these links, the user may be brought to a page on the linked-to site on which there appears a further link to the DeCSS software. If the user then clicks on the DeCSS link, download of the software begins. This page may or may not contain content other than the DeCSS link. Alternatively, the user may be brought to a page on the linked-to site that does not itself purport to link to DeCSS, but that links, either directly or via a series of other pages on the site, to another page on the site on which there appears a link to the DeCSS software. Finally, the user may be brought directly to the DeCSS link on the linked-to site such that download of DeCSS begins immediately without further user intervention....

[18] .... In January 2000, the studios filed this lawsuit against defendant Eric Corley and two others....

[19] Following the issuance of [a] preliminary injunction, defendants removed DeCSS from the 2600.com web site. In what they termed an act of "electronic civil disobedience," however, they continued to support links to other web sites purporting to offer DeCSS for download, a list which had grown to nearly five hundred by July 2000....

[20] .... [T]he availability of DeCSS on the Internet effectively has compromised plaintiffs' system of copyright protection for DVDs, requiring them either to tolerate increased piracy or to expend resources to develop and

implement a replacement system unless the availability of DeCSS is terminated. It is analogous to the publication of a bank vault combination in a national newspaper. Even if no one uses the combination to open the vault, its mere publication has the effect of defeating the bank's security system, forcing the bank to reprogram the lock. Development and implementation of a new DVD copy protection system, however, is far more difficult and costly than reprogramming a combination lock and may carry with it the added problem of rendering the existing installed base of compliant DVD players obsolete....

II. The Digital Millennium Copyright Act ...

[21] The DMCA contains two principal anticircumvention provisions. The first, Section 1201(a)(1), governs "[t]he act of circumventing a technological protection measure put in place by a copyright owner to control access to a copyrighted work," an act described by Congress as "the electronic equivalent of breaking into a locked room in order to obtain a copy of a book." The second, Section 1201(a)(2), which is the focus of this case, "supplements the prohibition against the act of circumvention in paragraph (a)(1) with prohibitions on creating and making available certain technologies ... developed or advertised to defeat technological protections against unauthorized access to a work." As defendants are accused here only of posting and linking to other sites posting DeCSS, and not of using it themselves to bypass plaintiffs' access controls, it is principally the second of the anticircumvention provisions that is at issue in this case.

B. Posting of DeCSS

1. Violation of Anti–Trafficking Provision

[22] Section 1201(a)(2) of the Copyright Act, part of the DMCA, provides that:

No person shall ... offer to the public, provide or otherwise traffic in any technology ... that—

> *(A) is primarily designed or produced for the purpose of circumventing a technological measure that effectively controls access to a work protected under [the Copyright Act];*
> *(B) has only limited commercially significant purpose or use other than to circumvent a technological measure that effectively controls access to a work protected under [the Copyright Act]; or*
> *(C) is marketed by that person or another acting in concert with that person with that person's knowledge for use in circumventing a technological measure that effectively controls access to a work protected under [the Copyright Act]."*

[23] In this case, defendants concededly offered and provided and, absent a court order, would continue to offer and provide DeCSS to the public by making it available for download on the 2600.com web site. DeCSS, a computer program, unquestionably is "technology" within the meaning of the statute. "[C]ircumvent a technological measure" is defined to mean descrambling a scrambled work, decrypting an encrypted work, or "otherwise to avoid, bypass, remove, deactivate, or impair a technological measure, without the authority of the copyright owner," 17 U.S.C. § 1201(a)(3)(A), so DeCSS clearly is a means of circumventing a technological access control measure.[137] In consequence, if CSS otherwise falls within paragraphs (A), (B) or (C) of Section

---

[137] Decryption or avoidance of an access control measure is not "circumvention" within the meaning of the statute unless it occurs "without the authority of the copyright owner." 17 U.S.C. § 1201(a)(3)(A). Defendants posit that purchasers of a DVD acquire the right "to perform all acts with it that are not exclusively granted to the copyright holder." Based on this premise, they argue that DeCSS does not circumvent CSS within the meaning of the statute because the Copyright Act does not grant the copyright holder the right to prohibit purchasers from decrypting. As the copyright holder has no statutory right to prohibit decryption, the argument goes, decryption cannot be understood as unlawful circumvention.

1201(a)(2), and if none of the statutory exceptions applies to their actions, defendants have violated and, unless enjoined, will continue to violate the DMCA by posting DeCSS.

a. Section 1201(a)(2)(A) ...

[24] During pretrial proceedings and at trial, defendants attacked plaintiffs' Section 1201(a)(2)(A) claim, arguing that CSS, which is based on a 40-bit encryption key, is a weak cipher that does not "effectively control" access to plaintiffs' copyrighted works.... [T]he contention is indefensible as a matter of law.

[25] First, the statute expressly provides that "a technological measure 'effectively controls access to a work' if the measure, in the ordinary course of its operation, requires the application of information or a process or a treatment, with the authority of the copyright owner, to gain access to a work." 17 U.S.C. § 1201(a)(3)(B). One cannot gain access to a CSS-protected work on a DVD without application of the three keys that are required by the software. One cannot lawfully gain access to the keys except by entering into a license with the DVD [Copy Control Association] under authority granted by the copyright owners or by purchasing a DVD player or drive containing the keys pursuant to such a license. In consequence, under the express terms of the statute, CSS "effectively controls access" to copyrighted DVD movies. It does so, within the meaning of the statute, whether or not it is a strong means of protection....

[26] As CSS effectively controls access to plaintiffs' copyrighted works, the only remaining question under Section 1201(a)(2)(A) is whether DeCSS was designed primarily to circumvent CSS. The answer is perfectly obvious. By the admission of both Jon Johansen, the programmer who principally wrote DeCSS, and defendant Corley, DeCSS was created solely for the purpose of decrypting CSS—that is all it does. Hence, absent satisfaction of a statutory exception, defendants clearly violated Section 1201(a)(2)(A) by posting DeCSS to their web site....

[27] Perhaps the centerpiece of defendants' statutory position is the contention that DeCSS was not created for the purpose of pirating copyrighted motion pictures. Rather, they argue, it was written to further the development of a DVD player that would run under the Linux operating system, as there allegedly were no Linux compatible players on the market at the time....

[28] As the earlier discussion demonstrates, the question whether the development of a Linux DVD player motivated those who wrote DeCSS is immaterial to the question whether the defendants now before the Court violated the anti-trafficking provision of the DMCA. The inescapable facts are that (1) CSS is a technological means that effectively controls access to plaintiffs' copyrighted works, (2) the one and only function of DeCSS is to circumvent CSS, and (3) defendants offered and provided DeCSS by posting it on their web site. Whether defendants did so in order to infringe, or to permit or encourage others to infringe, copyrighted works in violation of other provisions of the Copyright Act simply does not matter for purposes of Section 1201(a)(2). The offering or provision of the program is the prohibited conduct—and it is prohibited irrespective of why the program was written, except to whatever extent motive may be germane to determining whether their conduct falls within one of the statutory exceptions.

The argument is pure sophistry. The DMCA proscribes trafficking in technology that decrypts or avoids an access control measure without the copyright holder consenting to the decryption or avoidance. Defendants' argument seems to be a corruption of the first sale doctrine, which holds that the copyright holder, notwithstanding the exclusive distribution right conferred by Section 106(3) of the Copyright Act is deemed by its "first sale" of a copy of the copyrighted work to have consented to subsequent sale of the copy.

2. Statutory Exceptions

[29] Earlier in the litigation, defendants contended that their activities came within several exceptions contained in the DMCA and the Copyright Act and constitute fair use under the Copyright Act. Their post-trial memorandum appears to confine their argument to the reverse engineering exception. In any case, all of their assertions are entirely without merit....

[30] Defendants claim to fall under Section 1201(f) of the statute, which provides in substance that one may circumvent, or develop and employ technological means to circumvent, access control measures in order to achieve interoperability with another computer program provided that doing so does not infringe another's copyright and, in addition, that one may make information acquired through such efforts "available to others, if the person [in question] ... provides such information solely for the purpose of enabling interoperability of an independently created computer program with other programs, and to the extent that doing so does not constitute infringement...." They contend that DeCSS is necessary to achieve interoperability between computers running the Linux operating system and DVDs and that this exception therefore is satisfied. This contention fails.

[31] First, Section 1201(f)(3) permits information acquired through reverse engineering to be made available to others only by the person who acquired the information. But these defendants did not do any reverse engineering. They simply took DeCSS off someone else's web site and posted it on their own.

[32] Defendants would be in no stronger position even if they had authored DeCSS. The right to make the information available extends only to dissemination "solely for the purpose" of achieving interoperability as defined in the statute. It does not apply to public dissemination of means of circumvention, as the legislative history confirms. These defendants, however, did not post DeCSS "solely" to achieve interoperability with Linux or anything else.

[33] Finally, it is important to recognize that even the creators of DeCSS cannot credibly maintain that the "sole" purpose of DeCSS was to create a Linux DVD player. DeCSS concededly was developed on and runs under Windows—a far more widely used operating system. The developers of DeCSS therefore knew that DeCSS could be used to decrypt and play DVD movies on Windows as well as Linux machines. They knew also that the decrypted files could be copied like any other unprotected computer file. Moreover, the Court does not credit Mr. Johansen's testimony that he created DeCSS solely for the purpose of building a Linux player....

[34] Section 1201(g)(4) provides in relevant part that:

> *Notwithstanding the provisions of subsection (a)(2), it is not a violation of that subsection for a person to—*
>
>> *(A) develop and employ technological means to circumvent a technological measure for the sole purpose of that person performing the acts of good faith encryption research described in paragraph (2); and*
>> *(B) provide the technological means to another person with whom he or she is working collaboratively for the purpose of conducting the acts of good faith encryption research described in paragraph (2) or for the purpose of having that other person verify his or her acts of good faith encryption research described in paragraph (2).*

[35] Paragraph (2) in relevant part permits circumvention of technological measures in the course of good faith encryption research if:

(A) the person lawfully obtained the encrypted copy, phonorecord, performance, or display of the published work;

(B) such act is necessary to conduct such encryption research;

(C) the person made a good faith effort to obtain authorization before the circumvention; and

(D) such act does not constitute infringement under this title....

[36] In determining whether one is engaged in good faith encryption research, the Court is instructed to consider factors including whether the results of the putative encryption research are disseminated in a manner designed to advance the state of knowledge of encryption technology versus facilitation of copyright infringement, whether the person in question is engaged in legitimate study of or work in encryption, and whether the results of the research are communicated in a timely fashion to the copyright owner.

[37] Neither of the defendants remaining in this case was or is involved in good faith encryption research. They posted DeCSS for all the world to see. There is no evidence that they made any effort to provide the results of the DeCSS effort to the copyright owners. Surely there is no suggestion that either of them made a good faith effort to obtain authorization from the copyright owners. Accordingly, defendants are not protected by Section 1201(g)....

[38] Finally, defendants rely on the doctrine of fair use. Stated in its most general terms, the doctrine, now codified in Section 107 of the Copyright Act, limits the exclusive rights of a copyright holder by permitting others to make limited use of portions of the copyrighted work, for appropriate purposes, free of liability for copyright infringement. For example, it is permissible for one other than the copyright owner to reprint or quote a suitable part of a copyrighted book or article in certain circumstances. The doctrine traditionally has facilitated literary and artistic criticism, teaching and scholarship, and other socially useful forms of expression. It has been viewed by courts as a safety valve that accommodates the exclusive rights conferred by copyright with the freedom of expression guaranteed by the First Amendment.

[39] The use of technological means of controlling access to a copyrighted work may affect the ability to make fair uses of the work. Focusing specifically on the facts of this case, the application of CSS to encrypt a copyrighted motion picture requires the use of a compliant DVD player to view or listen to the movie. Perhaps more significantly, it prevents exact copying of either the video or the audio portion of all or any part of the film. This latter point means that certain uses that might qualify as "fair" for purposes of copyright infringement—for example, the preparation by a film studies professor of a single CD-ROM or tape containing two scenes from different movies in order to illustrate a point in a lecture on cinematography, as opposed to showing relevant parts of two different DVDs—would be difficult or impossible absent circumvention of the CSS encryption. Defendants therefore argue that the DMCA cannot properly be construed to make it difficult or impossible to make any fair use of plaintiffs' copyrighted works and that the statute therefore does not reach their activities, which are simply a means to enable users of DeCSS to make such fair uses.

[40] Defendants have focused on a significant point. Access control measures such as CSS do involve some risk of preventing lawful as well as unlawful uses of copyrighted material. Congress, however, clearly faced up to and dealt with this question in enacting the DMCA.

[41] The Court begins its statutory analysis, as it must, with the language of the statute. Section 107 of the Copyright Act provides in critical part that certain uses of copyrighted works that otherwise would be wrongful are "not ... infringement[s] of copyright." Defendants, however, are not here sued for copyright infringement. They are sued for offering and providing technology designed to circumvent technological measures that control access to copyrighted works and otherwise violating Section 1201(a)(2) of the Act. If Congress had meant the fair use defense to apply to such actions, it would have said so. Indeed, as the

legislative history demonstrates, the decision not to make fair use a defense to a claim under Section 1201(a) was quite deliberate.

[42] Congress was well aware during the consideration of the DMCA of the traditional role of the fair use defense in accommodating the exclusive rights of copyright owners with the legitimate interests of noninfringing users of portions of copyrighted works. It recognized the contention, voiced by a range of constituencies concerned with the legislation, that technological controls on access to copyrighted works might erode fair use by preventing access even for uses that would be deemed "fair" if only access might be gained. And it struck a balance among the competing interests.

[43] The first element of the balance was the careful limitation of Section 1201(a)(1)'s prohibition of the act of circumvention to the act itself so as not to apply to subsequent actions of a person once he or she has obtained authorized access to a copy of a [copyrighted] work. By doing so, it left the traditional defenses to copyright infringement, including fair use, fully applicable provided the access is authorized.

[44] Second, Congress delayed the effective date of Section 1201(a)(1)'s prohibition of the act of circumvention for two years pending further investigation about how best to reconcile Section 1201(a)(1) with fair use concerns. Following that investigation, which is being carried out in the form of a rule-making by the Register of Copyright, the prohibition will not apply to users of particular classes of copyrighted works who demonstrate that their ability to make noninfringing uses of those classes of works would be affected adversely by Section 1201(a)(1).

[45] Third, it created a series of exceptions to aspects of Section 1201(a) for certain uses that Congress thought "fair," including reverse engineering, security testing, good faith encryption research, and certain uses by nonprofit libraries, archives and educational institutions.

[46] Defendants claim also that the possibility that DeCSS might be used for the purpose of gaining access to copyrighted works in order to make fair use of those works saves them under *Sony Corp. v. Universal City Studios, Inc.* But they are mistaken. *Sony* does not apply to the activities with which defendants here are charged. Even if it did, it would not govern here....

[47] When *Sony* was decided, the only question was whether the manufacturers could be held liable for infringement by those who purchased equipment from them in circumstances in which there were many noninfringing uses for their equipment. But that is not the question now before this Court. The question here is whether the possibility of noninfringing fair use by someone who gains access to a protected copyrighted work through a circumvention technology distributed by the defendants saves the defendants from liability under Section 1201. But nothing in Section 1201 so suggests. By prohibiting the provision of circumvention technology, the DMCA fundamentally altered the landscape. A given device or piece of technology might have a substantial noninfringing use, and hence be immune from attack under *Sony*'s construction of the Copyright Act—but nonetheless still be subject to suppression under Section 1201. Indeed, Congress explicitly noted that Section 1201 does not incorporate *Sony*.

[48] The policy concerns raised by defendants were considered by Congress. Having considered them, Congress crafted a statute that, so far as the applicability of the fair use defense to Section 1201(a) claims is concerned, is crystal clear. In such circumstances, courts may not undo what Congress so plainly has done by "construing" the words of a statute to accomplish a result that Congress rejected. The fact that Congress elected to leave technologically unsophisticated persons who wish to make fair use of encrypted copyrighted works without the technical means of doing so is a matter for Congress unless Congress' decision contravenes the Constitution, a matter to which the Court turns below. Defendants' statutory fair use argument therefore is entirely without merit.

C. Linking to Sites Offering DeCSS

[49] Plaintiffs seek also to enjoin defendants from "linking" their 2600.com web site to other sites that make DeCSS available to users. ... The dispositive question is whether linking to another web site containing DeCSS constitutes "offer[ing DeCSS] to the public" or "provid[ing] or otherwise traffic[king]" in it within the meaning of the DMCA. Answering this question requires careful consideration of the nature and types of linking....

[50] To the extent that defendants have linked to sites that automatically commence the process of downloading DeCSS upon a user being transferred by defendants' hyperlinks, there can be no serious question. Defendants are engaged in the functional equivalent of transferring the DeCSS code to the user themselves.

[51] Substantially the same is true of defendants' hyperlinks to web pages that display nothing more than the DeCSS code or present the user only with the choice of commencing a download of DeCSS and no other content. The only distinction is that the entity extending to the user the option of downloading the program is the transferee site rather than defendants, a distinction without a difference.

[52] Potentially more troublesome might be links to pages that offer a good deal of content other than DeCSS but that offer a hyperlink for downloading, or transferring to a page for downloading, DeCSS. If one assumed, for the purposes of argument, that the *Los Angeles Times* web site somewhere contained the DeCSS code, it would be wrong to say that anyone who linked to the *Los Angeles Times* web site, regardless of purpose or the manner in which the link was described, thereby offered, provided or otherwise trafficked in DeCSS merely because DeCSS happened to be available on a site to which one linked. But that is not this case. Defendants urged others to post DeCSS in an effort to disseminate DeCSS and to inform defendants that they were doing so. Defendants then linked their site to those "mirror" sites, after first checking to ensure that the mirror sites in fact were posting DeCSS or something that looked like it, and proclaimed on their own site that DeCSS could be had by clicking on the hyperlinks on defendants' site. By doing so, they offered, provided or otherwise trafficked in DeCSS, and they continue to do so to this day....

[53] Defendants argue that the DMCA, at least as applied to prevent the public dissemination of DeCSS, violates the First Amendment to the Constitution. They claim that it does so in two ways. First, they argue that computer code is protected speech and that the DMCA's prohibition of dissemination of DeCSS therefore violates defendants' First Amendment rights. Second, they contend that the DMCA is unconstitutionally overbroad, chiefly because its prohibition of the dissemination of decryption technology prevents third parties from making fair use of plaintiffs' encrypted works, and vague. They argue also that a prohibition on their linking to sites that make DeCSS available is unconstitutional for much the same reasons....

[54] Defendants' assertion that computer code is "protected" by the First Amendment is quite understandable.... All modes of expression are covered by the First Amendment in the sense that the constitutionality of their regulation must be determined by reference to First Amendment doctrine and analysis. Regulation of different categories of expression, however, is subject to varying levels of judicial scrutiny. Thus, to say that a particular form of expression is "protected" by the First Amendment means that the constitutionality of any regulation of it must be measured by reference to the First Amendment. In some circumstances, however, the phrase connotes also that the standard for measurement is the most exacting level available....

[55] Defendants first attack Section 1201(a)(2), the anti-trafficking provision, as applied to them on the theory that DeCSS is constitutionally protected expression and that the statute improperly prevents them from communicating it. Their attack presupposes that a characterization of code as constitutionally protected

subjects any regulation of code to the highest level of First Amendment scrutiny. As we have seen, however, this does not necessarily follow....

[56] Broadly speaking, restrictions on expression fall into two categories. Some are restrictions on the voicing of particular ideas, which typically are referred to as content based restrictions. Others have nothing to do with the content of the expression—i.e., they are content neutral—but they have the incidental effect of limiting expression.

[57] In general, government has no power to restrict expression because of its message, its ideas, its subject matter, or its content.... In consequence, content based restrictions on speech are permissible only if they serve compelling state interests by the least restrictive means available.

[58] Content neutral restrictions, in contrast, are measured against a less exacting standard. Because restrictions of this type are not motivated by a desire to limit the message, they will be upheld if they serve a substantial governmental interest and restrict First Amendment freedoms no more than necessary....

[59] The reason that Congress enacted the anti-trafficking provision of the DMCA had nothing to do with suppressing particular ideas of computer programmers and everything to do with functionality—with preventing people from circumventing technological access control measures—just as laws prohibiting the possession of burglar tools have nothing to do with preventing people from expressing themselves by accumulating what to them may be attractive assortments of implements and everything to do with preventing burglaries. Rather, it is focused squarely upon the effect of the distribution of the functional capability that the code provides. Any impact on the dissemination of programmers' ideas is purely incidental to the overriding concerns of promoting the distribution of copyrighted works in digital form while at the same time protecting those works from piracy and other violations of the exclusive rights of copyright holders....

[60] Congress is not powerless to adopt content neutral regulations that incidentally affect expression, including the dissemination of the functional capabilities of computer code. A sufficiently important governmental interest in seeing to it that computers are not instructed to perform particular functions may justify incidental restrictions on the dissemination of the expressive elements of a program. Such a regulation will be upheld if it furthers an important or substantial governmental interest; if the governmental interest is unrelated to the suppression of free expression; and if the incidental restriction on alleged First Amendment freedoms is no greater than is essential to the furtherance of that interest.

[61] Moreover, to satisfy this standard, a regulation need not be the least speech-restrictive means of advancing the Government's interests. Rather, the requirement of narrow tailoring is satisfied so long as the regulation promotes a substantial government interest that would be achieved less effectively absent the regulation.

[62] The anti-trafficking provision of the DMCA furthers an important governmental interest—the protection of copyrighted works stored on digital media from the vastly expanded risk of piracy in this electronic age. The substantiality of that interest is evident both from the fact that the Constitution specifically empowers Congress to provide for copyright protection and from the significance to our economy of trade in copyrighted materials. Indeed, the Supreme Court has made clear that copyright protection itself is the engine of free expression. That substantial interest, moreover, is unrelated to the suppression of particular views expressed in means of gaining access to protected copyrighted works. Nor is the incidental restraint on protected expression—the prohibition of trafficking in means that would circumvent controls limiting access to unprotected materials or to copyrighted materials for noninfringing purposes—broader than is necessary

to accomplish Congress' goals of preventing infringement and promoting the availability of content in digital form....

[63] Defendants' second focus is the contention that Section 1201(a)(2) is unconstitutional because it prevents others from making fair use of copyrighted works by depriving them of the means of circumventing plaintiffs' access control system. In substance, they contend that the anti-trafficking provision leaves those who lack sufficient technical expertise to circumvent CSS themselves without the means of acquiring circumvention technology that they need to make fair use of the content of plaintiffs' copyrighted DVDs....

[64] The DMCA does have a notable potential impact on uses that copy portions of a DVD movie because compliant DVD players are designed so as to prevent copying. In consequence, even though the fair use doctrine permits limited copying of copyrighted works in appropriate circumstances, the CSS encryption of DVD movies, coupled with the characteristics of licensed DVD players, limits such uses absent circumvention of CSS. Moreover, the anti-trafficking provision of the DMCA may prevent technologically unsophisticated persons who wish to copy portions of DVD movies for fair use from obtaining the means of doing so. It is the interests of these individuals upon which defendants rely most heavily in contending that the DMCA violates the First Amendment because it deprives such persons of an asserted constitutional right to make fair use of copyrighted materials.

[65] As the foregoing suggests, the interests of persons wishing to circumvent CSS in order to make lawful use of the copyrighted movies it protects are remarkably varied. Some presumably are technologically sophisticated and therefore capable of circumventing CSS without access to defendants' or other purveyors' decryption programs; many presumably are not. Many of the possible fair uses may be made without circumventing CSS while others, i.e., those requiring copying, may not. Hence, the question whether Section 1201(a)(2) as applied here substantially affects rights, much less constitutionally protected rights, of members of the "fair use community" cannot be decided *in bloc*, without consideration of the circumstances of each member or similarly situated groups of members. Thus, the prudential concern with ensuring that constitutional questions be decided only when the facts before the Court so require counsels against permitting defendants to mount an overbreadth challenge here....

NOTES

1. Do you agree with the court's characterization of CSS as an "access control"? Can (or should) the § 1201 category into which CSS falls be assessed separately from the holistic strategy of which CSS is a part? An aspect of that strategy was to license use of CSS only to manufacturers who agreed not to equip their DVD players with a digital output. So is CSS better characterized as part of a "rights control" strategy? If CSS were characterized as a "rights control" technology, what effect, if any, on the court's decision? For an argument that courts have treated such hybrid or "merged" anti-circumvention technologies as entitled to the legal protections afforded to *both* access and rights controls, see R. Anthony Reese, *Will Merging Access Controls and Rights Controls Undermine the Structure of Anticircumvention Law?*, 18 BERK. TECH. L.J. 619 (2003).

2. CSS also functions to enforce territorial restrictions on the playback of DVDs. That is, DVD players contain codes that restrict playback to DVDs marketed in certain territories. The purpose of the territorial restrictions is to enforce geographic price discrimination. For example, the copyright owner may charge a higher price for a motion picture on DVD in a relatively rich territory (such as North America), versus one that is less well-off (such as India). Is this a desirable use of technological protections? Does it advance the policy goals of the Copyright Act? Why or why not? For an argument that the DVD territorial restrictions are likely to restrict competition and harm social welfare, see Emily Dunt, Joshua S. Gans & Stephen P. King, *The Economic Consequences of DVD Regional Restrictions*, 21 ECON. PAPERS 32 (2002).

3. Review § 1201(a)(3), and also review § 1201(i). Now consider, in light of those provisions, the following questions. If a friend gives you his password to access the *New York Times* website, and you use that password to access the site without yourself purchasing an online subscription, are you circumventing a technological measure? What about if you read nine of the ten free monthly articles that the *New York Times* website permits you to access, and then clear your browser cache so that you can read more articles without purchasing a subscription? Have you circumvented a technological measure within the meaning of the statute? What about if you use Google Chrome's "Incognito Mode" to access articles on the *New York Times* website? Does your use of this feature, which prevents the *New York Times* from keeping count of the articles you view, constitute a circumvention of a technological measure?

4. Do you accept the *Reimerdes* court's argument that the anti-circumvention provisions are not limited by fair use? Review § 1201(c). Why do you think Congress included the language providing that "[n]othing in this section shall affect rights, remedies, limitations, or defenses to copyright infringement, including fair use, under this title"? On appeal, the Second Circuit gave this account of the function of § 1201(c): "[S]ubsection 1201(c)(1) ... simply clarifies that the DMCA targets the *circumvention* of digital walls guarding copyrighted material (and trafficking in circumvention tools), but does not concern itself with the *use* of those materials after circumvention has occurred." Universal City Studios, Inc. v. Corley, 273 F.3d 429, 443 (2d Cir. 2001). Do you agree with that interpretation?

5. The Second Circuit's decision on appeal in *Reimerdes*, Universal City Studios, Inc. v. Corley, 273 F.3d 429 (2d Cir. 2001), also explored the limits of fair use as a "right of access":

> [T]he Appellants have provided no support for their premise that fair use of DVD movies is constitutionally required to be made by copying the original work in its original format. Their examples of the fair uses that they believe others will be prevented from making all involve copying in a digital format those portions of a DVD movie amenable to fair use, a copying that would enable the fair user to manipulate the digitally copied portions.... We know of no authority for the proposition that fair use, as protected by the Copyright Act, much less the Constitution, guarantees copying by the optimum method or in the identical format of the original.... The fact that the resulting copy will not be as perfect or as manipulable as a digital copy obtained by having direct access to the DVD movie in its digital form, provides no basis for a claim of unconstitutional limitation of fair use. A film critic making fair use of a movie by quoting selected lines of dialogue has no constitutionally valid claim that the review (in print or on television) would be technologically superior if the reviewer had not been prevented from using a movie camera in the theater, nor has an art student a valid constitutional claim to fair use of a painting by photographing it in a museum. Fair use has never been held to be a guarantee of access to copyrighted material in order to copy it by the fair user's preferred technique or in the format of the original.

6. Note a potentially important imprecision in the text of § 1201. Specifically, § 1201(a)(1)(A) provides that "[n]o person shall circumvent a technological measure that effectively controls access to a work protected under this title." What does it mean for a technological measure to control access to "a work protected under this title"? The question becomes pressing when we consider whether an individual can circumvent access protections to copy a *public domain* work. Such a work is not "protected under this title," that is, under Title 17, in which the Copyright Act is codified. On one reading of the statutory text, individuals would be entitled to circumvent technological protections that control access to a public domain work. But perhaps there is another reading of the statute that focuses not on the work, but on the particular technological protection measure. If the measure controls access to "a"—that is, to *any*—work protected by copyright, then by this reading it is unlawful for an individual to circumvent it. Which reading of the statute do you think is correct?

And why?

3. Second-Generation DMCA Disputes

Unlike *Reimerdes*, which arose out of efforts to protect against the piracy of copyrighted works, a second wave of DMCA disputes, exemplified by the next two cases, featured use of the DMCA in a bid to limit competition in certain product markets—specifically, in aftermarkets for complementary products (replacement garage door opener remote controls in the first case and replacement inkjet printer cartridges in the second one).

> As you read these cases, ask yourself whether the use made of the DMCA is consistent with the policies underlying the Copyright Act. Is Congress likely to have either foreseen or approved such uses of the DMCA when it added the anti-circumvention provisions to the copyright law? Ask yourself also whether the ways in which the following opinions limit the scope of the DMCA are themselves subject to (metaphorical) circumvention by shifting legal and business strategies.

Chamberlain Group, Inc. v. Skylink Technologies, Inc.
381 F.3d 1178 (Fed. Cir. 2004)

GAJARSA, J.:

[1] The Chamberlain Group, Inc. appeals the ... summary judgment of the United States District Court for the Northern District of Illinois in favor of Skylink Technologies, Inc., finding that Skylink is not violating the anti-trafficking provisions of the Digital Millennium Copyright Act, and dismissing all other claims, including claims of patent infringement....

[2] Chamberlain's claims at issue stem from its allegation that the District Court incorrectly construed the DMCA as placing a burden upon Chamberlain to prove that the circumvention of its technological measures enabled unauthorized access to its copyrighted software. But Skylink's accused device enables only uses that copyright law explicitly authorizes, and is therefore presumptively legal. Chamberlain has neither proved nor alleged a connection between Skylink's accused circumvention device and the protections that the copyright laws afford Chamberlain capable of overcoming that presumption. Chamberlain's failure to meet this burden alone compels a legal ruling in Skylink's favor. We therefore affirm the District Court's summary judgment in favor of Skylink....

[3] .... The matter on appeal involves only Chamberlain's allegation that Skylink is violating the DMCA, specifically the anti-trafficking provision of § 1201(a)(2). The District Court first denied Chamberlain's motion for summary judgment of its DMCA claim, and then granted Skylink's motion for summary judgment on the DMCA claim....

[4] The technology at issue involves Garage Door Openers (GDOs). A GDO typically consists of a hand-held portable transmitter and a garage door opening device mounted in a homeowner's garage. The opening device, in turn, includes both a receiver with associated signal processing software and a motor to open or close the garage door. In order to open or close the garage door, a user must activate the transmitter, which

sends a radio frequency (RF) signal to the receiver located on the opening device. Once the opener receives a recognized signal, the signal processing software directs the motor to open or close the garage door.

[5] When a homeowner purchases a GDO system, the manufacturer provides both an opener and a transmitter. Homeowners who desire replacement or spare transmitters can purchase them in the aftermarket. Aftermarket consumers have long been able to purchase "universal transmitters" that they can program to interoperate with their GDO system regardless of make or model. Skylink and Chamberlain are the only significant distributors of universal GDO transmitters. Chamberlain places no explicit restrictions on the types of transmitter that the homeowner may use with its system at the time of purchase. Chamberlain's customers therefore assume that they enjoy all of the rights associated with the use of their GDOs and any software embedded therein that the copyright laws and other laws of commerce provide.

[6] This dispute involves Chamberlain's Security+ line of GDOs and Skylink's Model 39 universal transmitter. Chamberlain's Security+ GDOs incorporate a copyrighted "rolling code" computer program that constantly changes the transmitter signal needed to open the garage door. Skylink's Model 39 transmitter, which does not incorporate rolling code, nevertheless allows users to operate Security+ openers. Chamberlain alleges that Skylink's transmitter renders the Security+ insecure by allowing unauthorized users to circumvent the security inherent in rolling codes. Of greater legal significance, however, Chamberlain contends that because of this property of the Model 39, Skylink is in violation of the anti-trafficking clause of the DMCA's anticircumvention provisions, specifically § 1201(a)(2).

[7] The code in a standard (i.e., non-rolling code) GDO transmitter is unique but fixed. Thus, according to Chamberlain, the typical GDO is vulnerable to attack by burglars who can open the garage door using a "code grabber." According to Chamberlain, code grabbers allow burglars in close proximity to a homeowner operating her garage door to record the signal sent from the transmitter to the opener, and to return later, replay the recorded signal, and open the garage door. Chamberlain concedes, however, that code grabbers are more theoretical than practical burgling devices; none of its witnesses had either firsthand knowledge of a single code grabbing problem or familiarity with data demonstrating the existence of a problem. Nevertheless, Chamberlain claims to have developed its rolling code system specifically to prevent code grabbing.

[8] The essence of the rolling code system is that the transmitted signals are broken into fixed and variable (or "rolling") components. The entire transmitted signal is a bit string. The fixed component serves to identify the transmitter. The rolling component cycles through a lengthy cycle of bit strings only some of which are capable of opening the door at any given time, ostensibly so that a burglar replaying a grabbed code is unlikely to send a valid signal—and therefore unlikely to open the garage door.

[9] A user wishing to set up a new transmitter for use with her Security+ GDO must switch the opener to "program mode" and send a signal from the transmitter to the opener. The opener stores both the fixed and rolling components of the transmitted signal. When the user switches the opener back to "operate mode," the system is set and the user may operate the opener with the newly programmed transmitter. In Chamberlain's transmitter, a computer program increases the rolling code by a factor of three each time the user activates the transmitter. When the transmitted signal reaches the receiver, a program in the opener checks to see whether the rolling code received was identical to one of the most recently received 1,024 rolling codes (the "rear window"). If so, it will not activate the motor. If, on the other hand, the rolling code received is among the next 4,096 binary signals (the "forward window"), the receiver will activate the motor.

[10] Not all recognized binary rolling signals are in either the forward or rear windows. If the transmitter sends a *single* signal outside of either window, the receiver will ignore it. If, however, the transmitter sends *two* signals outside either window in rapid succession, the opener will again access its programming, this time to

determine whether the two signals together comprise a "resynchronization" sequence. If the signals differ by three, the receiver will reset the windows and activate the motor. According to Chamberlain, resynchronization accommodates the possibility that homeowners using the same transmitter for multiple residences may transmit so many signals while out of range of the opener that they exhaust the entire forward window.

[11] Skylink began marketing and selling universal transmitters in 1992. Skylink designed its Model 39, launched in August 2002, to interoperate with common GDOs, including both rolling code and non-rolling code GDOs. Although Chamberlain concedes that the Model 39 transmitter is capable of operating many different GDOs, it nevertheless asserts that Skylink markets the Model 39 transmitter for use in circumventing its copyrighted rolling code computer program. Chamberlain supports this allegation by pointing to the Model 39's setting that operates *only* Chamberlain's rolling code GDOs.

[12] Skylink's Model 39 *does not* use rolling code technology…. When the homeowner actually uses the transmitter, it broadcasts *three* fixed codes in rapid succession. The first binary signal combines the identifying component with an arbitrary binary sequence. The second binary signal subtracts 1800 from the first signal. The third signal adds three to the second signal. The combination of these three codes transmitted with every press of the Model 39 transmitter button will either cause the Chamberlain GDO to operate in response to the first fixed code or cause the GDO to resynchronize and operate in response to the second and third fixed codes. Chamberlain characterizes this procedure as a circumvention of an important security measure; a code grabber that recorded the Model 39's three codes could later play them back and activate a Chamberlain rolling code GDO without authorization.

[13] …. [I]t is … noteworthy that Chamberlain *has not* alleged either that Skylink infringed its copyright or that Skylink is liable for contributory copyright infringement. What Chamberlain *has* alleged is that because its opener and transmitter both incorporate computer programs "protected by copyright" and because rolling codes are a "technological measure" that "controls access" to those programs, Skylink is prima facie liable for violating § 1201(a)(2). In the District Court's words, "Chamberlain claims that the rolling code computer program has a protective measure that protects itself. Thus, only one computer program is at work here, but it has two functions: (1) to verify the rolling code; and (2) once the rolling code is verified, to activate the GDO motor, by sending instructions to a microprocessor in the GDO." …

[14] The essence of the DMCA's anticircumvention provisions is that §§ 1201(a), (b) establish causes of action for liability. They do not establish a new property right. The DMCA's text indicates that circumvention is not infringement, 17 U.S.C. § 1201(c)(1) ("Nothing in this section shall affect rights, remedies, limitations, or defenses to copyright infringement, including fair use, under this title."), and the statute's structure makes the point even clearer. This distinction between property and liability is critical. Whereas copyrights, like patents, are property, liability protection from unauthorized circumvention merely creates a new cause of action under which a defendant may be liable. The distinction between property and liability goes straight to the issue of authorization, the issue upon which the District Court both denied Chamberlain's and granted Skylink's motion for summary judgment.

[15] A plaintiff alleging copyright infringement need prove *only* (1) ownership of a valid copyright, and (2) copying of constituent elements of the work that are original. The existence of a license, exclusive or nonexclusive, creates an affirmative defense to a claim of copyright infringement. In other words, under Seventh Circuit copyright law, a plaintiff only needs to show that the defendant has used her property; the burden of proving that the use was authorized falls squarely on the defendant. The DMCA, however, *defines* circumvention as an activity undertaken "without the authority of the copyright owner." 17 U.S.C. § 1201(a)(3)(A). The plain language of the statute therefore requires a plaintiff alleging circumvention (or trafficking) to prove that the defendant's access was unauthorized—a significant burden where, as here, the

copyright laws authorize consumers to use the copy of Chamberlain's software embedded in the GDOs that they purchased....

[16] .... According to Chamberlain, the 1998 enactment of the DMCA .... overrode all pre-existing consumer expectations about the legitimate uses of products containing copyrighted embedded software. Chamberlain contends that Congress empowered manufacturers to prohibit consumers from using embedded software products in conjunction with competing products when it passed § 1201(a)(1). According to Chamberlain, *all* such uses of products containing copyrighted software to which a technological measure controlled access are now per se illegal under the DMCA unless the manufacturer provided consumers with *explicit* authorization....

[17] Such an exemption, however, is only plausible if the anticircumvention provisions established a new property right ...—which as we have already explained, they do not.... Contrary to Chamberlain's assertion, the DMCA emphatically *did not* "fundamentally alter" the legal landscape governing the reasonable expectations of consumers or competitors; *did not* "fundamentally alter" the ways that courts analyze industry practices; and *did not* render the pre-DMCA history of the GDO industry irrelevant.

[18] What the DMCA did was introduce new grounds for liability in the context of the unauthorized access of copyrighted material. The statute's plain language requires plaintiffs to prove that those circumventing their technological measures controlling access did so "without the authority of the copyright owner." 17 U.S.C. § 1201(3)(A). Our inquiry ends with that clear language. We note, however, that the statute's structure, legislative history, and context within the Copyright Act all support our construction. They also help to explain why Chamberlain's warranty conditions and website postings cannot render users of Skylink's Model 39 "unauthorized" users for the purposes of establishing trafficking liability under the DMCA....

[19] Though as noted, circumvention *is not* a new form of infringement but rather a new violation prohibiting actions or products that facilitate infringement, it is significant that virtually every clause of § 1201 that mentions "access" links "access" to "protection." ...

[20] Chamberlain urges us to read the DMCA as if Congress simply created a new protection for copyrighted works without any reference at all either to the protections that copyright owners already possess or to the rights that the Copyright Act grants to the public. Chamberlain has not alleged that Skylink's Model 39 infringes its copyrights, nor has it alleged that the Model 39 contributes to third-party infringement of its copyrights. Chamberlain's allegation is considerably more straightforward: The only way for the Model 39 to interoperate with a Security+ GDO is by "accessing" copyrighted software. Skylink has therefore committed a per se violation of the DMCA. Chamberlain urges us to conclude that no necessary connection exists between access and *copyrights*. Congress could not have intended such a broad reading of the DMCA.

[21] Chamberlain derives its strongest claimed support for its proposed construction from the trial court's opinion in *Reimerdes,* a case involving the same statutory provision. Though Chamberlain is correct in considering some of the *Reimerdes* language supportive, it is the differences between the cases, rather than their similarities, that is most instructive in demonstrating precisely what the DMCA permits and what it prohibits....

[22] Chamberlain's proposed construction of the DMCA ignores the significant differences between defendants whose accused products enable copying and those, like Skylink, whose accused products enable only legitimate uses of copyrighted software. Chamberlain's repeated reliance on language targeted at defendants trumpeting their "electronic civil disobedience" apparently led it to misconstrue significant portions of the DMCA. Many of Chamberlain's assertions in its brief to this court conflate the property right of copyright with the liability that the anticircumvention provisions impose.

[23] Chamberlain relies upon the DMCA's prohibition of "fair uses ... as well as foul" to argue that the enactment of the DMCA eliminated all existing consumer expectations about the public's rights to use purchased products because those products might include technological measures controlling access to a copyrighted work. But Chamberlain appears to have overlooked the obvious. The possibility that § 1201 might prohibit some otherwise noninfringing public uses of copyrighted material arises simply because the Congressional decision to create liability and consequent damages for making, using, or selling a "key" that essentially enables a *trespass* upon intellectual property need not be identical in scope to the liabilities and compensable damages for *infringing* that property; it is, instead, a rebalancing of interests that attempts to deal with special problems created by the so-called digital revolution....

[24] .... Were § 1201(a) to allow copyright owners to use technological measures to block *all* access to their copyrighted works, it would effectively create two distinct copyright regimes. In the first regime, the owners of a typical work protected by copyright would possess only the rights enumerated in 17 U.S.C. § 106, subject to the additions, exceptions, and limitations outlined throughout the rest of the Copyright Act—notably but not solely the fair use provisions of § 107. Owners who feel that technology has put those rights at risk, and who incorporate technological measures to protect those rights from technological encroachment, gain the additional ability to hold traffickers in circumvention devices liable under § 1201(b) for putting their rights back at risk by enabling circumventors who use these devices to infringe.

[25] Under the second regime that Chamberlain's proposed construction implies, the owners of a work protected by *both* copyright *and* a technological measure that effectively controls access to that work per § 1201(a) would possess *unlimited* rights to hold circumventors liable under § 1201(a) *merely for accessing that work,* even if that access enabled *only* rights that the Copyright Act grants to the public. This second implied regime would be problematic for a number of reasons. First, as the Supreme Court recently explained, "Congress' exercise of its Copyright Clause authority must be rational." Eldred v. Ashcroft, 537 U.S. 186, 205 n.10 (2003). In determining whether a particular aspect of the Copyright Act "is a rational exercise of the legislative authority conferred by the Copyright Clause ... we defer substantially to Congress. It is Congress that has been assigned the task of defining the scope of the limited monopoly that should be granted to authors ... *in order to give the public appropriate access* to their work product." *Id.* at 204–05 (emphasis added). Chamberlain's proposed construction of § 1201(a) implies that in enacting the DMCA, Congress attempted to "give the public appropriate access" to copyrighted works by allowing copyright owners to deny all access to the public. Even under the substantial deference due Congress, such a redefinition borders on the irrational.

[26] That apparent irrationality, however, is not the most significant problem that this second regime implies. Such a regime would be hard to reconcile with the DMCA's statutory prescription that "[n]othing in this section shall affect rights, remedies, limitations, or defenses to copyright infringement, including fair use, under this title." 17 U.S.C. § 1201(c)(1). A provision that prohibited access without regard to the rest of the Copyright Act would clearly affect rights and limitations, if not remedies and defenses....

[27] Chamberlain's proposed severance of "access" from "protection" in § 1201(a) creates numerous other problems.... Under Chamberlain's proposed construction, explicated at oral argument, disabling a burglar alarm to gain "access" to a home containing copyrighted books, music, art, and periodicals would violate the DMCA; anyone who did so would unquestionably have "circumvent[ed] a technological measure that effectively controls access to a work protected under [the Copyright Act]." § 1201(a)(1). The appropriate deterrents to this type of behavior lie in tort law and criminal law, *not* in copyright law. Yet, were we to read the statute's "plain language" as Chamberlain urges, disabling a burglar alarm would be a per se violation of the DMCA.

[28] In a similar vein, Chamberlain's proposed construction would allow any manufacturer of any product to add a single copyrighted sentence or software fragment to its product, wrap the copyrighted material in a

trivial "encryption" scheme, and thereby gain the right to restrict consumers' rights to use its products in conjunction with competing products. In other words, Chamberlain's construction of the DMCA would allow virtually any company to attempt to leverage its sales into aftermarket monopolies—a practice that both the antitrust laws and the doctrine of copyright misuse normally prohibit....

[29] Finally, the requisite "authorization," on which the District Court granted Skylink summary judgment, points to yet another inconsistency in Chamberlain's proposed construction. The notion of authorization is central to understanding § 1201(a). Underlying Chamberlain's argument on appeal that it has not granted such authorization lies the necessary assumption that Chamberlain is entitled to prohibit legitimate purchasers of its embedded software from "accessing" the software by using it. Such an entitlement, however, would go far beyond the idea that the DMCA allows copyright owner to prohibit "fair uses ... as well as foul." Chamberlain's proposed construction would allow copyright owners to prohibit *exclusively fair* uses even in the absence of any feared foul use. It would therefore allow any copyright owner, through a combination of contractual terms and technological measures, to repeal the fair use doctrine with respect to an individual copyrighted work—or even selected copies of that copyrighted work. Again, this implication contradicts § 1201(c)(1) directly. Copyright law itself authorizes the public to make certain uses of copyrighted materials. Consumers who purchase a product containing a copy of embedded software have the inherent legal right to use that copy of the software. What the law authorizes, Chamberlain cannot revoke....

[30] We therefore reject Chamberlain's proposed construction in its entirety. We conclude that 17 U.S.C. § 1201 prohibits only forms of access that bear a reasonable relationship to the protections that the Copyright Act otherwise affords copyright owners. While such a rule of reason may create some uncertainty and consume some judicial resources, it is the only meaningful reading of the statute. Congress attempted to balance the legitimate interests of copyright owners with those of consumers of copyrighted products. *See* H.R. REP. No. 105–551, at 26 (1998). The courts must adhere to the language that Congress enacted to determine how it attempted to achieve that balance....

[31] The proper construction of § 1201(a)(2) therefore makes it clear that Chamberlain cannot prevail. A plaintiff alleging a violation of § 1201(a)(2) must prove: (1) ownership of a valid *copyright* on a work, (2) effectively controlled by a *technological measure*, which has been circumvented, (3) that third parties can now *access* (4) *without authorization*, in a manner that (5) infringes or facilitates infringing a right *protected* by the Copyright Act, because of a product that (6) the defendant either (i) *designed or produced* primarily for circumvention; (ii) made available despite only *limited commercial significance* other than circumvention; or (iii) *marketed* for use in circumvention of the controlling technological measure. A plaintiff incapable of establishing any one of elements (1) through (5) will have failed to prove a prima facie case. A plaintiff capable of proving elements (1) through (5) need prove only one of (6)(i), (ii), or (iii) to shift the burden back to the defendant. At that point, the various affirmative defenses enumerated throughout § 1201 become relevant....

[32] Chamberlain ... has failed to show not only the requisite lack of authorization, but also the necessary fifth element of its claim, the critical nexus between access and protection. Chamberlain neither alleged copyright infringement *nor explained how the access provided by the Model 39 transmitter facilitates the infringement of any right that the Copyright Act protects.* There can therefore be no reasonable relationship between the access that homeowners gain to Chamberlain's copyrighted software when using Skylink's Model 39 transmitter and the protections that the Copyright Act grants to Chamberlain. The Copyright Act authorized Chamberlain's customers to use the copy of Chamberlain's copyrighted software embedded in the GDOs that they purchased. Chamberlain's customers are therefore immune from § 1201(a)(1) circumvention liability. In the absence of allegations of either copyright infringement or § 1201(a)(1) circumvention, Skylink cannot be liable for § 1201(a)(2) trafficking. The District Court's grant of summary judgment in Skylink's favor was correct. Chamberlain failed to allege a claim under 17 U.S.C. § 1201....

[33] The DMCA does not create a new property right for copyright owners. Nor, for that matter, does it divest the public of the property rights that the Copyright Act has long granted to the public. The anticircumvention and anti-trafficking provisions of the DMCA create new grounds of liability. A copyright owner seeking to impose liability on an accused circumventor must demonstrate a reasonable relationship between the circumvention at issue and a use relating to a property right for which the Copyright Act permits the copyright owner to withhold authorization—as well as notice that authorization was withheld. A copyright owner seeking to impose liability on an accused trafficker must demonstrate that the trafficker's device enables either copyright infringement or a prohibited circumvention. Here, the District Court correctly ruled that Chamberlain pled no connection between unauthorized use of its copyrighted software and Skylink's accused transmitter. This connection is critical to sustaining a cause of action under the DMCA. We therefore affirm the District Court's summary judgment in favor of Skylink....

Lexmark International, Inc. v. Static Control Components, Inc.
387 F.3d 522 (6th Cir. 2005)

SUTTON, J.:

[1] This copyright dispute involves two computer programs, two federal statutes and three theories of liability. The first computer program, known as the "Toner Loading Program," calculates toner level in printers manufactured by Lexmark International. The second computer program, known as the "Printer Engine Program," controls various printer functions on Lexmark printers.

[2] The first statute, the general copyright statute, 17 U.S.C. § 101 *et seq.*, ... grants copyright protection to "original works of authorship fixed in any tangible medium of expression," but does not "extend to any idea, procedure, process, system, method of operation, concept, principle, or discovery." The second federal statute, the Digital Millennium Copyright Act, 17 U.S.C. § 1201 *et seq.*, was enacted in 1998 and proscribes the sale of products that may be used to "circumvent a technological measure that effectively controls access to a work" protected by the copyright statute.

[3] These statutes became relevant to these computer programs when Lexmark began selling discount toner cartridges for its printers that only Lexmark could re-fill and that contained a microchip designed to prevent Lexmark printers from functioning with toner cartridges that Lexmark had not re-filled. In an effort to support the market for competing toner cartridges, Static Control Components (SCC) mimicked Lexmark's computer chip and sold it to companies interested in selling remanufactured toner cartridges.

[4] Lexmark brought this action to enjoin the sale of SCC's computer chips and raised three theories of liability in doing so. Lexmark claimed that SCC's chip copied the Toner Loading Program in violation of the federal copyright statute. It claimed that SCC's chip violated the DMCA by circumventing a technological measure designed to control access to the Toner Loading Program. And it claimed that SCC's chip violated the DMCA by circumventing a technological measure designed to control access to the Printer Engine Program.

[5] After an evidentiary hearing, the district court decided that Lexmark had shown a likelihood of success on each claim and entered a preliminary injunction against SCC. As we view Lexmark's prospects for success on each of these claims differently, we vacate the preliminary injunction and remand the case for further proceedings....

[6] **The Parties.** Headquartered in Lexington, Kentucky, Lexmark is a leading manufacturer of laser and inkjet printers and has sold printers and toner cartridges for its printers since 1991. Lexmark is a publicly traded corporation and reported $4.8 billion in revenue for 2003.

[7] Static Control Components is a privately held company headquartered in Sanford, North Carolina. Started in 1987, it currently employs approximately 1,000 workers and makes a wide range of technology products, including microchips that it sells to third-party companies for use in remanufactured toner cartridges.

[8] **The Two Computer Programs.** The first program at issue is Lexmark's "Toner Loading Program," which measures the amount of toner remaining in the cartridge based on the amount of torque (rotational force) sensed on the toner cartridge wheel.... The Toner Loading Program for [one set of] printers comprises 33 program instructions and occupies 37 bytes of memory, while the Toner Loading Program for [another set of] printers comprises 45 program commands and uses 55 bytes of memory. To illustrate the modest size of this computer program, the phrase "Lexmark International, Inc. vs. Static Control Components, Inc." in ASCII format would occupy more memory than either version of the Toner Loading Program. The Toner Loading Program is located on a microchip contained in Lexmark's toner cartridges.

[9] The second program is Lexmark's "Printer Engine Program." The Printer Engine Program occupies far more memory than the Toner Loading Program and translates into over 20 printed pages of program commands. The program controls a variety of functions on each printer—e.g., paper feed and movement, and printer motor control. Unlike the Toner Loading Program, the Printer Engine Program is located within Lexmark's printers.

[10] Lexmark obtained Certificates of Registration from the Copyright Office for both programs. Neither program is encrypted and each can be read (and copied) directly from its respective memory chip.

[11] **Lexmark's Prebate and Non-Prebate Cartridges.** Lexmark markets two types of toner cartridges for its laser printers: "Prebate" and "Non-Prebate." Prebate cartridges are sold to business consumers at an up-front discount. In exchange, consumers agree to use the cartridge just once, then return the empty unit to Lexmark; a "shrink-wrap" agreement on the top of each cartridge box spells out these restrictions and confirms that using the cartridge constitutes acceptance of these terms. Non-Prebate cartridges are sold without any discount, are not subject to any restrictive agreements and may be re-filled with toner and reused by the consumer or a third-party remanufacturer.

[12] To ensure that consumers adhere to the Prebate agreement, Lexmark uses an "authentication sequence" that performs a "secret handshake" between each Lexmark printer and a microchip on each Lexmark toner cartridge. Both the printer and the chip employ a publicly available encryption algorithm known as "Secure Hash Algorigthm–1" or "SHA–1," which calculates a "Message Authentication Code" based on data in the microchip's memory. If the code calculated by the microchip matches the code calculated by the printer, the printer functions normally. If the two values do not match, the printer returns an error message and will not operate, blocking consumers from using toner cartridges that Lexmark has not authorized.

[13] **SCC's Competing Microchip.** SCC sells its own microchip—the "SMARTEK" chip—that permits consumers to satisfy Lexmark's authentication sequence each time it would otherwise be performed, *i.e.*, when the printer is turned on or the printer door is opened and shut. SCC's advertising boasts that its chip breaks Lexmark's "secret code" (the authentication sequence), which "even on the fastest computer available today ... would take **Years** to run through all of the possible 8–byte combinations to break." SCC sells these chips to third-party cartridge remanufacturers, permitting them to replace Lexmark's chip with the SMARTEK chip on refurbished Prebate cartridges. These recycled cartridges are in turn sold to consumers as a low-cost alternative to new Lexmark toner cartridges.

[14] Each of SCC's SMARTEK chips also contains a copy of Lexmark's Toner Loading Program, which SCC claims is necessary to make its product compatible with Lexmark's printers. The SMARTEK chips thus contain an identical copy of the Toner Loading Program that is appropriate for each Lexmark printer, and SCC acknowledges that it "slavishly copied" the Toner Loading Program "in the exact format and order" found on Lexmark's cartridge chip....

{In a part of the opinion, omitted here, the court found that the district court had erred in finding that Lexmark's Toner Loading Program was copyrightable. The court found that the program was functional, that elements of the program were likely scenes a faire or merged with functional aspects, that any creativity that remained was likely de minimis, and that in any event SCC's use was likely fair use.}

[15] In filing its complaint and in its motion for a preliminary injunction, Lexmark invoked ... the ban on distributing devices that circumvent access-control measures placed on copyrighted works. *See* 17 U.S.C. § 1201(a)(2). According to Lexmark, SCC's SMARTEK chip is a "device" marketed and sold by SCC that "circumvents" Lexmark's "technological measure" ... which "effectively controls access" to its copyrighted works (the Toner Loading Program and Printer Engine Program). Lexmark claims that the SMARTEK chip meets all three tests for liability under § 1201(a)(2): (1) the chip "is primarily designed or produced for the purpose of circumventing" Lexmark's authentication sequence, 17 U.S.C. § 1201(a)(2)(A); (2) the chip "has only limited commercially significant purpose or use other than to circumvent" the authentication sequence, *id.* § 1201(a)(2)(B); and (3) SCC "market[s]" the chip "for use in circumventing" the authentication sequence, *id.* § 1201(a)(2)(C). The district court agreed and concluded that Lexmark had shown a likelihood of success under all three provisions....

[16] We initially consider Lexmark's DMCA claim concerning the Printer Engine Program, which (the parties agree) is protected by the general copyright statute. In deciding that Lexmark's authentication sequence "effectively controls access to a work protected under [the copyright provisions]," the district court relied on a definition in the DMCA saying that a measure "effectively controls access to a work" if, "in the ordinary course of operation," it "requires the application of information, or a process or treatment, with the authority of the copyright owner, to gain access to the work." 17 U.S.C. § 1201(a)(3). Because Congress did not explain what it means to "gain access to the work," the district court relied on the "ordinary, customary meaning" of "access": "the ability to enter, to obtain, or to make use of." Based on this definition, the court concluded that "Lexmark's authentication sequence effectively 'controls access' to the Printer Engine Program because it controls the consumer's ability to *make use of* these programs."

[17] We disagree. It is not Lexmark's authentication sequence that "controls access" to the Printer Engine Program. It is the purchase of a Lexmark printer that allows "access" to the program. Anyone who buys a Lexmark printer may read the literal code of the Printer Engine Program directly from the printer memory, with or without the benefit of the authentication sequence, and the data from the program may be translated into readable source code after which copies may be freely distributed. No security device, in other words, protects access to the Printer Engine Program Code and no security device accordingly must be circumvented to obtain access to that program code.

[18] The authentication sequence, it is true, may well block one form of "access"—the "ability to ... make use of" the Printer Engine Program by preventing the printer from functioning. But it does not block another relevant form of "access"—the "ability to [] obtain" a copy of the work or to "make use of" the literal elements of the program (its code). Because the statute refers to "control[ling] access to a work protected under this title," it does not naturally apply when the "work protected under this title" is otherwise accessible. Just as one would not say that a lock on the back door of a house "controls access" to a house whose front door does not contain a lock and just as one would not say that a lock on any door of a house "controls access" to the house after its purchaser receives the key to the lock, it does not make sense to say that this provision of the

DMCA applies to otherwise-readily-accessible copyrighted works. Add to this the fact that the DMCA not only requires the technological measure to "control[] access" but also requires the measure to control that access "effectively," 17 U.S.C. § 1201(a)(2), and it seems clear that this provision does not naturally extend to a technological measure that restricts one form of access but leaves another route wide open....

[19] ... Lexmark counters that several cases have embraced a "to make use of" definition of "access" in applying the DMCA. While Lexmark is partially correct, these cases (and others as well) ultimately illustrate the liability line that the statute draws and in the end explain why access to the Printer Engine Program is not covered.

[20] In the essential setting where the DMCA applies, the copyright protection operates on two planes: in the literal code governing the work and in the visual or audio manifestation generated by the code's execution. For example, the encoded data on CDs translates into music and on DVDs into motion pictures, while the program commands in software for video games or computers translate into some other visual and audio manifestation. In the cases upon which Lexmark relies, restricting "use" of the work means restricting consumers from making use of the copyrightable expression in the work....

[21] The copyrightable expression in the Printer Engine Program, by contrast, operates on only one plane: in the literal elements of the program, its source and object code. Unlike the code underlying video games or DVDs, "using" or executing the Printer Engine Program does not in turn create any protected expression. Instead, the program's output is purely functional: the Printer Engine Program controls a number of operations in the Lexmark printer such as paper feed, paper movement, and motor control. And unlike the code underlying video games or DVDs, no encryption or other technological measure prevents access to the Printer Engine Program. Presumably, it is precisely because the Printer Engine Program is not a conduit to protectable expression that explains why Lexmark (or any other printer company) would not block access to the computer software that makes the printer work. Because Lexmark's authentication sequence does not restrict access to this literal code, the DMCA does not apply.

[22] Lexmark next argues that access-control measures may "effectively control access" to a copyrighted work within the meaning of the DMCA even though the measure may be evaded by an enterprising end-user. Doubtless, Lexmark is correct that a precondition for DMCA liability is not the creation of an impervious shield to the copyrighted work. Otherwise, the DMCA would apply only when it is not needed.

[23] But our reasoning does not turn on the *degree* to which a measure controls access to a work. It turns on the textual requirement that the challenged circumvention device must indeed circumvent *something*, which did not happen with the Printer Engine Program. Because Lexmark has not directed any of its security efforts, through its authentication sequence or otherwise, to ensuring that its copyrighted work (the Printer Engine Program) cannot be read and copied, it cannot lay claim to having put in place a "technological measure that effectively controls access to a work protected under [the copyright statute]." 17 U.S.C. § 1201(a)(2)(B).

[24] Nor can Lexmark tenably claim that this reading of the statute fails to respect Congress's purpose in enacting it. Congress enacted the DMCA to implement the Copyright Treaty of the World Intellectual Property Organization, and in doing so expressed concerns about the threat of "massive piracy" of digital works due to "the ease with which [they] can be copied and distributed worldwide virtually instantaneously." S. REP. NO. 105–190, at 8 (1998). As Congress saw it, "copyrighted works will most likely be encrypted and made available to consumers once payment is made for access to a copy of the work. [People] will try to profit from the works of others by decoding the encrypted codes protecting copyrighted works, or engaging in the business of providing devices or services to enable others to do so." H.R. REP. NO. 105–551, pt. 1, at 10. Backing with legal sanctions "the efforts of copyright owners to protect their works from piracy behind digital

walls such as encryption codes or password protections," Congress noted, would encourage copyright owners to make digital works more readily available, *see* S. REP. No. 105–190, at 8.

[25] Nowhere in its deliberations over the DMCA did Congress express an interest in creating liability for the circumvention of technological measures designed to prevent consumers from using consumer goods while leaving the copyrightable content of a work unprotected....

[26] In view of our conclusion regarding the Printer Engine Program, we can dispose quickly of Lexmark's DMCA claim regarding the Toner Loading Program. The SCC chip does not provide "access" to the Toner Loading Program but replaces the program. And to the extent a copy of the Toner Loading Program appears on the Printer Engine Program, Lexmark fails to overcome the same problem that undermines its DMCA claim with respect to the Printer Engine Program: Namely, it is not the SCC chip that permits access to the Printer Engine Program but the consumer's purchase of the printer. One other point deserves mention. All three liability provisions of this section of the DMCA require the claimant to show that the "technological measure" at issue "controls access to *a work protected under this title*," *see* 17 U.S.C. § 1201(a)(2)(A)-(C), which is to say a work protected under the general copyright statute. To the extent the Toner Loading Program is not a "work protected under [the copyright statute]," ... the DMCA necessarily would not protect it....

[27] Because Lexmark failed to establish a likelihood of success on any of its claims, whether under the general copyright statute or under the DMCA, we vacate the district court's preliminary injunction and remand the case for further proceedings consistent with this opinion.

MERRITT, J., concurring. ...

[28] I write separately to emphasize that our holding should not be limited to the narrow facts surrounding either the Toner Loading Program or the Printer Engine Program. We should make clear that in the future companies like Lexmark cannot use the DMCA in conjunction with copyright law to create monopolies of manufactured goods for themselves just by tweaking the facts of this case: by, for example, creating a Toner Loading Program that is more complex and "creative" than the one here, or by cutting off other access to the Printer Engine Program. The crucial point is that the DMCA forbids anyone from trafficking in any technology that "is primarily designed or produced for the purpose of circumventing a technological measure that effectively controls access to a [protected] work." 17 U.S.C. § 1201(2)(A) (emphasis added). The key question is the "purpose" of the circumvention technology. The microchip in SCC's toner cartridges is intended not to reap any benefit from the Toner Loading Program—SCC's microchip is not designed to measure toner levels—but only for the purpose of making SCC's competing toner cartridges work with printers manufactured by Lexmark.

[29] By contrast, Lexmark would have us read this statute in such a way that any time a manufacturer intentionally circumvents any technological measure and accesses a protected work it necessarily violates the statute regardless of its "purpose." Such a reading would ignore the precise language—"for the purpose of"—as well as the main point of the DMCA—to prohibit the pirating of copyright-protected works such as movies, music, and computer programs. If we were to adopt Lexmark's reading of the statute, manufacturers could potentially create monopolies for replacement parts simply by using similar, but more creative, lock-out codes. Automobile manufacturers, for example, could control the entire market of replacement parts for their vehicles by including lock-out chips. Congress did not intend to allow the DMCA to be used offensively in this manner, but rather only sought to reach those who circumvented protective measures "for the purpose" of pirating works protected by the copyright statute. Unless a plaintiff can show that a defendant circumvented protective measures for such a purpose, its claim should not be allowed to go forward. If Lexmark wishes to utilize DMCA protections for (allegedly) copyrightable works, it should not use such works to prevent competing cartridges from working with its printer....

FEIKENS, J., Concurring in part and Dissenting in part. {omitted}

NOTES

1. *Chamberlain* reads § 1201 to bar access only when the access is related to infringement. In *MDY Industries, LLC v. Blizzard Entertainment, Inc.*, 629 F.3d 928 (9th Cir. 2011), the Ninth Circuit rejected that reading of the statute. *MDY* concluded that § 1201(a) extends "a new form of protection, i.e., the right to prevent circumvention of access controls" to copyrighted works without regard to whether access is connected to infringement. *Id.* at 945. Which court's interpretation is a better fit with the text of § 1201? Which court's approach is more consistent with the goals of copyright law?

2. *Chamberlain* also holds that the plaintiff has in effect "authorized" the defendant's customers to access and use their copyrighted software. Do you agree with this holding? Is there anything the plaintiff could do to evade its effect?

3. *Lexmark* holds that Lexmark's identification sequence does not control access to the Printer Engine Program, because that program is itself not encrypted and may be copied directly from the printer memory. Do you agree with this holding? Again, is there anything the plaintiff could do to evade its effect?

4. The plaintiffs in both *Chamberlain* and *Lexmark* were attempting to use the DMCA not principally to protect valuable copyrighted works but as a lever to limit competition. How do you think that fact affected the courts' interpretations of the meaning of § 1201? Do you see any reason to distinguish between the strategy employed by Chamberlain and the one employed by Lexmark?

5. Note that the DMCA also provides legal protection for so-called "copyright management information" (CMI), as discussed in Chapter V with regard to attribution. Recall that the statute defines "copyright management information" to include such information or "metadata" about a copyrighted work as the information in the copyright notice (©, year of creation, and identity of the copyright owner), the title, the identity of the author (if different from the copyright owner), and the terms of use. The DMCA's CMI protections, codified in § 1202, provide as follows:

> *(a) False Copyright Management Information.—No person shall knowingly and with the intent to induce, enable, facilitate, or conceal infringement—(1) provide copyright management information that is false, or (2) distribute or import for distribution copyright management information that is false.*

> *(b) Removal or Alteration of Copyright Management Information.—No person shall, without the authority of the copyright owner or the law—(1) intentionally remove or alter any copyright management information, (2) distribute or import for distribution copyright management information knowing that the copyright management information has been removed or altered without authority of the copyright owner or the law, or (3) distribute, import for distribution, or publicly perform works, copies of works, or phonorecords, knowing that copyright management information has been removed or altered without authority of the copyright owner or the law— knowing, or, with respect to civil remedies under section 1203, having reasonable grounds to know, that it will induce, enable, facilitate, or conceal an infringement of any right under this title.*

Some courts have read § 1202 to apply only to CMI located *on or in* a copyrighted work, and not such information that is merely *associated with* a copyrighted work. In *Kelly v. Arriba Soft Corp.*, 77 F. Supp. 2d 1116, 1121-22 (C.D. Cal. 1999), *rev'd and remanded in part on other grounds*, 336 F.3d 811 (9th Cir. 2003), the plaintiff photographer included CMI adjacent to his photographs, but not directly on them. The court granted summary judgment in favor of the defendant, whose copies of the photographs had removed the CMI. The court held that "[b]ased on the language and the structure of the statute, ... this provision applies only to the removal of copyright management information on a plaintiff's product or original work." *Id.* at 1122. But other courts have disagreed. Notably, in *Murphy v. Millennium Radio Group L.L.C.*, 650 F.3d 295, 305, 310 (3d Cir. 2011), the Third Circuit concluded that the location of the photographer's name in the printed "gutter" credit did not prevent it from qualifying as CMI, and that the defendant's removal of the information could trigger liability under § 1202.

In *Mango v. Buzzfeed, Inc.*, 970 F.3d 167 (2d Cir. 2020), the Second Circuit clarified the knowledge required to support civil liability under § 1202 for the removal or alteration of CMI. In that case, Buzzfeed distributed Gregory Mango's photograph knowing that the valid CMI had been removed and replaced with improper CMI. The court held that the statutory language does not require knowledge that removal of the CMI would facilitate third-party infringement. Rather, the statute requires (1) knowledge that CMI has been removed and altered, and (2) knowledge that the removal or alteration will conceal "an infringement." The court found that Buzzfeed's distribution of Mango's photograph with knowledge that the CMI was removed and replaced with improper credit satisfied the first knowledge element. And Buzzfeed's knowing distribution of the photo with false attribution, which implied BuzzFeed had proper authorization to publish the photo and concealed its own infringement, satisfied the second knowledge element.

Finally, it appears that § 1202 claims have become more common in recent years. This may be because § 1203 of the Copyright Act makes statutory damages available for successful claims under § 1202 without regard to whether the relevant copyright was timely registered. *See* 17 U.S.C. § 1203(c)(3)(B) ("At any time before final judgment is entered, a complaining party may elect to recover an award of statutory damages for each violation of section 1202 in the sum of not less than $2,500 or more than $25,000.").

X. Copyright's Relationship to Contract and Other State Laws

In this chapter, you will learn about copyright's relationship to contract law and other state laws. First, we will study the particular rules and concerns surrounding the formation and interpretation of contracts governing copyright rights. Then, we will investigate what happens when people agree, via contract, to not engage in behavior that copyright law permits them to do (such as fair uses). We will also study whether certain contracting or other behavior by a copyright holder known as **copyright misuse** can lead to the unenforceability of the copyright against others. Finally, we will examine the circumstances in which copyright law preempts the enforcement of contracts. This introduction to copyright **preemption** provides a window to assess the viability of other state laws that abut copyright law.

A. Forming and Interpreting Contracts in Copyright

In this section, you'll learn about the basic rules that govern contracts and licenses involving copyrights. Then, you'll explore tools for interpreting contractual language in these agreements.

Copyright law allows authors to transfer their copyrights in whole or in part. Section 201(d) of the Copyright Act specifies:

> *(d) Transfer of Ownership.—*
>
> *(1) The ownership of a copyright may be transferred in whole or in part by any means of conveyance or by operation of law, and may be bequeathed by will or pass as personal property by the applicable laws of intestate succession.*
>
> *(2) Any of the exclusive rights comprised in a copyright, including any subdivision of any of the rights specified by section 106, may be transferred as provided by clause (1) and owned separately. The owner of any particular exclusive right is entitled, to the extent of that right, to all of the protection and remedies accorded to the copyright owner by this title.*

Recognize that § 201(d)(2) provides that each right in the bundle of copyright rights conferred by § 106 may be transferred and owned separately. A "transfer of copyright ownership" is broadly defined in § 101:

> A "transfer of copyright ownership" is an assignment, mortgage, exclusive license, or any other conveyance, alienation, or hypothecation of a copyright or of any of the exclusive rights comprised in a copyright, whether or not it is limited in time or place of effect, but not including a nonexclusive license.

Note that a transfer of copyright ownership does not include a nonexclusive license. Why do you think that is? More broadly, as a matter of copyright policy, is it a good idea to allow authors to transfer their copyright interests, or would it be better to require authors to retain control of their copyright interests? Does the free alienability of copyright rights tell you anything about copyright law's purposes?

Section 204(a) specifies how to execute a valid transfer of copyright:

> A transfer of copyright ownership, other than by operation of law, is not valid unless an instrument of conveyance, or a note or memorandum of the transfer, is in writing and signed by the owner of the rights conveyed or such owner's duly authorized agent.

Note the three requirements for the transfer, other than by operation of law, to be valid: (1) a writing, (2) signed, (3) by the owner or the owner's duly authorized agent. The writing need not be signed by the transferee. Nor need it contain any magic words; it is necessary only that the writing give evidence of the transferor's intent to transfer the copyright interest. As the Ninth Circuit has explained, "[s]ection 204's writing requirement not only protects authors from fraudulent claims" much like a statute of frauds, but it "also enhances predictability and certainty of ownership." Konigsberg Int'l Inc. v. Rice, 16 F.3d 355, 357 (9th Cir. 1994).

While courts have been consistent with respect to the required content of the writing, they have divided over the question of the writing's timing—in particular, whether the writing must be contemporaneous with the transfer or can instead later memorialize an earlier transfer. *Compare, e.g., id.* (requiring a contemporaneous writing for a copyright transfer to be valid), *with, e.g.,* Barefoot Architect, Inc. v. Bunge, 632 F.3d 822 (3d Cir. 2011) ("Under the statute's plain terms it is clear that an oral transfer can be given legal effect by a subsequent signed writing.").

Recall from Chapter IV that transfers of copyright ownership can be recorded with the Copyright Office. *See* 17 U.S.C. § 205. So long as the document specifically identifies the work and the work has been registered, the recordation serves as "constructive notice of the facts stated in the recorded document." *Id.* § 205(c). An unrecorded transfer is void against a subsequent bona fide purchaser for value who records first. *Id.* § 205(d). What do you think are the policy interests underlying the recordation provisions of the Copyright Act? Why might it be helpful to have the Copyright Office record transfers?

> Given that nonexclusive licenses are deemed not to be transfers of copyright ownership, such licenses can be effective even without a writing—that is, they can be created orally or implied through conduct. As you read the following case, consider when the law ought to infer an implied nonexclusive license from the parties' behavior. In such situations, how should a court infer the license's specific terms?

Asset Marketing Systems, Inc. v. Kevin Gagnon
542 F.3d 748 (9th Cir. 2008)

M. SMITH, J.: ...

[1] AMS [(Asset Marketing Systems, Inc.)] is a field marketing organization offering sales and marketing support to insurance marketing entities. From May 1999 to September 2003, [Kevin] Gagnon [doing business as Mister Computer] was an at-will, independent contractor for AMS, hired to assist with its information technology needs. Subsequently, Gagnon was asked to develop custom software for AMS. AMS was Gagnon's largest client, accounting for 98% of his business. Jay Akerstein, a partner at AMS who later became the Chief Operating Officer, was Gagnon's primary contact. Over the course of their four-year relationship, AMS paid Gagnon over $2 million, $250,000 of which was for custom software development and computer classes. Gagnon developed six computer programs for AMS.

[2] In May 2000, AMS and Gagnon entered a Technical Services Agreement (TSA), which was scheduled to expire on April 30, 2001. The TSA, printed on Mister Computer letterhead, set forth Gagnon's fees and the services to be provided. The services included "Custom Application Programming—Consultant will provide Contractor with specific add-on products to enhance Contractor's current in-house database application," and mentioned nothing about a license. The TSA was not renewed, though the relationship continued.

[3] AMS claims that on June 12, 2002, Gagnon signed a Vendor Nondisclosure Agreement (NDA). The NDA would have given AMS ownership of all intellectual property developed for AMS by Gagnon. Gagnon claims that the document is a forgery and that his signature cannot be authenticated.

[4] In June 2003, Gagnon proposed that AMS execute an Outside Vendor Agreement (OVA). The OVA included a Proprietary Rights clause providing:

> Client agrees that all designs, plans, specifications, drawings, inventions, processes, and other information or items produced by Contractor while performing services under this agreement will be the property of Contractor and will be licensed to Client on a non-exclusive basis as will any copyrights, patents, or trademarks obtained by Contractor while performing services under this agreement. On request and at Contractor's expense, Client agrees to help Contractor obtain patents and copyrights for any new developments. This includes providing data, plans, specifications, descriptions, documentation, and other information, as well as assisting Contractor in completing any required application or registration. Any source code or intellectual property will remain the property of Contractor. Trademarks, service marks, or any items identifying said Company shall remain the Company's said property. Contractor will allow Company non exclusive, unlimited licensing of software developed for Company.

[5] Akerstein declined to execute the OVA, but countered with a redlined version of the OVA, which substantially rewrote the Proprietary Rights clause to read:

> Contractor agrees that all designs, plans, specifications, drawings, inventions, processes, and other information or items produced by Contractor while performing services under this agreement will be the sole property of Client. Any source code or intellectual property agreed to and documented as Contractor's will remain the property of Contractor.

[6] By the end of June 2003, AMS had decided to terminate Gagnon's services. AMS extended an employment offer to Gagnon, but he declined to accept the offer. AMS and Gagnon then discussed an exit strategy, and by late July, the parties had set a target exit date of September 15, 2003.

[7] In August 2003, Gagnon responded to Akerstein's redlined OVA draft with a letter asserting that his "position has always been that Asset Marketing Systems shall be entitled to unlimited software licensing as long as my company had a business relationship with Asset Marketing Systems." The parties never executed the OVA.

[8] In a letter to AMS dated September 18, 2003, Gagnon demanded $1.75 million for AMS to have the right to continue to use the programs and $2 million for Gagnon's agreement not to sell or disclose the programs to AMS's competitors.

[9] In a letter dated September 23, 2003, AMS terminated its relationship with Gagnon. According to AMS, a consultant identified numerous problems with Gagnon's work. It also stated:

> Recently, we had discussed employee and intellectual property issues which have yet to be resolved. Despite the foregoing, I learned that we did not have copies of the source code for the software we developed and that copies of our SalesLogix software and our entire database may be maintained by you and your agents offsite.

[10] The letter then demanded:

In connection with that separation, you must immediately provide any and all copies of the source code for all software developed by and on behalf of Asset Marketing Systems immediately. You are not authorized to utilize that software which we believe is owned and all copyrights belong to Asset Marketing Systems....

[11] Specifically at issue are the six programs that Gagnon created for AMS. He included a copyright notice, "copyright Mister Computer," in the splash screens for each program.

[12] According to a declaration by one of Gagnon's former employees, the programs were designed to work with AMS's databases and included "detailed information concerning AMS' network of sales persons, including information related to AMS' agent lists, their territories, and the criteria used by AMS to qualify an agent or create a territory." The source code for these programs was installed on several of AMS's development computers, which were located at AMS's facilities.[2] The employee was not instructed by Gagnon to maintain the source code at any location other than AMS, and Gagnon made no attempt to hide the source code from AMS employees.

[13] In his deposition, Gagnon admitted that after he hired employees, the source code was stored on AMS computers in the development room. The room could not be accessed without a pass that Gagnon's software developers and a few key AMS personnel, including Akerstein, possessed....

[14] A week prior to his termination, Gagnon registered the copyright for these six programs with the United States Copyright Office....

[15] .... [In an ensuing suit for copyright infringement, t]he court found that Gagnon had granted AMS an implied, nonexclusive license to use, modify, and retain the source code of the programs....

[16] Gagnon alleges that AMS's continued use of the six programs constitutes copyright infringement because the programs were used by AMS without its obtaining a license or Gagnon's permission. AMS asserts three defenses to Gagnon's copyright infringement claim: an implied license, a transfer of copyright ownership via the NDA, and 17 U.S.C. § 117. We hold that AMS has an implied unlimited license for the programs, and we do not reach the other defenses asserted by AMS.

[17] Though exclusive licenses must be in writing, grants of nonexclusive licenses need not be in writing, and may be granted orally or by implication....

[18] ... [W]e have held that an implied license is granted when (1) a person (the licensee) requests the creation of a work, (2) the creator (the licensor) makes that particular work and delivers it to the licensee who requested it, and (3) the licensor intends that the licensee-requestor copy and distribute his work.... The last prong of the ... test, however, is not limited to copying and distribution; instead we look at the protected right at issue—here, whether Gagnon intended that AMS use, retain, and modify the programs.

1. AMS Requested the Creation of the Programs

[19] Gagnon argues that AMS never specifically requested that he create the programs, but rather relayed its needs to Mr. Gagnon and he satisfied them by providing either computer hardware or computer software at his discretion. We find this interpretation of "request" to be strained. Gagnon did not create the programs on his own initiative and market them to AMS; rather, he created them in response to AMS's requests. Moreover, after prototype software was developed, he made changes to the programs in response to Akerstein and

---

[2] Gagnon disputes that the source code was ever stored on the AMS server.

other AMS employees' requests. No genuine issue of material fact remains as to whether AMS requested the programs.

2. Gagnon Created the Software for AMS and Delivered It

[20] Though Gagnon argues that the programs could be converted for use by another company, Gagnon admitted that the programs were created specifically for AMS and that AMS paid for the work related to drafting of the programs as well as some related costs. It is, therefore, undisputed that Gagnon created these programs for AMS.

[21] The remaining question is whether Gagnon delivered the programs to AMS. We agree with the district court that Gagnon delivered them when he installed them onto the AMS computers and stored the source code on-site at AMS. Gagnon argues that even if he had installed the programs onto the AMS computers, he never delivered the source code so that AMS could modify the code. If AMS did not have the right to modify the code, it may have infringed Gagnon's copyright by exceeding the scope of its license. Gagnon primarily points to AMS's inability to locate the code on its own computer systems after his services were terminated to show that AMS did not possess the code. But, as we explain below, Gagnon's conduct manifested an objective intent to give AMS an unlimited license at the time of creation; thus, when he stored the source code at AMS, the code was delivered.

3. Gagnon's Intent as Manifested by His Conduct

[22] Gagnon argues that he never intended that AMS would retain and modify the programs he delivered. Gagnon misunderstands the inquiry into intent, and we conclude that his conduct did manifest an intent to grant a license. The relevant intent is the licensor's objective intent at the time of the creation and delivery of the software as manifested by the parties' conduct....

[23] Gagnon and AMS had an ongoing service relationship in which Gagnon provided technical support for all computer-related problems at AMS; he also created certain custom software applications at AMS's request. The relationship of the parties indicates neither an intent to grant nor deny a license without Gagnon's future involvement.

[24] Several documents exist, however, that reflect the parties' objective intent: the TSA, signed by both parties, the OVA submitted by Gagnon, and Gagnon's letter objecting to Akerstein's proposed changes to the OVA.[6] Courts have looked to contracts, even if unexecuted, as evidence of the intent of the party submitting the contract.

[25] The TSA, signed by both parties in 2000 and printed on Mister Computer letterhead, stated only that Gagnon "will provide" AMS "specific add-on products." Nothing in the TSA indicates Gagnon's understanding or intent that continued use of the custom application programming undertaken by Gagnon would be prohibited after the TSA terminated. The TSA also provided that AMS would be billed for Gagnon's services at an hourly rate.... Gagnon was well paid for his services. Under the circumstances, it defies logic that AMS would have paid Gagnon for his programming services if AMS could not have used the programs without further payment pursuant to a separate licensing arrangement that was never mentioned in the TSA, and never otherwise requested at the time. This is especially so because custom software is far less valuable without the ability to modify it and because the TSA was set to expire in one year; one would expect some indication of the need for future licensing if the custom programs were to become unusable after the TSA expired.

---

[6] We do not consider the NDA, allegedly signed by Gagnon, because Gagnon contests its validity and argues that his signature was forged, creating a factual dispute inappropriate for resolution on summary judgment.

[26] The OVA submitted by Gagnon, but never executed, did not evidence any intent by Gagnon to limit AMS's use of the programs. Gagnon argues that the clause, "Client agrees that [intellectual property] produced by Contractor while performing services under this agreement will be the property of Contractor and will be licensed to Client on a non-exclusive basis as will any copyrights, patents, or trademarks obtained by Contractor while performing services under this agreement ...," means that his license was conditioned on a continuing relationship with AMS. We disagree. The clause "while performing services under this agreement" modifies the production of the intellectual property and the obtainment of copyrights. Furthermore, the contract then expressly stated, "Contractor will allow Company non-exclusive, unlimited licensing of software developed for Company," eliminating any ambiguity.

[27] Moreover, Gagnon and AMS did not discuss a licensing agreement until their relationship was ending. Gagnon delivered the software without any caveats or limitations on AMS's use of the programs. Even if Gagnon and his employees maintained the software and had primary control over the code, they programmed on-site at AMS on AMS computers to which key AMS personnel had access-conduct that does not demonstrate an intent to retain sole control. The first time Gagnon expressed a contrary intent was in his letter to Akers[tein] *after* AMS had decided to terminate Gagnon's services.

[28] Finally, the splash screens containing the copyright notice do not negate AMS's license to use the product. The splash screens speak to Gagnon's intent to retain copyright ownership over the programs, not to his intent to grant or not grant a license as would be his right as the copyright owner.

[29] Gagnon had to express an intent to retain control over the programs and limit AMS's license if he intended to do so. A belated statement that the programs could not be used after Gagnon's departure, made after the termination decision and well after the creation and delivery of the programs for which substantial sums were paid, was not sufficient to negate all other objective manifestations of intent to grant AMS an unlimited license.

4. Scope and Irrevocability of Implied License

[30] For the reasons outlined, we hold that Gagnon granted AMS an unlimited, nonexclusive license to retain, use, and modify the software. Furthermore, because AMS paid consideration, this license is irrevocable. A nonexclusive license supported by consideration is a contract. If an implied license accompanied by consideration were revocable at will, the contract would be illusory.

[31] We affirm the district court's grant of summary judgment on the copyright infringement claim....

NOTES

1. Some courts emphasize that the three factors set out in *Asset Marketing Systems* are not necessarily the only relevant ones to consider whether there is an implied license. For example, the Fifth Circuit has stated that an implied license might "arise in other circumstances where the totality of the parties' conduct supported such an outcome." Baisden v. I'm Ready Prods., Inc., 693 F.3d 491, 501 (5th Cir. 2012). Are there other factors you think might be relevant to inferring a nonexclusive license?

2. Christopher Newman has explained that "a license is not a contractual obligation assumed by a licensor, but rather a form of limited property interest granted by one, as an exercise of one of the powers of title." Christopher M. Newman, *"What Exactly Are You Implying?": The Elusive Nature of the Implied Copyright License*, 32 Cardozo Arts & Ent. L.J. 501, 502 (2014). In light of this understanding, Newman argues that notions from property law are more suitable to making sense of implied licenses to copyrighted material than are principles from contract law:

The law of implied copyright licenses presents something of an explanatory challenge for this approach. If licenses are an exercise of the owner's power, how can they arise in circumstances where the owner made no effort to exercise it? In addition, there are clearly circumstances in which we think implied licenses should be irrevocable, and yet property formalities generally require a written grant to achieve this result. Does this mean that implied licenses, which by definition are not reduced to writing, must be contracts after all? Or perhaps that some of them are, while others are something else? ... [C]onsistent application of a property framework does a better job of rationalizing this area of law than the courts' various halfhearted invocations of contract law.

Newman goes on to situate implied copyright licenses "not in contract doctrine, but in the implied consent that is recognized as providing a defense to property and other torts." *See also* Christopher M. Newman, *A License Is Not a "Contract Not to Sue": Disentangling Property and Contract in the Law of Copyright Licenses*, 98 IOWA L. REV. 1101 (2013).

3. When a nonexclusive license is implied, can it be terminated under copyright law as per the termination provisions you studied in Chapter IV? The Eleventh Circuit has said that such a license can be terminated. Korman v. HBC Florida, Inc., 182 F.3d 1291 (11th Cir. 1999). The court reasoned that "[t]he plain language of section 203 covers all nonexclusive grants of a license that are executed after the specified date, and nothing in the statute excludes those that are implied."

4. The licensee of five tattoo designs inked on three different NBA players—Eric Bledsoe, LeBron James, and Kenyon Martin—sued the developer and publisher of the NBA 2K series of basketball simulation videogames for depicting animated versions of these players that included the licensed tattoos, as shown in Figure 125. The district court granted the defendants' motion for summary judgment on the ground that they had an implied license to feature the tattoos in representing the players' likenesses. Solid Oak Sketches, LLC v. 2K Games, Inc., 449 F. Supp. 3d 333 (S.D.N.Y. 2020). The court reasoned that "(i) the Players each requested the creation of the Tattoos, (ii) the tattooists created the Tattoos and delivered them to the Players by inking the designs onto their skin, and (iii) the tattooists intended the Players to copy and distribute the Tattoos as elements of their likenesses, each knowing that the Players were likely to appear in public, on television, in commercials, or in other forms of media." Are you convinced by each of the three parts of the court's reasoning?

Figure 125: LeBron James's likeness in NBA 2K videogame

Given that the duration of contracts or licenses over copyrights can be lengthy due to copyright's long duration, these agreements often must be interpreted well after they were first drafted and executed. In the period between the drafting and later interpretation of an agreement, technologies of distribution and the forms that works take might have changed in important ways.

> As you read the following case, consider the tools courts deploy to interpret the parties' agreements. Which party gets the benefit of the new use at issue? Is that a sensible result as a matter of copyright policy? As a matter of contract interpretation?

Margret Rey v. Richard G.D. Lafferty
990 F.2d 1379 (1st Cir. 1993)

CYR, J.: ...

I – BACKGROUND

[1] "Curious George" is an imaginary monkey whose antics are chronicled in seven books, written by Margret and H.A. Rey, which have entertained readers since the 1940s. A mischievous personality consistently lands Curious George in amusing scrapes and predicaments. The more recent "monkey business"—leading to the present litigation—began in 1977 when Margret Rey granted Milktrain Productions an option to produce and televise 104 animated "Curious George" film episodes. The option agreement was contingent on Milktrain's obtaining financing for the film project ....

A. The Original Film Agreements.

[2] Milktrain approached [Lafferty Harwood & Partners (LHP)], a Canadian investment firm, to obtain financing for the project. LHP agreed to fund the venture by selling shares in the project to investors (hereinafter: the "Milktrain Agreement"); LHP and its investors were to divide a 50% share of Milktrain's profits on the films and on any future ancillary products.

[3] With the financing commitment in place, Rey granted Milktrain and LHP a limited license "to produce (within a two-year period from the date of exercise) one hundred and four (104) four minute film episodes based on the [Curious George] character solely for broadcast on television" (hereinafter: the "Rey License"). Rey was to receive a fee for assisting with the editing and production of the episodes, and an additional royalty amounting to 10% of the revenues from any film telecasts....

B. The Revised Agreements.

[4] The film project soon encountered delays and financial setbacks. By early 1979, though only 32 of the 104 episodes had been completed, the original investment funds had been virtually exhausted. In order to rescue the project and complete the films to Rey's satisfaction, LHP offered to arrange additional financing. In consideration, LHP insisted that the Milktrain Agreement be revised to permit LHP to assume control of the film production process and to receive higher royalties on the completed episodes. Milktrain assented to these revisions, and the revised Milktrain Agreement (hereinafter: the "RMA") was signed on November 5, 1979.

[5] As prelude to its description of the new obligations between Milktrain and LHP, the RMA recited that Milktrain and LHP owned "the rights to Curious George which have been obtained from ... Rey" under the Rey License. The RMA further stated that:

> *Investors acquiring the episodes shall acquire all right, title and interest therein, without limitation or reserve, including the original negative....*
>
> *LHP shall have the right to participate on an equal basis with [Milktrain] in their right of first refusal after the present agency rights expire to undertake the exploitation of other rights to Curious George, including manufacturing, food, licensing and the publication of the 104 episodes in book form ... in accordance with the rights granted to [Milktrain] and LHP [by Rey] in [the Revised Rey License].[1]*

[6] Simultaneously with the negotiation of the RMA, LHP proposed several changes in the Rey License, including language which would have granted LHP the immediate right to "undertake the exploitation of other rights to 'Curious George,' including manufacturing, food, licensing and the publication of the 104 episodes in book form." Rey rejected the LHP proposal in a letter to Richard G.D. Lafferty (president and C.E.O. of LHP): "I have repeatedly stated to Milktrain and to you that I will not consider negotiating such rights before the films are done." Rey did consent, however, to certain changes to the royalty arrangements, whereby Rey would receive a 10% share of film revenues only "after the investors have recouped [their investment] and certain soft dollar commitments ... have been paid."

[7] On November 5, 1979, concurrently with the execution of the Revised Milktrain Agreement, a revised version of the Rey License (hereinafter: the "RRL") was executed, incorporating these changes, and superseding the original Rey License. The RRL recited that the original Rey License had granted Milktrain and LHP the right to produce and distribute animated "Curious George" films "for television viewing," but made no mention of the "ancillary product" rights unsuccessfully sought by LHP.

[8] As agreed, LHP undertook to arrange further financing to complete the film project. On November 23, 1979, LHP released another prospectus (hereinafter: the "1979 Private Placement Memorandum") to which it attached the Revised Milktrain Agreement. The 1979 Private Placement Memorandum again stressed the prospect of eventual revenues from ancillary products but noted that these rights "have yet to be negotiated" with Rey.

C. The Ancillary Products Agreement.

[9] Production of the 104 TV episodes was completed in 1982. On January 3, 1983, an Ancillary Products Agreement (or "APA") was signed by Rey and LHP, granting LHP a general right to license "Curious George" in spin-off ("ancillary") products for a renewable term of five years. The APA defined "ancillary products" as:

> *All tangible goods ... excluding books, films, tapes, records, or video productions.... However, for stories already owned by [LHP] and which have been produced as 104 episodes under the license granted in the January, 1978 agreement and the November 5, 1979 revision of that agreement, [LHP] shall have the right to produce books, films, tapes, records and video productions of these episodes under this Agreement, subject to [Rey's] prior approval ... which prior approval shall not be unreasonably withheld.*

---

[1] Shortly thereafter, Milktrain apparently assigned its share of ancillary product licensing rights to LHP, leaving LHP the sole owner of these rights.

[10] In return for these rights, Rey was to receive one-third of the royalties on the licensed products, with certain minimum annual payments guaranteed. Rey retained the right to disapprove *any product*, and to propose changes which would make a disapproved product acceptable to her. The APA provided, *inter alia*, that Rey's approval would not be withheld "unreasonably." ...

[11] Following the execution of the Ancillary Products Agreement, LHP assigned its licensing rights to a new subsidiary, Curgeo Enterprises, which turned its attention to licensing the "Curious George" character in various product forms....

E. Other Product Licenses.

[12] .... Beginning in 1983, the "Curious George" TV episodes were licensed to Sony Corporation, which transferred the images from the television film negatives to videotape. LHP takes the position that the Sony video license was entered pursuant to the RRL; Rey claims it is subject to the APA....

F. The Ancillary Products Agreement Renewal.

[13] ... LHP earned less money than it anticipated from ancillary products. When the APA came up for renewal in January 1988, LHP declined to exercise its option for an additional five-year term. Instead, the parties agreed to renew on a month-to-month basis, terminable by either party on one month's notice. Rey's royalty rate was increased to 50% (effective January 3, 1988), but with no guaranteed minimum payment. On April 10, 1989, Rey terminated the APA. LHP responded by advising that Curgeo would "continue to administer those licenses which [remained] outstanding and report to you from time to time accordingly." LHP thereupon continued to market the Sony videos ....

G. "Curious George" Goes to Court.

[14] On February 8, 1991, Rey filed suit against [Richard G.D.] Lafferty [(president and C.E.O. of LHP)], Curgeo and LHP, in connection with LHP's continuing, allegedly unauthorized production of ... Sony videos. Rey's complaint alleged violations of federal copyright ... [and] breach of contract ...; it sought to enjoin further violations and to recover unpaid royalties on the ... videos....

[15] After a four-day bench trial, the district court found for Rey on her claims for breach of contract, ruling that the ... video licenses were governed by the APA and that Rey was entitled to recover $256,327 in royalties....

II – DISCUSSION ...

[16] The Rey complaint alleged that LHP's only right to publish the "Curious George" TV episodes in ... video form derived from the Ancillary Products Agreement, was subject to the APA's royalty provisions, and expired when Rey terminated the APA in 1989. LHP responds that the ... video rights to the TV episodes were governed by the parties' other agreements, specifically the Revised Rey License, which (according to LHP) incorporated the Revised Milktrain Agreement. According to LHP, these other agreements continued in effect notwithstanding termination of the APA; moreover, these agreements provided that no royalties were due Rey before LHP's investors recovered their investment in the 104 TV films. The district court accepted the interpretation urged by Rey, based on the language of the various contracts and the circumstances surrounding their execution. We agree....

[17] The Ancillary Products Agreement provided, *inter alia*, that

for stories already owned by [LHP] ... which have been produced as 104 episodes under the license granted in the January, 1978 agreement and the November 5, 1979 revision of that agreement, [LHP] shall have the right to produce books, films, tapes, records and *video productions* of these episodes *under this Agreement*, subject to [Rey's] prior approval ...

(emphases added). Throughout the document the term "this Agreement," utilizing the capital letter "A", refers to the APA. Thus, the plain language of the operative provision clearly contemplates that the APA was to govern the licensing of any books and "video productions" arising from the 104 films.

[18] LHP argues, nonetheless, that a narrow meaning must be ascribed to the quoted APA language, insofar as the RMA purported to grant investors "all right, title and interest [to the 104 film episodes], without limitation or reserve, including the original negative." The problem with LHP's argument is that Rey never signed the RMA. LHP concedes this, but argues that the RMA and RRL were negotiated and executed simultaneously by LHP, and must be interpreted *in pari materia*. The Massachusetts courts sometimes have held that the party to be bound need not have signed each component part of an integrated agreement where it is the "sense" of the transaction, as supported by reliable indicia in the writings which were signed by the party to be bound, that a unitary transaction was contemplated by the parties. On this theory, LHP contends, Rey's signature on the RRL bound her to the language of the RMA, and authorized LHP to transfer the television episodes to [video] form ....

[19] However, where contract language contains no unambiguous indicia of the parties' mutual intent to enter into a unitary transaction, we review for "clear error" the fact-dominant determination whether their separate documents were intended by the parties as an integrated agreement.

[20] In the present case, we find no "clear error" in the district court's determination that the parties contemplated separate (though related) transactions for film rights and financing. The evidence cut both ways. On the one hand, the RMA and the RRL were executed at approximately the same time, with some overlap in their internal references and subject matter. On the other hand, their respective provisions are less in unison than parallel. Most importantly, the written and circumstantial indicia sharply contradict any suggestion of a meeting of the minds relating to the licensing of ancillary products. Rey did not participate in negotiating the RMA, did not sign it, was never made a party to its terms, and expressly refused, during the RRL negotiations, to license "Curious George" for the "ancillary" purposes now urged by LHP. Moreover, the 1979 Private Placement Memorandum prepared by LHP acknowledges Rey's nonacceptance by attaching the RRL as an exhibit and noting that ancillary product rights "have yet to be negotiated" with Rey. Finally, the ... record shows that LHP paid Rey royalties on the ... videos on several occasions at the 33% rate required under the APA, rather than the 10% rate prescribed by the RRL ...:

[21] LHP's claim to the Sony video royalties is ... complicated: assuming the videos were not covered by the contractual clause in the RMA, might they nonetheless have been covered by the grant of rights in the RRL, which licensed LHP to produce the 104 episodes "for television viewing"? The district court thought not: the parties' "reference to television viewing ... in a licensing agreement ... does not include [video technology] ... which probably was not in existence at the time that the rights were given." ...

[22] For purposes of the present appeal, we accept the uncontested district court finding that the relevant video technology "was not in existence at the time that the rights" were granted under the RRL in January 1979. Consequently, it must be inferred that the parties did not specifically contemplate television "viewing" of the "Curious George" films in videocassette form at the time the RRL was signed. Such absence of specific intent typifies cases which address "new uses" of licensed materials, i.e., novel technological developments which generate unforeseen applications for a previously licensed work.

[23] Normally, in such situations, the courts have sought at the outset to identify any indicia of a mutual general intent to apportion rights to "new uses," insofar as such general intent can be discerned from the language of the license, the surrounding circumstances, and trade usage. *See, e.g.,* Murphy v. Warner Bros. Pictures, Inc., 112 F.2d 746, 748 (9th Cir. 1940) (grant of "complete and entire" motion picture rights to licensed work held to encompass later-developed sound motion picture technology); Filmvideo Releasing Corp. v. Hastings, 446 F. Supp. 725 (S.D.N.Y. 1978) (author's explicit retention of "all" television rights to licensed work, in grant of motion picture rights predating technological advances permitting movies to be shown on television, included retention of right to show motion picture on television). Where no reliable indicia of general intent are discernible, however, courts have resorted to one of several interpretive methods to resolve the issue on policy grounds.

[24] Under the preferred method, ... the court will conclude, absent contrary indicia of the parties' intent, that the licensee may properly pursue any uses which may reasonably be said to fall within the medium as described in the license. Under this interpretive method, the courts will presume that at least the possibility of nonspecific "new uses" was foreseeable by the contracting parties at the time the licensing agreement was drafted; accordingly, the burden and risk of drafting licenses whose language anticipates the possibility of any particular "new use" are apportioned equally between licensor and licensee.

[25] An alternative interpretive method is to assume that a license of rights in a given medium (e.g., "motion picture rights") includes only such uses as fall within the unambiguous core meaning of the term ... and excludes any uses which lie within the ambiguous penumbra (e.g., exhibition of motion picture film on television). Thus any rights not expressly (in this case meaning unambiguously) granted are reserved.

[26] This method is intended to prevent licensees from reaping the entire windfall associated with the new medium, and is particularly appropriate in situations which involve overreaching or exploitation of unequal bargaining power by a licensee in negotiating the contract. It may also be appropriate where a particular "new use" was completely unforeseeable and therefore could not possibly have formed part of the bargain between the parties at the time of the original grant. Obviously, this method may be less appropriate in arm's-length transactions between sophisticated parties involving foreseeable technological developments; in such situations, narrow construction of license grants may afford an unjustifiable windfall to the licensor, who would retain blanket rights to analogous "new uses" of copyright material notwithstanding the breadth of the bargained-for grant.[7] ...

[27] These fine-tuned interpretive methods have led to divergent results in cases considering the extension of television rights to new video forms. Thus, for example, in *Rooney v. Columbia Pictures Industries, Inc.*, 538 F. Supp. 211 (S.D.N.Y.), *aff'd*, 714 F.2d 117 (2d Cir. 1982), the court determined that a series of contracts granting motion picture distributors a general license to exhibit plaintiffs' films "by any present or future methods or means" and "by any means now known or unknown" fairly encompassed the right to distribute the films by means of later-developed video technology. The contracts in question gave defendants extremely broad rights in the distribution and exhibition of pre-1960 films, plainly intending that such rights would be without limitation unless otherwise specified and further indicating that future technological advances in methods of reproduction, transmission and exhibition would inure to the benefit of defendants....

---

[7] The problem becomes particularly acute when the analogous technology develops so rapidly as to supplant the originally contemplated application of the licensed work, rendering the parties' original bargain obsolete. Thus, for example, broad grants of "motion picture rights," made before technological advances permitted the combination of moving images with sound, later were held, typically, to encompass the rights to sound motion picture technology; a narrower holding would have left the original license virtually worthless, despite its broad language, and would have provided the licensor with an undeserved windfall.

[28] By contrast, in *Cohen v. Paramount Pictures Corp.*, 845 F.2d 851 (9th Cir. 1988), the Ninth Circuit concluded that a 1969 contract granting rights to "[t]he exhibition of [a] motion picture [containing a licensed work] ... by means of television," but containing a broad restriction reserving to the licensor "all rights and uses in and to said musical composition, except those herein granted," did not encompass the right to revenues derived from sales of the film in videocassette form. After deciding that the general tenor of the contract section in which the granting clause was found contemplated some sort of broadcasting or centralized distribution, not distribution by sale or rental of individual copies to the general public, the court stressed that the playing of videocassettes, with their greater viewer control and decentralized access on an individual basis, did not constitute "exhibition" in the sense contemplated by the contract.

> .... *Television and videocassette display ... have very little in common besides the fact that a conventional monitor of a television set may be used both to receive television signals and to exhibit a videocassette. It is in light of this fact that Paramount argues that VCRs are equivalent to "exhibition by means of television." Yet, even that assertion is flawed. Playing a videocassette on a VCR does not require a standard television set capable of receiving television signals by cable or by broadcast; it is only necessary to have a monitor capable of displaying the material on the magnetized tape....*

[29] Although the question is extremely close, under the interpretive methodology outlined above we conclude that the RRL's grant of rights to the 104 film episodes "for television viewing" did not encompass the right to distribute the "Curious George" films in videocassette form.

[30] First, unlike the contract[] in *Rooney* ..., the RRL contained no general grant of rights in technologies yet to be developed, and no explicit reference to "future methods" of exhibition. Rather, the RRL appears to contemplate a comparatively limited and particular grant of rights, encompassing only the 104 film episodes and leaving future uses of "Curious George" to later negotiation in the ancillary products agreement. Although the RRL conversely contains no specific limiting language, we believe such limitation is reasonably inferable from the situation of the parties and the general tenor of the section in which the "television viewing" rights were granted.

[31] Second, "television viewing" and "videocassette viewing" are not coextensive terms. Even though videocassettes may be, and often are, viewed by means of VCRs on home television screens, still, ... a standard television set capable of receiving television signals is not strictly required for videocassette viewing. It is only necessary to have a monitor capable of displaying the material on the magnetized tape. Indeed, a number of non-television monitors recently marketed in the United States permit videocassette viewing on computer screens, flat-panel displays, and the like. Thus, we find insufficient reliable indicia of a contrary mutual intent on the part of Rey and LHP to warrant disturbing the district court's implicit determination that the language of the RRL is not broad enough to cover the new use.

[32] Finally, any lingering concerns about the correctness of the district court's interpretation are dispelled by the evidence that the RRL (including its "television viewing" clause) was drafted and proposed by LHP, a professional investment firm accustomed to licensing agreements. Rey, an elderly woman, does not appear to have participated in its drafting, and, indeed, does not appear to have been represented by counsel during the larger part of the transaction. Under these circumstances, ... ambiguities in the drafting instrument are traditionally construed against the licensor and the drafter.

[33] Accordingly, as the Sony videocassette sales were not encompassed by the RRL, but governed exclusively by the APA, we find no conflict between the terms of the documents, and we affirm the award of royalties to Rey under the APA.

NOTE

1. Is it possible to ascertain the parties' intent in an agreement as to new use of a work? If not, does copyright policy dictate an outcome that is preferable? If that result is at odds with general rules of contract interpretation, is there something to be said in favor of a federal common law of contract interpretation for copyright agreements? For a discussion about the federal underpinnings of copyright licenses and contracts, see Mark A. Lemley, *Beyond Preemption: The Law and Policy of Intellectual Property Licensing*, 87 CALIF. L. REV. 111 (1999).

B. Modifying Copyright Law by Contract

In this section, we address what happens when people agree, via contract or license, to not engage in behavior that copyright law permits them to do, such as take advantage of the first-sale doctrine (or engage in fair use of a copyrighted work, as discussed below in section D). Should the law enforce those agreements?

There are two quite different situations in which this issue typically arises, both regarding mass user licenses to a copyrighted work. The first is with regard to mass-marketed copyrighted material—typically, software products, but more recently other types of digital content as well. Many of these products contain end-user license agreements—typically in the form of shrink-wrap, click-wrap, or browse-wrap—that forbid users from engaging in a variety of practices, some of which would be permissible under the Copyright Act.

In the past two decades, a second form of mass user license agreement has emerged by which authors seek to ensure the public availability of their works on terms that they set. Creative Commons licenses are the most well-known form of this so-called "copyleft" agreement for copyrighted works that are not software. The open-source licenses that you read about in Chapter II—such as the GNU General Public License and the Apache License—are common forms of this sort of agreement for software works.

Creative Commons is a project formed by a group of activists, academics, and content creators to give rightsholders choices about how their works may be used that are meant to supplement the "all rights reserved" default of the formal copyright law. Creative Commons provides a variety of "some rights reserved" licenses, including licenses allowing free use with attribution, noncommercial use, use without the right to make derivative works, and use with the requirement that the user make freely usable any derivative work created using the original source material (referred to as the "share-alike" license, which is similar in purpose to the GNU General Public License). Creative Commons also provides a "no rights reserved" public domain dedication license, which provides a perpetual and unconditional license "for the benefit of each member of the public at large and to the detriment of Affirmer's heirs and successors."

Why would an author want to use any of these Creative Commons licenses rather than merely announcing that their work is in the public domain? Can you see how the Creative Commons and open-source licenses grant freedoms to users by embracing copyright law—which is typically conceptualized as restricting rather than actuating user freedoms?

As you read the following case involving a shrink-wrap license to software, consider how each party would like to characterize the transfers of software copies that have occurred and what the implications of each position are for copyright law. What test does the court use to evaluate how to characterize the transfers of software copies?

Timothy S. Vernor v. Autodesk, Inc.
621 F.3d 1102 (9th Cir. 2010)

CALLAHAN, J.: ...

[1] .... Autodesk makes computer-aided design software used by architects, engineers, and manufacturers.... It holds registered copyrights in all versions of the software including the discontinued Release 14 version, which is at issue in this case. It provided Release 14 to customers on CD-ROMs.

[2] Since at least 1986, Autodesk has offered AutoCAD to customers pursuant to an accompanying software license agreement ("SLA"), which customers must accept before installing the software. A customer who does not accept the SLA can return the software for a full refund. Autodesk offers SLAs with different terms for commercial, educational institution, and student users. The commercial license, which is the most expensive, imposes the fewest restrictions on users and allows them software upgrades at discounted prices.

[3] The SLA for Release 14 first recites that Autodesk retains title to all copies. Second, it states that the customer has a nonexclusive and nontransferable license to use Release 14. Third, it imposes transfer restrictions, prohibiting customers from renting, leasing, or transferring the software without Autodesk's prior consent and from electronically or physically transferring the software out of the Western Hemisphere. Fourth, it imposes significant use restrictions:

> YOU MAY NOT: (1) modify, translate, reverse-engineer, decompile, or disassemble the Software ... (3) remove any proprietary notices, labels, or marks from the Software or Documentation; (4) use ... the Software outside of the Western Hemisphere; (5) utilize any computer software or hardware designed to defeat any hardware copy-protection device, should the software you have licensed be equipped with such protection; or (6) use the Software for commercial or other revenue-generating purposes if the Software has been licensed or labeled for educational use only.

[4] Fifth, the SLA provides for license termination if the user copies the software without authorization or does not comply with the SLA's restrictions. Finally, the SLA provides that if the software is an upgrade of a previous version:

> [Y]ou must destroy the software previously licensed to you, including any copies resident on your hard disk drive ... within sixty (60) days of the purchase of the license to use the upgrade or update.... Autodesk reserves the right to require you to show satisfactory proof that previous copies of the software have been destroyed.

[5] Autodesk takes measures to enforce these license requirements. It assigns a serial number to each copy of AutoCAD and tracks registered licensees. It requires customers to input "activation codes" within one month after installation to continue using the software. The customer obtains the code by providing the product's serial number to Autodesk. Autodesk issues the activation code after confirming that the serial number is

authentic, the copy is not registered to a different customer, and the product has not been upgraded. Once a customer has an activation code, he or she may use it to activate the software on additional computers without notifying Autodesk....

[6] In March 1999, Autodesk reached a settlement agreement with its customer Cardwell/Thomas & Associates, Inc. ("CTA"), which Autodesk had accused of unauthorized use of its software. As part of the settlement, Autodesk licensed ten copies of Release 14 to CTA. CTA agreed to the SLA, which appeared (1) on each Release 14 package that Autodesk provided to CTA; (2) in the settlement agreement; and (3) on-screen, while the software is being installed.

[7] CTA later upgraded to the newer, fifteenth version of the AutoCAD program, AutoCAD 2000. It paid $495 per upgrade license, compared to $3,750 for each new license. The SLA for AutoCAD 2000, like the SLA for Release 14, required destruction of copies of previous versions of the software, with proof to be furnished to Autodesk on request. However, rather than destroying its Release 14 copies, CTA sold them to [Timothy] Vernor at an office sale with the handwritten activation codes necessary to use the software....

[8] .... In May 2005, [Vernor] purchased an authentic used copy of Release 14 at a garage sale from an unspecified seller. He never agreed to the SLA's terms, opened a sealed software packet, or installed the Release 14 software. Though he was aware of the SLA's existence, he believed that he was not bound by its terms. He posted the software copy for sale on eBay.

[9] Autodesk filed a Digital Millennium Copyright Act take-down notice with eBay claiming that Vernor's sale infringed its copyright, and eBay terminated Vernor's auction. Autodesk advised Vernor that it conveyed its software copies pursuant to non-transferable licenses, and resale of its software was copyright infringement. Vernor filed a DMCA counter-notice with eBay contesting the validity of Autodesk's copyright claim. Autodesk did not respond to the counter-notice. eBay reinstated the auction, and Vernor sold the software to another eBay user.

[10] In April 2007, Vernor purchased four authentic used copies of Release 14 at CTA's office sale. The authorization codes were handwritten on the outside of the box. He listed the four copies on eBay sequentially, representing, "This software is not currently installed on any computer." On each of the first three occasions, the same DMCA process ensued. Autodesk filed a DMCA take-down notice with eBay, and eBay removed Vernor's auction. Vernor submitted a counter-notice to which Autodesk did not respond, and eBay reinstated the auction.

[11] When Vernor listed his fourth, final copy of Release 14, Autodesk again filed a DMCA take-down notice with eBay. This time, eBay suspended Vernor's account because of Autodesk's repeated charges of infringement. Vernor also wrote to Autodesk, claiming that he was entitled to sell his Release 14 copies pursuant to the first sale doctrine, because he never installed the software or agreed to the SLA. In response, Autodesk's counsel directed Vernor to stop selling the software. Vernor filed a final counter-notice with eBay. When Autodesk again did not respond to Vernor's counter-notice, eBay reinstated Vernor's account. At that point, Vernor's eBay account had been suspended for one month, during which he was unable to earn income on eBay.

[12] Vernor currently has two additional copies of Release 14 that he wishes to sell on eBay. Although the record is not clear, it appears that Vernor sold two of the software packages that he purchased from CTA, for roughly $600 each, but did not sell the final two to avoid risking further suspension of his eBay account....

[13] In August 2007, Vernor brought a declaratory action against Autodesk to establish that his resales of used Release 14 software are protected by the first sale doctrine and do not infringe Autodesk's copyright....

[14] This case requires us to decide whether Autodesk sold Release 14 copies to its customers or licensed the copies to its customers. If CTA owned its copies of Release 14, then both its sales to Vernor and Vernor's subsequent sales were non-infringing under the first sale doctrine.[6] However, if Autodesk only licensed CTA to use copies of Release 14, then CTA's and Vernor's sales of those copies are not protected by the first sale doctrine and would therefore infringe Autodesk's exclusive distribution right....

[15] .... In its current form, [the first-sale doctrine] allows the "owner of a particular copy" of a copyrighted work to sell or dispose of his copy without the copyright owner's authorization. 17 U.S.C. § 109(a). The first sale doctrine does not apply to a person who possesses a copy of the copyrighted work without owning it, such as a licensee. *See id.* § 109(d)....

[16] In *United States v. Wise*, 550 F.2d 1180 (9th Cir. 1977), a criminal copyright infringement case, we considered whether copyright owners who transferred copies of their motion pictures pursuant to written distribution agreements had executed first sales. The defendant was found guilty of copyright infringement based on his for-profit sales of motion picture prints. The copyright owners distributed their films to third parties pursuant to written agreements that restricted their use and transfer. On appeal, the defendant argued that the government failed to prove the absence of a first sale for each film. If the copyright owners' initial transfers of the films were first sales, then the defendant's resales were protected by the first sale doctrine and thus were not copyright infringement.

[17] To determine whether a first sale occurred, we considered multiple factors pertaining to each film distribution agreement. Specifically, we considered whether the agreement (a) was labeled a license, (b) provided that the copyright owner retained title to the prints, (c) required the return or destruction of the prints, (d) forbade duplication of prints, or (e) required the transferee to maintain possession of the prints for the agreement's duration. Our use of these several considerations, none dispositive, may be seen in our treatment of each film print.

[18] For example, we reversed the defendant's conviction with respect to *Camelot*. It was unclear whether the *Camelot* print sold by the defendant had been subject to a first sale. Copyright owner Warner Brothers distributed *Camelot* prints pursuant to multiple agreements, and the government did not prove the absence of a first sale with respect to each agreement. We noted that, in one agreement, Warner Brothers had retained title to the prints, required possessor National Broadcasting Company ("NBC") to return the prints if the parties could select a mutual agreeable price, and if not, required NBC's certification that the prints were destroyed. We held that these factors created a license rather than a first sale.

[19] We further noted, however, that Warner Brothers had also furnished another *Camelot* print to actress Vanessa Redgrave. The print was provided to Redgrave at cost, and her use of the print was subject to several restrictions. She had to retain possession of the print and was not allowed to sell, license, reproduce, or publicly exhibit the print. She had no obligation to return the print to Warner Brothers. We concluded, "While the provision for payment for the cost of the film, standing alone, does not establish a sale, when taken with the rest of the language of the agreement, it reveals a transaction strongly resembling a sale with restrictions on the use of the print." There was no evidence of the print's whereabouts, and we held that "[i]n the absence of such proof," the government failed to prove the absence of a first sale with respect to this Redgrave print. Since it was unclear which copy the defendant had obtained and resold, his conviction for sale of *Camelot* had to be reversed.

---

[6] If Autodesk's transfer of Release 14 copies to CTA was a first sale, then CTA's resale of the software in violation of the SLA's terms would be a breach of contract, but would not result in copyright liability. *See* United States v. Wise, 550 F.2d 1180, 1187 (9th Cir.1977) ("[T]he exclusive right to vend the transferred copy rests with the vendee, who is not restricted by statute from further transfers of that copy, even though in breach of an agreement restricting its sale.").

[20] Thus, under *Wise*, where a transferee receives a particular copy of a copyrighted work pursuant to a written agreement, we consider all of the provisions of the agreement to determine whether the transferee became an owner of the copy or received a license. We may consider (1) whether the agreement was labeled a license and (2) whether the copyright owner retained title to the copy, required its return or destruction, forbade its duplication, or required the transferee to maintain possession of the copy for the agreement's duration. We did not find any one factor dispositive in *Wise*: we did not hold that the copyright owner's retention of title itself established the absence of a first sale or that a transferee's right to indefinite possession itself established a first sale....

[21] We hold today that a software user is a licensee rather than an owner of a copy where the copyright owner (1) specifies that the user is granted a license; (2) significantly restricts the user's ability to transfer the software; and (3) imposes notable use restrictions. Applying our holding to Autodesk's SLA, we conclude that CTA was a licensee rather than an owner of copies of Release 14 and thus was not entitled to invoke the first sale doctrine or the essential step defense.

[22] Autodesk retained title to the software and imposed significant transfer restrictions: it stated that the license is nontransferable, the software could not be transferred or leased without Autodesk's written consent, and the software could not be transferred outside the Western Hemisphere. The SLA also imposed use restrictions against the use of the software outside the Western Hemisphere and against modifying, translating, or reverse-engineering the software, removing any proprietary marks from the software or documentation, or defeating any copy protection device. Furthermore, the SLA provided for termination of the license upon the licensee's unauthorized copying or failure to comply with other license restrictions. Thus, because Autodesk reserved title to Release 14 copies and imposed significant transfer and use restrictions, we conclude that its customers are licensees of their copies of Release 14 rather than owners.

[23] CTA was a licensee rather than an "owner of a particular copy" of Release 14, and it was not entitled to resell its Release 14 copies to Vernor under the first sale doctrine. Therefore, Vernor did not receive title to the copies from CTA and accordingly could not pass ownership on to others. Both CTA's and Vernor's sales infringed Autodesk's exclusive right to distribute copies of its work.

[24] Because Vernor was not an owner, his customers are also not owners of Release 14 copies. Therefore, when they install Release 14 on their computers, the copies of the software that they make during installation infringe Autodesk's exclusive reproduction right because they too are not entitled to the benefit of the essential step defense.[13] 17 U.S.C. §§ 106(1), 117(a)(1) ....

[25] ... Vernor contends that "economic realities" demonstrate that Autodesk makes "first sales" to its customers, because Autodesk allows its customers to possess their copies of the software indefinitely and does not require recurring license payments. We held *supra* that neither of these factors is dispositive. Vernor cites no first sale doctrine case in support of this proposition....

[26] Although our holding today is controlled by our precedent, we recognize the significant policy considerations raised by the parties and amici on both sides of this appeal.

[27] Autodesk, the Software & Information Industry Association ("SIIA"), and the Motion Picture Association of America ("MPAA") have presented policy arguments that favor our result. For instance, Autodesk argues in

---

[13] It may seem intuitive that every lawful user of a copyrighted software program, whether they own their copies or are merely licensed to use them, should be entitled to an "essential step defense" that provides that they do not infringe simply by using a computer program that they lawfully acquired. However, the Copyright Act confers this defense only on owners of software copies. *See* 17 U.S.C. § 117. In contrast, a licensee's right to use the software, including the right to copy the software into RAM, is conferred by the terms of its license agreement.

favor of judicial enforcement of software license agreements that restrict transfers of copies of the work. Autodesk contends that this (1) allows for tiered pricing for different software markets, such as reduced pricing for students or educational institutions; (2) increases software companies' sales; (3) lowers prices for all consumers by spreading costs among a large number of purchasers; and (4) reduces the incidence of piracy by allowing copyright owners to bring infringement actions against unauthorized resellers. SIIA argues that a license can exist even where a customer (1) receives his copy of the work after making a single payment and (2) can indefinitely possess a software copy, because it is the software code and associated rights that are valuable rather than the inexpensive discs on which the code may be stored. Also, the MPAA argues that a customer's ability to possess a copyrighted work indefinitely should not compel a finding of a first sale, because there is often no practically feasible way for a consumer to return a copy to the copyright owner.

[28] Vernor, eBay, and the American Library Association ("ALA") have presented policy arguments against our decision. Vernor contends that our decision (1) does not vindicate the law's aversion to restraints on alienation of personal property; (2) may force everyone purchasing copyrighted property to trace the chain of title to ensure that a first sale occurred; and (3) ignores the economic realities of the relevant transactions, in which the copyright owner permanently released software copies into the stream of commerce without expectation of return in exchange for upfront payment of the full software price. eBay contends that a broad view of the first sale doctrine is necessary to facilitate the creation of secondary markets for copyrighted works, which contributes to the public good by (1) giving consumers additional opportunities to purchase and sell copyrighted works, often at below-retail prices; (2) allowing consumers to obtain copies of works after a copyright owner has ceased distribution; and (3) allowing the proliferation of businesses.

[29] The ALA contends that the first sale doctrine facilitates the availability of copyrighted works after their commercial lifespan, by *inter alia* enabling the existence of libraries, used bookstores, and hand-to-hand exchanges of copyrighted materials. The ALA further contends that judicial enforcement of software license agreements, which are often contracts of adhesion, could eliminate the software resale market, require used computer sellers to delete legitimate software prior to sale, and increase prices for consumers by reducing price competition for software vendors. It contends that Autodesk's position (1) undermines 17 U.S.C. § 109(b)(2), which permits non-profit libraries to lend software for non-commercial purposes, and (2) would hamper efforts by non-profits to collect and preserve out-of-print software. The ALA fears that the software industry's licensing practices could be adopted by other copyright owners, including book publishers, record labels, and movie studios.

[30] These are serious contentions on both sides, but they do not alter our conclusion that our precedent ... requires the result we reach. Congress is free, of course, to modify the first sale doctrine and the essential step defense if it deems these or other policy considerations to require a different approach....

NOTES

1. Reflect on the policy considerations in favor of labeling the transfers here as a license and those in favor of labeling them as a sale. Does copyright policy clearly favor one of these positions over the other? For thoughts on this question, see Aaron Perzanowski & Jason Schultz, *Reconciling Intellectual and Personal Property*, 90 NOTRE DAME L. REV. 1211 (2015). How do you weigh the importance of maintaining a broadly applicable first-sale doctrine against the importance of respecting contractual agreements that might seek to limit it? For an argument in favor of retaining property rights in products "bought" in the digital marketplace, including traditional copyright subject matter like books and music, see AARON PERZANOWSKI & JASON SCHULTZ, THE END OF OWNERSHIP: PERSONAL PROPERTY IN THE DIGITAL ECONOMY (2016), https://mitpress.mit.edu/books/end-ownership.

2. Shortly after *Vernor*, the Ninth Circuit issued another ruling on whether to understand a transfer of copies as a license or a sale of those copies, but this time concluded that the transfer was a sale. UMG Recordings, Inc. v. Augusto, 628 F.3d 1175 (9th Cir. 2011). In this case, UMG Recordings, one of the world's largest music companies, would

> ship[] specially-produced promotional CDs to a large group of individuals, such as music critics and radio programmers, that it has selected. There is no prior agreement or request by the recipients to receive the CDs. UMG does not seek or receive payment for the CDs, the content and design of which often differs from that of their commercial counterparts.... Relatively few of the recipients refuse delivery of the CDs or return them to UMG, and UMG destroys those that are returned.

Most of these CDs bore a statement like the following:

> This CD is the property of the record company and is licensed to the intended recipient for personal use only. Acceptance of this CD shall constitute an agreement to comply with the terms of the license. Resale or transfer of possession is not allowed and may be punishable under federal and state laws.

Defendant Troy Augusto was not a direct recipient of promotional CDs from UMG, but he was able to acquire some of these CDs, which he sold on eBay. UMG sued Augusto for copyright infringement, particularly for violating its exclusive right to distribute the CDs, which UMG argued it retained because the CDs had only been licensed, not sold, to their recipients.

The Ninth Circuit disagreed, ruling that UMG had effected a sale by distributing the CDs to the original recipients. The court reasoned:

> Our conclusion that the recipients acquired ownership of the CDs is based largely on the nature of UMG's distribution. First, the promotional CDs are dispatched to the recipients without any prior arrangement as to those particular copies. The CDs are not numbered, and no attempt is made to keep track of where particular copies are or what use is made of them.... [A]lthough UMG places written restrictions in the labels of the CDs, it has not established that the restrictions on the CDs create a license agreement....

> Because the record here is devoid of any indication that the recipients agreed to a license, there is no evidence to support a conclusion that licenses were established under the terms of the promotional statement. Accordingly, we conclude that UMG's transfer of possession to the recipients, without meaningful control or even knowledge of the status of the CDs after shipment, accomplished a transfer of title.

Given that there was a first sale, the recipients and later Augusto were entitled—pursuant to the first-sale doctrine—to dispose of the CDs as they saw fit.

As you read the following case, consider which goals the court is trying to serve in its interpretation of the open-source license at issue. How does the court interpret the license in light of these particular goals?

Robert Jacobsen v. Matthew Katzer

535 F.3d 1373 (Fed. Cir. 2008)

HOCHBERG, J.:

[1] We consider here the ability of a copyright holder to dedicate certain work to free public use and yet enforce an "open source" copyright license to control the future distribution and modification of that work. Appellant Robert Jacobsen appeals from an order denying a motion for preliminary injunction. Jacobsen holds a copyright to computer programming code. He makes that code available for public download from a website without a financial fee pursuant to the Artistic License, an "open source" or public license. Appellees Matthew Katzer and Kamind Associates, Inc. develop commercial software products for the model train industry and hobbyists. Jacobsen accused Katzer/Kamind of copying certain materials from Jacobsen's website and incorporating them into one of Katzer/Kamind's software packages without following the terms of the Artistic License. Jacobsen brought an action for copyright infringement and moved for a preliminary injunction.

[2] The District Court held that the open source Artistic License created an "intentionally broad" nonexclusive license which was unlimited in scope and thus did not create liability for copyright infringement.

[3] On this basis, the District Court denied the motion for a preliminary injunction. We vacate and remand.

[4] Jacobsen manages an open source software group called Java Model Railroad Interface ("JMRI"). Through the collective work of many participants, JMRI created a computer programming application called DecoderPro, which allows model railroad enthusiasts to use their computers to program the decoder chips that control model trains. DecoderPro files are available for download and use by the public free of charge from an open source incubator website called SourceForge; Jacobsen maintains the JMRI site on SourceForge. The downloadable files contain copyright notices and refer the user to a "COPYING" file, which clearly sets forth the terms of the Artistic License.

[5] Katzer/Kamind offers a competing software product, Decoder Commander, which is also used to program decoder chips. During development of Decoder Commander, one of Katzer/Kamind's predecessors or employees is alleged to have downloaded the decoder definition files from DecoderPro and used portions of these files as part of the Decoder Commander software. The Decoder Commander software files that used DecoderPro definition files did not comply with the terms of the Artistic License. Specifically, the Decoder Commander software did not include (1) the author[] names, (2) JMRI copyright notices, (3) references to the COPYING file, (4) an identification of SourceForge or JMRI as the original source of the definition files, and (5) a description of how the files or computer code had been changed from the original source code. The Decoder Commander software also changed various computer file names of DecoderPro files without providing a reference to the original JMRI files or information on where to get the Standard Version.

[6] Jacobsen moved for a preliminary injunction, arguing that the violation of the terms of the Artistic License constituted copyright infringement and that, under Ninth Circuit law, irreparable harm could be presumed in a copyright infringement case. The District Court .... denied the motion for a preliminary injunction....

[7] Public licenses, often referred to as "open source" licenses, are used by artists, authors, educators, software developers, and scientists who wish to create collaborative projects and to dedicate certain works to the public. Several types of public licenses have been designed to provide creators of copyrighted materials a means to protect and control their copyrights. Creative Commons, one of the amici curiae, provides free copyright licenses to allow parties to dedicate their works to the public or to license certain uses of their works while keeping some rights reserved.

[8] Open source licensing has become a widely used method of creative collaboration that serves to advance the arts and sciences in a manner and at a pace that few could have imagined just a few decades ago. For example, the Massachusetts Institute of Technology uses a Creative Commons public license for an OpenCourseWare project that licenses all 1800 MIT courses. Other public licenses support the GNU/Linux operating system, the Perl programming language, the Apache web server programs, the Firefox web browser, and a collaborative web-based encyclopedia called Wikipedia. Creative Commons notes that, by some estimates, there are close to 100,000,000 works licensed under various Creative Commons licenses. The Wikimedia Foundation, another of the amici curiae, estimates that the Wikipedia website has more than 75,000 active contributors working on some 9,000,000 articles in more than 250 languages.

[9] Open Source software projects invite computer programmers from around the world to view software code and make changes and improvements to it. Through such collaboration, software programs can often be written and debugged faster and at lower cost than if the copyright holder were required to do all of the work independently. In exchange and in consideration for this collaborative work, the copyright holder permits users to copy, modify and distribute the software code subject to conditions that serve to protect downstream users and to keep the code accessible.[2] By requiring that users copy and restate the license and attribution information, a copyright holder can ensure that recipients of the redistributed computer code know the identity of the owner as well as the scope of the license granted by the original owner. The Artistic License in this case also requires that changes to the computer code be tracked so that downstream users know what part of the computer code is the original code created by the copyright holder and what part has been newly added or altered by another collaborator.

[10] Traditionally, copyright owners sold their copyrighted material in exchange for money. The lack of money changing hands in open source licensing should not be presumed to mean that there is no economic consideration, however. There are substantial benefits, including economic benefits, to the creation and distribution of copyrighted works under public licenses that range far beyond traditional license royalties. For example, program creators may generate market share for their programs by providing certain components free of charge. Similarly, a programmer or company may increase its national or international reputation by incubating open source projects. Improvement to a product can come rapidly and free of charge from an expert not even known to the copyright holder....

[11] The parties do not dispute that Jacobsen is the holder of a copyright for certain materials distributed through his website. Katzer/Kamind also admits that portions of the DecoderPro software were copied, modified, and distributed as part of the Decoder Commander software. Accordingly, Jacobsen has made out a prima facie case of copyright infringement. Katzer/Kamind argues that they cannot be liable for copyright infringement because they had a license to use the material. Thus, the Court must evaluate whether the use by Katzer/Kamind was outside the scope of the license. The copyrighted materials in this case are downloadable by any user and are labeled to include a copyright notification and a COPYING file that includes the text of the Artistic License. The Artistic License grants users the right to copy, modify, and distribute the software:

---

[2] For example, the GNU General Public License, which is used for the Linux operating system, prohibits downstream users from charging for a license to the software.

provided that [the user] insert a prominent notice in each changed file stating how and when [the user] changed that file, and provided that [the user] do at least ONE of the following:

a) place [the user's] modifications in the Public Domain or otherwise make them Freely Available, such as by posting said modifications to Usenet or an equivalent medium, or placing the modifications on a major archive site such as ftp.uu.net, or by allowing the Copyright Holder to include [the user's] modifications in the Standard Version of the Package.

b) use the modified Package only within [the user's] corporation or organization.

c) rename any non-standard executables so the names do not conflict with the standard executables, which must also be provided, and provide a separate manual page for each nonstandard executable that clearly documents how it differs from the Standard Version, or

d) make other distribution arrangements with the Copyright Holder.

[12] The heart of the argument on appeal concerns whether the terms of the Artistic License are conditions of, or merely covenants to, the copyright license. Generally, a copyright owner who grants a nonexclusive license to use his copyrighted material waives his right to sue the licensee for copyright infringement and can sue only for breach of contract. If, however, a license is limited in scope and the licensee acts outside the scope, the licensor can bring an action for copyright infringement.

[13] Thus, if the terms of the Artistic License allegedly violated are both covenants and conditions, they may serve to limit the scope of the license and are governed by copyright law. If they are merely covenants, by contrast, they are governed by contract law. The District Court did not expressly state whether the limitations in the Artistic License are independent covenants or, rather, conditions to the scope; its analysis, however, clearly treated the license limitations as contractual covenants rather than conditions of the copyright license.[3]

[14] Jacobsen argues that the terms of the Artistic License define the scope of the license and that any use outside of these restrictions is copyright infringement. Katzer/Kamind argues that these terms do not limit the scope of the license and are merely covenants providing contractual terms for the use of the materials, and that his violation of them is neither compensable in damages nor subject to injunctive relief. Katzer/Kamind's argument is premised upon the assumption that Jacobsen's copyright gave him no economic rights because he made his computer code available to the public at no charge. From this assumption, Katzer/Kamind argues that copyright law does not recognize a cause of action for non-economic rights, relying on *Gilliam v. ABC*, 538 F.2d 14, 20–21 (2d Cir.1976) ("American copyright law, as presently written, does not recognize moral rights or provide a cause of action for their violation, since the law seeks to vindicate the economic, rather than the personal rights of authors."). The District Court based its opinion on the breadth of the Artistic License terms, to which we now turn....

[15] The Artistic License states on its face that the document creates conditions: "The intent of this document is to state the *conditions* under which a Package may be copied." (emphasis added) The Artistic License also uses the traditional language of conditions by noting that the rights to copy, modify, and distribute are

---

3 The District Court held that "Defendants' alleged violation of the conditions of the license may have constituted a breach of the nonexclusive license ... [and] the Court finds that Plaintiff's claim properly sounds in contract." Thus, despite the use of the word "conditions," the District Court treated the terms of the Artistic License as contractual covenants which did not limit the scope of the license.

granted "*provided that*" the conditions are met. Under California contract law, "provided that" typically denotes a condition.

[16] The conditions set forth in the Artistic License are vital to enable the copyright holder to retain the ability to benefit from the work of downstream users. By requiring that users who modify or distribute the copyrighted material retain the reference to the original source files, downstream users are directed to Jacobsen's website. Thus, downstream users know about the collaborative effort to improve and expand the SourceForge project once they learn of the "upstream" project from a "downstream" distribution, and they may join in that effort.

[17] The District Court interpreted the Artistic License to permit a user to "modify the material in any way" and did not find that any of the "provided that" limitations in the Artistic License served to limit this grant. The District Court's interpretation of the conditions of the Artistic License does not credit the explicit restrictions in the license that govern a downloader's right to modify and distribute the copyrighted work. The copyright holder here expressly stated the terms upon which the right to modify and distribute the material depended and invited direct contact if a downloader wished to negotiate other terms. These restrictions were both clear and necessary to accomplish the objectives of the open source licensing collaboration, including economic benefit. Moreover, the District Court did not address the other restrictions of the license, such as the requirement that all modification from the original be clearly shown with a new name and a separate page for any such modification that shows how it differs from the original.

[18] Copyright holders who engage in open source licensing have the right to control the modification and distribution of copyrighted material. As the Second Circuit explained in *Gilliam v. ABC*, 538 F.2d 14, 21 (2d Cir.1976), the "unauthorized editing of the underlying work, if proven, would constitute an infringement of the copyright in that work similar to any other use of a work that exceeded the license granted by the proprietor of the copyright." Copyright licenses are designed to support the right to exclude; money damages alone do not support or enforce that right. The choice to exact consideration in the form of compliance with the open source requirements of disclosure and explanation of changes, rather than as a dollar-denominated fee, is entitled to no less legal recognition. Indeed, because a calculation of damages is inherently speculative, these types of license restrictions might well be rendered meaningless absent the ability to enforce through injunctive relief.

[19] In this case, a user who downloads the JMRI copyrighted materials is authorized to make modifications and to distribute the materials "provided that" the user follows the restrictive terms of the Artistic License. A copyright holder can grant the right to make certain modifications, yet retain his right to prevent other modifications. Indeed, such a goal is exactly the purpose of adding conditions to a license grant. The Artistic License, like many other common copyright licenses, requires that any copies that are distributed contain the copyright notices and the COPYING file.

[20] It is outside the scope of the Artistic License to modify and distribute the copyrighted materials without copyright notices and a tracking of modifications from the original computer files. If a [downloader] does not assent to these conditions stated in the COPYING file, he is instructed to "make other arrangements with the Copyright Holder." Katzer/Kamind did not make any such "other arrangements." The clear language of the Artistic License creates conditions to protect the economic rights at issue in the granting of a public license. These conditions govern the rights to modify and distribute the computer programs and files included in the downloadable software package. The attribution and modification transparency requirements directly serve to drive traffic to the open source incubation page and to inform downstream users of the project, which is a significant economic goal of the copyright holder that the law will enforce. Through this controlled spread of information, the copyright holder gains creative collaborators to the open source project; by requiring that changes made by downstream users be visible to the copyright holder and others, the copyright holder learns

about the uses for his software and gains others' knowledge that can be used to advance future software releases....

[21] .... Having determined that the terms of the Artistic License are enforceable copyright conditions, we remand to ... the District Court ....

C. Copyright Misuse

The cases you just read seem to suggest that copyright holders can limit all sorts of sub-uses of their copyrighted works, but can they upset the balance of copyright law using contracts or other mechanisms? In this section, we'll discuss that question through the lens of the doctrine of copyright misuse and, in the next section, we'll do the same with regard to preemption doctrine.

Copyright misuse is loosely analogous to the doctrine of patent misuse in patent law, where it is a "defense to infringement claims when a patentee uses its patent as the effective means of restraining competition[, such as] with its sale of an unpatented article." Ill. Tool Works Inc. v. Independent Ink, Inc., 547 U.S. 28, 38 (2006). Construed generally, copyright misuse tends to be asserted as a defense to infringement when "copyright ... holders assert their rights, not to protect from market harm to their protected works, but to protect other aspects of their market by using the protected work." Jeanne C. Fromer, *Should the Law Care Why Intellectual Property Rights Have Been Asserted?*, 53 HOUS. L. REV. 549, 565 (2015).

> As you read this case, consider the theory of copyright misuse the defendant here is asserting. Is the defendant claiming to be a direct victim of this purported misuse? Does that matter? Consider carefully also the effect of a court's finding of copyright misuse on the infringement case and on the copyright's validity.

Video Pipeline, Inc. v. Buena Vista Home Entertainment, Inc.
342 F.3d 191 (3d Cir. 2003)

AMBRO, J.: ...

[1] Video Pipeline compiles movie trailers onto videotape for home video retailers to display in their stores. To obtain the right to distribute the trailers used in the compilations, Video Pipeline enters into agreements with various entertainment companies. It entered into such an agreement, the Master Clip License Agreement, with Disney in 1988, and Disney thereafter provided Video Pipeline with over 500 trailers for its movies.

[2] In 1997, Video Pipeline took its business to the web .... The company maintains a database accessible from VideoPipeline.net, which contains movie trailers Video Pipeline has received throughout the years. Video Pipeline's internet clients—retail web sites selling home videos—use VideoPipeline.net to display trailers to site visitors.... The operators of the web sites from which the trailers are accessed—Video Pipeline's internet clients—pay a fee to have the trailers streamed [to site visitors] based on the number of megabytes shown to site visitors. Video Pipeline has agreements to stream trailers with approximately 25 online retailers, including Yahoo!, Amazon, and Best Buy....

[3] Video Pipeline included in its online database trailers it received under the License Agreement from Disney. Because the License Agreement did not permit this use, Disney requested that Video Pipeline remove the trailers from the database. It complied with that request.

[4] On October 24, 2000, however, Video Pipeline filed a complaint in the District Court for the District of New Jersey seeking a declaratory judgment that its online use of the trailers did not violate federal copyright law. Disney shortly thereafter terminated the License Agreement.

[5] Video Pipeline decided to replace some of the trailers it had removed at Disney's request from its database. In order to do so, it copied approximately two minutes from each of at least 62 Disney movies to create its own clip previews of the movies. (Again, to distinguish between the previews created under the copyright holder's authority and those created by Video Pipeline, we call the former "trailers" and the latter "clip previews" or "clips." We use the term "previews" generically.) ...

[6] Disney also makes its trailers available online. It displays them on its own web sites in order to attract and to keep users there (a concept called "stickiness") and then takes advantage of the users' presence to advertise and sell other products. Disney has also entered into agreements to link its trailers with other businesses, and, for example, has such a link with the Apple Computer home page.

[7] Video Pipeline amended its complaint to seek a declaratory judgment allowing it to use the clip previews. Disney filed a counterclaim alleging copyright infringement. The District Court entered a preliminary injunction, later revised, prohibiting Video Pipeline from displaying clip previews of Disney films on the internet....

[8] Video Pipeline ... contends that Disney has misused its copyright and, as a result, should not receive the protection of copyright law. Video Pipeline points to certain licensing agreements that Disney has entered into with three companies and sought to enter into with a number of other companies operating web sites. Each of these licensing agreements provides that Disney, the licensor, will deliver trailers by way of hyperlinks for display on the licensee's web site. The Agreements further state:

> *The Website in which the Trailers are used may not be derogatory to or critical of the entertainment industry or of [Disney] (and its officers, directors, agents, employees, affiliates, divisions and subsidiaries) or of any motion picture produced or distributed by [Disney] ... [or] of the materials from which the Trailers were taken or of any person involved with the production of the Underlying Works. Any breach of this paragraph will render this license null and void and Licensee will be liable to all parties concerned for defamation and copyright infringement, as well as breach of contract....*

[9] As Video Pipeline sees it, such licensing agreements seek to use copyright law to suppress criticism and, in so doing, misuse those laws, triggering the copyright misuse doctrine.

[10] Neither the Supreme Court nor this Court has affirmatively recognized the copyright misuse doctrine. There is, however, a well-established patent misuse doctrine, and, as noted below, other courts of appeals have extended the doctrine to the copyright context.

[11] The misuse doctrine extends from the equitable principle that courts may appropriately withhold their aid where the plaintiff is using the right asserted contrary to the public interest. Misuse is not cause to invalidate the copyright or patent, but instead precludes its enforcement during the period of misuse. To defend on misuse grounds, the alleged infringer need not be subject to the purported misuse.

[12] Misuse often exists where the patent or copyright holder has engaged in some form of anti-competitive behavior. *See, e.g.,* Morton Salt Co. v. G.S. Suppiger Co., 314 U.S. 488 (1942) (explaining that public policy "forbids the use of the patent to secure an exclusive right or limited monopoly not granted by the Patent Office"); Practice Management Info. Corp. v. Am. Med. Ass'n, 121 F.3d 516 (9th Cir. 1997) (finding copyright misuse where license to use copyrighted good prohibited licensee from using competing goods); Lasercomb Am., Inc. v. Reynolds, 911 F.2d 970 (4th Cir. 1990) (holding the copyright holder misused its copyright by including in licensing agreements a provision that neither the licensee company nor its officers, employees, *et al.*, could develop competing goods for the term of the agreement, ninety-nine years). More on point, however, is the underlying policy rationale for the misuse doctrine set out in the Constitution's Copyright and Patent Clause: "to promote the Progress of Science and useful Arts." The ultimate aim of copyright law is to stimulate artistic creativity for the general public good. Put simply, our Constitution emphasizes the purpose and value of copyrights and patents. Harm caused by their misuse undermines their usefulness.

[13] Anti-competitive licensing agreements may conflict with the purpose behind a copyright's protection by depriving the public of the would-be competitor's creativity. The fair use doctrine and the refusal to copyright facts and ideas also address applications of copyright protection that would otherwise conflict with a copyright's constitutional goal. But it is possible that a copyright holder could leverage its copyright to restrain the creative expression of another without engaging in anti-competitive behavior or implicating the fair use and idea/expression doctrines.

[14] For instance, the concurring opinion, written for a majority of the judges, in *Rosemont Enters., Inc. v. Random House, Inc.*, 366 F.2d 303 (2d Cir. 1966), concluded that pursuant to the unclean hands doctrine the District Court should not have entered a preliminary injunction against an alleged copyright infringer where the copyright holder sought to use his copyright "to restrict the dissemination of information." In *Rosemont Enters.*, a corporation acting for the publicity-shy Howard Hughes purchased the copyright to an article about Hughes solely to bring an infringement suit to enjoin the publication of a forthcoming biography on Hughes. The concurring opinion reasoned:

> The spirit of the First Amendment applies to the copyright laws at least to the extent that the courts should not tolerate any attempted interference with the public's right to be informed regarding matters of general interest when anyone seeks to use the copyright statute which was designed to protect interests of quite a different nature.

[15] Although *Rosemont Enters.* did not concern an anti-competitive licensing agreement as in the typical misuse case, it focused—as do the misuse cases—on the copyright holder's attempt to disrupt a copyright's goal to increase the store of creative expression for the public good. A copyright holder's attempt to restrict expression that is critical of it (or of its copyrighted good, or the industry in which it operates, etc.) may, in context, subvert—as do anti-competitive restrictions—a copyright's policy goal to encourage the creation and dissemination to the public of creative activity.

[16] The licensing agreements in this case do seek to restrict expression by licensing the Disney trailers for use on the internet only so long as the web sites on which the trailers will appear do not derogate Disney, the entertainment industry, etc. But we nonetheless cannot conclude on this record that the agreements are likely to interfere with creative expression to such a degree that they affect in any significant way the policy interest in increasing the public store of creative activity. The licensing agreements do not, for instance, interfere with the licensee's opportunity to express such criticism on other web sites or elsewhere. There is no evidence that the public will find it any more difficult to obtain criticism of Disney and its interests, or even that the public is considerably less likely to come across this criticism, if it is not displayed on the same site as the trailers.... Finally, copyright law, and the misuse doctrine in particular, should not be interpreted to require Disney, if it licenses its trailers for display on any web sites but its own, to do so willy-nilly regardless of the

content displayed with its copyrighted works. Indeed such an application of the misuse doctrine would likely decrease the public's access to Disney's works because it might as a result refuse to license at all online display of its works.

[17] Thus, while we extend the patent misuse doctrine to copyright, and recognize that it might operate beyond its traditional anti-competition context, we hold it inapplicable here. On this record Disney's licensing agreements do not interfere significantly with copyright policy (while holding to the contrary might, in fact, do so). The District Court therefore correctly held that Video Pipeline will not likely succeed on its copyright misuse defense....

NOTES

1. Kathryn Judge criticizes existing copyright misuse doctrine, and:

> calls for a clarification of the policy goals protected by misuse and for the adoption, where possible, of rules (or standards) to protect the identified policy goals. Copyright misuse already has been most accepted in an area where we have a clear policy goal and a defined line to protect it—competition and antitrust law. Yet many of the cases invoking copyright misuse, while rationalized as necessary to protect copyright policy, fail to specify the public policy at stake and how the copyright holder's misuse undermines that policy. This clarification should not only assist courts in adjudicating copyright misuse claims, but should also enhance the doctrine's efficacy by putting copyright holders on notice of what constitutes misuse.

> Examination of the cases applying and commentary discussing copyright misuse suggests that recognizing one additional policy aim and a couple of guidelines to protect it should be sufficient to encompass the great majority of violations the doctrine has thus far been asked to address. That policy is the protection of the values embodied in the First Amendment and the protective guidelines are the idea/expression distinction and fair use. Specifically, ... any attempt by a copyright holder to expand the scope of his copyright to gain control over an idea or to deter fair use should constitute misuse.

Note, Kathryn Judge, *Rethinking Copyright Misuse*, 57 STAN. L. REV. 901, 904-05 (2004). Do you agree with Judge's assessment? How would applying her recommendations affect the outcome in *Video Pipeline*? For an argument that "copyright misuse should be decoupled from its basis in antitrust principles and instead should be based primarily in First Amendment speech principles," see David S. Olson, *First Amendment Based Copyright Misuse*, 52 WM. & MARY L. REV. 537 (2010).

2. Is the copyright misuse defense necessary if the copyright holder is acting anticompetitively in violation of the antitrust laws? When?

As you read the following case, consider a theory of how Omega might be misusing its copyright and how that theory relates to those considered in *Video Pipeline*.

Omega S.A. v. Costco Wholesale Corp.
776 F.3d 692 (9th Cir. 2015)

{Before the *Kirtsaeng* case you studied in Chapter V on the importation right, the U.S. Supreme Court had granted certiorari in this case to address the same issue about the first-sale doctrine's applicability with regard to the importation right. In this case, Costco had bought Omega watches abroad for less than their sale price in the United States, whereupon Costco sold them more cheaply in the United States than that sale price. The Supreme Court, sitting without Justice Kagan, deadlocked 4-4 on whether the first-sale doctrine applied to imports, which left the earlier Ninth Circuit decision in place that had held that it did not (which the Supreme Court later overturned in *Kirtsaeng*). On remand, the district court granted summary judgment to Costco on the ground that Omega misused its copyright.}

NELSON, J.: ...

[1] Omega manufactures luxury watches in Switzerland, which it distributes around the world. One of Omega's high-end watches, the Seamaster, sometimes bears an engraving of the Omega Globe Design. Omega obtained a copyright for the Omega Globe in March 2003. Omega began selling some Seamaster watches with engraved reproductions of the Omega Globe in September 2003.

[2] Omega distributes its watches, including the Seamaster, through authorized distributors and dealers throughout the world, including the United States. In 2003, Costco and Omega discussed the possibility of Costco carrying Omega watches. The parties did not come to an agreement and Costco never became an authorized Omega retailer.

[3] In 2004, Costco purchased 117 Seamaster watches bearing the Omega Globe on the so-called "gray market." First, Omega sold the watches to authorized foreign distributors. Next, unidentified third parties purchased the watches and sold them to ENE Limited, a New York company. Costco purchased the watches from ENE Limited. Costco then sold 43 of those watches to its members in California. Omega undoubtedly authorized the initial sale of the watches but did not approve the importation of the watches into the United States or Costco's later sale of the watches.

[4] Omega sued Costco for copyright infringement, specifically the importation of copyrighted work without the copyright holder's permission....

[5] On remand [from the Supreme Court], the district court again granted summary judgment to Costco, finding that Omega misused its copyright of the Omega Globe to expand its limited monopoly impermissibly....

[6] While briefing in this matter was pending, the Supreme Court revisited the first sale doctrine in *Kirtsaeng*, 133 S. Ct. at 1355....

[7] It is clear [from the *Kirtsaeng* ruling] that Omega has no infringement cause of action against Costco. Omega's only allegation is that Costco violated Omega's copyright-based importation and distribution rights by selling gray market watches without a prior authorized first sale in the United States. Omega concedes

that it authorized a first sale of the watches in a foreign jurisdiction. Omega's right to control importation and distribution of its copyrighted Omega Globe expired after that authorized first sale, and Costco's subsequent sale of the watches did not constitute copyright infringement....

WARDLAW, J., concurring in the judgment:

[8] The district court granted summary judgment ... to Costco based on the defense of copyright misuse. The majority affirms the district court relying upon the *Kirtsaeng*-resurrected first sale doctrine .... I concur in the judgment affirming the district court, but do so based on the district court's rationale for granting summary judgment—copyright misuse—and the arguments actually presented to us....

[9] The majority opinion fails to do justice to the facts presented by this unique lawsuit. Costco is one of America's largest retailers. It is well known that Costco's discount warehouses sell everything from pallets of toilet paper to slices of pizza. But only card-carrying members know that Costco also sells a wide range of luxury goods, including Dom Pérignon Champagne, Waterford crystal, Dolce & Gabbana handbags, and, until this lawsuit was filed, Omega watches.

Omega sued Costco for copyright infringement because Costco sold, without Omega's permission, forty-three genuine Omega watches in the United States. Each watch Costco sold was engraved with a copyrighted Omega design, which Costco did not have permission to use. The district court concluded, however, that because Omega placed the Globe Design on its watches at least in part to control the importation and sale of Omega watches in the United States, Omega had misused its copyright. In District Court Judge Terry Hatter's words, Omega impermissibly "used the defensive shield of copyright as an offensive sword." ...

[10] Omega is a Swiss luxury watchmaker which distributes and sells its watches around the world through authorized distributors and retailers. It is also a wholly-owned subsidiary of the Swiss corporation the Swatch Group, Ltd. The Swatch Group (U.S.), Inc. is Omega's authorized and exclusive distributor in the United States. Costco, a U.S. corporation, operates membership warehouse clubs which sell merchandise, including brand-name watches, to their members at lower prices than are available through many other retailers.

[11] Sometime before March 2003, Swatch U.S.A. learned that Costco was selling genuine Omega watches in the United States without Omega's authorization. Costco had circumvented Omega's distribution model and procured the Omega watches through the "gray market." Gray market goods, or parallel imports, are genuine brand-name products typically manufactured abroad, purchased, and imported into the United States by third parties. Retailers are able to sell these products at a discount through arbitrage, e.g., if Omega's watches retail for less in Morocco than in the United States, and Costco procures the watches at the Moroccan price and then imports them into the United States, Costco can undercut the authorized U.S. retailers. Costco was only the latest in a series of unauthorized retailers selling Omega watches in the United States. Because Costco and the other "unauthorized" retailers were selling Omega watches at far lower prices than Omega's suggested retail price, Swatch U.S.A. began to receive complaints from authorized Omega retailers.[3] Swatch U.S.A.'s then-president was faced with a mounting distribution problem. To increase Swatch U.S.A.'s control over Omega watches in the United States, Swatch U.S.A.'s president took action "to stem the tide of the gray market."

[12] Swatch U.S.A.'s legal department devised a strategy to use copyright protection to strengthen Omega's control over the importation of Omega watches into the United States. On March 12, 2003, Omega registered its "Globe Design" for U.S. copyright protection, and then began engraving a miniscule Globe Design on the

---

[3] When this lawsuit was filed in 2004, Omega's suggested retail price for the Omega "Seamaster," one of the brand's best-selling watches and the watch that is at the center of this copyright dispute, was $1,995. Costco sold the watch for the price of $1,299.

underside of the best-selling Seamaster watch. Although the Omega Seamaster was the first product line engraved with the Globe Design, Omega's plan was to eventually place copyrighted engravings on many of Swatch U.S.A.'s product lines and use the design's copyright protection to prevent unauthorized retailers from selling Omega's watches.[4]

[13] On remand [from the U.S. Supreme Court in the ensuing lawsuit], the parties ... cross-moved for summary judgment.... [T]he district court granted Costco's motion for summary judgment, based on the equitable defense of copyright misuse. The district court found that the purpose of Omega's lawsuit was to "stem the tide of the grey market" and the "unauthorized importation of Omega watches into the U.S." Omega had conceded that it had affixed the copyrighted Globe Design to the underside of its watches to take advantage of section 602 of the Copyright Act, which makes the importation of copyrighted goods into the United States without the copyright owner's authorization a violation of the owner's exclusive right to distribute. The district court concluded that Omega misused its copyright in the Globe Design by leveraging its limited monopoly over the design to control the importation and sale of Seamaster watches....

Figure 126: Omega watch globe, as compared with U.S. Quarter

[14] Because Omega's watches are useful articles, they are not copyrightable, with some possible exceptions not before us. Because the watches are not the proper subject of copyright protection, Omega does not argue that Costco infringed copyrights protecting its watches, the argument upon which the majority rests its opinion. Instead, it argues that Costco infringed its limited monopoly over the copyrighted Globe Design, which was engraved on the watches that Costco sold.

[15] Inherent in granting a copyright owner the exclusive right to reproduce his works is the risk that he will abuse the limited monopoly his copyright provides by restricting competition in a market that is beyond the scope of his copyright. An owner's attempt to impermissibly expand his lawful protection from competition contravenes not only the policy of the copyright laws, but also the central purpose of the antitrust laws. Copyright misuse is a judicially crafted affirmative defense to copyright infringement designed to combat the impermissible extension of a copyright's limited monopoly. Its purpose is to prevent holders of copyrights from leveraging their limited monopoly to allow them control of areas outside the monopoly.

---

[4] Although Omega had been engraving artistic designs, such as its "Seahorse," on the underside of its watches for decades as "a mark of prestige and luxury and identification," the Globe Design was markedly different. By contrast to the "Seahorse," which was prominently displayed on the watch's underside, the Globe Design measured only one-eighth of an inch in diameter—roughly the size of the hole in a Cheerio. Also, unlike it had with the "Seahorse," Omega neither advertised nor promoted the Globe Design.

[16] The defense of copyright misuse, however, is not limited to discouraging anti-competitive behavior. Indeed, the question is not whether the copyright is being used in a manner violative of antitrust law, but whether the copyright is being used in a manner violative of the public policy embodied in the grant of a copyright.... [C]opyright misuse does not invalidate a copyright, but precludes its enforcement during the period of misuse.

[17] The copyright misuse doctrine forbids the use of the copyright to secure an exclusive right or limited monopoly not granted by the Copyright Office. The defense is often applied when a defendant can prove either: (1) a violation of the antitrust laws; (2) that the copyright owner otherwise illegally extended its monopoly; or (3) that the copyright owner violated the public policies underlying the copyright laws. We have discussed copyright misuse in only a handful of published opinions. But while we have applied the doctrine sparingly, copyright misuse is a valid defense, the contours of which are still being defined....

[18] .... This appeal presents the novel issue whether Omega's attempted use of its Globe Design copyright to control imports and restrict competition from unauthorized retailers of its watches, which are neither copyrightable nor copyrighted, constitutes copyright misuse....

[19] The district court correctly held that Omega misused its copyright "by leveraging its limited monopoly in being able to control the importation of [the Globe Design] to control the importation of its Seamaster watches." The district court did not clearly err in finding that: (1) Omega copyrighted the Globe Design, at the advice of its legal department, to control the importation and distribution of Omega watches into the United States; and (2) Omega told its authorized distributors that the purpose of suing Costco was to "stem the tide of the grey market" and the "unauthorized importation of Omega watches into the U.S." In other words, Omega attempted to use the copyrighted Globe Design to decrease competition in the U.S. importation and distribution of its watches by it and its authorized dealers—an obvious leveraging of a copyright to control an area outside its limited monopoly on the design.

[20] Omega argues that its anti-competitive motives are irrelevant to the issue of copyright misuse. According to Omega, our inquiry should instead focus on the copyright holder's objective conduct or use. But Omega's semantic hairsplitting is unpersuasive. By definition, "use" includes an inquiry into purpose. *See* BLACK'S LAW DICTIONARY 1681 (9th ed. 2009) (defining "use" as "The application or employment of something; esp., a long-continued possession and employment of a thing *for a purpose* for which it is adapted") (emphasis added). However, we need not decide whether Omega's motives are sufficient to establish copyright misuse. The undisputed record shows that before this lawsuit consumers were able to a buy a genuine Omega Seamaster watch from Costco for 35% less than Omega's suggested retail price. This is no longer the case. Thus, at least one consequence of Omega's lawsuit has been a reduction of intrabrand price competition for uncopyrightable Omega watches in the United States.

[21] Lastly, because copyright misuse is an equitable defense to an infringement action, the core of our inquiry is whether equity may rightly withhold its assistance from such a use of the copyright by declining to entertain a suit for infringement until the improper practice has been abandoned and the consequences of the misuse of the copyright have been dissipated. If Omega was using its copyright in a manner contrary to public policy, we, as a court of equity, may refuse to aid such misuse.

[22] Equity supports the district court's refusal to enforce Omega's copyright in its Globe Design against Costco during the period of Omega's misuse. Omega wielded its copyrighted Globe Design to restrict unauthorized retailers from selling genuine Omega watches procured from the gray market. Indeed, in his deposition, Swatch U.S.A.'s president agreed that the "whole purpose" of creating the Globe Design in the first place was to prevent unauthorized retailers from selling Omega watches. Because unauthorized retailers, such as Costco, were selling gray market Omega watches in the United States below Omega's suggested

retail price, Omega attempted to maintain the price of its watches sold in the United States by inconspicuously engraving the copyrighted Globe Design on the underside of its Seamaster watches. Even drawing all reasonable inferences in Omega's favor, there is no genuine dispute as to whether Omega sued Costco for copyright infringement at least in part to control the unauthorized importation and sale of Omega watches. Thus, the district court did not err in granting Costco's motion for summary judgment on the copyright misuse defense....

[23] Omega's right to control distribution of its copyrighted work is not limitless. The Supreme Court has made clear that the property right granted by copyright law cannot be used with impunity to extend power in the marketplace beyond what Congress intended. Copyright misuse bars a culpable plaintiff from prevailing on an action for the infringement of the misused copyright. The Copyright Office granted Omega the exclusive right to control the importation and distribution of the Globe Design into the United States. It did not empower Omega to restrict competition from unauthorized retailers selling genuine, gray market Seamaster watches in the United States. Although the Globe Design engraved on the underside of the Seamaster watches was copyrighted, Omega misused its copyright when it used its intellectual property protection to obtain a copyright-like monopoly over uncopyrightable Seamaster watches. Omega's expansion of its copyright-like monopoly eliminated competition from unauthorized watch retailers like Costco, thereby allowing Omega to control—through its exclusive distributor, Swatch U.S.A.—the retail pricing of Seamaster watches sold in the United States. If the copyright law allowed Omega to use its copyright to combat the importation and sale of all gray market watches that are stamped with the Globe Design, it would effectively grant Omega a copyright-like monopoly over the distribution and sale of Omega watches in the United States. Because such an outcome directly controverts the aims of copyright law, it is impermissible....

[24] .... Even when drawing all reasonable inferences in Omega's favor, there is no genuine dispute concerning whether restricting retail competition was one of the reasons Omega sued Costco for copyright infringement.

[25] Omega had other available remedies. It could have terminated its distribution agreements with the distributors that sold Omega watches outside of their designated territories. Or, if Omega believed that Costco, or intermediaries like ENE Limited, were inducing distributors to breach their contracts, Omega may have been able to sue them for tortious interference. Instead, Omega improvidently decided to sue Costco for copyright infringement. By doing so, Omega misused the Congressionally limited power of copyright protection to address a problem better left for other avenues of relief.

[26] .... Because the district court correctly held that Omega misused its copyright in the Globe Design by attempting to leverage its limited monopoly over the design to control the importation and sale of Seamaster watches, I would affirm the district court on the issue of copyright misuse.

NOTES

1. For purposes of assessing copyright misuse (or any other copyright doctrine, for that matter), does it and should it matter why a copyright holder is asserting its rights? Jeanne Fromer observes that not all those who assert infringement of their copyright are doing so because they think they've experienced copyright harm: "a not insignificant number of assertions of copyright ... rights against third parties seek not to protect these interests, but others, such as privacy, protection of ancillary markets, or mere extraction of rents without making a sufficient contribution to society." Jeanne C. Fromer, *Should the Law Care Why Intellectual Property Rights Have Been Asserted?*, 53 HOUS. L. REV. 549, 551 (2015). Fromer reasons that "assertions of rights with ill-fitting motivations are sufficiently worrisome that courts ought to strongly consider weighing these motivations before granting relief." Why? She elaborates:

The biggest worry is that these assertions will distort the intellectual property system, causing harm to society. There are two related worries of distortion and harm. First, ... copyright ... law[is] calibrated to offer up incentive to create and disseminate valuable works to benefit society, but limited in time and scope to ameliorate the costs that the incentive of exclusive rights imposes on society. On this view, copyright ... law[was] designed with particular scenarios in mind, and [its] costs and benefits are attuned to those scenarios. Assertions of intellectual property outside of these scenarios can impose greater cost on society than the intellectual property laws had anticipated without concomitant benefit.... Allowing copyright ... claims to succeed[, for example,] when the rightsholder has not contributed much to societal progress in ways that matter to the law's foundations are troubling, because they impose the cost of protection on society without a corresponding gain. Similarly, assertions of protection for markets beyond the protected market—be they in relation to privacy and reputational interests or more generally—raise the specter of great cost to society. If rights are protected in those cases, they are likely to impose an additional cost on society because they will be imposing restrictions on market interests outside of the copyright ... system in addition to those within. On this reasoning, it makes sense for courts to screen out assertions of copyright ... rights by plaintiffs with motivations unrelated to the intellectual property system.

More subtly, there is another distortion and harm that can be imposed by assertions of intellectual property with motives mismatched to copyright ... laws.... [C]ourts' interpretations of ... copyright laws can be influenced by the plaintiff's mismatched motivation. These interpretations, if not carefully and explicitly tailored to the particular circumstances of the plaintiff's motivation for asserting rights, can affect others with more typical motivations for asserting their rights.

Do you agree that a plaintiff's motivations for asserting copyright sometimes ought to affect a court's decision? If so, how should courts respond to assertions of copyright infringement with ill-fitting motivations?

2. A party who has engaged in copyright misuse is restrained from enforcing the copyright or copyrights that have been misused, and such restraint is imposed until the misuse has been "cured." A recent case is instructive on how a plaintiff can cure copyright misuse. In this case, Disney had been distributing some of its movies in Combo Packs, which included a Blu-Ray disc, a DVD, and an alphanumeric code that could be redeemed online to stream or download a digital copy. Small print on the outside of the Combo Pack boxes stated that "Codes are not for sale or transfer." Even finer print on the boxes' bottom stated that "Terms and Conditions apply" with regard to the digital codes. The download code includes instructions for download and also states that "Codes are not for sale or transfer." The download website states—along with other terms—that by redeeming a code, the user "represents that [he] is the owner of the physical product that accompanied the digital code at the time of purchase. The redemption of a digital code sold or transferred separate from the original physical product is prohibited."

Disney sued Redbox for contributory copyright infringement for purchasing Disney's Combo Packs, disaggregating the three items in the packs, and then offering each for separate distribution (including the download codes for sale). Disney maintained that Redbox's resale of Combo Pack digital download codes encouraged end users to make unauthorized reproductions of Disney's copyrighted works.

The district court denied Disney a preliminary injunction on the ground that it was unlikely to succeed on the merits due to its commission of copyright misuse. Disney Enters., Inc. v. Redbox Automated Retail, LLC, No. CV 17–08655 DDP (AGRx), 2018 WL 1942139 (C.D. Cal. Feb. 20, 2018). The court elaborated:

Disney's copyrights do not give it the power to prevent consumers from selling or otherwise transferring the Blu-ray discs and DVDs contained within Combo Packs.... Nevertheless, the terms of [the] digital download services' license agreements purport to give Disney a power specifically denied to copyright holders by § 109(a). [They] require[] redeemers to represent that they are currently the owner of the physical product that accompanied the digital code at the time of purchase .... Thus, Combo Pack purchasers cannot access digital movie content, for which they have already paid, without exceeding the scope of the license agreement unless they forego their statutorily-guaranteed right to distribute their physical copies of that same movie as they see fit. This improper leveraging of Disney's copyright in the digital content to restrict secondary transfers of physical copies directly implicates and conflicts with public policy enshrined in the Copyright Act, and constitutes copyright misuse.

(Note that the court finds copyright misuse even though all of the content that Disney seeks to control is protected by copyright law, by contrast with *Omega*.) Disney responded by expeditiously revising its terms in an attempt to cure the misuse (and bolster its copyright infringement claim). Among other things, the new terms no longer required physical possession of the physical products contained in the Combo Packs to download but instead required that the digital code "may be redeemed only by an individual who obtains the code in the original combination disc + code package" and that "[d]igital codes are not authorized for redemption if sold separately." The district court thought that, in light of this and other changed language, Disney had now shown a likelihood of success on its claim for copyright infringement and granted a preliminary injunction against Redbox. Disney Enters., Inc. v. Redbox Automated Retail, LLC, 336 F. Supp. 3d 1146 (C.D. Cal. 2018). In so doing, the court ruled that Disney could move forward to enforce its copyrights because it was no longer misusing its copyrights. The court explained that Disney's "revised terms do not encroach upon disc owners' alienation rights or improperly expand Disney's power beyond the sphere of copyright. Under the revised terms, Combo Pack purchasers and recipients continue to enjoy digital access regardless whether they keep or dispose of the physical discs."

3. Do you think copyright misuse is better left as an affirmative defense to copyright infringement? Or would it be preferable to create an affirmative cause of action that can be brought for copyright misuse?

4. Can copyright non-use ever constitute copyright misuse? If not, should the defense be expanded to include it under appropriate circumstances?

D. Preemption

In addition to copyright misuse, courts might also restrict the operation of contract law by invoking preemption when the state law of contracts conflicts in certain ways with the operation of the federal copyright law. Contract law is not the only state law that can conflict with copyright law, and we will also touch on the ways that copyright law can preempt the operation of other state laws. Usually, these state laws expand copyright protection, but the relevant state laws might theoretically also contract copyright protection. Both categories of state law raise preemption issues.

Think for a moment about many of the categories of material you've already learned about that copyright law has been held not to protect: these include (just to name a few) databases lacking originality, soundalike sound recordings, ideas, historical facts, and many useful articles. Can state law protect these categories in spite of their lack of protection under federal copyright law, either by providing outright protection to these categories or by enforcing contracts between private parties that provide a form of this protection between the contracting parties?

Chapter X – Contract & Other State Laws

Recall that the Constitution grants Congress authority "To promote the Progress of Science and useful Arts, by securing for limited Times to Authors and Inventors the exclusive Right to their respective Writings and Discoveries." Pursuant to this grant of power, Congress has enacted copyright law. Take a step back for a moment to consider why the Framers might have been motivated to federalize copyright law in the first instance. The primary rationale was to provide a uniform national copyright law. Previously, a number of states had had copyright laws, but the differences inhibited the development of national markets: the substantive rules could vary from state to state—meaning, for example, that the authors of a work might be different depending on the state—and the administrative burdens were greater, with a need to register copyright in each state or bring suit in each state. The 1790 Act aimed to displace state copyright laws and bring published authors into the federal copyright protection scheme. Uniformity was also a strong motivator for bringing unpublished works into federal copyright law in the 1976 Act.

Does this desire for uniformity in copyright law indicate that states can play no role in supplementing or changing copyright law at all? This question is analyzed under the rubric of preemption. The Supremacy Clause of the Constitution provides a basis for preemption of state law by federal law. The Clause provides that "[t]h[e] Constitution, and the Laws of the United States which shall be made in pursuance thereof; and all treaties made, or which shall be made, under the authority of the United States, shall be the supreme law of the land." U.S. CONST. art. IV, cl. 2.

Generally, the Supreme Court has classified three different types of preemption of state law: **express preemption**, **field preemption**, and **conflict preemption**. Pac. Gas & Elec. Co. v. State Energy Res. Conservation & Dev. Comm'n, 461 U.S. 190 (1983). Express preemption occurs when Congress legislates, in a lawful exercise of authority, to state explicitly how its laws preempt state laws. The other two forms of preemption are implicit. Field preemption dictates that federal law supersedes state law when there is a "scheme of federal regulation so pervasive as to make reasonable the inference that Congress left no room to supplement it," either "because the federal interest [in the field] is so dominant or because the object sought to be obtained by the federal law and the character of obligations imposed by it may reveal the same purpose." *Id.* at 204. Conflict preemption "arises when compliance with both federal and state regulations is a physical impossibility or where state law stands as an obstacle to the accomplishment and execution of the full purposes and objectives of Congress." *Id.* A state law is preempted by federal law if any one or more of these three categories of preemption is found.

Consider first field preemption in the context of copyright law. The Supreme Court's rulings seem to reject the possibility of field preemption for copyright law. In particular, in *Goldstein v. California*, 412 U.S. 546 (1973), the Court rejected a preemption challenge to a California law criminalizing unauthorized copying of sound recordings with intent to sell them, at a time when federal copyright law did not yet confer protection on sound recordings. The Court reasoned that "[a]lthough the Copyright Clause ... recognizes the potential benefits of a national system, it does not indicate that all writings are of national interest or that state legislation is, in all cases, unnecessary or precluded." This statement seems to reject field preemption for copyright law.

Now consider conflict preemption in the context of federal intellectual property laws. Conflict preemption can be complex and hard to model, but to give you a feel for it, let's look at two Supreme Court decisions on conflict preemption, one that concludes that there isn't conflict preemption and one that concludes that there is.

In *Aronson v. Quick Point Pencil Co.*, 440 U.S. 257 (1979), the Supreme Court held that the federal patent laws did not preempt state contract law "to preclude enforcement of a contract to pay royalties to a patent applicant, on sales of articles embodying the putative invention, for so long as the contracting party sells them, if a patent is not granted." In that case, the parties had contracted for a specific royalty rate, which would be de-escalated by half were no patent to issue within five years. The Court thought that the contract at issue complemented, rather than interfered with, the balance effectuated by the federal patent scheme. It thought that the royalty contract provided an extra incentive to innovate, did not discourage patenting, promoted disclosure by encouraging the invention's commercialization, and did not remove any unpatented invention from the public domain (as the invention had not truly been in the public domain at the time of contracting and remained available to anyone else to use freely once the patent was not granted).

The Supreme Court considered patent law's preemptive effect again in *Bonito Boats, Inc. v. Thunder Craft Boats, Inc.*, 489 U.S. 141 (1989), in ruling on the constitutionality of a Florida law prohibiting the use of direct molding to duplicate for sale any manufactured vessel hull or component thereof without permission. The Court held that federal patent law preempted the state law. It reasoned that the U.S. Constitution's Intellectual Property Clause "reflects a balance between the need to encourage innovation and the avoidance of monopolies which stifle competition without any concomitant advance in the 'Progress of Science and useful Arts.'" As such, the Court continued, progress of science and useful arts is promoted—and authorized— only when rights of limited duration are granted and when the public domain is guarded against removals of material therein. To the Court, the patent laws effectuate this balance with its requirements of novelty and nonobviousness, which ensure that the public domain is the norm rather than the exception, and patent law's disclosure rules, which induce a public sharing of information for the benefit of the public domain. Through this analytical lens, the Court reasoned that the Florida law was preempted, as it upset this balance. For one thing, the state law's purpose was the same as that set out in the Intellectual Property Clause: to promote technological progress. Additionally, it sought to accomplish that goal by upsetting patent law's balance between promoting innovation through rights and competition, by providing producers with protection over unpatentable designs, which by the federal scheme, ought to be in the public domain.

In explaining the different result in *Aronson*, the *Bonito Boats* Court observed:

> We have ... reaffirmed the pragmatic approach which [we] take[] to the pre-emption of state laws dealing with the protection of intellectual property. See Aronson, 440 U.S. at 262 ("State law is not displaced merely because the contract relates to intellectual property which may or may not be patentable; the states are free to regulate the use of such intellectual property in any manner not inconsistent with federal law."). At the same time, we have consistently reiterated the teaching of [other cases] that ideas once placed before the public without the protection of a valid patent are subject to appropriation without significant restraint.

Do you think that *Aronson* and *Bonito Boats* are reconcilable in their approaches? For an argument that they are, see Paul Heald, *Federal Intellectual Property Law and the Economics of Preemption*, 76 IOWA L. REV. 959 (1991).

If nothing else, the different results in *Aronson* and *Bonito Boats*—not to mention many other decisions on conflict preemption by federal intellectual property laws—might underscore that even if the general framework for evaluating conflict preemption is clear, its application is not always evident. For an argument that courts' analyses of conflict preemption would be clarified and sharpened were courts to take account of the Intellectual Property Clause in their analyses, see Jeanne C. Fromer, *The Intellectual Property Clause's Preemptive Effect*, in INTELLECTUAL PROPERTY AND THE COMMON LAW 265 (Shyamkrishna Balganesh ed., 2013). In particular, Fromer argues that "state laws are preempted when they both fall within the IP Clause's preemptive scope and upset the IP Clause's balance, as instantiated by federal law."

Express preemption is also relevant to copyright law. In its 1976 revision of copyright law, Congress included a preemption provision in § 301. Section 301(a) provides that state laws are preempted when two conditions are met: (1) they confer "legal or equitable rights that are equivalent to any of the exclusive rights" provided by federal copyright law; and (2) they protect "works of authorship that are fixed in a tangible medium of expression and come within the subject matter of copyright as specified by sections 102 and 103" of the copyright laws. Section 301 was intended to clarify copyright's preemptive reach. (For a thorough history of this provision, see Howard B. Abrams, *Copyright, Misappropriation, and Preemption: Constitutional and Statutory Limits of State Law Protection*, 1983 SUP. CT. REV. 509.)

Despite the seeming determinacy of the Copyright Act's express preemption provision, the often-conflicting judicial decisions construing and applying § 301 underscore that, however express the preemption, analysis of the preemption provision's scope is anything but clear. In particular, when is a state right equivalent to copyright's exclusive rights, as the first factor requires? Most courts find that a state right is not preempted under § 301 when it contains an "extra element" not found under federal copyright protection. For example, the Sixth Circuit holds:

> *Equivalency exists if the right defined by state law may be abridged by an act which in and of itself would infringe one of the exclusive rights. Conversely, if an extra element is required instead of or in addition to the acts of reproduction, performance, distribution or display in order to constitute a state-created cause of action, there is no preemption, provided that the extra element changes the nature of the action so that it is qualitatively different from a copyright infringement claim.*

Wrench LLC v. Taco Bell Corp., 256 F.3d 446 (6th Cir. 2001). Under this framework, most state rights, including laws of contract, trade secrecy, and rights of publicity, are not likely to be preempted by § 301, as they have additional elements that copyright law does not. By contrast, a minority of courts hold that a state law is "equivalent to any of the exclusive rights" in § 106 if a copyright holder violates the state law merely by exercising any of his or her exclusive rights. *See, e.g.*, Baltimore Orioles, Inc. v. Major League Baseball Players Ass'n, 805 F.2d 663 (7th Cir. 1986). From this second framework, state laws can more easily be preempted under § 301.

In light of copyright law's express-preemption provision in § 301, many courts begin and end their analysis of copyright preemption with that section. However, to the extent that a state law causes an actual conflict or creates a sufficient obstacle to the goals of federal law, the Supremacy Clause, as understood by the Supreme Court, should nonetheless nullify that state law pursuant to principles of conflict preemption. This is true even if the express preemption provision in § 301 does not nullify that state law: the Supreme Court has rejected the "argument that the presence of [an] express pre-emption provision entirely foreclose[s] the possibility of conflict pre-emption," Geier v. Am. Honda Motor Co., 529 U.S. 861, 872 (2000), thereby suggesting that courts should always proceed with an analysis of conflict preemption by federal copyright law even if § 301 does not preempt the state law at hand.

With this background on preemption doctrine, let's consider whether contracts modifying copyright law's rules are ever preempted by copyright law. You may already be familiar with *ProCD, Inc. v. Zeidenberg*, 86 F.3d 1447 (7th Cir. 1996). In that case, ProCD had created a searchable database from 3,000 telephone directories. Probably fearing that the database would not be original (and therefore not copyrightable) post-*Feist*, it included a mass-market shrink-wrap license with the CD-ROM discs it sold to consumers. Although the license for consumers forbade it, the court stated that purchaser Matthew Zeidenberg sought to resell the data contained in the database for a profit. (A higher-priced version of the electronic database—intended for businesses—contained no such contractual restriction.) ProCD sued Zeidenberg for breach of contract, and the Seventh Circuit held that the contract was enforceable and not preempted by copyright law. *ProCD* became an influential case, and indeed, you'll see that the next case discusses it.

As you read the following case, think about the best argument you can make under express- and conflict-preemption principles for preemption of the contract at issue here, and against preemption of it. How does your framing of the case differ depending on your stance? Also, is there a material difference for preemption between a state law modifying copyright law and a contractual agreement doing the same?

Bowers v. Baystate Technologies, Inc.

320 F.3d 1317 (Fed. Cir. 2003) (en banc)

RADER, J.: ...

[1] Harold L. Bowers created a template to improve computer aided design (CAD) software....

[2] .... Mr. Bowers bundled [software] together as the Designer's Toolkit. Mr. Bowers sold the Designer's Toolkit with a shrink-wrap license that, *inter alia*, prohibited any reverse engineering.

[3] In 1989, Baystate also developed and marketed other [CAD] tools .... In 1988 and 1989, Mr. Bowers offered to establish a formal relationship with Baystate .... Baystate rejected that offer, however, telling Mr. Bowers that it believed it had "the in-house capability to develop the type of products you have proposed."

[4] In 1990, Mr. Bowers released Designer's Toolkit. By January 1991, Baystate had obtained copies of that product. Three months later, Baystate introduced the substantially revised Draft–Pak version 3, incorporating many of the features of Designer's Toolkit....

[5] Baystate sued Mr. Bowers for declaratory judgment that 1) Baystate's products do not infringe [Bowers' patent], 2) the patent is invalid, and 3) the patent is unenforceable. Mr. Bowers filed counterclaims for copyright infringement, patent infringement, and breach of contract.

[6] Following trial, the jury found for Mr. Bowers and awarded $1,948,869 for copyright infringement, $3,831,025 for breach of contract, and $232,977 for patent infringement. The district court, however, set aside the copyright damages as duplicative of the contract damages and entered judgment for $5,270,142 ....

[7] Baystate contends that the Copyright Act preempts the prohibition of reverse engineering embodied in Mr. Bowers' shrink-wrap license agreements. Swayed by this argument, the district court considered Mr. Bowers' contract and copyright claims coextensive. The district court instructed the jury that "reverse engineering violates the license agreement only if Baystate's product that resulted from reverse engineering infringes Bowers' copyright because it copies protectable expression." Mr. Bowers lodged a timely objection to this instruction. This court holds that the Copyright Act does not preempt or narrow the scope of Mr. Bowers' contract claim.

[8] .... The Copyright Act provides that "all legal or equitable rights that are equivalent to any of the exclusive rights within the general scope of copyright ... are governed exclusively by this title." 17 U.S.C. § 301(a). [We] do[] not interpret this language to require preemption as long as a state cause of action requires an extra element, beyond mere copying, preparation of derivative works, performance, distribution or display. Nevertheless, not every extra element of a state law claim will establish a qualitative variance between the rights protected by federal copyright law and those protected by state law....

[9] .... [T]he Copyright Act does not preempt the state contract action in this case. Indeed, most courts to examine this issue have found that the Copyright Act does not preempt contractual constraints on copyrighted articles. *See, e.g.,* ProCD, Inc. v. Zeidenberg, 86 F.3d 1447 (7th Cir. 1996) (holding that a shrink-wrap license was not preempted by federal copyright law).

[10] In *ProCD*, for example, the court found that the mutual assent and consideration required by a contract claim render that claim qualitatively different from copyright infringement.... [T]he court in *ProCD* reasoned: "A copyright is a right against the world. Contracts, by contrast, generally affect only their parties; strangers may do as they please, so contracts do not create 'exclusive rights.'" ... [W]e follow the reasoning of *ProCD* and the majority of other courts to consider this issue. This court, therefore, holds that the Copyright Act does not preempt Mr. Bowers' contract claims.

[11] In making this determination, this court has left untouched the conclusions reached in [other cases] regarding reverse engineering as a statutory fair use exception to copyright infringement.... Likewise, this claim distinction does not conflict with the expressly defined circumstances in which reverse engineering is not copyright infringement under 17 U.S.C. § 1201(f) (section of the Digital Millennium Copyright Act) ....

[12] Moreover, while the Fifth Circuit has held a state law prohibiting all copying of a computer program is preempted by the federal Copyright Act, *Vault Corp. v. Quaid Software, Ltd.*, 847 F.2d 255 (5th Cir. 1988), no evidence suggests the First Circuit {whose case law governs on this issue} would extend this concept to include private contractual agreements supported by mutual assent and consideration. The First Circuit recognizes contractual waiver of affirmative defenses and statutory rights.... [P]rivate parties are free to contractually forego the limited ability to reverse engineer a software product under the exemptions of the Copyright Act. Of course, a party bound by such a contract may elect to efficiently breach the agreement in order to ascertain ideas in a computer program unprotected by copyright law. Under such circumstances, the breaching party must weigh the benefits of breach against the arguably de minimus damages arising from merely discerning non-protected code....

DYK, J., concurring in part and dissenting in part:

[13] I join the majority opinion except insofar as it holds that the contract claim is not preempted by federal law.... By holding that shrinkwrap licenses that override the fair use defense are not preempted by the Copyright Act, the majority has rendered a decision in conflict with the only other federal court of appeals decision that has addressed the issue—the Fifth Circuit decision in *Vault Corp. v. Quaid Software Ltd.*, 847 F.2d 255 (5th Cir. 1988). The majority's approach permits state law to eviscerate an important federal copyright policy reflected in the fair use defense, and the majority's logic threatens other federal copyright policies as well. I respectfully dissent....

[14] Congress has made the Copyright Act the exclusive means for protecting copyright. The Act provides that "all legal or equitable rights that are equivalent to any of the exclusive rights within the general scope of copyright ... are governed exclusively by this title." 17 U.S.C. § 301(a). All other laws, including the common law, are preempted....

[15] The test for preemption by copyright law ... should be whether the state law "substantially impedes the public use of the otherwise unprotected" material. Bonito Boats, Inc. v. Thunder Craft Boats, Inc., 489 U.S. 141, 157, 167 (1989). That test seeks to determine whether the state cause of action contains an additional element not present in the copyright right, such as scienter. If the state cause of action contains such an extra element, it is not preempted by the Copyright Act. However, such an action is equivalent in substance to a copyright infringement claim and thus preempted by the Copyright Act where the additional element merely concerns the extent to which authors and their licensees can prohibit unauthorized copying by third parties....

[16] The fair use defense is an important limitation on copyright....

[17] .... [T]he fair use defense for reverse engineering is necessary so that copyright protection does not "extend to any idea, procedure, process, system, method of operation, concept, principle, or discovery, regardless of the form in which it is described, explained, illustrated, or embodied in such work," as proscribed by the Copyright Act....

[18] A state is not free to eliminate the fair use defense. Enforcement of a total ban on reverse engineering would conflict with the Copyright Act itself by protecting otherwise unprotectable material. If state law provided that a copyright holder could bar fair use of the copyrighted material by placing a black dot on each copy of the work offered for sale, there would be no question but that the state law would be preempted. A state law that allowed a copyright holder to simply label its products so as to eliminate a fair use defense would "substantially impede" the public's right to fair use and allow the copyright holder, through state law, to protect material that the Congress has determined must be free to all under the Copyright Act. *See Bonito Boats*, 489 U.S. at 157.

[19] I nonetheless agree with the majority opinion that a state can permit parties to contract away a fair use defense or to agree not to engage in uses of copyrighted material that are permitted by the copyright law, if the contract is freely negotiated. A freely negotiated agreement represents the "extra element" that prevents preemption of a state law claim that would otherwise be identical to the infringement claim barred by the fair use defense of reverse engineering.

[20] However, state law giving effect to shrinkwrap licenses is no different in substance from a hypothetical black dot law. Like any other contract of adhesion, the only choice offered to the purchaser is to avoid making the purchase in the first place. State law thus gives the copyright holder the ability to eliminate the fair use defense in each and every instance at its option. In doing so, as the majority concedes, it authorizes "shrinkwrap agreements ... [that] are far broader than the protection afforded by copyright law." ...

[21] There is, moreover, no logical stopping point to the majority's reasoning. The amici rightly question whether under our original opinion the first sale doctrine and a host of other limitations on copyright protection might be eliminated by shrinkwrap licenses in just this fashion. If by printing a few words on the outside of its product a party can eliminate the fair use defense, then it can also, by the same means, restrict a purchaser from asserting the "first sale" defense, embodied in 17 U.S.C. § 109(a), or any other of the protections Congress has afforded the public in the Copyright Act. That means that, under the majority's reasoning, state law could extensively undermine the protections of the Copyright Act....

[22] The Fifth Circuit's decision in *Vault* directly supports preemption of the shrinkwrap limitation. The majority states that *Vault* held that "a state law prohibiting all copying of a computer program is preempted by the federal Copyright Act" and then states that "no evidence suggests the First Circuit would extend this concept to include private contractual agreements supported by mutual assent and consideration." But, in fact, the Fifth Circuit held that the specific provision of state law that authorized contracts prohibiting reverse engineering, decompilation, or disassembly of computer programs was preempted by federal law because it conflicted with a portion of the Copyright Act and because it "touched upon an area of federal copyright law." From a preemption standpoint, there is no distinction between a state law that explicitly validates a contract that restricts reverse engineering (*Vault*) and general common law that permits such a restriction (as here). On the contrary, the preemption clause of the Copyright Act makes clear that it covers "any such right or equivalent right in any such work *under the common law or statutes of any State.*" 17 U.S.C. § 301(a) (emphasis added).

[23] I do not read *ProCD, Inc. v. Zeidenberg*, 86 F.3d 1447 (7th Cir. 1996), the only other court of appeals shrinkwrap case, as being to the contrary, even though it contains broad language stating that "a simple two-party contract is not 'equivalent to any of the exclusive rights within the general scope of copyright.'" In *ProCD*, the Seventh Circuit validated a shrinkwrap license that restricted the use of a CD-ROM to non-commercial purposes, which the defendant had violated by charging users a fee to access the CD-ROM over the Internet. The court held that the restriction to non-commercial use of the program was not equivalent to any rights protected by the Copyright Act. Rather, the "contract reflect[ed] private ordering, essential to efficient functioning of markets." The court saw the licensor as legitimately seeking to distinguish between personal and commercial use. "ProCD offers software and data for two prices: one for personal use, a higher prices for commercial use," the court said. The defendant "wants to use the data without paying the seller's price." The court also emphasized that the license "would not withdraw any information from the public domain" because all of the information on the CD-ROM was publicly available.

[24] The case before us is different from *ProCD*. The Copyright Act does not confer a right to pay the same amount for commercial and personal use. It does, however, confer a right to fair use, 17 U.S.C. § 107, which we have held encompasses reverse engineering....

[25] I conclude that *Vault* states the correct rule; that state law authorizing shrinkwrap licenses that prohibit reverse engineering is preempted; and that the First Circuit would so hold because the extra element here merely concerns *the extent to which* authors and their licensees can prohibit unauthorized copying by third parties. I respectfully dissent.

NOTES

1. Whether one thinks principles of conflict preemption have a hefty role to play in invalidating state contract laws in favor of federal copyright law is influenced heavily by one's view on whether copyright law provides default rules that parties are free to contract around, or instead whether copyright law crafts an intricate balance between providing and restricting rights to promote the progress of arts and culture, a balance which would be upset by parties varying copyright's rules in contracts. *See* Jeanne C. Fromer, *The Intellectual Property Clause's Preemptive Effect*, *in* INTELLECTUAL PROPERTY AND THE COMMON LAW 265 (Shyamkrishna Balganesh ed., 2013); Dennis S. Karjala, *Federal Preemption of Shrinkwrap and On-Line Licenses*, 22 U. DAYTON L. REV. 511 (1997); Maureen O'Rourke, *Drawing the Boundary Between Copyright and Contract: Copyright Preemption of Software License Terms*, 45 DUKE L.J. 479 (1995). For thoughts on the tensions between freedom of contract and the public benefits of freer uses of information, see J.H. Reichman & Jonathan A. Franklin, *Privately Legislated Intellectual Property Rights: Reconciling Freedom of Contract with Public Good Uses of Information*, 147 U. PA. L. REV. 875 (1999).

2. Should the fact that the copyright restrictions in the contract in *Bowers* were not negotiated matter to the analysis? For an argument that it should, see Viva R. Moffat, *Super-Copyright: Contracts, Preemption, and the Structure of Copyright Policymaking*, 41 U.C. DAVIS L. REV. 45 (2007).

3. Christina Bohannon argues that "preemption law seems ill-suited to contract claims." Christina Bohannon, *Copyright Preemption of Contracts*, 67 MD. L. REV. 616, 619 (2008). She suggests that

> *preemption cases are concerned with whether a state regulatory scheme is likely to supplant a federal scheme. In cases dealing with preemption of contracts, however, that is not ordinarily the issue. State law is necessary to enforce contracts, but the obligations are voluntarily assumed. Thus, the issue is really whether individuals should be able to contract away rights granted by the federal Copyright Act.*

As a consequence, she maintains that "in analyzing the Copyright Act's preemption of contracts, courts should draw more from the law related to contractual waiver of statutory rights." *Id.* Does this analysis help you make better sense of *Bowers*?

4. An empirical study of contracting terms finds substantial increases in reverse-engineering restrictions in contracts post-*Bowers*. Florencia Marotta-Wurgler & Robert Taylor, *Set in Stone? Change and Innovation in Consumer Standard-Form Contracts*, 88 N.Y.U. L. REV. 240 (2013). Does this finding have any bearing on how to evaluate preemption of contracts by copyright law?

Either way, Guy Rub argues that any such contracting changes following decisions like *Bowers* are irrelevant in practice: he maintains that litigation following *ProCD* has principally involved not non-negotiated mass consumer contracts modifying contract terms, but sophisticated parties and their individually negotiated contracts. For that reason, he concludes that "[c]ontracts do not seem to pose a significant risk to copyright policy." Guy A. Rub, *Copyright Survives: Rethinking the Copyright-Contract Conflict*, 103 VA. L. REV. 1141 (2017). Are you convinced by this argument?

5. Could you resolve the preemption claim in *Bowers* instead using principles of copyright misuse?

Most states extend to individuals, either by statute or as a matter of common law, a right of publicity, which is a property-like interest in the use of their name, image, voice, signature, or other personal characteristics in commerce or advertising. These laws are quite different than the contract laws on which this chapter is focused. Are these claims ever preempted by copyright law? To give a flavor of claims of preemption of state laws beyond contract claims, consider the following case.

Patrick Maloney v. T3Media, Inc.
853 F.3d 1004 (9th Cir. 2017)

M. SMITH, J.:

[1] Former student-athletes Patrick Maloney and Tim Judge allege that defendant T3Media, Inc. exploited their likenesses commercially by selling non-exclusive licenses permitting consumers to download photographs from the National Collegiate Athletic Association's (NCAA) Photo Library for non-commercial art use. Maloney and Judge assert statutory and common law publicity-right claims ... under California law. The district court held that the federal Copyright Act preempts plaintiffs' claims .... We affirm....

[2] Plaintiffs Patrick Maloney and Tim Judge are former NCAA student-athletes who played for the Catholic University (CU) men's basketball team between 1997 and 2001. In their final year at CU, they made it all the way to the Division III national championship game, and helped lead the underdog Cardinals to an upset 76–62 victory over the William Paterson University Pioneers. The game's drama was captured in a series of photographs depicting the plaintiffs in play, and later posing as members of the team with CU's first-ever national championship trophy. The NCAA owns or controls the copyright to these photographs. It accordingly placed them into its collection, the NCAA Photo Library.

[3] T3Media provides storage, hosting, and licensing services for a wide variety of digital content. In 2012, it contracted with the NCAA to store, host, and license the images in the NCAA Photo Library. The NCAA Photo Library itself contains thousands of photographs chronicling seventy years of NCAA sports history. Until 2014, T3Media made the photographs available to the public through its website, Paya.com.

[4] Consumers could view digital thumbnails of the images contained in the NCAA Photo Library on Paya.com, and obtain for $20 to $30 a non-exclusive license permitting them to download a copy of a chosen photograph. Brief descriptions of the events depicted in the images accompanied the digital thumbnails. Users were also required to assent to a "Content License Agreement" in order to download one of the photographs. Pursuant to that agreement, consumers could "use a single copy of the image for non-commercial art use." Consumers did not obtain "any right or license to use the name or likeness of any individual (including any athlete, announcer, or coach) appearing in the Content in connection with or as an express or implied endorsement of any product or service." ...

[5] Plaintiffs commenced this action in the Central District of California in June 2014. They allege that T3Media exploited their names and likenesses commercially by selling photographs on Paya.com depicting their 2001 triumph. They purport to represent a putative class "of all current and former NCAA student-athletes whose names, images, and likenesses have been used without their consent by [T3Media] for the purpose of advertising, selling, or soliciting purchases of the photographs themselves." The complaint asserts claims for violation of California's statutory right of publicity, Cal. Civ. Code § 3344, common law right of publicity, and [other claims].[2]

[6] .... T3Media argued that the federal Copyright Act preempts plaintiffs' claims ..... The district court ... [held] that the Copyright Act preempts plaintiffs' claims ....

[7] According to the district court, the plaintiffs asserted rights that fell within the subject matter of copyright because their claims derived from the licensing of copyrighted photographs, which were original works of authorship fixed in a tangible medium of expression under the circumstances. The court rejected plaintiffs' argument that a publicity-right claim involving a photograph is not subject to preemption. It distinguished between claims derived from "selling a copyrighted photograph containing an athlete's likeness," which it said require preemption, and claims based on "using the athlete's likeness contained in the photograph for some other purpose," which it said do not. The district court also concluded that plaintiffs were asserting rights equivalent to the exclusive rights contained in the Copyright Act because they did not identify a use of their names or likenesses "independent of the display, reproduction, and distribution of the copyrighted images in which they are depicted." ...

[8] Section 301 of the Act seeks "to preempt and abolish any rights under the common law or statutes of a State that are equivalent to copyright and that extend to works," so long as the rights fall "within the scope of the Federal copyright law." H.R. Rep. No. 94–1476, at 130 (1976). We have adopted a two-part test, in accordance with section 301, to determine whether a state law claim is preempted by the Act. First, we decide whether the subject matter of the state law claim falls within the subject matter of copyright as described in 17 U.S.C. §§ 102 and 103. Second, assuming it does, we determine whether the rights asserted under state law are equivalent to the rights contained in 17 U.S.C. § 106, which articulates the exclusive rights of copyright holders.

---

[2] A common law cause of action for appropriation of name or likeness may be pleaded by alleging (1) the defendant's use of the plaintiff's identity; (2) the appropriation of plaintiff's name or likeness to defendant's advantage, commercially or otherwise; (3) lack of consent; and (4) resulting injury. In addition, to plead the statutory remedy provided in Civil Code section 3344, there must also be an allegation of a knowing use of the plaintiff's name, photograph or likeness for purposes of advertising or solicitation or purchases. Further, judicial construction of section 3344 has imposed an additional requirement. A "direct" connection must be alleged between the use and the commercial purpose....

[9] Here, the parties joust solely with respect to step one and assert competing rules that seek to define the boundary between copyright preemption and state law rights of publicity. Plaintiffs maintain that photograph-based publicity-right claims categorically fall outside the subject matter of copyright because such claims protect an individual's persona, which itself cannot be fixed in a tangible medium of expression. T3Media, by contrast, insists that the publicity right protects against the non-consensual use of one's name or likeness on merchandise or in advertising. T3Media would permit publicity-right claims to proceed in those contexts, but find preemption where, as here, a likeness has been captured in an artistic work and the work itself is being distributed for personal use.

[10] The right of publicity seeks to prevent commercial exploitation of an individual's identity without that person's consent. Mindful of that premise, we conclude that a publicity-right claim is not preempted when it targets non-consensual use of one's name or likeness on merchandise or in advertising. But when a likeness has been captured in a copyrighted artistic visual work and the work itself is being distributed for personal use, a publicity-right claim interferes with the exclusive rights of the copyright holder, and is preempted by section 301 of the Copyright Act.

[11] Here, Maloney and Judge do not contend that their likenesses were ever used on merchandise or in advertising. They challenge instead the copyright holder's decision to distribute the copyrighted images themselves by selling consumers a non-exclusive license to download a chosen photograph from the NCAA Photo Library for noncommercial art use. Under these circumstances, the publicity-right claims ... challenge control of the artistic work itself. Because plaintiffs seek to hold T3Media liable for exercising rights governed exclusively by copyright law, the claims are preempted by section 301 of the Copyright Act....

[12] The "subject matter of copyright" embodies "original works of authorship fixed in any tangible medium of expression ... from which they can be perceived, reproduced, or otherwise communicated, either directly or with the aid of a machine or device." 17 U.S.C. § 102(a). "Works of authorship include," among other things, "pictorial" works. Id. §§ 102(a), (a)(5). Additionally, "[a] work is 'fixed' in a tangible medium of expression when its embodiment in a copy ... is sufficiently permanent or stable to permit it to be perceived, reproduced, or otherwise communicated for a period of time of more than transitory duration." Id. § 101.

[13] Here, the publicity-right claims arise from the licensing of photographs, which plaintiffs concede are expressive "pictorial" works to which "[a] photographer contributes some original elements."4 There is also no doubt that a photograph is "sufficiently permanent" to permit it to be perceived "for more than transitory duration." 17 U.S.C. § 101. The subject matter of the state law claims—the photographs—therefore appears to fall within the subject matter of copyright.

[14] Plaintiffs resist this conclusion by drilling down on the content of a publicity-right claim. Plaintiffs maintain that the right of publicity—as it pertains to photographs—protects against exploitation of an individual's "likeness" or "persona." Since those attributes exist independent of any single photograph, plaintiffs argue that photograph-based publicity-right claims categorically fall outside the "subject matter of copyright." In other words, plaintiffs insist they do not assert any right in the particular photographic "works of authorship" at issue here. Instead, they claim that the personal attributes protected by the right of publicity cannot be fixed in copyrightable form in the same way as an actor's performance or an author's writings.

[15] Plaintiffs draw support for their position primarily from *Downing v. Abercrombie & Fitch*, 265 F.3d 994 (9th Cir. 2001). There, clothing retailer Abercrombie & Fitch developed a surfing theme for its catalog, which was the company's largest advertising vehicle. As part of the campaign, Abercrombie purchased photographs depicting the plaintiffs taking part in the 1965 Makaha International Surf Championship in Hawaii. Abercrombie used the photographs in a section of the catalog entitled "Surf Nekkid." It also decided to create t-shirts, exactly like those worn by the plaintiffs in the photograph, for sale in the upcoming issue. These

"Final Heat Tees" appeared in the catalog for sale two pages after the pictures of the plaintiffs. Abercrombie did not obtain at any time the plaintiffs' permission to use the photographs in the catalog.

[16] We held that section 301 of the Copyright Act did not preempt plaintiffs' publicity-right claims. We reasoned that "it is not the publication of the photograph itself, as a creative work of authorship, that is the basis for [plaintiffs'] claims, but rather, it is the use of the [plaintiffs'] likenesses and their names pictured in the published photograph." We observed that "[a] person's name or likeness is not a work of authorship within the meaning of 17 U.S.C. § 102." "This is true," we said, "notwithstanding the fact that [plaintiffs'] names and likenesses are embodied in a copyrightable photograph."

[17] Contrary to plaintiffs' argument, *Downing* did not mint a categorical rule that publicity-right claims relating to a likeness in a photograph are not subject to preemption. Instead, we said that when the use of a likeness forms the basis of a publicity-right claim, the claim is not preempted. We did not state that a likeness is the basis of a publicity-right claim any time it is fixed in a photograph. The crux of the issue is thus deciding when a publicity-right claim seeks to vindicate misuse of an individual's likeness, as opposed to merely interfering with the distribution, display, or performance of a copyrighted work.

[18] On that point, plaintiffs rely almost entirely on the idea that a theoretical line should separate publicity-right claims based on photographs from other works protected by the Copyright Act. They insist that "[a] different preemption rule applies to right-of-publicity claims arising from performances in film and sound recordings as opposed to those arising from a mere likeness in a photograph," and that the latter type of claim is not subject to preemption because "[u]nlike a performance, a person's mere likeness is not a copyrightable contribution to a photograph."

[19] The text of the Copyright Act does not support plaintiffs' construction. Section 301 draws no distinction among different types of copyrighted works when it comes to federal preemption. It directs attention to sections 102 and 103, which list the categories of works in which copyright protection subsists, suggesting that the same preemption rule applies to all works that are contained within the "subject matter of copyright." Given that "pictorial" works appear on that list alongside "motion pictures" and "sound recordings," there is no textual basis to carve out a preemption rule that applies solely to photographs.

[20] Moreover, our precedents clarify that the distinction pertinent to the preemption of a publicity-right claim is not the type of copyrightable work at issue, but rather the way in which one's name or likeness is affected by the use of the copyrighted work.

[21] For example, in *Downing*, the publicity-right claim was not permitted to proceed simply because an individual's likeness was fixed in a photograph. Indeed, it was not the publication of the photograph itself, as a creative work of authorship, that formed the basis of the publicity-right claim. Instead, it was the unauthorized use of the plaintiffs' likenesses to advertise Abercrombie products, and the creation of t-shirts, exactly like those worn by the plaintiffs in the photograph, for sale in Abercrombie's catalog. The plaintiffs sustained injury to their individual personas because their likenesses were exploited commercially without their consent. The plaintiffs were not seeking to use the right of publicity simply to prevent publication of an artistic, visual work.

[22] *Laws* [v. Sony Music Entm't, 448 F.3d 1134 (9th Cir. 2006),] bolsters the interpretation that preemption turns on how a copyrighted photograph is used. In particular, *Laws* distinguished *Downing* as a case "involv[ing] photographs *used in advertising*." (emphasis added). We observed that "Abercrombie went well beyond the mere republication of the photograph.... Rather, it published the photo in connection with a broad surf-themed advertising campaign, identified the plaintiffs-surfers by name, and offered for sale the same t-shirts worn by the plaintiffs in the photo." Importantly, we said that "[Abercrombie] had suggested that the

surfers had *endorsed* Abercrombie's t-shirts. Accordingly, [*Downing*] concluded that 'it is not the publication of the photograph itself ... that is the basis for [plaintiffs'] claims, but rather, it is the use of the [plaintiffs'] likenesses and their names pictured in the published photographs.'" (emphasis added). *Laws* strongly implies that misuse of an individual's likeness is the basis of a publicity-right claim when the name or image is exploited in advertising or on merchandise. It correspondingly implies that one's likeness does not form the basis of a publicity-right claim when the tort action challenges control of the artistic work itself or involves the mere republication of the photograph.

[23] In further support of this interpretation, *Laws* appears to reject plaintiffs' reading of *Fleet v. CBS Inc.*, 50 Cal. App. 4th 1911, 58 Cal. Rptr.2d 645 (1996). In *Fleet*, the plaintiffs were actors in a film, *White Dragon*, to which the defendant, CBS, Inc., owned the copyright. Having been denied certain compensation, plaintiffs sued CBS alleging that CBS did not have permission to utilize their names, pictures, or likenesses in conjunction with any exploitation of the film. CBS released the film anyway and included a picture of one of the plaintiffs on the packaging and in advertising materials. The court held that section 301 of the Copyright Act preempted the plaintiffs' publicity-right claims. It agreed that as a general proposition Civil Code section 3344 is intended to protect rights which cannot be copyrighted. But it found that the "[plaintiffs'] analysis crumbles in the face of one obvious fact: their individual performances in the film *White Dragon* were copyrightable." Once the "performances were put on film, they became 'dramatic work[s]' 'fixed in [a] tangible medium of expression.'" (quoting 17 U.S.C. § 102(a)). "At that point," the court said, "the performances came within the scope or subject matter of copyright law protection." Given that the publicity-right claims sought "only to prevent CBS from reproducing and distributing [plaintiffs'] performances in the film," the court concluded that "the[] claims must be preempted by federal copyright law."

[24] Maloney and Judge read *Fleet*'s holding to be limited to preemption of dramatic performances, and not to include photographs, because it observes that "[t]he celebrity who has merely had his picture taken has not engaged in a 'dramatic work' or other 'work of authorship,' and, as Professor Nimmer said, would be afforded no protection under federal copyright law." They believe *Fleet* supports their line between photographs and dramatic performances because *Fleet* adds "*if not for state law*, [the celebrity who had his picture taken] would have no remedy against those who would misappropriate his image for their own gain." (emphasis added). The "state law," of course, is the right of publicity, so plaintiffs read *Fleet* to support a dichotomy between likenesses in photographs and likenesses in other copyrightable works.

[25] *Laws* explains that in *Fleet*, however, "[s]ince CBS's *use* of plaintiffs' likenesses did not extend beyond the use of the copyrighted material it held, there was no right of publicity at issue, aside from the actors' performances." (emphasis added). *Laws* does not read *Fleet*, as plaintiffs contend, to draw a line between photographs and performances. Instead, it endorses the practice of looking at how one's likeness is affected by the use of the copyrighted material—whether that material is a photograph or something else....

[26] In sum, our cases clarify that a publicity-right claim may proceed when a likeness is used non-consensually on merchandise or in advertising. But where a likeness has been captured in a copyrighted artistic visual work and the work itself is being distributed for personal use, a publicity-right claim is little more than a thinly disguised copyright claim because it seeks to hold a copyright holder liable for exercising his exclusive rights under the Copyright Act.[9] ...

[27] As noted, Maloney and Judge do not allege that their names and likenesses were ever used in connection with the sale of any merchandise. Nor do they contend that their likenesses were ever used in any advertising.

---

[9] The fact that the non-exclusive licenses were sold for a profit and their price does not alter our analysis.... More to the point, T3Media's decision to license expressive works for a fee does not change the fact that the publicity-right claims target the display and distribution of copyrighted photographs for personal use. Moreover, copyright holders are allowed to commercially exploit their copyrights by exercising their exclusive rights under the Copyright Act.

Instead, the copyrighted images themselves were licensed to individuals for "non-commercial art use." Moreover, the licensees of the Maloney and Judge photos did not obtain "any right or license to use the name or likeness of any individual ... in connection with or as an express or implied endorsement of any product or service."

[28] Plaintiffs' publicity-right claims ... challenge control of the artistic work itself. Pursuant to *Laws*, the subject matter of the state law claims therefore falls within the subject matter of copyright.

[29] We believe that our holding strikes the right balance by permitting athletes to control the use of their names or likenesses on merchandise or in advertising, while permitting photographers, the visual content licensing industry, art print services, the media, and the public, to use these culturally important images for expressive purposes. Plaintiffs' position, by contrast, would give the subject of every photograph a de facto veto over the artist's rights under the Copyright Act, and destroy the exclusivity of rights that Congress sought to protect by enacting the Copyright Act....

[30] At the second step, we determine whether the rights plaintiffs assert under state law are equivalent to rights within the general scope of copyright as specified by section 106 of the Copyright Act. Section 106 affords copyright owners the "exclusive rights" to display, perform, reproduce, or distribute copies of a copyrighted work, to authorize others to do those things, and to prepare derivative works based upon the copyrighted work. 17 U.S.C. § 106. To survive preemption, the state cause of action must protect rights which are qualitatively different from the copyright rights. The state claim must have an extra element which changes the nature of the action.

[31] As a threshold matter, plaintiffs waived any argument that the rights they assert are not equivalent to rights within the general scope of copyright. They did not argue the issue in their briefs, and we do not review issues raised only by amicus curiae. Even had they made the argument, the district court nonetheless was correct to conclude that the rights plaintiffs assert are no different than the rights contained within the general scope of the Copyright Act.

[32] The complaint asserts statutory and common law publicity-right claims .... Plaintiffs, however, do not identify any use of their likenesses independent of the display, reproduction, and distribution of the copyrighted material in which they are depicted. We have held that under those circumstances, none of plaintiffs' claims is qualitatively different from a copyright claim.[16] ...

[33] Under the circumstances presented here, the subject matter of the state law claims falls within the subject matter of copyright and the rights asserted under state law are equivalent to the rights contained in 17 U.S.C. § 106. The federal Copyright Act therefore preempts the plaintiffs' publicity-right claims .... In light of that holding, plaintiffs' cannot demonstrate a reasonable probability of prevailing on their challenged claims. The district court did not err in [its ruling]....

NOTES

1. In *Wendt v. Host Int'l, Inc.*, 125 F.3d 806 (9th Cir. 1997), George Wendt and John Ratzenberger, actors from the television series *Cheers* who played the characters Norm and Cliff, respectively, sued for a violation of their right of publicity based on animatronic robotic figures named Bob and Hank but based (loosely) on their likenesses and placed in airport bars modeled on the bar in the television series. Both are shown in Figure 127.

---

[16] The elements of a common law right-of-publicity claim are subsumed within those of a statutory claim. Thus, *Laws* necessarily concluded that the singer's common law publicity-right claim asserted rights equivalent to copyright rights.

Figure 127: Norm and Cliff characters in *Cheers* television series (top), and robot figures in Cheers Airport Bar (bottom)

The Ninth Circuit rejected the defendants' argument that the claim was preempted on the basis that "the figures appropriate only the identities of the characters Norm and Cliff, to which Paramount owns the copyrights, and not the identities of Wendt and Ratzenberger, who merely portrayed those characters on television and retain no licensing rights to them. They argue that appellants may not claim an appropriation of identity by relying upon indicia, such as the Cheers Bar set, that are the property of, or licensee of, a copyright owner." In response, Wendt and Ratzenberger "concede[d] that they retain no rights to the characters Norm and Cliff; they argue .... that it is the physical likeness to Wendt and Ratzenberger, not Paramount's characters, that has commercial value to [the defendant]." The court accepted this characterization and ruled that this claim was not preempted by federal copyright law because it contained elements different in kind from copyright infringement.

Is this ruling in conflict with *Maloney*? Are you more convinced by one or the other decision?

As the right of publicity has expanded to protect persona, some scholars worry about its interference with federal copyright law. For example, Jennifer Rothman argues that "persona should be thought of as the idea of a person rather than the expression of that person," yet "[c]opyright law explicitly precludes copyright holders from protecting ideas." Jennifer E. Rothman, *Copyright Preemption and the Right of Publicity*, 36 U.C. DAVIS L. REV. 199, 205-06 (2002). She would therefore "set forth three situations in which the right must yield to copyright law: first, when a publicity holder's action is based solely on the use of his or her persona rather than on the publicity holder's name or likeness; second, when the use at issue was licensed or authorized by a copyright holder who received consent from the publicity holder for the original work; and finally, when the use at issue is explicitly authorized by the Copyright Act." For more on preemption and the right of publicity, see Rebecca Tushnet, *Raising Walls Against Overlapping Rights: Preemption and the Right of Publicity*, 92 NOTRE DAME L. REV. 1539 (2017).

2. In addition to considering express preemption of a right of publicity law by federal copyright law, a recent Second Circuit decision also considered whether there was conflict preemption of the right of publicity law. In a lawsuit by hip hop recording artist 50 Cent against hip hop recording artist Rick Ross alleging a right of publicity violation under Connecticut law for Ross's release of a mixtape using 50 Cent's voice performing his song "In Da Club," as well as 50 Cent's stage name in the identification of the song, the Second Circuit found the state claim to be preempted by copyright law, both due to conflict preemption and express preemption. In re Jackson, 972 F.3d 25 (2d Cir. 2020). With regard to conflict preemption, the court first observed that "[f]ederal copyright law does not entirely divest the states of authority to limit the exploitation of a work within copyright's subject matter in furtherance of sufficiently substantial state interests, such as protecting a person's privacy, compensating for fraud or defamation, or regulating unauthorized use of its citizens' personas." The court emphasized that the important question underpinning conflict preemption is "whether the state law claim furthers substantial state law interests that are distinct from the interests served by the federal law which may preempt the claim." The court concluded that even though some right of publicity claims will survive this analysis, as they, say, "target false endorsements, and as such vindicate a state's interest in preventing consumer confusion" or "vindicate privacy or reputational interests," 50 Cent's claim "constitutes little more than a thinly disguised effort to exert control over an unauthorized production of a sample of his work," such that "[a]llowing [his] right of publicity suit to proceed would interfere with the functioning of the copyright system."

3. In *Nat'l Basketball Ass'n v. Motorola, Inc.*, 105 F.3d 841 (2d Cir. 1997), the National Basketball Association (NBA) sued Motorola over its handheld Sportstrax pagers that provided real-time information regarding professional basketball games in progress. One of its claims was commercial misappropriation under New York law. The Second Circuit ruled that while misappropriation claims are generally preempted by copyright law, "a narrow 'hot-news' misappropriation claim survives preemption for actions concerning material within the realm of copyright." It reasoned that there were extra elements beyond a copyright infringement claim that allowed it to survive preemption: "(i) the time-sensitive value of factual information, (ii) the free-riding by a defendant, and (iii) the threat to the very existence of the product or service provided by the plaintiff." The court then concluded that Motorola had not engaged in unlawful "hot-news" misappropriation because some of the elements of the claim were not shown, including free-riding because Motorola collects these scores on its own from the NBA's games, not by taking from the NBA's similar service.

In a subsequent case, the Second Circuit held that copyright law preempted financial services companies' "hot news" misappropriation claim against an online subscription news service that was copying and sharing these firms' equity research recommendations. The court reasoned that § 301 preempts the plaintiffs' claim because it is about copyrightable subject matter and implicates the exclusive rights set out in § 106, plus the defendant was not free-riding on the plaintiffs because "[i]t is collecting, collating and disseminating factual information—the facts that [plaintiffs] and others in the securities business have made recommendations with respect to the value of and the wisdom of purchasing or selling securities—and attributing the information to its source. The [plaintiffs] are making the news; [the defendant], despite the [plaintiffs'] understandable desire to protect their business model, is breaking it." Barclays Capital Inc. v. Theflyonthewall.com, Inc., 650 F.3d 876, 902 (2d Cir. 2011). What does it mean to "free-ride" on someone else here? Is anything left to state law claims of misappropriation after these rulings?

For an argument that courts have misunderstood the basis of the misappropriation doctrine with regard to news, see Shyamkrishna Balganesh, *"Hot News": The Enduring Myth of Property in News*, 111 COLUM. L. REV. 419 (2011). In particular, Balganesh argues that "the misappropriation doctrine (including its hot news variant) is incapable of creating a property interest, even in traditional intellectual property form, in news. While the doctrine is directed at deterring free riding, it does so in the context of solving a collective action problem that was and is unique to the newspaper industry, related to the practice of cooperative newsgathering." He then concludes that "[m]isappropriation is … a framework for recovery that draws on unfair competition and unjust enrichment law." If Balganesh is right, what does that mean for preemption of "hot news" misappropriation claims by copyright law?

4. Is state law protection of ideas preempted by federal copyright law? Recall that ideas are specifically deemed to be unprotected under § 102(b) of copyright law. How would you analyze preemption under § 301? As a matter of conflict preemption? For an argument that idea protection laws are not preempted, see Arthur R. Miller, *Common Law Protection for Products of the Mind: An "Idea" Whose Time Has Come*, 119 HARV. L. REV. 703 (2006). Miller reasons that:

> [P]reemption analysis … establishes the upper permissible limit on state idea protection, embodying a fundamental balance struck between creators' incentives and the public benefit. The Constitution and the Copyright Act articulate this balance. Beneath this federally imposed ceiling, states are free to choose not to give legal status to ideas at all or to regulate as they choose.… [A] regime [c]ould protect mental creativity, taking into account today's economy, notions of fairness and proper allocation of benefit, and the extent to which major segments of society profit from viable ideas.

Do you agree?

5. Recall resale royalties from our discussion in Chapter IV of terminations of transfer. Artist resale royalty rights grant artists a percentage of the proceeds on the resale of their works. Like termination, resale royalty schemes allow artists to benefit down the line should their works become more valuable. Unlike termination, resale royalties provide this benefit by allowing artists to share in the appreciated value of their work but without any renegotiation. A California law passed in 1976 guarantees artists five percent of the profits in a later sale of their artwork. Cal. Civ. Code § 986(a). The Ninth Circuit has held that the California law is almost entirely preempted by the 1976 Act pursuant to § 301. Close v. Sotheby's, Inc., 894 F.3d 1061 (9th Cir. 2018). The court first reasoned that the "plaintiffs' claims under [California law] for resale royalties on works of 'fine art'—defined as original paintings, sculptures, drawings, or works in glass—fall within the subject matter of copyright." Next, the court determined that the "plaintiffs' [resale royalty] claims assert rights equivalent to the federal distribution right codified in § 106(3), as limited by the first sale doctrine codified in § 109(a)." The court thought that the state and federal rights were not "coextensive," yet were equivalent: "The two rights differ in that one grants artists the right to receive a percentage payment on all sales of artwork after the first, while the other grants artists the right to receive full payment on the first (and only the first) sale. But, at root, both concern the distribution of copies of artwork and define artists' right (or lack thereof) to payment on downstream sales of those copies." Yet the court thought the state law was not preempted by the 1909 Act, which did not contain an express-preemption provision and which it analyzed under principles of conflict preemption. Do you agree with the court's reasoning?

6. In this chapter, you have learned how parties might—and might not—modify copyright rules by contract. You have also gotten a taste of how states might—and might not—vary or supplement federal copyright law with its own laws. Should the ways individuals and states seek to vary or supplement copyright law affect federal copyright policy? Or should federal copyright policy be determined independently of these others' actions?

Made in the USA
Las Vegas, NV
20 December 2022

63670843R00385